Chambers
Essential Password

**English | Portuguese
semi-bilingual dictionary
for elementary learners**

Tabela de pronúncia

Consoantes

[b]	but [bʌt]
[d]	dab [dæb]
[dʒ]	jam [dʒæm]; gem [dʒem]
[f]	fat [fæt]
[g]	go [gəʊ]
[h]	hat [hæt]
[j]	yet [jet]
[k]	cat [kæt]
[l]	lad [læd]
[m]	mat [mæt]
[n]	no [nəʊ]
[ŋ]	bang [bæŋ]
[p]	pat [pæt]
[r]	rat [ræt]
[(r)]	far [fɑ:(r)]
[s]	sat [sæt]
[ʃ]	sham [ʃæm]
[t]	tap [tæp]
[tʃ]	chat [tʃæt]
[θ]	thatch [θætʃ]
[ð]	that [ðæt]
[v]	vat [væt]
[w]	wall [wɔ:l]
[z]	zinc [zɪŋk]
[ʒ]	pleasure [pleʒə(r)]
[χ]	loch [lɒχ]

Vogais

[æ]	bat [bæt]
[ɑ:]	art [ɑ:t]
[e]	bet [bet]
[ɜ:]	curl [kɜ:l]
[ə]	amend [ə'mend]
[i:]	bee [bi:]
[ɪ]	bit [bɪt]
[ɒ]	wad [wɒd]
[ɔ:]	all [ɔ:l]
[ʊ]	put [pʊt]
[u:]	shoe [ʃu:]
[ʌ]	cut [kʌt]

Ditongos

[aɪ]	life [laɪf]
[au]	house [haʊs]
[eə]	there [ðeə(r)]
[eɪ]	date [deɪt]
[əʊ]	low [ləʊ]
[ɪə]	beer [bɪə(r)]
[ɔɪ]	boil [bɔɪl]
[ʊə]	poor [pʊə(r)]

Chambers
Essential Password

**English | Portuguese
semi-bilingual dictionary
for elementary learners**

Tradução Luciana Garcia

martins fontes
selo martins

Chambers Essential Password : English/Portuguese
semi-bilingual dictionary for elementary learners

© 2015 Martins Editora Livraria Ltda., São Paulo, para a presente edição.
© 2009 Chambers Harrap Publishers Ltd.
www.chambersharrap.co.uk
Imagens reproduzidas com a autorização de QA International, www.qa-international.com
a partir do livro "The Visual Dictionary" QA internacional. 2009. Todos os direitos reservados.
Chambers® é uma marca registrada da Chambers Harrap Publishers Ltd. Todos os direitos reservados.
Chambers Publishing Ltd é uma empresa do grupo Hachette.

Publisher *Evandro Mendonça Martins Fontes*
Coordenação editorial *Vanessa Faleck*
Produção editorial *Susana Leal*
Preparação *Juliana Amato*
Revisão *Lucas Torrisi*
Ellen Barros

Dados Internacionais de Catalogação na Publicação (CIP)
(Câmara Brasileira do Livro, SP, Brasil)

Chambers Essential Password : English/Portuguese semi-bilingual dictionary
for elementary learners / tradução de Luciana Garcia. – 1. ed. – São Paulo : Martins
Fontes - selo Martins, 2014.

ISBN 978-85-8063-138-8

1. Inglês - Dicionários - Português 2. Português - Dicionários - Inglês.

14-03059

CDD-423.69
-469.32

Índices para catálogo sistemático:
1. Inglês : Dicionários : Português 423.69
2. Português : Dicionários : Inglês 469.32

Todos os direitos desta edição para o Brasil reservados à
Martins Editora Livraria Ltda.
Av. Dr. Arnaldo, 2076
01255-000 São Paulo SP Brasil
Tel. (11) 3116 0000
info@emartinsfontes.com.br
www.emartinsfontes.com.br

Impressão e acabamento: Yangraf Gráfica e Editora

Sumário

Prefácio	7
Como usar este dicionário	8
Indicações gramaticais	10
Gramática no dicionário	11
Uso especial de certas palavras	12
Inglês britânico e inglês americano	12
Ampliando o seu vocabulário	13
Collocations	14
Páginas de estudo	17
Chambers Essential Password	1

Prefácio

O *Chambers Essential Password* é um dicionário novo para quem está aprendendo inglês. Ele contém todas as palavras importantes que você precisará para estudar, trabalhar ou simplesmente viver, explicadas de um modo simples e claro, usando expressões que você já conhece.

Ao abrir o livro, você provavelmente notará o símbolo ⊞ em muitos verbetes. Esse sinal serve para mostrar um dos aspectos mais importantes da língua inglesa: certas associações comuns de palavras em um contexto (*collocation,* em inglês). A palavra *collocation* indica o modo como as palavras geralmente se combinam em determinada situação. Por exemplo, se há muitos carros na rua e o trânsito fica lento por esse motivo, dizemos que há "**heavy traffic**" (congestionamento), e se alguém faz alguma coisa ilegal, dizemos que essa pessoa "**commit a crime**" (comete um crime). Essas combinações frequentemente são impossíveis de concluir, mas aprendê-las é uma das coisas mais importantes que você pode fazer para tornar o seu inglês mais fluente e natural, e este dicionário o ajudará com isso.

Ao contrário de muitos dicionários para principiantes, o *Chambers Essential Password* não possui códigos gramaticais complicados, mas todas as palavras mais importantes e comuns têm exemplos que mostram claramente como usá-las. Por ter sido escrito por professores experientes, neste livro você também encontrará observações que o ajudarão a evitar erros comuns.

As informações deste dicionário são baseadas nas evidências fornecidas pela *Chambers Harrap Corpus*, uma coleção de milhões de palavras da língua inglesa retiradas de todos os tipos de linguagens, desde jornais a romances e conversas coloquiais. Isso nos ajuda a entender como as palavras são usadas no cotidiano e nos dá a certeza de que o dicionário está completamente atualizado.

Você também encontrará uma Seção de Estudo, que fornece informações e ajuda com a gramática inglesa. Esperamos que você faça bom proveito do *Chambers Essential Password* em casa, nas aulas ou onde quer que esteja!

Como usar este dicionário

Os **verbetes** estão em ordem alfabética.

laugh¹ /lɑːf/ VERB [laughs, laughing, laughed]
to make a sound of enjoyment when you think something is funny □ + *at* She laughed at my jokes. □ + *about* We can laugh about the whole thing now. ▣ It really *made* me *laugh*. ▣ They *burst out laughing* (= suddenly laughed loudly). (**rir**)
♦ PHRASAL VERB **laugh at someone/something**
to laugh or say something rude because you think someone or something is stupid □ *Wallis just laughed at the suggestion.*

Todas as **formas verbais** são mostradas.

Os **phrasal verbs** são exibidos após o verbo principal do verbete.

Os números indicam os diferentes **significados** de uma palavra.

laugh² /lɑːf/ NOUN [plural laughs]
1 when you laugh, or the sound that you make when you laugh ▣ He *gave* a nervous *laugh*. □ *He has a very loud laugh.* (**riso**)

2 have a laugh an informal phrase that means to have fun and enjoy yourself □ *We all have such a laugh together.* (**dar risada**)

O **plural** de cada palavra é mostrado.

As **expressões idiomáticas** comuns geralmente são mostradas na primeira palavra apresentada no verbete.

laughter /ˈlɑːftə(r)/ NOUN, NO PLURAL when someone laughs or the sound that they make when they laugh □ *I could hear laughter in the next room.* (**risada**)

Toda palavra tem uma **indicação gramatical**, mostrando se é um substantivo, verbo, adjetivo etc.

As palavras indicadas desta forma são as de **uso mais comum e útil**.

eager /ˈiːɡə(r)/ ADJECTIVE wanting very much to do or have something □ **+ to do something** *Imran seems eager to learn.* (**ávido**)

Padrões gramaticais simples são apresentados para palavras comuns. São sempre seguidos de um exemplo, mostrando claramente como usar a palavra. Para uma explicação de todos os códigos gramaticais, ver página 11.

Cada verbete apresenta a **pronúncia** com base no Alfabeto Fonético Internacional. Você pode encontrar a explicação dos símbolos na página 2 do dicionário.

thoughtful /ˈθɔːtfʊl/ ADJECTIVE
1 a thoughtful person is kind and thinks of other people □ *It was very thoughtful of you to phone.* (**atencioso**)
2 if someone looks thoughtful, they look as if they are thinking (**pensativo**)
thoughtfully /ˈθɔːtfʊli/ ADVERB in a thoughtful way □ *She stared thoughtfully at the letter.* □ *She'd very thoughtfully left drinks and sandwiches on the kitchen table for us.* (**atenciosamente**)

Este dicionário tem milhares de **exemplos de frases** mostrando os usos típicos dos verbetes.

As palavras de uma **mesma família** são exibidas abaixo da palavra principal, se estiverem em ordem alfabética.

Algumas palavras podem ter mais de uma **grafia** possível.

hairdryer *or* **hairdrier** /ˈheədraɪə(r)/ NOUN [plural **hairdryers** *or* **hairdriers**] a piece of electrical equipment that dries your hair by blowing hot air over it (**secador de cabelo**)

Como usar este dicionário 9

Collocations (certas associações comuns de palavras) são uma característica muito importante deste dicionário. Para mais informações, ver página 14.

lonely /ˈləʊnli/ ADJECTIVE [lonelier, loneliest] unhappy because you are alone, with no friends around you ▫ *She suddenly felt very lonely.* ▫ *I get lonely at the weekends.* (**solitário**)

Os adjetivos e os advérbios nos graus **comparativo de superioridade e superlativo** são mostrados. Essas formas são usadas quando você quer dizer que alguma coisa ou alguém tem mais intensamente uma qualidade ao ser comparado com outros.

Como este dicionário foi projetado para ser usado na escola e em casa, palavras usadas nas **disciplinas escolares** de matemática, física, biologia, geografia e computação são identificadas.

desktop /ˈdesktɒp/ NOUN [plural desktops] a computer screen that shows the icons (= small pictures) for programs you can use. A computing word. (**área de trabalho**)

Este dicionário usa palavras simples em todos os verbetes, mas, quando há uma palavra mais difícil, fornece uma breve explicação.

microscope /ˈmaɪkrəskəʊp/ NOUN [plural microscopes] a piece of equipment with lenses (= curved pieces of glass) that makes very small objects look much larger so that you can study them closely (**microscópio**)

Se uma palavra é sempre usada em determinada **expressão**, essa expressão é mostrada antes da explicação, e tal explicação descreve a expressão completa.

beg /beg/ VERB [begs, begging, begged]
1 to ask someone for something in an eager or emotional way because you want it very much ▫ *I begged him to come home.* (**implorar**)
2 to ask people for money in the street because you are very poor (**mendigar**)
3 I beg your pardon (a) a formal way of saying sorry when you have made a mistake ▫ *Oh, I beg your pardon, I didn't realize this pen was yours.* (b) a formal way of asking someone to repeat what they have just said because you did not hear it ▫ *'I'm going now.' 'I beg your pardon.' 'I said, I'm going now.'* (**desculpar-se**)

Se você precisar identificar se uma palavra, por exemplo, é mais formal ou informal, isso é indicado em uma explicação. Para uma lista de palavras que descrevem essas características, ver página 12.

Usage notes orientam sobre o uso de uma palavra. Elas ajudam você a evitar erros que os estudantes iniciantes de inglês cometem com frequência.

picnic¹ /ˈpɪknɪk/ NOUN [plural picnics] a meal that you take with you to eat outdoors ▫ *We had a picnic on the beach.* ▫ *There's a beautiful picnic area in the forest.* (**piquenique**)

> Note that you **have** a picnic. You do not 'make' a picnic:
> ✓ We had a picnic in the park.
> ✗ We made a picnic in the park.

diaper /ˈdaɪəpə(r)/ NOUN [plural diapers] the US word for **nappy** (**fralda [EUA]**)

Este dicionário é escrito em inglês britânico. A grafia nas explicações e nos exemplos é britânica. Entretanto, grafias e palavras americanas comuns são identificadas.

O **Thesaurus** ajuda você a saber mais sobre palavras com significados semelhantes.

> **THESAURUS:** If you are **absent**, you are not at a place where you are expected to be. For example, you might be absent from school or work because you are ill. If you are **away** from work, you might be out of the office on business or on holiday. If a person is **missing**, they are not where you expect them to be, and you do not know where they are. If a person or thing has **gone**, it was in a place, but now it is no longer there.

Indicações gramaticais

Estas são as classificações gramaticais usadas neste dicionário.

abbreviation	forma simplificada das palavras, usando suas primeiras letras, abreviação	l (litre), UK (United Kingdom)
adjective	palavra que descreve um substantivo, adjetivo	pretty, hot, uncomfortable
adverb	palavra que descreve um verbo ou um adjetivo, advérbio	slowly, extremely, well
auxiliary verb	verbos utilizados para formar tempos verbais, formas negativas e interrogativas, verbo auxiliar	be, do, have
conjunction	palavra que une partes de uma oração, conjunção	but, however
determiner	palavra usada antes de um substantivo para mostrar como ele está sendo usado, determinante	the, this, those
exclamation	alguma coisa que se diz de repente ou em voz alta, exclamação	hey, ouch
modal verb	um verbo usado para expressar ideias tais como ser possível, necessário, correto etc., verbo modal	might, ought, will
noun	palavra que indica uma pessoa, coisa ou qualidade, substantivo	dog, table, car
noun no plural	substantivo que não pode ser usado no plural	air, happiness, ham
number	numeral	eleven, twenty, million
past participle	particípio passado	sung, watched, eaten
past tense	o verbo indicado no tempo passado	sang, watched, ate
plural noun	substantivo plural	trousers, outskirts
prefix	letras adicionadas no início de uma palavra para modificar seu significado, prefixo	anti-, eco-, hydro-
preposition	palavra usada para expressar noções como as de tempo, posição ou método, preposição	by, under, with
pronoun	palavra que pode substituir um substantivo, pronome	they, it, those
suffix	letras adicionadas no final de uma palavra para modificar seu significado, sufixo	-ful, -able
verb	palavra que indica ação ou estado de alguém ou de alguma coisa, verbo	speak, increase, allow

Gramática no dicionário

Para simplificar o uso deste dicionário, os códigos gramaticais são usados apenas para as palavras mais importantes ou mais comuns. A razão disso é que essas são as palavras que você provavelmente mais usará.

Você verá que, onde houver um código gramatical, haverá também um exemplo mostrando seu significado.

Esta é a lista dos códigos usados neste dicionário:

+ ing	a palavra é seguida de um verbo usando a forma -ing	e.g. + ing: *I like playing computer games*
+ question word	a palavra é seguida de palavras como *who, what, why*	e.g. + question word: *I don't understand why he is so upset*
+ that	a palavra é seguida por parte de uma oração começando com *that*	e.g. + that: *I promise that I'll pay you back later*
+ to do something	a palavra é seguida por um verbo no infinitivo	e.g. + to do something: *I forgot to lock the door*
no plural	este sentido da palavra não pode ser usado na forma plural, mesmo que outros sentidos da mesma palavra possam	e.g. no plural: *all the hairs that grow on your head*
+ in/over/up etc.	esta palavra é seguida por uma preposição	e.g.: truth + about: *We're determined to learn the truth about his disapearance*

Uso especial de certas palavras

Algumas vezes, uma palavra que pode ser usada em determinada situação não é adequada para uma situação diferente (quando escrevemos um artigo não usamos a mesma linguagem que falamos com nossos amigos).

Essas diferenças são claramente mostradas nas explicações deste dicionário. Estas são as palavras que usamos para descrevê-las:

formal – palavras formais são adequadas para um texto escrito e situações oficiais. Elas parecerão ligeiramente estranhas se você usá-las em uma conversa comum.

> **furthermore** /ˌfɜːðəˈmɔː(r)/ ADVERB a formal word used when you are adding something to what you have already said □ *His plans will be very expensive. Furthermore, they will cause a lot of disruption.* (**além disso**)

informal – palavras informais não são adequadas para textos escritos ou para situações oficiais. É mais natural usá-las com pessoas que você conheça bem.

> **dumb** /dʌm/ ADJECTIVE [dumber, dumbest]
> **1** stupid. An informal word □ *He kept asking me dumb questions.* (**idiota**)
> **2** not able to speak (**mudo**)

old-fashioned (antigo) – este dicionário não inclui palavras que não são mais usadas, mas existem algumas palavras que ainda estão em uso, embora não façam parte da linguagem comum dos jovens.

> **centigrade** /ˈsentɪɡreɪd/ ADJECTIVE an old-fashioned word for **Celsius** □ *forty degrees centigrade*

literary (literário) – palavras normalmente encontradas em poemas ou romances.

> **riches** /ˈrɪtʃɪz/ PLURAL NOUN a word used in stories meaning a lot of money and expensive things (**riqueza**)
>
> > ► THESAURUS: Money is a general word for coins and paper notes that you use for buying things. Riches is a literary word meaning a lot of money and expensive things. For example, you might talk about a king's riches in a story. Someone's wealth is all the money and expensive things that they have. A fortune is a very large amount of money.

Inglês britânico e inglês americano

Este dicionário é escrito em inglês britânico. A grafia e as palavras nas explicações e as frases de exemplos são britânicas. Entretanto, palavras americanas comuns também estão incluídas:

> **sidewalk** /ˈsaɪdwɔːk/ NOUN [*plural* sidewalks] the US word for **pavement** (**calçada**)

Ampliando o seu vocabulário 13

Algumas vezes, apenas um dos sentidos de uma palavra é americano. Por exemplo, o sentido do item de número 4:

---
regular /ˈregjʊlə(r)/ ADJECTIVE
1 happening often or doing something often ▣ *We all know the benefits of regular exercise.* ▣ *I keep in regular contact with my family.* ▣ *He writes to me on a regular basis.* □ *She was a regular visitor to the museum.* (**regular**)
2 having the same amount of time or space between each thing □ *He has a regular heartbeat.* ▣ *I still see the doctor at regular intervals.* (**regular**)
3 following the usual rules of grammar □ *'Cat' has a regular plural.* ▣ *'Pick' is a regular verb.* (**regular**)
4 a US word meaning usual □ *My regular doctor was away.* (**habitual**)

Muitas palavras têm grafias diferentes no inglês britânico e no inglês americano, e isto é explicado no dicionário:

---
cancel /ˈkænsəl/ VERB [**cancels, cancelling**/*US* **canceling, cancelled**/*US* **canceled**] to say that a planned event will not happen □ *The match was cancelled because of the snow.* (**cancelar**)

Ampliando o seu vocabulário

A língua inglesa possui um grande vocabulário, e este dicionário pode ajudar você a aumentar o seu. Alguns verbetes contêm um quadro **Thesaurus**. Esses quadros informam sobre palavras semelhantes à palavra principal. Com frequência, os quadros Thesaurus informam sobre palavras que possuem um sentido menos geral do que a palavra principal. Usando esse tipo de palavras, você pode tornar o seu inglês mais interessante e preciso:

➤ **THESAURUS:** If you are happy or cheerful, you are pleased, and feel that a situation is good. Delighted means very happy. If you are glad, you are happy because of something that has happened. Often you are glad because a bad or difficult situation has ended or because something bad has not happened. For example, you might be glad to be home after a long journey, or glad that your exams are finished.

Algumas vezes, os quadros Thesaurus explicam as diferenças entre as palavras que os alunos consideram confusas:

➤ **THESAURUS:** To leave means to go away from a place. The words depart and set off have a similar meaning, but are especially used to describe the start of a journey. For example we can say that a train departs at a particular time. Depart is a more formal word than set off.

Collocations

O que são *collocations*?

Collocations são conhecidas como "palavras associadas", pois são palavras que se combinam em certas situações. Por exemplo, se está chovendo muito forte, podemos falar em "*heavy* rain", e se duas pessoas se amam muito, podemos dizer que estão "*madly* in love".

Essas palavras aparecem juntas mais frequentemente do que apareceriam por acaso, ou simplesmente apenas por seus significados. Por exemplo, é correto dizer "steal a car", mas isso não é o que chamamos de *collocation*, porque o verbo "steal" pode ser usado com muitos substantivos diferentes. Entretanto, se nos referimos sobre alguém "*committing* a crime", estamos usando uma *collocation*, porque essas palavras se combinam mais fortemente e, se você precisar de um verbo que combine com a palavra "crime", deve escolher "commit" – um outro verbo como "do" não estaria correto.

Algumas vezes, conseguimos descobrir as *collocations* que queremos, mas geralmente é difícil. Por que "*pay* attention", ou "*draw* conclusions"? Por que "*tell* lies" mas "*make* promise"?

É por essa razão que tivemos o cuidado de mostrar as *collocations* das palavras mais úteis do dicionário. As *collocations* são indicadas pelo símbolo ⊞ para facilitar que você veja as palavras que melhor combinam com aquela que você está pesquisando.

Por que é tão importante aprender as *collocations*?

As palavras geralmente não são usadas sozinhas. Além de aprender uma palavra, você precisa saber as palavras que se aproximam dela: as palavras que permitem a você usá-la de maneira clara e natural.

Saber as *collocations* ajudará você a falar e a escrever um inglês mais natural e fluente. Por exemplo, você deve saber o significado da palavra "exam", mas também é importante saber quais verbos usar com ela. Embora seja possível dizer "I have to do an exam at the end of the year", é muito mais natural dizer "I have to *take* an exam at the end of the year". E, embora as pessoas entendam se você disser "I was successful in my exam", um falante nativo inglês provavelmente não diria desse modo; ele diria "I passed my exam".

Conhecer as *collocations* tornará o seu inglês mais interessante e ajudará você a se expressar melhor. Por exemplo, fica ótimo dizer "I was very disappointed", mas, se você souber dizer "I was *bitterly* disappointed", sua frase terá muito mais força e impressionará mais.

Conhecer as *collocations* ajudará você a evitar erros. Embora seja possível, algumas vezes, concluir quais palavras usar, ao mesmo tempo é fácil se enganar. Por exemplo, muitos estudantes de inglês dizem: "We decided to make a party for him". Isso não é o inglês correto; deve-se dizer: "We decided to *have* a party for him", ou, ainda melhor: "We decided to *throw* a party for him".

Saber as *collocations* melhorará os seus resultados nos exames. Muitos exames comuns de inglês testam o seu conhecimento sobre as *collocations*. Você perderá pontos se usar as incorretas, e ganhará pontos se optar pelas corretas e interessantes.

Encontrar e aprender as *collocations*

As *collocations* são uma parte muito importante do aprendizado do idioma, por isso é uma boa ideia aprendê-las corretamente desde o começo.

Veja as seguintes frases simples, por exemplo, para entender quão importantes elas são, até mesmo para o tipo de ideias e atividades sobre as quais conversamos quase diariamente:

- *I **brush** my **teeth** every morning.*
- *I need to **do** my **homework**.*
- *He **watches TV** every evening.*

Collocations 15

- It was **raining heavily** yesterday.
- My sister **wears glasses**.

Quando você pesquisar uma palavra no dicionário, tente verificar as *collocations* que se referem a ela e aprendê-las com a palavra.

Quais tipos de *collocations* existem?

adjective + noun	e.g. strong accent, detailed account, heavy traffic
verb + noun	e.g. gain acceptance, open an account, commit a crime
verb + adverb	e.g. go abroad, chop finely
noun + verb	e.g. standards slip, war breaks out
adverb + adjective	e.g. hopelessly lost, pleasantly surprised
verb + adjective	e.g. fall asleep, get married
noun + preposition + noun	e.g. a sense of achievement, a piece of advice
noun + noun	e.g. travel arrangements, management skills

Collocations adverbiais de intensidade

Se você pesquisar no dicionário, verá que há, frequentemente, modos muito mais interessantes de dizer "very" ou "extremely".

Por exemplo, se alguém estiver muito doente (very ill), podemos dizer que está "seriously ill"; e, se alguém for muito tímido (very shy), podemos dizer que é "painfully shy". Advérbios como "seriously" e "painfully" são chamados de advérbios intensificadores, pois deixam as palavras mais fortes ou intensas em seu significado. Essas são *collocations* bastante úteis para você aprender, porque podem deixar o seu inglês mais interessante.

Chambers Essential Password: Páginas de estudo

Tabelas dos verbos regulares

Present simple tense:

I	look
you	look
he/she/it	looks
we	look
they	look

*They **work** in my office.*
*I **enjoy** swimming.*
*Yukiko **wants** to make a phone call.*

Lembre-se de acrescentar um -s no final do verbo no tempo present simple na 3ª pessoa do singular (he/she/it).

Negative form:

I	don't look
you	don't look
he/she/it	doesn't look
we	don't look
they	don't look

*I **don't like** eggs.*
*He **doesn't speak** English.*
*We **don't want** to buy it.*

Question form:

Do	I	look?
Do	you	look?
Does	he/she/it	look?
Do	we	look?
Do	they	look?

***Do** you **work** on Saturdays?*
***Does** Carlos **want** a drink?*
***Do** you **like** football?*

Use o present simple:

- para indicar ações que expressem uma verdade ou que aconteçam com frequência:

  *The Earth **moves** round the sun.*

*If you **heat** water to 100°C, it **boils**.*
*My birthday **is** in April.*

- para expressar ações que acontecem por um longo tempo:

*Maria **wears** nice clothes.*
*We **live** in London.*
*He **works** in an office.*
*Sara **is** a doctor.*

- para indicar hábitos, rotinas e horários programados:

*Juan always **goes** to the gym after work.*
*They **collect** the rubbish on Mondays.*
*The train **arrives** at 8.30.*

- com alguns verbos especiais. Nós não usamos esses verbos nos continuous tenses (tempos contínuos), mas há exceções:

verbos que descrevem sentimentos ou ações ligados ao pensamento: *believe, dislike, feel, forget, hate, know, like, look, love, mean, need, prefer, remember, seem, think, understand, want*

*I **think** your mum is very friendly.*
*I **like** her very much.*

verbos dos sentidos: *taste, hear, see*

*This meat **tastes** strange.*
*I **hear** the phone ringing.*

verbos que indicam noção de posse: *have* (quando indicar posse), *own, belong*

*Pablo **has** two sisters.*
*They **own** five cars and a motorbike.*
*That phone **belongs** to me.*

Present continuous tense:

I	am	looking
you	are	looking
he/she/it	is	looking
we	are	looking
they	are	looking

Usamos com frequência as abreviações *I'm, you're, he's, she's, it's, we're, they're* com esse tempo.

*I'**m reading** a good book.*
*He'**s working** at the moment.*

Negative form:

I	am not	looking
you	are not	looking
he/she/it	is not	looking
we	are not	looking
they	are not	looking

I'm not staying in this hotel.
John's not living here at the moment – he's away at university.

Question form:

Am	I	looking?
Are	you	looking?
Is	he/she/it	looking?
Are	we	looking?
Are	they	looking?

***Are** you **working**?*
***Is** Sally **watching** TV?*

Usamos o present continuous:

- para expressar coisas que estão acontecendo agora:

  *He's **listening** to the radio.*
  *Where is Jenny? She's **brushing** her teeth.*

- para expressar situações temporárias:

  *I'm **living** in London for 6 months.*
  *I'm **studying** at Manchester University.*

- para indicar planejamentos:

  *I'm **seeing** John tonight.*
  *We're **meeting** the bank manager on Friday.*

Present perfect tense:

I	have	looked
you	have	looked
he/she/it	has	looked
we	have	looked
they	have	looked

Usamos com frequência as abreviações *I've, you've, he's, we've and they've* com esse tempo.

*I've **lived** in New York since September.*
*Anna **has travelled** all over the world.*

Negative form:

I	have not	looked
you	have not	looked
he/she/it	has not	looked
we	have not	looked
they	have not	looked

*I can't go out. I **haven't finished** my homework yet.*
*They **haven't visited** me for a long time.*

Tabelas dos verbos regulares

Question form:

Have	I	looked?
Have	you	looked?
Has	he/she/it	looked?
Have	we	looked?
Have	they	looked?

Have you ever visited this museum?
Has your brother finished his breakfast yet?

Usamos o present perfect:

- para indicar ações que se iniciaram no passado e ainda estão acontecendo:

    I've lived here for 5 years. (= and I still live here now)
    I haven't done the washing-up yet. (= the dishes are still dirty)

- para indicar ações que já terminaram de acontecer e cujo resultado ocorre no presente:

    I've finished my homework. (= so now we can go out)

- para indicar experiências passadas com referência ao presente:

    Have you ever been to New York? (= can you tell me about it now?)

Past simple tense:

I	looked
you	looked
he/she/it	looked
we	looked
they	looked

Lembre-se de que, se o verbo terminar em -e, você apenas acrescenta -d para formar o past simple:

*I **lived** in Rome for many years.*

Negative form:

I	didn't look
You	didn't look
He/she/it	didn't look
We	didn't look
They	didn't look

*They **didn't phone** me.*
*I **didn't want** to go to the party.*
*He **didn't help** me.*

Question form:

Did	I	look?
Did	you	look?

Did	he/she/it	look?
Did	we	look?
Did	they	look?

Did you **enjoy** the film?
Did Lola **come** to the party?

Usamos o past simple:

- para indicar ações e situações que se iniciaram e terminaram no tempo passado:

    I **walked** to the supermarket.
    Marco **lived** in Paris for 3 years.

Past continuous tense:

I	was	looking
you	were	looking
he/she/it	was	looking
we	were	looking
they	were	looking

I **was walking** down the road when I saw her.
He **was having** a bath when the phone rang.

Negative form:

I	was not	looking
you	were not	looking
he/she/it	was not	looking
we	were not	looking
they	were not	looking

Usamos com frequência as abreviações *wasn't* and *weren't* neste tempo.

It **wasn't raining**, so we didn't take our coats.
Helena **wasn't expecting** to see him at the party.

Question form:

Was	I	looking?
Were	you	looking?
Was	he/she/it	looking?
Were	we	looking?
Were	they	looking?

Were you **eating** dinner when I called?
Was Abdul **listening** to the teacher?

Usamos o past continuous:

- para indicar ações que estavam acontecendo quando outra ação ocorreu, ou em um momento específico no passado:

*While I **was watching** TV the doorbell rang.*
*We **were waiting** for a bus when it started to rain.*
*At midnight, Miguel **was** still **playing** games on the computer.*

- para indicar que duas ações estavam acontecendo ao mesmo tempo:

  *While I **was cooking**, my mother **was looking after** the children.*
  ***Were** you **listening** to what I **was saying**?*

Future simple tense:

I	will	look
you	will	look
he/she/it	will	look
we	will	look
they	will	look

Usamos com frequência as abreviações *I'll, you'll, he'll, we'll* and *they'll* neste tempo.

*I'**ll help** you to look for the book.*
*It **will be** an interesting trip.*

Negative form:

I	will not	look
you	will not	look
he/she/it	will not	look
we	will not	look
they	will not	look

Usamos com frequência a abreviação *won't* com este tempo.

*They **won't come** with me.*
*I **won't tell** anyone your secret.*

Question form:

Will	I	look?
Will	you	look?
Will	he/she/it	look?
Will	we	look?
Will	they	look?

***Will** you **call** me when you arrive?*
***Will** he **go away** for a long time?*

Usamos o simple future tense:

- para indicar que alguma coisa acontecerá no futuro:

  *I'**ll do** it later.*
  *Jack **will be** back this afternoon.*
  *The wedding **will begin** at 4 o'clock.*

- para expressar promessas:

  *I'll **love** you forever.*
  *He'll never **forget** your kindness.*

- para fazer oferecimentos ou solicitações:

  *I'll **help** you carry that box.*
  ***Will** you **open** a window, please?*

- para fazer previsões sobre o futuro (geralmente, quando não há evidências no presente):

  *I'm sure this **will be** a good year.*

Principais verbos irregulares:

infinitive	past tense	past participle
be	was/were	been
beat	beat	beaten
become	became	become
begin	began	begun
bend	bent	bent
bite	bit	bitten
bleed	bled	bled
blow	blew	blown
break	broke	broken
bring	brought	brought
build	built	built
burn	burned/burnt	burned/burnt
buy	bought	bought
catch	caught	caught
choose	chose	chosen
come	came	come
cost	cost	cost
cut	cut	cut
dig	dug	dug
do	did	done
draw	drew	drawn
drink	drank	drunk
drive	drove	driven
eat	ate	eaten
fall	fell	fallen
feel	felt	felt
fight	fought	fought
find	found	found
fly	flew	flown
forbid	forbade	forbidden
forget	forgot	forgotten
freeze	froze	frozen
get	got	got (US: gotten)
give	gave	given
go	went	gone
grow	grew	grown
have	had	had
hear	heard	heard

Principais verbos irregulares: 25

infinitive	past tense	past participle
hide	hid	hidden
hit	hit	hit
hold	held	held
hurt	hurt	hurt
keep	kept	kept
know	knew	known
lay	laid	laid
learn	learned/learnt	learned/learnt
leave	left	left
lend	lent	lent
let	let	let
lose	lost	lost
make	made	made
mean	meant	meant
meet	met	met
pay	paid	paid
put	put	put
read	read	read
ride	rode	ridden
ring	rang	rung
rise	rose	risen
run	ran	run
say	said	said
see	saw	seen
sell	sold	sold
send	sent	sent
set	set	set
shake	shook	shaken
shine	shone	shone
show	showed	shown
shut	shut	shut
sing	sang	sung
sink	sank	sunk
sit	sat	sat
sleep	slept	slept
smell	smelt	smelt
speak	spoke	spoken
spend	spent	spent
spoil	spoiled/spoilt	spoiled/spoilt
stand	stood	stood

26 Principais verbos irregulares:

infinitive	past tense	past participle
steal	stole	stolen
swim	swam	swum
take	took	taken
teach	taught	taught
tell	told	told
think	thought	thought
throw	threw	thrown
understand	understood	understood
wake	woke	woken
wear	wore	worn
win	won	won
write	wrote	written

Habilidades com o dicionário

Ordem alfabética

Esta é a ordem alfabética:

ABCDEFGHIJKLMNOPQRSTUVWXYZ
abcdefghijklmnopqrstuvwxyz

Todas as palavras do dicionário estão em ordem alfabética. As palavras que você procura no dicionário são chamadas de **verbetes**. Quando as primeiras letras de dois verbetes são iguais, as segundas e depois as terceiras letras também estão em ordem alfabética. Assim, a palavra *apple* vem antes de *carrot*, e a palavra *carrot* vem antes de *potato*. A palavra *animal* vem antes da palavra *apple*, e *apricot* vem depois de *apple* no dicionário.

Exercício 1
Coloque as palavras seguintes em ordem alfabética. Depois, confira suas respostas, procurando os verbetes no dicionário.

teacher
sun
keyboard
cat
goose
American
microphone
wind
bicycle
burglar

Exercício 2
Coloque as palavras seguintes em ordem alfabética. Depois, confira suas respostas, procurando os verbetes no dicionário.

bouquet
birthday
broccoli
ballet
building
bridge
blouse
biology
biscuit
box

Alguns verbetes são formados por duas ou mais palavras. São as palavras **compostas**. Da mesma forma que os verbetes comuns, os compostos também seguem a ordem alfabética no dicionário.

Exercício 3
Coloque as palavras seguintes em ordem alfabética. Depois, confira suas respostas, procurando os verbetes no dicionário.

28 Ordem alfabética

mineral water
midnight
modal verb
MP3 player
make-up
mother-in-law
mobile phone
microwave oven
middle class
moonlight

Alguns verbetes são abreviações (forma abreviada de palavras longas). Eles também estão em ordem alfabética.

Exercício 4
Coloque as palavras seguintes em ordem alfabética. Depois, confira suas respostas, procurando os verbetes no dicionário.

Christmas tree
certificate
traffic lights
ID
traffic jam
cm
mm
Boxing Day
HQ
BBC

Phrasal verbs são verbos formados por duas ou mais palavras, sendo um verbo e uma preposição ou um advérbio. Você deve considerar o phrasal verb como um todo para entender o seu significado. Os phrasal verbs vêm depois da entrada do verbo principal e estão organizados em ordem alfabética.

Exercício 5
Coloque os phrasal verbs seguintes em ordem alfabética e, depois, procure-os no dicionário para conferir as suas respostas.

get through
get through something
get up
get round to doing something
get on
get out of something
get over something
get away with

Homônimos

Algumas palavras possuem mais de uma classe gramatical. Por exemplo, a palavra *record* pode ser um *noun* (*He has a criminal **record***) ou um *verb* (*The band **are recording** a new album*). A palavra *record* também pode ser um *adjective*: (*He ran the race in **record** time*). Cada um dos três significados é um *homonym* (homônimo) da palavra *record*. Você precisa conhecer a classe gramatical em inglês de uma palavra para encontrar seu significado correto no dicionário. Neste dicionário, cada homonym é uma entrada de verbete separada. Então, a palavra *record* tem três verbetes homônimos: um para o substantivo (noun), um para o verbo (verb) e um para o adjetivo (adjective).

Exercício 6
Observe as frases seguintes: para cada frase, escolha a classe gramatical correta da palavra em **negrito**:

a	The loud noise **alarmed** him.	noun/verb
	My **alarm** goes off at 6 o'clock.	noun/verb
b	He has an **American** accent	noun/adjective
	Junko is an **American**, but her parents are Japanese.	noun/adjective
c	I received a job **offer** this morning.	noun/verb
	Ricardo **offered** to help me with my work.	noun/verb
d	I only went to his house **once**.	conjunction/adverb
	Once you finish your homework, you can watch TV.	conjunction/adverb
e	Could you **peel** the potatoes for me, please?	noun/verb
	Put the **peel** in the bin when you've finished.	noun/verb

Exercício 7
Nas frases seguintes, indique a que classe gramatical pertence cada palavra em **negrito**. Escreva *n* para o *noun*, *v* para o *verb*, e *a* para o *adjective*. Depois, verifique as palavras no dicionário e indique o número correto do homônimo de cada palavra.

Exemplo:

> I'll **phone** you in the morning. <u>v, phone 2</u>
> I can't talk at the moment, I'm on the **phone**. <u>n, phone 1</u>

a Maria **picked** some flowers from the garden. _____
   There are three dresses – please take your **pick**. _____

b The soldiers **pinned** him to the ground. _____
   There are some **pins** by the sewing machine. _____

c Oscar came in third **place** in the race. _____
   Nadia **placed** the cup carefully on the table. _____

d Have you got any **plastic** bags? _____
   These chairs are made of **plastic**. _____

e He was **presented** with a gold medal. _____
   Ana gave me a lovely **present** for my birthday. _____
   The **present** system for organizing the files works very well. _____

Palavras homófonas

Em inglês, algumas palavras têm a mesma pronúncia, mas são escritas com grafias diferentes. Elas são chamadas **homophones** (palavras homófonas). Você precisa ter a certeza da grafia da palavra antes de procurá-la no dicionário.

Exercício 8

Em cada frase abaixo, escolha a palavra correta para preencher o espaço. Cada par de palavras tem a mesma pronúncia. Confira suas respostas pesquisando as palavras no dicionário.

a Would you like an apple or a _____ ?   pair/pear
   I've just bought a new _____ of trousers.   pair/pear

b Would you like some more _____ on your pasta?   sauce/source
   The country's main _____ of energy is oil.   sauce/source

c _____ coat is yours?   which/witch
   The _____ in the story wore a big black hat.   which/witch

d My _____ leaves at 4.30, so I must leave now.   plain/plane
   We've painted the walls _____ white.   plain/plane

e Yukiko loves _____ music.   sole/soul
   The _____ of my shoe is worn out.   sole/soul

f There's a _____ in my new jumper.   hole/whole
   The economic problems are affecting the _____ world.   hole/whole

Encontrando a definição correta

Definition (definição) é a explicação do significado de uma palavra no dicionário. Ao encontrar o verbete correto, você pode achar mais de uma definição. Neste dicionário, as definições estão em ordem de frequência: as mais comuns vêm em primeiro lugar e assim por diante.

Exercício 9
Observe novamente as frases do exercício 7. Em cada frase, escreva o número da definição correta. Se houver apenas uma definição, escreva 1.

Exercício 10
Observe as seguintes frases. Depois, procure as aplicações de set no dicionário e decida a melhor para se adequar a cada frase.

a   Our teacher has set us some exercises for homework.

b   The sun sets at 8pm.

c   Wait for the glue to set before you paint it.

d   When are you going to set a date for your wedding?

e   I have to catch a plane tomorrow, so I've set my alarm for 7am.

f   The film is set in Rome and New York.

g   I set up my business in 1995.

h   He was set free after 15 years in prison.

Usando o dicionário para aprender mais informações sobre as palavras

O dicionário pode oferecer-lhe mais informações a respeito de uma palavra. Por exemplo, você pode aprender quais outras palavras são usadas com um verbete e suas informações gramaticais. Você pode procurar nas definições e nos quadros de explicações extras.

Exercício 11
Use o dicionário para descobrir as respostas para estas perguntas. A palavra que você precisa pesquisar no dicionário está em **negrito**.

a   Which of these sentences is wrong, and why?
    Our holiday was **absolutely** wonderful.
    Our holiday was **absolutely** OK.

b   Which word is needed to complete the sentence below?
    He told me the secret _____ **accident**.

c   What is wrong with the following sentence?
    We **accompanied** him at the airport.

d   Find three things that you can **protect** somebody from.

e   What is the difference between a **hedge** and a **fence**?

f   Find two things that can be **first-class**.

g   Name two things that you can **roast**.

h   Does the Earth **roll**, spin or revolve around the sun?

i   Which is bigger, a **van** or a truck?

j   What is the plural of the word **accommodation**?

k   Which word completes the following sentence?
    I'm going to _____ a **rest** before I go to the shops.

l   Name three places where you might make a **reservation**.

m   Complete the following sentences using expressions with the word **hand**.
    They walked _____ _____ down the street.
    You must _____ _____ with your mother when you cross the road.
    Let me _____ you a _____ with that heavy suitcase.
    You should _____ _____ with him when you meet him for the first time.

Exercício 12
O dicionário também pode ajudar você a encontrar as preposições indicadas para cada palavra. Verifique os seguintes verbos no dicionário e escolha a preposição correta para preencher os espaços. Use a mesma preposição para preencher os espaços das frases de exemplos.

Verbo + Preposição (verb + preposition)
a   accuse someone _____ sth
    The police accused him _____ murder.

Usando o dicionário para aprender mais informações sobre as palavras 33

b agree _____ someone
Janet agrees _____ me.

c apply _____ something
I have applied _____ a job in Australia.

d approve _____ something
They didn't approve _____ my behaviour.

e argue _____ someone
Katerina argues _____ her boyfriend about everything!

f ask _____ something
Shall I ask the waiter _____ some water?

g blame someone _____ something
Alex blamed me _____ the accident.

h borrow something _____ someone
Can I borrow £10 _____ you?

i hope _____ something
I'm hoping _____ good weather for our holidays.

j insist _____ something
His parents always insist _____ good behaviour.

k lend something _____ someone
It was raining, so Max lent his umbrella _____ me.

l listen _____ something/someone
Please listen _____ me when I'm talking!

m pay _____ something
My uncle paid _____ my plane ticket and hotel room.

n prepare _____ something
We need to prepare _____ the bad weather.

o prevent someone _____ doing something
The police prevented them _____ entering the building.

p provide someone _____ something
The hotel provides its guests _____ all meals.

q suffer _____ something
He's suffered _____ a bad back for many years.

r talk _____ someone
If you need to talk _____ someone, please call me.

s thank someone _____ something
I thanked them _____ their kindness.

t wait _____ someone/something
I'll wait _____ you outside the cinema.

u worry _____ something
Susie's very worried _____ her exams, but she'll be fine!

34 Usando o dicionário para aprender mais informações sobre as palavras

Exercício 13
Adjetivo + preposição (adjective + preposition)
Procure os seguintes adjetivos no dicionário e escolha a preposição correta para preencher os espaços. Use a mesma preposição para preencher os espaços nas frases de exemplos.

a afraid _____ something/someone
  The children are afraid _____ the dark.

b ashamed _____ someone/something
  You behaved very badly, and I'm ashamed _____ you.

c aware _____ something
  Mina was not aware _____ the time and missed her train.

d different _____ something
  I like this dress – it's different _____ all the others.

e fond _____ something/someone
  Mr Morrison is very fond _____ his grandchildren.

f good _____ something
  Elizabeth is very good _____ maths.

g guilty _____ something
  He told the judge that he was not guilty _____ the crime.

h interested _____ something
  Mia is very interested _____ horses.

i keen _____ something
  Joe is keen _____ riding his bike.

j proud _____ something/someone
  Cathy's son came first in the exam. She's very proud _____ him.

k sick _____ something
  I'm sick _____ this terrible weather!

l similar _____ something
  Your shoes are very similar _____ mine.

m tired _____ something
  We're tired _____ going to the same place on holiday every year. We want to go somewhere different.

Exercício 14
Substantivo + preposição (noun + preposition)
Procure os seguintes substantivos no dicionário e escolha a preposição correta para preencher os espaços. Use a mesma preposição para preencher os espaços nas frases de exemplos.

a answer _____
  Do you know the answer _____ question 3?

b attack _____
  There has been an attack _____ the airport.

c _____ average
  _____ average, I get about 7 hours' sleep every night.

Usando o dicionário para aprender mais informações sobre as palavras

d decrease _____
There has been a decrease _____ unemployment this month.

e disadvantage _____
One disadvantage _____ living here is that the weather is terrible.

f _____ a hurry
I was _____ such a hurry that I forgot my keys.

g increase _____
There's been a big increase _____ the number of homeless people.

h need _____
There is a need _____ more food for the people in the earthquake area.

i reaction _____
What was her reaction _____ the news?

j reason _____
Noriko didn't give any reason _____ her behaviour.

k result _____
Have you got the result _____ your tests yet?

l solution _____
There is no easy solution _____ this problem.

Exercício 15

O dicionário também pode indicar-lhe outras palavras que acompanhem o verbete. As palavras *make* e *do* frequentemente trazem problemas para os estudantes de inglês porque, em alguns idiomas, apenas uma palavra é usada para ambos os verbos (é o caso da língua portuguesa). Procure as seguintes palavras no dicionário e indique quais delas são usadas com *make* e *do*.

a _____ an **arrangement**

b _____ your **best**

c _____ **business**

d _____ a **decision**

e _____ someone a **favour**

f _____ **friends**

g _____ **homework**

h _____ a **job**

i _____ a **mess**

j _____ a **mistake**

k _____ **money**

l _____ a **noise**

m _____ a **phone call**

n _____ the **washing-up**

Pronúncia

O dicionário pode mostrar-lhe a pronúncia de uma palavra. Depois de cada verbete, você verá os símbolos de sua pronúncia. Há uma tabela completa desses símbolos na **página 2 deste dicionário**. Esses símbolos são muito úteis porque pode ser difícil descobrir a pronúncia de uma palavras apenas por sua grafia.

Exercício 16
Usando a tabela de pronúncia no **página 2**, descubra quais são as palavras a seguir. Tenha cuidado com a grafia, – especialmente a das vogais.

a /blæk/ _____
b /ˈzebrə/ _____
c /sʌm/ _____
d /ˈkɑːpɪt/ _____
e /pleɪt/ _____
f /əˈbʌv/ _____
g /dʒiːnz/ _____
h /ˈjeləʊ/ _____
i /ʃɔːt/ _____
j /ˈiːzɪ/ _____

Fonema diferentes, mesma pronúncia

Exercício 17
As palavras seguintes têm exatamente a mesma grafia, mas são pronunciadas de forma diferente quando indicam sentidos diferentes. Use o guia de pronúncia no **página 2** e o dicionário para decidir a pronúncia correta.

a /liːd/ /led/

The inside of your pencil is called the **lead**. _____
You must keep yo ur dog on a **lead** in the park. _____

b /kləʊz/ /kləʊs/

Please **close** the door behind you. _____
Don't sit too **close** to the fire. _____

c /wɪnd/ /waɪnd/

Wind the scarf around your neck to keep you warm. _____
Listen to the **wind** in the trees. _____

d /tɪə(r)z/ /teə(r)z/

There were large **tears** in the curtains. _____
Magda burst into **tears** when she heard the news. _____

Pronúncia 37

e /rəʊ/ /raʊ/

Jack and Sophie had a huge **row** last night. _____
There was a **row** of empty seats in front of us. _____

Exercício 18
Os seguintes pares de palavras têm grafias semelhantes, mas pronúncias diferentes entre si. Para cada palavra, decida qual som de vogal as letras em **negrito** possuem. Confira suas respostas consultando as palavras no dicionário. Use o guia de pronúncia na **página 2**.

c**o**mb b**o**mb
br**ea**k w**ea**k
n**ow** l**ow**
p**o**se l**o**se
sh**oe** t**oe**
l**o**rd w**o**rd
c**ou**gh t**ou**gh
m**ea**t gr**ea**t
w**o**rk f**o**rk

a /ɒ/ _____

b /ʌ/ _____

c /ɜː/ _____

d /iː/ _____

e /ɔː/ _____

f /uː/ _____

g /aʊ/ _____

h /əʊ/ _____

i /eɪ/ _____

Diferentes grafias, mesma pronúncia

Exercício 19
Você pode observar no exercício 8 que alguns sons possuem diferentes grafias. Escolha duas palavras para cada som de vogal abaixo. O som das vogais nas palavras estão em **negrito**.

b**ir**d   n**ea**t
d**ay**   p**ai**n
bl**ue**   r**u**n
fl**oo**d   thr**ough**
gr**ee**t   w**o**rd

a /ʌ/ _____

b /ɜː/_____

38 Pronúncia

c /iː/ _____

d /uː/ _____

e /eɪ/ _____

Mudanças da sílaba tônica

O dicionário também pode mostrar-lhe onde cai o acento tônico de uma palavra. O símbolo ['] mostra que o acento tônico ocorre na sílaba (parte da palavra) seguinte ao sinal. Por exemplo, se você verificar a pronúncia da palavra *abandon*, pode notar que o acento tônico cai na segunda sílaba.

/əˈbændən/ = a-**ban**-don

Exercício 20

Algumas palavras com mais de uma classe gramatical possuem o mesmo som, mas acento tônico diferente para cada uma dessas classes. Nas seguintes frases, encontre a classe gramatical correta para a palavra em **negrito** e depois anote a pronúncia correta (incluindo os sinais do acento tônico) no exercício.

	part of speech	pronunciation
1	I gave her a Christmas **present**.	_____
2	Who is going to **present** the prize?	_____
3	He visited the **desert** when he was in Morrocco.	_____
4	How could he **desert** his family?	_____
5	He broke the world **record**.	_____
6	You need to **record** the results in this chart.	_____
7	The countries of the Middle East **produce** much of the world's oil.	_____
8	They sell their **produce** at local markets.	_____

Letras mudas

Exercício 21

Algumas palavras em inglês possuem letras sem nenhuma pronúncia. Por exemplo, a letra "b" na palavra *thumb* é uma letra muda. Em cada palavra a seguir, descubra qual letra é muda. Verifique a pronúncia no dicionário para descobrir as respostas.

a castle

b comb

c honest

d listen

e wrong

Phrasal verbs

Phrasal verbs são verbos formados por uma ou mais palavras. *Get up* é um phrasal verb. No exercício 5, nós explicamos que os phrasal verbs aparecem depois da entrada do verbete, em ordem alfabética.

Os phrasal verbs podem ser difíceis para os estudantes usarem adequadamente, mas o dicionário pode ajudá-los. Há diferentes tipos de phrasal verbs, e eles funcionam de modos diferentes. Observe abaixo os phrasal verbs que aparecem com o verbo *get* no dicionário:

◆ PHRASAL VERBS **get away with something** to avoid being punished or criticized ☐ *I'm hoping to miss the next meeting, if I can get away with it.* **get on 1** to make progress ☐ *+ with I need to get on with my work.* ☐ *How are you getting on in your new job?* **2** to be friendly ☐ *Pierre and Alex don't really get on.* **get out of something** to avoid doing something ☐ *He'll do anything to get out of the washing up.* **get over something** to feel better after being ill or unhappy ☐ *He never really got over his wife's death.* **get round to doing something** to do something that you have been intending to do ☐ *I'd like to do more exercise, but I never seem to get round to it.* **get through** to manage to talk to someone on the telephone ☐ *I tried to ring her, but I couldn't get through.* **get through something** to reach the end of a difficult situation ☐ *It was a terrible illness, but his determination helped to get him through it.* **get (someone) up** to wake up and get out of bed ☐ *I always get up early.* ☐ *My Dad gets me up in the morning.*

---

a. phrasal verbs intransitivos (intransitive phrasal verbs)

get through (*manage to talk to someone on the telephone* = conseguir entrar em contato com alguém por telefone) é um *intransitive verb* (**verbo intransitivo**); ele não possui um objeto direto. No dicionário, você pode verificar os intransitivos *phrasal verbs* porque eles não se direcionam para alguém ou para alguma coisa no verbete.

Quais outros phrasal verbs do verbo *get* são intransitivos?

b. phrasal verbs transitivos (transitive phrasal verbs)

Outros phrasal verbs são **transitivos**: possuem um objeto direto. Existem três tipos principais de (phrasal verbs transitivos) *transitive phrasal verbs*:

get over something é um phrasal verb **inseparável** (*inseparable*). Seu objeto (alguma coisa) sempre se coloca **depois** do phrasal verb. You **get over an illness**, you do not ~~get an illness over~~.

Você pode verificar os phrasal verbs inseparáveis no dicionário porque eles se direcionam a alguma coisa ou a alguém **depois** deles.

Quais outros phrasal verbs do verbo *get* são inseparáveis?

Outros phrasal verbs são **separáveis** (*separable*). O objeto desses verbos pode se colocar **no meio** do phrasal verb ou **depois** dele. Quando o objeto for um pronome (he / she / it etc.), sempre ocorre no meio do phrasal verb. Não há phrasal verbs separáveis com o verbo *get*. Entretanto, se você procurar com o verbo *do*, encontrará um phrasal verb separável:

Pronúncia

◆ PHRASAL VERBS **do something up**
1 to fasten a piece of clothing ▫ *Do your jacket up.*
2 to repair or decorate a room or building **do without (something)** to manage without some thing

do something up é um phrasal verb separável. Você pode verificar isso no dicionário porque **alguma coisa** aparece no meio do phrasal verb. Assim, você pode dizer "*Do your jacket up*" ou "*Do up your jacket*", mas você deve dizer sempre "*Do it up*", e "*não Do up it*"

Alguns phrasal verbs podem ser usados com ou sem um objeto direto. Nesses verbos, os objetos aparecem entre parênteses no verbete. *Get (someone) up* é um exemplo. Você também pode observar que este verbo tem um objeto e é separável, porque a palavra *someone* está no meio do phrasal verb. Você pode ver nos exemplos como devemos usar este verbo:

I always get up early. (no object)
My Dad gets me up in the morning. (object)

do without é usado também com ou sem um objeto, mas é inseparável, de modo que o objeto sempre apareça depois do phrasal verb.

We didn't have much money for luxuries, so we did without. (sem objeto)
We didn't have much money, so we did without a car. (objeto depois do phrasal verb)
We couldn't afford the car, so we did without it. (pronome objeto depois do phrasal verb)
We couldn't afford the car, so we did it without.

Exercício 22

Procure a seção de phrasal verbs do verbo *take* neste dicionário. Use as informações acima e as informações do dicionário para indicar se as frases abaixo estão corretas ou não. Se estiverem incorretas, corrija-as. Os phrasal verbs estão em **negrito** nas frases abaixo:

a   The plane **took off** the ground.
b   Noah **took off** his shoes and sat down.
c   He **takes** his father **after**. They both have a great sense of humour.
d   I love riding horses. I **took up** it when I was a child.
e   I **took up** yoga when I had a bad back.
f   Oh that's the doorbell. Could you **take** this **over** while I answer it?
g   I **took** his phone number **down** on a piece of paper.
h   The police **took down** our names.
i   What time does your flight **take off**?
j   Are you hot in your coat? Why don't you **take** it **off**?

Referências cruzadas

Em algumas entradas de verbetes, você encontrará **referências cruzadas** (*cross references*). Essas referências mostram onde no dicionário você poderá encontrar mais informações sobre determinada palavra. Um dos tipos de *cross reference* mostra onde você pode encontrar mais informações sobre expressões idiomáticas ou locuções. Essa tarefa pode ser difícil se você não souber qual palavra procurar. Por exemplo, no verbete *have* há uma *cross reference* com *cake*.

---

have³ /hæv/ VERB [has, having, had]
1 used for describing someone or something ▫ *He has got black hair.* ▫ *The room had patches of damp on the walls.* ▫ *The soup had a delicious flavour.* (**ter**)
2 to own something ▫ *He has a house in Spain.* ▫ *I have got three brothers.* ▫ *She has the determination to win.* (**ter**)

Isso significa que você deve procurar o ícone **idiom** *have your cake and eat it* no verbete *cake*. Se você buscar por *cake*, irá descobrir o significado da expressão:

---

cake /keɪk/ NOUN [*plural* cakes] a sweet food made from a baked mixture, usually of flour, sugar, butter and eggs ▫ *a birthday cake* ▫ *He made a cake for the school fair.* ▫ *Would you like another slice of chocolate cake?* (**bolo**)

♦ IDIOM **have your cake and eat it** to get all the advantages of a situation in a way that is unfair (**levar todas as vantagens**)

Exercício 23
Procure cada uma destas palavras no dicionário. Em cada verbete, você encontrará uma *cross reference* para uma expressão idiomática. Anote abaixo a expressão e, depois, use a *cross reference* para descobrir uma definição para essa mesma expressão.

	idiom	definition
heart		
catch		
pull		
take		
turn¹		

Algumas *cross references* informam sobre algumas palavras americanas. Os falantes do inglês britânico e os do inglês americano às vezes usam palavras diferentes para descrever a mesma coisa. Se você procurar uma palavra americana neste dicionário, geralmente encontrará uma *cross reference* para uma palavra britânica, na qual poderá descobrir a definição.

Exercício 24
Use seu dicionário para encontrar as palavras britânicas correspondentes às palavras americanas a seguir:

a   candy

b   chip

42 Referências cruzadas

c grade
d homicide
e jelly
f line

Exercício 25

Algumas vezes, a referência cruzada ou a definição indicam a você que a grafia em inglês britânico é diferente. Novamente a informação principal estará na entrada da palavra britânica. Qual é a grafia britânica para as seguintes palavras? Use o dicionário para obter ajuda.

a favorite
b gray
c theater

Resolução dos exercícios

Exercício 1
American
bicycle
burglar
cat
goose
keyboard
microphone
sun
teacher
wind

Exercício 2
ballet
biology
birthday
biscuit
blouse
bouquet
box
bridge
broccoli
building

Exercício 3
make-up
microwave oven
middle class
midnight
mineral water
mobile phone
modal verb
moonlight
mother-in-law
MP3 player

Exercício 4
BBC
Boxing Day
certificate
Christmas tree
cm
HQ
ID
mm
traffic jam
traffic lights

Exercício 5
get away with
get on
get out of something
get over something
get round to doing something
get through
get through something
get up

Exercício 6
a verb
   noun

b adjective
   noun

c noun
   verb

d adverb
   conjunction

e verb
   noun

Exercício 7

a v, pick 1
   n, pick 2

b v, pin 2
   n, pin 1

c n, place 1
   v, place 2

d a, plastic 2
   n, plastic 1

e v, present 3
   n, present 1
   a, present 2

Exercício 8

a Would you like an apple or a pear?
   I've just bought a new pair of trousers.

b Would you like some more sauce on your pasta?
   The country's main source of energy is oil.

c Which coat is yours?
   The witch in the story wore a big black hat.

d My plane leaves at 4.30, so I must leave now.
   We've painted the walls plain white.

e Yukiko loves soul music.
   The sole of my shoe is worn out.

f There's a hole in my new jumper.
   The economic problems are affecting the whole world.

Exercício 9

a definition 2, definition 1

b definition 2, definition 1

c definition 6, definition 1

d definition 1, definition 1

e definition 1, definition 1, definition 2

Exercício 10

a 7
b 6
c 10
d 2
e 5
f 4
g phrasal verb *set something up*
h 9

Exercício 11

a A frase 2 está errada. A palavra "*absolutely*" significando "extremely" só é usada antes de adjetivos com sentidos muito fortes. Então, "*absolutely wonderful*" está correto, mas "*absolutely OK*" está errado.

b by accident (sense 2)

c The correct preposition is *to* (sense 1): *We accompanied him **to** the airport*.

d harm, danger (in definition), frost (in example)

e a hedge is made of bushes or trees, a fence is made of wood or metal.

f a ticket, a stamp (in examples)

g meat, vegetables (in definition)

h The Earth *revolves* around the sun (see the Thesaurus box).

i a truck (in definition)

j it has no plural (in part of speech and in usage box)

Resolução dos exercícios 45

k *I'm going to **have** a rest.* (in example for definition 2)

l a restaurant, a hotel, a plane (in definition)

m *hand in hand, hold hands, give you a hand, shake hands*

Exercício 12
a of
b with
c for
d of
e with
f for
g for
h from
i for
j on
k to
l to
m for
n for
o from
p with
q from
r to
s for
t for
u about

Exercício 13
a of
b of
c of
d from
e of
f at
g of
h in
i on
j of
k of
l to
m of

Exercício 14
a to
b on
c on
d in
e of
f in
g in
h for
i to
j for
k of
l to

Exercício 15
a make
b do
c do
d make
e do
f make
g do
h do
i make
j make
k make
l make
m make
n do

Exercício 16
a black
b zebra
c sum
d carpet
e plate
f above
g jeans
h yellow
i short
j easy

Resolução dos exercícios

Exercício 17
a /led/, /liːd/
b /kləʊz/, /kləʊs/
c /waɪnd/, /wɪnd/
d /teə(r)z/, /tɪə(r)z/
e /raʊ/, /rəʊ/

Exercício 18
a bomb, cough
b tough
c word, work
d weak, meat
e lord, fork
f lose, shoe
g now
h comb, low, pose, toe
i break, great

Exercício 19
a flood, run
b bird, word
c greet, neat
d blue, through
e day, pain

Exercício 20

		part of speech	pronunciation
1	I gave her a Christmas **present**.	noun	/ˈprezənt/
2	Who is going to **present** the prize?	verb	/prɪˈzent/
3	He visited the **desert** when he was in Morrocco.	noun	/dɪˈzɜːt/
4	How could he **desert** his family?	verb	/ˈdezət/
5	He broke the world **record**.	noun	/ˈrekɔːd/
6	You need to **record** the results in this chart.	verb	/rɪˈkɔːd/
7	The countries of the Middle East **produce** much of the world's oil.	verb	/prəˈdjuːs/
8	They sell their **produce** at local markets.	noun	/ˈprɒdjuːs/

Exercício 21
a castle – silent t
b comb – silent b
c honest – silent h
d listen – silent t
e wrong – silent w

Exercício 22
a *The plane took off.* (*take off* é um verbo intransitivo, portanto, não possui um objeto direto)
b correto (*take off* é separável neste sentido, de modo que o objeto vai para o meio ou para o final do phrasal verb quando não for um pronome.)
c *He takes after his father.* (*take after* é inseparável, o objeto deve estar após o phrasal verb.)

Resolução dos exercícios 47

d   *I took it up when I was a child.* (*take up* é separável, então o pronome vai sempre para o meio do phrasal verb.)

e   correto (o objeto pode ir para o meio ou para depois do verbo se não for um pronome.)

f   *Could you take over while I answer it?* (*take over* é um verbo intransitivo, de modo que não possui um objeto direto.)

g   correto (*take down* é separável, de modo que o objeto pode ir para o meio ou para depois do verbo se não for um pronome.)

h   correto (*take down* é separável, de modo que o objeto pode ir para o meio ou para depois do verbo se não for um pronome.)

i   correto (*take off* é intransitivo neste sentido, não possuindo, então, objeto direto.)

j   correto (*take off* é separável, de modo que o pronome vai sempre para o meio do phrasal verb.)

Exercício 23

	idiom	definition
heart	break someone's heart	to make someone very unhappy
catch	catch someone's eye	if something catches your eye, you notice it
pull	pull your socks up	to try to improve your behaviour or work
take	take your breath away	to surprise you very much
turn¹	turn your nose up at something	to refuse to accept something because you do not think it is good enough for you

Exercício 24

a   sweet   c   form   e   jam
b   crisp   d   murder   f   queue

Exercício 25

a   favourite   b   grey   c   theatre

A a

A ou **a** /eɪ/ the first letter of the alphabet (a primeira letra do alfabeto)

a ou **an** /ən/ DETERMINER
1 used before a noun to refer to one person or thing but not a particular person or thing □ *I need a pen.* □ *I'd love to have a baby.* (um, uma)
2 one □ *a hundred miles* (um, uma)
3 each or every □ *He gets £5 a week.* (por)

> ➤ Remember to use **an** (and not **a**) before a word that begins with a vowel, or a word that sounds as if it begins with a vowel □ *a bag* □ *an apple* □ *an hour*

abandon /əˈbændən/ VERB [**abandons, abandoning, abandoned**] to leave someone or something, often not intending to go back □ *He abandoned the car and walked the rest of the way.* □ *How could she abandon her family like that?* (abandonar)

abbreviation /əˌbriːviˈeɪʃən/ NOUN [plural **abbreviations**] a short form of a word or phrase □ + *of UK is an abbreviation of United Kingdom.* (abreviação)

ABC /ˌeɪbiːˈsiː/ NOUN [plural **ABCs**] the alphabet □ *The children were learning their ABC.* (abecedário)

abdomen /ˈæbdəmən/ NOUN [plural **abdomens**] the part of an animal or person's body that contains the stomach (abdome)

abduct /æbˈdʌkt/ VERB [**abducts, abducting, abducted**] to take someone away by using force □ *Two more tourists have been abducted from their hotel room.* (raptar)

ability /əˈbɪlɪti/ NOUN [plural **abilities**] someone who has the ability to do something is able to do it or has the skill to do it □ + *to do something Not everyone has the ability to play a musical instrument.* (capacidade)

> ➤ Remember that **ability** is followed by the structure *to do something*:
> ✓ her ability to drive
> ✗ her ability of driving

able /ˈeɪbəl/ ADJECTIVE **able to do something** if you are able to do something, you can do it □ *He wasn't able to run fast enough.* □ *Will you be able to help me?* (capaz)

abnormal /æbˈnɔːməl/ ADJECTIVE not normal, especially in a way that worries you □ *This is abnormal behaviour for a five-year-old.* (anormal)

abolish /əˈbɒlɪʃ/ VERB [**abolishes, abolishing, abolished**] to get rid of a rule or a way of doing something □ *The school has abolished its uniform.* (abolir)

abolition /ˌæbəˈlɪʃən/ NOUN, NO PLURAL getting rid of a law or a way of doing something □ *the abolition of slavery* (abolição)

about¹ /əˈbaʊt/ PREPOSITION
1 on the subject of □ *a book about bats* □ *a talk about Spain* (sobre)
2 in different parts of a place □ *Clothes were scattered about the room.* (aqui e ali, por)
3 What about/How about something? used to make a suggestion □ *How about going for a walk?* (que tal?)

about² /əˈbaʊt/ ADVERB
1 not exactly but almost the number or amount given □ *about five years ago* □ *about four centimetres* (cerca de)
2 in or to different parts of a place □ *We started moving things about.* □ *They were running about all day.* (por)
3 about to do something if you are about to do something, you are going to do it very soon □ *I was about to leave when the phone rang.* □ *I think it's about to rain.* (estar prestes a)

above /əˈbʌv/ PREPOSITION, ADVERB
1 in a higher position than something else □ *the shelf above the sink* □ *clouds in the sky above* (cima, acima)
2 more than an amount or level □ *two degrees above zero* □ *in the class above me* (acima de)
3 above all more than anything else □ *Above all, I'm grateful to my parents.* (acima de tudo)

abroad /əˈbrɔːd/ ADVERB in or to a foreign country 🔂 *We always go abroad for our holidays.* □ *She's abroad at the moment.* (no exterior)

abrupt /əˈbrʌpt/ ADJECTIVE
1 sudden and unexpected □ *The driver made an abrupt change of direction.* (abrupto, repentino)
2 rude and unfriendly 🔂 *She has rather an abrupt manner.* (abrupto, rude)

absence /ˈæbsəns/ NOUN [plural **absences**] being away from a place □ *Your absence from the meeting was noticed.* (ausência)

absent

absent /ˈæbsənt/ ADJECTIVE not at a place where you are expected to be □ *+ from She has been absent from school twice this week.* □ *Is anyone absent today?* (ausente)

> THESAURUS: If you are absent, you are not at a place where you are expected to be. For example, you might be absent from school or work because you are ill. If you are **away** from work, you might be out of the office on business or on holiday. If a person is **missing**, they are not where you expect them to be, and you do not know where they are. If a person or thing has **gone**, it was in a place, but now it is no longer there.

absolute /ˈæbsəluːt/ ADJECTIVE complete □ *I have absolute trust in her.* □ *That's absolute rubbish!* (absoluto)

absolutely /ˈæbsəluːtli/ ADVERB
1 completely □ *Are you absolutely sure you locked the door?* (absolutamente)
2 extremely □ *This cake is absolutely delicious!* □ *That's absolutely ridiculous!* (absolutamente, extremamente)
3 used to agree or to give permission □ *'We should write and thank them'. 'Absolutely'.* (absolutamente)

> **Absolutely** meaning 'extremely' is only used before adjectives with very strong meanings:
> ✓ *That's absolutely crazy.*
> ✗ *That's absolutely silly.*
> ✓ *She's absolutely beautiful.*
> ✗ *She's absolutely pretty.*

absorb /əbˈsɔːb/ VERB [absorbs, absorbing, absorbed] to take up liquid and keep it inside □ *The bath mat will absorb the splashes.* (absorver)

absorbent /əbˈsɔːbənt/ ADJECTIVE an absorbent material is able to take up liquid and keep it inside □ *absorbent kitchen towels* (absorvente)

absorbing /əbˈsɔːbɪŋ/ ADJECTIVE very interesting and taking all your attention □ *an absorbing puzzle* (cativante, interessante)

absurd /əbˈsɜːd/ ADJECTIVE very silly □ *What an absurd idea!* (absurdo)

abuse¹ /əˈbjuːs/ NOUN [plural abuses]
1 using something the wrong way for a bad reason □ *This is an abuse of power.* □ *alcohol abuse* (= drinking too much alcohol) (abuso)
2 violence or bad treatment □ *child abuse* (maustratos)
3 insults □ *They shouted abuse at us.* (injurioso)
• **abusive** /əˈbjuːsɪv/ ADJECTIVE rude or insulting □ *abusive language* (injurioso)

abuse² /əˈbjuːz/ VERB [abuses, abusing, abused]
1 to use something the wrong way for a bad purpose □ *She abused people's trust in order to steal money from them.* (abusar)
2 to hurt someone or to treat them badly □ *He was abused in prison.* (abusar de, insultar)

> The noun **abuse** ends with an **ss** sound. The verb **abuse** ends with a **z** sound.

access

academic /ˌækəˈdemɪk/ ADJECTIVE to do with studying and education □ *academic qualifications* □ *the academic year* (acadêmico)

academy /əˈkædəmi/ NOUN [plural academies]
1 a school or college where you learn about a particular subject □ *a science academy* (academia)
2 an organization that supports a particular subject □ *the Academy of Ancient Music* (academia)

accelerate /əkˈseləreɪt/ VERB [accelerates, accelerating, accelerated] to drive faster □ *She accelerated round the corner.* (acelerar)

accent /ˈæksent/ NOUN [plural accents]
1 the way people from a particular area pronounce words □ *I have a Scottish accent.* □ *I speak German with a strong English accent.* (sotaque)
2 a mark over a letter that shows how to pronounce it, for example in the word 'café' (sotaque)

> THESAURUS: Your **accent** is the way that you say words, according to where you come from. For example, you may speak English with a Scottish accent or a German accent. **Pronunciation** is the sound of a word or a letter. **Tone** refers to the feeling with which you speak a word, for example, your **tone** of voice may be angry or kind.

accept /əkˈsept/ VERB [accepts, accepting, accepted]
1 to take something that someone offers you □ *+ from He accepted some food from us.* □ *She won't accept help from anyone.* (aceitar)
2 to say yes to an invitation □ *We've accepted his invitation to lunch.* (aceitar)
3 to agree that something is true □ *+ that I accept that I was wrong and I'm sorry.* (aceitar)

acceptable /əkˈseptəbəl/ ADJECTIVE good enough □ *This kind of behaviour isn't acceptable!* (aceitável)

acceptance /əkˈseptəns/ NOUN, NO PLURAL
1 taking something that is given or offered to you □ *We are delighted about her acceptance of the job.* (aceitação)
2 when you agree that something is true, good or necessary □ *His ideas on education never gained acceptance.* (aceitação)

access /ˈækses/ NOUN, NO PLURAL
1 when you are able to see or use something □ *+to They don't have access to a doctor.* □ *Do you have Internet access?* (acesso)
2 a way of getting to or entering a place □ *+to The builders will need access to the house while you're out at work.* (acesso)
• **accessible** /əkˈsesəbəl/ ADJECTIVE
1 easy to get to □ *The house is not very accessible.* (acessível)
2 easy to see and use □ *We make the information accessible to the public.* (acessível)
3 easy to understand □ *Make sure you use clear, accessible language.* (acessível)

accident

accident /ˈæksɪdənt/ NOUN [plural **accidents**]
1 a bad thing that happens that is not intended ▫ *Don's had an accident.* ▫ *a serious/fatal accident* ▫ *She was injured in a road traffic accident.* ▫ *I'm sorry I broke your clock – it was an accident.* (acidente)
2 by accident if something happens by accident, it is not intended ▫ *I dropped the glass by accident and it smashed.* (por acidente)

accidental /ˌæksɪˈdentəl/ ADJECTIVE not intended ▫ *There was a lot of accidental damage.* (acidental)

accidentally /ˌæksɪˈdentəli/ ADVERB by accident ▫ *I accidentally shut the car door and locked my keys inside.* (acidentalmente)

accommodate /əˈkɒmədeɪt/ VERB [**accommodates, accommodating, accommodated**]
1 to find someone a place to stay ▫ *The whole group can be accommodated in the same hotel.* (acomodar)
2 to be big enough for someone or something ▫ *This room could easily accommodate ten people.* (acomodar)

accommodation /əˌkɒməˈdeɪʃən/ NOUN, NO PLURAL somewhere to stay or live ▫ *She's staying in rented accommodation.* ▫ *Does the college provide accommodation?* (acomodação)

> In UK English **accommodation** is never used in the plural:
> ✓ Accommodation is very expensive.
> ✗ Accommodations are very expensive.

accompany /əˈkʌmpəni/ VERB [**accompanies, accompanying, accompanied**]
1 to go with someone ▫ +*to* *We accompanied him to the station.* (acompanhar)
2 to play an instrument, especially the piano, while someone else sings a song or plays another instrument ▫ *Her sister usually accompanies her on the piano.* (acompanhar)

accomplish /əˈkʌmplɪʃ/ VERB [**accomplishes, accomplishing, accomplished**] to manage to do something ▫ *The children accomplished the task in a few minutes.* (realizar)

accomplishment /əˈkʌmplɪʃmənt/ NOUN [plural **accomplishments**] when you finish something successfully (realização)

according to /əˈkɔːdɪŋ tuː/ PREPOSITION
1 as said or written by someone ▫ *Hannah's ill, according to Lucy.* ▫ *According to the dictionary, there are two m's in 'accommodation'.* (de acordo com)
2 using a particular measurement or system ▫ *You'll be paid according to how much work you have done.* ▫ *Everything went according to plan* (= happened as intended). (de acordo)

account /əˈkaʊnt/ NOUN [plural **accounts**]
1 a description of something that has happened ▫ *He gave an account of his journey.* (conta)
2 an arrangement with a bank to keep money there ▫ *I opened a savings account.* ▫ *Which account do you want to pay this cheque into?* (conta)

3 take something into account to consider something when you are thinking about a situation or a decision ▫ *Will they take my age into account when they decide who can go?* (levar algo em conta)
4 on no account certainly not ▫ *On no account are you to stay out after ten o'clock.* (sem chance)

> **THESAURUS:** An account or a description is something you write or say. A report is usually more formal and may be spoken (for example, a news report) or written. For example, teachers write reports on their students. A statement is an official report of something, which is often written. For example, a witness might make a statement to the police describing what they saw.

◆ PHRASAL VERB [**accounts, accounting, accounted**]
account for something to be the reason for something ▫ *The fact that it's her birthday accounts for all the visitors she's had today.* (contar por algo)

accounts /əˈkaʊnts/ PLURAL NOUN written records of the money received and spent by a person or organization (contas)

accumulate /əˈkjuːmjʊleɪt/ VERB [**accumulates, accumulating, accumulated**] to collect a number or amount of something, or to increase in number or amount ▫ *Greenhouse gases are accumulating in the Earth's atmosphere.* (acumular)

accuracy /ˈækjʊrəsi/ NOUN, NO PLURAL being exactly correct ▫ *Please check the accuracy of this measurement.* (precisão)

accurate /ˈækjʊrət/ ADJECTIVE exactly correct ▫ *an accurate description* ▫ *accurate measurements* ▫ *What they said was pretty accurate.* (correto)

accusation /ˌækjuːˈzeɪʃən/ NOUN [plural **accusations**] a statement saying that someone has done something bad ▫ *She has made some accusations against me.* ▫ *These are serious accusations.* (acusação)

accuse /əˈkjuːz/ VERB [**accuses, accusing, accused**] to say that someone has done something bad ▫ +*of* *He was accused of murder.* ▫ *Are you accusing me of lying?* (acusar)

ace /eɪs/ NOUN [plural **aces**] a playing card with one symbol on it which has the highest or lowest value in games ▫ *the ace of spades* (ás)

ache¹ /eɪk/ NOUN [plural **aches**] a pain which is not strong but continues for a long time ▫ *I started getting aches and pains.* ▫ *She could feel an ache in her back.* (dor)

ache² /eɪk/ VERB [**aches, aching, ached**] to hurt for a long time, especially in a way which is not strong ▫ *My arm aches from playing too much tennis.* (doer)

achieve /əˈtʃiːv/ VERB [**achieves, achieving, achieved**] to succeed in doing or getting something good, especially by trying hard ▫ *We have achieved* everything we wanted to do. □ *She has achieved a very high standard.* (**conquistar**)

achievement /əˈtʃiːvmənt/ NOUN [plural **achievements**] a success or a good result □ *Reaching the finals is a great achievement.* (**conquista**)

acid /ˈæsɪd/ NOUN [plural **acids**] a type of chemical. Strong acids can dissolve metals. A chemistry word. (**ácido**)

acknowledge /əkˈnɒlɪdʒ/ VERB [**acknowledges, acknowledging, acknowledged**]
1 to admit that something is true □ *I acknowledge that you were right.* (**admitir**)
2 to tell someone that you have got something they sent you □ *They never acknowledge my letters.* (**reconhecer**)

acquire /əˈkwaɪə(r)/ VERB [**acquires, acquiring, acquired**] a formal word meaning to get or to buy something □ *I managed to acquire a copy of the tape.* □ *A Russian billionaire recently acquired 25% of the company.* (**adquirir**)

acre /ˈeɪkə(r)/ NOUN [plural **acres**] a unit for measuring the area of land, equal to 4047 square metres (**acre**)

acrobat /ˈækrəbæt/ NOUN [plural **acrobats**] someone who performs skilful physical movements, like jumping and balancing, to entertain people (**acrobata**)

across /əˈkrɒs/ PREPOSITION, ADVERB
1 from one side of something to the other □ *a bridge across the river* □ *I ran across the road* □ *Don't run, but walk across quickly.* □ *clouds moving across the sky* (**transversalmente**)
2 on the opposite side □ *Their house is across the river from ours.* (**do lado oposto**)

act¹ /ækt/ VERB [**acts, acting, acted**]
1 to behave in a particular way □ *Stop acting like a baby!* ▣ *Police thought the man was acting suspiciously.* (**agir**)
2 to do something ▣ *The hospital acted quickly to solve the problem.* □ *We must act now to save the planet!* (**agir**)
3 to perform in a film or in the theatre +**in** *He has acted in more than 50 films.* (**atuar**)
♦ PHRASAL VERB **act as something** to have a particular effect or to do a particular job. □ *Our driver also acted as interpreter.* □ *The sheet acted as a curtain.* (**desempenhar a função de**)

act² /ækt/ NOUN [plural **acts**]
1 something that someone does ▣ *a terrorist act* ▣ *He was accused of committing a criminal act.* □ +**of** *an act of kindness* (**ato**)
2 a part of a theatre performance □ *He appears in the third act of the play.* (**ato**)
3 a short performance, or the people in the performance □ *a comedy act* (**ato**)

acting /ˈæktɪŋ/ NOUN, NO PLURAL performing in films or in the theatre □ *There was some brilliant acting in the film.* (**representação**)

action /ˈækʃən/ NOUN [plural **actions**]
1 something you do ▣ *We must take action to prevent a disaster.* ▣ *They need to decide on a course of action* (= what to do). □ *He has to take responsibility for his actions.* (**ação**)
2 the action what happens in the story of a film, book or theatre play ▣ *Most of the action takes place in America.* (**ação**)
3 out of action not working □ *My car's out of action at the moment.* (**quebrado**)

activate /ˈæktɪveɪt/ VERB [**activates, activating, activated**] to make something start working □ *Someone activated the fire alarm.* (**ativar**)

active /ˈæktɪv/ ADJECTIVE
1 busy doing things or involved in an activity □ +**in** *Her mum's very active in the drama club.* ▣ *He remained politically active throughout his life.* ▣ *Fathers are taking a more active role in their children's lives.* (**ativo**)
2 moving around a lot ▣ *She's still physically active.* ▣ *Try to keep active as you grow older.* (**ativo**)
3 in grammar, an active verb or sentence has a subject that performs the action of the verb, for example in the sentence 'The cat chased the mouse'. (**ativo**)

activist /ˈæktɪvɪst/ NOUN [plural **activists**] someone who tries to change society by doing things that people notice □ *animal rights activists* (**ativista**)

activity /ækˈtɪvəti/ NOUN [plural **activities**]
1 something you do, especially something you do for fun, in an organized way ▣ *Outdoor activities include sailing and horse riding.* ▣ *a variety of sporting activities* (**atividade**)
2 no plural being active or busy generally ▣ *Children need regular physical activity.* ▣ *There was a flurry of activity* (= a lot of things happening) *for a few days.* (**atividade**)

actor /ˈæktə(r)/ NOUN [plural **actors**] someone who performs in a film or in the theatre (**ator**)

actress /ˈæktrɪs/ NOUN [plural **actresses**] a woman who performs in a film or in the theatre (**atriz**)

actual /ˈæktʃuəl/ ADJECTIVE really true or exact ▣ *We guessed there were about 100 people but the actual number was 110.* (**real**)

> ➤ **Actual** means 'true' or 'exact'. It does not mean 'existing now'. Adjectives that mean 'existing now' are 'present' and 'current':
> ✓ *My current job involves a lot of travel.*
> ✗ *My actual job involves a lot of travel.*

actually /ˈæktʃuəli/ ADVERB
1 used to emphasize what is true □ *Actually, I haven't read any of his books.* □ *We haven't actually chosen a name yet.* (**na verdade**)
2 used to emphasize something surprising □ *Instead of improving, things have actually got worse.* (**na verdade**)

acute /ə'kju:t/ ADJECTIVE
1 an acute problem, especially an illness, is very bad □ *acute appendicitis* (agudo)
2 an acute angle is less than 90°. A mathematics word. (agudo)

AD /ˌeɪ'di:/ ABBREVIATION used before or after a date to show that the date was after the birth of Jesus Christ □ *95 AD (Anno Domini,* d.C. [depois de Cristo])
→ *go to* **BC**

ad /æd/ NOUN [plural **ads**] an informal short way to say or write **advertisement** (anúncio)

adapt /ə'dæpt/ VERB [**adapts, adapting, adapted**]
1 to change so that you become more happy or comfortable in a new situation □ *It didn't take long to adapt to the heat.* (adaptar)
2 to change something to make it more suitable □ *The design can be adapted for use in a variety of situations.* (ajustar)

adaptable /ə'dæptəbəl/ ADJECTIVE able to deal with new or different situations (adaptável)

add /æd/ VERB [adds, adding, added]
1 to put things together □ **+to** *Add the sugar to the egg mixture.* (adicionar)
2 to put two or more numbers or amounts together □ *Add two and two.* (somar)
3 to say or write something more □ *'You could take the letter yourself – if you don't mind?' he added.* □ **+ that** *A police spokesman added that the two arrests weren't linked.* (acrescentar)
◆ PHRASAL VERB **add (something) up** to find the total of numbers put together □ *Can you add these numbers up in your head?* (somar)

addict /'ædɪkt/ NOUN [plural **addicts**] someone who cannot stop taking a drug 🔁 *a drug addict* (viciado)

addiction /ə'dɪkʃən/ NOUN [plural **addictions**] not being able to stop taking a drug □ *alcohol addiction* (vício)

addition /ə'dɪʃən/ NOUN [plural additions]
1 in addition (to something) extra or added to something □ *The schools offer extra subjects in addition to the basic curriculum.* (além de)
2 no plural the process of adding numbers together □ *The pupils are learning simple addition.* (adição)
3 something that has been added or when something is added 🔁 *There are four new additions to our menu.* 🔁 *The changes include the addition of a swimming pool.* (acréscimos a)

address¹ /ə'dres/ NOUN [plural addresses]
1 the details of the building, the street and the town where someone lives □ *I'll give you my address and telephone number.* 🔁 *Here is a list of the names and addresses of all the members.* (endereço)
2 the numbers, letters and symbols that are used to send e-mails or to find pages on the Internet. A computing word 🔁 *What's your e-mail address?* 🔁 *Our web address is in the brochure.* (endereço de email)

address² /ə'dres/ VERB [addresses, addressing, addressed]
1 to write an address on an envelope (endereçar)
2 to speak to someone □ *Were you addressing me?* (dirigir-se a)

adequate /'ædɪkwət/ ADJECTIVE enough □ *Three rooms should be adequate for our family.* □ *There's an adequate supply of clean water.* (adequado)

adjective /'ædʒɪktɪv/ NOUN [plural adjectives]
a word that tells you something about a noun. For example, *difficult, good* and *stupid* are adjectives. (adjetivo)

adjust /ə'dʒʌst/ VERB [adjusts, adjusting, adjusted]
1 to change something slightly □ *I adjusted the clock by two minutes.* (ajustar)
2 to get used to a new situation □ *It was difficult to adjust to living in a flat.* (adaptar)

admiral /'ædmərəl/ NOUN [plural **admirals**] one of the most important officers in the navy (almirante)

admiration /ˌædmə'reɪʃən/ NOUN, NO PLURAL a feeling of admiring someone or something □ **+ for** *I have great admiration for her work.* (admiração)

admire /əd'maɪə(r)/ VERB [**admires, admiring, admired**]
1 to like and respect someone or something very much □ *He was someone I admired greatly.* □ **+ for** *I admired her for her courage in speaking out.* (admirar)
2 to enjoy looking at something 🔁 *We stopped at the top of the hill to admire the view.* (apreciar)

admission /əd'mɪʃən/ NOUN [plural admissions]
1 when someone goes into a place or joins a university or other organization □ *A sign on the door said 'No admission'.* □ *the university admissions process* (admissão)
2 no plural the cost of going into a place □ *We don't charge admission here.* □ *Adult admission is £10.* (ingresso)

admit /əd'mɪt/ VERB [admits, admitting, admitted]
1 to agree that you have done something bad □ **+ (that)** *I admit that I should have told you sooner.* □ **+to** *She admitted to cheating.* □ *He admitted his mistake.* (confessar)
2 to agree that something is true □ *I admit that this is a difficult exercise, but do your best.* (reconhecer)
3 to allow someone to go into a place or to take someone to hospital □ *They won't admit anyone wearing trainers.* □ **+ to** *The next morning he was admitted to hospital.* (permitir)

adolescence /ˌædə'lesəns/ ADJECTIVE to do with the period of your life between being a child and becoming an adult □ *Martha had a difficult adolescence.* (adolescência)

adolescent /ˌædə'lesənt/ NOUN [plural **adolescents**] someone older than a child, but not yet an adult □ *adolescent girls/boys* (adolescente)

adopt /ə'dɒpt/ VERB [**adopts, adopting, adopted**] to take someone else's child into your family and

adore /əˈdɔː(r)/ VERB [adores, adoring, adored] to love something or someone very much □ *She adores her father.* (**idolatrar**)

adult¹ /ˈædʌlt/ NOUN [plural adults] someone who is no longer a child □ *The activity is suitable for adults and children.* (**adulto**)

adult² /ˈædʌlt/ ADJECTIVE to do with or for adults □ *adult sizes* □ *The film is aimed at an adult audience.* (**adulto**)

advance¹ /ədˈvɑːns/ NOUN [plural advances]
1 in advance before something is needed or before a particular time □ *I arrived in advance to make sure everything was ready.* □ *We prepared all the food in advance.* (**adiantado**)
2 progress or new things □ *technological advances* □ *We have to keep up with the latest advances in medicine.* (**avanço**)
3 a movement towards a place by an army □ *The troops continued their advance on the city.* (**marcha**)

advance² /ədˈvɑːns/ VERB [advances, advancing, advanced]
1 to make progress □ *Technology is advancing rapidly.* (**progredir**)
2 to move forwards □ *The crowd advanced towards us.* □ *The army is advancing on our borders.* (**avançar**)

advanced /ədˈvɑːnst/ ADJECTIVE
1 the newest or most developed □ *the most technologically advanced facilities* (**desenvolvido**)
2 at a high academic level □ *an advanced Spanish course* □ *advanced students* (**avançado**)

advantage /ədˈvɑːntɪdʒ/ NOUN [plural advantages]
1 something good or helpful about a situation □ *+ of the advantages of working from home* □ *Being tall does have some advantages.* (**vantagem**)
2 something that helps you to succeed □ *+ over Max had an advantage over the others as he already spoke Italian.* ▣ *Her long legs give her an advantage in the high jump.* ▣ *an unfair advantage* (**vantagem**)
3 take advantage of something to use a situation well □ *We took advantage of the sunshine to get the clothes dry.* (**tirar vantagem**)
4 take advantage of someone to get what you want from someone in an unfair way □ *She's very generous and her children take advantage of her.* (**aproveitar**)

adventure /ədˈventʃə(r)/ NOUN [plural adventures] something exciting that happens to you □ *A visit to the jungle would be a real adventure for us.* (**aventura**)

adventurous /ədˈventʃərəs/ ADJECTIVE an adventurous person likes to do exciting new things □ *He's more adventurous than his brother.* (**ousado**)

adverb /ˈædvɜːb/ NOUN [plural adverbs] a word that you use to describe a verb or an adjective. For example, *really, badly, abroad* and *often* are adverbs. (**advérbio**)

advert /ˈædvɜːt/ NOUN [plural adverts] a short word for an **advertisement** (**propaganda**)

advertise /ˈædvətaɪz/ VERB [advertises, advertising, advertised] to tell people about something in order to persuade them to buy it or use it □ *They advertise their products in magazines.* (**anunciar**)

advertisement /ədˈvɜːtɪsmənt/ NOUN [plural advertisements] a picture, short article or film about something to persuade people to buy it or use it ▣ *a television/newspaper advertisement* □ *+ for I saw an advertisement for a new chocolate bar.* (**propaganda**)

advertising /ˈædvətaɪzɪŋ/ NOUN, NO PLURAL the business of making advertisements □ *She works in advertising.* ▣ *an advertising campaign* (**publicidade**)

advice /ədˈvaɪs/ NOUN, NO PLURAL suggestions about what you think someone should do ▣ *She gave me some good advice.* ▣ *I decided to take Jane's advice and go to the doctor's.* ▣ *May I offer a piece of advice?* □ *+ on They provide expert advice on career development.* (**conselho**)

> Remember that **advice** with a **c** is a noun and **advise** with an **s** is a verb □ *Can you give me some advice?* □ *Can you advise me?*

> Remember also that you say **any/some advice** and not 'an advice':
> ✓ *Can I give you some advice?*
> ✗ *Can I give you an advice?*
> To talk about one particular suggestion, use **piece of advice**: □ *Can I give you a piece of advice?*

advise /ədˈvaɪz/ VERB [advises, advising, advised] to tell someone what you think they should do □ *+ to do something They are advising motorists to drive carefully.* □ *+ against We advise against all travel to the region.* □ *+ on He advises us on financial matters.* (**aconselhar**)

aerial /ˈeəriəl/ NOUN [plural aerials] a piece of metal equipment for getting or sending radio or television signals ▣ *a television aerial* (**antena**)

aerobics /eəˈrəʊbɪks/ PLURAL NOUN exercises for the whole body that make your heart and lungs work hard (**aeróbica**)

aeroplane /ˈeərəpleɪn/ NOUN [plural aeroplanes] a flying vehicle that has wings and an engine □ *The aeroplane took off at midday.* (**avião**)

aerosol /ˈeərəsɒl/ NOUN [plural aerosols] a container with a part that you press to force out very small drops of liquid (**aerossol**)

affair /əˈfeə(r)/ NOUN [plural affairs]
1 affairs events or activities in a particular area of life, business, politics, etc. ▣ *He is very interested in foreign affairs* (= international politics). ▣ *She was responsible for the financial affairs of the club.* (**negócios**)

2 a situation or an event, especially a problem or something bad □ *Some people have criticized the way he handled the affair.* (questão)
3 a sexual relationship between two people, especially when one or both of them is married to someone else 🔲 *She had an affair with an older man.* (teve um romance)

affect /əˈfekt/ VERB [affects, affecting, affected]
to change, influence or cause harm to someone or something □ *The accident affected his eyesight.* □ *Were you affected by the floods?* (afetar)

> Be careful not to confuse **affect**, which is a verb, with **effect**, which is a noun □ *One thing affects another.* □ *One thing has an effect on another.*

affection /əˈfekʃən/ NOUN, NO PLURAL a strong feeling of liking someone or something □ *I have great affection for the town.* □ *My father rarely showed his affection.* (afeição)

affectionate /əˈfekʃənət/ ADJECTIVE showing that you like or love someone □ *Her mother gave her an affectionate kiss.* (carinhoso)

afford /əˈfɔːd/ VERB [affords, affording, afforded]
if you can afford something, you have enough money to pay for it □ *I can't afford a new dress.* □ **+ to do something** *We couldn't afford to go abroad.* (dispor)

afraid /əˈfreɪd/ ADJECTIVE
1 frightened or worried □ *There's no need to be afraid.* □ **+ of** *Small children are often afraid of dogs.* □ **+ that** *I was afraid that I'd fall.* □ **+ to do something** *Don't be afraid to tell me if you don't understand.* (amedrontado)
2 I'm afraid used to tell someone in a polite way that you cannot do something or to give them bad news □ *I'm afraid I don't know.* □ *Helen can't come, I'm afraid.* □ **+ that** *I'm afraid that I can't tell you any more now.* (recear)

African[1] /ˈæfrɪkən/ ADJECTIVE belonging to or from Africa □ *an African country* (africano)
African[2] /ˈæfrɪkən/ NOUN [plural **Africans**] a person from Africa (africano)

after[1] /ˈɑːftə(r)/ PREPOSITION
1 when something has happened □ *I'll do it after dinner.* □ *It rained day after day.* (após)
2 after an hour/three days, etc. when an hour/three days, etc. have passed (depois de)
3 following in order □ *Your name's after mine on the list.* (seguinte)
4 following someone or something □ *We ran after the man.* (atrás)
5 after all used to talk about something that happened or was true although you did not expect it to be □ *I decided to go to the party after all.* (afinal)

after[2] /ˈɑːftə(r)/ CONJUNCTION when
something has happened □ *Mrs Shaw died after we moved.* □ *After we'd said goodbye, we felt quite sad.* (logo que)

> Use the phrases **a week/month, etc. from now** or **in a week's/month's, etc. time** to talk about a time in the future that you are measuring from now. Do not say 'after a week/month, etc.' to mean this:
> ✓ *A week from now my exams will all be finished.*
> ✓ *In a week's time my exams will all be finished.*
> ✗ *After a week my exams will all be finished.*

after[3] /ˈɑːftə(r)/ ADVERB following in time □ *Can you come the week after?* (depois, seguinte)

afternoon /ˌɑːftəˈnuːn/ NOUN [plural **afternoons**]
1 the time between the middle of the day and the evening □ *I saw him on Monday afternoon.* □ *We finish at 4 o'clock in the afternoon.* 🔲 *What are you doing this afternoon?* (tarde)
2 Good afternoon used to say 'hello' when you meet someone in the afternoon (Boa tarde)

afterwards /ˈɑːftəwədz/ ADVERB later or after something else □ *He's busy now but I'll speak to him afterwards.* □ *They moved to Paris and soon afterwards they got married.* (posteriormente)

again /əˈgen/ ADVERB
1 once more □ *Do it again!* □ *Will I see you again?* (de novo)
2 in the same place or situation as before □ *Can we go home again now?* (de novo)
3 again and again many times □ *I've told you again and again to tidy your room!* (muitas vezes)

> Remember that **again** meaning 'once more' usually comes after the object in a sentence:
> ✓ *I'd like to visit France again.*
> ✗ *I'd like to visit again France.*
> ✓ *We could have pizza again.*
> ✗ *We could have again pizza.*

against /əˈgenst/ PREPOSITION
1 leaning on, touching or hitting something □ *She was throwing a ball against the wall.* □ *He was sitting with his back against a tree.* (contra)
2 competing or fighting with someone □ *Liverpool are playing against Barcelona.* □ *We all support the fight against racism.* (contra)
3 disagreeing with a plan or situation □ *I'm against the ban on hunting.* (contrário)
4 against the law/rules not allowed by the laws/rules □ *Smoking on the train is against the law.* (contra as regras/leis)

age /eɪdʒ/ NOUN [plural **ages**]
1 how old someone or something is 🔲 *Zoe will start school at the age of four.* 🔲 *He's 19 years of age.* □ **+of** *Do you know the age of the building?* 🔲 *It's suitable for children of all ages.* (idade)

2 ages an informal word meaning a very long time □ *I haven't seen Alex for ages.* 🔁 *You took ages to finish.* □ *The tickets sold out ages ago.* (era)
3 a period of time in history □ *the Stone Age* (idade)

• **aged** /eɪdʒd/ ADJECTIVE used to say how many years old someone is □ *They have two children aged eight and three.* 🔁 *young people aged between 18 and 25* (com idade de/entre)

agency /ˈeɪdʒənsi/ NOUN [plural **agencies**]
a business that provides a particular service □ *an employment agency* □ *an advertising agency* (agência)

agenda /əˈdʒendə/ NOUN [plural **agendas**] a list of things to be discussed at a meeting 🔁 *What's on the agenda today?* (em pauta)

agent /ˈeɪdʒənt/ NOUN [plural **agents**]
1 someone who does business for another person or company □ *Our agents sell the books for us.* (representante)
2 someone who collects secret information for a government 🔁 *a secret agent* (agente)
→ go to **travel agent**, **estate agent**

aggression /əˈɡreʃən/ NOUN, NO PLURAL behaviour that is angry and threatening (agressão)
aggressive /əˈɡresɪv/ ADJECTIVE angry and threatening 🔁 *aggressive behaviour* (agressivo)

ago /əˈɡəʊ/ ADVERB used to say how long in the past something happened □ *I last saw Lily ten years ago.* 🔁 *That all seems a long time ago.* (atrás)

agony /ˈæɡəni/ NOUN, NO PLURAL very great pain □ *You could see he was in agony.* (agonia)

agree /əˈɡriː/ VERB [**agrees, agreeing, agreed**]
1 to have the same opinion as someone else about some thing □ + *with She never agrees with him about anything.* □ + *about I'm glad we agree about something.* (concordar)
2 to say that you will do what someone has asked you to □ + *to do something I only agreed to come if you came too.* (concordar)
3 to decide something together with someone □ + *on They couldn't agree on a name for the baby.* □ *Doctors have agreed a pay deal.* (concordar)

agreement /əˈɡriːmənt/ NOUN [plural **agreements**]
1 a decision or a promise between two or more people □ + *between a trade agreement between Canada and the US* □ + *with We have an agreement with the local sports club.* 🔁 *The two companies have reached an agreement.* (acordo)
2 no plural when people have the same opinion □ *There was no agreement about what to do.* (entendimento)
3 in agreement if people are in agreement, they agree with each other (concordância)

agriculture /ˈæɡrɪˌkʌltʃə(r)/ NOUN, NO PLURAL the work of farming (agricultura)

ahead /əˈhed/ ADVERB
1 in front □ *Run on ahead and tell them we're coming.* 🔁 *Our house is straight ahead.* (em frente, bem em frente)
2 in the future □ + *of We've got a long journey ahead of us.* 🔁 *We're planning for the year ahead.* (à frente, adiante)
3 in a better position in a race, competition, etc. □ + *of They are four points ahead of their main rivals.* □ *United were ahead after a goal in the first half.* (à frente)

aid¹ /eɪd/ NOUN [plural **aids**]
1 help 🔁 *He can walk with the aid of a stick.* 🔁 *Mr Oliver came to our aid* (= helped us). (auxílio)
2 money, food, etc. that is sent to places that need it □ *Many countries will send aid to the disaster area.* (ajuda)

aid² /eɪd/ VERB [**aids, aiding, aided**] to help someone □ *Gentle exercise will aid your recovery.* (ajudar)

AIDS ou **Aids** /eɪdz/ ABBREVIATION Acquired Immune Deficiency Syndrome; an illness that makes the body unable to fight disease (AIDS, síndrome de imunodeficiência adquirida)

aim¹ /eɪm/ VERB [**aims, aiming, aimed**]
1 to intend or to hope to do something □ + *to do something We aim to help all our customers.* □ + *for She's aiming for a medal at the next Olympics.* (almejar)
2 to point a weapon at someone or something □ + *at Paul was aiming at the target but missed it completely.* (apontar)

aim² /eɪm/ NOUN [plural **aims**]
1 what you are trying to achieve □ + *of The aim of the project is to encourage healthy eating.* 🔁 *My main aim is to get fit.* 🔁 *We have achieved our aim.* (objetivo)
2 take aim to point a weapon at someone or something □ + *at He took aim at the open window.* (visar)

ain't /eɪnt/ an informal short way to say and write 'am not', 'are not', 'is not', 'has not' or 'have not' □ *Ain't he clever?* □ *You ain't lived yet.* (ver **be**)

air¹ /eə(r)/ NOUN
1 no plural the gases around us that we breathe in 🔁 *Kelly went outside to get some fresh air.* □ *The air carries the seeds for miles.* (ar)
2 the air the space above you □ *He put his hand in the air.* □ *Police fired into the air.* (atmosfera)
3 no plural travel in an aircraft □ *The food is transported by air.* 🔁 *air travel* (avião)

air² /eə(r)/ VERB [**airs, airing, aired**] to allow some fresh air into a room (ventilar)

aircraft /ˈeəkrɑːft/ NOUN [plural **aircraft**] a vehicle that can fly 🔁 *a commercial aircraft* 🔁 *a military aircraft* (aeronave)

air force /ˈeə fɔːs/ NOUN [plural **air forces**] a military organization that uses aircraft (força aérea)

airline /ˈeəlaɪn/ NOUN [plural **airlines**] a company that takes people or goods to places by plane 🔁 *an airline ticket* 🔁 *an airline pilot* (companhia aérea)

airmail /ˈeəmeɪl/ NOUN, NO PLURAL the system of sending letters and packages by aeroplane □ *I'll send you the book by airmail.* (correio aéreo)

airport · all right

airport /'eəpɔ:t/ NOUN [plural **airports**] a place where passengers get on and off aircraft □ She arrived at the city's international airport. (**aeroporto**)

aisle /aɪl/ NOUN [plural **aisles**] the space that you can walk along between rows of seats or shelves in a church, supermarket, etc. (**corredor**)

alarm¹ /ə'lɑ:m/ NOUN [plural **alarms**]
1 a loud noise to warn people about something ⊕ the fire alarm ⊕ My alarm goes off at 7 o'clock. (**alarme**)
2 no plural a sudden feeling of fear and worry □ He jumped back in alarm. ⊕ Everyone stay calm, there's no cause for alarm. (**temor**)

alarm² /ə'lɑ:m/ VERB [**alarms, alarming, alarmed**] to frighten and worry someone suddenly □ It's okay, don't be alarmed. (**assustar**)

alarm clock /ə'lɑ:m ˌklɒk/ NOUN [plural **alarm clocks**] a clock that makes a noise to wake you up ⊕ His alarm clock went off (= rang) at 6 am. (**despertador**)

alarming /ə'lɑ:mɪŋ/ ADJECTIVE frightening and making you worry □ alarming reports (**alarmante**)

album /'ælbəm/ NOUN [plural **albums**]
1 a book for keeping photographs, stamps, etc. ⊕ a photo album (**álbum de fotografia**)
2 a collection of songs or pieces of music on a CD, record, etc. □ the band's new album (**disco**)

alcohol /'ælkəhɒl/ NOUN, NO PLURAL
1 drinks like wine and beer that can make you drunk ⊕ He doesn't drink alcohol. (**álcool**)
2 a substance in wine and beer that is also in some chemicals and medicines. A chemistry word. (**álcool**)

alcoholic /ˌælkə'hɒlɪk/ ADJECTIVE containing alcohol ⊕ alcoholic drinks (**alcoólico, bebidas alcoólicas**)

alert¹ /ə'lɜ:t/ ADJECTIVE quick to notice what is around you and to react to it □ Stay alert – the enemy could attack at any time. (**alerta**)

alert² /ə'lɜ:t/ NOUN [plural **alerts**]
1 a warning about something ⊕ Weather experts issued a flood alert. (**alerta**)
2 on alert ready to deal with problems ⊕ Security forces are on full/high alert. (**em alerta**)

alert³ /ə'lɜ:t/ VERB [**alerts, alerting, alerted**] to warn someone about a danger □ If you see a suspicious package, alert the police at once. (**alertar**)

alien¹ /'eɪliən/ NOUN [plural **aliens**]
1 a creature from another planet (**alienígena**)
2 someone who is not from the country they are living in ⊕ an illegal alien (**estrangeiro**)

alien² /'eɪliən/ ADJECTIVE
1 strange and not familiar □ The idea of taking orders from a woman was totally alien to him. (**estranheiro**)
2 to do with creatures from another planet □ an alien spaceship (**alienígena**)

alike¹ /ə'laɪk/ ADJECTIVE like one another □ The twins aren't alike in character. (**parecido**)

alike² /ə'laɪk/ ADVERB in the same way □ Dad treats us both alike. (**da mesma maneira**)

alive /ə'laɪv/ ADJECTIVE living □ He was seriously injured, but still alive. □ She didn't know whether he was alive or dead. (**vivo**)

all¹ /ɔ:l/ PRONOUN, DETERMINER
1 every one □ All the children stood up. □ I want to see them all. □ + of All of the animals were healthy. (**todos**)
2 every part □ We ate all the cake. □ Don't spend it all. □ We've been working all day. (**todo**)
3 the only thing □ All he's interested in is football. (**tudo**)
4 at all used to emphasize a negative statement □ You haven't eaten anything at all. (**absolutamente**)

all² /ɔ:l/ ADVERB
1 completely □ His shirt was all dirty. (**totalmente**)
2 all over (a) in every place or part of something □ His clothes were all over the place. (b) finished □ I'll be glad when it's all over. (**por todo, terminado**)

Allah /'ælə/ NOUN the Muslim name for God (**Alá**)

allege /ə'ledʒ/ VERB [**alleges, alleging, alleged**] to say that someone has done something wrong or illegal □ The police allege that he stole the car. (**alegar**)

allergic /ə'lɜ:dʒɪk/ ADJECTIVE having a condition where your body reacts badly to something you touch, breathe, eat or drink ⊕ an allergic reaction □ I'm allergic to cats. (**alérgico**)

allergy /'ælədʒi/ NOUN [plural **allergies**] a condition where your body reacts badly to something you touch, breathe, eat or drink □ a peanut allergy ⊕ I have an allergy to dairy products. (**alergia**)

alley /'æli/ or **alleyway** /'æliweɪ/ NOUN [plural **alleys**] a narrow passage between buildings (**ruela**)

alliance /ə'laɪəns/ NOUN [plural **alliances**] an agreement between organizations or countries to work together ⊕ The US car maker has formed an alliance with a Chinese manufacturer. (**aliança**)

alligator /'ælɪɡeɪtə(r)/ NOUN [plural **alligators**] a large reptile with thick skin, a long body and a big mouth with sharp teeth (**jacaré**)

allow /ə'laʊ/ VERB [**allows, allowing, allowed**]
1 to give permission for something □ + to do something Will you allow me to come in now? □ We do not allow smoking in the house. □ Prisoners are allowed out to exercise. (**permitir**)
2 to make something possible □ + to do something The new technology allows them to stay in touch with their families. (**permitir**)

> Do not use the phrase **it is not allowed to do something** as this is not correct English. Instead use either of these phrases □ **You are not allowed to** talk in a written exam. □ **Talking is not allowed** in a written exam.

all right¹ /ˌɔ:l 'raɪt/ ADJECTIVE, ADVERB
1 quite good but not very good □ The party was all right I suppose. (**bom**)

2 safe or well ▢ *I'm all right. How are you?* ▢ *I'm glad you're all right – we heard there was an accident.* (bem)

3 acceptable or not a problem ▢ *Is it all right if I go out tonight?* ▢ *It's all right – it wasn't your fault.* (tudo bem)

4 That's all right. used when someone has thanked you for something (tudo bem)

all right² /ɔːˈraɪt/ EXCLAMATION used to agree to some thing ▢ *All right, I'll go then.* (tudo bem)

ally NOUN /ˈælaɪ/ [**allies**] a person or country that supports another ▣ *He is one of the president's closest allies.* ▢ *Britain has been a strong political ally of the United States.* (aliado)

almost /ˈɔːlməʊst/ ADVERB not quite or not completely ▢ *She is almost ten years old.* ▣ *Almost all the children go to state schools.* ▢ *He's almost as tall as his father.* ▢ *It's almost impossible to predict.* ▢ *I almost missed my flight.* (quase)

alone /əˈləʊn/ ADJECTIVE, ADVERB

1 without anyone else ▢ *I live alone.* ▣ *I was all alone with no one to talk to.* ▢ *A young woman sat alone in the waiting room.* ▢ *I felt completely alone.* (só)

2 used to emphasize that only one person or thing is involved ▢ *The ticket alone will use up all my money.* (só)

3 leave something alone to not touch something ▢ *Leave my sweets alone!* (deixar em paz)

4 leave someone alone to not talk to or annoy some one ▢ *Leave her alone – she's had enough of your complaints.* (deixar em paz)

> Note that **alone** only means 'without anyone else'. It does not mean 'feeling sad because you are without other people'. The word for this is **lonely** ▢ *I was alone in the house.* ▢ *I felt lonely without my family around me.*

along¹ /əˈlɒŋ/ PREPOSITION

1 from one part of something to another ▢ *Shona walked along the street.* (ao longo)

2 by the side of something long ▢ *Hari's house is somewhere along this street.* (ao longo)

along² /əˈlɒŋ/ ADVERB

1 forwards ▢ *Move along, please.* ▢ *He was driving along, singing.* (para a frente)

2 with someone ▣ *We're going swimming – why don't you come along?* ▣ *Adam brought a friend along.* (junto)

3 along with together with ▢ *We'd packed drinks along with the sandwiches.* (junto com)

aloud /əˈlaʊd/ ADVERB so that other people can hear ▣ *She almost laughed aloud.* ▣ *Edith read the letter aloud to the boys.* (alto)

alphabet /ˈælfəbet/ NOUN [plural **alphabets**] all the written letters of a language ▣ *Z is the last letter of the alphabet.* (alfabeto)

alphabetical /ˌælfəˈbetɪkəl/ ADJECTIVE with the first letters in the order of the alphabet ▣ *The books are in alphabetical order.* ▢ *an alphabetical index* (alfabético)

already /ɔːlˈredi/ ADVERB

1 before now or before a particular time ▢ *I had already gone when Bob arrived.* ▢ *We've already booked our summer holiday.* (já)

2 now, before the expected time ▢ *Is he here already?* ▢ *I'm already tired.* (já)

also /ˈɔːlsəʊ/ ADVERB in addition ▢ *Bernie speaks French and also Italian.* ▢ *My sister also attends this school.* ▣ *The process is not only slow, but also very expensive.* (também)

altar /ˈɔːltə(r)/ NOUN [plural **altars**] a special table used for religious ceremonies in a church (altar)

alter /ˈɔːltə(r)/ VERB [**alters, altering, altered**] to change, or to change something ▢ *The town has altered a lot recently.* ▢ *Can you alter this skirt to fit me?* (alterar)

alteration /ˌɔːltəˈreɪʃən/ NOUN [plural **alterations**] a change, or the process of being changed ▢ *There have been a few alterations to our plans.* ▢ *The museum is closed for alteration.* (alteração)

alternate¹ /ɔːlˈtɜːnət/ ADJECTIVE

1 happening on one day, week, etc. but not the next ▢ *I have to work on alternate Saturdays.* (alternado)

2 with one thing, then another, then the first thing again, in a repeated pattern ▢ *alternate stripes of red and green* (alternado)

alternate² /ˈɔːltəneɪt/ VERB [**alternates, alternating, alternated**] if two things alternate, one happens or is used first, then the other, then the first again, etc. ▢ *She alternates between being too strict and being too soft.* ▢ *He alternates between the guitar and the violin.* (alternar)

alternative¹ /ɔːlˈtɜːnətɪv/ ADJECTIVE giving you another choice or possibility ▢ *If you cannot come on Tuesday you can suggest an alternative day.* ▢ *Drivers are advised to use an alternative route.* (alternativo)

alternative² /ɔːlˈtɜːnətɪv/ NOUN [plural **alternatives**] another possibility or choice ▢ *Is there an alternative to chips on the menu?* ▢ *There are cheaper alternatives.* (alternativa)

although /ɔːlˈðəʊ/ CONJUNCTION

1 despite the fact that ▢ *Although he was a clever boy, he didn't do well in exams.* ▢ *I went to the show, although I had said I wouldn't.* (embora)

2 but ▢ *He's retired from professional athletics, although he's still very fit.* (embora)

altogether /ˌɔːltəˈgeðə(r)/ ADVERB

1 completely ▢ *Finally, he stopped altogether.* ▣ *I'm not altogether happy.* (completamente)

2 in total ▢ *We raised £100 altogether.* ▢ *There are six of us altogether.* (no total)

aluminium — amusement

aluminium /ˌæljuˈmɪniəm/ NOUN, NO PLURAL a very light metal that is a silver colour (alumínio)

aluminum /əˈluːmɪnəm/ NOUN, NO PLURAL the US word for **aluminium** (alumínio)

always /ˈɔːlweɪz/ ADVERB
1 at all times □ *I always work hard.* ▣ *You look lovely, as always.* (sempre)
2 at all times in the past □ *She's always lived in the same village.* □ *He hasn't always been so successful.* (sempre)
3 forever □ *I'll always remember that day.* (sempre)
4 repeatedly □ + *ing* *I'm always getting this wrong.* (sempre)

> THESAURUS: **Always** means 'at all times'. For example, if you are very careful about your appearance, you might **always** look smart. If you do something **regularly**, or if something happens **regularly**, it happens often, and often with the same amount of time between each thing. For example, you might go swimming **regularly**. If you do something **repeatedly**, you do it many times. This word is often used to describe something which is bad or annoying. For example, you might say that you complain about something **repeatedly**.

am¹ /æm/ VERB the present tense of the verb **be** when it is used with with **I** □ *I am happy.* (ver be)

> Note that instead of **I am**, people often say and write the short form **I'm** □ *I'm very pleased.*

am² /eɪˈem/ ou **a.m.** ABBREVIATION used after the time to show that it is in the morning □ *My flight is at 6 am.* (abreviação de manhã)

amateur¹ /ˈæmətə(r)/ NOUN [plural amateurs] someone who does something because they enjoy it, not for money □ *The team is made up of enthusiastic amateurs.* (amador)

amateur² /ˈæmətə(r)/ ADJECTIVE doing something for fun and not to be paid □ *an amateur photographer* □ *amateur athletics* (amador)

amaze /əˈmeɪz/ VERB [amazes, amazing, amazed] to surprise someone very much □ *It amazes me how stupid you can be.* (surpreender)

amazed /əˈmeɪzd/ ADJECTIVE very surprised □ + *at* *We were all amazed at how easy it was.* □ + *that* *I'm amazed that no one was hurt.* □ *Mum looked amazed when he walked in.* (surpreso)

amazement /əˈmeɪzmənt/ NOUN, NO PLURAL great surprise ▣ *To my amazement, Dad agreed with me.* □ *He shook his head in amazement.* (surpresa)

amazing /əˈmeɪzɪŋ/ ADJECTIVE
1 very surprising □ *an amazing sight* □ *It's amazing how quickly the weather can change.* (surpreendente)
2 very pleasant, exciting or enjoyable □ *We saw an amazing sunset.* □ *It's a pretty amazing feeling.* (maravilhoso)

ambassador /æmˈbæsədə(r)/ NOUN [plural ambassadors] someone who officially represents their government in a foreign country □ *the British ambassador to Japan* (embaixador)

ambition /æmˈbɪʃən/ NOUN [plural ambitions]
1 something that you want to achieve ▣ *I have an ambition to see the pyramids.* ▣ *He achieved his ambition of becoming a doctor.* (ambição)
2 no plural wanting to be very successful □ *He shows a lack of ambition.* (ambição)

ambitious /æmˈbɪʃəs/ ADJECTIVE wanting to be very successful in life □ *an ambitious and talented young player* (ambicioso)

ambulance /ˈæmbjʊləns/ NOUN [plural ambulances] a vehicle for taking ill or injured people to hospital (ambulância)

American¹ /əˈmerɪkən/ ADJECTIVE belonging to or from America, especially the United States of America □ *an American accent* (americano)

American² /əˈmerɪkən/ NOUN [plural Americans] a person from America, especially the United States of America (norte-americano)

ammunition /ˌæmjʊˈnɪʃən/ NOUN, NO PLURAL bullets or bombs that you can fire from a weapon (munição)

among /əˈmʌŋ/ ou **amongst** /əˈmʌŋst/ PREPOSITION
1 surrounded by or in the middle of □ *You are among friends.* (entre)
2 between people in a group □ *Divide the chocolate among yourselves.* (entre)
3 in a group of □ *The band is popular among teenagers.* (entre)

amount /əˈmaʊnt/ NOUN [plural amounts] a quantity □ + *of* *a small amount of money* □ *These drinks contain large amounts of sugar.* (montante)

> Remember that 'large' and 'small' are used before the word **amount**, but not 'big' or 'little' □ *A large amount of this food is wasted.* □ *A small amount of salt is necessary.*

ample /ˈæmpəl/ ADJECTIVE enough or more than enough □ *We had ample opportunity to ask questions.* □ *an ample supply of water* (amplo)

amuse /əˈmjuːz/ VERB [amuses, amusing, amused] to make someone smile or laugh □ *He told jokes to amuse his classmates.* (divertir)

amused /əˈmjuːzd/ ADJECTIVE finding something funny □ *He smiled, amused at John's silly mistake.* □ *an amused expression* (divertido)

amusement /əˈmjuːzmənt/ NOUN [plural amusements] the feeling that makes you smile or laugh □ *He smiled with obvious amusement.* (diversão)

amusing /əˈmjuːzɪŋ/ ADJECTIVE making you want to smile or laugh □ *an amusing story* ▣ *She found the whole thing quite amusing.* (**divertido**)

an /ən/ DETERMINER used instead of **a** before words beginning with a vowel, or before words beginning with 'h' when it is not pronounced □ *an apple* □ *an elephant* □ *an honest person* (**um, uma**)

analysis /əˈnæləsɪs/ NOUN [plural **analyses**] when you examine something carefully in order to understand it ▣ *a statistical analysis* ▣ *We carried out a detailed analysis of the project.* (**análise**)

analyze *ou* **analyse** /ˈænəlaɪz/ VERB [**analyzes, analyzing, analyzed**] to examine something carefully in order to understand it ▣ *We need to analyze the data.* □ *Researchers analyzed a thousand samples.* (**analisar**)

ancestor /ˈænsestə(r)/ NOUN [plural **ancestors**] a member of your family who lived in the past □ *His distant ancestors came from India.* (**ancestral**)

anchor[1] /ˈæŋkə(r)/ NOUN [plural **anchors**] a heavy piece of metal attached to a boat that is dropped into the water to stop it from moving away. (**âncora**)

anchor[2] /ˈæŋkə(r)/ VERB [**anchors, anchoring, anchored**] to drop the anchor of a boat to stop it moving away □ *The ship is anchored in Sydney harbour.* (**ancorar**)

ancient /ˈeɪnʃənt/ ADJECTIVE from a very long time ago ▣ *ancient history* ▣ *the remains of an ancient civilization* (**antigo**)

and /ænd/ CONJUNCTION
1 a word that is used to join parts of sentences □ *bread and butter* □ *I saw Alice and Peter.* □ *Go and get ready.* (**e**)
2 added to □ *Two and two make four.* (**mais**)

angel /ˈeɪndʒəl/ NOUN [plural **angels**] a creature, usually shown like a person with wings, which is believed to bring messages from God. (**anjo**)

anger /ˈæŋɡə(r)/ NOUN, NO PLURAL the strong, bad feeling you get about someone or something that annoys you □ *The fans expressed their anger at the decision.* □ *There's a lot of anger among local people.* □ *He was shaking with anger.* (**raiva**)

angle /ˈæŋɡəl/ NOUN [plural **angles**] the shape that is made at the point where two straight lines meet, measured in degrees □ *a 90-degree angle* (**ângulo**)

angrily /ˈæŋɡrəli/ ADVERB in an angry way □ *A young woman came in, shouting angrily.* □ *He reacted angrily.* (**furiosamente**)

angry /ˈæŋɡri/ ADJECTIVE [**angrier, angriest**] very annoyed □ + *about* *They're angry about the way they were treated.* □ + *with* *I'm not angry with you.* □ *an angry crowd* ▣ *Then Mike got very angry.* ▣ *That kind of thing makes me so angry.* (**irritado**)

➤ THESAURUS: If you are angry, you dislike something or feel very impatient about it. **Annoyed** and **cross** have a similar meaning, but are not so strong. If you are **furious**, you are very angry. For example, you might be **annoyed** if a train is 5 minutes late, angry if you miss a meeting because your train doesn't arrive, and **furious** if you lose your job because you miss the meeting.

animal /ˈænɪməl/ NOUN [plural **animals**] a living creature that is not a human ▣ *a wild animal* ▣ *a farm animal* □ *The charity helps to protect endangered animals.* (**animal**)

ankle /ˈæŋkəl/ NOUN [plural **ankles**] the place where your foot joins your leg □ *She fell over and broke her left ankle.* (**tornozelo**)

annex[1] *ou* **annexe** /ˈæneks/ NOUN [plural **annexes**] an extra part of a building that is added on to it. (**anexo**)

annex[2] /əˈneks/ VERB [**annexes, annexing, annexed**] to take control of an area or country next to your own □ *After the war, the region was annexed by the Soviet Union.* (**anexar**)

anniversary /ˌænɪˈvɜːsəri/ NOUN [plural **anniversaries**] a date when you celebrate something that happened on the same date in the past ▣ *a wedding anniversary* □ + *of* *Today is the anniversary of the King's death.* ▣ *The celebrations will mark the 60th anniversary of the country's independence.* (**aniversário**)

announce /əˈnaʊns/ VERB [**announces, announcing, announced**] to tell people something, especially loudly or forcefully ▣ *The government has announced plans to build four new hospitals.* ▣ *Have they announced their engagement yet?* □ + *that* *The minister has announced that he is retiring.* (**anunciar**)

announcement /əˈnaʊnsmənt/ NOUN [plural **announcements**] something that people are told, especially publicly or officially ▣ *I want to make an announcement.* ▣ *a formal/official announcement* (**notificação**)

announcer /əˈnaʊnsə(r)/ NOUN [plural **announcers**] someone who introduces programmes on television or the radio. (**locutor**)

annoy /əˈnɔɪ/ VERB [**annoys, annoying, annoyed**] to make someone angry □ *It really annoys me when she wastes food.* (**irritar**)

annoyed /əˈnɔɪd/ ADJECTIVE angry □ + *with* *I could see that he was annoyed with me.* (**irritado**)

annoying /əˈnɔɪɪŋ/ ADJECTIVE making you feel annoyed ▣ *an annoying habit* □ *Jo can be so annoying!* (**irritante**)

annual¹ /ˈænjuəl/ ADJECTIVE an annual event happens once every year ◻ *an annual meeting of shareholders* (anual)

- **annually** /ˈænjuəli/ ADVERB happening once every year (anualmente)

annual² /ˈænjuəl/ NOUN [plural **annuals**] a book that is published every year (anuário)

another /əˈnʌðə(r)/ DETERMINER, PRONOUN
1 one more person or thing ◻ *Have another piece of chocolate.* ◻ *He had two gold medals and now he has another.* (outro)
2 a different person or thing ◻ *We'll finish this game another time.* ◻ *If that pen's broken, use another one.* ◻ *I lost my coat and I haven't got another.* (outro)

answer¹ /ˈɑːnsə(r)/ VERB [**answers, answering, answered**]
1 to reply when someone asks you a question or sends you a letter ◻ *I waited for him to answer.* ◻ *She tried to answer truthfully.* ◻ *I'm just going to answer his letter.* (responder)
2 to pick up the telephone when it rings, or to open the door when someone is there ◻ *A child answered the telephone.* ◻ *I knocked at the door and an old woman answered.* (responder)

answer² /ˈɑːnsə(r)/ NOUN [plural **answers**]
1 a reply ◻ + **to** *I couldn't find an answer to my question.* ▣ *He gave a detailed answer.* (resposta)
2 the solution to a problem ◻ *If you can't afford a car, a car sharing scheme could be the answer.* (resposta)
3 what you write or say to answer a question in an exam or a competition ▣ *the correct/wrong answer* (resposta certa/errada)

> Remember to use the preposition **to** after the noun **answer**:
> ✓ *What's the answer to question six?*
> ✗ *What's the answer for question six?*

answerphone /ˈɑːnsəˌfəʊn/ ou **answering machine** /ˈɑːnsərɪŋ məˌʃiːn/ NOUN [plural **answerphones** or **answering machines**] a machine that automatically answers your telephone and records messages for you (secretária eletrônica)

ant /ænt/ NOUN [plural **ants**] a small, usually black, insect that lives in organized groups (formiga)

Antarctic¹ /ænˈtɑːktɪk/ NOUN **the Antarctic** the area of the world round the South Pole (Antártica)

Antarctic² /ænˈtɑːktɪk/ ADJECTIVE to do with the Antarctic ◻ *Antarctic exploration* ◻ *the Antarctic winter* (antártica)

antenna /ænˈtenə/ NOUN [plural **antennae** ou **antennas**]
1 one of two long thin parts on the head of an insect or a sea animal, used for feeling (antena)
2 a thin piece of metal that is used for getting television or radio signals (antena)

anthem /ˈænθəm/ NOUN [plural **anthems**] a song that praises a country or an organization, for example a football team (hino)

anti- /ˈænti/ PREFIX anti- is added to the beginning of words to mean 'against' or 'preventing' ◻ *antisocial* ◻ *antifreeze* (anti-)

antibiotic /ˌæntibaɪˈɒtɪk/ NOUN [plural **antibiotics**] a medicine that kills bacteria that can cause infections ◻ *The doctor's put me on antibiotics.* (antibiótico)

anticipate /ænˈtɪsɪˌpeɪt/ VERB [**anticipates, anticipating, anticipated**] to expect something to happen, and often to prepare for it ◻ *We don't anticipate any problems.* (antecipar)

antique¹ /ænˈtiːk/ NOUN [plural **antiques**] an object that is old and valuable ◻ *a collector of antiques* (antiguidade)

antique² /ænˈtiːk/ ADJECTIVE old and valuable ◻ *antique jewellery* (antigo)

> Remember that **antique** is used for old objects, such as furniture and jewellery. It is not used for old buildings. For buildings, use **old** or **ancient** ◻ *They have a lot of very valuable antique furniture.* ◻ *We visited the ancient monuments.*

antonym /ˈæntənɪm/ NOUN [plural **antonyms**] a word that means the opposite of another word (antônimo)

anxiety /æŋˈzaɪəti/ NOUN [plural **anxieties**] a feeling of worry ◻ *The parents of these soldiers suffered a lot of anxiety.* (ansiedade)

anxious /ˈæŋkʃəs/ ADJECTIVE worried ◻ + **about** *He's anxious about missing his train.* ◻ *She gave me an anxious glance.* (ansioso)

any¹ /ˈeni/ DETERMINER, PRONOUN
1 used in questions and negative statements to mean 'some' ◻ *Have we got any sweets?* ◻ *We had lots of food, but there isn't any left now.* (algum/nenhum)
2 one or a piece of something, but not a particular one ◻ *Let me know if you have any questions.* ◻ *Choose any colour you like.* ◻ *The children all know the answers – ask any of them.* (qualquer)

any² /ˈeni/ ADVERB
1 at all ◻ *Are you feeling any better?* ◻ *Can't you walk any faster?* (um pouco)
2 any more if something does not happen any more, it has stopped happening ◻ *Ricky doesn't work here any more.* ◻ *The children don't get free milk any more.* (não mais)

anybody /ˈeniˌbɒdi/ PRONOUN
1 used in questions and negatives to mean 'a person' or 'people' ◻ *Has anybody seen my glasses?* ◻ *I didn't speak to anybody.* (alguém)
2 any person ◻ *Anybody is allowed to enter.* (qualquer um)

anyhow

anyhow /ˈenɪhaʊ/ ADVERB
1 used to add another reason to what you have just said □ *I missed lunch but I wasn't hungry anyhow.* (de qualquer maneira)
2 despite that □ *Two of our players are injured, but anyhow we have a very good team.* (de qualquer maneira)

anyone /ˈenɪwʌn/ PRONOUN
1 used in questions and negatives to mean 'a person' or 'people' □ *Has anyone got a mobile?* □ *There isn't anyone left.* (alguém)
2 any person □ *Anyone can bake a cake.* □ *He'll talk to anyone.* (qualquer um)

> Remember that 'anyone' is singular so the verb following it must be singular □ *If anyone calls, tell them I'll be back in ten minutes.* □ *Anyone is welcome to come.*

anything /ˈenɪθɪŋ/ PRONOUN
1 used in questions and negative statements to mean 'something' □ *We didn't have anything to eat.* □ *Is there anything I can do to help?* ▣ *Is there anything else I should know?* (algo)
2 something of any type □ *He's capable of anything.* □ *We can do anything we like while our teacher is away.* (qualquer coisa)

anyway /ˈenɪweɪ/ ADVERB
1 used to add another reason to what you have just said □ *I can give you a lift. I'm going that way anyway.* (de qualquer maneira)
2 despite that □ *Leon couldn't go with me but I enjoyed the party anyway.* (de todo jeito)
3 used to start a new part of a conversation □ *Anyway, how have you been lately?* (de qualquer maneira)

anywhere /ˈenɪweə(r)/ ADVERB
1 in or to any place □ *I'm willing to travel anywhere.* □ *You can buy these anywhere in the world.* □ *Don't go anywhere near Dad – he's in a terrible mood.* (qualquer lugar)
2 used in questions and negative statements to mean 'a place' □ *Have you got anywhere to stay?* □ *There isn't anywhere to hide.* (algum lugar)

apart /əˈpɑːt/ ADVERB
1 separated by distance or time □ *Stand with your feet apart.* □ *We had two classes, a week apart.* (separado)
2 into pieces ▣ *The seams of this jacket have come apart.* □ *We had to take the lamp apart to mend it.* (em pedaços)
3 apart from except for □ *Apart from us, nobody's interested.* □ *I've had nothing to eat apart from a biscuit.* (à parte de)
4 tell apart if you cannot tell two people apart, you cannot see any differences in their appearance (distinguir)

apartment /əˈpɑːtmənt/ NOUN [plural **apartments**] a mainly US word for **flat** (= set of rooms on one level) □ *an apartment block* (apartamento)

appear

ape /eɪp/ NOUN [plural **apes**] a large animal like a monkey with no tail (macaco)

apologize ou **apologise** /əˈpɒlədʒaɪz/ VERB [**apologizes, apologizing, apologized**] to say sorry for doing something wrong □ **+ for** *I had to apologize for being late.* (pedir desculpas)

apology /əˈpɒlədʒɪ/ NOUN [plural **apologies**] when someone says sorry for doing something wrong ▣ *He made a public apology.* ▣ *She demanded an apology from the newspaper's editor.* □ **+ for** *I owe you an apology for forgetting your birthday again.* (desculpa)

apostrophe /əˈpɒstrəfɪ/ NOUN [plural **apostrophes**]
1 the symbol (') that shows where a letter or letters have been missed out □ *Jane's* (= Jane is) *late again.* □ *I think it'll* (= it will) *rain later.* (apóstrofo)
2 the symbol (') that is used before the letters to show who something belongs to □ *I borrowed Ralf's bicycle.* (apóstrofo)

apparatus /ˌæpəˈreɪtəs/ NOUN, NO PLURAL the equipment that you need for a particular task □ *breathing apparatus* (aparelho)

apparent /əˈpærənt/ ADJECTIVE easy to see ▣ *Then, for no apparent reason, he began to cry.* (aparente)

apparently /əˈpærəntlɪ/ ADVERB used to tell people about something you have been told, although you are not sure if it is true □ *Apparently there's going to be an announcement later.* (aparentemente)

appeal¹ /əˈpiːl/ VERB [**appeals, appealing, appealed**]
1 to ask for something, often forcefully or publicly □ *The police have appealed to the public for more information.* (pedir)
2 if something appeals to you, you think you would enjoy it □ *Diving doesn't appeal to me at all.* (agradar)

appeal² /əˈpiːl/ NOUN [plural **appeals**]
1 when someone asks for something, often forcefully or publicly □ *Their appeals for calm were ignored.* □ *Their appeal raised £3,000 for the hospital.* (apelo)
2 the quality that makes something attractive □ *I don't understand the appeal of stamp collecting.* (atração)

appear /əˈpɪə(r)/ VERB [**appears, appearing, appeared**]
1 to seem □ **+ that** *It appears that his wife knew nothing of his crimes.* □ **+ to do something** *The man appeared to hit his victim.* ▣ *I appear to be the only one who has read the book.* □ *He appears determined to win.* (parecer)
2 to arrive or start to be able to be seen □ *Greta appeared round the corner.* □ *A car appeared in the distance.* (aparecer)
3 if an actor appears in a film or a play, they are in it (aparecer)

appearance

appearance /əˈpɪərəns/ NOUN [plural **appearances**]
1 the way someone or something looks □ *He was of Asian appearance.* □ *We thought carefully about the appearance of the room.* (**aparência**)
2 when someone appears in public ▣ *He is making his first appearance for AC Milan.* ▣ *This is her first public appearance since her divorce.* (**aparição**)
3 when someone or something arrives or starts to be seen □ *We were thrilled by the appearance of dolphins near our boat.* □ *The appearance of a police officer frightened the youths away.* (**aparição**)

appendix[1] /əˈpendɪks/ NOUN [plural **appendixes**] a small body part that has no purpose, just below the stomach. A biology word. (**apêndice**)

appendix[2] /əˈpendɪks/ NOUN [plural **appendices**] an extra part at the end of a book or document that gives more details about something (**apêndice**)

appetite /ˈæpɪtaɪt/ NOUN [plural **appetites**] the feeling of being hungry ▣ *Elly has lost her appetite since she's been ill.* ▣ *You'll spoil your appetite if you eat all those biscuits.* (**apetite**)

applaud /əˈplɔːd/ VERB [applauds, applauding, applauded] to hit your hands together to show that you enjoyed something □ *The audience applauded loudly.* (**aplaudir**)

> **THESAURUS:** When you **clap**, you hit your hands together to show appreciation, or to get someone's attention. To applaud means to clap in order to show appreciation, for example in a theatre or at a concert. If you **cheer**, you shout to show appreciation, or to encourage or praise someone. You might **cheer** at a rock concert, or at a sports event. When you **congratulate** someone, you tell them that you are happy about something that has happened to them. You might **congratulate** someone on getting married, passing an exam, or having a baby.

applause /əˈplɔːz/ NOUN, NO PLURAL when people hit their hands together to show that they enjoyed something (**aplauso**)

apple /ˈæpəl/ NOUN [plural **apples**] a hard, round fruit with red, green or yellow skin (**maçã**)
♦ IDIOM **the apple of someone's eye** if someone is the apple of your eye, you love them and are very proud of them (**menina dos olhos**)

appliance /əˈplaɪəns/ NOUN [plural **appliances**] a piece of electrical equipment ▣ *kitchen appliances* (**aparelho**)

applicant /ˈæplɪkənt/ NOUN [plural **applicants**] someone who applies for something such as a job or university place (**candidato**)

application /ˌæplɪˈkeɪʃən/ NOUN [plural **applications**] a written document asking for something such as a job (**solicitação**)

approach

apply /əˈplaɪ/ VERB [applies, applying, applied]
1 to officially ask for something, especially a job or a place on a course □ + **for** *I've applied for a new job.* □ + **to** *Maria's applying to university this year.* (**requerer**)
2 to spread a substance on a surface □ *Apply the cream to your skin three times a day.* (**aplicar**)
3 to affect a particular person or people □ + **to** *Do these rules apply to all of us?* (**aplicar**)

appoint /əˈpɔɪnt/ VERB [appoints, appointing, appointed] to officially give someone a job □ *The committee has appointed Mark Burns as manager.* (**nomear**)

appointment /əˈpɔɪntmənt/ NOUN [plural **appointments**] a time when you have arranged to meet someone ▣ *I've made an appointment with the nurse.* ▣ *I have a doctor's appointment.* ▣ *I've arranged a dental appointment.* (**encontro**)

> An **appointment** is an arranged meeting with a doctor, dentist, etc. It is not a meeting with a friend. To say that you are meeting a friend, say **I'm seeing x** or **I have arranged to see x**:
> ✓ *I'm seeing Maria this afternoon.*
> ✗ *I have an appointment with Maria this afternoon.*

> **THESAURUS:** A **date** is an arrangement to see someone that you are having a romantic relationship with. A **meeting** is a time when people come together to discuss something, for example at work. An **interview** is a meeting where you answer questions to find out if you are suitable for a job. You can also use **interview** to describe a meeting between a journalist and a famous person, where the famous person answers questions about their life or work.

appreciate /əˈpriːʃieɪt/ VERB [appreciates, appreciating, appreciated] to feel grateful for something □ *I really appreciate all the time you've spent on this.* (**estimar**)

appreciation /əˌpriːʃiˈeɪʃən/ NOUN, NO PLURAL when you are grateful to someone □ *Here's a little gift to show our appreciation of all your help.* (**estima**)

apprentice /əˈprentɪs/ NOUN [plural **apprentices**] someone who is learning how to do a skilled job from someone who can already do it (**aprendiz**)

approach[1] /əˈprəʊtʃ/ VERB [approaches, approaching, approached]
1 to come towards a place, person or thing □ *Approach the animals very slowly.* □ *The plane was approaching Paris from the south.* (**aproximar-se**)
2 to deal with something □ *What's the best way to approach the problem?* (**abordar**)

approach[2] /əˈprəʊtʃ/ NOUN [plural **approaches**]
1 a way of trying to deal with something □ + **to** *It's*

a sensible approach to the problem. ▣ *We could take a different approach.* (abordagem)
2 when something or someone gets closer □ *the approach of spring* □ *At the approach of the train, everyone pushed forward.* (aproximação)

appropriate /əˈprəʊpriət/ ADJECTIVE suitable □ *Please wear appropriate clothing.* (apropriado)

approval /əˈpruːvəl/ NOUN, NO PLURAL when someone thinks something is good □ *I've always wanted my father's approval.* (aprovação)

approve əˈpruːv/ VERB [approves, approving, approved] **approve of something/someone** to think something or someone is good □ *They don't approve of her boyfriend.* (aprovar)

approximate /əˈprɒksɪmət/ ADJECTIVE not exact but close □ *Can you tell me the approximate number of chairs we'll need?* □ *This is the approximate size of the rug.* (aproximado)

approximately /əˈprɒksɪmətli/ ADVERB not exactly although close to □ *There will be approximately sixty people there.* (aproximadamente)

apricot /ˈeɪprɪkɒt/ NOUN [plural apricots] a small light orange fruit with a soft skin and a stone inside (damasco)

April /ˈeɪprəl/ NOUN [plural Aprils] the fourth month of the year, after March and before May □ *We're getting married in April.* (abril)

apron /ˈeɪprən/ NOUN [plural aprons] something that you wear over your normal clothes, especially when you are cooking, which keeps your clothes clean (avental)

arch¹ /ɑːtʃ/ NOUN [plural arches] a curved structure that sometimes gives support to something, for example a bridge (arco)

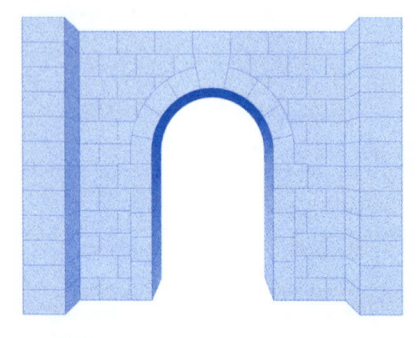

arch² /ɑːtʃ/ VERB [arches, arching, arched] to make a curved shape □ *The cat arched its back.* (arquear)

archaeologist /ˌɑːkiˈɒlədʒɪst/ NOUN [plural archaeologists] someone who studies things from ancient societies that have been found (arqueólogo)

archaeology /ˌɑːkiˈɒlədʒi/ NOUN, NO PLURAL the study of ancient societies by looking at things from that time that have been found (arqueologia)

archbishop /ˌɑːtʃˈbɪʃəp/ NOUN [plural archbishops] the most important priest in some Christian churches (arcebispo)

architect /ˈɑːkɪtekt/ NOUN [plural architects] someone whose job is to design buildings (arquiteto)

architecture /ˈɑːkɪtektʃə(r)/ NOUN, NO PLURAL
1 designing buildings □ *He studied architecture.* (arquitetura)
2 a style of building □ *modern architecture* (arquitetura)

Arctic¹ /ˈɑːktɪk/ NOUN **the Arctic** the area of the world around the North Pole (Ártico)

Arctic² /ˈɑːktɪk/ ADJECTIVE to do with the Arctic □ *the Arctic Ocean* (ártico)

are /ɑː(r)/ VERB the present tense of the verb **be** when it is used with **you**, **we** and **they** □ *They are hungry.* □ *Are we late?*

> Note that instead of **you are**, **we are** and **they are**, people often say or write the short forms, **you're**, **we're** and **they're** □ *You're late.* □ *We're here!* □ *They're over there.*

area /ˈeəriə/ NOUN [plural areas]
1 a part of a place □ *There are a lot of farms in this area.* □ *We work with children from poor areas of the city.* (área)
2 the size of a surface, that you measure in square units of measurement □ *A carpet that is 5 metres by 5 metres has an area of 25 square metres.* (área)

arena /əˈriːnə/ NOUN [plural arenas] a large space for sports or concerts with seats all around it (arena)

aren't /ɑːnt/ a short way to say and write 'are not' □ *These aren't my boots.* (ver **be**)

argue /ˈɑːɡjuː/ VERB [argues, arguing, argued] to speak in an angry way with someone because you disagree with them □ **+ with** *The children never stop arguing with each other.* □ **+ about/over** *They were arguing about where to go on holiday.* (discutir)

argument /ˈɑːɡjumənt/ NOUN [plural arguments] an angry discussion ▣ *The kids were having an argument.* ▣ *a heated argument* (= a very angry argument) □ **+ about** *an argument about money* (discussão)

> THESAURUS: A **discussion** is when two people talk about something. An **argument** is an angry discussion about something. **Quarrel** has a similar meaning, but a **quarrel** is usually less serious than an argument. For example, two children might have a **quarrel** about toys. A **dispute** is a serious argument. We often use this word to describe an argument about work, for example between managers and workers in a company. A **debate** is a formal discussion about something, for example between politicians.

arise /əˈraɪz/ VERB [arises, arising, arose, arisen] to happen □ *A small problem has arisen.* (surgir)

arithmetic

arithmetic /əˈrɪθmətɪk/ NOUN, NO PLURAL mathematics that involves processes such as adding and multiplying ☐ *simple arithmetic* (**aritmética**)

arm¹ /ɑːm/ NOUN [plural **arms**]
1 the part of your body between your shoulder and your hand ☐ *I put my arm round his shoulder.* ☐ *She folded her arms* (= crossed one over the other close to her body). (**braço**)
2 arm in arm holding someone's arm ☐ *They walked arm in arm along the beach.* (**braços dados**)

arm² /ɑːm/ VERB [**arms, arming, armed**] to give someone a weapon to fight with ☐ *The crowd was armed with sticks and knives.* (**armar-se**)

armchair /ˈɑːmtʃeə(r)/ NOUN [plural **armchairs**]
a comfortable chair with sides for resting your arms on (**poltrona**)

armed /ɑːmd/ ADJECTIVE carrying a weapon
☐ *heavily armed* ☐ *armed robbery/burglary* (**armado**)

armed forces /ɑːmd ˈfɔːsɪz/ PLURAL NOUN **the armed forces** the military groups of a country, for example its army (**forças armadas**)

armour /ˈɑːmə(r)/ NOUN, NO PLURAL metal covers worn by soldiers in the past to protect their bodies ☐ *a suit of armour* (**armadura**)

armpit /ˈɑːmpɪt/ NOUN [plural **armpits**] the part under your arm where it joins your body (**axila**)

army /ˈɑːmi/ NOUN [plural **armies**] an
organization of soldiers ☐ *He joined the army after leaving school.* ☐ *the US army* ☐ *an army officer* (**exército**)

arose /əˈrəʊz/ PAST TENSE OF **arise** (ver **arise**)

around /əˈraʊnd/ PREPOSITION, ADVERB
1 on all sides ☐ *We were sitting around the table.* (**ao redor**)
2 in or to different parts of a place ☐ *We walked around the city.* ☐ *There were clothes lying around everywhere.* ☐ *The children are allowed to run around all over the place.* (**ao redor**)
3 to several different people ☐ *We passed the drinks around.* (**ao redor**)
4 about ☐ *They should arrive at around 4 o'clock.* ☐ *I weigh around sixty kilos.* (**aproximadamente**)
5 to face the opposite direction ☐ *He turned around and pointed the gun at me.* (**em direção oposta**)
6 in a circular movement ☐ *Twist the knife around in the hole.* (**em círculo**)
7 near ☐ *Is there a teacher around?* (**perto**)

arrange /əˈreɪndʒ/ VERB [**arranges, arranging, arranged**]
1 to make plans to prepare for something ☐ *Who is arranging the wedding?* ☐ **+ to do something** *He's arranged to go out with his friends tonight.*

☐ **+ for** *I've arranged for a taxi to pick him up later.* (**planejar**)
2 to put things in a particular order ☐ *Arrange the flowers in the vase.* ☐ *All his books are arranged in alphabetical order.* (**arrumar**)

arrangement /əˈreɪndʒmənt/ NOUN [plural **arrangements**] a plan that is made so that
something can happen the way you want it to ☐ *They made arrangements to meet back at the car.* ☐ *If he's not back in time, we'll have to make other arrangements.* (**providência**)

array /əˈreɪ/ NOUN [plural **arrays**] a large group of things ☐ *He owns a vast array of electronic equipment.* (**conjunto**)

arrest¹ /əˈrest/ VERB [**arrests, arresting, arrested**] if the police arrest someone, they take them
to the police station because they may have committed a crime ☐ **+ for** *He was arrested for robbery.* (**prender**)

> **THESAURUS:** If the police arrest someone, they take them to the police station to ask them questions. We use **charge** when the police officially accuse someone of committing a crime. **Capture** is a more general word to describe catching someone or something and not letting it go. For example, you might **capture** an animal, or a soldier.

arrest² /əˈrest/ NOUN [plural **arrests**]
1 when the police arrest someone ☐ *Police have made three arrests in connection with the murder.* (**prisão**)
2 under arrest someone is under arrest when the police are keeping them because they may have committed a crime (**detido**)

arrival /əˈraɪvəl/ NOUN [plural **arrivals**] no plural when someone reaches a place ☐ *We are all looking forward to Alice's arrival.* (**chegada**)

arrive /əˈraɪv/ VERB [**arrives, arriving, arrived**]
to reach a place ☐ **+ at** *Please arrive at the station by 5.30.* ☐ **+ in** *We arrived in Warsaw on Friday.* ☐ *If they don't arrive soon, we'll have to go without them.* (**chegar**)

> Remember that you **arrive in** a city or country:
> ✓ *We arrived in Madrid at 10 o'clock that night.*
> ✗ *We arrived to Madrid at 10 o'clock that night.*

> **THESAURUS:** If you arrive somewhere, you reach that place. For example, you can arrive at a party, or in a city, or at work. If you **enter** a place, you go into a place, often a building or a room. If you **turn up** at a place, you arrive there, often unexpectedly or very late.

arrow /ˈærəʊ/ NOUN [plural arrows]
1 a pointed shape used to show a particular direction □ *Follow the red arrows to the X-ray department.* (seta)
2 a thin, pointed stick that is used as a weapon (flecha)

art /ɑːt/ NOUN [plural arts]
1 *no plural* the beautiful things that people make and invent in painting, music, writing, etc. (arte)
2 a skill that you use to do or make something □ *the art of conversation* (arte)
3 the arts subjects that you can study that are not sciences (humanidades)

artery /ˈɑːtəri/ NOUN [plural arteries] a tube that leads from your heart to the rest of your body. A biology word. (artéria)

article /ˈɑːtɪkəl/ NOUN [plural articles]
1 a piece of writing in a magazine or newspaper 🔲 *Maya wrote an article for the school magazine.* 🔲 *I read an interesting article in the newspaper.* □ *+ about/on an article about farming* (artigo)
2 a thing 🔲 *There were a few articles of clothing on the floor.* (peça)
3 in grammar, the words 'a', 'an' and 'the' (artigo)

> **THESAURUS:** An **article** is a piece of writing for a newspaper or a magazine. An **essay** is a piece of writing by a student about a particular subject. A **story** is a piece of writing, often about invented things. For example, we often read **stories** to children before they go to bed. **Story** can also be used to describe a report in a newspaper or on television about something that has happened.

artificial /ˌɑːtɪˈfɪʃəl/ ADJECTIVE looking natural, but made by a person or machine □ *artificial snow* (artificial)

artist /ˈɑːtɪst/ NOUN [plural artists]
1 someone who paints or draws things □ *the wellknown French artist, Claude Monet* (artista)
2 a performer, for example a singer or a dancer (artista)

artistic /ɑːˈtɪstɪk/ ADJECTIVE
1 to do with art □ *The ballet was one of his greatest artistic achievements.* (artístico)
2 good at art □ *Emma's very artistic.* (artístico)

as /əz/ CONJUNCTION, PREPOSITION
1 as ... as used to compare things □ *Are you as tall as me?* □ *This restaurant's not as cheap as the other one.* (tão... como)
2 while □ *As we climbed, the air got colder.* (conforme)
3 used to talk about the purpose or job of something or someone □ *She works as a teacher.* □ *I use this room as my study.* (como)
4 as if/as though used to talk about how something seems □ *He looks as if he's going to faint.* □ *She cried as though her heart was broken.* (como se)
5 because □ *I went first as I was the youngest.* (porque)

ash /æʃ/ NOUN [plural ashes] the white powder that remains after something is burnt (cinza)

ashamed /əˈʃeɪmd/ ADJECTIVE feeling embarrassed or guilty about something □ *+of I am deeply ashamed of everything I said, and I apologize.* 🔲 *You should be ashamed of yourself, behaving like that.* □ *+ that I felt ashamed that I had never visited him in hospital.* (envergonhado)

ashore /əˈʃɔː(r)/ ADVERB onto the land at the edge of a sea, river, etc. □ *We went ashore for dinner and returned to the ship later.* (na praia)

Asian[1] /ˈeɪʒən, ˈeɪʃən/ ADJECTIVE to do with Asia, or from Asia □ *Asian art* (asiático)

Asian[2] /ˈeɪʒən, ˈeɪʃən/ NOUN [plural Asians] someone who comes from Asia (asiático)

aside /əˈsaɪd/ ADVERB to or on one side 🔲 *Please stand aside and let us through.* (ao lado)

ask /ɑːsk/ VERB [asks, asking, asked]
1 to say something as a question □ *She asked how old I was.* □ *+ about They asked us about our families.* (perguntar)
2 to say that you want someone to give you something □ *+ for I asked Joanne for some food.* (pedir)
3 to say that you want someone to do something □ *+ to do something He asked me to close the door.* (pedir)
4 to invite □ *+ to We've asked twenty people to our party.* (convidar)

> Remember that you **ask someone**. You do not **ask to someone**:
> ✓ *He asked me the time.*
> ✗ *He asked to me the time.*

> **THESAURUS :** **Ask** is a general word. **Inquire** is a more formal word, and is used if you ask for information about something. For example, you might **inquire** about a job. If you have a **query**, you ask questions about something, often because you think that there has been a mistake or because you need more information. For example, you might have a **query** about a bill. If you **question** someone, you ask them questions, often officially. For example, the police might **question** someone about a crime.

asleep

asleep /əˈsliːp/ ADJECTIVE
1 if you are asleep, you are sleeping □ *Don't wake her if she's asleep.* ☐ *The baby was fast asleep* (= deeply asleep) *in her pram.* ☐ *She got out of bed, still half asleep* (= very tired). **(adormecido)**
2 fall asleep to start sleeping □ *He fell asleep in front of the television.* **(adormecer)**

aspect /ˈæspekt/ NOUN [plural **aspects**] a part of a situation or subject □ *Newspapers have examined every aspect of her life.* **(aspecto)**

aspiration /ˌæspəˈreɪʃən/ NOUN [plural **aspirations**] a hope that you will get or achieve something □ *She has aspirations to be a lawyer.* **(anseio)**

aspirin /ˈæsprɪn/ NOUN [plural **aspirin** or **aspirins**]
1 *no plural* a medicine that stops pain ☐ *He takes aspirin every day.* **(aspirina)**
2 a pill that contains this medicine ☐ *I've taken a couple of aspirins for my headache.* **(aspirinas)**

assassin /əˈsæsɪn/ NOUN [plural **assassins**] someone who kills an important person, for example a politician **(assassino)**

assassinate /əˈsæsɪneɪt/ VERB [**assassinates, assassinating, assassinated**] to kill a famous person **(assassinar)**

assassination /əˌsæsɪˈneɪʃən/ NOUN [plural **assassinations**] the murder of a famous person **(assassino)**

assault¹ /əˈsɔːlt/ NOUN [plural **assaults**] an attack ☐ *It was a violent assault on an elderly woman.* **(assalto)**

assault² /əˈsɔːlt/ VERB [**assaults, assaulting, assaulted**] to attack someone **(assaltar)**

assemble /əˈsembəl/ VERB [**assembles, assembling, assembled**]
1 to bring several things or people together □ *We've assembled a choir for the concert.* **(reunir)**
2 to make something by putting several parts together □ *Where are the instructions for assembling the bookcase?* **(agregar)**

assembly /əˈsemblɪ/ NOUN [plural **assemblies**]
1 a regular meeting for everyone in a school **(reunião)**
2 a group of people who make decisions for a country or an organization □ *the General Assembly of the United Nations* **(assembleia)**

assess /əˈses/ VERB [**assesses, assessing, assessed**] to examine something and make a judgment about it □ *One of our agents will assess the damage to your car.* **(avaliar)**

assignment /əˈsaɪnmənt/ NOUN [plural **assignments**] a job someone has given you to do □ *I've got three homework assignments to finish by Friday.* **(tarefa)**

assist /əˈsɪst/ VERB [**assists, assisting, assisted**] to help □ *Villagers assisted in the search for the girl.* **(auxiliar)**

assistance /əˈsɪstəns/ NOUN, NO PLURAL help ☐ *The charity provides financial assistance to people in need.* ☐ *Can I be of any assistance* (= can I help)? **(auxílio)**

assistant /əˈsɪstənt/ NOUN [plural **assistants**]
1 someone whose job is to help someone else ☐ *She's a teaching assistant at the local school.* ☐ *You can speak to the assistant manager.* **(auxiliar, assistente)**
2 someone who works in a shop ☐ *She worked as a shop assistant.* **(vendedor)**

> **THESAURUS :** An assistant is someone who helps you to do a job. For example, a teaching assistant helps a teacher in a classroom. A shop assistant helps customers in a shop. A **supporter** is someone who wants someone else to succeed. For example, you can be a **supporter** of a politician, or of a football team. A **colleague** is a person that you work with. An **ally** is a person or a country that supports another person or country.

associate VERB /əˈsoʊʃieɪt/ [**associates, associating, associated**] to be related to or caused by something □ *Heavy pollution is associated with increased road travel.* **(associar)**

association /əˌsoʊsiˈeɪʃən/ NOUN [plural **associations**] an organization for people with similar interests □ *a professional association for teachers* **(associação)**

assume /əˈsjuːm/ VERB [**assumes, assuming, assumed**] to think something is true, although you have no proof □ *Oh sorry, I assumed that you had met each other before.* **(supor)**

assure /əˈʃʊə(r)/ VERB [**assures, assuring, assured**] to tell someone that something is certainly true or will certainly happen □ *Mr Harris has assured us that the car will be ready tomorrow.* **(assegurar)**

asthma /ˈæsmə/ NOUN, NO PLURAL an illness that makes breathing difficult **(asma)**

astonish /əˈstɒnɪʃ/ VERB [**astonishes, astonishing, astonished**] to surprise someone very much □ *His arrest astonished his neighbours and friends.* **(surpreender)**

astonishment /əˈstɒnɪʃmənt/ NOUN, NO PLURAL the state of being very surprised □ *To my astonishment, she agreed that I could stay.* □ *We stared in astonishment at the painting.* **(surpresa)**

astronaut /ˈæstrənɔːt/ NOUN [plural **astronauts**] someone who travels into space **(astronauta)**

astronomer /əˈstrɒnəmə(r)/ NOUN [plural **astronomers**] someone who studies stars and planets **(astrônomo)**

astronomy /əˈstrɒnəmɪ/ NOUN, NO PLURAL the study of stars and planets **(astronomia)**

asylum /əˈsaɪləm/ NOUN, NO PLURAL when someone is allowed to stay in a country because they are in danger in their own country ☐ *Many people seek asylum in this country.* ☐ *He was granted asylum in 2006.* **(asilo)**

at

at /æt/ PREPOSITION
1 used to show the position of someone or something □ *Meet me at the station.* □ *The car is at Clara's house.* □ *He's still at work.* **(em)**
2 used to show the time or period that something happens □ *School finishes at 4 o'clock.* □ *Will you be here at the weekend?* □ *I always visit my parents at Christmas.* **(em)**
3 towards □ *He threw a bucket of water at me.* □ *Look at me!* □ *She drove the car straight at him.* **(para)**

4 bad/good at something used to show someone's level of ability □ *He's good at football.* (bom/ruim em algo)
5 used to show the price, speed, level, etc. of something □ *We bought four bottles at 75p each.* □ *The car was travelling at 70 miles an hour.* (a)
6 used to describe someone's reaction □ *He broke down at the news.* (por causa de)
7 at all used for emphasis, for example when talking about something that does not exist □ *Doesn't he have any friends at all?* □ *I'm not looking forward to the party at all.* (absolutamente)

ate /eɪt/ PAST TENSE OF **eat** (*ver* eat)

athlete /ˈæθliːt/ NOUN [plural **athletes**] someone who is good at sports such as running ▣ *She is one of the country's top athletes.* ▣ *He was an Olympic athlete in 1928.* (atleta)

athletics /æθˈletɪks/ NOUN, NO PLURAL the sports that include running, jumping and throwing □ *Lee is very good at athletics.* (atletismo)

atlas /ˈætləs/ NOUN [plural **atlases**] a book of maps (atlas)

atmosphere /ˈætməsfɪə(r)/ NOUN [plural **atmospheres**]
1 the feeling that a place or situation has □ *The atmosphere in the company was very friendly.* □ + *of Increased crime is creating an atmosphere of fear.* (atmosfera)
2 the air around a planet □ *the Earth's atmosphere* (atmosfera)

atom /ˈætəm/ NOUN [plural **atoms**] the smallest part of a chemical element □ *Water contains two hydrogen atoms and one oxygen atom.* (átomo)

atomic /əˈtɒmɪk/ ADJECTIVE using the power that is created when atoms are broken ▣ *an atomic bomb* ▣ *atomic energy* (atômico)

attach /əˈtætʃ/ VERB [**attaches, attaching, attached**]
1 to join one thing to another thing □ + *to They attached a rope to the car.* (prender)
2 if you attach a document to an e-mail, you send the document with the e-mail. A computing word. (anexar)

attachment /əˈtætʃmənt/ NOUN [plural **attachments**] a document or picture that you send with an e-mail. A computing word. ▣ *Don't open an attachment if you don't know who it's from.* (anexo)

attack¹ /əˈtæk/ VERB [**attacks, attacking, attacked**]
1 to suddenly try to hurt someone □ + *with He attacked her with a knife.* □ *A man was attacked and robbed on Friday.* (atacar)
2 to try to destroy a place using weapons □ *A violent crowd tried to attack the embassy.* (atacar)
3 to criticize someone or something □ *He attacked the government for failing to improve standards in schools.* (atacar)

attack² /əˈtæk/ NOUN [plural **attacks**]
1 a violent act against a place or person ▣ *The attack was carried out by four men.* ▣ *Terrorist attacks have killed thousands of people.* □ + *on The attack on police officers began when an angry crowd started throwing bottles.* (ataque realizado)
2 strong criticism □ + *on He launched a personal attack on the President.* (ataque)

> **THESAURUS:** An attack may involve any number of people. An **invasion** is when the army of one country enters another country. A **raid** is a short or sudden attack, usually with a particular purpose. For example, a bank **raid** is an attack on a bank to steal money, and in a police **raid**, the police visit a place without warning and often use force to enter it.

attacker /əˈtækə(r)/ NOUN [plural **attackers**] a person who tries to hurt someone violently □ *Ravi was able to describe his attacker to police.* (agressor)

attempt¹ /əˈtempt/ VERB [**attempts, attempting, attempted**] to try to do something □ + *to do something He attempted to explain what he meant.* (tentar)

attempt² /əˈtempt/ NOUN [plural **attempts**] when you try to do something ▣ *Doctors made a desperate attempt to save her life.* ▣ *She made no attempt to escape.* □ + *to do something His attempt to climb Mount Everest failed.* (tentativa)

attend /əˈtend/ VERB [**attends, attending, attended**] to go to an event. A formal word. □ *More than 100 people attended the meeting.* (comparecer)

> People **attend** formal meetings but people usually **come to** or **go to** parties, friends' houses, football matches, etc.:
> ✓ *Did Jamie come to the wedding?*
> ✗ *Did Jamie attend the wedding?*

attendance /əˈtendəns/ NOUN, NO PLURAL being present somewhere □ *She was given an award for 100% attendance at school.* (presença)

attention /əˈtenʃən/ NOUN, NO PLURAL
1 pay attention to listen or watch carefully □ + *to Pay attention to what I'm saying, please.* (prestar atenção)
2 interest and thought that you give to something ▣ *The story attracted attention from all over the world.* (atenção)
3 get someone's attention to make someone notice you □ *I waved at her to get her attention.* (atrair atenção de alguém)

attic /ˈætɪk/ NOUN [plural **attics**] the space in the roof of a house (sótão)

attitude

attitude /ˈætɪtjuːd/ NOUN [plural **attitudes**] the way someone thinks about something ▣ *He has a very positive attitude.* ▣ *He needs to change his attitude and start working hard.* □ **+ to/towards** *Jane has a relaxed attitude to life.* (**atitude**)

attract /əˈtrækt/ VERB [**attracts, attracting, attracted**]
1 to make someone feel interested in or like someone or something □ *It was his smile that first attracted me.* □ **+ to** *They were attracted to the idea of filming in Sydney because of the weather.* (**atrair**)
2 to make people come somewhere or do something □ *The museum attracts visitors from all around the world.* □ *The programme attracted 15 million viewers.* (**atrair**)

attraction /əˈtrækʃən/ NOUN [plural **attractions**]
1 *no plural* a feeling of liking someone and finding them physically attractive □ **+ between** *The attraction between them was immediate.* (**atração**)
2 something that people want to visit or do ▣ *The Eiffel Tower is a popular tourist attraction.* ▣ *The town's main attraction is its castle.* (**atração**)

attractive /əˈtræktɪv/ ADJECTIVE nice to look at □ *She was an attractive woman.* □ *The hotel is set in attractive gardens.* (**atraente**)

> **THESAURUS:** Attractive means 'pleasant to look at', and we use it to describe people and things. For example, a building may be attractive. Both men and women can be attractive. Good-looking can also be used to talk about men and women who have attractive faces. Pretty is usually used to talk about women and girls, and handsome is usually used to talk about men.

attribute[1] /əˈtrɪbjuːt/
♦ PHRASAL VERBS [**attributes, attributing, attributed**]
attribute something to someone to think that something was made, painted, written, etc. by a particular person □ *The statue had been wrongly attributed to Bernini.* **attribute something to something** to say that something is caused by some thing □ *He attributed his success to determination.* (**atribuir**)
attribute[2] /ˈætrɪbjuːt/ NOUN [plural **attributes**] a quality or feature □ *He was chosen for his physical attributes rather than his acting ability.* (**atributo**)

auction /ˈɔːkʃən/ NOUN [plural **auctions**] a sale in which the person who offers the most money buys some thing (**leilão**)

audience /ˈɔːdɪəns/ NOUN [plural **audiences**]
the people who listen to or watch a performance ▣ *My father was in the audience tonight.* ▣ *Many audience members left before the end of the show.* (**plateia**)

> **THESAURUS:** The audience is all the people who listen to or watch a performance, for example in the theatre or the cinema. A spectator is a person who watches an event, often a sports event such as a football match. A fan is someone who likes a person or thing very much. For example, you can be a fan of a football team, or of a pop star. A viewer is a person who watches television.

audition /ɔːˈdɪʃən/ NOUN [plural **auditions**] a short performance that an actor, dancer, etc. does so that someone else can decide if they are good enough to be in a play, musical group, etc. ▣ *They're holding auditions for the show next week.* (**audição**)

August /ˈɔːɡəst/ NOUN [plural **Augusts**] the eighth month of the year, after July and before September □ *We'll visit you in August.* (**agosto**)

aunt /ɑːnt/ *ou* **auntie** *ou* **aunty** /ˈɑːnti/ NOUN [plural **aunts** or **aunties**]
1 the sister of one of your parents □ *My aunt and uncle live in Canada.* □ *Auntie Emily came to stay.* (**tia**)
2 your uncle's wife (**tia**)

authentic /ɔːˈθentɪk/ ADJECTIVE real □ *an authentic wartime uniform* (**autêntico**)

author /ˈɔːθə(r)/ NOUN [plural **authors**] a writer □ *Atkinson is the author of four novels.* (**autor**)

authority /ɔːˈθɒrəti/ NOUN [plural **authorities**]
1 *no plural* power and control ▣ *People who are in a position of authority must behave appropriately.* □ **+ to do something** *The chairman has the authority to make decisions.* □ **+ over** *This law gives the government more authority over the police force.* (**autoridade**)
2 an official organization or government department that controls something ▣ *Some local authorities do not have enough money for repairing roads.* (**autoridade**)
3 the authorities the police and people who have the power to make people obey laws □ *The British authorities raised concerns over the deal.* (**autoridades**)

auto /ˈɔːtəʊ/ ADJECTIVE to do with cars □ *the American auto industry* (**automóvel**)

autograph /ˈɔːtəɡrɑːf/ NOUN [plural **autographs**] the name of a famous person, written by them ▣ *Please can I have your autograph?* (**autógrafo**)

automatic /ˌɔːtəˈmætɪk/ ADJECTIVE (**automático**)
1 an automatic machine works without a person operating it ▣ *automatic doors* ▣ *Our heating system is fully automatic.* (**automático**)
2 an automatic action is something you do without thinking □ *My automatic response was to cover my face.* (**automático**)

automatically /ˌɔːtəˈmætɪkəli/ ADVERB
1 without a person operating something □ *The doors open automatically.* (**automaticamente**)

2 without thinking □ *When I saw the stone coming I automatically ducked.* (**automaticamente**)

autumn /ˈɔːtəm/ NOUN [plural autumns]
the season after summer, when the leaves change colour and fall □ *I love the colours of autumn leaves.* (**outono**)

availability /əˌveɪləˈbɪləti/ NOUN, NO PLURAL
1 how possible it is to get something □ *Please can you check the availability of tickets for Thursday?* (**disponibilidade**)
2 the times when someone is free to do something (**disponibilidade**)

available /əˈveɪləbəl/ ADJECTIVE
1 if something is available, you can get it or buy it 🔲 *Guns are readily available* (= easy to get) *here.* 🔲 *The government plans to make more college places available to poor students.* (**disponível**)
2 if someone is available, they are free to do something □ + **to do something** *I'm sorry, there's nobody available to help you at the moment.* (**disponível**)

avalanche /ˈævəlɑːnʃ/ NOUN [plural avalanches]
a large amount of snow and rocks sliding down the side of a mountain (**avalanche**)

avenue /ˈævənjuː/ NOUN [plural avenues]
a wide street, usually with trees on both sides (**avenida**)

average¹ /ˈævərɪdʒ/ ADJECTIVE
1 usual or ordinary □ *How much do you earn in an average week?* (**normal**)
2 an average amount is the amount you get by adding amounts together and dividing by the number of amounts □ *average temperatures* □ *the average wage* (**média**)

average² /ˈævərɪdʒ/ NOUN [plural averages]
1 the amount you get by adding amounts together and dividing by the number of amounts. (**média**)
2 on average usually, or based on an average amount □ *On average, adults in this country watch three hours of TV every day.* (**em média**)
3 above/below average more/less than the average amount □ *Temperatures are below average for the time of year.* (**acima/abaixo da média**)

avoid /əˈvɔɪd/ VERB [avoids, avoiding, avoided]
to stay away from somewhere or someone □ *Have you been avoiding me?* □ *I left early to avoid the rush hour traffic.* (**evitar**)

await /əˈweɪt/ VERB [awaits, awaiting, awaited]
to wait for something or someone 🔲 *He is in prison, awaiting trial for murder.* (**aguardar**)

awake /əˈweɪk/ ADJECTIVE
not sleeping □ *I tried to stay awake.* 🔲 *Stop talking – you're keeping me awake.* 🔲 *She's wide awake* (= completely awake) *by six every morning.* (**acordado**)

> **Awake** is used mainly as an adjective. The verb **awake** is formal and not often used. Instead, use the phrasal verb **wake up**:
> ✓ *I woke up early this morning.*
> ✗ *I awoke early this morning.*

award¹ /əˈwɔːd/ NOUN [plural awards]
a prize for someone who has achieved something 🔲 *Joe won an award for his contribution to football.* (**prêmio, prêmios**)

award² /əˈwɔːd/ VERB [awards, awarding, awarded]
to give someone a prize or something good because of what they have achieved □ *She was awarded the Nobel Prize for literature.* (**premiar**)

aware /əˈweə(r)/ ADJECTIVE
if you are aware of something, you know about it □ + **of** *Katya became aware of someone else in the room.* □ + **that** *I'm perfectly aware that you've been waiting a long time.* (**ciente**)

away¹ /əˈweɪ/ ADVERB
1 to a different place or in a different place □ *He walked away.* □ *We'll be away for three weeks.* (**fora**)
2 at a distance □ *How far away is the school?* □ *The exam is only a week away.* (**a distância**)
3 not at work or school □ *Tina was away today.* (**fora**)
4 in the place where something is kept □ *Could you put the books away, please?* (**para longe**)

away² /əˈweɪ/ ADJECTIVE
an away game or match is one a team has to travel to (**campo adversário**)

awful /ˈɔːfʊl/ ADJECTIVE
1 very bad □ *an awful headache* 🔲 *The food was absolutely awful.* (**horrível**)
2 very great □ *There is an awful lot of ice on the roads.* □ *Looking after their dogs is an awful nuisance.* (**impressionante**)

awkward /ˈɔːkwəd/ ADJECTIVE
1 difficult to manage or use □ *I find this keyboard a bit awkward.* (**complicado**)
2 embarrassed or embarrassing □ *I feel really awkward when she asks me for money.* □ *an awkward silence* (**desagradável**)
3 awkward movements are not easy and relaxed (**desajeitado**)

awoke /əˈwəʊk/ PAST TENSE OF awake (ver awake)
awoken /əˈwəʊkən/ PAST PARTICIPLE OF awake (ver awake)

axe¹ /æks/ NOUN [plural axes]
a tool for cutting wood (**machado**)

axe² /æks/ VERB [axes, axing, axed]
to stop a plan or a service, close a business or get rid of workers □ *Thousands of jobs were axed.* (**despedir**)

B b

B ou b /biː/ the second letter of the alphabet (a segunda letra do alfabeto)

baby /ˈbeɪbi/ NOUN [plural babies] a very young child ▢ *Paola has had a baby.* ▢ *a baby boy* (**bebê**)

babysit /ˈbeɪbiˌsɪt/ VERB [babysits, babysitting, babysat] to look after a baby or child when its parents are not in the house ▢ *Could you babysit for me on Saturday?* (**ficar de babá**)

babysitter /ˈbeɪbiˌsɪtə(r)/ NOUN [plural babysitters] someone who looks after a baby or a child when its parents are not in the house (**babá**)

bachelor /ˈbætʃələ(r)/ NOUN [plural bachelors] a man who has never married (**solteiro**)

back¹ /bæk/ NOUN [plural backs]
1 the part of something that is furthest away from the front ▢ *Nina hid her diary at the back of a drawer.* (**fundo**)
2 the part of the body that goes from the shoulders to the bottom ▢ *I always sleep on my back.* (**costas**)
♦ IDIOM **back to front** the wrong way, so that the part that should be at the back is now at the front ▢ *You've got your sweater on back to front!* (**de trás para frente**)

back² /bæk/ VERB [backs, backing, backed]
1 to support or help someone or something ▢ *He is backing the female candidate in the election.* (**ajudar**)
2 to move backwards, usually in a car ▢ *She backed into the drive.* (**mover para trás**)
♦ PHRASAL VERBS **back someone up** to support someone ▢ *If you complain to the teacher, I'll back you up.* **back something up** to make an extra copy of information on a computer. A computing word. ▢ *Are the files all backed up?* **back down** to admit that you are wrong ▢ *He backed down when I showed him that his calculations were wrong.*

back³ /bæk/ ADVERB
1 to the place where a person or thing was before ▢ *What time is he coming back?* ▢ *Could you give Maria her book back, please?* (**de volta**)
2 in the direction that is the opposite of forwards ▢ *I stood back to let her pass.* ▢ *She sat back in her chair.* (**para trás**)
3 as a reply to something ▢ *Can I call you back in an hour?* (**de volta**)
4 to the condition someone or something was in before ▢ *I went back to sleep.* (**de volta**)
5 to an earlier time ▢ *Thinking back to that day, she was obviously unhappy.* (**anteriormente**)

back⁴ /bæk/ ADJECTIVE away from the front ▢ *Ben's had one of his back teeth taken out.* (**de trás**)

backbone /ˈbækbəʊn/ NOUN [plural backbones] the row of bones down the middle of your back (**coluna vertebral**)

backdrop /ˈbækdrɒp/ NOUN [plural backdrops]
1 the things you can see behind the main thing you are looking at ▢ *The hotel is set against a backdrop of beautiful mountains.* (**pano de fundo**)
2 a cloth with a picture on it that is hung at the back of a stage in a theatre (**pano de fundo**)

background /ˈbækɡraʊnd/ NOUN [plural backgrounds]
1 the part of a picture which is behind the main people or objects ▢ *Here's a photo of us with Mount Fuji in the background.* (**em segundo plano**)
2 a person's background is their family and the things they have done in the past ▢ *These children are from very poor backgrounds.* (**experiência**)
3 the background of an event is all the things that happened before it and caused it to happen ▢ *+ to the background to the English civil war.* (**acontecimento**)

backpack /ˈbækpæk/ NOUN [plural backpacks] a large bag that you carry on your back ▢ *I was carrying the tent in my backpack.* (**mochila**)

backspace /ˈbækspeɪs/ VERB [backspaces, backspacing, backspaced] to move back one space by pressing a key on a computer. A computing word. (**voltar um espaço**)

backup /ˈbækʌp/ NOUN [plural **backups**] an extra copy of information on a computer. A computing word. (cópia reserva)

backward /ˈbækwəd/ ADJECTIVE towards the back □ *a backward look* (para trás)

backwards /ˈbækwədz/ ADVERB

1 in the direction behind you □ *I stepped backwards to give her some room.* (para trás)
2 in the wrong position, with the back part at the front □ *I think my skirt is on backwards.* (de trás para a frente)
3 in the opposite way to the usual way □ *Tom can say the alphabet backwards.* (de trás para a frente)

bacon /ˈbeɪkən/ NOUN, NO PLURAL thin pieces of salty meat from a pig (bacon)

bacteria /bækˈtɪərɪə/ PLURAL NOUN very small living things that sometimes cause disease in humans and animals (bactéria)

bad /bæd/ ADJECTIVE [worse, worst]

1 not of a good standard □ *I've had a really bad haircut.* □ *The food was so bad I couldn't eat it.* (ruim)
2 unpleasant, causing problems or worry □ *Bad weather can spoil a holiday.* □ *I had some bad news this morning.* (ruim)
3 not bad satisfactory or good enough □ *We made over three hundred pounds so that's not bad.* □ *'How are you doing, Maria?' 'Not bad, thanks.'* (nada mal)
4 bad for someone harmful to your body, making you not healthy □ *It's bad for you to eat too much sugar.* (mal para alguém)
5 bad at something not able to do something well □ *I'm very bad at maths.* (ruim em algo)
6 food which is bad does not taste or smell good because it is old □ *This meat is bad – throw it away.* (estragado)
7 evil or cruel □ *He's not a bad man.* (ruim)

> Remember that **bad** is an adjective and not an adverb. To describe the way that someone does something, use the adverb **badly**:
> ✓ He behaved very badly.
> ✗ He behaved very bad.

bade /bæd, beɪd/ PAST TENSE OF **bid²** □ *I bade him goodbye.* (ver **bid**)

badge /bædʒ/ NOUN [plural **badges**] a small object with words or pictures that you put on your clothes to show something, for example your name (crachá)

badly /ˈbædlɪ/ ADVERB [worse, worst]

1 seriously □ *The car was badly damaged in the crash.* (seriamente)
2 in a way that is not good □ *Both children behaved badly.* (de modo ruim)
3 very much □ *I badly wanted a new pair of shoes.* (muito)

bag /bæg/ NOUN [plural **bags**] an object that you put things in and carry with you □ *a leather bag* □ *a bag of crisps* (bolsa)

> THESAURUS: **Bag** is a general word for an object that you use for carrying things. A **backpack** is a large bag that you carry on your back. For example, you might use a **backpack** if you go camping. A **handbag** is a bag that a woman uses to carry things like money and keys. We use a **suitcase** to carry our clothes in when we are travelling.

baggage /ˈbægɪdʒ/ NOUN, NO PLURAL the cases and bags that a person takes with them when they travel □ *The baggage is stored in the back of the coach.* (bagagem)

> Remember that the noun **baggage** is never used in the plural:
> ✓ I had so much baggage.
> ✗ I had so many baggages.

bail¹ /beɪl/ NOUN, NO PLURAL money that must be paid to a court so that someone who has been arrested for a crime can leave a prison until their trial □ *He was released on bail.* (fiança)

bail² /beɪl/ VERB [**bails, bailing, bailed**] to allow someone to go free because bail has been paid (afiançar)

bait /beɪt/ NOUN, NO PLURAL food that you use for catching a fish or an animal (isca)

bake /beɪk/ VERB [**bakes, baking, baked**] to cook things like bread, cakes or biscuits in an oven □ *I baked a cake this afternoon.* □ *I love to bake with the children.* (assar)

balance¹ /ˈbæləns/ NOUN, NO PLURAL

1 when you have the same amount of weight on each side of the body so that you do not fall over □ *I lost my balance and fell over.* □ *I find it hard to keep my balance in high heels.* (equilíbrio)
2 a good situation in which you have or do the right amount of two or more things □ *I try to achieve a balance between work and family life.* (equilíbrio)
3 the amount of money that is in a bank account (saldo)

**balance² ** /ˈbæləns/ VERB [balances, balancing, balanced] to stay in a position where you do not fall to either side, or to put something in a position where it will not fall ▢ Lisa balanced the book on her head. (equilibrar)

balcony /ˈbælkəni/ NOUN [plural balconies]
1 a part of a high building which is on the outside wall. You can sit or stand in it ▢ We sat on the balcony and watched the sun go down. (sacada)
2 in a theatre, the area upstairs where the seats are above the rest of the audience (camarote)

bald /bɔːld/ ADJECTIVE [balder, baldest] with little or no hair on the head ▣ He's going bald. (careca)

ball /bɔːl/ NOUN [plural balls]
1 a round object that you use for playing games like football and tennis (bola)
2 anything that has a round shape ▢ a ball of string ▢ The hedgehog rolled itself into a ball. (bola)
3 a big formal party where people dance (baile)

ballet /ˈbæleɪ/ NOUN [plural ballets]
1 no plural a type of dancing that tells a story and uses smooth, attractive movements which are very difficult to do ▣ a ballet dancer ▢ Sarah does ballet and tap dancing. (balé)
2 a story which is told using ballet ▢ My favourite ballets are The Nutcracker and Swan Lake. (balé)

balloon /bəˈluːn/ NOUN [plural balloons] a very light, round, rubber object that is filled with air or gas ▢ The children were holding balloons. (balão)

ballot /ˈbælət/ NOUN [plural ballots] a way of voting in secret by marking a paper and putting it into a special box ▣ They held a ballot to decide who would be leader. (votação)

bamboo /bæmˈbuː/ NOUN, NO PLURAL a tall grass that has hard, hollow stems that are used to make furniture (bambu)

ban /bæn/ NOUN [plural bans] an order that people are not allowed to do something ▢ There's a ban on smoking in public places. (proibição)

banana /bəˈnɑːnə/ NOUN [plural bananas] a long, curved, yellow fruit which is white inside ▣ I watched him peel a banana. (banana)

band /bænd/ NOUN [plural bands]
1 a group of musicians who play together a rock band (banda)
2 a long, thin piece of material used for putting round something ▣ a rubber band (fita)
3 a group ▢ a band of robbers (bando)

bandage¹ /ˈbændɪdʒ/ NOUN [plural bandages] a long piece of cloth that you put around a part of your body that has been cut or hurt ▢ He had a bandage around his arm. (bandagem)

bandage² /ˈbændɪdʒ/ VERB [bandages, bandaging, bandaged] to put a bandage around a part of your body ▢ The nurse bandaged his wrist. (enfaixar)

bandit /ˈbændɪt/ NOUN [plural bandits] some one who attacks people who are travelling and takes money and possessions from them (bandido)

bang¹ /bæŋ/ NOUN [plural bangs]
1 a sudden loud noise ▢ There was a loud bang and all the lights went out. (estrondo)
2 when you knock part of your body against something ▢ She's had a bang on the head and is feeling a bit dizzy. (pancada)

bang² /bæŋ/ VERB [bangs, banging, banged]
1 to make a sudden loud noise by hitting against something ▢ The door banged shut in the wind. (bater)
2 to knock part of your body against something ▢ Neil banged his head on the shelf. (bater)

banish /ˈbænɪʃ/ VERB [banishes, banishing, banished] to make someone leave their country or their home as a punishment (banir)

bank¹ /bæŋk/ NOUN [plural banks]
1 a business that looks after other people's money and also lends money ▣ I must go to the bank. (banco)
2 an area of ground which is next to a river or lake ▢ We camped on the banks of Loch Lomond. (margem)

> **THESAURUS:** The bank of a river or a lake is the area of land next to it. The area of land next to the sea is called the shore. A slope is the side of a hill or mountain. Side and edge are more general words. You can talk about the side of a river, but also the side of a building or a road. Edge is often used to talk about the very end or outer part of something. For example, you might talk about the edge of a cliff or the edge of a city.

bank² /bæŋk/ VERB [banks, banking, banked] to have a bank account with a particular bank ▢ I've banked with them for years. (depositar)
♦ PHRASAL VERB **bank on something** to depend on something ▢ He might help you but don't bank on it.

bank account /bæŋk əˈkaʊnt/ NOUN [plural bank accounts] an arrangement that you have with a bank for keeping money there, and for taking it out when you need it ▣ I must open a bank account. (conta bancária)

bank balance /bæŋk ˈbæləns/ NOUN [plural bank balances] the amount of money you have in a bank account (saldo bancário)

banking /ˈbæŋkɪŋ/ NOUN, NO PLURAL the business that banks do (negócio bancário)

banknote /ˈbæŋknəʊt/ NOUN [plural banknotes] a piece of paper money ▢ a £20 banknote (nota de dinheiro)

bankrupt /ˈbæŋkrʌpt/ ADJECTIVE if a person or business is bankrupt, they are not able to pay the money they owe ▣ The business went bankrupt because costs rose. (falido)

banner /'bænə(r)/ NOUN [plural **banners**] a large piece of cloth with writing on it which people carry on poles ☐ *The anti-war protesters were carrying banners.* (**faixa**)

bar¹ /bɑː(r)/ NOUN [plural **bars**]
1 a place that sells alcoholic drinks ☐ *The city is full of cafe's and bars.* (**bar**)
2 a long narrow piece of metal ☐ *an iron bar* (**barra**)
3 a large piece of something such as chocolate or soap ☐ *+ of a bar of chocolate* (**barra**)

bar² /bɑː(r)/ VERB [**bars, barring, barred**]
1 if someone is barred from a place or barred from doing something, they are not allowed in or are not allowed to do it ☐ *+ from Anyone over the age of 12 is barred from the competition.* (**barrar**)
2 to prevent someone from going somewhere by standing in their way ☐ *Over a hundred protestors barred the entrance to the building.* (**barrar**)
3 to lock a door or window by putting a metal bar across it (**barrar**)

barbecue¹ /'bɑːbɪkjuː/ NOUN [plural **barbecues**]
1 a piece of equipment used for cooking food outdoors ☐ *She was trying to light the barbecue.* 🔲 *Put some more sausages on the barbecue.* (**grelha**)
2 a party or meal outdoors where food is cooked on a barbecue 🔲 *We're having a barbecue tonight.* (**churrasco**)

barbecue² /'bɑːbɪkjuː/ VERB [**barbecues, barbecuing, barbecued**] to cook food on a barbecue (**assar, grelhar**)

barber /'bɑːbə(r)/ NOUN [plural **barbers**]
1 a man whose job is to cut men's hair (**barbeiro**)
2 barber's a shop where men have their hair cut (**barbeiro**)

bare /beə(r)/ ADJECTIVE [**barer, barest**] not covered with anything 🔲 *It's too cold to go out with bare legs.* ☐ *The wall looks really bare without any pictures on it.* (**nu**)

barely /'beəli/ ADVERB almost not ☐ *She was old and barely able to walk.* ☐ *They had barely arrived when they had to leave again.* (**mal**)

bargain /'bɑːgɪn/ NOUN [plural **bargains**]
1 something that is cheap or cheaper than usual ☐ *These jeans were a real bargain.* (**pechincha**)
2 an agreement in which each person or group promises to do something 🔲 *She tried to strike a bargain with* (= make an agreement with) *him.* (**fazer um acordo com**)

barge /bɑːdʒ/ NOUN [plural **barges**] a boat with a flat bottom, used on canals (= passages of water) and rivers (**barcaça**)

bark¹ /bɑːk/ NOUN [plural **barks**]
1 the short, loud sound that a dog makes (**latido**)
2 the rough wood on the outside of a tree (**córtex**)

bark² /bɑːk/ VERB [**barks, barking, barked**] when a dog barks, it makes a short, loud sound (**latir**)

barn /bɑːn/ NOUN [plural **barns**] a large building on a farm, for keeping crops or animals in (**celeiro**)

barracks /'bærəks/ PLURAL NOUN a group of buildings where soldiers live and work (**quartel**)

barrel /'bærəl/ NOUN [plural **barrels**]
1 a wooden or metal container with curved sides, used for holding liquids such as beer (**barril**)
2 the barrel of a gun is the metal tube through which the bullet is fired (**cano**)

barrier /'bæriə(r)/ NOUN [plural **barriers**]
1 a gate or fence used to stop people getting past ☐ *There is a barrier at the exit of the car park, and you need a ticket to get out.* (**barreira**)
2 something that stops you from making progress or stops you from being successful ☐ *Nowadays, being a woman isn't a barrier to a career in the navy.* (**barreira**)

> **THESAURUS:** A **barrier** is a thing which stops people moving forward. For example, there might be a barrier at the entrance or exit of a car park or a station to check tickets. A **wall** is a structure that separates two areas or goes round an area. You might have a **wall** around your garden. **Walls** are usually made of something hard such as brick or concrete. A **fence** goes around land, and is usually made of wood or metal. You might have a **fence** around a garden or a field. A **railing** is a fence made of vertical metal bars. You often see **railings** around parks in cities.

barrister /'bærɪstə(r)/ NOUN [plural **barristers**] a lawyer who works in a court (**advogado**)

base¹ /beɪs/ NOUN [plural **bases**]
1 the lowest part of something ☐ *+ of He broke a bone at the base of his spine.* (**base**)
2 something which is under something else and which supports it ☐ *The shed stood on a concrete base.* (**base**)
3 the main place where someone works or stays ☐ *+ for The hotel is an ideal base for walking holidays.* (**base**)

base² /beɪs/ VERB [**bases, basing, based**] if a person or organization is based in a particular place, that is where they live or do their work ☐ *usually passive The company is based in Moscow.* (**estabelecer**)
◆ PHRASAL VERB **base something on something** to use an idea, situation, fact etc. as the thing that you develop something else from ☐ *often passive The court's decision was based on facts.*

baseball /'beɪsbɔːl/ NOUN [plural **baseballs**]
1 *no plural* a game for two teams who hit a ball with a long bat (= wooden stick) and run to four different places 🔲 *He taught me how to play baseball.* ☐ *a baseball game* (**beisebol**)
2 a small ball used in the game of baseball (**bola de beisebol**)

basement /'beɪsmənt/ NOUN [plural **basements**] the lowest level of a building, under the ground ☐ *There is a restaurant in the basement* ☐ *a basement flat* (**porão**)

bases /'beɪsiːz/ PLURAL OF **basis** and **base** (**ver basis, base**)

basic

basic /ˈbeɪsɪk/ ADJECTIVE
1 being the main or most important part of something □ *He taught us the basic principles of karate.* □ *basic training/skills* (**básico**)
2 without any extra or special features □ *The cottage was pretty basic – it didn't even have a proper bath.* (**básico**)

basin /ˈbeɪsən/ NOUN [plural **basins**]
1 a bowl with taps (= objects you turn to get water) for washing your hands and face in (**bacia**)
2 a bowl used in the kitchen for holding food □ *a pudding basin* (**bacias**)

> **THESAURUS:** We usually call the bowl that we use for washing in the bathroom a **basin**. The bowl which we use for washing things in the kitchen is usually called a **sink**. **Basin** is also a word for a bowl that we use for preparing food. **Bowl** is a more general word, and a **bowl** can be large or small. We use **bowls** for eating from and also for cooking. **Dish** is also a general word, and can be a **plate** or a **bowl**.

basis /ˈbeɪsɪs/ NOUN [plural **bases**]
1 on a regular/part-time/unpaid, etc. basis used to express the method or system used for arranging or organizing something □ *The team meets on a weekly basis.* □ *I work there on a voluntary basis.* (**base**)
2 the thing on which something is based □ *Sweets can be eaten occasionally but should not form the basis of your diet.* (**base**)

basket /ˈbɑːskɪt/ NOUN [plural **baskets**] a container for storing or carrying things, made of thin pieces of material such as wood or plastic □ *a shopping basket* □ *+ of a basket of fruit* (**cesta**)

basketball /ˈbɑːskɪtbɔːl/ NOUN [plural **basketballs**]
1 no plural a game played by two teams who try to throw a ball through a net (**basquete**)
2 a large ball used to play basketball (**bola de basquete**)

bat¹ /bæt/ NOUN [plural **bats**]
1 a piece of wood used for hitting the ball in sports such as cricket and baseball (**bastão**)
2 an animal that flies around at night, and looks like a mouse with wings (**morcego**)

bat² /bæt/ VERB [bats, batting, batted] to use the bat in games such as cricket and baseball □ *It's Gary's turn to bat next.* (**bater**)

batch /bætʃ/ NOUN [plural **batches**] several people or things that are dealt with as a group □ *He tied a batch of papers together.* (**grupo**)

bath¹ /bɑːθ/ NOUN [plural **baths**]
1 a long container that you fill with water and sit or lie in to wash yourself □ *Russell's in the bath.* □ *She went upstairs and ran a bath* (= put water in it). (**banheira**)
2 when you sit or lie in a long container filled with water so that you can wash yourself □ *I think I'll have a bath.* (**banho**)

bath² /bɑːθ/ VERB [baths, bathing, bathed] to wash someone in a bath (**dar banho em**)

bathroom /ˈbɑːθruːm/ NOUN [plural **bathrooms**] the room that you wash yourself in □ *The hotel rooms all have a private bathroom.* □ *a bathroom mirror* (**banheiro**)

batsman /ˈbætsmən/ NOUN [plural **batsmen**] a man who is hitting the ball in cricket (**batedor**)
batter¹ /ˈbætə(r)/ VERB [batters, battering, battered] to hit someone or something very hard several times □ *He was battered to death with a hammer.* □ *Waves battered the shore.* (**espancar**)
• **battered** /ˈbætəd/ ADJECTIVE damaged □ *a battered leather suitcase* (**danificado**)
batter² /ˈbætə(r)/ NOUN, NO PLURAL a mixture of flour, milk and eggs, used for covering food before it is fried (**massa**)
• **battered** /ˈbætəd/ ADJECTIVE covered in batter □ *battered cod* (**coberto por massa**)
battery /ˈbætəri/ NOUN [plural **batteries**] a device to supply electrical power to things like watches, cameras and car engines □ *The car wouldn't start because the battery was flat* (= the battery did not work). (**bateria**)

battle /ˈbætəl/ NOUN [plural **battles**] a fight between two armies □ *the Battle of Hastings* □ *His father was killed in battle.* (**batalha**)

> **THESAURUS:** A **battle** is a fight between two armies. A **war** describes a longer period of fighting between two armies, groups or countries. A **war** may include a number of different **battles**. **Fight** is a more general word. A **fight** can be a situation where people use force to hurt each other, or an argument between people.

battlefield /ˈbætəlfiːld/ NOUN [plural **battlefields**] a place where armies fight (**campo de batalha**)

bay /beɪ/ NOUN [plural **bays**] a piece of land on the coast that curves in □ *the Bay of Biscay* (**baía**)

BBC /ˌbiːbiːˈsiː/ ABBREVIATION British Broadcasting Corporation; the television and radio company paid for by the public in the UK (**BBC**)

BC /ˌbiːˈsiː/ ABBREVIATION before Christ; used after a date to show that it was before the birth of Jesus Christ. □ *450 BC* (**a.C.**)
L go to **AD**

be¹ /biː/ VERB
1 used for giving information about someone or something □ *He's French.* □ *Are you hungry?* □ *Her brother's an accountant.* (**ser, estar**)
2 there are/is/were, etc. used for saying

that something exists or existed □ *There are a lot of people here.* □ *Is there anything else to eat?* (haver)

be² /biː/ AUXILIARY VERB (verbo auxiliar)
1 used with the present participle of another verb to talk about actions that were or are continuous □ *I am enjoying my course.* □ *What are you doing?* □ *He is not doing very well at school*
2 used with the present participle of another verb to talk about actions in the future □ *He is going to London next week.* □ *They are opening a new shop.* □ *I am coming back again later.*
3 used with the past participle of another verb to make passive sentences □ *She was taken to hospital.* □ *They have been warned before.* □ *The animals will be kept in a zoo.*

beach /biːtʃ/ NOUN [plural beaches] an area of sand or stones at the edge of the sea □ *We spent the day on the beach.* ▣ *The town has a beautiful sandy beach.* (praia)

> THESAURUS: A beach is an area of sand or stones next to the sea. People often go to a beach to play or swim. The **shore** describes the area of land where water such as sea or a lake reaches the land. People may not be able to go on a particular part of a **shore**, for example if it is very rocky. **Coast** describes any area next to the sea and involves a bigger area than shore. For example, we can say that a town is on the **coast**, or that a road travels along a **coast**.

bead /biːd/ NOUN [plural beads] a small round piece of glass, plastic or wood with a hole through it, used for making jewellery (conta)

beak /biːk/ NOUN [plural beaks] a bird's beak is its hard pointed mouth (bica, bico)

beam¹ /biːm/ NOUN [plural beams]
1 a line of light □ *the beam of the car's headlights* (feixe de luz)
2 a long thick piece of wood or metal that is used to support the weight of a building (viga)
3 a big smile (sorriso)

beam² /biːm/ VERB [beams, beaming, beamed] to smile a big smile □ *Meg beamed at him gratefully.* (sorri)

bean /biːn/ NOUN [plural beans] a vegetable that is the large seed of some plants □ *kidney beans* (vagem)

bear¹ /beə(r)/ VERB [bears, bearing, bore, born or borne]
1 to accept something unpleasant or painful ▣ *I can't bear the thought of him suffering.* □ *+ to do something Stephanie can't bear to leave her children.* □ *Can you bear to wait a bit longer for dinner?* (suportar)
2 bear something in mind to remember that something is important □ *Please bear in mind that you only have an hour to write your essay.* (ter em mente)
3 to carry something in your hand □ *Hassan appeared, bearing a cup of coffee.* (carregar)
• **bearable** /ˈbeərəbəl/ ADJECTIVE if something is bearable, you can accept it, despite the fact that it is bad □ *The warmer weather made life a bit more bearable.* (suportável)

bear² /beə(r)/ NOUN [plural bears] a large, strong animal with thick fur (urso)

beard /bɪəd/ NOUN [plural beards] the hair that grows on a man's chin ▣ *He wanted to grow a beard.* ▣ *Dieter shaved off his beard.* (barba)

beast /biːst/ NOUN [plural beasts]
1 an animal, especially a large one (besta)
2 an old-fashioned word meaning a cruel person (besta)

beat¹ /biːt/ VERB [beats, beating, beat, beaten]
1 to defeat someone in a game or competition □ *England were beaten 3-0 by Italy.* □ *+ at She beat me at squash.* (bater)
2 to hit someone or something many times □ *He was beaten and robbed by two men.* (bater)
3 to make a regular sound or movement □ *He could hear his heart beating.* (bater)
4 to mix food together very quickly □ *Beat the eggs.* (bater)
♦ PHRASAL VERB **beat someone up** to hit or kick someone until they are badly injured □ *He was beaten up by some boys in his class.* (surrar)

beat² /biːt/ NOUN [plural beats]
1 a regular sound or movement like that made by your heart □ *+ of I could hear the rapid beat of her heart.* (batida)
2 a regular rhythm in music (ritmo)

beautiful /ˈbjuːtɪfʊl/ ADJECTIVE
1 very attractive □ *She was a very beautiful young woman.* ▣ *She looked beautiful in her long blue dress.* □ *beautiful countryside* □ *beautiful music* (bonito)
2 very sunny and bright □ *It was a cold but beautiful day.* (bonito)

beauty /ˈbjuːti/ NOUN, NO PLURAL the quality of being very attractive ▣ *The area is noted for its natural beauty.* □ *+ of the beauty of her face* (beleza)

became /bɪˈkeɪm/ PAST TENSE OF **become** (ver become)

because /bɪˈkɒz/ CONJUNCTION
1 used for giving the reason for something □ *We chose the hotel because it was easy for everyone to get to.* □ *You can't borrow my bike because there's something wrong with the brakes.* (porque)
2 because of as a result of □ *Because of your rudeness, we've lost the job.* □ *We decided not to go because of the rain.* (por causa de)

become /bɪˈkʌm/ VERB [becomes, becoming, became, become]
1 to begin to be something □ *She'd become old and frail.* □ *He became prime minister in 1997.* (tornar-se)

2 what became of someone/something used to ask what has happened to someone or something □ *Do you remember the woman with the pink coat? I wonder what became of her?* (**acontecer com**)

bed /bed/ NOUN [plural **beds**]

1 a piece of furniture that you sleep on □ *He was ill and spent the day in bed.* □ *I got out of bed and went downstairs.* □ *What time do you usually go to bed?* □ *I need to make the bed* (= put the sheets on it). □ *The room had a double bed* (= bed for two people) *in it.* (**cama**)
2 the bottom of a river, a lake or the sea □ *the sea bed* (**leito**)
3 an area in a garden that contains flowers and other plants □ *He was weeding the flower bed.* (**canteiro**)

> **THESAURUS:** Bed is a general word for the piece of furniture that you sleep on. A **single bed** is a bed for one person. A **double bed** is a bed for two people. A **cot** is a bed with high sides that a baby sleeps in. The **mattress** is the soft part of the bed, that you lie on.

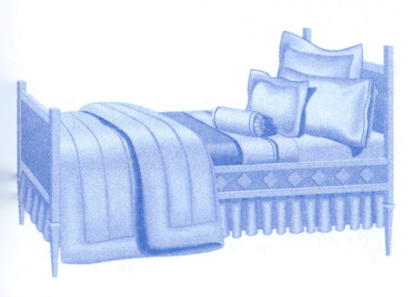

bedroom /'bedrʊm/ NOUN [plural **bedrooms**]
a room that you sleep in □ *We have a spare bedroom so you can come and stay.* □ *bedroom furniture* (**quarto**)

bee /biː/ NOUN [plural **bees**]
a black and yellow insect that makes honey (**abelha**)

beef /biːf/ NOUN, NO PLURAL
meat from a cow □ *We had roast beef for dinner.* (**carne**)

been /biːn/ PAST PARTICIPLE OF **be**
□ *I have been thinking.* (**ver be**)

beer /bɪə(r)/ NOUN [plural **beers**]
1 *no plural* an alcoholic drink made from a type of grain □ *He had a pint of beer in his hand.* □ *empty beer bottles* (**cerveja**)
2 a glass of this drink □ *I'll have a beer please.* (**cerveja**)

beetle /'biːtəl/ NOUN [plural **beetles**]
a black insect with a hard back (**besouro**)

before¹ /bɪ'fɔː(r)/ PREPOSITION

1 earlier than something □ *He lost his job just before Christmas.* □ *I posted the letter the day before yesterday.* □ *+ ing He tidied the house before going to bed.* (**antes**)
2 if one place is before another place, you get to that place first □ *Our house is just before the turning on the left.* (**antes**)
3 before long soon □ *Before long, we became good friends.* (**logo**)

before² /bɪ'fɔː(r)/ CONJUNCTION
earlier than the time when something will happen □ *Wash your hands before you come to the table.* (**antes de**)

before³ /bɪ'fɔː(r)/ ADVERB
at an earlier time □ *I don't think we've met before.* □ *We had all been to the beach the day before.* (**anterior**)

beg /beg/ VERB [**begs, begging, begged**]
1 to ask someone for something in an eager or emotional way because you want it very much □ *I begged him to come home.* (**implorar**)
2 to ask people for money in the street because you are very poor (**mendigar**)
3 I beg your pardon (a) a formal way of saying sorry when you have made a mistake □ *Oh, I beg your pardon, I didn't realize this pen was yours.* (b) a formal way of asking someone to repeat what they have just said because you did not hear it □ *'I'm going now.' 'I beg your pardon.' 'I said, I'm going now.'* (**desculpar-se**)

began /bɪ'gæn/ PAST TENSE OF **begin** (**ver begin**)

beggar /'begə(r)/ NOUN [plural **beggars**] someone who asks people for money in the street (**mendigo**)

begin /bɪ'gɪn/ VERB [**begins, beginning, began, begun**]
1 to start □ *The concert began at 7.30 and finished at 9.30.* □ *+ to do something I was beginning to feel better.* □ *+ ing She began walking towards the door.* □ *+ with The year began with a big disappointment.* (**começar**)
2 to begin with at the start of something □ *Lorna didn't like her new school to begin with.* (**antes de tudo**)

beginner /bɪ'gɪnə(r)/ NOUN [plural **beginners**]
someone who has just started to do or to learn something □ *a guitar class for beginners* (**novato**)

> **THESAURUS:** A beginner is someone who is starting to do or learn something. A **learner** is also learning to do something, but a **learner** may or may not be a beginner. For example, you can be a language **learner** for many years. A **recruit** is someone who has just joined a company or an organization. New soldiers are also called **recruits**.

beginning /bɪ'gɪnɪŋ/ NOUN, NO PLURAL
the start of something or the first part of something □ *My birthday is at the beginning of July.* □ *He led from*

the beginning of the race. ◨ *In the beginning*, I didn't like her very much. (começo)

begun /bɪˈɡʌn/ PAST PARTICIPLE OF **begin** (ver **begin**)

behalf /bɪˈhɑːf/ NOUN **on someone's behalf /on behalf of someone** for someone else ◻ *Petra spoke on behalf of the other students.* (em nome de)

behave /bɪˈheɪv/ VERB [behaves, behaving, behaved]
1 to do things in a particular way ◨ *I'm sorry – I've behaved badly.* ◨ *He was behaving like a child!* (comportar-se)
2 to be polite and not do anything that you should not do ◻ *Did the children behave?* ◨ *I hope Harry behaved himself.* (comportar-se)

behavior /bɪˈheɪvjə(r)/ NOUN, NO PLURAL the US spelling of **behaviour** (comportamento)

behaviour /bɪˈheɪvjə(r)/ NOUN, NO PLURAL
the way you behave ◨ *Children should be rewarded for good behaviour.* ◨ *I've never seen such bad behaviour.* ◻ + **towards** *His behaviour towards Sarah was appalling.* (comportamento)

> Remember that the noun **behaviour** is never used in the plural:
> ✓ *The children's behaviour was awful.*
> ✗ *The children's behaviours were awful.*

behind¹ /bɪˈhaɪnd/ PREPOSITION
1 at the back of something or someone ◻ *Look behind the sofa.* ◻ *Rachel peeped out from behind the curtains.* ◻ *Shut the door behind you, please.* (atrás de)
2 making less progress than other people ◨ *Roberto's fallen behind the rest of the class* (atrasado)
3 behind someone's back without someone knowing ◻ *I don't like people talking about me behind my back.* (pelas costas de alguém)

behind² /bɪˈhaɪnd/ ADVERB
1 at the back ◨ *The car was hit from behind.* (atrás)
2 late doing something ◻ *I'm behind with my work.* (atrasado)
3 in the place where you were ◨ *I stayed behind after the class to talk to my teacher.* ◨ *I left my bag behind.* (para trás)

beige /beɪʒ/ ADJECTIVE having a light brown colour ◻ *They chose a beige carpet.* (bege)

being¹ /ˈbiːɪŋ/ VERB the present participle of the verb **be** ◻ *Help! I'm being attacked!* (ver **be**)

being² /ˈbiːɪŋ/ NOUN [plural **beings**] a person or creature ◻ *a being from another planet* (ser)

belief /bɪˈliːf/ NOUN [plural beliefs]
something you believe, especially something that you think is true or something that you think exists ◨ *religious beliefs* ◻ + **that** *There is a widespread belief that the economy will improve.* ◻ + **in** *His belief in God remained with him all his life.* (crença)

believe /bɪˈliːv/ VERB [believes, believing, believed]
1 to think that something is true ◻ *I believed his story.* ◻ *I found his excuses difficult to believe.* ◻ + **that** *I can't believe that you did that!* (acreditar)
2 to think that something is true although you are not completely sure. A formal word. ◻ + **that** *I believe that they're getting married.* (acreditar)
◆ PHRASAL VERB **believe in something**
1 to think that something exists ◻ *I don't believe in ghosts.* **2** to think that something is important or acceptable ◻ *I don't believe in hitting children.*

believer /bɪˈliːvə(r)/ NOUN [plural **believers**] someone who believes something, especially someone who believes in a particular religion (crente)

bell /bel/ NOUN [plural bells]
1 a hollow metal object that makes a ringing sound when it moves ◨ *The church bells were ringing.* (sinos)
2 a device that makes a ringing sound when you press it ◻ *a bicycle bell* ◨ *She walked up to the front door and rang the bell.* (sino)

belly /ˈbeli/ NOUN [plural **bellies**] an informal word for the stomach (barriga)

belong /bɪˈlɒŋ/
◆ PHRASAL VERBS [belongs, belonging, belonged]
belong to someone if something belongs to you, you own it ◻ *Who does this suitcase belong to?*
belong to something to be a member of an organization ◻ *Peter belongs to the local tennis club.* (pertence)

belongings /bɪˈlɒŋɪŋz/ PLURAL NOUN
the things you own ◨ *They returned to the hotel to collect their belongings.* ◨ *The bag contained a few personal belongings.* (pertences)

> THESAURUS: Your **belongings** are the things that you own, especially when you are carrying them with you. **Possessions** and **property** are more general words to describe the things that you own. Your **stuff** or your **things** are more informal words for this. **Goods** are things that have been made to sell. For example, a lorry delivers **goods** to a shop.

beloved /bɪˈlʌvɪd/ ADJECTIVE loved very much ◻ *I lost my beloved old teddy bear.* (amado)

below¹ /bɪˈləʊ/ PREPOSITION
1 in a lower place or position ◻ *The plane was flying below the clouds.* ◻ *Simon was in the class below me in school.* (abaixo)
2 less than a particular amount or level ◻ *Audience numbers never fell below 1000.* ◨ *The results were below average.* (abaixo)

below² /bɪˈləʊ/ ADVERB
at or to a lower place ◻ *We climbed to the top of the hill and looked down*

belt / better

on the valley below. ◻ Write your name and address below. (abaixo)

belt /belt/ NOUN [plural **belts**] a narrow piece of leather or cloth that you wear around your waist 🔲 Karim undid his belt. (cinto)

bench /bentʃ/ NOUN [plural **benches**] a long seat 🔲 a park bench (banco)

> **THESAURUS:** A bench is a long seat which may have arms and a back. We often see benches outdoors, for example in a park. A sofa is a long comfortable seat for more than one person. A chair is a piece of furniture for one person, with a back. It may be hard or soft. A stool is a seat without a back. You sit on a stool to play the piano. Seat is a more general word to describe any object that you sit on. A seat may be a chair, a bench outside, or it may be the place where you sit in a vehicle such as a car or a plane.

bend¹ /bend/ VERB [bends, bending, bent]
1 to move the top part of your body to a lower position ◻ She bent down to pick up some paper she'd dropped. (inclinar-se)
2 to move a part of your body so that it is no longer straight 🔲 Bend your knees slightly. (dobrar-se)
3 to curve ◻ He bent the wire around the post. ◻ The road bends to the right up ahead. (curvar-se)

bend² /bend/ NOUN [plural **bends**] a curve 🔲 There was a sharp bend in the road. (curva)

beneath /bɪˈniːθ/ PREPOSITION, PREPOSITION below or under something ◻ He lay on the ground beneath the tree. ◻ I didn't realize there was another layer of chocolates beneath. (abaixo)

beneficial /ˌbenɪˈfɪʃəl/ ADJECTIVE having a good effect on someone or something 🔲 Improved diet had a beneficial effect on patients. (benéfico)

benefit¹ /ˈbenɪfɪt/ NOUN [plural **benefits**] an advantage that you get from something 🔲 Most patients get some benefit from the treatment. 🔲 The centre is run for the benefit of (= in order to help) the community. (benefício)

benefit² /ˈbenɪfɪt/ VERB [benefits, benefiting/ US benefitting, benefited/US benefitted] if you benefit from something, or if something benefits you, it helps you ◻ + **from** I think you'll benefit from the extra lessons. (beneficiar)

bent¹ /bent/ PAST TENSE AND PAST PARTICIPLE OF bend¹ (ver bend)
bent² /bent/ ADJECTIVE not straight ◻ a bent pin (curvado)

berry /ˈberi/ NOUN [plural **berries**] a small soft fruit containing seeds ◻ Holly has red berries. (fruto)

beside /bɪˈsaɪd/ PREPOSITION next to or at the side of someone or something ◻ There was a chair beside the bed. ◻ Go and stand beside Billy. (ao lado)

besides¹ /bɪˈsaɪdz/ PREPOSITION as well as ◻ Besides playing the piano, she sings in a choir. (além de)
besides² /bɪˈsaɪdz/ ADVERB also ◻ It's too wet to go out. Besides, I'm really tired. (além disso)

best¹ /best/ ADJECTIVE better than everyone or everything else 🔲 Mia is my best friend. 🔲 What's the best way to cook this fish? ◻ It is probably best to arrive a little early. (melhor)

best² /best/ NOUN
1 the best the person or thing that is better than all others ◻ Which of these computers is the best? (o melhor)
2 do/try your best to do something as well as you can ◻ It doesn't matter if you don't win, just do your best. (fazer/tentar o melhor)

best³ /best/ ADVERB
1 more than everything else 🔲 What food do you like best? 🔲 The area is best known for its wine. (mais)
2 in the most satisfactory way ◻ She performs best when she is slightly nervous. (melhor)

bet¹ /bet/ VERB [bets, betting, bet or betted]
1 I bet (a) used for saying what you think will happen or what you think is true ◻ I bet he'll forget to come. ◻ I bet Jane wasn't pleased about that. **(b)** used for saying that you understand why someone feels the way they do ◻ 'I was really upset when he told me.' 'I bet you were!' (apostar)
2 to try to win money by guessing the result of a competition, etc. ◻ My uncle bets on horse races. ◻ I bet him 50p that I could climb the tree. (apostar)

bet² /bet/ NOUN [plural **bets**] money that you risk by trying to guess the result of a competition 🔲 I put a bet on the winning horse. (aposta)

betray /bɪˈtreɪ/ VERB [betrays, betraying, betrayed] to do something which harms someone who trusts you ◻ He betrayed me by telling everyone my secret. (trair)

better¹ /ˈbetə(r)/ ADJECTIVE
1 of a higher standard or more suitable or enjoyable ◻ I want to buy a better computer. 🔲 Is his work getting any better? 🔲 His French is much better than mine. ◻ It's better to buy spices from an Asian shop. (melhor)
2 not as ill 🔲 I hope you get better soon. 🔲 Are you feeling better now? (melhor)
3 the bigger/faster, etc. the better the more big/fast, etc. something is, the more you will like it (quanto maior/mais rápido etc., melhor)

better² /ˈbetə(r)/ ADVERB
1 in a more enjoyable or suitable way or to a higher standard ◻ Which do you like better, the green one or the blue one? ◻ Try to do better next time. ◻ I wish I could swim better. (mais)

2 I/he, etc. had better used to say that someone ought to do something □ *I'd better hurry, or I'll be late.* □ *I think you had better apologize.* (melhor) **3 better off** (a) richer □ *We're better off now than we were ten years ago.* (b) in a better situation □ *You'd be better off hiring a car rather than buying one.* (em melhor)

between /bɪ'twiːn/ PREPOSITION, ADVERB

1 in the area that divides two people, things or places □ *What letter comes between Q and S in the alphabet?* □ *I had to stand between Dan and Shona.* □ *We were on the road between San Francisco and Los Angeles.* (entre)
2 in the period of time that separates two times □ *The shop is closed between 2 and 3.* □ *There was only a week between the wedding and their house move.* (entre)
3 used to show a range of amounts or measurements □ *We usually have between 2 and 4 centimetres of rainfall in January.* (entre)
4 used to show the people or groups involved in something □ *There was an interesting discussion between Angela and Kim.* □ *The match between Leeds and Arsenal has been cancelled.* □ *Between us, we cleaned the whole house.* (entre)
5 used to show the differences of two things, people or groups □ *Can you see the difference between the real jewels and the fakes?* (entre)
6 used to show how something is divided □ *Russell and Colin divided the work between them.* (entre)

beware /bɪ'weə(r)/ VERB used for warning someone about something □ *The sign on the gate said 'Beware of the dog'.* (cuidado)

> The verb **beware** does not have different forms or tenses like other verbs, because it is only used when you are telling people what to do or giving them a warning.

beyond /bɪ'jɒnd/ PREPOSITION, ADVERB

1 on the other side of something □ *Turn right just beyond the bridge.* □ *She had never travelled beyond Europe.* □ *I stared out of the window at the hills beyond.* (além de)
2 after a particular time □ *The strike is likely to continue beyond Christmas.* (depois de)

bias /'baɪəs/ NOUN [plural **biases**] when someone supports one person or thing in a way that is unfair □ *She felt there was a bias against female employees.* (preconceito)
Bible /'baɪbəl/ NOUN [plural **Bibles**] the holy book of the Christian religion (Bíblia)
biblical /'bɪblɪkəl/ ADJECTIVE to do with the Bible, or in the Bible □ *a biblical character* (bíblico)

bicycle /'baɪsɪkəl/ NOUN [plural bicycles] a

vehicle you sit on and turn the wheels by pressing the pedals (= parts your feet go on) □ *I learned to ride a bicycle when I was six.* (bicicleta)

bid¹ /bɪd/ NOUN [plural **bids**] an amount of money that you offer to pay for something that a lot of people want to buy □ *The highest bid for the house was £300,000.* (lance)
bid² /bɪd/ VERB [**bids, bidding, bid**] to offer to pay a particular amount of money for something □ *Will someone bid £5 for this beautiful old chair?* (oferecer)
bid³ /bɪd/ VERB [**bids, bidding, bid** or **bade, bidden** or **bid**] to say something such as 'good morning' or 'good night' to someone. An old-fashioned word. □ *He bade me goodnight.* (dizer)

big /bɪg/ ADJECTIVE [bigger, biggest]

1 large in size □ *a big car* □ *It was the biggest fish he'd ever seen.* □ *They live in a great big* (= very big) *house.* (grande)
2 important and having a large effect □ *a big decision* □ *a big mistake* □ *There's a big match on TV tonight.* (grande)
3 big brother/sister a brother or sister who is older than you □ *I've got a big sister and a little brother.* (irmão, irmã mais velho[a])

bike /baɪk/ NOUN [plural bikes] a bicycle □ *Can you ride a bike?* □ *We went on a bike ride.* □ *The road has a separate bike lane.* (bicicleta)

bikini /bɪ'kiːni/ NOUN [plural **bikinis**] a piece of clothing in two parts that women wear for swimming (biquíni)

bill /bɪl/ NOUN [plural bills]

1 a piece of paper showing how much you must pay for something □ *Have you paid the phone bill?* □ *a gas bill* (pagou a conta)
2 a suggestion for a new law that people in a government vote for or against □ *The government have passed a bill* (= made a law) *which will restrict Internet gambling.* (lei)
3 the US word for **note**₁ (= piece of paper money) □ *a $100 bill* (nota)

> THESAURUS: A **bill** is a piece of paper which tells you how much money you must pay for something such as electricity or the telephone. An **account** is an arrangement with a bank to keep your money there. A **statement** is a piece of paper which tells you how much money you have in your bank account.

billion /'bɪljən/ NUMBER [plural **billions**] the number 1,000,000,000 □ *The government gets billions of pounds a year from taxes.* (**bilhão**)

billionaire /ˌbɪljəˈneə(r)/ NOUN [plural **billionaires**] someone who has a billion pounds or a billion dollars or more (**bilionário**)

bin /bɪn/ NOUN [plural **bins**] a container for putting rubbish in 🔊 *a rubbish bin* 🔊 *You should put paper in the recycling bin.* (**lata de lixo**)

bind /baɪnd/ VERB [**binds, binding, bound**] to tie something together □ *The robbers bound his hands and feet with tape.* (**amarrar**)

bingo /'bɪŋɡəʊ/ NOUN, NO PLURAL a game in which you mark numbers on a card when someone shouts those numbers. You win if you are the first person to mark all the numbers on your card. (**bingo**)

binoculars /bɪ'nɒkjʊləz/ PLURAL NOUN a piece of equipment that you hold up to your eyes to help you see things that are a long way away □ *She was watching the birds with a pair of binoculars.* (**binóculo**)

biography /baɪ'ɒɡrəfi/ NOUN [plural **biographies**] a book about a real person's life □ *+ of She wrote a biography of Napoleon.* (**biografia**)

biological /ˌbaɪə'lɒdʒɪkəl/ ADJECTIVE to do with living things and the way they grow and behave □ *a biological process* (**biológico**)

biologist /baɪ'ɒlədʒɪst/ NOUN [plural **biologists**] a person who studies biology (**biologista**)

biology /baɪ'ɒlədʒi/ NOUN, NO PLURAL the study of living things (**biologia**)

bird /bɜːd/ NOUN [plural **birds**] a creature with wings and feathers that produces eggs □ *wild birds* □ *There was a bird's nest in the tree.* (**pássaro**)

birth /bɜːθ/ NOUN [plural **births**]
1 the time when someone is born □ *He was there at the births of all his children.* 🔊 *What is your date of birth (= the date when you were born)?* (**nascimento**)
2 give birth if a woman gives birth, a baby comes out of her body □ *She gave birth to a healthy baby boy.* (**dar à luz**)

birthday /'bɜːθdeɪ/ NOUN [plural **birthdays**] the date you were born which happens each year □ *It's my mother's 60th birthday next week.* 🔊 *Happy Birthday John!* 🔊 *I'm going to his birthday party* 🔊 *Did you get a lot of birthday presents?* (**aniversário**)

biscuit /'bɪskɪt/ NOUN [plural **biscuits**] a flat hard cake □ *He was eating a chocolate biscuit.* 🔊 *a packet of biscuits* (**biscoito**)

bishop /'bɪʃəp/ NOUN [plural **bishops**] an important priest in some Christian churches (**bispo, bispos**)

bit[1] /bɪt/ NOUN [plural **bits**]
1 a bit (a) slightly □ *I'm a bit tired today.* 🔊 *He looks a bit like David Beckham.* (b) a short time □ *We had to wait a bit for the bus.* 🔊 *I don't mind looking after her for a bit* (c) a small amount □ *'Would you like some more fish?' 'Yes, just a bit, please.'* □ *+ of I need a bit of help with my homework.* (**um pouco**)
2 a piece or part of something bigger □ *+ of There were some bits of the book that I enjoyed.* (**parte**)
3 quite a bit a lot □ *He's quite a bit taller than his wife.* (**bem**)

> The phrase **a bit** meaning 'slightly' is used a lot in spoken English but is too informal for formal written English. If you are writing an essay, it is better to use the words **slightly** or **a little**:
> ✓ *Attitudes to this subject have changed slightly.*
> ✗ *Attitudes to this subject have changed a bit.*

bit[2] /bɪt/ PAST TENSE OF **bite**[1] (ver **bite**[1])

bite[1] /baɪt/ VERB [**bites, biting, bit, bitten**]
1 to use your teeth to cut through something □ *+ into Guy bit into the apple.* 🔊 *A lot of people bite their nails.* (**roer**)
2 if an animal bites, it injures someone with its teeth □ *She was badly bitten by a dog.* (**morder**)

bite[2] /baɪt/ NOUN [plural **bites**]
1 when you bite food with your teeth 🔊 *Ali took a bite of the sausage.* (**mordida**)
2 an injury on your skin where an animal or insect has bitten you 🔊 *an insect bite* □ *a mosquito bite* (**mordida/picada de inseto**)

bitten /'bɪtən/ PAST PARTICIPLE OF **bite**[1] (ver **bite**[1])

bitter /'bɪtə(r)/ ADJECTIVE
1 angry because you feel someone has treated you badly □ *He turned into a bitter old man.* (**triste**)
2 having a strong taste such as you find in strong coffee □ *Dark chocolate is too bitter for me.* (**amargo**)
3 if the weather is bitter, it is extremely cold □ *It's bitter out there!* (**congelante**)

black[1] /blæk/ ADJECTIVE
1 having the colour of coal or the sky at night □ *I bought a black coat.* (**preto**)
2 black people are of a race that have dark brown skin □ *We need more black police officers.* (**negro**)
3 black tea or coffee has no milk in it (**preto**)

black[2] /blæk/ NOUN, NO PLURAL the colour of coal or the sky at night (**preto**)

blackboard

blackboard /'blæk‚bɔːd/ NOUN [plural **blackboards**] a dark board that a teacher writes on in a classroom (quadro-negro)

black hole /‚blæk'həʊl/ NOUN [plural **black holes**] an area in outer space that pulls everything into it. Nothing can escape from a black hole. (buraco negro)

blade /bleɪd/ NOUN [plural **blades**]
1 the sharp part of a knife or tool which cuts ⌑ *a razor blade* (lâmina)
2 a blade of grass a long thin piece of grass (lâmina)

blame¹ /bleɪm/ VERB [**blames, blaming, blamed**] to say that something is someone's fault □ + *for He blamed me for the accident.* (responsabilizar)

blame² /bleɪm/ NOUN, NO PLURAL responsibility for something bad that has happened ⌑ *Why do I always get the blame for everything?* ⌑ *I'm not going to take the blame for someone else's mistake.* (culpa)

blank /blæŋk/ ADJECTIVE
1 with no writing on, or with no sound or pictures on ⌑ *a blank sheet of paper* □ *a blank CD* (em branco)
2 showing no emotion or no understanding ⌑ *She gave me a blank stare.* (olhar vago)

blanket /'blæŋkɪt/ NOUN [plural **blankets**]
1 a cover for a bed, usually made of wool □ *a wool blanket* (cobertor)
2 a layer that covers everything □ + *of A blanket of snow covered the roads.* (cobertor)

> **THESAURUS:** A **blanket** is a cover for a bed and is usually made of wool. A **sheet** is also used on a bed, but is thin, and is usually made of cotton. A **duvet** is a cotton bag, usually filled with feathers. A **cover** is something that you put on the top of something else to protect it. A duvet **cover** is a bag made of cotton that you put around a duvet to protect it and for decoration.

blast¹ /blɑːst/ NOUN [plural **blasts**]
1 an explosion ⌑ *They were killed in a bomb blast.* □ *Three people survived the blast.* (explosão)
2 a sudden strong movement of air □ *The door opened, letting in a blast of freezing air.* (rajada)
3 a loud sound from something such as a horn □ *The lorry driver gave a couple of blasts on his horn.* (toque)

blast² /blɑːst/ VERB [**blasts, blasting, blasted**]
1 to make a lot of loud noise □ *Music was blasting out of the open windows.* (explodir)
2 to use explosives to break up something such as rock (explodir)
♦ PHRASAL VERB **blast off** if a rocket (= type of spacecraft) blasts off, it starts to go up into the air (ser lançado)

blaze¹ /bleɪz/ NOUN [plural **blazes**] a big fire ⌑ *Firefighters put out the blaze.* (chama)

block

blaze² /bleɪz/ VERB [**blazes, blazing, blazed**] to burn or shine brightly □ *Her eyes were blazing with anger.* (brilhar)

bleak /bliːk/ ADJECTIVE [**bleaker, bleakest**]
1 without hope or happiness □ *The economic situation looks bleak.* ⌑ *a bleak future/outlook* (desanimador)
2 a bleak place is cold, empty and not pleasant □ *a bleak winter landscape* (deserto)

bleed /bliːd/ VERB [**bleeds, bleeding, bled**] when you bleed, blood comes out of a cut on your body □ *He was bleeding from a cut on his head.* ⌑ *My head was bleeding profusely* (= very much). (sangrar)

blend¹ /blend/ VERB [**blends, blending, blended**] to mix things together completely □ *Blend the butter and the sugar.* (misturar)

blend² /blend/ NOUN [plural **blends**] a mixture of two or more things □ *Banana milkshake is a blend of milk, banana and ice cream.* (mistura)

blender /'blendə(r)/ NOUN [plural **blenders**] a machine used for mixing food (liquidificador)

bless /bles/ VERB [**blesses, blessing, blessed**] to ask God to protect someone or to make something holy □ *The priest blessed the bread and the wine.* (abençoar)
♦ IDIOM **Bless you!** something you say when someone sneezes (= suddenly blows out air from their nose and mouth in a way that they cannot control)

blew /bluː/ PAST TENSE OF **blow¹** (ver **blow¹**)

blind¹ /blaɪnd/ ADJECTIVE not able to see ⌑ *He went blind* (= became blind) *at the age of five.* (cego)

blind² /blaɪnd/ NOUN [plural **blinds**]
1 the blind people who are blind (o cego)
2 a covering that you pull down over a window (cortina)

blink /blɪŋk/ VERB [**blinks, blinking, blinked**] to close and open your eyes quickly □ *He was blinking in the strong sunlight.* □ *Emma tried to blink away the tears.* (piscar)

blister /'blɪstər/ NOUN [plural **blisters**] a swollen area filled with liquid on your skin where it has been burned or rubbed (bolha)

blizzard /'blɪzəd/ NOUN [plural **blizzards**] a storm with strong winds and snow (nevasca)

block¹ /blɒk/ NOUN [plural **blocks**]
1 a solid, usually square piece of something □ *Cut the wood into blocks.* □ + *of a block of ice* (bloco)
2 a large building with a lot of offices or homes in it ⌑ *a block of flats* ⌑ *a fifteen-storey office block* (conjunto)

block² /blɒk/ VERB [**blocks, blocking, blocked**]
1 to stop people or things from getting through □ *The road was blocked by a tree.* ⌑ *A large police officer blocked our path/exit.* □ + *up The stream was blocked up with sticks.* (bloquear)
2 to be in front of someone so that they cannot see something or light cannot get to them ⌑ *A tall man in front was blocking my view.* (bloquear)
♦ PHRASAL VERB **block something off** to close

something such as a path or an entrance by placing something across it □ *The police had blocked off the road.* (**bloquear algo**)

blog[1] /blɒg/ NOUN [*plural* **blogs**] a record of someone's activities and opinions that they put on the Internet for other people to read. A computing word. (**blog**)

blog[2] /blɒg/ VERB [**blogs, blogging, blogged**] to write a blog. A computing word. (**blogar**)

blogger /ˈblɒgə(r)/ NOUN [*plural* **bloggers**] someone who writes a record of their activities and opinions and puts it on the Internet for other people to read. A computing word. (**blogueiro**)

bloke /bləʊk/ NOUN [*plural* **blokes**] an informal word meaning man □ *He's a nice bloke.* (**homem, sujeito**)

blond[1] or **blonde** /blɒnd/ ADJECTIVE [**blonder, blondest**] blond hair is pale yellow □ *She had long blonde hair.* (**loiro**)

blond[2] or **blonde** /blɒnd/ NOUN [*plural* **blonds** or **blondes**] a person with pale yellow hair (**loiro**)

blood /blʌd/ NOUN, NO PLURAL the red liquid that is inside your body □ *Your heart pumps blood around your body.* 🖻 *A blood test will show if you have an infection.* (**sangue**)

bloom[1] /bluːm/ NOUN [*plural* **blooms**] a flower □ *The stems are covered in large white blooms.* (**flor**)

bloom[2] /bluːm/ VERB [**blooms, blooming, bloomed**] to produce flowers □ *A lot of plants have bloomed early this year.* (**florescer**)

blossom[1] /ˈblɒsəm/ NOUN [*plural* **blossoms**] the flowers that appear on a fruit tree before the fruit grows (**flor**)

> **THESAURUS:** Blossom is the flowers that appear on fruit trees such as apples and cherries before the fruit grows. A bud is the part of a plant that the flower grows from. Flower is a more general word to describe the coloured part of a plant that turns into fruit and where seeds are produced.

blossom[2] /ˈblɒsəm/ VERB [**blossoms, blossoming, blossomed**] to produce blossom (**florescer**)

blouse /blaʊz/ NOUN [*plural* **blouses**] a woman's shirt □ *a school blouse* (**blusa**)

blow[1] /bləʊ/ VERB [**blows, blowing, blew, blown**]
1 wind blows when it moves around □ *A cold wind was blowing from the east.* (**soprar**)
2 to push out air from your mouth onto something or into something □ *Blow on your soup – it's hot.* (**soprar**)
3 to breathe into something such as a musical instrument in order to make a sound □ *When I blow this whistle, I want you all to stop.* (**soprar**)
4 blow your nose to get the liquid out of your nose by forcing air through it (**assoar o nariz**)
◆ PHRASAL VERBS **blow over** if an argument blows over, people forget about it **blow something up** to destroy something with an explosion □ *He was planning to blow up the aeroplane and all its passengers.* (**parar/explodir**)

blow[2] /bləʊ/ NOUN [*plural* **blows**]
1 a hard knock □ + **to** *He suffered a blow to the face.* (**soco**)
2 something disappointing that happens □ *It was a blow not being able to go to the concert.* (**golpe**)

blown /bləʊn/ PAST PARTICIPLE OF **blow**[1] (ver **blow**[1])

blue[1] /bluː/ ADJECTIVE having the colour of the sky 🖻 *She was wearing a dark blue dress.* 🖻 *He has a pale blue shirt on.* (**azul**)

blue[2] /bluː/ NOUN [*plural* **blues**] the colour of the sky □ *The sea was a deep blue.* (**azul**)
◆ IDIOM **out of the blue** not expected at all □ *Out of the blue, he announced that he was leaving.* (**inesperadamente**)

blunt /blʌnt/ ADJECTIVE [**blunter, bluntest**] with an edge or point that is not sharp □ *This knife is blunt.* (**sem corte**)

blush /blʌʃ/ VERB [**blushes, blushing, blushed**] to start to have a red face because you are embarrassed □ *Everyone turned to look at Philip, who blushed.* (**corar**)

board[1] /bɔːd/ NOUN [*plural* **boards**]
1 a flat piece of wood 🖻 *Please use a bread board for cutting on.* 🖻 *I lifted the carpets to look at the floor boards.* (**tábuas**)
2 a flat piece of wood or cardboard with marks on it, used to play a game □ *a chess board* (**tabuleiro**)
3 a surface on the wall of a classroom where the teacher writes □ *The answers are on the board.* (**quadro**)
4 a group of people who control a company or other organization 🖻 *the board of directors* 🖻 *a board meeting* (**conselho, diretoria, conselho**)
5 on board on a ship, aircraft or other vehicle □ *There were 197 passengers on board.* (**a bordo**)

board[2] /bɔːd/ VERB [**boards, boarding, boarded**] to get on a ship or an aeroplane □ *Could all remaining passengers please board the plane.* (**embarcar**)

boarder /ˈbɔːdə(r)/ NOUN [*plural* **boarders**] a student who lives at his or her school □ *The school has day students and boarders.* (**aluno interno**)

boarding pass /ˈbɔːdɪŋ ˌpɑːs/ or **boarding card** /ˈbɔːdɪŋ ˌkɑːd/ NOUN [*plural* **boarding passes** or **boarding cards**] a card that you need to show someone before you can get on an aeroplane or a ship □ *Passengers should have their boarding passes ready.* (**passagem**)

boarding school /ˈbɔːdɪŋ ˌskuːl/ NOUN [*plural* **boarding schools**] a school in which students can live (**internato**)

boast /bəʊst/ VERB [**boasts, boasting, boasted**] to talk proudly about yourself in a way that other people find annoying □ *He's always boasting about the famous people he knows.* (**vangloriar-se**)

boastful /'bəʊstfʊl/ ADJECTIVE often talking proudly about the good things you have done or the expensive things you own (**orgulhoso**)

boat /bəʊt/ NOUN [plural **boats**] a vehicle for travelling over water □ *a fishing boat* (**barco**)
♦ IDIOM **in the same boat** having the same problems as other people □ *Don't worry, we're all in the same boat.* (**no mesmo barco**)

> THESAURUS: Boat is a general word to describe any vehicle that travels on water. Very large boats are usually called **ships**. For example, **ships** transport goods around the world. A **ferry** is a boat which carries passengers between two places, and can be large or small. A **barge** is a long, narrow boat used to carry goods on a canal. A **yacht** is a boat with sails. We use **yachts** for racing or for pleasure.

bob /bɒb/ VERB [**bobs, bobbing, bobbed**] to move up and down quickly □ *She watched the little boats bobbing on the lake.* (**agitar, agita, agitando, agitado**)

body /'bɒdɪ/ NOUN [plural **bodies**]
1 the whole physical form of a person or animal □ *I had red spots all over my body.* (**corpo**)
2 a dead person □ *His body was never found.* (**corpo**)

bodyguard /'bɒdɪgɑːd/ NOUN [plural **bodyguards**] someone whose job is to protect an important or famous person (**guarda-costas**)

boil /bɔɪl/ VERB [**boils, boiling, boiled**]
1 a liquid boils when it is heated until it produces bubbles and turns into gas □ *Is the water boiling yet?* □ *Boil some water in a pan and add the pasta.* (**ferver**)
2 to cook food in boiling water □ *I'm going to boil some eggs.* (**ferver**)
3 to heat a container of liquid until it is boiling □ *Shall I boil the kettle?* (**ferver**)

bold /bəʊld/ ADJECTIVE [**bolder, boldest**]
1 not afraid to take a risk □ *Calling an election was a bold move* (= a brave thing to do) *for the president.* □ *It was rather bold of him to ask that question.* (**movimento corajoso**)
2 bold type or print is thick dark letters **like this** □ *Her name is written in bold type at the top of the page.* (**negrito**)

bolt[1] /bəʊlt/ NOUN [plural **bolts**]
1 a metal bar that you push across a door to lock it □ *She slid back the bolts and opened the door.* (**trinco**)
2 a metal object with small, raised lines that you use with a nut (= metal object with a hole in the middle) to fasten pieces of wood or metal together (**parafuso**)

bolt[2] /bəʊlt/ VERB [**bolts, bolting, bolted**]
1 to lock a door using a bolt □ *We bolted all the doors before we went to bed.* (**trancar**)

2 to run away very fast □ *Beth's horse bolted when it heard the noise.* (**disparar**)

bomb[1] /bɒm/ NOUN [plural **bombs**] a weapon that explodes to cause serious damage to buildings, people, etc. □ *The bomb went off in a crowded market.* (**bomba**)

bomb[2] /bɒm/ VERB [**bombs, bombing, bombed**] to attack a place using bombs □ *Enemy aircraft bombed every town and village in the area.* (**bombardear**)

bone /bəʊn/ NOUN [plural **bones**] one of the hard parts that form the frame inside the body of an animal or person □ *Brian broke a bone in his arm.* (**osso**)

bonnet /'bɒnɪt/ NOUN [plural **bonnets**]
1 the part at the front of a car that covers the engine (**capô**)
2 a woman's or child's hat that you tie under the chin (**gorro**)

bonus /'bəʊnəs/ NOUN [plural **bonuses**]
1 something good that you get in addition to something else good □ *The food is great, and has the added bonus of being healthy too.* (**bônus**)
2 extra money that people sometimes get in addition to their usual payment □ *a Christmas bonus* (**bônus**)

> THESAURUS: A bonus is extra money that you sometimes get at work, in addition to your usual payment. You might get a bonus if your work is very good. A **reward** is money that you get for doing something good. You might get a **reward** if you help to catch a criminal. A **tip** is money that you get for helping someone as part of your job, for example if you are a waiter. A **prize** is something that you get for winning a competition. A **gift** or a **present** is something that you give to someone, for example because it is their birthday.

boo /buː/ VERB [**boos, booing, booed**] people in an audience boo when they make loud noises because they do not think the performance is good (**vaiar**)

book[1] /bʊk/ NOUN [plural **books**] a set of pages joined together inside a cover □ *a library book* □ *Have you read Dan Brown's new book?* □ *I'm reading a really interesting book about Mexico.* (**livro**)

> THESAURUS : Book is a general word for pages joined together inside a cover. An **atlas** is a book of maps. A **guidebook** is a book that contains information for people visiting a place. It might contain maps and information about things to see. A **manual** is a book that tells you how to do something. We use **manuals** to help us use machines. A **textbook** is a book that students use to help them with their studies. For example, you might have a geography **textbook**.

book[2] /bʊk/ VERB [**books, booking, booked**] to buy tickets for something or to arrange to have or use something in the future □ *I'd like to book a* table for four, please. □ *We've booked a family holiday in Majorca.* (reservar)

> THESAURUS: If you **book** something or **reserve** something, you buy tickets or arrange to use something in the future. For example, you can reserve seats on a train, or you can book a holiday. If you **order** something, you pay for it and arrange for someone to deliver it to you. For example you can order food in a restaurant and you can order a book on the Internet.

bookshop /ˈbʊkʃɒp/ NOUN [*plural* **bookshops**] a shop that sells books (livraria)

boom[1] /buːm/ NOUN [*plural* **booms**]
1 a situation in which a company or country sells a lot of products and makes a lot of money □ *an economic boom* (crescimento)
2 a loud noise like the sound of a big drum (estrondo)

boom[2] /buːm/ VERB [**booms, booming, boomed**]
1 if a business or the economy booms, it becomes very successful (expandir-se)
2 to make a loud noise like the sound of a drum (estrondear)

boost[1] /buːst/ NOUN [*plural* **boosts**] something that makes something larger or more successful □ *The school funds got a boost from the money raised at the summer fair.* (impulso)

boost[2] /buːst/ VERB [**boosts, boosting, boosted**] to make something larger or more successful □ *Extra lessons will help to boost her confidence.* (impulsionar)

boot /buːt/ NOUN [*plural* **boots**]
1 a type of shoe that covers the ankle and often part of the leg (bota)
2 the covered place at the back of a car for storing bags, etc. (porta-malas)

booth /buːð/ NOUN [*plural* **booths**] a small place with walls around it where you can do something privately, for example make a telephone call (cabine)

border /ˈbɔːdə(r)/ NOUN [*plural* **borders**]
1 the line which separates two countries or areas □ *They lived near the Canadian border.* (fronteira)
2 a strip around the edge of something, often for decoration □ *a pillowcase with a pretty lace border* (borda)

bore[1] /bɔː(r)/ VERB [**bores, boring, bored**]
1 to make someone feel bored □ *The speech bored him.* (entediar)
2 to make a hole in something with a sharp tool (cavar)

• **boredom** /ˈbɔːdəm/ NOUN, NO PLURAL the feeling of being bored (tédio)

bore[2] /bɔː(r)/ PAST TENSE OF **bear**[1] (ver **bear**[1])

bored /bɔːd/ ADJECTIVE feeling that something is not interesting or that you have nothing to do □ *+ with I'm really bored with my clothes.* □ *The others enjoyed the show, but I was bored stiff* (= extremely bored). (entediado)

boring /ˈbɔːrɪŋ/ ADJECTIVE not at all interesting □ *My course is really boring.* (chato)

> Remember the difference between the words **boring** and **bored**. **Boring** means 'not interesting'. **Bored** is how you feel when something is not interesting □ *What a boring film!* □ *I was so bored during the film, I fell asleep.*

born[1] /bɔːn/ VERB **be born** (a) a person or animal is born when it comes out of its mother's body □ *My sister was born in 1989.* □ *He was born with a heart problem.* (b) something is born when it starts to exist □ *The idea for the film was born over dinner at Jack's house.* (nascido)

> Remember that the verb is **be born** and not just **born**:
> ✓ *I was born in Germany.*
> ✗ *I born in Germany.*

born[2] /bɔːn/ ADJECTIVE a born leader/performer, etc. is a very good leader/performer, etc. □ *Zoe's a born entertainer.* (nato)

borne /bɔːn/ PAST PARTICIPLE OF **bear**[1] (ver **bear**[1])

borrow /ˈbɒrəʊ/ VERB [**borrows, borrowing, borrowed**] to use something that belongs to someone else and give it back to them later □ *Can I borrow your pencil for a minute, please?* □ *+ from She borrowed £100 from her Dad.* (pegar emprestado)

> Remember that when you **borrow** something, you use something that belongs to someone else. When you give something to someone else to use, the verb is **lend** □ *I borrowed Dan's mobile.* □ *Dan lent me his mobile.*

boss /bɒs/ NOUN [*plural* **bosses**] someone who is in charge of other people at work □ *I'm going to ask my boss for a pay rise.* (chefe)

♦ PHRASAL VERB [**bosses, bossing, bossed**] **boss someone around/about** to tell other people what to do, in a way that annoys them □ *I wish Amy would stop bossing us all around.*

bossy /ˈbɒsi/ ADJECTIVE always telling other people what to do □ *Stop being so bossy – you're not in charge here.* (mandão)

both /bəʊθ/ PRONOUN, DETERMINER used for saying that the same thing is true for two people or things □ *She ate both cakes, and I didn't get one.* □ *+ of Both of the boys are good at tennis.* □ *Both the men wore black suits.* □ *We both like classical music.* □ *The book is both interesting and informative.* (ambos)

bother

bother /ˈbɒðə(r)/ VERB [bothers, bothering, bothered]
1 to do something that annoys or interrupts someone □ *Stop bothering me, I'm busy.* (incomodar)
2 can't be bothered if you can't be bothered to do something, you feel too lazy to do it □ *I can't be bothered to cook just for myself.* (vontade)
3 to make you feel unhappy or worried □ *He said that losing the match didn't bother him.* (preocupar)
4 to take the time or make an effort to do something □ *Don't bother tidying up yet.* (dar-se ao trabalho)

bottle /ˈbɒtəl/ NOUN [plural bottles] a glass or plastic container used for holding liquids, often with a narrow part at the top □ **+ of** *a bottle of mineral water* □ *a wine bottle* (garrafa)

bottom¹ /ˈbɒtəm/ NOUN [plural bottoms]
1 the lowest part of something □ **+ of** *He stood at the bottom of the stairs* □ *the bottom of the sea* (fundo)
2 the surface on the lowest part of something □ *There were holes in the bottom of his shoes.* (fundo)
3 the lowest level of success □ *My team is at the bottom of the league.* (último)
4 the part of something that is furthest away □ *the bottom of the road/garden* (fundo)
5 the part of your body that you sit on □ *Always keep your baby's bottom clean and dry.* (traseiro)

bottom² /ˈbɒtəm/ ADJECTIVE
1 in the lowest position □ *Put the biggest books on the bottom shelf.* (último)
2 at the lowest level of success ▣ *She came bottom in the exam.* (último)

bought /bɔːt/ PAST TENSE AND PAST PARTICIPLE OF **buy** (ver **buy**)
boulder /ˈbəʊldə(r)/ NOUN [plural boulders] a very big stone (rocha)
bounce /baʊns/ VERB [bounces, bouncing, bounced]
1 to hit a hard surface and move away again □ *The ball bounced high into the air.* (quicar)
2 to jump up and down on a soft surface □ *The children were bouncing on the bed.* (saltar)

bouncy /ˈbaʊnsi/ ADJECTIVE [bouncier, bounciest]
1 able to hit a hard surface and move away again easily □ *a bouncy ball* (pulo)
2 a bouncy surface moves up and down when you move or jump on it (ímpeto)

bound¹ /baʊnd/ VERB [bounds, bounding, bounded] to run with long jumping steps □ *The dogs bounded into the room, barking excitedly.* (saltar)

bound² /baʊnd/ NOUN [plural bounds]
1 a jump □ *The deer jumped over the fence in a single bound.* (salto)
2 out of bounds if a place is out of bounds, you are not allowed to go there (interditado)

bound³ /baʊnd/ PAST TENSE AND PAST PARTICIPLE OF **bind** (ver **bind**)

box

boundary /ˈbaʊndəri/ NOUN [plural boundaries] a line that divides two places □ *We live on the boundary between the city and the countryside.* (limite)

bouquet /buˈkeɪ/ NOUN [plural bouquets] flowers that have been tied together in an attractive way (buquê)

bow¹ /baʊ/ VERB [bows, bowing, bowed] to bend your head or the top part of your body forward to say hello to someone politely or to show them respect □ *Everyone bowed to the king and queen.* (curvar-se)

bow² /baʊ/ NOUN [plural bows]
1 when you bow ▣ *The pianist came back on stage to take a bow.* (reverência)
2 the pointed front part of a ship (proa)

bow³ /bəʊ/ NOUN [plural bows]
1 a knot with two circular ends, used to tie shoes or for decoration □ *Tie the ribbon in a bow.* (laço)
2 a weapon made from a long piece of wood, used for shooting arrows (arco)
3 a long, straight piece of wood with horse hair stretched along it, used for playing some musical instruments □ *a violin bow* (arco)

bowl /bəʊl/ NOUN [plural bowls] a round, open container, used for holding food □ *a soup bowl* □ *a bowl of cornflakes* (tigela)

bowler /ˈbəʊlə(r)/ NOUN [plural bowlers] the person who bowls in sports such as cricket and baseball (lançador)

bowling /ˈbəʊlɪŋ/ NOUN, NO PLURAL a game in which players roll a large heavy ball along a track and try to knock over objects shaped like bottles (boliche)

box¹ /bɒks/ NOUN [plural boxes]
1 a container, sometimes with a lid, used for holding or storing things (caixa)
2 a small square on a page with information in it or with a space where you must write ▣ *Tick the relevant box.* (ticar o quadro)

box² /bɒks/ VERB [boxes, boxing, boxed] to take part in the sport of boxing (lutar boxe)

• **boxer** /ˈbɒksə(r)/ NOUN [plural boxers] someone who takes part in the sport of boxing (boxeador)

boxing /ˈbɒksɪŋ/ NOUN, NO PLURAL a sport in which two people fight by hitting each other while wearing heavy gloves (= coverings for your hands) (boxe)

Boxing Day /ˈbɒksɪŋ ˌdeɪ/ NOUN the day after Christmas Day (dia seguinte ao Natal)

box office /ˈbɒks ˌɒfɪs/ NOUN [plural **box offices**] the place at a theatre or cinema where you buy tickets (bilheteria)

boy /bɔɪ/ NOUN [plural **boys**] a male child □ *a six-year-old boy* □ *They've got two boys and a girl.* □ *When I was a little boy I wanted to be a train driver.* (menino)

boycott[1] /ˈbɔɪkɒt/ VERB [**boycotts, boycotting, boycotted**] to refuse to take part in an activity or to buy a particular product (boicotar)

boycott[2] /ˈbɔɪkɒt/ NOUN [plural **boycotts**] a situation in which someone boycotts an activity or product (boicote)

boyfriend /ˈbɔɪfrend/ NOUN [plural **boyfriends**] a man or boy who you are having a romantic relationship with □ *Emily has got a new boyfriend.* (namorado)

bra /brɑː/ NOUN [plural **bras**] a piece of underwear that women wear to support their breasts (sutiã)

brace /breɪs/ NOUN [plural **braces**] a piece of wire that you have on your teeth to pull them into a straight position (braçadeira)

bracelet /ˈbreɪslɪt/ NOUN [plural **bracelets**] a piece of jewellery that you wear around your arm □ *a diamond bracelet* (pulseira)

bracket /ˈbrækɪt/ NOUN [plural **brackets**] one of a pair of marks ( ) or [ ], used to separate information from the main text 🔹 *She added her own comments in brackets after each point.* (colchete, parênteses)

brag /bræg/ VERB [**brags, bragging, bragged**] to talk about your achievements or possessions in a proud way that annoys people □ *Kate's always bragging about the expensive gifts he gives her.* (gabar-se)

brain /breɪn/ NOUN [plural **brains**] the organ inside your head that controls all the other parts of your body, and that you think with □ *the human brain* (cérebro)

brake[1] /breɪk/ NOUN [plural **brakes**] the part in a vehicle that you press to stop the vehicle or make it go slower □ *Have you checked your brakes?* 🔹 *a brake pedal* (freio)

brake[2] /breɪk/ VERB [**brakes, braking, braked**] to use a brake to stop a vehicle or make it go slower □ *Dad braked suddenly and we were all thrown forward.* (frear)

branch /brɑːntʃ/ NOUN [plural **branches**]
1 one of the smaller parts of a tree that grow out from the main straight part □ *Crows build their nests high in the branches of trees.* (ramo)

2 one of the shops or businesses that belong to a larger organization 🔹 *the local branch of the bank* 🔹 *They're opening a new branch in Livingston.* (filial)

brand /brænd/ NOUN [plural **brands**] a product that has a particular name, and that is made by a particular company □ *This isn't my usual brand of shampoo.* (marca)

brand-new /ˌbræn dˈnjuː/ ADJECTIVE completely new □ *a brand-new car* (novo em folha)

brass[1] /brɑːs/ NOUN, NO PLURAL a yellow metal used for making things such as musical instruments (latão)

brass[2] /brɑːs/ ADJECTIVE made of brass □ *a brass candlestick* (de latão)

brave /breɪv/ ADJECTIVE [**braver, bravest**] able to deal with danger without being afraid, or able to suffer pain without complaining □ **+ of** *It was very brave of her to jump in the water and save the child.* □ *This might hurt a little – just try to be brave.* (valente)

♦ IDIOM **put a brave face on something** to behave as if you are not afraid or worried, although you feel afraid or worried (mostrar valentia perante algo)

bravery /ˈbreɪvəri/ NOUN, NO PLURAL being brave □ *an award for bravery* (valentia)

bread /bred/ NOUN, NO PLURAL a basic food made with flour and water that is baked in an oven. It is often sold in a large piece and then cut into smaller pieces. 🔹 *a loaf of bread* 🔹 *a slice of bread* 🔹 *brown/white bread* (pão)

break[1] /breɪk/ VERB [**breaks, breaking, broke, broken**]
1 to separate into pieces or to make something separate into pieces □ *The vase fell to the floor and broke.* □ *Be careful, you'll break that glass.* □ **+ off** *I broke a piece off the biscuit.* □ **+ up** *The company was broken up and sold in several parts.* (quebrar)
2 to damage something or to become damaged □ *My camera broke.* □ *I've broken my umbrella.* (quebrar)

break

3 break your arm/leg, etc. to damage a bone so that it cracks (**quebrar**)
4 break the rules/the law/your promise, etc. to not do what you should do, for example because it is a rule or you have made a promise (**quebrar**)
• **breakable** /ˈbreɪkəbəl/ ADJECTIVE able to be broken easily (**quebradiço**)
♦ IDIOM **break someone's heart** to make someone very unhappy □ *It breaks my heart to see the children suffer.* (**partir o coração de alguém**)
♦ PHRASAL VERBS **break down** if a machine or vehicle breaks down, it stops working □ *Sorry I'm late; the car broke down.* **break in** to get into a place by using force □ *Thieves broke in using a hammer.* **break out** to start suddenly 🗗 *Fighting broke out during a football match.* 🗗 *Fire broke out in the factory.* (**irromper**) **break up 1** if two people break up, they end their relationship □ *She's broken up with her boyfriend.* (**romper**) **2** a school breaks up when the term finishes and the holiday starts (**interromper atividades**)

> THESAURUS: Break is a general word. If you break something into small pieces, for example by dropping it, you can use the words smash and shatter. For example, you might smash or shatter a plate if you drop it. If you damage something thin such as paper or cloth by pulling it apart, you use the word tear. If something splits or if you split it, it breaks apart. For example, you might split a piece of wood with an axe.

break² /breɪk/ NOUN [plural breaks]
1 a short period of time in which someone stops an activity 🗗 *Shall we have/take a break?* 🗗 *What time is your lunch break?* □ + **from** *I need a break from the children.* (**intervalo**)
2 an opening or crack in something □ + **in** *a break in the clouds* □ *She suffered a nasty break in her leg.* (**abertura**)

breakdown /ˈbreɪkdaʊn/ NOUN [plural breakdowns]
1 when a machine or vehicle stops working □ *We had a breakdown on the motorway.* (**avaria**)
2 when something fails in a situation □ *a breakdown in communication* □ *Stress contributed to the breakdown of his marriage.* (**crise**)
3 a period of mental illness when someone is too upset or sad to deal with life 🗗 *She suffered a breakdown after her divorce.* 🗗 *a nervous breakdown* (**colapso**)

breakfast /ˈbrekfəst/ NOUN [plural breakfasts]
the first meal that you eat in the morning □ *What do you usually have for breakfast?* (**café da manhã**)

breast /brest/ NOUN [plural breasts]
1 one of the two organs on the front of a woman's body that produce milk when she has a baby 🗗 *breast milk* 🗗 *breast cancer* (**seio**)
2 the front part of a bird's body, or the meat from this part 🗗 *chicken breasts* (**peito**)

breath /breθ/ NOUN [plural breaths]
1 when you fill your lungs with air and then allow the air out again 🗗 *Take a deep breath.* (**respiração**)
2 the air that comes out of your mouth □ *We could see our breath in the freezing air.* (**hálito**)
3 be out of breath to be breathing fast because you have been running or working hard □ *You shouldn't be out of breath after walking upstairs.* (**fôlego**)
4 hold your breath to breathe in but not breathe out again □ *They have to hold their breath for a long time under the water.* (**respiração**)
5 under your breath if you say something under your breath, you say it very quietly (**sussurrar**)
♦ IDIOM **take your breath away** to surprise you very much □ *His kindness took my breath away.* (**deixar alguém boquiaberto**)

breathe /briːð/ VERB [breathes, breathing, breathed]
to take air into and out of your lungs □ *He was so quiet, I thought he had stopped breathing.* □ *It feels good to breathe some clean air again.* (**respirar**)
♦ PHRASAL VERBS **breathe in** to take air into your lungs □ *Breathe in through your nose.* **breathe out** to allow air out of your lungs □ *Now breathe out through your mouth.* (**inspirar, expirar**)

> Remember that the verb breathe has an e at the end, while the noun breath does not. Be careful not to confuse the spellings of the verb breathes and the noun plural breaths.

breed¹ /briːd/ VERB [breeds, breeding, bred]
1 when animals breed they produce young animals □ *The birds breed across Europe and Asia.* (**reproduzir[-se]**)
2 to produce young animals from dogs, cows, sheep, etc. □ *These dogs are bred for hunting.* (**gerar**)

breed² /briːd/ NOUN [plural breeds]
a particular type of animal □ *The Aberdeen Angus is a famous Scottish breed of cattle.* (**raça**)

breeze /briːz/ NOUN [plural breezes] a light wind □ *a cool/gentle breeze* (**brisa**)
bribe /braɪb/ NOUN [plural bribes] money that is offered to someone so that they will do something dishonest 🗗 *accept/take a bribe* (**suborno**)

brick /brɪk/ NOUN [plural bricks]
a block used for building walls □ *Someone threw a brick through the window.* 🗗 *a brick wall* (**tijolo**)

bride /braɪd/ NOUN [plural **brides**] a woman who is getting married (**noiva**)

bridge /brɪdʒ/ NOUN [plural **bridges**]

1 a structure that is built over a river or a road to allow people or vehicles to cross from one side to the other ◻ *We drove across the bridge.* 🖻 *a railway bridge* (**ponte**)
2 a card game for four people playing in pairs (**ponte**)

brief /briːf/ ADJECTIVE [**briefer**, **briefest**] short
◻ *We had a brief telephone conversation.* ◻ *He wrote her a brief note.* (**breve**)

briefcase /ˈbriːfkeɪs/ NOUN [plural **briefcases**] a flat case for carrying business documents (**pasta**)

briefly /ˈbriːfli/ ADVERB in or for a short amount of time ◻ *Tell us briefly what you want us to do.* ◻ *They stopped briefly to get petrol.* (**brevemente**)

brigade /brɪˈɡeɪd/ NOUN [plural **brigades**] a group of soldiers that forms part of a group in the army
→ go to **fire brigade** (**brigada**)

bright /braɪt/ ADJECTIVE [**brighter**, **brightest**]

1 producing a lot of light ◻ *We could see the bright lights of the city.* (**brilhante**)
2 full of light ◻ *This is a nice bright bedroom.* (**iluminado**)
3 a bright colour is strong and clear ◻ *His eyes were bright blue.* (**vivo**)
4 clever ◻ *He was always the brightest child in our family.* (**brilhante**)

brighten /ˈbraɪtən/ VERB [**brightens**, **brightening**, **brightened**] to become brighter or to make something brighter ◻ *The weather brightened up and we went out for a walk.* ◻ *A coat of paint would brighten the walls.* (**clarear**)

brilliant /ˈbrɪljənt/ ADJECTIVE
1 very clever, or showing great skill ◻ *Fiona gave a brilliant speech.* (**brilhante**)
2 very bright 🖻 *brilliant sunshine* (**brilhante**)

bring /brɪŋ/ VERB [**brings**, **bringing**, **brought**]

1 to take or carry a person or thing with you when you go somewhere ◻ + **to** *You can bring all your friends to the party.* ◻ *He brought a couple of jigsaws downstairs.* ◻ + **back** *He never brought back the book he borrowed.* (**trazer**)
2 to cause a feeling or a situation ◻ + **to** *The new leaders brought peace to the area.* ◻ *Our grandchildren have brought us great happiness.* (**trazer**)

> Use **bring** when you are talking about taking a person or thing towards you (the person speaking). Use **take** when you are talking about taking a person or thing away from you (the person speaking), or away from the place where you are now ◻ *Could you bring my mobile when you come?* ◻ *I'll take some flowers to the hospital.*

◆ PHRASAL VERBS **bring something about** to cause something to happen ◻ *Motherhood had brought about enormous changes.* **bring something up 1** to mention a subject ◻ *Did anyone bring up the subject of payment?* (**provocar**) **2** to make food come up from your stomach and out of your mouth **bring someone up** to look after a child until they are old enough to look after themselves ◻ *My parents brought me up to be polite and considerate.*

brink /brɪŋk/ NOUN **on the brink of something** if you are on the brink of something, it is going to happen very soon ◻ *Noreen was on the brink of tears.* (**beira**)

Brit /brɪt/ NOUN [plural **Brits**] a British person. An informal word ◻ *There are a lot of Brits in Majorca in the summer.* (**britânico**)

Britain /ˈbrɪtən/ NOUN England, Scotland and Wales (**Bretanha**)

British¹ /ˈbrɪtɪʃ/ ADJECTIVE belonging to or coming from Britain ◻ *British industry* (**britânico**)

British² /ˈbrɪtɪʃ/ NOUN **the British** the people who come from Britain (**britânicos**)

Briton /ˈbrɪtən/ NOUN [plural **Britons**] a person who comes from Britain ◻ *Several Britons were killed in the accident.* (**britânico**)

broad /brɔːd/ ADJECTIVE [**broader**, **broadest**]

1 wide 🖻 *He was a tall man with broad shoulders.* 🖻 *She gave us a broad smile.* (**largo**)
2 including many different things 🖻 *We discussed a broad range of subjects.* (**amplo**)

broadcast¹ /ˈbrɔːdkɑːst/ NOUN [plural **broadcasts**] a programme sent out on television or radio 🖻 *We watched a live broadcast of the World Cup Final.* (**transmissão**)

broadcast² /ˈbrɔːdkɑːst/ VERB [**broadcasts**, **broadcasting**, **broadcast**] to send out information or programmes on television or radio ◻ *The interview was broadcast on Sunday.* ◻ *The BBC broadcast the event live.* (**transmitir**)

broaden /ˈbrɔːdən/ VERB [**broadens**, **broadening**, **broadened**]
1 to become wider, or to make something wider ◻ *They've broadened the road.* ◻ *Her smile broadened.* (**ampliar**)
2 to include more things or people ◻ *The socialist party will have to broaden its appeal.* (**ampliar**)
◆ IDIOM **broaden your mind** to give you more knowledge about the world and make you accept different people more ◻ *They say that travel broadens the mind.* (**ampliar a mente/horizonte**)
→ go to **broaden your horizon**

broccoli /ˈbrɒkəli/ NOUN, NO PLURAL a vegetable with a lot of very small green or purple flowers growing from a thick stem (**brócolis**)

brochure /ˈbrəʊʃə(r)/ NOUN [plural **brochures**] a small book containing information about particular products or services, often with pictures □ *a holiday brochure* (**folheto**)

broke /brəʊk/ PAST TENSE OF **break**¹ (ver **break**)

broken¹ /ˈbrəʊkən/ PAST PARTICIPLE OF **break**¹ (ver **break**¹)

broken² /ˈbrəʊkən/ ADJECTIVE
1 damaged, and often in several pieces ▣ *broken glass* ▣ *a broken bone* (**quebrado**)
2 if a machine is broken, it is not working □ *The washing machine is broken.* (**quebrado**)
3 if someone's heart is broken, they are very sad, especially because someone they loved has gone away or died ▣ *They say she died of a broken heart.* (**partido**)

bronze /brɒnz/ NOUN [plural **bronzes**]
1 a dark red-brown metal □ *The statue was made of bronze.* (**bronze**)
2 a bronze medal (= prize for coming third in a competition or race) □ *Williams came first, Miller came second, and Lewis got the bronze.* (**bronze**)

brooch /brəʊtʃ/ NOUN [plural **brooches**] a piece of jewellery with a pin on the back that you fasten to the front of a dress or jacket (**broche**)

brother /ˈbrʌðə(r)/ NOUN [plural **brothers**] a boy or man who has the same parents as you ▣ *I share a bedroom with my little brother.* ▣ *Do you have any brothers and sisters?* (**irmão**)

brother-in-law /ˈbrʌðərɪnlɔː/ NOUN [plural **brothers-in-law**] your sister's husband or the brother of your husband or wife (**cunhado**)

brought /brɔːt/ PAST TENSE AND PAST PARTICIPLE OF **bring** (ver **bring**)

brow /braʊ/ NOUN [plural **brows**] the part of your face above your eyes □ *She wrinkled her brow in confusion.* (**testa**)

brown¹ /braʊn/ ADJECTIVE having the colour of soil or wood ▣ *She has light brown hair.* ▣ *They painted the walls dark brown.* (**castanho**)

brown² /braʊn/ NOUN [plural **browns**] the colour of soil or wood □ *We chose a dark brown for the sofa.* (**marrom**)

bruise¹ /bruːz/ NOUN [plural **bruises**] a dark mark that you get on your skin if it is hit □ *Joe's got a big black bruise under his eye.* (**contusão**)

bruise² /bruːz/ VERB [**bruises, bruising, bruised**] to make a bruise on someone's skin □ *Daniel bruised his knee when he fell.* (**machucar**)

brush¹ /brʌʃ/ VERB [**brushes, brushing, brushed**] to make something tidy or clean using a brush ▣ *Have you brushed your teeth?* ▣ *Make sure you brush your hair before you go out.* (**escovar**)

brush² /brʌʃ/ NOUN [plural **brushes**] an object with short hairs or thin pieces of plastic, wire, etc. fixed to a handle, used for tidying your hair, painting or cleaning □ *You'll need a brush to get the mud off those shoes.* □ *An artist needs a range of different brushes.* (**escova**)

brutal /ˈbruːtəl/ ADJECTIVE very cruel □ *a brutal murder* (**brutal**)

bubble¹ /ˈbʌbəl/ NOUN [plural **bubbles**] a very thin light ball of liquid filled with air ▣ *soap bubbles* ▣ *The children were blowing bubbles in the garden.* (**bolha**)

bubble² /ˈbʌbəl/ VERB [**bubbles, bubbling, bubbled**] liquid bubbles when small balls of air form in it, usually because it is boiling □ *A big pot of soup was bubbling on the stove.* (**borbulhar**)

bucket /ˈbʌkɪt/ NOUN [plural **buckets**] a round open container with a handle, used for carrying water, or substances such as soil or sand ▣ *a bucket of water* □ *You'll need about four buckets of water to wash the car.* (**balde**)

buckle¹ /ˈbʌkəl/ NOUN [plural **buckles**] a metal object on the end of a belt, used for fastening it (**fivela**)

buckle² /ˈbʌkəl/ VERB [**buckles, buckling, buckled**] to fasten something with a buckle □ *She buckled her belt tightly around her waist.* (**afivelar**)

bud /bʌd/ NOUN [plural **buds**] the part of a plant from which a leaf or flower develops (**broto**)

Buddhism /ˈbʊdɪzəm/ NOUN, NO PLURAL a religion that is practised in many parts of the world, which follows the teaching of Buddha □ *He gave up politics, and went to Tibet to study Buddhism.* (**budismo**)

Buddhist¹ /ˈbʊdɪst/ NOUN [plural **Buddhists**] someone who practises Buddhism (**budista**)

Buddhist² /ˈbʊdɪst/ ADJECTIVE to do with Buddhism or Buddhists ▣ *a Buddhist monk* (**budista**)

budget¹ /ˈbʌdʒɪt/ NOUN [plural **budgets**] an amount of money that a person, company or government has available to spend □ *We offer holidays to suit all budgets.* ▣ *They were on a tight budget* (= did not have much money). □ *The*

budget

company is cutting its marketing budget. □ *the education budget* (**orçamento**)
budget² /ˈbʌdʒɪt/ ADJECTIVE cheap □ *budget flights* (**barato**)

buffet¹ /ˈbʊfeɪ/ NOUN [plural **buffets**] a meal where different types of food are put on a table from which people can choose what they want (**bufê**)

buffet² /ˈbʌfɪt/ VERB [**buffets, buffeting, buffeted**] to knock someone or something about roughly □ *The little boat was buffeted by the storm.* (**esbofetear**)

bug /bʌg/ NOUN [plural **bugs**]
1 an informal word for an infectious illness 🔲 *She's got a tummy bug.* (**infecção**)
2 a fault in a computer program 🔲 *She is trying to fix a bug in the program.* (**defeito**)
3 a small insect (**inseto**)

build /bɪld/ VERB [**builds, building, built**] to make something by putting materials or parts together □ *He's planning to build his own house.* □ *The walls are built of wood.* (**construir**)

builder /ˈbɪldə(r)/ [plural **builders**] someone whose job is to build and repair houses and other structures (**construtor**)

building /ˈbɪldɪŋ/ [plural **buildings**]
1 a structure with walls and a roof, for example a house or a church □ *What's the tallest building in the world?* (**edifício**)
2 no plural the activity of building houses and other structures □ *There is a lot of building going on in this street.* (**construção**)

> THESAURUS: Building is a general word for any structure with a roof and walls. A house is a general word for a place where people live, often for one family. A flat is a set of rooms that someone lives in, which is part of a larger building. Flats usually have no stairs inside. A set of flats in a building is called a block of flats. Flats are sometimes called apartments, especially in American English. A cottage is a small house in the countryside or in a village.

building society /ˈbɪldɪŋ səˈsaɪəti/ NOUN [plural **building societies**] an organization similar to a bank, from which people can borrow money to buy a house (**sociedade de crédito**)
built /bɪlt/ PAST TENSE AND PAST PARTICIPLE OF **build** (ver **build**)

bulb /bʌlb/ NOUN [plural **bulbs**] a glass object that you put in an electric light to make it work □ *I need a new bulb for my lamp.* (**bulbo**)

bulge /bʌldʒ/ VERB [**bulges, bulging, bulged**]
1 if someone's eyes or muscles bulge, they stick out □ *His eyes bulged in horror.* (**inchar**)
2 if a container is bulging, it is very full □ *His sack was bulging with presents.* (**inchar**)
bulk /bʌlk/ NOUN
1 the bulk of something most of something

43

bun

□ *The bulk of his pocket money was spent on computer games.* (**a maior parte**)
2 in bulk you buy in bulk when you buy something in large quantities □ *It's much cheaper to buy household goods in bulk.* (**em grande quantidade**)

bull /bʊl/ NOUN [plural **bulls**]
1 an adult male cow (**touro**)
2 the male of some other animals, such as the elephant (**macho**)

bulldozer /ˈbʊldəʊzə(r)/ NOUN [plural **bulldozers**] a large vehicle with a heavy metal container at the front, used for moving large amounts of earth and stones (**escavadeira**)

bullet /ˈbʊlɪt/ NOUN [plural **bullets**] a small piece of metal that is shot from a gun □ *a bullet wound* 🔲 *Several people were in the room when the bullets were fired.* (**bala**)

bully¹ /ˈbʊli/ NOUN [plural **bullies**] a person who frightens or hurts people who are smaller or weaker than they are (**valentão**)
bully² /ˈbʊli/ VERB [**bullies, bullying, bullied**] to frighten or hurt smaller or weaker people (**intimidar**)
• **bullying** /ˈbʊliɪŋ/ NOUN, NO PLURAL when someone bullies another person (**intimidação**)
bump¹ /bʌmp/ VERB [**bumps, bumping, bumped**] to knock against something by accident *The baby bumped her head on the table.* □ *I bumped into the wall.* (**bater**)
♦ PHRASAL VERB **bump into someone** to meet someone by chance □ *I bumped into Sarah in town today.* (**topar com alguém**)
bump² /bʌmp/ NOUN [plural **bumps**]
1 a raised part on a surface □ *He had a nasty bump on the back of his head.* □ *There were a lot of bumps in the road.* (**protuberância**)
2 a knock □ *I felt a gentle bump against my leg* (**batida**)
bumper¹ /ˈbʌmpə(r)/ NOUN [plural **bumpers**] a long bar fixed to the front and back of a car that protects it if it hits something (**para-choque**)
bumper² /ˈbʌmpə(r)/ ADJECTIVE bigger than usual 🔲 *We had a bumper crop of tomatoes this year.* (**abundante**)
bun /bʌn/ NOUN [plural **buns**]
1 a small round sweet cake □ *a currant bun* (**bolinho**)
2 bread in the form of a round shape □ *a hamburger in a bun* (**pãozinho**)
3 a hairstyle in which the hair is twisted into a tight ball and fixed at the back of the head (**coque**)

bunch /bʌntʃ/ NOUN [plural **bunches**]
1 a group of things tied or held together ▫ *a bunch of flowers* ▫ *The caretaker has a big bunch of keys.* (**grupo, punhado**)
2 a group of things that grow together ▫ *a bunch of grapes/bananas* (**cacho**)

bundle /ˈbʌndəl/ NOUN [plural **bundles**] a group of things fastened together ▫ *a bundle of newspapers* (**maço**)

bungalow /ˈbʌŋɡələʊ/ NOUN [plural **bungalows**] a house that is all on one level (**bangalô**)

buoy /bɔɪ/ NOUN [plural **buoys**] a large object that floats in the sea, used to warn people or ships of danger (**boia**)

burden /ˈbɜːdən/ NOUN [plural **burdens**] something unpleasant or difficult that someone has to deal with ▫ *He offered to share the burden of the work.* ▫ *Running two homes is a big financial burden.* (**fardo**)

burger /ˈbɜːɡə(r)/ NOUN [plural **burgers**] a type of flat round food made from small pieces of meat that have been pressed together ▫ *I'll have a burger with fries and a coke, please.* (**hambúrguer**)

burglar /ˈbɜːɡlə(r)/ NOUN [plural **burglars**] someone who illegally enters a building in order to steal things ▫ *The burglars broke in through a downstairs window.* (**ladrão**)

burglary /ˈbɜːɡləri/ NOUN [plural **burglaries**] the crime of going into a building and stealing things ▫ *He called the police to report a burglary.* (**roubo**)

burial /ˈberiəl/ NOUN [plural **burials**] when a dead person is put in the ground (**enterro**)

burn¹ /bɜːn/ VERB [**burns, burning, burnt** or **burned**]
1 to destroy something by setting fire to it, or to be destroyed in this way ▫ *We burn all our garden waste.* ▫ *Both houses burnt to the ground.* (**queimar**)
2 to be on fire ▫ *We could see the grass burning from miles away.* (**queimar**)
3 to injure yourself by touching fire or heat ▫ *I burnt my hand on the cooker.* (**queimar**)
♦ PHRASAL VERB **burn down** if a building burns down, it is completely destroyed in a fire ▫ *The old school burnt down.* (**ser destruído**)

burn² /bɜːn/ NOUN [plural **burns**] an injury or mark left after touching fire or something very hot (**queimadura**)

burst /bɜːst/ VERB [**bursts, bursting, burst**]
1 to break or tear, especially from having too much pressure inside ▫ *The pipe had burst and water was running everywhere.* ▫ *He was bursting all the balloons with a pin.* (**estourar**)
2 burst into flames to suddenly start to burn a lot (**irromper em chamas**)
3 burst into tears to suddenly start to cry (**desatar a chorar**)
♦ PHRASAL VERB **burst out crying/laughing** to suddenly start to cry or laugh (**desatar a chorar, rir**)

bury /ˈberi/ VERB [**buries, burying, buried**] to put in the ground, especially a dead person ▫ *She was buried in the village where she was born.* ▫ *They buried the treasure.* (**enterrar**)

bus /bʌs/ NOUN [plural **buses**] a large vehicle with a lot of seats for passengers ▫ *I caught the bus into town.* ▫ *a school bus* ▫ *a bus driver* (**ônibus**)

bush /bʊʃ/ NOUN [plural **bushes**] a type of small tree ▫ *a rose bush* (**arbusto**)

business /ˈbɪznɪs/ NOUN [plural **businesses**]
1 no plural buying and selling, and the work of producing things that people will buy ▫ *He went into business* (= started buying and selling) *with his brother.* ▫ *In 2004 her company went out of business* (= ended because they had no money). ▫ *They do a lot of business with Asia* (= They sell a lot to Asia). (**negócios**)
2 a company that makes and sells goods, or that sells services ▫ *He runs the business with his wife.* (**negócios**)
3 on business working ▫ *He travels a lot on business.* (**a negócios**)

> Remember that you travel/go somewhere **on business**:
> ✓ *I was recently in Paris on business.*
> ✗ *I was recently in Paris for business.*

♦ IDIOM **Mind your own business!** used as a rude way of refusing to answer a personal question ▫ *'What's your boyfriend's name?' 'Mind your own business!'* (**cuide de sua vida!**)

businessman /ˈbɪznɪsmæn/ NOUN [plural **businessmen**] a man who works in business, usually in a high position (**homem de negócios**)

businesswoman /ˈbɪznɪsˌwʊmən/ NOUN [plural **businesswomen**] a woman who works in business, usually in a high position (**mulher de negócios**)

bus stop /ˈbʌs ˌstɒp/ NOUN [plural **bus stops**] a place where a bus stops to allow passengers to get on or off ▫ *I saw Fiona standing at the bus stop.* (**ponto de ônibus**)

busy /ˈbɪzi/ ADJECTIVE [**busier, busiest**]
1 doing a lot of things ▫ + **with** *They're busy with wedding preparations.* ▫ + **doing something** *I was*

busy getting dinner ready. 🔲 *That report should keep him busy today.* 🔲 *I've had a very busy day.* (**mais ocupado**)
2 full of people or traffic 🔲 *We live on a busy street.* ◻ *Were the shops busy this morning?* (**movimentado**)

but /bʌt/ CONJUNCTION used for joining two parts of a sentence which say different or opposite things ◻ *She eats fish but not meat.* ◻ *He's not very attractive but he's a nice guy.* ◻ *I can cycle but I can't drive.* ◻ *I'd like to come but I haven't got time.* (**mas**)

butcher /ˈbʊtʃə(r)/ NOUN [plural **butchers**]
1 someone whose job is to cut up and sell raw meat (**açougueiro**)
2 butcher's a shop that sells raw meat (**açougue**)

butter /ˈbʌtə(r)/ NOUN, NO PLURAL a yellow food made from milk, used for spreading on bread or for cooking 🔲 *a slice of bread and butter* (**manteiga**)

butterfly /ˈbʌtəflaɪ/ NOUN [plural **butterflies**] a type of insect with large brightly coloured wings (**borboleta**)
♦ IDIOM **get/have butterflies (in your stomach)** to have an uncomfortable feeling in your stomach because you are nervous (**frio na barriga**)

button /ˈbʌtən/ NOUN [plural **buttons**]
1 a small object that you press in order to make a machine work 🔲 *I pressed the button to call the lift.* ◻ *Press the start button.* (**botão**)
2 a small round object used for fastening clothes 🔲 *He did up/undid* (= fastened/unfastened) *his buttons.* (**botão**)

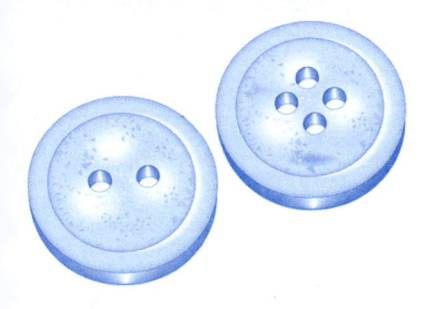

buy /baɪ/ VERB [**buys, buying, bought**] to get something by giving money for it ◻ *I've bought the tickets.* ◻ *Have you bought him a present?* ◻ **+ from** *We buy most of our food from the supermarket.* (**comprar**)

buyer /ˈbaɪə(r)/ NOUN [plural **buyers**] someone who buys something ◻ *Have they found a buyer for their house?* (**comprador**)

buzz[1] /bʌz/ NOUN, NO PLURAL the continuous sound that a large flying insect makes ◻ *The constant buzz of insects disturbed his sleep.* (**zumbido**)
buzz[2] /bʌz/ VERB [**buzzes, buzzing, buzzed**] to make a continuous sound like a large flying insect ◻ *Flies buzzed round our heads.* (**zumbir**)

by[1] /baɪ/ PREPOSITION
1 shows who or what does something ◻ *a painting by Picasso* ◻ *The house was built by her grandfather.* (**por**)
2 near or next to something ◻ *There's a cafe' by the station.* (**perto de**)
3 using something ◻ *We came by train.* ◻ *All their clothes are made by hand.* ◻ *Can I pay by credit card?* ◻ **+ doing something** *By buying food from local shops you are supporting your community.* (**de, a, com**)
4 past ◻ *A tall boy ran by me.* (**por**)
5 by accident/chance without intending to ◻ *We met by chance.* ◻ *I only discovered it by accident.* (**por acaso**)
6 by 20%/£500, etc. shows how much something has increased or decreased ◻ *Prices have risen by 20 percent.* (**com**)
7 by the arm/coat, etc. shows which part of someone you take in your hand ◻ *She grabbed me by the hand.* (**por**)
8 before ◻ *I'll be home by 7.30.* (**antes**)
9 used when giving measurements of length and width ◻ *The room is 5 metres by 3 metres.* (**por**)

by[2] /baɪ/ ADVERB past ◻ *A car went speeding by.* (**por aqui**)
♦ IDIOM **by the way** used before you say something that is not related to what you were saying before (**a propósito**)

bye /baɪ/ EXCLAMATION an informal word that means goodbye ◻ *Bye – see you later!* (**tchau**)
bypass /ˈbaɪpɑːs/ NOUN [plural **by passes**] a road around a town or city (**desvio**)

Cc

C¹ ou **C** /si:/ the third letter of the alphabet (a terceira letra do alfabeto)

C² /si:/ ABBREVIATION
1 Celsius (**Celsius**)
2 centigrade (**centígrado**)

cab /kæb/ NOUN [plural **cabs**] a taxi ▢ *We took a cab to the airport.* (**táxi**)

cabbage /'kæbɪdʒ/ NOUN [plural **cabbages**] a large round green vegetable formed of tight layers of leaves (**repolho**)

cabin /'kæbɪn/ NOUN [plural **cabins**]
1 a simple wooden house ▢ *He built a log cabin in the forest.* (**cabana**)
2 a small room for sleeping in on a ship (**cabine**)
3 the part of an aeroplane which the passengers sit in (**cabine**)

cabinet /'kæbɪnɪt/ NOUN [plural **cabinets**]
1 **Cabinet** a group of people with important government jobs who decide what the government will do ▢ *She became a member of the Cabinet in 1990.* ▢ *a Cabinet meeting* (**gabinete**)
2 a cupboard with shelves, used for storing things or for showing attractive objects ▢ *a bathroom cabinet* (**armário**)

cable /'keɪbəl/ NOUN [plural **cables**]
1 a tube containing wires that carry electricity or electronic signals ▢ *a telephone cable* (**cabo**)
2 thick, strong metal rope ▢ *Miles of cable were used to build the bridge.* (**cabo**)
3 *no plural* a television service in which programmes are sent along underground wires ▢ *We can't get cable or satellite here.* (**cabo**)

café /'kæfeɪ/ NOUN [plural **cafés**] a small restaurant that serves drinks and things to eat (**café**)

cafeteria /ˌkæfɪ'tɪərɪə/ NOUN [plural **cafeterias**] a restaurant where the customers buy food and drink and take it to a table to eat it (**cantina**)

cage /keɪdʒ/ NOUN [plural **cages**] a box or an area with bars around it for keeping birds or animals in ▢ *The pet shop sells bird cages and hamster cages.* (**gaiola**)

cake /keɪk/ NOUN [plural **cakes**] a sweet food made from a baked mixture, usually of flour, sugar, butter and eggs ▢ *a birthday cake* ▢ *He made a cake for the school fair.* ▢ *Would you like another slice of chocolate cake?* (**bolo**)

◆ IDIOM **have your cake and eat it** to get all the advantages of a situation in a way that is unfair (**levar todas as vantagens**)

calculate /'kælkjʊleɪt/ VERB [**calculates, calculating, calculated**] to find out an amount by using mathematics ▢ *One apple costs 13p. Calculate the cost of 174 apples.* ▢ *Do you understand how they calculate tax?* (**calcular**)

calculation /ˌkælkjʊ'leɪʃən/ NOUN [plural **calculations**] when you use mathematics to find out an amount ▢ *I did some quick calculations to work out the total cost.* ▢ *By my calculation, we should finish by Tuesday.* (**cálculo**)

calculator /'kælkjʊleɪtə(r)/ NOUN [plural **calculators**] an electronic machine that you use for doing mathematical calculations ▢ *a pocket calculator* (**calculadora**)

calendar /'kælɪndə(r)/ NOUN [plural **calendars**] something that shows all the days, weeks and months of the year ▢ *She looked on the calendar to see what date it would be on Monday.* (**calendário**)

calf /kɑːf/ NOUN [plural **calves**]
1 the back part of your leg below the knee (**panturrilha**)
2 a young cow (**bezerro**)

call¹ /kɔːl/ VERB [**calls, calling, called**]
1 if a person or thing is called something, that is their name ▢ *He's called Jonathan James.* (**chamar**)
2 to shout ▢ *I heard him calling my name.* (**gritar**)
3 to ask someone to come to you ▢ *Call the children in from the garden.* (**chamar**)
4 to telephone someone ▢ *Have you called your mother yet?* (**ligar**)
5 to visit someone ▢ + **in** *We called in to see Maria this morning.* (**visitar**)

> Remember that the verb **call** meaning 'telephone' is used without 'to':
> ✓ *I called my brother to wish him happy birthday.*
> ✗ *I called to my brother to wish him happy birthday.*

◆ PHRASAL VERBS **call for someone** to go to someone's house in order to go somewhere with them ▢ *I'll call for you at seven.* **call something off** to stop a plan or an activity ▢ *The search has* been called off. **call someone up** a US word meaning to telephone someone □ *He called me up in the middle of the night.*

call² /kɔːl/ NOUN [plural **calls**]
1 when you contact someone by telephone 🔁 *Give me a call tomor row.* 🔁 *I'm sure I can find someone to fix you car – let me make a few calls.* (chamada)
2 a shout □ *They ignored his calls for help.* (gritos)
3 a short visit 🔁 *I thought I might pay you a call tomorrow.* (visita)

calm¹ /kɑːm/ ADJECTIVE [**calmer, calmest**]
1 not nervous, excited or upset □ *Try to stay calm.* □ *'Yes', he said in a calm voice.* (calmo)
2 if the sea is calm, it is flat with no big waves (calmo)

calm² /kɑːm/
◆ PHRASAL VERB [**calms, calming, calmed**] **calm (someone) down** to stop someone being angry, excited or upset, or to stop being angry, excited or upset 🔁 *She took a couple of deep breaths to calm herself down.* □ *Just calm down! Nobody's going to hurt you.* (acalmar)

calmly /'kɑːmlɪ/ ADVERB without seeming nervous or excited □ *Grace walked calmly on to the stage.* (calmamente)

calves /kɑːvz/ PLURAL OF **calf** (ver bezerros)
came /keɪm/ PAST TENSE OF **come** (ver come)

camel /'kæməl/ NOUN [plural **camels**] a large animal that lives in the desert and has one or two humps (= tall rounded parts) on its back (camelo)

camera /'kæmərə/ NOUN [plural **cameras**] a device for taking photographs, or for making television programmes or films 🔁 *I have a digital camera.* 🔁 *He's very confident in front of the television cameras.* (câmera)

camp¹ /kæmp/ NOUN [plural **camps**] a place where people live in tents or temporary shelters, usually for a short time 🔁 *a holiday camp* 🔁 *a refugee camp* (acampamento)

camp² /kæmp/ VERB [**camps, camping, camped**] to stay somewhere for a short time in a tent or caravan (= vehicle for living in) □ *We camped next to the lake.* (acampar)

campaign /kæm'peɪn/ NOUN [plural **campaigns**] a series of activities designed to achieve something □ *an advertising campaign* □ *an election campaign* (campanha)

camping /'kæmpɪŋ/ NOUN, NO PLURAL the activity of staying in a tent 🔁 *We went camping in France last summer.* 🔁 *The boys are on a camping trip.* (camping)

campsite /'kæmpsaɪt/ NOUN [plural **campsites**] a place where people stay in tents for a holiday □ *We found a good campsite near the river.* (área para camping)

campus /'kæmpəs/ NOUN [plural **campuses**] the land and buildings that form a university or college (campus)

can¹ /kæn/ MODAL VERB
1 to be able to do something □ *Can you swim? Yes, I can.* □ *Can you see my keys anywhere?* (poder)
2 to be allowed to □ *Can I go swimming? Yes, you can.*
3 used to ask someone to do something or give you something □ *Can you open the window, please?* □ *Can you lend me some money?* (poder)
4 used to say if something is possible or not □ *Can you buy tickets here?* □ *Tiredness can cause accidents.* (poder)

➤ **Can** is the present tense form. Use **could** for the past tense.

➤ To ask for something politely, do not use **can** but instead use **could** □ *Could I use this chair, please?*

can² /kæn/ NOUN [plural **cans**]
1 a closed metal container that keeps food or drink fresh 🔁 *a beer can* 🔁 *Do you recycle your tin cans?* □ *She opened a can of beans.* (lata)
2 a container used for liquid or other substances □ *a paint can* (lata)

can³ /kæn/ VERB [**cans, canning, canned**] to put food or drink in closed metal cans that keep it fresh (enlatar)

canal /kə'næl/ NOUN [plural **canals**] a long passage filled with water, made for boats to travel along □ *the Panama Canal* (canal)

cancel /'kænsəl/ VERB [**cancels, cancelling/US canceling, cancelled/US canceled**] to say that a planned event will not happen □ *The match was cancelled because of the snow.* (cancelar)

cancer /'kænsə(r)/ NOUN, NO PLURAL a serious disease in which some cells in the body start to grow very quickly □ *Smoking can cause lung cancer.* 🔁 *Use sun cream – you don't want to get skin cancer.* 🔁 *The drug is used to treat cancer patients.* (câncer)

candidate /'kændɪdət/ NOUN [plural **candidates**]
1 someone who is trying to get a job □ **+ for** *There are three candidates for the job.* □ *The Democratic candidate for the US presidency is Barack Obama.* (candidato)
2 someone who is taking an exam □ *All our GCSE candidates were successful.* (candidato)

candle /'kæ ndəl/ NOUN [plural **candles**] a stick of wax with a piece of string through the middle which produces a flame when you burn it 🔁 *I must light the candles on the dinner table.* 🔁 *Don't forget to blow out the candle.* (vela)

candy /'kændɪ/ NOUN [plural **candi es**] the US word for **sweet²** (sense 1) (doce)

cane /keɪn/ NOUN [plural **canes**] a stick that someone uses to help them walk (vara)

cannon

cannon /'kænən/ NOUN [plural **cannons**] a large gun that fires big metal balls or other large explosives (**canhão**)

cannot /'kænɒt/ MODAL VERB the negative form of can □ *I just cannot do it.* (**ver can**)

> In spoken English, **can't** is usually used instead of 'cannot' □ *I can't come tonight.*

canoe /kə'nu:/ NOUN [plural **canoes**] a light boat with pointed ends which you move through the water using a paddle (= stick with wide flat ends) (**canoa**)

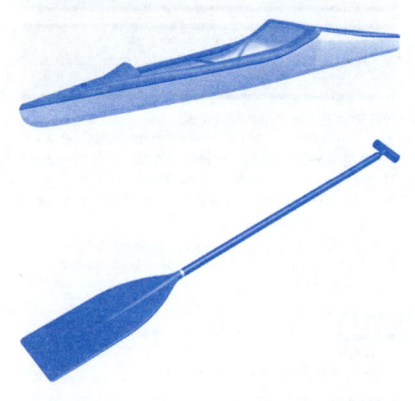

can't /kɑ:nt/ a short way to say and write **cannot** □ *I can't hear you.* (ver **cannot**)

canteen /ˌkæn'ti:n/ NOUN [plural **canteens**] a restaurant in a school or work place □ *I had lunch with my friends in the school canteen.* (**cantina**)

canvas /'kænvəs/ NOUN [plural **canvases**]
1 a piece of strong cloth stretched on a frame for an artist to paint on (**tela**)
2 strong cloth used to make tents and sails (**lona**)

canyon /'kænjən/ NOUN [plural **canyons**] a deep valley with steep sides. A geography word □ *the Grand Canyon* (**desfiladeiro**)

cap /kæp/ NOUN [plural **caps**]
1 a soft hat, often with a flat part that sticks out at the front □ *a baseball cap* (**boné**)
2 a small top for a bottle, tube or pen □ *The pen will dry up if you leave the cap off.* (**tampa**)

capability /ˌkeɪpə'bɪlɪti/ NOUN [plural **capabilities**] ability or power to do something ▣ *The task is simply beyond his capabilities.* (**capacidade**)

capable /'keɪpəbəl/ ADJECTIVE
1 if you are capable of something, you are able to do it □ *The old lady isn't capable of looking after herself any more.* (**capaz**)
2 able to do things and deal with problems without help □ *She's a very capable person.* (**capaz**)

> Note that the structure that comes after **capable** is **of doing something**:
> ✓ *She isn't **capable of** looking after a small child.*
> ✗ *She isn't capable to look after a small child.*

capacitor /kə'pæsɪtə(r)/ NOUN [plural **capacitors**] a device used to store electrical charge. A physics word. (**capacitor**)

capacity /kə'pæsɪti/ NOUN [plural **capacities**]
1 the total amount that a container or building will hold ▣ *The hall has a seating capacity of 300.* □ *Each barrel has a capacity of 100 litres.* (**capacidade**)
2 someone's ability to do or experience something □ *Flynn has the capacity to be a great leader.* (**capacidade**)

capital /'kæpɪtəl/ NOUN [plural **capitals**]
1 the city where the government of a state or country is □ + *of London is the capital of England.* (**capital**)
2 a large letter such as *B* that you write at the beginning of a sentence, or at the beginning of a name □ *Write your name in capitals at the top of the page.* ▣ *The notice was typed in capital letters.* (**maiúscula**)

captain /'kæptɪn/ NOUN [plural **captains**]
1 the person in charge of a ship or an aircraft □ *Everyone must obey the captain's orders.* (**capitão**)
2 the person in charge of a sports team □ *He is the new England captain.* (**capitão**)
3 a person of middle rank in the army, high rank in the navy or high rank in the US police □ *Captain Jones* (**capitão**)

captive /'kæptɪv/ NOUN [plural **captives**] a prisoner (**prisioneiro**)

captivity /kæp'tɪvɪti/ NOUN, NO PLURAL when a person or animal is kept in a place which they are not allowed to leave □ *The bear spent its whole life in captivity.* (**cativeiro**)

capture¹ /'kæptʃə(r)/ VERB [**captures, capturing, captured**]
1 to catch an animal or person and not allow them to escape □ *Many soldiers were captured by the enemy.* (**capturar**)
2 to get control of a place or equipment by force □ *Armed soldiers have captured the airport.* (**capturar**)

capture² /'kæptʃə(r)/ NOUN, NO PLURAL
1 when you catch someone or something ▣ *How long can the killer avoid capture?* (**captura**)
2 when you take or get control of a place or equipment □ *the capture of enemy tanks* (**captura**)

car /kɑ:(r)/ NOUN [plural **cars**] a vehicle with an engine and seats for a small number of passengers □ *Many children travel to school by car.* ▣ *You need a licence before you can drive a car.* ▣ *Where did you park the car?* ▣ *I've lost the car keys.* (**carro**)

caravan /'kærəvæn/ NOUN [plural **caravans**] a vehicle for living in, especially on holiday, which can be pulled behind a car (**reboque, trailer**)

carbohydrate   carpet

carbohydrate /ˌkɑːbəʊˈhaɪdreɪt/ NOUN [plural carbohydrates] a substance in foods such as potatoes and bread which gives your body energy (**carboidrato**)

carbon /ˈkɑːbən/ NOUN, NO PLURAL a chemical element which is in all living things and in substances such as coal and oil. A chemistry word. (**carbono**)

carbon dioxide /ˌkɑːbən daɪˈɒksaɪd/ NOUN, NO PLURAL a gas that is produced when people and animals breathe out and when carbon is burned. A chemistry word. (**gás carbônico**)

card /kɑːd/ NOUN [plural cards]
1 a piece of stiff paper with a picture and a message ▣ a birthday/Christmas card ▣ I must send her a card. (**cartão**)
2 no plural thick stiff paper □ coloured card (**cartão**)
3 a small flat piece of plastic that you can use in shops and machines to pay for things □ Can I pay by card? ▣ a bank card (**cartão de banco**)
4 a small piece of stiff paper or plastic with information on it □ a library card □ Here's my business card. (**cartão**)
5 one of a set of rectangular pieces of card used for playing games ▣ I bought a pack of cards. (**baralho**)
6 cards games that are played with a set of cards ▣ Do you like playing cards? (**baralho**)

cardboard /ˈkɑːdbɔːd/ NOUN, NO PLURAL very stiff thick paper used to make boxes and packages for goods ▣ a cardboard box (**papelão**)

cardiac /ˈkɑːdiæk/ ADJECTIVE to do with the heart. A biology word □ a cardiac surgeon (**cardíaco**)

cardigan /ˈkɑːdɪɡən/ NOUN [plural cardigans] a piece of clothing for your upper body that is made from wool and fastens with buttons down the front (**cardigã**)

cardinal¹ /ˈkɑːdɪnəl/ NOUN [plural cardinals] a priest of high rank in the Roman Catholic Church (**cardeal**)

cardinal² /ˈkɑːdɪnəl/ ADJECTIVE cardinal numbers are numbers like one, two, three, not first, second, third. A mathematics word. (**cardinais**)

care¹ /keə(r)/ NOUN, NO PLURAL
1 looking after someone ▣ They need urgent medical care. ▣ The care he received in hospital was excellent. (**cuidado**)
2 take care of someone/something to look after someone or something □ Their aunt took care of them after their parents died. (**tomar conta**)
3 when you give something a lot of attention or effort ▣ Meg does her work with great care. ▣ She took a lot of care over her appearance. (**cuidado**)
4 take care to be careful not to have an accident or make a mistake □ You must take care to lock all the doors. □ Take care – the roads are very icy! (**tomar cuidado**)

care² /keə(r)/ VERB [cares, caring, cared]
1 to think that something is interesting or important □ + question word He said he didn't care what happened. □ + about I don't care about your holiday plans – we've got work to do! (**preocupar-se**)
2 to feel love or affection for someone □ + for He really cares for his staff. (**cuidar de alguém/algo**)
◆ PHRASAL VERB **care for someone/something** to look after a person or an animal □ Sarah wants to be a vet so that she can care for sick animals.

career /kəˈrɪə(r)/ NOUN [plural careers] a job or type of work that you train for and continue doing for a long time □ + in a career in the police force □ a teaching career □ We both chose law as a career. (**carreira**)

> **THESAURUS:** A career is something that you train for and do for a long time. The word **profession** is similar, and is usually used for jobs which need special qualifications. For example, medicine, teaching and law are all professions. A **trade** is a job using your hands that involves special skills or training. Plumbers work in a trade. **Job** is a general word to describe the work that someone does for money.

careful /ˈkeəfʊl/ ADJECTIVE making sure that you do something correctly or safely ▣ Be careful when you cross the road. □ + to do something Dad is always careful to lock all the doors. (**cuidadoso**)

carefully /ˈkeəfʊli/ ADVERB without making mistakes or causing damage □ Greta wrapped up the glass carefully in tissue paper. (**cuidadosamente**)

careless /ˈkeəlɪs/ ADJECTIVE not being careful ▣ a careless mistake □ Alex is a bit careless with his money. (**displicente**)

carelessly /ˈkeəlɪsli/ ADVERB in a careless way □ He threw the letter aside carelessly. (**displicentemente**)

cargo /ˈkɑːɡəʊ/ NOUN [plural cargoes] the things that a vehicle is carrying □ The ship had a cargo of sugar and coffee. (**carga**)

carnival /ˈkɑːnɪvəl/ NOUN [plural carnivals] a celebration when people sing and dance outdoors wearing special clothes (**carnaval**)

carp¹ /kɑːp/ NOUN [plural carp] a large fish that lives in lakes and rivers (**carpa**)

carp² /kɑːp/ VERB [carps, carping, carped] to complain a lot in a way that is annoying □ He was carping about the cost of everything. (**reclamar**)

car park /ˈkɑːr ˌpɑːk/ NOUN [plural car parks] a building or place where cars can be left □ The car park was full. (**estacionamento**)

carpenter /ˈkɑːpəntə(r)/ NOUN [plural carpenters] someone whose job is to make things from wood (**carpinteiro**)

carpentry /ˈkɑːpəntri/ NOUN, NO PLURAL making things from wood (**carpintaria**)

carpet /ˈkɑːpɪt/ NOUN [plural carpets] a covering for a floor made of wool or a similar material □ Don't get mud on the carpet. (**tapete**)

carriage /ˈkærɪdʒ/ NOUN [plural **carriages**]
1 one of the long parts of a train where passengers sit (**vagão**)
2 a vehicle with wheels that is pulled by horses (**carruagem**)

> **THESAURUS:** A carriage is one of the parts of a train where people sit. The words carriage and coach also describe vehicles that are pulled by horses. People used carriages and coaches for travelling in the past. Coaches were usually used for long journeys. Nowadays, a coach is a bus for long journeys. Note that a car is a vehicle with an engine and seats for a small number of passengers. Vehicle is a general word for something that carries people or goods. Cars, buses and trains are all vehicles.

carrot /ˈkærət/ NOUN [plural **carrots**] a long orange vegetable that grows under the ground (**cenoura**)

carry /ˈkæri/ VERB [**carries, carrying, carried**]
1 to pick something up and take it somewhere □ *This suitcase is too heavy for me to carry.* □ *You may only carry one bag onto the plane.* (**carregar**)
2 to have something with you in your hand, your pocket, etc. □ *The robber was carrying a gun.* □ *Why were you carrying so much cash on you?* □ + *around Do you have to carry that umbrella around with you?* (**carregar**)
♦ PHRASAL VERBS **carry on** to continue □ + *with Carry on with your work while I go and see the headmaster.* □ + *ing When the noise stopped, our guide was able to carry on speaking.* **carry out something 1** to do a task □ *carry out research/an experiment* **2** to do something that you have said you will do 🔄 *Will the terrorists manage to carry out their threat?*

cart /kɑːt/ NOUN [plural **carts**] a vehicle for goods which is pulled by a horse 🔄 *a horse and cart*

carton /ˈkɑːtən/ NOUN [plural **cartons**] a box for food or drink that is made of cardboard □ *a carton of milk* (**caixa de papelão**)

cartoon /kɑːˈtuːn/ NOUN [plural **cartoons**]
1 a funny drawing or series of drawings in a newspaper or magazine (**cartum**)
2 a film made from a long series of drawings 🔄 *Mickey Mouse is a cartoon character.* (**desenho animado**)

carve /kɑːv/ VERB [**carves, carving, carved**]
1 to make something by cutting wood, stone, etc. □ *There are angels carved out of stone.* (**entalhar**)
2 to cut meat into thin flat pieces using a sharp knife (**trinchar**)

> **THESAURUS:** If you cut something, you use a knife to divide it into pieces. Cut is a general word. If you cut thin pieces from a large piece of meat, such as a chicken, you can use the word carve. Slice has a similar meaning, but we usually use slice when a whole thing is cut into thin, flat pieces. For example, you can slice a loaf of bread or an onion. When you cut something into lots of small pieces you use the word chop.

case /keɪs/ NOUN [plural **cases**]
1 a situation or an example of a particular situation □ *Inspectors are examining several cases of cruelty to animals.* 🔄 *You haven't got any money? In that case, you'd better get a job.* (**caso**)
2 (**just**) **in case** because of the possibility of something □ *I don't think it's going to rain, but I'll take my umbrella just in case.* (**se por acaso**)
3 a crime that the police are trying to solve □ *a murder case* (**caso**)
4 something that is being decided in a court 🔄 *a court case* (**caso**)
5 a container for something □ *a violin case* □ *The crown jewels are in a glass case.* (**estojo**)
6 a suitcase (= large container for carrying clothes on holiday) 🔄 *Have you packed your case yet?* (**mala**)

cash¹ /kæʃ/ NOUN, NO PLURAL
1 money in the form of paper money and coins □ *The gardener likes to be paid in cash.* (**dinheiro**)
2 money 🔄 *I'm rather short of cash* (= I haven't got much money). (**dinheiro**)

> **THESAURUS:** You use money for buying things. Cash is a word to describe money in the form of notes and coins. A note is a piece of paper money. A coin is a piece of metal money, which is usually round. Change is extra money which is given back to you when you pay for something. For example, if you are buying something that costs £4.50 and you use a £5.00 note to pay for it, you will get 50p change.

cash² /kæʃ/ VERB [**cashes, cashing, cashed**] to cash a cheque is to change it for paper money or coins (**descontar**)

cashpoint /ˈkæʃpɔɪnt/ NOUN [plural **cashpoints**] a machine, usually in the wall outside a bank, where you can get money using a small plastic card (**caixa eletrônico**)

casino /kəˈsiːnəʊ/ NOUN [plural **casinos**] a building where people play games in which they lose or win money (**cassino**)

cast¹ /kɑːst/ VERB [**casts, casting, cast**]
1 to choose the actors who will be in a play or a film □ *He was cast as Hamlet.* (**designar**)
2 if something casts light or a shadow somewhere, it makes it go there □ *The lamp cast light onto the desk.* (**lançar**)
3 when you cast your vote, you vote for someone or something (**dar**)
4 cast a spell on someone/something to use magic on someone or something (**lançar um feitiço em alguém/algo**)

cast² /kɑːst/ NOUN [plural **casts**]
1 the actors in a play or a film □ *a member of the cast* (**elenco**)
2 a hard covering that is put on a broken arm or leg (**molde**)

castle

castle /ˈkɑːsəl/ NOUN [plural **castles**] a large building with high walls and towers, which was built to protect people from attack □ *Edinburgh Castle stands high above the city.* □ *We visited a ruined castle.* (**castelo**)

casual /ˈkæʒuəl/ ADJECTIVE
1 not formal □ *casual clothes* □ *She runs the hotel in quite a casual and relaxed style.* (**informal**)
2 not serious □ *He has had several casual relationships since his divorce.* □ *I worry about Sarita's casual attitude to her work.* (**casual**)

casualty /ˈkæʒjuəlti/ NOUN [plural **casualties**] someone who has been injured or killed □ *Ambulances rushed the casualties to hospital.* (**baixa**)

cat /kæt/ NOUN [plural **cats**]
1 an animal which people keep as a pet, which catches mice and birds □ *I stroked the cat and it purred happily.* (**gato**)
2 a wild animals such as a lion, that belongs to the same family as the cat 🔁 *One of my favourite big cats is the leopard.* (**felino**)
→ *go to* **let** *the cat out of the bag*

catalog /ˈkætəlɒg/ NOUN [plural **catalogs**] the US spelling of **catalogue** (**catálogo [EUA]**)

catalogue /ˈkætəlɒg/ NOUN [plural **catalogues**]
1 a book that shows the products you can buy from a company 🔁 *Mum got me some jeans from a mail order catalogue.* (**catálogo**)
2 a list of all the books or objects in a collection (**catálogo**)

> **THESAURUS:** There are several words to describe books that contain lists of useful information. A **catalogue** is a book that shows products that you can buy from a company. A **brochure** is similar, and is often used for selling holidays, or other things that you do not buy in a shop and take home, such as kitchens. A **directory** is a book that contains a list of names and telephone numbers in alphabetical order. An **index** is the section at the end of a book which tells you which page to look on for information.

catastrophe /kəˈtæstrəfi/ NOUN [plural **catastrophes**] an event that causes a lot of damage or suffering □ *The government has plans for dealing with floods and other natural catastrophes.* (**catástrofe**)

catch[1] /kætʃ/ VERB [**catches, catching, caught**]
1 to stop and hold something that is moving through the air □ *Throw the ball and I'll try to catch it.* (**apanhar**)
2 to stop a person or animal from escaping □ *James caught a huge fish.* □ *Police managed to catch the escaped prisoners.* (**apanhar**)
3 to get an illness □ *Most people catch between two and four colds a year.* (**apanhar**)
4 to get on a bus, train, etc. □ *I left early so that I could catch the 8.30 train.* (**apanhar**)
5 to become stuck on something, or to make something become stuck on something else □ *Sam caught his sleeve on the door handle.* (**prender**)
6 catch fire to start burning □ *The plane caught fire after its tyre burst on landing.* (**pegar fogo**)
7 catch sight of someone/something to see someone or something for a short time □ *I just managed to catch sight of the queen.* (**avistar alguém/algo**)
→ *go to* **catch someone's eye**
♦ PHRASAL VERB **catch (someone/something) up**
1 to reach someone or something that is in front of you by moving faster than them □ *We ran to catch the others up.* **2** to get to the same level as someone or something □ *When children miss a lot of school, it can be difficult for them to catch up with the others.*

catch[2] /kætʃ/ NOUN [plural **catches**] when someone stops and holds something that was moving through the air □ *That was a brilliant catch!* (**pegada**)

category /ˈkætəˌgɔri/ NOUN [plural **categories**] a group of people or things of the same type 🔁 *Our members tend to fall into one of three categories.* (**categoria**)

cathedral /kəˈθiːdrəl/ NOUN [plural **cathedrals**] a large and important church □ *St Paul's Cathedral in London* (**catedral**)

Catholic[1] /ˈkæθlɪk/ ADJECTIVE to do with, or belonging to, the Roman Catholic Church □ *a Catholic priest* (**católico**)

• **Catholicism** /kəˈθɒlɪˌsɪzəm/ NOUN, NO PLURAL the beliefs and practices of Catholics (**catolicismo**)

Catholic[2] /ˈkæθlɪk/ NOUN [plural **Catholics**] a member of the Roman Catholic Church (**católico**)

cattle /ˈkætəl/ PLURAL NOUN male and female cows on a farm □ *cattle farmers* (**gado**)

caught /kɔːt/ PAST TENSE AND PAST PARTICIPLE OF **catch**[1] (ver **catch**[1])

cauliflower /ˈkɒlɪˌflaʊə(r)/ NOUN [plural **cauliflowers**] a round vegetable with green leaves around a hard white centre (**couve-flor**)

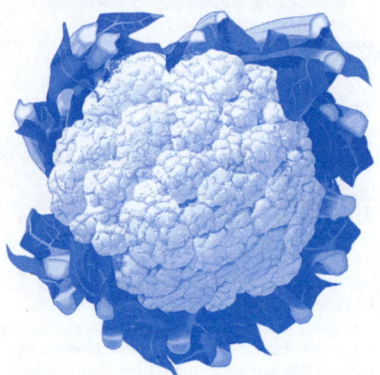

cause¹ /kɔːz/ VERB [**causes, causing, caused**] to make something happen ▢ *Do they know what caused the accident?* ▢ *Strong winds caused problems on the roads.* ▢ + **to do something** *Unfortunately the delay caused me to miss my appointment.* (**causar**)

cause² /kɔːz/ NOUN [plural **causes**]
1 what makes something happen ▢ *There are many causes of poverty.* ▢ *The engineer can't find the cause of the problem.* (**causa**)
2 something that people support because they believe it is good or useful ▣ *She collects money for many good causes.* (**razão**)

caution /ˈkɔːʃən/ NOUN, NO PLURAL when you take care to avoid danger or risk ▢ *Please drive with caution.* (**cuidado**)

cautious /ˈkɔːʃəs/ ADJECTIVE very careful to avoid danger or risk ▢ *He's very cautious with his money.* (**cauteloso**)

cave /keɪv/ NOUN [plural **caves**] a large hole in a mountain or under the ground ▢ *The cave was dark and damp.* (**gruta**)

CD /ˌsiːˈdiː/ ABBREVIATION **compact disc**; a disc with sound recorded on it ▢ *He bought a CD of Scottish folk songs.* (**CD**)

CD-ROM /ˌsiːdiːˈrɒm/ ABBREVIATION **compact disc read-only memory**; a type of CD that stores a lot of information which you play on a computer ▢ *The dictionary is available on CD-ROM.* (**CD-ROM**)

cease /siːs/ VERB [**ceases, ceasing, ceased**] a formal word meaning to stop (**cessar**)

ceasefire /ˌsiːsˈfaɪə(r)/ NOUN [plural **ceasefires**] an agreement between two armies to stop fighting for a period of time (**cessar-fogo**)

ceiling /ˈsiːlɪŋ/ NOUN [plural **ceilings**] the surface at the top of a room ▢ *This house has very high ceilings.* (**teto**)

celebrate /ˈselɪbreɪt/ VERB [**celebrates, celebrating, celebrated**] when you celebrate an event you have a party or do other special things because of it ▣ *Dad took a day off work to celebrate his 50th birthday.* ▣ *We like to celebrate Christmas in a traditional way.* ▣ *Mark passed his driving test, so we're going out to celebrate!* (**celebrar**)

celebration /ˌselɪˈbreɪʃən/ NOUN [plural **celebrations**] a party or something special that is done to celebrate an event ▢ *a wedding celebration* (**celebração**)

> THESAURUS: Celebration is a general word for a party or other event that is held to celebrate a special event. An **anniversary** is a date when you celebrate something that happened on the same date in the past. For example, you might celebrate your wedding **anniversary**. Note that in English, the celebration of the date of your birth is called your **birthday**, not your anniversary. A **party** is a special event where people get together to dance, drink and eat.

celebrity /sɪˈlebrɪti/ NOUN [plural **celebrities**] someone who is famous ▢ *Will there be any celebrities at the party?* (**celebridade**)

celery /ˈseləri/ NOUN, NO PLURAL a vegetable with long, pale green stems, usually eaten raw (**aipo**)

cell /sel/ NOUN [plural **cells**]
1 the smallest part of a living thing ▢ *cancerous cells* (**célula**)
2 a small room that a prisoner is kept in or that a monk (= religious man) lives in (**cela**)

cellar /ˈselə(r)/ NOUN [plural **cellars**] an underground room used for storing things (**porão, adega**)

cellphone /ˈselfəʊn/ NOUN [plural **cellphones**] the US word for **mobile phone** (**telefone celular**)

Celsius /ˈselsiəs/ ADJECTIVE measured using the temperature measurement at which water freezes at 0 degrees and boils at 100 degrees ▢ *57 degrees Celsius* (**Celsius**)

cement /sɪˈment/ NOUN, NO PLURAL a grey powder that is mixed with sand and water for use in building (**cimento**)

cemetery /ˈsemɪtəri/ NOUN [plural **cemeteries**] a place where dead people are buried (**cemitério**)

cent /sent/ NOUN [plural **cents**] a unit of money worth 1/100 of a dollar (**cêntimo**)

center /ˈsentə(r)/ NOUN [plural **centers**] the US spelling of **centre** (**centro**)

centigrade /ˈsentɪɡreɪd/ ADJECTIVE an old-fashioned word for **Celsius** ▢ *forty degrees centigrade* (**centígrado**)

centimetre /ˈsentɪmiːtə(r)/ NOUN [plural **centimetres**] a unit for measuring length, equal to 10 millimetres. This is often written **cm** ▢ *The card measures eight centimetres across.* ▢ *These heels are 8cm high.* (**centímetro**)

central /ˈsentrəl/ ADJECTIVE near or in the centre of an object or a place ▢ *He works in central London.* (**central**)

central heating /ˌsentrəl ˈhiːtɪŋ/ NOUN, NO PLURAL
a system used for heating houses where heated water goes through pipes to each room (**aquecimento central**)

centre /ˈsentə(r)/ NOUN [plural centres]
1 the middle point or part of something □ *It is difficult to park in the city centre.* □ *These chocolates have soft centres.* □ **+ of** *He stood in the centre of the field.* (**centro**)
2 the most important part of something □ **+ of** *The woman at the centre of the dispute is refusing to speak to journalists.* □ *The idea is at the centre of the project.* (**centro**)
3 a place or a building used for a particular activity □ *a sports centre* □ *The centre carries out research into breast cancer.* (**centro**)

century /ˈsentʃʊri/ NOUN [plural centuries]
a hundred years □ *She lived in the fifteenth century.* □ *a twentieth-century building* (**século**)

cereal /ˈsɪəriəl/ NOUN [plural cereals]
1 a plant such as rice, that is grown in order to use the grains for food □ *Wheat is a cereal used for making bread and pasta.* (**cereal**)
2 food made from cereal crops, especially one eaten for breakfast 🔄 *breakfast cereals* (**cereais**)

ceremony /ˈserɪməni/ NOUN [plural ceremonies]
a formal event where special or traditional words or actions are used 🔄 *a wedding ceremony* 🔄 *The graduation ceremony was held at the cathedral.* 🔄 *Who will be attending the award ceremony this year?* (**cerimônia**)

certain /ˈsɜːtən/ ADJECTIVE
1 with no doubts □ **+ about** *Dad wasn't certain about the time of the train.* □ **+ question word** *I'm not certain how it works.* □ **+ that** *I'm certain that I saw someone in the garden.* (**certo**)
2 sure to happen or be true □ **+ that** *It seems certain that he will get the job.* 🔄 *Make certain that the rope is tight.* □ **+ to do something** *She says you're certain to pass the exam.* (**seguro**)
3 used to talk about someone or something without saying exactly which person or thing you are talking about □ *There are certain rules which you must obey.* □ *Certain people have been asked to leave.* (**certo**)

certainly /ˈsɜːtənli/ ADVERB
1 used to show that there is no doubt about something □ *Joe certainly knows a lot about birds.* □ *'Can I stay up until midnight?' 'Certainly not!'* (**certamente**)
2 used to agree to something □ *'May I borrow your lawnmower?' 'Certainly.'* (**com certeza**)

certificate /səˈtɪfɪkət/ NOUN [plural certificates]
an official document that shows something is true 🔄 *They asked to see my birth certificate.* □ *We each received a certificate for completing the course.* (**certidão**)

> **THESAURUS:** A **document** is a general word for a piece of paper with official information on it. For example, travel **documents** might include passport, tickets and visas. A **certificate** is an official piece of paper that shows that something is true. For example, you get a certificate to show that you have passed an examination. A **licence** is a document which gives you official permission to do something. A driving **licence** shows that you are allowed to drive a car. A **passport** is an official document which you carry with you when you travel to other countries to show who you are.

chain¹ /tʃeɪn/ NOUN [plural chains]
1 metal rings that are connected in a line □ *He wore a gold chain around his neck.* □ *The chain came off my bicycle.* (**corrente**)
2 a group of similar shops, restaurants, etc. that have the same owner □ **+ of** *She owns a chain of restaurants.* (**cadeia**)

chain² /tʃeɪn/ VERB [chains, chaining, chained]
to fasten something or someone with a chain □ *often passive* *The bicycle was chained to the fence.* (**acorrentar**)

chair¹ /tʃeə(r)/ NOUN [plural chairs]
1 a piece of furniture that has a back and which one person sits on (**cadeira**)
2 the person who is in charge of a meeting, business or organization (**presidência**)

chair² /tʃeə(r)/ VERB [chairs, chairing, chaired]
to be officially in charge of a meeting (**presidir**)

chairman /ˈtʃeəmən/ NOUN [plural chairmen]
1 the person who is in charge of a company, group or organization □ *the chairman of the board* (**presidente**)
2 the person who is in charge of a meeting (**presidente**)

chairwoman

chairwoman /ˈtʃeəwʊmən/ NOUN [plural **chairwomen**]
1 a woman who is in charge of a company, group or organization (**presidenta**)
2 a woman who is in charge of a meeting (**presidenta**)

chalk /tʃɔːk/ NOUN, NO PLURAL
1 a type of soft white stone ◻ *crumbling chalk cliffs* (**greda, giz**)
2 pieces of this stone that you use to draw with ◻ *She wrote on the blackboard with chalk.* (**giz**)

challenge¹ /ˈtʃælɪndʒ/ NOUN [plural **challenges**]
1 something that is difficult to do ▣ *The world faces a huge challenge in tackling climate change.* ▣ *Crime poses/presents a serious challenge to our community.* (**desafio**)
2 when you try to change a rule, or do not accept a decision or someone's authority ▣ *There is likely to be a legal challenge to this decison.* (**contestação**)
3 when you ask someone to fight or compete with you ◻ *The approach of their army was a clear challenge.* (**desafio**)

challenge² /ˈtʃælɪndʒ/ VERB [**challenges, challenging, challenged**]
1 to try to change a rule, or to say that you do not accept a decision or someone's authority ◻ *We will challenge this decision in the courts.* (**contestar**)
2 to ask someone to compete or fight ◻ **+ to** *He challenged his enemy to a fight.* (**desafiar**)
3 if something challenges you, you find it difficult to do ◻ *This exam will challenge even our best pupils.* (**desafiar**)
• **challenger** /ˈtʃælɪndʒə(r)/ NOUN [plural **challengers**] someone who wants to try and beat another person in a game, election, etc. (**desafiante**)

champagne /ʃæmˈpeɪn/ NOUN, NO PLURAL a pale French wine with lots of bubbles, often drunk to celebrate something ◻ *Let's open a bottle of champagne.* (**champanhe**)

champion /ˈtʃæmpɪən/ NOUN [plural **champions**] a person or team that has beaten all the others in a competition ◻ *He became world boxing champion at twenty-six.* (**campeão**)

championship /ˈtʃæmpɪənʃɪp/ NOUN [plural **championships**] a competition to decide who is the best at a game or sport (**campeonato**)

chance /tʃɑːns/ NOUN [plural **chances**]
1 a possibility that something will happen ◻ **+ that** *There is a good chance that she is still alive.* ◻ **+ of** *Our school has no chance of winning the match.* (**chance**)
2 an opportunity ◻ **+ to do something** *I haven't had a chance to check yet.* ▣ *You didn't give me a chance to answer.* ▣ *This is your last chance to buy a ticket.* (**chance**)
3 by chance in a way that is not planned or expected ◻ *I saw him by chance at the supermarket.* (**por sorte**)

change

4 take a chance to take a risk ◻ *I took a chance on the weather staying dry and left my coat at home.* (**arriscar-se**)

▸ Note that **chance** meaning 'a possibility that something will happen' is followed by **that** or **of doing something** ◻ *What are the chances that they will win?* ◻ *What are the chances of them winning?*

chancellor /ˈtʃɑːnsələ(r)/ NOUN [plural **chancellors**]
1 the British government official who is in charge of finance (**chanceler**)
2 the leader of the government of some European countries ◻ *the German chancellor* (**chanceler**)

change¹ /tʃeɪndʒ/ VERB [**changes, changing, changed**]
1 to become different, or to make something different ◻ **+ into** *It has changed from a liquid into a gas.* ◻ **+ from** *The leaves changed from green to gold.* (**mudar**)
2 to stop having or using one thing and start having or using another instead ◻ *We need to change the batteries.* ◻ *My daughter changed schools last term.* ▣ *Don't try to change the subject* (= start talking about something else). ◻ **+ to** *I'm changing to a new dentist.* (**mudar**)
3 to put on different clothes ▣ *I must get changed* (= change my clothes) *for work.* ◻ **+ into** *I will just change into my jeans.* (**trocar de roupa**)
4 change your mind to start to think or plan something different from before ◻ *I've changed my mind – I'll have soup not pasta, please.* (**mudar de ideia**)

▸ **THESAURUS:** Change is a general word to talk about when you stop using one thing and start using something else. You can also use that word **swap** when you stop having or using one thing and take or use something else instead. For example, you might **swap** a book with a friend (you give a book to your friend and your friend gives you another book in return). **Replace** is used when you put one thing in the place of another. For example, if the batteries in a radio run out, you **replace** them with new batteries.

change² /tʃeɪndʒ/ NOUN [plural **changes**]
1 a difference ▣ *I have made some changes to the timetable.* ◻ **+ in** *Let's wait until there is a change in the weather.* (**mudança**)
2 a change something that is enjoyable because it is new and different ◻ *I didn't hate my old job – I just fancied a change.* (**mudança**)
3 for a change instead of the usual thing ◻ *Could you just stop complaining for a change?* (**para variar**)
4 no plural the extra money that is given back to you when you have paid for something ▣ *I told the taxi driver to keep the change.* (**troco**)

channel /ˈtʃænəl/ NOUN [plural channels]
1 a television or radio station ▫ *May I change channels, or are you watching this?* (mudar de canal)
2 a narrow piece of sea ▫ *the English Channel* (canal)

chant /tʃɑːnt/ VERB [chants, chanting, chanted] to shout or sing something repeatedly (entoar)

chaos /ˈkeɪɒs/ NOUN, NO PLURAL great confusion ▫ *There was chaos in town when the traffic lights stopped working.* (caos)

chap /tʃæp/ NOUN [plural chaps] an informal word for a man ▫ *He's a nice chap.* (sujeito)

chapel /ˈtʃæpəl/ NOUN [plural chapels] a small church, or a room used as a church ▫ *the hospital chapel* (capela)

chapter /ˈtʃæptə(r)/ NOUN [plural chapters] one of the parts that a book is divided into ▫ *Turn to Chapter 3 in your history books.* ▫ *Can I just finish (= finish reading) this chapter?* (capítulo)

character /ˈkærəktə(r)/ NOUN [plural characters]
1 what someone or something is like and the qualities that they have ▫ *Can you describe her character? Is she reliable?* ▫ *It isn't in his character to stay angry for long.* (caráter)
2 a person in a story, film or play ▫ *Harry Potter is a fictional character.* ▫ *Who is your favourite character in the book?* (personagem)

charge¹ /tʃɑːdʒ/ VERB [charges, charging, charged]
1 to ask a particular amount of money for something ▫ **+ for** *How much do you charge for a haircut?* ▫ *The shopkeeper charged me $20 too much.* (cobrar)
2 if the police charge someone with a crime, they accuse them officially ▫ **+ with** *He was charged with murder.* (acusar)
3 to move forward quickly and suddenly ▫ *The boys came charging into the room.* ▫ *We charged down the hill towards them.* (investir)
4 to fill a battery or piece of electrical equipment with electricity ▫ *Where can I charge my phone?* (carregar)

charge² /tʃɑːdʒ/ NOUN [plural charges]
1 the amount of money that you have to pay ▫ *You can have another cup of coffee free of charge (= without paying).* ▫ *There will be a small charge for postage and packing.* (preço)
2 in charge controlling or managing something or someone ▫ *I am in charge while the boss is away.* ▫ *Ms Handy is in charge of the sales department.* (responsável por)
3 take charge to take control of something or someone ▫ *Can you take charge of the food preparation?* (tomar a direção)
4 when someone is accused of a crime ▫ *He was arrested on a charge of robbery.* (acusação)

▸ **THESAURUS:** The **charge** for something is the amount of money that you have to pay for it. We usually use **charge** to talk about a service and **price** to talk about goods. So, we talk about the **price** of goods in shops, but the **charge** for supplying electricity to your house. A **fee** is an amount of money that you pay for a particular service. You use **rate** to talk about how much you pay someone for a service. For example, a lawyer's **rate** is how much they cost per hour or per day, but their **fee** is the total amount you pay them for a particular job.

charity /ˈtʃærəti/ NOUN [plural charities] an organization that gives money or other help to people who need it (caridade)

charm /tʃɑːm/ NOUN [plural charms]
1 a quality that makes someone pleasant and attractive to other people (encanto)
2 an object that is believed to be lucky

charming /ˈtʃɑːmɪŋ/ ADJECTIVE extremely pleasant ▫ *What a charming young man your son is.* (encantador)

chart /tʃɑːt/ NOUN [plural charts]
1 a drawing that shows information ▫ *This chart shows the population growth over the last fifty years.* (gráfico)
2 the charts a list of the most popular music ▫ *Their new record went straight to the top of the charts.* (parada de sucessos)
3 a map of the sea used by sailors (carta, mapa)

▸ **THESAURUS:** **Chart** and **diagram** are words for a drawing that shows information. **Diagrams** often show how something works, for example a machine. A **graph** is a chart which shows how things compare to each other or how something changes. A **graph** is usually made of lines between different points. A **map** is a drawing of a particular area which shows rivers, roads and hills. You can use a **map** to help you find your way. A **plan** is a drawing to show you how to build something. For example, architects draw **plans** when they are designing a new house.

chase¹ /tʃeɪs/ VERB [chases, chasing, chased] to run after someone or something to try and catch them ▫ *A police officer chased the thief down the High Street.* ▫ *Our dog was chasing a rabbit.* (perseguir)

▸ **THESAURUS:** If you **chase** someone, you run after them and try to catch them. If you **follow** someone, you go where they go, moving behind them. You can **follow** someone in secret. If you look for something or someone, you can use the word **hunt**. For example, the police might **hunt** a criminal, or you might **hunt** for something that you have lost. We also use **hunt** to talk about chasing and killing an animal for sport or for food.

chase² /tʃeɪs/ NOUN [plural chases] when someone or something is chased ▫ *A man was arrested following a high-speed car chase.* (perseguição)

chat 56 **chemical**

chat¹ /tʃæt/ VERB [chats, chatting, chatted] to talk to someone in a friendly way □ + *to* *She was chatting to her friend on the phone.* (bater papo)

chat² /tʃæt/ NOUN [*plural* chats] a friendly talk 🔁 *Come round later and we can have a chat.* (papo, bater um papo)

cheap /tʃiːp/ ADJECTIVE [cheaper, cheapest] not costing a lot □ *a cheap air ticket* □ *It is cheaper to buy vegetables at the market.* (barato)

> THESAURUS: Cheap is a general word to describe something which does not cost a lot of money. A bargain is something which costs less than usual. Your budget is the total amount of money that you can spend on something. For example, you might have a budget for a holiday.

cheat¹ /tʃiːt/ VERB [cheats, cheating, cheated] to behave dishonestly in order to succeed at something or get something □ *It's cheating to look at someone else's cards.* □ *Hey, you're cheating! That's against the rules.* (trapacear)

cheat² /tʃiːt/ NOUN [*plural* cheats] someone who cheats (trapaceiro)

check¹ /tʃek/ VERB [checks, checking, checked]
1 to make sure that something is correct □ *Please check your work carefully before you hand it in.* □ *I think my appointment is at 10.30, but I'll check in my diary.* (conferir)
2 to find out □ + *question word* *Could you check whether the post has arrived?* □ *He is just checking how many copies we need.* (verificar, checar)
3 to make sure that something is working correctly □ *The engineer came to check the fire alarm.* (verificar)
♦ PHRASAL VERBS **check in** to tell the people at a hotel or airport that you have arrived □ *Please check in two hours before the flight.* **check out** to pay for your stay at a hotel and leave □ *You must check out before 10 am.*

check² /tʃek/ NOUN [*plural* checks]
1 a test to see that something is correct or is working correctly 🔁 *a health/safety check* 🔁 *The police did fingerprint checks on the document.* (verificação)
2 a pattern of squares □ *black-and-white check*
3 the US spelling of cheque (cheque [EUA])
4 the US word for tick¹ (sense 1) (ticar)
5 the US word for a bill in a restaurant (conta [EUA])

> THESAURUS: A check or a test is something you do to find out if something is working properly or that it is correct. An inspection is an official visit by a person to check that a place is working properly. For example, restaurants have inspections to make sure that the kitchens are clean and safe. An examination is a test of someone's knowledge about a subject. Most students take examinations.

check-in /tʃekɪn/ NOUN [*plural* check-ins]
1 a desk at an airport where passengers' tickets are checked
2 *no plural* the process that happens when you arrive at an airport

checkout /tʃekaʊt/ NOUN [*plural* checkouts]
1 the place where you pay at a supermarket □ *There was a big queue at the checkout.* (caixa)
2 the place on a website where you pay for things you have bought. A computing word. (caixa)

checkpoint /tʃekpɔɪnt/ NOUN [*plural* checkpoints] a place where soldiers or police stop vehicles or people (posto de controle)

cheek /tʃiːk/ NOUN [*plural* cheeks] one of the two areas on each side of your face below your eyes 🔁 *She has lovely rosy cheeks.* (bochecha)

cheeky /tʃiːki/ ADJECTIVE [cheekier, cheekiest] a bit rude, often in a funny way □ *You cheeky boy!* □ *a cheeky grin* (atrevido)

cheer¹ /tʃɪə(r)/ VERB [cheers, cheering, cheered] to shout loudly to praise or encourage someone □ *We cheered loudly when he came onto the stage.* □ *The spectators cheered each runner as they ran past.* (ovacionar)
♦ PHRASAL VERB **cheer (someone) up** to feel happier, or to make someone feel happier □ *Cheer up! Don't look so miserable!* □ *I've got some news that will cheer you up.* (animar alguém)

cheer² /tʃɪə(r)/ NOUN [*plural* cheers] a loud shout to show that you are pleased □ *When he caught the ball there was a big cheer from the crowd.* (viva)

cheerful /tʃɪəfʊl/ ADJECTIVE happy □ *You're very cheerful this morning.* (alegre)

cheerio /ˌtʃɪəriˈəʊ/ EXCLAMATION an informal word meaning goodbye □ *Cheerio, see you tomorrow.* (até logo!)

cheers /tʃɪəz/ EXCLAMATION
1 a word used to express your good wishes to other people when you are drinking alcohol together □ *Cheers, everyone. Happy New Year!* (saúde)
2 an informal word meaning thank you □ *'Here's your book back'. 'Cheers'.* (obrigado!)

cheese /tʃiːz/ NOUN [*plural* cheeses] a solid white or yellow food made from milk □ *cheese sauce* 🔁 *Would you like some cheese and biscuits?* 🔁 *Sprinkle some grated cheese on the top.* (queijo)

chef /ʃef/ NOUN [*plural* chefs] someone whose job is to cook in a restaurant or a hotel □ *Please tell the chef that was delicious.* (chefe de cozinha)

chemical¹ /ˈkemɪkəl/ NOUN [*plural* chemicals] a substance that is formed by or used in chemistry 🔁 *The lorry contained dangerous chemicals.* □ *The hydrochloric acid and other chemicals are kept in the laboratory.* (produto químico)

chemical² /ˈkemɪkəl/ ADJECTIVE involving or produced by chemistry 🔁 *a chemical reaction* (químico)

chemist — choice

chemist /'kemɪst/ NOUN [plural **chemists**]
1 someone who prepares medicines □ *Could you ask the chemist if my prescription is ready?* (**farmacêutico**)
2 **chemist's** a shop where medicines and products for washing, etc. are sold (**farmácia**)
3 someone who studies chemistry (**químico**)

chemistry /'kemɪstri/ NOUN, NO PLURAL the study of chemical elements and how they react with each other □ *She studied physics and chemistry at A level.* (**química**)

cheque /tʃek/ NOUN [plural **cheques**] a piece of printed paper that you sign and use as a way of paying for things 🔁 *I wrote him a cheque for £50.* 🔁 *Our last customer paid by cheque.* (**cheque**)

cherry /'tʃeri/ NOUN [plural **cherries**] a small round red fruit with a hard seed inside (**cereja**)

chess /tʃes/ NOUN, NO PLURAL a game where two players move pieces on a board with black and white squares 🔁 *a chess board* 🔁 *Tom plays chess almost every day.* (**xadrez**)

chest /tʃest/ NOUN [plural **chests**]
1 the front of your body between your neck and your stomach □ *a hairy chest* □ *chest pains* (**peito**)
2 a large box for storing things □ *a treasure chest* (**arca**)

chew /tʃuː/ VERB [**chews, chewing, chewed**] to break up food inside your mouth with your teeth □ *My tooth is sore and it hurts to chew.* □ *He bit off a piece of bread and chewed it slowly.* (**mascar**)

chewing gum /'tʃuːɪŋ ˌɡʌm/ NOUN, NO PLURAL a sweet substance that you chew but do not swallow (**chiclete**)

chick /tʃɪk/ NOUN [plural **chicks**] a baby bird (**filhote de ave**)

chicken /'tʃɪkɪn/ NOUN [plural **chickens**]
1 a bird that is kept on farms to produce eggs and to be eaten 🔁 *The farmer keeps a few chickens.* 🔁 *This chicken has stopped laying* (= producing eggs).
2 no plural the meat from this bird □ *roast chicken* (**frango**)

chief¹ /tʃiːf/ ADJECTIVE biggest or most important □ *the chief city of the region* □ *My chief worry is the cost.* (**chefe**)

chief² /tʃiːf/ NOUN [plural **chiefs**]
1 a person in charge of a group or organization □ *We heard a speech by the new police chief.* □ *Industry chiefs met today in London.* (**chefe**)
2 a ruler of a tribe (= large group of related people) □ *an African tribal chief* (**chefe, líder**)

child /tʃaɪld/ NOUN [plural **children**]
1 a young human □ *When my Dad was a child, he lived in New York.* □ *There are thirty children in my class.* (**criança**)
2 a son or daughter 🔁 *Sue never had* (= gave birth to) *any children.* □ *Our children are grown up now.* (**filho ou filha**)

> **THESAURUS:** Child is a general word to describe someone who is not an adult. We usually use the word **teenager** to describe older children aged between 13 and 19. A very young child who cannot walk is a **baby**. **Kid** is an informal word for a child.

childhood /'tʃaɪldˌhʊd/ NOUN, NO PLURAL the time in your life when you are a child □ *My memories of childhood are very happy.* (**infância**)

children /'tʃɪldrən/ PLURAL OF **child** (ver **child**)

chilly /'tʃɪli/ ADJECTIVE [**chillier, chilliest**] cold □ *It's a bit chilly in here.* (**frio**)

chimney /'tʃɪmni/ NOUN [plural **chimneys**] a pipe above a fire that allows smoke to escape □ *a factory chimney* (**chaminé**)

chimpanzee /ˌtʃɪmpæn'ziː/ NOUN [plural **chimpanzees**] a small African ape (= large monkey) with black fur, a flat face and large brown eyes (**chimpanzé**)

chin /tʃɪn/ NOUN [plural **chins**] the part of your face that is below your mouth (**queixo**)

china /'tʃaɪnə/ NOUN, NO PLURAL
1 clay used for making things like cups and plates (**porcelana**)
2 cups, plates, etc. which are made from this clay (**porcelana**)

chip¹ /tʃɪp/ NOUN [plural **chips**]
1 a long thin piece of potato that is fried and eaten hot 🔁 *fish and chips* (**batata frita**)
2 the US word for **crisp²** (= a very thin piece of potato cooked in oil and eaten cold) □ *a bag of chips* (ver **crisp²**)
3 a small piece broken off a hard object, or the place where a small piece has broken off □ *The plate had a chip in it.* (**rachadura**)
4 a very small part in a computer or other electronic equipment that contains a circuit (= system of wires) and stores information (**chip**)

chip² /tʃɪp/ VERB [**chips, chipping, chipped**] to break a small piece off something □ *Roy chipped one of his teeth playing rugby.* (**rachar**)

chocolate /'tʃɒkələt/ NOUN [plural **chocolates**]
1 no plural a sweet brown food made from the seeds of a tropical tree 🔁 *milk/dark chocolate* 🔁 *a bar of chocolate* (**chocolate**)
2 one of many small sweets made with chocolate that are sold together 🔁 *a box of chocolates* (**chocolates**)
3 a sweet drink made with chocolate 🔁 *a hot chocolate* (**chocolate quente**)

choice /tʃɔɪs/ NOUN [plural **choices**]
1 when you can choose between different things 🔁 *If I had a choice, I'd work from home.* 🔁 *I had to leave – I had no choice.* (**escolha**)
2 a decision to choose a person or thing 🔁 *In the end I had to make a choice.* 🔁 *It was a hard choice to make.* (**escolha**)
3 the different things you can choose from □ **+ of** *We were given a choice of meat or fish.* 🔁 *The bag is available in a wide choice of colours.* (**escolha**)

choir /ˈkwaɪə(r)/ NOUN [plural **choirs**] a group of singers ☐ *She sings in the church choir.* (**coro**)

choke /tʃəʊk/ VERB [**chokes, choking, choked**] to not be able to breathe because something is blocking your throat ☐ *She choked on a fish bone.* (**sufocar**)

choose /tʃuːz/ VERB [**chooses, choosing, chose, chosen**] to take one particular thing or person from a group of people or things ☐ *Can you help me choose a present for grandma?* ☐ *Kitty chose a slice of chocolate cake.* ☐ **+ between** *I can't choose between the red one and the pink one.* ☐ **+ question word** *How do you choose which charity to give money to?* ☐ **+ to do something** *She chose to attend a university near home.* (**escolher**)

chop[1] /tʃɒp/ VERB [**chops, chopping, chopped**] to cut something into pieces ☐ *Chop the onion into large chunks.* ☐ *He was chopping wood for the fire.* (**picar**)
◆ PHRASAL VERBS **chop something down** to cut the main part of a tree or big plant so that it falls down **chop something off** to remove a part of something by cutting it ☐ *He accidentally chopped his finger off.* (**abater, cortar**)

chop[2] /tʃɒp/ NOUN [plural **chops**] a piece of meat, usually with a bone ☐ *lamb chops* (**costeleta**)

chorus /ˈkɔːrəs/ NOUN [plural **choruses**]
1 the part of a song that you repeat several times ☐ *We all joined in with the chorus.* (**refrão**)
2 a large group of people who regularly sing together (**coro**)

chosen /ˈtʃəʊzən/ PAST PARTICIPLE OF **choose** (ver **choose**)

Christ /kraɪst/ NOUN Jesus Christ, the holy man that Christians believe is the Son of God (**Cristo**)

Christian[1] /ˈkrɪstʃən/ NOUN [plural **Christians**] someone who is a member of the religion that is based on the ideas of Jesus Christ and the Bible (**cristão**)

Christian[2] /ˈkrɪstʃən/ ADJECTIVE to do with Christianity or Christians (**cristão**)

Christianity /ˌkrɪstiˈænəti/ NOUN, NO PLURAL the religion that is based on the ideas of Jesus Christ and the Bible (**cristianismo**)

Christmas[1] /ˈkrɪsməs/ NOUN, NO PLURAL 25 December, the day Christians celebrate the birth of Christ each year ☐ *Happy Christmas!* (**Natal**)

Christmas[2] /ˈkrɪsməs/ ADJECTIVE for or to do with Christmas ☐ *Christmas decorations/presents* (**natalino**)

Christmas Day /ˌkrɪsməs ˈdeɪ/ NOUN, NO PLURAL 25 December, the day on which Christmas is celebrated (**dia de Natal**)

Christmas Eve /ˌkrɪsməs ˈiːv/ NOUN, NO PLURAL 24 December, the day before Christmas Day (**véspera de Natal**)

Christmas tree /ˈkrɪsməs ˌtriː/ NOUN [plural **Christmas trees**] a tree that you cover with decorations and lights and put in your house during the Christmas period (**árvore de Natal**)

chronic /ˈkrɒnɪk/ ADJECTIVE a chronic disease is one that continues for a long time (**crônico**)

chuckle /ˈtʃʌkəl/ VERB [**chuckles, chuckling, chuckled**] to laugh quietly ☐ *The story made me chuckle to myself.* (**risadinha**)

chunk /tʃʌŋk/ NOUN [plural **chunks**] a thick piece of something ☐ *a chunk of cheese* ☐ *pineapple chunks* (**naco**)

church /tʃɜːtʃ/ NOUN [plural **churches**] a building where people, especially Christians, go to pray ☐ *Do you go to church?* (**igreja**)

cigar /sɪˈɡɑː(r)/ NOUN [plural **cigars**] a thick tube made from dried tobacco leaves that people smoke (**charuto, cigarro**)

cigarette /ˌsɪɡəˈret/ NOUN [plural **cigarettes**] a thin tube of paper filled with tobacco that people smoke (**cigarro**)

cinema /ˈsɪnəmə/ NOUN [plural **cinemas**] a place where you go to watch a film on a big screen ☐ *We went to the cinema last night.* (**cinema**)

circle[1] /ˈsɜːkəl/ NOUN [plural **circles**]
1 a flat shape whose outside edge is a continuous curved line which is always the same distance away from a central point ☐ *Draw one circle for the head and another for the body.* ☐ *Form a circle in the centre of the room.* (**círculo**)
2 a group of people who know each other or do a particular activity together ☐ *a sewing circle* ☐ *He's not part of my circle of friends.* (**círculo**)
3 the circle the upper area of seats in a theatre or cinema (**balcão**)

circle[2] /ˈsɜːkəl/ VERB [**circles, circling, circled**]
1 to move in a circle ☐ *Birds circled overhead.* ☐ *Several planes were circling the airport.* (**cercar, rodear**)
2 to draw a circle around something ☐ *She circled the area on the map with a red pen.* (**circular**)

circuit /ˈsɜːkɪt/ NOUN [plural **circuits**]
1 a path, route or track that forms a circle ☐ *He drove five laps of the circuit.* (**circuito**)
2 the path that electricity goes along between two points (**circuito**)

circular[1] /ˈsɜːkjʊlə(r)/ ADJECTIVE
1 in the shape of a circle ☐ *a circular window* (**circular**)
2 a circular journey or route finishes in the same place that it started (**circular**)

circular[2] /ˈsɜːkjʊlə(r)/ NOUN [plural **circulars**] a letter or advertisement that is sent to a lot of different people (**circular**)

circulate /ˈsɜːkjuleɪt/ VERB [circulates, circulating, circulated] to move around or through something □ *Water circulates in the central heating system.* □ *Details of the meeting will be circulated to all members of staff.* (**circular**)

circulation /ˌsɜːkjuˈleɪʃən/ NOUN, NO PLURAL
1 the movement of blood around your body. A biology word □ *I have very poor circulation.* (**circulação**)
2 movement around or through something □ *This system controls the circulation of air.* (**circulação**)

circumstances /ˈsɜːkəmˌstænsɪz/ PLURAL NOUN
1 the events or conditions that affect or cause a particular situation 🗈 *His reaction was understandable under the circumstances* (= when you consider the situation). (**circunstâncias**)
2 under no circumstances used for saying that something must not happen □ *Under no circumstances should you attempt to climb without a rope.* (**circunstância**)

circus /ˈsɜːkəs/ NOUN [plural circuses] a show performed in a big tent by people and often trained animals □ *We're taking the children to the circus tonight.* (**circo**)

citizen /ˈsɪtɪzən/ NOUN [plural citizens] someone who has the right to live in a particular country permanently □ *He lives in Singapore but he's an Australian citizen.* (**cidadão**)

city /ˈsɪti/ NOUN [plural cities] a large, important town 🗈 *Paris is the capital city of France.* □ *the city streets* (**cidade**)

civic /ˈsɪvɪk/ ADJECTIVE to do with a city or the people who live in it □ *civic pride* (**cívico**)

civilian /sɪˈvɪljən/ NOUN [plural civilians] a person who is not a member of a military organization or the police (**civil**)

civilization ou **civilisation** /ˌsɪvɪlaɪˈzeɪʃən/ NOUN [plural civilizations] a society that has its own culture and organizations □ *ancient civilizations* (**civilização**)

civil rights /ˌsɪvəl ˈraɪts/ PLURAL NOUN your basic rights to be treated fairly in society, to express yourself, and to practise your religion (**direitos civis**)

civil servant /ˌsɪvəlˈsɜːvənt/ NOUN [plural civil servants] someone who works in the government departments of a country (**funcionário público**)

civil service /ˌsɪvəl ˈsɜːvɪs/ the civil service all the departments of the government and the people who work in them (**serviço público**)

civil war /ˌsɪvəl ˈwɔː(r)/ NOUN [plural civil wars] a war between different groups within the same country (**guerra civil**)

claim¹ /kleɪm/ VERB [claims, claiming, claimed]
1 to say that something is true, although there is no clear proof □ *Marco claims he saw a flying saucer.* □ *The group claims to represent over a million workers.* (**afirmar**)
2 to officially ask for something as your right or to say that it is yours □ *You'll need to fill in this form to claim unemployment benefit.* □ *If no one claims the lost items they will be sold for charity.* (**reclamar**)

claim² /kleɪm/ NOUN [plural claims]
1 a statement that something is true although it has not been proved 🗈 *The government has rejected claims that pensions will fall.* 🗈 *He denied claims of racism.* (**reclamação**)
2 when you ask for something that you have a right to or that you say is yours 🗈 *compensation claims* 🗈 *insurance claims* (**reivindicação**)

clap¹ /klæp/ VERB [claps, clapping, clapped] to hit your hands together, especially to show that you like or admire someone or something □ *The audience clapped and cheered.* □ *We all clapped in time to the music.* (**aplaudir**)

clap² /klæp/ NOUN [plural claps]
1 when you clap your hands 🗈 *Let's all give Adam a clap.* (**aplauso**)
2 a clap of thunder a sudden very loud sound made by thunder (**trovoada**)

clarify /ˈklærɪfaɪ/ VERB [clarifies, clarifying, clarified] to make something clearer or easier to understand □ *I asked her to clarify her remarks.* (**esclarecer**)

clash¹ /klæʃ/ VERB [clashes, clashing, clashed]
1 if two people or groups clash, they fight or disagree angrily with each other □ *Protesters clashed with the police.* (**embater-se**)
2 if two events clash, they happen at the same time □ *Unfortunately the meeting clashes with my piano exam.* (**entrechocar-se**)
3 if two colours clash, they do not look good together □ *The purple clashes with the red.* (**não combinar**)

clash² /klæʃ/ NOUN [plural clashes]
1 an angry disagreement or fight □ *There were violent clashes between students and the police today.* (**choque**)
2 a sound made when two metal objects hit against each other. (**estrondo**)

clasp /klɑːsp/ VERB [clasps, clasping, clasped] to hold something or someone tightly □ *Jenny was clasping a baby in her arms.* (**segurar**)

class /klɑːs/ NOUN [plural classes]
1 a group of students who are taught together, or a period of time during which a particular subject is taught 🗈 *Hannah's in my class at school.* □ *I'm going to my aerobics class tonight.* (**aula**)
2 one of the social groups into which people can be divided according to their family, income, job, etc. □ *the working class* (**classe**)
3 a group of animals or plants that are related to each other or have similar qualities (**categoria**)

classic¹ /ˈklæsɪk/ NOUN [plural classics] a great book or other work of art that is admired for a long time after it was written or made □ *great film classics* (**clássico**)

classic² /ˈklæsɪk/ ADJECTIVE very good and popular for a long time ☐ *classic children's stories* (**clássico**)

classical /ˈklæsɪkəl/ ADJECTIVE
1 belonging to the style or culture of ancient Greece or Rome ☐ *classical architecture* (**clássico**)
2 traditional ☐ *classical ballet* (**clássico**)

classical music /ˌklæsɪkəl ˈmjuːzɪk/ NOUN, NO PLURAL traditional, serious music written by people like Beethoven and Verdi (**música clássica**)

classify /ˈklæsɪfaɪ/ VERB [**classifies, classifying, classified**] to put people or things into groups or classes according to what qualities they have ☐ *The books are classified by subject.* (**classificar**)

classmate /ˈklɑːsmeɪt/ NOUN [**plural classmates**] someone in your school or college class (**colega de classe**)

classroom /ˈklɑːsruːm/ NOUN [**plural classrooms**] a room where students have lessons (**sala de aula**)

clause /klɔːz/ NOUN [**plural clauses**] a group of words that makes up a sentence or part of a sentence ☐ *a relative clause* (**oração**)

claw /klɔː/ NOUN [**plural claws**]
1 one of the long pointed nails on the toes of some animals and birds (**garra**)
2 a long part at the end of the leg of some sea creatures and insects, that is used for holding things (**presa**)

clay /kleɪ/ NOUN, NO PLURAL a soft sticky substance in the ground that goes hard when it is baked and is used for making cups and bowls ☐ *clay pots* (**barro**)

clean¹ /kliːn/ ADJECTIVE [**cleaner, cleanest**] not dirty ☐ *clean hands* ☐ *a clean kitchen* ☐ *clean air* ☐ *clean drinking water* 🔄 *Everywhere looked clean and tidy.* (**limpo**)

• **cleanly** /ˈkliːnli/ ADVERB if something breaks cleanly, it breaks completely and in a tidy way ☐ *The log split cleanly in half.* (**perfeitamente**)

clean² /kliːn/ VERB [**cleans, cleaning, cleaned**] to remove the dirt from something ☐ *I've just been cleaning the kitchen.* ☐ *Have you cleaned your teeth?* (**limpar**)
♦ PHRASAL VERB **clean (something) up** to make a place clean and tidy, removing any rubbish ☐ *I'll start cleaning up this mess.* (**limpar [algo]**)

> **THESAURUS**: Clean is a general word to describe removing dirt from something. If you clean something with a brush, you can use the word **sweep**. If you rub the surface of something to clean it, you can use the word **wipe**. For example, you **wipe** the table after a meal. If you **scrub** something such as a dirty pan, you rub it very hard to get it clean. If something has a layer of fine powder on it, you might **dust** it with a cloth.

cleaner /ˈkliːnə(r)/ NOUN [**plural cleaners**] someone whose job is to clean places ☐ *The cleaner comes in once a week.* (**limpador, faxineiro**)

clear¹ /klɪə(r)/ ADJECTIVE [**clearer, clearest**]
1 easy to understand ☐ *I gave clear instructions.* ☐ *He drew a very clear map.* (**claro**)
2 obvious ☐ *+ that It was clear that she wasn't happy.* 🔄 *Sally made her feelings very clear.* (**claro**)
3 easy to see or hear ☐ *The recording wasn't very clear.* (**claro**)
4 transparent ☐ *clear glass* (**claro**)
5 not blocked or covered by anything ☐ *a clear sky* ☐ *a clear view of the stage* ☐ *+ of The road was clear of traffic.* (**desimpedido**)

clear² /klɪə(r)/ VERB [**clears, clearing, cleared**] to remove people or things from a place ☐ *I'll just clear these dishes.* ☐ *Police cleared the streets around the car bomb.* (**desimpedir**)
♦ PHRASAL VERBS **clear something away** to remove things that you have finished using in order to make a place tidy ☐ *I'll just clear away my papers.* **clear (something) up** to make a place tidy ☐ *I helped to clear up after the party.* **clear up** to get better ☐ *Her skin problem has cleared up.* ☐ *The weather has cleared up.*

clearly /ˈklɪəli/ ADVERB
1 in a way that is easy to see, hear, or understand ☐ *You can see it quite clearly in the photo.* ☐ *She explained it very clearly.* (**claramente**)
2 obviously ☐ *Clearly, we can't do the job without enough people.* (**claramente**)

cleric /ˈklerɪk/ NOUN [**plural clerics**] a member of the clergy (= priests) (**clérigo**)

clerk /klɑːk/ NOUN [**plural clerks**] an office worker whose job is to write letters, store documents, or keep financial records (**empregado de escritório**)

clever /ˈklevə(r)/ ADJECTIVE [**cleverer, cleverest**] good at learning and understanding things ☐ *He was a very clever boy.* (**esperto**)

click¹ /klɪk/ VERB [**clicks, clicking, clicked**]
1 to press a button on a computer mouse in order to make the computer do something. A computing word ☐ *Just type your message and click 'Send'.* ☐ *+ on Click on the icon to open the program.* (**clicar**)
2 to make a short, sharp sound ☐ *We could hear her heels clicking on the stone floor.* (**estalar**)

click² /klɪk/ NOUN [**plural clicks**]
1 a short, sharp sound ☐ *The box closed with a click.* (**clique**)
2 when you press a button on a computer mouse to make the computer do something. A computing word ☐ *You can place your order with just one click.* (**clique**)

client /ˈklaɪənt/ NOUN [**plural clients**] someone who pays someone else for a service (**cliente**)

cliff — clothes

cliff /klɪf/ NOUN [plural **cliffs**] the high, steep side of a piece of land, usually next to the sea (**penhasco**)

climate /ˈklaɪmɪt/ NOUN [plural **climates**] the type of weather that a country or area usually gets ☐ *These plants only grow in hot climates.* (**clima**)

> **THESAURUS:** The climate of a place is the type of weather that it usually gets. For example, a place might have a wet climate if it often rains there. **Weather** describes the particular conditions in a place at a particular time, for example how hot it is, or whether it is raining. The **temperature** of a place is how hot or cold it is. We usually measure **temperature** in degrees Celsius.

climb[1] /klaɪm/ VERB [**climbs, climbing, climbed**]
1 to go up or to go towards the top, often using your hands and feet ☐ *He likes to climb trees.* ☐ *It's a very difficult mountain to climb.* (**escalar**)
2 to increase in number ☐ *Last year, the number of people without a job climbed to 2 million.* (**subir**)

climb[2] /klaɪm/ NOUN [plural **climbs**] an act of climbing or the distance you climb ☐ *We had a steep climb to the top.* (**escalada**)

climber /ˈklaɪmə(r)/ NOUN [plural **climbers**] someone who climbs, often as a hobby or sport ☐ *a very experienced climber* (**alpinista**)

cling /klɪŋ/ VERB [**clings, clinging, clung**] to hold on to something tightly, usually because you are afraid ☐ *The child clung to her mother.* (**agarrar[-se]**)

clinic /ˈklɪnɪk/ NOUN [plural **clinics**] a place where people can see doctors to get treatment and advice ☐ *an eye clinic* (**clínica**)

clip[1] /klɪp/ VERB [**clips, clipping, clipped**]
1 to cut small or short parts off something ☐ *He was busy clipping the hedge.* (**podar, tosquiar**)
2 to fasten something to something else with a pin ☐ *He had a badge clipped to his lapel.* (**prender**)

clip[2] /klɪp/ NOUN [plural **clips**] a small object that fastens something together or to something else ⊞ *a paper clip* ⊞ *a hair clip* (**clipe, grampo, presilha**)

cloak /kləʊk/ NOUN [plural **cloaks**] a loose coat without sleeves that hangs down from the shoulders (**capa**)

cloakroom /ˈkləʊkruːm/ NOUN [plural **cloakrooms**] a room or area in a building where visitors can leave their coats, hats and bags (**vestiário**)

clock /klɒk/ NOUN [plural **clocks**] an object which shows the time ☐ *an alarm clock* ☐ *There's a clock on the kitchen wall.* (**relógio**)

close[1] /kləʊz/ VERB [**closes, closing, closed**]
1 to shut ☐ *Could you close the door, please?* ☐ *The door closed behind him.* ☐ *Close your eyes and go to sleep.* (**fechar**)
2 if a shop, restaurant, etc. closes, it stops serving people, for example at the end of a day ☐ *Supermarkets close around 8 o'clock.* (**fechar**)
3 to stop operating as a business, permanently ☐ *A lot of shops in this area have closed.* (**fechar**)
4 to finish using a computer program or document and make it go off your screen. A computing word. (**fechar**)
◆ PHRASAL VERB **close (something) down** to stop operating as a business, or make something stop operating as a business ☐ *A lot of small businesses are closing down.* (**encerrar**)

close[2] /kləʊz/ NOUN, NO PLURAL the end of something ☐ *The pound was weak at the close of trading.* ⊞ *She quickly brought the meeting to a close.* (**fim**)

close[3] /kləʊs/ ADJECTIVE [**closer, closest**]
1 near in distance or time ☐ + **to** *The flat is close to the shops.* ☐ *It was close to midnight when he got back.* (**perto**)
2 if you are close to someone, you know and like them well ☐ + **to** *I'm very close to my younger sister.* ⊞ *We invited a few close friends.* (**íntimo**)
3 a close relation is someone such as your mother, father, sister or brother (**próximo**)
4 looking or listening carefully ⊞ *Pay close attention to what he says.* ⊞ *I kept a close eye on the time.* (**bastante**)

close[4] /kləʊs/ ADVERB [**closer, closest**]
1 near ☐ *Her mother was standing close by.* (**perto**)
2 be/come close to doing something to almost do something ☐ *He came close to winning.* (**chegar**)

close[5] /kləʊs/ NOUN [plural **closes**] a street that cars can go into only at one end ☐ *They live at 16 Cathedral Close.* (**beco sem saída**)

closed /kləʊzd/ ADJECTIVE not open ☐ *Laura kept her eyes closed.* ☐ *The banks are closed on Sundays.* (**fechado**)

closely /ˈkləʊsli/ ADVERB
1 carefully ☐ *Police are examining the scene closely.* (**rigorosamente**)
2 with little distance between two things ⊞ *He entered, closely followed by his parents.* (**de perto**)
3 if two things are closely connected, they are very similar or have a strong connection ☐ *Humans are very closely related to apes.* (**estreitamente**)

closure /ˈkləʊʒə(r)/ NOUN [plural **closures**] when a business, organization, etc. stops operating ☐ *school closures* (**fechamento, fechamentos**)

cloth /klɒθ/ NOUN [plural **cloths**]
1 *no plural* material made of wool, cotton, etc., used for making clothes, etc. ☐ *cotton cloth* ☐ *a cloth bag* (**nuvem**)
2 a piece of cloth used for cleaning or drying ☐ *She wiped the table with a damp cloth.* (**nuvem**)

clothes /kləʊðz/ PLURAL NOUN the things people wear to cover their bodies ⊞ *She wears very interesting clothes.* ☐ *baby clothes* ☐ *a clothes shop* (**roupa**)

> **THESAURUS:** Clothes is a general word. An outfit is a set of clothes that go together. You might buy a new outfit to wear to a party. A costume is a set of clothes that you wear to make you look like another person, an animal or another creature. Children often dress up in costumes. A disguise is something you wear so that people will not know who you are, or to make you look like someone else. A famous person might wear a disguise so that people will not know who she is. Garment is a word for a piece of clothing. It is quite a formal word.

clothing
/'kləʊðɪŋ/ NOUN, NO PLURAL clothes, especially for a particular activity □ *waterproof clothing* □ *Please bring a change of clothing.* a piece of clothing (**roupa**)

cloud
/klaʊd/ NOUN [plural clouds]
1 a white or grey mass of small water drops that is in the sky □ *rain clouds* □ *dark clouds* (**nuvem**)
2 a mass of smoke, dust, sand, etc. in the air □ *a cloud of flies* □ *Clouds of smoke were pouring out of the factory.* (**nuvem**)

> **THESAURUS:** A cloud is a white or grey mass of small water drops in the sky. Rain falls from clouds. Mist is small drops of water in the air that make it difficult to see. If mist is very thick, we call it fog.

cloudy
/'klaʊdi/ ADJECTIVE [cloudier, cloudiest] full of clouds a *cloudy sky* (**nublado**)

clown
/klaʊn/ NOUN [plural clowns] someone who wears funny clothes, has a painted face, and does silly things to make people laugh (**palhaço**)

club
/klʌb/ NOUN [plural clubs]
1 an organization of people who meet regularly to do a particular activity, or the place where they meet *She belongs to a golf club.* *I've joined a tennis club.* (**clube**)
2 a place where people go at night to dance and drink (**boate**)
3 one of the sticks used in golf to hit the ball (**taco**)
4 clubs one of the four types of playing card, which have the symbol (♣) printed on them □ *the four of clubs* (**paus**)

clue
/kluː/ NOUN [plural clues] a sign or piece of information that helps solve a problem, mystery or crime □ *a crossword clue* □ *The police are looking for clues.* (**chave, pista**)
◆ IDIOM **not have a clue** an informal phrase meaning to know or understand nothing about something □ *I didn't have a clue what she meant.* (**não ter a menor ideia**)

clumsy
/'klʌmzi/ ADJECTIVE [clumsier, clumsiest] a clumsy person is awkward in the way they move, often dropping things or knocking into things (**desajeitado**)

clung
/klʌŋ/ PAST TENSE AND PAST PARTICIPLE OF **cling** (ver **cling**)

clutch
/klʌtʃ/ VERB [clutches, clutching, clutched] to hold something tightly in your hand or hands □ *She clutched her mother's hand.* (**apertar**)

cm
ABBREVIATION **centimetre** or **centimetres** (cm [**centímetro**])

Co
ABBREVIATION **company**, used in the name of a business □ *Smith, Jenkins and Co.* (**Cia** [**companhia**])

coach¹
/kəʊtʃ/ NOUN [plural coaches]
1 a comfortable bus for long journeys □ *a coach station* a *coach trip* (**ônibus**)
2 someone who helps people to improve a skill, often a sport, or who gives extra teaching in a school subject □ *a rugby coach* □ *a singing coach* (**treinador**)
3 in the past, a vehicle that was pulled by horses (**coche**)

coach²
/kəʊtʃ/ VERB [coaches, coaching, coached] to help someone to improve a skill, often a sport, or to give extra teaching to someone in a school subject □ *He's being coached by an ex-Olympic champion.* (**treinar**)

coal
/kəʊl/ NOUN, NO PLURAL a hard black substance that is dug out of the ground and burnt to give heat (**carvão mineral**)

coast
/kəʊst/ NOUN [plural coasts] the area of land next to the sea □ *It's a town on the west coast of Ireland.* □ *They've gone for a trip to the coast.* (**costa**)
◆ IDIOM **the coast is clear** if the coast is clear, there is no one around to see you or stop you doing something (**a barra está limpa**)

coastline
/'kəʊstl aɪn/ NOUN [plural coastline] the edge of a coast □ *the beautiful Scottish coastline* (**litoral**)

coat
/kəʊt/ NOUN [plural coats]
1 a piece of clothing with sleeves that you wear over your other clothes when you go out □ *He was wearing a thick winter coat.* (**casaco**)
2 a layer of a substance a *coat of paint* (**demão**)
3 the fur of an animal (**pelagem**)

cockpit
/'kɒkpɪt/ NOUN [plural cockpits] the area in an aeroplane where the pilot sits (**cockpit**)

cocktail
/'kɒkteɪl/ NOUN [plural cocktails] an alcoholic drink made with two or more types of drink mixed together (**coquetel**)

cocoa
/'kəʊkəʊ/ NOUN, NO PLURAL
1 a brown powder made from the seeds of a tropical tree, used to make chocolate (**cacau**)
2 a hot drink made from cocoa powder mixed with milk (**cacau**)

coconut / collection

coconut /ˈkəʊkəˌnʌt/ NOUN [plural **coconuts**] a large nut with a brown outer part with hair on, and white flesh and liquid inside ⊞ *coconut milk* (**coco**)

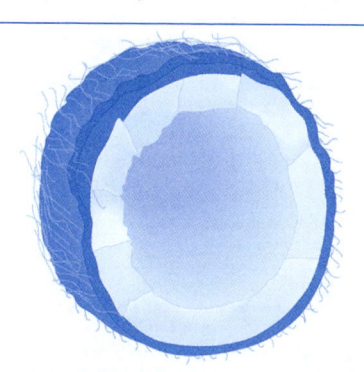

cod /kɒd/ NOUN [plural **cod**] a large sea fish that you can eat (**bacalhau**)

code /kəʊd/ NOUN [plural **codes**]
1 a set of signs or letters used instead of normal writing to send a secret message □ *The letter was written in code.* ⊞ *They managed to break the code* (= understand it). (**código**)
2 the first part of a telephone number that tells you the area or the country □ *What's the code for the UK?* (**código**)

coffee /ˈkɒfi/ NOUN [plural **coffees**]
1 *no plural* a drink made from the beans of a tropical plant □ *I don't drink coffee.* ⊞ *Let's have a cup of coffee.* ⊞ *black/white coffee* (= coffee without/with milk) (**café**)
2 a cup of this drink □ *Two black coffees, please.* (**café**)

coffin /ˈkɒfɪn/ NOUN [plural **coffins**] a long wooden box that a dead body is put into to be buried (**caixão**)

coin /kɔɪn/ NOUN [plural **coins**] a round, flat piece of metal money ⊞ *a gold coin* ⊞ *a pound coin* (**moeda**)

coincide /ˌkəʊ ɪnˈsaɪd/ VERB [**coincides, coinciding, coincided**] when events coincide with each other, they happen at the same time □ *The carnival will coincide with the beginning of the school holidays.* (**coincidir**)

coincidence /kəʊˈɪnsɪdəns/ NOUN [plural **coincidences**] when two things happen at the same time by chance □ *It was coincidence that I was on the train that day.* □ *By coincidence, his father had also worked in China.* (**coincidência**)

cola /ˈkəʊlə/ NOUN [plural **colas**] a dark brown, sweet fizzy (= with bubbles) drink (**coca**)

cold¹ /kəʊld/ ADJECTIVE [**colder, coldest**] low in temperature □ *a cold drink* □ *She hated cold weather.* ⊞ *It's freezing cold outside.* ⊞ *His hands felt cold.* (**frio**)

▶ **THESAURUS:** Cold is a general word to talk about things that are low in temperature. If you say that something such as the weather or a room is **chilly**, you mean that it is quite cold, in an unpleasant way. If something is quite cold in a pleasant way, you use the word **cool**. For example, people might enjoy a **cool** breeze in a very hot place. If something is **freezing**, it is very cold.

cold² /kəʊld/ NOUN [plural **colds**]
1 a common illness that makes you cough and blocks your nose ⊞ *Hannah's got a cold.* ⊞ *I caught a cold while I was away.* (**resfriado**)
2 the cold cold weather or a low temperature □ *We waited around in the cold for an hour.* (**frio**)

collapse¹ /kəˈlæps/ VERB [**collapses, collapsing, collapsed**]
1 if a building or structure collapses, it falls down because it is too weak □ *The bridge collapsed under the lorry's weight.* (**ruir, desmoronar**)
2 if a person collapses, they fall down because they are ill or very tired □ *He collapsed from exhaustion.* □ *I put down my bags and collapsed on the sofa.* (**desmaiar**)

collapse² /kəˈlæps/ NOUN [plural **collapses**]
1 when a building, structure or person falls down □ *After her collapse, she went to Switzerland to recover.* (**queda**)
2 when a business, government, plan, etc. fails □ *The country faces economic collapse.* (**fracasso**)

collar /ˈkɒlə(r)/ NOUN [plural **collars**]
1 the piece of material on a shirt or jacket that fits round your neck □ *I unbuttoned my shirt collar.* (**gola**)
2 a piece of leather or other material fastened round an animal's neck (**coleira**)

colleague /ˈkɒliːg/ NOUN [plural **colleagues**] a person who you work with □ *A colleague of mine told me about it.* (**colega**)

collect /kəˈlekt/ VERB [**collects, collecting, collected**]
1 to get things from different places and put them together □ *The survey collected data from 500 people.* □ *+ up Could you collect up all the plates, please?* (**coletar**)
2 to get and keep things of a particular type as a hobby □ *Ted collects unusual postcards.* (**colecionar**)
3 to go to a place to get someone or something □ *George collected me from the airport.* □ *The following items are collected for recycling.* (**apanhar**)
4 to take money from people □ *I'm collecting donations for charity.* (**arrecadar**)

collection /kəˈlekʃən/ NOUN [plural **collections**]
1 things that have been collected together ⊞ *a private art collection* □ *+ of a collection of rare photographs* □ *The book is a collection of short stories.* (**coleção**)

2 when you go to get something from a place □ *There were two parcels waiting for collection.* □ *weekly rubbish collections* (**coleta**)
3 money collected from different people □ *We had a collection for Bob's retirement.* (**coleta**)

college /ˈkɒlɪdʒ/ NOUN [plural colleges]
in the UK, a place where people go to learn after they have left school ▣ *She went to college to do catering.* (**faculdade**)

collide /kəˈlaɪd/ VERB [collides, colliding, collided] when moving objects collide, they hit each other □ *The bus collided with a car.* (**colidir**)

collision /kəˈlɪʒən/ NOUN [plural collisions] a crash between moving vehicles or objects □ *A collision between two lorries has closed the road.* (**colisão, trombada**)

colon /ˈkəʊlən/ NOUN [plural colons] a mark (:) used to separate parts of a sentence or used before a list (**dois-pontos**)

colonel /ˈkɜːnəl/ NOUN [plural colonels] an officer with a high rank in the army or air force (**coronel**)

colony /ˈkɒləni/ NOUN [plural colonies] a country or area that is controlled by another country ▣ *The French established a colony there in the 19th century.* (**colônia**)

colour¹ /ˈkʌlə(r)/ NOUN [plural colours]
red, blue, green, black, etc. □ **+ of** *Look at the colour of the sky.* □ *What colour are your eyes?* □ *The sea was a lovely colour.* ▣ *There is a range of designs in bright colours.* (**cor**)

> When you say the colour of something or ask about the colour of something, remember to use the verb **be** and not **have**:
> ✓ *Your jacket is a lovely colour.*
> ✗ *Your jacket has a lovely colour.*
> ✓ *What colour is your coat?*
> ✗ *What colour has your coat?*

> Note also that when you say the colour of something, you do not usually use the word 'colour' after the name of the colour:
> ✓ *My new car is red.*
> ✗ *My new car is red colour.*

colour² /ˈkʌlə(r)/ VERB [colours, colouring, coloured] to make something a particular colour or to become a particular colour □ *Does she colour her hair?* □ *Colour the sun yellow.* □ **+ in** *Would you like to colour in your picture?* (**colorir, pintar**)

colour³ /ˈkʌlə(r)/ ADJECTIVE
having or using colour □ *a colour TV* □ *a colour photograph* (**colorido**)

coloured /ˈkʌləd/ ADJECTIVE
having a colour or colours, not just black and white ▣ *a brightly coloured scarf* □ *Use different coloured pens.* (**colorido**)

colourful /ˈkʌləfʊl/ ADJECTIVE
having lots of bright colours □ *dancers in colourful costumes* □ *The garden was full of colourful flowers.* (**colorido**)

colourless /ˈkʌləlɪs/ ADJECTIVE
having no colour □ *Water is a colourless liquid.* (**incolor**)

column /ˈkɒləm/ NOUN [plural columns]
1 a tall, thick post, usually made of stone □ *Huge columns support the roof.* (**coluna**)
2 a piece of writing in a newspaper that appears regularly and is usually written by the same person ▣ *He writes a weekly newspaper column.* (**coluna**)
3 numbers or words written one under the other on a page □ **+ of** *a column of figures* □ *Add up the numbers in the right-hand column.* (**coluna**)
4 something with a long or tall narrow shape □ **+ of** *Columns of smoke and dust rose from the erupting volcano.* (**coluna**)

comb¹ /kəʊm/ NOUN [plural combs]
an object with a row of very narrow parts along one side that you use to tidy your hair (**pente**)

comb² /kəʊm/ VERB [combs, combing, combed]
to tidy your hair using a comb □ *She combed her hair.* (**pentear**)

combat¹ /ˈkɒmbæt/ NOUN, NO PLURAL fighting, especially in a war □ *The two soldiers died in combat.* (**combate**)

combat² /ˈkɒmbæt/ VERB [combats, combatting, combatted] to try to stop something bad or harmful □ *The government brought in new laws to combat terrorism.* □ *He will receive treatment to combat the infection.* (**combater**)

combination /ˌkɒmbɪˈneɪʃən/ NOUN [plural combinations]
several things that have been joined or mixed together □ **+ of** *The problem is due to a combination of factors.* (**combinação**)

combine /kəmˈbaɪn/ VERB [combines, combining, combined]
to join or mix things together □ *Combine all the ingredients in a mixing bowl.* □ **+ with** *Carbon dioxide combines with water to form an acid.* (**associar[-se]**)

come /kʌm/ VERB [comes, coming, came, come]
1 to move towards someone or a place □ *Come here!* □ *Here comes Julia.* □ *He came back to see me later.* □ *She came in and said hello.* (**vir**)
2 to go with someone □ **+ with** *Are you coming with us or not?* □ *We're going swimming – do you want to come?* (**vir**)
3 to arrive □ *Has my parcel come yet?* (**chegar**)
4 to move in a particular direction or to a particular (**baixar, desabrochar, nascer**) level □ *Prices have come down.* □ *All the flowers have come up.* □ *We watched the sun come up.*
5 come second/last/before, etc. to have a particular position in a competition or a list □ *P comes before Q in the alphabet.* □ *Philippe came first in the English exam.* (**ser**)
6 come apart/off, etc. to become separated from something □ *I picked up the jug and the handle came off.* (**desfazer-se**)
7 How come …? used to ask for an explanation □ *How come Penny isn't here?* (**por que**)

> Remember that the verb **come** means 'to move towards the speaker' or 'to move with the speaker'. For movements away from the speaker, use **go** □ *Come here!* □ *Eva came to see us last night.* □ *Are you coming to the supermarket with me?*

◆ PHRASAL VERBS **come along 1** to arrive □ *Luckily a police officer came along at that moment.* **2** to go with someone □ *Do you mind if I come along?* **come from somewhere** to be born somewhere or to live somewhere □ *She comes from Brazil.* **Come on!** used to encourage someone or to make them go faster □ *Come on, we're going to be late for school!* **come round** to become conscious again □ *When he came round, he could remember nothing about the accident.* **come to something** to be a particular amount of money □ *Six bananas and a bag of apples – that comes to £2.80, please.* **come up** to happen □ *If the opportunity to travel comes up, you should take it.* □ *If any problems come up, just phone me.*

comedian /kəˈmiːdiən/ NOUN [plural **comedians**] a performer who tells jokes and funny stories (**cômico**)

comedy /ˈkɒmədi/ NOUN [plural **comedies**] entertainment that makes you laugh □ *His latest movie is a comedy.* □ *a comedy sketch* (**comédia**)

comet /ˈkɒmɪt/ NOUN [plural **comets**] a type of star that travels across the sky with a line of light behind it (**cometa**)

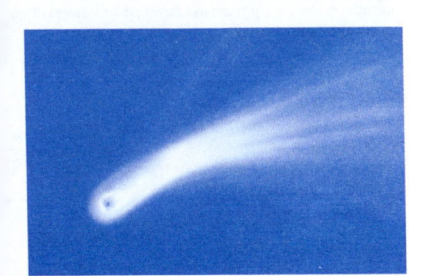

comfort¹ /ˈkʌmfət/ NOUN, NO PLURAL a feeling of being relaxed and without pain or other unpleasant feelings □ *I prefer to travel in comfort, flying first class.* □ *When I buy shoes, I choose comfort before fashion.* 🔁 *People can now shop online in the comfort of their own home.* (**conforto**)

comfort² /ˈkʌmfət/ VERB [**comforts, comforting, comforted**] to make someone feel happier by or doing nice things □ *After she heard the news, she was being comforted by relatives.* saying (**consolar**)

comfortable /ˈkʌmfətəbəl/ ADJECTIVE
1 relaxed and without pain □ *Are you comfortable there?* 🔁 *I was in a lot of pain and couldn't get comfortable.* 🔁 *He immediately made me feel comfortable.* (**confortável**)
2 feeling pleasant and not causing any pain □ *a comfortable chair* □ *They're the most comfortable shoes I've got.* (**confortável**)

comic¹ /ˈkɒmɪk/ ADJECTIVE to do with comedy 🔁 *a comic actor* □ *He has great comic timing.* (**cômico**)

comic² /ˈkɒmɪk/ NOUN [plural **comics**] (**história em quadrinhos**)
1 a magazine, especially for children, that has picture stories (**história em quadrinhos**)
2 someone whose job is to tell jokes and make people laugh (**cômico**)

comma /ˈkɒmə/ NOUN [plural **commas**] a mark (,) used to separate parts of a sentence (**vírgula**)

command¹ /kəˈmɑːnd/ VERB [**commands, commanding, commanded**]
1 to be in control of someone or something, especially in a military organization □ *He eventually commanded the regiment.* (**comandar**)
2 to order someone to do something □ *'Stand up straight!' he commanded.* □ **+ to do something** *An officer commanded him to go back to his unit.* (**ordenar**)

• **commander** /kəˈmɑːndə(r)/ NOUN [plural **commanders**] someone who is in charge, especially in the police or a military organization (**comandante**)

command² /kəˈmɑːnd/ NOUN [plural **commands**]
1 an order to do something 🔁 *You must obey commands.* 🔁 *He gave the command to shoot.* (**ordem**)
2 *no plural* control of someone or something □ **+ of** *He took command of the expedition.* (**comando**)
3 in command in control of a group of people □ *Who's the officer in command?* (**no comando**)

comment¹ /ˈkɒment/ NOUN [plural **comments**] something you say to give your opinion □ *I'd welcome any comments about the revised schedule.* 🔁 *He made the comments in a meeting.* (**comentário**)

comment² /ˈkɒment/ VERB [**comments, commenting, commented**] to give your opinion about something □ *'That was a waste of time',* Sally commented. □ *A spokesman refused to comment on the reports.* (**comentar**)

commentary /ˈkɒməntəri/ NOUN [plural **commentaries**] a description or explanation of an event as it happens □ *There will be live radio commentary of every match.* (**comentário**)

commentator /ˈkɒmənteɪtə(r)/ NOUN [plural **commentators**] someone who gives a description or explanation of an event as it happens □ *a football commentator* (**comentarista**)

commerce /'kɒmɜːs/ NOUN, NO PLURAL the buying and selling of goods and services □ *international commerce* (**comércio**)

commercial /kə'mɜːʃəl/ ADJECTIVE to do with business and selling things □ *commercial and residential buildings* □ *a commercial airline* (**comercial**)

commit /kə'mɪt/ VERB [**commits, committing, committed**] to do something bad or illegal ▣ *He went on to commit more serious crimes.* ▣ *What makes people commit murder?* ▣ *to commit suicide* (**cometer**)

commitment /kə'mɪtmənt/ NOUN [plural **commitments**]
1 a promise to do something ▣ *Viran made a definite commitment to be there.* (**compromisso**)
2 *no plural* strong support, effort and enthusiasm for something ▣ *She has demonstrated great commitment to the job.* (**compromisso**)

committee /kə'mɪti/ NOUN [plural **committees**] a group of people chosen to do a particular job or to make decisions about something □ *I'm on the committee for the summer fair.* (**comissão**)

common /'kɒmən/ ADJECTIVE [**commoner, commonest**]
1 existing or happening often and in many places ▣ *Traffic jams are a common occurrence in cities.*
□ + **among** *The condition is common among older people.* □ *Chickenpox is one of the commonest childhood diseases.* (**comum**)
2 shared by several people ▣ *We share a common language.* ▣ *It's common knowledge* (= everyone knows) *that Ann's leaving.* (**comum**)

common sense /ˌkɒmən 'sens/ NOUN, NO PLURAL the ability to think and behave in a sensible, practical way ▣ *Use your common sense.* □ *He tries to take a common sense approach to his work.* (**bom-senso**)

communicate /kə'mjuːnɪkeɪt/ VERB [**communicates, communicating, communicated**] to share information, opinions, feelings, etc. with other people by speaking, writing, etc. □ + **with** *We are looking for new ways to communicate with our customers.* □ + **by** *We communicate mainly by telephone and e-mail.* □ *He failed to communicate important information.* (**comunicar**)

communication /kəˌmjuːnɪ'keɪʃən/ NOUN, NO PLURAL sharing of information ▣ *Text messaging is a common form of communication.* □ + **with** *We want to improve communication with the public.* □ + **between** *There was poor communication between departments.* (**comunicação**)

communism /'kɒmjuˌnɪzəm/ NOUN, NO PLURAL a political system in which the government owns all industry and everyone is treated equally (**comunismo**)

community /kə'mjuːnəti/ NOUN [plural **communities**] people living in a particular area ▣ *The school serves the local community.* □ *He grew up in a small fishing community.* (**comunidade**)

compact /kəm'pækt/ ADJECTIVE small and taking up very little space □ *a compact camera* □ *The equipment is very compact and easy to carry.* (**compacto**)

compact disc /ˌkɒmpækt'dɪsk/ NOUN [plural **compact discs**] a disc with sound recorded on it (**CD**)

companion /kəm'pænjən/ NOUN [plural **companions**] someone who is with you □ *Who is her companion?* (**companheiro**)

company /'kʌmpəni/ NOUN [plural **companies**]
1 a business organization □ *an insurance company* □ *He works for a small web design company.* (**companhia**)
2 *no plural* being with other people or the people you spend time with ▣ *He's very good company* (= fun to spend time with). (**companhia**)
3 keep someone company to stay with someone or go somewhere with them □ *Jon came along to keep me company.* (**fazer companhia**)

comparative¹ /kəm'pærətɪv/ ADJECTIVE in grammar, a comparative adjective or adverb usually ends with *-er* or is used with *more*. For example *better, happier* and *more dangerous* are comparative forms. (**comparativo**)

comparative² /kəm'pærətɪv/ NOUN [plural **comparatives**] a comparative form of an adjective or adverb (**comparativo**)

compare /kəm'peə(r)/ VERB [**compares, comparing, compared**] to consider how two or more things are similar or different, or which is better □ + **to** *The weather today is lovely compared to last week.* □ + **with** *The figure is slightly low compared with the national average.* □ *Researchers compared the performance of the four groups.* (**comparar**)

comparison /kəm'pærɪsən/ NOUN [plural **comparisons**] when you compare things ▣ *Many people have drawn a comparison between the two players.* □ + **between** *Teachers were always making comparisons between me and my brother.* ▣ *There's no comparison between shop cakes and homemade cakes* (= homemade cakes are much better). ▣ *Taxes are low in comparison with other countries.* (**comparação**)

compartment /kəm'pɑːtmənt/ NOUN [plural **compartments**]
1 a separate part within a container, piece of furniture, etc. □ *There was a secret compartment at the back of the desk.* (**compartimento**)
2 a separate area, especially in a train ▣ *the first-class compartment* (**cabine**)

compass

compass /ˈkʌmpəs/ NOUN [plural compasses]
1 a piece of equipment that shows the direction of north, which you can use to find your way (**bússola**)
2 compasses a piece of equipment used for drawing circles (**compasso**)

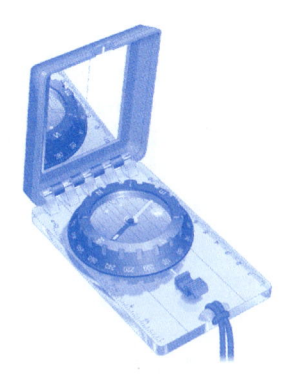

compel /kəmˈpel/ VERB [compels, compelling, compell ed] a formal word meaning to force someone to do something 🔁 *I felt compelled to get involved.* (**obrigar**)

compensate /ˈkɒmpənseɪt/ VERB [compensates, compensating, compensated] to pay someone money in exchange for something they have lost or suffered ◻ *We were compensated for the extra hours we had to work.* (**compensar**)

compete /kəmˈpiːt/ VERB [competes, competing, competed] to take part in a race, competition, etc. ◻ *I always dreamed of competing in the Olympics.* ◻ **+ against** *We'll be competing against some top teams.* ◻ **+ for** *Twenty-five players are competing for the title.* ◻ *He has the ability to compete at the highest level.* (**competir**)

competition /ˌkɒmpɪˈtɪʃən/ NOUN [plural competitions] an event at which people try to win or to be better than the others 🔁 *She entered a competition to win a holiday.* 🔁 *He won a singing competition.* (**competição**)

> **THESAURUS:** A **competition** or a **contest** is an event in which people try to win something or be better than others. A **match** is a sports competition between two players or two teams. A **game** is more general, and is any activity with rules that people do for enjoyment. A **race** is a competition to see who can do something fastest or get somewhere fastest.

competitive /kəmˈpetɪtɪv/ ADJECTIVE
1 to do with or involving competition 🔁 *a competitive sport* (**competitivo**)
2 liking to compete and win ◻ *I'm a very competitive person.* (**competitivo**)

compliment

competitor /kəmˈpetɪtə(r)/ NOUN [plural competitors] someone taking part in a competition ◻ *He's the oldest competitor in the race.* (**competidor**)

> **THESAURUS:** A **competitor** or **contestant** is a person who takes part in a competition. A **candidate** is a person who takes part in an examination or someone who is trying to get a job or win an election.

complain /kəmˈpleɪn/ VERB [complains, complaining, complained] to say that you are not happy or satisfied about something ◻ **+ that** *He complained that it was too hot.* ◻ **+ about** *Our neighbours complained about the noise.* (**queixar-se**)

complaint /kəmˈpleɪnt/ NOUN [plural complaints] when you complain about something ◻ **+ about** *We've received several complaints about his behaviour.* 🔁 *I wish to make a complaint.* (**queixa**)

complete¹ /kəmˈpliːt/ VERB [completes, completing, completed] to finish something ◻ *You must complete the test in 15 minutes.* ◻ *She completed a 10-week English course.* ◻ *The work should be completed by the end of March.* ◻ *Complete the sentence using one word in each gap.* (**completar**)

complete² /kəmˈpliːt/ ADJECTIVE
1 including all parts ◻ *a complete set of golf clubs* ◻ *Here's the complete list of winners.* ◻ **+ with** *It's a 5-star hotel complete with indoor pool and spa.* (**completo**)
2 used to emphasize what you are saying ◻ *I felt a complete fool.* ◻ *It was a complete surprise to me.* 🔁 *She received a letter from a complete stranger.* (**completo**)

completely /kəmˈpliːtlɪ/ ADVERB in every way or with every part finished ◻ *I agree completely.* ◻ *The whole day was completely ruined.* ◻ *This job is completely different from what I did before.* ◻ *They had completely cleaned the whole house.* (**completamente**)

> Note that **completely** comes before adjectives that have strong meanings. Before adjectives that are less strong, use **very** or **extremely** ◻ *It's completely ridiculous.* ◻ *It's very silly.* ◻ *It's completely exhausting.* ◻ *It's very tiring.*

complex /ˈkɒmpleks/ ADJECTIVE with many different parts and difficult to understand ◻ *These are complex issues.* ◻ *The situation has become increasingly complex.* (**complexo**)

complicated /ˈkɒmplɪkeɪtɪd/ ADJECTIVE difficult to understand or to deal with ◻ *a complicated calculation* ◻ *The situation has become more complicated.* (**complicado**)

compliment /ˈkɒmplɪmənt/ NOUN [plural compliments] something that you say that praises someone 🔁 *Otto paid me a compliment for once.* (**cumprimento, elogio**)

> **THESAURUS:** Praise is when you tell someone that they have done something well. A compliment is what you say to praise someone. Congratulations are what you say to tell someone that you are happy about their good news. For example, you might say 'Congratulations' to someone if they have a new baby or if it is their birthday. Admiration is what you feel when you have great respect for someone or if you think that they have done something very special.

compose /kəmˈpəʊz/ VERB [composes, composing, composed]
1 to write a piece of music □ *He has composed the music for a number of movies.* (compor)
2 if something is composed of something, it is formed of it □ *The team is composed of three men and three women.* (compor)

composer /kəmˈpəʊzə(r)/ NOUN [plural composers] someone who writes music (compositor)

composition /ˌkɒmpəˈzɪʃən/ NOUN [plural compositions]
1 a piece of music (composição)
2 an essay □ *We had to write a composition on the nature of love.* (composição)

compound /ˈkɒmpaʊnd/ NOUN [plural compounds]
1 a substance formed from two or more parts or substances. A chemistry word □ *a chemical compound* (um composto químico)
2 a word made of two or more other words. The words *airport* and *car park* are compounds. (composto)

comprehensive /ˌkɒmprɪˈhensɪv/ NOUN [plural comprehensives] a comprehensive school (abrangente)

compromise /ˈkɒmprəmaɪz/ VERB [compromises, compromising, compromised] to give up some part of what you want so that an agreement can be made □ *I'm not willing to compromise on this issue.* (comprometer)

computer /kəmˈpjuːtə(r)/ NOUN [plural computers] an electronic machine that can store and deal with very large amounts of information ▣ *a personal computer* ▣ *I mostly use my computer to send emails.* (computador)

computing /kəmˈpjuːtɪŋ/ NOUN, NO PLURAL the use of computers or the skill of working with computers □ *He studied computing.* (informática)

conceal /kənˈsiːl/ VERB [conceals, concealing, concealed] to hide something or to keep it secret □ *She concealed herself behind a bush.* □ *He couldn't conceal his disappointment.* (dissimular)

concentrate /ˈkɒnsəntreɪt/ VERB [concentrates, concentrating, concentrated] to give all your attention to something □ *+ on Try to concentrate on one thing at a time.* ▣ *I had to concentrate hard to understand what he said.* (concentrar)

concept /ˈkɒnsept/ NOUN [plural concepts] an idea or principle □ *the concept of democracy* □ *We teach some of the basic concepts of web design.* (conceito)

concern[1] /kənˈsɜːn/ VERB [concerns, concerning, concerned]
1 to worry someone □ *His disappearance was beginning to concern us.* □ *Which issue concerns you most right now?* (preocupar)
2 to affect or to be important to someone □ *Don't interfere in things that don't concern you.* (interessar)
3 to be about something □ *The research concerns the long-term effects of poor diet.* (dizer respeito)

concern[2] /kənˈsɜːn/ NOUN [plural concerns]
1 something that worries you or a feeling of worry □ *If you have any concerns about the exam, speak to your teacher.* ▣ *He expressed concern about the safety of the vehicle.* ▣ *There is widespread concern about fuel shortages.* □ *They showed no concern for the law.* (preocupação)
2 something that affects you or is important to you ▣ *My main concern is getting a job.* (preocupação)

concerned /kənˈsɜːnd/ ADJECTIVE
1 worried or caring about someone or something □ *concerned parents* □ *Many people are concerned about the environmental impact of flying.* (preocupado)
2 as far as I'm/he's, etc. concerned used to show someone's opinion □ *As far as I'm concerned, he can go ahead.* (na opinião de [alguém])

concerning /kənˈsɜːnɪŋ/ PREPOSITION about or involving someone or something □ *There are serious allegations concerning his behaviour.* (a respeito de)

concert /ˈkɒnsət/ NOUN [plural concerts] a musical performance ▣ *a rock concert* (concerto)

conclude /kənˈkluːd/ VERB [concludes, concluding, concluded]
1 to decide something after thinking carefully about it □ *He concluded that she was lying.* □ *The researchers concluded that the risk is very low.* (condenar)
2 a formal word meaning to end □ *The drama course concluded with a performance.* (condenado à morte)

conclusion /kənˈkluːʒən/ NOUN [plural conclusions]
1 a decision you make after thinking carefully about something □ *+of What was the main conclusion of the study?* ▣ *I've come to the conclusion that she just doesn't care.* ▣ *You can reach your own conclusion about that.* ▣ *It's difficult to draw any conclusions from one small survey.* (conclusão)
2 the last part of something □ *+ of I just have to write the conclusion of my essay.* □ *He spoke to reporters at the conclusion of the meeting.* (conclusão)

concrete /ˈkɒŋkriːt/ NOUN, NO PLURAL a strong, hard building material made by mixing sand, cement (= grey powder), small stones and water □ *a slab of concrete* (concreto)

condemn /kənˈdem/ VERB [condemns, condemning, condemned]

condition

1 to say that someone or something is wrong or bad □ *The President has condemned the violence.* (condenar)
2 if someone is condemned to a serious punishment, they are given it by a court 🔁 *He was condemned to death.* (condenar)

condition /kənˈdɪʃən/ NOUN [plural conditions]
1 the state that someone or something is in □ + **of** *There were concerns over the condition of the plane.* 🔁 *He was taken to hospital in a critical condition.* 🔁 *The house was in a poor condition.* 🔁 *The flight was cancelled due to bad weather conditions.* (condição)
2 something that has to happen before something else does, especially as part of an agreement □ + **of** *He broke the conditions of his licence.* 🔁 *I'll go on the condition that you come too.* (condição)

conduct¹ VERB /kənˈdʌkt/ [conducts, conducting, conducted]
1 to organize or do something 🔁 *Doctors are conducting further tests.* □ *We are conducting a full investigation into the accident.* (conduzir)
2 to stand in front of an orchestra (= large group of musicians) to control their performance □ *Sarah Hobbs conducted the orchestra.* (reger)

conduct² NOUN, NO PLURAL /ˈkɒndʌkt/
1 the way someone behaves □ *Their reckless conduct was the cause of the accident.* (comportamento)
2 the way something is organized or done □ *An independent body is supervising the conduct of the election.* (condução, transmissão)

conductor /kənˈdʌktə(r)/ NOUN [plural conductors] someone who stands in front of an orchestra (= large group of musicians) to control their performance (condutor)

cone /kəʊn/ NOUN [plural cones]
1 a solid shape with a round base and sides that slope up to a point at the top, or an object with this shape 🔁 *a traffic cone* (cone)
2 a hard fruit of some trees □ *a pine cone* (pinha)

conference /ˈkɒnfərəns/ NOUN [plural conferences]
a large meeting of people to discuss a particular subject □ + **on** *a UN conference on climate change* 🔁 *The union is holding its annual conference this week.* (conferência)

confess /kənˈfes/ VERB [confesses, confessing, confessed] to admit to other people that you have done something wrong □ *He confessed to stealing the money.* □ *'I forgot his name', she confessed.* (confessar)

confession /kənˈfeʃən/ NOUN [plural confessions] when you admit that you are guilty of a crime or something wrong 🔁 *I've got a confession to make.* 🔁 *He made a full confession to the police.* (confissão)

confidence /ˈkɒnfɪdəns/ NOUN, NO PLURAL
being sure of yourself and your abilities □ + **to do something** *It gave me the confidence to try again.* 🔁 *We're growing in confidence.* 🔁 *I totally lost my confidence.* (confiança)

confident /ˈkɒnfɪdənt/ ADJECTIVE
sure of yourself or your abilities □ + **in** *I'm confident in my own ability.* 🔁 *I'm feeling pretty confident.* □ *She's a very confident swimmer.* (confiante)

confidential /ˌkɒnfɪˈdenʃəl/ ADJECTIVE secret or private 🔁 *He had access to confidential information.* 🔁 *highly/strictly confidential* (confidencial, sigiloso)

confine /kənˈfaɪn/ VERB [confines, confining, confined] to keep someone or something within limits or shut inside a place □ *The soldiers were confined to barracks.* □ *Please confine your remarks to the subject under discussion.* (confinar)

confirm /kənˈfɜːm/ VERB [confirms, confirming, confirmed]
1 to say or to make sure that something is correct or true □ *Police would not confirm the identity of the woman.* □ + **that** *A company spokesman confirmed that the director had resigned.* □ + **question word** *She refused to confirm whether the rumour was true.* □ + **as** *Robinson was confirmed as England captain yesterday.* (confirmar)
2 to say that something will happen as arranged □ + **that** *Please confirm that you will be able to come to the meeting.* □ *I'm writing to confirm the booking.* (confirmar)

conflict /ˈkɒnflɪkt/ NOUN [plural conflicts] an argument or a disagreement 🔁 *We help to resolve conflicts between neighbours.* 🔁 *There is an armed conflict in the region.* (conflito)

confront /kənˈfrʌnt/ VERB [confronts, confronting, confronted] if you are confronted with a problem or a difficult situation, it appears and you have to deal with it □ *She was confronted with a difficult choice.* □ *How would you react if you were confronted by a real emergency?* (confrontar)

confuse /kənˈfjuːz/ VERB [confuses, confusing, confused]
1 to make someone unable to think clearly or to understand something □ *I think it will confuse people if we make changes.* (confundir)
2 to think one thing or person is something or someone else □ *I think you're confusing the two brothers.* □ + **with** *A podcast should not be confused with a webcast.* (confundir)

confusion /kənˈfjuːʒən/ NOUN, NO PLURAL
a feeling of being confused 🔁 *The new rules caused confusion among tourists.* 🔁 *I saw the look of confusion on her face.* (confusão)

congratulate /kənˈɡrætʃʊˌeɪt/ VERB [congratulates, congratulating, congratulated] to tell someone you are happy about their achievements or their good news □ *I congratulated her on her exam results.* (congratular)

congratulations /kənˌɡrætʃʊˈleɪʃənz/ PLURAL NOUN
something you say to someone to show that you are happy about their achievements or their

good news □ *Congratulations! That's great news.* □ **+ on** *Congratulations on passing your exams.* (**parabéns, congratulações**)

> Remember that the preposition you use after the noun **congratulations** is **on** □ *Congratulations **on** your marriage!* □ *Congratulations **on** passing your driving test!*

conjunction /kənˈdʒʌŋkʃən/ NOUN [plural **conjunctions**] in grammar, a word that connects other words or parts of a sentence. For example, *and*, *but* and *or* are conjunctions. (**conjunção**)

connect /kəˈnekt/ VERB [**connects, connecting, connected**] to join two things together □ *The Channel Tunnel connects Britain and France.* □ *The two parts of the building are connected by a corridor.* (**conectar**)

connection /kəˈnekʃən/ NOUN [plural **connections**]
1 the relationship between two people, things or events □ **+ between** *They researched the connection between diet and certain diseases.* □ **+ with** *There is a possible connection with corruption.* □ **+ to** *I have a personal connection to the town.* (**relação**)
2 something that connects telephones, computers, etc. □ *a high-speed broadband connection* □ *a wireless Internet connection* (**conexão**)
3 something that joins two things together ▣ *a loose electrical connection* (**conexão**)

conquer /ˈkɒŋkə(r)/ VERB [**conquers, conquering, conquered**] to take control of a country or an area, especially in a war □ *Napoleon tried to conquer Egypt.* (**conquistar**)

conqueror /ˈkɒŋkərə(r)/ NOUN [plural **conquerors**] someone who takes control of a country or an area, especially in a war (**conquistador**)

conquest /ˈkɒŋkwest/ NOUN [plural **conquests**] when someone takes control of a country or an area, especially in a war □ *the Spanish conquest of Mexico* (**conquista**)

conscience /ˈkɒnʃəns/ NOUN [plural **consciences**] your feeling of what is right and wrong □ *You should follow your conscience.* ▣ *Now I can relax with a clear conscience* (= without feeling guilty). ▣ *He clearly had a guilty conscience.* (**consciência**)

conscious /ˈkɒnʃəs/ ADJECTIVE awake and aware of what is around you ▣ *He is now fully conscious following the operation.* □ *He had to fight to remain conscious.* (**consciente**)

consent /kənˈsent/ NOUN, NO PLURAL when you agree to or allow something ▣ *Patients must give their consent for the treatment.* (**consentimento**)

consequence /ˈkɒnsɪkwəns/ NOUN [plural **consequences**] something that is the result of something else □ *She didn't realize the consequences of her actions.* ▣ *If you eat too much, you'll suffer the consequences.* ▣ *They could face serious health consequences if they don't change their lifestyles.* (**consequência**)

consequently /ˈkɒnsɪkwəntli/ ADVERB as a result □ *He injured his ankle and, consequently, he had to withdraw from the match.* (**consequentemente**)

conservation /ˌkɒnsəˈveɪʃən/ NOUN, NO PLURAL looking after something to prevent it being damaged or destroyed ▣ *nature conservation* (**conservação**)

conservative /kənˈsɜːvətɪv/ ADJECTIVE a conservative person does not like changes or new ideas □ *He's a very conservative dresser.* (**conservador**)

consider /kənˈsɪdə(r)/ VERB [**considers, considering, considered**]
1 to think about something carefully □ *I'll consider your idea.* □ *We're considering all the options.* □ **+ whether** *I'm considering whether to go or not.* □ **+ ing** *Have you considered hiring a car?* (**considerar**)
2 to have a particular opinion about someone or something □ *I consider him to be a true friend.* □ *We will delete anything we consider inappropriate.* □ *I consider myself to be very lucky.* (**considerar**)

> Note that when **consider** (meaning 'to think about something carefully') is followed by a verb, that verb is in the -ing form:
> ✓ *She's considering leaving her job.*
> ✗ *She's considering to leave her job.*

considerable /kənˈsɪdərəbəl/ ADJECTIVE quite large or important □ *a considerable distance* □ *We've spent a considerable amount of money already.* (**considerável**)

consideration /kənˌsɪdəˈreɪʃən/ NOUN [plural **considerations**]
1 thinking carefully about things ▣ *The idea deserves serious consideration.* ▣ *We will give consideration to the request.* (**atenção**)
2 take something into consideration to think about something while you are making a decision or a plan □ *We will take all views into consideration.* (**levar em consideração**)
3 thinking about other people and what they want □ *We all want to be treated with consideration and respect.* □ *They showed little consideration for her privacy.* (**consideração**)

consist /kənˈsɪst/
♦ PHRASAL VERB [**consists, consisting, consisted**] **consist of something** to be made of two or more things □ *It was a simple meal, consisting of bread and cheese.* ▣ *His diet consists mainly of meat and potatoes.* (**consistir**)

console[1] /kənˈsəʊl/ VERB [**consoles, consoling, consoled**] to make someone who is sad or disappointed feel better (**consolar**)

console[2] /ˈkɒnsəʊl/ NOUN [plural **consoles**] a piece of equipment that you connect to a television to play video games on ▣ *a games console* (**console**)

consonant /ˈkɒnsənənt/ NOUN [plural **consonants**] any letter of the alphabet except *a, e, i, o*, or *u* (**consoante**)
→ *go to* **vowel**

constant /'kɒnstənt/ ADJECTIVE never stopping □ *He was in constant pain.* □ *The city is under constant threat of attack.* (constante)

constituency /kən'stɪtjuənsi/ NOUN [plural **constituencies**] a part of a country that elects someone to a parliament (circunscrição eleitoral)

construct /kən'strʌkt/ VERB [constructs, constructing, constructed] to build something □ *The building was constructed in 1974.* (construir)

construction /kən'strʌkʃən/ NOUN [plural **constructions**] the process of building something □ *The substance is used in road construction.* (construção)

consul /'kɒnsəl/ NOUN [plural **consuls**] a government official who works in a foreign city and helps visitors from his or her own country □ *The British consul in Barcelona arranged for him to have a temporary passport.* (cônsul)

consult /kən'sʌlt/ VERB [consults, consulting, consulted] to speak to someone or to look at something in order to get information or advice □ *If symptoms persist, consult a doctor.* □ *Anna stopped to consult the map.* (consultar)

consume /kən'sju:m/ VERB [consumes, consuming, consumed] to use something such as energy or time *Cities consume 75% of the world's energy.* (consumir)

consumer /kən'sju:mə(r)/ NOUN [plural **consumers**] someone who buys and uses something □ *Consumers want choice and competitive prices.* (consumidor)

consumption /kən'sʌmpʃən/ NOUN, NO PLURAL the use of things such as energy, fuel, water, etc. ▣ *The newer model of car offers better fuel consumption.* □ *The programme suggests ways of reducing water consumption.* (consumo)

contact¹ /'kɒntækt/ NOUN, NO PLURAL
1 when you write to someone or speak to them by telephone □ **+ with** *I've had no contact with my brother for over a year.* ▣ *I've lost contact with most of the people I went to school with.* ▣ *I keep in contact with all my ex-colleagues.* (contato)
2 in contact if you are in contact with someone, you write to them or speak to them by telephone □ *Have you been in contact with Adrian recently?* (em contato)
3 when two things or people touch each other ▣ *There was no physical contact between them.* ▣ *She became ill after coming into contact with infected chickens.* (contato)

contact² /'kɒntækt/ VERB [contacts, contacting, contacted] to write to someone or to speak to them on the telephone □ *Anyone with information about the fire should contact police.* (contatar)

contain /kən'teɪn/ VERB [contacts, containing, contained]
1 to include something or have it as a part □ *The document contained important personal information.* □ *Oranges contain a lot of vitamin C.* (conter)
2 to have something inside □ *The bag contained some money.* (conter)

> Note that the verb **contain** is never used in the -ing form. It is always used in simple tenses:
> ✓ *The bag contained my passport.*
> ✗ *The bag was containing my passport.*

container /kən'teɪnə(r)/ NOUN [plural **containers**] something for putting things in, for example a box ▣ *She put the food in a plastic container.* □ **+ of** *a container of milk* (recipiente)

contemplate /'kɒntəmpleɪt/ VERB [contemplates, contemplating, contemplated] to think seriously about something □ *We're contemplating moving to France.* (considerar)

content¹ /'kɒntent/ NOUN, NO PLURAL
1 the subject or ideas that a magazine, television programme, etc. deals with □ *The content is not suitable for children.* (conteúdo)
2 the amount of a substance that something contains ▣ *Pizzas have a very high fat content.* (conteúdo)
→ go to **contents**

content² /kən'tent/ ADJECTIVE happy □ *Tatsuya was quite content to let Mai help him.* (contente)
• **contented** /kən'tentɪd/ ADJECTIVE happy and satisfied □ *a contented smile* □ *Gemma was a contented baby.* (feliz, satisfeito)

contents /'kɒntentz/ PLURAL NOUN the things that are inside something □ *She emptied the contents of her bag onto the table.* □ *The newspaper revealed the contents of the Prince's letter.* (conteúdo)

> **THESAURUS:** The **contents** of a something are the things that are inside it. For example, you can talk about the contents of a bag or the contents of a book. The **parts** of a thing are all of the different small things that you use to make a bigger thing, such as a machine. For example, you can talk about the parts of a car. **Ingredients** are the different foods that you use to cook something. For example the ingredients of a cake include flour, butter and eggs.

contest /ˈkɒntest/ NOUN [plural **contests**] a competition 🔲 *She entered a singing contest.* (**disputa**)

contestant /kənˈtestənt/ NOUN [plural **contestants**] someone who is taking part in a competition (**disputante**)

context /ˈkɒntekst/ NOUN [plural **contexts**]
1 the situation in which something happens and all the events that caused it 🔲 *These events need to be seen in the context of the decade in which they happened.* (**contexto**)
2 the words before and after a word which help you to understand its meaning (**contexto**)

continent /ˈkɒntɪnənt/ NOUN [plural **continents**] one of the large areas that the Earth's land is divided into. The continents are Africa, Antarctica, North America, South America, Asia, Australia and Europe (**continente**)
• **continental** /ˌkɒntɪˈnentəl/ ADJECTIVE to do with continents (**continental**)

continue /kənˈtɪnjuː/ VERB [**continues, continuing, continued**]
1 to keep happening, existing, or doing something without stopping 🔲 + **for** *This disagreement has continued for many years.* 🔲 + **to do something** *Jake continued to do well at school.* 🔲 + **ing** *She continued working past retirement age.* 🔲 + **with** *He said he would continue with his campaign.* (**continuar**)
2 to start doing something again 🔲 *Police will continue the search in the morning.* (**continuar**)
3 to go further in the same direction 🔲 + **along** *They continued along the road until they reached the village.* (**continuar**)

continuous /kənˈtɪnjuəs/ ADJECTIVE
1 existing or happening without stopping 🔲 *There has been a continuous improvement in exam results.* (**contínuo**)
2 in grammar, the continuous form of a verb shows that something is continuing to happen 🔲 *The sentence 'They are playing football' is in the continuous form.* (**contínuo**)

contract¹ /ˈkɒntrækt/ NOUN [plural **contracts**] an official written agreement 🔲 *She signed a contract to design clothes for a top store.* 🔲 *The company has won a contract to supply books to schools.* (**contrato**)

contrary¹ /ˈkɒntrəri/ ADJECTIVE completely different to something else 🔲 *They have contrary views on the subject.* 🔲 *Contrary to popular belief* (= although many people believe this)*, hair does not grow quicker if you cut it.* (**contrário**)
contrary² /ˈkɒntrəri/ NOUN, NO PLURAL
1 the contrary the opposite 🔲 *He's not a nervous person. Quite the contrary, in fact.* (**o contrário**)
2 on the contrary used for emphasizing that the opposite is true 🔲 *The situation isn't depressing. On the contrary, there's a new feeling of hope.* (**pelo contrário**)

contrast¹ /ˈkɒntrɑːst/ NOUN [plural **contrasts**] a big difference 🔲 *The contrast between the two men could not be greater.* (**contraste**)
contrast² /kənˈtrɑːst/ VERB [**contrasts, contrasting, contrasted**]
1 if two things contrast, they are very different from each other 🔲 *His comments contrast sharply with those of his colleagues.* (**contrastar**)
2 to compare two things and show the differences between them 🔲 *She contrasted her experiences of working in China with her time in India.* (**comparar**)

contribute /kənˈtrɪbjuːt, ˈkɒntrɪbjuːt/ VERB [**contributes, contributing, contributed**] to give something in order to buy or achieve something together with other people 🔲 *We all contributed towards Paul's present.* 🔲 *He contributed a lot to the discussion.* (**contribuir**)

contribution /ˌkɒntrɪˈbjuːʃən/ NOUN [plural **contributions**] something that you give or do to help achieve something 🔲 *She has made a significant contribution to the project.* (**contribuição**)

control¹ /kənˈtrəʊl/ NOUN [plural **controls**]
1 no plural the power or ability to make someone or something do what you want 🔲 + **over** *He has no control over his children.* 🔲 *Brock lost control of the car and it hit a tree.* 🔲 *The army has taken control of the city.* (**controle**)
2 in control having the power to make decisions in an organization, country etc. 🔲 *He remains in control of the company.* (**no controle**)
3 under control if something is under control, someone's dealing with it 🔲 *The situation is under control.* 🔲 *It took three hours to get the fire under control.* (**sob controle**)
4 out of control unable to be controlled 🔲 *The situation is getting out of control.* (**fora de controle**)
5 controls the handles, buttons etc. you use to make a vehicle or machine work (**controle**)

control² /kənˈtrəʊl/ VERB [**controls, controlling, controlled**]
1 to have the power to make decisions 🔲 *Congress was controlled by the Democrats.* (**controlar**)
2 to make someone or something do what you want 🔲 *To be a good football player you must be able to control the ball.* (**controlar**)

controversial /ˌkɒntrəˈvɜːʃəl/ ADJECTIVE causing disagreement 🔲 *Nuclear power is a highly controversial issue.* (**controverso/polêmico**)

convenience /kənˈviːnjəns/ NOUN, NO PLURAL the state of being easy to use, reach or do 🔲 *I like the convenience of living so close to the shops.* 🔲 *For everyone's convenience, we will meet after school.* (**conveniência**)

convenient /kənˈviːnjənt/ ADJECTIVE
1 suitable and easy 🔲 *Drinking fruit juice is a convenient way for children to get vitamin C.* (**conveniente**)
2 very close and easy to get to 🔲 + **for** *Our house is very convenient for the school.* (**conveniente**)

conversation /ˌkɒnvəˈseɪʃən/ NOUN [plural **conversations**] a talk between people 🔷 *We had a long conversation about music.* □ **+ with** *I had a nice conversation with my Dad last night.* 🔷 *I overheard a conversation between my brother and his girlfriend.* (**conversa**)

converse¹ /kənˈvɜːs/ VERB [**converses, conversing, conversed**] when people converse, they talk to each other. A formal word. (**conversar**)

converse² /ˈkɒnvɜːs/ NOUN, NO PLURAL **the converse** the opposite of a statement, fact etc. (**inverso**)

• **conversely** /kənˈvɜːsli/ ADVERB in the opposite way, or from the opposite point of view (**inversamente**)

conversion /kənˈvɜːʃən/ NOUN [plural **conversions**]
1 when you change something from one thing to another □ *the conversion from analogue to digital television* (**conversão**)
2 when someone changes to a different religion □ *her conversion from Christianity to Islam* (**conversão**)

convert /kənˈvɜːt/ VERB [**converts, converting, converted**]
1 to change something into something else □ *Convert this sum of money from pounds into dollars.* (**converter**)
2 to change from one religion to another one (**converter**)

convey /kənˈveɪ/ VERB [**conveys, conveying, conveyed**] to communicate information, ideas or feelings □ *What are you trying to convey in this poem?* (**expressar**)

convict /ˈkɒnvɪkt/ NOUN [plural **convicts**] someone who has been found guilty of a crime and sent to prison (**condenado**)

convince /kənˈvɪns/ VERB [**convinces, convincing, convinced**] to make someone believe that something is true □ *Vijay tried to convince his parents that he was too ill to go to school.* (**convencer**)

convoy /ˈkɒnvɔɪ/ NOUN [plural **convoys**] a line of vehicles which are travelling together (**comboio**)

cook¹ /kʊk/ VERB [**cooks, cooking, cooked**]
1 to prepare and heat food so that it is ready to eat 🔷 *I offered to cook a meal for her.* 🔷 *Ben was cooking dinner.* □ *Cook the pasta in a pan of boiling water.* (**cozinhar**)
2 food cooks when it heats up and becomes ready to eat □ *While the potatoes are cooking, prepare the other vegetables.* (**cozinhar**)

> **THESAURUS:** Cook is a general word. If you **bake** something, you cook it in an oven. You **bake** cakes and bread. When you cook meat or vegetables in an oven, using fat, you use the word **roast**. When you **grill** food, you cook it on a barbecue or under direct heat. If you cook food in fat in a pan, you **fry** it. When you use hot water to cook food in a pan, you **boil** it. To **simmer** food means to boil it very gently.

cook² /kʊk/ NOUN [plural **cooks**] someone who prepares and cooks food 🔷 *Emma's a really good cook.* □ *He works as a hospital cook.* (**cozinheiro**)

cooker /ˈkʊkə(r)/ NOUN [plural **cookers**] a piece of kitchen equipment used for cooking food □ *a gas cooker* (**fogão**)

> Note that a **cook** is someone who prepares and cooks food and a **cooker** is a piece of equipment used for cooking food.

cookery /ˈkʊkəri/ NOUN, NO PLURAL the skill or activity of cooking food □ *She's doing a cookery course.* (**culinária**)

cookie /ˈkʊki/ NOUN [plural **cookies**] a biscuit □ *a chocolate chip cookie* (**biscoito**)

cooking /ˈkʊkɪŋ/ NOUN, NO PLURAL
1 when someone cooks food □ *Cooking is my main interest.* (**cozinhar**)
2 the type of food that is cooked □ *I love my grandma's cooking.* (**cozinhar**)

cool¹ /kuːl/ ADJECTIVE [**cooler, coolest**]
1 slightly cold 🔷 *There was a cool breeze.* 🔷 *I need a cool drink.* (**fresco**)
2 an informal word meaning great □ *He has a really cool haircut.* □ *'I've got a new mobile'. 'Cool!'* (**legal**)
3 calm 🔷 *Try to stay cool in a dangerous situation.* (**calmo**)

cool² /kuːl/ VERB [**cools, cooling, cooled**] to become cooler or to make something cooler □ *Have a drink to help you cool down.* (**esfriar**)

cooperate /kəʊˈɒpəˌreɪt/ VERB [**cooperates, cooperating, cooperated**] to work together with other people to achieve something □ *The two countries are cooperating with each other in the fight against terrorism.* (**cooperar**)

cooperation /kəʊˌɒpəˈreɪʃən/ NOUN, NO PLURAL working with others so that something can be done or achieved (**cooperação**)

cooperative /kəʊˈɒpərətɪv/ ADJECTIVE willing to do what someone asks you to do (**cooperativo**)

coordinate /kəʊˈɔːdɪneɪt/ VERB [**coordinates, coordinating, coordinated**] to organize all the different parts of something □ *He is coordinating the research project.* (**coordenar**)

cop /kɒp/ NOUN [plural **cops**] an informal word for a police officer □ *a New York cop* (**guarda**)

copper¹ /ˈkɒpə(r)/ NOUN, NO PLURAL a red-brown metal (cobre)

copper² /ˈkɒpə(r)/ ADJECTIVE
1 made of copper ▢ *a copper kettle* (de cobre)
2 having the colour of copper ▢ *She had beautiful copper hair.* (cobre)

copy¹ /ˈkɒpɪ/ NOUN [plural copies]
1 something that is made so that it looks exactly the same as something else 🔁 *Rick bought a CD and made a copy from that.* ▢ + *of He sent a copy of her death certificate.* (cópia)
2 one book, magazine, etc. from many the same that have been produced ▢ + *of I bought a copy of her new book.* (exemplar)

copy² /ˈkɒpɪ/ VERB [copies, copying, copied]
1 to make something that is exactly the same as something else ▢ *She copied the file onto a CD.* (copiar)
2 to write down words or information that you have found somewhere ▢ *I copied the train times into my notebook.* ▢ *She tried to copy my answers in the exam.* (copiar)
◆ PHRASAL VERB **copy something down** to write something that someone has told you or that is written somewhere ▢ *Copy down these questions and do them for homework.*

copyright /ˈkɒpɪˌraɪt/ NOUN, NO PLURAL the legal right to copy or use a book, film, etc. 🔁 *The company owns the copyright to thousands of songs.* (direitos autorais)

coral¹ /ˈkɒrəl/ NOUN, NO PLURAL a hard pink or white substance formed from the bones of small sea creatures (coral)

coral² /ˈkɒrəl/ ADJECTIVE made of coral ▢ *a coral island* ▢ *a coral necklace* (coral)

cord /kɔːd/ NOUN [plural cords]
1 a piece of thick string ▢ *The prisoner's hands were tied with cord.* (cordão)
2 wire covered with plastic that connects a piece of equipment to an electrical supply (fio)

core /kɔː(r)/ NOUN [plural cores]
1 the most important part of something 🔁 *This area is at the core of the Chinese manufacturing industry.* (centro)
2 the hard part with seeds in the middle of fruit like apples ▢ *an apple core* (núcleo)

cork /kɔːk/ NOUN [plural corks]
1 *no plural* a light material from the outside part of a tree (cortiça)
2 a piece of cork, which is put inside the top of a wine bottle (rolha)

corn /kɔːn/ NOUN, NO PLURAL a crop that is grown for grain (grão)

corner /ˈkɔːnə(r)/ NOUN [plural corners]
1 a point where two walls, edges or lines meet 🔁 *It was a large room with a table in the corner* ▢ + *of The corner of the page was torn.* (canto)
2 the point where two roads meet 🔁 *There's a hairdresser's on the corner* 🔁 *The school is just round the corner.* ▢ + *of I'll meet you at the corner of George Street and Alexander Road.* (esquina)

coronation /ˌkɒrəˈneɪʃən/ NOUN [plural coronations] a ceremony in which someone becomes a king or queen (coroação)

corporation /ˌkɔːpəˈreɪʃən/ NOUN [plural corporations] a large company (corporação)

corpse /kɔːps/ NOUN [plural corpses] a dead body (cadáver)

correct¹ /kəˈrekt/ ADJECTIVE right, not wrong 🔁 *The correct answer is 15.* ▢ *What is the correct pronunciation of that word?* (correto, certo)
• **correctly** /kəˈrektlɪ/ ADVERB in a way that is correct ▢ *Make sure you enter your password correctly.* (corretamente)

correct² /kəˈrekt/ VERB [corrects, correcting, corrected]
1 to make something right ▢ *He had an operation on his ankle to correct the problem.* (corrigir)
2 to show someone the mistakes they have made in speaking or writing ▢ *He interrupted me to correct my grammar.* (corrigir)

correction /kəˈrekʃən/ NOUN [plural corrections] a change that makes something right 🔁 *They have made corrections to their report.* (correção)

correspond /ˌkɒrɪˈspɒnd/ VERB [corresponds, corresponding, corresponded]
1 if two things correspond, they are the same ▢ *Let's see if what he told you corresponds with what he told me.* (corresponder)
2 if people correspond, they write to each other. A formal word. (corresponder)

correspondence /ˌkɒrɪˈspɒndəns/ NOUN, NO PLURAL letters that people write to each other, or the activity of writing letters (correspondência)

correspondent /ˌkɒrɪˈspɒndənt/ NOUN [plural correspondents] someone who writes news reports about a particular subject ▢ *a political correspondent* (correspondente)

corridor /ˈkɒrɪdɔː(r)/ NOUN [plural corridors] a passage in a building with doors on one or both sides 🔁 *a long corridor* ▢ *I was chatting to her in the corridor.* (corredor)

corrupt /kəˈrʌpt/ ADJECTIVE being dishonest in order to get money or power ▢ *corrupt officials* (corrupto)

cost¹ /kɒst/ VERB [costs, costing, cost] to have particular price ▢ *The ticket cost £35.* ▢ *How much does a litre of milk cost?* ▢ *This coat cost me a lot of money.* ▢ + **to do something** *It cost £10,000 to fix the roof.* (custar)

cost² /kɒst/ NOUN [plural costs]
1 the amount of money that you need in order to buy or do something ▢ + *of The average cost of house in this area is £350,000.* 🔁 *the high cost of*

fuel ⬚ There has been an increase in the cost of living (= the price of food, clothes, etc.). (**custo de vida**)
2 damage that is done to someone or something □ + **to** There's a great cost to the environment when we burn carbon fuels. (**custo**)
♦ IDIOM **at all costs** used for saying that you will do something even if it is difficult or even if people suffer □ Yushi was determined to succeed at all costs. (**a qualquer custo**)

co-star /'kəʊ,stɑː(r)/ NOUN [plural **co-stars**] one of two famous actors in a film or play (**coadjuvante**)

costly /'kɒstlɪ/ ADJECTIVE expensi ve □ The building was costly to repair. (**caro**)

costume /'kɒstjuːm/ NOUN [plural **costumes**]
1 a set of clothes that you wear to make you look like a different person or like an animal or other creature □ The costumes in the film were beautiful. □ He was in a clown's costume at Amy's party. (**traje**)
2 the traditional clothes from a country or from a time in the past ⬚ The children were dressed in national costume for the parade. □ Elizabethan costumes (**traje**)

cosy /'kəʊzɪ/ ADJECTIVE [**cosier**, **cosiest**] warm and comfortable □ a cosy little bedroom □ I'm nice and cosy sitting here by the fire. (**aconchegante**)

cot /kɒt/ NOUN [plural **cots**] a bed with high sides that a baby sleeps in (**berço**)

cottage /'kɒtɪdʒ/ NOUN [plural **cottages**] a small house in the countryside or in a village □ They've bought one of the cottages in the village. (**casa de campo**)

cotton /'kɒtən/ NOUN, NO PLURAL
1 a common type of cloth made from a plant □ a white cotton shirt □ cotton sheets (**algodão**)
2 a plant that produces a soft white substance, used for making cloth □ cotton farmers (**algodão**)

couch /kaʊtʃ/ NOUN [plural **couches**] a long, comfortable chair that two or more people can sit on (**divã, sofá**)

cough¹ /kɒf/ VERB [**coughs, coughing, coughed**]
to make a loud rough sound in your throat as air comes out of your lungs □ He was coughing and sneezing. (**tossir**)

cough² /kɒf/ NOUN [plural **coughs**]
1 the noise you make when you cough ⬚ She gave a little cough and looked up. (**tosse**)
2 an illness that causes you to cough ⬚ I have got a bad cough. ⬚ You need some cough medicine. (**tosse**)

could /kʊd/ MODAL VERB
1 used as the past tense of **can¹** □ We could see into the building. □ He could run very fast when he was young. □ He said we could go. (**podia**)
2 used to ask for something or to ask someone to do something □ Could I have a glass of water, please? □ Could you pass me the butter? (**poderia**)
3 used to make a suggestion □ You could try texting her. □ We could go for a walk. (**poderia**)
4 used to say that something is possible □ The weather could get better later. □ The disease could be prevented with good hygiene. (**poderia**)

couldn't /'kʊdənt/ a short way to say and write 'could not' (**não poderia**)

could've /'kʊdəv/ a short way to say and write 'could have' (**poderia**)

council /'kaʊnsəl/ NOUN [plural **councils**] a group of people who are elected to control a town or city ⬚ Local councils are responsible for repairing roads. □ council leaders (**conselho**)

count¹ /kaʊnt/ VERB [**counts, counting, counted**]
1 to find out the total of something □ He was busy counting his money. (**contar**)
2 to say numbers in order □ Can you count backwards from 10? (**contar**)
3 to be important □ He played well when it counted. (**contar**)
♦ PHRASAL VERBS **count on someone** to depend on someone □ I was counting on him to help.
count up something to find out the total of something □ She counted up how many people there were.

count² /kaʊnt/ NOUN [plural **counts**]
1 the process of counting, or the total you get ⬚ She did a quick count of the people present. (**contagem**)
2 keep count to know how many of something there is (**contagem**)
3 lose count to stop knowing how many of something there is (**perder a conta**)

countable noun /ˌkaʊntəbəl 'naʊn/ NOUN [plural **countable nouns**] in grammar, a noun that can form a plural, e.g. dog, table or car (**substantivo contável**)

countdown /'kaʊnt,daʊn/ NOUN, NO PLURAL
1 the time just before something important and exciting happens □ The countdown to the World Cup has begun. (**contagem regressiva**)
2 when people count backwards to zero before something happens (**contagem regressiva**)

counter /'kaʊntə(r)/ NOUN [plural **counters**]
1 the place where people are served in a shop or bank □ She worked on the perfume counter. (**balcão**)
2 a small plastic disc used in some games that are played on a board (**ficha**)

count noun /'kaʊnt ˌnaʊn/ NOUN [plural **count nouns**] in grammar, a noun that can form a plural, e.g. dog, table or car (**substantivo contável**)

country¹ /'kʌntrɪ/ NOUN [plural **countries**]
1 an area of land with its own government and national borders □ We don't have the death penalty in this country. ⬚ Have you ever lived in a foreign country? (**exterior**)
2 the country areas that are away from towns and cities □ I prefer living in the country. (**interior**)

country² /ˈkʌntri/ ADJECTIVE in or from the countryside ◻ *country lanes* ◻ *The Prime Minister's country house is located on Lake Mousseau.* (campo)

countryside /ˈkʌntrisaɪd/ NOUN, NO PLURAL land that is away from towns and cities ▣ *The hotel is surrounded by open countryside.* (campo)

> THESAURUS: The countryside or the country is land that is away from towns and cities. Scenery is what you can see when you look around, especially natural things such as trees and rivers in the countryside. A landscape is a view of a large area of land, and may be in a city or in the country.

county /ˈkaʊnti/ NOUN [plural **counties**] an area of a country or state that has its own local government ◻ *Yorkshire is a huge county.* (condado)

coup /kuː/ NOUN [plural **coups**] when a group of people suddenly take control of a country without an election ▣ *a military coup* (golpe)

couple /ˈkʌpəl/ NOUN [plural **couples**]
1 two or approximately two ◻ **+ of** *I haven't seen him for a couple of months.* ◻ *She relaxed after the first couple of games.* ◻ *Who ate all the chocolates? I only had a couple.* (par)
2 a husband and wife, or two people who have a similar close relationship ▣ *Most people on the holiday were married couples.* ▣ *Many young couples can't afford to buy a house.* (casal)

courage /ˈkʌrɪdʒ/ NOUN, NO PLURAL the ability to do difficult or frightening things ▣ *He didn't have the courage to tell her what he really thought.* ▣ *John showed great courage throughout his ordeal.* ▣ *I haven't plucked up the courage* (= found the cour age) *to leave my job yet.* (coragem)

courageous /kəˈreɪdʒəs/ ADJECTIVE brave ◻ *a courageous decision* (corajoso)

course /kɔːs/ NOUN [plural **courses**]
1 of course (a) used for saying yes ◻ *'Can I borrow your pen?' 'Of course you can'.* (b) used for saying that what happened was what you expected ◻ *We went on holiday and of course it rained the whole time.* (evidentemente, obviamente)
2 of course not used for emphasizing the word no ◻ *'Did you leave the keys in the car?' 'No, of course not'.* (evidentemente não)
3 a set of lessons on a particular subject ▣ *I'm doing a French course.* ▣ *There was a four-year training course to become a teacher.* ◻ **+ in** *a part-time course in business studies* (curso)
4 one of the parts of a meal ▣ *For the main course we had roast chicken.* (prato)
5 the direction that a vehicle is travelling in ▣ *The pilot had to change course and land in Berlin.* (curso)
6 a piece of land that a race is run on or a game of golf is played on ◻ *a golf course* (pista)

> Remember that **course** (sense 3) is followed by the preposition **in** ◻ *She's doing a four-day course in travel writing.*

> THESAURUS: A class or a lesson is a period of time when a group of students learn something from a teacher. A set of lessons on a subject is called a course. A lecture is a talk by a teacher, particularly for older students. Often, a large number of students listen to a lecture together.

court /kɔːt/ NOUN [plural **courts**]
1 the room where legal trials take place ▣ *He will appear in court charged with murder.* (tribunal)
2 an area where you play sports such as tennis ◻ *an indoor basketball court* (quadra)
3 the home of a king or queen and the people who live with them (corte)

courtyard /ˈkɔːtjɑːd/ NOUN [plural **courtyards**] an open area that is surrounded by walls, usually next to a building (pátio)

cousin /ˈkʌzən/ NOUN [plural **cousins**] the son or daughter of your aunt or uncle ◻ *Clare and I are cousins.* (primo)

cover¹ /ˈkʌvə(r)/ VERB [**covers, covering, covered**]
1 to put something over something else to hide or protect it ◻ **+ with** *Mum had covered the table with a clean cloth.* ◻ **+ up** *We covered up the broken window with a board.* ◻ *Cover your mouth when you cough, please.* (cobrir)
2 to form a layer on the surface of something ◻ *The mountains were covered in snow.* ◻ *The carpets are covered in mud.* (cobrir)
3 to deal with or to include a subject or some information ◻ *The local newspaper covered the story.* ◻ *The course covers every aspect of childcare.* ◻ *This law only covers UK residents.* (cobrir)
◆ PHRASAL VERB **cover something up** to stop people from discovering something bad you have done ◻ *He set fire to the house in an attempt to cover up his crime.*

cover² /ˈkʌvə(r)/ NOUN [plural **covers**]
1 something that you put on top of or around something to protect it ◻ *a duvet cover* (coberta)
2 the outer part of a book or magazine ▣ *There was a photograph of him on the front cover.* (capa)
3 *no plural* protection from attack or bad weather ▣ *We took cover in an old church.* (cobertura)

cow /kaʊ/ NOUN [plural **cows**] a large animal kept on farms for its milk or meat ▣ *The farmer had large herd of cows.* (vaca)

coward /ˈkaʊəd/ NOUN [plural **cowards**] someone who has no courage (covarde)

cowardly   creative

cowardly /'kaʊədli/ ADJECTIVE behaving like a person who has no courage (**covarde**)

cowboy /'kaʊbɔɪ/ NOUN [plural **cowboys**] a man who rides a horse and looks after cows in the US (**caubói**)

crab /kræb/ NOUN [plural **crabs**] a sea creature with a round shell and ten legs, whose pink meat is eaten (**caranguejo**)

crack¹ /kræk/ VERB [cracks, cracking, cracked]
1 to break something so that a line appears on the surface, or to break in this way □ *I'm sorry, I've cracked this cup.* □ *The ice had started to crack.* (**rachar**)
2 if you crack an egg or a nut, you break it open (**quebrar**)

crack² /kræk/ NOUN [plural **cracks**]
1 a narrow break □ *This mug has a crack in it.* □ *The ceiling had lots of cracks in it.* (**rachadura**)
2 a narrow space between two parts of something □ *The sun was coming in through a crack in the curtain.* (**fresta**)
3 a sudden short sound □ *the crack of a whip* (**estalo**)

cracker /'krækə(r)/ NOUN [plural **crackers**]
1 a paper tube with a toy inside that you pull apart at Christmas (**embrulho em forma de tubo**)
2 a plain, dry biscuit that you eat with cheese (**bolacha**)

cradle /'kreɪdəl/ NOUN [plural **cradles**] a baby's bed that can move from side to side (**berço**)

craft¹ /krɑːft/ NOUN [plural **crafts**] a skill in which you make something with your hands □ *They teach traditional crafts such as pottery and sewing.* (**artesanato**)

craft² /krɑːft/ VERB [crafts, crafting, crafted] to make something using skill □ *The statues were crafted from marble.* (**elaborar**)

craft³ /krɑːft/ NOUN [plural **craft**] a boat (**barco**)

cram /kræm/ VERB [crams, cramming, crammed] to push people or things into a small space □ *Elizabeth tried to cram everything into her bags.* □ *We all crammed into the car.* (**abarrotar**)

crane /kreɪn/ NOUN [plural **cranes**] a tall machine used to lift and move heavy things (**guindaste**)

crash¹ /kræʃ/ VERB [crashes, crashing, crashed]
1 if a vehicle crashes, or you crash it, it hits something by accident □ *A plane had crashed into the mountain.* □ *Jane crashed her car last night.* (**colidir**)
2 to make a loud noise, often by hitting something □ *The crystal vase crashed to the floor.* □ *The waves were crashing against the rocks.* (**espatifar[-se]**)
3 if a computer crashes, it suddenly stops working. A computing word. (**pifar [informática]**)

crash² /kræʃ/ ADJECTIVE done in a short time to get results quickly □ *a crash diet* □ *I took a crash course in French.* (**intensivo**)

crash³ /kræʃ/ NOUN [plural **crashes**]
1 an accident in which a vehicle hits something □ *Her parents were killed in a plane crash.* (**acidente**)
2 a loud noise made when something breaks or falls □ *the crash of breaking glass* (**barulho**)

crawl /krɔːl/ VERB [crawls, crawling, crawled]
1 to move on your hands and knees □ *The baby has just learnt to crawl.* (**engatinhar**)
2 insects crawl when they move around on their legs □ *There's a spider crawling up the wall behind you.* (**rastejar**)

crayon /'kreɪɒn/ NOUN [plural **crayons**] a stick of coloured wax or a coloured pencil for drawing with (**giz de cera/lápis de cor**)

crazy /'kreɪzi/ ADJECTIVE [crazier, craziest]
1 silly or stupid □ *a crazy idea* □ *Have you gone crazy?* (**louco**)
2 angry □ *Mum will go crazy when she finds out.* □ *His stupid questions drive me crazy.* (**nervoso**)
3 be crazy about someone/something to like someone or something very much □ *As a child, she was crazy about horses.* (**ficar louco por algo ou alguém**)

creak /kriːk/ VERB [creaks, creaking, creaked] if a door or a piece of wood creaks, it makes a long low sound □ *The floorboards creaked as he crossed the room.* (**ranger**)

cream¹ /kriːm/ NOUN [plural **creams**]
1 *no plural* a thick yellow-white liquid that forms on top of milk □ *strawberries and cream* (**nata**)
2 a soft substance that you put on your skin or hair □ *suntan cream* (**creme**)
3 *no plural* a yellow-white colour (**creme**)

cream² /kriːm/ ADJECTIVE having a yellow-white colour □ *a cream leather sofa* (**creme**)

create /kriːˈeɪt/ VERB [creates, creating, created] to make something happen or exist □ *We are hoping to create an environmentally friendly building.* □ *Snow created problems for drivers today.* □ *He hoped to create a good impression by arriving on time.* (**criar**)

creation /kriːˈeɪʃən/ NOUN [plural **creations**]
1 the act or process of creating something □ *He opposed the creation of a new department.* (**criação**)
2 something that has been made □ *This dress is one of the designer's latest creations.* (**criação**)

creative /kriːˈeɪtɪv/ ADJECTIVE good at imagining and making new things, especially works of art □ *She's a very creative artist.* (**criativo**)

creature

creature /'kri:tʃə(r)/ NOUN [plural **creatures**] any living thing that is not a plant (criatura)

credible /'kredəbəl/ ADJECTIVE able to be believed □ *a credible story* (crível)

credit¹ /'kredɪt/ NOUN, NO PLURAL
1 a way of buying goods or services and paying for them later □ *I bought the car on credit.* (crédito)
2 praise that people give you for something you have done ▣ *We all worked hard but Ben got most of the credit.* ▣ *I can't take all the credit for the success of the film.* (crédito)
3 in credit your bank account is in credit when you have money in it (ter saldo [positivo])

credit² /'kredɪt/ VERB [**credits, crediting, credited**] to put some money into a bank account (creditar)

credit card /'kredɪt ˌkɑːd/ NOUN [plural **credit cards**] a small plastic card that allows you to buy things when you want them and to pay for them later □ *Can I pay by credit card?* (cartão de crédito)

creep /kri:p/ VERB [**creeps, creeping, crept**] to move slowly and quietly so that nobody hears you □ *He crept downstairs in the middle of the night.* (insinuar-se)

crept /krept/ PAST TENSE AND PAST PARTICIPLE OF **creep** (ver **creep**)

crest /krest/ NOUN [plural **crests**]
1 the highest point of a hill or wave (crista)
2 the feathers that point upwards on the top of some birds' heads (crista)

crew /kru:/ NOUN [plural **crews**] a group of people who work together on a ship, aeroplane or train □ *The lifeboat has a crew of five.* (bando)

cricket /'krɪkɪt/ NOUN [plural **crickets**]
1 *no plural* a game played outdoors between two teams of eleven players who score points by hitting a ball □ *a cricket bat* (críquete)
2 a small insect that lives in grass and makes a noise by rubbing its wings together (grilo)

cried /kraɪd/ PAST TENSE AND PAST PARTICIPLE OF **cry¹** (ver **cry¹**)

crime /kraɪm/ NOUN [plural **crimes**]
1 *no plural* illegal activities □ *a life of crime* ▣ *The government is introducing new measures to fight crime.* ▣ *Violent crime is increasing.* (crime)
2 an illegal activity □ *minor crimes like shoplifting* ▣ *Have you ever committed a crime?* ▣ *The police never managed to solve the crime* (= discover who did it). (crime)

> Note that a person **commits** a crime. A person does not **make** or **do** a crime.

criminal¹ /'krɪmɪnəl/ NOUN [plural **criminals**] someone who has committed a crime □ *a dangerous criminal* (criminoso)

cross

criminal² /'krɪmɪnəl/ ADJECTIVE to do with crime or criminals ▣ *He has a criminal record.* (criminal)

crisis /'kraɪsɪs/ NOUN [plural **crises**] a very difficult or dangerous time or event □ *a financial crisis* □ *the growing crisis in the housing market* (crise)

crisp¹ /krɪsp/ ADJECTIVE [**crisper, crispest**]
1 crisp food is pleasantly hard or fresh □ *crisp salad leaves* □ *crisp pastry* (fresco)
2 crisp weather is cold and dry □ *a crisp spring morning* (fresco)

crisp² /krɪsp/ NOUN [plural **crisps**] a very thin piece of potato that is cooked in oil and eaten cold ▣ *a bag of crisps* (batata frita)

critic /'krɪtɪk/ NOUN [plural **critics**] someone whose job is to give their opinion of new books, films, plays, etc. □ *He was the film critic for the Times.* (crítico)

critical /'krɪtɪkəl/ ADJECTIVE
1 saying that you think something is bad or wrong ▣ *The report was highly critical of her work.* □ *critical remarks/comments* (crítico)
2 very important □ *The talks have reached a critical stage.* □ *Good hygiene is of critical importance.* (crítico)

criticism /'krɪtɪsɪzəm/ NOUN, NO PLURAL when you say what is bad about someone or something ▣ *There has been widespread criticism of the new laws.* ▣ *The company has faced criticism from environmental campaigners.* (crítica)

criticize *or* **criticise** /'krɪtɪsaɪz/ VERB [**criticizes, criticizing, criticized**] to say what you think is bad about someone or something □ *It always hurts when you criticize me.* □ *+ for They were criticized for leaving the children alone.* (criticar)

crockery /'krɒkəri/ NOUN, NO PLURAL plates, bowls, cups, etc. (louça)

crocodile /'krɒkədaɪl/ NOUN [plural **crocodiles**] a large reptile with a long tail and a big mouth that lives in rivers and lakes (crocodilo)

crook /krʊk/ NOUN [plural **crooks**] an informal word for a criminal or someone who tricks people (ladrão)

crooked /'krʊkɪd/ ADJECTIVE
1 not straight or even □ *crooked teeth* □ *That picture's crooked.* (torto)
2 an informal word meaning not honest □ *crooked cops* (desonesto)

crop /krɒp/ NOUN [plural **crops**] a plant that is grown for food □ *They grow crops such as corn and maize.* (produto agrícola)

cross¹ /krɒs/ NOUN [plural **crosses**]
1 the symbol 'x', used to show when an answer is wrong, or used to show someone where to write something on a document (cruz)
2 a symbol used in the Christian religion to represent the cross on which Christ died (cruz)

cross² /krɒs/ ADJECTIVE [crosser, crossest] angry □ **+ with** *I got very cross with him for not doing his homework.* (**zangado, irritado**)

cross³ /krɒs/ VERB [crosses, crossing, crossed]
1 to go from one side of something to the other 🔲 *Find a safe place to cross the road.* □ *A bridge crosses the river at that point.* □ *Troops crossed the border at dawn.* (**atravessar**)
2 if two things cross, they go across each other □ *The accident happened where the road and railway line cross.* (**cruzar**)
3 cross your arms/fingers/legs to put one arm/finger/leg over the top of the other □ *She is sitting quietly, with her arms crossed.* (**cruzar os braços**)
◆ PHRASAL VERB **cross something out** to draw a line through something, usually because it is wrong □ *He crossed out his answer and started again.*

crossing /ˈkrɒsɪŋ/ NOUN [plural crossings] a place where you can cross a road or a river □ *Be sure to cross at the crossing.* (**travessia**)

crossroads /ˈkrɒsrəʊdz/ NOUN [plural crossroads] a place where two roads meet and cross each other □ *Turn left at the crossroads up ahead.* (**encruzilhada**)

crouch /kraʊtʃ/ VERB [crouches, crouching, crouched] to bend your legs and back so that your body is close to the ground □ *She crouched down to tie her shoe lace.* (**agachar-se**)

crow /krəʊ/ NOUN [plural crows] a large black bird that makes a loud, rough sound (**coroa**)

crowd¹ /kraʊd/ NOUN [plural crowds] a large number of people or things together in one place □ *a football crowd* □ *crowds of shoppers* 🔲 *A crowd had gathered at the scene.* (**multidão**)

crowd² /kraʊd/ VERB [crowds, crowding, crowded] if a large number of people crowd somewhere, they fill that place □ *People crowded the streets.* (**abarrotar**)

crowded /ˈkraʊdɪd/ ADJECTIVE full of people □ *crowded shops* (**abarrotado**)

crown /kraʊn/ NOUN [plural crowns] a circle made of gold and valuable stones that a king or queen wears on their head at formal occasions (**coroa**)

crucial /ˈkruːʃəl/ ADJECTIVE very important □ *The talks are now at a crucial stage.* □ *crucial information* (**crucial**)

crude /kruːd/ ADJECTIVE [cruder, crudest]
1 made or done in a simple, rough way showing little skill □ *I had a rather crude map that Josh had quickly drawn.*
2 rude □ *a crude joke* (**rude**)

cruel /krʊəl/ ADJECTIVE [crueller, cruellest] causing pain or suffering to people or animals without caring □ **+ to do something** *It's cruel to keep an animal in such a small cage.* □ **+ to** *He was cruel to his children.* (**cruel**)

cruelty /ˈkrʊəltɪ/ NOUN, NO PLURAL when someone is cruel □ *They were accused of cruelty to animals.* (**crueldade**)

cruise¹ /kruːz/ VERB [cruises, cruising, cruised] to travel in a car, boat, etc. at the same speed (**viajar**)

cruise² /kruːz/ NOUN [plural cruises] a holiday spent on a ship, travelling to a lot of different places (**cruzeiro**)

crumble /ˈkrʌmbəl/ VERB [crumbles, crumbling, crumbled] to break into very small pieces □ *The walls of the old house were crumbling.* □ *Crumble the biscuit on top of the fruit.* (**despedaçar**)

crunch /krʌntʃ/ VERB [crunches, crunching, crunched]
1 to make a noise as you bite and eat something hard □ *She was crunching on a carrot stick.* (**mastigar ruidosamente**)
2 to make the sound of something being crushed □ *The snow crunched under our feet.* (**ranger**)

crunchy /ˈkrʌntʃɪ/ ADJECTIVE [crunchier, crunchiest] crunchy food is pleasantly hard and makes a noise when you bite it □ *a crunchy biscuit* (**crocante**)

crush /krʌʃ/ VERB [crushes, crushing, crushed] to press something so that it is broken or in small pieces □ *His leg was crushed by a falling rock.* □ *Crush two cloves of garlic.* (**esmagar**)

crust /krʌst/ NOUN [plural crusts] the hard surface on the outside of bread or some other baked foods □ *Cut the crusts off two slices of bread.* (**crosta**)

cry¹ /kraɪ/ VERB [cries, crying, cried]
1 to produce liquid from your eyes because you are sad or in pain □ *I could hear a baby crying in the next room.* (**chorar**)
2 to shout □ **+ out** *She cried out in pain.* (**gritar**)

cry² /kraɪ/ NOUN [plural cries] a shout □ **+ for** *No one heard her cries for help.* (**grito**)

crystal /ˈkrɪstəl/ NOUN [plural crystals]
1 a small regular shape that some substances form when they become solid, for example salt, ice or a mineral □ *sugar crystals* (**cristal**)
2 *no plural* a type of high quality glass □ *crystal wine glasses* (**cristal**)

cub /kʌb/ NOUN [plural cubs] a baby animal, for example a lion or bear (**filhote**)

cube /kjuːb/ NOUN [plural cubes] a solid shape with six equal square sides □ *sugar cubes* (**cubo**)

cucumber /ˈkjuːkʌmbə(r)/ NOUN [plural cucumbers] a long vegetable with a green skin that you eat raw in salads (**pepino**)

cuddle /ˈkʌdəl/ VERB [cuddles, cuddling, cuddled] to hold someone in your arms to show that you love them □ *They were kissing and cuddling on the sofa.* (**aconchegar**)

cultivate /ˈkʌltɪˌveɪt/ VERB [cultivates, cultivating, cultivated]

1 to prepare land so that you can grow crops on it □ *Peasants used to cultivate the land.* (cultivar)
2 to grow a crop to eat or to sell □ *Rice is cultivated in India.* (cultivar)

cultivation /ˌkʌltɪˈveɪʃən/ NOUN, NO PLURAL
1 the process of preparing land to grow crops (cultivo)
2 the process of growing crops (cultivo)

cultural /ˈkʌltʃərəl/ ADJECTIVE to do with culture, especially art, music and literature □ *cultural activities* (cultural)

culture /ˈkʌltʃə(r)/ NOUN [*plural* cultures]
1 the customs and beliefs of a particular group or society that make it different from other people or societies □ *The school has students from many different cultures.* (cultura)
2 *no plural* music, literature, art, etc. (cultura)

cunning /ˈkʌnɪŋ/ ADJECTIVE clever in a dishonest way □ *I have a cunning plan.* (astuto)

cup /kʌp/ NOUN [*plural* cups]
1 a small container with a handle that you drink from □ *cups and saucers* □ *Let's have a cup of tea.* (xícara)
2 a metal cup given as a prize in a competition, or the competition itself □ *the World Cup* (taça)
◆ IDIOM **not be someone's cup of tea** if something is not your cup of tea, you do not like it or are not interested in it □ *Graphic novels aren't my cup of tea.* (não fazer o gênero de alguém)

cupboard /ˈkʌbəd/ NOUN [*plural* cupboards] a piece of furniture with shelves and a door, used to store things in □ *a kitchen cupboard* □ *The plates are in the cupboard.* (armário)

cure¹ /kjʊə(r)/ VERB [cures, curing, cured] to make someone with an illness healthy again □ **+ of** *The treatment cured her of her insomnia.* (curar)

cure² /kjʊə(r)/ NOUN [*plural* cures] some thing that makes an illness end or go away □ **+ for** *a cure for cancer* (cura)

curfew /ˈkɜːfjuː/ NOUN [*plural* curfews] a law that says that people must stay in their houses after a particular time (toque de recolher)

curiosity /ˌkjʊəriˈɒsəti/ NOUN, NO PLURAL the feeling of wanting to discover facts about something □ *Children have a natural curiosity about the world.* (curiosidade)

curious /ˈkjʊəriəs/ ADJECTIVE wanting to know about something □ **+ about** *He was very curious about my past.* (curioso)

curl¹ /kɜːl/ NOUN [*plural* curls] a piece of hair that forms a curved shape □ *blonde curls* (cacho)

curl² /kɜːl/ VERB [curls, curling, curled] to form curves or to make something form curves □ *Do you curl your hair or is it natural?* (encaracolar)
◆ PHRASAL VERB **curl up** to sit or lie with your arms and legs close to your body □ *Jenny curled up on the sofa and fell asleep.* (cachear)

curly /ˈkɜːli/ ADJECTIVE [curlier, curliest] shaped like a curl or with a lot of curls 🔁 *curly hair* □ *a curly tail* (cacheado)

currency /ˈkʌrənsi/ NOUN [*plural* currencies] the money used in a particular country 🔁 *foreign currency* □ *The euro is the European currency.* (moeda)

current¹ /ˈkʌrənt/ ADJECTIVE existing or happening now □ *The current situation is not acceptable.* (corrente)

current² /ˈkʌrənt/ NOUN [*plural* currents]
1 a flow of water or air going in one direction 🔁 *Strong currents swept them out to sea.* (corrente)
2 a flow of electricity through a wire (corrente)

curriculum /kəˈrɪkjələm/ NOUN [*plural* curriculums or curricula] a course of study or all the courses of study at a school or college (currículo)

curry /ˈkʌri/ NOUN [*plural* curries] a type of food cooked with spices □ *chicken curry* (curry)

curse¹ /kɜːs/ NOUN [*plural* curses] magic words which are intended to make someone have bad luck 🔁 *She put a curse on the family.* (maldição)
curse² /kɜːs/ VERB [curses, cursing, cursed]
1 to use rude words (maldizer)
2 to say angry things about someone or something □ *I was cursing him for leaving the car so dirty.* (praguejar)

curtain /ˈkɜːtən/ NOUN [*plural* curtains] a long piece of material that can be pulled across a window 🔁 *Could you draw the curtains* (= open or close the curtains), *please?* (cortina)

curve¹ /kɜːv/ NOUN [*plural* curves] a line that bends (curva)

curve² /kɜːv/ VERB [curves, curving, curved] to form a curve or make something form a curve □ *The wall curves round the end of the garden.* (vira)

cushion /ˈkʊʃən/ NOUN [plural **cushions**] a cloth bag filled with something soft that you sit on or rest against to be comfortable ▢ *There were some cushions on the sofa.* (**almofada**)

custody /ˈkʌstədɪ/ NOUN, NO PLURAL
1 when someone is kept in prison until their trial for a crime ▣ *He was held in custody for several weeks.* (**custódia**)
2 the legal right to have a child living with you, especially after parents separate ▣ *She lost/won custody of the children.* (**guarda**)

custom /ˈkʌstəm/ NOUN [plural **customs**]
something that people usually do or that is a tradition ▢ *Japanese customs* ▢ *It is my custom to walk to the station each morning.* (**costume**)

customer /ˈkʌstəmə(r)/ NOUN [plural **customers**]
a person who buys things or services from a shop or business ▢ *The business attracts customers from all over the country.* ▢ *This office handles customer complaints.* (**cliente, freguês**)

customs /ˈkʌstəmz/ NOUN, NO PLURAL the place at an airport or port where officials check your bags to make sure they do not contain anything illegal ▢ *a customs officer* (**alfândega**)

cut[1] /kʌt/ VERB [**cuts, cutting, cut**]
1 to use a knife or a sharp tool to divide something or remove a piece from something ▢ *Cut the cake into six pieces.* ▢ *Ben tried to cut the wood in two.* ▢ + *off She's cut off all her hair.* ▢ + *up Shall I help you cut up your food?* (**cortar**)
2 to injure yourself by rubbing or hitting your skin with something sharp ▢ *I cut my finger on the can lid.* (**cortar**)
3 to reduce the amount or level of something ▢ *Mum and Dad have cut my allowance.* (**cortar**)
4 to remove an amount of text from a computer document (**cortar**)

♦ PHRASAL VERBS **cut down (on something)** to reduce the amount or number of something or to do something less ▢ *The doctor told her to cut down on red meat.* **cut someone off** if you are cut off on the telephone, the connection is broken before the call ends **cut someone/something off**
1 to stop people from leaving a place ▢ *The whole town was cut off by the flooding.* **2** to stop the supply of something ▢ *If you don't pay your bill, the electricity will be cut off.* **cut something out** to stop eating or drinking something ▢ *I feel much better since I cut meat out of my diet.*

cut[2] /kʌt/ NOUN [plural **cuts**]
1 an opening or injury made by something sharp ▢ *She's got a nasty cut on her forehead.* ▢ *He made two cuts in the fabric.* (**corte**)
2 a reduction in something ▢ *a price cut* ▢ *job cuts* (**corte**)

cute /kjuːt/ ADJECTIVE [**cuter, cutest**] attractive or pretty ▢ *a cute little puppy* (**engraçadinho, fofo**)

cutlery /ˈkʌtləri/ NOUN, NO PLURAL knives, forks and spoons (**faqueiro**)

cycle[1] /ˈsaɪkəl/ NOUN [plural **cycles**]
1 a series of things that happen one after the other and then start again ▢ *He seems to be trapped in a cycle of stealing and prison.* (**ciclo**)
2 a bicycle (**bicicleta**)

cycle[2] /ˈsaɪkəl/ VERB [**cycles, cycling, cycled**]
to ride a bicycle ▢ *I always cycle to school.* (**andar de bicicleta**)

cyclist /ˈsaɪklɪst/ NOUN [plural **cyclists**] someone who rides a bicycle (**ciclista**)

cyclone /ˈsaɪkləʊn/ NOUN [plural **cyclones**] a large storm that happens in tropical countries, with strong winds moving in a circle (**ciclone**)

cylinder /ˈsɪlɪndə(r)/ NOUN [plural **cylinders**] a solid shape with a circular top and bottom and long straight sides (**cilindro**)

cylindrical /sɪˈlɪndrɪkəl/ ADJECTIVE having a circular top and bottom and long straight sides (**cilíndrico**)

Dd

D ou **d** /di:/ the fourth letter of the alphabet (a quarta letra do alfabeto)

dad ou **Dad** /dæd/ NOUN [plural **dads** or **Dads**] an informal word that means father and that you use for talking to your father □ *Hey Dad, I scored a goal today!* □ *It was really nice of your dad to help.* (papai)

daddy ou **Daddy** /'dædi/ NOUN [plural **daddies** or **Daddies**] a word that children use for talking to or about their father □ *Read me another story, Daddy!* □ *I gave my daddy a big hug.* (papai)

daft /dɑːft/ ADJECTIVE [**dafter, daftest**] silly □ *What a daft thing to do.* □ *Don't be daft – you can't do that!* (ridículo)

dagger /'dægə(r)/ NOUN [plural **daggers**] a small knife that is used as a weapon (punhal)

daily[1] /'deɪli/ ADJECTIVE happening or done every day 🔁 *Exercise is part of my daily routine.* □ *Two tablets is the correct daily dose.* (diária)

daily[2] /'deɪli/ ADVERB every day □ *We have fresh bread delivered daily.* (diariamente)

dairy[1] /'deəri/ ADJECTIVE
1 to do with keeping cows to produce milk 🔁 *a dairy farmer* (leiteria)
2 dairy foods contain milk or are made from milk 🔁 *She can't eat dairy products.* (laticínio)

dairy[2] /'deəri/ NOUN [plural **dairies**] a place where foods such as butter and cheese are made from milk (fábrica de laticínios)

dam /dæm/ NOUN [plural **dams**] a wall across a river that holds a lot of the water back (barragem)

damage[1] /'dæmɪdʒ/ NOUN, NO PLURAL harm that is done by something 🔁 *The storm caused a lot of damage.* □ **+ to** *The storm did some damage to the roof.* (dano)

> Note the verbs that are used with the noun **damage**. Something **causes** damage or **does** damage:
> ✓ *The fire caused a lot of damage.*
> ✗ *The fire made a lot of damage.*

damage[2] /'dæmɪdʒ/ VERB [**damages, damaging, damaged**] to spoil or break something □ *The book was damaged in the post.* (danificar)

> Note that the verb **damage** is used for *things* and not *people*. For people, use **hurt** or **injure**
> □ *The car was badly damaged in the accident.*
> □ *Both men were injured in the accident.*

damp /dæmp/ ADJECTIVE [**damper, dampest**] slightly wet □ *Wipe with a damp cloth.* (úmido)

dance[1] /dɑːns/ VERB [**dances, dancing, danced**] to move your feet and body to music □ *Let's dance!* □ *She danced with her boyfriend all evening.* □ *Will you teach me how to dance the tango?* (dançar)

dance[2] /dɑːns/ NOUN [plural **dances**]
1 when you dance 🔁 *Why don't you have a dance with your dad?* (dança)
2 a particular set of steps that you do to music □ *The first dance we learnt was the waltz.* (dança)
3 a party for dancing (baile)

dancer /'dɑːnsə(r)/ NOUN [plural **dancers**] someone who dances (dançarino)

dancing /'dɑːnsɪŋ/ NOUN, NO PLURAL the activity of moving your feet and body to music □ *I love dancing.* (dança)

danger /'deɪndʒə(r)/ NOUN [plural **dangers**]
1 a situation where something may harm you □ *Danger! Keep out!* (perigo)
2 in danger in a situation where something could harm you □ *He wasn't in danger at any point.* (em perigo)
3 something or someone that may harm you □ **+ of** *the dangers of smoking* □ **+ to** *This man is a serious danger to the public.* (perigo)

dangerous /'deɪndʒərəs/ ADJECTIVE if something is dangerous, it may harm you □ *a dangerous substance* (perigoso)

dangerously /'deɪndʒərəsli/ ADVERB in a dangerous way □ *He was driving dangerously close to the edge.* (perigosamente)

dare /deə(r)/ VERB [**dares, daring, dared**]
1 dare (to) do something to be brave enough to do something □ *Rachel wouldn't dare argue with the boss.* □ *I never thought I'd dare to jump out of a plane.* (desafiar)
2 to ask someone to do something dangerous or frightening 🔁 *I dare you* to climb to the top. (desafiar)

daring   dead

3 How dare you/he, etc. do something! something you say when someone has done something that upsets you very much ☐ *How dare you speak to me like that!* (**como se atreve a [fazer algo]**)
4 Don't you dare! used to tell someone that if they do something you will be very angry with them ☐ *Don't you dare throw that at me!* (**não se atreva!**)

daring /ˈdeərɪŋ/ ADJECTIVE brave ☐ *a daring rescue attempt* (**audacioso**)

dark¹ /dɑːk/ ADJECTIVE [**darker, darkest**]
1 without light ☐ *When we looked outside it was getting dark.* ☐ *All of a sudden it went dark.* (**escuro**)
2 not light in colour and nearer to black than to white ☐ *dark blue* ☐ *Ruth has dark hair.* (**escuro**)

dark² /dɑːk/ NOUN, NO PLURAL
1 where there is no light ☐ *I'm not afraid of the dark.* (**escuridão**)
2 the time when it becomes dark outside ☐ *Don't go out after dark without a torch.* (**escuridão**)

darkness /ˈdɑːknɪs/ NOUN, NO PLURAL where there is no light (**escuridão**)

darling /ˈdɑːlɪŋ/ NOUN [*plural* **darlings**] a word used for talking to someone you love ☐ *What's the matter, darling?* (**querido**)

dart /dɑːt/ VERB [**darts, darting, darted**] to move somewhere fast ☐ *A child darted out of the door as I came in.* (**disparar**)

dash¹ /dæʃ/ VERB [**dashes, dashing, dashed**] to hurry somewhere ☐ *I've got to dash to the shops.* ☐ *Mary came in but then she dashed off again.* (**arremeter**)

dash² /dæʃ/ NOUN [*plural* **dashes**]
1 a line '–' that is sometimes used in writing between parts of a sentence (**travessão**)
2 when you hurry to get somewhere ☐ *The two boys made a dash for the door.* ☐ *In our mad dash to catch the plane we forgot the presents.* (**arremetida**)

data /ˈdeɪtə/ NOUN, NO PLURAL information ☐ *The hospital keeps a lot of personal data on its patients.* ☐ *We collected data over a five-year period.* (**dados**)

database /ˈdeɪtəbeɪs/ NOUN [*plural* **databases**] information that is stored on a computer in an organized form ☐ *Details of known criminals are stored on a national computer database.* (**banco de dados**)

date¹ /deɪt/ NOUN [*plural* **dates**]
1 the number of the day of the month, the month and the year ☐ *The date today is 30 July.* (**data**)
2 a particular day of a particular month and year ☐ *What is your date of birth?* ☐ *Shall we fix/set a date for our next meeting?* (**data**)
3 an arrangement to meet someone that you are having a romantic relationship with or who you may start a romantic relationship with ☐ *Polly's got another date with Chris tonight.* (**encontro**)
4 a small, brown, sticky fruit (**tâmara**)

date² /deɪt/ VERB [**dates, dating, dated**]
to write a date on a letter or other document ☐ *The letter was dated 3rd May.* (**datar**)

2 to have a romantic relationship with someone and meet them regularly ☐ *How long have you and Kelly been dating?* (**namorar**)

daughter /ˈdɔːtə(r)/ NOUN [*plural* **daughters**] someone's female child ☐ *She was the daughter of a poet.* ☐ *Dave and Maria have a new baby daughter.* (**filha**)

daughter-in-law /ˈdɔːtərɪnˌlɔː/ NOUN [*plural* **daughters-in-law**] your son's wife ☐ *Have you met my daughter-in-law, Sandra?* (**nora**)

dawn /dɔːn/ NOUN [*plural* **dawns**] the beginning of the day, when it gets light (**alvorada**)

day /deɪ/ NOUN [*plural* **days**]
1 the twenty-four hours between one midnight (= 12 am) and another ☐ *There are 365 days in a year.* ☐ *I do five hours' work a day.* ☐ *I try to do some exercise every day.* (**dia**)
2 the time when there is light from the sun, or when you are awake ☐ *We spent the whole day on the beach.* ☐ *I spent all day cleaning the house.* ☐ *Did you have a good day at work?* (**dia**)
3 a time or period ☐ *in my grandfather's day* ☐ *In those days we didn't have computers.* (**tempo**)
4 one day used to talk about something that happened in the past or something that will happen in the future ☐ *One day I came home to discover my car had been stolen.* ☐ *I hope to have my own business one day.* (**algum dia**)
5 the other day a few days ago ☐ *I saw Julio the other day.* (**outro dia**)
6 these days used to talk about what things are like now ☐ *These days I don't play much tennis.* (**hoje em dia**)

daylight /ˈdeɪlaɪt/ NOUN, NO PLURAL
1 the light that comes from the sun during the day ☐ *In the daylight she looked pale.* (**luz do dia**)
2 the part of the day when there is light ☐ *I'd like to get home in daylight.* (**luz do dia**)

day-to-day /ˌdeɪtəˈdeɪ/ ADJECTIVE happening or done regularly, every day ☐ *These attacks now happen on a day-to-day basis* (= every day). ☐ *Diane is in charge of the day-to-day running of the department.* (**diário**)

dead¹ /ded/ ADJECTIVE
1 not now living ☐ *I could see he was dead.* ☐ *He dropped dead* (= died suddenly) *on the tennis court.* ☐ *a dead body* (**morto**)
2 no longer working ☐ *My phone's gone dead.* ☐ *The batteries are dead.* (**inerte**)

dead² /ded/ NOUN **the dead** people who have died (**os mortos**)

dead³ /ded/ ADVERB
1 exactly ☐ *They were standing dead in the centre of the circle.* (**completamente**)
2 an informal word meaning very ☐ *dead boring/easy* (**muito**)

deadline /ˈdedlaɪn/ NOUN [plural **deadlines**] the time when something must be finished ▫ *You'll miss the deadline if you delay.* (prazo final)

deadly /ˈdedli/ ADJECTIVE [**deadlier, deadliest**] able to kill ▫ *a deadly weapon* ▫ *a deadly poison* (mortal)

deaf /def/ ADJECTIVE [**deafer, deafest**] not able to hear, or not able to hear well ▫ *Grandma is getting a bit deaf.* (surdo)
• **deafness** /ˈdefnɪs/ NOUN, NO PLURAL being deaf (surdez)

deal¹ /diːl/ NOUN [plural **deals**]
1 an agreement, especially in business or politics ▫ *make/strike a deal* ▫ *We are about to sign a deal with a major record producer.* ▫ *I got a good deal* (= a cheap price) *on my new car.* (transação)
2 a great deal a large amount ▫ *We spent a great deal of money on solar panels.* (uma boa quantia)

deal² /diːl/ VERB [**deals, dealing, dealt**] to give cards to players in a game ▫ *You deal the cards this time.* (cartear)
◆ PHRASAL VERB **deal with something/someone**
1 to take action, especially to solve a problem or to get something done ▫ *New houses were built to deal with the problem of homelessness.* ▫ *You take the boy to another room – I'll deal with his father.* ▫ *I need to deal with all these letters.* **2** to learn to accept a difficult situation ▫ *I'm finding it hard to deal with his death.* **3** to be about a particular subject ▫ *The programme deals with the true cost of cheap labour.*

dealer /ˈdiːlə(r)/ NOUN [plural **dealers**] someone who buys and sells things ▫ *an antiques dealer* (negociante)

dear¹ /dɪə(r)/ ADJECTIVE [**dearer, dearest**]
1 The word you use with a name or title at the beginning of a letter ▫ *Dear Max* ▫ *Dear Sir* (caro, prezado)
2 loved ▫ *a very dear friend* (querido)
3 expensive ▫ *The shoes were beautiful but very dear.* (caro)

dear² /dɪə(r)/ EXCLAMATION **Oh dear!** something you say when something slightly bad has happened ▫ *Oh dear! I'm late again.* (Oh, meu Deus!)

death /deθ/ NOUN [plural **deaths**] the time when a person or animal stops living ▫ *He wrote this just before his death in 1875.* ▫ + **from** *The number of deaths from cancer is decreasing all the time.* ▫ *The cause of death was unknown.* (morte)

death penalty /ˈdeθ ˌpenəlti/ NOUN [plural **death penalties**] when someone is killed as a legal punishment for a crime (pena de morte)

debate¹ /dɪˈbeɪt/ NOUN [plural **debates**] a big or formal discussion about something ▫ *a parliamentary debate* (debate)

debate² /dɪˈbeɪt/ VERB [**debates, debating, debated**] to have a debate about something (debater)

debris /ˈdeɪbriː/ NOUN, NO PLURAL the parts of something that has broken into pieces ▫ *Debris from the crashed aircraft lay all around.* (escombros)

debt /det/ NOUN [plural **debts**]
1 an amount of money that one person owes to another ▫ *I always pay off my debts.* (dívida)
2 in debt owing someone money (em dívida)

decade /ˈdekeɪd/ NOUN [plural **decades**] a period of ten years ▫ *This is the first decade of the twenty-first century.* (década)

decay¹ /dɪˈkeɪ/ NOUN, NO PLURAL when something becomes rotten or breaks into pieces ▫ *This toothpaste helps prevent tooth decay.* (deterioração)

decay² /dɪˈkeɪ/ VERB [**decays, decaying, decayed**] to go rotten or break into pieces ▫ *The bins were full of decaying food.* (deteriorar)

deceive /dɪˈsiːv/ VERB [**deceives, deceiving, deceived**] to make someone believe something that is not true ▫ + **by** *Don't be deceived by his friendly manner.* ▫ + **into** *She was deceived into thinking she'd won a holiday.* ▫ *If she thinks Keith actually loves her, she's deceiving herself.* (enganar)

December /dɪˈsembə(r)/ NOUN [plural **Decembers**] the twelfth month of the year, after November and before January ▫ *Her birthday is in December.* (dezembro)

decent /ˈdiːsənt/ ADJECTIVE
1 acceptable or good enough ▫ *Is there a decent butcher's near here?* ▫ *I think they have a decent chance of winning.* (decente)
2 good, honest and of a high moral standard ▫ *He's a very decent bloke.* (decente)

decide /dɪˈsaɪd/ VERB [**decides, deciding, decided**] to choose what you are going to do ▫ + **to do something** *Greg decided to buy a computer.* ▫ + **that** *She decided that she would go with him.* ▫ *I can't decide what to do.* (decidir)

decimal¹ /ˈdesɪməl/ ADJECTIVE a decimal system is a way of counting based on the number ten (decimal)

decimal² /ˈdesɪməl/ NOUN [plural **decimals**] a fraction (= number that is less than a whole number) written as a decimal point (.) followed by numbers. A mathematics word ▫ *A half, written a a decimal, is 0.5.* (decimal, decimais)

decision /dɪˈsɪʒ ən/ NOUN [plural **decisions**] when you decide something ▫ *I will let you know when I have made my decision.* ▫ *Finally we took the difficult decision to sell the house.* ▫ *Most of us think the directors came to the right decision.* (decisão)

> **THESAURUS:** When you choose what you are going to do, you make a decision. A **conclusion** is a decision that you make after you have thought about it very carefully. You also write a **conclusion** at the end of an essay. A **verdict** is the decision that a jury or a judge makes in court when they decide if someone is guilty of a crime.

deck

deck /dek/ NOUN [plural **decks**]
1 the flat part that you walk on on the outside of a boat □ *Let's take a walk up on deck.* (**convés**)
2 one of the levels of a boat or bus 🔊 *There are more seats on the upper deck.* (**piso**)

declaration /ˌdekləˈreɪʃən/ NOUN [plural **declarations**] an announcement □ *a declaration of war* (**declaração**)

declare /dɪˈkleə(r)/ VERB [**declares, declaring, declared**] to announce something firmly or officially 🔊 *Britain declared war on Germany.* □ *She suddenly declared that she was leaving.* (**declarar**)

decline /dɪˈklaɪn/ VERB [**declines, declining, declined**]
1 to become weaker or smaller □ *His popularity has declined sharply.* (**declinar**)
2 a formal word that means to refuse □ *I'm afraid I must decline your kind invitation.* □ *The minister declined to comment.* (**recusar**)

decorate /ˈdekəreɪt/ VERB [**decorates, decorating, decorated**]
1 to put things on or around something to make it look more attractive □ *We'll decorate the cake with sugar roses.* (**decorar**)
2 to put paint or paper on the inside walls of a room □ *We've just decorated the dining room.* (**decorar**)

decoration /ˌdekəˈreɪʃən/ NOUN [plural **decorations**]
1 when you add something to make something more attractive, or the thing you add 🔊 *Christmas/ party decorations* (**decoração**)
2 *no plural* putting paint or paper on the inside walls of a room □ *The whole house is in need of decoration.* (**decoração**)

decorator /ˈdekəreɪtə(r)/ NOUN [plural **decorators**] someone whose job is to decorate rooms (**decorador**)

decrease¹ /dɪˈkriːs/ VERB [**decreases, decreasing, decreased**] to make something less or to become less □ *A healthy diet helps to decrease the risk of heart disease.* □ *Josh's interest in football decreased as he got older.* (**diminuir**)

decrease² /ˈdiːkriːs/ NOUN [plural **decreases**] an amount by which something is smaller □ *+ in There was a decrease in violent crime in the area.* □ *+ of They saw a decrease of 5% in sales.* (**diminuição**)

dedicate /ˈdedɪkeɪt/ VERB [**dedicates, dedicating, dedicated**] to spend a particular amount of time doing something □ *She dedicated her whole life to music.* (**dedicar**)

deep¹ /diːp/ ADJECTIVE [**deeper, deepest**]
1 going a long way down from the top □ *Is the pond very deep?* □ *The sea was 30 metres deep at that point.* (**profundo**)
2 deep feelings and emotions are very strong □ *I have a deep dislike of dogs.* (**profundo**)
3 deep colours are strong and dark □ *I painted the walls deep blue.* (**intenso**)
4 a deep sound is very low 🔊 *a deep voice* (**grave**)
5 a deep breath a big breath that fills your lungs □ *Take a deep breath then jump into the water.* (**respiração profunda**)

deep² /diːp/ ADVERB [**deeper, deepest**] a long way from the top of something □ *They swam deep beneath the ocean.* (**profundamente**)

deeply /ˈdiːpli/ ADVERB
1 very much □ *I deeply regret my actions.* (**profundamente**)
2 if you breathe deeply, you take a lot of air into your lungs (**profundamente**)

deer /dɪə(r)/ NOUN [plural **deer**] a large wild animal that has antlers (= parts like branches) on the head of the males (**veado**)

defeat¹ /dɪˈfiːt/ VERB [**defeats, defeating, defeated**] to beat someone in a war or competition 🔊 *We shall defeat the enemy and restore peace.* □ *The visiting team were defeated 3-0.* (**derrotar**)

defeat² /dɪˈfiːt/ NOUN [plural **defeats**] a game, fight, war, etc. that you have lost 🔊 *The king suffered a defeat by the rebel army.* 🔊 *England had another heavy defeat in the cricket.* (**derrota**)

defect¹ /ˈdiːfekt/ NOUN [plural **defects**] a fault that stops something from working correctly □ *He has a serious heart defect.*

> **THESAURUS:** A **defect** is a problem or a fault which stops something from working properly. For example, you can have a defect in your body or in a machine. A **flaw** is a bad quality in a person or a thing. You might talk about a flaw in someone's character or a flaw in the design of a building. An **error** or a **mistake** is something wrong that you do. Usually, a mistake is smaller or less important than an error.

defect² /dɪˈfekt/ VERB [**defects, defecting, defected**] to leave a country or organization and go to live or work in an enemy country or organization □ *The spy defected to the United States.* (**desertar**)

• **defection** /dɪˈfekʃən/ NOUN [plural **defections**] when someone defects □ *There were three more defections when the athletes were in Canada.* (**deserção**)

defence /dɪˈfens/ NOUN [plural **defences**]
1 *no plural* the act of protecting someone or something from attack, harm, criticism, etc. 🔊 *His bodyguards leaped to his defence.* 🔊 *The prime minister spoke out in defence of the chancellor.* (**defesa**)
2 something that protects something or someone from attack, harm, criticism, etc. □ *They have built massive defences against the tide.* (**defesa**)

defend /dɪˈfend/ VERB [defends, defending, defended] to protect someone or something from attack, harm, criticism, etc. □ + *against* Heavy armour on the tanks defends them against gunfire. □ Kim always defends his brother if people say he's too quiet. (**defender**)

defense /dɪˈfens/ NOUN [plural **defenses**] the US spelling of **defence** (**defesa [EUA]**)

define /dɪˈfaɪn/ VERB [defines, defining, defined] to show or explain exactly what something is □ Researchers have defined the problem. □ The aims of the project were poorly defined. (**definir**)

definite /ˈdefɪnɪt/ ADJECTIVE certain □ It's not definite, but the wedding will probably be in August. □ I've noticed a definite improvement in his condition. (**definitivo**)

definite article /ˌdefɪnɪt ˈɑːtɪkəl/ NOUN [plural **definite articles**] the name used in grammar for the word **the** (**artigo definido**)

> There are two kinds of article in English grammar: **the** is the *definite article* and **a** or **an** is the *indefinite article*.

definitely /ˈdefɪnɪtli/ ADVERB certainly □ We'll definitely be back by 10 o'clock. □ 'Do you think she'll pass the exam?' 'Oh yes, definitely'. □ I definitely want to go back there. (**definitivamente**)

definition /ˌdefɪˈnɪʃən/ NOUN [plural **definitions**] an explanation of the meaning of a word or phrase □ Look up the definition of 'magic' in your dictionary. (**definição**)

defy /dɪˈfaɪ/ VERB [defies, defying, defied] to refuse to obey someone or something □ Defying his mother, he left the house. (**desafiar**)

degree /dɪˈgriː/ NOUN [plural **degrees**]
1 a unit for measuring temperature, shown by the symbol ° □ It's 30° (degrees) here today. (**grau**)
2 a unit for measuring angles, shown by the symbol ° □ An angle of 90 ° (degrees) is a right angle. (**grau**)
3 a qualification that students can study for at a university or college □ He's got a degree in German. 🔳 He *did* his *degree* at Cambridge. (**diploma**)

delay¹ /dɪˈleɪ/ NOUN [plural **delays**] the extra time you have to wait if something happens later than expected □ There was a delay of half an hour before take-off. 🔳 Please return to your seats *without delay*. (**atraso**)

delay² /dɪˈleɪ/ VERB [delays, delaying, delayed]
1 to do something or make something happen later than was planned or expected □ We delayed our holidays until after the strike. □ Buy now! Don't delay! (**atrasar**)
2 to make someone or something late □ I was delayed by the arrival of an unexpected visitor. (**atrasar**)

> THESAURUS: To **delay** or **postpone** something means to decide to do it later than planned. You could **postpone** a meeting or a holiday, for example. **Put off** has the same meaning, but is less formal. To **cancel** something means to stop something from happening as planned. You might **cancel** a football match if it is snowing, for example. **Call off** has the same meaning, but is less formal.

delegate /ˈdelɪgət/ NOUN [plural **delegates**] someone who goes to a meeting to represent someone else (**delegado, representante**)

delete /dɪˈliːt/ VERB [deletes, deleting, deleted]
1 to remove something from a piece of writing □ Someone has deleted your name from the list. □ I think we should delete the last paragraph. (**suprimir**)
2 to remove something such as a file that is stored on a computer. A computing word □ I've accidentally deleted all their addresses. (**deletar**)

deliberate¹ /dɪˈlɪbərət/ ADJECTIVE done on purpose □ He said it was an accident, but I'm sure it was deliberate. 🔳 It was a *deliberate attempt* to confuse his opponent. (**deliberado**)

deliberate² /dɪˈlɪbəreɪt/ VERB [deliberates, deliberating, deliberated] to think carefully about something □ They deliberated for three hours over their decision. (**deliberar**)

deliberately /dɪˈlɪbərətli/ ADVERB on purpose □ You deliberately dropped that so that you wouldn't have to eat it! (**deliberadamente**)

delicate /ˈdelɪkət/ ADJECTIVE
1 easily damaged □ This china is very delicate. 🔳 We must respect the *delicate balance* between humans and nature. (**delicado**)
2 not strong 🔳 a *delicate flavour* 🔳 a *delicate fragrance* (**delicado**)

delicious /dɪˈlɪʃəs/ ADJECTIVE tasting very good 🔳 Mum's homemade soup *tastes absolutely delicious*. □ That was a delicious meal. (**delicioso**)

delight¹ /dɪˈlaɪt/ NOUN [plural **delights**] great pleasure □ The baby squealed with delight when he saw his mother. □ It was such a delight to see her. (**deleite**)

delight² /dɪˈlaɪt/ VERB [delights, delighting, delighted] to please someone very much (**deleitar-se, encantar**)

delighted /dɪˈlaɪtɪd/ ADJECTIVE very pleased 🔳 That's great news – I'm *absolutely delighted!* □ + *to do something* We'd be delighted to come to the party. (**encantado**)

delightful /dɪˈlaɪtful/ ADJECTIVE very pleasant □ What a delightful surprise! (**encantador**)
• **delightfully** /dɪˈlaɪtfuli/ ADVERB in a delightful way □ a delightfully funny book (**deliciosamente**)

deliver /dɪˈlɪvə(r)/ VERB [delivers, delivering, delivered]

1 to take something, especially letters, packages or something you have bought, to a place □ *We're delivering leaflets to all the houses in this area.* □ *Our new washing machine is being delivered next week.* (entregar)
2 if someone delivers a baby, they help the baby to be born (fazer o parto)

> **THESAURUS:** To deliver something means to take it to a place. Deliver is usually used to talk about letters, parcels and things that you have bought. If you **send** something to a place, you arrange for it to go there. For example, you can **send** a letter or an email. To **supply** something means to provide it. For example, you can say that a company **supplies** a shop with bread. If you **give** someone something, you let them have it.

delivery /dɪˈlɪvəri/ NOUN [plural deliveries]
1 no plural when something is delivered □ *The price includes free delivery.* (entrega)
2 something that has been delivered or will be delivered □ *We are expecting a delivery of bricks.* (entrega)
3 when a baby is born □ *It was a straightforward delivery.* (parto)

demand¹ /dɪˈmɑːnd/ VERB [demands, demanding, demanded]
to ask for something in a forceful way that shows you do not expect to be refused □ *They are demanding the release of all political prisoners.* □ *He demanded an apology from the journalist.* □ + **to do something** *I demanded to see the manager.* □ + **that** *The group is demanding that the law should be changed.* (exigir)

demand² /dɪˈmɑːnd/ NOUN [plural demands]
1 when someone asks for something in a very forceful way □ + **for** *I gave in to his demands for a new computer.* □ *Employers say they can't meet the union's demands.* (exigência)
2 in demand wanted by a lot of people □ *His skills are in demand all over the world.* (solicitado)

democracy /dɪˈmɒkrəsi/ NOUN [plural democracies]
a form of government or a country where people elect their leaders □ *The allies plan to introduce democracy to the country.* □ *We live in a democracy.* (democracia)

democratic /ˌdeməˈkrætɪk/ ADJECTIVE
based on a form of government where people elect their leaders □ *democratic elections* (democrata)

demolish /dɪˈmɒlɪʃ/ VERB [demolishes, demolishing, demolished]
to destroy something, especially a building □ *The flats will be demolished immediately.* (demolir)

demolition /ˌdeməˈlɪʃən/ NOUN, NO PLURAL
when something is destroyed, especially a building □ *We watched the demolition of the old sports centre.* (demolição)

demon /ˈdiːmən/ NOUN [plural demons]
an evil spirit (demônio)

demonstrate /ˈdemənstreɪt/ VERB [demonstrates, demonstrating, demonstrated]
1 to show that something exists or is true □ *Her success demonstrates that women can do well in business.* (demonstrar)
2 to show someone how to do something or how something works □ *Can you demonstrate how the ice cream maker works?* (demonstrar)
3 to march or stand with a group of other people to show that you support or disagree with something □ *They are demonstrating against the war.* (manifestar[-se], protestar)

demonstration /ˌdemənˈstreɪʃən/ NOUN [plural demonstrations]
1 an event where a group of people stand or march together to show that they support or disagree with something □ *Supporters of the prisoners held a demonstration outside the court.* □ *Over 5,000 people took part in the demonstration.* □ + **against** *They organized a peaceful demonstration against the war.* (manifestação)
2 when someone shows you how to do something or how something works □ *a cookery demonstration* □ *The sales assistant gave us a demonstration of the phone's features.* (demonstração)

den /den/ NOUN [plural **dens**] the home of a wild animal □ *a lion's den* (covil)

denial /dɪˈnaɪəl/ NOUN [plural **denials**] when you say that something is not true □ *He repeated his denial of his guilt.* (recusa)

denim /ˈdenɪm/ NOUN, NO PLURAL a strong cotton cloth, usually blue, that is used to make clothes □ *Joe was wearing a denim jacket.* (brim)

dense /dens/ ADJECTIVE [denser, densest]
1 containing a lot of people or things very close together □ *a dense forest* (denso)
2 thick and difficult to see through □ *Dense fog filled the valley.* (denso)

dent /dent/ NOUN [plural **dents**] a hollow in a hard surface where it has been hit □ *There's a dent in the car bumper.* (amassado)

dental /ˈdentəl/ ADJECTIVE to do with teeth □ *Children get free dental care.* (dentário)

dentist /ˈdentɪst/ NOUN [plural dentists]
someone whose job is to look after people's teeth (dentista)

deny /dɪˈnaɪ/ VERB [denies, denying, denied]
to say that something is not true □ + **that** *Nina denied that she had stolen the bag.* □ + **ing** *He denies doing anything wrong.* □ *She denied any involvement in the crime.* (negar)

> **THESAURUS:** To deny doing something means to say that something is not true. For example, a criminal might deny committing a crime. To **oppose** means to disagree with someone's plans or ideas and try to stop or change them. For example, a group of people might **oppose** plans to build a factory in their village. To **disagree** means to have a different opinion from someone else.

depart /dɪˈpɑːt/ VERB [departs, departing, departed] to leave a place, especially to start a journey □ *Flight BA123 is now departing.* □ *+ from The Oxford train departs from platform 8.* (partir)

department /dɪˈpɑːtmənt/ NOUN [plural departments] a part of a school, shop, business or government that deals with a particular subject or area of work □ *the sales department* □ *The college has a very fine modern languages department.* (departamento)

department store /dɪˈpɑːtmənt ˌstɔː(r)/ NOUN [plural department stores] a large shop that has different departments which sell different types of product (loja de departamento)

departure /dɪˈpɑːtʃə(r)/ NOUN [plural departures] when someone or something leaves a place □ *All departures are shown on the timetable.* □ *We were shocked by her sudden departure from the school.* (partida)

depend /dɪˈpend/ VERB [depends, depending, depended] **it/that depends** used to say that you are not certain because something else affects the situati on □ *'Do you want to come to the film?' 'It depends how late it goes on'.* □ *'Are you going to invite Rick?' 'That depends. I think he's still angry with me.'* (depender)

◆ PHRASAL VERB **depend on someone/something**
1 to need the help of someone or something □ *Millions of children depend on charity for their educat ion.* □ *The farm depends on government subsidie s.* **2** if what happens depends on something else, it is affected by it and may change because of it □ *A lot will depend on how well you do in your exams.* **3** to be able to trust someone to do what you want or need □ *I can depend on my family to help me.*

dependant /dɪˈpendənt/ NOUN [plural dependants] someone whose food, clothes, house, etc. you have to pay for □ *Fill in the names of all your dependants.* (dependente)

dependent¹ /dɪˈpendənt/ ADJECTIVE needing something or someone to live or exist □ *She's totally dependent on her car to get around.* (dependente)

dependent² /dɪˈpendənt/ NOUN [plural dependents] the US spelling of **dependant** (dependente [EUA])

deport /dɪˈpɔːt/ VERB [deports, deporting, deported] to force a foreign person to leave a country □ *He will be deported when he finishes his prison sentence.* (deportar, expulsar)

deposit¹ /dɪˈpɒzɪt/ NOUN [plural deposits]
1 part of the price of something that you pay before you buy the thing, and that you will lose if you do not buy it 🔲 *We've put down a deposit on a flat.* (depósito)
2 an amount of money that you pay into a bank account 🔲 *He made several large deposits.* (depósito)
3 an amount of money that you pay when you rent something, that you get back if you return the thing without any damage (depósito, sinal)

deposit² /dɪˈpɒzɪt/ VERB [deposits, depositing, deposited] to put money into a bank account □ *I'm hoping to deposit £50 a month into a savings account.* (depositar)

depot /ˈdepəʊ/ NOUN [plural depots]
1 a place where vehicles like buses or trains are kept when they are not being used (garagem)
2 a building where goods are stored □ *a weapons depot* (armazém)

depressed /dɪˈprest/ ADJECTIVE unhappy □ *I felt a bit depressed about how much weight I'd put on.* (deprimido)

deprive /dɪˈpraɪv/ VERB [deprives, depriving, deprived] to take something important or necessary away from someone □ *She's been deprived of sleep for days.* (privar)

depth /depθ/ NOUN [plural depths]
1 the distance from the top to the bottom of something □ *This instrument measures the depth of the water.* □ *+ of We dug down to a depth of around 2 metres.* □ *The swimming pool was only 2 metres in depth.* (profundidade)
2 in depth in a lot of detail □ *We discussed the situation in great depth.* (a fundo)

deputy /ˈdepjuti/ NOUN [plural deputies] someone who has the job that is next in importance to another job □ *He is deputy sales manager.* (substituto)

descend /dɪˈsend/ VERB [descends, descending, descended] to go or climb down. A formal word □ *They descended the stairs.* □ *The road descended steeply.* (descer)

descendant /dɪˈsendənt/ NOUN [plural descendants] someone who is related to a person who lived in the past □ *a direct descendant of Genghis Khan* (descendente)

descent /dɪˈsent/ NOUN [plural descents] a movement down □ *the descent of the mountain* □ *The plane started its descent.* (descida)

describe /dɪˈskraɪb/ VERB [describes, describing, described] to say what happened or what someone or something is like □ *A reporter described the scene in detail.* □ *+ question word Can you describe what you saw?* □ *+ as He described his daughter as kind and caring.* 🔲 *She describes herself as a feminist.* (descrever)

description /dɪˈskrɪpʃən/ NOUN [plural descriptions] when you describe someone or something □ *+ of There's a description of the hotel* 🔲 *She gave a detailed description of the man.* 🔲 *He fitted the general description of the attacker* (= his appearance was the same as what was described). 🔲 *a job description* (descrição)

desert

desert¹ /dɪˈzɜːt/ VERB [deserts, deserting, deserted] to go away and leave someone or something, especially the army ☐ The soldier was shot for deserting. ☐ She deserted her young family. (abandonar, desertar)

desert² /ˈdezət/ NOUN [plural deserts] an area of land where it rains very little so the ground is very dry ☐ the Sahara desert (deserto)

deserve /dɪˈzɜːv/ VERB [deserves, deserving, deserved] if you deserve something, you should have it because of your behaviour ☐ I'm pleased Molly won the prize – she deserves it. ☐ + to do something Samir deserves to be promoted. (merecer)

design¹ /dɪˈzaɪn/ VERB [designs, designing, designed] to plan something before it is built or made ☐ The concert hall was designed by architect Frank Gehry. ☐ She designs clothes for a top fashion store. ☐ We design software to control robots. (projetar)

design² /dɪˈzaɪn/ NOUN [plural designs]
1 a plan or drawing of something that could be made ☐ + for a design for a new racing car ☐ She has won awards for her designs. (desenho)
2 a pattern ☐ They wore dresses in bright floral designs. (padrão)

designer¹ /dɪˈzaɪnə(r)/ NOUN [plural designers] someone whose job is to design things ☐ a fashion designer ☐ a web designer (projetista, desenhista)

designer² /dɪˈzaɪnə(r)/ ADJECTIVE expensive and fashionable and made by a famous company ☐ designer clothes ☐ designer sunglasses (designer)

desire¹ /dɪˈzaɪə(r)/ NOUN [plural desires] a strong feeling of wanting something ☐ He had a burning desire (= very much wanted) to become a doctor. ☐ We respect his desire for privacy. (desejo)

desire² /dɪˈzaɪə(r)/ VERB [desires, desiring, desired] to want something very much. A formal word ☐ You can have any model you desire. (desejar)

desk /desk/ NOUN [plural desks] a table for writing or working at ☐ Andrew sat at his desk. ☐ There was a big pile of papers on her desk. (escrivaninha)

desktop /ˈdesktɒp/ NOUN [plural desktops] a computer screen that shows the icons (= small pictures) for programs you can use. A computing word. (área de trabalho)

despair /dɪˈspeə(r)/ NOUN, NO PLURAL a feeling of having no hope ☐ We were in deep despair. ☐ There's a growing sense of despair among local people. (desespero)

desperate /ˈdespərət/ ADJECTIVE
1 feeling very worried and that you will do anything to improve your situation ☐ He made a desperate attempt to escape. (desesperado)
2 needing something very much ☐ Farmers are desperate for workers. ☐ He was desperate to win. (desesperado)

despise /dɪˈspaɪz/ VERB [despises, despising, despised] to hate someone or something very much ☐ The two men despised each other. (desprezar)

determined D

despite /dɪˈspaɪt/ PREPOSITION used to say that something happens or is true, although something else makes it seem unlikely ☐ Despite the rain, we enjoyed the picnic. ☐ I think that she'll be very good, despite the fact that she doesn't have much experience. ☐ + ing The team remained positive, despite losing their first two games. (apesar de)

dessert /dɪˈzɜːt/ NOUN [plural desserts] sweet food eaten at the end of a meal ☐ We had ice cream for dessert. (sobremesa)

destination /ˌdestɪˈneɪʃən/ NOUN [plural destinations] the place someone is travelling to ☐ We were very tired when we finally reached our destination. ☐ The town is a popular tourist destination. (destino)

destroy /dɪˈstrɔɪ/ VERB [destroys, destroying, destroyed] to damage something so badly that it no longer exists or cannot be used ☐ Thousands of homes were destroyed by the earthquake. ☐ A fire destroyed dozens of paintings at the museum. (destruir)

destruction /dɪˈstrʌkʃən/ NOUN, NO PLURAL when something is destroyed ☐ + of We need to stop the destruction of the rainforest. ☐ The storms caused widespread destruction. (destruição)

detail /ˈdiːteɪl/ NOUN [plural details]
1 a small part, fact, or piece of information about something ☐ + of They provided details of the plans. ☐ + about We learnt more details about the incident. ☐ For further details, see our website. ☐ She didn't give any details. (detalhe)
2 in detail including all the information or facts about something ☐ She described in detail what had happened. ☐ We need to examine it in detail. (detalhadamente)

detect /dɪˈtekt/ VERB [detects, detecting, detected] to discover something that is difficult to find ☐ The dogs are trained to detect explosives. ☐ The test can detect cancer at an early stage. (detectar)

detective /dɪˈtektɪv/ NOUN [plural detectives] someone whose job is to try to find out information about a crime ☐ a private detective ☐ a retired police detective ☐ She told detectives that she'd seen a man leaving the building. (detetive)

deteriorate /dɪˈtɪəriəreɪt/ VERB [deteriorates, deteriorating, deteriorated] to get worse ☐ Joe's health is deteriorating rapidly. (deteriorar)

determination /dɪˌtɜːmɪˈneɪʃən/ NOUN, NO PLURAL a strong feeling that you want to do something, even when it is difficult ☐ They showed great determination. ☐ + to do something He has a determination to win. (determinação)

determined /dɪˈtɜːmɪnd/ ADJECTIVE having or showing determination ☐ + to do something The team was determined to finish first. ☐ She's a very determined young woman. 🔁 He's made a *determined effort* to lose weight. (**determinado**)

detonate /ˈdetəneɪt/ VERB [**detonates, detonating, detonated**] to explode or to make something explode ☐ The bomb was detonated from across the street. (**detonar**)

devastate /ˈdevəsteɪt/ VERB [**devastates, devastating, devastated**] to destroy something or damage it very badly ☐ The storm devastated much of the city. (**devastar**)

devastated /ˈdevəsteɪtɪd/ ADJECTIVE
1 very shocked and upset ☐ We were absolutely devastated by the news. (**arrasar**)
2 completely destroyed ☐ The minister visited the devastated area. (**devastar**)

devastating /ˈdevəsteɪtɪŋ/ ADJECTIVE
1 making someone very shocked and upset ☐ *devastating news* (**devastador**)
2 causing a lot of damage ☐ *devastating floods* (**devastador**)

develop /dɪˈveləp/ VERB [**develops, developing, developed**]
1 to grow or change, or to make something grow bigger, better or more advanced ☐ The young animals develop very quickly. ☐ **+ into** The eggs develop into adult insects. ☐ There are plans to develop tourism in the area. ☐ The process has developed over time. (**desenvolver**)
2 to design and create something new ☐ Researchers are developing new technologies. ☐ We need to develop strategies to deal with this problem. (**desenvolver**)
3 to start to happen or exist ☐ The disease develops gradually. ☐ A close friendship developed between the two women. (**desenvolver**)
4 to make a photograph on a film into a picture (**revelar**)

developing /dɪˈveləpɪŋ/ ADJECTIVE
1 a developing country is quite poor and its economy is not very advanced (**em desenvolvimento**)
2 in the process of happening or growing ☐ We're reporting on two developing news stories. (**em desenvolvimento**)

development /dɪˈveləpmənt/ NOUN [*plural* **developments**]
1 when something becomes bigger, better or more advanced 🔁 There has been rapid *economic development*. ☐ **+ of** The condition affects the normal development of the brain. (**desenvolvimento**)
2 when something new is created ☐ **+ of** This research may aid the development of new treatments. ☐ The project is still in the early stages of development. 🔁 *New developments* in mobile phone technology have made communication easier. (**avanço**)

device /dɪˈvaɪs/ NOUN [*plural* **devices**] a tool or piece of equipment ☐ *a device for cleaning keyboards* (**instrumento**)

> **THESAURUS:** A **tool** is a thing that you use to do a particular job. Hammers and drills are **tools**. A **device** is a tool or a piece of equipment that you use to do something. For example, a remote control is a device for changing the television channel. An **instrument** is a tool that you use for doing a particular task, particularly in science or medicine.

devil /ˈdevəl/ NOUN [*plural* **devils**]
1 The Devil the most powerful evil spirit in some religions (**diabo**)
2 an evil spirit (**demônio**)

devise /dɪˈvaɪz/ VERB [**devises, devising, devised**] to design a plan or way of doing something 🔁 We need to *devise a plan*. 🔁 He *devised* a *method of measuring earthquakes*. (**inventar**)

devote /dɪˈvəʊt/ (**dedicar**)
◆ PHRASAL VERB [**devotes, devoting, devoted**]
devote yourself to someone/something to give all your time and interest to someone or something ☐ She devoted herself to helping the poor. (**dedicar**)

diabetes /ˌdaɪəˈbiːtiːz/ NOUN, NO PLURAL a serious illness in which your body cannot control the amount of sugar in your blood (**diabetes**)

diagnose /ˌdaɪəgˈnəʊz/ VERB [**diagnoses, diagnosing, diagnosed**] to decide what is wrong with a person or a piece of equipment ☐ She was diagnosed with cancer last year. ☐ It's important to diagnose the disease early. ☐ An engineer diagnosed the problem and fixed it. (**diagnosticar**)

diagram /ˈdaɪəgræm/ NOUN [*plural* **diagrams**] a drawing that explains something 🔁 He *drew a diagram* of the building. (**diagrama**)

dial¹ /ˈdaɪəl/ NOUN [*plural* **dials**]
1 the round part on a clock or a machine that shows the time or a measurement (**mostrador**)
2 a round control on a radio or other machine that you turn to operate it ☐ *I turned the radio dial.* (**mostrador**)

dial² /ˈdaɪəl/ VERB [**dials, dialling**/US **dialing, dialled**/US **dialed**] to call a telephone number 🔁 She picked up the phone and *dialled* the *number*. ☐ In an emergency, dial 999. (**discar**)

> **THESAURUS:** When you **dial** a telephone number, you put the number into your telephone and start making a call. If you **call** someone, **ring** someone, or **phone** someone, you make a telephone call to them. These words all have the same meaning. When you put the phone down at the end of your conversation, you **hang up**.

dialogue /ˈdaɪəlɒg/ NOUN [*plural* **dialogues**] the words or conversation of characters in a book, film, etc. (**diálogo**)

diameter /daɪˈæmɪtə(r)/ NOUN [plural **diameters**] a straight line from one side of a circle to the other through its centre, or this measurement. A mathematics word ▫ *the diameter of the pipe* (**diâmetro**)

diamond /ˈdaɪəmənd/ NOUN [plural **diamonds**]
1 a very hard, clear stone that is very valuable ▫ *a diamond ring* (**diamante**)
2 a four-sided pointed shape (2) (**ouros**)
3 diamonds one of the four types of playing card, with a diamond symbol printed on them ▫ *the eight of diamonds* (**ouros**)

diaper /ˈdaɪəpə(r)/ NOUN [plural **diapers**] the US word for **nappy** (**fralda [EUA]**)

diary /ˈdaɪəri/ NOUN [plural **diaries**] a book with spaces for all the dates of the year where you can write things down ▫ *I've put the appointment in my diary.* ▫ *I'll check my diary.* 🔊 *He kept a diary.* (**diário**)

dice /daɪs/ NOUN [plural **dice**] a small object with six square sides with different numbers of small round marks on each side that you use in games 🔊 *Each player rolls the dice.* (**dado**)

dictate /dɪkˈteɪt/ VERB [**dictates, dictating, dictated**] to say words for someone to write down ▫ *I have to type the letters that my boss dictates.* (**ditar**)

dictation /dɪkˈteɪʃən/ NOUN [plural **dictations**] a piece of text that a teacher reads for students to write down, or the process of doing this (**ditado**)

dictator /dɪkˈteɪtə(r)/ NOUN [plural **dictators**] a person who has complete power over a country ▫ *a fascist dictator* (**ditador**)

dictionary /ˈdɪkʃənəri/ NOUN [plural **dictionaries**] a book that gives words in alphabetical order and their meanings ▫ *a French dictionary* ▫ + *of a dictionary of medical terms* (**dicionário**)

did /dɪd/ PAST TENSE OF **do** (**ver do**)

didn't /ˈdɪdənt/ a short way to say 'did not' (**ver do**)

die /daɪ/ VERB [**dies, dying, died**]
1 to stop living ▫ *Her father died suddenly at the age of 56.* ▫ + *of Six people died in the crash.* ▫ + *of He died of heart failure.* ▫ + *from He was taken to hospital, but died from his injuries.* (**morrer**)
2 to disappear or stop existing ▫ *My love for him will never die.* (**desaparecer**)
◆ IDIOM **be dying for something/to do something** an informal phrase meaning you want to have something or do something very much and you do not want to wait ▫ *I'm dying for a cold drink.* ▫ *The kids were dying to get outside.*
◆ PHRASAL VERB **die down** to gradually become quieter or less active ▫ *She waited until the applause had died down.* ▫ *All the attention seems to have died down now.*

diesel /ˈdiːzəl/ NOUN, NO PLURAL a heavy type of oil that is used as fuel (**diesel**)

diet¹ /ˈdaɪət/ NOUN [plural **diets**]
1 the food that a person eats 🔊 *Do you have a healthy diet?* 🔊 *You need to eat a balanced diet.* ▫ + *of They live on a basic diet of rice and beans.* (**dieta**)
2 a limited amount or range of foods that someone eats, for example to lose weight 🔊 *Maybe you need to go on a diet.* (**regime**)

diet² /ˈdaɪət/ VERB [**diets, dieting, dieted**] to eat less food in order to lose weight ▫ *I've never dieted, but I do do a lot of exercise.* (**fazer regime**)

differ /ˈdɪfə(r)/ VERB [**differs, differing, differed**] to not be the same as something else ▫ + *from His working methods differ from other TV producers.* ▫ + *in The males and females differ in size.* (**diferir**)

difference /ˈdɪfrəns/ NOUN [plural **differences**]
1 the way in which two people or things are not the same ▫ + *between Is there a difference between male and female players?* ▫ + *in There was a difference in the children's behaviour.* 🔊 *There are big differences between the two cultures.* 🔊 *They don't know the difference between right and wrong.* (**diferença**)
2 make a difference to have an effect on something ▫ + *to This will make a difference to people's lives.* ▫ *Working harder didn't make any difference – we still couldn't manage.* (**fazer diferença**)

different /ˈdɪfrənt/ ADJECTIVE not the same as someone or something else ▫ + *from He seems quite different from the rest of the boys.* ▫ + *in The two girls are very different in appearance and personality.* 🔊 *Each case is completely different.* ▫ *We listen to different types of music.* (**diferente**)

difficult /ˈdɪfɪkəlt/ ADJECTIVE
1 not easy to do or understand ▫ *That's a very difficult question.* ▫ + *to do something It's becoming increasingly difficult to find a parking space.* ▫ + *for It's difficult for anyone to understand.* 🔊 *Many people are finding it difficult to get jobs.* (**difícil**)
2 not friendly or easy to please ▫ *a difficult customer* (**difícil**)

difficulty /ˈdɪfɪkəlti/ NOUN, NO PLURAL when something is difficult to do or understand ▫ *You should be able to do this without difficulty.* ▫ + *ing She has difficulty sleeping.* ▫ + *in He was having difficulty in breathing.* ▫ + *with My grandmother now has difficulty with everyday tasks.* 🔊 *With great difficulty, he managed to pull himself out of the water.* (**dificuldade**)

dig /dɪg/ VERB [**digs, digging, dug**]
1 to make a hole, especially in the ground 🔊 *They dug a hole in the snow.* ▫ *They're digging a tunnel.* (**cavar**)
2 to lift up and turn over soil with a spade (= tool with a flat, metal part that you push into the soil) ▫ *He's digging in the garden.* (**cavoucar**)
◆ PHRASAL VERB **dig something up** to remove

something from under the ground by digging □ *We dug up some vegetables.* (desenterrar algo)

> **THESAURUS:** If you dig, you make a hole, usually in the ground. For example, you might dig in your garden when you are planting something. When you scoop, you lift something in your curved hands, or with a spoon or similar tool. You might scoop ice cream out of a container, for example. When someone digs a big hole in the ground in order to get something out, we use the word mine. You mine diamonds and coal, for example.

digest /daɪˈdʒest/ VERB [digests, digesting, digested] when the body digests food, it changes it into substances that it can use ▣ *Bacteria in the stomach help to digest food.* (digerir)

digital /ˈdɪdʒɪtəl/ ADJECTIVE
1 storing information, sounds and pictures as sets of numbers or electronic signals ▣ *a digital camera* ▣ *a digital radio* ▣ *There's been a growth in digital music sales.* (digital)
2 a digital clock or watch shows the time as numbers (digital)

dignity /ˈdɪgnɪti/ NOUN, NO PLURAL calm, controlled behaviour, especially in a difficult situati on □ *She showed great dignity through a difficult period.* (dignidade)

dilemma /dɪˈlemə/ NOUN [plural dilemmas] when you have to decide which of two or more things to do and you are finding this decision difficult ▣ *I'm in a dilemma over whether to go or not.* ▣ *a moral dilemma* (dilema)

dim /dɪm/ ADJECTIVE [dimmer, dimmest] not bright or clear ▣ *We couldn't see much in the dim light.* □ *I made my way along the dim corridor.* (turvo/ vago)

diminish /dɪˈmɪnɪʃ/ VERB [diminishes, diminishing, diminished] to become less or smaller, or to make something less or smaller □ *I don't want to diminish the importance of this meeting.* □ *Recently, their power has diminished.* (diminuir)

dine /daɪn/ VERB [dines, dining, dined] to eat dinner (= main meal). A formal word □ *They regularly dine at the best restaurants.* (jantar)

dining room /ˈdaɪnɪŋ ˌruːm/ NOUN [plural dining rooms] the room in a house or hotel where you have your meals (sala de jantar)

dinner /ˈdɪnə(r)/ NOUN [plural dinners] a main meal in the evening or in the middle of the day □ *We had fish for dinner.* ▣ *We sat down to eat dinner.* ▣ *Alice is cooking dinner.* (jantar)

dinosaur /ˈdaɪnəsɔː(r)/ NOUN [plural dinosaurs] a very large type of animal that lived millions of years ago and no longer exists (dinossauro)

dip /dɪp/ VERB [dips, dipping, dipped] to put something in and out of a liquid quickly □ *Dip the clothes in the dye.* □ *She dipped a toe into the water.* (mergulhar)

diploma /dɪˈpləʊmə/ NOUN [plural diplomas] a qualification that someone can study for in a particular subject □ **+ in** *She has a diploma in Journalism Studies.* (diploma)

dire /daɪə(r)/ ADJECTIVE very bad, serious or extreme ▣ *a dire warning* ▣ *These people are in dire need of help.* ▣ *If these spending cuts go ahead, they will have dire consequences.* (perigoso)

direct[1] /dɪˈrekt/ ADJECTIVE
1 straight from one place to another ▣ *It's the shortest, most direct route.* ▣ *a direct flight between London and Beijing* (direto)
2 involving two people or things with nothing else between ▣ *We had no direct contact with Mr Ellis.* ▣ *They found a direct link between computer usage and back pain.* (direto)

direct[2] /dɪˈrekt/ VERB [directs, directing, directed]
1 to tell the actors in a film or play what to do ▣ *The film was directed by Clint Eastwood.* □ *She directed the new production of the musical.* (dirigir)
2 to tell someone how to get somewhere □ *Could you direct me to the post office, please?* (orientar)

direction /dɪˈrekʃən/ NOUN [plural directions]
1 the place or point a thing or person is going or facing to wards □ *In which direction was she going – towards town or away?* □ **+ of** *He pointed in the direction of the kitchen.* ▣ *The bus was travelling in the opposite direction.* ▣ *They all walked off in different directions.* ▣ *The wind has changed direction.* (direção)
2 directions instructions for getting somewhere or doing something ▣ *I followed his directions as we drove out of town.* □ *Make sure you read the directions for use carefully.* (instrução)

> **THESAURUS:** A direction is the place or point a thing or person is moving or pointing towards. Your route is the way you take to get somewhere. So, a bus route is the roads that the bus uses to get from the start to the end of its journey. Way is a more general word, which can have a similar meaning to direction: □ *Which way did she go? North or south?*, or a similar meaning to route: □ *What is the best way to get to the station?* Note that in English, the surface that vehicles travel on is called a road.

directly /dɪˈrektli/ ADVERB with no other person or thing between or involved □ *It plugs directly into your computer.* □ *Did you talk directly to him?* ▣ *He wasn't directly involved in the project.* ▣ *She wasn't directly responsible for the error.* (diretamente)

direct object /dɪˌrekt ˈɒbdʒɪkt/ NOUN [plural direct objects] the noun or pronoun that is affected by the action of a verb. For example, in *He gave the boy a book*, the direct object is *a book*. (objeto direto)

director

director /dɪˌrektə(r)/ NOUN [plural **directors**]
1 the manager of a business, organization or department □ + *of the director of the CIA* 🔾 *the institute's executive director* 🔾 *the supermarket's finance director* (**diretor**)
2 someone who makes a film or organizes a stage show 🔾 *a Hollywood film director* □ + *of She's the artistic director of the Sydney Theatre Company.* (**diretor**)

directory /dɪˈrektəri/ NOUN [plural **directories**]
a book containing an alphabetical list of names, numbers or other information 🔾 *a telephone directory* (**catálogo, lista**)

direct speech /dɪˌrekt ˈspiːtʃ/ NOUN, NO PLURAL
in a story or report, the exact words that a person said (**discurso direto**)

dirt /dɜːt/ NOUN, NO PLURAL any substance that is not clean or that makes something become not clean □ *Rinse under water to remove any dirt.* □ *She brushed the dirt from the surface.* (**sujeira**)

dirty /ˈdɜːti/ ADJECTIVE [**dirtier, dirtiest**]
not clean □ *dirty hands* □ *I cleared all the dirty dishes.* 🔾 *Try not to get your clothes dirty.* 🔾 *a pile of dirty laundry* (**sujo**)

disability /ˌdɪsəˈbɪləti/ NOUN [plural **disabilities**]
a physical or mental problem that makes some parts of life difficult 🔾 *a physical disability* □ *Buildings should be accessible to people with disabilities.* (**invalidez, deficiência**)

disabled¹ /dɪsˈeɪbəld/ ADJECTIVE having a disability 🔾 *We provide support for disabled people.* 🔾 *Our son is severely disabled.* (**inválido**)

disabled² /dɪsˈeɪbəld/ NOUN **the disabled**
people who are disabled (**os deficientes**)

disadvantage /ˌdɪsədˈvɑːntɪdʒ/ NOUN [plural **disadvantages**] something that makes something less attractive, less successful or more difficult □ + *of The only disadvantage of the plan is that it could be too expensive.* □ *The advantages outweigh the disadvantages.* (**desvantagem**)

disagree /ˌdɪsəˈɡriː/ VERB [**disagrees, disagreeing, disagreed**] to have a different opinion from someone else about something □ + *with I completely disagree with you about that.* □ + *about Doctors disagree about how effective the treatment is.* □ + *over Ministers disagree over who is to blame.* □ + *on They disagree on almost everything.* (**discordar**)

◆ PHRASAL VERB **disagree with something** to disapprove of something □ *Many people disagree with the death penalty.*

disagreement /ˌdɪsəˈɡriːmənt/ NOUN [plural **disagreements**] when people have different opinions or argue 🔾 *We've had several disagreements on this subject.* □ *There are still some areas of disagreement.* □ + *between There was some disagreement between John and Robert.* □ + *over There are disagreements over money.* (**discordância**)

discard

disappear /ˌdɪsəˈpɪə(r)/ VERB [**disappears, disappearing, disappeared**]
1 if someone or something disappears, they go somewhere where they cannot be seen or found □ + *from The woman disappeared from her home in April.* □ *He disappeared into the crowd.* □ *The car disappeared down the street.* (**desaparecer**)
2 to stop existing □ *The symptoms usually disappear within a couple of days.* □ *Finally the light disappeared altogether.* (**desaparecer**)

disappoint /ˌdɪsəˈpɔɪnt/ VERB [**disappoints, disappointing, disappointed**] to make someone feel unhappy because something is not how they had hoped or expected □ *I'm sorry to disappoint you, but I can't come to your party.* □ *We don't want to disappoint our fans.* (**decepcionar**)

disappointed /ˌdɪsəˈpɔɪntɪd/ ADJECTIVE
unhappy because something is not how you had hoped or expected □ + *that I'm disappointed that he can't come.* □ + *with I'm very disappointed with the result.* (**decepcionado**)

disappointing /ˌdɪsəˈpɔɪntɪŋ/ ADJECTIVE not as good as you hoped or expected 🔾 *It was a disappointing performance by the team.* □ *It's extremely disappointing that we haven't made any progress.* (**decepcionante**)

disappointment /ˌdɪsəˈpɔɪntmənt/ NOUN [plural **disappointments**] a feeling of being disappointed or something that makes you disappointed 🔾 *The hotel was a big disappointment.* 🔾 *She expressed her disappointment at the decision.* (**decepção**)

disapproval /ˌdɪsəˈpruːvəl/ NOUN, NO PLURAL
when you think something is bad, wrong or not suitable □ + *of She ignored the disapproval of her family.* 🔾 *His parents expressed their disapproval of the planned marriage.* (**desaprovação**)

disapprove /ˌdɪsəˈpruːv/ VERB [**disapproves, disapproving, disapproved**] to think that something or someone is bad, wrong or not suitable □ + *of My parents definitely disapproved of my new friend.* □ *We were wearing short skirts and he clearly disapproved.* (**desaprovar**)

disaster /dɪˈzɑːstə(r)/ NOUN [plural **disasters**]
something that causes a lot of damage, injuries or deaths 🔾 *They help victims of natural disasters such as earthquakes.* 🔾 *The flight had just taken off when disaster struck.* (**desastre**)

disc /dɪsk/ NOUN [plural **discs**]
1 something flat and round □ *a small metal disc* □ *a disc of yellow plastic* (**disco**)
2 a record (= flat plastic object with music recorded on it) or CD (= small flat metal object with music or information recorded on it) (**disco**)

discard /dɪˈskɑːd/ VERB [**discards, discarding, discarded**] to throw something away □ *a discarded wrapper* □ *Discard the herbs before serving.* (**descartar**)

discipline[1] /ˈdɪsɪplɪn/ NOUN, NO PLURAL when people are made to obey rules and behave in a particular way ◻ *We're concerned about the lack of discipline in the school.* (**disciplina**)

discipline[2] /ˈdɪsɪplɪn/ VERB [**disciplines, disciplining, disciplined**] to punish someone ◻ *Parents were asked how they discipline their children.* (**punir**)

disc jockey /ˈdɪsk ˌdʒɒkɪ/ NOUN [plural **disc jockeys**] someone who plays recorded music on the radio or at a club (**disc-jóquei**)

disco /ˈdɪskəʊ/ NOUN [plural **discos**] a place or party where people dance to recorded music (**discoteca**)

discount /ˈdɪskaʊnt/ NOUN [plural **discounts**] a reduction in the price of something ◻ **+ on** *There's a 10% discount on all goods.* ◻ *I got a £5 discount.* ◻ *The company offers discounts to students.* (**desconto**)

discourage /dɪˈskʌrɪdʒ/ VERB [**discourages, discouraging, discouraged**] to try to stop something happening or to persuade someone not to do something ◻ *They introduced new laws to discourage smoking.* ◻ *We want to discourage people from driving into the city centre.* (**desencorajar**)

discover /dɪˈskʌvə(r)/ VERB [**discovers, discovering, discovered**] to find information, a place or an object, especially for the first time ◻ *The settlers discovered gold in the mountains.* ◻ *The man's body was discovered yesterday.* ◻ *She finally discovered the truth.* ◻ **+ that** *We discovered that the paint wouldn't mix with water.* ◻ **+ question word** *Scientists hope to discover why numbers of the birds have dropped.* (**descobrir**)

discovery /dɪˈskʌvərɪ/ NOUN [plural **discoveries**] when someone discovers something, or the thing they discover ◻ **+ of** *the discovery of America* ◻ *He made a surprising discovery.* (**descoberta**)

discriminate /dɪˈskrɪmɪneɪt/ VERB [**discriminates, discriminating, discriminated**] to treat someone unfairly because of their colour, religion, sex, etc. ◻ *Some employers were accused of discriminating against women.* (**discriminar**)

discrimination /dɪsˌkrɪmɪˈneɪʃən/ NOUN, NO PLURAL treating people unfairly because of their colour, religion, sex, etc. ◻ *racial discrimination* ◻ *They have suffered discrimination.* (**discriminação**)

discuss /dɪˈskʌs/ VERB [**discusses, discussing, discussed**] to talk about something ◻ *You should try to discuss these issues with your wife.* ◻ **+ question word** *We have been discussing what to do.* (**discutir**)

> Note that when you use the verb **discuss**, you must say what you are discussing:
> ✓ I must discuss the problem with Angela.
> ✗ I must discuss with Angela.

discussion /dɪˈskʌʃən/ NOUN [plural **discussions**] when people discuss something ◻ **+ about** *We got into a discussion about politics.* ◻ **+ between** *There have been weeks of discussion between US and Chinese officials.* ◻ *The two sides have agreed to hold discussions next week.* (**discussão**)

disease /dɪˈziːz/ NOUN [plural **diseases**] an illness ◻ *He developed heart disease.* ◻ *The infection can cause liver disease.* (**doença**)

> **THESAURUS:** Disease and **illness** are similar in meaning, but disease is more general. A disease can affect a person, an animal or a plant. An **illness** affects a person. An **infection** is a disease that is caused by bacteria or a virus. For example, you might have an ear **infection** or a skin **infection**. The word **sickness** is usually used in a general way. For example you can say that someone has time off work because of **sickness** (the person may have several different illnesses or infections).

disgrace[1] /dɪsˈɡreɪs/ NOUN, NO PLURAL
1 when someone loses respect because of something they have done ◻ *It's no disgrace to come last if you tried hard.* ◻ *You have brought disgrace to your family.* (**desonra**)
2 in disgrace if you are in disgrace, other people are angry with you ◻ *Debbie's in disgrace for staying out all night.* (**desgraça**)

disgrace[2] /dɪsˈɡreɪs/ VERB [**disgraces, disgracing, disgraced**] to lose other people's respect because of your behaviour ◻ *I disgraced myself and my family.* (**envergonhar**)

disgraceful /dɪsˈɡreɪsfʊl/ ADJECTIVE very bad or shocking ◻ *Their behaviour was absolutely disgraceful.* (**vergonhoso**)

• **disgracefully** /dɪsˈɡreɪsfʊlɪ/ ADVERB very badly ◻ *They treated him disgracefully.* (**vergonhosamente**)

disguise[1] /dɪsˈɡaɪz/ NOUN [plural **disguises**] something you wear to change your appearance so that people do not recognize you ◻ *He left the hotel in disguise.* (**disfarce**)

disguise[2] /dɪsˈɡaɪz/ VERB [**disguises, disguising, disguised**] to make something or someone look, sound or seem like something or someone else ◻ *He had a bomb disguised as a laptop computer.* ◻ *She disguised herself as a tourist.* (**disfarçar**)

disgust[1] /dɪsˈɡʌst/ NOUN, NO PLURAL a strong feeling that you do not like or approve of something ◻ *The sight of the worms filled Luisa with disgust.* (**repugnância**)

disgust[2] /dɪsˈɡʌst/ VERB [**disgusts, disgusting, disgusted**] to make someone feel disgust ◻ *They were disgusted by what they saw.* ◻ *It disgusts me that people can behave that way.* (**repugnar, enojar**)

disgusting /dɪsˈɡʌstɪŋ/ ADJECTIVE extremely bad or unpleasant ◻ *a disgusting mess* ◻ *It tasted absolutely disgusting.* ◻ *disgusting behaviour* (**repugnante**)

dish /dɪʃ/ NOUN [plural **dishes**]
1 a plate or bowl for food ◻ *Cover the dish with a*

dishonest — distinguish

lid. 🔷 *a pile of dirty dishes* 🔷 *I'll wash the dishes.* (prato, travessa)
2 food that has been prepared for eating ▫ *a fish dish* 🔷 *The restaurant serves traditional dishes.* (prato)

dishonest /dɪsˈɒnɪst/ ADJECTIVE not telling the truth, or doing things that are wrong or illegal ▫ *I didn't do anything dishonest.* ▫ *It would be dishonest to hide it from him.* (desonesto)

dishwasher /ˈdɪʃwɒʃə(r)/ NOUN [plural **dishwashers**] a machine for washing things such as plates, cups, etc. after a meal (lava-louças)

disk /dɪsk/ NOUN [plural **disks**]
1 a round flat object that computers use to store information on. A computing word. ▫ *Insert a disk into drive D.* 🔷 *It requires at least 600MB of disk space.* (disco)
2 the US spelling of **disc** (disco [EUA])

dislike¹ /dɪsˈlaɪk/ VERB [**dislikes, disliking, disliked**] to not like someone or something ▫ *She disliked the idea of the children travelling alone.* ▫ *He disliked dentists intensely.* ▫ *+ ing I dislike getting up early.* (detestar)

dislike² /dɪsˈlaɪk/ NOUN [plural **dislikes**] something you dislike or the feeling of disliking something or someone ▫ *He had a dislike of crowds.* 🔷 *They took an instant dislike to each other.* (aversão)

dismay /dɪsˈmeɪ/ NOUN, NO PLURAL an unpleasant feeling of surprise and worry ▫ *We watched in dismay as Ted fell into the water.* 🔷 *To her dismay, she found her foot was stuck.* 🔷 *Campaigners expressed dismay at the decision.* (consternação)

dismiss /dɪsˈmɪs/ VERB [**dismisses, dismissing, dismissed**]
1 to make someone leave their job ▫ *She was dismissed for misconduct.* ▫ *He was dismissed from the army.* (demitir)
2 to send someone away ▫ *The class were dismissed by the teacher early today.* (demitir)

> **THESAURUS:** If you **fire** someone, you tell someone that they must leave their job. **Dismiss** has a similar meaning to **fire**, but is more formal. You can also say that someone gets the **sack**. These words are all used when someone has done something wrong or if their work is not good enough.

dispatch /dɪsˈpætʃ/ VERB [**dispatches, dispatching, dispatched**] a formal word meaning to send something or someone somewhere ▫ *The parcel was dispatched on the 29th.* ▫ *The navy dispatched a helicopter to help in the search.* (despachar)

display¹ /dɪˈspleɪ/ NOUN [plural **displays**]
1 things which are arranged or presented for people to look at ▫ *+ of a display of the children's work* 🔷 *a fireworks display* (exibição)
2 on display arranged for people to look at ▫ *The painting is on display at the National Gallery.* (em exposição)

display² /dɪˈspleɪ/ VERB [**displays, displaying, displayed**] to arrange things for people to look at ▫ *The treasure will be displayed in the museum for two months.* ▫ *All offices must display no smoking signs.* (expor)

disposal /dɪˈspəʊzəl/ NOUN, NO PLURAL getting rid of something 🔷 *We are using new methods of waste disposal.* ▫ *There are strict regulations about the disposal of chemicals.* (descarte)

dispose /dɪˈspəʊz/
♦ PHRASAL VERB [**disposes, disposing, disposed**] **dispose of something** to get rid of something ▫ *Where can I dispose of my old fridge?* (dispõe)

dispute¹ /dɪˈspjuːt/ NOUN [plural **disputes**] a serious disagreement about something ▫ *They went on strike in a dispute over pay.* 🔷 *They are trying to resolve their dispute.* (disputa)

dispute² /dɪˈspjuːt/ VERB [**disputes, disputing, disputed**] to say that something is not true or correct ▫ *They dispute that they have been treated fairly.* (contestar)

disrupt /dɪsˈrʌpt/ VERB [**disrupts, disrupting, disrupted**] to stop something continuing as usual ▫ *Traffic was disrupted because of the march.* (perturbar)

dissolve /dɪˈzɒlv/ VERB [**dissolves, dissolving, dissolved**] to melt or be melted in liquid ▫ *Keep stirring until the sugar dissolves completely.* ▫ *Stir to dissolve the sugar.* (dissolver)

> **THESAURUS:** If a solid **dissolves**, it disappears when you mix it with water. Salt and sugar dissolve in water. If something **melts**, or if you **melt** it, it changes from a solid to a liquid when you heat it. Snow melts in the sun, and you can melt butter in a pan. If you **soften** something, or if it **softens**, it becomes soft, but not liquid. You can soften butter by keeping it out of the fridge.

distance /ˈdɪstəns/ NOUN [plural **distances**]
1 the space between things ▫ *+ between Measure the distance between the lines.* ▫ *+ from The hotel is only a short distance from the city centre.* 🔷 *He doesn't like driving long distances.* (distância)
2 in the distance if you see or hear something in the distance you see or hear it but it is a long way away ▫ *I could hear the sound of a train in the distance.* (ao longe)

distant /ˈdɪstənt/ ADJECTIVE far away in space or time ▫ *He heard distant voices which were getting closer.* 🔷 *The holiday seems like a distant memory now.* 🔷 *the distant past* (distante)

distinct /dɪˈstɪŋkt/ ADJECTIVE
1 easy to see, hear, smell etc. ▫ *Green tea has a distinct flavour.* (nítido)
2 different ▫ *The two languages are quite distinct.* (diferente)

distinguish /dɪˈstɪŋgwɪʃ/ VERB [**distinguishes, distinguishing, distinguished**] to see a difference between things ▫ *If you're colour blind, you have difficulties distinguishing green from red.* (distinto)

distract /dɪˈstrækt/ VERB [distracts, distracting, distracted] to take someone's attention away from something □ Advertisements at the side of the road can distract drivers. (**distrair**)

distress /dɪˈstres/ NOUN, NO PLURAL when someone is upset □ I didn't want to cause them any distress. (**aflição**)

distressing /dɪˈstresɪŋ/ ADJECTIVE making someone feel very upset □ It has been a very distressing time for me and my family. (**aflitivo**)

distribute /dɪˈstrɪbjuːt/ VERB [distributes, distributing, distributed] to give something to a lot of people or places □ Please distribute the leaflets to your friends. □ The company manufactures and distributes drinks. (**distribuir**)

distribution /ˌdɪstrɪˈbjuːʃən/ NOUN, NO PLURAL the process of giving something to a group of people □ He organized the distribution of food among the refugees. (**distribuição**)

district /ˈdɪstrɪkt/ NOUN [plural districts] a part of a country or city □ Shanghai's business district (**bairro, distrito**)

disturb /dɪˈstɜːb/ VERB [disturbs, disturbing, disturbed]
1 to interrupt what someone is doing □ I'm sorry to disturb you, but I need to ask you a question. (**incomodar**)
2 to upset or worry someone □ The incident disturbed him. (**perturbar**)
3 to move something and change its position □ Someone had disturbed the papers at my desk. (**desarranjar**)

ditch /dɪtʃ/ NOUN [plural ditches] a long narrow hole at the side of a field or road (**vala**)

dive[1] /daɪv/ VERB [dives, diving, dived]
1 to jump into water with your arms and head first □ + **into** Sasha dived into the pool. (**mergulhar**)
2 to swim under water using special equipment (**mergulhar**)

• **diver** /ˈdaɪvə(r)/ NOUN [plural divers] someone who swims under water using special equipment (**mergulhadores**)

dive[2] /daɪv/ NOUN [plural dives]
1 a jump into water with your arms and head first (**mergulho**)
2 a time when you swim under water using special equipment (**mergulho**)

diverse /daɪˈvɜːs/ ADJECTIVE of very different types □ He has appeared in a diverse range of films. (**diverso**)

diversion /daɪˈvɜːʃən/ NOUN [plural diversions] a different route for traffic because the usual one is closed (**desvio**)

diversity /daɪˈvɜːsəti/ NOUN, NO PLURAL when there are many different types of people or things □ Australia's cultural diversity (**diversidade**)

divert /daɪˈvɜːt/ VERB [diverts, diverting, diverted] to make something go in a different direction □ Traffic was diverted because of an accident. (**desviar**)

divide /dɪˈvaɪd/ VERB [divides, dividing, divided]
1 to separate into parts, or to separate something into parts □ + **into** Divide the class into teams of five. □ The cell divides and becomes two cells. (**dividir**)
2 to separate something and give a part of it to several people □ + **up** They divided up the money. □ + **between** She divided the cake between the children. (**dividir**)
3 to find how many times one number contains another number. A mathematics word □ + **by** If you divide 12 by 3, you get 4. □ 12 divided by 3 is 4. (**dividir**)

divine /dɪˈvaɪn/ ADJECTIVE coming from God, or to do with God □ divine punishment (**divino**)

division /dɪˈvɪʒən/ NOUN [plural divisions]
1 no plural the process of separating people or things into groups or parts □ cell division (**divisão**)
2 no plural the way something is shared between people □ + **of** We need a more equal division of power between governments. (**divisão**)
3 no plural when you calculate how many times one number contains another number. A mathematics word. (**divisão**)
4 a group within a large organization □ He heads the company's sales and marketing division. (**divisão**)

divorce[1] /dɪˈvɔːs/ NOUN [plural divorces] the legal ending of a marriage ▣ We're getting a divorce. (**divórcio**)

divorce[2] /dɪˈvɔːs/ VERB [divorces, divorcing, divorced] to end your marriage legally □ His parents divorced when he was six. □ Julia is divorcing her husband. (**divorciar-se**)

DIY /ˌdiːaɪˈwaɪ/ ABBREVIATION **do-it-yourself**; when you make or repair things in the home yourself □ DIY stores (**faça você mesmo**)

dizzy /ˈdɪzi/ ADJECTIVE [dizzier, dizziest] feeling as if everything around you is moving and you are going to fall ▣ You'll get dizzy if you spin round like that. (**tonto**)

DJ /ˌdiːˈdʒeɪ/ ABBREVIATION **disc jockey**; someone who plays music in a club or on the radio (**DJ**)

do · domestic

do¹ /du:/ AUXILIARY VERB [does, doing, did, done]
1 used with another verb to make questions and negative sentences □ *Do you want another drink?* □ *I don't* (= do not) *like her husband.* □ *She doesn't* (= does not) *play tennis.*
2 used to avoid repeating a verb □ *'I love chocolate'. 'So do I'.* □ *They spent a lot more money than I did.*
3 used to emphasize the main verb □ *I do love Paris.* □ *She does want to come, but she's very busy.*
4 used at the end of a sentence to make it into a question □ *Lucy goes to this school, doesn't she?*

> Notice that instead of **do not**, people often say or write the short form **don't** and instead of **does not**, people often say or write the short form **doesn't**.

do² /du:/ VERB [does, doing, did, done]
1 to perform an action □ *What are you doing?* □ *Make sure you do your homework.* □ *What does your mother do* (= what is her job)? □ + **with** *What have you done with the map* (= where is it)? (**fazer**)
2 to study a subject □ *I'm doing English and French.* (**fazer**)
3 do badly/well to make bad/good progress □ *Oleg's doing well with his swimming.* (**ir**)
4 How are you doing? an informal way of asking someone about their health and situation □ *Hi Carlos – how are you doing?* (**ir**)
5 something will do something will be enough or be suitable □ *If you haven't got walking boots, trainers will do.* (**dar certo**)
6 to do with something connected with something □ *He's writing a book – something to do with astronomy.* (**ter a ver com**)
7 someone could do with something someone needs something. An informal phrase □ *I could do with a hot drink.* (**bem que eu gostaria de**)

◆ PHRASAL VERBS **do something up**
1 to fasten a piece of clothing □ *Do your jacket up.*
2 to repair or decorate a room or building **do without (something)** to manage without some thing

dock¹ /dɒk/ NOUN [plural **docks**] the place where ships stop so goods can be taken on and off (**doca**)
dock² /dɒk/ VERB [**docks, docking, docked**] a ship docks when it goes into a dock (**atracar**)

doctor /'dɒktə(r)/ NOUN [plural doctors]
1 someone whose job is to treat people who are ill 🔳 *You should see a doctor if your symptoms don't improve.* □ *Could I make an appointment with Doctor Kennedy, please?* (**médico**)
2 the doctor's the place where a doctor works □ *Go to the doctor's if your cough isn't any better.* (**clínica**)

document /'dɒkjumənt/ NOUN [plural documents]
1 a paper with official information on it □ *Make sure you have all your travel documents with you.* 🔳 *She had to sign some legal documents.* (**documento**)
2 something that you write and keep on a computer. A computing word. 🔳 *How do I open a new document?* (**documento**)

documentary¹ /ˌdɒkju'mentəri/ NOUN [plural **documentaries**] a film or television programme about real people or real events □ *They made a documentary on global warming.* (**documentário**)
documentary² /ˌdɒkju'mentəri/ ADJECTIVE a documentary programme or film is about real people or real events 🔳 *It's a new documentary series set in a school.* (**documentário**)
dodge /dɒdʒ/ VERB [**dodges, dodging, dodged**]
1 to move quickly to avoid something □ *Graeme managed to dodge out of the way before the ball hit him.* (**esquivar**)
2 to avoid doing something or talking about something 🔳 *He dodged questions about his private life.* (**esquivar**)
does /dʌz/ VERB the form of the verb **do** that is used with **he**, **she** and **it** (**ver do**)
doesn't /'dʌznt/ a short way to say and write 'does not' (**ver do**)

dog /dɒg/ NOUN [plural dogs] an animal with four legs that is kept as a pet, for hunting or for guarding buildings 🔳 *The dog barks whenever anyone comes to the house.* 🔳 *He walks the dog every evening.* (**cão, cachorro**)

doll /dɒl/ NOUN [plural dolls] a toy in the shape of a person (**boneca**)

dollar /'dɒlə(r)/ NOUN [plural dollars] the unit of money in many countries including the US, Canada, Australia and New Zealand. The written symbol is $ □ *They've spent millions of dollars on the project.* (**dólar**)

dolphin /'dɒlfɪn/ NOUN [plural dolphins] an intelligent sea mammal that has grey skin and a long pointed mouth (**golfinho**)

dome /dəʊm/ NOUN [plural **domes**] a raised round roof on a building (**cúpula**)
domestic /də'mestɪk/ ADJECTIVE
1 to do with your home, or happening in your home □ *I hate domestic tasks like cleaning and cooking.* 🔳 *She was the victim of domestic violence.* (**doméstico**)
2 to do with one particular country and not international □ *the government's domestic policies* 🔳 *At Boston, he took a domestic flight to Seattle.* (**doméstico**)
3 a domestic animal is kept as a pet or on a farm (**doméstico**)

dominance /'dɒmɪnəns/ NOUN, NO PLURAL
when someone has more influence, power, and control than other people □ *The company's dominance of the home phone market is declining.* (**dominância**)

dominate /'dɒmɪneɪt/ VERB [dominates, dominating, dominated] to have more influence, power, or success than others □ *The company dominates the insurance market.* □ *He dominated to conversation.* (**dominar**)

donate /də'neɪt/ VERB [donates, donating, donated] to give something, especially money, to someone who needs it □ *He donated money to a local charity.* (**doar**)

donation /də'neɪʃən/ NOUN [plural donations] something, especially money, that you give to help a person or an organization □ *He was asked whether he would like to make a donation.* 🔁 *She made generous donations to various charities.* (**doação**)

> **THESAURUS:** A donation is something, especially money, that you give to help a person or organization. A contribution is something that you give or do to help to achieves something. You might make a contribution to a project, or you might make a contribution to help to buy something. Gift and present are words to describe a thing that you give to someone. For example, you might give someone a gift or a present on their birthday.

done /dʌn/ PAST PARTICIPLE OF do (**ver do**)
donkey /'dɒŋki/ NOUN [plural donkeys] an animal that looks like a small horse with longears (**burro**)
donor /'dəʊnə(r)/ NOUN [plural donors] someone who gives something to help a person or organization 🔁 *An anonymous donor has offered £5,000 to help find the girl's killer.* 🔁 *Blood donors are urgently needed.* (**doador**)
don't /dəʊnt/ a short way to say and write 'do not' (**ver do**)

door /dɔː(r)/ NOUN [plural doors]
1 the thing you open to get into a building, room, cupboard or vehicle 🔁 *Janie opened the door and went in.* 🔁 *She quickly closed the door.* 🔁 *There was a bell by the front door.* 🔁 *Just go and knock on the door.* □ *She closed the car door.* (**porta**)
2 the space in a wall where you go into a building or room □ *He was so fat he could barely get through the door.* (**porta**)
3 at the door if there is someone at the door, someone is waiting for you to open the door so they can come inside □ *Mum, there's someone at the door.* (**porta**)

doorbell /'dɔːbel/ NOUN [plural doorbells] a button on the door of a building that you press to ring a bell to tell the people inside that you are there (**campainha**)
doorway /'dɔːweɪ/ NOUN [plural doorways] the entrance to a room or building □ *He was standing in the doorway.* (**vão da porta**)
dose /dəʊs/ NOUN [plural doses] an amount of medicine that you take at one time 🔁 *You may get problems if you take a high dose of the drug.* (**dose**)
dot¹ /dɒt/ NOUN [plural dots]
1 a small round mark (**ponto**)
2 the symbol (.) in an Internet or email address □ *Is it 'al dot wood'? (= Is it 'al.wood'?)* (**ponto**)
dot² /dɒt/ VERB [dots, dotting, dotted] if a large area is dotted with things, there are a lot of them with spaces between each thing □ *The hillside was dotted with sheep.* (**pontilhar**)

double¹ /'dʌbəl/ ADJECTIVE
1 twice as much or twice as many □ *He was given a double dose of medicine.* (**duplo**)
2 having or involving two parts or things which are the same □ *double doors* □ *She's a double Olympic medallist.* (**duplo**)
3 suitable for two people 🔁 *It costs £100 a night for a double room.* (**duplo**)
4 used when you are saying that a particular number or letter is repeated □ *You spell 'marry' m-a-double-r-y.* (**duplo**)

double² /'dʌbəl/ DETERMINER twice as big or twice as much □ *She earns double the amount I do.* (**duas vezes**)

double³ /'dʌbəl/ VERB [doubles, doubling, doubled] to become twice as big, or to make something become twice as big □ + **in** *The shares have doubled in value.* □ *The drug doubles your risk of having a heart attack.* (**duplicar**)

doubt¹ /daʊt/ NOUN [plural doubts]
1 a feeling of not being certain about something 🔁 *Leo had serious doubts about the plan.* 🔁 *I have no doubt that you will succeed.* (**dúvida**)
2 be in doubt if something is in doubt, it is not certain that it will succeed or continue to exist □ *His future at the club is in doubt.* (**estar em dúvida**)
3 no doubt used for emphasizing that something seems very certain □ *No doubt he'll be late as usual.* (**sem dúvida**)

doubt² /daʊt/ VERB [doubts, doubting, doubted]
to think that something is probably not true or will probably not happen □ + **that** *I doubt that he will agree.* 🔁 *'Do you think Rebecca will come?' 'I doubt it'.* (**duvidar**)

doubtful /ˈdaʊtfʊl/ ADJECTIVE probably not true, or probably not going to happen ▫ *It's doubtful whether she'll take the job.* (**incerto**)

dough /dəʊ/ NOUN, NO PLURAL a mixture of flour and water for making bread (**massa**)

dove /dʌv/ NOUN [*plural* doves] a white bird, used as a sign of peace (**pomba, rolinha**)

down¹ /daʊn/ ADVERB

1 towards or in a lower position ▫ *He was sitting down.* ▫ *She bent down to speak to the child.* ▫ *I'll put the box down here.* (**para baixo**)

2 to a smaller size, amount or level ▫ *He cut the picture down to fit the frame.* ▫ *Can you turn the television down, please?* (**para baixo**)

3 along ▫ *I'm just going down to the post office.* (**ao longo de**)

4 in or towards the south ▫ *We're driving down from Edinburgh tonight.* (**para o sul**)

down² /daʊn/ ADJECTIVE

1 unhappy. An informal word ▫ *You seem a bit down.* (**deprimido**)

2 if a computer or website is down, it is not working. A computing word ▫ *I can't book the tickets because the website's down.* (**pane**)

down³ /daʊn/ PREPOSITION

1 towards or in a lower part ▫ *There were tears running down his face.* (**para baixo**)

2 along ▫ *Rachel was walking down the road.*

downhill /ˌdaʊnˈhɪl/ ADVERB down a slope ▫ *The car rolled downhill.* (**em declive**)

download¹ /ˌdaʊnˈləʊd/ VERB [downloads, downloading, downloaded] to copy information, such as pictures or music, onto your computer from the Internet or another computer. A computing word. ▫ *You can download music for free.* ▫ *The file is downloading now.* (**baixar arquivo [informática]**)

download² /ˈdaʊnləʊd/ NOUN [*plural* downloads] something that you have copied onto your computer from the Internet or another computer. A computing word. (**arquivo baixado [informática]**)

downstairs¹ ADVERB /ˌdaʊnˈsteəz/ to or on a lower level of a building ▫ *He went downstairs to get breakfast.* ▫ *The kids were all downstairs.* (**andar de baixo**)

downstairs² ADJECTIVE /ˈdaʊnˌsteəz/ on a lower level in a building ▫ *a downstairs bathroom* (**no andar de baixo**)

downward /ˈdaʊnwəd/ ADJECTIVE towards a lower place or position ▫ *a downward slope* (**para baixo**)

downwards /ˈdaʊnwədz/ *or* **downward** /ˈdaʊnwəd/ ADVERB towards a lower place or position ▫ *The path winds downwards to the lake.* (**para baixo**)

dozen /ˈdʌzən/ NOUN [*plural* dozens]

1 twelve ▫ *a dozen eggs* ▫ *There were about two dozen (= 24) people at the party.* ▫ *I read half a dozen (= 6) pages.* (**dúzia**)

2 dozens of something a lot of something. An informal phrase ▫ *He's been in dozens of films.* (**dúzias de [algo]**)

Dr ABBREVIATION **doctor**. The abbreviation is used in writing ▫ *Dr Smith* (**dr.**)

draft /drɑːft/ VERB [drafts, drafting, drafted] to write something that you will change before you finish it ▫ *He was drafting a letter to his boss.* (**esboçar**)

drag /dræɡ/ VERB [drags, dragging, dragged]

1 to pull something along the ground ▫ *Thomas came out of school, dragging his school bag behind him.* (**puxar**)

2 to move words or pictures on a computer screen by pulling them with a mouse. A computing word. (**arrastar**)

> **THESAURUS: Pull** is a general word to describe the action of holding something and moving it towards you. If you drag something, you pull it along the ground, often because it is heavy. If you tow something, you pull it along behind you with a rope or a chain. Tow is often used to talk about vehicles. If you tug something, you pull it suddenly and firmly. For example, a child might tug another child's hair.

dragon /ˈdræɡən/ NOUN [*plural* dragons] a big imaginary animal with wings, that breathes fire from its mouth (**dragão**)

drain¹ /dreɪn/ VERB [drains, draining, drained]

1 to make the liquid in something flow away ▫ *They had to drain the tank.* ▫ *Drain the pasta and serve with the sauce.* (**escoar**)

2 if a liquid drains, it flows away ▫ *She watched the water drain down the sink.* (**drenar**)

drain² /dreɪn/ NOUN [*plural* drains] a pipe or hole that allows waste water to flow away ▫ *The drain was blocked.* (**canal de escoamento**)

> **THESAURUS:** A **pipe** is a metal or plastic tube that water or gas can flow through. A drain is a pipe or a hole that takes waste water away. For example, sinks have a drain, and there are drains in the street to take rain water away. A **ditch** is a long narrow hole at the side of a road or a field to collect waste water.

drainpipe /ˈdreɪnpaɪp/ NOUN [*plural* drainpipes] a pipe on the outside of a building, that takes waste water down into the ground (**cano de esgoto**)

drama /ˈdrɑːmə/ NOUN [*plural* dramas]

1 a play at the theatre or on television ▫ *a TV drama* ▫ *an Australian drama series* (**drama**)

2 no plural plays and acting in general ▫ *Dan studied drama at Birmingham University.* ▫ *She went to drama school.* (**arte dramática**)

3 something exciting which happens ▫ *They watched the drama unfold (= happen) from her bedroom window.* (**acontecimento**)

dramatic /drəˈmætɪk/ ADJECTIVE

1 sudden, exciting or unexpected ▫ *There has been a dramatic increase in the number of exam passes.* ▫ *Computers have led to dramatic changes in work habits.* ▫ *He described his dramatic rescue from the sinking boat.* (**espetacular**)

2 to do with plays and the theatre ▫ *the dramatic works of an author* (**dramático**)

drank /dræŋk/ PAST TENSE OF **drink**¹ (ver **drink**¹)

draught /drɑːft/ NOUN [plural **draughts**]
1 a movement of air in a room which feels cold (**corrente de ar**)
2 draughts a game for two people who move flat, round pieces on a board that has black and white squares on it (**damas**)

draw¹ /drɔː/ VERB [**draws, drawing, drew, drawn**]
1 to make a picture with a pencil or pen □ *Ellie was drawing*. ▣ *She drew a lovely picture of a horse*. (**desenhar**)
2 to pull something from somewhere or pull something in a particular direction. A literary word □ *He drew a small piece of paper from his pocket*. (**puxar**)
3 to score the same number of points as someone else in a game □ *We drew 2-2*. (**empatar**)
4 draw closer/near to move closer in time or distance □ *As they drew closer she saw a path*. □ *Election day is drawing near*. (**mover-se**)
5 draw the curtains to pull curtains so that they cover a window or do not cover a window (**puxar**)
◆ PHRASAL VERB **draw up** if a vehicle draws up, it stops □ *A taxi drew up outside the house.*

draw² /drɔː/ NOUN [plural **draws**] a game that ends with both players or teams having the same score ▣ *The game ended in a draw*. (**empate**)

drawer /drɔː(r)/ NOUN [plural **drawers**] a part of a piece of furniture that you pull out and keep things in ▣ *He opened the drawer and got out some paper.* ▣ *The pens are in the top drawer*. (**gaveta**)

drawing /ˈdrɔːɪŋ/ NOUN [plural **drawings**]
1 a picture done with a pencil or pen ▣ *She did a few drawings*. □ *+ of a drawing of a house* (**desenho**)
2 no plural making pictures using a pencil or pen □ *Most children like drawing*. (**desenho**)

drawn /drɔːn/ PAST PARTICIPLE OF **draw**¹ (ver **draw**¹)

dreadful /ˈdredfʊl/ ADJECTIVE very bad □ *dreadful news* □ *a dreadful film*. (**terrível**)

dream¹ /driːm/ NOUN [plural **dreams**]
1 the things you think and see in your mind while you sleep ▣ *I had a very strange dream last night.* □ *+ about I had a dream about you*. ▣ *a bad dream* (**sonho**)
2 something you hope will happen □ *It was always her dream to go to Hollywood*. (**sonho**)

dream² /driːm/ VERB [**dreams, dreaming, dreamt or dreamed**]
1 to think about and see something in your mind while you sleep □ *+ that Last night I dreamt that I was lying on a beach.* □ *+ about I often dream about flying*. (**sonhar**)
2 to imagine something that you would like to happen □ *+ of I've always dreamt of moving to the coast*. (**sonhar**)

> Note that sense 2 of the verb **dream** is followed by **of** + the ing-form of the verb:
> ✓ *I've always dreamt of owning a restaurant.*
> ✗ *I've always dreamt to own a restaurant.*

dress¹ /dres/ NOUN [plural **dresses**]
1 a piece of clothing for girls or women like a top and skirt joined together □ *She was wearing a black dress*. ▣ *a wedding dress* (**vestido**)
2 no plural clothes of a particular type ▣ *The dancers were wearing traditional Highland dress*. (**roupa**)

dress² /dres/ VERB [**dresses, dressing, dressed**]
1 to put clothes on yourself or someone else ▣ *She got dressed and had breakfast.* □ *I'll dress the children*. (**vestir**)
2 to wear a particular style of clothes □ *She always dresses smartly*. (**vestir**)

> Note that when you put clothes on yourself, you **get dressed**:
> ✓ *I get dressed in the dark.*
> ✗ *I dress myself in the dark.*

◆ PHRASAL VERB **dress up 1** to put on clothes that make you look like someone else □ *Oliver is going to dress up as a pirate*. **2** to wear clothes that are more formal than the clothes you usually wear □ *Can I go in jeans, or do I need to dress up?*

dresser /ˈdresə(r)/ NOUN [plural **dressers**] a piece of furniture with a cupboard at the bottom and shelves above for keeping plates on (**armário de cozinha**)

dressing /ˈdresɪŋ/ NOUN [plural **dressings**] a sauce for a salad ▣ *a salad dressing*. (**tempero**)

drew /druː/ PAST TENSE OF **draw**¹ (ver **draw**¹)

dried¹ /draɪd/ PAST TENSE AND PAST PARTICIPLE OF **dry**¹ □ *Jill dried the glasses with a soft cloth.* (ver **dry**²)

dried² /draɪd/ ADJECTIVE dried food or flowers have had the water taken out of them ▣ *dried fruit* □ *dried herbs* (**seco**)

drift /drɪft/ VERB [**drifts, drifting, drifted**] to move with a current of water or air □ *Smoke drifted over the city*. (**ser levado**)

drill¹ /drɪl/ NOUN [plural **drills**] a tool for making holes in something hard, such as stone □ *an electric drill* (**broca, furadeira**)

drill² /drɪl/ VERB [**drills, drilling, drilled**] to make a hole in something hard ▣ *She drilled a hole in the wall.* □ *They had to drill through rock*. (**perfurar**)

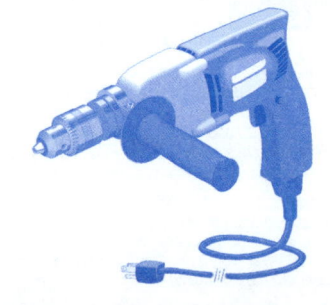

drink

drink¹ /drɪŋk/ VERB [drinks, drinking, drank, drunk]
1 to swallow a liquid □ *I drink a lot of coffee.* ▣ *I'll get you something to drink.* (beber)
2 to drink alcohol □ *Mark doesn't drink.* (beber)

> **THESAURUS:** If you **swallow** food or drink, you make it go down your throat. Drink is a general word for swallowing a liquid. If you **sip**, you drink something slowly, taking only a small amount at a time. For example, you might **sip** a drink which is very hot.

drink² /drɪŋk/ NOUN [plural drinks] a liquid that you swallow ▣ *Can I have a drink, please?* □ *+ of Would you like a drink of water?* (bebida)

drip /drɪp/ VERB [drips, dripping, dripped]
1 if a liquid drips, it falls in drops □ *Water was dripping from the trees.* (pingar)
2 to produce drops of liquid □ *I can hear a tap dripping somewhere.* (gotejar)

> **THESAURUS:** If a liquid **drips**, it falls in small drops. If a liquid **splashes**, or if you **splash** it, it hits something with a quick movement, often making a noise. Children enjoy **splashing** in water, and you might **splash** water on your face. If a liquid **trickles**, it flows in a slow, thin stream. For example, blood might **trickle** down your arm if you cut yourself. If a liquid or gas **leaks**, it escapes from the place where it should be. For example, a pipe might **leak** in your house.

drive¹ /draɪv/ VERB [drives, driving, drove, driven] to make a car, bus, etc. move and control where it goes and how fast it moves □ *Can you drive?* □ *I had to drive my mother's car.* □ *We drove to Spain.* □ *She drove me to the airport.* (dirigir)

drive² /draɪv/ NOUN [plural drives]
1 a journey in a car ▣ *We went for a drive in the country.* ▣ *He began the long drive home.* □ *It's a two-hour drive to the coast.* (passeio de carro)
2 an area in front of a house where you can put your car □ *There were two cars on the drive.* (caminho)
3 a part of a computer that stores information. A computing word □ *The PC has a standard DVD drive.* (drive)

driven /ˈdrɪvən/ PAST PARTICIPLE OF **drive¹** (ver **drive¹**)

driver /ˈdraɪvə(r)/ NOUN [plural drivers] a person who drives a car, etc. □ *a taxi driver* □ *She's a good driver.* (motorista)

driving /ˈdraɪvɪŋ/ NOUN, NO PLURAL when you drive a car, etc. or the way that you drive ▣ *Jane's having driving lessons.* □ *He was arrested for dangerous driving.* (direção)

driving licence /ˈdraɪvɪŋ ˌlaɪsəns/ NOUN [plural driving licences] an official document that shows you are allowed to drive □ *He didn't have a driving licence.* ▣ *A clean driving licence* (= showing that you have never done anything wrong while driving) *is essential for the job.* (carteira de motorista)

droop /druːp/ VERB [droops, drooping, drooped] to hang down □ *The flowers were starting to droop.* □ *Her head drooped slightly forwards.* (pender)

drop¹ /drɒp/ VERB [drops, dropping, dropped]
1 to fall to the ground, or to allow something to fall to the ground □ *She tripped and dropped her glass.* □ *The ball dropped into the hole.* (cair)
2 to change to a lower level or amount □ *The temperature drops at night.* □ *+ from The exam pass rate has dropped from 75% to 60%.* (cair)
3 if you drop someone somewhere, you take them there in your car, and then drive somewhere else yourself □ *I'll drop you at the doctor's on my way to the supermarket.* (deixar)
♦ PHRASAL VERBS **drop by/in/round** to visit someone for a short time □ *Why don't you drop round for a coffee later?* **drop someone/something off** to take someone or something to a place □ *I've got to drop this bag off at my Mum's house.* **drop out** to stop doing something before you have finished □ *She dropped out of school at the age of fifteen.*

drop² /drɒp/ NOUN [plural drops]
1 a very small amount of a liquid □ *+ of Was that a drop of rain?* □ *There were some drops of blood on the floor.* (gota)
2 no plural a decrease ▣ *There has been a sharp drop* (= big decrease) *in profits.* □ *+ in There was a small drop in the number of tourists last year.* (queda)

drought /draʊt/ NOUN [plural droughts] a time when very little rain falls ▣ *The country is currently suffering from a severe drought.* (seca)

drove /drəʊv/ PAST TENSE OF **drive¹** (ver **drive¹**)

drown /draʊn/ VERB [drowns, drowning, drowned] to die because of being under water and not able to breathe □ *Three soldiers drowned when their truck fell into a river.* (afogar-se)

drug /drʌɡ/ NOUN [plural drugs]
1 a medicine ▣ *Doctors usually prescribe the drug for children.* (remédio)
2 an illegal substance that people take to change the way they feel ▣ *He was on drugs* (= regularly taking drugs). ▣ *I've never taken drugs.* ▣ *a drug addict* (droga)

drum¹ /drʌm/ NOUN [plural drums]
1 an instrument that is round and has a skin stretched over it that you hit to make a rhythm ▣ *He plays the drums in a band.* ▣ *a drum kit* (= a set of drums) (tambor)
2 a tall round container for liquids ▣ *an oil drum* (tambor)

drum² /drʌm/ VERB [drums, drumming, drummed] to hit something in a regular rhythm □ *Rain was drumming on the roof.* □ *He was drumming impatiently on the table.* (tamborilar)

drummer /ˈdrʌmə(r)/ NOUN [plural drummers] someone who plays the drums (baterista)

drunk¹ /drʌŋk/ PAST PARTICIPLE OF **drink¹** (ver **drink¹**)

drunk² /drʌŋk/ ADJECTIVE having drunk too much alcohol □ *He got drunk at the party.* (bêbado)

drunken /'drʌŋkən/ ADJECTIVE having drunk too much alcohol, or involving people who have drunk too much alcohol □ *a drunken brawl* (bêbado)

dry¹ /draɪ/ ADJECTIVE [drier, driest]
1 not wet □ *Are the clothes dry yet?* (seco)
2 with little rain □ *dry weather* □ *a hot, dry summer* (seco)

dry² /draɪ/ VERB [dries, drying, dried] to make something dry, or to become dry □ *He dried his hands on the towel.* □ *She hung the clothes out to dry.* (secar)
◆ PHRASAL VERB **dry (something) up** to dry plates, bowls, etc. after someone has washed them (enxugar)

dry-clean /ˌdraɪ'kliːn/ VERB [dry-cleans, dry-cleaning, dry-cleaned] to clean clothes with chemicals instead of water (lavar a seco)

dry cleaner /ˌdraɪ'kliːnə(r)/ NOUN [plural dry cleaners] a shop where clothes are cleaned with chemicals instead of water (tinturaria)

dry cleaning /ˌdraɪ'kliːnɪŋ/ NOUN, NO PLURAL
1 clothes that are cleaned with chemicals instead of water (lavagem a seco)
2 cleaning clothes using chemicals instead of water (lavagem a seco)

dual /'djuːəl/ ADJECTIVE having two parts □ *Hening has dual Belgian/French nationality.* (dupla)

dub /dʌb/ VERB [dubs, dubbing, dubbed] to change the language in a film or television programme into a different language □ *The film has been dubbed into Russian.* (dublar)

duck¹ /dʌk/ NOUN [plural ducks]
1 a water bird with short legs and a wide, flat beak □ *wild ducks* (pato)
2 no plural the meat from a duck □ *roast duck* (pato)

duck² /dʌk/ VERB [ducks, ducking, ducked] to lower your head or body so that you are not hit or seen □ *Hamish ducked his head to get through the low doorway.* □ *+ behind He ducked behind a car when the shooting began.* (esquivar-se)

due /djuː/ ADJECTIVE
1 expected to arrive or happen □ *+ at The train is due at 10:15.* □ *+ in Their baby is due in March.* □ *+ to do something The project is due to start next month.* (esperado)
2 needing to be paid □ *The rent is due at the beginning of the month.* (devido)
3 due to something because of something □ *The plane was delayed due to bad weather.* (devido a)
4 be due for something if you are due for something, it is time to have that thing □ *I'm due for a pay rise.* (merecer algo)

dug /dʌg/ PAST TENSE AND PAST PARTICIPLE OF **dig** (ver **dig**)

duke /djuːk/ NOUN [plural dukes] a title for a man with a very high social rank (duque)

dull /dʌl/ ADJECTIVE [duller, dullest]
1 boring □ *It was the dullest job you could imagine.* □ *Life is never dull when John's around.* (maçante)
2 not bright □ *It was a dull, grey day.* (sombrio)

dumb /dʌm/ ADJECTIVE [dumber, dumbest]
1 stupid. An informal word □ *He kept asking me dumb questions.* (idiota)
2 not able to speak (mudo)

dump¹ /dʌmp/ VERB [dumps, dumping, dumped]
1 to put something somewhere quickly □ *He dumped his bag in the hall and ran upstairs.* (largar)
2 to leave something somewhere because you do not want it □ *It is not acceptable to dump toxic waste in the sea.* (despejar)

dump² /dʌmp/ NOUN [plural dumps] a place where people can leave things they do not want □ *I'm going to take the old sofa to the dump.* (despejo)

dune /djuːn/ NOUN [plural dunes] a hill of sand (duna)

duo /'djuːəʊ/ NOUN [plural duos] two people who perform together □ *a comedy duo*

duplicate¹ /'djuːplɪkət/ NOUN [plural duplicates] an exact copy □ *She sent a duplicate of the photo.* (cópia)

duplicate² /'djuːplɪkət/ ADJECTIVE exactly the same □ *a duplicate key* (duplicata)

duration /djʊ'reɪʃən/ NOUN, NO PLURAL the length of time that something continues. A formal word □ *Hotel guests are offered a car for the duration of their stay.* (duração)

during /'djʊərɪŋ/ PREPOSITION
1 at one point in a period of time □ *My grandfather was killed during the war.* (durante)
2 through the whole of a period of time □ *The garden looks beautiful during the summer.* (durante)

> Remember that **during** is not used to talk about how long something happens. Use **for** for this:
> ✓ *I studied English for three years.*
> ✗ *I studied English during three years.*

dusk /dʌsk/ NOUN, NO PLURAL the time in the evening when it starts to get dark □ *Dusk was falling.* (penumbra)

dust¹ /dʌst/ NOUN, NO PLURAL a powder of dirt on a surface or in the air □ *A thin layer of dust covered the desk.* □ *The horses kicked up a cloud of dust.* (pó)

dust² /dʌst/ VERB [dusts, dusting, dusted] to clean dust from something using a cloth □ *I've dusted the shelves.* (limpar o pó, desempoeirar)

dustbin /'dʌstbɪn/ NOUN [plural dustbins] a container for rubbish, which is outside your house □ *She threw the empty boxes in the dustbin.* (lata de lixo)

dusty /'dʌsti/ ADJECTIVE [dustier, dustiest] covered with dust □ *a dusty floor* □ *Children played in the dusty streets.* (poeirento)

duty /ˈdjuːtɪ/ NOUN [plural **duties**]
1 something that you do because other people expect you to do it or because it is morally right to do it ▣ *He felt he had a moral duty to help her.* □ + **to do something** *Society has a duty to protect children.* (**dever**)
2 on/off duty if someone such as a doctor, police officer etc. is on duty, they are working, and if they are off duty, they are not working □ *Which doctor is on duty tonight?* (**estar/não estar de plantão**)

duty-free /ˌdjuːtɪˈfriː/ ADJECTIVE duty-free products are cheaper because you can bring them into a country without paying tax □ *duty-free perfume* ▣ *We went to the duty-free shop at the airport.* (**isento de taxa**)

duvet /ˈduːveɪ/ NOUN [plural **duvets**] a thick warm cover for your bed □ *He pulled the duvet over his head.* ▣ *a duvet cover* (**acolchoado**)

DVD /ˌdiːviːˈdiː/ ABBREVIATION **digital versatile disk**; a type of disk with pictures and sound recorded on it □ *The movie is available on DVD.* ▣ *a DVD player* ▣ *The children were watching a DVD.* (**DVD**)

dwarf[1] /dwɔːf/ NOUN [plural **dwarfs** or **dwarves**] an imaginary creature in children's stories, which looks like a very small man (**anão, gnomo, duende**)

dwarf[2] /dwɔːf/ ADJECTIVE dwarf plants are much smaller than the usual type □ *dwarf apple trees* (**anão**)

dye[1] /daɪ/ NOUN [plural **dyes**] a substance used for changing the colour of cloth or hair (**tintura**)

dye[2] /daɪ/ VERB [**dyes, dyeing, dyed**] to use a substance to change the colour of cloth or hair □ *Emma dyed her hair red.* (**tingir**)

dynamic /daɪˈnæmɪk/ ADJECTIVE full of energy and new ideas □ *a dynamic young manager.* (**dinâmico**)

E e

E¹ ou **e** /iː/ the fifth letter of the alphabet (**a quinta letra do alfabeto**)
E² /iː/ ABBREVIATION **east**² (**leste**)
e- /iː/ PREFIX e- is added to the beginning of words to mean 'electronic' or to do with the Internet □ *e-commerce* (**eletrônico**)

each /iːtʃ/ DETERMINER, PRONOUN
1 every separate person or thing □ *We had to pay £5 each.* □ **+ of** *Each of the soldiers was given a gun.* □ *He had a heavy suitcase in each hand.* (**cada**)
2 each other used to show that each person or thing in a group of two or more does something to the others □ *The team all hugged each other.* □ *The cat and dog don't like each other much.* (**mutuamente, um ao outro**)

> Remember that **each** is followed by a singular noun: □ *Each person starts the game with five cards.*

eager /ˈiːɡə(r)/ ADJECTIVE wanting very much to do or have something □ **+ to do something** *Imran seems eager to learn.* (**ávido**)

eagle /ˈiːɡəl/ NOUN [*plural* **eagles**] a large bird with a curved beak that hunts small birds and animals (**águia**)

ear /ɪə(r)/ NOUN [*plural* **ears**]
1 one of the two parts on each side of your head that you hear with □ *He whispered something in my ear.* (**orelha, ouvido**)
2 the part at the top of the stem of some plants where the grains grow □ *an ear of corn* (**espiga**)

earache /ˈɪəreɪk/ NOUN, NO PLURAL pain inside your ear (**dor de ouvido**)

early /ˈɜːlɪ/ ADJECTIVE, ADVERB [**earlier, earliest**]
1 happening or arriving before others or before the expected or normal time □ *Nick had taken an earlier train.* □ *I'm tired so I'm going to bed early tonight.* (**cedo**)
2 near the beginning of something □ *It's so quiet here in the early morning.* □ *She showed musical talent early in life.* ▣ *The police were in the early stages of the investigation.* (**início**)
3 early on in the first part of something □ *He played really well early on in the match.* (**logo no começo**)

earn /ɜːn/ VERB [**earns, earning, earned**]
1 to get money for work that you do □ *He earns about £45,000 a year.* ▣ *Does she earn her living* (= get all the money she needs to live) *as an artist?* (**ganhar**)
2 to get something good, such as praise, because you have done something well □ *He worked hard and earned the respect of his colleagues.* (**merecer**)

> Remember that you **earn** money for work that you do. You **win** money in a competition: □ *He earns a very good salary.* □ *He won a million pounds on the lottery.*

earnings /ˈɜːnɪŋz/ PLURAL NOUN money that you get from working (**vencimento**)

earring /ˈɪərɪŋ/ NOUN [*plural* **earrings**] a piece of jewellery for the ear □ *a pair of earrings* □ *diamond earrings* (**brinco**)

earth /ɜːθ/ NOUN [*plural* **earths**]
1 Earth the planet we live on ▣ *life on Earth* □ *The Earth rotates around the sun.* (**Terra**)
2 no plural soil □ *a pile of earth* (**terra**)
◆ IDIOM **how/what/where/why on earth?** used to emphasize a question, usually when you are very surprised □ *How on earth did that happen?* □ *What on earth was he wearing?*

earthquake /ˈɜːθkweɪk/ NOUN [*plural* **earthquakes**] when the ground suddenly moves, often causing serious damage to buildings (**terremoto**)

ease¹ /iːz/ NOUN, NO PLURAL
1 with ease easily □ *She won the race with ease.* (**facilidade**)
2 at ease relaxed □ *He's never completely at ease talking to strangers.* (**sentir-se à vontade**)

ease[2] /iːz/ VERB [eases, easing, eased] to become less difficult or painful, or to make something less difficult or painful ▣ These tablets should ease the pain. ▢ Tensions in the area have gradually eased. (aliviar)

easily /ˈiːzɪli/ ADVERB with no effort or difficulty ▢ Chelsea won easily. (facilmente)

east[1] /iːst/ NOUN, NO PLURAL the direction that you look towards to see the sunrise ▢ Which way is east? ▢ York is to the east of Harrogate. (leste)

east[2] /iːst/ ADJECTIVE, ADVERB in or towards the east ▢ the east coast ▢ East London ▢ We headed east. ([para] leste)

Easter /ˈiːstə(r)/ NOUN, NO PLURAL a Christian holiday in March or April to celebrate when Christ came back to life from the dead ▢ the Easter holidays ▢ Easter Sunday (Páscoa)

eastern /ˈiːstən/ ADJECTIVE in or from the east part of a country or area ▢ the eastern coast of America ▢ Eastern England (oriental)

easy[1] /ˈiːzi/ ADJECTIVE [easier, easiest] not difficult to do ▢ an easy exam paper (fácil)

easy[2] /ˈiːzi/ ADVERB [easier, easiest] **take it easy** to relax and not work hard ▢ Grandad's taking it easy in the garden. (sossegado)
♦ IDIOMS **Easier said than done.** used to say that something is difficult to do ▢ I know I should get the kids to help but that's easier said than done. **go easy on someone** to treat someone more gently ▢ Go easy on Matt, he's having a hard time at the moment. **go easy on something** to eat or use only a little of something ▢ My doctor said I should go easy on the red meat.

eat /iːt/ VERB [eats, eating, ate, eaten]
1 to put food in your mouth and swallow it ▢ We've eaten all the bread. ▢ He ate a huge meal. ▣ Do you fancy something to eat? (comer)
2 to have a meal ▢ What time would you like to eat? (comer)
♦ PHRASAL VERBS **eat out** to have a meal in a restaurant ▢ We eat out about twice a month. **eat something up** to eat all of an amount of food ▢ Eat up your vegetables, Maisie.

eBay /ˈiːbeɪ/ NOUN, NO PLURAL a website where you can buy and sell things. A trademark. ▣ She buys a lot of clothes on eBay. (e-Bay)

echo[1] /ˈekəʊ/ VERB [echoes, echoing, echoed] a sound echoes when it comes back and you hear it again ▢ Their laughter echoed in the empty concert hall. (ecoar)

echo[2] /ˈekəʊ/ NOUN [plural echoes] a sound that you hear again after it is sent back off a surface such as a wall (eco)

ecology /ɪˈkɒlədʒi/ NOUN, NO PLURAL the study of how plants and animals exist together and how their environment affects them (ecologia)

economic /ˌiːkəˈnɒmɪk/ ADJECTIVE to do with money, business and industry ▣ More economic growth is predicted. ▣ economic development ▢ an economic forecast (econômico)

economics /ˌiːkəˈnɒmɪks/ NOUN, NO PLURAL the study of how money, business and industry are organized ▢ a degree in economics (economia)

economy /ɪˈkɒnəmi/ NOUN [plural economies] all the money a country or area creates through producing and selling goods and services, and the way that money is used ▢ Canada's economy grew fast. ▢ Tourism benefits the local economy. (economia)

ecosystem /ˈiːkəʊˌsɪstəm/ NOUN [plural ecosystems] all the plants and animals in an area and the way they depend on each other and on their environment to live (ecossistema)

edge /edʒ/ NOUN [plural edges]
1 the outer part or end of something ▢ We stood on the edge of the cliff. ▢ I live on the outer edge of the city. ▢ Trim off all the rough edges. (beira)
2 a side of something that is sharp enough to cut (gume)
3 on edge nervous and slightly bad-tempered (impaciente)

edit /ˈedɪt/ VERB [edits, editing, edited] to prepare a book, document, film, etc. by correcting mistakes and making any changes that are needed (editar)

edition /ɪˈdɪʃən/ NOUN [plural editions] the copies of a book, newspaper, etc. that are printed at the same time ▢ The story was in the early editions of the newspaper. ▢ I bought the hardback edition of her first novel. (edição)

editor /ˈedɪtə(r)/ NOUN [plural editors] someone whose job is to prepare a book, document, newspaper, etc. to be published by correcting mistakes and making any changes that are needed ▢ He thanked his editor for all her help. (editor, organizador)

educate /ˈedjʊkeɪt/ VERB [educates, educating, educated]
1 to teach someone ▢ He was educated at the local school. (educar, ensinar, instruir)
2 to give people information about something so that they understand it more ▢ + **about** We need to educate people about the importance of exercise. (educar)

education /ˌedjʊˈkeɪʃən/ NOUN, NO PLURAL the process of teaching, especially in schools or colleges ▢ Our students receive a good standard of education. ▢ secondary education (educação, instrução, formação)

> **THESAURUS:** Education is a general word for the process of teaching and learning things. Teaching is the work that a teacher does. Training is the process of teaching someone how to do something. For example, you might get training in how to use a computer or how to do a new job.

educational /ˌedjuˈkeɪʃənəl/ ADJECTIVE to do with teaching and learning ◘ *She organized an educational visit to the museum.* ◻ *He works for a company which makes educational toys.* (**educacional**)

effect /ɪˈfekt/ NOUN [plural **effects**] if one thing has an effect on another, it influences it or causes something to happen to it ◻ **+ on** *His asthma has no effect on his ability as a footballer.* ◻ *She was suffering from the effects of a long plane journey.* (**efeito**)

> Be careful not to confuse **effect**, which is a noun, with **affect**, which is a verb: ◻ *One thing has an effect on another.* ◻ *One thing affects another.*

effective /ɪˈfektɪv/ ADJECTIVE working well or producing the results you want ◻ *This is an effective treatment for the common cold.* ◻ *Do you know of an effective way of removing chewing gum from a carpet?* (**eficaz**)

> **THESAURUS:** You might describe a medicine as effective if it makes you feel better. If something is **efficient**, it works well and does not waste time or energy. You might describe a factory as **efficient** if it produces things that are good quality in a short time. If a teacher describes your work as **adequate**, it is good enough, but not very good. If something is **useful**, it helps you to do something. For example, a map is **useful** in a city that you do not know.

efficient /ɪˈfɪʃənt/ ADJECTIVE working well and not wasting any time or energy ◻ *The questionnaire was an efficient method of collecting information.* ◻ *This is not an efficient use of resources.* (**eficiente**)

effort /ˈefət/ NOUN [plural **efforts**] the physical or mental energy that you need to do something ◘ *She made a real effort to be friendly.* ◘ *You must put some more effort into your school work.* ◻ **+ to do something** *It takes a lot of effort to be an athlete.* (**esforço**)

eg or **e.g.** /ˌiːˈdʒiː/ ABBREVIATION for example ◻ *The zoo specializes in African animals, eg the lion and the giraffe.* (**por exemplo**)

egg /eg/ NOUN [plural **eggs**]
1 an oval object with a shell or case, in which a baby bird, reptile or fish develops ◘ *The cuckoo lays its eggs in another bird's nest.* (**ovo**)
2 an oval object with a shell produced by a chicken or similar bird that we eat as food ◘ *a boiled/fried egg* ◘ *Beat two egg yolks with a little milk.* (**ovo**)

ego /ˈiːgəʊ/ NOUN [plural **egos**] the opinion you have of yourself ◻ *All the attention and praise was good for her ego.* (**ego**)

eight /eɪt/ NUMBER [plural **eights**] the number 8 (**oito**)

eighteen /ˌeɪˈtiːn/ NUMBER the number 18 (**dezoito**)

eighteenth /ˌeɪˈtiːnθ/ NUMBER 18th written as a word (**dezoito avos**)

eighth¹ /eɪtθ/ NUMBER 8th written as a word ◻ *the eighth book in the series* ◻ *Our team finished eighth.* (**oitavo**)

eighth² /eɪtθ/ NOUN [plural **eighths**] 1/8; one of eight equal parts of something (**oitavo**)

eightieth /ˈeɪtiəθ/ NUMBER 80th written as a word (**octogésimo**)

eighty /ˈeɪti/ NUMBER [plural **eighties**] the number 80 (**oitenta**)

either¹ /ˈaɪðə(r)/ ADVERB used in negative sentences to mean 'as well' ◻ *If you don't go, I won't go either.* ◻ *Dan doesn't like cheese either.* (**também não**)

either² /ˈaɪðə(r)/ DETERMINER, PRONOUN
1 one or the other ◻ *She can write with either hand.* ◻ **+ of** *I can't afford either of them.* (**um ou outro**)
2 both ◘ *They stood on either side of the Queen.* (**cada um dos dois**)

either³ /ˈaɪðə(r)/ CONJUNCTION **either ... or** used to show a choice ◻ *You can have either a video game or a CD.* (**ou... ou**)

elaborate /ɪˈlæbərət/ ADJECTIVE involving complicated detail or decoration ◻ *an elaborate plan* ◻ *elaborate costumes* (**complexo**)

elbow /ˈelbəʊ/ NOUN [plural **elbows**] the part in the middle of your arm where it bends (**cotovelo**)

elder¹ /ˈeldə(r)/ ADJECTIVE older ◻ *She has an elder brother.* (**mais velho**)

elder² /ˈeldə(r)/ NOUN, NO PLURAL **the elder** the older of two people ◻ *She's the elder of two sisters.* (**mais velho**)

elderly¹ /ˈeldəli/ ADJECTIVE old ◻ *an elderly lady* (**idoso**)

elderly | 107 | e-mail

> **THESAURUS:** Old is a general word to describe people or things that have existed for a long time. When you are talking about people, the word elderly is more polite than the word old. We do not use elderly to talk about things. Aged is used to say how old a person is. To talk about how old a thing is, we usually use the word old. For example, you can say that a child is aged three, or that he is three years old. You say that a house is ten years old, not aged ten.

elderly² /ˈeldəlɪ/ NOUN **the elderly** people who are old □ *Sarah works in a care home for the elderly.* (idosos)

eldest¹ /ˈeldɪst/ ADJECTIVE oldest □ *Alex is my eldest child.* (mais velho)

eldest² /ˈeldɪst/ NOUN, NO PLURAL **the eldest** the person who is the oldest □ *Fiona is the eldest of three sisters.* (o mais velho)

elect /ɪˈlekt/ VERB [**elects, electing, elected**] to choose someone for a particular job or position in an organization by voting □ *The committee has to elect a chairperson.* □ *The president was elected in 2004.* (eleger)

> **THESAURUS:** If you elect a person, you choose them to do a job, by voting. For example, we elect politicians. If you appoint someone, you officially give that person a job. Pick and choose are more general words to describe taking one thing or person from a group. For example, you might pick or choose paint for your kitchen, or people to invite to a party.

election /ɪˈlekʃən/ NOUN [plural **elections**] when people choose someone by voting 🔁 *Nobody knows when he will decide to hold the election.* 🔁 *Her party won the election.* (eleição)

electric /ɪˈlektrɪk/ ADJECTIVE made or worked by electricity □ *an electric spark* □ *an electric light* □ *electric current* (elétrico)

electrical /ɪˈlektrɪkəl/ ADJECTIVE to do with electricity □ *She's studying electrical engineering.* □ *The shop sells small electrical appliances like kettles and irons.* (elétrico)

electricity /ɪˌlekˈtrɪsətɪ/ NOUN, NO PLURAL a type of energy used to make light and heat and to make machines work □ *We're trying to save electricity by turning off our computers at night.* (eletricidade)

electron /ɪˈlektrɒn/ NOUN [plural **electrons**] one of the parts of an atom that move around the nucleus and have a negative electrical charge. A chemistry and physics word. (elétron)

electronic /ɪˌlekˈtrɒnɪk/ ADJECTIVE using electricity and very small electrical parts to work 🔁 *an electronic device* 🔁 *They sell computers and other electronic equipment.* (eletrônico)

electronics /ɪˌlekˈtrɒnɪks/ NOUN, NO PLURAL the study of how electricity flows and how it can be used in machinery (eletrônica)

element /ˈelɪmənt/ NOUN [plural **elements**]
1 a part of something □ *They are unhappy about some elements of the course.* □ *His work has a political element.* (elemento)
2 a substance that cannot be divided into smaller chemical substances, for example oxygen and carbon. A chemistry word. (elemento)

elementary /ˌelɪˈmentərɪ/ ADJECTIVE basic □ *You have forgotten the elementary principles of journalism.* □ *He makes too many elementary mistakes.* □ *elementary maths* □ *students at elementary level* (elementar)

elephant /ˈelɪfənt/ NOUN [plural **elephants**] a very large animal with a long nose, large ears and thick grey skin (elefante)

eleven /ɪˈlevən/ NUMBER [plural **elevens**] the number 11 (onze)

eleventh /ɪˈlevənθ/ NUMBER 11th written as a word (décimo primeiro, undécimo)

eliminate /ɪˈlɪmɪneɪt/ VERB [**eliminates, eliminating, eliminated**] to get rid of something completely □ *We aim to eliminate poverty.* 🔁 *The new technology eliminates the need for ID cards and passwords.* (eliminar)

elite¹ /ɪˈliːt/ NOUN [plural **elites**] the best, most important or most powerful people in a society or group □ *the country's ruling elite* □ *the sporting elite* (elite)

elite² /ɪˈliːt/ ADJECTIVE of very high quality □ *an elite athlete* (de elite)

else /els/ ADVERB
1 as well as the thing or person that has been talked about 🔁 *Promise not to tell anyone else.* 🔁 *You must wait in the queue, the same as everybody else.* 🔁 *There's something else I need to tell you.* (mais, outro)
2 different from something or someone 🔁 *I had to leave. What else could I do?* 🔁 *I hate swimming. Can we do something else instead?* 🔁 *He must be angry. Why else would he react like that?* (mais, outro)
3 or else used to say that a bad thing will happen if another thing does not happen □ *Put on a jumper or else you'll get cold.* (ou então)

elsewhere /elsˈweə(r)/ ADVERB in or to another place □ *It's too expensive here, we'll have to look elsewhere.* (em outro lugar)

e-mail¹ ou **email** /ˈiːmeɪl/ NOUN [plural **e-mails** or **emails**]
1 no plural the system for sending messages between computers □ *They keep in touch by*

e-mail. □ *Are you on e-mail?* 🔄 *What's your e-mail address?* (e-mail)
2 a written message sent between computers 🔄 *He sends me an e-mail every day.* (e-mail)

e-mail² or **email** /ˈiːmeɪl/ VERB [e-mails, emailing, e-mailed or emails, emailing, emailed] to send someone an e-mail □ *I'll e-mail you the address.* (enviar um e-mail)

embarrass /ɪmˈbærəs/ VERB [embarrasses, embarrassing, embarrassed] to make someone feel ashamed or stupid □ *Stop it! You're embarrassing me!* □ *The information could embarrass the president if it gets out.* (embaraçar)

embarrassed /ɪmˈbærəst/ ADJECTIVE looking or feeling ashamed or stupid □ *an embarrassed silence* 🔄 *Quinn felt embarrassed.* □ **+ about** *They're very embarrassed about what's happened.* □ **+ by** *She looked a little embarrassed by all the attention.*

> **THESAURUS:** If you are embarrassed, you feel ashamed or silly about something that you have done or said. If you feel **shy**, you do not feel comfortable or confident when you speak to other people. If someone **humiliates** you, they make you feel stupid or ashamed about something, and you feel **humiliated**. This is a stronger word than embarrassed.

embarrassing /ɪmˈbærəsɪŋ/ ADJECTIVE making you feel embarrassed □ *It was an embarrassing moment.* 🔄 *a highly embarrassing photo* □ **+ for** *The incident was very embarrassing for the government.* (embaraçoso)

embarrassment /ɪmˈbærəsmənt/ NOUN, NO PLURAL a feeling of being embarrassed 🔄 *Check the price in advance to avoid embarrassment.* 🔄 *I don't want to cause her any embarrassment.* (embaraço)

embassy /ˈembəsi/ NOUN [plural embassies] a group of officials who represent their government in a foreign country, or the building where they work □ *the Australian embassy in Washington* (embaixada)

embrace /ɪmˈbreɪs/ VERB [embraces, embracing, embraced] to put your arms around someone and hold them as a sign of love or being friends □ *The two friends embraced warmly.* (abraçar)

embryo /ˈembriəʊ/ NOUN [plural embryos] a baby or animal when it starts growing inside its mother's body. A biology word. (embrião)

emerge /ɪˈmɜːdʒ/ VERB [emerges, emerging, emerged] to come out of something or from behind something □ *The baby crocodiles emerge from the eggs.* □ *Al emerged from the tent.* (emergir)

emergency¹ /ɪˈmɜːdʒənsi/ NOUN [plural emergencies] a sudden, unexpected and usually dangerous event that needs immediate action 🔄 *In an emergency, call my husband's number.* 🔄 *I always take my mobile with me in case of emergencies.* 🔄 *a medical emergency* (emergência)

emergency² /ɪˈmɜːdʒənsi/ ADJECTIVE to do with an emergency □ *emergency surgery* □ *The plane made an emergency landing.* ([de] emergência)

emit /ɪˈmɪt/ VERB [emits, emitting, emitted] to send light, heat, gas or a sound out into the air. A formal word. □ *The substance emits light.* □ *The machine emitted a high-pitched noise.* (emitir, emanar)

emotion /ɪˈməʊʃən/ NOUN [plural emotions] a feeling, such as love, hate, fear or anger 🔄 *He showed no emotion throughout the trial.* □ *Anya struggled to control her emotions.* 🔄 *I've got mixed emotions* (= good and bad feelings) *about the place.* (emoção, afeto)

emotional /ɪˈməʊʃənəl/ ADJECTIVE showing or having strong feelings □ *an emotional speech* 🔄 *I get emotional just talking about it.* □ *He was in a highly emotional state.* (emotivo)

emperor /ˈempərə(r)/ NOUN [plural emperors] the ruler of a group of countries governed by one leader or government (imperador)

emphasis /ˈemfəsɪs/ NOUN [plural emphases] special importance or attention you give to something 🔄 *Schools put too much emphasis on exams.* (ênfase)

emphasize or **emphasise** /ˈemfəsaɪz/ VERB [emphasizes, emphasizing, emphasized] to give special importance or attention to something 🔄 *I want to emphasize the importance of road safety.* □ *She emphasized that she had been treated very well.* (enfatizar)

empire /ˈempaɪə(r)/ NOUN [plural empires] a group of countries governed by one leader or government □ *the Roman empire* (império)

employ /ɪmˈplɔɪ/ VERB [employs, employing, employed] to pay someone to work for you □ *The company employs skilled workers.* □ **+ as** *He was employed as a teacher.* □ **+ to do something** *We employed a local builder to do the work.* (empregador)

employee /ɪmˈplɔɪiː/ NOUN [plural employees] someone who works for a company or another person 🔄 *The company has 16 full-time employees.* □ **+ of** *We spoke to a former employee of the firm.* (empregador)

employer /ɪmˈplɔɪə(r)/ NOUN [plural employers] a company or person who employs people □ *It's a chance for students to meet potential employers.* □ *The factory is the area's largest employer.* (empregador)

employment /ɪmˈplɔɪmənt/ NOUN, NO PLURAL paid work for a company or person 🔄 *Are you in*

empty | 109 | **engineering**

full-time employment? 🔹 *He found employment as a security guard.* (**emprego**)

empty¹ /ˈempti/ ADJECTIVE [emptier, emptiest]
containing nothing or no one □ *an empty box* 🔹 *There was an empty space between the two buildings.* □ *The restaurant was almost empty.* □ + *of The streets were empty of traffic.* (**vazio**)

empty² /ˈempti/ VERB [empties, emptying, emptied]
to become empty, or to make something empty □ *Empty your pockets.* □ *The theatre slowly emptied.* (**esvaziar**)

enable /ɪˈneɪbəl/ VERB [enables, enabling, enabled] to make it possible for someone to do something □ *The software enables users to download music.* (**possibilitar**)

enclose /ɪnˈkloʊz/ VERB [encloses, enclosing, enclosed]
1 to put something in an envelope with a letter □ *I'm enclosing a copy of the certificate.* (**incluir**)
2 to be all around something □ *The children's play area is enclosed by a wooden fence.* (**cercar**)

encourage /ɪnˈkʌrɪdʒ/ VERB [encourages, encouraging, encouraged]
to support someone and make them feel confident about doing something □ + *to do something We encourage students to work together.* □ *My parents encouraged me to write.* □ *We have been encouraged by recent successes.* (**incentivar**)

encouragement /ɪnˈkʌrɪdʒmənt/ NOUN,
NO PLURAL when you encourage someone or something □ *The crowd shouted encouragement to the team.* □ + *to do something She needed no encouragement to dive into the pool.* (**incentivo**)

end¹ /end/ NOUN [plural ends]
1 the last part of something □ *The end of the book is very sad.* □ *I'll come back at the end of the week.* (**fim**)
2 the part of something that is furthest away from the middle □ *He poked me with the end of a stick.* 🔹 *There is a church at the other end of this street.* 🔹 *We sat at opposite ends of the table.* (**fim, extremidade**)
3 when something does not exist any more 🔹 *We were sad when our holiday came to an end.* (**fim**)
4 in the end after a long period of time □ *The train was delayed, but we got there in the end.* (**no fim**)

end² /end/ VERB [ends, ending, ended]
to finish □ *Our holiday ends tomorrow.* □ + *with He ended his speech with a joke.* □ *The word cough ends with a 'f' sound.* (**terminar**)

♦ PHRASAL VERB **end up somewhere/doing something** to have to do something or to finish in a bad situation □ *I knew he'd end up in prison.* □ *I ended up catching a later train.*

endanger /ɪnˈdeɪndʒə(r)/ VERB [endangers, endangering, endangered] to cause someone to be in a dangerous situation 🔹 *His actions could have endangered the lives of people nearby.* □ *These chemicals could endanger public health.* (**pôr em perigo**)

ending /ˈendɪŋ/ NOUN [plural endings]
the last part of a story 🔹 *The story had a happy ending.* □ + *of I don't want to spoil the ending of the film.*

endless /ˈendləs/ ADJECTIVE seeming to never finish □ *The task seemed endless.* 🔹 *There's an endless supply of cheap workers.* (**sem fim**)

enemy /ˈenəmi/ NOUN [plural enemies]
1 someone who is against you and wants to harm you 🔹 *He made a few enemies while he was there.* □ + *of They are viewed as enemies of the regime.* (**inimigo**)
2 the enemy in a war, the people or country you are fighting against □ *We will defend ourselves and defeat the enemy.* (**o inimigo**)

> **THESAURUS:** An **enemy** is someone who is trying to harm you, or a country that is fighting against yours. An **opponent** is someone that you compete against in a competition or game. For example, you might have an **opponent** in an election, or in a boxing match. A **rival** is a person or an organization that is competing against you, for example in business.

energetic /ˌenəˈdʒetɪk/ ADJECTIVE
very active and full of energy □ *an energetic dance* □ *I feel a lot more energetic.* (**enérgico**)

energy /ˈenədʒi/ NOUN [plural energies]
1 the strength or power you have to work or to be active □ *Young children have loads of energy.* □ *My boss has tremendous energy and enthusiasm.* □ + *to do something I didn't have the energy to walk home.* (**energia**)
2 a form of power, such as heat or electricity 🔹 *Turn off lights to save energy.* 🔹 *nuclear energy* 🔹 *renewable sources of energy* □ *energy efficiency* (**energia**)

engaged /ɪnˈgeɪdʒd/ ADJECTIVE
1 if two people are engaged, they have promised to marry each other □ + *to She's engaged to actor Alex Donovan.* 🔹 *The couple got engaged last month.* (**comprometido**)
2 if a telephone or toilet is engaged, it is being used (**ocupado**)

engine /ˈendʒɪn/ NOUN [plural engines]
a part of a machine that uses energy to produce movement □ *a car with a diesel engine* 🔹 *He closed the door and started the engine.* (**motor**)

engineer /ˌendʒɪˈnɪə(r)/ NOUN [plural engineers]
someone who designs, makes or repairs things like bridges, roads or machines □ *a telephone engineer* (**engenheiro, mecânico**)

engineering /ˌendʒɪˈnɪərɪŋ/ NOUN, NO PLURAL
the study or work of designing and making machines, roads, bridges, etc. 🔹 *He graduated in mechanical engineering.* (**engenharia**)

English¹ /'ɪŋglɪʃ/ ADJECTIVE
1 belonging to or from England ▢ *the English countryside* (**inglês**)
2 to do with the English language *an English translation* (**inglês**)

English² /'ɪŋglɪʃ/ NOUN
1 *no plural* the main language of Britain, North America and Australia, and an official language in some other countries ▢ *She speaks English very well.* (**inglês**)
2 the English people from England (**os ingleses**)

Englishman /'ɪŋglɪʃmən/ NOUN [*plural* **Englishmen**] a man who comes from England, or who has English parents (**inglês**)

enhance /ɪn'hɑ:ns/ VERB [**enhances, enhancing, enhanced**] to improve something ▢ *He has never used drugs to enhance his performance.* (**ressaltar**)

enjoy /ɪn'dʒɔɪ/ VERB [enjoys, enjoying, enjoyed]
1 to like doing something ▢ *They seemed to enjoy the concert.* ▢ *Enjoy your meal!* ▢ **+ ing** *I enjoy playing tennis.* (**gosta de**)
2 enjoy yourself to have a good time doing something ▢ *We enjoyed ourselves at the party.* ▢ *He was clearly enjoying himself.* (**divertir-se**)

enjoyable /ɪn'dʒɔɪəbəl/ ADJECTIVE fun and
giving you pleasure ▢ *The whole trip was a really enjoyable experience.* (**agradável**)

enjoyment /ɪn'dʒɔɪmənt/ NOUN, NO PLURAL
when you enjoy something ▣ *I get tremendous enjoyment out of the sport.* ▢ **+ of** *I don't let the illness affect my enjoyment of life.* (**prazer**)

enormous /ɪ'nɔ:məs/ ADJECTIVE very big or great
▢ *an enormous tree* ▣ *It cost an enormous amount of money.* ▢ *The staff were under enormous pressure.* (**enorme**)

enough¹ /ɪ'nʌf/ DETERMINER, PRONOUN as much
or as many as you need or want ▢ *Have you all had enough to eat?* ▢ *We need some more oil – there isn't enough here.* ▢ *I've got enough problems without this!* (**suficiente**)

enough² /ɪ'nʌf/ ADVERB as much as is needed or
wanted ▢ *She's not pretty enough to be a model.* ▢ *Stop when you think you've written enough.* (**o bastante**)

enquiry /en'kwaɪəri/ NOUN [plural enquiries]
another spelling of **inquiry** (ver **inquiry**)

enter /'entə(r)/ VERB [enters, entering, entered]
1 to go into a place ▢ *A tall man entered the room.* ▢ *He entered hospital at 3pm.* ▢ *The bullet entered his chest.* ▢ *They entered the country illegally.* (**entrar em**)
2 to put information in a book, document, computer, etc. ▢ *Enter your name here.* ▢ *The data is entered in a special computerized system.* (**registrar**)
3 to take part in a competition or an exam ▢ *My mum agreed to enter the mother's race.* (**inscrever-se**)

entertain /ˌentə'teɪn/ VERB [entertains, entertaining, entertained]
1 to do something which people find interesting and enjoyable ▢ *Emily entertained us by telling a few jokes.* ▢ *A band entertained the crowd.* (**entreter**)
2 to invite people as your guests for a meal or a drink ▢ *Tom tends to cook when we're entertaining.* (**receber**)

entertaining /ˌentə'teɪnɪŋ/ ADJECTIVE
interesting and enjoyable ▢ *She gave an entertaining account of her trip.* ▢ *It was a highly entertaining match.* (**divertido**)

entertainment /ˌentə'teɪnmənt/ NOUN [plural entertainments]
something that entertains people ▢ *There's live entertainment every night.* ▣ *Traditional dancers provided the entertainment.* ▣ *There are new forms of entertainment developing on the Internet.* (**espetáculo, entretenimento**)

enthusiasm /ɪn'θju:ziæzəm/ NOUN, NO PLURAL
when you are very interested in something or want to do it very much ▢ **+ for** *Her enthusiasm for her subject remains strong.* ▣ *There was a general lack of enthusiasm for the project.* (**entusiasmo**)

enthusiastic /ɪnˌθju:zɪ'æstɪk/ ADJECTIVE
showing enthusiasm ▢ **+ about** *Not everyone is enthusiastic about the idea.* ▢ *You don't sound very enthusiastic.* (**entusiasmado**)

entire /ɪn'taɪə(r)/ ADJECTIVE all of something ▢ *He lived his entire life in the same town.* (**inteiro**)

entrance /'entrəns/ NOUN [plural entrances]
the part of a building where you go into it ▣ *I'll meet you outside the main entrance.* ▢ **+ of** *There are security staff at the entrance of the building.* ▢ **+ to** *There were clear signs at the entrance to the tunnel.* (**entrada**)

> **THESAURUS:** An **entrance** is the way into a building. A **door** is the thing that you open in order to go into a building, a room, a cupboard or a car. A **gate** is part of a fence or a wall that opens like a door. You might go through a **gate** to get into a garden, for example.

entrepreneur /ˌɒntrəprə'nɜ:(r)/ NOUN
[plural **entrepreneurs**] a person who starts a business using their own ideas and usually their own money ▢ *China's young entrepreneurs* (**empreendedor**)

entry /'entri/ NOUN [plural entries]
1 when you go into a place ▣ *They were refused entry into the country.* ▣ *We gained entry (= got in) through an open window.* ▢ **+ to** *This card gives you free entry to most museums.* ▢ **+ into** *They were allowed entry into the area.* (**entrada**)
2 no entry a phrase used on signs to show that you must not go into a place. (**proibida a entrada**)
3 something that you have done to try to win a competition ▣ *The winning entries will be announced next week.* (**inscrição**)

envelope /ˈenvələup/ NOUN [plural **envelopes**]
a folded paper cover for a letter, especially one that is sent by post □ *a brown A4 envelope* ▣ *You haven't opened the envelope.* (**envelope**)

environment /ɪnˈvaɪərənmənt/ NOUN [plural **environments**]
1 the environment all the things, such as air, land, sea, animals and plants, that make up the natural world around us ▣ *Our main aim is to protect the environment.* (**ambiente**)
2 the things that surround you where you live, work or do something ▣ *We want to create a positive working environment.* □ *It provides a safe environment for young children to play.* (**ambiente**)

> **THESAURUS:** The **environment** is all of the things that make up the world around us, such as the air, land and sea. Your **surroundings** are the area around a person or a place. **Nature** describes everything in the world that was not made or changed by man such as animals and plants.

envoy /ˈenvɔɪ/ NOUN [plural **envoys**] a government official sent to another country to meet with a foreign government □ *the United Nations envoy to Bosnia* (**enviado**)

envy¹ /ˈenvɪ/ NOUN, NO PLURAL a feeling of wanting what someone else has □ *I felt a little envy at her success.* (**inveja**)

envy² /ˈenvɪ/ VERB [**envies, envying, envied**] to want what someone else has □ *We envied him because he didn't have to go to school.* (**invejar**)

enzyme /ˈenzaɪm/ NOUN [plural **enzymes**] a chemical substance made in both animals and plants, which causes chemical changes. A biology word. (**enzima**)

epic /ˈepɪk/ NOUN [plural **epics**] a long story, poem or film about great events or exciting adventures □ *His new film is a historical epic.* (**épico, epopeia**)

epidemic /ˌepɪˈdemɪk/ NOUN [plural **epidemics**]
a situation in which a disease spreads quickly and many people become ill at the same time □ *a flu epidemic* (**epidemia**)

episode /ˈepɪsəud/ NOUN [plural **episodes**]
one separate part of a story that is broadcast on the radio or television over a period of time (**episódio**)

> **THESAURUS:** An **episode** is one part of a longer story that is shown on the television or the radio. A **chapter** is one of the parts that a book is divided into. A **scene** is a short part of a play, book or film that happens in one place. A **passage** is a short part of a piece of writing or music.

equal¹ /ˈiːkwəl/ ADJECTIVE
1 of the same size, value or amount □ *Cut the cake into four roughly equal slices.* (**igual**)
2 having or deserving the same rights as other people □ *Men and women were finally regarded as equal.* ▣ *equal rights for all* (**igual**)

equal² /ˈiːkwəl/ NOUN [plural **equals**] someone who has the same rights or importance as another person □ *The women expect to be treated as equals.* (**igual**)

equal³ /ˈiːkwəl/ VERB [**equals, equalling/** US **equaling, equalled/** US **equaled**]
1 to be the same in size, value or amount □ *Two plus two equals four.* (**igualar**)
2 to achieve as much as someone else □ *She equalled the world record.* (**igualar**)

equality /iːˈkwɒlɪtɪ/ NOUN, NO PLURAL when everyone has the same rights and importance ▣ *racial equality* ▣ *sexual equality* (**igualdade**)

equation /ɪˈkweɪʒən/ NOUN [plural **equations**] a mathematical statement that shows that two sets of numbers are equal (**equação**)

equator /ɪˈkweɪtə(r)/ NOUN, NO PLURAL **the equator** the line drawn on maps that goes around the middle of the Earth □ *Kampala is just north of the equator.* (**equador**)

equipment /ɪˈkwɪpmənt/ NOUN, NO PLURAL the machines, furniture, etc. that you need in order to do a particular activity or job □ *camping equipment* □ *office equipment* ▣ *a piece of equipment* (**equipamento**)

> Remember that **equipment** is never used in the plural:
> ✓ We need more equipment.
> ✗ We need more equipments.

equivalent¹ /ɪˈkwɪvələnt/ NOUN [plural **equivalents**] something that has the same value, use, meaning or effect as something else □ *The Internet has become the modern equivalent of a telephone or a daily newspaper.* □ *Children eat the equivalent of almost twelve bags of sugar every year.* (**equivalente**)

equivalent² /ɪˈkwɪvələnt/ ADJECTIVE having the same value, use, meaning or effect □ *The average temperature of Mars is roughly equivalent to* *the temperature in Antarctica.* (equivalente)

-er /-ər/ SUFFIX
1 -er is added to the end of words to mean 'a person or thing that does something' □ *teacher*
2 -er is added to the end of some adjectives to make a comparative form □ *brighter*

era /'ɪərə/ NOUN [plural **eras**] a period of time ◨ *The country is entering a new era of peace.* (era)

erase /ɪ'reɪz/ VERB [**erases, erasing, erased**] to remove information or files from a computer □ *The file had somehow been erased.* (apagar)

eraser /ɪ'reɪzə(r)/ NOUN [plural **erasers**] a small piece of rubber used to remove pencil marks from paper (borracha)

erect /ɪ'rekt/ VERB [**erects, erecting, erected**] to build something or put it together. A formal word. □ *They erected a monument to their leader.* □ *A barrier was erected around the area.* □ *We had to erect the tent in the dark.* (erigir, erguer)

erode /ɪ'rəʊd/ VERB [**erodes, eroding, eroded**] if something erodes or is eroded, its surface is gradually removed by wind or water, for example □ *Houses are falling into the sea as the coastline erodes.* (erodir)

error /'erə(r)/ NOUN [plural **errors**] a mistake ◨ *He admits making some errors.* ◨ *The report blamed human error for the air crash.* (erro)

erupt /ɪ'rʌpt/ VERB [**erupts, erupting, erupted**] a volcano erupts when hot rocks, flames and dust suddenly come out of it (explodir, entrar em erupção)

> **THESAURUS:** We usually use erupt to talk about volcanoes. If something explodes, it breaks open suddenly so that parts fly out, making a loud noise. For example, you say that a bomb explodes. If something bursts, it also breaks open suddenly, but with less violence. A water pipe might burst, ora balloon.

escalate /'eskəleɪt/ VERB [**escalates, escalating, escalated**] to make or become worse or more serio us □ *The violence has escalated in recent weeks.* (subir, escalar)

escalator /'eskəleɪtə(r)/ NOUN [plural **escalators**] a set of moving stairs for carrying people between the levels of a building ◨ *Shall we take the escalator?* (escada rolante)

escape¹ /ɪ'skeɪp/ VERB [**escapes, escaping, escaped**]
1 to get away from a place where you are being kept □ **+ from** *The lion had escaped from its cage.* (escapar, fugir)
2 to get away from a dangerous place or situation □ **+ from** *He escaped from the country hidden in a lorry.* □ *When fire broke out, we managed to escape through the window.* (safar-se de)

escape² /ɪ'skeɪp/ NOUN [plural **escapes**] when someone gets away from a place or a bad situation □ **+ from** *He wrote a book about his daring escape from prison.* (fuga)

escort¹ /ɪ'skɔːt/ VERB [**escorts, escorting, escorted**] to go somewhere with someone in order to look after them □ *Airport staff will escort your child to the boarding gate.* (acompanhar, escoltar)

escort² /'eskɔːt/ NOUN [plural **escorts**] someone who goes somewhere with another person in order to look after them ◨ *The players needed a police escort to get to the bus.* (acompanhante, escolta)

especially /ɪ'speʃəli/ ADVERB
1 very, more than anything or anyone else □ *I was especially impressed by the food.* □ *He wasn't especially clever.* □ *The children, especially the younger ones, were tired.* (especialmente)
2 for one person or purpose only □ **+ for** *I bought it especially for you.* □ **+ to do something** *I came here especially to see you.* (especialmente)

essay /'eseɪ/ NOUN [plural **essays**] a piece of writing by a student about a particular subject □ **+ on** *Students are required to write a 4,000-word essay on a topic of their choice.* (redação, ensaio)

essence /'esəns/ NOUN, NO PLURAL **the essence of something** the most important part of something, or its true character □ *The film captures the essence of life in 18th-century Paris.* (a essência de algo)

essential /ɪ'senʃəl/ ADJECTIVE if something is essential, you must do it or have it □ **+ that** *It is essential that we all stay together.* ◨ *Fat is an essential part of our diet.* □ *A car is useful, but not essential.* (essencial)

establish /ɪ'stæblɪʃ/ VERB [**establishes, establishing, established**] to start an organization or business □ *He established a small bakery.* (fundar, estabelecer)

estate /ɪ'steɪt/ NOUN [plural **estates**] a large area with a lot of buildings on it ◨ *an industrial estate* ◨ *a housing estate* (loteamento, propriedade)

estate agent /ɪ'steɪt ˌeɪdʒənt/ NOUN [plural **estate agents**] someone whose job is to help people to buy and sell houses and apartments (corretor de imóveis)

estimate¹ /'estɪmeɪt/ VERB [**estimates, estimating, estimated**] to try to judge the size, amount or value of something, using the information that you have □ *The government estimated the cost at over £5 million.* □ *Experts estimate that thousands of deaths every year are caused by unhealthy diets.* (estimar)

estimate² /'estɪmət/ NOUN [plural **estimates**] when you estimate something (estimativa)

etc *or* **etc.** /ɪt'setərə/ ABBREVIATION used after a list to show that there are other similar things that you have not mentioned □ *The art shop sells paints, canvases, brushes, etc.* (etc)

ethnic /'eθnɪk/ ADJECTIVE to do with a group of people who have the same race and culture

EU

🔹 The Pashtuns form the main ethnic group of Afghanistan. (étnico)

EU /ˌiːˈjuː/ ABBREVIATION the EU the European Union; a political and economic organization of European countries (**UE**)

euro /ˈjʊərəʊ/ NOUN [plural euros] the main unit of money in many European countries □ There are 100 cents in a euro. (**euro**)

European¹ /ˌjʊərəˈpiːən/ ADJECTIVE belonging to or from Europe (**europeu**)

European² /ˌjʊərəˈpiːən/ NOUN [plural Europeans] a person from Europe (**europeu**)

European Union /ˌjʊərəˌpiːən ˈjuːnjən/ NOUN, NO PLURAL the European Union a political and economic organization of European countries (**a União Europeia**)

evacuate /ɪˈvækjueɪt/ VERB [evacuates, evacuating, evacuated] to leave a place because it is dangerous, or to make people leave a place because it is dangerous □ Hundreds of people had to evacuate their homes during the floods. □ Residents were evacuated from the areas affected by the fires. (**evacuar**)

eve /iːv/ NOUN [plural eves]
1 the day or evening before a particular day □ He died on the eve of his 80th birthday. (**véspera**)
2 Eve used in the names of some days that come before an important day □ Christmas Eve □ New Year's Eve (**véspera**)

even¹ /ˈiːvən/ ADVERB
1 used to emphasize another word □ It was even colder the next morning. □ Max is even better than Adam at football. □ Even Pia seemed to be enjoying herself. (**até**)
2 even though although □ She still tried to help him, even though he was so rude to her. (**ainda que, mesmo que**)
3 even if used to say that what you are going to say next would not change anything □ Grandad wouldn't go on holiday even if we paid for it. (**mesmo que**)

even² /ˈiːvən/ ADJECTIVE
1 an even surface is level and smooth (**liso**)
2 equal □ The scores were even. (**quite**)
3 an even number is one that can be divided by 2 (**par**)

evening /ˈiːvnɪŋ/ NOUN [plural evenings] the last part of the day, before the night begins 🔹 What are you doing this evening? 🔹 We're going to the cinema on Friday evening. 🔹 They usually watch TV in the evening. 🔹 What time do you usually have your evening meal? (**noite**)

event /ɪˈvent/ NOUN [plural events] something that happens 🔹 These events occurred in the 19th century. 🔹 Recent events have made it necessary to introduce new rules. 🔹 Millions of people watched the events unfold (= happen) on TV. (**acontecimento, evento**)

eventual /ɪˈventʃuəl/ ADJECTIVE happening at the end of a period of time or as a result of a process □ They lost the match to the eventual winners, Liverpool. (**final**)

ever /ˈevə(r)/ ADVERB
1 at any time or at all □ Have you ever been to France? □ Nobody ever offers to help me. □ It was the most delicious meal ever. □ If you are ever in Edinburgh, do come and see me. (**jamais**)
2 ever since since the time when □ He's been unhappy ever since he started at his new school. (**desde**)
3 for ever for all future time □ I'm sure we'll be friends forever. (**sempre**)

every /ˈevrɪ/ DETERMINER
1 all the people or things □ Every runner will get a medal for taking part. □ There were eight cakes on the plate, and she ate every one. (**todo**)
2 every day/week/three hours, etc. used to show how often something happens □ He does 200 press-ups every day. (**todo**)

> Remember that **every** is followed by a singular noun: □ Every student in the group owns a mobile phone.

everybody /ˈevrɪˌbɒdɪ/ PRONOUN everyone □ I thought everybody liked ice cream. □ Could everybody listen, please? (**todo mundo**)

everyone /ˈevrɪwʌn/ PRONOUN every person □ Everyone likes Jonathan. □ I knew everyone at the party. 🔹 Everyone else (= all other people) had left by this point. (**todo mundo**)

everything /ˈevrɪθɪŋ/ PRONOUN all the things in a place or situation □ Everything in the room was covered in dust. 🔹 We kept the books, and threw everything else in the bin. (**tudo**)

everywhere /ˈevrɪweə(r)/ ADVERB in or to every place □ We looked everywhere but couldn't find it. □ They go everywhere together. (**em todo lugar, por toda a parte**)

evidence /ˈevɪdəns/ NOUN, NO PLURAL facts or objects that help to prove something □ His body was examined and no evidence of the disease found. (**prova**)

evident /ˈevɪdənt/ ADJECTIVE obvious or easy to understand □ It was evident that she was unhappy. (**evidente**)

evil¹ /ˈiːvəl/ ADJECTIVE morally very bad and cruel □ an evil man □ This was an evil act. (**mau**)

evil² /ˈiːvəl/ NOUN, NO PLURAL evil actions generally □ So are we all capable of evil? (**mal**)

evolution /ˌiːvəˈluːʃən/ NOUN, NO PLURAL the process by which animals and plants change over many thousands of years in order to suit their environment (**evolução**)

exact

exact /ɪgˈzækt/ ADJECTIVE accurate in every way ☐ Those were his exact words. ☐ I don't recall the exact date. ☐ They never mentioned the exact amount of money. ☐ This is an exact copy of the document. (exato)

exactly /ɪgˈzæktli/ ADVERB
1 used when saying prices, amounts, the time, etc. that are completely accurate ☐ That comes to £10 exactly. ☐ It's five o'clock exactly. (exatamente)
2 in every way ☐ That's exactly what I was thinking. ☐ He looks exactly like his father. ☐ The coats look exactly the same to me. (exatamente)
3 used for agreeing strongly with what someone has said ☐ 'She should be pleased she's got a job.' 'Exactly.' (exatamente)

exaggerate /ɪgˈzædʒəreɪt/ VERB [exaggerates, exaggerating, exaggerated] to say that something is more extreme than it really is ☐ He's not that fat – you're exaggerating! ☐ The media have exaggerated the problem. (exagerar)

exam /ɪgˈzæm/ NOUN [plural exams] an important test of someone's knowledge or ability ☐ I'm taking my final exams in June. ☐ She passed her exams. ☐ What if he fails his exams? (exame)

examination /ɪgˌzæmɪˈneɪʃən/ NOUN [plural examinations]
1 a formal word that means exam (exame)
2 no plural when someone looks carefully at something ☐ On closer examination, the painting turned out to be a copy. (exame)

examine /ɪgˈzæmɪn/ VERB [examines, examining, examined]
1 to look at something carefully ☐ The sample was examined under a microscope. (examinar)
2 if a doctor examines you, he or she looks carefully at your body to see if there is anything wrong ☐ The doctor examined her throat and ears. (examinar)

example /ɪgˈzɑːmpəl/ NOUN [plural examples]
1 something which has all the features or qualities of the type of thing that you are talking about ☐ This is a typical example of a building from this period. ☐ Let me give you an example of what I mean. (exemplo)
2 for example used for giving an example of something ☐ People drive unnecessarily. Jo, for example, drives to her friend's house which is 10 minutes' walk away. (por exemplo)

exceed /ɪkˈsiːd/ VERB [exceeds, exceeding, exceeded] to be greater than a particular limit or amount ☐ He exceeded the speed limit by 30 kilometres per hour. (exceto)

excellent /ˈeksələnt/ ADJECTIVE extremely good or of a very high standard ☐ Her work is excellent. (excelente)

except /ɪkˈsept/ PREPOSITION, CONJUNCTION not including something ☐ He works every day except Sunday. ☐ + that I feel better now, except that my head still hurts a bit. ☐ + for Everyone stayed, except for the children. (exceto)

exception /ɪkˈsepʃən/ NOUN [plural exceptions]
1 something that is not the same as the others in a group, and so cannot be included in a statement about them ☐ With a few exceptions, the people were very friendly. ☐ There is one exception to this rule. (exceção)
2 make an exception to say that one person does not have to follow a particular rule ☐ You're not supposed to leave the room during the lesson, but I'll make an exception for you. (fazer uma exceção)

excess^1 /ˈɪkses/ NOUN [plural excesses] too much of something ☐ There was an excess of fat in his blood. (excesso)

excess^2 /ˈekses/ ADJECTIVE more than you want, or more than is allowed ☐ Many airlines charge you for excess baggage. (excesso)

exchange^1 /ɪksˈtʃeɪndʒ/ VERB [exchanges, exchanging, exchanged] to give someone something and take something from them ☐ We exchanged rings as a sign of our friendship. ☐ They exchanged phone numbers. ☐ We only exchanged a few words (= spoke for a short time). ☐ This website enables us to exchange information. (trocar)

exchange^2 /ɪksˈtʃeɪndʒ/ NOUN [plural exchanges]
1 in exchange for something if you do something or give something in exchange for something, you do it or give it to get that thing ☐ He took money in exchange for passing on information. (em troca de algo)
2 when you give something to someone and take something from them ☐ + of The exchange of food is a symbol of our community. (troca)

excite /ɪkˈsaɪt/ VERB [excites, exciting, excited] to make someone feel excited (excitar)

excited /ɪkˈsaɪtɪd/ ADJECTIVE feeling very happy and not calm because something good is going to happen ☐ He was getting excited about the party. ☐ + about It was my first trip to the US and I was really excited about it. ☐ + to do something I'm excited to be part of the team. (excitado)

excitement /ɪkˈsaɪtmənt/ NOUN, NO PLURAL the feeling of being excited ☐ The news caused great excitement. ☐ In her excitement, she forgot something important. ☐ + of I still remember the excitement of winning the competition. (excitação)

exciting /ɪkˈsaɪtɪŋ/ ADJECTIVE making you feel excited ☐ an exciting opportunity ☐ + to do something The game was exciting to watch. (excitante)

> Remember the difference between the words **excited** and **exciting**. If you are **excited**, you are very happy because something good is going to happen. Something that is **exciting** makes you feel excited: ☐ I was so **excited** during the game. ☐ It was such an **exciting** game.

exclaim /ɪkˈskleɪm/ VERB [exclaims, exclaiming, exclaimed] to say something suddenly and loudly because you are surprised, angry, etc. ◻ 'What a wonderful surprise!', she exclaimed. (**exclamar**)

exclude /ɪkˈskluːd/ VERB [excludes, excluding, excluded]
1 to not allow someone to take part in something or go into a place ◻ Paul was excluded from school for a week as a punishment. (**excluir**)
2 to deliberately not include something ◻ The figures exclude children under the age of twelve. (**excluir**)

excuse[1] /ɪkˈskjuːs/ NOUN [plural excuses] a reason you give to explain why you did something wrong or did not do something ▣ I'm sick of you making excuses about your work. ▣ He's late again – he'd better have a good excuse this time! ▣ + for There's no excuse for this sort of behaviour. (**desculpa**)

excuse[2] /ɪkˈskjuːz/ VERB [excuses, excusing, excused]
1 excuse me (a) something that you say to get someone's attention ◻ Excuse me, could you tell me the way to the library? ◻ Excuse me, Susan, there's someone on the phone for you. (b) used to say sorry ◻ Oh, excuse me, I didn't realize this seat was taken. (**com licença**)
2 to forgive someone for doing something, especially something that is not serious ◻ Please excuse the mess in here. ◻ I hope you'll excuse us being late. (**desculpar**)
3 if you are excused something, you are allowed not to do it ◻ + from Could I be excused from tennis today, as I don't feel well? (**dispensar**)

execute /ˈeksɪkjuːt/ VERB [executes, executing, executed] to kill someone as an official punishment ◻ Many of the prisoners were executed. (**executar**)

execution /ˌeksɪˈkjuːʃən/ NOUN [plural executions] killing someone as an official punishment ◻ He is facing execution for his role in the terrorist bombings. (**execução**)

exercise[1] /ˈeksəsaɪz/ NOUN [plural exercises]
1 no plural physical activities done to keep your body strong and healthy ▣ We should all take more exercise. ▣ Regular exercise will help to control your weight. (**exercício**)
2 a particular movement done to make your body strong and healthy ◻ We did some stretching exercises. ◻ This exercise works the stomach muscles. (**exercício**)
3 a piece of written work you do when you are studying ◻ Please do exercise 4 in your grammar book. ◻ This exercise deals with prepositions. (**exercício**)

exercise[2] /ˈeksəsaɪz/ VERB [exercises, exercising, exercised] to do exercises to make you strong and healthy ▣ I try to exercise regularly. ◻ You should try to exercise the damaged joints. (**exercitar**)

exhaust[1] /ɪɡˈzɔːst/ VERB [exhausts, exhausting, exhausted] to make someone very tired ◻ That jog exhausted me. (**exaurir**)

exhaust[2] /ɪɡˈzɔːst/ NOUN [plural exhausts]
1 the pipe on a vehicle which waste gas come out of (**escapamento**)
2 no plural the waste gas that comes out of a vehicle ▣ exhaust fumes (**escapamento**)

exhausted /ɪɡˈzɔːstɪd/ ADJECTIVE extremely tired ◻ She was completely exhausted by the time she got home. (**exausto**)

exhausting /ɪɡˈzɔːstɪŋ/ ADJECTIVE making you feel extremely tired ◻ It was an exhausting climb. (**esgotante**)

exhaustion /ɪɡˈzɔːstʃən/ NOUN, NO PLURAL a feeling of extreme tiredness ◻ The singer cancelled his tour because of stress and exhaustion. (**exaustão**)

exhibit /ɪɡˈzɪbɪt/ VERB [exhibits, exhibiting, exhibited] to show something in a place such as a museum ◻ Julia exhibits her paintings at a small local gallery. (**expor**)

exhibition /ˌeksɪˈbɪʃən/ NOUN [plural exhibitions] a show where people go to see paintings, photographs, etc. ▣ an art exhibition ◻ + of The museum will be holding an exhibition of works by Monet. (**exposição**)

> **THESAURUS:** An **exhibition** is a show where people go to see paintings, photographs etc. A **demonstration** is when someone shows you how to do something or how it works. For example, you might go to a cookery **demonstration**. A **presentation** is a talk to a group of people to explain or describe something. For example, you might give a **presentation** to the people you work with.

exile[1] /ˈeksaɪl/ NOUN [plural exiles]
1 someone who has been forced to leave their country, usually for political reasons (**exilado**)
2 in exile if someone is in exile, they have been forced to live in a country that is not their own, for political reasons ◻ The former leader is now living in exile in Japan. (**em exílio**)

exile[2] /ˈeksaɪl/ VERB [exiles, exiling, exiled] if you are exiled, you are forced to leave your own country and live somewhere else, for political reasons (**exilar**)

exist /ɪɡˈzɪst/ VERB [exists, existing, existed] to be real, or to happen ◻ Does God really exist? ◻ Similar problems exist in Britain. (**existir**)

existence /ɪɡˈzɪstəns/ NOUN, NO PLURAL when someone or something exists ◻ The rule was in existence for almost 40 years. ◻ + of We can no longer deny the existence of global warming. (**existência**)

exit /ˈeksɪt/ NOUN [plural exits] a door you go through to leave a public building or vehicle ▣ The bus has an emergency exit at the back. (**saída**)

exotic /ɪɡˈzɒtɪk/ ADJECTIVE interesting and unusual, and often to do with a foreign country □ *exotic animals* □ *exotic holidays* (**exótico**)

expand /ɪkˈspænd/ VERB [**expands, expanding, expanded**] to become bigger, or to make something become bigger □ *Many cities are expanding very rapidly.* □ *The company plans to expand its range of products.* (**expandir[-se]**)

expansion /ɪkˈspænʃən/ NOUN, NO PLURAL when something increases in size or amount □ *The rapid expansion of the airline industry has led to cheap flights.* (**expansão**)

expect /ɪkˈspekt/ VERB [**expects, expecting, expected**]
1 to think that something will happen or be true □ *We're expecting an announcement soon.* □ *I expect he's forgotten the meeting.* □ *I didn't expect anything like this to happen.* □ + *to do something Sales are expected to fall next month.* □ + *that I expect that it will be hot in Portugal.* (**esperar, acreditar**)
2 to think that something or someone will arrive □ *I'm expecting a phone call from Mary.* (**esperar**)
3 to think that something ought to happen or that you have a right to it □ + *to do something I expect you to behave better than this.* □ *Our customers expect a first class service.* (**esperar**)
4 if you are expected to do something, you have to do it □ *We are expected to do 3 hours' homework a day.* (**esperar**)

expedition /ˌekspɪˈdɪʃən/ NOUN [**plural expeditions**] a long journey, especially to a dangerous place or to a place that has not been visited before □ *The group went on an expedition to the South Pole.* (**expedição**)

expel /ɪkˈspel/ VERB [**expels, expelling, expelled**] to make someone leave a school, country or organization because they have done something wrong □ *John was expelled from school for hitting a teacher.* (**expulsar**)

expense /ɪkˈspens/ NOUN [**plural expenses**] the money that you pay for something ▣ *medical/legal expenses* ▣ *The money he gave me will cover the expense of the transport.* ▣ *We have to pay our own travelling expenses.* (**despesa**)

expensive /ɪkˈspensɪv/ ADJECTIVE costing a lot of money □ *These clothes are too expensive for me.* □ *expensive gifts/equipment* (**caro**)

experience¹ /ɪkˈspɪəriəns/ NOUN [**plural experiences**]
1 no plural knowledge and skill that you get by doing something or by something happening to you ▣ *The players have been gaining experience over the last four years.* ▣ *She had no experience of looking after children.* □ + *of The company is looking for someone with experience of managing people.* (**experiência**)
2 something that happens to you ▣ *We had a bad experience on holiday.* ▣ *The whole experience was terrifying.* □ *Watching a baby being born was an amazing experience.* (**experiência**)

experience² /ɪkˈspɪəriəns/ VERB [**experiences, experiencing, experienced**] if you experience something, it happens to you or you feel it □ *Many customers were experiencing problems with Internet access.* □ *He had never experienced such pain.* (**experimentar**)

experienced /ɪkˈspɪəriənst/ ADJECTIVE having skill and knowledge because you have done something for a long time □ *an experienced teacher* (**experiente**)

experiment¹ /ɪkˈsperɪmənt/ NOUN [**plural experiments**] a scientific test to discover or prove something ▣ *Two experiments were conducted, using children suffering from heart problems.* ▣ *The experiment shows that lack of sleep affects people's performance of basic tasks.* (**experiência**)

experiment² /ɪkˈsperɪment/ VERB [**experiments, experimenting, experimented**] to do scientific tests to discover or prove something □ + *on The team experimented on rats.* (**fazer experiência**)

expert¹ /ˈekspɜːt/ NOUN [**plural experts**] someone who knows a lot about something □ *legal/health experts* □ + *on/in She's an expert on Middle East politics.* (**especialista, perito**)

expert² /ˈekspɜːt/ ADJECTIVE very good at something, or knowing a lot about something □ *expert skiers* (**especializado**)

expire /ɪkˈspaɪə(r)/ VERB [**expires, expiring, expired**] if an official document or agreement expires, the time when you can use it ends □ *Your passport expired last month.* (**expirar**)

explain /ɪkˈspleɪn/ VERB [**explains, explaining, explained**]
1 to give someone more or simpler information so that they can understand something □ + *question word Could you explain what you mean?* □ + *to She explained the rules of the game to me.* (**explicar**)
2 to give or to be a reason for something □ *He was asked to explain his absence.* □ *Having a bad childhood can explain the behaviour of some criminals.* □ + *that She explained that she had lost her keys.* (**explicação**)

> Note that you cannot *explain someone something*. You must *explain something to someone*:
> ✓ She explained the rules to me.
> ✗ She explained me the rules.

explanation /ˌekspləˈneɪʃən/ NOUN [**plural explanations**]
1 something you say or write to make something easy to understand ▣ *She gave an explanation of how to do it.* □ + *of The teacher started with an explanation of why plants are green.* (**explicação**)
2 a reason for something ▣ *The research offers several explanations for this behaviour.* □ + *for Is there a scientific explanation for this?* (**explicação**)

explicit /ɪkˈsplɪsɪt/ ADJECTIVE clear and exact □ Michael gave me explicit instructions about how to do it. (explicação)

explode /ɪkˈspləʊd/ VERB [explodes, exploding, exploded] to burst (= break suddenly so the parts fly out) and make a very loud noise ⊞ A bomb exploded in the centre of the city. □ The car exploded, killing two police officers. □ Fireworks exploded in every direction. (explodir)

> Note that a bomb **explodes**. When people make a bomb explode in a building, aeroplane, etc. they **blow up** that building, aeroplane, etc.: □ The bomb exploded in the centre of the building. □ They blew up the building.

exploit /ɪkˈsplɔɪt/ VERB [exploits, exploiting, exploited] to use someone unfairly to help you get what you want □ These people are often exploited as they will work for very little money. (explorar)

exploration /ˌeksplə'reɪʃən/ NOUN [plural explorations] going to a place to find out about it □ space exploration (exploração)

explore /ɪkˈsplɔː(r)/ VERB [explores, exploring, explored] to travel around a place and find out what it is like □ The hotel is a good base for exploring the region. □ Radar technology will help us to explore the planet Mars. (explorar)

explorer /ɪkˈsplɔːrə(r)/ NOUN [plural explorers] someone who travels to places that people have not been to before □ a Polar explorer. (explorador)

explosion /ɪkˈspləʊʒən/ NOUN [plural explosions] when something such as a bomb explodes □ The explosion happened inside the building. ⊞ Two soldiers were killed in a roadside bomb explosion. ⊞ He was seriously injured in a gas explosion. (explosão)

explosive¹ /ɪkˈspləʊsɪv/ ADJECTIVE able to cause an explosion □ a highly explosive gas ⊞ an explosive device (explosivo)

explosive² /ɪkˈspləʊsɪv/ NOUN [plural explosives] a substance that can cause an explosion (explosivo)

export¹ /ɪkˈspɔːt/ VERB [exports, exporting, exported] to sell goods to another country □ India exports rice and wheat to many countries. (exportar)
→ go to **import**

export² /ˈekspɔːt/ NOUN [plural exports]
1 a product that a country sells to another country □ Syria's main export is oil. (exportação)
2 no plural the process of selling goods to another country □ The country relies on the export of wool. (exportação)
→ L go to **import**

expose /ɪkˈspəʊz/ VERB [exposes, exposing, exposed] to show something that was covered or hidden □ He pulled up his shirt to expose his stomach. (expor)

express¹ /ɪkˈspres/ VERB [expresses, expressing, expressed] to show or tell people what you are thinking or feeling ⊞ He expressed his concerns about the safety of the equipment. ⊞ She expressed strong views about education. ⊞ Amy expressed surprise at his comments. □ He was unable to express himself clearly. (expressar)

express² /ɪkˈspres/ NOUN [plural expresses] a train or bus that is fast because it does not stop at many places □ We caught the express to Leeds. (expresso)

express³ /ɪkˈspres/ ADJECTIVE travelling fast from one place to another ⊞ an express train □ The package arrived express delivery. (expresso)

expression /ɪkˈspreʃən/ NOUN [plural expressions]
1 a look on your face that shows what you are thinking or feeling ⊞ I could tell by the expression on his face that he didn't believe me. ⊞ I couldn't read her facial expression. (expressão)
2 a word or phrase ⊞ Dieter always uses very old-fashioned expressions. (expressão)

extend /ɪkˈstend/ VERB [extends, extending, extended]
1 to make something bigger □ We're having our kitchen extended. □ The airport has plans to extend the runway. (ampliar)
2 to make something continue for longer □ The contract was extended by three months. (extender)

extension /ɪkˈstenʃən/ NOUN [plural extensions]
1 a part added to a building □ They're building an extension at the side of the house. (extensão)
2 a telephone line to a particular person in an office □ Can I have extension 4321, please? (extensão)

extensive /ɪkˈstensɪv/ ADJECTIVE large in size or amount ⊞ The fire caused extensive damage. ⊞ He has an extensive collection of rare books. (extenso)

extent /ɪkˈstent/ NOUN, NO PLURAL
1 the size or degree of something □ What's the extent of the damage? (extensão)
2 to some extent/to a certain extent in some ways □ The situation has improved to some extent. (até certo ponto)

exterior /ɪkˈstɪəriə(r)/ NOUN [plural exteriors] the outside of something □ The house had a very impressive exterior. (exterior)
→ go to **interior¹**

external /ɪkˈstɜːnəl/ ADJECTIVE on the outside of a person or thing □ The building has external lighting. (externo)

extinct /ɪkˈstɪŋkt/ ADJECTIVE a type of animal or plant which is extinct no longer exists □ Many types of frog have already become extinct. (extinto)

extinguish /ɪkˈstɪŋgwɪʃ/ VERB [extinguishes, extinguishing, extinguished] a formal word meaning to make a fire stop burning or to make a light stop shining □ Firefighters tried to extinguish the flames. (apagar)

extra¹
/'ekstrə/ ADJECTIVE more or more than usual ☐ The extra money will be used to buy books. ☐ The teacher gives Raj extra help with maths. ☐ The room is £70 but meals are extra (= meals are not included in the price). (**adicional**)

extra²
/'ekstrə/ ADVERB more than usual ☐ I get paid extra for working at weekends. ☐ I bought an extra large box of chocolates. (**extra**)

extract /ɪk'strækt/ VERB [extracts, extracting, extracted] a formal word meaning to remove something from a place ☐ No dentist will extract a tooth that could be saved. (**extrair**)

extraordinary
/ɪk'strɔːdənrɪ/ ADJECTIVE very special, unusual or surprising ☐ Ann told me the most extraordinary story. ☐ He knew he had seen something quite extraordinary (= very extraordinary). ☐ + that It's extraordinary that he survived the accident. (**extraordinário, notável**)

extravagant /ɪk'strævəgənt/ ADJECTIVE spending or costing too much money, or using too much of something ☐ an extravagant lifestyle ☐ Don't be too extravagant with the paper – we haven't much left. (**gastador, extravagante**)

extreme
/ɪk'striːm/ ADJECTIVE
1 very great ☐ The roads are icy, and motorists should drive with extreme caution. ☐ We were working under extreme pressure. (**extremo**)
2 very unusual or severe ☐ Planes cannot take off or land in extreme weather conditions. ☐ In extreme cases, the illness can cause death. (**extremo**)
3 at the furthest edge of something ☐ My mother is on the extreme right of the picture. (**extremo**)

extremely
/ɪk'striːmlɪ/ ADVERB very ☐ He found it extremely difficult to relax. ☐ Education is extremely important. ☐ Ben did extremely well in the test. (**extremamente**)

> **Extremely** is not used before adjectives which have a strong meaning:
> ✓ It was extremely difficult to hear.
> ✗ It was extremely impossible to hear. If you are using an adjective with a strong meaning, put an adverb such as **completely** or **absolutely** before it: ☐ It was absolutely impossible to hear.

eye
/aɪ/ NOUN [plural eyes]
1 one of the two things on your face which you see with ☐ I have blonde hair and blue eyes. ☐ John closed his eyes and tried to sleep. ☐ When she opened her eyes again, he'd gone. (**olho**)
2 the hole in a needle that you put the thread through (**buraco**)
♦ IDIOMS **catch someone's eye** if something catches your eye, you notice it ☐ A sudden movement caught my eye. **keep an eye on someone/ something** to look after someone or something to make sure they are safe ☐ Could you keep an eye on the children for me? **not see eye to eye** to disagree with someone about something ☐ We don't see eye to eye about religion.

eyebrow /'aɪbraʊ/ NOUN [plural eyebrows] one of the two lines of hair above your eyes (**sobrancelha**)
eyelash /'aɪlæʃ/ NOUN [plural eyelashes] one of the many hairs round the edges of your eyes (**cílio**)
eyelid /'aɪlɪd/ NOUN [plural eyelids] one of the pieces of skin that cover your eyes when your eyes are closed (**pálpebra**)

Ff

F¹ or **f** /ef/ the sixth letter of the alphabet (a sexta letra do alfabeto)

F² /ef/ ABBREVIATION Fahrenheit (Fahrenheit)

fabric /ˈfæbrɪk/ NOUN [plural **fabrics**] cloth □ *They are made of natural fabrics such as cotton or linen.* (tecido)

fabulous /ˈfæbjʊləs/ ADJECTIVE extremely good □ *The weather was fabulous.* □ *You look fabulous in that dress.* (fabuloso)

face¹ /feɪs/ NOUN [plural **faces**]
1 the front of your head where your eyes, nose, and mouth are □ *She had a huge smile on her face.* (rosto)
2 the part of a clock or watch where the numbers are (face)

face² /feɪs/ VERB [**faces, facing, faced**]
1 to be in a particular direction □ *My house faces the park.* □ *She turned to face him.* (dar de frente para)
2 to have to deal with a difficult situation □ *She has faced many difficulties in her life.* (enfrentar)
3 can't face doing something if you can't face doing something, it is too unpleasant for you to do □ *I just can't face cooking this evening.* (não aguentar)

facility /fəˈsɪlɪti/ NOUN [plural **facilities**]
facilities buildings, rooms or equipment that you can use for doing something ▣ *The university has excellent sports facilities.* □ *The company provides childcare facilities for employees.* (instalação)

fact /fækt/ NOUN [plural **facts**]
1 something that you know is true □ **+ about** *We don't yet know all the facts about the accident.* ▣ *I know for a fact* (= I'm certain) *that he was in London last week.* ▣ *The fact is, I'm too scared to talk to him.* ▣ *The fact that she's ill means she can't work full-time.* (fato)
2 in fact/as a matter of fact used to give more information about something □ *They know each other well; in fact they went to school together.* (de fato)
3 in fact used to say what is really true □ *He said he was ill, when in fact he was at the football match.* (na verdade)

faction /ˈfækʃən/ NOUN [plural **factions**] a group that is part of a larger group but has different opinions from others in that group (facção)

factor /ˈfæktə(r)/ NOUN [plural **factors**] something that causes or influences a situation □ *The weather is often one of the main factors in choosing where to go for a holiday.* ▣ *Price is an important factor for many people.* (fator)

factory /ˈfæktəri/ NOUN [plural **factories**] a building where something is made in large quantities □ *a chocolate factory* (fábrica)

fade /feɪd/ VERB [**fades, fading, faded**]
1 to disappear or become less strong gradually □ *Hopes of finding him were starting to fade.* □ *His smile faded.* □ *Their voices faded into the background.* (enfraquecer)
2 to lose colour and become less bright □ *These jeans have faded.* □ *The light was fading.* (enfraquecer)

Fahrenheit /ˈfærənhaɪt/ NOUN, NO PLURAL a system for measuring temperature in which water freezes at 32 degrees and boils at 212 degrees (Fahrenheit)

fail¹ /feɪl/ VERB [**fails, failing, failed**]
1 to not be successful □ **+ in** *They failed in their attempt to sail round the world.* □ **+ to do something** *The business failed to attract enough customers.* □ *After four years, the marriage failed.* (fracassar)
2 if you fail an exam or test, you do not pass it □ *My brother failed his driving test.* (reprovar, fracassar)
3 to not do something that is expected or needed □ **+ to do something** *The parcel failed to arrive.* □ *Yesterday's announcement failed to address the main problems.* □ *They failed to provide enough food for the animals.* (fracassar)

fail² /feɪl/ NOUN, NO PLURAL **without fail** (a) used to show that something always happens in a particular way or at a particular time □ *He visits me every day, without fail* (b) used to emphasize that something must be done □ *I want your homework in tomorrow, without fail!* (sem falta)

failure /ˈfeɪljə(r)/ NOUN [plural **failures**]
1 when something is not successful ▣ *Their first attempt ended in failure.* □ **+ of** *After the failure of his business, he went to live abroad.* (fracasso)
2 someone or something that is not successful □ *She felt like a failure.* □ *The party was a complete failure.* (fraco)

faint¹ /feɪnt/ ADJECTIVE [**fainter, faintest**]
1 difficult to see, hear or smell □ *There's a faint mark on the carpet.* □ *the faint sound of footsteps* □ *He gave a faint smile.* (fraco)
2 if you feel faint, you feel that you might become unconscious ▣ *I suddenly felt faint.* (fraco)

• **faintly** /ˈfeɪntli/ ADVERB in a way that is difficult to see, hear or smell □ *'Yes,' she said faintly.* □

The room smelled faintly of smoke. (**vagamente, ligeiramente**)

faint² /feɪnt/ VERB [**faints, fainting, fainted**] to suddenly become unconscious and fall to the ground □ *Richard fainted when he saw the blood.* (**desmaiar**)

fair¹ /feə(r)/ ADJECTIVE [**fairer, fairest**]
1 treating everyone in the same, reasonable way ▣ *It's not fair! Ella got more cake than me.* ▣ *a fair trial/elec tion* ▣ *Make sure Patsy does her fair share of the work.* (**justo**)
2 fair skin or hair is light in colour (**loiro**)
3 fair weather is pleasant, with no rain (**claro**)
4 quite good but not very good □ *Joe's work is only fair.* (**médio**)
• **fairly** /ˈfeəli/ ADVERB
1 quite a lot, but not extremely □ *He is fairly well paid.* □ *It's fairly obvious that she is lying.* (**bastante**)
2 in a fair way □ *They treat their staff fairly.* □ *The money was divided fairly between them.* (**imparcialmente**)

fair² /feə(r)/ NOUN [*plural* **fairs**] an event held outdoors, where you can ride on machines, play games, etc. (**quermesse, feira**)

fairy /ˈfeəri/ NOUN [*plural* **fairies**] an imaginary creature which looks like a small person with wings (**fada**)

faith /feɪθ/ NOUN [*plural* **faiths**]
1 *no plural* great trust and belief in someone or some thing ▣ *I have a lot of faith in him.* ▣ *I've lost faith in the whole system.* (**fé, confiança**)
2 a religion □ *the Christian faith* □ *people of different faiths* (**fé**)
3 *no plural* religious belief generally □ *He was a man of deep faith.* (**fé**)

faithful /ˈfeɪθfʊl/ ADJECTIVE loyal and keeping your promises □ *a faithful friend* □ *He was faithful to his wife.* (**fé**)

faithfully /ˈfeɪθfʊli/ ADVERB **Yours faithfully** something you write at the end of a formal letter that begins with 'Dear Sir' or 'Dear Madam' (**fielmente**)

fake /feɪk/ ADJECTIVE not real, but copying something else □ *fake fur* □ *He was travelling on a fake passport.* (**fielmente**)

fall¹ /fɔːl/ VERB [**falls, falling, fell, fallen**]
1 to drop down to the ground □ *The apples fell from the tree.* □ *Snow fell all morning.* (**cair**)
2 to suddenly go down to the ground by accident □ *Ben fell downstairs.* □ + **off** *He fell off a fence and broke his arm.* (**cair**)
3 fall apart/off/out, etc. to become separated □ *The doll's arms fell off.* □ *All his hair fell out.* (**desprender**)
4 if an amount, price or temperature falls, it goes down □ + **by** *The temperature has fallen by several degree s.* □ + **to** *Prices fell to their lowest levels since June.* (**cair**)
5 to start being in a particular state ▣ *They fell in love.* ▣ *I often fall asleep at the cinema.* ▣ *He fell ill on holiday.* (**ficar**)
♦ PHRASAL VERBS **fall for someone** to start to love someone **fall for something** to be tricked by something □ *I told her I'd give her the money later and she fell for it!* **fall over** to fall to the ground or onto one side □ *I fell over and cut my knee.* **fall out** to stop being friends □ *Carlos and Sergei have fallen out.* **fall through** to fail or not happen □ *Their plans for a holiday have fallen through.*

> **THESAURUS:** If you **fall**, or **fall over**, you drop to the ground. If you **trip**, you hit your foot on something and fall, or almost fall. For example, you might **trip** on a carpet. If you **collapse**, you fall over because you are ill or very tired.

fall² /fɔːl/ NOUN [*plural* **falls**]
1 when someone falls by accident □ *My grandmother had a serious fall last week.* (**queda**)
2 a decrease in a price, amount or temperature □ + **in** *There has been a fall in unemployment.* (**queda**)
3 the US word for **autumn** (**outono**)

false /fɔːls/ ADJECTIVE
1 not true or based on information that is not correct □ *He made a false statement to the police.* □ *These claims are completely false.* ▣ *We had a false sense of security.* ▣ *We don't want to give people false hope.* (**falso**)
2 not real or natural ▣ *false teeth* □ *a false passport* (**falso**)

fame /feɪm/ NOUN, NO PLURAL the state of being known by a lot of people ▣ *She found fame in a hit TV series.* ▣ *He achieved international fame as a novelist.* ▣ *Young actors go to Hollywood seeking fame and fortune* (= *fame and money*). (**fama**)

familiar /fəˈmɪljə(r)/ ADJECTIVE
1 known to you □ *His voice sounded familiar.* ▣ *There were a few familiar faces* (= *people you know*) *at the party.* (**família**)
2 be familiar with something to have seen or used something before □ *I'm not familiar with this software.* □ *If you're familiar with the area, it's just next to the big park.* (**familiarizado com algo**)

family /ˈfæmɪli/ NOUN [*plural* **families**] a group of people who are related to each other ▣ *I invited my whole family to the wedding.* ▣ *I met her parents and several other family members.* ▣ *She discussed the decision with family and friends.* □ *The minister met the families of the victims.* (**família**)

> **Family** can be used with a singular or plural verb in British English: □ *The family next door has a dog.* □ *The family next door have a dog.*

famine /ˈfæmɪn/ NOUN [*plural* **famines**] a situation in which many people in an area do not have enough food and may die □ *The country was hit by a severe drought and famine.* (fome, escassez)

famous /ˈfeɪməs/ ADJECTIVE known by a lot of people □ *a famous actor* □ *a famous painting* □ **+ for** *She is most famous for her role in Star Wars.* □ **+ as** *He later became famous as a children's writer.* (famoso)

fan¹ /fæn/ NOUN [plural **fans**]
1 someone who likes or admires a person or thing very much □ *football fans* □ *She's a big fan of Madonna.* (fã)
2 a machine with thin blades that turn round and make the air cooler □ *There was a ceiling fan in our room.* (ventilador)
3 something that you move in front of your face to make you feel cooler (leque)

fan² /fæn/ VERB [**fans, fanning, fanned**] to move something in front of your face to make you feel cooler □ *He fanned himself with his cap.* (abanar)

fancy¹ /ˈfænsi/ VERB [**fancies, fancying, fancied**]
1 an informal word meaning to want to have or do something □ *Do you fancy going to the cinema?* □ *I really fancy a curry.* (ter vontade de)
2 an informal word meaning to be attracted to someone □ *My friend fancies you.* (desejar)

fancy² /ˈfænsi/ ADJECTIVE [**fancier, fanciest**] fashionable or expensive □ *fancy clothes* □ *We went for a meal at a fancy restaurant.* (na moda)

fantastic /fænˈtæstɪk/ ADJECTIVE an informal word meaning extremely good □ *We had a fantastic time in Rome.* □ *This is a fantastic opportunity for us.* □ *You look fantastic!* (fantástico)

far¹ /fɑː(r)/ ADVERB [**farther** or **further, farthest** or **furthest**]
1 a long distance □ *Don't go too far.* □ **+ away** *Is the hotel very far away?* □ **+ to** *It's not far to Paris.* □ **+ from** *He lives not far from the church.* (longe)
2 much □ *She's a far better swimmer than I am.* □ *He's far more interested in football.* □ *These trousers are far too small for me.* (muito)
3 **as far as I know/can remember, etc.** used to say what you think is true □ *As far as I can remember, there aren't any very steep hills.* (até, tanto quanto [sei/me lembro etc.])
4 **by far** used to emphasize the quality you are talking about □ *He's by far the most talented of our dancers.* (de longe)
5 **so far** until now □ *So far, there haven't been any accidents.* (até agora, por enquanto)

> Note that **far**, meaning 'a long distance', is mainly used in questions and in negative sentences: □ *How far is it to the town centre?* □ *It's not far from the town centre.* In positive sentences, we usually say **a long way**: □ *It's a long way from the town centre.*

far² /fɑː(r)/ ADJECTIVE the far part of something is the part that is the greatest distance from you □ *The house is on the far side of the lake.* (distante)

fare /feə(r)/ NOUN [plural **fares**] the price of a journey by bus, train, aeroplane, etc. □ *The train fare to London is £33.* □ *Cheap air fares make travel much easier.* (passagem)

farm¹ /fɑːm/ NOUN [plural **farms**] an area of land where crops are grown and animals are kept □ *a dairy farm* (= which keeps cows for milk) □ *a farm animal* □ *He works on a farm.* (fazenda)

farm² /fɑːm/ VERB [**farms, farming, farmed**] to use land for growing crops or keeping animals for meat □ *They have farmed the land here for generations.* (cultivar)

farmer /ˈfɑːmə(r)/ NOUN [plural **farmers**] someone who owns and works on a farm □ *a local sheep farmer* (fazendeiro)

farmhouse /ˈfɑːmhaʊs/ NOUN [plural **farmhouses**] a house on a farm where the farmer lives (casa de fazenda)

farming /ˈfɑːmɪŋ/ NOUN, NO PLURAL the activity or business of working on and managing a farm □ *The organization promotes organic farming.* □ *He grew up in a small farming community.* (agricultura, lavoura)

fascinate /ˈfæsɪneɪt/ VERB [**fascinates, fascinating, fascinated**] to interest and attract someone very much □ *The story of Tutankhamun has fascinated people for many years.* □ *The thing that fascinates me is the variety of shapes and colours.* (fascinar)

fascinated /ˈfæsɪneɪtɪd/ ADJECTIVE very interested and attracted by something □ *As a kid I was fascinated by the stars.* □ *She watched the fascinated expressions of the children.* (fascinado)

fascinating /ˈfæsɪneɪtɪŋ/ ADJECTIVE very interesting □ *a fascinating story* □ *It's the island's wildlife that I find fascinating.* (fascinante)

fashion /ˈfæʃən/ NOUN [plural **fashions**] something, especially a piece of clothing, that is very popular at a particular time □ **+ for** *There was a fashion for tight jeans.* □ *Short skirts were in fashion then.* □ *She wears all the latest fashions.* (moda)

fashionable /ˈfæʃənəbəl/ ADJECTIVE popular with many people at a particular time □ *a fashionable restaurant* □ *The area has become fashionable with students.* □ **+ to do something** *It's fashionable to play team sports again.* (na moda)

fast¹ /fɑːst/ ADJECTIVE [**faster, fastest**]
1 quick □ *a fast car* □ *He was the fastest runner.* (rápido)
2 if a clock or watch is fast, it shows a time that is later than the correct time (adiantado)

fast² /fɑːst/ ADVERB [faster, fastest]
1 quickly □ *She can run very fast.* □ *We're working as fast as we can.* □ *The population has grown faster than in any other region.* (**depressa**)
2 fast asleep completely asleep □ *The boys are fast asleep.* (**profundamente**)
3 firmly or tightly ▣ *The door was stuck fast.* (**firme**)

fast³ /fɑːst/ VERB [fasts, fasting, fasted] to not eat any food for a period of time, often for religious reasons □ *I am fasting because it is Ramadan.* (**jejuar**)

fast⁴ /fɑːst/ NOUN [plural fasts] a time when you fast (**jejum**)

fasten /ˈfɑːsən/ VERB [fastens, fastening, fastened] to join or fix two things or parts together ▣ *Please fasten your seat belts.* □ *+ to The phone was fastened to the wall.* □ *She fastened the papers together with a stapler.* □ *The dress fastens at the back.* (**apertar**)

fastener /ˈfɑːsənə(r)/ NOUN [plural fasteners] something that is used to join two things together (**prendedor, fecho**)

fast food /fɑːst ˈfuːd/ NOUN, NO PLURAL food that is prepared and served quickly in a restaurant, often to take away (**refeição, fast-food**)

fat¹ /fæt/ ADJECTIVE [fatter, fattest]
1 a fat person has too much flesh, usually because they eat too much ▣ *George is getting fat, isn't he?* ▣ *Do these jeans make me look fat?* □ *Fat children are often teased.* (**gordo**)
2 thick or large □ *a big, fat book* (**gordo**)

> It is not polite to describe someone as **fat**. To sound less rude, use the words **big** or **overweight**: □ *She's quite big at the moment and unhappy about it.*

fat² /fæt/ NOUN [plural fats]
1 no plural a soft white substance that forms a layer under your skin ▣ *Can exercise reduce body fat?* (**gordura**)
2 a substance like oil that is in food or used in cooking □ *Limit the amount of fat you eat.* ▣ *Hard cheese has a higher fat content.* (**gordura**)

fatal /ˈfeɪtəl/ ADJECTIVE causing someone's death ▣ *a fatal accident* (**fatal**)

fate /feɪt/ NOUN, NO PLURAL
1 the things that happen to someone, especially bad things ▣ *I hope that the others don't suffer the same fate.* ▣ *The High Court will decide the fate of the three men.* (**destino**)
2 a power that seems to control what happens □ *She believes that fate brought them together.* (**destino, sorte**)

father /ˈfɑːðə(r)/ NOUN [plural fathers] your male parent □ *I'll speak to my father.* (**pai**)

> **Father** is a formal way of speaking or referring to your male parent. Most young people use the word **Dad** instead and young children often use the word **Daddy**.

Father Christmas /ˌfɑːðə ˈkrɪsməs/ NOUN an imaginary old man with a white beard in a red coat who children believe brings presents on Christmas Eve (**Papai Noel**)

father-in-law /ˈfɑːðər ɪn ˌlɔː/ NOUN [plural fathers-in-law] the father of your wife or husband (**sogro**)

fatigue /fəˈtiːɡ/ NOUN, NO PLURAL extreme tiredness □ *The illness can cause fatigue.* (**fadiga**)

fault /fɔːlt/ NOUN [plural faults]
1 the fact of being responsible for something bad or wrong □ *Sorry, that's my fault – I left it unlocked.* □ *+ of This is not the fault of the teachers.* □ *The driver was not at fault.* (**culpa**)
2 a mistake, problem or bad feature □ *The plane developed a technical fault.* □ *+ with There was a fault with the design.* (**defeito**)

faulty /ˈfɔːlti/ ADJECTIVE not working correctly □ *a faulty computer* (**defeituoso**)

favor /ˈfeɪvə(r)/ NOUN [plural favors], VERB [favors, favoring, favored] the US spelling of **favour** (**favor**)

favorite /ˈfeɪvrɪt/ ADJECTIVE, NOUN [plural favorites] the US spelling of **favourite** (**favorito**)

favour /ˈfeɪvə(r)/ NOUN [plural favours]
1 something you do for someone to help them ▣ *Could you do me a favour and check my homework?* ▣ *I need to ask you a favour.* ▣ *As a special favour, Bill's fixing my car.* (**favor**)
2 in favour of something supporting something as a good idea □ *I'm in favour of higher pay for nurses.* □ *Workers have voted in favour of strike action.* (**a favor**)

favourite¹ /ˈfeɪvrɪt/ ADJECTIVE your favourite person or thing is the one you like best □ *My favourite colour is purple.* □ *Who's your favourite player?* (**favorito**)

favourite² /ˈfeɪvrɪt/ NOUN [plural favourites] the person or thing you like best □ *I love all cheese, but brie is my favourite.* (**favorito**)

fax¹ /fæks/ NOUN [plural faxes]
1 a written message that is sent by a machine over a telephone line ▣ *I sent a fax to the bank.* (**fax**)
2 a machine used for sending a fax message (**aparelho de fax**)

fax² /fæks/ VERB [faxes, faxing, faxed] to send someone a fax (**enviar um fax**)

fear¹ /fɪə(r)/ NOUN [plural fears]
1 no plural the feeling of being very frightened □ *She was shaking with fear.* ▣ *They live in constant fear of attack.* (**medo**)
2 a feeling of being frightened or worried about a particular thing □ *+ of John has a fear of spiders.* □ *+ about He has raised fears about the future of the company.* □ *+ for She expressed fears for their safety.* ▣ *The news confirmed her worst fears.* (**medo**)

fear² /fɪə(r)/ VERB [fears, fearing, feared] to be afraid of or worried about someone or something ◻ *Experts fear the virus could spread.* ◻ **+ that** *He feared that she was already too late.* ◻ **+ for** *He feared for his safety.* 🔳 *She feared for her life* (= thought she might die). **(ter medo de)**

fearless /ˈfɪəlɪs/ ADJECTIVE not frightened by anything ◻ *a fearless fighter* **(destemido)**

feast /fiːst/ NOUN [plural feasts] a large meal for a special occasion **(banquete)**

feat /fiːt/ NOUN [plural feats] something someone does that needs a lot of skill, strength or courage ◻ *a feat of strength and endurance* **(proeza)**

feather /ˈfeðə(r)/ NOUN [plural feathers] one of the long light things that cover a bird's body **(pena)**

feature /ˈfiːtʃə(r)/ NOUN [plural features]
1 a part or quality of something ◻ **+ of** *One of the key features of the system is its flexibility.* 🔳 *The phone's other features include a camera, radio and MP3 player.* ◻ *The school buses have special safety features.* **(característica)**
2 a part of your face, such as your eyes, nose or mouth 🔳 *She described the man's hair colour and facial features.* **(traço)**

February /ˈfebruəri/ NOUN [plural Februarys] the second month of the year, after January and before March ◻ *I started my new job in February.* **(fevereiro)**

fed /fed/ PAST TENSE AND PAST PARTICIPLE OF **feed** (ver **feed**)

federal /ˈfedərəl/ ADJECTIVE to do with a group of states which make some of their own laws but also have a national government ◻ *a federal system* **(federal)**

fed up /ˌfed ˈʌp/ ADJECTIVE annoyed or bored with something that has been happening for a long time ◻ *I've been peeling potatoes all morning and I'm fed up now.* ◻ *We're fed up with your moaning.* **(farto, cheio)**

fee /fiː/ NOUN [plural fees] an amount of money that you pay for a service ◻ **+ for** *They charge a monthly fee for unlimited Internet access.* 🔳 *Companies pay a fee to advertise on the site.* **(honorário)**

feed /fiːd/ VERB [feeds, feeding, fed] to give food to a person or an animal ◻ *Dad was feeding the baby.* ◻ *I don't earn enough money to feed my family.* ◻ *Can you feed my cat while I'm on holiday?* **(alimentar)**

feedback /ˈfiːdbæk/ NOUN, NO PLURAL opinions from people about work you are doing or have done, intended to help you do it better 🔳 *It's always good to get feedback from customers.* **(retorno)**

feel /fiːl/ VERB [feels, feeling, felt]
1 to have an emotion or to be in a particular state ◻ *I feel tired.* ◻ *Do you feel better today?* ◻ *How are you feeling?* ◻ *I don't feel any anger towards them.* **(sentir)**
2 to touch something with your fingers to see what it is like ◻ *Feel how soft her fur is!* **(apalpar)**
3 to experience something touching you or happening to you ◻ *Suddenly, she felt a hand on her shoulder.* ◻ *He could feel himself falling.* ◻ *I felt a pain in my leg.* **(sentir)**
4 if something feels a certain way, that is how it seems to you ◻ *Your forehead feels hot.* ◻ *It feels strange to be back here.* ◻ *It feels as though nobody is interested.* **(parecer)**
5 to think or believe something ◻ *I feel he should have asked my opinion first.* **(achar)**
6 feel like something to want something or want to do something ◻ **+ ing** *Do you feel like going for a swim?* **(estar com vontade de)**

feeling /ˈfiːlɪŋ/ NOUN [plural feelings]
1 an emotion ◻ *There was a feeling of excitement amongst the children.* **(sentimento)**
2 something that you experience physically, or the ability to experience it ◻ *I don't like the feeling of being under water.* 🔳 *I lost the feeling in my toes.* **(sensibilidade)**
3 a belief that something is true 🔳 *I have the feeling that she's avoiding me.* **(sensação)**
→ *go to* **hurt¹** someone's feelings

feet /fiːt/ PLURAL OF **foot** (pé)

fell¹ /fel/ PAST TENSE OF **fall¹** (ver **fall¹**)

fell² /fel/ VERB [fells, felling, felled] if you fell a tree, you cut it down **(derrubar)**

fellow¹ /ˈfeləʊ/ NOUN [plural fellows] an old-fashioned word for a boy or man ◻ *He's an unusual fellow.* **(sujeito)**

fellow² /ˈfeləʊ/ ADJECTIVE used to refer to a person who is similar to you in some way ◻ *He chatted with fellow passengers.* **(colega)**

felt¹ /felt/ NOUN, NO PLURAL a type of cloth made of rolled and pressed wool **(feltro)**

felt² /felt/ PAST TENSE AND PAST PARTICIPLE OF **feel** (ver **feel**)

female¹ /ˈfiːmeɪl/ ADJECTIVE belonging to the sex which can give birth or lay eggs ◻ *a female athlete* ◻ *She won the award for best female artist.* ◻ *A female lion is called a lioness.* **(fêmea, mulher)**

female² /ˈfiːmeɪl/ NOUN [plural females] a female animal or person ◻ *We saw an adult female with three cubs.* **(fêmea)**

feminine /ˈfemɪnɪn/ ADJECTIVE
1 to do with women, or having qualities that are typical of a woman ◻ *a feminine voice* ◻ *This outfit feels more feminine.* **(feminino)**
2 in English grammar, feminine forms of words refer to females. For example, *she* is a feminine pronoun. **(feminino)**

fence /fens/ NOUN [plural fences] a wooden or metal structure that goes around or separates land ◻ *He put up a fence around the garden.* **(cerca)**

ferocious

ferocious /fəˈrəʊʃəs/ ADJECTIVE extremely violent, strong or dangerous □ *a ferocious dog* □ *a ferocious storm* (**feroz**)

ferry /ˈferi/ NOUN [plural **ferries**] a boat that carries people and vehicles ▣ *a passenger ferry* ▣ *We took a ferry to a smaller island.* (**balsa**)

fertile /ˈfɜːtaɪl/ ADJECTIVE
1 fertile land is good for growing crops on □ *fertile soil* (**fértil**)
2 a fertile person or animal is able to produce children or young animals (**fértil**)

fertilizer *or* **fertiliser** /ˈfɜːtɪlaɪzə(r)/ NOUN [plural **fertilizers**] a substance you put on soil to make plants grow better (**fertilizante**)

festival /ˈfestɪvəl/ NOUN [plural **festivals**]
1 a series of special events of a particular type ▣ *a film festival* ▣ *a five-day music festival* □ *+ of an annual festival of traditional music* (**festival**)
2 a special time or day when people celebrate some thing ▣ *a religious festival* □ *+ of the Muslim festival of Eid* (**festa**)

fetch /fetʃ/ VERB [**fetches, fetching, fetched**] to go somewhere and bring something or someone back with you □ *Could you fetch the newspaper for me, please?* □ *I'll come and fetch you.* □ *The women fetch water from the river.* (**buscar**)

fever /ˈfiːvə(r)/ NOUN [plural **fevers**] if you have a fever, your body temperature is higher than normal because you are ill ▣ *He had a high fever.* (**febre**)

few /fjuː/ DETERMINER, PRONOUN [**fewer, fewest**]
1 a small number □ *I packed a few apples and some bread.* □ *A few people tried to help him.* □ *I visit her every few days.* □ *The past few weeks have been very difficult.* (**alguns**)
2 some but not many □ *We only had a few replies to our advert.* □ *Few of the children had seen a cow before.* ▣ *Very few people know her real name.* (**poucos**)
3 **quite a few** quite a lot □ *There were quite a few mistakes in his work.* (**muitos**)

fiancé /fiˈɒnseɪ/ NOUN [plural **fiancés**] a woman's fiancé is the man she has promised to marry □ *She will marry her fiancé in April.* (**noivo**)

fiancée /fiˈɒnseɪ/ NOUN [plural **fiancées**] a man's fiancée is the woman he has promised to marry □ *Tom's fiancée is a teacher.* (**noiva**)

fibre /ˈfaɪbə(r)/ NOUN [plural **fibres**]
1 a substance in food which your body cannot digest, and which helps your bowels work well □ *Brown bread is high in fibre.* (**fibra**)
2 a thin thread of something □ *Fibres from the girl's clothing were found in his car.* (**fibra**)

fiction /ˈfɪkʃən/ NOUN, NO PLURAL books about imaginary people and situations ▣ *He enjoys reading crime fiction.* ▣ *JK Rowling is one of the most famous children's fiction writers.* (**ficção**)

field /fiːld/ NOUN [plural **fields**] an area of land used for growing crops or keeping animals on □ *There were lots of cows in the field.* □ *+ of We saw a lovely field of poppies.* (**campo**)

fierce /fɪəs/ ADJECTIVE [**fiercer, fiercest**] violent and angry □ *a fierce animal* □ *fierce fighting* (**feroz**)

fifteen /ˌfɪfˈtiːn/ NUMBER the number 15 (**quinze**)
fifteenth /ˌfɪfˈtiːnθ/ NUMBER 15th written as a word (**décimo quinto**)

fifth¹ /fɪfθ/ NUMBER 5th written as a word □ *Today is their fifth wedding anniversary.* (**quinto**)

fifth² /fɪfθ/ NOUN [plural **fifths**] 1/5; one of five equal parts of something □ *A fifth of the money is mine.* (**quinto**)

fiftieth /ˈfɪftiəθ/ NUMBER 50th written as a word (**quinquagésimo**)

fifty /ˈfɪfti/ NUMBER [plural **fifties**]
1 the number 50 (**cinquenta**)
2 **the fifties** the years between 1950 and 1959 (**os anos 1950**)

fight¹ /faɪt/ VERB [**fights, fighting, fought**]
1 to use your body or weapons to try to defeat someone □ *They started fighting.* □ *My great-grandfather fought in the second world war.* □ *Troops fought a fierce battle in the desert.* (**lutar**)
2 to argue with someone □ *+ about They're fighting about who should do the washing up.* □ *+ over They're fighting over her money* (= arguing about who should have it). (**brigar, discutir**)

fight² /faɪt/ NOUN [plural **fights**]
1 when people use physical force to hurt each other □ *+ between There was a fight between local gangs.* (**luta**)
2 when people argue with each other □ *I had a fight with my Mum about staying out late.* ▣ *Josh is always trying to pick a fight* (= start an argument). (**briga, discussão**)
3 when people try hard to achieve something □ *+ for His book describes the long fight for justice.* (**luta**)

fighter /ˈfaɪtə(r)/ NOUN [plural **fighters**] someone who is fighting (**lutador**)

figure /ˈfɪɡə(r)/ NOUN [plural **figures**]
1 a number that tells you an amount, especially in official documents ▣ *official/government figures* ▣ *The latest unemployment figures were released* (= told to the public) *today.* ▣ *Figures show that unemployment has increased.* (**soma**)
2 a number □ *He paid a four figure sum* (= over £1,000). ▣ *The number of deaths has reached double figures* (= is at least 10). (**dígito**)
3 the shape of your body □ *She's got a lovely figure.* (**figura**)
4 a person that you do not know or cannot see clearly □ *There was a shadowy figure in the doorway.* (**figura**)

file¹ /faɪl/ NOUN [plural **files**]
1 a place for storing information on a computer.

file | fine

A computing word. □ *I've created a new file for the accounts.* □ *I downloaded some image files.* (**arquivos**)
2 a piece of folded card for keeping documents in (**arquivo**)
3 a tool with a rough edge for making things smooth (**lima**)

file² /faɪl/ VERB [files, filing, filed]
1 to put documents into a file □ *Please file these application forms under 'rejects'.* (**arquivar**)
2 to walk somewhere, one person behind another □ *The children filed into the hall.* (**andar em fila**)
3 to make something smooth using a file (**limar**)

fill /fɪl/ VERB [fills, filling, filled]
1 to make a container or space full □ + **with** *The waiter filled our glasses with wine.* □ *The room was filled with smoke* □ + **up** *She filled up the pan with water.* (**encher**)
2 to become full □ + **with** *The concert hall quickly filled with people.* □ + **up** *The room had filled up by the time we got back.* (**encher-se**)
◆ PHRASAL VERB **fill something in/out** to write information in the spaces on an official document ▣ *To apply for a place on the course, you need to fill in this form.* (**preencher algo**)

filling /ˈfɪlɪŋ/ ADJECTIVE food that is filling makes your stomach feel full (**recheio**)

film¹ /fɪlm/ NOUN [plural films]
1 a story that you watch in a cinema or on television ▣ *Have you seen this James Bond film?* ▣ *He was watching a film on television.* ▣ *They made a film about his life.* ▣ *a film star* (= a famous actor who has been in many films) (**filme**)
2 something you put inside a camera so you can take photographs ▣ *I need a new roll of film.* (**filme**)

> THESAURUS: A film or a movie is a general word for a story that you watch in a cinema or on television. Movie is the usual word in American English. A documentary is a film about real people or real events. A cartoon is a film made from a long series of drawings.

film² /fɪlm/ VERB [films, filming, filmed]
to make a film of something □ *They were filming scenes for her new movie.* □ *'Brokeback Mountain' was filmed in Canada.* (**filmar**)

filter¹ /ˈfɪltə(r)/ NOUN [plural filters] a device that you put a liquid or gas through in order to remove solid substances □ *a water filter* (**filtro**)
filter² /ˈfɪltə(r)/ VERB [filters, filtered, filtering] to put something through a filter (**filtrar**)

final¹ /ˈfaɪnəl/ ADJECTIVE
coming at the end □ *I'm reading the final chapter of the book.* □ *On the final day of his tour, the Prime Minister visited a school.* (**final, último**)

final² /ˈfaɪnəl/ NOUN [plural finals]
the last game in a competition, which decides who will win □ *Federer will play Henman in the final.* □ *The team are through to the finals.* (**final**)

finale NOUN [plural finales] the last part of a show or piece of music (**ato final**)
finally ADVERB
1 after a long time □ *When he finally arrived, it was after midnight.* (**finalmente**)
2 used to introduce the last in a list of things □ *Finally, I would like to thank everyone who has helped.* (**finalmente**)

finance¹ /ˈfaɪnæns/ NOUN [plural finances]
things that are to do with money, especially in a government or company □ *John is an expert in finance.* ▣ *She's the company's finance director.* (**finança**)

finance² /faɪˈnæns/ VERB [finances, financing, financed]
to provide the money for something, especially in business □ *They took out a loan to finance the project.* (**financiar**)

financial /faɪˈnænʃəl/ ADJECTIVE
to do with money ▣ *banks and other financial institutions* ▣ *Many companies are facing financial difficulties.* (**financeiro**)

find /faɪnd/ VERB [finds, finding, found]
1 to discover or see something or someone you have been looking for □ *I can't find my pencil case.* □ *The murderer was never found.* (**achar, encontrar**)
2 to discover something by chance □ *A jogger found the body by the river last night.* □ *I found a beetle in my soup.* (**achar**)
3 to discover that something has happened or that something is true □ *The survey found a link between birth weight and intelligence.* □ + **that** *I find that it is best to call her in the mornings.* □ *I found I had forgotten my phone.* (**descobrir**)
4 to discover an answer, a reason or a way of doing something ▣ *We found a way to stop the leak.* ▣ *We are trying to find a solution to the problem of litter.* (**descobrir**)
5 find someone guilty/not guilty to say that someone is guilty/not guilty in a court □ *He was found guilty of murder and sentenced to life in prison.* (**considerar alguém culpado/inocente**)
◆ PHRASAL VERB **find out (something)** to discover information or the truth about something □ + **that** *We found out that they had been stealing from us.* □ + **about** *She used the Internet to find out about bees.* □ *I need to find out how to set up a website.*

fine¹ /faɪn/ ADJECTIVE [finer, finest]
1 good or acceptable □ *'Let's meet at seven.' 'OK, that sounds fine.'* □ *'Is the water hot enough?' 'Yes, it's fine, thanks.'* (**ótimo**)
2 healthy or happy □ *'How are you?' 'I'm fine, thanks.'* ▣ *Don't worry, I'm absolutely fine.* (**bem**)
3 of a very good quality □ *The museum has many fine examples of Japanese art.* □ *It was a fine performance.* (**ótimo**)
4 very thin, or made of very small pieces *a fine needle* □ *fine powder* (**fino**)
5 sunny, with no rain ▣ *The fine weather brought many people to the coast.* (**lindo**)
● **finely** /ˈfaɪnli/ ADVERB
1 into very thin small pieces ▣ *Chop the onion finely.* (**finamente**)

2 in a beautiful way ▢ *The palace was finely decorated.* (otimamente)

> Note that the adjective **fine**, meaning 'healthy or happy' never has the word 'very' before it:
> ✓ *'How are you, Lilia?' 'I'm fine, thanks.'*
> ✗ *'How are you, Lilia?' 'I'm very fine, thanks.'*

fine² /faɪn/ VERB [**fines, fining, fined**] to make someone pay a fine ▢ *He was fined for dropping litter.* (multar)

fine³ /faɪn/ NOUN [*plural* **fines**] money that someone must pay as a punishment ▣ *He was given a parking fine.* ▣ *She was ordered to pay a fine of £60 for speeding.* (multa)

finger /ˈfɪŋgə(r)/ NOUN [*plural* **fingers**] one of the five long parts at the end of your hand ▣ *Sam had a cut on his little finger* (= smallest finger). (dedo)

♦ IDIOMS **(keep your) fingers crossed** used for saying that you hope something will happen ▢ *We're keeping our fingers crossed that he passes the exam.* ▢ *Fingers crossed the train arrives on time.* **put your finger on something** to understand exactly what is wrong, different etc. ▢ *Something wasn't right but I couldn't put my finger on it.*

fingernail /ˈfɪŋgəneɪl/ NOUN [*plural* **fingernails**] the hard part at the top of each finger ▢ *He bites his fingernails.* (unha)

fingerprint /ˈfɪŋgəprɪnt/ NOUN [*plural* **fingerprints**] the mark that your finger leaves when you touch something ▢ *The police took his fingerprints.* (impressão digital)

fingertip /ˈfɪŋgətɪp/ NOUN [*plural* **fingertips**] the top end of each finger (ponta do dedo)

finish¹ /ˈfɪnɪʃ/ VERB [**finishes, finishing, finished**]
1 to complete something ▢ *Have you finished your homework?* ▢ + *ing* *I've finished cleaning the bathroom.* (terminar)
2 to come to an end ▢ *What time did the film finish?* (acabar)
3 to use, eat or drink all of something ▢ *I've finished the bread.* (acabar)

♦ PHRASAL VERBS **finish something off 1** to complete the last part of something ▢ *I just need to finish off the housework.* **2** to eat, drink or use the last part of something ▢ *The children finished off all the sausages.* **finish with something** to stop using or needing something ▢ *Have you finished with the bread knife?*

finish² /ˈfɪnɪʃ/ NOUN [*plural* **finishes**] the last part of something ▣ *The course was badly planned from start to finish.* (chegada)

fire¹ /ˈfaɪə(r)/ NOUN [*plural* **fires**]
1 no plural flames and heat that are caused by something burning ▢ *The building was destroyed by fire.* (fogo)
2 when something burns in a way that is not intended ▣ *Fire broke out* (= started) *in the warehouse.* ▣ *We used buckets of water to put out the fire.* ▣ *The curtains caught fire* (= started to burn).
3 on fire burning ▢ *Soon the whole building was on fire.* (em chamas)
4 set fire to something to make something burn (colocar fogo)
5 a pile of wood, coal, etc. that is burned to provide heat ▣ *I lit a fire in the bedroom.* (fogo)

> THESAURUS: A **fire** is the heat and flames caused by burning something. You can have a fire in your house to keep you warm, or it can be an accident. A **flame** is the hot orange gas that you see in a fire. A **blaze** is a big fire.

fire² /ˈfaɪə(r)/ VERB [**fires, firing, fired**]
1 to fire a gun is to shoot a bullet from it (atirar)
2 an informal word meaning to tell someone that they must leave their job ▢ *She was fired for bullying her colleagues.* (demitir)

firearm /ˈfaɪərɑːm/ NOUN [*plural* **firearms**] a formal word meaning a gun (arma de fogo)

fire brigade /ˈfaɪə brɪˌgeɪd/ NOUN [*plural* **fire brigades**] the group of people whose job is to stop fires burning (corpo de bombeiros)

fire engine /ˈfaɪər ˌendʒɪn/ NOUN [*plural* **fire engines**] a vehicle that carries fire fighters and their equipment (carro de bombeiros)

firefighter /ˈfaɪəˌfaɪtə(r)/ NOUN [*plural* **firefighters**] someone whose job is to stop fires burning ▢ *Firefighters battled for two hours to get the blaze under control.* (bombeiro)

fireman /ˈfaɪəmən/ NOUN [*plural* **firemen**] a man whose job is to stop fires burning (bombeiro)

fireplace /ˈfaɪəpleɪs/ NOUN [*plural* **fireplaces**] the space for a fire in the wall of a room, or the frame around this space (lareira)

firework /ˈfaɪəwɜːk/ NOUN [*plural* **fireworks**] something which explodes and makes bright lights in the sky for entertainment ▣ *The festival ended with a spectacular fireworks display.* (fogo de artifício)

firm¹ /fɜːm/ ADJECTIVE [**firmer, firmest**]
1 not soft ▢ *a firm bed* (firme)
2 showing that you are in control and that you mean what you say ▢ *She spoke in a quiet but firm voice.* ▢ *She is a very firm leader.* ▢ + *with* *You should be more firm with the children.* (firme)
3 tight, strong and not going to move ▢ *Betsy took a firm hold on the tray.* (firme)

firm² /fɜːm/ NOUN [*plural* **firms**] a company ▢ *Sally works for a law firm.* ▢ *a software firm* (firma)

first¹ /fɜːst/ DETERMINER, NUMBER
1 coming before everyone or everything else ▢ *His was the first name on the list.* ▢ *The first time I went skiing, I hated it.* ▢ *Take the first road on the left.* (primeiro)
2 1st written as a word (primeiro)

first 127 **flag**

first² /fɜːst/ PRONOUN, NOUN, NO PLURAL the person or thing that comes before all others □ *She was the first to realise how the drug could be used.* □ *This is the first in a series of Beethoven concerts.* □ *The doctor's ready now. Who's first?* (primeiro)

first³ /fɜːst/ ADVERB
1 before anyone or anything else □ *You can phone Josh, but eat your dinner first.* □ *First you need to dig the foundations.* (primeiro)
2 for the first time □ *We first met at university.* □ *I first became aware of the problem last week.* (pela primeira vez)
3 doing better than everyone else in a competition, exam, etc. ▣ *Philip came first in the cookery competition.* (primeiro)
4 at first at the beginning □ *At first I couldn't speak French at all.* (inicialmente)

first-class¹ /ˌfɜːstˈklɑːs/ ADJECTIVE used about travel when you pay more for a better seat etc., and about post when you pay more for a quicker service □ *a first-class train ticket* □ *a first-class stamp* (primeira classe)

first-class² /ˌfɜːstˈklɑːs/ ADVERB using the best or most expensive type □ *Len always travels first-class.* (de primeira classe)

first name /ˈfɜːst ˌneɪm/ NOUN [plural **first names**] the name that comes before your family name □ *Her first name's 'Jane' and her surname is 'Smith'.* ([pre]nome)

fish¹ /fɪʃ/ NOUN [plural **fish** or **fishes**]
1 an animal that lives and swims in water ▣ *They were trying to catch fish in the stream.* (peixe)
2 *no plural* the meat from this animal eaten as food □ *We had fish for dinner.* (peixe)

> Note that the plural form of **fish** is usually **fish**. **Fishes** is not common but is sometimes used when talking about different types of fish:
> ✓ *We caught a lot of fish.*
> ✗ *We caught a lot of fishes.*

fish² /fɪʃ/ VERB [**fishes, fishing, fished**] to try to catch fish □ + **for** *The men were fishing for salmon.* (pescar)

fisherman /ˈfɪʃəmən/ NOUN [plural **fishermen**] someone who catches fish as a job or sport (pescador)

fishing /ˈfɪʃɪŋ/ NOUN, NO PLURAL the sport or job of catching fish ▣ *We're going fishing at the weekend.* ▣ *the fishing industry* (pesca)

fist /fɪst/ NOUN [plural **fists**] your hand when it is closed tightly □ *Don't shake your fist at me!* (punho)

fit¹ /fɪt/ VERB [**fits, fitting, fitted**]
1 to be the right shape or size for someone or something □ *The dress fits you perfectly.* □ *The cupboard will fit in the corner.* (ajustar[-se])
2 to have enough room to put something or someone somewhere, or to be small enough to go somewhere □ *I can't fit any more documents in this file.* □ *We tried to get the piano up the stairs, but it wouldn't fit.* (ajustar)
3 to fix something in a place □ *We're having a new kitchen fitted next week.* □ **+ with** *He was fitted with a pacemaker.* (aquipar)
♦ PHRASAL VERBS **fit in** to become accepted by a group of people □ *They were all very sporty, and I didn't really fit in.* **fit someone/something in** to have time to see someone or do something □ *We can fit you in to see the doctor at ten.*

fit² /fɪt/ ADJECTIVE [**fitter, fittest**]
1 healthy, especially because of doing exercise ▣ *I'm trying to get fit.* (em forma)
2 suitable or good enough □ **+ to do something** *This food isn't fit to eat.* (adequado)

five /faɪv/ NUMBER [plural **fives**] the number 5 (cinco)

fix /fɪks/ VERB [**fixes, fixing, fixed**]
1 to attach something to something else □ **+ to** *She fixed the shelves to the wall.* (fixar)
2 to repair something □ *He's trying to fix the roof.* ▣ *I need to get the car fixed.* ▣ *All our staff are working to fix the problem.* (consertar)
3 to decide something ▣ *Have you fixed a date for the wedding?* (marcar)
♦ PHRASAL VERB **fix something up** to arrange something such as a meeting or visit □ *They fixed up a meeting for the following week.*

> **THESAURUS:** If you **fix** or **mend** something you repair it. If you **adjust** something, you change it slightly. For example, you might **adjust** a clock if it is fast or slow. If you **correct** something, you make it right or show someone the mistakes that they have made. For example, a teacher might **correct** a student's writing.

flag /flæg/ NOUN [plural **flags**] a piece of cloth with a pattern on it, used as the symbol of a country or organization □ *The American flag has stars and stripes on it.* ▣ *Hundreds of people were waving* *flags as the Queen arrived.* 🔼 *Flags were flying on the castle.* (bandeira)

flame /fleɪm/ NOUN [plural **flames**]
1 the hot orange gas you see in a fire ▫ *Flames leapt from the roof.* 🔼 *Firefighters tried to put out the flames.* (chama)
2 in flames burning ▫ *The building was in flames.* (em chamas)
3 burst into flames/go up in flames to suddenly start burning ▫ *The plane skidded off the runway and burst into flames.* (explodir em chamas)

flap¹ /flæp/ VERB [**flaps, flapping, flapped**] if a bird flaps its wings, it moves them up and down (bater [asas], adejar)

flap² /flæp/ NOUN [plural **flaps**] a piece of something that hangs down over an opening ▫ *He closed the tent flaps.* (aba)

flash¹ /flæʃ/ VERB [**flashes, flashing, flashed**]
1 if a light flashes, it goes on and off quickly ▫ *The warning light was flashing.* 🔼 *a flashing light* (lampejar)
2 to make a light go on and off quickly ▫ *He flashed his car lights to warn other drivers of the danger.* (piscar)
3 to appear for a short time and then disappear ▫ *Some important news suddenly flashed up on the screen.* (em um piscar de olhos)

flash² /flæʃ/ NOUN [plural **flashes**]
1 a sudden bright light 🔼 *a flash of lightning* (lampejo)
2 a light on a camera that you use when you are taking photographs indoors (flash)
3 in a flash an informal phrase meaning very quickly ▫ *She was out of the door in a flash.* (em um piscar de olhos)

> **THESAURUS:** A flash is a sudden bright light. For example, we talk about a flash of lightning. If something shines with small flashes of light, we can say that it **glitters**. Diamonds **glitter**, for example. A **spark** is a small burning piece that is sent out of a fire. A **glow** is a warm or soft light. A fire might **glow**, especially when it is not burning very strongly.

flat¹ /flæt/ ADJECTIVE [**flatter, flattest**]
1 level, smooth and not sloping ▫ *a flat roof* ▫ *Place the box on a flat surface.* ▫ *I'd like to have a flatter stomach.* (plano, raso)
2 a flat tyre does not have enough air in it (vazio)

flat² /flæt/ ADVERB in a way that is level, smooth and not sloping ▫ *I spread the carpet flat on the floor.* ▫ *Omar was lying flat on his back.* (horizontalmente)

flat³ /flæt/ NOUN [plural **flats**] a set of rooms that someone lives in, which are part of a larger building (apartamento)

flatten /ˈflætən/ VERB [**flattens, flattening, flattened**] to make something become flat (aplanar)

flatter /ˈflætə(r)/ VERB [**flatters, flattering, flattered**] to say nice things to someone because you want to please them, especially when you are not being sincere ▫ *I'm sure he's just flattering me when he said he enjoyed reading my article.* (adular)

flavour /ˈfleɪvə(r)/ NOUN [plural **flavours**] the taste that something has ▫ *Chocolate is my favourite ice cream flavour.* ▫ *Brown rice has a wonderful nutty flavour.* (sabor)

flaw /flɔː/ NOUN [plural **flaws**] a fault in someone or something ▫ *The building has some serious design flaws.* (defeito)

fled /fled/ PAST TENSE AND PAST PARTICIPLE OF **flee** (ver **flee**)

flee /fliː/ VERB [**flees, fleeing, fled**] a formal word meaning to run away or to escape ▫ *Nina turned and fled.* (fugir)

fleet /fliːt/ NOUN [plural **fleets**] a group of ships or vehicles ▫ *a fleet of boats* (frota)

flesh /fleʃ/ NOUN, NO PLURAL the part of a person's or animal's body between the skin and the bones ▫ *The salmon's flesh should be pink and firm.* (carne)

flew /fluː/ PAST TENSE OF **fly**¹ (ver **fly**¹)

flexibility /ˌfleksəˈbɪləti/ NOUN, NO PLURAL
1 the quality of being able to change to suit different people or situations ▫ *We appreciate your flexibility about the time of the meeting.* (flexibilidade)
2 the quality of being easy to bend (flexibilidade)

flexible /ˈfleksəbəl/ ADJECTIVE
1 able to change to suit different people or situations ▫ *flexible arrangements* (flexível)
2 easy to bend ▫ *flexible wires* (flexível)

flick /flɪk/ VERB [**flicks, flicking, flicked**] to send something through the air quickly and suddenly, often with your fingers ▫ *She flicked the fly off her coat.* ▫ *He flicked the ball back to me.* (fazer um movimento rápido)
♦ PHRASAL VERB **flick through something** to look quickly at each page in a magazine, book, etc.

flight /flaɪt/ NOUN [plural **flights**]
1 a journey in an aircraft ▫ + *from a direct flight from Heathrow to Singapore* 🔼 *He boarded a flight to Tokyo.* (voo)
2 a set of stairs 🔼 *We walked up several flights of stairs.* 🔼 *a flight of steps* ▫ *She climbed the five flights to her apartment.* (lance, andar)

fling /flɪŋ/ VERB [**flings, flinging, flung**] to throw or move something using a lot of force ▫ *He flung his racket down.* ▫ *She flung her arms round him.* ▫ *She flung herself down in the chair, completely exhausted.* (arremessar)

flip /flɪp/ VERB [**flips, flipping, flipped**] to turn over quickly or to make something turn over quickly ▫ *The car ran off the road and flipped over.* ▫ *After a couple of minutes, flip the fish over to cook the other side.* (lançar)

flirt

flirt /flɜːt/ VERB [flirts, flirting, flirted] to behave as if you think someone is attractive □ *Emma was flirting with her sister's boyfriend.* (flertar)

float /fləʊt/ VERB [floats, floating, floated]
1 to move slowly or to stay on the surface of a liquid and not sink □ *Leaves were floating on the surface of the water.* □ *The boat floated slowly down the river.* (flutuar)
2 to stay in the air or to move slowly through the air □ *He let go of the balloon and it floated away.* □ *Voices floated down the stairs.* (flutuar)

flock /flɒk/ NOUN [plural flocks] a group of sheep or birds (bando, rebanho)

flood¹ /flʌd/ NOUN [plural floods] a lot of water covering a place that is usually dry □ *Two days of heavy rain caused floods.* (inundação)

flood² /flʌd/ VERB [floods, flooding, flooded] if water floods a place or if a place floods, it becomes covered in a lot of water □ *Large parts of the town were flooded.* □ *The river has flooded its banks.* (inundar)

floor /flɔː(r)/ NOUN [plural floors]
1 the surface that you stand on in a room □ *There were toys all over the kitchen floor.* □ *The hall has a wooden floor.* (piso, assoalho)
2 one of the levels in a building □ *Which floor is your apartment on?* □ *Our office is on the top floor of the building.* (andar)

floppy disk /ˌflɒpi ˈdɪsk/ NOUN [plural floppy disks] a disk inside a flat piece of plastic that is used for copying information from a computer. A computing word (disquete)

flour /flaʊə(r)/ NOUN, NO PLURAL powder made from wheat (= grain), used for making bread and cakes (farinha)

flourish /ˈflʌrɪʃ/ VERB [flourishes, flourishing, flourished] to develop quickly and well □ *Her new business is flourishing.* □ *Wildlife is once again flourishing in the area.* (florescer)

flow¹ /fləʊ/ VERB [flows, flowing, flowed] if a liquid flows, it moves along □ **+ through** *The River Thames flows through London.* □ **+ into** *The water flows into the sea.* □ *Tears flowed down her face.* (correr)

flow² /fləʊ/ NOUN [plural flows] a continuous movement of something □ **+ of** *We used bandages to stop the flow of blood.* □ *a steady flow of tourists* (fluxo)

> THESAURUS: A flow is a continuous movement of something, especially liquid. A **current** is a flow of water or air moving in one direction. A **tide** is the regular rise and fall of the level of the sea. At high **tide**, the sea covers the beach. At low **tide**, the sea does not cover the beach. A **flood** is a lot of water covering a place that is usually dry. If there is a lot of rain, it can cause a flood.

fly

flower /ˈflaʊə(r)/ NOUN [plural flowers] the coloured part of a plant □ *Tulips are my favourite flower.* □ *We picked some wild flowers.* □ *They gave her a bunch of flowers.* (flor)

flown /fləʊn/ PAST PARTICIPLE OF **fly¹** (ver fly¹)

flu /fluː/ NOUN, NO PLURAL an illness like a very bad cold which makes you feel hot and tired □ *Last month she caught flu.* □ *I had a bout of flu.* (gripe, influenza)

fluent /ˈfluːənt/ ADJECTIVE able to speak a language easily and well □ *She speaks fluent German.* (fluente)

fluid¹ /ˈfluːɪd/ NOUN [plural fluids] a liquid □ *Runners should drink plenty of fluids.* (fluido, líquido)

fluid² /ˈfluːɪd/ ADJECTIVE able to flow like a liquid □ *Blood is a fluid substance.* (fluido)

flung /flʌŋ/ PAST TENSE AND PAST PARTICIPLE OF **fling** (ver fling)

flush /flʌʃ/ VERB [flushes, flushing, flushed]
1 to press or pull a handle to make water go down a toilet □ *I can't flush the toilet.* (dar descarga)
2 to become red in the face □ *He flushed with embarrassment.* (corar)

flute /fluːt/ NOUN [plural flutes] a musical instrument you play by holding it sideways against your mouth and blowing into it (flauta)

flutter /ˈflʌtə(r)/ VERB [flutters, fluttering, fluttered] to move quickly up and down or from side to side □ *Her eyelids fluttered.* □ *The flags fluttered in the breeze.* (adejar)

fly¹ /flaɪ/ VERB [flies, flying, flew, flown]
1 to travel in an aircraft □ **+ to** *He flew to Miami.* □ *She flew in by helicopter.* (voar)
2 to move through the air using wings □ *A robin flew across the garden.* □ *A plane flew overhead.* (voar)
3 to control an aircraft □ *She learned to fly a helicopter.* (pilotar)
4 to move very quickly □ *A bullet flew past my head.* □ *The door flew open.* (mover-se rapidamente, abrir-se de repente)

> **THESAURUS:** Fly is a general word for moving above the earth. Planes and birds can fly. To **float** means to stay in the air or move slowly through the air. A balloon **floats** in the air. If something **hovers**, it stays still in the air. A helicopter can **hover**, and some birds can **hover**.

fly² /flaɪ/ NOUN [plural **flies**] a small insect that flies (**mosca**)

foam /fəʊm/ NOUN, NO PLURAL a mass of small bubbles on top of a liquid ☐ *I like to eat the foam off my coffee with a spoon.* (**espuma**)

focus¹ /ˈfəʊkəs/ VERB [**focuses, focusing, focused**]
1 to concentrate on one particular thing ☐ *The report focused on the need to improve standards.* 🔁 *She wants to focus attention on the problem.* (**concentrar**)
2 to make small changes to equipment such as a camera so that you get a clear picture (**focalizar**)

focus² /ˈfəʊkəs/ NOUN, NO PLURAL
1 when you focus on one thing, or the thing you focus on 🔁 *My main focus is to play well.* 🔁 *She soon became the focus of media attention.* (**foco**)
2 in focus if an image is in focus, it can be seen clearly ☐ *Make sure the faces are in focus.* (**em foco**)
3 out of focus if an image is out of focus, it cannot be seen clearly ☐ *Some of the photos were out of focus.* (**fora de foco**)

foe /fəʊ/ NOUN [plural **foes**] a formal word for an enemy ☐ *The two men are old foes.* (**adversário**)

fog /fɒg/ NOUN, NO PLURAL thick, low cloud that makes it difficult to see 🔁 *The flight was delayed due to thick fog.* ☐ *The fog lifted slightly.* (**neblina, névoa**)

foggy /ˈfɒgi/ ADJECTIVE [**foggier, foggiest**] having a lot of fog ☐ *a foggy day* ☐ *foggy weather* (**enevoado**)
♦ IDIOM **not have the foggiest (idea)** used to emphasize that you do not know anything about something ☐ *I haven't got the foggiest idea where he is.*

fold¹ /fəʊld/ VERB [**folds, folding, folded**]
1 to bend one part of something so that it covers another part ☐ *Dan folded the letter and put it in the envelope.* ☐ *He folded the clothes neatly.* (**dobrar**)
2 to make something smaller by bending parts of it ☐ + **up** *He folded up his laptop and put it in his bag.* ☐ *The back seats fold down to give more luggage space.* (**dobrar**)
3 fold your arms to cross your arms over your chest (**cruzar os braços**)

fold² /fəʊld/ NOUN [plural **folds**] a line or mark where something is folded (**dobra**)

folder /ˈfəʊldə(r)/ NOUN [plural **folders**]
1 a cardboard or plastic cover for holding papers (**pastas**)
2 a place where you keep documents on a computer. A computing word. (**pasta**)

folk¹ /fəʊk/ PLURAL NOUN people ☐ *He has more money than most folk around here.* 🔁 *Babies and old folk are most at risk.* (**povo**)

folk² /fəʊk/ ADJECTIVE to do with the traditions and culture of the people of a country or area 🔁 *an Irish folk song* 🔁 *Russian folk tales* (**popular, folclórico**)

folk music /ˈfəʊk ˌmjuːzɪk/ NOUN, NO PLURAL traditional music from a particular country or area (**música popular**)

follow /ˈfɒləʊ/ VERB [**follows, following, followed**]
1 to go behind someone or something and go where they go ☐ *He followed her down the street.* (**seguir**)
2 to happen after something ☐ *The meal was followed by a dance.* (**seguir**)
3 to do what a person or a rule, law, etc. says you should do 🔁 *We decided to follow his advice and catch the train.* 🔁 *Just open the letter and follow the instructions in it.* (**seguir**)
4 if you follow a road, you go along it ☐ *Follow the path to the end and turn right.* (**seguir**)
5 to understand what someone is saying ☐ *Do you follow me?* (**acompanhar**)

following /ˈfɒləʊɪŋ/ ADJECTIVE the following day, week, year, etc. is the next one ☐ *I finished work on Friday and we went on holiday the following Wednesday.* (**seguinte**)

fond /fɒnd/ ADJECTIVE [**fonder, fondest**] **fond of someone/something** liking someone or something ☐ + **ing** *We're very fond of walking in the countryside.* ☐ *He is particularly fond of chocolate.* 🔁 *I've grown very fond of the children.* (**mais querido**)

food /fuːd/ NOUN [plural **foods**] *no plural* things that people and animals eat ☐ *They didn't have enough food.* ☐ *We often eat Chinese food.* 🔁 *pet food* (**comida**)

> Note that **food** is not usually used in the plural. **Foods** is sometimes used when talking about different types of food but is not common:
> ✓ *I buy most of our food at the supermarket.*
> ✗ *I buy most of our foods at the supermarket.*

fool¹ /fuːl/ NOUN [plural **fools**]
1 a stupid or silly person ☐ *I'm not a complete fool.* ☐ *I didn't want to look a fool.* (**tolo**)
2 make a fool of yourself to do something that makes people think you are silly ☐ *They're going to make fools of themselves.* (**fazer papel de bobo**)

fool² /fuːl/ VERB [**fools, fooling, fooled**] to trick someone ☐ *His story didn't fool anyone.* ☐ *Don't be fooled by cheap copies.* (**lograr**)

foolish /ˈfuːlɪʃ/ ADJECTIVE silly or stupid □ *a foolish mistake* □ *He didn't want to appear foolish.* (**idiota, tolo**)

foot /fʊt/ NOUN [plural **feet**]
1 one of the parts of your body that you stand on □ *He has a broken foot.* □ *We got to our feet* (= stood up) *when she came in.* □ *I've been on my feet* (= standing up) *all day.* (**pé**)
2 a unit for measuring length, equal to 30.48 centimetres. This is often written **ft**. (**pé**)
3 the foot of the bottom of something □ *We camped at the foot of the mountain.* (**pé, base**)
4 on foot if you travel on foot, you walk (**a pé**)
♦ IDIOM **put your feet up** to rest and relax

footage /ˈfʊtɪdʒ/ NOUN, NO PLURAL a filmed record of an event □ *We bring you live footage of the ceremony.* (**filmagem**)

football /ˈfʊtbɔːl/ NOUN [plural **footballs**]
1 no plural a sport played by two teams who try to kick a ball into a goal □ *The boys are playing football outside.* □ *a football match* □ *a game of football* □ *a football team* (**futebol**)
2 the ball used for playing football □ *Some kids were kicking a football about.* (**bola de futebol**)

footballer /ˈfʊtbɔːlə(r)/ NOUN [plural **footballers**] someone who plays football, especially as their job (**jogador de futebol**)

footprint /ˈfʊtprɪnt/ NOUN [plural **footprints**] a mark that your foot leaves on the ground □ *footprints in the snow* (**pegada**)

footstep /ˈfʊtstep/ NOUN [plural **footsteps**] the sound of someone walking □ *I could hear footsteps.* (**passo**)

for /fɔː(r)/ PREPOSITION
1 to be received or used by someone, or to help some one □ *There's a letter for you.* □ *She made a cake for her Mum.* □ *I did all the ironing for Peter.* (**para**)
2 in order to do something or to get something □ *He asked me for money.* □ *Let's go for a walk.* □ *I went to the supermarket for some eggs.* (**por**)
3 used to show a reason or what something is intended to do □ *What's this switch for?* □ *He was arrested for shoplifting.* □ *I gave her a necklace for her birthday.* (**para**)
4 used to show an amount of time, distance, money, etc. □ *I've lived here for eight years.* □ *We walked for two miles.* □ *I got these trainers for £30.* (**por**)
5 meaning something □ *What's the word for 'girl' in French?* (**para**)
6 supporting or agreeing with someone or something □ *I voted for her.* □ *Are you for or against the new airport?* (**a favor**)

> When you are explaining why someone does something, remember to use the infinitive **to do** something. Do not use **for**:
> ✓ *I went home to see my mother.*
> ✗ *I went home for seeing my mother.*

forbid /fəˈbɪd/ VERB [**forbids, forbidding, forbade, forbidden**] to tell someone that they must not do something □ **+ to do something** *They forbade their daughter to see Henry any more.* □ **+ from** *He is forbidden from discussing the case.* □ *The school rules forbid the use of mobile phones in class.* (**proibir**)

forbidden /fəˈbɪdən/ ADJECTIVE not allowed □ *Smoking is forbidden throughout the hospital.* □ *Alcohol is strictly forbidden.* (**proibido**)

force¹ /fɔːs/ NOUN [plural **forces**]
1 no plural power or physical strength □ *The force of the explosion damaged many buildings.* (**força**)
2 by force by violent physical action □ *They took the land by force.* (**à força**)
3 a group of people, such as police or soldiers, who are trained to work together □ *the armed forces* □ *A defence force was sent into the region.* (**força**)

force² /fɔːs/ VERB [**forces, forcing, forced**]
1 to make someone do something □ **+ to do something** *He forced me to give him money.* (**forçar, obrigar**)
□ *often passive She was forced to move house.*
2 to make something move by using your strength □ *The police had to force the door open.* (**forçar**)

forecast¹ /ˈfɔːkɑːst/ NOUN [plural **forecasts**] a statement about what you think will happen in the future, based on information □ *a weather forecast* □ **+ of** *We had a forecast of heavy rain.* (**previsão**)

forecast² /ˈfɔːkɑːst/ VERB [**forecasts, forecasting, forecast**] to make a forecast □ *Rain is forecast for the weekend.* □ *The company has forecast record profits.* (**prever**)

forehead /ˈfɔːhed/ NOUN [plural **foreheads**] the top part of your face above your eyes (**testa**)

foreign /ˈfɒrən/ ADJECTIVE from a country that is not your country □ *a foreign language* □ *a group of foreign tourists* (**estrangeiro**)

> THESAURUS: Something or someone that is **foreign** is from a country that is not your country. Something that is **international** involves several countries. You might talk about an **international** conference, for example. An **immigrant** is someone who comes to live in a country that is not their own country.

foreigner /ˈfɒrənə(r)/ NOUN [plural **foreigners**] someone who comes from a country that is not your country (**estrangeiro**)

forest /ˈfɒrɪst/ NOUN [plural **forests**] a place where a lot of trees are growing together □ *We stayed at a camp deep in the forest.* (**floresta**)

forever /fəˈrevə(r)/ ADVERB for all future time □ *You can't stay in your room forever.* □ *Their lives have been changed forever.* (**para sempre**)

forgave /fəˈgeɪv/ PAST TENSE OF **forgive** (ver **forgive**)

forget /fəˈget/ VERB [**forgets, forgetting, forgot, forgotten**]
1 to be unable to remember something □ *I've forgotten her name.* □ + *that I forgot that you had been there before.* □ + *about I had forgotten about the heat here.* (esquecer)
2 to not remember to do something or that something is happening □ + *to do something I forgot to feed the dog.* □ + *that He forgot that Milo was coming.* □ *Don't forget to lock the door.* □ *I completely forgot her birthday.* (esquecer)
3 to stop thinking or caring about something □ *Forget about your exams and come to the party.* (esquecer)

forgetful /fəˈgetfʊl/ ADJECTIVE often forgetting things (esquecido, distraído)

forgive /fəˈgɪv/ VERB [**forgives, forgiving, forgave, forgiven**] to stop being angry with someone for something they have done □ + *for Have you forgiven him for breaking the window?* □ *His family can never forgive the killers.* □ *If anything happens to her, I'll never forgive myself.* (perdoar)

forgot /fəˈgɒt/ PAST TENSE OF **forget** (ver **forget**)
forgotten /fəˈgɒtən/ PAST PARTICIPLE OF **forget** (ver **forget**)

fork¹ /fɔːk/ NOUN [plural **forks**]
1 an object with a handle and points that you use for lifting food to your mouth □ *a knife and fork* (garfo, forcado)
2 a place where a road or river divides and goes in two different directions □ *We came to a fork in the road.* (bifurcação)
3 a tool with a long handle and points that you use for digging (garfo)

fork² /fɔːk/ VERB [**forks, forking, forked**] if a road or a river forks, it divides into two parts going in different directions □ *Just after the bridge, the road forks.* (bifurcar)

form¹ /fɔːm/ NOUN [plural **forms**]
1 a type of something □ *What form of transport do you use?* □ *I have tried various forms of exercise.* □ *You need to use some form of wrist support.* (tipo)
2 a document with questions and spaces to write your answers □ *You have to fill in a form to get a passport.* □ *Can you sign this form, please?* (formulário)
3 the shape of someone or something □ *I saw his lifeless form on the floor.* (forma)
4 a class at school □ *Which form are you in?* (série)

> THESAURUS: A *document* is a general word for an official piece of paper. A *form* is a document with questions on it that you have to complete. For example, you have to fill in a form to get a passport. A *questionnaire* is a list of questions that several people answer in order to get information. A business might use a *questionnaire* to find out what customers think about their products.

form² /fɔːm/ VERB [**forms, forming, formed**]
1 to start to exist or to make something start to exist □ *How was the Earth formed?* □ *An idea formed in his mind.* □ *I formed a good impression of his work.* □ *His party is likely to form the next government.* (formar)
2 to be something or the thing that something is made of □ *This article could form the basis of a book.* □ *The area forms part of a safari park.* (constituir)
3 to make a particular shape □ *The children held hands and formed a circle.* (fazer)

formal /ˈfɔːməl/ ADJECTIVE
1 following rules about what is polite and correct, not friendly and relaxed □ *a formal dinner party* □ *The atmosphere was very formal.* (formal)
2 public or official, or following official rules or methods □ *A formal announcement is expected tomorrow.* □ *I wish to make a formal complaint.* (formal)

format /ˈfɔːmæt/ NOUN [plural **formats**] the way something is designed or arranged □ *Please send two photographs in digital format.* □ *There are plans to change the format of the competition.* (formato)

former¹ /ˈfɔːmə(r)/ ADJECTIVE existing or true in the past but not now □ *the former President* □ *In former times, people did not travel so much.* (passado)

former² /ˈfɔːmə(r)/ NOUN, NO PLURAL **the former** the first of two people or things you mention □ *We visited America and Canada but stayed longer in the former.* (primeiro)

formerly /ˈfɔːməlɪ/ ADVERB in the past but not now □ *Their house was formerly a shop.*
formula /ˈfɔːmjʊlə/ NOUN [plural **formulas** or **formulae**]
1 in mathematics or chemistry, a set of letters, numbers or symbols that represent a rule, structure, etc. □ *What's the formula for calculating the area of a circle?* □ *a mathematical formula* (fórmula)
2 the combination of substances used to make something (fórmula)

fort /fɔːt/ NOUN [plural **forts**] a strong building used by soldiers to defend a place from attack (forte)
forthcoming /ˌfɔːθˈkʌmɪŋ/ ADJECTIVE happening soon □ *forthcoming events* □ *They played some tracks from their forthcoming album.* (futuro)
fortieth /ˈfɔːtɪəθ/ NUMBER 40th written as a word (quadragésico)

fortnight /ˈfɔːtnaɪt/ NOUN [plural **fortnights**] a period of two weeks □ *We're going to Greece for a fortnight.* □ *I've been very busy over the past fortnight.* □ *He visits her once a fortnight.* (quinzena)

fortunate /ˈfɔːtʃənət/ ADJECTIVE lucky □ *We were fortunate to catch our train, we were so late.* □ *It's extremely fortunate that no one was hurt.* □ *We should help people who are less fortunate than ourselves.* (afortunado)

fortunately /ˈfɔːtʃənətli/ ADVERB used to say that something lucky has happened □ *Fortunately, nobody was injured.* (**afortunadamente**)

fortune /ˈfɔːtʃuːn/ NOUN [plural **fortunes**]
1 a very large amount of money □ *His uncle died and left him a fortune.* ▣ *He made his fortune in the oil industry.* ▣ *They spent a fortune on it.* (**fortuna**)
2 no plural good luck □ *Sue had the good fortune to win first prize.* (**sorte**)

forty /ˈfɔːti/ NUMBER [plural **forties**] the number 40 (**quarenta, os anos 1940**)

forum /ˈfɔːrəm/ NOUN [plural **forums**] a place or situation in which people can discuss things and express their opinions □ *an online forum* □ *The programme is intended to be a forum for public debate.* (**fórum**)

forward¹ /ˈfɔːwəd/ ADJECTIVE in the direction that is in front of you □ *a forward movement* (**para a frente**)

forward² /ˈfɔːwəd/ or **forwards** /ˈfɔːwədz/ ADVERB in the direction that is in front of you □ *The car moved slowly forwards.* □ *Amy leaned forward.* ▣ *He rocked backwards and forwards.* (**para a frente**)

forward³ /ˈfɔːwəd/ VERB [**forwards, forwarding, forwarded**] to send a letter or e-mail you have received to someone else □ *He forwarded the email to several colleagues.* (**expedir**)

fossil /ˈfɒsəl/ NOUN [plural **fossils**] a dead animal or plant that has been kept in a piece of rock for thousands of years (**fóssil**)

fought /fɔːt/ PAST TENSE AND PAST PARTICIPLE OF **fight¹** (ver **fight¹**)

foul /faʊl/ ADJECTIVE [**fouler, foulest**]
1 very dirty or with a bad smell or taste □ *The tea tasted foul.* (**nojento**)
2 very unpleasant ▣ *foul weather* ▣ *He's in a foul mood.* (**abominável**)

found¹ /faʊnd/ VERB [**founds, founding, founded**] to start an organization □ *The college was founded in 1950.* (**fundar**)

found² /faʊnd/ PAST TENSE AND PAST PARTICIPLE OF **find** (ver **find**)

foundation /faʊnˈdeɪʃən/ NOUN [plural **foundations**]
1 foundations the part of a building that is under the ground and which supports it ▣ *They have dug the foundations for our new home.* (**fundação**)
2 when an organization, business or country is started □ *She has worked here since the company's foundation in 1997.* (**fundação**)

fountain /ˈfaʊntɪn/ NOUN [plural **fountains**] a structure that pushes water up into the air for decoration in a garden or park (**fonte**)

> **THESAURUS:** A **fountain** is a structure that pushes water up into the air for decoration. A **spring** is a place where water flows out of the ground. A **well** is a deep hole in the ground where you can get water, oil or gas. A **reservoir** is a large lake where water is collected and stored in order to be used by people.

four /fɔː(r)/ NUMBER [plural **fours**] the number 4 (**quatro**)

fourteen /ˌfɔːˈtiːn/ NUMBER the number 14 (**quatorze**)

fourteenth /ˌfɔːˈtiːnθ/ NUMBER 14th written as a word (**décimo quarto**)

fourth /fɔːθ/ NUMBER 4th written as a word □ *You are fourth on the list.* □ *Mario finished fourth in the race.* (**quarto**)

fox /fɒks/ NOUN [plural **foxes**] a wild animal that looks like a dog, with red fur and a thick tail (**raposa**)

fraction /ˈfrækʃən/ NOUN [plural **fractions**] an amount, such as 1/2 or 3/8, that is part of a whole number (**fração**)

fracture¹ /ˈfræktʃə(r)/ VERB [**fractures, fracturing, fractured**] to crack or break something, especially a bone in your body □ *Emma's fractured her arm.* (**fraturar**)

fracture² /ˈfræktʃə(r)/ NOUN [plural **fractures**] a crack or break in something, especially a bone in your body (**fratura**)

fragile /ˈfrædʒaɪl/ ADJECTIVE not very strong and can easily be broken, damaged or destroyed □ *The bones become fragile and more likely to break.* □ *a fragile peace* (**frágil**)

fragment /ˈfrægmənt/ NOUN [plural **fragments**] a small piece that has broken off something □ *There were fragments of glass on the floor.* (**pedaço**)

> **THESAURUS:** A **fragment** is a small piece that has broken off something. A **scrap** is a small piece or amount of something. We often talk about a **scrap** of paper, a **scrap** of material or a **scrap** of food. A **chip** is a small piece which has broken off something hard, such as a plate.

fragrance /ˈfreɪɡrəns/ NOUN [plural **fragrances**] a pleasant smell □ *the sweet fragrance of jasmine flowers* (**fragrância, perfume**)

fragrant /ˈfreɪɡrənt/ ADJECTIVE smelling pleasant □ *fragrant flowers* (**perfumado**)

frail /freɪl/ ADJECTIVE [**frailer, frailest**] thin and weak □ *a frail old man* (**frágil**)

frame¹ /freɪm/ NOUN [plural **frames**]
1 a structure that fits around the edge of something, for example a picture or a window (**moldura**)
2 a structure that supports something, and around which the thing is built □ *My bike has a lightweight frame.* (**armação**)
3 frames the part that holds the glass parts in a pair of glasses (**emoldurado**)

frame² /freɪm/ VERB [**frames, framing, framed**] to put something such as a picture in a frame □ *I'm going to get this photo framed.* (**emoldurar**)

framework /ˈfreɪmwɜːk/ NOUN [plural **frameworks**] the basic ideas or principles that something is based on □ *This provides a framework for sustainable development.* (**estrutura**)

frank /fræŋk/ ADJECTIVE [franker, frankest] honest and saying what you think 🔹 *We had a fairly frank discussion.* 🔹 *To be quite frank, I don't think it'll work.* (**franco**)

fraud /frɔːd/ NOUN, NO PLURAL the crime of tricking people to get money □ *He was found guilty of credit card fraud.* (**fraude**)

freak /friːk/ NOUN [plural freaks] a very strange person or a person who looks very strange (**excêntrico**)

free¹ /friː/ ADJECTIVE

1 not costing any money □ *It's free to get into the museum.* □ *I've got two free tickets for the show.* (**gratuito**)

2 not controlled by people or laws □ *We were given free access to all the files.* □ *The country needs to hold free and fair elections.* □ **+ to do something** *You are free to leave whenever you wish.* (**livre**)

3 available to be used □ *Is this seat free?* (**livre**)

4 not busy □ *Are you free this evening?* (**livre**)

5 free time time when you are not busy and can do what you want (**tempo livre**)

6 not a prisoner □ *He is once more a free man.* 🔹 *They broke into the prison and set the prisoners free.* (**livre**)

> **THESAURUS:** If something is free, it is available to be used. You might ask someone if a seat on a train is free if you want to sit there. Vacant has a similar meaning but is a more formal word. If something is spare, it is extra, and available to be used. You might have a spare bedroom in your house for guests to use. If something is empty, it contains nothing or no one. You might say that a room is empty if it contains no furniture, or no people.

free² /friː/ VERB [frees, freeing, freed]
to allow a person or animal out of a prison or place where they were being kept □ *The hostages were freed this morning.* (**libertar**)

free³ /friː/ ADVERB

1 without any payment □ *Children under 5 travel free.* (**livremente**)

2 out of a place where a person or animal is being kept or tied up □ *They struggled to get free.* 🔹 *They managed to break free of their chains.* (**livre**)

freedom /ˈfriːdəm/ NOUN, NO PLURAL

1 the right to do what you want 🔹 *freedom of speech/movement* (**liberdade**)

2 the state of not being a prisoner (**liberdade**)

freely /ˈfriːli/ ADVERB without being limited or controlled 🔹 *The information is freely available.* □ *You can speak freely to me.* (**livremente**)

freeway /ˈfriːweɪ/ NOUN [plural freeways] the US word for **motorway** (**autoestrada**)

freeze /friːz/ VERB [freezes, freezing, froze, frozen]

1 to become very cold and hard, or to turn into ice □ *The lake freezes in winter.* □ **+ over** *The river froze over* (= became covered in ice). (**congelar**)

2 to store food at a very cold temperature so it keeps for a long time □ *We'll eat some and freeze the rest.* (**congelar**)

freezer /ˈfriːzə(r)/ NOUN [plural freezers]
a machine for keeping food very cold (**congelador**)

freezing /ˈfriːzɪŋ/ ADJECTIVE very cold □ *It's freezing in here!* 🔹 *It was freezing cold outside.* (**gelado**)

French fries /ˌfrentʃ ˈfraɪz/ PLURAL NOUN
long thin pieces of potato, fried in oil □ *a burger with French fries* (**batata frita**)

frenzy /ˈfrenzi/ NOUN, NO PLURAL a state or period of great excitement, activity and emotion 🔹 *a frenzy of activity* 🔹 *Their engagement has created a media frenzy.* (**frenesi**)

frequency /ˈfriːkwənsi/ NOUN, NO PLURAL how often something happens □ *Global warming may increase the frequency of severe hurricanes.* (**frequência**)

frequent /ˈfriːkwənt/ ADJECTIVE
happening often □ *Dave makes frequent visits to his grandmother.* □ *His e-mails are becoming more frequent.* (**frequente**)

frequently /ˈfriːkwəntli/ ADVERB often □ *Lee is frequently late for work.* □ *She frequently appears in women's magazines.* (**frequentemente**)

fresh /freʃ/ ADJECTIVE [fresher, freshest]

1 fresh food is not old, and has not been dried, frozen, etc. 🔹 *fresh fruit/vegetables* □ *This salad will stay fresh for a day or two.* (**fresco**)

2 new and different 🔹 *They hope to make a fresh start in Australia.* □ *I'll put some fresh sheets on the bed.* (**novo**)

3 fresh air is clean air in outside areas 🔹 *I'm going for a walk to get some fresh air.* (**fresco**)

> **THESAURUS:** If you describe food as fresh, it is not old, and has not been dried or frozen. Food which is raw is not cooked. Food which is natural has not been made by people or machines and has not had artificial things added to it.

Friday /ˈfraɪdi/ NOUN [plural Fridays] the day of the week after Thursday and before Saturday □ *It's my birthday on Friday.* (**sexta-feira**)

fridge /frɪdʒ/ NOUN [plural fridges]
a machine that you store food or drink in to keep it cold and fresh □ *He opened the fridge to get some milk.* □ *There's some chocolate in the fridge.* (**refrigerador**)

fried¹ /fraɪd/ PAST TENSE AND PAST PARTICIPLE OF **fry**
□ *She fried the fish in butter.* (**ver fry**)

fried² /fraɪd/ ADJECTIVE cooked in hot oil or fat □ *a fried egg* (**frito**)

friend /frend/ NOUN [plural friends]
1 someone who you know well and like □ **+ of** *She's a friend of mine.* 🗨 *Lindsay is my best friend.* 🗨 *They only told their family and close friends.* (amigo)
2 make friends (with someone) to meet and become friends with someone □ *She soon made friends.* □ *I made friends with Alex at college.* (tornar-se amigo)

friendly /ˈfrendlɪ/ ADJECTIVE [friendlier, friendliest]
kind and pleasant towards someone □ **+ to** *She's friendly to everyone.* □ *a friendly smile* □ *The staff are friendly and helpful.* (amigável)

fright /fraɪt/ NOUN [plural frights]
a sudden feeling of fear 🗨 *You gave me a fright, jumping out like that!* 🗨 *I got a fright when I saw it.* (pavor, susto)

frighten /ˈfraɪtən/ VERB [frightens, frightening, frightened]
to make someone feel afraid or worried □ *A sudden noise frightened the horses.* □ *You'll frighten the baby!* (amedrontar)

frightened /ˈfraɪtənd/ ADJECTIVE
afraid or very worried □ **+ of** *He's frightened of dogs.* □ **+ to do something** *He was too frightened to tell his parents.* 🗨 *I felt very frightened.* □ *a frightened expression* (apavorado)

frightening /ˈfraɪtənɪŋ/ ADJECTIVE
making you feel afraid or very worried □ *a frightening experience* □ *They look very frightening.* □ *That's a frightening thought!* (assustador)

fringe /frɪndʒ/ NOUN [plural fringes]
1 hair that hangs down over the top of your face (franja)
2 loose threads that hang down from the edge of something as decoration (franja)

frog /frɒg/ NOUN [plural frogs]
a small brown or green animal that can jump and swim and lives near water (rã)

from /frɒm/ PREPOSITION
1 used to show where or when something started or where it was before □ *She's driving up from London.* □ *The shops are open from nine to five.* □ *He took a photograph from the drawer.* □ *You can get batteries from the shop over the road.* □ *He stole some money from his parents.* (de)
2 used to show who gave or sent something □ *I had a lovely card from Julie.* (de)
3 used to show where someone was born or lives □ *I'm from Taiwan.* (de)
4 used to show how far something is □ *Do you live far from here?* □ *We are 15 miles from the nearest super market.* (de)
5 used to show what something is made of or what has caused something □ *Yogurt is made from milk.* □ *He was shivering from the cold.* (de)
6 from now on starting now and continuing into the future □ *From now on I'll be much more careful about locking the house.* (de agora em diante)

front¹ /frʌnt/ NOUN [plural fronts]
1 the part of something that faces forwards, or the part that is furthest forwards □ *The house has a red front.* □ *The front of the car was badly damaged.* (frente)
2 in front of someone/something (a) next to the front part of something □ *Please don't park in front of the gates.* □ *He stood right in front of me.* □ *She jumped in front of the moving train.* (b) where someone can see or hear you □ *He hit the children in front of their parents.* □ *She loves performing in front of a large audience.* (diante de alguém/algo)
3 in front further forward than someone or something □ *I was driving along when the car in front suddenly stopped.* (em frente)

front² /frʌnt/ ADJECTIVE
at the front of something 🗨 *I knocked on the front door.* 🗨 *We sat in the front row.* (frente)

frontier /ˈfrʌntɪə(r)/ NOUN [plural frontiers]
a dividing line between two countries □ *Pakistan's western frontier* □ **+ of** *He extended the frontiers of his empire.* □ **+ with** *The mountains mark Nepal's frontier with India.* (fronteira)

> **THESAURUS:** A **frontier** or a **border** is a line which separates two countries. You can also talk about a **border** between places where there is no passport check. For example, we talk about the **border** between Scotland and England. The **outskirts** are the outer parts of a town or city.

frost /frɒst/ NOUN [plural frosts] no plural
a very thin layer of white ice that forms on surfaces outside when the weather is cold □ *There's frost on the ground.* (geada)

frosty /ˈfrɒstɪ/ ADJECTIVE [frostier, frostiest]
when it is frosty, everything is covered in frost (= a thin, white layer of ice) □ *a frosty morning* (coberto de geada)

frown /fraʊn/ VERB [frowns, frowning, frowned]
to look as if you are angry, worried or thinking a lot by moving your eyebrows (= lines of hair above your eyes) down □ *She frowned when I suggested it.* (franzir a testa)

froze /frəʊz/ PAST TENSE OF freeze
□ *The milk froze in the fridge.* (ver **freeze**)

frozen¹ /ˈfrəʊzən/ PAST PARTICIPLE OF freeze
□ *It was so cold that the lake had frozen.* (ver **freeze**)

frozen² /ˈfrəʊzən/ ADJECTIVE
frozen food is stored at a very cold temperature to make it last for a long time □ *a packet of frozen peas* (congelado)

fruit /fruːt/ NOUN, NO PLURAL
a food such as an apple which grows on a plant and contains the seeds of the plant 🗨 *fruit and vegetables* 🗨 *We eat plenty of fresh fruit.* 🗨 *I usually have a piece of fruit for breakfast.* (fruta)

> Note that **fruit** is not usually used in the plural. Sometimes the plural **fruits** is used, meaning 'types of fruit' but it is not common:
> ✓ *You should eat more fruit.*
> ✗ *You should eat more fruits.*

fry /fraɪ/ VERB [fries, frying, fried] to cook something in hot oil or fat □ *Fry the onions in a little olive oil.* (fritar)

frying pan /ˈfraɪɪŋ ˌpæn/ NOUN [plural frying pans] a flat pan with a long handle for frying food □ *Heat the oil in a large frying pan.* (frigideira)
♦ IDIOM **out of the frying pan into the fire** used for saying that someone has left one bad situation but is now in a different and much worse situation

ft /ˌefˈtiː/ ABBREVIATION **foot** (= measurement) or **feet** (pé)

fuel /fjʊəl/ NOUN [plural fuels] a substance such as gas, wood or coal that burns to give heat, light or power □ *The trains run on diesel fuel.* ▣ *fuel consumption* (combustível)

fulfil /fʊlˈfɪl/ VERB [fulfils, fulfilling, fulfilled] to do a particular job or something you are expected to do ▣ *He fulfils an important role within the team.* ▣ *He failed to fulfil his financial obligations.* (cumprir)

fulfill /fʊlˈfɪl/ VERB [fulfills, fulfilling, fulfilled] the US spelling of **fulfil**

full /fʊl/ ADJECTIVE [fuller, fullest]
1 containing as much as possible □ *The train was full.* □ *He gave me a full bottle of milk.* □ *The jug was only half full.* (cheio)
2 containing a lot of something □ *Your work is full of mistakes.* □ *My socks are full of holes.* (cheio)
3 complete ▣ *He told me the full story.* ▣ *She made a full recovery.* (completo)
4 having eaten enough □ + *up* *No more cake for me, thanks – I'm full up.* (cheio)
→ L go to **give full rein to something**

full stop /ˌfʊl ˈstɒp/ NOUN [plural full stops] the mark (.) used for showing where a sentence ends (ponto-final)

full-time /ˌfʊl-ˈtaɪm/ ADJECTIVE, ADVERB working for all the hours of a normal job, not part of the time ▣ *a full-time job* ▣ *a full-time employee* ▣ *We both work full-time.* (em tempo integral)

fun /fʌn/ NOUN, NO PLURAL
1 enjoyment and pleasure ▣ *Skateboarding is really good fun.* ▣ *It was great fun!* ▣ *We had a lot of fun at the party.* □ *That sounds like fun.* (divertimento)
2 **make fun of someone/something** to make jokes about someone or something, in a way that is not kind □ *They're always making fun of my accent.* (caçoar de alguém/algo)

function¹ /ˈfʌŋkʃən/ NOUN [plural functions] the purpose of someone or something ▣ *Proteins perform different functions in the body.* ▣ *The operating system controls the basic functions of a computer.* (função)

function² /ˈfʌŋkʃən/ VERB [functions, functioning, functioned] to work in the correct way ▣ *In some patients these cells don't function properly.* ▣ *The system seems to be functioning normally.* (funcionar)

fund¹ /fʌnd/ NOUN [plural funds] an amount of money for a particular purpose □ *a pension fund* □ *We set up a fund for victims of the earthquake.* (fundo)

fund² /fʌnd/ VERB [funds, funding, funded] to provide money for a particular purpose □ *The research was funded by the Medical Research Council.* (financiar)

fundamental /ˌfʌndəˈmentəl/ ADJECTIVE basic and important □ *the fundamental rules of management* □ *This raises some fundamental questions.* (fundamental)

funeral /ˈfjuːnərəl/ NOUN [plural funerals] a ceremony for a person who has recently died in which the body of the dead person is buried or burned ▣ *I didn't go to her funeral.* (funeral)

fungus /ˈfʌŋɡəs/ NOUN [plural fungi] a plant with no leaves or flowers, for example a mushroom (= plant that you can eat, with a stem and a flat or round top) (fungo)

funny /ˈfʌni/ ADJECTIVE [funnier, funniest]
1 making you laugh □ *I don't find him very funny.* □ *They looked so funny that she had to smile.* ▣ *Luckily, he saw the funny side of the situation.* (engraçado)
2 strange, surprising or unusual □ *There was a funny noise coming from the engine.* ▣ *The funny thing is, I was just about to call him when he called me.* (esquisito)

> Do not confuse the adjective **funny** with the noun **fun**. Something that is **funny** makes you laugh. Something that you describe as **fun** is very enjoyable although it may not make you laugh: □ *That was such a funny film - I laughed all the way through.* □ *Skating is fun.*

fur /fɜː(r)/ NOUN, NO PLURAL the soft hair on some animals □ *a rabbit with soft, brown fur* (pelo)

furious /ˈfjʊəriəs/ ADJECTIVE extremely angry □ *We're absolutely furious about this.* □ *I had a furious row with Charlotte.* (furioso)

furnish /ˈfɜːnɪʃ/ VERB [furnishes, furnishing, furnished] to put furniture in a house or room □ *The six large rooms are furnished with antiques.* (mobiliar)

furniture /ˈfɜːnɪtʃə(r)/ NOUN, NO PLURAL objects such as beds, tables and chairs that you put in a room ▣ *A small bed and an old wardrobe were the only pieces of furniture in the room.* (mobília)

> Remember that **furniture** is an uncountable noun:
> ✓ *We don't have any furniture.*
> ✗ *We don't have any furnitures.*

further¹ /ˈfɜːðə(r)/ ADJECTIVE, ADVERB
1 at or to a greater distance away □ + *from* *Which is further from here, London or Aberdeen?* □ + *up* *Santa Monica is a few miles further up the coast.* □ *I walked further than I needed.* □ *We travelled further north.* (mais longe)

2 more or extra 🔂 *If you need further information, please ask.* □ *He refused to comment further* (= say more). 🔂 *Prices may rise even further.* (**mais**)

further² /ˈfɜː.ðə(r)/ VERB [furthers, furthering, furthered] to help something be successful □ *These qualifications will help further your career.* (**avançar**)

furthermore /ˌfɜː.ðəˈmɔː(r)/ ADVERB a formal word used when you are adding something to what you have already said □ *His plans will be very expensive. Furthermore, they will cause a lot of disruption.* (**além disso**)

furthest /ˈfɜː.ðəst/ ADVERB, ADJECTIVE at or to the greatest distance or amount □ *Who can throw the ball the furthest?* □ + **from** *They sat in the corner furthest from the door.* □ *We reached the furthest point south.* (**o mais longe**)

fury /ˈfjʊəri/ NOUN, NO PLURAL a very strong feeling of anger □ *The announcement sparked fury from unions.* (**fúria**)

fuss /fʌs/ NOUN, NO PLURAL
1 unnecessary worry, excitement or anger about something □ *I don't know what all the fuss is about.* 🔂 *I don't want to make a fuss about it.* (**rebuliço**)
2 make a fuss of someone to give someone a lot of attention □ *He made a great fuss of her when she visited.* (**fazer muita onda com alguém**)

fussy /ˈfʌsi/ ADJECTIVE [fussier, fussiest]
1 worrying too much about small details that are not important (**caprichoso**)
2 only liking particular things □ *Children can be so fussy about food.* 🔂 *a fussy eater* (**caprichoso**)

future¹ /ˈfjuː.tʃə(r)/ NOUN [plural futures]
1 the future the time to come after now □ *You can't know what will happen to you in the future.* 🔂 *We expect a decision in the near future.* (**futuro**)
2 in future in the time from now on □ *In future, please be more careful.* (**no futuro**)

future² /ˈfjuː.tʃə(r)/ ADJECTIVE happening or existing in a time after now □ *future plans* □ *We need to preserve the planet for future generations.* (**futuro**)

future tense /ˌfjuː.tʃə ˈtens/ NOUN [plural future tenses] the form of a verb that you use when you are talking about what will happen in the future (**tempo futuro**)

Gg

G or **g** /dʒiː/ the seventh letter of the alphabet (a sétima letra do alfabeto)

g /dʒiː/ ABBREVIATION **gram** or **grams** (grama)

gadget /'gædʒɪt/ NOUN [plural **gadgets**] a tool or small piece of equipment ☐ *I've got a gadget to unblock the sink.* (dispositivo)

gain /ɡeɪn/ VERB [**gains, gaining, gained**]
1 to get or achieve something ☐ *You gain twenty extra points for that move.* ▣ *We could not gain access* (= get in) *to the building.* ▣ *Soldiers have fought to gain control of the area.* (ganhar)
2 to increase in amount, speed, weight, etc. ☐ *I gained over 20 kilos when I was pregnant.* (ganhar)

galaxy /'gæləksɪ/ NOUN [plural **galaxies**] a very large group of stars in the universe ☐ *Our galaxy is the Milky Way.* (galáxia)

gale /ɡeɪl/ NOUN [plural **gales**] a very strong wind ☐ *The old apple tree blew down in a gale.* (vendaval)

gallery /'gælərɪ/ NOUN [plural **galleries**] a large building or a shop where works of art are shown to the public (galeria)

gallon /'ɡælən/ NOUN [plural **gallons**] a unit for measuring liquids, equal to about 4.5 litres (galão)

gallop /'ɡæləp/ VERB [**gallops, galloping, galloped**] a horse gallops when it runs at its fastest speed with all four feet off the ground at the same time (galopar)

gamble¹ /'ɡæmbəl/ VERB [**gambles, gambling, gambled**] to risk money on the result of a game, race or competition ☐ *He enjoyed gambling on horse races.* (jogar, apostar)
◆ PHRASAL VERB **gamble on something** to take a risk, hoping that something will happen ☐ *We've decided to gamble on the rain stopping before we have our barbecue.*

gamble² /'ɡæmbəl/ NOUN [plural **gambles**] something you decide to do that is a risk ▣ *We took a gamble on the weather.* ▣ *Their gamble paid off* (= was successful). (risco)

gambler /'ɡæmblə(r)/ NOUN [plural **gamblers**] someone who risks money on the result of a race or game (jogador)

game /ɡeɪm/ NOUN [plural **games**]
1 an activity that people do for enjoyment, that has rules, often needs skill, and is usually won or lost ☐ *a computer game* ▣ *After dinner, we all played games.* ☐ *a game of tennis/chess* (jogo)
2 *no plural* wild animals and birds that are hunted for their meat (caça)

gang /ɡæŋ/ NOUN [plural **gangs**]
1 a group of young people who spend time together and often cause trouble ☐ *Her son got involved in a gang.* (gangue)
2 an organized group of criminals ☐ *Police have arrested a gang of bank robbers.* (gangue)
3 an informal word meaning a group of friends who meet regularly ☐ *I'm meeting up with the gang tonight.* (equipe)

> **THESAURUS:** A **gang** is a group of young people who spend time together and often cause trouble. We can also talk about a gang of criminals. A **team** is a group of people who work together, especially in sports. You can talk about a football or baseball team. You can also talk about a team of engineers or a team of managers. A **crew** is a group of people who work together on a ship, aeroplane or train.

gangster /'ɡæŋstə(r)/ NOUN [plural **gangsters**] a member of a group of criminals (gângster)

gap /ɡæp/ NOUN [plural **gaps**]
1 an opening or space in the middle of something or between things ☐ *The fox got through a gap in the wall.* ☐ *He has a gap between his front teeth.* (brecha)
2 a difference between two things ☐ *The gap between rich and poor is widening.* ▣ *There's a big age gap between her two children.* (diferença)
3 something missing ☐ *There's a gap in his memory around the time of the accident.* (lacuna, vazio)
4 a period of time when something stops ☐ *He's going back to university after a three-year gap.* (intervalo)

garage /'ɡærɑːʒ, 'ɡærɪdʒ/ NOUN [plural **garages**]
1 a small building that you keep your car in (garagem)
2 a place where vehicles are repaired, or a shop selling petrol (oficina)

garbage /'ɡɑːbɪdʒ/ NOUN, NO PLURAL the US word for **rubbish** (lixo)

garden /'ɡɑːdən/ NOUN [plural **gardens**]
1 a piece of land next to a house where flowers, trees and vegetables are grown ▣ *The front garden is mainly grass.* (jardim)

2 gardens a large area of grass, trees, flowers, etc. for the public to use or around a big house □ *I always like to visit gardens when I go on holidays.* (jardim)

> THESAURUS: A garden is an area of land around a house where flowers, trees, vegetables and grass grow. A **park** is an area of grass and trees in a town where people can go to relax. A **field** is an area of land used for growing crops or keeping animals, often as part of a farm.

gardener /ˈgɑːdnə(r)/ NOUN [plural **gardeners**] someone who works in a garden (jardineiro)

gardening /ˈgɑːdnɪŋ/ NOUN, NO PLURAL the activity of working in and taking care of a garden (jardinagem)

garlic /ˈgɑːlɪk/ NOUN, NO PLURAL a plant like a small onion with a strong taste and smell used in cooking to add flavour 🔲 *Crush two cloves of garlic with the spices.* (alho)

garment /ˈgɑːmənt/ NOUN [plural **garments**] a formal word meaning a piece of clothing □ *Garments, such as suits, may be hung up in special bags.* (roupa)

gas /gæs/ NOUN [plural **gases** or **gasses**]
1 a substance that is not liquid or solid and that moves about like air □ *Oxygen and carbon dioxide are two of the gases that make up air.* (gás)
2 *no plural* a gas or mixture of gases that burns easily and is used for cooking or heating □ *a gas fire* (gás)
3 *no plural* the US word for **petrol** (gasolina)

gasp¹ /gɑːsp/ VERB [**gasps, gasping, gasped**]
1 to take a short sudden breath in through your open mouth because you are shocked or surprised □ *They all gasped in horror.* (engasgar)
2 to find it hard to breathe 🔲 *He fell to the floor, gasping for breath.* (arfar)

gasp² /gɑːsp/ NOUN [plural **gasps**] the sound of a sudden short breath (sobressalto)

gate /geɪt/ NOUN [plural **gates**]
1 the part of a fence, wall etc. that opens and closes like a door □ *Please close the gate.* (porteira, cancela)
2 the place where passengers get on or off a plane at an airport □ *Flight BA123 to Rome is now boarding at Gate 12.* (portão)

gather /ˈgæðə(r)/ VERB [**gathers, gathering, gathered**]
1 if people gather or are gathered, they come together or are brought together in a group 🔲 *A crowd gathered at the airport.* □ *The teachers gathered all the children together in the dining hall.* (aglomerar-se)
2 to collect things or bring them together □ *Police are gathering as much information as they can about the attacker.* □ *The lecturer gathered together all her papers.* (colher)

gave /geɪv/ PAST TENSE OF **give** (ver **give**)

gay /geɪ/ ADJECTIVE [**gayer, gayest**] homosexual or to do with homosexuals □ *a gay bar* □ *a gay marriage* (homossexual)

gaze¹ /geɪz/ VERB [**gazes, gazing, gazed**] to look at something or someone for a long time, especially because they are interesting or attractive □ *The children gazed at the toys in the window.* (fitar)

> THESAURUS: To **look** at something means to turn your eyes in order to see something. **Look** is a general word. If you **watch** something, you look at it for a while. For example, we **watch** television. To gaze at something means to look at something or someone for a long time, especially because they are interesting or attractive. You might gaze at a beautiful painting or a nice view, for example. To **stare** at something means to look at it for a long time.

gaze² /geɪz/ NOUN, NO PLURAL a long look □ *Her gaze was fixed on a tree in the distance.* (olhar fixo)

GB /ˌdʒiːˈbiː/ ABBREVIATION Great Britain (GB)

GCSE /ˌdʒiːsiːesˈiː/ ABBREVIATION General Certificate of Secondary Education; an exam taken by students in England and Wales at around the age of 16 □ *He's doing GCSE maths.* (GCSE)

gear /gɪə(r)/ NOUN [plural **gears**]
1 the set of parts in a car or bicycle that controls how fast the wheels turn □ *Our new car has five gears.* (marcha)
2 a particular position of the gears on a vehicle 🔲 *She still finds it hard to change gear.* 🔲 *Put the car into first gear and move off.* (marcha)
3 *no plural* the clothes and equipment you use for a particular sport or job □ *tennis gear* (equipamento)

geese /giːs/ PLURAL OF **goose** (ver **goose**)

gel /dʒel/ NOUN [plural **gels**] a thick clear substance that is between a liquid and a solid 🔲 *shower gel* 🔲 *Do you use hair gel?* (gel)

gem /dʒem/ NOUN [plural **gems**] a valuable stone that is used in jewellery (pedra preciosa)

gender /ˈdʒendə(r)/ NOUN [plural **genders**] the state of being male or female □ *The job application form asks you to say which gender you are.* (gênero)

gene /dʒiːn/ NOUN [plural **genes**] a part of a living cell that is passed on from parents to children and that controls things like hair or skin colour. A biology word. (gene)

general¹ /ˈdʒenərəl/ ADJECTIVE
1 involving or affecting most people or things □ *There was a general feeling of gloom.* 🔲 *Sales to the general public* (= ordinary people) *will begin on July 11.* (geral)
2 not detailed or exact, but giving the most important information □ *Can you give me a*

general idea of what it will cost? 🔲 I understand economics in general terms. 🔲 As a general rule (= in most situations) I use two eggs for every 125g flour. (geral)
3 in general (a) considering the whole of something or someone ☐ Schools are achieving better results in general. ☐ There is agreement among the population in general. (b) in most situations ☐ In general, I think it's better to travel by train. (em geral)
4 dealing with a lot of activities, subjects or parts of a subject ☐ He does general household repairs. ☐ I'm looking for a general introduction to Western art. (geral)

general² /ˈdʒenərəl/ NOUN [plural generals] an important army officer (general)

general election /ˌdʒenərəl ɪˈlekʃən/ NOUN [plural general elections] an election in which all the people in a country vote to choose the people who will be in the next government (eleição geral)

generally /ˈdʒenərəli/ ADVERB
1 by most people or in most cases ☐ She's generally considered Britain's greatest actor. ☐ They were generally well dressed. (geralmente)
2 usually ☐ Children generally start school at about the age of five. (geralmente)

general practitioner /ˌdʒenərəl prækˈtɪʃənə(r)/ NOUN [plural general practitioners] a doctor who looks after people from a particular area and treats them for a lot of different illnesses (clínico geral)

> You will often see the abbreviation for general practitioner, which is GP.

generate /ˈdʒenəreɪt/ VERB [generates, generating, generated] to create or produce some thing ☐ His work generated a lot of interest. ☐ The house uses solar power to generate electricity. (suscitar)

generation /ˌdʒenəˈreɪʃən/ NOUN [plural generations] all the people in a family or society who were born at about the same time 🔲 the younger generation ☐ There were four generations of the family at the wedding. (geração)

generosity /ˌdʒenəˈrɒsəti/ NOUN, NO PLURAL the quality of being generous (generosidade)

generous /ˈdʒenərəs/ ADJECTIVE giving a lot of money, presents or time to others ☐ The locals are kind and generous people. (generoso)

genetic /dʒɪˈnetɪk/ ADJECTIVE to do with the part of a living cell that is passed on from parents to their children and that controls things like hair or skin colour, or the scientific study of these cells. A biology word ☐ a genetic defect (genético)

genetics /dʒɪˈnetɪks/ NOUN, NO PLURAL the scientific study of how living things develop as a result of the qualities parents pass on to their children in part of their cells (genética)

genius /ˈdʒiːniəs/ NOUN [plural geniuses] someone who is extremely clever or skilful (gênio)

gentle /ˈdʒentəl/ ADJECTIVE [gentler, gentlest]
1 careful not to hurt or upset anyone or anything ☐ He was a gentle man. ☐ She gave him a gentle tap on his shoulder. (gentil)
2 not strong, severe or violent ☐ a gentle breeze (suave)

> **THESAURUS:** If you are gentle, you are careful not to hurt or upset anyone or anything. If you are **kind**, you behave in a way that shows that you care about people and want to make them happy. Note that **sympathetic** does not mean the same as kind. If you are **sympathetic**, you show that you feel sorry for someone who is unhappy or suffering.

gentleman /ˈdʒentəlmən/ NOUN [plural gentlemen]
1 a word used to refer politely to a man ☐ Good morning, gentlemen. 🔲 Ladies and gentlemen, welcome to the show. (senhor)
2 a man who is polite and treats people with respect ☐ Her husband's a real gentleman. (cavalheiro)

gently /ˈdʒentli/ ADVERB in a gentle way ☐ He picked the injured bird up gently. (suavemente)

genuine /ˈdʒenjuɪn/ ADJECTIVE real or true ☐ a genuine work of art (autêntico)

geography /dʒiˈɒgrəfi/ NOUN, NO PLURAL the study of the Earth's surface and the countries, weather and people of the world ☐ human geography (geografia)

geology /dʒiˈɒlədʒi/ NOUN, NO PLURAL the study of the Earth's rocks and soil (geologia)

germ /dʒɜːm/ NOUN [plural germs] a very small living thing that can cause disease ☐ This product kills most germs. (germe)

gesture /ˈdʒestʃə(r)/ NOUN [plural gestures] a movement made with your hand, arm or head to express what you think or feel 🔲 The driver made a rude gesture out of the car window. (gesto)

get /get/ VERB [gets, getting, got]
1 to take, receive or buy something ☐ Isabel got lots of birthday presents. ☐ Did you get my letter? ☐ I got a new dress today. (ganhar, alcançar, comprar)
2 to go somewhere and then bring something back ☐ Could you get me a drink? ☐ I'll go and get the money. (conseguir)
3 get away/in/out, etc. to move in a particular

direction □ We managed to get over the wall. □ All the chickens have got out. □ Catch a bus, and get off near the cathedral. (sair, escapar)
4 to become □ The baby's getting bigger every day. □ I got wet in the rain. □ If I mention money, he always gets angry. □ The wine glasses got broken. (tornar-se)
5 if you get somewhere, you arrive there □ We got to New York at 5 o'clock in the morning. □ What time will you get home? □ The train gets in at three thirty. (chegar)
6 if you get a bus, train, etc., that is how you travel. □ I usually get the train to work. (pegar)
7 to become ill with a particular illness □ They had an injection to stop them getting measles. (contrair)
♦ PHRASAL VERBS **get away with something** to avoid being punished or criticized □ I'm hoping to miss the next meeting, if I can get away with it. **get on 1** to make progress □ + **with** I need to get on with my work. □ How are you getting on in your new job? **2** to be friendly □ Pierre and Alex don't really get on. **get out of something** to avoid doing something □ He'll do anything to get out of the washing up. **get over something** to feel better after being ill or unhappy □ He never really got over his wife's death. **get round to doing something** to do something that you have been intending to do □ I'd like to do more exercise, but I never seem to get round to it. **get through** to manage to talk to someone on the telephone □ I tried to ring her, but I couldn't get through. **get through something** to reach the end of a difficult situation □ It was a terrible illness, but his determination helped to get him through it. **get (someone) up** to wake up and get out of bed □ I always get up early. □ My Dad gets me up in the morning.

ghost /gəʊst/ NOUN [plural **ghosts**] the spirit of a dead person which some people think they can see □ Do you believe in ghosts? (fantasma)

giant[1] /ˈdʒaɪənt/ NOUN [plural **giants**] in stories, a man who is extremely tall and strong (gigante)

giant[2] /ˈdʒaɪənt/ ADJECTIVE much bigger than usual □ a giant crane □ a giant tortoise (gigante)

gift /gɪft/ NOUN [plural **gifts**]
1 a present 🔲 a wedding gift 🔲 Many children give gifts to their teacher at the end of term. 🔲 a gift shop □ + **from** The necklace had been a gift from her boyfriend. (presente)
2 a natural ability □ + **for** Adam has a gift for languages. (dom)

gigantic /dʒaɪˈɡæntɪk/ ADJECTIVE extremely big □ a gigantic statue (gigantesco)

giggle[1] /ˈɡɪɡəl/ VERB [**giggles, giggling, giggled**] to laugh in a silly or nervous way (dar risadinha)

giggle[2] /ˈɡɪɡəl/ NOUN [plural **giggles**] a silly or nervous laugh (risadinha)

ginger[1] /ˈdʒɪndʒə(r)/ NOUN, NO PLURAL a root that has a spicy taste and is used in cooking (gengibre)

ginger[2] /ˈdʒɪndʒə(r)/ ADJECTIVE ginger hair is a redbrown colour (amarelo-avermelhado)

giraffe /dʒɪˈrɑːf/ NOUN [plural **giraffes**] an African animal with a very long neck and long legs (girafa)

girl /ɡɜːl/ NOUN [plural **girls**] a female child or young woman □ Police are searching for a missing 10-year-old girl. 🔲 a teenage girl 🔲 There were two little girls (= very young girls) playing in the garden. (menina, garota)

girlfriend /ˈɡɜːlfrend/ NOUN [plural **girlfriends**]
1 a girl or woman that you are having a romantic relationship with □ Dan has a new girlfriend. (namorada)
2 a female friend that a girl or woman has □ I go out with my girlfriends once a week. (amiga)

give /ɡɪv/ VERB [**gives, giving, gave, given**]
1 to let someone have something □ Give your bags to the porter. □ Make sure you give back all the books you borrowed. □ Let me give you some advice. □ This news gives us hope. □ He gave us permission to visit the temple. □ Could you give us some information about hotels? (dar)
2 to make someone have something □ They were given a severe punishment. □ Our boss gives us too much work. □ The sudden noise gave me a fright. (dar)
3 **give evidence/a performance/a speech, etc.** to say something or to perform in public □ She gave evidence at his trial. □ He gave a wonderful performance of Beethoven's Moonlight Sonata. (dar)
4 to make a sound or a movement □ He gave a shout of joy. □ She gave her brother a kick. (dar)
♦ PHRASAL VERBS **give something away 1** to allow someone to have something without paying for it □ I gave away all my old toys. **2** to tell a secret □ The party was meant to be a surprise, but Billy gave it away. **give in** to agree to something you did not want to agree to □ I kept asking for the new computer game, and eventually Dad gave in and bought it for me. **give something out** to give something to a group of people □ Can you give out the reading books please, Kazuo? **give up (something) 1** if you give up a habit, you stop doing it □ She's managed to give up smoking. **2** to stop doing something before it is finished, because it is too difficult □ I've given up trying to keep this room tidy. □ Don't give up – only another mile to go!

> **THESAURUS:** If you give something to someone, you let them have it. If you **deliver** something, you take it to a place. For example, postmen **deliver** letters to people's homes. If you **hand** something **over** you give something to someone. Often, this is something that you do not want to give. For example, a bank worker might **hand over** money to a robber. If you **award** something to someone, you give the person a prize because they have done something good.

given[1] /ˈɡɪvən/ ADJECTIVE decided or agreed □ You have a given time to complete each question. □ On any given day, there are several accidents. (dado)

given² /ˈɡɪvən/ PAST PARTICIPLE OF give (ver **give**)

given³ /ˈɡɪvən/ PREPOSITION considering the fact that □ *Given that they don't have much money, their offer is extremely generous.* (**dado**)

glacier /ˈɡlæsɪə(r)/ NOUN [plural **glaciers**] a large mass of ice that moves slowly down a mountain valley (**geleira**)

glad /ɡlæd/ ADJECTIVE [**gladder, gladdest**] pleased and happy because of something □ + *that I'm just glad that the exams are over.* □ + *to do something I'm so glad to see you.* (**feliz, alegre**)

glamorous /ˈɡlæmərəs/ ADJECTIVE attractive, fashionable and exciting □ *She was looking very glamorous in a black dress.* □ *a glamorous lifestyle* (**glamoroso**)

glamour /ˈɡlæmə(r)/ NOUN, NO PLURAL a special quality that makes someone or something seem attractive, fashionable and exciting □ *She will add some glamour to the show.* (**glamour, sedução**)

glance¹ /ɡlɑːns/ VERB [**glances, glancing, glanced**] to look at something or someone for a very short time □ + *at Anselm glanced nervously at his watch.* □ + *around He glanced around to see if anyone was looking.* (**dar uma olhada, lançar os olhos**)

> **THESAURUS:** If you glance at something, you look at it for a very short time. You might glance at your watch. If you **glimpse** something, you see it for a very short time. You might **glimpse** a famous person in a big crowd.

glance² /ɡlɑːns/ NOUN [plural **glances**] a quick look 🖼 *He cast a nervous glance at Yvonne.* 🖼 *Richard and I exchanged glances* (= we looked at each other for a short time). (**olhadela**)

glare¹ /ɡleə(r)/ VERB [**glares, glaring, glared**] to look at someone in a way that shows you are very angry □ *Mia glared at him.* (**fulminar com os olhos**)

glare² /ɡleə(r)/ NOUN [plural **glares**]
1 very strong bright light that makes your eyes hurt □ *He stood in the glare of the car's headlights.* (**brilho ofuscante**)
2 an angry look (**olhar fulminante**)

glaring /ˈɡleərɪŋ/ ADJECTIVE
1 very obvious 🖼 *a glaring mistake* (**flagrante**)
2 very bright, and making your eyes hurt □ *the glaring sun* (**ofuscante**)

glass¹ /ɡlɑːs/ NOUN [plural **glasses**]
1 *no plural* a hard transparent material, used for making bottles, windows, etc. 🖼 *There was broken glass all over the pavement.* 🖼 *She stepped on a piece of glass and cut her foot.* (**vidro**)
2 a container made of glass, which you drink from □ *a tall glass* 🖼 *a wine glass* □ + *of She drank three glasses of milk.* 🖼 *Betsy poured a glass of juice.* (**copo, taça**)
3 glasses something you wear to help you see better, which consists of two pieces of plastic or glass in a frame 🖼 *I need a new pair of glasses.* 🖼 *My Dad wears glasses.* (**óculos**)

glass² /ɡlɑːs/ ADJECTIVE made of glass □ *a glass bowl* (**de vidro**)

gleam /ɡliːm/ VERB [**gleams, gleaming, gleamed**] to shine □ *A light gleamed in the distance.* (**raio, brilho**)

glide /ɡlaɪd/ VERB [**glides, gliding, glided**] to move in a smooth and quiet way □ *The waiters glide between the tables.* (**deslizar**)

glider /ˈɡlaɪdə(r)/ NOUN [plural **gliders**] an aeroplane with no engine which moves on air currents (**planador**)

glimpse /ɡlɪmps/ NOUN [plural **glimpses**] when you see someone or something only for a very short time 🖼 *People climbed on fences, hoping to catch a glimpse of* (= see) *the princess.* (**vislumbre, lampejo**)

glitter /ˈɡlɪtə(r)/ VERB [**glitters, glittering, glittered**] to shine with small flashes of light □ *His eyes glittered in the light.* (**cintilar**)

global /ˈɡləʊbəl/ ADJECTIVE to do with or involving the whole world □ *Global sales rose by 20%.* □ *global climate change* (**universal**)

global warming /ˌɡləʊbəl ˈwɔːmɪŋ/ NOUN, NO PLURAL the gradual increase in the Earth's temperature caused by pollution (**aquecimento global**)

globe /ɡləʊb/ NOUN [plural **globes**]
1 a large ball with a map of the Earth printed on it (**globo terrestre**)
2 the globe the world □ *The company has offices around the globe.* (**globo**)

glorious /ˈɡlɔːriəs/ ADJECTIVE
1 extremely beautiful or good □ *glorious sunshine* □ *The hotel is surrounded by glorious countryside.* (**esplêndido**)
2 deserving or receiving praise □ *a glorious victory* (**glorioso**)

glory /ˈɡlɔːri/ NOUN [plural **glories**] praise and admiration □ *His moment of glory came when he won the championship.* (**glória**)

glossy /ˈɡlɒsi/ ADJECTIVE [**glossier, glossiest**] smooth and shiny 🖼 *glossy hair* □ *a glossy surface* (**lustroso**)

glove /ɡlʌv/ NOUN [plural **gloves**] something you wear to cover your hand 🖼 *a pair of gloves* 🖼 *I wear gloves in the winter.* 🖼 *It's a good idea to wear rubber gloves when you're cleaning.* (**luva**)

glow

glow¹ /gləʊ/ NOUN, NO PLURAL
1 warm or soft light ▫ *the glow of the fire* (incandescência)
2 a glow of satisfaction/pride etc. a good feeling of being satisfied, proud, etc. ▫ *He felt a glow of satisfaction when he looked at his work.* (arrebatamento)

glow² /gləʊ/ VERB [glows, glowing, glowed]
1 to burn or shine with a soft light ▫ *A fire glowed in the corner of the room.* (corar)
2 glow with pride/satisfaction/confidence, etc. to show that you are very proud, satisfied, etc. ▫ *She was glowing with pride as she watched her son accept the award.*

glue¹ /gluː/ NOUN [plural **glues**] a substance used for sticking things together ▫ *Use glue to stick the fabric onto the paper.* (cola)

glue² /gluː/ VERB [glues, gluing or glueing, glued] to stick something using glue ▫ *He glued the two pieces of wood together.* (colar)

go¹ /gəʊ/ VERB [goes, going, went, gone]
1 to travel or move somewhere ▫ *I'm going home now.* ▫ **+ to** *We're going to France for our holiday.* ▫ *He went into the other room.* ▫ *I wish she'd go away.* ▫ *He left home at 18 and never went back.* (ir)
2 to travel or move somewhere so that you can do something ▫ **+ to** *She goes to school in the next village.* ▫ **+ for** *Shall we go for a swim?* ▫ *We all went cycling.* (ir)
3 to leave or disappear ▫ *It's six o'clock, so I'll have to go soon.* ▫ *I'm sure I left my coat here, but it's gone.* ▫ *The food all went very quickly.* (sumir, partir)
4 if a road or path goes somewhere, it leads there ▫ *Does this road go to Edinburgh?* (ir)
5 the place where something goes is where it fits or is kept ▫ *That piece of the jigsaw goes at the top.* ▫ *The cups go on the top shelf.* (ser)
6 to become ▫ *Her face went pale.* ▫ *Your soup's gone cold.* (tornar-se)
7 to happen in a particular way ▫ *The concert went well.* ▫ *How's your new job going?* (transcorrer)
8 be going to do something (a) to intend to do something ▫ *I'm going to write to Molly.* ▫ *What were you going to say?* (b) to be expected to happen ▫ *I think it's going to rain.* (ir fazer algo)
◆ PHRASAL VERBS **go by** if time goes by, it passes **go down** to become lower in level ▫ *His temperature has gone down a bit.* **go off 1** if food goes off, it becomes rotten **2** to explode ▫ *A bomb has gone off in a busy London street.* **go off someone/ something** to stop liking someone or something ▫ *I've gone off spicy food.* **go on 1** to continue for a period of time ▫ *His speech went on for hours.* **2** to continue doing something ▫ **+ ing** *He went on singing, despite the noise.* ▫ **+ with** *Go on with your work.* **3** if something is going on, it is happening ▫ *What's going on?* **go out** to leave your house, especially for a social activity ▫ *Are you going out tonight?* **go round** to be enough for everyone ▫ *Is there enough bread to go round?* **go through something** to experience something ▫ *She went through agony during the illness.* **go up** to become higher in level ▫ *Prices have gone up again.*

go² /gəʊ/ NOUN [plural **goes**]
1 an attempt ▫ *It doesn't matter if you can't climb to the top – just have a go.* (tentativa)
2 when it is your turn to do something, especially in a game ▫ *Pick up a card, Adam – it's your go.* (vez)

goal /gəʊl/ NOUN [plural **goals**]
1 something that you want to achieve ▫ *If she works hard, she should achieve her goal.* ▫ *The government's long-term goal is to reduce the number of people in prison.* (objetivo, meta)
2 a point scored when a ball goes into the net in a game such as football ▫ *Cahill scored the first goal.* ▫ *Giggs scored the winning goal.* (gol)
3 the area where the ball must go to score a point in a game such as football ▫ *He was standing in front of the goal.* (gol)

goalkeeper /ˈgəʊlˌkiːpə(r)/ NOUN [plural **goalkeepers**] the player who stands in front of the net in a game such as football and who tries to stop the ball going into the net (goleiro)

goat /gəʊt/ NOUN [plural **goats**] an animal with horns and long hair under its chin ▫ *The cheese is made from goat's milk.* (cabra, bode)

god /gɒd/ NOUN [plural **gods**]
1 God no plural the spirit that Christians, Muslims and Jews pray to ▫ *Do you believe in God?* (Deus)
2 a spirit that some people believe controls nature or represents a particular quality ▫ *Greek and Roman gods* ▫ **+ of** *Thor was the Viking god of thunder.* (deus)

goddess /ˈgɒdɪs/ NOUN [plural **goddesses**] a female god (deusa)

goes /gəʊz/ VERB the present tense of the verb **go¹** when it is used with 'he', 'she', or 'it' ▫ *He goes to work at eight o'clock.* (ver **go**)

gold¹ /gəʊld/ NOUN [plural **golds**]
1 no plural a valuable pale yellow metal, used to make jewellery ▫ *bars of gold* (ouro)
2 a gold medal (= prize for coming first in a competition or race) ▫ *He won gold in the long jump.* (ouro)

gold² /gəʊld/ ADJECTIVE
1 made of gold ▫ *a gold ring* (ouro)
2 having the colour of gold ▫ *a gold leather handbag* (ouro)

golden /ˈgəʊldən/ ADJECTIVE
1 made of gold ▫ *a golden crown* (de ouro)
2 having the colour of gold ▫ *golden hair* (dourado)

golf /gɒlf/ NOUN, NO PLURAL a game in which you have to hit a small ball into holes in the ground ▫ *a golf ball* ▫ *My Dad plays golf.* ▫ *an 18-hole golf* *course* 🔲 *Professional golfers have someone to carry their golf clubs* (= sticks used for hitting the ball). **(golfe)**

gone /gɒn/ PAST PARTICIPLE OF **go** (ver **go**)

good¹ /gʊd/ ADJECTIVE [better, best]

1 suitable or of a high standard ☐ *That's a good idea.* ☐ *I've got some good news for you.* ☐ *She has been a good friend to me.* ☐ *I know a good way to cook rice.* **(bom)**

2 enjoyable or pleasant ☐ *Did you have a good holiday?* ☐ *We had a good time in Moscow.* **(bom, agradável)**

3 able to do something well ☐ + *at Mark's very good at fixing cars.* ☐ *Ben's a pretty good cook.* **(bom)**

4 something you say to show you are pleased ☐ *Oh, good – Harry's arrived.* **(bom)**

5 good for you something that is good for you makes you healthy or makes your life better ☐ *Eat your vegetables – they're good for you.* **(bom)**

6 a good child or animal behaves well ☐ *The children have been very good.* **(bom)**

> Remember that **good** is an adjective and not an adverb. Use the adverb **well** to say that someone does something in a way that is good:
> ✓ She is a good cook.
> ✓ She cooks very well.
> ✗ She cooks very **good**.

good² /gʊd/ NOUN, NO PLURAL

1 something that produces an advantage 🔲 *Cleaning it with water won't do any good – you need soap.* 🔲 *I know this medicine tastes bad, but it's for your own good.* **(bem, proveitoso)**

2 no good/not any good not of good quality, or not helpful ☐ *These gloves are no good – they're too thin.* ☐ *It's no good phoning her – she never has her phone switched on.* **(inútil)**

3 do someone good to make someone feel better or to make their life better ☐ *Have a day off work – it will do you good.* **(bem)**

4 what is morally right ☐ *We recognize the difference between good and evil.* **(bem)**

◆ IDIOM **for good** forever ☐ *I left home for good when I was 18.*

good afternoon /gʊd ˌɑːftəˈnuːn/ EXCLAMATION something that you say when you meet someone in the afternoon **(boa tarde)**

goodbye /gʊdˈbaɪ/ EXCLAMATION something you say when you are leaving or when other people are leaving ☐ *Goodbye, Anna. See you next week.* 🔲 *I felt sad when it was time to say goodbye.* **(até logo, adeus)**

good evening /gʊd ˈiːvnɪŋ/ EXCLAMATION a formal way of saying 'hello' when you see someone in the evening ☐ *Good evening ladies and gentlemen, and welcome to the show.* **(boa noite)**

good-looking /ˈgʊdlʊkɪŋ/ ADJECTIVE someone who is good-looking has an attractive face ☐ *Amy's new boyfriend is really good-looking.* **(bonito)**

good morning /gʊd ˈmɔːnɪŋ/ EXCLAMATION a formal way of saying 'hello' when you see someone in the morning ☐ *Good morning, everyone.* **(bom dia)**

goodness /ˈgʊdnɪs/ NOUN, NO PLURAL

1 being good and kind **(bondade)**

2 things in food that will make you healthy when you eat it ☐ *Tomatoes are full of goodness.* **(valor nutritivo)**

◆ IDIOMS **for goodness' sake** something you say when you are annoyed ☐ *For goodness sake, Dave, just open the door!* **Goodness (me)!** something you say when you are surprised ☐ *Goodness me, it's five o'clock already.*

good night /gʊd ˈnaɪt/ EXCLAMATION

1 something you say to someone just before you go to sleep at night ☐ *Good night, Mum.* 🔲 *He's upstairs saying good night to the children.* **(boa noite)**

2 a formal way of saying 'goodbye' to people late in the evening ☐ *Good night. Thanks for coming.* **(boa noite)**

goods /gʊdz/ PLURAL NOUN things that have been made to sell ☐ *electrical goods* ☐ *cars, jewellery and other luxury goods* 🔲 *Sales of household goods have fallen.* **(artigos)**

goose /guːs/ NOUN [plural **geese**] a large white or grey bird **(ganso)**

gorgeous /ˈgɔːdʒəs/ ADJECTIVE very beautiful or pleasant ☐ *The baby's absolutely gorgeous.* ☐ *gorgeous weather* **(deslumbrante, esplêndido)**

gorilla /gəˈrɪlə/ NOUN [plural **gorillas**] an animal that looks like a very large monkey **(gorila)**

gossip¹ /ˈgɒsɪp/ NOUN [plural **gossips**]

1 informal talk about other people, often about their private lives ☐ *She told me all the latest gossip.* ☐ *Tim loves a good gossip.* **(fofoca)**

2 someone who enjoys talking about other people's lives, in a way that you disapprove of **(fofoqueiro)**

gossip² /ˈgɒsɪp/ VERB [**gossips, gossiping, gossiped**] to talk about other people, often about their private lives **(mexericar, fofocar)**

got /gɒt/ PAST TENSE AND PAST PARTICIPLE OF **get** (ver **get**)

> In North America the past participle of 'get' is **gotten** and not 'got'. ☐ *She'd gotten mad at him.*

govern /ˈgʌvən/ VERB [governs, governing, governed] to officially control a country or area ☐ *The country was governed by the Republicans.* ☐ *the governing party* **(governar)**

> **THESAURUS:** If a political party governs a country or area, it officially controls that place. **Rule** and **reign** have a similar meaning, but **rule** is also used to talk about kings and queens. **Reign** is only used to talk about kings and queens. If you **lead** a group of people, you control them. You can **lead** a team of workers or a political party, for example.

government /ˈgʌvənmənt/ NOUN [plural **governments**] the group of people who control a country or area ▫ The party will form the next government. ▫ The government has announced an increase in taxes. ▫ a government department ▫ He criticized government policies. (**governo**)

governor /ˈgʌvənə(r)/ NOUN [plural **governors**] someone who is in charge of a place or organization ▫ the governor of Arkansas ▫ a school governor (**diretor**)

gown /gaʊn/ NOUN [plural **gowns**] (**vestido longo**)
1 a long formal dress that women wear on special occasions (**vestido longo**)
2 a loose piece of clothing worn in hospital ▫ a hospital gown (**avental**)

GP /ˌdʒiːˈpiː/ ABBREVIATION **general practitioner**; a doctor who looks after people from a particular area and treats them for a lot of different illnesses (**clínico geral**)

grab /græb/ VERB [**grabs, grabbing, grabbed**] to take something suddenly or violently ▫ He grabbed my bag and ran away. ▫ She grabbed my arm as I fell. (**agarrar**)

grace /greɪs/ NOUN, NO PLURAL
1 a smooth and attractive way of moving ▫ He kicks the ball with effortless grace. (**graça**)
2 a prayer that some people say before a meal ▫ Dad said grace. (**graça**)

graceful /ˈgreɪsfʊl/ ADJECTIVE smooth and attractive in shape or in the way you move ▫ He watched her graceful movements. ▫ the graceful curve of the dome (**gracioso**)
• **gracefully** /ˈgreɪsfʊli/ ADVERB in a graceful way

gracious /ˈgreɪʃəs/ ADJECTIVE polite and kind ▫ It was very gracious of you to apologize. (**graciosamente**)

grade¹ /greɪd/ NOUN [plural **grades**]
1 a number or letter that shows how good a student's work is ▫ She got a grade A in her English exam. ▫ He achieved top grades in his exams. (**nota**)
2 a level of quality or importance ▫ The jewellery is made from a lower grade of gold. ▫ He had been promoted to a higher grade at work. (**categoria**)
3 the US word for **form¹** (= school class) (**classificado**)

grade² /greɪd/ VERB [**grades, grading, graded**] to separate things into groups of similar size or quality ▫ Hotels are graded according to the facilities they offer. ▫ a grading system (**classificar**)

gradual /ˈgrædʒuəl/ ADJECTIVE happening slowly over a long period ▫ There has been a gradual improvement in his work. ▫ Recovery will be a very gradual process. (**gradual**)

gradually /ˈgrædʒuəli/ ADVERB slowly over a long period ▫ His health has gradually improved. ▫ Gradually, her life began to return to normal. (**gradualmente**)

graduate¹ /ˈgrædʒuət/ NOUN [plural **graduates**] someone who has a degree (= qualification) from a university or college ▫ George is a graduate of Edinburgh University. (**diplomado, graduado**)

graduate² /ˈgrædʒueɪt/ VERB [**graduates, graduating, graduated**] to get a degree (= qualification) from a university or college (**diplomar-se**)

graduation /ˌgrædʒuˈeɪʃən/ NOUN, NO PLURAL when you finish a university course and get a degree (= qualification) ▫ a graduation ceremony (**formatura**)

grain /greɪn/ NOUN [plural **grains**]
1 no plural the seeds of crops such as rice ▫ They export grain to Russia. (**grão**)
2 a seed from a crop such as rice ▫ + of a grain of wheat (**grão**)
3 one of the very small pieces of something such as sugar, salt, etc. ▫ + of grains of sand (**grão**)
4 the pattern of lines on the surface of wood (**grão**)

gram /græm/ NOUN [plural **grams**] a unit for measuring weight. There are one thousand grams in a kilogram. Gram is often written **g**. (**grama**)

grammar /ˈgræmə(r)/ NOUN **no plural** the rules of a particular language, for example how words are formed and how words are put together in a sentence ▫ French grammar (**gramática**)

grammatical /grəˈmætɪkəl/ ADJECTIVE
1 to do with grammar ▫ grammatical rules ▫ a grammatical error (**gramatical**)
2 correct according to the rules of grammar ▫ That sentence isn't grammatical, is it? (**gramaticamente correto**)

gramme /græm/ NOUN [plural **grammes**] another spelling of **gram** (**grama**)

grand /grænd/ ADJECTIVE [**grander, grandest**] very large, expensive or special, making you feel admiration ▫ The house was very grand. (**grandioso**)

grandad /ˈgrændæd/ NOUN [plural **grandads**] an informal word for grandfather (**vovô**)

grandchild /ˈgræntʃaɪld/ NOUN [plural **grandchildren**] a child of your son or daughter ▫ We've got three grown-up children and five grandchildren. (**neto**)

granddaughter /ˈgrændɔːtə(r)/ NOUN [plural **granddaughters**] the daughter of your son or daughter (**neta**)

grandfather /ˈgrænd fɑːðə(r)/ NOUN [plural **grandfathers**] the father of your mother or father ▫ my paternal grandfather (= father's father) ▫ my maternal grandfather (= mother's father) ▫ He recently became a grandfather. (**avô**)

grandma /ˈgrænmɑː/ NOUN [plural **grandmas**] an informal word for grandmother ▫ At the weekend I usually visit my grandma. (**avó**)

grandmother
/ˈɡrænmʌðə(r)/ NOUN [plural **grandmothers**] the mother of your mother or father ▫ my *maternal grandmother* (= mother's mother) ▫ my *paternal grandmother* (= father's mother) ▫ *We called in to see my grandmother.* (**avó**)

grandpa
/ˈɡrænpɑː/ NOUN [plural **grandpas**] an informal word for grandfather ▫ *My grandpa loved singing.* (**vovô**)

grandparent
/ˈɡrænpeərənt/ NOUN [plural **grandparents**] a parent of your father or your mother ▫ *I went to stay with my elderly grandparents.* (**avô, avó**)

grandson
/ˈɡrænsʌn/ NOUN [plural **grandsons**] the son of your son or daughter (**neto**)

granny /ˈɡrænɪ/ NOUN [plural **grannies**] an informal word for grandmother (**vovó**)

grant¹
/ɡrɑːnt/ VERB [**grants, granting, granted**]
1 to officially allow someone to have or to do something they have asked for ▫ *The judge granted him permission to appeal.* ▫ *His request was granted.* (**conceder**)
2 take something/someone for granted to expect something or someone to be there as usual and to forget that you are lucky to have them ▫ *We take our health for granted.* (**pressupor, assumir, presumir**)
3 take something for granted to expect something to happen without checking or thinking much about it ▫ *You can't take anything for granted.* ▫ *She took it for granted that I would agree.* (**dar por certo**)

grant²
/ɡrɑːnt/ NOUN [plural **grants**] an amount of money that has been given to you for a special purpose ▫ *The college received a grant of £20,000 to improve computer facilities.* ▫ *She applied for a research grant.* (**subvenção**)

grape
/ɡreɪp/ NOUN [plural **grapes**] a small, pale green or dark red fruit that grows in groups and is used to make wine ▫ *a bunch of grapes* (**uva**)

graph /ɡrɑːf/ NOUN [plural **graphs**] a picture with lines drawn between different points, used to show how things compare to each other or how something changes (**gráfico**)

grasp /ɡrɑːsp/ VERB [**grasps, grasping, grasped**]
1 to take hold of something tightly ▫ *She saw the dog and grasped my hand.* ▫ *He grasped the rope and began to climb.* (**agarrar**)
2 to understand an idea ▫ *I still couldn't grasp what he was trying to tell me.* ▫ *It might be difficult for children to grasp this concept.* (**compreender**)

grass
/ɡrɑːs/ NOUN, NO PLURAL a plant with very thin green leaves which covers gardens and fields ▫ *I cut the grass at the weekend.* ▫ *a blade of grass* (= one leaf) (**capim, grama**)

◆ IDIOM **the grass is (always) greener on the other side** the situation somewhere else or for someone else always seems better than your own

grate¹ /ɡreɪt/ VERB [**grates, grating, grated**] to cut food into small, thin pieces by rubbing it against a grater (= kitchen tool) ▫ *grated cheese* (**ralar**)

> **THESAURUS:** If you **grate** food such as cheese or carrots, you cut it into small thin pieces by rubbing it against a kitchen tool called a grater. If you **grind** something, you crush it into a powder. For example, we often **grind** pepper and coffee. If you **mince** something, you cut it into very small pieces using a machine. We often **mince** meat such as beef before cooking it.

grate² /ɡreɪt/ NOUN [plural **grates**] a frame of metal bars which holds the wood, coal, etc. in a fireplace (= space for a fire in the wall of a room) (**grelha**)

grateful
/ˈɡreɪtfʊl/ ADJECTIVE pleased with someone and wanting to thank them because they have done something for you ▫ + *for I'm very grateful for all your kindness.* ▫ + *to I felt so grateful to him for stopping to help.* ▫ *She gave me a grateful smile.* (**grato**)

gratitude /ˈɡrætɪtjuːd/ NOUN, NO PLURAL a feeling of being grateful to someone ▫ *She expressed her gratitude to the hospital.* (**gratidão**)

grave¹ /ɡreɪv/ NOUN [plural **graves**] a place where a dead body is buried (**túmulo**)

grave² /ɡreɪv/ ADJECTIVE [**graver, gravest**] very serious ▫ *a grave mistake* ▫ *You are in grave danger.* ▫ *He expressed grave concern about the situation.* (**grave**)

gravity /ˈɡrævətɪ/ NOUN, NO PLURAL
1 the force that pulls things towards the earth and makes them fall to the ground (**gravidade**)
2 a formal word meaning how serious something is ▫ *We appreciate the gravity of the situation.* (**gravidade**)

gray /ɡreɪ/ ADJECTIVE, NOUN [plural **grays**] the US spelling of **grey** (**cinza**)

graze /greɪz/ VERB [grazes, grazing, grazed]
1 if animals graze, they move around eating grass and other plants (pastar)
2 to hurt your skin by rubbing it against something hard and rough □ *I fell and grazed my knees.* (esfolar)

grease /gri:s/ NOUN, NO PLURAL a substance such as fat or thick oil □ *a grease stain* (gordura, graxa)

greasy /ˈgri:si/ ADJECTIVE [greasier, greasiest] covered in or containing thick fat or oil □ *greasy food* □ *He wiped his greasy fingers on his jeans.* (engordurado)

great /greɪt/ ADJECTIVE [greater, greatest]
1 very good □ *This is a great opportunity for you to travel.* □ *Our builders have done a great job.* □ *Your hair looks great like that.* □ *I've had a great idea!* □ *We had a great time in Venice.* (grande)
2 very large in size, amount or level □ *The elephant lifted one of its great feet.* 🔲 *We had a great deal of* (= a lot of) *trouble getting the information we needed.* 🔲 *His dinner party was a great success.* □ *They were in great danger.* (grande)
3 important and powerful □ *great armies* □ *a great nation* (grande)
4 a slightly informal way of expressing pleasure or agreement □ *'We'll meet you at seven.' 'Great – see you then!'* (ótimo)

Great Britain /ˌgreɪt ˈbrɪtən/ NOUN England, Scotland and Wales (Grã-Bretanha)

great-grand-daughter /ˌgreɪtˈgrændɔ:tə(r)/ NOUN [plural great-grand-daughters] your grandchild's daughter (bisneta)

great-grandfather /ˌgreɪtˈgrændfɑ:ðə(r)/ NOUN [plural great-grandfathers] your grandmother's or grandfather's father (bisavô)

great-grandmother /ˌgreɪtˈgrænmʌðə(r)/ NOUN [plural great-grandmothers] your grandmother's or grandfather's mother (bisavó)

great-grandson /ˌgreɪtˈgrænsʌn/ NOUN [plural great-grandsons] your grandchild's son (bisneto)

greed /gri:d/ NOUN, NO PLURAL when you want more of something than you need, especially food or money □ *Big businesses are often accused of greed and selfishness.* (ganância)

greedy /ˈgri:di/ ADJECTIVE [greedier, greediest] wanting more of something than you need □ *You greedy pig! You've eaten it all.* (ganancioso)

> **THESAURUS:** If someone is greedy, they want more of something such as food or money than they need. If you are **hungry**, you have a feeling of wanting to eat. If you are **starving** you are ill because you do not have enough to eat.

green¹ /gri:n/ ADJECTIVE
1 having the colour of leaves or grass □ *He's wearing a green coat.* □ *The curtains were dark green.* (verde)
2 to do with protecting the environment □ *She's involved in green politics.* □ *We're trying to be green by cycling to work.* (verde)
3 green spaces places with grass and plants (espaço verde)

green² /gri:n/ NOUN [plural greens] the colour of leaves and grass (verde, verdura)

greengrocer /ˈgri:nˌgrəʊsə(r)/ NOUN [plural greengrocers]
1 someone who sells fruit and vegetables (verde)
2 greengrocer's a shop selling fruit and vegetables (quitanda)

greenhouse /ˈgri:nhaʊs/ NOUN [plural greenhouses] a building with glass walls and a glass roof that stays warm and is used for growing plants in (estufa)

greenhouse gas /ˈgri:nhaʊs ˌgæs/ NOUN [plural greenhouse gases] a gas that stops heat from leaving the atmosphere, causing the temperature of Earth to increase □ *Greenhouse gases include carbon dioxide and methane.* (gás estufa)

greet /gri:t/ VERB [greets, greeting, greeted] to say something to someone when they arrive or when you meet them □ *She went outside to greet her visitors.* □ *He was greeted by a crowd of fans at the airport.* (saudar)

greeting /ˈgri:tɪŋ/ NOUN [plural greetings] something polite or friendly that you say when you meet someone or send a message to someone □ *They exchanged friendly greetings.* □ *John sends his warmest greetings.* (saudação)

grenade /grəˈneɪd/ NOUN [plural grenades] a small bomb that explodes a few seconds after someone throws it (granada)

grew /gru:/ PAST TENSE OF **grow** (ver grow)

grey¹ /greɪ/ ADJECTIVE having the colour you get when you mix black and white □ *The sheets were grey with dirt.* (cinza)

grey² /greɪ/ NOUN [plural greys] the colour that you get when you mix black and white (cinza)

grid /grɪd/ NOUN [plural grids] a pattern of lines that cross each other to form squares (rede)

grief /gri:f/ NOUN, NO PLURAL a feeling of great sadness, especially when someone has died □ *He expressed his grief at his baby daughter's death.* (pesar)
♦ IDIOM **come to grief** to fail or to have an accident □ *Drivers often come to grief on the mountain roads.*

grieve /gri:v/ VERB [grieves, grieving, grieved] to feel very sad, especially because someone has died □ *She was still grieving for her dead son.* (afligir)

grill¹ /grɪl/ VERB [grills, grilling, grilled] to cook food by putting it close to direct heat □ *Grill the fish for a couple of minutes on each side.* (grelhar)

grill² /grɪl/ NOUN [plural grills]
1 a piece of kitchen equipment which cooks food under a direct heat (grelha)

2 metal bars which food can be cooked on over a fire (**grelha**)

grim /grɪm/ ADJECTIVE [grimmer, grimmest]
1 very unpleasant, worrying or shocking □ *The situation looked pretty grim.* □ *The pictures illustrate the grim reality of life in the refugee camps.* (**sinistro**)
2 serious and unfriendly □ *The men wore grim expressions.* (**carrancudo**)

grin¹ /grɪn/ VERB [grins, grinning, grinned] to give a big smile □ *Ben was grinning broadly as he came out.* (**dar um sorriso largo**)
♦ IDIOM **grin and bear it** to accept a difficult situation without complaining □ *You'll just have to grin and bear it.* (**aguentar firme**)

grin² /grɪn/ NOUN [plural grins] a big smile □ *His face broke into a broad grin.* (**sorriso largo**)

grind /graɪnd/ VERB [grinds, grinding, ground]
1 to crush something solid into a powder □ *ground pepper* □ *The rocks are ground into dust.* (**triturar**)
2 to make something smooth or sharp by rubbing it against a hard surface (**carrancudo**)

grip¹ /grɪp/ VERB [grips, gripping, gripped] to hold something tightly □ *Martha gripped his arm.* □ *I gripped the steering wheel tighter.* (**segurar**)

grip² /grɪp/ NOUN [plural grips] when someone holds something tightly □ *He tightened his grip on her shoulder.* (**aperto**)

groan¹ /groʊn/ VERB [groans, groaning, groaned] to make a long deep sound to express pain, unhappiness, etc. □ *He groaned in pain.*

groan² /groʊn/ NOUN [plural groans] when you groan □ *She got slowly to her feet with a groan.* (**gemido**)

grocer /ˈgroʊsə(r)/ NOUN [plural grocers]
1 grocer's a shop selling food and things for the house (**mercearia**)
2 someone who runs a shop selling food and things for the house (**merceeiro**)

groceries /ˈgroʊsəriz/ PLURAL NOUN food and things for the house that you buy regularly □ *a bag of groceries* □ *More people now buy their groceries online.* (**secos e molhados, comestíveis**)

grocery /ˈgroʊsəri/ ADJECTIVE to do with food and things for the house that you buy regularly or the shop where you buy these things □ *grocery shopping* □ *a grocery list* (**relacionado a produtos de mercearia**)

groom /gruːm/ NOUN [plural grooms]
1 a bridegroom (= man who is getting married) (**noivo**)
2 someone whose job is to look after horses (**cavalariço**)

ground¹ /graʊnd/ NOUN [plural grounds]
1 the Earth's surface □ *The damaged satellite will fall to the ground next week.* □ *These plants grow best on higher ground.* (**solo**)
2 earth or soil □ *The ground is frozen.* □ *fertile ground* (**solo**)
3 an area where a particular sport is played □ *a football ground* (**terreno, campo**)

▸ **THESAURUS**: Ground, earth and soil all refer to the top layer of the land, where you can grow plants. Soil is the word that gardeners usually use for this, and ground and earth are more general. Dirt is any substance that is not clean or makes something become not clean. Dust is the layer of powder that you see on a surface that has not been cleaned for a long time.

ground² /graʊnd/ VERB [grounds, grounding, grounded] to stop an aircraft from leaving the ground (**impedir de decolar**)

ground³ /graʊnd/ PAST TENSE AND PAST PARTICIPLE OF **grind** (**ver grind**)

ground floor /ˌgraʊnd ˈflɔː(r)/ NOUN, NO PLURAL the floor of a building at the level of the ground outside □ *The electrical department is on the ground floor.* (**andar térreo**)

group¹ /gruːp/ NOUN [plural groups]
1 a number of people or things that are together or that belong together □ **+ of** *There was a small group of people waiting outside.* □ *We split the samples into three different groups.* (**grupo**) □ *Environmental groups have opposed the plans.* (**grupo**)
2 a number of people who perform music together □ *a pop group* (**conjunto, banda**)

group² /gruːp/ VERB [groups, grouping, grouped] to put people or things together in a group or groups □ *The children were grouped according to age.* (**agrupar[-se]**)

grouse¹ /graʊs/ NOUN [plural grouse] a type of fat bird that lives on open land and is hunted for sport (**galo silvestre**)

grouse² /graʊs/ VERB [grouses, grousing, groused] to complain about something □ *People always grouse about ticket prices.* (**queixar-se**)

grouse³ /graʊs/ NOUN [plural grouses] a complaint (**queixa**)

grow /groʊ/ VERB [grows, growing, grew, grown]
1 if a person, animal or plant grows, it becomes bigger or taller □ *He's grown as tall as his father.* □ *The grass has grown a lot this week.* (**crescer**)
2 if you grow plants, you put seeds in the ground and look after them □ *We grow vegetables in our garden.* □ *organically grown produce* (**crescer**)
3 if your hair or nails grow, they become longer
4 to increase in amount or size □ *The world's population is growing rapidly.* □ *Since he changed schools, his confidence has grown.* (**crescer**)
5 to become □ *It was growing dark.* □ *The sound grew louder.* (**crescer**)
♦ PHRASAL VERBS **grow out of something 1** if a child grows out of clothes, they become too big for them **2** to stop liking or doing something as you become older □ *I used to take a doll to bed, but I grew out of it in the end.* **grow up 1** to become older or to become an adult **2** to stop behaving

growl

like a child □ *I wish you'd grow up and take some responsibility!* **3** to develop □ *An unpleasant atmosphere grew up in the office.*

growl /graʊl/ VERB [growls, growling, growled] if an animal such as a dog growls, it makes a deep threatening noise in its throat □ *Two black guard dogs growled.* (rosnar)

grown /grəʊn/ PAST PARTICIPLE OF **grow** (ver **grow**)

grown-up¹ /ˈgrəʊnʌp/ NOUN [plural grown-ups] an adult □ *The grown-ups enjoyed themselves as much as the children.* (adulto)

grown-up² /ˈgrəʊnʌp/ ADJECTIVE adult □ *We have three grown-up children.* (adulto)

growth /grəʊθ/ NOUN [plural growths]

1 *no plural* when something grows, develops or gets bigger □ + *of the rapid growth of computer technology* □ + *in The company reported a growth in sales.* □ *economic growth* □ *Warmth brings about growth in the garden.* (crescimento)
2 a lump that grows on the body □ *A growth developed on his hand.* (tumor)

grumble /ˈgrʌmbəl/ VERB [grumbles, grumbling, grumbled] to complain in an unhappy way, especially about small things □ *She was grumbling about the food.* (rosnar, resmungar)

grunt /grʌnt/ VERB [grunts, grunting, grunted] to make a deep noise like a pig □ *He only grunted in response.* (grunhir)

guarantee¹ /ˌgærənˈtiː/ NOUN [plural guarantees]
1 a promise that something will certainly be done or will happen □ *I give a guarantee that we will do everything we can.* □ *Simply having talent is no guarantee of success.* (garantia)
2 a promise that a product will be repaired or replaced if there is something wrong with it □ *a money-back guarantee* □ *The equipment has a one year guarantee.* (garantia)

guarantee² /ˌgærənˈtiː/ VERB [guarantees, guaranteeing, guaranteed]
1 to make a promise that something will happen or be done □ *We couldn't guarantee his safety.* (garantir)
2 to give a guarantee for a product that is sold (garantir)

guard¹ /gɑːd/ NOUN [plural guards]

1 someone whose job is to protect a person or place, or to make sure that prisoners do not escape (guarda)
2 under guard being protected or prevented from escaping □ *He was taken to the prison under armed guard.* (sob guarda)
3 keep/stand guard to protect a person or place, or to make sure that prisoners do not escape □ *I stood guard over the money.* (vigiar, montar guarda)
4 on guard (a) responsible for protecting a person or place □ *There were no soldiers on guard that night.* (b) ready to deal with a difficult situation □ *You need to be on guard for suspicious phone calls.* (prevenido, alerta)

guard² /gɑːd/ VERB [guards, guarding, guarded]

1 to make sure that someone does not escape □ *You guard the back entrance.* (guardar, resguardar)
2 to protect someone or something □ *I guarded the children while he went for help.* (guardar)

guilty

guardian /ˈgɑːdiən/ NOUN [plural guardians] someone who is legally responsible for a child when its parents have died (guardião)

guerrilla /gəˈrɪlə/ NOUN [plural guerrillas] a fighter who is a member of a small or unofficial army fighting for political reasons (guerrilha)

guess¹ /ges/ VERB [guesses, guessing, guessed]

1 to give an answer or opinion without knowing all the facts □ + *question word Guess how old she is.* (adivinhar)
2 I guess a slightly informal phrase used to say that you think something is true □ *I guess we'll have to sell the car.* (adivinhar)

guess² /ges/ NOUN [plural guesses]

an answer or opinion made by guessing □ *At a rough guess, I'd say he's forty.* (palpite)

guest /gest/ NOUN [plural guests]

1 someone you invite to your house or to a party □ *a wedding guest* □ *She was one of 200 guests at the party.* (convidado)
2 someone staying in a hotel □ *Hotel guests can use the gym for free.* (hóspede)

> **THESAURUS:** A **guest** is someone who is staying in a place that is not their home. A guest can stay in someone's house or at a hotel. A **visitor** is someone who comes to your house to see you for a short time. They may or may not sleep in your house. A **lodger** is a person who pays money to live in a room in someone else's house.

guesthouse /ˈgesthaʊs/ NOUN [plural guesthouses] a small hotel (pensão)

guidance /ˈgaɪdəns/ NOUN, NO PLURAL advice about how you should do something □ *We provide guidance on environmental management.* (orientação)

guide¹ /gaɪd/ NOUN [plural guides]

1 someone whose job is to show places to people who are visiting □ *A guide showed us around the cathedral.* (guia)
2 a book that gives information about a place or tells you how to do something (guia)

guide² /gaɪd/ VERB [guides, guiding, guided]

to go with someone to show them where to go or tell them about a place (guiar)

guidebook /ˈgaɪdbʊk/ NOUN [plural guidebooks]

a book which contains information for people visiting a particular place (guia)

guilt /gɪlt/ NOUN, NO PLURAL

1 an unpleasant feeling you get when you know you have done something wrong □ *a sense of guilt* □ *She felt no guilt at what she had done.* (culpa)
2 the fact that you have done something wrong □ *He admitted his guilt and accepted the punishment.* (culpa)

guilty /ˈgɪlti/ ADJECTIVE [guiltier, guiltiest]
1 ashamed because you have done something wrong ▣ *I felt guilty about lying to them.* ▢ *I had a guilty conscience.* (**culpa**)
2 having committed a crime ▢ **+ of** *They are guilty of war crimes.* ▣ *He pleaded guilty to theft.* ▣ *He was found guilty of drug smuggling.* (**culpado**)

guitar /gɪˈtɑː(r)/ NOUN [plural guitars] an instrument with strings that you play with your fingers or a small piece of plastic ▣ *an electric guitar* (**violão**)

gulf /gʌlf/ NOUN [plural gulfs] a large area of sea almost surrounded by land ▢ *the Gulf of Taranto* (**golfo**)

gum /gʌm/ NOUN [plural gums]
1 the hard pink part in your mouth that your teeth grow from ▣ *gum disease* (**gengiva**)
2 *no plural* a soft sweet substance that you chew but do not swallow ▢ *a stick of gum* (**goma de mascar, chicle**)

gun /gʌn/ NOUN [plural guns] a weapon that fires bullets from a metal tube ▣ *The soldier quickly loaded his gun.* (**arma de fogo**)

gunfire /ˈgʌnfaɪə(r)/ NOUN, NO PLURAL when guns are fired or the sound that this makes ▢ *They suddenly heard gunfire in the distance.* (**tiroteio**)

gunman /ˈgʌnmən/ NOUN [plural gunmen] a man who uses a gun to steal from people or kill them ▢ *Two masked gunmen attacked him in his own home.* (**pistoleiro**)

gush /gʌʃ/ VERB [gushes, gushing, gushed] if liquid gushes, it flows out suddenly and in large amounts ▢ *Blood was gushing from a wound on her forehead.* (**jorrar**)

gust /gʌst/ NOUN [plural gusts] a sudden strong wind ▢ *A gust of wind blew her hat off.* (**rajada**)

gut /gʌt/ NOUN [plural guts]
1 the tube that takes food from your stomach to be passed out of your body as waste (**intestino**)
2 *guts* (a) courage and determination ▣ *It took guts to stand up to his father.* ▢ *He didn't have the guts to tell me he was leaving.* (b) the organs inside an animal's body (**coragem**)

guy /gaɪ/ NOUN [plural guys] an informal word for a man (**sujeito**)

gym /dʒɪm/ NOUN [plural gyms]
1 a room or building with equipment for doing exercises ▢ *I go to the gym three times a week.* (**ginásio**)
2 exercises that you do inside, especially at school ▢ *We have gym on Wednesday.* (**ginástica**)

gymnast /ˈdʒɪmnæst/ NOUN [plural gymnasts] someone trained to do a sport in which they use their body to bend, jump, etc. in a beautiful way (**ginasta**)

gymnastics /dʒɪmˈnæstɪks/ NOUN, NO PLURAL a sport in which people use their bodies to bend, jump, etc. in a beautiful way (**ginástica**)

H*h*

H *or* **h** /eɪtʃ/ the eighth letter of the alphabet (**a oitava letra do alfabeto**)

habit /ˈhæbɪt/ NOUN [plural **habits**] something that you do regularly, especially without thinking about it □ + *of* *We want to get kids into the habit of regular exercise.* 🔲 *Tommy has a bad habit of biting his fingernails.* 🔲 *We asked people about their eating habits.* (**hábito**)

habitat /ˈhæbɪtæt/ NOUN [plural **habitats**] the place where an animal or a plant lives or grows 🔲 *We wanted to study the lions in their natural habitat.* (**habitat**)

hack /hæk/ VERB [**hacks, hacking, hacked**]
1 to cut something roughly □ *They hacked their way through the thick jungle.* □ *She hacked off chunks of hair.* (**picar**)
2 to get into someone's computer illegally to look at information stored there. A computing word □ *He hacked into military computer systems.* (**hackear**)

had /hæd/ PAST TENSE AND PAST PARTICIPLE OF **have**³ (**ver have³**)

hadn't /ˈhædənt/ a short way to say and write had not □ *Laura hadn't expected to win.* (**ver have³**)

hail¹ /heɪl/ VERB [**hails, hailing, hailed**] if it hails, small white balls of frozen ice fall from the sky (**chover granizo**)

hail² /heɪl/ NOUN, NO PLURAL small white balls of frozen ice that fall from the sky □ *a hail storm* (**granizo**)

hair /heə(r)/ NOUN [plural **hairs**]
1 *no plural* all the thin threads that grow on your head 🔲 *long/short hair* 🔲 *straight/curly hair* 🔲 *She's tall with shoulder-length blonde hair.* 🔲 *I need to get my haircut.* (**cabelo**)
2 one of the thin threads that grow on the surface of the skin of animals and humans □ *It made the hairs on my arms stand up.* (**pelo**)

> Remember that 'hair' meaning 'all the hair on your head' is never used in the plural:
> ✓ She has short hair.
> ✗ She has short hairs.

◆ IDIOM **make someone's hair stand on end** to make someone very frightened or shocked □ *The thought of finding a snake makes my hair stand on end.*

hairbrush /ˈheəbrʌʃ/ NOUN [plural **hairbrushes**] a brush for brushing your hair (**escova de cabelo**)

haircut /ˈheəkʌt/ NOUN [plural **haircuts**]
1 when someone cuts your hair □ *You need a haircut.* (**corte de cabelo**)
2 the style in which your hair is cut □ *She's got a new haircut.* (**corte de cabelo**)

hairdresser /ˈheədresə(r)/ NOUN [plural **hairdressers**]
1 someone whose job is to cut, arrange and colour people's hair (**cabeleireiro**)
2 hairdresser's a place where a hairdresser works (**salão de cabeleireiro**)

hairdryer *or* **hairdrier** /ˈheədraɪə(r)/ NOUN [plural **hairdryers** *or* **hairdriers**] a piece of electrical equipment that dries your hair by blowing hot air over it (**secador de cabelo**)

hairstyle /ˈheəstaɪl/ NOUN [plural **hairstyles**] the style in which your hair has been cut and arranged □ *She showed off her new hairstyle.* (**penteado**)

hairy /ˈheərɪ/ ADJECTIVE [**hairier, hairiest**] covered with hair □ *a hairy chest* (**cabeludo, peludo**)

half¹ /hɑːf/ NOUN, DETERMINER [plural **halves**]
1 1/2; one of two equal parts of something □ *He ate half and I ate the other half.* □ *You have an hour and a half to play.* 🔲 *Meet us here in half an hour.* (**metade, meio**)
2 in half if you break, cut, etc. something in half, you divide it into two equal parts □ *We cut the cake in half.* (**metade, meio**)
3 half past one/two, etc. 30 minutes after one o'clock/two o'clock, etc. □ *He left at half past six.* (**meia**)

half² /hɑːf/ ADVERB
1 to the amount of a half □ *This glass is only half full.* □ *She is half Spanish* (= one of her parents is Spanish). (**meio**)
2 partly, but not completely □ *I was half asleep.* (**meio**)

half-brother /ˈhɑːfˌbrʌðə(r)/ NOUN [plural **half-brothers**] a male relative with either the same father or the same mother as you (**meio-irmão**)

hall /hɔːl/ NOUN [plural **halls**]
1 an area just inside the entrance to a house that you go through to get to other rooms or to the stairs (**saguão**)
□ *She checked her hair in the mirror in the hall.* 🔲 *The front door opens into a small entrance hall.*
2 a large building or room where meetings, concerts and other events are held 🔲 *a concert hall* 🔲 *a meeting at the village hall* (**salão**)

hallo /həˈləʊ/ EXCLAMATION another spelling of **hello** (**olá, ei**)

halt¹ /hɔːlt/ VERB [halts, halting, halted]
1 to stop moving or to make something stop moving ◻ *Traffic suddenly halted.* (**parar**)
2 to stop happening or developing or to stop something happening or developing ◻ *The government is taking measures to halt the spread of the disease.* ◻ *These attacks should halt immediately.* (**para**)

halt² /hɔːlt/ NOUN [plural halts]
1 when something stops moving ▣ *The car came to a sudden halt.* (**parada**)
2 when something stops happening or developing ▣ *He called a halt to the press conference and walked out.* (**parada**)

halve /hɑːv/ VERB [halves, halving, halved] to divide or cut something into two equal parts ◻ *Halve the mushrooms.* (**cortar ao meio**)

ham /hæm/ NOUN, NO PLURAL meat from the leg of a pig which has been cooked using salt or smoke (**presunto**)

hamburger /ˈhæmbɜːgə(r)/ NOUN [plural hamburgers] a round flat shape made from very small pieces of meat that is fried and usually eaten between pieces of bread (**hambúrguer**)

hammer¹ /ˈhæmə(r)/ NOUN [plural hammers] a tool with a heavy metal or wooden part at the end of a handle, used for hitting nails, etc. (**martelo**)

hammer² /ˈhæmə(r)/ VERB [hammers, hammering, hammered]
1 to hit something with a hammer ◻ *Hammer the nails in one by one.* (**martelar**)
2 to hit something hard ◻ **+ on** *He was hammering on the door with his fists.* ◻ *The region was hammered by powerful storms.* (**martelar**)

hamper¹ /ˈhæmpə(r)/ VERB [hampers, hampering, hampered] to make it difficult for someone or something to make progress ◻ *Rescue efforts were hampered by rain.* (**estorvar**)

hamper² /ˈhæmpə(r)/ NOUN [plural hampers] a large basket (= container made from very thin pieces of wood) with a lid, often used for carrying food (**cesta**)

hand¹ /hænd/ NOUN [plural hands]
1 the part of your body at the end of your arm ◻ *I took her by the hand.* ▣ *They walked hand in hand* (= with their hands joined together). ▣ *Hold hands with me while we cross the road.* ▣ *He refused to shake hands with my father.* (**mão**)
2 by hand (a) if something is made or done by hand, it is made or done by a person, not a machine (b) if a letter is delivered by hand, someone brings it to you without posting it (**à mão**)
3 help ▣ *Can I give you a hand with those bags?* ▣ *Do you need a hand with the washing up?* (**mão**)
4 the part of a watch or clock that points to the time (**ponteiro**)
♦ IDIOM **on the one hand... on the other hand** used to compare the advantages and disadvantages of something ◻ *On the one hand, working at home saves me a lot of time, on the other hand it can be rather lonely.*

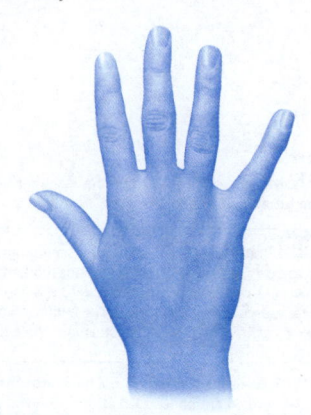

hand² /hænd/ VERB [hands, handing, handed] to give something to someone ◻ *Could you hand me a plate?* (**dar, entregar**)
♦ PHRASAL VERBS **hand something in** to give something to someone, for example a teacher ◻ *Have you handed in your homework?* **hand something out** to give something to everyone in a group ◻ *Can you hand out the textbooks?* **hand something over** to give something to someone ◻ *Hand over all your money.*

handbag /ˈhændbæg/ NOUN [plural handbags] a woman's bag for carrying things like money and keys ◻ *a black leather handbag* (**bolsa**)

handcuffs /ˈhændkʌfs/ PLURAL NOUN a pair of metal rings joined by a chain which police use to lock around a prisoner's wrists (= parts of the arms next to the hands) (**algemas**)

handful /ˈhændfʊl/ NOUN [plural handfuls]
1 an amount that you can hold in your hand ◻ *a handful of rice* (**punhado**)
2 a handful of something a small number of something ◻ *Only a handful of people turned up.* (**punhado**)
3 a handful an informal word for a child or an animal whose behaviour makes them difficult to deal with ◻ *Greta can be quite a handful.* (**insuportável**)

hand-held /ˈhænd held/ ADJECTIVE small enough to hold in your hand during use ◻ *It was filmed using a hand-held video camera.* (**portátil**)

handicap /ˈhændɪkæp/ NOUN [plural handicaps]
1 a disadvantage that prevents you doing something easily or as well as other people ◻ *Lack of qualifications can be a major handicap.* (**desvantagem**)
2 an old-fashioned word for a physical or mental injury or disability that prevents someone from living normally ◻ *A school for children with mental and physical handicaps.* (**deficiência**)

handkerchief / hard

handkerchief /'hæŋkətʃɪf/ NOUN [plural handkerchiefs] a small piece of cloth or thin, soft paper used for drying your nose or eyes (**lenço**)

handle¹ /'hændəl/ NOUN [plural handles]
1 the part of an object that you use to pick it up and hold it □ *a brush with a long handle* (**cabo**)
2 the part of a door that you hold when you open and close it 🔁 *a door handle* (**maçaneta**)

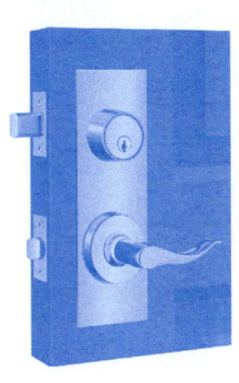

handle² /'hændəl/ VERB [handles, handling, handled]
1 to deal with something □ *Mr Peters is handling all the arrangements for the trip.* 🔁 *I would have handled the situation differently.* (**negociar, lidar**)
2 to touch something or to hold it with your hands □ *Try not to handle the fruit too much.* (**manipular**)

handsome /'hænsəm/ ADJECTIVE [handsomer, handsomest] attractive, especially used about a man □ *a handsome young actor* □ *He looked so handsome in his uniform.* (**bonito**)

handwriting /'hændraɪtɪŋ/ NOUN, NO PLURAL writing done with a pen or a pencil, not printed □ *The speech is written in a notebook in Dr King's own handwriting.* (**letra manuscrita, escrita**)

handy /'hændi/ ADJECTIVE [handier, handiest]
1 useful and easy to use □ *It's a handy size for carrying in your pocket.* (**prático**)
2 near and easy to reach □ *The house is handy for the station.* (**acessível**)
3 come in handy an informal phrase meaning to be useful □ *Bring the torch, it might come in handy.* (**ser útil**)

hang /hæŋ/ VERB [hangs, hanging, hung]
1 to attach something so that the top part is fixed and the lower part is able to move □ *Hang your jackets on the pegs.* □ *Joe was hanging upside down by his feet.* 🔁 *The branches hung down to the ground.* (**pendurar**)
2 to kill someone by tying a rope around their neck and making them drop so that the rope is tight □ *He hanged himself in his prison cell.* (**enforcar**)

◆ PHRASAL VERBS **hang about/around** to stay in a place, doing nothing □ *There was a group of boys hanging round outside our house.* **hang on 1** to hold something tightly □ *Hang on tight and we'll pull you up.* **2** an informal word meaning to wait □ *Hang on a minute!* **hang something up** to put something such as clothing in a place where it can hang □ *We hung up our coats in the hall.*

happen /'hæpən/ VERB [happens, happening, happened]
1 if something happens, it takes place, usually without being planned □ *The accident happened last week.* □ *I pressed the button but nothing happened.* 🔁 *He'll be pleased, whatever happens.* (**acontecer**)
2 happen to do something to do something by chance □ *She just happened to be there and saw the whole thing.* (**acontecer**)

happily /'hæpɪli/ ADVERB feeling, showing or expressing happiness □ *The girls were smiling happily.* 🔁 *They're happily married.* (**felizmente, alegremente**)

happiness /'hæpɪnɪs/ NOUN, NO PLURAL the state of being happy 🔁 *He has finally found happiness in his personal life.* □ *My children are my greatest source of happiness.* (**felicidade**)

happy /'hæpi/ ADJECTIVE [happier, happiest]
1 pleased and feeling that a situation is good □ *It was the happiest day of her life.* □ *He looked really happy.* 🔁 *More money won't make her happy.* (**feliz**)
2 making you feel happy □ *I had a very happy childhood.* □ *The story has a happy ending.* (**feliz**)
3 Happy Birthday/Christmas, etc. used to say that you hope someone will be happy on a special day (**feliz**)

> **THESAURUS:** If you are **happy** or **cheerful**, you are pleased, and feel that a situation is good. **Delighted** means very happy. If you are **glad**, you are happy because of something that has happened. Often you are **glad** because a bad or difficult situation has ended or because something bad has not happened. For example, you might be **glad** to be home after a long journey, or **glad** that your exams are finished.

harbor /'hɑːbə(r)/ NOUN [plural harbors] the US spelling of **harbour** (**porto [EUA]**)

harbour /'hɑːbə(r)/ NOUN [plural harbours] a safe area of water near the coast, usually protected by big walls, where ships come so that people can go onto the land □ *The ship sailed into Sydney harbour.* (**porto**)

hard¹ /hɑːd/ ADJECTIVE [harder, hardest]
1 firm and solid and not easy to bend or break □ *This bread is a bit hard.* □ *The ball will only bounce on a hard surface.* (**duro**)
2 difficult to do □ *+ to do something* It was hard to concentrate with all the noise. □ *The exam was really hard.* (**difícil**)

3 unpleasant or full of problems 🔹 *They had a hard life.* 🔹 *He had a hard time in the army.* (**difícil**)

hard² /hɑːd/ ADVERB [harder, hardest]
1 with a lot of effort 🔹 *They always work hard.* 🔹 *You need to try harder.* (**intensamente**)
2 with a lot of force □ *It was raining hard when we got there.* (**forte**)

hard disk /ˈhɑːdˌdɪsk/ *or* **hard drive** /ˈhɑːdˌdraɪv/ NOUN [plural hard disks *or* hard drives] a part inside a computer where information is stored. A computing word. (**disco rígido**)

harden /ˈhɑːdən/ VERB [hardens, hardening, hardened] to become hard or solid □ *The mixture hardens into a solid gel.* (**endurecer**)

hardly /ˈhɑːdli/ ADVERB only just or almost not □ *I hardly know him.* □ *He hardly spoke a word of English.* 🔹 *There were hardly any people there.* 🔹 *We hardly ever saw her.* 🔹 *He'd hardly put the key in the door when down came the rain.* (**mal**)

> Notice that the word **hardly** does not mean 'with a lot of effort' or 'with a lot of force'. For these two meanings, use the word **hard**:
> ✓ She works so hard.
> ✗ She works so hardly.
> ✓ It's raining hard.
> ✗ It's raining hardly.

hardware /ˈhɑːdweə(r)/ NOUN, NO PLURAL the machines and equipment that make up a computer system. A computing word □ *We need to update our computer hardware and software.* (**hardware**)

harm¹ /hɑːm/ VERB [harms, harming, harmed] to hurt, damage or cause problems for someone or some thing □ *You might harm your eyes if you sit too close to the TV.* □ *She believes that violent video games can harm children.* □ *We know that air travel harms the environment.* (**fazer mal**)

harm² /hɑːm/ NOUN, NO PLURAL
1 damage, injury or problems 🔹 *The knife wasn't sharp enough to cause much harm.* 🔹 *If you stay with me, you won't come to any harm.* 🔹 *It wouldn't do any harm to ask for advice.* (**mal**)
2 there's no harm in doing something used to say that an action will not cause problems and may help a situation □ *I don't think you'll be able to persuade him to come, but there's no harm in trying.* (**não há mal algum em**)

harmful /ˈhɑːmfʊl/ ADJECTIVE causing damage, injury or problems □ *Use a cream to protect your skin from the sun's harmful rays.* (**prejudicial**)

harmless /ˈhɑːmlɪs/ ADJECTIVE not causing any damage, injury or problems □ *This substance is harmless to animals.* (**inofensivo**)

harmony /ˈhɑːməni/ NOUN [plural harmonies]
1 when people live in a peaceful and friendly way □ *We live in harmony with our neighbours.* (**harmonia**)

2 a combination of musical notes that sound pleasant together □ *complex vocal harmonies* (**harmonia**)

harsh /hɑːʃ/ ADJECTIVE [harsher, harshest]
1 very cold, uncomfortable or difficult, etc. □ *a harsh climate* □ *a harsh winter* □ *The poor lived in very harsh conditions.* (**severo**)
2 cruel, severe and often unfair □ *a harsh punishment* 🔹 *harsh criticism* 🔹 *He had harsh words for his teammate.* (**severo**)

harvest¹ /ˈhɑːvɪst/ NOUN [plural harvests]
1 the activity of collecting crops □ *Heavy rains delayed the harvest.* (**colheita**)
2 the amount of a crop that is collected □ *The price rise is due to poor wheat harvests.* (**colheita**)

harvest² /ˈhɑːvɪst/ VERB [harvests, harvesting, harvested] to collect a crop □ *The apples are harvested in late summer.* (**colher**)

has /hæz/ VERB the present tense of the verb **have** when it is used with **he, she** and **it** □ *He has brown eyes.* (ver **have**)

hasn't /ˈhæzənt/ a short way to say and write **has not** □ *Anne hasn't arrived yet.* (ver **have**)

hat /hæt/ NOUN [plural hats] a covering you wear on your head □ *a straw hat* □ *a fur hat* (**chapéu**)

hatch /hætʃ/ VERB [hatches, hatching, hatched] baby birds or reptiles hatch when they break out of their eggs □ *We watched the chicks hatch.* (**chocar**)

hate¹ /heɪt/ VERB [hates, hating, hated] to dislike someone or something very much □ *+ ing I hate being late.* □ *I hate the idea of wasting all that money.* (**detestar, odiar**)

> **THESAURUS:** If you **dislike** something or someone, you do not like it. **Hate** and **loathe** both mean that you dislike something or someone very much.

hate² /heɪt/ NOUN, NO PLURAL a very strong feeling that you do not like someone or something □ *There was a look of real hate in his eyes.* (**ódio**)

hatred /'heɪtrɪd/ NOUN, NO PLURAL a very strong feeling that you do not like someone or something □ *I have a hatred of dogs.* 🗨 *He was accused of promoting racial hatred.* **(ódio)**

haul /hɔːl/ VERB [hauls, hauling, hauled] to pull someone or something using a lot of effort □ *He managed to haul himself up on to the boat.* **(puxar)**

haunt /hɔːnt/ VERB [haunts, haunting, haunted] if a ghost (= dead person's spirit) haunts a place, people think it appears there □ *People claim that the castle is haunted by the ghost of the young prince.* **(assombrar)**

haunted /'hɔːntɪd/ ADJECTIVE visited by ghosts (= spirits of dead people) □ *Some people believe that this room is haunted.* □ *a haunted castle* **(assombrado)**

have¹ /hæv/ AUXILIARY VERB [has, having, had] used with the past participle of another verb to form the present perfect tense or the past perfect tense □ *I have bought a new car.* □ *Have you fed the rabbit?* □ *She has been feeling tired recently.* □ *They had opened a restaurant in Athens.* **(ter)**

have² /hæv/ MODAL VERB [has, having, had]
1 have to do something if you have to do something, you must do it □ *I have to go away for a few days.* □ *You'll have to give him the money.* 🗨 *I don't have to go to work tomorrow.* **(ter de)**
2 used for telling someone how to do something □ *You have to press the green button.* **(ter de)**

➤ Notice that when **have to** (sense 1) is negative, the negative form is usually made with **do**: □ *I don't have to go.* □ *He doesn't have to work.* The question form of **have to** is also made with **do**: □ *Do you have to tell him?* □ *Do we have to come?*

have³ /hæv/ VERB [has, having, had]
1 used for describing someone or something □ *He has got black hair.* □ *The room had patches of damp on the walls.* □ *The soup had a delicious flavour.* **(ter)**
2 to own something □ *He has a house in Spain.* □ *I have got three brothers.* □ *She has the determination to win.* **(ter)**
3 used for saying that someone has something with them □ *Do you have a towel I could use?* □ *He had a large dog with him.* **(ter)**
4 to have an illness to suffer from it □ *She has cancer.* □ *I had a terrible headache.* **(ter)**
5 have a look/shower/walk, etc. to do a particular thing **(dar)**
6 to have food or drink is to eat it or drink it □ *You'll have lunch with us, won't you?* □ *I had a huge curry last night.* **(comer, beber)**
7 to experience something □ *We've had a lot of problems.* □ *I hope you have a great time in Mexico.* **(ter)**
→ *go to* **have your cake and eat it**

➤ Notice (sense 2) that **have** and **have got** are both used to mean 'to own something'. It is normal, especially in spoken English, to use the short forms of **have got** and **has got**: □ *I've got a dog.* (= I have got a dog). □ *She's got a dog.* (= She has got a dog).

haven't /'hævənt/ a short way to say and write *have not* □ *I haven't seen the film yet.* (ver **have¹**, **have²**, **have³**)

hawk /hɔːk/ NOUN [plural hawks] a bird that can see very well and hunts small animals for food **(falcão)**

hay /heɪ/ NOUN, NO PLURAL grass that has been cut and dried, used to feed animals **(feno)**

hazard /'hæzəd/ NOUN [plural hazards] something that could cause harm or damage 🗨 *Undercooked food is a potential health hazard.* 🗨 *a fire hazard* **(risco)**

➤ **THESAURUS:** A **hazard** is something that could cause harm or damage. For example, food that is not stored properly can be a health hazard. A **danger** is a situation where something may harm you. A **risk** is something that could cause problems in the future. For example, if the economic situation is bad, there is a risk that you will lose your job. An **accident** is a bad thing that happens that is not intended.

haze /heɪz/ NOUN [plural hazes] air that is difficult to see through because of heat, smoke, dust, etc. **(neblina)**

he /hiː/ PRONOUN used to talk or write about a man, boy or male animal that has already been mentioned □ *Everyone likes Ted because he is so funny.* □ *Don't worry – he won't bite.* **(ele)**

head¹ /hed/ NOUN [plural heads]
1 the part of the body that contains the brain, eyes, mouth, etc. □ *She suffered serious head injuries.* □ *He turned his head to look at the clock.* 🗨 *nod/shake your head* 🗨 *She was dressed in black from head to toe.* **(cabeça)**
2 your mind □ *The idea just popped into my head.* **(cabeça, mente)**
3 the person who is in charge of an organization or a group of people □ *He is the former head of the prison service.* **(cabeça, chefe)**
4 the top or front of something □ *Put your name at the head of each page.* □ *I went straight to the head of the queue.* **(topo, cabeceira)**
◆ IDIOMS **be over someone's head** to be too difficult for someone to understand □ *The stuff about economics was right over my head* **go to someone's head** if success, praise, etc. goes to someone's head, they become too proud **head over heels 1** if you fall head over heels, you fall in a sudden and forceful way □ *He slipped on the ice and went head over heels.* **2** if you are head over heels in love, you love someone very much **keep your head** to stay calm □ *She kept her head in a crisis.*

> **THESAURUS:** The head of an organization or a group of people is the person who is in charge. Chief has a similar meaning. We often use chief to talk about the most important police officer in a group. A manager is someone who is in charge of other people at work. Boss is a more informal word for this. A principal is the person who is in charge of a school, college or university.

head² /hed/ VERB [heads, heading, headed]
1 to go towards a particular place □ *It's time for us to head home.* □ *We were heading north along the motor way.* (**rumar para**)
2 to be in charge of an organization or a group of people □ *She heads the development team.* (**encabeçar**)
3 to hit a ball with your head (**cabecear**)

headache /ˈhedeɪk/ NOUN [plural headaches]
a pain in your head 🔁 *I've got a splitting headache.* 🔁 *That noise is giving me a headache.* (**dor de cabeça**)

headlight /ˈhedlaɪt/ NOUN [plural headlights]
one of the two big lights at the front of a vehicle (**farol dianteiro**)

headline /ˈhedlaɪn/ NOUN [plural headlines]
1 the words that are printed in large letters at the top of a newspaper article (**título**)
2 **headlines** the most important news stories that are reported at the beginning of a news programme on the television or radio □ *Here is Charlotte Green with today's headlines.* (**manchete**)

headquarters /ˈhedˌkwɔːtəz/ PLURAL NOUN
the central office from which a large business or organization is controlled □ *Our company headquarters are in London.* (**quartel-general**)

headteacher /ˌhedˈtiːtʃə(r)/ NOUN [plural headteachers]
a teacher who is in charge of a school (**diretor escolar**)

heal /hiːl/ VERB [heals, healing, healed]
to become healthy again, or to make a person or part of the body healthy again □ *The wound needs time to heal.* □ *The substance is used for healing cuts.* □ *With time, the body will heal itself.* (**curar**)

> **THESAURUS:** If something heals, it gets healthy again. For example, a wound heals. To cure means to make someone with an illness better again. Medicine can cure an illness. You can use the noun cure to talk about the thing that makes you better. A remedy is also something which treats an illness. We often use remedy to talk about things which are not medicine. For example, some people believe that drinking honey and lemon is a remedy for a cold.

health /helθ/ NOUN, NO PLURAL
how well your body is □ *Her health has been very poor recently.* 🔁 *Too much red meat is bad for your health.* 🔁 *He appeared to be in good health.* 🔁 *She was forced to leave due to ill health.* (**saúde**)

healthy /ˈhelθi/ ADJECTIVE [healthier, healthiest]
1 physically well and not ill in any way □ *Exercise and a good diet can help you stay healthy.* □ *She seems perfectly healthy.* (**saudável**)
2 having a good effect on your health 🔁 *healthy eating* 🔁 *She has a very healthy lifestyle.* (**saudável**)

heap /hiːp/ NOUN [plural heaps]
an untidy pile of things □ *I found a heap of dirty clothes at the top of the stairs.* 🔁 *His clothes were in a heap in the bottom of the wardrobe.* (**pilha**)

hear /hɪə(r)/ VERB [hears, hearing, heard]
1 to be aware of sounds through your ears □ *Can you hear that clicking noise?* □ *I heard the sound of an explosion.* □ *She screamed, but nobody heard her.* (**ouvir**)
2 to be told something □ **+ that** *I heard that she was unhappy in her job.* □ *The court heard that the men both used false passports.* □ **+ about** *Did you hear about Rob's accident?* (**ouvir**)
3 have heard of someone/something to know that someone or something exists □ *I'd never heard of him before.* (**ouvir falar de alguém**)
◆ PHRASAL VERB **hear from someone** to receive a letter, email, telephone call, etc. from someone □ *Have you heard from Joss recently?* (**ter notícias de alguém**)

> **THESAURUS:** If you hear something you are aware of sounds through your ears. If you listen to something, you pay attention to a sound so that you can hear it. If you overhear something, you hear something that someone says when they are not talking to you.

hearing /ˈhɪərɪŋ/ NOUN [plural hearings]
your ability to hear □ *My hearing was affected by the constant noise.* (**audição**)

heart /hɑːt/ NOUN [plural hearts]
1 the organ that sends blood around your body 🔁 *My heart was beating very fast.* 🔁 *He suffers from heart disease.* (**coração**)
2 the centre of something □ **+ of** *She lives in the heart of the city.* (**centro**)
3 the most important part of something □ **+ of** *Jealousy is at the heart of their problems.* 🔁 *I really tried to get to the heart of what was upsetting her.* (**centro**)
4 someone's feelings or character □ *She captured the hearts of the audience.* □ *Ken has a kind heart.* (**coração**)
5 a shape (♥) that represents the human heart and human love (**coração**)
6 hearts one of the four types of playing card, which have the symbol (♥) printed on them (**copas**)
◆ IDIOMS **know/learn something (off) by heart** to know or learn something so well that you do not have to read it □ *I learned the whole poem off by heart.* **not have the heart to do something** to be too kind to do something □ *I didn't have the heart to tell him his story was rubbish.* **someone's heart**

heart attack 157 **help**

sinks if someone's heart sinks, they are disappointed or expect that something bad will happen □ *My heart sank when I saw how dirty the holiday cottage was.*
→ L go to **break**¹ someone's heart

heart attack /'hɑːt əˌtæk/ NOUN [plural **heart attacks**] when someone's heart suddenly stops working □ *He died of a heart attack.* (**ataque cardíaco**)

heartbeat /'hɑːtbiːt/ NOUN [plural **heartbeats**] the regular sound or movement that your heart makes (**batimento cardíaco**)

heat¹ /hiːt/ NOUN [plural **heats**]
1 *no plural* the quality of being hot or how hot something is □ *The panels use heat from the sun.* □ *Turn up the heat until the soup is boiling.* (**calor**)
2 the heat very hot weather □ *I can't stand the heat in summer.* (**o calor**)
3 a game or a race to decide who goes on to the next stage of a competition □ *Ian won his heat and went through to the semi-final.* (**prova eliminatória**)

heat² /hiːt/ VERB [**heats, heating, heated**] to make something hot or hotter □ *We use solar energy to heat our water.* □ *Heat the oven to medium.* (**aquecer[-se]**)
◆ PHRASAL VERB **heat (something) up** to become hotter or to make something hotter □ *We heated up the soup over the fire.*

heater /'hiːtə(r)/ NOUN [plural **heaters**] a piece of equipment that heats water or a place □ *I'll turn this heater on.* (**aquecedor**)

heaven /'hevən/ NOUN, NO PLURAL in some religions, the place where God lives and where good people go when they die (**paraíso**)

heavily /'hevɪli/ ADVERB
1 a lot or to a large degree □ *The soldiers were heavily armed.* □ *His wife is heavily pregnant.* (**bem, muito**)
2 with a lot of force or weight □ *It was snowing heavily when we left.* □ *She fell heavily, twisting her ankle.* (**pesadamente**)

heavy /'hevi/ ADJECTIVE [**heavier, heaviest**]
1 something that is heavy weighs a lot □ *The bags were too heavy for me to carry.* (**pesado**)
2 if you say how heavy something is, you say how much it weighs □ *How heavy are these bricks?* (**pesado**)
3 large in amount or degree ▣ *heavy traffic* ▣ *heavy rain/snow* ▣ *There was heavy fighting in the region.* (**forte, abundante**)
4 a heavy smoker/drinker someone who smokes a lot/drinks a lot of alcohol (**muito**)

hectare /'hekteə(r)/ NOUN [plural **hectares**] a unit for measuring area equal to 10,000 square metres. This is often written **ha**. (**hectare**)

he'd /hiːd/ a short way to say and write he had or he would □ *He'd never been there before.* □ *He'd do it for me if I asked him.* (ver **have**)

hedge /hedʒ/ NOUN [plural **hedges**] a line of bushes or trees growing close together that separates one piece of land from another □ *A thick hedge surrounds the garden.* (**sebe**)

heel /hiːl/ NOUN [plural **heels**]
1 the back part of your foot □ *She was getting a blister on her heel.* (**calcanhar**)
2 the part of a shoe under the back of your foot ▣ *She was wearing high heels.* (**salto**)

height /haɪt/ NOUN [plural **heights**]
1 how tall or high someone or something is □ *He's of average height.* □ *I'd say the wall's about four metres in height.* (**altura**)
2 how far above the ground something is □ *We are now flying at a height of 11,000 metres.* (**altura**)

heir /eə(r)/ NOUN [plural **heirs**] the person who has a legal right to someone's money or property when they die □ *He is the heir to a large fortune.* (**herdeiro**)

held /held/ PAST TENSE AND PAST PARTICIPLE OF **hold¹** □ *She held my hand.* □ *We held the meeting in David's office.* (ver **hold¹**)

helicopter /'helɪkɒptə(r)/ NOUN [plural **helicopters**] a small aircraft without wings that is lifted into the air by long thin parts on top which turn round very fast (**helicóptero**)

he'll /hiːl/ a short way to say and write he will □ *He'll be here soon.* (ver **will**)

hell /hel/ NOUN, NO PLURAL
1 in some religions, the place where bad people go when they die (**inferno**)
2 a very unpleasant experience □ *The last few months of the relationship were hell.* (**inferno**)

hello /hə'ləʊ/ EXCLAMATION something you say when you meet someone or begin talking to someone on the telephone □ *Hello, Sophie. How are you?* □ *Hello, it's Mark.* (**olá, ei**)

helmet /'helmɪt/ NOUN [plural **helmets**] a hard hat worn to protect your head □ *a cycling helmet* □ *a fireman's helmet* (**capacete**)

help¹ /help/ VERB [**helps, helping, helped**]
1 to do something to make a situation or activity easier for someone □ + **to do something** *I helped him to find somewhere to stay.* □ *I find a warm bath helps to relax me.* □ + **with** *My Mum helped me with my homework.* (**ajudar**)
2 to make a situation better or easier □ *If you've got a cold, eating oranges might help.* □ *It helps if you put the heavier items at the bottom.* □ *I took some painkillers, but they didn't help much.* (**ajudar**)
3 can't help (doing) something if you can't help something, you cannot stop yourself from doing it or stop it happening □ *She couldn't help laughing when she saw his face.* (**deixar de, evitar**)

4 help yourself to take something without waiting for someone to give it to you □ *Help yourself to some food.* (**servir-se de**)

help² /help/ EXCLAMATION **Help!** used to shout for help in a serious situation (**socorro!**)

help³ /help/ NOUN [plural **helps**]
1 *no plural* when someone does something to make a situation or an activity easier for someone ⊞ *He needs help with his garden.* ⊞ *I was in debt, but I didn't know where to get help.* ⊞ *These children get extra help with their reading.* (**ajuda**)
2 someone or something that helps someone ⊞ *Thanks for the advice. It was a great help.* □ *I couldn't work out how to use the system, and the instructions weren't much help.* (**ajuda**)

helpful /ˈhelpfʊl/ ADJECTIVE
1 useful □ *helpful advice* (**útil**)
2 willing to help □ *There was a lot of tidying up, but the children were very helpful.* (**prestativo**)

helpless /ˈhelpləs/ ADJECTIVE not able to do anything for yourself, or to help other people in trouble □ *How could anyone rob a helpless old man?* (**desamparado**)

hen /hen/ NOUN [plural **hens**] a female chicken (**galinha**)

her¹ /hɜː(r)/ PRONOUN used as the object of a sentence to talk or write about a woman, girl or female animal that has already been mentioned □ *I'm looking for Mrs Peters. Have you seen her?* □ *I gave the letter to her.* (**ela, a**)

her² /hɜː(r)/ DETERMINER belonging to or to do with a woman, girl or female animal □ *Her hair is blonde.* □ *That's her problem, not mine.* (**seu, sua**)

herb /hɜːb/ NOUN [plural **herbs**] a plant that is used for giving flavour to food and for making medicines □ *herbs and spices* □ *a herb garden* (**erva**)

herd /hɜːd/ NOUN [plural **herds**] a large group of animals of one type that live as a group *a herd of cattle* (**rebanho, manada**)

here /hɪə(r)/ ADVERB
1 in or to this place □ *I like it here.* □ *Come here!* □ *You can leave your shoes here.* □ *He's American, but he's lived over here for years.* (**aqui**)
2 used to say that someone or something has arrived or has been found □ *Here's Tom at last.* □ *Here's the house we are looking for.* (**aí**)
3 used when you give someone something □ *Here, put on this jacket.* □ *Here you are – we saved some food for you.* (**aqui**)
4 here and there in a few different places □ *There were a few mistakes here and there.* (**aqui e ali**)

heritage /ˈherɪtɪdʒ/ NOUN, NO PLURAL the buildings, customs, culture, etc. of a country that are important because they have existed for a long time □ *Spain's cultural heritage* (**herança**)

hero /ˈhɪərəʊ/ NOUN [plural **heroes**]
1 someone who people admire because of the brave or difficult things they have done □ *Nelson Mandela is a hero to many of us.* (**herói**)
2 the most important male character in a story or film □ *The hero of the book is a New York detective.* (**herói**)

heroine /ˈherəʊɪn/ NOUN [plural **heroines**]
1 a woman or girl who people admire because of the brave or difficult things she has done (**heroína**)
2 the most important female character in a story or film (**heroína**)

hers /hɜːz/ PRONOUN used to talk or write about things belonging to or to do with a woman or girl that has already been mentioned □ *I gave Sandra my phone number and she gave me hers.* □ *'Was it your idea, or Ann's?'* *'It was hers.'* (**o seu, a sua**)

> Notice that there is no apostrophe between the **r** and the **s** in **hers**.

herself /hɜːˈself/ PRONOUN
1 the reflexive form of *her* □ *Did Barbara hurt herself when she fell down? She sang to herself as she worked.* (**ela mesma**)
2 used to show that she does something without any help from other people *She always answers every fan letter herself.* ⊞ *She's only 3 but she can get dressed all by herself.* (**ela mesma**)
3 used to emphasize the pronoun □ *I wanted to speak to Gina herself.* (**ela mesma**)
4 by herself not with or near other people □ *She always sits by herself.* (**sozinha**)

he's /hiːz/ a short way to say and write *he is* or *he has* □ *He's my brother.* □ *He's done all the work.*

hey /heɪ/ EXCLAMATION an word used to get someone's attention or show you are surprised □ *Hey, stop that!* □ *Hey, look at this!* (**ei**)

hi /haɪ/ EXCLAMATION hello □ *Hi, Charlotte!* □ *Hi, how are you?* (**oi**)

hide¹ /haɪd/ VERB [**hides, hiding, hid, hidden**]
1 to put or keep something or someone in a place where people cannot see or find them easily □ *I hid her presents under my bed.* □ *He kept his money hidden from his wife.* (**esconder[-se]**)
2 to go to a place where people cannot see you □ *Eva was hiding and the other children were looking for her.* □ *He hid behind a tree.* (**esconder[-se]**)
3 to not tell or show people your feelings or some information □ *Sarah didn't try to hide her disappointment at losing.* □ *I've got nothing to hide.* (**esconder**)

> **THESAURUS:** If you **hide** something, you put or keep something in a place where people cannot find it easily. If you **bury** something, you put it in the ground and cover it up. If you **disguise** something or someone, you make them look like something else so that people will not recognize them. If you **cover** something, you put something over something else in order to hide it or protect it.

hide² /haɪd/ NOUN [plural **hides**] the skin of an animal (**pele, couro**)

hiding /'haɪdɪŋ/ NOUN, NO PLURAL when someone stays in a secret place or changes their appearance so that no one will find them 🔁 *The ex-spy is believed to be in hiding in London.* 🔁 *He knew he would be arrested so he went into hiding.* (**esconderijo**)

high¹ /haɪ/ ADJECTIVE [higher, highest]

1 a large distance above the ground □ *The apples were too high to reach.* □ *It's best to keep medicines on a high shelf.* (**alto**)
2 a long distance from the bottom to the top □ *It is a very high building.* □ *They built a high wall around the house.* (**alto**)
3 having a particular height □ *The fence is 4 metres high.* □ *How high is Snowdon?* (**de altura**)
4 large in amount or level 🔁 *The temperature was unusually high.* 🔁 *We drove at high speed through the town.* 🔁 *We were shocked at the high cost of housing.* 🔁 *They found high levels of pollution in the area.* (**alto**)
5 a high sound or musical note is near the top of the range of sounds □ *We could hear the children's high voices.* (**altos níveis**)

> Remember that people who are big in height are described as **tall** and not **high**:
> ✓ *Her father is very tall.*
> ✗ *Her father is very high.*

high² /haɪ/ ADVERB [higher, highest]

1 at or to a large distance above the ground □ *She threw the ball high in the air.* □ *Dirty clothes were piled high in her bedroom.* □ *The village is located high above the sea.* (**alto**)
2 at or to a large amount or level □ *The temperature rose higher and higher.* □ *Prices remain high.* (**alto**)

highlight¹ /'haɪlaɪt/ VERB [**highlights, highlighting, highlighted**] to emphasize something □ *These figures highlight a growing problem.* (**realçar, ressaltar**)

highlight² /'haɪlaɪt/ NOUN [plural **highlights**] the best part of an event or period of time □ *His singing was the highlight of the concert.* (**ponto culminante, ponto alto**)

highly /'haɪli/ ADVERB very □ *highly qualified teachers* □ *This seems highly unlikely.* (**altamente, muito**)

high school /'haɪˌskuːl/ NOUN [plural **high schools**] in the US, a school for children aged between 14 and 18 (**escola secundária**)

high street /'haɪˌstriːt/ NOUN [plural **high streets**] the main street of a town, where the shops and banks are □ *Most of the high street banks will be raising their interest rates.* (**rua principal**)

high-tech /ˌhaɪ'tek/ ADJECTIVE using the most modern technology □ *high-tech security equipment* □ *high-tech computer graphics* (**high-tech**)

highway /'haɪweɪ/ NOUN [plural **highways**] a US word for a road between cities and towns (**estrada**)

hijack /'haɪdʒæk/ VERB [**hijacks, hijacking, hijacked**] to take control of an aeroplane by force □ *Two students hijacked the plane in Thailand.* (**sequestrar**)

hijacker /'haɪdʒækə(r)/ NOUN [plural **hijackers**] someone who takes control of an aeroplane by force □ *The hijackers were arrested by Australian police.* (**sequestrador**)

hike /haɪk/ NOUN [plural **hikes**] a long walk in the countryside (**caminhada**)

hill /hɪl/ NOUN [plural hills] a raised or high area of land, smaller than a mountain □ *We went walking in the Tuscan hills.* (**colina**)

◆ IDIOM **over the hill** if someone is over the hill, they are too old to do something

hilly /'hɪli/ ADJECTIVE [**hillier, hilliest**] a hilly area has a lot of hills (**montanhoso**)

him /hɪm/ PRONOUN used as the object of a sentence to talk or write about a man, boy or male animal that has already been mentioned □ *I'm looking for Mr Peters. Have you seen him anywhere?* □ *She threw the book at him.* (**ele, o**)

himself /hɪm'self/ PRONOUN

1 the reflexive form of *him* □ *He poked himself in the eye by mistake.* □ *The old man was muttering to himself.* (**mesmo, se**)
2 used to show that he does something without any help from other people □ *I was surprised he did all the cooking himself.* 🔁 *Jack can tie his shoelaces all by himself already.* (**ele mesmo, sozinho**)
3 used to emphasize the pronoun *him* □ *He's never been to London himself.* (**sozinho**)
4 by himself not with or near other people □ *He stood by himself in a corner.* (**sozinho**)

Hindu¹ /'hɪnduː/ NOUN [plural Hindus] a person whose religion is Hinduism (**hindu**)

Hindu² /'hɪnduː/ ADJECTIVE to do with Hinduism □ *The main Hindu gods are Brahma, Vishnu and Shiva.* (**hindus**)

Hinduism /'hɪnduːɪzəm/ NOUN, NO PLURAL a religion of India and parts of South East Asia, which has many gods and teaches that after people die they will return to life in another body (**hinduísmo**)

hint¹ /hɪnt/ NOUN [plural hints]

1 a helpful piece of advice □ *Can you give me any hints on how to learn vocabulary?* (**dica**)
2 something that suggests what you think or want but not in a direct way 🔁 *She dropped a hint that something exciting was about to happen.* 🔁 *He kept yawning but no one took the hint and went home.* (**dica, pista**)

> THESAURUS: A **hint** or a **tip** is a helpful piece of advice. A **suggestion** is a more general word for an idea that you mention. A **clue** is a piece of information that helps to solve a problem or a crime.

hint² /hɪnt/ VERB [hints, hinting, hinted] to suggest something in a way that is not clear or direct □ *Laura hinted that she might be leaving.* (**insinuar**)

hip /hɪp/ NOUN [plural hips] each of the two parts at the side of your body, below your waist and above your leg □ *Gran fell and broke her hip.* (**quadril**)

hip-hop /'hɪphɒp/ NOUN, NO PLURAL a type of pop music in which the words are about social problems and are spoken not sung □ *hip-hop groups* (**hip hop**)

hippopotamus /ˌhɪpə'pɒtəməs/ NOUN [plural **hippopotamuses** or **hippopotami**] a large African animal with a heavy body, small ears and short legs, that lives near or in rivers (**hipopótamo**)

hire¹ /'haɪə(r)/ VERB [hires, hiring, hired]
1 to pay to use something for a period of time, especially a short period, and then return it □ *We hired bikes while we were on holiday.* (**alugar**)
2 to begin to employ someone □ *I've decided to hire a cleaner.* (**contratar**)

▸ Notice (sense 1) that in British English you **hire** things usually for a short time, only paying once to use them. You **rent**, usually for a longer period, a house or an office, etc., paying every month or many times. In American English you always **rent** things. The verb **hire** is not used.

hire² /'haɪə(r)/ NOUN, NO PLURAL when you pay to use something for a period of time □ *The holiday price includes the hire of a car.* 🔹 *There are boats for hire on the lake.* (**aluguel**)

his¹ /hɪz/ DETERMINER belonging to or to do with to him □ *Julian has left his coat behind.* □ *Blame Harry. It was his idea.* (**seu, sua**)

his² /hɪz/ PRONOUN used to talk or write about things belonging to or to do with to a man, boy or male animal that has already been mentioned □ *I didn't have an umbrella so Grandad lent me his.* (**seu, sua**)

hiss¹ /hɪs/ VERB [hisses, hissing, hissed] to make a noise like a long 's' sound □ *a hissing snake* (**seu, sua**)

hiss² /hɪs/ NOUN [plural hisses] a sound like that made by a snake □ *We could hear the hiss of gas escaping from the pipe.* (**silvo, assobio**)

historic /hɪ'stɒrɪk/ ADJECTIVE important in history □ *a historic victory* (**histórico**)

historical /hɪ'stɒrɪkəl/ ADJECTIVE to do with history □ *historical records* (**histórico**)

▸ Notice the difference between **historic** and **historical**. **Historic** means 'important in history'. **Historical** means 'to do with history': □ *This was a historic moment.* □ *She writes historical novels.*

history /'hɪstəri/ NOUN [plural histories] all the things that happened in the past, or the study of things that happened in the past □ *local history* □ *modern European history* □ *He studied history at university.* □ *history books* (**história**)

hit¹ /hɪt/ VERB [hits, hitting, hit] to touch against someone or something with force □ *Stop hitting your brother!* □ *The plane hit the ground and burst into flames.* □ *I hit my head on the cupboard door.* □ *She hit him with a baseball bat.* □ *Storms hit the west coast last night.* (**bater**)

hit² /hɪt/ NOUN [plural hits]
1 something or someone that is very popular □ *The show was an instant hit.* □ *He's a big hit with the old ladies.* (**sucesso**)
2 when you touch against something with force □ *I got a hit on my arm.* (**golpe**)

HIV /ˌeɪtʃaɪ'viː/ ABBREVIATION human immunodeficiency virus; the virus that causes the disease AIDS (**HIV**)

hobby /'hɒbɪ/ NOUN [plural hobbies] something you like doing in your free time 🔹 *My Dad's favourite hobby is birdwatching.* 🔹 *It's my new hobby.* 🔹 *She didn't really have any hobbies.* (**passatempo**)

hockey /'hɒkɪ/ NOUN, NO PLURAL a game in which two teams use curved sticks to hit a ball into a net 🔹 *We play hockey at school.* 🔹 *a hockey stick* □ *a hockey team* (**hóquei**)

hold¹ /həʊld/ VERB [holds, holding, held]
1 to have something in your hand or hands □ *He was holding a big wooden box.* 🔹 *Hold tight – we're going over some rough ground.* (**segurar**)
2 to support something or to stop something moving □ *The pieces of wood are held together with nails.* 🔹 *Use glue to hold the cardboard in place.* (**segurar**)
3 to organize an event □ *We held the meeting in our office.* 🔹 *The general has promised to hold an election.* (**realizar**)
4 to have space for something □ *The room holds 300 people.* (**acomodar**)
5 to contain something □ *This rack holds my wine collection.* (**conter**)
6 to have a particular job or position in an organization □ *She holds the post of director.* (**ocupar**)
7 hold your breath to deliberately not breathe (**prender a respiração**)
8 hold hands to curve your hand around someone else's hand (**apertar a mão**)

◆ PHRASAL VERBS **hold something/someone back** to stop someone or something making progress □ *A lack of formal education did not hold her back.* **hold on 1** to hold something tightly □ *Hold on tight! We're coming to get you.* **2** to wait □ *Hold on a minute – I just need to check my email.* **hold someone/something up** to make something or someone slow or late □ *We got held up by the* *traffic.* □ *All these regulations are holding up progress.*

hold² /həʊld/ NOUN [plural holds]

1 when you hold something, or the way something is held 🔹 *I got hold of the handle and pulled it hard.* 🔹 *Try to catch hold of the rope.* 🔹 *My hands were so wet, I couldn't keep hold of the rail.* (**segurar, agarrar-se a**)
2 get hold of something to manage to get some thing □ *Do you know where I can get hold of some cheap bricks?* (**conseguir algo**)
3 get hold of someone to manage to speak to someone □ *I've been trying to get hold of her all morning.* (**contatar alguém**)
4 the place in a ship or an aeroplane where goods or bags are stored (**porão**)

hole /həʊl/ NOUN [plural holes]
a space in the surface of something □ + **in** *He had a hole in his sock.* □ *She drilled a hole in the wall.* (**buraco**)

> **THESAURUS:** Hole is a general word. A **tear** is a hole in something that has been pulled apart. We usually use **tear** to talk about thin things like paper or material. A **slot** is a small narrow hole in something, especially one where you put coins or bank cards. A **crack** is a narrow break in something. If a plate has a **crack** in it, it may still be in one piece, but it has a narrow break.

holiday /ˈhɒlɪdeɪ/ NOUN [plural holidays]

1 a time when you do not have to work or go to school 🔹 *What are you doing in the summer holidays?* 🔹 *The museum is very busy during school holidays.* (**férias**)
2 on holiday if you are on holiday, you are not working or not at school for a period □ *I'm on holiday next week.* (**de férias**)
3 a period of time when you stay in a different place to enjoy yourself 🔹 *We're going on holiday next week.* □ *a skiing holiday* 🔹 *Spain is a popular holiday destination for British travellers.* (**férias**)

> The word **holiday** is used by British speakers of English. North American speakers of English use the word **vacation**.

hollow /ˈhɒləʊ/ ADJECTIVE [hollower, hollowest]
having an empty space inside □ *hollow chocolate eggs* □ *a hollow tube* (**oco**)

holy /ˈhəʊli/ ADJECTIVE [holier, holiest]

1 to do with God or religion □ *The Koran is the Muslim holy book.* □ *The Golden Temple is a holy site in Punjab.* (**sagrado**)
2 having strong religious feelings □ *a holy man* (**santo**)

home¹ /həʊm/ NOUN [plural homes]

1 the place where you live or where you lived when you were a child □ *I left my watch at home.* 🔹 *He left home at the age of twenty.* 🔹 *Cambridge is my home town.* (**lar, casa**)
2 a place where people or animals who need care live □ *a children's home* □ *an old people's home*
♦ IDIOM **be/feel at home** to be very relaxed and confident in a place

home² /həʊm/ ADVERB

1 to the place where you live 🔹 *It's time to go home.* 🔹 *Thousands of soldiers are returning home this week.* □ *I met Freddie on my way home.* (**para casa**)
2 at the place where you live □ *Will you be home tomorrow?* (**em casa**)

> Notice that you **go home** or **get home**. You do not 'go to home' or 'get to home':
> ✓ *I usually get home late.*
> ✗ *I usually get to home late.*

homeless¹ /ˈhəʊmləs/ ADJECTIVE having nowhere to live □ *Thousands of people have been made homeless by the earthquake.* (**sem lar**)
homeless² /ˈhəʊmləs/ NOUN **the homeless** people who have nowhere to live □ *The charity provides meals for the homeless.* (**sem lar**)
homemade /ˌhəʊmˈmeɪd/ ADJECTIVE made in someone's home and not in a factory □ *homemade cakes* (**feito em casa**)

homework /ˈhəʊmwɜːk/ NOUN, NO PLURAL
school work that you have to do at home 🔹 *Have you done your maths homework yet?* 🔹 *The teacher gives us too much homework.* (**lição de casa**)

homicide /ˈhɒmɪsaɪd/ NOUN [plural homicides] a US or legal word for **murder** (= the crime of killing someone) (**homicídio**)

homosexual¹ /ˌhɒməˈsekʃuəl/ ADJECTIVE
attracted to people of the same sex (**homossexual**)

homosexual² /ˌhɒməˈsekʃuəl/ NOUN [plural homosexuals]
someone who is attracted to people of the same sex (**homossexual**)

honest /ˈɒnɪst/ ADJECTIVE

1 an honest person can be trusted and does not lie, cheat or steal □ *You can trust her – she's very honest.* (**honesto**)
2 to be honest used before you say what you really think □ *To be honest, I don't really want to go.* (**para ser honesto**)

honestly /ˈɒnɪstli/ ADVERB

1 in an honest way □ *Martin told me honestly what he thought.* □ *He behaved very honestly and handed the money in to the police.* (**honestamente**)
2 used for emphasizing that what you are saying is true despite the fact that it is surprising □ *I honestly didn't realize you were all waiting for me.* (**honestamente**)
3 something you say to show that you are annoyed □ *Honestly, I wish you'd listen to what I tell you.* (**francamente**)

honesty /ˈɒnɪsti/ NOUN, NO PLURAL
being honest □ *Thanks for telling me. I appreciate your honesty.* (**honestidade**)

honey

honey /'hʌnɪ/ NOUN, NO PLURAL a sweet food that bees make (mel)

honeymoon /'hʌnɪmuːn/ NOUN [plural honeymoons]
a holiday that a man and woman go on just after their wedding □ *Rob and Sarah went to Mexico for their honeymoon.* (lua de mel)

honor /'ɒnə(r)/ NOUN [plural honors] the US spelling of **honour** (honra)

honour

honour /'ɒnə(r)/ NOUN [plural honours]
1 *no plural* the respect that people have for someone who has behaved well or achieved something that people admire □ *I am fighting for my family's honour.* (honra)
2 something that makes you proud □ *It was an honour to meet him.* □ *It is a great honour to be here today.* (honra)
3 in someone's honour/in honour of someone in order to show respect to someone □ *I wrote the book in honour of my father.* (em homenagem)

hood /hʊd/ NOUN [plural hoods]
1 the part of a coat, etc. which you can pull up to cover the back of your head (capuz)
2 the US word for **bonnet** (= part of a car) (capô)

hook¹ /hʊk/ NOUN [plural hooks]
1 a bent piece of metal or plastic that you hang things on □ *Hang your coats on the hook.* (gancho)
2 a bent piece of metal used for catching fish (anzol)
3 off the hook if a telephone is off the hook, the part you speak into has not been put back correctly, so nobody can call you (fora de problema)

hook² /hʊk/ VERB [hooks, hooking, hooked] to hang or catch something using a hook (enganchar)

hoop /huːp/ NOUN [plural hoops] a ring of metal, plastic or wood (aro)

Hoover /'huːvə(r)/ NOUN [plural Hoovers] a machine that cleans floors by sucking up small bits. A trademark. (aspirador)

hoover /'huːvə(r)/ VERB [hoovers, hoovering, hoovered] to clean a floor using a machine that sucks up small bits □ *He hoovered up the salt he'd spilt.* (passar aspirador)

hop¹ /hɒp/ VERB [hops, hopping, hopped]
1 to jump on one leg (pular num pé só)
2 if a bird or animal hops, it moves by jumping □ *A little bird hopped onto the arm of the chair.* (saltitar)

hop² /hɒp/ NOUN [plural hops] a jump, especially on one leg (pulo num pé só)

hope¹

hope¹ /həʊp/ VERB [hopes, hoping, hoped] to think that something is possible and to wish for it to happen or be true □ **+ that** *I hope that David manages to get home for Christmas.* □ **+to do something** *I hope to start my own business next year.* □ **+ for** *I'm hoping for a new bike for my birthday.* ▣ *'Will the bank still be open?' 'I hope so!'* ▣ *'Is he coming with us?' 'I hope not.'* (esperar)

hope²

hope² /həʊp/ NOUN [plural hopes]
1 *no plural* a feeling that the future will be good or that something good will happen ▣ *The new centre offers hope to people with cancer.* ▣ *We knew it would be difficult to succeed, but we never lost hope.* (esperança)
2 something that you wish will happen or be true □ *My hope is that he will agree to lend us the money.* ▣ *News of the president's interest really raised our hopes.* (esperança)
3 something that gives you a chance of success ▣ *Going to court is our only hope of getting justice.* ▣ *There is little hope of finishing the work on time.* (esperança)
4 in the hope of something in order to try to get something or make something happen □ *I left work early in the hope of meeting Tom.* (na esperança de)

hopeful /'həʊpfʊl/ ADJECTIVE feeling that the future will be good or that something good will happen □ *I'm very hopeful that we can find a suitable house.* (esperançoso)
• **hopefully** /'həʊpfʊli/ ADVERB
1 used to say that you hope something will happen □ *Hopefully she'll have forgotten about our homework.* (tomara que)
2 showing hope □ *'Is there any more?' she asked hopefully.* (esperançosamente)

hopeless /'həʊplɪs/ ADJECTIVE
1 without any hope of succeeding □ *We tried to put out the flames, but it was hopeless.* (inútil)
2 an informal word meaning very bad □ *Chris was hopeless in goal.* (sofrível)
• **hopelessly** /'həʊplɪsli/ ADVERB extremely ▣ *We got hopelessly lost.* (irremediavelmente)

horizon /hə'raɪzən/ NOUN **the horizon** the line where the land and sky seem to meet (horizonte)

horizontal

horizontal /ˌhɒrɪ'zɒntəl/ ADJECTIVE straight and parallel to the ground ▣ *a horizontal line* □ *She was wearing a T-shirt with horizontal stripes.* (horizontal)

hormone /'hɔːməʊn/ NOUN [plural hormones] a chemical that your body makes, which controls things such as how the body grows. A biology word. (hormônio)

horn

horn /hɔːn/ NOUN [plural horns]
1 one of the two pointed things made of bone on the heads of some animals, such as a goat □ *a bull's horns* (chifre)
2 a device in a vehicle that you press to make a loud noise ▣ *He heard a car horn outside.* ▣ *Drivers sounded their horns as the men ran into the road.* (buzina)
3 a musical instrument made of metal that you blow into □ *the French horn* (corneta)

horrible

horrible /'hɒrəbəl/ ADJECTIVE very unpleasant □ *It was a horrible feeling to think I wouldn't see him again.* □ *a horrible situation* □ *Why are you being so horrible to everyone?* (horrível)

horrific /hɒ'rɪfɪk/ ADJECTIVE extremely bad, often involving death or injuries □ *a horrific car crash* □ *horrific scenes of violence* (horroroso)

horrified /'hɒrɪfaɪd/ ADJECTIVE extremely shocked and upset □ *He was horrified at the suggestion that he had cheated.* (horrorizar)

horrify

horrify /ˈhɒrɪfaɪ/ VERB [horrifies, horrifying, horrified] to shock and upset someone □ *It's a story that will horrify any parent.* (horrorizar, amedrontar)

horror¹ /ˈhɒrə(r)/ NOUN [plural horrors] a strong feeling of shock and upset □ *I watched in horror as the car burst into flames.* (horror)

horror² /ˈhɒrə(r)/ ADJECTIVE a horror film or story is very frightening and often unpleasant (terror)

horse /hɔːs/ NOUN [plural horses] a large animal which people ride or use for pulling things ⊞ *Have you ever ridden a horse?* ⊞ *The horse galloped (= ran) across the field.* (cavalo)

hose /həʊz/ NOUN [plural hoses] a long tube used for putting water on fires or gardens (mangueira)

hospital /ˈhɒspɪtəl/ NOUN [plural hospitals] a building where people go for medical treatment when they are ill or injured □ *Jane is in hospital having an operation.* ⊞ *She was taken to hospital after being stabbed.* ⊞ *He's recovered and is coming out of hospital tomorrow.* □ *a psychiatric hospital* ⊞ *Many hospital wards (= rooms where people stay) have been closed.* (hospital)

> **THESAURUS:** A **doctor** is a person who treats people when they are ill. **Doctors** may work in a hospital or in a **surgery**. A **nurse** is a person who looks after people when they are ill, especially in a hospital. A **surgeon** is a doctor who does operations. A **patient** is someone who is being treated by a doctor or a nurse.

hospitality /ˌhɒspɪˈtælɪti/ NOUN, NO PLURAL being friendly to visitors, liking to provide food and a pleasant place to stay □ *The hotel is known for its warm hospitality.* (hospitalidade)

host /həʊst/ NOUN [plural hosts] the person at a party or meal who has invited you and arranged everything (anfitrião)

hostage /ˈhɒstɪdʒ/ NOUN [plural hostages] someone who is kept as a prisoner until the people holding them get what they want ⊞ *He was taken hostage by a group of militants.* (refém)

hostel /ˈhɒstəl/ NOUN [plural hostels] a cheap place for people to stay □ *a youth hostel* □ *He was staying in a hostel for homeless people.* (albergue, alojamento)

hostile /ˈhɒstaɪl/ ADJECTIVE unfriendly or showing strong dislike □ *a hostile reaction* □ *Hostile crowds booed at the Prime Minister.* (hostil)

hot /hɒt/ ADJECTIVE [hotter, hottest]
1 having a high temperature □ *Don't touch the oven. It's very hot.* □ *Is there any hot water left?* □ *It was a very hot summer.* ⊞ *It was a boiling hot day.* (quente)
2 spicy □ *hot curries* (picante)

hotel /həʊˈtel/ NOUN [plural hotels] a building that you pay to stay in when you are travelling or on holiday ⊞ *We stayed in a five-star hotel.*

⊞ *Our hotel room didn't even have a television.*
⊞ *Hotel guests have free use of the swimming pool.* (hotel)

hound /haʊnd/ NOUN [plural hounds] a dog used for hunting (cão de caça)

hour /ˈaʊə(r)/ NOUN [plural hours]
1 a period of time that lasts 60 minutes. There are 24 hours in one day □ *Each lesson lasts an hour.* □ *An hour later, they had all gone.* □ *I do an hour's exercise every day.* ⊞ *I'll be about half an hour.* (hora)
2 the period of time when something happens □ *What hours do you work?* ⊞ *Our opening hours are 9–5.* ⊞ *Shall we meet up in the lunch hour?* (hora)
3 hours an informal word meaning a long time ⊞ *We spent hours talking on the phone.* (horas)

house /haʊs/ NOUN [plural houses] a building in which people, especially one family, live □ *Our house is the one with the yellow door.* ⊞ *We moved house last year.* (casa)

household /ˈhaʊshəʊld/ NOUN [plural households] all the people who live in the same house □ *Most UK households have access to the Internet.* (lar)

housewife /ˈhaʊswaɪf/ NOUN [plural housewives] a woman who stays at home to look after her family and house, and does not have a paid job □ *She tried to be the perfect housewife.* (dona de casa)

housework /ˈhaʊswɜːk/ NOUN, NO PLURAL the work you do to keep your house clean and tidy ⊞ *She hated doing the housework.* (serviço doméstico)

> Remember that **housework** is not used in the plural:
> ✓ *Who does most of the housework?*
> ✗ *Who does most of the houseworks?*

hover /ˈhɒvə(r)/ VERB [hovers, hovering, hovered] to stay still in the air □ *Police helicopters hovered overhead.* (pairar)

hovercraft /ˈhɒvəkrɑːft/ NOUN [plural hovercrafts] a vehicle that travels across water or land, and has a cushion (= soft bag) of air under it (hovercraft)

how /haʊ/ ADVERB

1 used for asking or talking about the way something is done □ + **to do something** I'll show you how to tie a knot. □ How will we get there? □ Do you know how to turn the oven on? (como)
2 used for asking or talking about size, amount, level or age □ I don't know how old Maurice is exactly. □ How strong do you like your tea? 🔊 How much is that DVD player? 🔊 How many brothers and sisters have you got? (quanto)
3 used for asking or talking about what something is like or what form or condition it is in □ How do you want this money – cash or cheque? □ How's work? □ How's the new extension going? (como)
4 used for asking or talking about someone's health 🔊 Hello, how are you today? □ How's your leg now? (como)
5 How about ...? used for making a suggestion □ How about asking the children to help? (que tal)
6 used to emphasize an adjective or an adverb □ How odd that she didn't phone. □ He died? Oh, how sad. (que)

> Remember that **how** is not used with **like** to ask someone to describe someone or something. The correct phrase for this is **what is someone/something like?**:
> ✓ What is your new teacher like?
> ✗ How is your new teacher like?

however /haʊˈevə(r)/ CONJUNCTION, ADVERB

1 used for saying that something does not affect a situation □ However hard he tried, he couldn't do it. 🔊 She wanted to travel to Australia however much it cost. □ Your donation, however small, will make an important difference. (por mais que)
2 despite what has just been said □ The business had been successful. Over the past few years, however, sales had started to fall. □ People were saying that the school was going to close. However, the school denied the rumours. (no entanto)

howl[1] /haʊl/ VERB [howls, howling, howled]

1 if a dog howls, it makes a long, high noise (uivar)
2 if the wind howls, it makes a lot of noise □ The wind howled in off the sea. (uivar)

howl[2] /haʊl/ NOUN [plural **howls**] a long, loud sound made by a dog or similar animal (uivo)

HQ /ˌeɪtʃˈkjuː/ ABBREVIATION **headquarters** (QG)

hug[1] /hʌɡ/ VERB [hugs, hugging, hugged] to put your arms around someone and hold them □ My mother was always hugging and kissing us. □ Everyone was crying and hugging each other. (abraçar)

hug[2] /hʌɡ/ NOUN [plural **hugs**] the action of putting your arms around someone and holding them 🔊 I could see she was upset so I gave her a hug. (abraço)

huge /hjuːdʒ/ ADJECTIVE very big □ The school has spent a huge amount of money on the project. □ The film was a huge success. □ I'm a huge fan of his music. □ The house was huge. (enorme)

hum /hʌm/ VERB [hums, humming, hummed]

1 to sing with your mouth closed □ She hummed quietly to herself as she worked. (cantarolar)
2 to make a low continuous noise like someone humming □ He turned the key and the engine hummed into life. (zumbir)

human[1] /ˈhjuːmən/ ADJECTIVE to do with people and the way that people behave 🔊 They appeared to have no respect for human life. 🔊 Everyone wants to win: it's human nature. 🔊 The human brain can process huge amounts of information. (humano)

human[2] /ˈhjuːmən/ or **human being** /ˌhjuːmən ˈbiːɪŋ/ NOUN [plural **humans** or **human beings**] a person □ Is there a vaccine to protect humans from the disease? □ Technology has enabled human beings to survive longer. (ser humano)

humanity /hjuːˈmænətɪ/ NOUN, NO PLURAL all the people in the world □ We must act now to save humanity. (humanidade)

human rights /ˌhjuːmən ˈraɪts/ PLURAL NOUN basic rights such as freedom and fair treatment, especially by a government □ The organization promotes human rights for all. (direitos humanos)

humble /ˈhʌmbəl/ ADJECTIVE [humbler, humblest]

1 not believing you are important (humilde)
2 having a low social position □ He comes from a humble background. (humilde)

humiliate /hjuːˈmɪlɪeɪt/ VERB [humiliates, humiliating, humiliated] to make someone feel stupid or ashamed □ His wife accused him of humiliating her in public. (humilhar)

humorous /ˈhjuːmərəs/ ADJECTIVE funny 🔊 He told us a humorous story about a man on his wedding day. 🔊 The President made a humorous remark. (humorístico)

humour /ˈhjuːmə(r)/ NOUN, NO PLURAL

1 the quality that makes something funny □ She suddenly saw the humour in the situation and laughed loudly. (cômico)
2 the ability to know when something is funny, or to say things that make people laugh □ He loved her for her humour and her quiet determination. 🔊 We share the same sense of humour. (humor)

hundred /ˈhʌndrəd/ NUMBER [plural **hundreds**]

1 the number 100 (cem)
2 hundreds a large number. An informal word □ + **of** There were hundreds of people queuing for tickets. (centena)

hundredth[1] /ˈhʌndrədθ/ NUMBER 100th written as a word (centésimo)

hundredth[2] /ˈhʌndrədθ/ NOUN [plural **hundredths**] 1/100; one of a hundred equal parts of some thing □ He lost the race by two hundredths of a second. (centésimo)

hung /hʌŋ/ PAST TENSE AND PAST PARTICIPLE OF **hang** (ver **hang**)

hunger /ˈhʌŋɡə(r)/ NOUN, NO PLURAL

1 a feeling that you want to eat □ It seemed that nothing would satisfy his hunger. (fome)
2 not having enough food □ These children are dying of hunger. (fome)

hungry /'hʌŋgri/ ADJECTIVE [hungrier, hungriest] having a feeling of wanting to eat ▫ *The children were starting to get hungry.* (**faminto, esfomeado**)

hunt /hʌnt/ VERB [hunts, hunting, hunted]
1 to chase and kill animals for food or for sport ▫ *The men hunt seals and the women fish.* ▫ *+ for They were out hunting for rabbits.* (**caçar**)
2 to try to find someone or something ▫ *+ for More than 40 officers are hunting for the killer.* ▫ *Investigators are hunting for more clues.* (**caçar**)

hunter /'hʌntə(r)/ NOUN [plural **hunters**] a person or animal that hunts (**caçador**)

hurdle /'hɜːdəl/ NOUN [plural **hurdles**] a problem that needs to be solved in order to make progress 🔁 *Finding enough money was a major hurdle for our business.* 🔁 *He had to face many hurdles in his career.* (**obstáculo**)

hurricane /'hʌrɪkən/ NOUN [plural **hurricanes**] a storm with very strong winds (**furacão**)

hurry¹ /'hʌri/ VERB [hurries, hurrying, hurried]
1 to go somewhere quickly ▫ *She turned and hurried back along the path.* ▫ *The streets were full of people hurrying home to their families.* (**apressar[-se]**)
2 to do something more quickly ▫ *You'll have to hurry if you want to leave at six.* (**apressar[-se]**)
♦ PHRASAL VERB **hurry up** to start moving somewhere or doing something more quickly ▫ *Hurry up! We're going to be late.* ▫ *I wish he'd hurry up in the bathroom.* (**apressar[-se]**)

hurry² /'hʌri/ NOUN, NO PLURAL
1 in a hurry doing something or going somewhere quickly, because you do not have much time ▫ *We had to finish the job in a hurry.* ▫ *I can't talk now – I'm in a hurry.* (**apressadamente, apressado**)
2 there's no hurry used for telling someone that they do not need to do something quickly because you have a lot of time ▫ *Call me back when you're ready; there's no hurry.* (**pressa**)

hurt¹ /hɜːt/ VERB [hurts, hurting, hurt]
1 to cause pain or injury to someone ▫ *She fell and hurt her ankle.* ▫ *Will the injection hurt?* (**ferir, machucar**)
2 to be painful ▫ *My shoulder hurts.* (**doer**)
3 to make someone feel upset ▫ *The truth can hurt sometimes.* ▫ *His criticism really hurt her.* (**ferir, magoar**)
♦ IDIOM **hurt someone's feelings** to make someone feel upset ▫ *If you don't visit her, you'll hurt her feelings.*

hurt² /hɜːt/ ADJECTIVE
1 injured 🔁 *Be careful – someone could get hurt.* (**ferido**)
2 upset 🔁 *I was deeply hurt by his lack of appreciation.* (**ferido, machucado**)

husband /'hʌzbənd/ NOUN [plural **husbands**] the man that a woman is married to ▫ *Her husband died five years ago.* (**marido**)

husky¹ /'hʌski/ ADJECTIVE [huskier, huskiest] a husky voice is deep and rough (**rouco**)
husky² /'hʌski/ NOUN [plural **huskies**] a type of large dog that is used to pull heavy things over snow (**cão esquimó de puxar trenós**)

hut /hʌt/ NOUN [plural **huts**] a small, simple building made of wood, mud or metal (**cabana**)

hydrofoil /'haɪdrəfɔɪl/ NOUN [plural **hydrofoils**] a type of boat that rises slightly above the surface of the water when it is moving fast (**hidrofólio**)

hydrogen /'haɪdrədʒən/ NOUN, NO PLURAL the lightest gas that exists, which combines with oxygen to make water. A chemistry word. (**hidrogênio**)

hygiene /'haɪdʒiːn/ NOUN, NO PLURAL keeping yourself and the things around you clean, so that you stay healthy ▫ *The best way to avoid infection is to practise good hygiene.* 🔁 *Poor food hygiene can cause disease.* (**higiene**)

hymn /hɪm/ NOUN [plural **hymns**] a song sung by Christians to praise God (**hino**)

hyphen /'haɪfən/ NOUN [plural **hyphens**] the short line (-) used for joining two words together, or for showing that a word has been divided and part of it is on the next line (**hífen**)

I i

I¹ or **i** /aɪ/ the ninth letter of the alphabet (**a nona letra do alfabeto**)

I² /aɪ/ PRONOUN used to talk or write about yourself ▫ *I live near Edinburgh.* ▫ *I didn't forget your birthday, did I?* (**eu**)

ice /aɪs/ NOUN, NO PLURAL frozen water ▫ *The ice melted and the water began to rise.* ▫ *Her hand felt like a block of ice.* (**gelo**)

iceberg /ˈaɪsbɜːɡ/ NOUN [plural **icebergs**] a large mass of ice floating in the sea (**iceberg**)

ice cream /ˌaɪs ˈkriːm/ NOUN [plural **ice creams**]
1 *no plural* a sweet frozen food made from milk or cream ▫ *I'll have some strawberry ice cream, please.* (**sorvete**)
2 an amount of ice cream for one person ▫ *Would you like an ice cream?* (**sorvete**)

ice hockey /ˈaɪs ˌhɒki/ NOUN, NO PLURAL a sport played on ice in which two teams use curved sticks to try to hit a small round object into a net (**ícone**)

icon /ˈaɪkɒn/ NOUN [plural **icons**] a small symbol on a computer screen that represents a program or a file. A computing word. ▫ *Click on the browser icon on your desktop.* (**ícone**)

icy /ˈaɪsi/ ADJECTIVE [**icier, iciest**]
1 covered with ice ▫ *Drivers lost control of their cars on the icy roads.* (**gelado**)
2 extremely cold ▫ *An icy wind was blowing.* ▫ *She threw off her jacket and jumped into the icy water.* (**gelado**)

ID /ˌaɪ ˈdiː/ ABBREVIATION identification; an official document that proves who you are ▫ *We'll need some form of ID.* (**identidade**)

I'd /aɪd/ a short way to say and write I would or I had ▫ *I'd like another drink, please.* ▫ *I'd just gone to bed when the phone rang.*

idea /aɪˈdɪə/ NOUN [plural **ideas**]
1 a thought or plan about something you could do ▫ *It was a good/brilliant idea to look online.* ▫ *Taking six children swimming was a bad idea.* ▫ *I've had an idea about how to fix the fence.* ▫ **+ to do something** *It was Kate's idea to buy a van.* (**ideia**)
2 *no plural* knowledge about something ▫ *I had no idea what was happening.* ▫ *Can you give us some idea of how many people are coming?* ▫ *Do you have any idea how to switch the heating on?* (**ideia**)

ideal /aɪˈdɪəl/ ADJECTIVE exactly right for a particular purpose ▫ *It's an ideal house for a family.* ▫ *The meeting was an ideal opportunity to make my announcement.* (**ideal**)

identical /aɪˈdentɪkəl/ ADJECTIVE exactly the same ▫ *She gave birth to identical twins.* ▫ *The room was identical to his own.* (**idêntico**)

identification /aɪˌdentɪfɪˈkeɪʃən/ NOUN, NO PLURAL an official document that gives details such as your name and your date of birth, sometimes with a photograph of you on it, to prove who you are ▫ *The men wore their uniforms and carried official identification.* (**identificação**)

identify /aɪˈdentɪfaɪ/ VERB [**identifies, identifying, identified**] to recognize someone or something and to say who or what they are ▫ *She had to identify the body.* ▫ *Maps helped them identify the buildings.* ▫ *We were taught how to identify the signs of mental illness.* (**identidade**)

identity /aɪˈdentəti/ NOUN [plural **identities**] who someone is ▫ *Police are trying to discover the identity of the thief.* (**identidade**)

idiom /ˈɪdiəm/ NOUN [plural **idioms**] a phrase that has a meaning that you cannot understand simply by knowing the meaning of the separate words ▫ *The idiom 'once in a blue moon' means 'very rarely'.* (**expressão idiomática**)

idiot /ˈɪdiət/ NOUN [plural **idiots**] a stupid person ▫ *I felt like a complete idiot.* (**idiota**)

idle /ˈaɪdəl/ ADJECTIVE [**idler, idlest**]
1 if a machine is idle, it is not being used (**inativo, ocioso**)
2 lazy ▫ *Those children are just bone idle* (= very lazy). (**preguiçoso**)

i.e. /ˌaɪ ˈiː/ ABBREVIATION used for giving more information to show what you mean ▫ *The whole trip, i.e. food, travel and hotel, cost £500.* (**isto é**)

if /ɪf/ CONJUNCTION
1 used to say that something must happen before something else can happen or be true ▫ *If we leave now, we should catch the train.* ▫ *If you do your homework now, you can go out later.* (**se**)
2 used to say that something will be the result of something that might happen or be true ▫ *He will have to go into hospital if his condition gets worse.* ▫ *I hope the bricks will arrive tomorrow. If not, the builders won't be able to work.* ▫ *Will you be at home tomorrow? If so* (= if you are)*, would you mind taking in a parcel for me?* (**se**)

3 whether □ *I don't know if I can come on Thursday.* □ *He asked me if I minded him smoking.* (se)
4 every time □ *I always call in at his house if I'm passing.* (se)
5 if only used to talk about something you wish would happen or be true □ *If only he'd listen to your advice!* (se pelo menos)

ignite /ɪɡˈnaɪt/ VERB [ignites, igniting, ignited] to start to burn or to make something start to burn □ *The fuel ignited, causing a massive fire.* □ *Lightning and high winds ignited the dry wood.* (inflamar[-se])

ignorance /ˈɪɡnərəns/ NOUN, NO PLURAL not knowing about a subject or a situation □ *The report suggests that there is widespread ignorance about the disease.* (ignorância)

ignorant /ˈɪɡnərənt/ ADJECTIVE not knowing about something □ *Many people are ignorant of the dangers.* (ignorante)

ignore /ɪɡˈnɔː(r)/ VERB [ignores, ignoring, ignored] to not pay attention to someone or something □ *He ignored all my advice.* □ *The sport has been generally ignored by the media.* (ignorar)

> **THESAURUS:** If you **ignore** someone or take no notice of them, you do not pay attention to them. If you **neglect** or **reject** someone, you do not give them enough love and attention.

I'll /aɪl/ a short way to say and write I will □ *I'll be back next week.* □ *I'll carry these things for you.*

ill /ɪl/ ADJECTIVE suffering from an illness 🔹 *Do you feel ill?* 🔹 *She fell ill after eating chicken that was not cooked properly.* 🔹 *He is seriously ill with cancer.* (doente)

> Notice that you use **seriously ill** and not 'badly ill' to describe someone with a very bad illness.

> **THESAURUS:** If you are **ill**, you are suffering from an illness. **Sick** can have the same meaning, but in British English, it often also means that you feel as if you are going to vomit. If you are **unhealthy**, you do not have good health.

illegal /ɪˈliːɡəl/ ADJECTIVE not allowed by the law □ *It is illegal to sell alcohol to children.* □ *They are involved in illegal activitites.* (ilegal)

> **THESAURUS:** If something is **illegal**, it is not allowed by law. It is illegal to drive a car without a licence. If something is **forbidden**, it is not allowed. For example a small child may be forbidden from playing with scissors.

illegally /ɪˈliːɡəli/ ADVERB in an illegal way □ *Your car is parked illegally.* □ *He was found guilty of illegally possessing a firearm.* (ilegalmente)

illness /ˈɪlnɪs/ NOUN [plural illnesses]
1 a disease 🔹 *He is suffering from a serious illness.* 🔹 *Measles was once a common childhood illness.* □ *The illness is caused by a virus.* (doença)
2 *no plural* bad health □ *Illness prevented him from competing in the championship.* (doença)

illusion /ɪˈluːʒən/ NOUN [plural illusions]
1 a false idea or belief 🔹 *He's under the illusion that it's easy to get a job.* 🔹 *She had no illusions about her son's abilities.* (ilusão)
2 something that is not really what it seems to be 🔹 *Try using mirrors to create an illusion of space.* (ilusão)

illustrate /ˈɪləstreɪt/ VERB [illustrates, illustrating, illustrated] to draw pictures to go in books, magazines, etc. □ *She illustrated several books for children.* (ilustrar)

illustration /ˌɪləˈstreɪʃən/ NOUN [plural illustrations] a picture in a book, magazine, etc. (ilustração)

I'm /aɪm/ a short way to say and write I am □ *I'm hungry.* □ *I'm going to New York tomorrow.* (ver **be**)

image /ˈɪmɪdʒ/ NOUN [plural images]
1 an idea or opinion that people have about someone or something 🔹 *The agency is aiming to create an image of a dynamic, modern city.* (imagem)
2 a picture, especially one on television, film or on a computer □ *We have new images of accident.* 🔹 *A special camera was used to capture images of the child in its mother's womb.* (imagem)
3 a picture that you have in your mind □ *Disturbing images filled his head.* (imagem)

imaginary /ɪˈmædʒɪnəri/ ADJECTIVE existing in your mind but not real □ *It is perfectly normal for children to have imaginary friends.* (imaginário)

imagination /ɪˌmædʒɪˈneɪʃən/ NOUN, NO PLURAL your ability to think of new ideas or to form interesting pictures and stories in your mind. 🔹 *Rory has a very vivid imagination.* 🔹 *Reading encourages children to use their imagination.* (imaginação)

imagine /ɪˈmædʒɪn/ VERB [imagines, imagining, imagined]
1 to form a picture of someone or something in your mind □ + **question word** *I tried to imagine what he would look like.* □ + **that** *Imagine that you're the manager of a large company.* □ + **ing** *Imagine having your own aeroplane!* (imaginar)
2 to think that something exists or is true when it does not or is not □ *I keep imagining I can hear voices.* (imaginar)

imitate /ˈɪmɪteɪt/ VERB [imitates, imitating, imitated]
1 to copy someone or something because you like

them or it □ *He tries to imitate the style of famous artists.* (**imitar**)
2 to copy the way someone speaks or behaves as a joke □ *He's always imitating my friend's voice.* (**imitar**)

immediate /ɪˈmiːdɪət/ ADJECTIVE happening now, and without delay ▣ *I can't give you an immediate response.* □ *They demanded the immediate withdrawal of troops.* (**imediato**)

immediately¹ /ɪˈmiːdɪətli/ CONJUNCTION as soon as □ *Immediately I got the message, I ran to tell father.* (**assim que**)

immediately² /ɪˈmiːdɪətli/ ADVERB now or without delay □ *Come here immediately!* □ *I rang the doctor immediately.* (**imediatamente**)

immense /ɪˈmens/ ADJECTIVE extremely large in size, amount or degree □ *Some children are under immense pressure to succeed.* □ *He used his immense wealth to help a lot of people.* (**imenso**)

immigrant /ˈɪmɪɡrənt/ NOUN [plural **immigrants**] someone who has come to live in a country from another country (**imigrante**)

immigration /ˌɪmɪˈɡreɪʃən/ NOUN, NO PLURAL when people come to live in a foreign country □ *Immigration rose sharply in 2007.* ▣ *The government has announced new immigration laws.* (**imigrantes**)

imminent /ˈɪmɪnənt/ ADJECTIVE something that is imminent is going to happen very soon ▣ *Her life is in imminent danger.* ▣ *There is no imminent threat to health.* (**iminente**)

immoral /ɪˈmɒrəl/ ADJECTIVE morally wrong □ *He accused her of immoral conduct.* (**imoral**)

immune /ɪˈmjuːn/ ADJECTIVE unable to be infected by a particular disease. A biology word □ *Some people are naturally immune to the virus.* (**imune**)

immunity /ɪˈmjuːnəti/ NOUN, NO PLURAL your ability to avoid getting a particular disease. A biology word □ *Catching chickenpox gives lifelong immunity against the virus.* (**imunidade**)

impact¹ /ˈɪmpækt/ NOUN [plural **impacts**] the effect that something has □ *The changes will have a significant impact on schools.* (**impacto**)

impact² /ɪmˈpækt/ VERB [**impacts, impacting, impacted**] to have an effect on something □ *A long journey could impact on the team's performance.* (**apertar**)

imperative /ɪmˈperətɪv/ NOUN, NO PLURAL **the imperative** a verb form that you use to tell someone to do something (**imperativo**)

implant¹ /ɪmˈplɑːnt/ VERB [**implants, implanting, implanted**] to put something into someone's body to make it work or look better □ *A device is implanted in the heart which regulates the heartbeat.* (**implantar**)

implant² /ˈɪmplɑːnt/ NOUN [plural **implants**] something that is put in someone's body to make it work or look better □ *dental implants* (**implante**)

imply /ɪmˈplaɪ/ VERB [**implies, implying, implied**] to suggest that something is true without saying it directly □ *Are you implying that he lied?* (**insinuar**)

import¹ /ɪmˈpɔːt/ VERB [**imports, importing, imported**]
1 to bring a product from another country into your country in order to sell it □ **+ into** *The cars had been imported into the UK.* □ **+ from** *Many electrical goods are imported from Japan.* (**importar**)
2 to copy computer information from another place. A computing word. (**importar**)
→ L go to **export**

import² /ˈɪmpɔːt/ NOUN [plural **imports**] a product that is brought from another country into your country in order to sell □ *The country is dependent on oil imports.* (**importação**)
→ L go to **export²**

importance /ɪmˈpɔːtəns/ NOUN, NO PLURAL when something is important □ **+ of** *This just shows the importance of education.* ▣ *She stressed the importance of eating healthily.* (**importância**)

important /ɪmˈpɔːtənt/ ADJECTIVE
1 necessary or having a big effect on something □ *Books are an important part of our culture.* □ **+to do something** *It's important to listen to what the teacher is saying.* □ **+ that** *It's important that people are given this information.* □ **+ to** *Amy's career is very important to her.* ▣ *For me, the most important thing is to be happy.* (**importante**)
2 an important person has a lot of power or influence □ *The Prime Minister is the most important person in government.* (**importante**)

> Remember that something is **important to** someone and not **important for** someone:
> ✓ *My family is very important to me.*
> ✗ *My family is very important for me.*

importantly /ɪmˈpɔːtəntli/ ADVERB **more/most importantly** used before saying something that is more important or the most important thing □ *I love it here in Hong Kong and more importantly, the children love it too.* (**importantemente**)

impossible /ɪmˈpɒsəbəl/ ADJECTIVE not possible ▣ *an impossible task* □ **+ to do something** *It's impossible to explain.* ▣ *Ink stains are almost impossible to get rid of.* ▣ *Rain made it impossible for the game to continue.* (**impossível**)

impress /ɪmˈpres/ VERB [**impresses, impressing, impressed**] to make someone feel admiration □ *He was trying to impress his friends in his new car.* □ *Her attitude impressed me.* (**impressionar**)

impression /ɪmˈpreʃən/ NOUN [plural **impressions**]
1 an idea or feeling that you get about someone or something ▣ *I got the impression that he wasn't*

impressive / income tax

happy. 🔊 *She gives the impression of not really caring.* (**impressão**)

2 the effect that someone or something has on you 🔊 *The film made a big impression on me* (**impressão**)

impressive /ɪmˈpresɪv/ ADJECTIVE making you feel admirat ion □ *an impressive performance* □ *She's a very impressive woman.* (**impressionante**)

imprison /ɪmˈprɪzən/ VERB [**imprisons, imprisoning, imprisoned**] to put someone in prison or in a place they cannot escape from □ *He was imprisoned for fraud.* (**prender, aprisionar**)

improve /ɪmˈpruːv/ VERB [**improves, improving, improved**]

1 to become better □ *I hope the weather improves soon.* □ *The situation has slowly improved.* (**aperfeiçoar**)

2 to make something better □ *Exercise can improve your health.* □ *The new law is intended to improve road safety.* □ *This treatment will improve the quality of life for many cancer sufferers.* (**melhorar, aperfeiçoar**)

> THESAURUS: If you improve something you make it better than it was before. If you mend something, you fix it when it is broken. If you reform something, you make changes to it in order to improve it. A government might reform the education system, for example. If you correct something, you make it right or show someone the mistakes in it. A teacher might correct the mistakes in an essay, for example.

improvement /ɪmˈpruːvmənt/ NOUN [plural **improvements**] the process of becoming better or of making something better 🔊 *His test results have shown a great improvement.* 🔊 *We have seen no improvement in the health service.* 🔊 *There has been a significant improvement in living standards.* □ + **in** *an improvement in behaviour* (**aperfeiçoamento**)

improvise /ˈɪmprəˌvaɪz/ VERB [**improvises, improvising, improvised**] to decide what to say or do at the time when you are saying or doing it and not before □ *I had forgotten the notes for my talk so I had to improvise.* (**improvisar**)

impulse /ˈɪmpʌls/ NOUN [plural **impulses**]

1 a sudden feeling that makes you want to do some thing □ *He resisted the impulse to hit the man.* (**impulso**)

2 on impulse without thinking first □ *On impulse, he put his arm around her.* (**impulso**)

impulsive /ɪmˈpʌlsɪv/ ADJECTIVE doing things suddenly without thinking first □ *Jane is very impulsive.* (**impulsivo**)

in¹ /ɪn/ PREPOSITION

1 inside something □ *He keeps his keys in the drawer.* □ *The books are in my bedroom.* (**em**)
2 at a place □ *They live in Nottingham.* (**em**)
3 being part of something □ *There's a hole in my trousers.* □ *There was a strange smell in the air.* (**em**)
4 at a particular time □ *It's my birthday in May.* (**em**)
5 after a period of time □ *I'll be back in a few minutes.* (**em**)
6 wearing particular clothes □ *Who's the woman in the red dress?* (**em**)
7 shown as part of something □ *I looked in the dictionary to find the spelling of 'weird'.* (**em**)
8 using a particular thing □ *They were speaking in Japanese.* □ *The letter was written in purple ink.* (**em**)

in² /ɪn/ ADVERB

1 into a place or towards the inside of something □ *Come in and sit down.* □ *Push the needle in.* □ *A wide belt will hold your tummy in.* (**para dentro**)
2 at your home or place of work □ *I'm sorry, Dad's not in. Can I take a message?* 🔊 *I usually get in at around eight.* (**em, aqui, aí**)

in³ /ɪn/ ABBREVIATION **inch** or **inches**

inappropriate /ˌɪnəˈprəʊpriət/ ADJECTIVE not suitable for a particular situation or occasion □ *inappropriate behaviour* (**inadequado**)

inch /ɪntʃ/ NOUN [plural **inches**] a unit for measuring length, equal to about 2.5 centimetres □ *The ruler was 12 inches long.* (**polegada**)

include /ɪnˈkluːd/ VERB [**includes, including, included**]

1 if one thing includes another thing, the second thing is part of the first thing □ *The price of the ticket includes dinner.* □ *The guest list included many famous people.* □ *Ryan's films include 'Sleepless in Seattle' and 'Against the Ropes'.* (**incluir**)
2 to allow someone to be part of a group □ + **in** *Students are included in making decisions.* (**incluir**)

including /ɪnˈkluːdɪŋ/ PREPOSITION a word used to show that a person or thing is part of a larger group □ *We went to all the museums, including the new one.* □ *Seven people, including two young girls, died in the accident.* (**inclusive**)

income /ˈɪŋkʌm/ NOUN [plural **incomes**]

1 the amount of money you earn 🔊 *He had an annual income of £35,000.* 🔊 *The average household income has increased.* □ + **from** *She has had income from the sale of two houses.* (**rendimento**)
2 on a high/low income earning a lot/not much money □ *There aren't enough houses for people on low incomes.* (**com rendimento alto/baixo**)

> THESAURUS: Your pay is how much money you earn from your job. A wage is the money that you are paid for doing your job, especially when you are paid every week. When you are paid every month, we usually use the word salary. We also use salary and income to talk about how much someone earns in a year. Profit is the money you make when you sell something for more than you paid for it.

income tax /ˈɪŋkʌm ˌtæks/ NOUN, NO PLURAL tax that you have to pay on the money you earn (**imposto sobre a renda**)

inconvenience /ˌɪnkənˈviːnjəns/ NOUN [plural **inconveniences**] problems that something or someone causes you □ We apologize for the delay and for any inconvenience caused. (**incômodo**)

inconvenient /ˌɪnkənˈviːnjənt/ ADJECTIVE causing problems □ Have I called at an inconvenient time? (**inconveniente**)

incorrect /ˌɪnkəˈrekt/ ADJECTIVE wrong □ The answer to number three is incorrect. □ He'd been given incorrect information. (**incorreto**)

increase¹ /ɪnˈkriːs/ VERB [**increases, increasing, increased**]
1 to become become bigger in size or amount ⧉ The number of students has increased dramatically over the last ten years. □ + in The house has increased in value. □ + by Their wages will increase by 4%. (**aumentar**)
2 to make something become bigger in size or amount ⧉ Being overweight increases the risk of heart disease. ⧉ The government plans to increase the number of police officers. (**aumentar**)

increase² /ˈɪnkriːs/ NOUN [plural **increases**] a rise in amount or size □ price increases □ + in There's been a big increase in sales. (**aumento**)

increasingly /ɪnˈkriːsɪŋli/ ADVERB more and more □ The need to reduce car use is becoming increasingly important. (**cada vez mais**)

incredible /ɪnˈkredəbəl/ ADJECTIVE
1 extremely good or great □ To reach the finals is an incredible achievement. □ He showed incredible strength. (**incrível**)
2 difficult to believe □ It's incredible that he didn't realize he was so ill. (**incrível**)

indeed /ɪnˈdiːd/ ADVERB
1 used to emphasize what you are saying □ He was driving very fast indeed. □ It was indeed a mistake. (**mesmo**)
2 a formal word used to add something which supports what you have just said □ The Internet has become very popular. Indeed most people now have Internet access at home. (**de fato**)

indefinite article /ɪnˌdefɪnɪt ˈɑːtɪkəl/ NOUN [plural **indefinite articles**] the word a or the word an (**artigo definido**)

> There are two types of article in English grammar: **a** or **an** is the *indefinite article* and **the** is the *definite article*.

indefinitely /ɪnˈdefɪnɪtli/ ADVERB for a period of time with no fixed limits □ The game was postponed indefinitely. (**indefinidamente**)

independence /ˌɪndɪˈpendəns/ NOUN, NO PLURAL
1 when a country is not controlled by another country ⧉ East Timor gained independence in 2002. (**independência**)
2 when someone does not depend on other people for help □ financial independence (**independente**)

independent /ˌɪndɪˈpendənt/ ADJECTIVE
1 not controlled by another government or organization □ independent companies □ + from Mozambique became independent from Portugal in 1975. □ + of The council will be independent of the government. (**independente**)
2 not depending on other people for help □ My great-grandmother's 90 but she's very independent. ⧉ Some students are financially independent. (**independente**)

index /ˈɪndeks/ NOUN [plural **indexes** or **indices**] an alphabetical list in a book that tells you what page you can find information on □ Look up 'wild flowers' in the index. (**índice**)

indicate /ˈɪndɪkeɪt/ VERB [**indicates, indicating, indicated**]
1 to show that something is true or that something exists □ The study indicates that 70% of road accidents happen on country roads. (**indicar**)
2 to show someone what they should look at or where they should go □ There was an arrow indicating where to go. (**indicar, sinalizar**)
3 to show which way you are going to turn in a vehicle □ Always indicate before turning. (**indicar**)

indirect /ˌɪndɪˈrekt/ ADJECTIVE
1 not directly caused by something, or not directly related to something □ indirect effects (**indireto**)
2 not going the shortest way □ an indirect route (**indireto**)

indirect object /ˌɪndɪrekt ˈɒbdʒɪkt/ NOUN [plural **indirect objects**] in grammar, the person that something is given to, done to, etc. □ In the sentence 'I bought my mother a watch.', 'mother' is the indirect object. (**objeto indireto**)

indirect speech /ˌɪndɪrektˈspiːtʃ/ NOUN, NO PLURAL reporting what someone said without repeating their exact words □ 'He said he would come with me' is an example of indirect speech. (**discurso indireto**)

individual¹ /ˌɪndɪˈvɪdʒuəl/ ADJECTIVE for or relating to one person only □ The choice you make depends on your individual circumstances. (**individual**)

• **individually** /ˌɪndɪˈvɪdʒuəli/ ADVERB not with other things or people □ Wrap each glass individually. □ He talked to each student individually. (**individualmente**)

individual² /ˌɪndɪˈvɪdʒuəl/ NOUN [plural **individuals**] one person □ The medical study included 100 healthy individuals. (**indivíduo**)

indoor /ˈɪndɔː(r)/ ADJECTIVE inside a building □ an indoor swimming pool □ indoor activities □ indoor plants (**interno**)

indoors /ˌɪnˈdɔːz/ ADVERB into or inside a building □ It was cooler indoors. ⧉ Police warned people to stay indoors. ⧉ We went indoors because it started to rain. (**dentro**)

industrial /ɪnˈdʌstrɪəl/ ADJECTIVE relating to industry and factories □ industrial laws □ Industrial *production fell last month.* □ *Pollution is caused by industrial processes.* (**industrial**)

industry /ˈɪndəstri/ NOUN [plural **industries**]
1 no plural the production of goods, especially in a factory □ *The chemical is widely used in industry.* ▣ *Heavy industry* (= production of large goods) *has almost disappeared from the area.* (**indústria**)
2 all the companies involved in one particular type of trade or service □ *She had a successful career in the music industry.* □ *The violence has damaged the country's tourism industry.* □ *Electricity and gas industries are facing rising costs.* (**indústria**)

inevitable /ɪnˈevɪtəbəl/ ADJECTIVE certain to happen and not possible to avoid □ *Further conflict in the region is inevitable.* (**inevitável**)

infamous /ˈɪnfəməs/ ADJECTIVE famous for doing something bad (**infame**)

infect /ɪnˈfekt/ VERB [**infects, infecting, infected**]
1 to give someone an illness □ + **with** *Several patients were infected with the virus.* (**contaminar, infeccionar**)
2 if a computer is infected with a virus (= harmful program), it is damaged because of it. A computing word. (**infectar**)

> **THESAURUS:** If something such as a virus infects a person, it gives them an illness. To pollute means to make the air, land or water dirty and dangerous to live in because of harmful substances. To poison means to add a dangerous substance to something or kill or harm someone with a dangerous substance.

infection /ɪnˈfekʃən/ NOUN [plural **infections**] a disease that is caused by bacteria, a virus, etc. □ *an ear infection* (**infecção**)

infectious /ɪnˈfekʃəs/ ADJECTIVE an infectious disease can be passed from one person to another ▣ *The virus is highly infectious.* (**infeccioso**)

inferior /ɪnˈfɪərɪə(r)/ ADJECTIVE not as good as someone or something else □ *Amy often felt inferior to the other women in the office.* □ *This cake was made with inferior ingredients.* (**inferior**)

infinite /ˈɪnfɪnət/ ADJECTIVE without any limits or end □ *The universe is infinite.* (**infinito**)

infinitive /ɪnˈfɪnətɪv/ NOUN [plural **infinitives**]
the basic form of a verb that can be used to make all the other forms, for example *to play* or *to eat* (**infinitivo**)

inflammation /ˌɪnfləˈmeɪʃən/ NOUN [plural **inflammations**] swelling, pain and sometimes red skin in part of your body □ *The drug will reduce the inflammation in your joints.* (**inflamação**)

inflate /ɪnˈfleɪt/ VERB [**inflates, inflating, inflated**] to fill something with air □ *The tyres need to be inflated.* (**encher**)

inflict /ɪnˈflɪkt/ VERB [**inflicts, inflicting, inflicted**]
to make someone suffer something unpleasant or painful □ *The home team inflicted a heavy defeat on the visitors.* (**infligir**)

influence¹ /ˈɪnfluəns/ NOUN [plural **influences**]
1 the power to affect other people or things □ + **over** *He has considerable influence over his colleagues.* □ + **on** *Exchange rates have a big influence on our business.* (**influência**)
2 someone or something that has an effect on other people or things □ *Ann is a good influence on you.* □ *Her films reflect her many cultural influences.* (**influência**)

influence² /ˈɪnfluəns/ VERB [**influences, influencing, influenced**]
to have an effect on someone or something □ *His advice influenced my decision.* □ *My early work was influenced by Samuel Beckett.* (**influenciar**)

influential /ˌɪnfluˈenʃəl/ ADJECTIVE having a lot of influence ▣ *He was one of the most influential figures in Hollywood at that time.* (**influente**)

influenza /ˌɪnfluˈenzə/ NOUN, NO PLURAL a formal word for flu (= illness like a very bad cold) (**gripe**)

inform /ɪnˈfɔːm/ VERB [**informs, informing, informed**]
to tell someone about something, especially officially □ *If you come here again I'll inform the police.* □ + **that** *We were informed that our luggage had been lost.* □ + **of** *I'll inform you of my decision.* ▣ *Please keep me informed of your plans.* (**informar**)

informal /ɪnˈfɔːməl/ ADJECTIVE relaxed and friendly, or suitable for relaxed occasions □ *The meeting was informal.* □ *We can wear informal clothes to the office at weekends.* (**informal**)

information /ˌɪnfəˈmeɪʃən/ NOUN, NO PLURAL
facts about someone or something □ + **on** *Have you got any information on things to do in the area?* □ + **about** *I gave him some information about our services.* ▣ *The report provides a lot of information about medical errors.* ▣ *For further information visit our website.* ▣ *That is a very interesting piece of information.* (**informação**)

> Remember that **information** cannot be used in the plural:
> ✓ *I got some* **information** *off the Internet.*
> ✗ *I got some* **informations** *off the Internet.*
> To talk about one fact about a subject and not many facts, use the phrase **piece of information**: □ *Here's a useful* **piece of information**.

information technology /ˌɪnfəˌmeɪʃən tekˈnɒlədʒi/ NOUN, NO PLURAL the study or use of computers to store, send or use information (**tecnologia da informação**)

> You will often see the abbreviation for information technology, which is **IT**.

infrared /ˌɪnfrəˈred/ ADJECTIVE infrared light cannot be seen but gives out heat (**infravermelho**)

ingredient /ɪnˈɡriːdiənt/ NOUN [plural **ingredients**]
1 one of the things you use to make a particular food □ *Mix the dry ingredients in a bowl.* (**ingrediente**)
2 one of the qualities something needs to be successful □ *Music is an essential ingredient of most teenagers' lives.* (**ingrediente**)

inhabit /ɪnˈhæbɪt/ VERB [**inhabits, inhabiting, inhabited**] to live in a particular place □ *The series looks at the creatures that inhabit our planet.* (**habitar**)

inhabitant /ɪnˈhæbɪtənt/ NOUN [plural **inhabitants**] someone who lives in a place □ *There are differences between the inhabitants of the two islands.* (**habitar**)

> THESAURUS: An **inhabitant** is someone who lives in a place. You can talk about the inhabitants of a town or a country. A **native** is someone who was born in a particular place. You can be a **native** of a town or a region or a country. A **citizen** is someone who has the right to live in a particular country permanently. You may become a **citizen** of a country where you were not born.

inhale /ɪnˈheɪl/ VERB [**inhales, inhaling, inhaled**] to breathe air, smoke, etc. into your lungs □ *She inhaled deeply.* (**inalar**)

inherit /ɪnˈherɪt/ VERB [**inherits, inheriting, inherited**] to receive money or other possessions from someone who has died □ *Imogen inherited the house from her father.* (**herdar**)

inheritance /ɪnˈherɪtəns/ NOUN [plural **inheritances**] money or possessions that you receive from someone who has died □ *She lived on a small inheritance from her grandmother.* (**herança**)

initial[1] /ɪˈnɪʃəl/ ADJECTIVE at the beginning ▣ *Initial reports* suggest the crash was caused by engine failure. ▣ *My initial reaction was horror.* (**inicial**)
• **initially** /ɪˈnɪʃəli/ ADVERB in the beginning □ *Initially, things were very difficult.* (**inicialmente**)

initial[2] /ɪˈnɪʃəl/ NOUN [plural **initials**] the first letter of a word, especially someone's name □ *His initials are J.C.* (**inicial**)

inject /ɪnˈdʒekt/ VERB [**injects, injecting, injected**] to put a substance into someone's body using a needle □ *She has to inject herself with insulin every day.* (**injetar**)

injection /ɪnˈdʒekʃən/ NOUN [plural **injections**] when a substance is put into someone's body using a needle □ *insulin injections* (**injeção**)

injure /ˈɪndʒə(r)/ VERB [**injures, injuring, injured**] to hurt someone or something □ *Matt injured his knee in a skiing accident.* (**ferir**)

injured /ˈɪndʒəd/ ADJECTIVE hurt □ *Fiona was badly injured in a road accident.* (**magoado, ferido**)

injury /ˈɪndʒəri/ NOUN [plural **injuries**] damage to part of your body ▣ *a serious head injury* ▣ *He was lucky to suffer only minor injuries in the crash.* (**lesão, ferimento**)

> THESAURUS: An **injury** is damage to a part of your body. Injuries can be on the outside or the inside of your body. A **wound** or a **cut** is an injury where your skin is broken. A **wound** is often more serious than a **cut**. A **fracture** is a break, especially to a bone in your body.

injustice /ɪnˈdʒʌstɪs/ NOUN [plural **injustices**] when people are treated unfairly or an action that is unfair □ *I was hurt by the injustice of her criticism.* (**injustiça**)

ink /ɪŋk/ NOUN [plural **inks**] a coloured liquid used for writing or printing (**tinta**)

inn /ɪn/ NOUN [plural **inns**] a small hotel or pub, especially in the countryside (**albergue**)

inner /ˈɪnə(r)/ ADJECTIVE on the inside or close to the centre of something □ *She kept her purse in the inner pocket of her bag.* □ *inner London* (**interno**)

innocence /ˈɪnəsəns/ NOUN, NO PLURAL when someone is not guilty of a crime □ *New evidence proved his innocence.* (**inocência**)

innocent /ˈɪnəsənt/ ADJECTIVE not guilty of a crime □ *An innocent man had been hanged.* □ *She claims she is innocent of the crime.* (**inocente**)

innovation /ˌɪnəˈveɪʃən/ NOUN [plural **innovations**] something completely new, especially a new method of doing something □ *He keeps up with all the latest innovations in medicine.* (**inovação**)

inquire /ɪnˈkwaɪə(r)/ VERB [**inquires, inquiring, inquired**] to ask for information about something □ *He inquired how to get to the library.* □ *I'm inquiring about the job advertised in the paper.* (**indagar**)

inquiry /ɪnˈkwaɪəri/ NOUN [plural **inquiries**] a question you ask in order to get information □ *We've had a number of inquiries about new cars.* (**interrogatório**)

insane /ɪnˈseɪn/ ADJECTIVE
1 having a serious mental illness (**louco**)
2 very silly □ *Her work schedule is just insane.* (**insensato**)

insect /ˈɪnsekt/ NOUN [plural **insects**] a small creature with six legs and often wings, for example a bee or a fly (**inseto**)

insert /ɪnˈsɜːt/ VERB [**inserts, inserting, inserted**] to put something into something else □ *He inserted some coins into the meter.* □ *You need to insert a few more examples.* (**inserir**)

inside[1] /ɪnˈsaɪd/ PREPOSITION in or into a building, container or area □ *She put the book inside her bag.* □ *Draw a cross inside the box.* (**interior**)

inside² /ɪnˈsaɪd/ NOUN [plural insides]

1 the inside the part that is in the middle and not on the outside □ *The inside of his jacket was torn.* (**interior**)

2 inside out if clothes are inside out, the part that should be on the inside is on the outside □ *You've got your socks on inside out.* (**avesso**)

> THESAURUS: The inside of something is the part that is in the middle and not on the outside. Inside is a general word. The **interior** of something is the inside, especially of a room or a building. The **contents** are what is inside something. We often talk about the **contents** of a book or a bag. The **core** of something is the central part. For example, the **core** of an apple is the hard part with seeds.

inside³ /ɪnˈsaɪd/ ADJECTIVE
in or facing the middle of something □ *Keep it in an inside pocket.* (**interno**)

inside⁴ /ɪnˈsaɪd/ ADVERB

1 in or into a building □ *Come inside – you'll get cold.*

2 in or into a container or an area □ *Has that tin got anything inside?* (**dentro**)

insist /ɪnˈsɪst/ VERB [insists, insisting, insisted]

1 to say firmly that something must happen or be done □ **+ on** *I always insist on a single room.* □ **+ on** *Fay insisted on paying.* □ **+ that** *The school insists that all students must wear full uniform.* (**insistir**)

2 to keep saying firmly that something is true □ **+ that** *Mark insists that he hasn't done anything wrong.* (**insistir**)

inspect /ɪnˈspekt/ VERB [inspects, inspecting, inspected]
to look very carefully at someone or some thing □ *He inspected our documents closely.* (**inspetor**)

inspection /ɪnˈspekʃən/ NOUN [plural inspections]

1 when you look very carefully at someone or something 🔁 *On close inspection, I realized the note wasn't in Josh's handwriting.* (**inspeção**)

2 an official visit to a place to check that it is working properly 🔁 *Public health officers carry out regular inspections of restaurants.* (**vistoria**)

inspector /ɪnˈspektə(r)/ NOUN [plural inspectors]

1 someone whose job is to look very carefully at a place such as a school or restaurant (**inspetor**)

2 a police officer with quite a high rank (**inspetor**)

inspire /ɪnˈspaɪə(r)/ VERB [inspires, inspiring, inspired]
to give someone ideas and enthusiasm □ *My mother inspired me to write stories.*

install or instal /ɪnˈstɔːl/ VERB [installs or instals, installing, installed]

1 to put a piece of equipment in place and make it ready to use □ *We have installed central heating.* (**instalar**)

2 to put software on to a computer to be used. A computing word □ *I installed the software and began the work.* (**instalar**)

instance /ˈɪnstəns/ NOUN [plural instances] **for instance** for example □ *Some birds, penguins for instance, cannot fly at all.* (**exemplo**)

instant¹ /ˈɪnstənt/ ADJECTIVE

1 happening immediately □ *The film was an instant success.* (**instantâneo**)

2 able to be prepared very quickly □ *instant coffee* (**instantâneo**)

instant² /ˈɪnstənt/ NOUN [plural instants]

1 a very short time □ *The doctor will be with you in an instant.* (**instante**)

2 a particular moment in time □ *At that very instant, the phone rang.* (**instante**)

instantly /ˈɪnstəntliː/ ADVERB
immediately □ *I recognized him instantly.* (**instantaneamente**)

instead /ɪnˈsted/ ADVERB
in place of someone or something else □ *Bob was ill so Joe went instead.* □ **+ of** *You could use a pencil instead of a pen.* □ *Instead of moaning you could actually help.* (**em substituição**)

> Notice that when you put a verb after **instead**, you need the preposition **of** before the verb. Also, the verb must be in the *-ing* form: □ *Instead of lying in bed all day, you could work.*

instinct /ˈɪnstɪŋkt/ NOUN [plural instincts]
the natural way you react or behave without thinking or being taught □ *These animals have a strong survival instinct.* □ *My first instinct was to run away.* (**instinto**)

institute /ˈɪnstɪtjuːt/ NOUN [plural institutes]
an organization where people study a particular subject □ *We have a training institute in Florida.* (**instituto**)

institution /ˌɪnstɪˈtjuːʃən/ NOUN [plural institutions]
a large organization □ *I have worked for several banks and other financial institutions.* (**instituição**)

instruct /ɪnˈstrʌkt/ VERB [instructs, instructing, instructed]

1 to tell someone to do something □ *I instructed her to go straight home.* (**instruir**)

2 to teach someone □ *Staff will be instructed in the correct use of the machinery.* (**instruir**)

instruction

instruction /ɪnˈstrʌkʃən/ NOUN [plural **instructions**] **instructions** printed information about how to do something □ *Read the instructions before you begin.* ▣ *Make sure you follow the instructions.* (instrução)

instructor /ɪnˈstrʌktə(r)/ NOUN [plural **instructors**] someone who teaches a sport or a skill □ *a driving instructor* (instrutor)

instrument /ˈɪnstrəmənt/ NOUN [plural **instruments**]
1 something used for making music, for example a guitar or a piano ▣ *She plays several musical instruments.* (instrumento)
2 a tool for doing a particular task □ *surgical instruments* (instrumentos)

insufficient /ˌɪnsəˈfɪʃənt/ ADJECTIVE not enough □ *There was insufficient evidence to make an arrest.* (insufiente)

insult¹ /ɪnˈsʌlt/ VERB [**insults, insulting, insulted**] to say or do something rude that offends someone □ *He was fired for insulting his manager.* (insultar)

insult² /ˈɪnsʌlt/ NOUN [plural **insults**] a remark or action that is rude and offends someone □ *The crowd were hurling insults at the referee.* □ *To sell the jewellery is an insult to her memory.* (insulto)

insurance /ɪnˈʃɔːrəns/ NOUN, NO PLURAL an arrangement in which you pay a company money and they pay the costs if you have an accident or are ill, or if something you own is damaged or stolen □ *car insurance* ▣ *I've taken out health insurance.* (seguro)

insure /ɪnˈʃɔː(r)/ VERB [**insures, insuring, insured**] to pay money to a company who will pay the costs if you have an accident or are ill, or if something you own is damaged or stolen □ + **for** *She insured her jewellery for £50,000.* □ + **against** *Are you insured against loss of earnings?* (segurar)

intact /ɪnˈtækt/ ADJECTIVE not broken or damaged □ *One of the mosaic floors has been preserved intact.* (intacto)

integrity /ɪnˈtegrɪti/ NOUN, NO PLURAL the quality of being honest and having high moral standards □ *Colleagues praised his integrity.* (integridade)

intelligence /ɪnˈtelɪdʒəns/ NOUN, NO PLURAL your ability to learn and understand things □ *No one is questioning your son's intelligence.* (inteligência)

intelligent /ɪnˈtelɪdʒənt/ ADJECTIVE clever and able to understand things quickly ▣ *These students are highly intelligent.* (inteligente)

intelligently /ɪnˈtelɪdʒəntli/ ADVERB in an intelligent way □ *He spoke intelligently about politics.* (inteligentemente)

intend /ɪnˈtend/ VERB [**intends, intending, intended**] to plan to do something □ + **to do something** *I intend to visit Will when I'm in Seattle. I intend staying longer but their money ran out.* (tencionar)

intensive /ɪnˈtensɪv/ ADJECTIVE involving a lot of effort or activity in a short time □ *an intensive language course* (intensivo)

intent /ɪnˈtent/ NOUN, NO PLURAL when you intend to do something □ *It was not my intent to offend him.* (intento)

intention /ɪnˈtenʃən/ NOUN [plural **intentions**] the thing you plan to do □ + **to do something** *It is my intention to finish before 5 o'clock.* ▣ *He had no intention of obeying his father.* (intenção)

interact /ˌɪntərˈækt/ VERB [**interacts, interacting, interacted**] to talk to other people and do things with them □ *Joe always interacted well with other children.* (interagir)

interest¹ /ˈɪntrəst/ NOUN [plural **interests**]
1 *no plural* the feeling of wanting to know about something or give your attention to something □ + **in** *I have no interest in cricket.* ▣ *I try to take an interest in my husband's work.* ▣ *In the end, I lost interest in my studies.* (interesse)
2 something that you enjoy doing or learning about □ *My main interests are sport and reading.* (interesse)
3 *no plural* extra money that you have to pay back when you have borrowed money, or that a bank pays you for having your money □ + **on** *The interest on the car payments was huge.* ▣ *I had to pay interest on the loan.* ▣ *They charge 10% interest.*

interest² /ˈɪntrəst/ VERB [**interests, interesting, interested**] to make someone want to know about something or do an activity □ + **in** *I'm trying to interest him in Chinese music.* □ *Can I interest you in a boat ride?* (interessar)

interested /ˈɪntrəstɪd/ ADJECTIVE
1 having or showing interest □ + **in** *Dan is very interested in old cars.* □ + **to do something** *I'd be interested to hear her side of the story.* (interessado)
2 wanting to do something □ + **in** *I'm not interested in making money. I'm interested in buying a bike.* (interessado)

interesting /ˈɪntrəstɪŋ/ ADJECTIVE making you feel interested □ *It was a very interesting story.* □ *It is interesting to note that he had never been to Egypt.* (interessante)

> Remember the difference between the words **interesting** and **interested**. **Interesting** means 'making you feel interested'. **Interested** is how you feel when something is interesting: □ *It's a very interesting subject.* □ *I'm very interested in the subject.*

interest rate /ˈɪntrəst ˌreɪt/ NOUN [plural **interest rates**] the amount of extra money that you

interfere /ˌɪntəˈfɪə(r)/ VERB [**interferes, interfering, interfered**] to get involved in a situation where you are not wanted □ *Many teenagers feel their parents interfere too much in their lives.* (**interferir**)

◆ PHRASAL VERB **interfere with something** to affect something in a bad way □ *The illness doesn't interfere with my ability to do the job.* (**interferir**)

interior[1] /ɪnˈtɪərɪə(r)/ NOUN [*plural* **interiors**] the inside of something □ *The interior of the house was beautifully decorated.* (**interior**)

interior[2] /ɪnˈtɪərɪə(r)/ ADJECTIVE on or for the inside of something □ *an interior wall* (**interior**)
L *go to* **exterior**

intermediate /ˌɪntəˈmiːdɪət/ ADJECTIVE

between a basic and advanced level in a subject □ *an intermediate English course* 🔂 *The book is for students studying maths at an intermediate level.* (**intermediário**)

internal /ɪnˈtɜːnəl/ ADJECTIVE
1 inside your body □ *internal injuries* □ *internal organs* (**interno**)
2 within an organization or country □ *an internal investigation* □ *internal flights* (**interno**)

international /ˌɪntəˈnæʃənəl/ ADJECTIVE

involving several countries □ *international law* □ *an international conference* □ *international trade* (**internacional**)

> **THESAURUS:** Something that is international involves several countries. Something that is global or universal affects or involves the whole world.

Internet[1] /ˈɪntənet/ NOUN, NO PLURAL **the Internet** a computer system that allows people around the world to share information □ *I found this hotel on the Internet.* (**Internet**)

Internet[2] /ˈɪntənet/ ADJECTIVE to do with the Internet 🔂 *Most homes now have Internet access.* 🔂 *Internet users* (**Internet**)

interpret /ɪnˈtɜːprɪt/ VERB [interprets, interpreting, interpreted]

to change what someone has said into a different language □ *If you don't speak French, we can provide someone to interpret for you.* (**interpretar**)

interpreter /ɪnˈtɜːprɪtə(r)/ NOUN [*plural* **interpreters**] someone whose job is to change what someone says into a different language (**intérprete**)

interrupt /ˌɪntəˈrʌpt/ VERB [interrupts, interrupting, interrupted]

to stop someone when they are in the middle of saying or doing something □ *I'm sorry to interrupt, but what time do we have to leave?* □ *Could I just interrupt you for a moment?* (**interromper**)

interruption /ˌɪntəˈrʌpʃən/ NOUN [*plural* interruptions]

something that stops you doing or saying something □ *I can't work with all these interruptions.* (**interrupção**)

interval /ˈɪntəvəl/ NOUN [*plural* intervals]

1 a period of time between two things □ *Her husband died in 1990, and after a decent interval, she married again.* 🔂 *After a short interval the police arrived.* □ **+ of** *an interval of two weeks* (**intervalo**)

2 at weekly/monthly etc. intervals used for saying how often something happens □ *Meetings are held at regular intervals.* □ *You should have a dental check-up at six-month intervals.* (**de tempos em tempos**)

interview[1] /ˈɪntəvjuː/ NOUN [*plural* interviews]

1 a meeting in which someone asks you a lot of questions to find out if you are suitable for a job or a place on a course 🔂 *I have got an interview this afternoon.* 🔂 *I wear this suit for job interviews.* □ **+ for** *I didn't even get an interview for the job.* (**entrevista**)

2 a meeting in which someone asks a famous person questions 🔂 *Most reporters are nervous if they do an interview with the Queen.* 🔂 *The singer doesn't give interviews very often.* 🔂 *In an exclusive interview with this paper, she talks openly about her marriage.* (**entrevista**)

interview[2] /ˈɪntəvjuː/ VERB [interviews, interviewing, interviewed]

to ask someone questions at an interview □ *The driver was interviewed by police.* (**entrevistar**)

intimidate /ɪnˈtɪmɪdeɪt/ VERB [**intimidates, intimidating, intimidated**] to frighten someone, especially by threatening them □ *He won't let his attackers intimidate him into moving away from the area.* (**intimidar**)

into /ˈɪntʊ/ PREPOSITION

1 towards the inside of a room, container, area, etc. □ *We went into the house.* □ *I got into bed.* □ *He put earth into the hole.* (**dentro**)
2 towards the lower part of a substance □ *Our feet sank into the soft sand.* □ *He fell into the water.* (**dentro**)
3 hitting against something □ *I drove into a wall.* (**contra**)
4 used for saying how something or someone changes □ *She cut the pizza into four pieces.* □ *The caterpillar changed into a butterfly.* (**em**)
5 towards a particular thing □ *He looked into my eyes.* □ *She gazed into the mirror.* (**em**)
6 to do with a particular subject or situation □ *How did we get into this mess?* □ *We are holding an investigation into child poverty.* (**em, dentro**)
7 used when talking about dividing one number by another □ *2 into 4 goes twice.* (**em**)

introduce /ˌɪntrəˈdjuːs/ VERB [introduces, introducing, introduced]

1 if you introduce two people who do not know each other, you tell each of them the other person's

introduction | irony

name □ + *to He introduced me to his sister.* □ *Have you two been introduced?* (**apresentar**)
2 to make something start to happen or be used □ *The new law was introduced in 1999.* (**introduzir**)

> **THESAURUS:** If you **introduce** something, you make it start to happen or be used. If you **launch** a new product, you start to sell it. If you **establish** a business or organization, you start it. **Start** and **begin** are more general words to describe these actions.

introduction /ˌɪntrəˈdʌkʃən/ NOUN [plural introductions]
1 *no plural* when something is started or begins to be used □ *They opposed the introduction of identity cards.* (**introdução**)
2 the first part of a book, speech or piece of music (**introdução**)

invade /ɪnˈveɪd/ VERB [invades, invading, invaded]
to enter a country with an army, and try to take control of it □ *7000 troops invaded the country.* (**invadir**)

invalid¹ /ɪnˈvælɪd/ ADJECTIVE not acceptable because of a law or rule □ *an invalid bus pass* (**inválido**)
invalid² /ˈɪnvəlɪd/ NOUN [plural **invalids**] someone who is ill or unable to look after themselves (**doente**)

invasion /ɪnˈveɪʒən/ NOUN [plural invasions]
an attack on a country by an army entering it □ + *of The government decided to launch an invasion of the country.* (**invasão**)

invent /ɪnˈvent/ VERB [invents, inventing, invented]
to design or create a new type of thing □ *Thomas Edison invented the electric light bulb.* □ *There was a lot of argument about who had invented the word.* (**inventar**)

invention /ɪnˈvenʃən/ NOUN [plural inventions]
1 a new type of thing which someone has designed or created □ *The washing machine was a brilliant invention.* (**invenção**)
2 *no plural* when someone designs or creates a new type of thing □ + *of The invention of the computer would change the world forever.* (**invenção**)

inventor /ɪnˈventə(r)/ NOUN [plural **inventors**] someone who has invented something new (**inventor**)
invest /ɪnˈvest/ VERB [invests, investing, invested] to put money in a bank or business in order to make more money □ *My Dad has invested some money in the business.* (**investir**)
investigate /ɪnˈvestɪgeɪt/ VERB [investigates, investigating, investigated] to try to find out about something such as an accident or crime □ *Police are investigating his death.* (**investigar**)
investigation /ɪnˌvestɪˈgeɪʃən/ NOUN [plural **investigations**] an attempt to find out about something such as an accident or a crime

□ *Officials have launched an investigation into what happened.* (**investigação**)
invisible /ɪnˈvɪzəbəl/ ADJECTIVE impossible to see □ *The star is almost invisible.* (**invisível**)

invitation /ˌɪnvɪˈteɪʃən/ NOUN [plural invitations]
when someone asks you if you would like to go somewhere or do something □ + *to We've had an invitation to William and Charlotte's wedding.* □ + *to do something He accepted an invitation to meet the President.* (**convite**)

invite /ɪnˈvaɪt/ VERB [invites, inviting, invited]
to ask someone if they would like to do something or go somewhere □ + *for We've invited some friends round for dinner.* □ + *to Raj has invited me to his birthday party.* □ + *to do something Beth was invited to speak at the conference.* (**convidar**)
♦ PHRASAL VERB **invite someone over/round** to ask someone to come to your house, for example to have a meal with you □ *I've invited Ann round tonight.*

involve /ɪnˈvɒlv/ VERB [involves, involving, involved]
1 if an activity or situation involves something, that thing is a part of it □ *The treatment involves a slight risk.* □ + *ing The job involves selling Internet space to companies.* (**acarretar**)
2 to affect someone or something □ *Crimes involving children are very rare.* □ *Five vehicles were involved in the accident.* (**envolver**)
3 to allow someone to take part in something □ + *in The school tries to involve students in decision-making.* (**envolver**)

Irish¹ /ˈaɪrɪʃ/ ADJECTIVE belonging to or from Ireland (**Irlandês**)
Irish² /ˈaɪrɪʃ/ NOUN **the Irish** people from Ireland (**Irlandês**)

iron¹ /ˈaɪən/ NOUN [plural irons]
1 *no plural* a hard strong metal that is also found in small amounts in your blood and some food □ *The railings were made from iron.* □ *Spinach contains vitamin C and iron.* (**ferro**)
2 a piece of electrical equipment that you press on clothes to make them smooth □ *Have you switched the iron off?* (**ferro de passar**)

iron² /ˈaɪən/ VERB [irons, ironing, ironed]
to make clothes smooth using an iron □ *Ben was ironing some shirts.* (**passar a ferro**)

iron³ /ˈaɪən/ ADJECTIVE
made from iron □ *iron gates* (**ferro**)

ironic /aɪˈrɒnɪk/ ADJECTIVE an ironic situation is surprising, often because it is the opposite of what you expected □ *It's ironic that a man who spent his life treating heart disease should die of a heart attack.* (**Irônico**)
irony /ˈaɪrəni/ NOUN [plural **ironies**] a situation that is surprising because it is the opposite of what

irregular — itself

you expected 🔹 *The irony is that the man who cooks all this marvellous food can no longer taste it.* (**ironia**)

irregular /ɪˈregjulə(r)/ ADJECTIVE
1 having a different amount of time or space between separate things 🔹 *an irregular heartbeat* □ *The trees had been planted at irregular intervals.* (**irregular**)
2 not smooth or even □ *irregular shapes* (**irregular**)
3 not following the usual rules of grammar □ *irregular verbs* (**irregular**)

irritate /ˈɪrɪteɪt/ VERB [**irritates, irritating, irritated**]
1 to make someone feel annoyed □ *It irritates me that he never helps with the washing up.* (**irritar**)
2 to make something such as your skin or eyes sore □ *Some sun creams can irritate your skin.* (**irritar**)

is /ɪz/ VERB the present tense of the verb **be** that is used with **he**, **she**, or **it** □ *He is tall.* □ *It is too hot.* (**verbo be**)

> Note that instead of **he is**, **she is** and **it is**, people often say and write the short forms, **he's**, **she's** and **it's**: □ *He's here.* □ *She's tall.* □ *It's great.*

-ish /ɪʃ/ SUFFIX -ish is added to the end of words to mean 'slightly' □ *reddish* (= slightly red) (**[sufixo] levemente**)

Islam /ˈɪzlɑːm/ NOUN, NO PLURAL the Muslim religion that was started by Mohammed (**Islã**)

Islamic /ɪzˈlæmɪk/ ADJECTIVE to do with Islam □ *Islamic law* □ *the Islamic faith* (**islâmico**)

island /ˈaɪlənd/ NOUN [*plural* **islands**] an area of land surrounded by sea □ *There are lots of unusual plants on the island.* □ *the Caribbean island of Trinidad* 🔹 *a remote island in the Pacific Ocean* □ *the Channel Islands* (**ilha**)

isn't /ˈɪzənt/ a short way to say and write is not □ *It isn't fair.*

isolate /ˈaɪsəleɪt/ VERB [**isolates, isolating, isolated**] to separate someone or something from other people or things □ *The infected animals were isolated in a field.* (**isola**)

• **isolated** /ˈaɪsəleɪtɪd/ ADJECTIVE
1 feeling alone and sad that you do not meet other people □ *Old people often feel isolated.* (**isolado**)
2 far away from other places □ *an isolated farmhouse* (**isolado**)

issue¹ /ˈɪʃuː/ NOUN [*plural* **issues**]
1 a subject that people discuss or that causes problems □ *+ of* *We discussed the issue of money.* 🔹 *Polly raised the issue of transport.* 🔹 *The environment is a key issue in this election campaign.* 🔹 *The issue arose because one of the children made a complaint.* (**assunto**)
2 a newspaper or magazine that is one of a number printed and sold at the same time □ *Have you seen this week's issue of the magazine?* (**número**)

issue² /ˈɪʃuː/ VERB [**issues, issuing, issued**]
1 to say something to the public in an official way 🔹 *issue a statement/warning* (**publicar**)
2 to supply someone with something □ *+ with* *We were all issued with pens.* (**distribuir**)

IT /ˌaɪˈtiː/ ABBREVIATION **information technology** (**TI**)

it /ɪt/ PRONOUN (**isso, isto, aquilo, o, a**)
1 used to talk or write about something that has already been mentioned □ *I've lost my book. Have you seen it?* □ *It was a great day.*
2 used to talk about a fact or opinion □ *It's expensive to travel by train.* □ *It's very quiet here, isn't it?* □ *What's it like in Spain?*
3 used to talk about the weather, time and dates □ *It rained yesterday.* □ *What time is it?* □ *It's 3 o'clock.*
4 used to talk about distance □ *It's a long way to the coast.* □ *How far is it to your house?*
5 used to tell someone who is there, on the telephone, etc. □ *Hello, it's Pat here.* □ *It's your brother at the door.*

itch /ɪtʃ/ VERB [**itches, itching, itched**] if part of your body itches, it feels uncomfortable and makes you want to scratch it (**coçar**)
♦ IDIOM **be itching to do something** an informal phrase meaning to want to do something very much □ *I was itching to play football again.*

itchy /ˈɪtʃi/ ADJECTIVE an itchy part of your body feels uncomfortable and makes you want to scratch it (**coceira**)

it'd /ˈɪtəd/ a short way to say and write it would or it had □ *It'd be good if you could come.* □ *It'd been raining all day.* (**ver have, would**)

item /ˈaɪtəm/ NOUN [*plural* **items**] one thing which is part of a group or is on a list □ *There were several items on the list.* 🔹 *He left his mobile phone and other personal items in the car.* 🔹 *She had some very expensive items of clothing in her wardrobe.* (**item**)

it'll /ˈɪtəl/ a short way to say and write it will □ *It'll be nice to see you.* (**ver will**)

it's /ɪts/ a short way to say and write it is or it has □ *It's snowing.* □ *It's been a long time since I saw you.* (**ver be, have**)

> Try not to confuse the spellings of **its** and **it's**. **Its** is the possessive form of **it**, and tells you something belongs to **it**: *The bird built its nest.* **It's** is a short form of two words put together: *I think it's going to rain.*

its /ɪts/ ADJECTIVE belonging to or to do with it □ *Keep the hat in its box.* 🔹 *The school has its own tennis courts.* (**seu, sua, seus, suas**)

itself /ɪtˈself/ PRONOUN
1 the reflexive form of *it* □ *The school has transformed itself.* □ *Australia has found itself in a difficult position.* (**si mesmo**)

2 used to show that a thing or animal does something without any help from anyone or anything else □ *The cut soon healed itself.* ◻ *The dog managed to get free all by itself.* (**sozinho**)
3 used to emphasize the pronoun *it* □ *I don't dislike the building itself.* (**em si**)

4 by itself not with or near other things □ *The cottage stood by itself on a hillside.* □ *Talent by itself is not enough to make you successful.* (**sozinho**)

I've /aɪv/ a short way to say and write I have □ *I've finished my homework.* □ *I've got six cats.* (ver **have**)

J or **j** /dʒeɪ/ the tenth letter of the alphabet (a décima letra do alfabeto)

jab /dʒæb/ NOUN [plural **jabs**] when you quickly push something sharp into or towards something □ *She gave him a jab in the ribs with her elbow.* (cutucão, pontada)

jacket /'dʒækɪt/ NOUN [plural **jackets**] a short coat, usually with long sleeves □ *a leather jacket* □ *a denim jacket* (jaqueta)

jail /dʒeɪl/ NOUN [plural **jails**] a building where criminals are kept □ *She was sentenced to 12 months in jail.* ⊞ *He's just been released from jail.* (cadeia)

jam¹ /dʒæm/ NOUN [plural **jams**]
1 a sweet, sticky food made of fruit and sugar that you spread on bread □ *strawberry jam* (geleia)
2 a line of vehicles that are not moving or are moving very slowly ⊞ *I got stuck in a traffic jam.* (engarrafamento)

jam² /dʒæm/ VERB [**jams, jamming, jammed**]
1 to push something into a space so that it fits very tightly □ *She jammed the clothes into her suitcase.* (espremer)
2 to become or to make something become unable to move or work □ *I tried to open the door but it was jammed.* (emperrar)
3 to fill a place completely with people or things □ **+ with** *The M6 was jammed with traffic after an accident.* ⊞ *All the cupboards were jammed full of clothes.* (abarrotar)

January /'dʒænjuəri/ NOUN [plural **Januarys**] the first month of the year, after December and before February □ *My birthday is in January.* (janeiro)

jar /dʒɑː(r)/ NOUN [plural **jars**] a glass container with a wide neck and a lid, used for storing food □ *a jam jar* □ *a jar of coffee* (pote)

> **THESAURUS:** A **jar** is a glass container with a wide neck and a lid. It is used for storing food. For example, we keep jam in a jar. A **pot** is a round container with or without a lid, used for storing things in, for cooking or for growing plants in. A **jug** is a container with a handle used for pouring liquids. A **vase** is a container for flowers.

jaw /dʒɔː/ NOUN [plural **jaws**] the lower part of your face made up of two bones that your teeth grow in (maxilar)
♦ IDIOM **someone's jaw drops** if someone's jaw drops, they show with their face that they are extremely surprised □ *She told us what she earned and our jaws dropped.*

jazz /dʒæz/ NOUN, NO PLURAL a type of music with a strong beat that is often changed or added to as it is played □ *modern jazz* (jazz)

jealous /'dʒeləs/ ADJECTIVE
1 feeling angry and unhappy because someone has something you want or because you want to be like someone else □ **+ of** *He's jealous of his brother's success.* ⊞ *She made me jealous by going out with her other friends.* (invejoso)
2 feeling upset and angry because you think someone you love is in love with someone else □ *a jealous wife* (ciumento)

jealousy /'dʒeləsi/ NOUN, NO PLURAL jealous feelings (com ciúme)

jeans /dʒiːnz/ PLURAL NOUN trousers made of denim (= thick, usually blue, cotton) (jeans)

jelly /'dʒeli/ NOUN [plural **jellies**]
1 a soft, sweet food with a fruit flavour that shakes when you move it and is eaten cold □ *a bowl of jelly and ice cream* (gelatina)
2 a US word for **jam¹** (geleia)

jellyfish /'dʒelifɪʃ/ NOUN [plural **jellyfish** or **jellyfishes**] a sea animal with a soft transparent body that can sting you (= hurt you by putting poison into your skin) (água-viva)

jerk /dʒɜːk/ VERB [jerks, jerking, jerked]
1 to make a short sudden movement □ *The driver started the engine and the old bus jerked forward.* (sacudir)
2 to pull something with a sudden rough movement □ *He jerked his hand away.* (sacudir)

jersey /ˈdʒɜːzɪ/ NOUN [plural jerseys] a warm piece of clothing with sleeves that you pull on over your head and wear on the top half of your body (camisa de malha)

Jesus /ˈdʒiːzəs/ or **Jesus Christ** /ˌdʒiːzəs ˈkraɪst/ NOUN the man who Christians believe to be the son of God and on whose teaching Christianity is based (Jesus Cristo)

jet /dʒet/ NOUN [plural jets]
1 a fast plane with powerful engines □ *a passenger jet* (avião a jato)
2 a strong fast flow of liquid or gas forced through a small hole □ *The printer releases jets of coloured ink.* (sacudir)

Jew /dʒuː/ NOUN [plural Jews] someone whose religion is Judaism or whose family originally came from the ancient Hebrew people of Israel (judeu)

jewel /ˈdʒuːəl/ NOUN [plural jewels] a valuable stone, used to make jewellery □ *a ring set with precious jewels* (pedra preciosa)

jewellery /ˈdʒuːəlrɪ/ NOUN, NO PLURAL things that you wear to decorate your body and clothes, often made of metal and valuable stones □ *She wears a lot of gold jewellery.* 🔁 *a beautiful piece of jewellery* (joias)

jewelry /ˈdʒuːəlrɪ/ NOUN, NO PLURAL the US spelling of **jewellery** (joias)

Jewish /ˈdʒuːɪʃ/ ADJECTIVE to do with Jews or Judaism □ *a Jewish religious festival* □ *Jewish history* (judaica)

job /dʒɒb/ NOUN [plural jobs]
1 the work someone does regularly for money 🔁 *He needs to get a job.* 🔁 *They offered me a job in the shop.* 🔁 *He lost his job because of the illness.* □ *+ as She got a job as a chef.* 🔁 *a part-time/full-time job* (trabalho)
2 a piece of work □ *There are plenty of jobs to do about the house.* (trabalho)
3 a good/bad, etc. job the standard of work someone has done □ *You've made a good job of that painting.* □ *The builders did a great job.* (trabalho)

> If you want to ask someone what type of job they do, the usual question is **What do you do?** or **What do you do for a living?**. People do not usually ask 'What is your job?'.

jobless /ˈdʒɒblɪs/ PLURAL NOUN **the jobless** people who do not have a job (desempregado)

jockey /ˈdʒɒkɪ/ NOUN [plural jockeys] someone who rides a horse in races □ *a champion jockey* (jóquei)

jog¹ /dʒɒg/ VERB [jogs, jogging, jogged] to run slowly, especially for exercise □ *She jogs around the park every morning.* (fazer cooper)

jog² /dʒɒg/ NOUN [plural jogs] a slow run for exercise □ *They've gone for a jog along the beach.* (cooper)

join /dʒɔɪn/ VERB [joins, joining, joined]
1 to become a member of a group or organization □ *I've joined a rowing club.* □ *He joined the army last year.* □ *I joined the company in 1999.* (associar-se)
2 to connect things together □ *+ to You have to join the metal part to the wood.* (ligar)
3 to come together at a particular point □ *The track joins the main road just around this corner.* (juntar-se)
4 to come together with other people □ *Please welcome Jill Smith, who joins us from London.* □ *Would you like to join us for lunch?* (juntar-se)
5 join hands to hold someone's hand with your hand (juntar as mãos)
◆ PHRASAL VERB **join in** to take part in an activity with other people □ *He didn't join in with the singing.*

joint¹ /dʒɔɪnt/ NOUN [plural joints]
1 a place in your body where two bones meet □ *painful hip joints* (articulação)
2 a large piece of meat that is cooked whole □ *a joint of beef* (carne com osso)
3 a place where two or more things join □ *Water was leaking from a joint in the pipe.* (junta)

joint² /dʒɔɪnt/ ADJECTIVE done or owned together 🔁 *The project was a joint effort between Tom and Sue.* 🔁 *Some married couples have a joint account.* (conjunto)

joke¹ /dʒəʊk/ NOUN [plural jokes] something that someone says or does to make people laugh 🔁 *Matt is always telling jokes.* (piada, brincadeira)

joke² /dʒəʊk/ VERB [jokes, joking, joked]
1 to make a joke □ *The kids were laughing and joking about him missing the goal.* (caçoar)
2 Just/Only joking! something you say meaning that what you have just said is not true and was intended to be funny □ *There's a big rip in your trousers. Only joking!* (brincar)
3 You're joking! something you say when someone says something extremely surprising □ *'She's only twenty.' 'You're joking! I thought she was nearer forty!'* (brincar)

jolly /ˈdʒɒlɪ/ ADJECTIVE [jollier, jolliest] happy □ *a man with a jolly face* (jovial)

journal /ˈdʒɜːnəl/ NOUN [plural journals]
1 a magazine about a particular subject □ *He subscribes to several political journals.* (revistas)
2 a book in which someone writes what they have done each day (diário)

journalism   jump

> THESAURUS: Publication is a general word for something that is printed and sold. A magazine is a thin book with pictures in it which is published every week or every month. There are lots of different kinds of magazines, for example fashion magazines and gardening magazines. A journal is a magazine about a particular subject, for professional people or people who study a particular subject. If you are a doctor, you might read a medical journal. A newspaper is a publication with reports and pictures about recent events. Newspapers are sold every day or every week.

journalism /'dʒɜ:nəlɪzəm/ NOUN, NO PLURAL
the work of writing articles for newspapers, magazines, television or radio ☐ a career in journalism (**jornalismo**)

journalist /'dʒɜ:nəlɪst/ NOUN [plural **journalists**]
someone whose job is to write articles for newspapers, magazines, television or radio (**jornalista**)

journey /'dʒɜ:ni/ NOUN [plural **journeys**] when you travel from one place to another, especially a long distance ☐ He has a two-hour journey to work each day. ☐ The train journey was very pleasant. (**viagem**)

> THESAURUS: A journey is when you travel from one place to another, especially a long distance. A drive is a journey in a car. The words outing and trip describe going somewhere, doing something, and then coming back. An outing is for pleasure, and is usually quite short. A trip can be for work or for pleasure, and may be longer than an outing. For example you might go on an outing or a trip to the beach. You might go on a business trip to a foreign country. Travel is a more general word to describe the activity of going from one place to another. Note that the word travel is not usually used in the plural.

joy /dʒɔɪ/ NOUN [plural **joys**]
1 a feeling of being very happy ☐ She finally experienced the joy of holding her child. (**alegria**)
2 something that makes you very happy ☐ The new model is a joy to drive. (**alegria**)

Judaism /'dʒu:deɪɪzəm/ NOUN, NO PLURAL the Jewish religion which is based on the Old Testament of the Bible (**judaísmo**)

judge¹ /dʒʌdʒ/ VERB [**judges, judging, judged**]
1 to form an opinion about someone or something ☐ **+ on** I tend to judge books on their story rather than their use of language. ☐ **+ by** It's wrong to judge people by what clothes they wear. ☐ The event was judged a success. (**julgar**)
2 to decide who or what is the winner of a competition ☐ I was asked to judge the competition. (**arbitrar**)

judge² /dʒʌdʒ/ NOUN [plural **judges**]
1 someone who is in charge of a trial in court and decides what punishments should be given (**juiz**)
2 someone who judges a competition (**árbitro**)

judgement or **judgment** /'dʒʌdʒmənt/ NOUN [plural **judgements** or **judgments**]
1 the ability to make good decisions or form correct opinions ☐ When it comes to education, I trust her judgement. ☐ I can't tell you exactly how much salt to add – just use your judgement. (**discernimento**)
2 an opinion about someone or something ☐ In my judgement, it wouldn't be a very sensible thing to do. ☐ You will have to make a judgement about whether or not to trust her. (**opinião**)
3 the decision made by a judge in a court ☐ He is due to pass judgment on Wednesday. (**julgamento**)

jug /dʒʌg/ NOUN [plural **jugs**] a container with a handle used for pouring liquids ☐ a milk jug ☐ a jug of cream (**cântaro**)

juggle /'dʒʌgəl/ VERB [**juggles, juggling, juggled**]
to keep several balls, etc. in the air by repeatedly throwing them up and catching them (**fazer malabarismo**)

juice /dʒu:s/ NOUN [plural **juices**] the liquid in fruit or vegetables, often used as a drink ☐ a glass of orange juice (**suco**)

juicy /'dʒu:si/ ADJECTIVE [**juicier, juiciest**] full of juice ☐ a nice juicy peach (**suculento**)

July /dʒu:'laɪ/ NOUN [plural **Julys**] the seventh month of the year, after June and before August ☐ Clara will be 11 in July. (**julho**)

jump¹ /dʒʌmp/ VERB [**jumps, jumping, jumped**]
1 to push yourself off the ground or other surface with your legs ☐ We jumped up and down in excitement. ☐ **+ over** The dog jumped over the wall. ☐ He jumped down from the tree. (**pular, saltar**)
2 to go over something by pushing yourself into the air with your legs ☐ The horse jumped the fence. (**saltar**)
3 to move or go somewhere quickly ☐ As soon as I heard the news, I jumped on a train to Scotland. ☐ He jumped to his feet when she came in. (**saltar**)

jump

4 to make a movement because you are suddenly afraid ▣ *The noise of the bell made me jump.*
♦ PHRASAL VERB **jump at something** to accept an opportunity in a very eager way ▣ *He jumped at the chance to work in Africa.*

jump² /dʒʌmp/ NOUN [plural **jumps**] when you push yourself off the ground with your legs ▢ *Do three more jumps.* (**pulo, salto**)

jumper /'dʒʌmpə(r)/ NOUN [plural **jumpers**] a warm piece of clothing with sleeves that you pull on over your head and wear on the top half of your body (**blusão**)

junction /'dʒʌŋkʃən/ NOUN [plural **junctions**] a place where roads or railway lines meet and cross ▢ *Turn right at the junction ahead.* (**entroncamento**)

June /dʒu:n/ NOUN [plural **Junes**] the sixth month of the year, after May and before July ▢ *We're moving house in June.* (**junho**)

jungle /'dʒʌŋgəl/ NOUN [plural **jungles**] a thick forest in a hot country ▢ *the Peruvian jungle* (**selva**)

junior /'dʒu:niə(r)/ ADJECTIVE

1 having a lower position in an organization ▢ *junior staff* ▢ *She's a junior minister at the Foreign Office.* (**subalterno, hierarquicamente inferior**)

2 of or for younger people ▢ *junior members of the tennis club* ▢ *junior classes* (**júnior, mais novo**)

junk /dʒʌŋk/ NOUN, NO PLURAL old things with little use or value ▢ *Most of this is junk and we can just get rid of it.* (**refugo, traste**)

junk food /'dʒʌŋk ˌfu:d/ NOUN, NO PLURAL food that is not good for your health but that you can eat or prepare quickly (**lanche sem valor nutritivo**)

juror /'dʒʊərə(r)/ NOUN [plural **jurors**] one of the people in a court of law who listen to the facts and decide if someone is guilty of a crime or not (**jurado**)

jury /'dʒʊəri/ NOUN [plural **juries**] a group of people in a court of law who listen to the facts and decide if someone is guilty of a crime or not (**júri**)

just¹ /dʒʌst/ ADVERB

1 at this time, or at a particular time in the past ▢ *I'm just getting dressed.* ▢ *We were just sitting down to dinner.* ▣ *Just then, a man came in.* ▣ *I can't talk to you just now.* (**justamente**)

2 a very short time ago ▢ *I've just finished work.* ▢ *The clock's just struck five.* (**há pouco**)

3 only ▢ *I'll just have a sandwich.* ▢ *It was just a joke.* ▢ *I just want to go home.* (**só, apenas**)

4 almost not ▣ *I could only just see him.* ▢ *We just managed to swim to the shore.* ▢ *She was just ahead of me.* (**apenas**)

5 used to emphasize what you are saying ▢ *I was just devastated by the news.* ▢ *A cold drink was just what I needed.* (**simplesmente**)

6 just about almost ▢ *I've just about finished here.* (**mais ou menos**)

7 be just about to do something to be going to do something very soon ▢ *I was just about to phone you.* (**justamente**)

8 just as at the same time as ▢ *Just as we got there, the fire alarm went off.* (**exatamente**)

just² /dʒʌst/ ADJECTIVE fair ▢ *a just decision* (**justo**)

justice /'dʒʌstɪs/ NOUN, NO PLURAL

1 fair treatment of people by the law ▢ *The group is fighting for justice for all.* (**justiça**)

2 the system of laws which judges and punishes people ▢ *the criminal justice system* (**justiça**)

K k

K¹ or **k** /keɪ/ the 11th letter of the alphabet (a décima primeira letra do alfabeto)

K² /keɪ/ ABBREVIATION one thousand □ *She earns £30K a year.* (mil)

kangaroo /ˌkæŋɡəˈruː/ NOUN [plural **kangaroos**] an Australian animal that moves by jumping, and carries its baby in a pouch (= a pocket at the front of its body) (canguru)

keen /kiːn/ ADJECTIVE [keener, keenest]

1 interested in or enjoying a particular activity very much □ *Jim's a keen swimmer.* □ **+ on** *She's very keen on riding.* ▣ *She has a keen interest in art.*
2 wanting to do something □ **+ to do something** *Everyone seemed very keen to help.* (ardoroso)

keep /kiːp/ VERB [keeps, keeping, kept]

1 to make someone or something stay in a particular state □ *Keep the door closed.* □ *The noise kept me awake.* □ *Keep still!* □ *Keep your mouth shut!* (manter-se)
2 to prevent someone or something going to a particular place □ *Keep the children away from the fire.* □ *I tried to keep the sun off my face.* □ *A high fence kept out strangers.* (manter)
3 keep doing something to continue to do something, or to do something repeatedly □ *It's hard to keep going when you're so tired.* □ *I keep forgetting to lock the door.* (prosseguir)
4 to continue to have or own something □ *You can keep the book.* □ *The company has promised that they will keep their jobs.* (guardar, conservar)
5 to put something in a particular place when you are not using it □ *I keep my diary in a drawer.* ▣ *This ring is valuable – make sure you keep it in a safe place.* (guardar, guarde em local seguro)
6 to make someone stay in a particular place □ *They're keeping him in hospital for a few more days.* □ *She was kept in after school.* (reter)
7 keep a promise to do what you have promised to do (manter uma promessa)
8 keep a secret to not tell anyone a secret
→ go to **keep an eye on someone/something** (guardar um segredo)

◆ PHRASAL VERBS **keep on doing something** to continue to do something, or to do something repeatedly □ *He ignored the cries and kept on walking.* □ *They keep on waking me up.* **keep up 1** to move at the same speed as someone else □ *She walks so fast I can hardly keep up.* **2** to make the same amount of progress as someone or something else □ *Their rivals invested in new technology, and they failed to keep up.* **keep up something** to continue to do something □ *I've been keeping up my exercise programme.*

> **THESAURUS:** If you **keep** something, you put something in a particular place when you are not using it. You might keep your keys in a bag. If you **preserve** something, you keep it the same and stop it from being lost or destroyed. For example, you can **preserve** things in a museum. If you **collect** something, you get things from different places and put them together. Some people **collect** stamps. If you **store** something, you keep it somewhere, for example, you can **store** information on a computer and you can **store** food in a cupboard.

kept /kept/ PAST TENSE AND PAST PARTICIPLE OF **keep** (ver **keep**)

kettle /ˈketəl/ NOUN [plural kettles]
a container with a lid and a handle, used for boiling water ▣ *I've put the kettle on (= I am heating water in a kettle) for a cup of tea* (chaleira)

key /kiː/ NOUN [plural keys]

1 a small metal object used for locking something such as a door or window, or for starting the engine of a vehicle ▣ *I switched the light off and turned the key in the lock.* ▣ *Have you seen my car keys?* ▣ *a bunch of keys* (chave)
2 a button on a computer keyboard or a telephone ▣ *Use the arrow keys to move from one image to the next.* □ *Press any key to continue.* (tecla)
3 the main thing that helps you to achieve something □ **+ to** *Confidence is the key to success in this business.* (tecla)
4 one of the white or black parts you press on a piano or a similar instrument to make a sound (tecla)
5 a list of answers to questions in an exercise or test (resposta)

keyboard /ˈkiːbɔːd/ NOUN [plural keyboards]

1 a piece of computer equipment with keys (= buttons) on it that you press to put information into the computer (teclado)
2 the set of keys on a musical instrument such as a piano □ *a piano keyboard* (teclado)

kg /ˌkeɪˈdʒiː/ ABBREVIATION **kilogram** or **kilograms** (kg)

kick¹ /kɪk/ VERB [kicks, kicking, kicked]

1 to hit someone or something with your foot □ *Jane kicked the ball over the fence.* □ *He kicked me in the leg.* (chutar)

2 to move your legs quickly and with force □ *She was carried, kicking and screaming, to the car.* (**chutar**)

◆ PHRASAL VERBS **kick (something) off** to start something □ *We kicked off the meeting with a discussion about love.* **kick someone out** to make someone leave a place □ *He was kicked out of the army for laziness.*

kick² /kɪk/ NOUN [plural **kicks**]
1 when you kick, or kick something □ *I gave him a kick in the leg.* (**pontapé**)
2 an informal word meaning a feeling of pleasure or excitement 🔁 *He gets a kick out of driving fast.* (**prazer**)

kick-off /'kɪkɒf/ NOUN [plural **kick-offs**] the start of a football game (**pontapé inicial**)

kid /kɪd/ NOUN [plural **kids**]
1 an informal word meaning child □ *Have they got any kids?* □ *You can't expect him to look after the baby – he's just a kid.* (**garoto**)
2 a young goat (**garoto**)

kidnap /'kɪdnæp/ VERB [**kidnaps, kidnapping, kidnapped**] to take someone away using force, and to ask their family or the government for something such as money in exchange for their safe return □ *The journalist was kidnapped three weeks ago.* (**sequestrar, raptar**)

> **THESAURUS:** If you **kidnap** someone, you take them away using force and ask for money from their family or a government in exchange for their safe return. If you **hijack** a plane, you take control of it by force. If you **capture** someone or something, you catch them and do not allow them to escape.

kidnapper /'kɪdnæpə(r)/ NOUN [plural **kidnappers**] a person who takes someone away using force, and asks for money in exchange for their safe return □ *The kidnappers have demanded a ransom of £2 million.* (**raptor, sequestrador**)

kidney /'kɪdni/ NOUN [plural **kidneys**] one of the two organs in your body that clean your blood and remove waste from it. A biology word. (**rim, rins**)

kill /kɪl/ VERB [**kills, killing, killed**] to make a person or animal die □ *Two people were killed in the crash.* □ *The explosion killed six people.* □ *He tried to kill himself.* (**matar**)

> **THESAURUS:** If you **kill** a person or an animal, they make it die. If a person **murders** someone, they kill that person deliberately. To **execute** someone means to kill someone as an official punishment. To **assassinate** someone means to kill a famous person, often a politician. President Abraham Lincoln was **assassinated**, for example.

killer /'kɪlə(r)/ NOUN [plural **killers**] a person who kills someone □ *Police have appealed for more information to help catch the killer.* (**matador, assassino**)

◆ IDIOM **make a killing** to make a lot of money

kilo /'kiːləʊ/ NOUN [plural **kilos**] a short way to say and write **kilogram** (**quilo**)

kilogram or **kilogramme** /'kɪləˌgræm/ NOUN [plural **kilograms** or **kilogrammes**] a unit for measuring weight, equal to 1000 grams. This is often written **kg**. □ *Katherine weighs 60 kilograms.* (**quilograma**)

kilometre /'kɪləmiːtə(r), kɪ'lɒmɪtə(r)/ NOUN [plural **kilometres**] a unit for measuring distance, equal to 1000 metres. This is often written **km**. □ *We live 20 kilometres from the coast.* (**quilômetro**)

kind¹ /kaɪnd/ NOUN [plural **kinds**]
1 a type of person or thing □ **+ of** *What kind of dog have you got?* 🔁 *Encourage children to try different kinds of fruit.* 🔁 *There are all kinds of styles to choose from.* (**espécie, tipo**)
2 kind of an informal phrase that means slightly □ *It's kind of like Sara's dress.* (**de certo modo**)

kind² /kaɪnd/ ADJECTIVE [**kinder, kindest**] behaving in a way that shows you care about people and want to make them happy □ *She's the kindest person I know.* □ **+ to** *You've all been very kind to me.* □ **+ of** *It was kind of you to help us.* □ *Thank you for your kind offer.* (**gentil**)

kindergarten /'kɪndəgɑːtən/ NOUN [plural **kindergartens**]
1 in the UK, a school for children under five (**jardim de infância**)
2 in the US, the first year of school education for children aged five or six (**jardim de infância**)

kindness /'kaɪndnɪs/ NOUN, NO PLURAL when someone is kind □ *What I like most about him is his kindness.* (**gentileza**)

king /kɪŋ/ NOUN [plural **kings**] a man who rules a country, being the most important male member of its royal family □ *He's the future king of Great Britain.* (**rei**)

kingdom /'kɪŋdəm/ NOUN [plural **kingdoms**] a country ruled by a king or queen □ *the United Kingdom* □ *the kingdom of Denmark* (**reino**)

kiosk /'kiːɒsk/ NOUN [plural **kiosks**] a small shop that sells things such as newspapers, drinks and sweets (**quiosque**)

kiss¹ /kɪs/ VERB [**kisses, kissing, kissed**] to touch someone with your lips, especially on their mouth or face, to show that you feel love or affection for them 🔁 *He kissed her goodbye and got into the car.* □ *She leaned towards him and kissed his cheek.* (**beijar**)

kiss

kiss² /kɪs/ NOUN [plural **kisses**] when you kiss someone ▣ *He gave her a kiss.* □ *+ on a kiss on the lips* (**beijo**)

kit /kɪt/ NOUN [plural **kits**]
1 the clothes that you need for a particular activity ▣ *I brought my football kit home for washing.* (**material**)
2 a set of tools or equipment that you need for a particular activity □ *a first aid kit* □ *a bicycle repair kit* (**material**)
3 a set of parts that you can put together to make something □ *I got a model boat kit for my birthday.* (**kit**)

kitchen /ˈkɪtʃɪn/ NOUN [plural **kitchens**] a room where you prepare and cook food, and sometimes eat food □ *John is in the kitchen.* ▣ *I sat at the kitchen table and drank my coffee.* (**cozinha**)

kitten /ˈkɪtən/ NOUN [plural **kittens**] a young cat (**gatinho**)

km ABBREVIATION **kilometre** or **kilometer** (**km**)

knee /niː/ NOUN [plural **knees**] the part in the middle of your leg where the leg bends □ *a knee injury* (**joelho**)

kneel /niːl/ VERB [**kneels, kneeling, knelt**] to move into a position in which your knees and lower legs are on the ground, or to be in this position □ *+ down She knelt down beside me and stroked my hair.* □ *He was kneeling by the bed, praying.* (**ajoelhar**)

knelt /nelt/ PAST TENSE AND PAST PARTICIPLE OF **kneel** (ver **kneel**)

knew /njuː/ PAST TENSE OF **know** (ver **know**)

knickers /ˈnɪkəz/ PLURAL NOUN a piece of underwear for women or girls, which covers the bottom (**calcinha**)

knife /naɪf/ NOUN [plural **knives**] a tool with a blade and a handle, used especially for cutting food ▣ *Have we got enough knives and forks?* ▣ *a sharp knife* (**faca**)

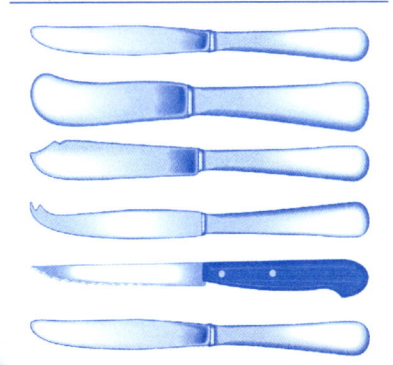

knight /naɪt/ NOUN [plural **knights**]
1 in the past, a soldier of a high social class who rode a horse (**cavaleiro**)
2 a man who has been given an honour by a British king or queen that allows him to use the title 'Sir' (**cavaleiro**)

know

knit /nɪt/ VERB [**knits, knitting, knitted**] to make something, for example a piece of clothing, using two long knitting needles (= pointed metal or wooden sticks) and wool □ *I'm knitting a scarf.* (**tricotar**)

knives /naɪvz/ PLURAL OF **knife** (ver **knife**)

knock¹ /nɒk/ VERB [**knocks, knocking, knocked**]
1 to hit someone or something so that it moves or falls □ *+ over The cat knocked over the vase.* □ *The blast knocked us off our feet.* □ *I fell and knocked my tooth out.* (**derrubar**)
2 to hit a hard surface, especially a door, with your hand in order to get attention □ *Knock before you come in.* □ *+ on I knocked on the door but nobody answered.* (**bater**)
◆ PHRASAL VERB **knock someone out 1** to make someone become unconscious **2** to defeat a person or a team in a competition □ *+ of Liverpool have been knocked out of the competition.*

knock² /nɒk/ NOUN [plural **knocks**] the sound of someone or something knocking on a hard surface □ *There was a knock at the door.* (**pancada**)

knot¹ /nɒt/ NOUN [plural **knots**]
1 a join made by tying two ends of string, rope or cloth together ▣ *to tie a knot* (**nó**)
2 a mass of untidy, twisted threads of hair, string, etc. that are difficult to separate □ *Let's comb these knots out of your hair.* (**nó**)
3 a unit for measuring how fast a ship is travelling (**nó**)

knot² /nɒt/ VERB [**knots, knotting, knotted**] to tie something with a knot □ *A scarf was knotted around his neck.* (**atar**)

> **THESAURUS:** To **tie** two things means to join them together using string, rope etc. To **knot** something means to tie two ends of string, rope etc together. To **knit** means to make something, for example clothing, using wool and special long needles. To **weave** means to make cloth by passing threads over and under each other on a special frame called a loom.

know /nəʊ/ VERB [**knows, knowing, knew, known**]
1 to have information or knowledge about something □ *I didn't know the answer to her questions.* ▣ *'What's the capital of Hungary?' 'I don't know.'* □ *+ question word Do you know where he lives?* □ *She knows how to make me happy.* □ *+ about I didn't know about the course.* (**saber, conhecer**)
2 to be familiar with a person □ *I didn't know anyone at the party.* ▣ *I got to know her when I was a student.* ▣ *I don't know him very well.* (**conhecer**)
3 to be familiar with a place or a thing because you have been there, seen it, used it, etc. □ *Do you know Berlin well?* □ *I know his work.* (**conhecer**)
4 let someone know to tell someone something □ *I'm going to be late – could you let John know, please?* (**avisar**)

> Remember that to **know** something means to *have* knowledge about something. To **find out** something is to *get* knowledge about something:
> ✓ I called Annie to find out when she was leaving.
> ✗ I called Annie to know when she was leaving.

knowledge /ˈnɒlɪdʒ/ NOUN, NO PLURAL the information that you know about something ▫ Candidates need to show that they have a *basic knowledge* of English. ▫ It's *common knowledge* (= everyone knows) that he has health problems. ▫ **+ of** She has a good knowledge of sport. (**conhecimento**)

known¹ /nəʊn/ PAST PARTICIPLE OF **know** (ver **know**)
known² /nəʊn/ ADJECTIVE
1 that people know about ▫ There is no known cure for the disease. (**conhecido**)
2 famous ▫ She is known for her performance in the film 'The Red Shoes'. (**conhecido, famoso**)

Koran /kəˈrɑːn/ NOUN **the Koran** the holy book of the Islamic religion (**alcorão**)

L l

L or **l** /el/ the 12th letter of the alphabet (**a décima segunda letra do alfabeto**)

lab /læb/ NOUN [plural **labs**] a short way to say and write **laboratory**

label[1] /ˈleɪbəl/ NOUN [plural **labels**] a small piece of paper or cloth that is fixed to something and gives information about it □ *The washing instructions are on the label.* □ *I looked at the ingredients on the label.* (**rótulo, etiqueta**)

> THESAURUS: A **label** or a **tag** is a small piece of paper or cloth that is fixed to something and gives information about it. Goods in shops usually have a price **tag** on them, and clothes usually have a **label** inside to tell you how to clean them. A **ticket** is a small piece of paper that shows that you have paid to do something. You might have a train **ticket** or a theatre **ticket**, for example.

label[2] /ˈleɪbəl/ VERB [**labels, labelling**/ US **labeling, labelled**/ US **labeled**] to fix a label to something □ *All the boxes have been carefully labelled.* □ *Manufacturers should label their products more clearly.* (**rotular**)

laboratory /ləˈbɒrətəri/ NOUN [plural **laboratories**] a room containing equipment for scientific work □ *a laboratory experiment* □ *Tests were carried out at a laboratory.* (**laboratório**)

labour /ˈleɪbə(r)/ NOUN, NO PLURAL
1 workers, especially in a particular country or type of work ▣ *There is a shortage of skilled labour.* (**mão de obra**)
□ *the rising cost of labour* ▣ *the labour market*
2 work, especially hard, physical work ▣ *He was used to hard, manual labour.* (**trabalho**)

labourer /ˈleɪbərə(r)/ NOUN [plural **labourers**] a person who does hard physical work □ *a farm labourer* (**trabalhador**)

Labour Party /ˈleɪbər ˌpɑːti/ NOUN, NO PLURAL in the UK, one of the main political parties (**Partido Trabalhista**)

lace /leɪs/ NOUN [plural **laces**]
1 a decorative cloth with delicate patterns of many holes □ *a collar trimmed with lace* (**renda**)
2 a piece of string for tying up shoes or other clothing ▣ *He bent down to tie his shoe laces.* (**cordão**)

lack[1] /læk/ VERB [**lacks, lacking, lacked**] to be without something or not to not have enough of some thing □ *Audrey lacks a sense of humour.* □ *We lack the resources to deal with all the requests.* (**ter falta de**)

lack[2] /læk/ NOUN, NO PLURAL when you do not have something, or you do not have enough of something □ + *of He was suffering from lack of sleep.* ▣ *He shows a complete lack of understanding.* (**falta**)

ladder /ˈlædə(r)/ NOUN [plural **ladders**] a set of steps that you use for climbing up to high places and can move around to different places □ *He had to climb a ladder to reach the top cupboard.* (**escada**)

ladies /ˈleɪdɪz/ PLURAL NOUN a public toilet for women and girls □ *Where is the ladies, please?* (**banheiro feminino**)

lady /ˈleɪdɪ/ NOUN [plural **ladies**]
1 a polite word for a woman □ *Ask that lady if the seat by her is free.* ▣ *Good evening ladies and gentlemen.* (**senhora**)
2 in the UK, a title for a woman with a high social rank (**senhora**)

laid /leɪd/ PAST TENSE AND PAST PARTICIPLE OF **lay**[1] □ *She laid the baby on the blanket.* (**ver lay**[1])

lain /leɪn/ PAST PARTICIPLE OF **lie**[3] (= put your body in a flat position) □ *I had lain down for a moment and fallen fast asleep.* (**ver lie**[3])

lake /leɪk/ NOUN [plural **lakes**] a large area of water with land all around it □ *Lake Como* (**lago**)

> THESAURUS: A **lake** is a large area of water with land all around it. Lakes can be natural or created by people. A **reservoir** is a large lake where water is collected and stored in order to be used by people. A **pond** is a small area of water, smaller than a lake. Some people have a **pond** in their garden.

lamb /læm/ NOUN [plural **lambs**]
1 a young sheep (**cordeiro**)
2 *no plural* meat from a young sheep □ *roast lamb* □ *lamb chops* (**cordeiro**)

lame /leɪm/ ADJECTIVE [**lamer, lamest**] not able to walk well because of an injury □ *a lame horse* (**manco**)

lamp /læmp/ NOUN [plural **lamps**] a light, especially one which stands on a table □ *a table lamp* □ *a bedside lamp* □ *an old oil lamp* (**lampião**)

land[1] /lænd/ NOUN [plural **lands**]
1 *no plural* an area of ground □ *an acre of land* ▣ *agricultural land* (**terra**)

2 *no plural* the part of the Earth not covered by water 🔲 *It's good to be back on dry land.* (terra)
3 a word for a country used especially in stories 🔲 *He talked of his adventures in foreign lands.* (terra)

land² /lænd/ VERB [lands, landing, landed]
1 when an aircraft lands, it arrives on the ground after a flight 🔲 *The plane landed around 3pm.* (aterrissar)
🔲 *The flight landed safely at Glasgow airport.*
2 to stop somewhere after flying or falling 🔲 *The bird landed on a branch.* 🔲 *The book fell off the table and landed on the floor.* 🔲 *I slipped but managed to land on my feet.* (aterrissar)

landing /'lændɪŋ/ NOUN [plural landings]
1 the process of moving a plane down to the ground 🔲 *The helicopter made an emergency landing.* (aterrissagem, desembarque)
2 the floor at the top of some stairs or the floor between two sets of stairs 🔲 *She reached the second-floor landing.* (patamar)

landlady /'lændleɪdɪ/ NOUN [plural landladies] a woman who owns a house that someone else pays to live in (senhoria)

landlord /'lændlɔːd/ NOUN [plural landlords] a man who owns a house that someone else pays to live in 🔲 *Her landlord raised the rent.* (senhorio)

landmark /'lændmɑːk/ NOUN [plural landmarks] a place, especially a building, that helps you know where you are because you can easily recognize it 🔲 *The tower is one of the city's most famous landmarks.* 🔲 *He spotted a familiar landmark.* (marco, ponto de referência)

landscape /'lændskeɪp/ NOUN [plural landscapes] a view of a large area of land 🔲 *He looked out at the beautiful landscape.* 🔲 *a snowy landscape* (paisagem)

lane /leɪn/ NOUN [plural lanes]
1 a narrow road 🔲 *We drove along narrow country lanes.* (caminho)
2 a strip of a road separated by painted lines 🔲 *She pulled out into the fast lane.* 🔲 *The northbound lane of the motorway was closed after an accident.* (pista)

language /'læŋgwɪdʒ/ NOUN [plural languages]
1 *no plural* communication using speech and writing 🔲 *formal language* 🔲 *He used some interesting language to describe the scene.* 🔲 *+ of the language of diplomacy* (linguagem)
2 the words used by a particular group, especially the people that live in one country 🔲 *the English language* 🔲 *All children should learn a foreign language.* 🔲 *Do you speak any other languages?* (língua)

> **THESAURUS:** Language refers to communication using speech and writing. **Speech** refers to the ability to speak or the way that someone speaks. Your **accent** is the way that you say words, according to where you come from.

lap /læp/ NOUN [plural laps]
1 the top part of a person's legs when they are in a sitting position 🔲 *Jessie sat on her mother's lap.* (colo)
2 one complete journey around a race track 🔲 *He crashed on the first lap of the race.* (volta)

laptop /'læptɒp/ NOUN [plural laptops] a small computer that can be carried easily. A computing word. (laptop)

large /lɑːdʒ/ ADJECTIVE [larger, largest] big or bigger than normal in size or amount 🔲 *a large house* 🔲 *A large number of people were waiting.* 🔲 *Large parts of the country are without power.* (grande)

laser /'leɪzə(r)/ NOUN [plural lasers] a very narrow, powerful beam of light 🔲 *a laser beam* 🔲 *The surgery uses lasers.* (laser)

last¹ /lɑːst/ ADJECTIVE, DETERMINER
1 most recent 🔲 *We moved house last October.* 🔲 *In the last few months we have been very busy.* 🔲 *On my last birthday, he gave me a necklace.* 🔲 *The last time I ate fish, I was ill.* 🔲 *Their last album was a huge success.* (último)
2 coming after all the others 🔲 *We caught the last train to Cambridge.* 🔲 *This is the last time I will ever help you.* 🔲 *That was her last public appearance.* (último)
3 the last moment/minute the latest possible time before something 🔲 *Our flight was cancelled at the last moment.* 🔲 *Don't leave it to the last minute to book a hotel.* (último momento/minuto)
4 the final one remaining 🔲 *She ate my last toffee.* (último)

last² /lɑːst/ VERB [lasts, lasting, lasted]
1 to continue for a period of time 🔲 *The lesson seemed to last for ever.* 🔲 *The film lasted over three hours.* (durar)
2 to remain in good condition 🔲 *These boots have lasted well.* (durar)
3 to be enough 🔲 *The food lasted for three days.* (durar)

last³ /lɑːst/ ADVERB
1 after all the others 🔲 *She arrived last.* 🔲 *Make sure you add the sugar last.* 🔲 *I came last in the swimming race.* (por último)
2 most recently 🔲 *When did you last see Anna?* (por último)

lasting /'lɑːstɪŋ/ ADJECTIVE continuing to exist for a long time 🔲 *They hope to achieve a lasting peace.* 🔲 *His book made a lasting impression on me.* (duradouro)

lastly /'lɑːstlɪ/ ADVERB after all other people or things 🔲 *Lastly, I just want to thank my wife.* (enfim)

late /leɪt/ ADJECTIVE, ADVERB [later, latest]
1 after the time that is expected or necessary 🔲 *The bus was late.* 🔲 *+ for If you don't hurry, you'll be late for work.* 🔲 *I was too late to help him.* 🔲 *I'm coming to the meeting, but I might be a bit late.* (atrasado)
2 near the end of the day 🔲 *The children stayed up late to watch a movie.* 🔲 *Will the party go on late?* 🔲 *It's getting late – we should leave.* (tarde)
3 near the end of a period of time 🔲 *the late 18th*

lately /ˈleɪtlɪ/ ADVERB recently ◻ *I haven't been to many parties lately.* (**ultimamente**)

later /ˈleɪtə(r)/ ADJECTIVE, ADVERB after the time you have been talking about ◻ *Later, he married an artist.* ◻ *She rang me later to apologize.* ◻ *Two years later I received a letter from him.* ◻ *Is there a later train?* (**mais tarde**)

latest /ˈleɪtɪst/ ADJECTIVE most recent ◻ *I regularly check the Internet for the latest news.* ◻ *We stock all the latest fashions.* (**mais recente, mais novo**)

Latin /ˈlætɪn/ NOUN, NO PLURAL the language of the ancient Romans (**latim**)

latitude /ˈlætɪtjuːd/ NOUN [plural **latitudes**] the position of a place along imaginary lines around the Earth north and south of the equator (= line around the middle of the Earth). It is measured in degrees north and south. (**latitude**)

latter /ˈlætə(r)/ ADJECTIVE nearer the end of a period of time than the beginning ▣ *the latter part of the 19th century* (**final**)

laugh¹ /lɑːf/ VERB [**laughs, laughing, laughed**] to make a sound of enjoyment when you think something is funny ◻ + *at* *She laughed at my jokes.* ◻ + *about* *We can laugh about the whole thing now.* ▣ *It really made me laugh.* ▣ *They burst out laughing* (= suddenly laughed loudly). (**rir**)

♦ PHRASAL VERB **laugh at someone/something** to laugh or say something rude because you think someone or something is stupid ◻ *Wallis just laughed at the suggestion.*

laugh² /lɑːf/ NOUN [plural **laughs**] **1** when you laugh, or the sound that you make when you laugh ▣ *He gave a nervous laugh.* ◻ *He has a very loud laugh.* (**riso**)
2 have a laugh an informal phrase that means to have fun and enjoy yourself ◻ *We all have such a laugh together.* (**dar risada**)

laughter /ˈlɑːftə(r)/ NOUN, NO PLURAL when someone laughs or the sound that they make when they laugh ◻ *I could hear laughter in the next room.* (**risada**)

launch /lɔːntʃ/ VERB [**launches, launching, launched**]
1 to put a boat or ship in the water for the first time (**lançar**)
2 to send a spacecraft into the sky ◻ *The first Sputnik satellite was launched into space in 1957.* (**lançar**)
3 to start to sell a new product ◻ *The latest model will be launched next month.* (**lançar**)

laundry /ˈlɔːndrɪ/ NOUN, NO PLURAL clothes that are going to be washed, or have just been washed ◻ *a pile of dirty laundry* ◻ *a laundry basket* ▣ *I've done the laundry.* (**roupa lavada**)

lava /ˈlɑːvə/ NOUN, NO PLURAL the hot liquid rock that comes out of a volcano (= mountain that explodes) and becomes solid as it cools down. A geography word. (**lava**)

lavatory /ˈlævətrɪ/ NOUN [plural **lavatories**] a formal word for toilet ◻ *a public lavatory* (**sanitário**)

law /lɔː/ NOUN [plural **laws**]
1 an official rule in a country or state that everyone must obey ◻ + *against* *laws against discrimination* (**lei**)
2 the law an official set of rules that everyone in a country or state must obey ▣ *They have broken the law.* (**lei**)
3 by law if you have to do something by law, there is an official rule which says that you must do it ◻ *You are required by law to provide this information.* (**pela lei**)
4 be against the law to not be allowed by law ◻ *Driving at the age of 13 is against the law.* (**ser contra a lei**)

▶ **THESAURUS:** A **rule** is an instruction about what is allowed or what is not allowed. Games have **rules**, and schools have **rules** about how students must behave. A **law** is an official set of rules that everyone in a country must obey. An **order** is an instruction to do something. Soldiers give **orders** to other soldiers.

lawn /lɔːn/ NOUN [plural **lawns**] an area of short grass in a garden ▣ *I need to mow the lawn* (= cut the grass with a machine). (**gramado**)

lawyer /ˈlɔːjə(r)/ NOUN [plural **lawyers**] someone whose job is to advise people about the law and to act for other people in legal situations ▣ *a defence lawyer* ◻ *His lawyer said he would appeal against the sentence.* (**advogado**)

lay¹ /leɪ/ VERB [**lays, laying, laid**]
1 to put something down carefully ◻ + *on* *She laid the book on the table.* ◻ + *down* *Slowly, he laid down the gun.* ◻ *I went to lay flowers on his grave.* (**pousar**)
2 lay the table to put knives, forks, etc. on a table to prepare for a meal (**levar**)
3 if a bird lays an egg, it produces it (**estar à frente**)

▶ Try not to confuse the verbs **lay** and **lie**. To **lay** something somewhere is to put something down. To **lie** somewhere is to be in a flat position: ◻ *She looked for a place to lay the baby.* ◻ *Why don't you lie on the sofa and watch TV?*

lay² /leɪ/ PAST TENSE OF **lie³** (**ver lie³**)

layer /ˈleɪə(r)/ NOUN [plural **layers**] an amount of a substance that covers something or is between other things ◻ + *of* *The grass was covered with a layer of snow.* ▣ *Remove the outer layers of the onion.* ◻ *Wear several layers of clothing.* ◻ *Dust had settled in a thin layer over everything.* (**camada**)

lead¹ /liːd/ VERB [**leads, leading, led**]
1 to show someone where to go by going first or

going with them □ *You lead and I'll follow on my bike.* □ *She led me into a large room.* (**conduzir**)
2 if a road, path, etc. leads somewhere, that is where it goes □ **+ to** *This road leads to London.* (**levar**)
3 to be winning in a race or competition, or to be the most successful at something □ *Liverpool were leading 2-0 at the end of the first half.* □ **+ by** *They are leading by three goals to one.* 🔁 *Our company leads the world in computer technology.* (**estar à frente**)
4 to direct or control an activity or a group of people □ *The team should be led by someone with a lot of experience.* □ *A new officer is leading the investigation.* (**conduzir**)
5 lead a comfortable/full/normal, etc. life to live in a particular way (**levar a vida**)
6 lead the way to be the first to do something □ *This university led the way in introducing schemes to attract poorer students.* (**mostrar o caminho**)
◆ PHRASAL VERB **lead to something** to cause something to happen or exist □ *Long hours at work led to the breakdown of his marriage.* □ *Using the mouse too much can lead to wrist problems.*

lead² /liːd/ NOUN [plural **leads**]
1 the position in a race or competition where you are winning □ *Jenkins has been in the lead for most of the race.* 🔁 *Juventus took the lead after 23 minutes.* (**liderança**)
2 a long, narrow piece of leather attached to a dog's collar in order to hold it. 🔁 *All dogs must be kept on a lead.* (**trela, correia**)
3 a wire that connects a piece of electrical equipment to an electricity supply (**fio**)

lead³ /led/ NOUN [plural **leads**]
1 a soft, dark grey metal (**chumbo**)
2 the dark grey inside part of a pencil (**mina**)

leader /ˈliːdə(r)/ NOUN [plural **leaders**] a person who is in charge of a group of people □ **+ of** *the leader of the expedition* 🔁 *a religious leader* 🔁 *the country's political leaders* □ *the Republican Party leader* (**chefe, líder**)

leading /ˈliːdɪŋ/ ADJECTIVE most important or most successful □ *He is one of Scotland's leading playwrights.* □ *the team's leading scorer* (**principal, mais importante**)

leaf /liːf/ NOUN [plural **leaves**] a flat green part of a plant or tree that grows out from a stem or a branch □ *The sun shone through the leaves.* □ *a plate of salad leaves* (**folha**)

leaflet /ˈliːflɪt/ NOUN [plural **leaflets**] a piece of paper that gives printed information about something □ *a leaflet about recycling* (**folheto**)

league /liːg/ NOUN [plural **leagues**]
1 a group of teams that play sports matches against each other □ *the professional basketball league* 🔁 *I'm still hoping we can win the league this season.* 🔁 *They're top of the league table.* (**liga**)
2 a group of people or countries who agree to work together (**liga**)

leak¹ /liːk/ NOUN [plural **leaks**] a hole that liquid or gas can escape or enter through, or the gas or liquid that escapes □ *There could be a leak in the pipe.* 🔁 *a gas leak* (**vazamento**)

leak² /liːk/ VERB [**leaks, leaking, leaked**] if liquid or gas leaks, it escapes from or enters something and if an object leaks, gas or liquid escapes from or enters it through a hole □ *Gas was leaking from somewhere under the floor.* □ *My boots leak.* (**vazar**)

leaky /ˈliːki/ ADJECTIVE [**leakier, leakiest**] having small holes or cracks which a gas or liquid can escape from □ *a leaky roof* (**furado**)

lean¹ /liːn/ VERB [**leans, leaning, leant** *or* **leaned**]
1 to move your body in a particular direction by bending at the waist □ **+ forward** *He leaned forward to kiss her.* □ **+ back** *She leaned back in her chair.* □ **+ over** *Could you lean over and get the salt for me?* □ **+ out** *She leaned out of the window.* (**inclinar[-se]**)
2 to put something against something so that it is supported by it, or to be in this position □ **+ on** *She leaned her head on his shoulder.* □ **+ against** *A bike was leaning against the wall.* (**apoiar[-se]**)

lean² /liːn/ ADJECTIVE [**leaner, leanest**] with no fat or little fat □ *I only buy lean meat.* (**magro**)

> **THESAURUS:** We usually use lean to talk about meat, although it is sometimes used to talk about people. If you want to say that a person has little fat, the word is **thin**. If someone is thin in an attractive way, you can use the words **slim** or **slender**, especially for women. **Skinny** means very thin, often in an unattractive way. **Skinny** is an informal word.

leap¹ /liːp/ VERB [**leaps, leaping, leapt** *or* **leaped**]
1 to move suddenly and quickly □ *She leapt up and ran to the door.* □ *I leapt out of bed.* (**pular**)
2 to jump high or a long distance □ *We saw dolphins leaping out of the water.* □ *The dancer leapt into the air.* (**saltar**)

leap² /liːp/ NOUN [plural **leaps**] a big jump □ *He took an impressive leap over the fence.* (**pulo**)

leap year /ˈliːpjɪə(r)/ NOUN [plural **leap years**] a year that happens every four years and has 366 days. The extra day is February 29. (**ano bissexto**)

learn /lɜːn/ VERB [**learns, learning, learnt** *or* **learned**]
1 to get to know about something or get to know how to do something □ **+ to do something** *He's learning to drive.* □ *She wanted to learn English.* □ **+ question word** *I learned how to cook from my mother.* □ **+ about** *We learnt about the local culture.* □ **+ from** *I've learnt from my mistakes.* (**aprender**)
2 to find out some news or information □ **+ that** *I was surprised to learn that she'd already left.* □ **+ whether** *Today he will learn whether he needs surgery.* (**ficar sabendo**)

learner /ˈlɜːnə(r)/ NOUN [plural **learners**] a person who is learning something ▢ *It's a book for young language learners.* ▣ *He was a quick learner.* (aprendiz)

lease /liːs/ VERB [**leases, leasing, leased**] to rent something to someone ▢ *They lease the land from the local council.* (arrendar)

least¹ /liːst/ ADVERB

1 less than anyone or anything else in size, amount or degree ▢ *She chose the least expensive trousers.* ▢ *He always turns up when you least expect him.* ▢ *These price rises will affect those who are least able to afford them.* (menos)
2 at least (a) not less than ▢ *She must be at least 50.* ▢ *It will take at least two hours to get there.* (b) used before you add a positive statement after talking about something bad ▢ *She was very late, but at least she phoned to let us know.* (c) used to correct what you have just said or to make it less certain ▢ *I saw her in the library – at least, I think it was her.* (pelo menos)

least² /liːst/ DETERMINER, PRONOUN

1 the smallest amount, size or degree ▢ *The person who had the least difficulty was the tallest.* ▢ *Of everyone here, I know least about the subject.* ▢ *He is the richest, but he gave the least.* (o mínimo)
2 not in the least (bit)/not the least bit not at all ▢ *He wasn't the least bit sorry for all the trouble he caused.* (nem um pouco)

leather /ˈleðə(r)/ NOUN, NO PLURAL a strong material for making shoes, bags and clothes that is made from the skin of an animal ▢ *a leather jacket* ▢ *a pair of black leather boots* (couro)

leave¹ /liːv/ VERB [**leaves, leaving, left**]

1 to go away from a place ▢ *I left the office early.* ▢ *The train leaves at two.* ▢ *I left work at four thirty.* ▣ *I left home when I was 18.* (sair, partir)
2 to not take something with you when you go away ▢ *Maria left her umbrella on the bus.* ▢ *+ behind I left all my books behind.* (deixar)
3 to put something or someone somewhere ▢ *Leave your shoes by the door.* ▢ *I left the children with a neighbour.* (deixar)
4 to allow something to be in a particular position or state ▢ *Leave the conditioner in your hair for five minutes.* ▢ *She left the door unlocked.* (deixar)
5 to not use all of something ▢ *Is there any milk left?* (de sobra)
6 to not do something but do it later or let someone else do it ▢ *I'll leave the washing up and do it in the morning.* ▢ *+ to I left all the driving to her.* (deixar)
7 to give something to someone after your death ▢ *Her grandmother left Joy all her jewellery.* (deixar)
8 leave someone/something alone to stop touching something or talking to someone ▢ *Journalists wouldn't leave her alone.* ▢ *Leave my clothes alone.* (deixar em paz)

♦ PHRASAL VERBS **leave someone/something out** to not include someone or something ▢ *I told him what she said, but I left out the rude bits.* ▣ *Some of our members felt left out because they could not do the activities.* **leave something over** if something is left over, it is what remains when the rest of something has been used ▢ *There was a lot of food left over from the party.*

> **THESAURUS:** To **leave** means to go away from a place. The words **depart** and **set off** have a similar meaning, but are especially used to describe the start of a journey. For example we can say that a train **departs** at a particular time. **Depart** is a more formal word than **set off**.

leave² /liːv/ NOUN, NO PLURAL a period of holiday from work ▢ *I had a week's leave.* ▢ *He committed the crime while he was on leave from the army.* (licença)

leaves /liːvz/ PLURAL OF **leaf** (ver **leaf**)

lecture¹ /ˈlektʃə(r)/ NOUN [plural **lectures**] a talk by someone to a group of people to teach them about something ▢ *+ on a lecture on economics* ▣ *He was due to give a lect ure at Leeds University.* ▣ *He attended a lecture by Carl Jung.* (conferência)

lecture² /ˈlektʃə(r)/ VERB [**lectures, lecturing, lectured**] to give a lecture or lectures about a particular subject ▢ *He lectured on history at Cambridge University.* (dissertar, dar aula)

led /led/ PAST TENSE AND PAST PARTICIPLE OF **lead¹** ▢ *Connor led a wild life for many years.* ▢ *Where have you led us?* (ver **lead¹**)

left¹ /left/ ADJECTIVE, ADVERB on or towards the side of your body that is to the west if you are facing north ▣ *Can you write with your left hand?* ▣ *You stand on the left side of him.* ▣ *Now turn left.* ▢ *Click on the link in the top left corner of the screen.* (esquerdo)

left² /left/ NOUN, NO PLURAL the left side or direction ▢ *Stop just here on the left.* ▢ *Diana is standing to the left of Robert.* (esquerda)

left³ /left/ PAST TENSE AND PAST PARTICIPLE OF **leave¹** ▢ *She left early.* ▢ *I've left my book at home.* (ver **leave¹**)

left-handed /ˌleftˈhændɪd/ ADJECTIVE using your left hand to do things, especially to write ▢ *Are you left-handed?* ▢ *a left-handed batsman* (canhoto)

leg /leg/ NOUN [plural **legs**]

1 one of the parts of the body that animals and humans stand and walk on ▢ *I broke my leg skiing.* ▢ *How many legs do spiders have?* ▢ *Try standing on one leg.* (perna)
2 the part of a pair of trousers that covers one leg (perna)
3 one of the pieces that supports a table, chair, etc. (perna)

legal /ˈliːɡəl/ ADJECTIVE allowed by the law □ *Is it legal to ride your bike on the pavement?* (**legal**)

legend /ˈledʒənd/ NOUN [plural **legends**]
1 an old traditional story that is usually not true □ *the legend of St George and the dragon* (**lenda**)
2 a very famous person □ *Formula One legend, Ayrton Senna* (**lenda**)

leisure /ˈleʒə(r)/ NOUN, NO PLURAL time when you do not have to work □ *Families are spending more on leisure.* 🔊 *What do you do in your leisure time?* (**lazer**)
◆ IDIOM **at your leisure** when you have time □ *Take the brochure home and read it at your leisure.*

lemon /ˈlemən/ NOUN [plural **lemons**] an oval fruit with a hard, yellow skin and very sour juice □ *tea with a slice of lemon* □ *Add the juice of a lemon.* (**limão**)

lemonade /ˌleməˈneɪd/ NOUN [plural **lemonades**] a cold drink with a lemon flavour and a lot of bubbles □ *a bottle of lemonade* (**limonada**)

lend /lend/ VERB [**lends, lending, lent**] to allow someone to use something or have some money for a short time □ *Could you lend me £5, Mum?* □ + **to** *Adam has lent his MP3 player to Andy.* □ *The bank no longer lends to first-time buyers.* (**emprestar**)
◆ IDIOM **lend a hand** to help someone

> Remember that when you **lend** something, you give something to someone else to use. When you use something that belongs to someone else, the verb is **borrow** □ *Dan lent me his mobile* □ *I borrowed Dan's mobile.*

length /leŋθ/ NOUN [plural **lengths**]
1 how long something is from one end to the other end □ *Measure the table's length.* □ *The pieces of wood were all different lengths.* (**comprimento, extensão**)
2 **at length** if you talk at length, you talk for a long time □ *The doctor explained the different treatments at length.* (**encompridar**)

lengthen /ˈleŋθən/ VERB [**lengthens, lengthening, lengthened**] to become longer or to make something longer □ *I think you should lengthen that skirt.* □ *Shadows lengthened as the sun went down.* (**encompridar**)

lengthy /ˈleŋθi/ ADJECTIVE [**lengthier, lengthiest**] taking a long time □ *Getting a passport was a lengthy process.* (**comprido**)

lens /lenz/ NOUN [plural **lenses**] a curved piece of glass that you look through in glasses, cameras and scientific instruments □ *a zoom lens* □ *Adjust the lens in the telescope.* (**lente**)

lent /lent/ PAST TENSE AND PAST PARTICIPLE OF **lend** □ *I lent him a book.* □ *I've lent her some money.* (**ver lend**)

lentil /ˈlentɪl/ NOUN [plural **lentils**] a small orange, brown or green seed that is dried and cooked □ *lentil soup* (**lentilha**)

leopard /ˈlepəd/ NOUN [plural **leopards**] a large animal of the cat family with yellow fur and dark spots (**leopardo**)

less¹ /les/ DETERMINER, PRONOUN a smaller amount of □ *We'll have to spend less money.* □ *I have less time than Patrick.* □ *I had less on my plate than you.* □ + **of** *He spends less of his time with his children.* (**menos**)

> Notice that **less** is used with uncountable nouns, for example *time* and *money*. With the plural form of countable nouns, for example *cars* and *people* use **fewer**: □ *I have **less** money than I used to.* □ *I have **fewer** problems than I used to.*

less² /les/ PREPOSITION taking away a particular amount □ *The cost will be £100 less the discount.* (**menos**)

less³ /les/ ADVERB
1 used to make comparative forms of adjectives and adverbs, with the meaning 'not as much' □ *My clothes are less expensive.* 🔊 *I'm less patient than you.* 🔊 *These instructions are a lot less complicated.* 🔊 *I'm less and less interested in TV.* (**menos**)
2 to a smaller degree □ *I exercise less these days.* 🔊 *I eat less than I used to.* 🔊 *I see her less and less.* (**menos**)

-less /lɪs/ SUFFIX -less is added to the end of words to mean 'without' □ *hopeless* □ *thoughtless*

lessen /ˈlesən/ VERB [**lessens, lessening, lessened**] to become less or to make something less □ *The drugs should lessen the pain.* (**diminuir**)

lesson /ˈlesən/ NOUN [plural **lessons**] a period of time in which you learn something or teach someone something □ *When's your next lesson?* □ *a driving lesson* 🔊 *I'm taking swimming lessons.* (**aula**)

let /let/ VERB [**lets, letting, let**]
1 to allow someone to do something or something to happen □ *He won't let anyone use his tools.* □ *This card lets me travel free.* (**deixar**)
2 to allow someone or something to go somewhere □ + **in** *They won't let them in the building.* □ *She won't let the children out of her sight.* □ *These windows let in the rain.* (**deixar**)
3 **let's** used to make a suggestion about what to do □ *Let's go swimming.* □ *Let's get out of here.* (**vamos**)
4 **let go** to stop holding something □ *He grasped my hand and wouldn't let go.* □ *Now you can let go of the rope.* (**largar**)
5 **let someone know** to tell someone something □ *Could you let Mick know I'll be late?* □ *I want to let everyone know why I acted the way I did.* (**fazer com que**)
6 to rent a room, building, etc. to someone (**alugar**)
◆ PHRASAL VERBS **let someone down** to upset someone by behaving badly or not doing something

they expected you to do ▫ *Our suppliers have let us down.* ▫ *You've let yourself down and you've let your family down.* **let someone off** to not punish someone for something bad they have done

lethal /ˈliːθəl/ ADJECTIVE causing or able to cause death ▫ *a lethal weapon* ▫ *a lethal dose of the drug* (**mortal**)

letter /ˈletə(r)/ NOUN [plural letters]

1 a message that you write and send by post to another person ▣ *Why don't you write a letter?* ▣ *I got a letter from Laura this morning.* (**carta**)
2 one of the written shapes that you combine to write words, like *a*, *b* or *c* ▫ *the letters of the alphabet* (**letra**)

> THESAURUS: A **message** is a piece of written or spoken information sent from one person to another. A **letter** is a message that you write and send by post to another person. A **note** is a short informal letter, or a piece of writing to help you to remember something. For example, you might write a **note** to remind you to phone someone. A **memo** is a short note that you write to someone who works in the same company as you.

lettuce /ˈletɪs/ NOUN [plural lettuces]
a vegetable with large green leaves that are used in salads (**alface**)

level¹ /ˈlevəl/ ADJECTIVE
1 flat or horizontal ▫ *a piece of level ground* ▫ *Add a level tablespoonful of flour.* (**raso, plano**)
2 at the same height as something else ▫ + **with** *The picture needs to be level with the mirror next to it.* (**nivelado**)

level² /ˈlevəl/ VERB [levels, levelling/US leveling, levelled/US leveled]
to make something flat, smooth or horizontal ▫ *The ground will have to be levelled before they can build on it.* (**nivelar**)

level³ /ˈlevəl/ NOUN [plural levels]
1 the amount, size or number of something ▣ *Sudoku puzzles need a high level of concentration.* ▣ *Low levels of pollution were recorded.* ▫ *Unemployment has stayed at the same level for over three years.* (**nível**)
2 a particular height or distance above or below the ground ▫ *She hung the pictures at eye level.* ▫ *The water level was rising.* (**nível**)
3 the particular ability or standard of someone or something ▫ *It's best to start at beginners' level.* ▫ *He played squash at international level.* (**nível**)

lever /ˈliːvə(r)/ NOUN [plural levers]
1 a handle that operates a machine or engine ▫ *Push the lever up to start the engine.* ▫ *a gear lever* (**alavanca**)
2 a strong bar that you press on in order to move something heavy (**alavanca**)

liable /ˈlaɪəbəl/ ADJECTIVE **liable to do something** often doing something, especially something bad ▫ *She's liable to lose her temper.* (**suscetível**)

liar /ˈlaɪə(r)/ NOUN [plural liars] someone who tells lies (**mentiroso**)

liberal /ˈlɪbərəl/ ADJECTIVE accepting different ideas and types of behaviour ▫ *It's a very liberal society.* (**liberal, tolerante**)

liberty /ˈlɪbəti/ NOUN, NO PLURAL freedom to do, or go where you want or say what you want ▫ *Prisoners are deprived of their liberty.* (**liberal**)

librarian /laɪˈbreərɪən/ NOUN [plural librarians] someone who works in a library ▫ *the school librarian* (**bibliotecário**)

library /ˈlaɪbrəri/ NOUN [plural libraries] a building or room that has a lot of books, CDs or DVDs that you can borrow ▣ *library books* (**biblioteca**)

licence /ˈlaɪsəns/ NOUN [plural licences]
an official document that gives someone permission to do or have something ▫ *a driving licence* ▫ *a licence to sell alcohol* (**licença**)

license¹ /ˈlaɪsəns/ VERB [licenses, licensing, licensed]
to give someone official permission to do something ▫ *The restaurant is licensed to serve alcohol.* (**autorizar**)

license² /ˈlaɪsəns/ NOUN [plural licenses] the US spelling of **licence** (**licença**)

lick /lɪk/ VERB [licks, licking, licked] to move your tongue over something ▫ *The cat was licking its paws.* ▫ *She licked her lips nervously.* (**lamber**)

lid /lɪd/ NOUN [plural lids]
a cover that fits the top of a container ▫ *Can you get the lid off this jar?* (**tampa**)

lie¹ /laɪ/ VERB [lies, lying, lied]
to say something that you know is not true ▫ + **about** *He lied about his age.* ▫ + **to** *Did you lie to me?* (**mentir**)

lie² /laɪ/ NOUN [plural lies]
something that you say that is not true when you know that it is not true ▣ *He's always telling lies.* (**mentira**)

> Notice that people **tell lies**. They do not 'say lies':
> ✓ *Don't tell lies, Oliver.*
> ✗ *Don't say lies, Oliver.*

lie³ /laɪ/ VERB [lies, lying, lay, lain]
1 to be in a flat position, for example on the floor or on a bed, or to put your body in this position ▫ *She's been lying on a beach all day.* ▫ *Lie flat on your back.* ▫ *Go and lie on the couch.* (**deitar**)
2 to be in a particular position ▫ *The town lies to the east of Geneva.* ▫ *There were clothes lying all over the floor.* ▫ *Snow lay on the hills.* (**ficar**)

◆ PHRASAL VERB **lie down** to put your body into a flat position, especially to rest ▫ *I don't feel well – I'm going to lie down for a while.* (**deitar-se**)

> Notice that the past tense of **lie** when it means 'to say something that you know is not true' is **lied**. The past tense of **lie** when it means 'to be in a flat position' is **lay**.

lieutenant /lefˈtenənt/ NOUN [plural **lieutenants**] an officer in the army or navy (**tenente**)

life /laɪf/ NOUN [plural **lives**]
1 the time between being born and dying ▣ He spent his life helping others. ▣ I've had these problems my whole life. ▣ He lived in Glasgow all his life. ▢ Our lives have been ruined by this disease. (**vida**)
2 the way someone lives ▣ They live a simple life. ▣ We lead a quiet life. ▣ This course will change your life. (**vida**)
3 the existence of a person ▣ I'm not prepared to risk my life to save your dog. ▣ He saved my life. ▣ Hundreds of soldiers have lost their lives in this war. (**vida**)
4 no plural living things ▢ Is there human life anywhere else in the universe? ▢ plant life (**vida**)
5 energy and enthusiasm ▢ Try to put a bit more life into your singing. ▣ He's always full of life. (**vida**)

lifeboat /ˈlaɪfbəʊt/ NOUN [plural **lifeboats**] a boat used for saving people from dangerous situations at sea ▢ the lifeboat crew (**barco salva-vidas**)

lifestyle /ˈlaɪfstaɪl/ NOUN [plural **lifestyles**] the way that someone lives ▢ We try to have a healthy lifestyle. (**estilo de vida**)

lifetime /ˈlaɪftaɪm/ NOUN [plural **lifetimes**] the length of time that a particular person is alive ▢ These children will see such technological advances in their lifetime. (**vida, vidas**)

lift¹ /lɪft/ VERB [**lifts, lifting, lifted**] to move something upwards or raise it ▣ She lifted the baby out of his cot. ▣ He was so weak that he couldn't lift his head. (**erguer**)

lift² /lɪft/ NOUN [plural **lifts**]
1 a machine like a large box that carries people or things between floors in a tall building ▣ Take the lift to the sixth floor. (**elevadores**)
2 a ride in someone's car ▣ Could you give me a lift home? (**carona**)

light¹ /laɪt/ NOUN [plural **lights**]
1 no plural the energy from something such as the sun or a piece of electrical equipment that allows us to see ▢ There isn't enough light to read. ▣ A ray of light shone through the curtains. ▣ The room was filled with bright light. (**luz**)
2 a piece of equipment that produces light ▣ Don't forget to switch off the light. ▣ I turned on the light. ▣ Where is the light switch? (**luz**)
3 set light to something to make something burn (**pôr fogo em**)

light² /laɪt/ VERB [**lights, lighting, lit**]
1 to make something start to burn ▣ Let's light the fire. (**acender**)
2 to start burning ▢ Why won't the cooker light? (**acender**)
3 to light a place is to make it brighter ▢ The room was lit with candles. (**aluminar[-se]**)

> **THESAURUS:** If you **burn** something, you destroy it with fire. When you light a fire, you make it start to burn. You can also say that you **set fire to** something. Note that you light a fire, but **set fire to** the wood or coal that you want to burn. If you make a light work, you **turn** it **on** or **switch** it **on**.

light³ /laɪt/ ADJECTIVE [**lighter, lightest**]
1 bright or not dark ▢ It's still light enough to read. ▣ Mike got up as soon as it began to get light. (**claro**)
2 pale in colour ▢ light blue ▢ You can make colours lighter by adding white to them. (**claro**)
3 not heavy ▢ My bike has a very light frame. ▢ This bag feels light. (**leve**)
4 not strong or in large amounts ▣ Light winds reduced the temperature. ▣ Traffic is light around London tonight. ▢ I felt a light touch on my arm. (**claro, suave**)

light bulb /ˈlaɪt ˌbʌlb/ NOUN [plural **light bulbs**] a hollow glass object that contains a wire which produces light when electricity passes through it ▢ energy-saving light bulbs (**lâmpada elétrica**)

lighter /ˈlaɪtə(r)/ NOUN [plural **lighters**] a small object that produces a flame to make a cigarette start burning ▢ Do you have a lighter I could use? (**isqueiro**)

lighting /ˈlaɪtɪŋ/ NOUN, NO PLURAL the lights used in a room ▢ soft lighting (**iluminação**)

lightly /ˈlaɪtli/ ADVERB
1 gently ▢ She touched me lightly on the arm and smiled. (**levemente**)
2 not much ▢ a lightly boiled egg ▢ She was lightly tanned. (**ligeiramente**)

lightning /ˈlaɪtnɪŋ/ NOUN, NO PLURAL a bright flash of electricity in the sky that sometimes happens in a storm ▢ a flash of lightning ▣ thunder and lightning ▣ The church was struck by lightning in the storm. (**raio**)

like¹ /laɪk/ PREPOSITION
1 similar to ▢ Geraldine looks just like her mother.
2 in a similar way to ▢ She dances like a professional. (**como**)
3 if you ask what someone or something is like, you want someone to describe them ▢ What's your new teacher like? (**como**)
4 used to give examples ▢ I love sports like tennis and badminton. (**como**)

like² /laɪk/ CONJUNCTION
1 as if ▢ You look like you've seen a ghost. (**como**)
2 in the same way as. An informal word ▢ Tie the knot like I showed you. (**como**)

like³ /laɪk/ VERB [likes, liking, liked]
1 to think that something or someone is pleasant or enjoyable □ *I like pizza.* □ *I don't like football.* 🔁 *I like this house better than our old house.* 🔁 *I don't like the idea of eating raw fish.* 🔁 *He liked the way she talked.* □ *+ ing I don't like coming home after dark.* □ *+ to do something I like to get up early.* (gostar)
2 Would you like ...? used to offer someone something □ *Would you like a biscuit?* □ *Would you like to come with us?* (querer)
3 would like if you would like something, you want it □ *I'd like a cup of tea.* (querer)
4 would like to do something if you would like to do something, you want to do it □ *I'd like to go home now.* (querer)
5 if you like (a) used when you make an offer □ *I'll come with you if you like.* (b) used to say yes when someone suggests doing something □ *'Shall I bring some food?' 'Yes, if you like.'* (se você quiser)

> Notice that **would like** meaning 'want to do some thing' (sense 4) is followed by the verb form **to do something**:
> ✓ *I would like to go home.*
> ✗ *I would like that I go home.*

likelihood /ˈlaɪklɪhʊd/ NOUN, NO PLURAL
the possibility that something will happen □ *There's a strong likelihood of rain today.* (probabilidade)

likely /ˈlaɪkli/ ADJECTIVE
1 expected to happen □ *+ to do something People are more likely to come if the weather is good.* □ *+ that It's very likely that nobody will come.* (é provável que)
2 probably true □ *That seems the most likely explanation.* (provável)

limb /lɪm/ NOUN [plural limbs]
a leg or an arm (membro)

lime¹ /laɪm/ NOUN [plural limes]
1 a small, sour fruit that looks like a green lemon □ *Add the juice of two limes.* (lima)
2 no plural a white substance that is used to help plants grow and to make cement (= substance used in building) (lima)

lime² /laɪm/ ADJECTIVE
having a bright green colour □ *a lime green shirt* (cor de lima)

limit¹ /ˈlɪmɪt/ NOUN [plural limits]
1 the largest or smallest amount or level that is allowed or possible 🔁 *There's a time limit for this test* 🔁 *She had above the legal limit of alcohol in her blood.* 🔁 *Each person is allowed 10 kg of luggage, and you are over the limit.* □ *+ to There's a limit to how much I can help her.* (limite)
2 the outside edge of an area □ *the city limits* (limite)

limit² /ˈlɪmɪt/ VERB [limits, limiting, limited]
to keep someone or something below a particular amount or level □ *Places on the course are limited, so book early.* □ *People covered their windows to limit damage from the storm.* □ *+ to I shall have to limit you to one cake each.* (limitar)

limp¹ /lɪmp/ VERB [limps, limping, limped]
to walk with difficulty because your leg or foot hurts □ *Beckham limped off the pitch.* (mancar)

limp² /lɪmp/ NOUN, NO PLURAL
a way of walking that is not even and shows that someone's leg or foot hurts □ *He walked with a limp.* (manqueira)

line¹ /laɪn/ NOUN [plural lines]
1 a long thin mark □ *There are white lines in the middle of the road.* 🔁 *Draw a straight line from A to B.* 🔁 *Sign on the dotted line.* 🔁 *The first runners have already crossed the finishing line.* (linha)
2 a row of things or people □ *The children formed a line.* □ *There is a line of old oak trees by the road.* (fila)
3 a row of words on a page □ *Look at the first line of the poem.* (linha)
4 a piece of rope, wire, etc. used for a particular purpose □ *I was hanging the washing on the line.*
5 the US word for queue (fila)

line² /laɪn/ VERB [lines, lining, lined]
1 to be in a row along the sides of something □ *Police officers will line the route of the procession.* (alinhar)
2 to cover the inside of a piece of clothing or a container with something □ *The coat is lined with fur.* (encapar)

linen /ˈlɪnɪn/ NOUN, NO PLURAL
1 a type of cloth like a heavy, slightly rough, cotton that is made from a plant □ *a linen jacket* (linho)
2 things made of cloth used to cover beds or tables □ *table linen* (roupa-branca)

linger /ˈlɪŋɡə(r)/ VERB [lingers, lingering, lingered]
to stay somewhere for a long time □ *Fans were still lingering at the stage door.* □ *The smell of fish seemed to linger for days.* (subsistir)

lining /ˈlaɪnɪŋ/ NOUN [plural linings]
a covering on the inside of a piece of clothing or container □ *a jacket lining* □ *a silver box with a velvet lining* (forro)

link¹ /lɪŋk/ NOUN [plural links]
1 a relationship between two people or things □ *+ between Research soon proved the link between smoking and lung cancer.* □ *+ with It is thought that the group has links with terrorist organizations.* (elo, vínculo)
2 a connection between two files, especially on a website. A computing word. □ *Click on the link to reserve your tickets.* (link)
3 one of the rings of a chain (elo)

link² /lɪŋk/ VERB [links, linking, linked]
if two people or things are linked, they are connected to each other in some way □ *Were these two events linked in any way?* 🔁 *Diet and health are closely linked.* □ *A bridge links the two buildings.* (ligar)

lion /ˈlaɪən/ NOUN [plural lions]
a large, wild animal of the cat family, the male of which has thick hair around its head (leão)

lip /lɪp/ NOUN [plural **lips**] either the upper or the lower outside edge of your mouth ▫ *He kissed her lightly on the lips.* (**lábio**)

lipstick /ˈlɪpstɪk/ NOUN [plural **lipsticks**] make-up that women put on their lips to make the lips a different colour ▫ *She was wearing bright red lipstick.* (**batom**)

liquid¹ /ˈlɪkwɪd/ NOUN [plural **liquids**] a substance that can flow, such as water or oil ▫ *In hot weather make sure you drink plenty of liquids.* (**líquido**)

liquid² /ˈlɪkwɪd/ ADJECTIVE in the form of a liquid ▫ *a liquid soap* (**líquido**)

list¹ /lɪst/ NOUN [plural **lists**] a group of things such as names, numbers or prices, written one below the other ▫ *His name is on the list.* ▫ *a shopping list* ▫ *I've added your name to the list.* ▫ *You should make a list of things to do.* (**lista**)

> Notice the preposition. Something is **on** a list and not 'in' a list:
> ✓ *I'll put your name on the list.*
> ✗ *I'll put your name in the list.*

list² /lɪst/ VERB [**lists, listing, listed**] to write a list, or to give information in the form of a list ▫ *The players are listed alphabetically.* (**listar**)

listen /ˈlɪsən/ VERB [**listens, listening, listened**]
1 to pay attention to a sound so that you can hear it ▫ + *to Listen to me when I'm talking!* ▫ *Do you ever listen to classical music?* ▫ *I often listen to the radio.* (**escutar**)
2 to pay attention to someone's advice and do what they suggest ▫ *I told you to wear a coat but you wouldn't listen!* (**escutar**)

lit /lɪt/ PAST TENSE AND PAST PARTICIPLE OF **light**² ▫ *She lit the fire.* ▫ *I haven't lit the candles yet.* (ver **light**²)

literary /ˈlɪtərəri/ ADJECTIVE to do with books, writers and literature ▫ *a literary critic* ▫ *a literary magazine* (**literário**)

literature /ˈlɪtrətʃə(r)/ NOUN, NO PLURAL stories, poetry and plays ▫ *He's studying English literature.* ▫ *20th-century children's literature* (**literatura**)

litre /ˈliːtə(r)/ NOUN [plural **litres**] a unit for measuring liquid ▫ + *of a litre of water* ▫ *Petrol now costs more than £1 per litre.* (**litro**)

litter /ˈlɪtə(r)/ NOUN, NO PLURAL paper and other rubbish that people have thrown on the ground in a public place ▫ *You can be fined for dropping litter.* (**lixo**)

little¹ /ˈlɪtəl/ DETERMINER, PRONOUN, ADVERB [**less, least**]
1 not much ▫ *There is little hope of finding them alive.* ▫ *She cares so little for other people's opinions.* ▫ *It costs very little to go on a camping holiday.* ▫ + *of I remember very little of what he said.* (**pouco**)
2 a little a small amount or to a small degree ▫ *I added a little salt.* ▫ *'Would you like milk?' 'Just a little, please.'* ▫ *Jump up and down a little to keep warm.* ▫ *I'm feeling a little cold.* (**um pouco**)

little² /ˈlɪtəl/ ADJECTIVE [**littler, littlest**]
1 small ▫ *They stuck little pieces of cardboard all over it.* ▫ *He's got his own little bicycle.* ▫ *Can I have a little bit of butter?* (**pequeno, pouco**)
2 short in time or distance ▫ *It's only a little way to the hotel.* ▫ *He'll be here in a little while.*
3 young ▫ *a little boy/girl* ▫ *my little brother/sister* (**pequeno**)

live¹ /lɪv/ VERB [**lives, living, lived**]
1 to be alive ▫ *Cats don't usually live for much more than twenty years.* ▫ *People are living longer these days.* (**viver**)
2 to have your home in a certain place ▫ *How long have you lived in Madrid?* ▫ *I live next door to Sam.* (**morar**)
3 to pass your life in a certain way ▫ *She's used to living alone.* (**viver**)
◆ PHRASAL VERB **live on something 1** to eat a particular type of food ▫ *They live on nuts and insects.* **2** money you live on is money you use for the things you need ▫ *We managed to live on our savings for two years.*

live² /laɪv/ ADJECTIVE
1 not dead ▫ *We bought some live oysters.* (**vivo**)
2 a live broadcast is happening as you watch or hear it (**vivo**)

live³ /laɪv/ ADVERB if something is broadcast live, it is happening as you watch or hear it ▫ *We are going live to our correspondent in Berlin.* (**ao vivo**)

lively /ˈlaɪvli/ ADJECTIVE [**livelier, liveliest**] full of activity, interest or energy ▫ *a group of lively children* ▫ *There was a lively debate on the issue.* ▫ *The café' has great food and a lively atmosphere.* (**vivo**)

liver /ˈlɪvə(r)/ NOUN [plural **livers**] a large organ in your body that is very important for cleaning your blood. A biology word. (**fígado**)

living¹ /ˈlɪvɪŋ/ NOUN [plural **livings**] the money you earn from working and that you live on ▫ *I make my living as a professional actor.* ▫ *He earns a living by teaching the piano.* ▫ *I make a decent living* (= enough money). ▫ *What do you do for a living?* (= What is your job?) (**meio de vida**)

living² /ˈlɪvɪŋ/ ADJECTIVE alive ▫ *a living organism* ▫ *She has no living relatives.* (**vivo**)

living room /ˈlɪvɪŋ ˌruːm/ NOUN [plural **living rooms**] a room in a house for sitting and relaxing in ▫ *I was in the living room, watching television.* (**sala de estar**)

lizard /ˈlɪzəd/ NOUN [plural **lizards**] a reptile with four legs, a long body and a tail (**lagarto**)

load

load¹ /ləʊd/ VERB [loads, loading, loaded]
1 to put something into a vehicle, especially a ship or a truck ☐ + *up* *We loaded up the van with furniture.* ☐ + *onto* *The boxes are loaded onto a truck.* ☐ + *with* *A tanker loaded with oil has sunk off the coast.* (**carregar**)
2 to put something into a machine or piece of equipment ☐ *Have you loaded the dishwasher?* (**carregar**)
3 to put a program into a computer's memory so you can use it ☐ *The computer is loaded with anti-virus software.* (**carregar**)
4 to put bullets in a gun (**carregar**)

load² /ləʊd/ NOUN [plural loads]
1 the things that a vehicle or person is carrying or can carry 🔹 *The ship was carrying a load of new cars.* ☐ *There were two lorry loads of rubbish.* ☐ *Take another load upstairs.* (**carga**)
2 loads/a load an informal word meaning a large amount ☐ *We have loads to talk about.* ☐ + *of* *He brought a load of food with him.* (**um monte**)

loaf /ləʊf/ NOUN [plural loaves] a large piece of bread for cutting into smaller pieces ☐ + *of* *a loaf of bread* ☐ *a brown sliced loaf* (**pão**)

loan¹ /ləʊn/ NOUN [plural loans] money that you borrow 🔹 *He wasn't able to repay the loan.* 🔹 *They took out a loan* (= arranged to borrow money) *to extend the house.* 🔹 *a bank loan* (**empréstimo**)

loan² /ləʊn/ VERB [loans, loaning, loaned] to lend something to someone ☐ *My brother loaned me the money to buy a new car.* (**emprestar**)

loathe /ləʊð/ VERB [loathes, loathing, loathed] to hate someone or something ☐ *I loathe shopping.* (**abominar**)

loaves /ləʊvz/ PLURAL OF **loaf** (ver **loaf**)

lobster /ˈlɒbstə(r)/ NOUN [plural lobsters] a sea animal with a hard shell, two large claws (= hard curved parts) and eight legs (**lagosta**)

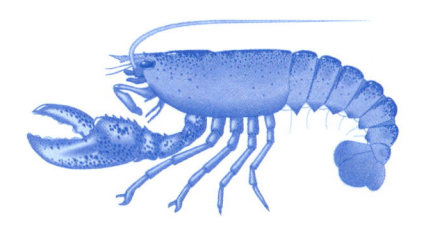

local /ˈləʊkəl/ ADJECTIVE to do with the area near to you ☐ *our local library* ☐ *a local newspaper*

🔹 *local government* 🔹 *Local residents are unhappy about the plans.* (**local**)

locally /ˈləʊkəli/ ADVERB in or from the area near to you ☐ *Most of our vegetables are grown locally.* ☐ *The hill is known locally as Old Misty.* (**localmente**)

locate /ləʊˈkeɪt/ VERB [locates, locating, located] **be located by/in/near, etc.** to be in a particular place ☐ *Their headquarters are located in Paris.* ☐ *The camps are mostly located near the border.* (**localizar**)

location /ləʊˈkeɪʃən/ NOUN [plural locations] a place or position ☐ + *of* *Nobody knows the exact location of the meeting.* ☐ *We have over 200 staff at 40 locations across the country.* (**localização**)

lock¹ /lɒk/ NOUN [plural locks] a device that fastens things such as doors and drawers, usually opened and closed using a key ☐ *There was no lock on the door.* ☐ *We had to change the lock on the front door.* (**fechadura**)

lock² /lɒk/ VERB [locks, locking, locked]
1 to fasten something such as a door with a key, or to be fastened this way 🔹 *Lock the door when you leave.* ☐ *This door doesn't lock.* (**trancar**)
2 to put something or someone in a place that is locked ☐ + *up* *He's a dangerous criminal who should be locked up.* ☐ + *away* *I locked all my jewellery away in a box.* ☐ + *in* *The medicines are locked in a cupboard.* (**encerrar**)

locker /ˈlɒkə(r)/ NOUN [plural lockers] a small cupboard, especially one that can be locked ☐ *I left my suitcase in a luggage locker at the station.* (**compartimento com chave**)

lodge /lɒdʒ/ VERB [lodges, lodging, lodged] to live in a room in someone else's house and pay them rent (**hospedar[-se]**)

loft /lɒft/ NOUN [plural lofts] the space between the roof of a house and the rooms ☐ *Our suitcases are stored in the loft.* (**sótão**)

log¹ /lɒɡ/ NOUN [plural logs] a part of a branch or tree that has been cut up (**tora**)

log² /lɒɡ/ VERB [logs, logging, logged] to make an official written record of something (**registrar no diário de bordo**)

♦ PHRASAL VERBS **log in/on** to start using a computer, website, etc. by typing in a word or code (= series of letters or numbers) **log off/out** to stop using a computer, website, etc. by clicking on something on the screen

logic /ˈlɒdʒɪk/ NOUN, NO PLURAL a way of thinking using facts and reason ☐ *I could see the logic of his argument.* (**lógica**)

logo /ˈləʊɡəʊ/ NOUN [plural logos] a design that is the symbol of a company or a product ☐ *The company has launched a new logo.* (**logotipo**)

lone /ləʊn/ ADJECTIVE alone, single or only ☐ *He was killed by a lone gunman.* 🔹 *She's a lone parent with two young children.* (**sozinho**)

loneliness /ˈləʊnlɪnɪs/ NOUN, NO PLURAL when you are unhappy because you are alone ☐ *He felt a growing sense of loneliness.* (solidão)

lonely
/ˈləʊnlɪ/ ADJECTIVE [lonelier, loneliest]
unhappy because you are alone, with no friends around you 🔹 *She suddenly felt very lonely.* 🔹 *I get lonely at the weekends.* (solitário)

long¹
/lɒŋ/ ADJECTIVE [longer, longest]
1 lasting a lot of time 🔹 *It took a long time to persuade her to come.* ☐ *There were long delays on the trains.* (longo)
2 measuring a long distance from one end to the other ☐ *She has very long hair.* ☐ *We went on a long journey.* ☐ *How long is the rope?* 🔹 *It's a long way from here.* (longo)
3 having a certain length ☐ *The garden is 50 m long.* ☐ *The film was three hours long.* (de duração)

long²
/lɒŋ/ ADVERB [longer, longest]
1 for a long time ☐ *Have you been waiting long?* ☐ *It won't be long till she starts school.* ☐ *The concert didn't last long.* (muito tempo)
2 much earlier or later than the time you are talking about 🔹 *The house was knocked down long ago.* 🔹 *He was a vegetarian long before I met him.* (longo, enquanto)
3 as long as used for saying that something must happen or be true before something else can happen or be true ☐ *You can borrow my jacket as long as you bring it back tomorrow.* (de duração)

long³ /lɒŋ/ VERB [longs, longing, longed] to want something very much ☐ *I was longing to sit down.* ☐ *They were longing for a chance to rest.* (cobiçar, desejar)

look¹
/lʊk/ VERB [looks, looking, looked]
1 to turn your eyes to see something ☐ + *at She was looking at the view.* ☐ *Look behind you.* ☐ *Oh look, there's a deer over there!* ☐ *Look where you're going!* (olhar)
2 to try to find something or someone ☐ + *for I'm looking for my passport.* (procurar)
3 to have a particular appearance ☐ *You look a bit tired.* ☐ *Kate looked fine when I saw her yesterday.* (parecer)
4 to seem ☐ *It looks as if Joe won't be coming.* ☐ *His job prospects are looking good.* (parecer)

> Notice the prepositions that are used with **look**. When you turn your eyes to see something (sense 1), you look **at** something:
> ✓ *I looked at the clock.*
> ✗ *I looked the clock.*

◆ PHRASAL VERBS **look after someone** to take care of someone or something ☐ *Her husband looks after the baby during the day.* **look forward to something** to feel pleased and excited about something that is going to happen ☐ *I'm really looking forward to meeting his family.*

> When *look forward to* is followed by a verb, the verb is in the *-ing* form:
> ✓ *We're looking forward to seeing you!*
> ✗ *We're looking forward to see you.*

look out to be careful because something might be dangerous ☐ *Look out! The path is very slippery.*
look something up to look in a book, on a computer, etc. to find information about something ☐ *I looked up the word 'digest' in the dictionary.*

look²
/lʊk/ NOUN [plural looks]
1 when you look at something or someone 🔹 *May I have a look at your watch?* 🔹 *Take a look at these documents.* 🔹 *I had a good look round their house.* (olhada)
2 when you try to find something or someone 🔹 *I had a look outside, but I couldn't see her.* (olhada)
3 an expression on someone's face ☐ *She gave me a warning look.* ☐ *There was a look of fear on his face.* (olhar)
4 the appearance of someone or something 🔹 *I don't like the look of those black clouds.* (aspecto)
5 someone's looks how attractive someone is ☐ *She is worried that she is losing her looks.* (beleza)

loom /luːm/ NOUN [plural looms] a machine for making cloth (tear)

loop /luːp/ NOUN [plural loops] a circle of something such as a thread, a piece of string or a narrow piece of cloth ☐ *Make a loop and pull one end through it.*

loose
/luːs/ ADJECTIVE [looser, loosest]
1 not tight or firmly fixed ☐ *a loose knot* ☐ *Wear loose, comfortable clothing.* 🔹 *One of the screws had come loose.* (frouxo)
2 not tied up or shut in ☐ *Her hair was hanging loose.* ☐ *Let the dogs run around loose.* (solto, livre)

loosen /ˈluːsən/ VERB [loosens, loosening, loosened] to make something less firm, fixed or tight ☐ *I had to loosen my belt.* ☐ *She loosened her grip on Frank's arm.* (afrouxar)

lord /lɔːd/ NOUN [plural lords]
1 used as the title of a man with a high social rank in the UK, or a man with this title ☐ *Lord Asquith* ☐ *the Lord Mayor of London* (Lorde)
2 Lord used in prayers as a way of addressing God (o Senhor)

lorry
/ˈlɒrɪ/ NOUN [plural lorries] a large vehicle for carrying heavy goods by road 🔹 *a lorry driver* (caminhão)

lose
/luːz/ VERB [loses, losing, lost]
1 to not be able to find someone or something ☐ *I've lost my keys.* (perder)
2 to have something taken away from you 🔹 *Fifty people have lost their jobs.* 🔹 *He was willing to lose his life for his beliefs.* (perder)
3 to have less of something than you had before 🔹 *She has lost weight recently.* 🔹 *The children soon lost interest in the animals.* 🔹 *The business is losing money.* (perder)

loss — **low**

4 to not have something you had before ▣ *I was so angry, I lost control and started shouting.* ▣ *I would hate to lose contact with my friends.* ▣ *I lost sight* (= stopped being able to see) *of the train.* (**perder**)
5 to be beaten in a competition, election, etc. □ *+ by I lost by 4 games to 6.* ▣ *We narrowly lost* (= only just lost) *the match.* (**perder**)

loss /lɒs/ NOUN [plural **losses**]
1 when you lose something □ *She was sacked over the loss of confidential documents.* □ *+ of He spoke about the loss of his home in a fire.* ▣ *There will be some job losses.* (**perda**)
2 when a business spends more money than it earns, or this amount of money □ *+ of The company announced a pre-tax loss of £2 million.* (**perda**)

lost¹ /lɒst/ ADJECTIVE
1 if something is lost, nobody knows where it is □ *The painting has been lost for centuries.* (**perdido**)
2 someone who is lost does not know where they are ▣ *How did you get lost when you had a map?* ▣ *We were hopelessly lost.* (**perdido**)

lost² /lɒst/ PAST TENSE OF **lose** (ver **lose**)

lot /lɒt/ NOUN [plural **lots**]
1 a lot/lots a large number or amount □ *+of There were a lot of people there.* □ *I bought lots of food.* □ *She doesn't eat a lot.* □ *We've got a lot to talk about.* (**muito**)
2 a lot better/happier/quicker, etc. much better/happier/quicker, etc. □ *You'd keep a lot warmer if you wore a hat.* (**muito**)

> Notice (*sense 1*) that **a** only goes before **lot** and not before **lots** □ *She has a lot of friends.* □ *She has lots of friends.*

lottery /'lɒtəri/ NOUN [plural **lotteries**] a game where people win money or prizes when their number or ticket is chosen by chance from many others ▣ *He looked like he'd won the lottery.* (**loteria**)

loud¹ /laʊd/ ADJECTIVE [**louder, loudest**] making a lot of sound ▣ *a loud noise* ▣ *She asked again in a louder voice.* □ *The music was too loud for me.* (**alto**)

loud² /laʊd/ ADVERB [**louder, loudest**]
1 making a lot of sound □ *Could you speak a little louder please?* □ *I screamed as loud as I could.* (**alto**)
2 out loud so that other people can hear you □ *I read the letter out loud.* □ *She laughed out loud.* (**em voz alta**)

loudly /'laʊdli/ ADVERB making a lot of sound □ *The crowds cheered loudly.* □ *I knocked again more loudly.* (**ruidosamente**)

lounge /laʊndʒ/ NOUN [plural **lounges**]
1 a room in a house where you sit and relax □ *I was watching TV in the lounge.* (**sala de estar**)
2 a room in a public building where people can sit to relax or to wait □ *a hotel lounge* ▣ *an airport lounge* (**sala de estardo aeroporto**)

love¹ /lʌv/ VERB [**loves, loving, loved**]
1 to have a strong romantic feeling for someone □ *I love you.* (**amar**)
2 to have a strong emotional feeling for a friend or family member who you like and care about □ *I loved my mother very much.* (**amar**)
3 to like or enjoy something very much □ *I love Chinese food.* □ *+ ing He loves playing with the children.* □ *+ to do something I'd love to be able to play the piano.* (**adorar, gostar**)

> **THESAURUS:** If you **like** someone, you think that they are pleasant. If you **love** or **adore** someone, you like them very much. If you **admire** someone, you like and respect them very much. Note that you can use all of these words to talk about things as well as people.

love² /lʌv/ NOUN [plural **loves**]
1 *no plural* a strong romantic feeling for someone ▣ *She fell in love with him at university.* ▣ *Within days, they were madly in love* (= loved each other very much). □ *+ for My love for him did not survive.* (**amor**)
2 *no plural* a strong emotional feeling for a friend or family member who you like and care about □ *+ for Her love for her children kept her going.* (**amor**)
3 *no plural* a feeling of liking or enjoying something very much □ *+ of I did not share her love of opera.* (**paixão**)
4 *no plural* used at the end of a letter □ *Hope to see you soon. Love, Emma.* □ *Have a great birthday. Lots of love, Mum.* (**amor**)

lovely /'lʌvli/ ADJECTIVE [**lovelier, loveliest**]
1 beautiful or attractive □ *She has lovely eyes.* ▣ *You look lovely in that dress.* (**encantador**)
2 enjoyable or pleasant □ *It was lovely to see you again.* □ *It was a lovely evening.* (**agradável**)
3 kind and friendly □ *She's a really lovely woman.* (**adorável**)

lover /'lʌvə(r)/ NOUN [plural **lovers**]
1 a person who is having a romantic relationship with someone else (**namorado**)
2 someone who is very interested in or enthusiastic about something □ *an art lover* □ *a music lover* □ *I've always been an animal lover.* (**apreciador**)

loving /'lʌvɪŋ/ ADJECTIVE
1 showing or expressing love □ *a loving look* □ *She has a very loving family.* (**amoroso**)
2 in loving memory used to remember someone who has died □ *In loving memory of my father, John.* (**em memória**)

low¹ /ləʊ/ ADJECTIVE [**lower, lowest**]
1 near to the ground or short in height □ *a low hedge* □ *I can reach the lowest branches.* (**baixo**)
2 less than usual in amount or level □ *We are experiencing very low temperatures.* □ *I try to look for the lowest prices.* □ *The risk of frost is very*

low now. □ **+ In** *Skimmed milk is low in fat.* (baixo)
3 a low sound or musical note is near the bottom of the range of sounds (baixo)
4 quiet □ *He spoke in a low voice.* (baixo)

low² /ləʊ/ ADVERB [lower, lowest] in or to a low position or level □ *Their supplies began to run low.* □ *They flew low over the desert.* (baixo)

lower /ˈləʊə(r)/ VERB [lowers, lowering, lowered]
1 to reduce something in amount or degree □ *They have lowered their prices.* ▣ *A good diet can lower your risk of heart disease.* ▣ *She lowered her voice to a whisper.* (abaixar)
2 to move something to a position nearer the bottom of something or nearer the ground □ **+ into** *They lowered the boat into the water.* □ *She lowered her head slightly.* (abaixar)

loyal /ˈlɔɪəl/ ADJECTIVE always supporting or being a friend to someone ▣ *a loyal fan* ▣ *We want to reward loyal customers.* ▣ *He remained loyal to the king.* (leal)

loyalty /ˈlɔɪəlti/ NOUN, NO PLURAL being loyal to some one ▣ *You always have a sense of loyalty to your home town.* □ **+ to** *The fans have demonstrated their loyalty to the team.* (lealdade)

Ltd ABBREVIATION Limited; used in the names of companies □ *Joe Bloggs Shoes Ltd* (ltda.)

luck /lʌk/ NOUN, NO PLURAL
1 when something good happens by chance ▣ *With a bit of luck, we'll be there by lunch time.* ▣ *Meeting Tim was a real piece of luck.* ▣ *I wished him luck with his exam.* (sorte, acaso)
2 the way things happen by chance ▣ *bad/good luck* □ *Whether or not you'll get on the course depends on your luck.* (sorte)
3 when you are successful at something ▣ *Have you had any luck selling your house?* □ *I've been trying to buy a wedding dress, but without any luck so far.* (sorte)
4 Good luck! used to tell someone that you hope they will succeed □ *Good luck with your exams.* (Boa sorte!)

lucky /ˈlʌki/ ADJECTIVE [luckier, luckiest]
1 a lucky person has good luck □ **+ to do something** *You're lucky to live so near the school.* □ **+ that** *It's lucky that they didn't discover the truth.* (com sorte)
2 bringing good luck ▣ *a lucky charm* (que dá sorte)

luggage /ˈlʌɡɪdʒ/ NOUN, NO PLURAL a traveller's bags and cases ▣ *I was only travelling with hand luggage.* ▣ *Each passenger can check in two pieces of luggage.* ▣ *a luggage rack* (bagagem)

> Remember that the noun **luggage** is not used in the plural:
> ✓ *I had so much luggage.*
> ✗ *I had so many luggages.*

lump /lʌmp/ NOUN [plural lumps]
1 a small piece of something without a clear shape □ **+ of** *a lump of coal* □ *a bowl of sugar lumps* (grumo, caroço)
2 a hard piece of tissue growing on or in your body □ *She found a lump in her breast.* (caroço)

lunch /lʌntʃ/ NOUN [plural lunches] the meal that you eat in the middle of the day ▣ *I had a sandwich for lunch.* ▣ *I had lunch with a friend.* ▣ *We ate lunch in a small café.* ▣ *I'll call you during my lunch break.* (almoço)

lunchtime /ˈlʌntʃtaɪm/ NOUN [plural lunchtimes] the time in the middle of the day when you have a meal □ *I'll meet you at lunchtime.* □ *They arrived yesterday lunchtime.* (hora do almoço)

lung /lʌŋ/ NOUN [plural lungs] one of the two organs inside your chest like bags that you use for breathing. A biology word. (pulmão)

lure /ljʊə(r)/ VERB [lures, luring, lured] to persuade a person or an animal to do something using a reward □ *Scraps of food are used to lure the animals.* □ *They're offering special deals to lure customers back.* (atrair)

lurk /lɜːk/ VERB [lurks, lurking, lurked] to wait secretly where you cannot be seen, especially because you are going to do something bad □ *Someone was lurking in the bushes.* (esconder-se)

luxurious /lʌɡˈʒʊəriəs/ ADJECTIVE very comfortable and expensive □ *The hotel room was very luxurious.* □ *She enjoyed a luxurious lifestyle.* (luxuoso)

luxury /ˈlʌkʃəri/ NOUN [plural luxuries]
1 a situation in which you are very comfortable, with expensive or beautiful things □ *They live in luxury.* □ *We stayed in five-star luxury.* □ *a luxury hotel* □ *luxury goods* (luxo)
2 something that is pleasant, and often expensive, but not necessary □ *We couldn't afford luxuries such as chocolate.* (luxos)

lyrics /ˈlɪrɪks/ PLURAL NOUN the words of a song □ *He wrote the lyrics for most of their songs.* (letra)

M m

M or m /em/ the 13th letter of the alphabet (a décima terceira letra do alfabeto)
m /em/ ABBREVIATION metre or metres or million

machine /mə'ʃi:n/ NOUN [plural machines]
a piece of equipment that uses power to do a particular job ☐ *a washing machine* ☐ *a coffee machine* ▣ *He used a fax machine in the office.* ☐ *Cows are usually milked by machine.* (máquina)

> THESAURUS: A machine is a piece of equipment that uses power to do a particular job. An engine is part of a machine that uses energy to produce movement. For example, a car is a machine which has an engine to make it move. A motor is a smaller type of engine. For example, a car's engine contains motors to make the various parts work.

machine gun /mə'ʃi:n ˌgʌn/ NOUN [plural machine guns] an automatic gun that fires a lot of bullets very quickly (metralhadora)

machinery /mə'ʃi:nəri/ NOUN, NO PLURAL
big machines ☐ *farm machinery* ▣ *Cranes and other heavy machinery were used to remove the rocks.* (maquinaria)

mad /mæd/ ADJECTIVE [madder, maddest]
1 an informal word meaning stupid ☐ *Swimming where you know there are sharks is a mad thing to do.* ☐ *I thought he was mad wanting to climb Everest.* (louco)
2 mentally ill ▣ *The poor woman went mad with grief.* (louco)
3 a mainly US word meaning very angry ☐ *I got mad at him for lying to me.* (louco)
4 **go mad** an informal phrase meaning to become very angry or behave in a way that is not controlled ☐ *She'll go mad if she finds out you tricked her.* (louco)
5 **be mad about/on someone/something** to like someone or something very much ☐ *He's mad about football.* (louco)
6 **like mad** (a) as quickly as possible and using a lot of energy ☐ *She was running like mad to keep up with the others.* (b) a lot ☐ *My arms were hurting like mad.* (como um louco)

madam /'mædəm/ NOUN [plural madams]
1 a formal and polite word used for talking to a woman, for example when serving her in a shop or restaurant ☐ *Can I help you, madam?* (senhora)
2 **Dear Madam** a way of beginning a formal letter to a woman when you do not know her name ☐ *Dear Madam, I'm writing to enquire about the job which was advertised in the newspaper.* (prezada senhora)

made /meɪd/ PAST TENSE AND PAST PARTICIPLE OF **make** (ver **make**)

madness /'mædnɪs/ NOUN, NO PLURAL stupid or dangerous behaviour ▣ *In a moment of madness he hit the other man.* (loucura)

magazine /ˌmægə'zi:n/ NOUN [plural magazines]
a thin book with pictures in it which is usually published every week or every month ▣ *Amy was reading a magazine.* ☐ *a fashion magazine* ☐ *a magazine article* (revista)

magic¹ /'mædʒɪk/ NOUN, NO PLURAL
1 a strange power that some people believe exists, causing strange things to happen that you cannot explain ▣ *Wizards use magic.* (magia)
2 tricks, such as making things disappear, which are done to entertain people ☐ *Children love watching magic.* (mágica)

magic² /'mædʒɪk/ ADJECTIVE
1 involving tricks such as making things disappear ▣ *magic tricks* ☐ *a magic show* (mágica)
2 able to make impossible things happen ☐ *a magic wand* ☐ *a magic potion* (mágica)

magical /'mædʒɪkəl/ ADJECTIVE
1 special and exciting or attractive ☐ *a magical atmosphere* ☐ *a magical place* (mágico)
2 done using magic, or having magic powers ☐ *magical powers* ☐ *magical healing* (mágico)
• **magically** /'mædʒɪkəli/ ADVERB using magic, or in a way that seems to be magic ☐ *The next morning, the missing books had magically reappeared on the shelf.* (magicamente)

magician /mə'dʒɪʃən/ NOUN [plural magicians]
1 someone who does magic tricks to entertain people (mágico)
2 someone who has magic powers, especially in stories (mágicos)

magistrate /'mædʒɪstreɪt/ NOUN [plural magistrates] a judge who deals with crimes which are not of the most serious type (magistrado)

magnet /'mægnɪt/ NOUN [plural **magnets**] a piece of iron which makes other metal objects move towards it (**ímã**)

magnetic /mæg'netɪk/ ADJECTIVE having the power to attract metal objects □ *Iron has magnetic properties.* □ *The satellite will measure the sun's magnetic field.* (**magnético**)

maid /meɪd/ NOUN [plural **maids**] a woman whose job is to keep the rooms clean and tidy in a hotel or house (**empregada doméstica**)

mail[1] /meɪl/ NOUN, NO PLURAL
1 letters and packages which are sent by post □ *My mail was delivered to the wrong address.* (**correspondência**)
2 the system of sending and delivering letters and packages □ *His passport was sent in the mail.* (**correio**)

> Remember that the noun **mail** is not used in the plural:
> ✓ *We get a lot of mail.*
> ✗ *We get a lot of mails.*

> **THESAURUS:** A **letter** is a message that you write and send to another person. A **parcel** is something wrapped in paper and sent somewhere. **Correspondence** is letters that people write to each other, or the activity of writing letters. The **mail** or the **post** is the service that collects and delivers letters and parcels, or the letters and parcels which are sent.

mail[2] /meɪl/ VERB [**mails, mailing, mailed**]
1 to send a letter or package in the post (**enviar pelo correio**)
2 to e-mail someone □ *I'll mail you some photos.* (**enviar e-mail**)

main /meɪn/ ADJECTIVE biggest or most important □ *The main reason I do sport is to improve my health.* □ *a main road* □ *Police guarded the main entrance of the building.* (**principal**)

mainly /'meɪnli/ ADVERB mostly or in most cases □ *Her job mainly involves organizing conferences.* □ *We chose Spain mainly because of the weather.* □ *The spice is used mainly in Indian cooking.* (**principalmente**)

maintain /meɪn'teɪn/ VERB
1 to make something continue at the same level or in the same way as before □ *Players need to maintain their fitness levels.* □ *The Republican Party has maintained control of the country.* (**manter**)
2 to keep a house or piece of equipment in good condition □ *The car wasn't maintained properly.* (**manter**)

maintenance /'meɪntənəns/ NOUN, NO PLURAL regular cleaning or repairs done to keep something in good condition ⚑ *The bridge has been closed for maintenance work.* (**manutenção**)

majesty /'mædʒəsti/ NOUN [plural **majesties**] **His/Her/Your Majesty** a title used when speaking to or about a king or queen □ *Her Majesty will be attending a Thanksgiving service next week.* (**Majestade**)

major[1] /'meɪdʒə(r)/ ADJECTIVE very big, serious or important □ *a major problem* □ *major changes* □ *The company has offices in all major cities.* (**principal**)

major[2] /'meɪdʒə(r)/ NOUN [plural **majors**] an army officer above the rank of captain (**major**)

majority /mə'dʒɒrəti/ NOUN [plural **majorities**] *no plural* most of the people or things in a group □ **+ of** *The study showed that a majority of people have access to the Internet.* □ *The illness is linked to diet in the majority of cases.* ⚑ *The vast majority of students agreed with the proposal.* (**maioria**)

make /meɪk/ VERB [**makes, making, made**]
1 to create or produce something □ *I'll make dinner.* □ *She makes all the children's clothes.* □ *They've made a film of the book.* □ *The children were making so much noise.* (**fazer**)
2 to cause someone to feel a particular emotion □ *It made me so angry.* □ *That film makes me cry.* (**fazer**)
3 to force someone to do something □ *My parents made me do my homework.* □ *No one is going to make you go if you don't want to.* (**fazer**)
4 used with some nouns to do with speech □ *May I make a suggestion?* □ *He made a very strange comment.* □ *I've made a complaint.* □ *He made an interesting point.* (**fazer**)
5 make a decision to decide something □ *Have you made a decision yet?* (**tomar uma decisão**)
6 make a mistake to do something wrong □ *Everyone makes mistakes.* (**cometer erro**)
7 to earn money □ *He makes about $90,000 a year.* □ *You can make a lot of money in banking.* (**ganhar**)
8 to be the total amount of two or more numbers added together □ *Six and six makes twelve.* (**perfazer**)
9 make do to accept or use something although it is not exactly what you wanted □ *If we can't borrow Andrew's van we'll have to make do with the car.* (**quebrar o galho**)
10 make it to manage to go somewhere or manage to arrive somewhere in time to do something □ *If we run we might just make it before the train leaves.* (**conseguir**)

◆ PHRASAL VERBS **make something into**

make-up

something to change something so that it becomes something else □ *We've made the spare room into an office.* **make something/someone out** to be able to see or hear something or someone although with difficulty □ *His voice was very low but I could just make out what he said.* **make up** to become friendly again after an argument **make up something** to give an explanation that is not true □ *He made up some excuse about the train being late.*

> THESAURUS: Make is a general word. To manufacture something means to make it in a factory. If you construct or build something, you make it by putting materials or parts together. Produce is also a general word for making or creating things. When we talk about growing things such as crops, we usually use the word produce. A tree produces fruit, for example.

make-up /'meɪkʌp/ NOUN, NO PLURAL coloured substances that you put on your face to improve or change your appearance 🔲 *A lot of women wear make-up.* 🔲 *She was putting on her make-up.* (**maquiagem**)

malaria /məˈleərɪə/ NOUN, NO PLURAL a serious tropical disease which people can get if they are bitten by a mosquito (= type of insect) (**malária**)

male¹ /meɪl/ ADJECTIVE belonging to the sex that does not have babies □ *male students* □ *a male swan* □ *The group's members are mostly male.* (**macho**)

male² /meɪl/ NOUN [plural **males**] a male person or animal □ *Thirty thousand adult males disappear every year.* (**macho**)

mall /mɔːl, mæl/ NOUN [plural **malls**] a shopping centre that is indoors (**shopping center**)

mammal /ˈmæməl/ NOUN [plural **mammals**] an animal that feeds its babies on milk from its own body □ *Humans, cows and dogs are mammals.* (**mamífero**)

man /mæn/ NOUN [plural **men**]
1 an adult male human □ *a young man* □ *an old man* □ *a married man* □ *I work mainly with men.* (**homem**)
2 no plural humans considered as a group □ *Man is closely related to the ape.* (**homem**)

manage /ˈmænɪdʒ/ VERB [**manages, managing, managed**]
1 to succeed in doing something □ + **to do** *some thing The prisoners managed to escape.* □ *We couldn't manage without your help.* □ *Emma managed a smile even though she didn't feel very happy.* (**conseguir**)
2 to be in charge of a business, team, etc. □ *Who manages the business for you?* □ *Alan is managing the new project.* (**administrar**)

management /ˈmænɪdʒmənt/ NOUN, NO PLURAL
1 the job of controlling a business or activity □ *a job in management* 🔲 *management skills* (**gestão, administração**)
2 the people who control a company □ *The management has agreed to further talks.* □ *The restaurant is under new management.* 🔲 *senior management* (**diretoria**)
3 the way that something is controlled □ + **of** *The government's successful management of the economy continues.* (**administração**)

manager /ˈmænɪdʒə(r)/ NOUN [plural **managers**] someone who is in charge of a company, team, etc. □ *a project manager* □ *a football manager* 🔲 *She's a senior manager for a law firm.* □ + **of** *Can I speak to the manager of the hotel, please?* (**gerente, diretor**)

• **manageress** /ˌmænɪdʒəˈres/ NOUN [plural **manageresses**] a woman who is in charge of a restaurant, shop, etc. (**dirigente, diretora**)

manipulate /məˈnɪpjʊleɪt/ VERB [**manipulates, manipulating, manipulated**] to control someone or something so that they do what you want, often in a dishonest way □ *He knew how to manipulate the media.* (**manipular**)

mankind /ˌmænˈkaɪnd/ NOUN, NO PLURAL all humans □ *This is one of the most terrible diseases in the history of mankind.* (**humanidade**)

man-made /ˌmænˈmeɪd/ ADJECTIVE made or caused by people and not natural □ *a man-made lake* □ *man-made disasters* (**artificial**)

manner /ˈmænə(r)/ NOUN [plural **manners**]
1 the way in which something happens or is done □ *The boys behaved in a very responsible manner.* □ + **of** *The manner of his death was extremely shocking.* (**maneira**)
2 manners polite ways of behaving in a social situation 🔲 *His parents taught him good manners.* 🔲 *It's bad manners* (= it is not polite) *to talk when your mouth is full of food.* 🔲 *She needs to learn some manners.* (**maneiras, boas maneiras**)

mansion /ˈmænʃən/ NOUN [plural **mansions**] a very large, expensive house (**mansão**)

manslaughter /ˈmænslɔːtə(r)/ NOUN, NO PLURAL the crime of killing someone but not intentionally (**homicídio involuntário**)

manual¹ /ˈmænjʊəl/ ADJECTIVE involving your hands or physical strength 🔲 *manual work* 🔲 *manual labour* (**manual**)

manual² /ˈmænjʊəl/ NOUN [plural **manuals**] a book that tells you how to do something such as use a machine (**manual**)

manufacture /ˌmænjʊˈfæktʃə(r)/ VERB [**manufactures, manufacturing, manufactured**] to make something in a factory □ *The company manufactures car parts.* (**fabricar**)

manufacturer /ˌmænjuˈfæktʃərə(r)/ NOUN [plural **manufacturers**] a company that makes something in a factory □ *food manufacturers* (**fabricar**)

many /ˈmeni/ DETERMINER, PRONOUN [plural **more, most**]
1 a lot or a large number □ *Were there many people at the party?* □ *We've had so many problems.* □ *There are too many people here.* □ *She doesn't have many friends.* (**muitos**)
2 how many used to ask about the number of something □ *How many chairs will you need?* (**quantos**)

> Remember that **many** is used with the plural forms of *countable* nouns. It is not used with *uncountable* nouns:
> *How **many** plates do we need?*
> How many food do we need?
> With uncountable nouns, the word **much** is used: □ *How **much** food do we need?*

map /mæp/ NOUN [plural **maps**] a drawing of an area which shows things such as roads, rivers and hills □ *Where's Tokyo on this map?* □ *Emma stopped the car and looked at the map.* □ *She drew a little map to show where her house was.* □ *a road map* □ + **of** *Have you got a map of France?* (**mapa**)

marathon /ˈmærəθən/ NOUN [plural **marathons**] a race in which people run approximately 26 miles or 42 kilometres □ *She ran her first marathon last year.* (**maratona**)

marble /ˈmɑːbəl/ NOUN [plural **marbles**]
1 *no plural* a type of smooth stone used for making things □ *a marble statue* (**mármore**)
2 a small glass ball that children play with (**bola de gude**)

March /mɑːtʃ/ NOUN [plural **Marches**] the third month of the year, after February and before April □ *I'm going to Chile in March.* (**março**)

march¹ /mɑːtʃ/ VERB [**marches, marching, marched**]
1 if soldiers march, they walk together with the same, regular steps (**marchar**)
2 to walk somewhere quickly in an angry, confident or determined way □ + **into/out of** *He marched into the office and demanded to speak to the manager.* (**marchar**)
3 to walk with many other people in order to protest (= show that you disagree) about something □ + **through** *Anti-war protesters marched through the streets.* (**marchar**)

march² /mɑːtʃ/ NOUN [plural **marches**]
1 an event in which a large group of people walk somewhere to protest (= show that they disagree) about something □ + **against** *2,000 people took part in a march against the new employment laws.* (**marcha**)
2 a walk with regular steps done by soldiers □ *a slow march* (**marcha**)

margin /ˈmɑːdʒɪn/ NOUN [plural **margins**] the empty space at the side of a page □ *The teacher had written some comments in the margin.* (**margem**)

marine¹ /məˈriːn/ ADJECTIVE to do with the sea and the animals that live there □ *marine animals* □ *the marine environment* (**marinho**)

marine² /məˈriːn/ NOUN [plural **marines**] a soldier who fights on land and at sea (**fuzileiro naval**)

mark¹ /mɑːk/ NOUN [plural **marks**]
1 an area of something that is a different colour from the thing it is on □ *There's a dirty mark on the sofa.* □ *The rabbit's fur is brown, with black marks.* □ *The bite marks have gone now.* (**marca**)
2 a number or letter that says how well you have done a piece of school work, exam, etc. □ *a high/low mark* □ *He got top marks* (= the best possible marks) *in all his exams.* (**nota**)

> THESAURUS: A **mark** is an area of something that is a different colour from the thing it is on. A **spot** is a round shape that is often part of a pattern. A **stain** is a dirty mark on something that is difficult to remove. A **scratch** is a mark left on a surface by something sharp.

mark² /mɑːk/ VERB [**marks, marking, marked**]
1 to judge the quality of and correct a student's work, exam, etc. (**corrigir**)
2 to make a mark on the surface of something □ *Shoes with black soles may mark this floor.* (**manchar**)
3 to write words or a symbol on something □ *I've marked on the list the people I want to see.* □ *Go along the path marked 'exit'.* (**marcar**)

market /ˈmɑːkɪt/ NOUN [plural **markets**]
1 a building or outside area where people sell things □ *a street market* □ *an outdoor market* □ *a fish market* □ *a market stall* (**feira, mercado**)
2 the people who want to buy something □ *There is a huge market for mobile phones.* □ *Our main market is in Europe.* □ *The magazine is aimed at the teenage market.* (**mercado**)
3 on the market available for people to buy □ *The house has been on the market for six months.* (**no mercado**)

marriage /ˈmærɪdʒ/ NOUN [plural **marriages**]
1 the legal relationship of being husband and wife □ *My parents had a long and happy marriage.* (**casamento**)
2 the ceremony in which a man and woman become husband and wife □ *The marriage took place in St Paul's Cathedral.* (**casado**)

> Notice that a **marriage** is a ceremony in which a man and woman become husband and wife. The occasion when two people become husband and wife, when friends and family dance and eat, etc. is called a **wedding**:
> ✓ *I was invited to the **wedding**.*
> ✗ *I was invited to the marriage.*

married /ˈmærɪd/ ADJECTIVE
1 having a husband or wife □ *a married man* □ *a married couple* □ **+ to** *Miranda is married to John.* 🔁 *They are getting married in June.* (**casado**)
2 to do with marriage □ *married life* (**casado**)

marry /ˈmæri/ VERB [marries, marrying, married]
1 to make someone your husband or wife in a special ceremony □ *Andrew has asked me to marry him.* □ *Her brother never married.* (**casar-se**)
2 to officially perform the ceremony that makes two people become husband and wife □ *They were married by the bishop.* (**casar**)

marsh /mɑːʃ/ NOUN [plural **marshes**] an area of land that is soft and wet all the time (**pântano**)

marvellous /ˈmɑːvələs/ ADJECTIVE extremely good □ *That's marvellous news!* (**ótimo, maravilhoso**)

masculine /ˈmæskjʊlɪn/ ADJECTIVE
1 to do with men, or having qualities that are typical of a man □ *a deep, masculine voice* (**masculino**)
2 in English grammar, masculine forms of words refer to males. For example, *he* is a masculine pronoun. (**masculino**)

mask¹ /mɑːsk/ NOUN [plural **masks**] something that you wear over your face in order to protect it, to hide or for decoration □ *a carnival mask* □ *The surgeon removed his mask to speak to her.* (**máscara**)

mask² /mɑːsk/ VERB [masks, masking, masked] to prevent something such as a feeling or smell from being noticed □ *She sprayed air freshener to mask the cooking smells.* (**mascarar**)

mass /mæs/ NOUN [plural masses]
1 a large lump or quantity of something with no clear shape □ **+ of** *After the crash, the car was a mass of tangled metal.* □ *The little girl had a mass of blonde curls.* (**massa**)
2 **masses** a lot of something. An informal word. □ *He's got masses of toys.* (**montes**)
3 **Mass** a ceremony in some Christian churches in which people eat bread and drink wine (**missa**)

massacre /ˈmæsəkə(r)/ NOUN [plural **massacres**] the killing of a large number of people (**massacre**)

massage¹ /ˈmæsɑːʒ/ VERB [massages, massaging, massaged] to rub parts of a person's body in order to make them relax or to make the muscles less painful □ *Could you massage my shoulders?* (**massagear**)

massage² /ˈmæsɑːʒ/ NOUN [plural **massages**] when someone rubs parts of a person's body in order to make them relax or to make the muscles less painful 🔁 *I gave her a foot massage.* (**massagem**)

massive /ˈmæsɪv/ ADJECTIVE very big □ *She earns a massive amount of money.* (**maciço**)

mast /mɑːst/ NOUN [plural **masts**]
1 a tall pole used for sending out radio, television or mobile phone signals (**torre**)
2 a tall pole for holding the sails of a boat or ship (**mastro**)

master¹ /ˈmɑːstə(r)/ NOUN [plural masters]
1 a man who has control over something □ *a dog and its master* (**patrão**)
2 someone who is very good at a particular activity □ *a master of disguise* (**mestre**)

master² /ˈmɑːstə(r)/ VERB [masters, mastering, mastered]
to learn how to do something well □ *Juggling needs quite a lot of practice before you master it.* (**dominar**)

mat /mæt/ NOUN [plural **mats**]
1 a flat piece of material for covering or protecting part of a floor □ *a door mat* (**capacho**)
2 a small piece of material for putting under something to protect a table's surface □ *a table mat* (**descanso para pratos**)

match¹ /mætʃ/ NOUN [plural matches]
1 a sports competition between two players or two teams 🔁 *a football match* 🔁 *Who won the match?* (**partida**)
2 a short, thin piece of wood with a substance on the end that produces fire when it is rubbed on a rough surface 🔁 *He struck a match to light a candle.* (**fósforo**)
3 something that is similar to another thing or suitable to be with another thing, especially in its colour or pattern □ *This isn't the same make of paint but it's a very good match.* (**combinação**)

match² /mætʃ/ VERB [matches, matching, matched]
1 to be the same colour or style □ *Her handbag matched her shoes.* □ *His handwriting matched that on the letter.* (**combinar com**)
2 to put two people or things together because they are suitable for each other □ **+ to** *Match the word on the left to its meaning on the right.* (**combinar com**)

mate¹ /meɪt/ NOUN [plural mates]
1 an informal word for a friend □ *He's a good mate of mine.* 🔁 *She's my best mate.* (**companheiro**)
2 the male or female that an animal breeds with (**parceiro**)

mate² /meɪt/ VERB [mates, mating, mated]
animals and birds mate when they have sex to produce babies □ *Swans mate for life.* (**acasalar**)

material /məˈtɪərɪəl/ NOUN [plural **materials**]
1 cloth ☐ *The jacket was made of a very thick material.* (**tecido**)
2 a substance used for making something else ☐ *building materials* ☐ *raw materials for the steel industry* (**material**)

maternal /məˈtɜːnəl/ ADJECTIVE
1 to do with, or typical of, a mother ☐ *maternal feelings* ⊕ *a maternal instinct* (**maternal**)
2 related through your mother's side of your family ☐ *your maternal grandmother* (**materno**)

math /mæθ/ NOUN, NO PLURAL the US word for **maths** (**matemática**)

mathematical /ˌmæθəˈmætɪkəl/ ADJECTIVE
to do with or using mathematics ☐ *a mathematical genius* ☐ *a mathematical calculation* (**matemático**)

mathematics /ˌmæθəˈmætɪks/ NOUN, NO PLURAL the study of measurements, numbers, quantities and shapes. A formal word. (**matemática**)

maths /mæθs/ NOUN, NO PLURAL a short way to say and write **mathematics** (**matemática**)

matinée /ˈmætɪneɪ/ NOUN [plural **matinées**]
a performance at a theatre or cinema in the afternoon (**matinê, vesperal**)

matter¹ /ˈmætə(r)/ NOUN [plural **matters**]
1 a subject or situation ☐ *He wants to see you to discuss a personal matter.* ☐ *We need to think about all the practical matters.* ☐ **+ for** *This is a matter for the police.* (**assunto**)
2 the matter used to talk about something that is wrong with something or causing a problem ⊕ *What's the matter with Rachel? She's very quiet.* ⊕ *I know something's the matter with Eve.* ☐ *What's the matter with these tomatoes? They look brown.* (**problema**)
3 no plural any substance that takes up space and is part of the physical universe (**matéria**)
4 as a matter of fact used to add information or to say that something that has just been said is wrong ☐ *As a matter of fact, he's one of the richest men in the country.* (**na verdade**)

matter² /ˈmætə(r)/ VERB [**matters, mattering, mattered**] to be important ⊕ *It doesn't matter if you're late – we can save you some food.* ☐ *Does it matter if the door isn't completely closed?* ☐ *Winning matters to him more than it should.* (**importar**)

mattress /ˈmætrɪs/ NOUN [plural **mattresses**] the thick, soft part of a bed, that you lie on (**colchão**)

mature¹ /məˈtjʊə(r)/ ADJECTIVE
1 completely grown or developed ☐ *a mature male elephant* ☐ *mature trees* (**maduro**)
2 behaving in a sensible way, like an adult ☐ *He's a very mature 13-year-old.* (**maduro**)

mature² /məˈtjʊə(r)/ VERB [**matures, maturing, matured**]
1 to become completely grown or developed (**amadurecer**)

2 to start to behave in a sensible way, like an adult (**amadurecer**)

maximum¹ /ˈmæksɪməm/ NOUN, NO PLURAL the greatest amount or degree that is possible or allowed ☐ *The maximum I'm prepared to pay is £200.* ☐ *The car will hold a maximum of five people.* (**máximo**)

maximum² /ˈmæksɪməm/ ADJECTIVE being the greatest amount or degree that is possible or allowed ☐ *The maximum speed limit is 40 mph on this road.* ☐ *The crime carries a maximum penalty of five years' imprisonment.* (**máximo**)

May /meɪ/ NOUN [plural **Mays**] the fifth month of the year, after April and before June ☐ *The weather was awful in May.* (**maio**)

may /meɪ/ MODAL VERB
1 used to talk about the possibility that something is true or something will happen ☐ *I may apply for the job, but I'm not sure yet.* ☐ *He thinks she may be lying.* (**ser possível**)
2 a formal word used for asking for or giving permission ☐ *May I ask what you're doing in my room?* ☐ *You may leave the table now.* (**poder**)

maybe /ˈmeɪbiː/ ADVERB possibly ☐ *Maybe she called earlier.* ☐ *Maybe they're not coming.* ☐ *It'll take two, maybe three, days to paint the room.* (**talvez**)

mayor /meə(r)/ NOUN [plural **mayors**] a man or woman elected as the official leader of a town or city (**prefeito**)

me /miː/ PRONOUN used as the object in a sentence to talk or write about yourself ☐ *Would you make me a cup of tea, please?* ☐ *Are there any letters for me?* ☐ *Hi, it's me. Sorry, but I'm going to be late.* (**eu, mim, me**)

➤ Remember that **me** is used after a verb or preposition. In a sentence in which you are doing the action, use **I** before the verb: ☐ *I gave her some flowers.* ☐ *He gave me some flowers.*

meal /miːl/ NOUN [plural **meals**] food that you eat at one time, for example breakfast ⊕ *We're going out for a meal on Saturday night.* ⊕ *I have my main meal in the evening.* (**refeição**)

➤ THESAURUS: Meal is a general word for food that you eat at a particular time. The first meal that you eat in the morning is called breakfast. The meal that you eat in the middle of the day is usually called lunch. This meal is also sometimes called dinner. Usually, dinner is the main meal in the evening. Some people call this meal tea. A lighter meal in the evening or in the afternoon is also called tea. A snack is a small amount of food that you eat between meals.

mean¹ /miːn/ VERB [**means, meaning, meant**]
1 to have a particular meaning ☐ *What does 'intrepid' mean?* ☐ *Her name means 'lucky' in Arabic.* (**significar**)

mean

2 to try to express an opinion or a fact ◻ *I didn't know what she meant when she told me to speak like a lady.* ◻ *What did she mean by 'too academic'?* 🔁 *I see what you mean about his bad temper.* (**querer dizer**)
3 to intend to do something ◻ + *to do something I'm sorry. I didn't mean to upset you.* ◻ *Did you mean to take this turning?* (**tencionar**)
4 to be a sign that something will happen, or to have a particular result ◻ + *that Higher wages meant that more people could afford cars.* ◻ *Dark clouds usually mean rain.* (**significar**)
5 be meant to do something if you are meant to do something, someone has said that you must do it ◻ *I'm meant to do my homework before I watch TV.* **deveria fazer algo**)

mean² /miːn/ ADJECTIVE [meaner, meanest]
1 a mean person does not like spending money or giving things to other people ◻ *She's too mean to pay to have her hair cut.* (**mesquinho**)
2 unkind ◻ *Mum, Adam's being mean to me!* (**mesquinho**)

mean³ /miːn/ NOUN [plural means] the average. A mathematics word. (**média**)
→ *go to* **means**

meaning /ˈmiːnɪŋ/ NOUN [plural meanings]
1 what a word or action expresses ◻ *The music conveys the meaning of the text.* ◻ *I didn't understand the meaning of his words.* ◻ *We searched for a hidden meaning in his letter.* (**sentido, significado**)
2 importance or purpose ◻ *We all want to understand the meaning of life.* ◻ *He helped me understand the meaning of these events.* (**sentido, significado**)

means /miːnz/ NOUN [plural means]
1 a way or method of doing something ◻ *a means of transport* ◻ *a means of payment* (**meios**)
2 money ◻ *Does he have the means to buy a car?* (**meios**)
3 by all means used to politely give someone permission to do something ◻ *'Can I have a look at your magazine?' 'By all means.'* (**sem dúvida**)
4 by no means not at all or in no way ◻ *It was by no means the worst talk I'd heard.* (**de jeito nenhum, nem um pouco**)

meant /ment/ PAST TENSE AND PAST PARTICIPLE OF **mean¹** ◻ *I meant every word I said.* ◻ *She had meant to tell him but forgot.* (ver **mean¹**)

meantime /ˈmiːntaɪm/ NOUN, NO PLURAL **in the meantime** in the time before something happens ◻ *We're having the car repaired but in the meantime we're borrowing my sister's.* (**nesse ínterim**)

meanwhile /ˈmiːnwaɪl/ ADVERB
1 in the time before something happens ◻ *I'll start the report once the sales figures are in. Meanwhile I've got plenty of work to do.* (**enquanto isso**)
2 at the same time ◻ *Tom was enjoying himself with his friends. Meanwhile, I was working like crazy back here.* (**enquanto isso**)

measles /ˈmiːzəlz/ NOUN, NO PLURAL an infectious disease, especially among children, in which you feel very hot and your skin is covered in red spots (**sarampo**)

measure¹ /ˈmeʒə(r)/ VERB [measures, measuring, measured]
1 to find how tall, long, wide, fast, etc. something is ◻ *She was measuring the window for some new curtains.* (**medir**)
2 to be a particular size ◻ *The room measures 3.5 metres from the door to the window.* (**medir**)

measure² /ˈmeʒə(r)/ NOUN [plural measures]
1 an official action done to achieve something or deal with something 🔁 *The school is being closed as a temporary measure.* 🔁 *The government is introducing new measures to fight crime.* (**medida**)
2 a unit used in measuring ◻ *A kilogram is a measure of weight, while a kilometre is a measure of distance or length.* (**medida**)

measurement /ˈmeʒəmənt/ NOUN [plural measurements] a size or amount found by measuring ◻ *Can you write down the exact measurements of the floor?* (**medição, medida**)

> **THESAURUS:** A **measurement** is a size or amount found by measuring. A thing's **size** is how big, small, long, wide etc. it is. **Length** is how long something is from one end to the other end. **Height** is how tall or high someone or something is. Note that we only use **height** to talk about people, not length. **Width** is how much a thing measures from side to side. **Depth** is the distance from the top to the bottom of something.

meat /miːt/ NOUN [plural meats] the flesh of animals eaten as food 🔁 *red meat* such as beef 🔁 *white meat* such as chicken (**carne**)

> **THESAURUS:** Meat is a general word for the flesh of animals eaten as food. The meat that we get from a cow is called **beef**. The meat that we get from a pig is called **pork**. Thin slices of salty meat from a pig are called **bacon**. Thin slices of cooked meat from the leg of a pig are called **ham**. The meat we get from a sheep is usually called **lamb**.

mechanic /mɪˈkænɪk/ NOUN [plural mechanics] someone whose job is to repair vehicles and machines 🔁 *a car mechanic* (**mecânico**)

mechanical /mɪˈkænɪkəl/ ADJECTIVE to do with machines ◻ *There must have been a mechanical failure.* ◻ *a mechanical device* (**mecânico**)

mechanism /ˈmekənɪzəm/ NOUN [plural mechanisms] a working part of a machine, or its system of working parts ◻ *The springs are part of the clock's mechanism.* (**mecanismo**)

medal /ˈmedəl/ NOUN [plural medals] a metal disk given as a prize in a competition or for brave actions 🔁 *an Olympic medal* 🔁 *a gold/silver/bronze medal* 🔁 *He was awarded a medal for bravery.* (**medalha**)

media /ˈmiːdɪə/ PLURAL NOUN the media newspapers, television and radio or other means of communicating information to the public ◻ There was nothing in the media about his speech. (**meios de comunicação**)

median /ˈmiːdɪən/ ADJECTIVE being the median. A mathematics word. ◻ the median price/age (**mediano**)

medical /ˈmedɪkəl/ ADJECTIVE to do with medicine or doctors and their work ◫ He did not need any medical treatment. ◫ She's receiving the best medical care. ◫ the medical staff ◫ a serious medical condition (**médico**)

medicine /ˈmedɪsɪn/ NOUN [plural medicines]
1 a substance used to treat or prevent illnesses ◻ cough medicine ◫ Have you taken your medicine? (**remédio**)
2 no plural the science of treating and preventing illnesses ◫ He studied medicine at the University of Melbourne. ◻ traditional Chinese medicine (**medicina**)

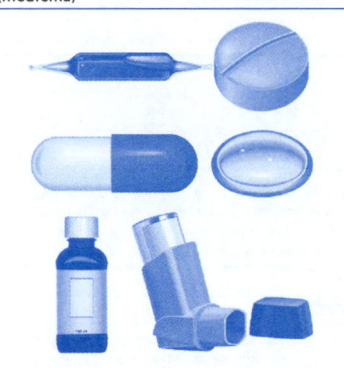

medieval /ˌmedɪˈiːvəl/ ADJECTIVE to do with the period of history from about 1000 to 1500 ◻ a medieval castle (**medieval**)

medium /ˈmiːdɪəm/ ADJECTIVE in the middle of a group of amounts or sizes ◻ He is dark and of medium height. ◻ Heat a large pan over a medium heat. ◫ Small and medium sized businesses will be affected. (**médio**)

meet /miːt/ VERB [meets, meeting, met]
1 to come to the same place as someone else by chance ◻ Guess who I met in town? (**encontrar**)
2 to come to the same place as someone else because you have arranged to see them ◻ Let's meet for a coffee next week. ◻ Is there anywhere we can meet privately? ◻ The committee meets once a month. (**encontrar-se**)
3 to wait for someone at a particular place where they will arrive ◻ We'll meet her at the airport. (**encontrar**)
4 to be with and speak to someone for the first time ◻ Have you met my big sister, Jane? ◫ I'm very pleased to meet you at last. (**conhecer**)
◆ PHRASAL VERB **meet up** to come together with other people in order to do something ◻ We meet up about once a week for a chat.

meeting /ˈmiːtɪŋ/ NOUN [plural meetings] a time when people come together, especially to discuss something ◻ We need to arrange a meeting to discuss this matter. ◻ Anne's in a meeting at the moment. (**reunião**)

melody /ˈmelədɪ/ NOUN [plural melodies] a tune, especially one that is pleasant to listen to ◻ The song had a lovely melody. (**melodia**)

melon /ˈmelən/ NOUN [plural melons] a large round fruit with a thick green or yellow skin and sweet, yellow or orange flesh (**melão**)

melt /melt/ VERB [melts, melting, melted] to become soft or liquid when heated ◻ By afternoon the snow had melted. ◻ Salt is used to melt ice on roads. ◻ Stir in the melted butter. (**derreter**)

member /ˈmembə(r)/ NOUN [plural members] a person who belongs to a group or organization ◻ + of He's the youngest member of the team. ◫ They celebrated with friends and family members. ◫ It was reported by a member of the public. ◫ The restaurant is open to members of staff. (**membro**)

membership /ˈmembəʃɪp/ NOUN [plural memberships]
1 no plural being a member ◻ + of Membership of the gym costs £600 a year. (**qualidade de membro, associação**)
2 all the people who are members of a group or organization ◻ The union membership voted to reject the offer. (**sócios**)

memo /ˈmeməʊ/ NOUN [plural memos] a short note that you send to someone who works in the same company or organization as you (**memento, memorando**)

memorable /ˈmemərəbəl/ ADJECTIVE a memorable event is one that you remember because it is special or important ◻ Their kiss was the most memorable moment of the film. (**memorável**)

memory /ˈmemərɪ/ NOUN [plural memories]
1 the ability to remember things ◻ There are several ways to improve your memory. ◻ + for I've got an awful memory for names (= I don't remember them). (**recordação**)
2 something you remember ◻ + of He has happy memories of his school days. ◫ The pictures brought back painful memories. (**recordação**)
3 no plural the part of a computer where information is stored. A computing word. ◻ 6GB of memory (**memória**)

> **THESAURUS:** A memory is a thing that you remember. A souvenir is a thing that you buy to help you remember a particular place or an occasion. For example, many people buy souvenirs when they go on holiday. If you write something down to help you to remember it, you can call this piece of paper a note.

men /men/ PLURAL OF man (ver **man**)

menace /ˈmenəs/ NOUN [plural menaces] something that causes or might cause trouble or danger ◻ These biting flies are a real menace. (**ameaça**)

mend

mend /mend/ VERB [mends, mending, mended] to repair something that is broken or damaged □ We need to mend the hole in the tent. □ I took my watch to be mended. (emendar)

mental /ˈmentəl/ ADJECTIVE to do with the mind or thinking □ mental arithmetic □ Does she have the mental strength to be a top player? 🔁 mental illness 🔁 mental health services (mental)

mention /ˈmenʃən/ VERB [mentions, mentioning, mentioned]
1 to talk or to write about something, but not in detail □ Nobody mentioned it before. □ + in His name was mentioned in the report. □ + to Don't mention it to Jonathan. □ + that You mentioned that he's got a new car. 🔁 As I mentioned earlier, I hadn't met him before. (mencionar)
2 don't mention it something you say to be polite when someone thanks you for something (não há de quê)

> THESAURUS: If you mention something, you talk or write about something, but not in detail. If you hint, you suggest something in a way that is not clear or direct. If you reveal something, you tell someone something that is secret or surprising. If you claim something, you say that it is true, although there is no clear proof.

menu /ˈmenjuː/ NOUN [plural menus]
1 a list of the food available in a restaurant □ Would you like to look at the menu? □ We have a three-course set menu. (cardápio)
2 on a computer, a list of choices on the screen that you can choose from. A computing word. 🔁 a dropdown menu (menu)

merchant /ˈmɜːtʃənt/ NOUN [plural merchants] someone who has a business buying and selling goods □ a wine merchant (comerciante)

mercy /ˈmɜːsɪ/ NOUN, NO PLURAL the quality of being kind and willing to forgive someone, especially someone you have power over 🔁 The judge showed no mercy to the killers. □ He ignored their pleas for mercy. (misericórdia)

merge /mɜːdʒ/ VERB [merges, merging, merged] if two things or organizations merge, they combine or join with each other □ Her work life seemed to be increasingly merging with her home life. □ The two companies merged in 1999. (fundir)

merit /ˈmerɪt/ NOUN [plural merits] a quality that makes something or someone valuable or important □ The film lacks artistic merit. □ Players are picked for the team on merit. (mérito)

mermaid /ˈmɜːmeɪd/ NOUN [plural mermaids] in stories, a beautiful creature who lives in the sea and is half a woman and half a fish (sereia)

merry /ˈmerɪ/ ADJECTIVE [merrier, merriest] happy and showing that you are enjoying yourself □ He whistled a merry tune. (alegre)

metre

mess /mes/ NOUN [plural messes]
1 an untidy or dirty state □ The kitchen's in a mess. (bagunça)
2 someone or something that is dirty or untidy □ I'd been gardening and I looked a right mess. □ Your room's a complete mess. (bagunça)
3 something that is in a confused state or that involves a lot of problems □ His whole life was in a mess. 🔁 He made a complete mess of the accounts. (bagunça)

◆ PHRASAL VERBS [messes, messing, messed] **mess about/around** to waste time with silly behaviour □ Stop messing about and get on with your work! **mess something up 1** to do something badly or to spoil something □ I messed up my French exam. **2** to make something untidy □ She messed up all my carefully arranged papers.

message /ˈmesɪdʒ/ NOUN [plural messages] a piece of written or spoken information sent from one person to another 🔁 I sent a message wishing him luck. 🔁 I left a message on her phone. 🔁 a text message □ + from She's received thousands of messages from her fans. □ + of messages of support (recado)

messenger /ˈmesɪndʒə(r)/ NOUN [plural messengers] someone who carries messages from one person to another (mensageiro)

messy /ˈmesɪ/ ADJECTIVE [messier, messiest]
1 untidy or dirty □ a messy room □ He had long, messy hair. (sujo)
2 complicated and unpleasant to deal with □ a messy divorce (sujo)

met /met/ PAST TENSE AND PAST PARTICIPLE OF **meet** (ver meet)

metal /ˈmetəl/ NOUN [plural metals] a hard shiny material such as iron, gold or silver □ The car was now a heap of twisted metal. 🔁 precious metals (metal)

metaphor /ˈmetəfə(r)/ NOUN [plural metaphors] a way of describing something by comparing it to something else □ To use a boxing metaphor, the minister got knocked out in the first round. (metáfora)

meter /ˈmiːtə(r)/ NOUN [plural meters]
1 a device that measures and records the amount of something 🔁 a gas meter □ Take a meter reading on the day you move in. (registro, contador)
2 the US spelling of **metre** (métodos)

method /ˈmeθəd/ NOUN [plural methods] a way of doing something, especially a planned or organized way □ + of methods of disease prevention □ + for We need to develop new methods for dealing with the problem. 🔁 Artists here use traditional methods. □ teaching methods □ farming methods (método)

metre /ˈmiːtə(r)/ NOUN [plural metres] a unit for measuring length, equal to 100 centimetres. □ + of Almost two metres of snow had fallen. □ It's suitable for boats up to three metres in length. □ He fell just ten metres from the finish line. □ a 400 metre runner 🔁 2500 square metres of office space (metro)

metric /'metrɪk/ ADJECTIVE to do with a system of measuring that uses units such as litres and grams, based on tens (**métrico**)

mg /ˌem'dʒiː/ ABBREVIATION milligram (mg)

miaow[1] /miːˈaʊ/ NOUN [plural miaows] the sound that a cat makes (**miado**)

miaow[2] /miːˈaʊ/ VERB [miaows, miaowing, miaowed] a cat miaows when it makes this sound (**miar**)

mice /maɪs/ PLURAL OF mouse (**ratos**)

microphone /'maɪkrəfəʊn/ NOUN [plural microphones] an electronic device used for recording sound or making sound louder □ Speak into the microphone. □ She took the microphone to address the crowd. (**microfone**)

microscope /'maɪkrəskəʊp/ NOUN [plural microscopes] a piece of equipment with lenses (= curved pieces of glass) that makes very small objects look much larger so that you can study them closely (**microscópio**)

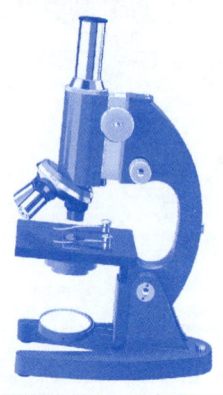

microwave /'maɪkrəweɪv/ NOUN [plural microwaves] a microwave oven (**micro-ondas**)

microwave oven /ˌmaɪkrəweɪv 'ʌvən/ NOUN [plural microwave ovens] an oven that cooks food very quickly using electrical and magnetic waves instead of heat (**forno de micro-ondas**)

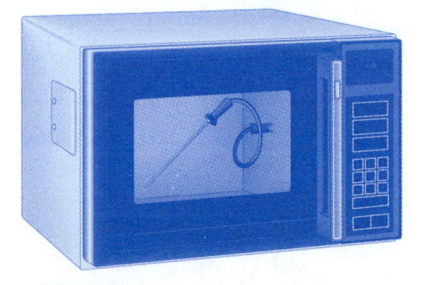

midday /ˌmɪd'deɪ/ NOUN, NO PLURAL twelve o'clock in the middle of the day, or around this time □ She arrived at midday yesterday. ◫ We waited in the hot midday sun. ◫ They had bread and cheese for their midday meal. (**meio-dia**)

middle[1] /'mɪdəl/ NOUN [plural middles]
1 the middle the point, position or part furthest from the sides or edges of something □ Let me sit in the middle. □ **+ of** They live on an island in the middle of the ocean. (**meio, centro**)
2 the point in a period of time that is half way through that period of time □ **+ of** I woke up in the middle of the night. □ He stood up and asked a question in the middle of the meeting. (**meio**)
3 be in the middle of doing something to be busy doing something □ I can't come to the phone – I'm in the middle of bathing the children. (**estar ocupado com**)

middle[2] /'mɪdəl/ ADJECTIVE in the central point or position of something □ I liked the middle section of the book. □ I was driving in the middle lane. □ He's the middle child of a family of five boys. (**do meio**)

middle-aged /ˌmɪdəl'eɪdʒd/ ADJECTIVE approximately between the ages of 45 and 60 □ a middle-aged man (**meia-idade**)

middle class[1] /ˌmɪdəl 'klɑːs/ NOUN [plural middle classes] the social class that consists mainly of educated people who have a good standard of living (**a classe média**)

middle class[2] /ˌmɪdəl 'klɑːs/ ADJECTIVE to do with the middle class □ a middle class family (**de classe média**)

midnight /'mɪdnaɪt/ NOUN, NO PLURAL twelve o'clock at night □ The competition closes at midnight tonight. □ It was past midnight when we finally got home. (**meia-noite**)

might[1] /maɪt/ MODAL VERB
1 used to talk about the possibility that something is true or something will happen □ He might stay. □ It might rain. (**poder**)
2 you might like/want to do something used to make polite suggestions □ You might want to take some extra food with you. (**poderia**)
3 might as well used to say that you should probably do something because there is nothing better to do □ If you can't be bothered to practise, you might as well give up the piano. (**poderia até**)

might[2] /maɪt/ NOUN, NO PLURAL a formal word meaning power or strength ◫ He pulled with all his might. (**força**)

mighty /'maɪti/ ADJECTIVE [mightier, mightiest] a formal word meaning big and powerful □ the mighty Mississippi River (**poderoso**)

migrate /maɪ'greɪt/ VERB [migrates, migrating, migrated]
1 if birds or animals migrate, they travel to a different part of the world at the same time

migration — mind

each year □ *The birds migrate northwards in spring.* (migrar)
2 to move to a different country to find work □ *His family migrated to Australia in 1918.* (migrar)

migration /maɪˈgreɪʃən/ NOUN, NO PLURAL when birds, animals or people travel to a different part of the world at the same time each year (migração)

mild /maɪld/ ADJECTIVE [**milder, mildest**]
1 mild weather is quite warm □ *The weather was unusually mild for November.* ▣ *The mild winter had prevented ice from forming on the lake.* (ameno)
2 not severe or not serious □ *The virus causes a relatively mild illness.* □ *She looked at him with mild annoyance.* (brando)
3 having a flavour that is not strong □ *mild cheese* □ *Chicken has a mild flavour.* (suave)

mile /maɪl/ NOUN [**plural miles**] a unit for measuring distance, equal to 1.6 kilometres □ *The ship was 20 miles off the coast.* ▣ *His car was travelling at a speed of 110 miles per hour.* ▣ *The traffic jam was six miles long.* (milha)

milestone /ˈmaɪlstəʊn/ NOUN [**plural milestones**] an important event in someone's life or in the development of something □ *The game was a milestone in British sporting history.* (marco)

military /ˈmɪlɪtərɪ/ ADJECTIVE to do with the army, navy or air force ▣ *Military forces invaded the country.* ▣ *Many soldiers were injured in military operations.* ▣ *a military base* □ *a military commander* (militar)

milk¹ /mɪlk/ NOUN, NO PLURAL a white liquid produced by female animals, which people drink or which is used to feed babies □ *Would you like a glass of milk?* □ *Breast milk contains important nutrients for babies.* (leite)

milk² /mɪlk/ VERB [**milks, milking, milked**] to take milk from a cow or goat □ *The cows are milked by machine.* (ordenhar)

mill /mɪl/ NOUN [**plural mills**]
1 a building with machinery for crushing grain □ *The wheat for our bread comes from a traditional mill* (moinho)
2 a factory that produces a particular material such as cotton, paper or wool □ *a paper mill* (fábrica)

millennium /mɪˈlenɪəm/ NOUN [**plural millennia**] a period of a thousand years (milênio)

milligram *or* **milligramme** /ˈmɪlɪgræm/ NOUN [**plural milligrams** *or* **milligrammes**] a unit for measuring weight, equal to 1/1000 of a gram. This is often written **mg** (miligrama, miligramas)

milliliter /ˈmɪlɪliːtə(r)/ NOUN the US spelling of **millilitre** (mililitro)

millilitre /ˈmɪlɪliːtə(r)/ NOUN [**plural millilitres**] a unit for measuring liquid, equal to 1/1000 of a litre. This is often written **ml**. (mililitro)

millimeter /ˈmɪlɪmiːtə(r)/ NOUN [**plural millimeters**] the US spelling of **millimetre** (milímetro)

millimetre /ˈmɪlɪmiːtə(r)/ NOUN [**plural millimetres**] a unit for measuring length, equal to 1/1000 of a metre. This is often written **mm**. (milímetro)

million /ˈmɪljən/ NUMBER [**plural millions** *or* **million**]
1 the number 1,000,000 (milhão)
2 millions a very large number. An informal word □ *+ of There were millions of flies crawling on the food.* (milhão)

millionaire /ˌmɪljəˈneə(r)/ NOUN [**plural millionaires**] someone who has £1,000,000 or $1,000,000 or more (milionário)

millionth¹ /ˈmɪljənθ/ NUMBER 1,000,000th written as a word (milionésimo)

millionth² /ˈmɪljənθ/ NOUN [**plural millionths**] 1/1,000,000; one of a million equal parts of something (milionésimo)

mimic /ˈmɪmɪk/ VERB [**mimics, mimicking, mimicked**] to copy the way someone speaks or behaves as a joke (imitar)

min /mɪn/ ABBREVIATION
1 minute¹; used in writing (minuto)
2 minimum¹ and³; used in writing (mínimo)

mince /mɪns/ VERB [**minces, mincing, minced**] to cut food into very small pieces using a machine □ *minced beef* (picar)

mind¹ /maɪnd/ NOUN [**plural minds**]
1 your brain, or your ability to think, understand, remember, etc. □ *All sorts of thoughts went through my mind.* (mente)
2 make up your mind to decide □ *I couldn't make up my mind whether to go to Paris or not.* (decidir-se)
3 on your mind if something is on your mind, you are thinking about it a lot and usually worrying about it □ *I've got a lot on my mind at the moment.* (em que pensar)
4 have someone/something in mind to be thinking of a particular person or thing □ *Do you have any particular colour in mind for the curtains?* (ter em mente)
◆ IDIOMS **be/go out of your mind** to become extremely worried or upset □ *We were out of our minds with worry for them.* **take your mind off something** to stop you thinking about something bad by making you think about something else □ *I'm in a lot of pain, but going dancing takes my mind off it.* (perder a razão/distrair, desviar a atenção)

mind² /maɪnd/ VERB [**minds, minding, minded**]
1 to be upset or annoyed by something □ *Do you mind if I smoke?* □ *I'm sure Sue wouldn't mind you borrowing her car.* (incomodar-se)

2 would you mind doing something used to ask someone politely to do something □ *Would you mind opening the window?* (**você se importaria**)
3 used to tell someone to be careful not to get hurt □ *Mind your head on that branch.* (**tomar cuidado**)
4 nevermind used to say that something is not important □ *'I haven't finished my homework.' 'Never mind, you can hand it in tomorrow.'* (**não tem importância**)
◆ PHRASAL VERB **mind out** used to tell someone to be careful not to get hurt □ *Mind out – there's a car coming!* (**cuidado!**)

mine¹ /maɪn/ PRONOUN used to talk or write about things belonging to or to do with you □ *Is this book yours or mine?* □ *Jan is a friend of mine.* (**meu, minha, meus, minhas**)

mine² /maɪn/ NOUN [plural **mines**]
1 a place where people dig something such as coal or gold from the ground □ *a coal mine* (**mina**)
2 a bomb that is hidden in the ground or in water, which explodes when someone touches it (**mina**)

mine³ /maɪn/ VERB [**mines, mining, mined**]
1 to dig into the ground in order to get something such as coal or gold □ *Diamonds are mined from the rocks.* (**extrair**)
2 to put bombs under the ground or in water

miner /ˈmaɪnə(r)/ NOUN [plural **miners**] someone who works in a mine (**mineiro**)

mineral /ˈmɪnərəl/ NOUN [plural **minerals**]
1 a natural substance in the earth, such as coal, salt or gold □ *Our mineral resources are not great.* (**mineral**)
2 a natural substance such as iron that your body needs to stay healthy 🔲 *Some vegetables contain a lot of vitamins and minerals.* (**mineral**)

mineral water /ˈmɪnərəl ˌwɔːtə(r)/ NOUN [plural **mineral waters**] water that you buy in bottles, which comes from under the ground □ *a bottle of mineral water* (**água mineral**)

miniature /ˈmɪnətʃə(r)/ ADJECTIVE very much smaller than normal □ *a miniature camera* (**miniatura**)

minibus /ˈmɪnibʌs/ NOUN [plural **minibuses**] a small bus for about 12 people (**micro-ônibus**)

minimal /ˈmɪnɪməl/ ADJECTIVE very small in amount or degree □ *The fire caused minimal damage.* (**mínimo**)

minimum¹ /ˈmɪnɪməm/ ADJECTIVE being the smallest amount or degree that is possible or allowed 🔲 *The minimum age for driving in the UK is 17.* □ *£250 was the minimum amount needed to open a bank account.* (**mínimo**)

minimum² /ˈmɪnɪməm/ NOUN, NO PLURAL the smallest amount or degree that is possible or allowed 🔲 *We need to keep costs to a minimum.* □ **+ of** *He did his duties with the minimum of fuss.* □ *The hotel costs a minimum of £200 a night.* (**mínimo**)

mining /ˈmaɪnɪŋ/ NOUN, NO PLURAL the job of digging something such as coal or gold from the ground □ *the mining industry* (**mineração**)

minister /ˈmɪnɪstə(r)/ NOUN [plural **ministers**]
1 a politician who is in charge of a government department 🔲 *Government ministers will visit China next week.* □ *the health minister* □ **+ of/for** *the Minister for Education* (**ministro**)
2 a priest in some Christian churches □ *a Methodist minister* (**ministro, pastor**)

ministry /ˈmɪnɪstri/ NOUN [plural **ministries**] a government department □ *the Ministry of Defence* □ *ministry officials* (**ministério**)

minor¹ /ˈmaɪnə(r)/ ADJECTIVE not serious or important 🔲 *He suffered minor injuries in the accident.* □ *I've made a few minor changes to the report.* 🔲 *The problems were relatively minor.* (**menor**)

minor² /ˈmaɪnə(r)/ NOUN [plural **minors**] someone who is legally a child (**menor**)

minority /maɪˈnɒrəti/ NOUN [plural **minorities**] a small group of people which is part of a much larger group 🔲 *A small minority of our students are from Africa.* (**minoria**)

mint /mɪnt/ NOUN [plural **mints**]
1 a plant with strong-smelling leaves, used in cooking (**menta**)
2 a type of sweet with a strong flavour (**bala de menta**)

minus /ˈmaɪnəs/ ADJECTIVE less than zero □ *minus ten degrees* (**negativo**)

minute¹ /ˈmɪnɪt/ NOUN [plural **minutes**]
1 a period of 60 seconds □ *The journey only lasted a few minutes.* □ *I loved every minute of my visit.* (**minuto**)
□ *Rendell scored in the eighth minute.* (**minuto**)
2 a short time □ *Wait a minute while I look for my keys.* □ *Just a minute – I need to phone Clara.* (**minuto**)
3 the exact time □ *I knew something was wrong the minute I saw him.* □ *At that very minute there was a loud explosion.* (**minuto**)
4 any minute very soon □ *Paul will be here any minute now.* □ *The bomb could explode at any minute.* (**qualquer minuto**)
5 this minute immediately □ *Come here this minute!* (**imediatamente**)
→ go to **minutes**

minute² /maɪˈnjuːt/ ADJECTIVE extremely small □ *Minute traces of blood were found on his clothes.* (**minúsculo**)

minutes /ˈmɪnɪts/ PLURAL NOUN a written record of a meeting 🔲 *Who is going to take the minutes?* (**ata**)

miracle /ˈmɪrəkəl/ NOUN [plural **miracles**]
1 something extremely lucky that happens and that no one would expect □ *It's a miracle that no one was killed in the accident.* □ *a miracle cure* (**milagre**)
2 something that happens which seems impossible and that people think God has done (**milagre**)

miraculous — mixture

miraculous /mɪˈrækjʊləs/ ADJECTIVE extremely lucky and not expected 🔁 *He made a miraculous recovery.* (milagroso)

mirror /ˈmɪrə(r)/ NOUN [plural mirrors] a piece of special glass that you look at to see an image of yourself □ *Ben was looking at himself in the mirror.* (espelho)

miserable /ˈmɪzərəbəl/ ADJECTIVE
1 very unhappy □ *She's miserable because all her friends are away.* □ *Dan looked pretty miserable.* (infeliz)
2 making you feel unhappy □ *What miserable weather!* □ *She'd had a miserable childhood.* (miserável)

misery /ˈmɪzəri/ NOUN, NO PLURAL great unhappiness or suffering □ *Bad weather has caused misery for thousands of travellers.* (miséria)

mislead /ˌmɪsˈliːd/ VERB [misleads, misleading, misled] to make someone believe something that is not true □ *The government deliberately misled the public about the state of the economy.* (enganar)

Miss /mɪs/ NOUN [plural Misses] a word used before the name of a girl or a woman who is not married □ *Miss Smith* □ *Miss Zoe Arnison* (moça, senhorita)

miss¹ /mɪs/ VERB [misses, missing, missed]
1 to fail to hit or catch something you are aiming at 🔁 *A bullet narrowly missed (= only just missed) his spine.* □ *He missed the penalty.* (errar)
2 to not go to something or experience something □ *I had to miss my daughter's school concert.* □ *Don't miss their new show!* (perder)
3 to miss a train, bus, plane, etc. is to not arrive in time to catch it (perder)
4 to feel sad because of someone you can no longer be with or something you can no longer have or do 🔁 *I missed my family terribly when I lived abroad.* □ *+ ing I miss being able to walk on the beach.* (sentir saudade)

◆ PHRASAL VERB **miss someone/something out** to not include someone or something □ *He read us the book, but he missed out all the rude words.*

> **THESAURUS:** If you **miss** something, you do not go to it or experience it. We often use this word for things or experiences that we want to go to or to experience, but cannot. If you **avoid** doing something, you stay away from it. If you **prevent** something, you stop it from happening, or stop someone from doing something. If you **skip** something, you do not do something that you should do, or something that you usually do. For example, you might **skip** a meal if you feel unwell.

miss² /mɪs/ NOUN [plural misses] when you do not hit something you are aiming at □ *His miss cost his team the match.* (falha)

◆ IDIOM **give something a miss** to decide not to do something □ *I was feeling tired, so I decided to give the party a miss.*

missile /ˈmɪsaɪl/ NOUN [plural missiles]
1 a weapon that travels long distances and explodes when it hits something □ *long-range missiles* (míssil)
2 an object that someone throws to hit someone or something □ *Police were hit by bottles, stones and other missiles.* (projétil)

missing /ˈmɪsɪŋ/ ADJECTIVE if someone or something is missing, they are not where you expect them to be and you do not know where they are 🔁 *Some important documents had gone missing.* □ *Rescue teams are looking for three missing climbers.* (desaparecido)

mist /mɪst/ NOUN [plural mists] very small drops of water in the air that make it difficult for you to see 🔁 *A fine mist hung over the city.* 🔁 *The morning mist had lifted.* (névoa)

mistake¹ /mɪˈsteɪk/ NOUN [plural mistakes]
1 something wrong that you do 🔁 *We've all made mistakes.* 🔁 *She knew that inviting him would be a big mistake.* 🔁 *There were lots of spelling mistakes in his writing.* □ *+ to do something It was a mistake to come here.* (erro)
2 by mistake by accident □ *He deleted the file by mistake.* □ *The letter was delivered to the wrong house by mistake.* (por engano)

> **THESAURUS:** A **mistake** is something wrong that you do. If something bad or wrong is your **fault**, you are responsible for it. If you take the **blame** for something bad that happens, you accept responsibility for it.

mistake² /mɪˈsteɪk/ VERB [mistakes, mistaking, mistook, mistaken] to understand something in the wrong way □ *No one could mistake his meaning.* (enganar-se)

◆ PHRASAL VERB **mistake someone/something for someone/something** to think wrongly that a person or thing is someone or something else □ *People often mistake Clare for her sister.* (confundir)

mistook /mɪˈstʊk/ PAST TENSE OF **mistake**² (ver mistake²)

mix /mɪks/ VERB [mixes, mixing, mixed]
1 to combine two or more substances □ *If you mix black paint and white paint, you get grey.* 🔁 *In a small bowl, mix together the garlic and butter.* □ *+ with Mix the powder with water.* (misturar)
2 to combine □ *Oil and water don't mix.* (misturar-se)
3 to talk to people and spend time with them socially □ *Marija was very shy and found it difficult to mix.* □ *+ with My Mum doesn't like the people I mix with.* (relacionar-se)

◆ PHRASAL VERBS **mix someone/something up** to think that a person or thing is someone or something else □ *The twins are very alike and the teacher often mixes them up.* **mix something up** to put a group of things in the wrong order □ *Somehow the pages have all got mixed up.* (confundir alguém ou algo / misturar)

mixture /ˈmɪkstʃə(r)/ NOUN [plural mixtures] a combination of different things 🔁 *The city is a* *strange mixture of old and new buildings.* □ *+ of I felt a mixture of anger and sadness.* □ *Stir the mixture until the sugar dissolves.* (mistura)

mm /ˌem 'em/ ABBREVIATION **millimetre**

moan /məʊn/ VERB [moans, moaning, moaned]
1 to complain about something, often in a way that annoys other people □ *Oh stop moaning!* □ *Tim was moaning about the weather.* (lamentar[-se])
2 to make a long, low sound, usually because you are in pain □ *I could hear the injured passengers moaning in pain.* (gemer)

mobile[1] /ˈməʊbaɪl/ ADJECTIVE able to move or be moved □ *He was older and less mobile than his wife.* □ *a mobile home* (móvel)

mobile[2] /ˈməʊbaɪl/ NOUN [plural mobiles] a telephone that you carry with you □ *Is your mobile switched on?* 🕮 *Have you got my mobile number?* (celular)

mobile phone /ˌməʊbaɪl 'fəʊn/ NOUN [plural mobile phones] a telephone that you carry with you (telefone celular)

mock /mɒk/ VERB [mocks, mocking, mocked] to be unkind to someone by making jokes about them or by copying what they say or do □ *Other people might mock David's voice, but I love it.* (zombar)

modal verb /ˌməʊdəl ˈvɜːb/ NOUN [plural modal verbs] a verb such as 'ought' or 'might' that is used to show ideas such as being possible, necessary, certain, etc. (verbo modal)

model[1] /ˈmɒdəl/ NOUN [plural models]
1 a small copy of something bigger □ *+ of On display was a model of the ship.* 🕮 *He enjoys making models of aeroplanes.* (modelo)
2 a person whose job is to wear clothes at fashion shows and for magazine photographs 🕮 *a fashion model* □ *a male model* (modelo)

model[2] /ˈmɒdəl/ ADJECTIVE a model car, building, etc. is a small copy of a real one □ *He enjoys making model planes.* (modelo)

model[3] /ˈmɒdəl/ VERB [models, modelling/US modeling, modelled/US modeled] to work as a model, wearing clothes at fashion shows and for magazine photographs (modelo)

moderate /ˈmɒdərət/ ADJECTIVE not extreme □ *moderate heat* □ *The doctor told him to take moderate exercise.* (moderado)

modern /ˈmɒdən/ ADJECTIVE to do with the present time and not the past 🕮 *In the modern world, most women go out to work.* 🕮 *Modern life is very busy.* 🕮 *modern art* (moderno)

> THESAURUS: Modern means to do with the present time and not the past. Something that is recent happened only a short time ago. Something that is current exists or is happening now.

modest /ˈmɒdɪst/ ADJECTIVE not talking about your skills and achievements even when you have been successful □ *Paul is very modest.* (modesto)

> THESAURUS: Someone who is modest does not talk about their skills and achievements even when they have been successful. Someone who is humble does not believe that they are important. Someone who is shy is nervous, and not confident when meeting and speaking to people.

Mohammed /məˈhæmɪd/ NOUN the holy man on whose ideas the religion of Islam is based (Maomé)

moist /mɔɪst/ ADJECTIVE [moister, moistest] slightly wet □ *moist air* (úmido, mais úmido, o mais úmido)

moisture /ˈmɔɪstʃə(r)/ NOUN, NO PLURAL a small amount of liquid in or on something □ *This helps keep the moisture in the soil.* (umidade)

moisturizer or **moisturiser** /ˈmɔɪstʃəraɪzə(r)/ NOUN [plural moisturizers] a cream you put on your skin to make it soft and not dry (hidratante, umedecedores)

mole /məʊl/ NOUN [plural moles]
1 a small brown spot on your skin which is permanent (pinta)
2 a small animal which lives underground and is almost blind (toupeira)

molecule /ˈmɒlɪkjuːl/ NOUN [plural molecules] the smallest unit that a chemical element or compound (= substance formed from two or more parts or substances) can be divided into. Molecules are made up of two or more atoms. A chemistry or physics word. (molécula)

mom /mɒm/ NOUN [plural moms] the US word for **mum** (mamãe)

moment /ˈməʊmənt/ NOUN [plural moments]
1 a short period of time □ *Stop what you're doing for a moment.* 🕮 *Wait a moment – I'm not ready.* 🕮 *Please take a moment* (= use a short period of time) *to read this information.* (momento)
2 a particular point in time □ *Just at that moment, she heard a door slam.* □ *Winning this competition has been the proudest moment in my athletics career.* (momento)
3 at the moment now □ *The house is empty at the moment.* (momento)
4 at any moment at any time soon □ *Doctors have said he could die at any moment.* (momento)
5 in a moment very soon □ *I'll explain what I mean in a moment.* □ *I'll be back in a moment.* (momento)

monarch /ˈmɒnək/ NOUN [plural monarchs] a king or queen (monarca)

monarchy /ˈmɒnəkɪ/ NOUN [plural monarchies] a country that has a king or queen □ *Britain is a monarchy.* (monarquia)

monastery /ˈmɒnəstərɪ/ NOUN [plural monasteries] a building where monks (= religious men) live (mosteiro)

Monday /ˈmʌndɪ/ NOUN [plural Mondays] the day of the week after Sunday and before Tuesday □ *On Monday, I went to London.* □ *See you next Monday.* (segunda-feira)

money

money /ˈmʌni/ NOUN, NO PLURAL
1 coins and paper notes that you use for buying things ◻ *We don't have the money for a new car.* ◻ *Dan spends most of his money on computer games.* ◻ *I'm trying to save some money.* ◻ *She earns a lot of money.* (**dinheiro**)
2 make money to earn money or to make a profit ◻ *He had never made much money from writing.* ◻ *She made a lot of money from the sale of the house.* (**ganhar dinheiro**)

monitor¹ /ˈmɒnɪtə(r)/ VERB [monitors, monitoring, monitored] to check something regularly to see how it changes ◻ *The school monitors the progress of all its students.* (**monitorar, controlar**)
monitor² /ˈmɒnɪtə(r)/ NOUN [plural **monitors**] a screen that is attached to a computer. A computing word ◻ *a computer monitor* (**monitor**)

monk /mʌŋk/ NOUN [plural **monks**] one of a group of religious men who live together (**monge**)

monkey /ˈmʌŋki/ NOUN [plural **monkeys**] an animal with a long tail that lives in trees in hot countries ◻ *The monkeys were trained to perform simple tasks.* (**macaco**)

monster /ˈmɒnstə(r)/ NOUN [plural **monsters**] in stories, a very big and frightening creature ◻ *My little boy thinks there are monsters under his bed.* (**monstro**)

month /mʌnθ/ NOUN [plural **months**] one of twelve periods that a year is divided into ◻ *the month of May* ◻ *the winter months* ◻ *I went to France last month.* ◻ *It's my birthday next month.* (**mês**)

monthly /ˈmʌnθli/ ADJECTIVE, ADVERB happening once a month ◻ *a monthly meeting* ◻ *He is paid monthly.* (**mensalmente, mensal**)

monument /ˈmɒnjumənt/ NOUN [plural **monuments**] something that has been built in memory of a person or event ◻ *They built a monument to Sir Walter Scott.* (**monumento**)

moo /muː/ VERB [moos, mooing, mooed] a cow moos when it makes a long low sound (**mugir**)

mood /muːd/ NOUN [plural **moods**] someone's feelings at a particular time ◻ *I woke up in a bad mood this morning.* ◻ *You're in a good mood today!* (**ânimo, humor**)

moody /ˈmuːdi/ ADJECTIVE [moodier, moodiest] often becoming angry or unhappy ◻ *moody teenagers* (**mal-humorado**)

moon /muːn/ NOUN [plural **moons**] **the moon** the round object that you see in the sky at night and which moves around the Earth ◻ *The moon shone brightly.* ◻ *Neil Armstrong made the first moon landing.* (**lua**)

moonlight /ˈmuːnlaɪt/ NOUN, NO PLURAL light that comes from the moon ◻ *His eyes shone in the moonlight.* (**luar**)

moreover

moor¹ /mɔː(r)/ NOUN [plural **moors**] a large high area of land that is covered with grass and bushes. A geography word. (**charneca**)
moor² /mɔː(r)/ VERB [moors, mooring, moored] to fasten a boat to something (**atracar**)

moral¹ /ˈmɒrəl/ ADJECTIVE to do with right and wrong and the way people should behave ◻ *She had high moral standards.* ◻ *He objected to the war for moral reasons.* (**virtuoso**)

moral² /ˈmɒrəl/ NOUN [plural **morals**] something that a story or experience teaches you about how to behave ◻ *The moral of the story is never give up.* → go to **morals** (**moral**)

morale /məˈrɑːl/ NOUN, NO PLURAL how confident or happy a person or group of people feel ◻ *Morale in the office is fairly low.* ◻ *Pay rises usually improve morale.* (**moral**)

morally /ˈmɒrəli/ ADVERB to do with what is right or wrong behaviour ◻ *Not paying your taxes is morally wrong.* (**moralmente**)

morals /ˈmɒrəlz/ PLURAL NOUN the beliefs someone has about what is right and wrong behaviour ◻ *His remarks have started a public debate on the nation's morals.* (**moral**)

more¹ /mɔː(r)/ DETERMINER, PRONOUN
1 a larger number or amount ◻ *He has more friends than anyone else I know.* ◻ *The bill was more than £10,000.* ◻ *He knows more about elephants than anyone else in the UK.* ◻ *More and more people are buying organic food.* (**mais**)
2 something in addition to what you have, what is there, or what you have talked about ◻ *Is there any more cake?* ◻ *Would you like some more coffee?* ◻ *You need to do more to help.* ◻ *8 people died, and at least twenty more were injured.* (**mais**)

more² /mɔː(r)/ ADVERB
1 used to make comparative forms of adjectives and adverbs, especially ones with 2 or more syllables ◻ *He's more patient than I am.* ◻ *More recently, I have begun to enjoy crime novels.* ◻ *Harry's a lot more emotional than his sister.* (**mais**)
2 to a greater degree ◻ *I exercise more than I used to.* ◻ *I like her more and more.* (**mais**)
3 more or less almost, but not exactly ◻ *We've more or less finished decorating the kitchen.* ◻ *She more or less said she didn't trust us.* (**mais ou menos**)
4 the more... the more/less used to say that if one thing increases, another thing will increase or decrease ◻ *The more I read about Cuba, the more I want to go there.* ◻ *The more I see her, the less I like her.* (**quanto mais... mais/menos**)

moreover /mɔːˈrəʊvə(r)/ ADVERB a formal word for **also** ◻ *We do not have the facilities for this project. Moreover, we do not have enough staff.* (**além disso**)

morning /ˈmɔːnɪŋ/ NOUN [plural mornings]
1 the early part of the day from when the sun rises to the middle of the day □ *He takes the dog for a walk every morning.* 🔷 *He was late this morning.* (**manhã**)
2 in the morning (a) in the early part of the day □ *I'm usually quite tired in the morning.* (b) tomorrow morning □ *See you in the morning.* (**de manhã**)
3 Good morning! used to say 'hello' when you meet someone in the morning (**Bom dia!**)

mortgage /ˈmɔːɡɪdʒ/ NOUN [plural mortgages] money that you borrow from a bank or financial organization in order to buy a house or land 🔷 *They've taken out a huge mortgage on the flat.* (**hipoteca**)

mosque /mɒsk/ NOUN [plural mosques] a place where Muslims meet and pray (**mesquita**)

mosquito /məˈskiːtəʊ/ NOUN [plural mosquitoes or mosquitos] an insect which feeds by biting people or animals and sucking their blood (**mosquito**)

most¹ /məʊst/ DETERMINER, PRONOUN
1 the largest number or amount □ *Most people support the policy.* □ *Which club has spent most money on new players this season?* □ *All three children eat a lot but Tom eats the most.* (**mais**)
2 almost all □ *Most of my friends are people I know from work.* □ *I like most types of fruit.* (**a maioria**)
3 at the most and not more □ *The trip should cost £500 at the most.* (**no máximo**)
4 make the most of something to get as much advantage as possible from something that may not continue □ *Make the most of the good weather while it lasts.* (**aproveitar ao máximo**)

most² /məʊst/ ADVERB
1 used to make superlative forms of adjectives and adverbs, especially ones with two or more syllables □ *Paul was the most intelligent boy in the class.* □ *Most importantly, he has learned to pay more attention in class.* (**o/a/os/as mais**)
2 more than anyone or anything else □ *What kind of music do you like most?* (**mais**)

mostly /ˈməʊstli/ ADVERB in most cases or most of the time □ *They mostly play indoors.* □ *The band plays mostly '70s music.* (**principalmente, quase sempre**)

motel /məʊˈtel/ NOUN [plural motels] a hotel near a main road for people who are travelling by car (**motel**)
moth /mɒθ/ NOUN [plural moths] an insect with large wings that flies at night (**mariposa**)

mother /ˈmʌðə(r)/ NOUN [plural mothers] the female parent of a person or animal □ *My mother was very tall.* □ *The animals learn to hunt from their mother.* (**mãe**)

mother-in-law /ˈmʌðərɪnlɔː/ NOUN [plural mothers-in-law] the mother of your husband or wife (**sogra**)
motion /ˈməʊʃən/ NOUN [plural motions] movement or how something moves □ *The motion of the waves made him sleepy.* 🔷 *Do not attempt to get off while the ride is in motion.* (**movimento**)
motive /ˈməʊtɪv/ NOUN [plural motives] the reason someone has for doing something □ *There seemed to be no motive for the attack.* (**motivo**)

> **THESAURUS:** The **reason** for something is why it happened, exists or is true. A **motive** is the reason that someone has for doing something. We often talk about the motive for committing a crime. A **cause** is what makes something happen. Your **purpose** is what you intend to achieve when you do something. Your **intention** is the thing that you plan to do.

motor /ˈməʊtə(r)/ NOUN [plural motors] the part of a machine that uses petrol, electricity, etc. to produce movement and make the machine work □ *an electric motor* (**motor**)

motorbike /ˈməʊtəbaɪk/ NOUN [plural motorbikes] a vehicle with two wheels and an engine. You sit on it like a bicycle. (**motocicleta**)

motorcycle /ˈməʊtəsaɪkəl/ NOUN [plural motorcycles] a motorbike or moped (**motocicleta**)

motorist /ˈməʊtərɪst/ NOUN [plural motorists] someone who drives a car □ *The motorist was driving above the speed limit.* (**motorista**)
motor racing /ˈməʊtə ˌreɪsɪŋ/ NOUN, NO PLURAL the sport of driving cars very fast around a track (**corrida automobilística**)

motorway /ˈməʊtəweɪ/ NOUN [plural motorways] a wide road for vehicles travelling fast over long distances (**rodovia, autoestrada**)

mould /məʊld/ NOUN [plural moulds]
1 a hollow container which a liquid is poured into so that the liquid has the same shape as the container when it is cool and firm □ *a jelly mould* (**molde, forma**)
2 a soft green or black substance that grows on old food or in wet conditions □ *The bathroom ceiling was covered in mould.* (**mofo, bolor**)

mouldy /ˈməʊldɪ/ ADJECTIVE [mouldier, mouldiest]
covered with a soft green or black substance that grows on old food or in wet conditions □ *The bread has gone mouldy.* (**mofado, embolorado**)

> **THESAURUS:** Food that is mouldy is covered in the soft green or black substance that grows on old food. Food that is **stale** is not fresh. Food that is **rotten** is decaying or decayed. Food that is **bad** does not taste or smell good because it is old.

mound /maʊnd/ NOUN [plural mounds]
1 a small hill or pile of earth or stones □ *a burial mound* (**montículo**)
2 a pile or large amount of something □ *a mound of ironing* (**montículo**)

Mount /maʊnt/ NOUN, NO PLURAL used before the names of mountains □ *the top of Mount Everest* (**monte**)

mount /maʊnt/ VERB [mounts, mounting, mounted]
1 if a feeling among a group of people mounts, it increases in level □ *Fears are mounting for the safety of the young climbers.* (**subir**)
2 to get on a horse or bicycle (**montar**)

◆ PHRASAL VERB **mount up** to gradually increase □ *The cost soon mounts up.*

mountain /ˈmaʊntɪn/ NOUN [plural mountains]
a very high hill □ *the Rocky Mountains* □ *We spent our holiday walking in the mountains.* □ *a mountain range* (**montanha**)

mourn /mɔːn/ VERB [mourns, mourning, mourned]
to be very sad because someone you love has died □ *She was still mourning for her husband.* (**prantear**)

mouse /maʊs/ NOUN [plural mice]
1 a small animal with grey or brown fur and a long tail (**rato**)
2 a small device that you move with your hand in order to make a computer do things. A computing word. (**mouse**)

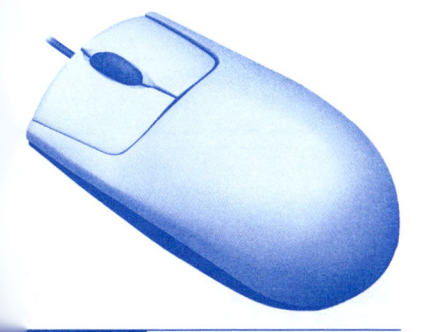

moustache /məˈstɑːʃ/ NOUN [plural moustaches]
a line of hair that some men grow above their top lip (**bigode**)

mouth /maʊθ/ NOUN [plural mouths]
1 the part of your face that you use for speaking and eating and which contains your tongue and teeth (**boca**)
2 the place where a river flows into the sea (**bocal, embocadura**)

mouthful /ˈmaʊθfʊl/ NOUN [plural mouthfuls]
an amount of food or drink that you put in your mouth at one time □ *She ate a few mouthfuls of soup.* (**bocado**)

move¹ /muːv/ VERB [moves, moving, moved]
1 to change position, or to change the position of something □ *Please move your bag off the kitchen table.* □ *He moved forwards to kick the ball.* □ *Nobody moved as the clock struck.* □ *I'm sure I saw the curtain move.* (**mover, mexer**)
2 if a person or an organization moves, they go to live or work in a different place □ + *to* *We moved to London in 2003.* □ *We moved house over ten times while I was a child.* □ *Our office is moving to Bristol.* (**mudar**)

◆ PHRASAL VERBS **move in** to begin to live in a new home or work in a new place □ *We moved in last year.* **move out** to leave the place where you have been living or working □ *I moved out of my parents' house when I was 18.*

move² /muːv/ NOUN [plural moves]
1 an action that achieves something □ *Buying a house turned out to be a good move.* □ *They made no move to help her.* □ *I've given him my phone number – it's up to him to make the next move.* (**movimento**)
2 when you go to live or work in another place □ *I've packed all my files ready for the office move.* □ *They split up after her move to London.* (**mudança**)
3 a change of position □ *The slightest move was painful.* (**mudança**)

◆ IDIOM **get a move on** an informal phrase meaning to hurry □ *Get a move on – we're going to be late!*

movement /ˈmuːvmənt/ NOUN [plural movements]
1 a change of position or place □ *I saw a slight movement of the curtain.* □ *Try to make slow, graceful movements of the arms.* □ *The police tracked the movements of all the suspects.* (**movimento**)
2 a group of people with the same interests or aims □ *the anti-war movement* (**movimento**)

movie /ˈmuːvi/ NOUN [plural movies]
1 a film □ *Do you have a favourite movie?* □ *a movie star* □ *a horror movie* (**filme**)
2 the movies a cinema □ *Let's go to the movies.* (**cinema**)

MP /ˌemˈpiː/ ABBREVIATION Member of Parliament; someone who has been elected to the British parliament (**membro do parlamento**)

MP3 /ˌempiːˈθriː/ NOUN [plural MP3s] a computer file that stores music and recorded speech (**MP3**)

MP3 player /ˌem piːˈθriː pleɪə(r)/ NOUN [plural MP3 players] a small piece of computer equipment for storing and playing music and recorded speech (**aparelho de MP3**)

mph /ˌempiːˈeɪtʃ/ ABBREVIATION miles per hour; a unit for measuring speed ▫ *The maximum speed on this road is 30 mph.* (**mph, milhas por hora**)

Mr /ˈmɪstə(r)/ NOUN a title used before a man's name ▫ *My art teacher is called Mr Jackson.* ▫ *Hello, Mr Rose.* (**sr.**)

Mrs /ˈmɪsɪz/ NOUN a title used before a married woman's name ▫ *That's my neighbour, Mrs Baker.* ▫ *Good morning, Mrs Clarke.* (**sra.**)

Ms /mɪz, məz/ NOUN a title sometimes used before a woman's name. It does not tell you if she is married or not. ▫ *Ms Duggan* (**sra.**)

much¹ /mʌtʃ/ DETERMINER, PRONOUN
1 how much used in questions about amounts ▫ *How much fruit do you eat each day?* ▫ *The pay depends on how much responsibility you take on.* ▫ *How much are (= what is the price of) these apples?* (**muito**)
2 used in negative sentences to say that there is not a large amount of something ▫ *A few more days won't make much difference.* ▫ *She doesn't say much.* ▫ *There isn't much to laugh about.* ▫ *'Do you have any money?' 'Not much.'* (**muito**)
3 too much more than is wanted, needed or acceptable ▫ *We bought far too much food.* ▫ *We've got too much work.* (**demais**)
4 so much used to emphasize the large amount of something ▫ *I have so much to do.* ▫ *Why did you give me so much food?* (**tanto**)
5 as much used to talk about amounts that are as large as something else ▫ *I hope I can give you as much support as you've given me.* (**tanto como, tanto quanto**)

> Remember that **much** is only used with uncountable nouns:
> ✓ *I've eaten too much food.*
> ✗ *There are too much cars on the road.* With countable nouns that are in the plural, the word **many** is used: ▫ *How many dogs do they have?*

much² /mʌtʃ/ ADVERB
1 often or a lot ▫ *Do you miss your old school much?* ▫ *Thanks very much – you've been a great help.* ▫ *He doesn't love her as much as she loves him.* ▫ *I had to work away from home too much in my last job.* (**muito**)
2 used to emphasize comparative adjectives ▫ *He's much taller than his brother.* ▫ *She's much more beautiful now she's older.* (**muito**)

mud /mʌd/ NOUN, NO PLURAL soft wet soil ▫ *His football boots were covered in mud.* (**lama**)

muddy /ˈmʌdi/ ADJECTIVE [**muddier, muddiest**] covered or filled with mud ▫ *The track through the woods was very muddy.* ▫ *Take off your muddy boots.* (**enlameado**)

mug /mʌg/ NOUN [plural **mugs**] a cup with straight sides and a handle ▫ *a mug of hot chocolate* (**caneca**)

multiple /ˈmʌltɪpəl/ ADJECTIVE many ▫ *She suffered multiple injuries in the crash.* (**múltiplo**)

multiply /ˈmʌltɪplaɪ/ VERB [**multiplies, multiplying, multiplied**] to increase a number by adding it to itself a particular number of times. A mathematics word ▫ *13 multiplied by 3 is 39.* (**multiplicar**)

mum /mʌm/ NOUN [plural **mums**] an informal word for mother ▫ *Can I have another cake, Mum?* ▫ *How's your mum?* (**mamãe**)

mumble /ˈmʌmbəl/ VERB [**mumbles, mumbling, mumbled**] to speak quietly or without opening your mouth enough, so that people cannot understand you ▫ *He mumbled something about not having enough money.* (**resmungar**)

mummy /ˈmʌmi/ NOUN [plural **mummies**] a child's word for mother ▫ *Mummy, can we go now?* ▫ *Where's your mummy, Jake?* (**mamãe**)

murder¹ /ˈmɜːdə(r)/ NOUN [plural **murders**] the crime of killing someone deliberately ▫ *He admitted committing the murder.* ▫ *He was charged with attempted murder (= trying to kill someone).* (**assassinato**)

murder² /ˈmɜːdə(r)/ VERB [**murders, murdering, murdered**] to kill someone deliberately ▫ *She denies murdering her husband.* (**assassinar**)

murderer /ˈmɜːdərə(r)/ NOUN [plural **murderers**] someone who has murdered another person (**assassino**)

murmur /ˈmɜːmə(r)/ VERB [**murmurs, murmuring, murmured**] to speak very quietly ▫ *He murmured something in her ear.* (**murmurar**)

> **THESAURUS:** To **murmur** means to speak very quietly. To **mutter** also means to speak quietly, but usually because you are angry or complaining about something. If you **whisper**, you talk very quietly to someone, so that other people cannot hear. If you **mumble**, you speak quietly or without opening your mouth enough so that people cannot understand you.

muscle /ˈmʌsəl/ NOUN [plural **muscles**] one of the parts in the body that are connected to bones and that cause the body to move by becoming shorter or longer ▫ *stomach muscles* ▫ *Joe has pulled a muscle (= injured the muscle) in his leg.* (**músculo**)

museum /mjuːˈziːəm/ NOUN [plural **museums**] a building where collections of interesting things are arranged for people to see ▫ *the Natural History Museum* (**museu**)

mushroom /ˈmʌʃrʊm/ NOUN [plural **mushrooms**] a type of fungus (= plant with no leaves or flowers) that you can eat, with a stem and a flat or round top □ *mushroom risotto* (cogumelo)

music /ˈmjuːzɪk/ NOUN, NO PLURAL
1 sounds arranged in patterns, sung or played by instruments 🔊 *Do you like classical music?* 🔊 *I've been listening to a lot of dance music recently.* □ *a music teacher* (música)
2 the written sounds that represent a piece of music 🔊 *I wish I could read music.* (música)

> Remember that the noun **music** is not used in the plural:
> ✓ *He listens to a lot of music.*
> ✗ *He listens to a lot of musics.*

musical¹ /ˈmjuːzɪkəl/ ADJECTIVE
1 to do with music □ *She has no musical training.* 🔊 *Do you play a musical instrument?* (musical)
2 good at playing or singing music □ *The whole family is very musical.* (musical)

musical² /ˈmjuːzɪkəl/ NOUN [plural musicals]
a play or film in which there is a lot of singing and dancing □ *He loves all the old Hollywood musicals.* (musical)

musician /mjuːˈzɪʃən/ NOUN [plural musicians]
someone who plays a musical instrument □ *She's one of our most talented young musicians.* (músico)

Muslim¹ /ˈmʊzlɪm/ or Moslem /ˈmɒzləm/ NOUN [plural Muslims or Moslems]
someone who believes in Islam (muçulmano)

Muslim² /ˈmʊzlɪm/ or Moslem /ˈmɒzləm/ ADJECTIVE
to do with Islam □ *Friday is the Muslim holy day.* (muçulmano)

must /məs, məst, stressed mʌst/ MODAL VERB
1 used to say that something is necessary □ *You must arrive for your interview on time.* (precisar)
2 used to say that you think something is true □ *You must be very tired after such a long journey.* □ *They must have known about the money.* (dever)
3 used to make an offer or a suggestion □ *You must come over for dinner.* □ *We must meet up soon.* (dever)

mustache /ˈmʌstæʃ/ NOUN [plural mustaches] a US spelling of moustache (bigode)

mustard /ˈmʌstəd/ NOUN, NO PLURAL
a cold yellow or brown sauce used to give food a hot taste (mostarda)

mustn't /ˈmʌsənt/
a short way to say and write must not □ *I mustn't forget.* (forma negativa de must)

> Note that **mustn't** means it is *necessary not to do something*. To say that it is *not necessary to do something*, use **don't need/have to**:
> ✓ *You mustn't walk on the railway line. It's dangerous.*
> ✓ *Come if you like but you don't need to.*
> ✗ *Come if you like but you mustn't to.*

mutter /ˈmʌtə(r)/ VERB [mutters, muttering, muttered]
to speak quietly, often when you are complaining □ *He muttered something about people never listening to him.* (murmurar)

my /maɪ/ DETERMINER
belonging to or to do with me □ *There's my son.* □ *Have you seen my boots anywhere?* (meu, minha, meus, minhas)

myself /maɪˈself/ PRONOUN
1 the reflexive form of I □ *I was washing myself.* □ *I cut myself on the glass.* □ *I felt really proud of myself.* (me, mim mesmo)
2 used to show that you do something without any help from other people □ *I suppose I'll have to do it myself if no one else can be bothered.* 🔊 *I can't take care of him all by myself.* (eu mesmo, sozinho)
3 used to emphasize the pronoun I □ *I have not seen the film myself.* (eu mesmo)
4 by myself not with or near other people □ *I live by myself.* (sozinho)

mysterious /mɪˈstɪəriəs/ ADJECTIVE
strange and difficult to understand or explain 🔊 *He died in mysterious circumstances.* □ *No one knows why she left – it's very mysterious.* (misterioso)

mystery /ˈmɪstəri/ NOUN [plural mysteries]
something strange which you do not understand and which cannot be explained 🔊 *She set out to solve the mystery of his disappearance.* (mistério)

> THESAURUS: A **mystery** is a strange thing that you do not understand and which cannot be explained. A **secret** is a piece of information that must not be told to other people. A **puzzle** is something that is difficult to understand.

myth /mɪθ/ NOUN [plural myths]
1 a story about ancient gods, heroes (= brave people) and monsters (= frightening creatures) □ *Greek and Roman myths* (mito)
2 something that many people believe, but which is not true □ *It's a myth that eating late at night makes you fat.* (mito)

mythology /mɪˈθɒlədʒi/ NOUN, NO PLURAL
stories about ancient gods and heroes (= brave people) (mitologia)

N n

N¹ *or* **n** /en/ the 14th letter of the alphabet (a décima quarta letra do alfabeto)
N² /en/ ABBREVIATION **north²** (N)

nail¹ /neɪl/ NOUN [*plural* nails]
1 the hard covering on top of the ends of your fingers and toes ▣ *You need to cut your nails.* ▣ *a pair of nail scissors* (unha)
2 a thin pointed piece of metal, used to join things together, especially pieces of wood (prego)

nail² /neɪl/ VERB [nails, nailing, nailed] to attach or join something with a nail or nails ▣ *Nail the number on the door.* (pregar)

naked /ˈneɪkɪd/ ADJECTIVE not wearing any clothes ▣ *He stripped naked to the waist to cut the grass.* ▣ *The children were running around stark naked in the sun.* (nu)

name¹ /neɪm/ NOUN [*plural* names] the word or words that you use to refer to a person, animal, place or thing ▣ *What's your name?* ▣ *Write your name and address here.* ▣ *I can't remember the name of the street.* ▣ *She changed her name when she got married.* (nome)

▶ THESAURUS: Name is a general word for the word or words that you use to refer to a person, animal, place or thing. Your surname is your last name or family name. You first name is the name that comes before your surname. Your parents usually choose your first name. A nickname is a name that you use for someone that is not their real name.

name² /neɪm/ VERB [names, naming, named]
1 to give someone or something a name ▣ *They've named their son Samuel.* ▣ *The ship has not been named yet.* (chamar, dar nome)
2 to say what the name of someone or something is ▣ *The dead men will not be named until their families have been informed.* (nomear)

▶ Note that to **name** someone is to give someone (often a baby) or something a name. To say the name of someone or something, use **be called**:
✓ *She is called Justina.*
✗ *She is named Justina.*

nanny /ˈnæni/ NOUN [*plural* nannies] a person whose job is to look after someone's child or children, usually in their own home (babá)

nappy /ˈnæpi/ NOUN [*plural* nappies] a thick piece of soft cloth or paper that you fasten around a baby's bottom ▣ *Could you change the baby's nappy?* (fralda)

narrow /ˈnærəʊ/ ADJECTIVE [narrower, narrowest]
1 not very wide ▣ *She found a narrow door in the garden wall.* ▣ *The road was too narrow for overtaking.* (estreito)
2 only just achieved ▣ *We had a narrow escape when our car went off the road.* (apertado, por pouco)

nasty /ˈnɑːsti/ ADJECTIVE [nastier, nastiest] very unpleasant or unkind ▣ *The drug left a nasty taste in my mouth.* ▣ *He's always saying nasty things about everybody.* (desagradável)

nation /ˈneɪʃən/ NOUN [*plural* nations]
1 a country with its own government ▣ *the African nations* (nação)
2 the people of a country ▣ *Today the nation is voting for a new government.* (povo)

national /ˈnæʃənəl/ ADJECTIVE
1 to do with the whole of a country ▣ *They report local, national and international news.* ▣ *House prices in the south-east are well above the national average.* (nacional)
2 typical of a particular country ▣ *Paella is the national dish of Spain.* ▣ *Dancers in national costume greeted the president.* (nacional)

nationality /ˌnæʃəˈnæləti/ NOUN [*plural* nationalities] the state of being a legal member of a particular country ▣ *Omar has British nationality.* ▣ *Louis has dual nationality because his mother is French and his father is American.* (nacionalidade)

native¹ /ˈneɪtɪv/ ADJECTIVE to do with the place you were born in ▣ *His native language is French.* ▣ *In 1965 he left his native Austria.* (natal)
native² /ˈneɪtɪv/ NOUN [*plural* natives] someone who was born in a particular place ▣ *She's a native of New South Wales.* (nativo)

natural /ˈnætʃərəl/ ADJECTIVE

1 to do with or made by nature, not by people or machines □ *the natural world* □ *an area of great natural beauty* 🔊 *An earthquake is an example of a natural disaster.* 🔊 *The old man had died of natural causes.* (**natural**)
2 normal or to be expected □ *It's only natural to be a little nervous before a test.* (**natural**)

naturally /ˈnætʃərəli/ ADVERB

1 as would be expected □ *Naturally, we were annoyed not to win.* (**naturalmente**)
2 in a way that is normal □ *Joe began to relax and act a bit more naturally.* (**naturalmente**)
3 without help from anything artificial □ *Let the skin heal naturally.* (**naturalmente**)

nature /ˈneɪtʃə(r)/ NOUN [plural natures]

1 *no plural* everything in the world that was not made or changed by people, such as animals, trees, the sea, etc. □ *I love watching programmes about nature.* □ *the forces of nature* (**natureza**)
2 a person's character or qualities 🔊 *It's human nature to protect one's family.* 🔊 *It's not in her nature to be unkind.* (**natureza**)

> Note that **nature** (sense 1) is never used with **the**:
> ✓ *I've always loved nature.*
> ✗ *I've always loved the nature.*

naughty /ˈnɔːti/ ADJECTIVE [naughtier, naughtiest] behaving badly or not doing what you are told to do □ *You've been a very naughty little boy.* (**malcriado**)

naval /ˈneɪvəl/ ADJECTIVE to do with the navy □ *an important naval base* (**naval**)

navigate /ˈnævɪgeɪt/ VERB [navigates, navigating, navigated] to use a map or other equipment to find your way somewhere in a vehicle □ *My mother always drove and my father had to navigate.* (**pilotar**)

navigation /ˌnævɪˈgeɪʃən/ NOUN, NO PLURAL the process of using maps or other equipment to find your way some where (**navegação**)

navigator /ˈnævɪgeɪtə(r)/ NOUN [plural navigators] someone who uses a map or other equipment to find the way somewhere in a vehicle (**piloto**)

navy¹ /ˈneɪvi/ NOUN [plural navies]

1 **the navy** military ships and the soldiers that work on them 🔊 *Matt is hoping to join the navy.* (**marinha**)
2 a very dark blue colour (**azul-marinho**)

navy² /ˈneɪvi/ ADJECTIVE of a very dark blue colour □ *a navy jacket*

near¹ /nɪə(r)/ PREPOSITION, ADVERB [nearer, nearest]

1 a short distance away □ *I live quite near Tom.* □ + *to* We rented a house near to the beach. □ *Stand a little nearer and you'll be able to see better.* □ *They took him to the nearest hospital.* (**perto**)
2 a short time in the future □ *I don't want to take on extra work so near my exams.* 🔊 *It's a bit early to plan the food – let's talk about it nearer the time.* (**perto**)

near² /nɪə(r)/ ADJECTIVE [nearer, nearest]

not far away in distance or time 🔊 *Will you be seeing Kate in the near future?* □ *He is a near neighbour of mine.* (**próximo**)

nearby /ˈnɪəbaɪ/ ADJECTIVE, ADVERB

quite close to where you are or the place you are talking about □ *We went to a nearby restaurant for dinner.* □ *Is there a bank nearby?* (**perto**)

> Note that **nearby** is not a preposition. The preposition with the same meaning is **near**:
> ✓ *Their apartment is very near the office.*
> ✗ *Their apartment is very nearby the office.*

nearly /ˈnɪəli/ ADVERB

almost but not completely □ *We're nearly there.* □ *Nearly everyone had a good time.* □ *They've lived there for nearly three years.* (**quase**)

neat /niːt/ ADJECTIVE [neater, neatest]

tidy and arranged carefully □ *Your handwriting's very neat.* 🔊 *Anna always keeps her room neat and tidy.* (**arrumado**)

necessarily /ˌnesəˈserɪli/ ADVERB

not necessarily not in every case □ *Men aren't necessarily stronger than women.* (**arrumado**)

necessary /ˈnesəsəri/ ADJECTIVE

needed in order to do something, get something or make something happen □ *The website lists the necessary skills for each job.* 🔊 *I can work late if necessary.* □ + **to do something** *Is it necessary to come early?* □ + **for** *Good English is necessary for this job.* (**necessário**)

necessity /nɪˈsesəti/ NOUN [plural necessities]

something that is needed □ *A warm coat is a necessity in this weather.* (**necessariamente**)

neck /nek/ NOUN [plural necks]

1 the part of your body between your head and your shoulders □ *She had her headphones around her neck.* (**pescoço**)
2 the opening in a piece of clothing that you put your head through □ *This T-shirt is too baggy around the neck.* (**gola**)
3 the narrow part of a bottle near its opening (**colarinho, gargalo**)

necklace /ˈneklɪs/ NOUN [plural necklaces] a piece of jewellery you wear around your neck □ *a diamond necklace* (**colar**)

need

need¹ /niːd/ VERB [needs, needing, needed]

1 if you need something, you must have it in order to exist or to do something □ *I need a sharp knife.* □ *I need your advice.* □ *Do you need any help?* □ *This provides the energy needed to heat the building.* (**necessitar**)

2 if you need to do something, you must do it, and if you need to have a particular quality, you must have it □ **+ to do something** *We all need to eat and drink.* □ *You need to make more effort with your studies.* □ *You need to be tough to be a doctor.* (**precisar**)

3 someone doesn't need to do something/ needn't do something it is not necessary for someone to do something □ *She doesn't need to pay me.* (**não precisar fazer algo**)

need² /niːd/ NOUN [plural needs]

1 something that it is necessary to have □ **+ for** *There is an urgent need for more nurses.* (**necessidade**)

2 something that it is necessary to do □ **+ to do something** *He recognizes the need to invest more money.* □ *There is no need to wait for me.* (**necessidade**)

3 be in need of something to need something □ *This house is in need of a thorough clean.* (**necessitar de algo**)

> Remember that the noun **need** takes the preposition **for**:
> ✓ There is a need **for** more housing.
> ✗ There is a need **of** more housing.

needle /ˈniːdəl/ NOUN [plural needles]

1 a small, pointed piece of metal used for sewing □ *a needle and thread* □ *Can you thread this needle for me?* (**agulha**)

2 a long thin piece of wood, metal or plastic that is used for knitting (= making something with wool and two long sticks) □ *a pair of knitting needles* (**agulha**)

3 the thin, sharp metal part of a medical instrument for putting a drug into someone's body or taking blood out (**agulha**)

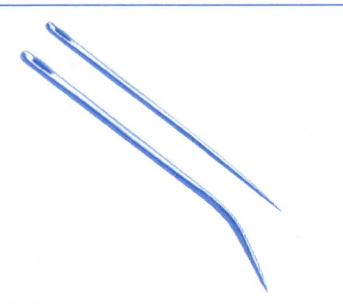

needn't /ˈniːdənt/ a short way to say and write need not (ver **need**)

negative¹ /ˈnegətɪv/ ADJECTIVE

1 not feeling hope or enthusiasm □ *Since his illness he's been feeling very negative.* □ *You'll never win until you lose that negative attitude.* (**negativo**)

2 bad or harmful □ *The drug has a number of negative effects.* (**negativo**)

3 a negative word or phrase expresses the meaning 'not' or 'no' □ *a negative sentence* □ *We got a negative reply to our request.* (**negativo**)

4 a negative number is less than zero, for example 25. A mathematics word. (**negativo**)

negative² /ˈnegətɪv/ NOUN [plural negatives] a film before it is printed, where light objects appear dark and dark objects appear light (**negativo**)

neglect¹ /nɪˈglekt/ VERB [neglects, neglecting, neglected] to not give someone or something enough care and attention □ *I've been neglecting the housework because I've been so busy.* □ *The couple are accused of neglecting their children.* (**negligenciar**)

neglect² /nɪˈglekt/ NOUN, NO PLURAL when someone or something does not get enough care or attention □ *The garden has suffered years of neglect.* (**negligência**)

negotiate /nɪˈgəʊʃieɪt/ VERB [negotiates, negotiating, negotiated] to try to make an agreement with someone by having discussions with them □ *Employees are currently negotiating with managers over a pay rise.* □ *The two parties are hoping to negotiate a settlement to the conflict.* (**negociar**)

neighbor /ˈneɪbə(r)/ NOUN [plural neighbors] the US spelling of **neighbour** (**vizinho**)

• **neighborhood** /ˈneɪbəhʊd/ NOUN [plural neighborhoods] the US spelling of **neighbourhood** (**bairro**)

neighbour /ˈneɪbə(r)/ NOUN [plural neighbours] someone who lives near you or in the next house to you □ *We asked a neighbour to feed the cat.* □ *Cecilia was our next-door neighbour for twelve years.* (**vizinho**)

neighbourhood /ˈneɪbəhʊd/ NOUN [plural neighbourhoods] an area of a town or city □ *This is a pretty neighbourhood with a lot of trees and parks.* (**bairro**)

nephew

neither¹ /ˈnaɪðə(r)/ DETERMINER, PRONOUN not either of two people or things □ *Neither woman seemed to understand English.* □ *Neither of us can go.* (**nem um nem outro, nenhum dos dois**)

neither² /ˈnaɪðə(r)/ ADVERB used to say that a negative statement is also true about someone or something else □ *I can't go and neither can Fay.* □ *'I don't like garlic.' 'Neither does Richard.'* □ *'I'm not working today.' 'Me neither, let's go out.'* (**nem, também não**)

neither³ /ˈnaɪðə(r)/ CONJUNCTION **neither... nor** used when something negative is true of two people or things □ *Neither Peter nor Michael turned up.* □ *I neither know, nor care, where he is.* (**nem... nem**)

nephew /ˈnefjuː/ NOUN [plural nephews] the son of your brother or sister, or the son of your wife's or husband's brother or sister (**sobrinho**)

nerve /nɜːv/ NOUN [plural **nerves**]
1 one of the connections like threads that carry messages between your brain and other parts of your body. A biology word □ *the optic nerve* □ *nerve endings* (**nervo**)
2 the courage you need to do something difficult or dangerous □ *+ to do something I didn't have the nerve to jump.* (**coragem**)
3 **nerves** nervous feelings ▣ *She went for a walk to calm her nerves.* (**nervos**)
♦ IDIOM **get on someone's nerves** to annoy someone, especially by doing the same thing many times □ *His constant complaints were getting on my nerves.*

nervous /ˈnɜːvəs/ ADJECTIVE
1 worried or frightened □ *I get terribly nervous just before I go on stage.* □ *a nervous laugh* □ *+ about She was very nervous about her interview.* (**nervoso**)
2 to do with the nerves in your body. A biology word □ *nervous disorders* (**nervoso**)

nervously /ˈnɜːvəsli/ ADVERB in a worried, slightly frightened, way □ *She giggled nervously.* (**nervosamente**)

nervousness /ˈnɜːvəsnɪs/ NOUN, NO PLURAL a worried, slightly frightened feeling □ *He struggled to hide his nervousness.* (**nervosismo**)

nervous system /ˈnɜːvəs ˌsɪstəm/ NOUN [plural **nervous systems**] all the nerves in your body and the way they connect to your brain to send messages about feeling and movement. A biology word. (**sistema nervoso**)

nest /nest/ NOUN [plural **nests**] a place where birds or some kinds of insects and animals live and have their babies □ *We found a bird's nest in a tree.* (**ninho**)

net /net/ NOUN [plural **nets**]
1 a material made of crossed string or rope with holes between, or something made from this and used for a particular purpose ▣ *a fishing net* ▣ *a mosquito net* ▣ *The acrobats performed without a safety net.* (**rede**)
2 a thin material made of crossed threads with holes between □ *net curtains* (**rede**)
3 **the Net** the Internet ▣ *She spends hours surfing the Net.* (**rede**)

network /ˈnetwɜːk/ NOUN [plural **networks**]
1 a system of roads, railways lines, etc. that cross and connect with one another □ *A strike has shut down the railway network.* (**rede**)
2 a group of people or companies that work together or help each other □ *She is lucky to have the support of a wide network of friends.* □ *The company has a network of dealers throughout the country.* (**rede**)
3 a system of computers that are all connected together so that they can share information (**rede**)

neutral /ˈnjuːtrəl/ ADJECTIVE
1 not supporting either side in an argument, war or competition □ *The referee must remain neutral.* (**neutro**)
2 a neutral colour is not strong or bright (**neutro**)

never /ˈnevə(r)/ ADVERB not ever □ *I've never been abroad.* □ *It's never too late to learn.* □ *I promise never to say that again.* □ *I would never do anything to hurt you.* (**nunca**)

> Note that **never** usually goes before a 'to infinitive'. It does not go between 'to' and the verb:
> ✓ *I promise never to do it again.*
> ✗ *I promise to never do it again.*

nevertheless /ˌnevəðəˈles/ ADVERB despite that □ *The car isn't perfect, but it's very good nevertheless.* (**apesar de tudo**)

new /njuː/ ADJECTIVE [**newer, newest**]
1 not existing before, or only recently made, bought, invented, etc. □ *A new hospital is being built in the city.* □ *We are creating new online materials.* ▣ *New technology has improved international communications.* □ *He bought a new jacket.* □ *I got a new bike for my birthday.*
2 different □ *I met my new boss today.* □ *He showed me a new way to make cheese sauce.* (**novo**)
3 not familiar □ *Working in a team is a new experience for me.* □ *+ to The business world is still new to her.* (**novo**)
4 **new to something** if you are new to an area or an activity, you have only recently come there or started to do it □ *She's still quite new to the job.* (**novato em**)

> THESAURUS: Something which is **new** did not exist before, or has recently been made, bought, invented etc. Something which is **fresh** is new and different, in a good way. For example, you might talk about putting fresh sheets on the bed. Food which is **fresh** is not old and has not been dried or frozen. Something which is **unused** has never been used.

newborn /ˈnjuːbɔːn/ ADJECTIVE a newborn baby has just been born (**recém-nascido**)
newly /ˈnjuːli/ ADVERB recently □ *the newly appointed London Mayor* (**recém**)

news /njuːz/ NOUN, NO PLURAL

1 new information □ + *about* Have you heard the news about Raj? □ + *of* News of her safe return was greeted with joy. □ + *on*Is there any news on the wedding date yet? 🔄 We've had some *good news*; Beth is pregnant. 🔄 I'm afraid I've got some *bad news*. (**novidade, notícia**)
2 the news information about important events on the radio or television, or in newspapers, etc. 🔄 the *local/national news* □ They always watch the news at 10 o'clock. (**noticiário**)

> Remember that **news** is used with a singular verb:
> ✓ The news is so bad at the moment.
> ✗ The news are so bad at the moment.

newsagent /ˈnjuːzeɪdʒənt/ NOUN [plural newsagents]

1 someone who sells newspapers and magazines (**jornaleiro**)
2 newsagent's a shop that sells newspapers and magazines and usually other things like sweets and cigarettes (**banca de jornal com loja de conveniência**)

newspaper /ˈnjuːzpeɪpə(r)/ NOUN [plural newspapers]

large folded pieces of paper printed with reports and pictures about recent events and sold every day or every week □ I saw your picture in the newspaper. 🔄 He started his career working on the *local newspaper*. (**jornal**)

New Year /ˌnjuː ˈjɪə(r)/ NOUN, NO PLURAL

the first few days of January, when people often celebrate □ They're having a New Year's party. □ Happy New Year! (**ano-novo**)

New Year's Day /ˌnjuː jɪəz ˈdeɪ/ NOUN [plural New Year's Days]

1 January, the first day of the year (**dia de ano-novo**)

New Year's Eve /ˌnjuː jɪəz ˈiːv/ NOUN [plural New Year's Eves]

31 December, the last day of the year (**véspera de ano-novo**)

next¹ /nekst/ ADJECTIVE

1 following or happening immediately after □ What's the next name on the list? □ I need to phone him in the next hour. □ The next morning he felt much better. □ Next time I see Sally, I'll ask her. (**próximo**)
2 next week/Saturday/year, etc. the week/Saturday/year, etc. after this one □ Do you want to come round next weekend? (**próximo**)
3 nearest to the place where you are now □ Take the next left. □ The next town is five miles away. (**próximo, seguinte**)

next² /nekst/ PRONOUN

1 the person or thing that follows or happens immediately after someone or something else □ Who's next to see the doctor? (**o seguinte**)
2 the week/Saturday/year, etc. after next two weeks/Saturdays/years, etc. from the present □ I'm going to New York the week after next. (**seguinte**)

next³ /nekst/ PREPOSITION

1 next to in a position at the side of someone or something □ I put the book down next to her. 🔄 Nobody wants to live *right next to* a motorway. (**ao lado de**)
2 next to nothing almost nothing □ I earn next to nothing from my writing. (**quase nada**)

next⁴ /nekst/ ADVERB

immediately after something else □ What will happen next? □ Next we need to paint the walls. (**logo em seguida**)

next door /ˌnekst ˈdɔː(r)/ ADJECTIVE, ADVERB

in the next house, building or room 🔄 We have very nice *next door neighbours*. □ Our office is next door to the station. □ We get on well with the people next door. (**vizinho**)

NHS /ˌen eɪtʃ ˈes/ ABBREVIATION

the NHS the National Health Service; the system which provides free medical treatment for people in the UK □ He had the operation done on the NHS. (**serviço nacional de saúde**)

nice /naɪs/ ADJECTIVE [nicer, nicest]

1 pleasant, good or attractive □ If the weather's nice, we can go for a walk. □ She took me to a really nice restaurant. 🔄 Have a *nice time* in Germany! (**bonito, agradável**)
2 kind or friendly □ That wasn't a very nice thing to do. □ + *to* She's always nice to the children. □ + *of* It was very nice of Rob to give me a lift. □ + *about* My tutor was really nice about my work. (**gentil, amável**)

> **THESAURUS:** Nice is a general word. If something or someone is nice to look at, you can say they are **attractive**. If an experience is nice, you can say that it is **pleasant** or **enjoyable**. If an experience is very nice, you can say that it is **great** or **fantastic**. If a person is nice because they are kind and pleasant, you can say that they are **friendly**.

nickname¹ /ˈnɪkneɪm/ NOUN [plural nicknames]

a name that you use for someone that is not their real name □ His nickname at school was 'President' because his real name's Kennedy. (**apelido**)

nickname² /ˈnɪkneɪm/ VERB [nicknames, nicknaming, nicknamed]

to call someone by a nickname □ They nicknamed him 'Scottie'. (**apelidar**)

niece /niːs/ NOUN [plural nieces]

the daughter of your brother or sister, or the daughter of your wife's or husband's brother or sister (**sobrinha**)

night /naɪt/ NOUN [plural nights]

1 the time when it is dark and when people usually sleep 🔄 I hardly slept *last night*. 🔄 I *spent the night* at my sister's. 🔄 The dog woke me up *in the middle of the night*. 🔄 He's been having *sleepless nights* worrying about work. (**noite**)
2 at night during the time when it is dark □ I don't walk the streets on my own at night. (**à noite**)
3 the part of the evening before you go to bed 🔄

nightclub

I went out with David last night. □ *Are you doing anything on Saturday night?* □ *I'm having a night out with my friends on Friday.* (**noite**)
4 Good night. something you say when you leave someone in the evening, or when you or they go to bed (**Boa noite**)

> Notice that we usually say **at night** to mean 'during the time when it is dark':
> ✓ *I never drive at night.*
> ✗ *I never drive in the night.*

nightclub /ˈnaɪtklʌb/ NOUN [plural **nightclubs**]
a place where people can dance and drink late at night (**boate**)

nightmare /ˈnaɪtmeə(r)/ NOUN [plural **nightmares**]
1 a frightening dream □ *Older children often have nightmares.* (**pesadelo**)
2 a very unpleasant experience □ *The drive home was a complete nightmare.* (**pesadelo**)

nine /naɪn/ NUMBER [plural **nines**] the number 9 (**nove**)

nineteen /ˌnaɪnˈtiːn/ NUMBE [plural **nineteens**]
the number 19 (**dezenove**)

nineteenth /ˌnaɪnˈtiːnθ/ NUMBER 19th written as a word (**décimo nono**)

ninetieth /ˈnaɪntiəθ/ NUMBER 90th written as a word (**nonagésimo**)

ninety /ˈnaɪnti/ NUMBER [plural **nineties**]
1 the number 90 (**noventa**)
2 **the nineties** the years between 1990 and 1999 (**os anos 1990**)

ninth¹ /naɪnθ/ NUMBER 9th written as a word (**nono**)

ninth² /naɪnθ/ NOUN [plural **ninths**] 1/9; one of nine equal parts of something (**nove avos**)

No. or **no.** /nəʊ/ ABBREVIATION **number¹** (n°)

no¹ /nəʊ/ EXCLAMATION
1 used to refuse, disagree or give a negative answer □ *'Can you give me a lift to the station?' 'No, sorry, I need to get straight home.'* □ *'Tim's really stupid.' 'No he isn't!'* □ *'Can I have some more cake?' 'No, you've had enough already.'* □ *'Are you all right?' 'No, I've got my foot stuck.'* (**não**)
2 used to agree with a negative statement □ *'The weather's not very good today.' 'No, it's a bit cold.'* (**não**)
3 used to express shock or surprise 🔁 *Oh no! I've left my passport at home!* □ *'Chris and Alice are getting married.' 'No! They've only known each other a few weeks!'* (**não**)

no² /nəʊ/ ADVERB not any □ *She's no better this morning.* 🔁 *No fewer than four players were sent off during the match.* □ *Payment is due no later than the 15th.* (**não**)

no³ /nəʊ/ DETERMINER
1 not any □ *They have no money.* □ *There is no need to bring a coat.* □ *No decisions have been taken yet.* (**nenhum**)
2 used to say that something is not allowed □ *No smoking.* (**proibido**)

noble /ˈnəʊbəl/ ADJECTIVE [**nobler, noblest**]
1 brave and honest, or helping other people in a way that people admire □ *We are doing important work for a noble cause.* (**nobre**)
2 belonging to a high social class □ *He comes from a noble family.* (**nobre**)

nobody /ˈnəʊbədi/ PRONOUN not any person □ *Nobody tells me what to do!* □ *There was nobody at home.* 🔁 *Nobody else noticed it.* (**ninguém**)

> Note that **nobody** is always followed by a singular verb:
> ✓ *Nobody has said anything.*
> ✗ *Nobody have said anything.*

nod¹ /nɒd/ VERB [**nods, nodding, nodded**] to move your head up and down, especially to agree or to say 'yes' 🔁 *He nodded his head enthusiastically.* 🔁 *His wife nodded in agreement.* (**acenar a cabeça**)

nod² /nɒd/ NOUN [plural **nods**] when you nod your head 🔁 *He gave a small nod.* (**aceno de cabeça**)

noise /nɔɪz/ NOUN [plural **noises**]
1 a sound 🔁 *Did you hear a noise outside?* 🔁 *The bird was making screeching noises.* 🔁 *There was a sudden, loud noise.* (**barulho**)
2 no plural sound that is loud or unpleasant □ + **of** *He shouted over the noise of the engine.* 🔁 *Could you please make a little less noise?* 🔁 *The background noise made it difficult to hear.* (**barulho**)

noisy /ˈnɔɪzi/ ADJECTIVE [**noisier, noisiest**]
making a lot of noise □ *a noisy party* □ *Some people complain about noisy neighbours.* □ *The fridge seems very noisy – is there something wrong with it?* (**barulhento**)

nominate /ˈnɒmɪneɪt/ VERB [**nominates, nominating, nominated**] to suggest someone for a job, position or prize □ *Charles nominated Peter as leader of the group.* □ *She was nominated for an Oscar.* (**nomear**)

non- /nɒn/ PREFIX non- is added to the beginning of words to mean 'not' □ *a non-smoker* (= someone who does not smoke) (**[prefixo] não-**)

none /nʌn/ PRONOUN not any □ + **of** *None of them are going to admit to being wrong.* □ *We looked for more biscuits but there were none left.* 🔁 *Most people there ate little food, or none at all* (**nenhum**)

nonetheless /ˌnʌnðəˈles/ ADVERB despite that □ *It was not easy; nonetheless, he tried his best.* □ *There have been one or two delays; the road will open on time, nonetheless.* (**apesar disso**)

nonsense /ˈnɒnsəns/ NOUN, NO PLURAL something that is not true or sensible 🔁 *His theory is a load of nonsense.* 🔁 *You're talking nonsense.* 🔁 *These reports are absolute nonsense.* (**disparate**)

noodle /ˈnuːdəl/ NOUN [plural **noodles**] a long thin piece of pasta (**talharim**)

noon /nuːn/ NOUN, NO PLURAL twelve o'clock in the middle of the day ▢ *We'll have our lunch at noon.* ▢ *It was a few minutes past noon.* (**meio-dia**)

no one *or* **no-one** /ˈnəʊwʌn/ PRONOUN not any person ▢ *No one's in at the moment.* ▢ *No one knows what happened.* ▢ *There was no one to ask.* ▣ *There was no one else in the building.* (**ninguém**)

> Note that **no one** is always followed by a singular verb:
> ✓ *No one tells me anything.*
> ✗ *No one tell me anything.*

nor /nɔː(r)/ CONJUNCTION
1 neither... nor used when something negative is true of two people or things ▢ *Neither Jack nor Jenny is at home.* ▢ *Neither the teachers nor the parents are happy with the situation.* (**nem... nem**)
2 used after a negative statement to say that the same is true for someone else ▢ *He didn't see anything unusual, and nor did any of his friends.* ▢ *I'm sure Jack wouldn't like that and nor would I.* (**nem**)

normal /ˈnɔːməl/ ADJECTIVE usual and expected ▢ **+ to do something** *It's normal to feel hungry at lunchtime.* ▢ **+ for** *This temperature is normal for August.* ▣ *He just wants to live a normal life.* ▣ *There's been a lot of building work, but we should be back to normal soon.* (**normal**)

> THESAURUS: Something that is normal is usual and expected. Something that is **common** exists or happens often and in many places. For example, you can say that traffic jams are **common** in large cities. If something is **typical**, it has the usual qualities of a particular person or thing. You can talk about the **typical** food of a particular region, for example. If something is **ordinary**, it is not unusual or different.

normally /ˈnɔːməli/ ADVERB
1 usually ▢ *We normally go to bed pretty early.* ▢ *Normally, I drive to work.* ▢ *I don't normally do this kind of thing.* (**normalmente**)
2 in the usual and expected way ▢ *This plant has developed normally, but the other one is diseased.* (**normalmente**)

north[1] /nɔːθ/ NOUN, NO PLURAL the direction that is to your left when you are facing the rising sun (**norte**)

north[2] /nɔːθ/ ADJECTIVE, ADVERB in or towards the north ▢ *the cold north wind* ▢ *We were travelling north on the motorway.* (**para o norte**)

north-east[1] /ˌnɔːθˈiːst/ NOUN, NO PLURAL the direction between north and east (**nordeste**)

north-east[2] /ˌnɔːθˈiːst/ ADJECTIVE, ADVERB in or towards the north-east ▢ *The north-east region of Spain.* (**para nordeste**)

northern /ˈnɔːðən/ ADJECTIVE in or from the north ▢ *the cold northern climate* ▢ *Northern districts will have some rain.* (**do norte**)

North Pole /ˌnɔːθ ˈpəʊl/ NOUN **the North Pole** the point on the Earth that is furthest north (**polo norte**)

north-west[1] /ˌnɔːθˈwest/ NOUN, NO PLURAL the direction between north and west (**noroeste**)

north-west[2] /ˌnɔːθˈwest/ ADJECTIVE, ADVERB in or towards the north-west (**para noroeste**)

nose /nəʊz/ NOUN [plural **noses**]
1 the part of your face that you breathe and smell through ▣ *I need to blow my nose.* ▣ *I had sore eyes and a runny nose.* (**nariz**)
2 the front part of something that sticks out, for example, the front of an aircraft (**nariz**)
◆ IDIOMS **turn your nose up at something** to refuse to accept something because you do not think it is good enough for you ▢ *She turned her nose up at my soup.* **under someone's nose** if something happens under someone's nose, they are there when it happens, but they do not notice ▢ *He was rescued from under the noses of his guards.*

nostril /ˈnɒstrɪl/ NOUN [plural **nostrils**] one of the two openings in your nose that you breathe and smell through (**narina**)

not /nɒt/ ADVERB
1 used after verbs like *be* and *do* and modal verbs to make negative sentences. It often becomes **n't** when it is added to verbs ▢ *I'm not going.* ▢ *They have not made a decision yet.* ▢ *It isn't fair.* ▢ *I can't hear you.* (**não**)
2 used to give the next words or phrase a negative meaning ▢ *I told her not to look.* ▢ *Not everyone was happy with the decision.* '*Are you ready?*' '*Not yet.*' ▢ '*Did it upset you?*' '*Not at all.*' ▢ *Let's not go there again.* (**não**)
3 used with verbs like *hope* and *suspect* or adverbs like *certainly* or *definitely* to make a negative reply ▢ '*Will you be much longer?*' '*I hope not.*' '*Can I borrow £5?*' '*Certainly not.*' (**não**)
4 or not used to express a negative possibility ▢ *I don't know if he'll be there or not.* (**ou não**)

> Note that **not** usually goes before a 'to infinitive'. It does not go between 'to' and the verb:
> ✓ *He told me **not to** be late*
> ✗ *He told me to not be late.*

notable /ˈnəʊtəbəl/ ADJECTIVE important and worth remembering ▢ *The most notable part of the evening was the music.* ▣ *The whole family were there, with one notable exception.* (**notável**)

note 227 **now**

note¹ /nəʊt/ NOUN [plural notes]
1 a short piece of writing to help you remember something ▫ I made a note of his phone number. □ I've got a note of all their names. (**nota**)
2 a short letter ▫ I wrote her a note to say how sorry I was. (**bilhete**)
3 notes information that you write down when you are reading a book, in a lesson, etc. ▫ There is a handout, so you don't need to take notes. (**anotações**)
4 a piece of paper money □ a five pound note. (**nota**)
5 a single musical sound or the written sign for it □ I can't reach the high notes. (**nota**)

note² /nəʊt/ VERB [notes, noting, noted]
to notice something or to pay attention to something □ + **that** I noted that she always wore red, and wondered why. □ We noted the absence of the prince. (**notar**)
♦ PHRASAL VERB **note something down** to write something down so that you will not forget it □ I noted down the train times.

notebook /ˈnəʊtbʊk/ NOUN [plural notebooks]
1 a small book that you use to write things down in (**caderno**)
2 a very small computer that you can carry around. A computing word. (**notebook**)

notepaper /ˈnəʊtpeɪpə(r)/ NOUN, NO PLURAL
plain paper that you use for writing letters on □ a sheet of headed notepaper (**papel de carta**)

nothing /ˈnʌθɪŋ/ PRONOUN
1 not anything □ There's nothing to eat. □ There's nothing wrong with me. □ He carried on as if nothing had happened. ▫ There was nothing else we could do. ▫ I've heard nothing but (= only) praise for her work. (**nada**)
2 for nothing (a) without being paid □ He mended my car for nothing. (b) with no successful result □ You mean we did all that work for nothing? (**de graça, para nada**)
3 nothing like not at all similar □ He's nothing like his brother. (**nada parecido**)

> Remember that **nothing** is not used with other negative words, such as 'not' and 'never':
> ✓ She said nothing.
> ✗ She didn't say nothing. □ She didn't say anything.

notice¹ /ˈnəʊtɪs/ VERB [notices, noticing, noticed]
to become aware of something because you see, hear, feel, smell or taste it □ I noticed a funny smell in the hall. □ Did you notice the way George was looking at Emily? □ + **that** I noticed that the kitchen window was open. □ + **question word** He noticed how she kept checking her mobile. (**notar**)

> Note that the verb **notice** is *not* used with the verbs 'can' and 'could':
> ✓ I noticed that she was thinner.
> ✗ I could notice that she was thinner.

notice² /ˈnəʊtɪs/ NOUN [plural notices]
1 a written sign □ a notice pinned on the board □ A notice on the door said 'Closed'. □ The council has put up warning notices next to the river. (**aviso**)
2 no plural attention ▫ No one took any notice of (= paid attention to) her. (**atenção**)

noticeable /ˈnəʊtɪsəbəl/ ADJECTIVE
obvious or easy to see □ There was a noticeable difference in his appearance. □ The most noticeable feature was the smell. (**visível**)

notify /ˈnəʊtɪfaɪ/ VERB [notifies, notifying, notified]
to officially tell someone about something □ You will be notified of the date. (**notificar**)

notion /ˈnəʊʃən/ NOUN [plural notions]
an idea or a belief □ This goes against the whole notion of free speech. (**opinião**)

notorious /nəʊˈtɔːriəs/ ADJECTIVE
famous for something bad □ a notorious criminal (**notório**)

noun /naʊn/ NOUN [plural nouns]
a word that refers to a person, a thing, or a quality. For example, *tree*, *Sue*, *air* and *happiness* are nouns. (**nome, substantivo**)

novel /ˈnɒvəl/ NOUN [plural novels]
a book that tells an invented story □ a historical/romantic novel (**romance**)

> THESAURUS: **Book** is a general word for pages joined together inside a cover. A **story** or a **tale** is a description of events, which can be real or invented. **Stories** and **tales** can be spoken or written. For example, 'Cinderella' is a **story**. A novel is a book that tells an invented story. For example, 'War and Peace' is a novel.

novelist /ˈnɒvəlɪst/ NOUN [plural novelists]
a person who writes books that tell an invented story (**romancista**)

November /nəʊˈvembə(r)/ NOUN [plural Novembers]
the eleventh month of the year, after October and before December □ What's the weather like in November? (**novembro**)

now /naʊ/ ADVERB
1 at the present time □ It is now five o'clock. □ I'm working as a teacher now. ▫ He has refused to speak until now. (**agora**)
2 from this moment □ Now I can see him. □ You can look at the answers now. ▫ From now on, I'll be giving you homework every day. □ Now I can afford to go on holiday. (**agora**)
3 immediately □ I'll do it now. ▫ I want to see you in my office right now! (**agora**)
4 used to start a sentence □ Now, can anyone tell me the last two kings of England? (**agora**)
5 (every) now and then sometimes, but not often □ Every now and then I treat myself to a really hot curry. (**de vez em quando**)

nowadays

6 just now a very short time ago □ *I saw Jim outside just now.* (agora mesmo)

nowadays /ˈnaʊəˌdeɪz/ ADVERB
at the present time, usually when compared to the past □ *Nowadays, women usually have their babies in hospital.* □ *There's much more for youngsters to do nowadays than there was 20 years ago.* (atualmente)

nowhere /ˈnəʊweə(r)/ ADVERB
1 not anywhere □ *We've got nowhere to go.* ▣ *These birds are found nowhere else in the world.* (em nenhum lugar)
2 nowhere near not at all close in distance, time or a quality □ *Paris is nowhere near Marseilles.* □ *The stadium was nowhere near full.* (nem de longe)

nuclear /ˈnjuːklɪə(r)/ ADJECTIVE
to do with the reaction that happens when atoms are divided or forced together ▣ *nuclear power* ▣ *a nuclear bomb* (nuclear)

nucleus /ˈnjuːklɪəs/ NOUN [*plural* **nuclei**] the central or most important part of something □ *The nucleus of the cell performs several important functions.* □ *The nucleus of the team hasn't changed.* (núcleo)

nude /njuːd/ ADJECTIVE not wearing any clothes □ *a nude woman* (nu)

nuisance /ˈnjuːsəns/ NOUN [*plural* **nuisances**] a person, thing or situation that annoys you or causes problems for you □ *The rabbits have become a nuisance to local gardeners.* ▣ *'I've locked myself out.' 'Oh, what a nuisance!'* (amolação)

numb /nʌm/ ADJECTIVE [**number, numbest**] if a part of your body is numb, you cannot feel it ▣ *I was so cold my hands had gone completely numb.* (dormente)

number¹ /ˈnʌmbə(r)/ NOUN [*plural* **numbers**]
1 a word or symbol showing how many of something there are or in what position something is in a series □ *the number four* □ *Please write down any three figure number.* □ *I was number eight on the list.* (número)
2 a quantity of things or people □ **+ of** *We hope to increase the number of customers.* ▣ *He keeps a large number of animals.* □ *A number of* (= several) *people have complained.* (número)
3 a number that represents something or someone, for example to show what they are or who they belong to □ *a membership number* □ *What is your account number?* (número)
4 a telephone number □ *I'll give you my number.* ▣ *I must have dialled the wrong number.* (número)

► **THESAURUS:** Number is a general word for a word or a symbol showing how many of something there are or in what position something is in a series. Figure is often used to refer to a number that tells you an amount, especially in official documents. For example, you can talk about unemployment figures (how many people are unemployed). A unit is a measure used to show an amount or level. For example, you can say that a centimetre is a unit of length.

number² /ˈnʌmbə(r)/ VERB [**numbers, numbering, numbered**]
to give a thing or a person a number as part of a series □ *The boxes are all clearly numbered.* □ *Have you numbered the pages?* (numerar)

numerous /ˈnjuːmərəs/ ADJECTIVE many □ *Numerous people have had the same experience.* ▣ *I've met him on numerous occasions.* (numeroso)
nun /nʌn/ NOUN [*plural* **nuns**] a member of a religious group of women who live away from other people (freira)

nurse¹ /nɜːs/ NOUN [*plural* **nurses**]
a person whose job is to look after people when they are ill or injured, especially in a hospital □ *She works as a nurse at the hospital.* (enfermeiro)

nurse² /nɜːs/ VERB [**nurses, nursing, nursed**]
to look after someone when they are ill or injured □ *He had nursed her back to health over several weeks.* (cuidar)

nursery /ˈnɜːsəri/ NOUN [*plural* **nurseries**]
1 a place where babies and young children are looked after while their parents are at work □ *Lizzie goes to a local nursery three days a week.* (creche)
2 a place where plants are grown and sold (viveiro)
nursing /ˈnɜːsɪŋ/ NOUN, NO PLURAL the job of being a nurse (enfermagem)

nut /nʌt/ NOUN [*plural* **nuts**]
1 the fruit of some trees that has a hard shell and an inside part that can often be eaten □ *a cashew nut* □ *a bag of mixed nuts* (noz)
2 a small piece of metal with a hole in the middle which fits onto the end of a bolt (= thin piece of metal) to hold things together □ *a wheel nut* (porca)

nutrient /ˈnjuːtriənt/ NOUN [*plural* **nutrients**] any substance in food that gives you energy and makes you healthy □ *Iron is an essential nutrient for many animals.* (nutriente)
nutrition /njuːˈtrɪʃən/ NOUN, NO PLURAL food and the way it affects your health □ *Good nutrition is necessary for a quick recovery.* □ *information about nutrition* (nutrição)

Oo

O or **o** /əʊ/ the 15th letter of the alphabet (**a décima quinta letra do alfabeto**)

oak /əʊk/ NOUN [plural **oaks**] a large tree with hard wood, or the wood from this tree (**carvalho**)

oasis /əʊˈeɪsɪs/ NOUN [plural **oases**] a place in a desert where there are plants and water (**oásis**)

oath /əʊθ/ NOUN [plural **oaths**] a formal promise ▣ Members *swear an oath* of secrecy about the group. (**juramento**)

obese /əʊˈbiːs/ ADJECTIVE extremely fat (**obeso**)

obey /əˈbeɪ/ VERB [obeys, obeying, obeyed] to do what a person or rule tells you to do ▢ He was taught to obey his parents. ▣ Drivers must *obey the law*. ▣ He *refused to obey* a court order. (**obedecer**)

object¹ /ˈɒbdʒɪkt/ NOUN [plural **objects**]
1 a thing that you can see or touch but not a person or animal ▢ There were various objects on the table. ▢ Keep sharp objects away from children. (**objeto**)
2 an aim or purpose ▢ His main object in life was to become rich. ▢ *+ of* The object of the exercise is to improve teaching standards. (**objetivo**)
3 in grammar, the person or thing that a verb affects ▢ In the sentence 'I ate the apple', 'apple' is the object. (**objeto**)

object² /əbˈdʒekt/ VERB [objects, objecting, objected] to say that you do not want something to happen ▢ Nobody objected to the original proposal. (**objetar**)

objection /əbˈdʒekʃən/ NOUN [plural **objections**] a reason you do not want something to happen ▢ My only objection is that he is too young. ▣ I *have no objections* to the changes. (**objeção**)

obligation /ˌɒblɪˈɡeɪʃən/ NOUN [plural **obligations**] a duty to do something ▣ Schools have a *legal obligation* to take good care of students. (**obrigação**)

observation /ˌɒbzəˈveɪʃən/ NOUN [plural **observations**] when you watch someone or something very carefully ▢ He has been kept in hospital for observation. (**observação**)

observe /əbˈzɜːv/ VERB [observes, observing, observed] to watch someone or something very carefully ▢ Police continued to observe his actions with interest. (**observar**)

obstacle /ˈɒbstəkəl/ NOUN [plural **obstacles**]
1 something that stops you from doing what you want to do ▢ He had overcome a lot of obstacles in his life. (**obstáculo**)
2 an object that is in front of you and that you must move or go around in order to go forward (**obstáculo**)

obstruct /əbˈstrʌkt/ VERB [obstructs, obstructing, obstructed]
1 to block somewhere such as a road, door or path, so that people cannot move along or through it ▢ The road was obstructed by a fallen tree. (**obstruir**)
2 to try to prevent something from happening ▢ He was arrested for obstructing the police investigation. (**obstruir**)

obtain /əbˈteɪn/ VERB [obtains, obtaining, obtained] a formal word meaning to get something ▢ Clients can obtain information from our website. (**obter**)

> Note that the word **obtain** is used mainly in formal situations and is not common. The usual word is **get**:
> ✓ Where did you get your jacket?
> ✗ Where did you obtain your jacket?

obvious /ˈɒbviəs/ ADJECTIVE easy to see or understand ▢ *+ that* It was obvious that she was unhappy. ▣ He started crying for no *obvious reason*. ▢ *+ to* It was obvious to anyone in the room that he was lying. (**óbvio**)

obviously /ˈɒbviəsli/ ADVERB used for giving information that you expect other people will already know or will agree with ▢ Obviously, I'll need some help. ▢ Obviously we're not happy with this situation. (**obviamente**)

occasion /əˈkeɪʒən/ NOUN [plural **occasions**]
1 a particular time when something happens ▢ I've met him on several occasions. ▣ He has run in the race on three previous occasions. (**ocasião**)
2 an important event ▣ She only wore the shoes for *special occasions*. (**ocasião**)

occasional /əˈkeɪʒənəl/ ADJECTIVE happening sometimes but not often ▢ They made occasional visits to Scotland. ▣ Eating *the occasional* ice cream won't make you fat. (**ocasional, eventual**)

• **occasionally** /əˈkeɪʒənəli/ ADVERB sometimes but not often ▢ I occasionally go to the theatre. (**ocasionalmente**)

occupation /ˌɒkjʊˈpeɪʃən/ NOUN [plural **occupations**]
1 a formal word meaning job ▢ Firefighting is a dangerous occupation. ▢ professional occupations (**ocupação, profissão**)
2 a formal word meaning something you like doing in your free time ▢ Reading is his favourite occupation. (**ocupação**)
3 *no plural* when an army enters a country or area

and takes control of it □ **+ of** *the Roman occupation of Britain* (ocupação)

occupy /'ɒkjupaɪ/ VERB [occupies, occupying, occupied]
1 to occupy a space is to fill it □ *A table occupied the centre of the room.* (ocupar)
2 if someone occupies a building, they live or work there □ *The building is occupied by several small companies.* (ocupar)
3 to keep someone busy □ *She has more than enough to occupy her.* □ *He occupied himself with the garden.* (ocupar)
4 to enter a country or area and take control of it with an army □ *Soldiers were occupying the town.* (ocupar)

occur /ə'kɜː(r)/ VERB [occurs, occurring, occurred] a formal word meaning to happen □ *The accident occurred last night.* (ocorrer)

◆ PHRASAL VERB **occur to someone** if something occurs to you, you suddenly think it □ *It never occurred to me that I should see a doctor about it.*

ocean /'əʊʃən/ NOUN [plural oceans] one of the 5 large areas of sea in the world □ *the Atlantic Ocean* (oceano)

> THESAURUS: Sea is the salt water that covers most of the Earth's surface. A sea is a large area of salt water. An ocean is one of the 5 large areas of sea in the world. A lake is a large area of fresh water with land all around it. A wave is a raised line of water that moves across the sea or other area of water. The tide is the regular rise and fall of the level of the sea.

o'clock /ə'klɒk/ ADVERB used after the numbers one to twelve to say what time of day it is □ *School starts at nine o'clock.* □ *'What time is it?' 'It's nearly 12 o'clock.'* (hora)

October /ɒk'təʊbə(r)/ NOUN [plural Octobers] the tenth month of the year, after September and before November □ *He retired in October.* (outubro)

odd /ɒd/ ADJECTIVE [odder, oddest]
1 strange □ *It seems an odd choice.* □ *He's very odd.* (estranho)
2 without the other one of a pair □ *an odd shoe* (avulso)
3 an odd number is a number that you cannot divide exactly by two □ *5 and 7 are odd numbers.* (ímpar)

of /ɒv/ PREPOSITION
1 used to show an amount or measurement □ *hundreds of people* □ *a pint of milk* □ *an increase of 13%* □ *I'm part of a team.* □ *I left home at the age of 16.* (de)
2 used to show which members of a group are affected or being talked about □ *I have some bananas, but none of them are ripe.* □ *Many of our members are over 60.* □ *All of the children will receive a present.* (de)
3 used to talk about the characteristics or qualities that someone or something has □ *Did you notice the size of their offices?* (de)
4 used after a noun to show a particular example of that thing □ *There have been several cases of cholera.* □ *I grew up in the town of Aylesbury.* □ *We worked together for a short period of time.* (de)
5 made from or caused by something □ *They constructed a building of ice.* □ *There was a large pile of newspapers in the corner.* □ *The whole house smelled of garlic.* □ *We could hear their shouts of joy.* □ *He died of hunger.* (de)
6 about something, showing something or to do with something □ *He told us stories of his adventures in India.* □ *I need a map of Berlin.* □ *I always carry a photograph of my children.* □ *You remind me of my sister.* □ *He was frightened of bees.* (de)
7 containing something □ *I gave her a box of chocolates.* □ *Would you like a glass of water?* □ *I read a book of his poems.* (de)
8 belonging to or experienced by someone or something □ *The furniture is the property of the school.* □ *I lost the lid of the box.* □ *We must consider the needs of the patients.* (de)
9 used to show the position of something or someone □ *We live just south of Edinburgh.* □ *I sat at the side of the bed.* □ *There is a large garden to the rear of the property.* (de)

off¹ /ɒf/ ADVERB, PREPOSITION
1 away from the top or surface of something □ *I took the book off the shelf.* □ *Keep off the grass.* □ *I'm trying to get the mud off my shoes.* □ *Make sure you don't fall off!* (distante)
2 no longer attached to something □ *The petals have all dropped off.* □ *Some tiles have come off the roof.* (fora, para fora)
3 away in distance, in time or from a place □ *We were drifting a few miles off the coast.* □ *The holiday seems a long way off.* □ *He walked off and left me.* (distante)
4 if you take clothes off, you stop wearing them □ *I took off my jacket.* □ *He had his shoes off.* (tirar a roupa)
5 out of a public vehicle □ *I got off the train in Padua.* □ *Take the number 7 bus and get off at the station.* (para fora)
6 not operating □ *I switched the heating off.* □ *Make sure your phones are off.* (desligar)
7 if a price has a particular amount off, it is reduced by that amount □ *All computer games are 20% off this week.* (desconto)
8 not at work or at school □ *Why don't you take the day off?* □ *She's off work today.* (de folga)
9 near to something, and usually connected to it □ *My office is off the main corridor.* □ *Our road is just off the main road.* (próximo de)

off² /ɒf/ ADJECTIVE if food is off, it is rotten and cannot be eaten □ *This milk is off.* (estragado)

offence /ə'fens/ NOUN [plural offences]
1 a crime □ *The police charged him with three offences.* 🔁 *He has committed several violent offences.* 🔁 *Burning the flag is a criminal offence in some countries.* (transgressão)

offend

2 no plural when you upset someone by saying or doing something ▫ *His comments certainly caused offence.* ▫ *Philip took offence* (= felt offended) *at the suggestion.* (ofensa)

offend /əˈfend/ VERB [offends, offending, offended] to make someone feel upset or angry by something you say or do ▫ *I hope I didn't offend anyone.* (ofender)

offense /əˈfens/ NOUN [plural offenses] the US spelling of offence (transgressão)

offensive /əˈfensɪv/ ADJECTIVE rude and insulting ▫ *offensive remarks* ▫ *He found the question deeply offensive.* (ofensivo)

offer¹ /ˈɒfə(r)/ VERB [offers, offering, offered]
1 to ask someone if they want something ▫ *She offered me another drink.* ▫ **+ to** *He offered the sweets to all the children in the class.* (oferecer)
2 to say that you will do something for someone ▫ **+ to do something** *She offered to carry my bag for me.* (oferecer[-se])

offer² /ˈɒfə(r)/ NOUN [plural offers]
1 when you ask someone if they want something or if you can do something for them ▫ *It was a very generous offer.* ▫ *I've had several job offers.* ▫ *She accepted his offer to drive her home.* ▫ **+ of** *an offer of help* (oferta, proposta)
2 an amount of money offered ▫ *They made an offer of £300,000 for the house.* (oferta)
3 on offer being sold at a lower price than usual ▫ *These chocolates were on offer.* (em oferta)

office /ˈɒfɪs/ NOUN [plural offices]
1 a building where people work for a company ▫ *Our head office* (= main office) *is in London.* ▫ *an office building* ▫ *office workers* (escritório)
2 a room or building used for a particular purpose ▫ *the tourist information office* ▫ *The ticket office opens at 8 o'clock.* ▫ *The manager is in her office.* (gabinete)

officer /ˈɒfɪsə(r)/ NOUN [plural officers]
1 a person in the army, navy or air force who is in charge of ordinary soldiers ▫ *senior army officers* (oficial)
2 someone who has a particular job in a government or organization ▫ *a prison officer* ▫ *immigration officers* ▫ *He's the chief executive officer of the company.* (funcionário)

official¹ /əˈfɪʃəl/ ADJECTIVE done or approved by a government or someone in authority ▫ *an official announcement* ▫ *Canada has two official languages.* ▫ *Official figures show that crime has risen by 10%.* (oficial)

▸ **THESAURUS:** Something which is **official** has been done or approved by a government or someone in authority. Something that is **proper** is correct and suitable. For example, you can talk about the **proper** equipment for a job. Something that is **legal** is permitted by law.

official² /əˈfɪʃəl/ NOUN [plural officials] someone who has an important job in an organization, especially a government ▫ *government officials* (funcionário graduado)

officially /əˈfɪʃəli/ ADVERB publicly and formally ▫ *The new library is now officially open.* ▫ *He will officially retire next week.* (oficialmente)

often /ˈɒfən, ˈɒftən/ ADVERB
1 many times ▫ *I often go to the cinema.* ▫ *I don't play tennis very often now.* ▫ *How often do you see Jess?* ▫ *I wish I could travel more often.* ▫ *He visits the area quite often.* (com frequência)
2 in many situations or cases ▫ *Jokes are often difficult to translate.* ▫ *Often, schools are unable to deal with problem students.* (com frequência)

oh /əʊ/ EXCLAMATION
1 used when you have just understood something ▫ *Oh, I see.* ▫ *Oh, so that's why she isn't here.* (oh)
2 used when you are disappointed or annoyed ▫ *Oh, that's a shame!* ▫ *Oh no, the computer has just crashed!* (oh)
3 used when you are very pleased or surprised ▫ *Oh, that's very kind!* ▫ *Oh, that's fantastic!* (oh)

oil¹ /ɔɪl/ NOUN, NO PLURAL
1 a thick, dark liquid under the ground that is used for making petrol ▫ *Oil prices have increased.* ▫ *the oil industry* ▫ *US oil production* (óleo)
2 a thick liquid from plants or animals, used in cooking ▫ *olive oil* ▫ *vegetable oil* ▫ *Heat the oil in a pan and fry the onions until soft.* (óleo)

oil² /ɔɪl/ VERB [oils, oiling, oiled] to put oil on something (lubrificar, olear)

oily /ˈɔɪli/ ADJECTIVE [oilier, oiliest] like oil, or covered with oil ▫ *an oily liquid* ▫ *an oily cloth* (oleoso)

OK¹ or **okay** /əʊˈkeɪ/ EXCLAMATION
1 an informal way of agreeing or asking someone if they agree ▫ *'I'll come over after work.' 'OK'.* ▫ *OK! I'll do it!* ▫ *You need to do your homework before Friday, OK?* (tudo bem)
2 used before you start talking, especially to many people ▫ *OK, first of all I'd like to welcome you all to the school.* (tudo bem)

OK² or **okay** /əʊˈkeɪ/ ADJECTIVE, ADVERB
1 an informal word meaning allowed or acceptable ▫ *Is it OK if I get there a bit later?* ▫ *I'm really sorry I forgot your birthday.' 'That's OK.'* ▫ **+ to do something** *Is it OK to open the window?* (tudo bem)
2 an informal word meaning healthy and happy ▫ *'How are you?' 'I'm OK, thanks.'* ▫ *Are you feeling OK now?* (bem)
3 an informal word meaning good enough ▫ *Do I look OK in this dress?* ▫ *I think I did OK in the exam.* (bem)

old /əʊld/ ADJECTIVE [older, oldest]
1 used to talk about someone's age ▫ *How old are you?* ▫ *He's nine years old.* (velho)

2 having lived or existed for a long time ◨ *an old man/woman* ◻ *an old church* ◻ *She's not old enough to vote.* ◻ *I'm too old to go out all night.* ◻ *My older brother* (= older than me) *is a builder.* **(velho)**
3 having been owned or used for a long time ◻ *I wore a pair of old shoes.* **(velho)**
4 used to talk about something or someone from a time before now ◻ *My old car didn't have air conditioning.* ◻ *The old road went through the town centre.* ◻ *I saw one of my old teachers yesterday.* **(antigo)**
5 an old friend someone who has been your friend for a long time **(velho amigo)**

old age /ˌəʊld ˈeɪdʒ/ NOUN, NO PLURAL the time when someone is old ◻ *He wrote poems in his old age.* **(velhice)**

old-fashioned /ˌəʊld ˈfæʃənd/ ADJECTIVE not modern or fashionable ◻ *old-fashioned clothes* ◻ *His ideas are very old-fashioned.* ◻ *He contacted her in the old-fashioned way, by writing a letter.* **(fora de moda)**

olive /ˈɒlɪv/ NOUN [plural **olives**] a small black or green fruit that is not sweet. It is eaten and is used to make oil for cooking. **(oliva, azeitona)**

Olympic Games /əˌlɪmpɪk ˈɡeɪmz/ or **Olympics** /əˈlɪmpɪks/ PLURAL NOUN **the Olympic Games/the Olympics** the international sports competition that takes place every four years in a different country **(jogos olímpicos)**

omelet /ˈɒmlɪt/ NOUN [plural **omelets**] the US spelling of **omelette (omelete)**

omelette /ˈɒmlɪt/ NOUN [plural **omelettes**] a food made by mixing eggs and frying them, often with other food inside ◻ *a cheese omelette* **(omelete)**

omit /əˈmɪt/ VERB [**omits, omitting, omitted**] to not include something ◻ *This detail was omitted from the documents.* **(omitir)**

on¹ /ɒn/ PREPOSITION

1 touching or supported by the top surface of something ◻ *The books are on the table.* ◻ *We built our house on a hill.* ◻ *I was standing on one leg.* **(sobre)**
2 onto something ◻ *Rain was falling on the crowd.* ◻ *I jumped on the bike.* **(em)**
3 sticking to or hanging from something ◻ *There were lots of pictures on the walls.* ◻ *Put your coat on the peg.* **(em)**
4 used to say what day or date something happens ◻ *He's coming to see us on Friday.* **(em)**
5 about ◻ *He gave me a book on Scottish history.* ◻ *I can't comment on her views.* **(sobre)**
6 using a particular form of transport ◻ *I came on the bus.* **(em)**
7 being performed or broadcast ◻ *The programme will be on TV next week.* **(em)**
8 used to say how much time or money you use for a particular thing ◻ *We spent £300 on flowers.* **(em)**
9 as a result of touching or hitting something ◻ *I tripped on a loose stone.* ◻ *She hit her head on the shelf.* **(em)**
10 using a particular machine or piece of equipment ◻ *He's on the phone at the moment.* ◻ *The letter was written on a typewriter.* **(em)**

on² /ɒn/ ADVERB

1 if you have a piece of clothing on, you are wearing it ◻ *Put your coat on.* **(em)**
2 if a machine or a piece of equipment is on, it is working or being used ◻ *Switch the light on.* ◻ *Shall we have the heating on?* **(ligado)**
3 used to show that an action continues ◻ *We worked on into the night.* ◻ *We all became bored as he droned on about football.* **(continuidade de uma ação)**
4 onto a vehicle ◻ *I got on at Cambridge station.* **(em)**
5 being performed or broadcast ◻ *What's on at the cinema?* **(passando [tv, cinema, etc.])**
6 going to take place ◻ *Is the party still on?*
7 forward ◻ *They moved on.* ◻ *We went on until we came to a river.* **(adiante)**
8 on and on continuing for a long time ◻ *The speeches went on and on.* **(sem parar)**

once¹ /wʌns/ ADVERB

1 one time only ◻ *He only did it once.* ◻ *It's the kind of opportunity you get once in your life.* ◻ *I only met him once.* **(uma vez)**
2 once a/every one time in every period of time ◻ *I wash my car once a week.* ◻ *We meet about once every four or five months.* **(uma vez)**
3 at a time in the past ◻ *People once lived in caves.* ◻ *They once owned the whole town.* ◻ *I was a communist once.* **(outrora)**
4 once again/more again, or one more time ◻ *I found myself alone once more.* ◻ *He is once again in prison.* ◻ *Basic errors have once again cost lives.* **(mais uma vez)**
5 at once (a) immediately ◻ *Miss Peters wants to see you at once.* (b) at the same time ◻ *I can't do two things at once.* **(imediatamente)**
6 once or twice a few times ◻ *I've met him once or twice.* **(algumas vezes)**

once² /wʌns/ CONJUNCTION as soon as ◻ *Once you've finished, you can go.* ◻ *Once I started getting into debt, I was always anxious.* **(uma vez que)**

one¹ /wʌn/ NUMBER [plural **ones**] the number 1 **(um)**

one² /wʌn/ DETERMINER

1 used to talk about one particular person or thing ◻ *We've only had one reply.* ◻ *+ of One of my friends came round.* ◨ *One or two of the apples were rotten.* **(um)**
2 one day/evening, etc. on a day/evening, etc. in the future that has not been decided ◻ *We must meet up for lunch one day.* **(um dia, uma noite etc.)**

one³ /wʌn/ PRONOUN [plural **ones**]

1 used to avoid repeating a word ◻ *These plums are delicious – would you like one?* ◻ *My fridge broke and I had to buy a new one.* ◻ *Our house is one of the ones with a yellow door.* **(um, aquele)**
2 a formal word meaning anyone or you ◻ *One can see the sea from here.* **(alguém)**

oneself

3 one another each other □ *They embraced one another.* □ *They have great respect for one another.* (um ao outro)
4 one by one one after the other □ *One by one, people began to get up and leave.* (um por um)

oneself /wʌnˈself/ PRONOUN the reflexive form of 'one' used for talking about yourself or people in general. A formal word □ *One can lie to oneself as well as to other people.* (si, si mesmo)

one-way /ˌwʌnˈweɪ/ ADJECTIVE
1 allowing cars to travel in one direction only 🔁 *It was a narrow one-way street.* 🔁 *The town had a very complicated one-way system.* (de mão única)
2 a one-way ticket, price, etc. is for travelling to a place but not coming back □ *The airline is offering one-way fares to Paris for £25.* (único, bilhete de ida)

onion /ˈʌnjən/ NOUN [plural **onions**] a round vegetable with many layers that makes your eyes hurt when you cut it □ *Fry the onions until they are soft.* □ *onion soup* (cebola)

online /ˌɒnˈlaɪn/ ADJECTIVE, ADVERB using the Internet □ *online advertising* □ *online videos* 🔁 *Younger people are more likely to go online for the news.* 🔁 *Many people now shop online.* (on-line)

only¹ /ˈəʊnli/ ADVERB
1 used to emphasize how small an amount, number, etc. is □ *There are only two weeks left.* □ *Only one of us can win.* □ *She left the job after only a week.* □ *This is only the beginning.* (apenas, somente)
2 nobody or nothing else □ *Only you can do it.* □ *I only use the best quality ingredients.* □ *She would only say that she was disappointed.* (apenas)
3 used to say that something is not important or not intended to be harmful □ *'What's that noise?' 'Oh, it's only the children.'* □ *I was only trying to help.* (apenas)
4 only just (a) a very short time ago □ *I've only just finished my essay.* (b) by a very small amount □ *He only just beat me.* (acabar de/só)

only² /ˈəʊnli/ CONJUNCTION used to say that something cannot happen or is not true □ *I'd like to come, only I have to work.* (só que)

only³ /ˈəʊnli/ ADJECTIVE without any others of the same type □ *It was the only book on keeping goats that I could find.* □ *His only son was killed in the war.* 🔁 *She was an only child* (= had no brothers or sisters). (único)

onto /ˈɒntuː/ PREPOSITION used for showing movement into a position in or on something □ *I climbed onto the roof.* □ *Jim got onto the bus.* □ *The dog rolled onto its side.* (para)

open¹ /ˈəʊpən/ ADJECTIVE
1 not shut or fastened 🔁 *The window was wide open.* □ *An open book lay on the table.* □ *The door burst open and Ella ran in.* □ *His eyes were open and he was still breathing.* (aberto, bem aberto)
2 available to be visited or used □ *We are open from 9–5.* □ *Is the restaurant open on Mondays?* □ *The new road will be open in June.* (aberto)
3 not covered, surrounded or blocked 🔁 *She had a love of open spaces.* □ *He had an open wound on his leg.* □ *The Oxford road is open again.* (aberto)
4 if a computer program or document is open, it is ready to be used. A computing word. (aberto)
5 honest and not keeping secrets □ *He was very open with me about his work.* □ *We would like to see a more open style of government.* (aberto)

> **THESAURUS:** Open is a general word. If you open something that is locked, for example a door, you can use the word **unlock**. If you open something that is fastened, you can use the words **undo** or **unfasten**. For example, you can **undo** a coat. If you open something that is folded, you can use the word **unfold**. For example, you can **unfold** a map or a T-shirt.

open² /ˈəʊpən/ ADJECTIVE
1 to move to a position that is not shut or fastened, or to make something do this □ *He opened the door.* □ *I opened my eyes.* □ *Open your books on page 34.* (abrir)
2 to remove the cover from a package, letter, etc. □ *I opened my birthday presents this morning.* □ *Have you opened the letter from the bank yet?* (abrir)
3 to become available to be visited or used, or to make something available to be visited or used □ *The new supermarket opened last week.* □ *They will be opening the new road in December.* □ *What time does the surgery open on Sundays?* □ *We don't open on Sundays.* (abrir[-se])
4 to make a computer program or document ready to use. A computing word. □ *Open the spreadsheet and click at the top of the column.* (abrir)
5 to begin something □ *He opened the meeting with a speech of welcome.* □ *Police have opened an enquiry into the shooting.* (abrir)
6 if you open a bank account, you make an arrangement with a bank to keep your money there (abrir)

opener /ˈəʊpənə(r)/ NOUN [plural **openers**] something that opens a container such as a bottle or a can □ *a tin opener* (abridor)

opening¹ /ˈəʊpənɪŋ/ NOUN [plural **openings**]
1 a hole or space □ *There was an opening in the fence.* (abertura)
2 an event to mark the start of a place, building, etc. being available to visit or use □ *We all went to the opening of the new museum.* (abertura)

opening² /ˈəʊpənɪŋ/ ADJECTIVE happening at the beginning of something 🔁 *I'd like to make a few* *opening remarks.* □ *The opening chapter is rather technical.* (abertura)

opera /ˈɒpərə/ NOUN [plural **operas**] a musical play in which the words are sung □ *an opera singer* (ópera)

operate /ˈɒpəreɪt/ VERB [**operates, operating, operated**]
1 if machinery or equipment operates, it works, and if you operate it, you make it work □ *The radio operates on batteries.* □ *My job was to operate the switch board.* (funcionar)
2 to cut into someone's body to repair or remove a part when someone is ill □ **+ on** *They operated on the boy to save his sight.* (operar)

operation /ˌɒpəˈreɪʃən/ NOUN [plural **operations**]
1 when a doctor cuts into someone's body in order to repair or remove part of it 🔁 *He has to have an operation on his heart.* 🔁 *a minor operation* (operação)
2 a carefully planned and organized action □ *a rescue operation* □ *It was a joint operation between British and Spanish troops.* (operação)

operator /ˈɒpəreɪtə(r)/ NOUN [plural **operators**]
1 someone whose job is to work a machine □ *a lift operator* (operador)
2 someone whose job is to connect telephone calls □ *Ask the operator to put you through to his extension.* (telefonista)
3 a person or company that does a particular type of business □ *a tour operator* (operador)

opinion /əˈpɪnjən/ NOUN [plural **opinions**] what you think or believe □ **+ of** *What's your opinion of the new arts centre?* □ **+ about** *My opinions about education have changed.* 🔁 *She has strong opinions about the war.* 🔁 *In my opinion, you did the right thing.* 🔁 *She didn't give* (= say) *her opinion of the film.* 🔁 *I have a very high/low* (= good/bad) *opinion of most of my colleagues.* (opinião)

> Note that you **give** (or **express**) an opinion. You do not 'say' an opinion:
> ✓ *Did she give her opinion of Claudia's work?*
> ✗ *Did she say her opinion of Claudia's work?*

opponent /əˈpəʊnənt/ NOUN [plural **opponents**] someone you compete against in a game or a competition □ *He beat his opponent by four points.* (adversário)

opportunity /ˌɒpəˈtjuːnəti/ NOUN [plural **opportunities**] a chance to do something or a situation when you can do something □ *She saw the trip as the opportunity of a lifetime.* □ **+ for** *There will be an opportunity for questions later.* □ **+ to do something** *I had the opportunity to travel a lot in Europe.* 🔁 *I took the opportunity to speak to the senator in private.* (oportunidade)

> THESAURUS: **Chance** is a general word to talk about things that might happen or when it is possible for you to do something that you want to do. An **opportunity** is a chance to do something or a situation when you can do something. You can say that you have a **chance** or an opportunity to go to America. A **possibility** is the chance that something might happen. For example, you can say that there is a **chance** or a **possibility** that it will rain.

oppose /əˈpəʊz/ VERB [**opposes, opposing, opposed**] to disagree with someone's ideas, plans or actions and try to change or stop them □ *Local people opposed the plan to expand the airport.* (opor-se)

opposite¹ /ˈɒpəzɪt/ ADJECTIVE
1 facing something or on the other side of something □ *The answers are on the opposite page.* □ *She lives on the opposite side of town.* (oposto)
2 completely different □ *Her remarks had the opposite effect to what she intended.* □ *They walked off in opposite directions.* (oposto, contrário)

opposite² /ˈɒpəzɪt/ NOUN [plural **opposites**] someone or something that is completely different from someone or something else □ *Hot is the opposite of cold.* □ *My sister and I are complete opposites.* (contrários)

optical /ˈɒptɪkəl/ ADJECTIVE to do with the eyes, sight or light □ *an optical instrument* (ótico)

optimism /ˈɒptɪmɪzəm/ NOUN, NO PLURAL when you believe that good things will happen □ *She was full of optimism about her new job.* (otimismo)

optimistic /ˌɒptɪˈmɪstɪk/ ADJECTIVE hoping or believing that good things will happen □ *I'm not feeling very optimistic about this exam.* (otimista)

option /ˈɒpʃən/ NOUN [plural **options**] something that you can choose or decide to do □ *There are several options open to me.* □ *Is there a vegetarian option on the menu?* □ *Our only option was to accept his offer.* □ **+ of doing something** *We have the option of buying or leasing a car.* (opção, escolha)

> THESAURUS: An **option** or a **choice** is something that you can choose or decide to do. An **alternative** is another possibility or choice. For example, if you usually go to work by car, you need to find an **alternative** if your car breaks down. A **preference** is when you prefer one thing to another or the thing that you like or prefer.

optional /ˈɒpʃənəl/ ADJECTIVE if something is optional, you can have it or do it if you want to, but you do not have to □ *Music was an optional subject at my school.* 🔁 *The car has a lot of optional extras.* (opcional)

-or /-ə(r)/ SUFFIX another way of spelling **-er** (ver **-er**)

or /ə:(r)/ CONJUNCTION
1 used to show possibilities or choices □ *Would you prefer tea or coffee?* □ *We could see a film or go for a walk.* □ *Their little girl must be seven or eight.* □ *Shall we have pizza, pasta or risotto?* (ou)
2 used after a negative verb to say not any of a list of things or people □ *I don't like him or his sister.* (ou)
3 used for saying what will happen if something is not done □ *I'd better go or I'll miss the last bus.* (senão)

oral /ˈɔːrəl/ ADJECTIVE spoken, not written □ *an oral examination* (oral)

orange¹ /ˈɒrɪndʒ/ ADJECTIVE having the colour you get if you mix red and yellow □ *This bush has tiny orange flowers in summer.* (alaranjado)

orange² /ˈɒrɪndʒ/ NOUN [plural **oranges**]
1 a round fruit with orange skin and a lot of juice □ *orange juice* (laranja)
2 the colour you get if you mix red and yellow (laranja, alaranjado)

orbit¹ /ˈɔːbɪt/ NOUN [plural **orbits**] the circular path along which something moves around a sun, moon or planet □ *The spaceship is in orbit round the moon.* (órbita)

> **THESAURUS:** A **circle** is a flat shape whose outside edge is a continuous curved line which is always the same distance away from a central point. An **orbit** is the circular path along which something moves around a sun, moon or planet. A **circuit** is a path, route or track that forms a circle. A **cycle** is a series of things that happen one after the other and then start again.

orbit² /ˈɔːbɪt/ VERB [**orbits, orbiting, orbited**] to go round a sun, moon or planet □ *The spacecraft is orbiting Earth.* (descrever uma órbita)

orchard /ˈɔːtʃəd/ NOUN [plural **orchards**] an area of land where fruit trees are grown □ *a cherry orchard* (pomar)

orchestra /ˈɔːkɪstrə/ NOUN [plural **orchestras**] a large group of musicians playing together □ *a symphony orchestra* (orquestra)

ordeal /ɔːˈdiːl/ NOUN [plural **ordeals**] a very unpleasant experience □ *He spent ten years in prison, but survived the ordeal with great courage.* (provação)

order¹ /ˈɔːdə(r)/ NOUN [plural **orders**]
1 an instruction to do something 🔷 *The soldier was given the order to shoot.* 🔷 *I refuse to take orders from that man.* 🔷 *They obeyed the order to retreat.* (ordem)
2 when you ask for food or goods that you will pay for. 🔷 *The waiter came to take our order.* (pedido)
3 the way things are arranged 🔷 *The books are in alphabetical order of their authors.* □ *List the options in your order of preference.* (ordem)
4 a state where everything is tidy or in its correct state □ *I need to get my accounts in order.* (ordem)
5 **in order to do something** so that something can happen or be done □ *She took the money in order to buy food.* □ *I phoned him in order to arrange a meeting.* (para)
6 **out of order** not working correctly □ *The toilets are out of order today.* (enguiçado)

order² /ˈɔːdə(r)/ VERB [**orders, ordering, ordered**]
1 to tell someone to do something □ + **to do something** *The doctor ordered her to rest for a few days.* □ *The government has ordered an enquiry into the accident.* (ordenar)
2 to ask for food or goods that you will pay for □ *I ordered some magazines from the newsagent.* □ *I ordered the pizza.* (encomendar)
3 to arrange things in a particular way □ *I ordered the CDs according to the type of music.* (ordenar)

ordinary /ˈɔːdɪnri/ ADJECTIVE
1 normal and not unusual or different □ *It was just an ordinary Monday morning.* □ *Ordinary people don't buy designer clothes.* (comum)
2 **out of the ordinary** unusual or different from normal □ *Your tests show nothing out of the ordinary.* (excepcional)

organ /ˈɔːgən/ NOUN [plural **organs**]
1 a part of your body that has a special purpose □ *an organ donor* (= someone who lets their organs be used after they die) (órgão)
2 a large musical instrument with keys like a piano and several long pipes that air is pushed through, often found in churches □ *She played the organ at our wedding.* (órgão)

organic /ɔːˈgænɪk/ ADJECTIVE
1 organic food is produced without using chemicals □ *I only buy organic vegetables.* (orgânico)
2 found in or made by living things □ *organic fertilizers* (orgânico)

organism /ˈɔːgənɪzəm/ NOUN [plural **organisms**] any living thing, especially one that is very small. A biology word. □ *Samples of marine organisms were collected from the sea bed.* (organismo)

organization or **organisation** /ˌɔːgənaɪˈzeɪʃən/ NOUN [plural **organizations**]
1 a group of people who work together for a purpose □ *He's working for a voluntary organization that helps ex-prisoners.* (organização)
2 the activity of arranging or preparing for an event or an activity □ *The festival took months of organization.* (organização)
3 the way in which something is arranged or organized □ *Paul's essays show a lack of organization.* (organização)

organize or **organise** /ˈɔːgənaɪz/ VERB [**organizes, organizing, organized**]
1 to arrange and prepare an event or an activity □ *We've organized a surprise party for his birthday.* (organizar)
2 to make something tidy or to put something in order □ *He organized all the papers into neat piles.* (organizar)

organized or organised /ˈɔːɡənaɪzd/
ADJECTIVE
1 involving a group of people who plan and do something together □ *We went on an organized tour of the city.* (**organizado**)
2 an organized person is good at planning and arranging things □ *I'm just not very organized.* (**organizado**)

organizer or organiser /ˈɔːɡənaɪzə(r)/ NOUN
[plural **organizers**] someone who organizes an event or an activity □ *a conference organizer* (**organizador**)

origin /ˈɒrɪdʒɪn/ NOUN [plural **origins**]
1 the cause of something or place where something starts □ *There are many theories about the origin of our solar system.* □ *The English language contains many words of Anglo-Saxon origin.* (**origem**)
2 the country, race, class etc. that someone comes from □ *Her family are Italian in origin.* ▣ *Please state your ethnic origin on the form.* (**origem**)

original /əˈrɪdʒɪnəl/ ADJECTIVE
1 existing from the beginning, or not having been changed □ *The original story had been changed over the centuries.* □ *Our house still has the original fireplaces.* (**original**)
2 new and interesting, and not like others of its type □ *a novel full of original ideas* ▣ *Her paintings are highly original.* (**original**)
3 done by the artist himself or herself □ *He owns an original drawing by Picasso.* (**original**)

> **THESAURUS:** If something such as a painting is done by the artist himself or herself, you can say that it is original. If you say that a painting is **authentic** or **genuine**, you are emphasizing that it is real or true and not a copy.

originally /əˈrɪdʒɪnəli/ ADVERB
in the beginning □ *His family comes from Scotland originally.* □ *The building was originally used as a store.* (**originalmente**)

orphan /ˈɔːfən/ NOUN [plural **orphans**] a child whose parents are both dead (**órfão**)

orphanage /ˈɔːfənɪdʒ/ NOUN [plural **orphanages**] a home for children whose parents are both dead (**orfanato**)

other¹ /ˈʌðə(r)/ ADJECTIVE
1 used to talk about something or someone else of a similar type □ *Do you have any other news to tell me?* □ *I have lots of other questions.* ▣ *I prefer living with other people.* ▣ *There were lots of other things to do.* (**outro**)
2 different from the thing or person you have been talking about □ *There must be some other reason.* □ *Does this dress come in any other colours?* ▣ *I thought Kate would be taller than Jo, but it was the other way round* (= the opposite). (**outro**)
3 used to talk about the second of two things or people, when the first has already been mentioned □ *Where is my other glove?* □ *I live on the other side of town.* ▣ *This vase is Chinese, and the other one is Japanese.* (**outro**)
4 used to talk about the remaining people or things □ *The other team members will arrive tomorrow.* (**outro**)
5 the other day/week, etc. a few days/weeks, etc. ago □ *I saw Adam the other day.* (**outro**)

other² /ˈʌðə(r)/ PRONOUN
1 the second of two □ *Here's one sock, but where is the other?* (**outro**)
2 others things or people of a similar type □ *I really enjoyed that book. Do you have any others by her?* (**outros**)
3 the others the remaining people or things □ *I've found some of her letters, but where are the others?* □ *Wait for the others to arrive.* (**os demais**)

otherwise /ˈʌðəwaɪz/ ADVERB
1 used to say what will happen if something is not done or is not true □ *You need to get up, otherwise you'll be late.* □ *I hope it won't be cold. Otherwise we'll need to take coats.* (**senão**)
2 if the thing that has just been mentioned is not true □ *He must have seen the letter, otherwise how could he have known the truth?* (**senão**)
3 except for the thing that has just been mentioned □ *I've got a cold, but I'm fine otherwise.* □ *One person raised his hand. Otherwise, nobody moved.* (**em outros aspectos**)
4 different to what has been said □ *Unless I hear otherwise, I'll be there at ten.* □ *I thought the food was fine, but Des thought otherwise.* (**de outra maneira**)

ought /ɔːt/ MODAL VERB **ought to do something** (a) used to say what is the best or right thing to do □ *I think we ought to call the police.* □ *He ought to wear glasses.* (b) used to say that you expect something to be true □ *They ought to reach Berlin by tomorrow.* □ *Three loaves ought to be enough.* (**dever**)

oughtn't /ˈɔːtənt/ a short way to say and write ought not □ *You really oughtn't to see him again.* (**não dever**)

ounce /aʊns/ NOUN [plural **ounces**] a unit for measuring weight, equal to equal to 28.35 grams. This is often written **oz**. (**onça**)

our /aʊə(r)/ ADJECTIVE
belonging to or to do with us □ *That is our car.* (**nosso**)

ours /aʊəz/ PRONOUN
used to talk or write about things belonging to or to do with us □ *That car is ours.* □ *These books are ours.* (**nosso**)

ourselves /aʊəˈselvz/ PRONOUN
1 the reflexive form of **we** □ *We saw ourselves in the mirror.* □ *We should keep some of the money for ourselves.* (**nos**)
2 used to show that we do something without any help from other people □ *We painted the room ourselves.* ▣ *We built the house all by ourselves.* (**nós mesmos**)
3 used to emphasize the pronoun **we** □ *We ourselves played no part in this.* (**nós mesmos**)
4 by ourselves not with or near other people □ *They left us by ourselves in a cold room.* (**sozinhos**)

out /aʊt/ ADVERB, PREPOSITION
1 from inside a container, hole, vehicle, etc. ◻ *She opened her bag and took out an umbrella.* ◻ **+ of** *He got out of the car.* ◻ *I opened the cupboard and a bag of rice fell out.* **(fora)**
2 away from your home or work for a social activity **(fora)**
3 away from your home or work ◻ *I phoned, but you were out.* ◻ *Are you going out tonight?* ◻ *I was out with Gerry last night.* **(fora, sair)**
4 away from a building or place ◻ *I stood out in the garden.* ◻ **+ of** *She was dragged out of the room by armed guards.* ◻ *He is not allowed to go out of the country.* **(fora)**
5 if a fire or light is out, it is not shining ◻ *When we reached the house, all the lights were out.* **(apagado)**
6 out of used to say what something is made from ◻ *The shelter was made out of sticks.* **(de)**
7 two/six, etc. out of ten/a hundred, etc. used to say how many people or things in a group are involved in or affected by something **(entre)**

outbreak /'aʊtbreɪk/ NOUN [plural **outbreaks**] when something such as war or a disease starts ◻ *There's been a fresh outbreak of measles in the area.* **(deflagração)**
outburst /'aʊtbɜːst/ NOUN [plural **outbursts**] when someone suddenly says something that shows strong emotion, especially anger ◻ *Her outburst shocked her colleagues.* **(explosão)**
outcome /'aʊtkʌm/ NOUN [plural **outcomes**] the final result of something ◻ *What was the outcome of your discussion?* **(resultado)**

> **THESAURUS: Result** is a general word for what happens because of something else. An **outcome** is the final result of something. A **conclusion** is a decision that you make after thinking carefully about something, or the last part of something. For example, you can talk about the **conclusion** of an essay. An **effect** is what happens as a result of something else. For example, the **effect** of eating too much junk food is that you may become overweight or ill.

outdoor /'aʊtdɔː(r)/ ADJECTIVE happening or done outside or for use outside ◻ *an outdoor swimming pool* ◻ *outdoor shoes* **(de sair)**

outdoors /ˌaʊt'dɔːz/ ADVERB outside ◻ *She sat outdoors in the sun.* ◻ *Don't go outdoors if it's raining.* **(fora, ao ar livre)**

outer /'aʊtə(r)/ ADJECTIVE
1 on or near the outside of something ◻ *Peel off the outer layers of the onion.* **(exterior)**
2 furthest away from the centre ◻ *the outer suburbs of Paris* **(exterior)**

outfit /'aʊtfɪt/ NOUN [plural **outfits**] a set of clothes that are worn together ◻ *I've bought myself a new outfit for the wedding.* ◻ *Jake got a cowboy outfit for his birthday.* **(traje)**

outgoing /'aʊtgəʊɪŋ/ ADJECTIVE friendly and liking to talk to other people ◻ *Sally's quite a confident, outgoing girl.* **(sociável)**
outing /'aʊtɪŋ/ NOUN [plural **outings**] a short journey made for pleasure ◻ *I took the kids on an outing to the seaside.* **(saída, passeio)**
outline /'aʊtlaɪn/ NOUN [plural **outlines**] a line that shows the shape of something ◻ *First he drew the outline of a church seen against the sky.* **(contorno)**
outlook /'aʊtlʊk/ NOUN [plural **outlooks**] what experts think may happen in the future ◻ *The outlook for the economy is poor.* **(previsão)**
outrage /'aʊtreɪdʒ/ VERB [**outrages, outraging, outraged**] to make someone feel shocked and angry ◻ *Fay was outraged by his behaviour.* **(ultrajar)**
outrageous /aʊt'reɪdʒəs/ ADJECTIVE shocking or very unreasonable ◻ *His behaviour was absolutely outrageous.* ◻ *This restaurant charges outrageous prices.* **(abusivo)**

outside¹ /aʊt'saɪd/ ADVERB not inside a building ◻ *Let's eat outside.* ◻ *He went outside for a cigarette.* **(fora)**

outside² /aʊt'saɪd, 'aʊtsaɪd/ NOUN **the outside** the outer surface or part of something ◻ *The outside of the house was painted white.* ◻ *The cake was burnt on the outside.* **(exterior)**

outside³ /aʊt'saɪd/ PREPOSITION not inside a building, room or area, but near it ◻ *He was standing outside our house.* ◻ *I come from a small village just outside York.* **(fora de)**

outskirts /'aʊtskɜːts/ PLURAL NOUN **the outskirts** the outer parts of a town or city ◻ *He lives on the outskirts of Edinburgh.* **(arredores, periferia)**
outspoken /ˌaʊt'spəʊkən/ ADJECTIVE saying exactly what you mean, even if it upsets people ◻ *She is an outspoken critic of the government.* **(franco, sem papas na língua)**
outstanding /ˌaʊt'stændɪŋ/ ADJECTIVE excellent ◻ *an outstanding student* **(notável)**

oval¹ /'əʊvəl/ ADJECTIVE shaped like a circle with the edges pressed slightly together ◻ *an oval table* **(oval)**

oval² /'əʊvəl/ NOUN [plural **ovals**] an oval shape ◻ *He drew an oval.* **(oval)**

oven /'ʌvən/ NOUN [plural **ovens**] the part of a cooker that is shaped like a box with a door and is used for cooking and heating food ◻ *Bake the cake in the centre of the oven for 30 minutes.* **(forno)**

over¹ /'əʊvə(r)/ PREPOSITION
1 above someone or something, or moving across the place above someone or something ◻ *His photograph hung over the fireplace.* ◻ *An eagle flew right over our heads.* **(acima de)**
2 more than ◻ *He's over 90 years old.* ◻ *She left school just over three years ago.* **(acima de)**

3 across □ *We ran over the bridge.* (por)
4 covering something or someone □ *I put a blanket over her legs.* □ *There was snow over the hills.* ▣ *You've got mud all over your clothes.* (sobre)
5 on the other side of something □ *There is a house just over that hill.* □ *The sun set over the horizon.* □ *My house is just over the road.* (por cima de)

over² /ˌəʊvə(r)/ ADVERB

1 moving across the place above someone or something □ *An aeroplane flew over.* (sobre)
2 from one side to the other □ *That bridge isn't safe – I'm not going over.* (sobre)
3 higher in number or amount □ *Children aged seven and over may swim alone.* (mais)
4 onto the other side □ *The dog rolled over in the mud.* □ *Turn your papers over.* (ao contrário [virar])
5 to a particular place □ *He walked over to speak to them.* □ *Would you like to come over for lunch?* (do outro lado)
6 towards the side □ *Could you stand a bit further over to the right?* □ *I moved over to make room for him.* (para o lado)
7 remaining □ *There were two cakes left over.* (de sobra)
8 all over again again, from the beginning □ *My computer crashed, and I had to do my essay all over again.* (outra vez)
9 over and over again and again □ *I told her over and over again not to talk to strangers.* (repetidas vezes)

overall¹ /ˌəʊvərˈɔːl/ ADVERB considering or including everything or everyone □ *Overall, I'm very pleased with the film.* (no total)
overall² /ˈəʊvərɔːl/ NOUN [plural **overalls**]
1 a piece of clothing like a thin coat worn over ordinary clothes to protect them □ *She wears an overall when cleaning the house.* (avental)
2 overalls a piece of clothing that covers the legs and body, worn to protect clothing during dirty work (macacão)
overboard /ˈəʊvəbɔːd/ ADVERB over the side of a ship or boat and into the water □ *He jumped overboard to save the drowning man.* □ *Man overboard!* (ao mar, pela borda fora)
◆ IDIOM **go overboard** to do something too much, often because you are excited about something □ *I think you've gone a bit overboard with the decorations.*
overcame /ˌəʊvəˈkeɪm/ PAST TENSE OF **overcome** (ver overcome)
overcome /ˌəʊvəˈkʌm/ VERB [**overcomes, overcoming, overcame, overcome**] to manage to deal successfully with a problem □ *She has struggled to overcome her depression.* (superar)
overdose /ˈəʊvədəʊs/ NOUN [plural **overdoses**] more of a drug or medicine than is safe □ *an overdose of sleeping pills* (overdose)
overdue /ˌəʊvəˈdjuː/ ADJECTIVE if something is overdue, it should have happened, been done, been paid, etc. before now □ *Our library books are overdue.* (em atraso)
overhead /ˌəʊvəˈhed/ ADVERB, ADJECTIVE above your head or high above the ground □ *A plane was flying overhead.* □ *overhead cables* (aéreo)

overhear /ˌəʊvəˈhɪə(r)/ VERB [**overhears, overhearing, overheard**] to hear what someone says when they are not talking to you □ *I overheard them talking about me.* (ouvir por acaso)
overlook /ˌəʊvəˈlʊk/ VERB [**overlooks, overlooking, overlooked**]
1 to fail to notice or consider something □ *You have overlooked one important detail.* (omitir)
2 to have a view over a place □ *The house overlooks the river.* (contemplar de cima)

overnight /ˌəʊvəˈnaɪt/ ADJECTIVE, ADVERB for or during the night □ *an overnight train* □ *The centre provides overnight accommodation.* ▣ *We stayed overnight in London.* (noturno)

overtake /ˌəʊvəˈteɪk/ VERB [**overtakes, overtaking, overtook, overtaken**] to move past a vehicle that is travelling in the same direction □ *He overtook a police car.* (ultrapassar)

overthrow /ˌəʊvəˈθrəʊ/ VERB [**overthrows, overthrowing, overthrew, overthrown**] to take power away from a leader or a government by force □ *They are plotting to overthrow the current regime.* (derrubar)
overtime /ˈəʊvətaɪm/ NOUN, NO PLURAL extra time spent working in addition to your normal working hours ▣ *We had to work overtime to get everything finished.* (hora extra)
overturn /ˌəʊvəˈtɜːn/ VERB [**overturns, overturning, overturned**] to turn something upside down or to turn upside down □ *Chairs were overturned and glasses were broken.* □ *The bus overturned in wet conditions.* (virar, emborcar)
overweight /ˌəʊvəˈweɪt/ ADJECTIVE an overweight person is too heavy □ *I'm about four kilos overweight.* (acima do peso)
overwhelm /ˌəʊvəˈwelm/ VERB [**overwhelms, overwhelming, overwhelmed**] to have a very strong and sudden effect on someone □ *We were overwhelmed with joy.* (esmagar)
overwhelming /ˌəʊvəˈwelmɪŋ/ ADJECTIVE
1 very large or important □ *They won an overwhelming victory over their rivals.* ▣ *An overwhelming majority of workers voted to strike.* (esmagador)
2 overwhelming emotions and feelings are very strong □ *There's an overwhelming feeling of relief.* □ *The temptation was almost overwhelming.* (irresistível)

owe /əʊ/ VERB [**owes, owing, owed**]

1 to have to pay money to someone □ *I owe Val £10.* □ **+ to** *He owes money to suppliers.* (dever)
2 to have something only because of someone or something □ **+ to** *He owes his success to his family.* (dever)

owing to /ˈəʊɪŋ tə/ PREPOSITION because of □ *He withdrew from the competition owing to a back injury.* □ *The club closed down owing to lack of funding.* (devido a)
owl /aʊl/ NOUN [plural **owls**] a large bird that hunts at night (coruja)

own   239   **ozone**

own¹ /əʊn/ ADJECTIVE
belonging to or done by the person mentioned □ *I need to spend more time with my own family.* □ *The rules are for your own safety.* □ *Is this all your own work?* □ *I'd love to have a horse of my very own.* (**próprio**)

own² /əʊn/ PRONOUN
1 used to show that something belongs to someone or something □ *I lent him a pencil, because he forgot to bring his own.* □ *There are plenty of showers – each bedroom has its own.* (**próprio**)

2 on your own (a) without help from anyone else □ *He managed to finish the work on his own.* □ *Did you do this all on your own?* (b) alone □ *I live on my own in a small flat.* (**completamente só**)

3 of your own if someone or something has something of its own, it belongs only to them □ *I'd love a bedroom of my own.* □ *Each apartment has a small garden of its own.* (**próprio**)

◆ IDIOM **get your own back** to do something unpleasant to someone who has done something unpleasant to you.

own³ /əʊn/ VERB [owns, owning, owned]
you own something if it belongs to you, especially if you have bought it □ *I own a car.* □ *He doesn't own a single book.* (**possuir**)

◆ PHRASAL VERB **own up** to admit that you did something wrong □ *Nobody owned up to breaking the chair.*

owner /'əʊnə(r)/ NOUN [plural owners]
a person who owns something (**proprietário**)

ownership /'əʊnəʃɪp/ NOUN, NO PLURAL
when someone owns something □ *Home ownership has risen.* (**propriedade**)

oxygen /'ɒksɪdʒən/ NOUN, NO PLURAL
a gas that has no taste, colour or smell, and forms part of the air. A chemistry word. (**oxigênio**)

oyster /'ɔɪstə(r)/ NOUN [plural oysters] a type of sea creature in a shell that can be eaten (**ostra**)

ozone /'əʊzəʊn/ NOUN, NO PLURAL a form of oxygen with a strong smell. A chemistry word. (**ozônio**)

Pp

P *or* **p** /piː/ the 16th letter of the alphabet (**a décima sétima letra do alfabeto**)

p /piː/ ABBREVIATION **page** *or* **pence**

pace /peɪs/ NOUN [plural **paces**] the speed at which something happens or at which someone does some thing □ *the pace of change* □ *He was walking at a very slow pace.* (**ritmo**)

pack¹ /pæk/ VERB [packs, packing, packed]

1 to put things in a bag or case ready for a journey □ *She packed hurriedly and caught the next train.* □ *Ben packed his bag for the holiday.* □ *Make sure you pack your swimming costume.* (**empacotar**)
2 to put something into a box so it can be moved, sold or stored □ *She has a job packing chocolates in a factory.* □ **+ in** *The food was packed in brown paper bags.* □ **+ up** *They packed up all their furniture ready for the house move.* (**embalar**)
3 if people pack a place, a lot of them go there and fill it □ *Reporters packed the courtroom.* □ **+ into** *More then 15,000 fans packed into the sports stadium.* (**amontoar-se**)
♦ PHRASAL VERB **pack (something) up** to put things into bags or boxes so that they can be moved □ *He packed up his belongings and left.* □ *We decided to pack up and go home.*

pack² /pæk/ NOUN [plural packs]

1 a set of documents that have been put together 🔄 *All new students will receive an information pack.* □ *If you are interested in the job, you can download an application pack.* (**pacote**)
2 a set of products that are sold together □ **+ of** *I bought a pack of 6 cakes.* □ *a pack of chewing gum* (**pacote**)
3 a set of 52 cards that you play games with □ **+ of** *a pack of cards* (**baralho**)
4 a group of animals that live and hunt together □ **+ of** *a pack of wolves* (**bando, matilha**)
5 a group of similar people, especially people you do not like □ **+ of** *There was a pack of kids standing outside the shop.* (**bando, quadrilha**)

package /ˈpækɪdʒ/ NOUN [plural **packages**] something that has been wrapped in paper or put in a box, especially so it can be sent by post □ *He sent the package to his brother.* □ *Police will destroy any suspicious packages.* (**pacote**)

packed /pækt/ ADJECTIVE very crowded □ *The train was packed.* (**abarrotado**)

packet /ˈpækɪt/ NOUN [plural packets]
a box or bag containing several of the same things □ *There were a lot of seeds in the packet.* 🔄 *He opened the packet and offered me some peanuts.* □ **+ of** *a packet of biscuits* □ *a packet of crisps* (**pacote**)

pact /pækt/ NOUN [plural **pacts**] an agreement between two people, groups or countries 🔄 *We made a pact never to tell anyone what happened.* (**pacto**)

pad₁ /pæd/ NOUN [plural **pads**]
1 a thick piece of soft material, used for protecting something or for making it more comfortable □ *I always wear knee pads and elbow pads when I'm roller skating.* (**almofada**)
2 a book of pieces of paper, used for writing or drawing on □ *a sketch pad* (**bloco**)

pad₂ /pæd/ VERB [**pads, padding, padded**] to fill or wrap something with a soft material □ *The horses' hooves had been padded with cloth to muffle the sound.* (**forrar, rechear**)

paddle /ˈpædəl/ NOUN [plural **paddles**] a short piece of wood with a flat end, used for rowing a boat (**remo**)

page /peɪdʒ/ NOUN [plural pages]

1 a piece of paper in a book, newspaper or magazine, or one side of it □ *The information can be found on page 135.* 🔄 *His picture was on the front page of the newspaper.* 🔄 *She turned the pages very slowly.* (**página**)
2 the writing or pictures that you see on a computer screen, especially as part of a website □ *You need to refresh the page to see the information.* 🔄 *Visit our information page to find out more.* (**página**)

paid /peɪd/ PAST TENSE AND PAST PARTICIPLE OF **pay¹** (ver **pay¹**)

pain /peɪn/ NOUN [plural pains]

1 the unpleasant feeling you have when part of your body hurts □ *stomach pains* 🔄 *He felt a stinging pain.* 🔄 *Aspirin is used to relieve pain* (= make pain less bad). 🔄 *Ann felt a sharp pain in her leg.* □ **+ in** *He had pains in his chest.* (**dor**)
2 be in pain to have an unpleasant feeling because part of your body hurts □ *Amy was in constant pain from a broken shoulder.* □ *He was obviously in great pain.* (**com dor**)

painful

3 no plural sadness 🔹 *She felt that seeing him would cause her too much pain.* 🔹 *Nothing I can say will ease the pain* (= make it less bad). □ **+ of** *The pain of leaving his wife behind was almost too much to bear.* (**dor**)
4 an informal word meaning someone or something that is annoying □ *Sometimes she can be a real pain.* (**insuportável**)

painful /ˈpeɪnfʊl/ ADJECTIVE causing pain □ *Is your knee still painful?* □ *She had a painful lump on her arm.* (**doloroso, dolorido**)

painkiller /ˈpeɪnkɪlə(r)/ NOUN [plural **painkillers**] a drug that reduces pain. (**analgésico**)

paint¹ /peɪnt/ NOUN [plural **paints**] a coloured substance that you put on a surface to change its colour or to make a picture □ *a tin of red paint* 🔹 *The ceiling needs a new coat of paint.* □ *a box of oil paints* (**tinta**)

paint² /peɪnt/ VERB [**paints, painting, painted**]
1 to put paint on a surface □ *Dan was painting the front door.* □ *The dining room was painted red.* (**pintar**)
2 to make a picture using paint □ *He painted a portrait of the queen.* (**pintar**)

painter /ˈpeɪntə(r)/ NOUN [plural **painters**]
1 an artist who makes pictures using paint (**pintura**)
2 someone whose job is to paint buildings and rooms 🔹 *My Dad is a painter and decorator.* (**pintor**)

painting /ˈpeɪntɪŋ/ NOUN [plural **paintings**]
1 a picture that someone has made using paint □ *They sold a painting by Monet.* (**pintura**)
2 no plural the activity of painting walls or pictures □ *I enjoy painting.* (**pintura**)

pair /peə(r)/ NOUN [plural **pairs**]
1 two things of the same kind that you use or keep together □ **+ of** *a pair of socks* □ *a pair of shoes* □ *a pair of china dogs.* (**par**)
2 a single thing made up of two parts □ *I bought a pair of jeans.* □ *a pair of glasses* □ *a pair of scissors* (**par**)
3 two people who do something together, or who are friends □ *The Australian pair won the game.* □ *The teacher asked us to work in pairs.* (**dupla**)

palace /ˈpæləs/ NOUN [plural **palaces**] a big, grand house where a king or queen lives □ *the presidential palace* □ *Crowds of people stood outside the palace gates.* (**palácio**)

pale /peɪl/ ADJECTIVE [**paler, palest**]
1 light in colour □ *She was wearing a pale blue Tshirt.* □ *the pale light of dawn* (**pálido**)
2 having very white skin, especially because you are ill or because you have had a shock □ *She looked very pale and thin.* 🔹 *He suddenly went very pale.* (**pálido**)

palm /pɑːm/ NOUN [plural **palms**]
1 the inside surface of your hand 🔹 *She kept wiping the palms of her hands on her skirt.* (**palma**)
2 a tree that grows in hot, dry places

pamphlet /ˈpæmflɪt/ NOUN [plural **pamphlets**] a thin book with a paper cover, which has information in it (**folheto**)

pan /pæn/ NOUN [plural **pans**] a metal container with a handle, used for cooking food □ *Cover the pan with a lid.* (**panela**)

> **THESAURUS:** Pan is a general word for a metal container with a handle, used for cooking food. A round pan with a handle, and often a lid, is called a saucepan. You might use a saucepan for cooking sauce, but also for boiling vegetables or pasta, for example. A frying pan is a flat pan with a long handle, used for frying food.

pancake /ˈpænkeɪk/ NOUN [plural **pancakes**] a thin food made by frying a mixture of milk, flour and eggs (**panqueca**)

panda /ˈpændə/ NOUN [plural **pandas**] a large animal from China which is black and white, and looks like a bear (**panda**)

pane /peɪn/ NOUN [plural **panes**] a piece of glass used in a window or door □ *a pane of glass* (**vidro, vidraça**)

panel /ˈpænəl/ NOUN [plural **panels**]
1 a usually rectangular piece of wood, glass, etc. that is part of a door, wall, etc. (**painel**)
2 a group of people who are chosen to discuss or judge something, or to answer questions □ *A panel of judges will decide on the winner.* (**grupo**)

panic¹ /ˈpænɪk/ NOUN, NO PLURAL a sudden strong feeling of fear or worry that makes you unable to think calmly 🔹 *The fire caused panic.* □ *People ran into the streets in panic when the earthquake struck.* (**pânico**)

panic² /ˈpænɪk/ VERB [**panics, panicking, panicked**] to be so frightened or worried that you cannot think calmly □ *There's no need to panic. We've got plenty of time.* (**entrar em pânico**)

pant /pænt/ VERB [**pants, panting, panted**] to breathe quickly and noisily, especially because you have been using a lot of physical effort □ *He was sweating and panting.* (**ofegar**)

pants /pænts/ PLURAL NOUN
1 a piece of underwear that covers your bottom 🔹 *a clean pair of pants* (**cueca**)
2 the US word for **trousers** (**calças**)

paper¹ /ˈpeɪpə(r)/ NOUN [plural papers]
1 no plural the thin material that you write on or draw on, or that you wrap things in 🔲 I wrote his address on a piece of paper. 🔲 The present was wrapped in pretty pink paper. (**papel**)
2 a newspaper 🔲 Have you read today's paper? 🔲 I saw the article in the local paper. (**jornal**)
3 an exam 🔲 an exam paper 🔲 He showed me last year's maths paper. L go to papers (**exame, prova**)

paper² /ˈpeɪpə(r)/ ADJECTIVE made from paper or cardboard 🔲 a paper bag 🔲 paper cups (**de papel**)

papers /ˈpeɪpəz/ PLURAL NOUN official documents 🔲 legal papers 🔲 He's signed the divorce papers. (**documentos, papéis**)

parachute /ˈpærəʃuːt/ NOUN [plural parachutes] a large piece of cloth attached to a person's body by strings that they use to help them fall safely if they jump from an aircraft (**paraquedas**)

parade¹ /pəˈreɪd/ NOUN [plural parades] an event in which people or vehicles move through an area to celebrate something, often with music, decorations, etc. 🔲 Hundreds of people took part in the carnival parade. (**desfile, parada**)

parade² /pəˈreɪd/ VERB [parades, parading, paraded] to walk with a lot of other people in order to celebrate something or to complain about something 🔲 Demonstrators paraded through the streets of the city. (**desfilar**)

paradise /ˈpærədaɪs/ NOUN, NO PLURAL
1 in some religions, the place good people go when they die (**paraíso**)
2 a perfect place or situation 🔲 The island is a paradise for birdwatchers. (**paraíso**)

paragraph /ˈpærəɡrɑːf/ NOUN [plural paragraphs] a part of a piece of writing that starts on a new line and contains one or more sentences 🔲 I read the first paragraph of the article. (**parágrafo**)

parallel /ˈpærəlel/ ADJECTIVE parallel lines have the same distance between them all the way along 🔲 She drew two parallel lines. 🔲 Lockwood Road runs parallel to Hollies Road. (**paralelo**)

paralyse /ˈpærəlaɪz/ VERB [paralyses, paralysing, paralysed] if someone is paralysed by something, they are unable to move their body, or are unable to move part of their body 🔲 He was paralysed by a skiing accident in which he broke his neck. (**paralisar**)

paralyze /ˈpærəlaɪz/ VERB [paralyzes, paralyzing, paralyzed] the US spelling of paralyse (**paralisar**)

paramedic /ˌpærəˈmedɪk/ NOUN [plural paramedics] someone who works in an ambulance (= medical emergency vehicle) and is trained to help ill or injured people (**paramédico**)

parcel /ˈpɑːsəl/ NOUN [plural parcels] something wrapped in paper and sent somewhere 🔲 A parcel arrived for you this morning. 🔲 She opened the parcel and there were three books inside. (**pacote**)

pardon /ˈpɑːdən/ EXCLAMATION
1 used to ask someone to repeat what they have just said because you did not hear it 🔲 'We're going to be late.' 'Pardon?' 'I said, we're going to be late.' (**perdão**)
2 pardon me used when you have just made a rude noise with your body (**desculpar-me**)

parent /ˈpeərənt/ NOUN [plural parents] your mother or father 🔲 My parents divorced last year. 🔲 Her proud parents watched as she received the award. (**pai, mãe, pais**)

parish /ˈpærɪʃ/ NOUN [plural parishes] an area that has its own church 🔲 a parish priest (**paróquia**)

park¹ /pɑːk/ NOUN [plural parks] an area of grass and trees in a town where people can go to relax 🔲 I went for a walk in the park. 🔲 They were sitting on a park bench. (**parque**)

park² /pɑːk/ VERB [parks, parking, parked] to leave a vehicle in a place, for example by the side of the road or in a car park 🔲 She parked the car outside the house. 🔲 Dad drove into town but couldn't find anywhere to park. (**estacionar**)

parking /ˈpɑːkɪŋ/ NOUN, NO PLURAL
1 space where you can park your vehicle 🔲 There is free parking for museum visitors. 🔲 She drove round, looking for a parking space. (**estacionamento**)
2 the process of putting a vehicle into a space and leaving it there 🔲 Many learner drivers find parking very difficult. (**estacionar**)

parking lot /ˈpɑːkɪŋ ˌlɒt/ NOUN [plural parking lots] the US word for car park

parliament /ˈpɑːləmənt/ NOUN [plural parliaments] a group of people who make the laws for a country 🔲 the Scottish parliament 🔲 He entered parliament (= was elected to a parliament) in 1981. (**parlamento**)

> **THESAURUS:** A parliament is a group of people who make the laws for a country. A government is a group of people who control a country or area. A party is an organized group of people who share the same political beliefs and try to get elected to the government. The members of one party may form a government, but the members of other political parties may also be part of the parliament.

parole /pəˈrəʊl/ NOUN, NO PLURAL an arrangement in which someone is allowed to leave prison early but must go back to prison if they do not behave well 🔲 Roberts was released on parole in 2005. (**liberdade condicional**)

parrot /ˈpærət/ NOUN [plural parrots] a tropical bird with brightly coloured feathers that can copy what people say (**papagaio**)

part¹ /pɑːt/ NOUN [plural parts]
1 one of the pieces, areas, amounts, etc. that

part   **party**

together make something □ *The pizza is cut into six equal parts.* □ *She lives in a remote part of Scotland.* □ *I spent part of the day working in the garden.* □ *They made me feel part of the family.* (parte)
2 take part to be involved in an activity with other people □ *Everyone can take part in the competition.* □ *She took part in a run for charity.* (tomar parte)
3 some, but not all of something □ **+ of** *Part of the problem is that he works such long hours.* □ *Part of me thinks we should just forget about her.* (parte)
4 a character in a play, film, etc. or the words or actions that the character has to say or do 🔊 *He's playing the part of Othello.* □ *I need to learn my part.* (papel)
5 a piece of a machine or a piece of equipment 🔊 *We took plenty of spare parts for the van.* (parte)

> **THESAURUS:** A part is one of the pieces, areas, amounts, etc. that together make something. Part, **piece** and **section** are very similar in meaning. Part is the most general of these words. You can talk about a part of a car, a part of your life or a part of a place, for example. A **section** is one of the parts that together make up something. For example, you can talk about a **section** of a newspaper. A **piece** is one of the parts that join together to make a particular thing. For example, you can talk about a **piece** of a car. A **portion** is a part of a total amount. We often use **portion** to talk about food. For example, you can talk about a **portion** of cake.

part² /pɑːt/ VERB [parts, parting, parted]
1 when people part, they go away from each other □ *We parted at the end of the street.* 🔊 *They parted company in Toronto.* □ *After ten years of marriage, they agreed to part.* (separar)
2 when two things part, they move away from each other to leave a space, and if you part two things, you make a space between them □ *Suddenly, the clouds parted and we had a wonderful view.* □ *We parted the curtains slightly.* (separar)

♦ PHRASAL VERB **part with something** to give something away, often when you do not want to □ *I couldn't bear to part with my books.*

partial /ˈpɑːʃəl/ ADJECTIVE not complete □ *a partial success* (parcial)
partially /ˈpɑːʃəli/ ADVERB not completely □ *a partially eaten biscuit* (parcialmente)
participant /pɑːˈtɪsɪpənt/ NOUN [plural participants] someone who takes part in an event or activity with other people □ *She was an active participant in the debate.* (participante)
participate /pɑːˈtɪsɪpeɪt/ VERB [participates, participating, participated] to take part in an event or activity □ *The programme aims to encourage more children to participate in sport.* (participar)

participle /ˈpɑːtɪsɪpəl/ NOUN [plural participles] a word formed from a verb and used as an adjective, or to form different tenses of the verb. The present participle usually ends in '-ing' and the past participle usually ends in '-ed'. (particípio)

particle /ˈpɑːtɪkəl/ NOUN [plural particles] a very small piece of something □ *a particle of dust* □ *tiny carbon particles* (partícula)

particular /pəˈtɪkjʊlə(r)/ ADJECTIVE
1 used to show that you are talking about one person or thing and not others □ *On that particular day I was early.* □ *Is there a particular person I should speak to about this?* (específico, determinado)
2 especially great □ *He took particular care when writing the letter.* □ *Aircraft safety is an area of particular concern.* (especial)

particularly /pəˈtɪkjʊləli/ ADVERB
1 very, or more than usual □ *The noise was particularly loud.* □ *Young babies are particularly vulnerable.* 🔊 *They were not particularly helpful.* (particularmente)
2 used to show that something is true for one person or thing more than others □ *Temperatures were very high this summer, particularly in July.* □ *The changes will affect those on low incomes, particularly the elderly.* (particularmente)

partly /ˈpɑːtli/ ADVERB in some ways or to some degree, but not completely □ *I was partly to blame for the mix-up.* □ *He had to leave his job, partly because of his health.* □ *That's only partly true.* (em parte)

partner /ˈpɑːtnə(r)/ NOUN [plural partners]
1 one of two people who do something together, such as dancing or playing a game 🔊 *a dance partner* □ *a tennis partner* (parceiro)
2 one of two or more people who own a business together 🔊 *She's a senior partner in a law firm.* 🔊 *his former business partner* (sócio)
3 someone you are married to or have a sexual relationship with □ *She lives with her long-term partner and their two children.* (parceiro)

part of speech /ˌpɑːt əv ˈspiːtʃ/ NOUN [plural parts of speech] in grammar, one of the groups that words belong to according to the job they do, such as noun, verb, adjective or adverb (categoria gramatical)

part-time /ˌpɑːtˈtaɪm/ ADJECTIVE, ADVERB working for only part of a full working day or week 🔊 *a part time job* 🔊 *She works part-time for the local newspaper.* (meio expediente)

party /ˈpɑːti/ NOUN [plural parties]
1 an event where people celebrate something or enjoy themselves together eating, drinking, dancing, etc. 🔊 *a birthday party* 🔊 *We're having a party next week.* 🔊 *He threw a huge party to celebrate.* (festa)
2 an organized group of people who share the

same political beliefs and try to get elected to the government 🔹 a *political party* 🔹 the *party leader* ◻ *He joined the Labour Party in 1936.* (**partido**)
3 a group of people travelling or doing something together ◻ **+ of** *The museum was busy with several parties of schoolchildren.* (**grupo**)

> Note that you **have** or **throw** a party (sense *1*): You do not 'make' a party:
> ✓ *We're having a party for Celia's 21st birthday.*
> ✗ *We're making a party for Celia's 21st birthday.*

pass¹ /pɑːs/ VERB [**passes, passing, passed**]
1 to go past something ◻ *The lorry passed us on a bend.* ◻ *I pass her house every morning.* (**passar**)
2 to move in a particular direction or to a particular place ◻ *The procession passed in front of the town hall.* ◻ *The road passes through a forest.* (**passar**)
3 to be successful in an exam ◻ *She passed her entrance exams.* ◻ *I've got my driving test tomorrow, but I don't think I'll pass.* (**passar**)
4 to give someone something with your hand ◻ *Pass me the butter, please.* ◻ **+ to** *He passed a note to his colleague.* (**passar**)
5 if time passes, it goes by ◻ *A whole year passed and she did not receive a letter from him.* ◻ *The morning passed slowly.* (**passar**)
6 pass the time to do something to use a period of time ◻ *I passed the time reading a book.*
7 to kick, hit or throw the ball to someone else on your team in a sport ◻ *He passed the ball to Edwards.* (**passar**)

> Remember that you **spend** a period of time somewhere. You do not 'pass' a period of time: ◻ *I spent the summer in Barcelona.* ◻ *I've spent all morning cleaning.* ◻ *We spent the holidays at my grandparents'.*

◆ PHRASAL VERBS **pass something around/round** to offer something to everyone in a group ◻ *She passed round the biscuits.* **pass away/on** to die **pass something on** to give someone something that has been given to you ◻ *Can you pass on a message for me?* ◻ *When you've finished with the book, could you pass it on to Paola?* **pass out** to become unconscious ◻ *When I saw the blood, I passed out.*

pass² /pɑːs/ NOUN [**plural passes**]
1 a successful result in an exam or on a course (**aprovação**)
2 a ticket or document that allows you to go into a place or to travel on a vehicle 🔹 *Have you got your bus pass?* (**passe**)
3 when you kick, hit or throw the ball to someone else on your team in a sport (**passe**)
4 a narrow path between mountains (**desfiladeiro**)

passage /ˈpæsɪdʒ/ NOUN [**plural passages**]
1 a long narrow room or area that connects rooms or places ◻ *He ran down a narrow passage between buildings.* ◻ *a secret underground passage* (**passagem**)
2 a part of a piece of writing or music ◻ *Read the next passage aloud.* ◻ **+ from** *He quoted a passage from the Bible.* (**passagem**)

passenger /ˈpæsɪndʒə(r)/ NOUN [**plural passengers**] someone travelling in a vehicle who is not the driver or someone who works on it 🔹 *an airline passenger* 🔹 *I sat in the passenger seat.* (**passageiro**)

passion /ˈpæʃən/ NOUN [**plural passions**]
1 very strong beliefs and opinions about something ◻ *He spoke with real passion.* 🔹 *Passions are running high* (= people are very angry and upset) *in the city.* (**paixão**)
2 a very strong feeling of love ◻ *He kissed her in a moment of passion.* (**paixão**)

passionate /ˈpæʃənɪt/ ADJECTIVE
1 showing strong emotions or beliefs ◻ *She's a passionate advocate of animal rights.* ◻ *I feel very passionate about this issue.* (**apaixonado**)
2 having a strong feeling of love ◻ *They had a very passionate relationship.* (**apaixonado**)

passive /ˈpæsɪv/ ADJECTIVE a passive verb is used when the person or thing that is the subject of the verb does not do the action but has something done to them, for example in the sentence *The leaves are being eaten by caterpillars.* (**passivo**)

passport /ˈpɑːspɔːt/ NOUN [**plural passports**] an official document with your photograph and personal details that you carry when you travel to a foreign country ◻ *a British passport* 🔹 *You have to show your passport.* ◻ *passport control* (**passaporte**)

password /ˈpɑːswɜːd/ NOUN [**plural passwords**] a secret word that you have to know before you are allowed into a place, or before you can use a computer or system 🔹 *Please enter your password.* (**senha**)

past¹ /pɑːst/ PREPOSITION, ADVERB
1 up to and further than ◻ *She dashed past me, gasping as she ran.* ◻ *He just walked past without saying hello.* ◻ *Bullets flew past my head.* ◻ *Follow the road past a cottage.* (**adiante**)
2 further than ◻ *Turn right just past the bridge.* ◻ *A few miles past the farm, we came to a turning.* (**além de**)
3 used for saying the time up to 30 minutes after an hour ◻ *It's ten past three.* ◻ *I'll meet you at half past ten.* (**mais de, além de**)

past² /pɑːst/ ADJECTIVE
1 having happened or existed in the time before the present ◻ *I have admitted my past mistakes.* (**passado, anterior**)
2 used to talk about a period of time just before the present ◻ *The past few days have been very difficult for all of us.* (**passado**)

past³ /pɑːst/ NOUN, NO PLURAL
1 the past the time before the present ◻ *I have met him a few times in the past.* ◻ *When we meet, we never talk about the past.* (**passado**)
2 someone's past is their life and experiences until

now, and a country's past is what has happened there and what its people have done ◻ *I don't know much about her past.* ◻ *The country is trying to forget its military past.* (**passado**)
3 the past the form of a verb that is used for talking about things that happened before the present (**passado**)

pasta /ˈpæstə/ NOUN, NO PLURAL a food made from flour, water and eggs and formed into different shapes ◻ *pasta with tomato sauce* (**massa**)

past participle /ˌpɑːst ˈpɑːtɪsɪpəl/ NOUN [plural **past participles**] the form of a verb that usually ends with '-ed' and is used to form the perfect tense, passive forms and sometimes adjectives (**particípio passado**)

pastry /ˈpeɪstri/ NOUN [plural **pastries**]
1 no plural a mixture of flour and fat made into a flat piece and baked with food inside (**massa**)
2 a cake made with pastry (**doce**)

past tense /ˌpɑːst ˈtens/ NOUN [plural **past tenses**] a form of a verb that you use when you are talking about what has happened in the past. For example, *relaxed* in *I relaxed after the race* is a past tense. (**passado**)

pasty[1] /ˈpeɪsti/ ADJECTIVE [**pastier, pastiest**] having skin that is unhealthy and looks unhealthy (**pálido**)

pasty[2] /ˈpæsti/ NOUN [plural **pasties**] a piece of pastry folded around food such as meat and vegetables (**torta**)

pat[1] /pæt/ VERB [**pats, patting, patted**] to touch or to hit someone or something gently with your flat hand in a friendly way ◻ *Celia patted his shoulder kindly.* ◻ *He patted the horse's neck.* (**afagar**)

♦ IDIOM **pat someone on the back** to praise someone for something they have done ◻ *I patted myself on the back for a job well done.*

> **THESAURUS:** To **pat** someone or something means to touch or to hit someone or something gently with your flat hand in a friendly way. You might pat a dog. To **stroke** something means to rub it gently with your hand. For example, you might stroke a cat. To **tap** means to knock gently or hit your fingers or feet gently against something. You might tap someone on the arm to get their attention. To **slap** means to hit something or someone with the flat part of your hand.

pat[2] /pæt/ NOUN [plural **pats**] when you pat someone or something ◻ *He gave the dog a pat on the head.* (**tapinha**)

♦ IDIOM **a pat on the back** praise for doing something ◻ *She deserves a pat on the back.*

patch[1] /pætʃ/ NOUN [plural **patches**]
1 a small area of something, especially that is different from what is around it ◻ *a patch of grass* 🔄 *a vegetable patch* (= area of ground where you grow vegetables) ◻ *There's a damp patch on the wall.* (**canteiro**)

2 a piece of material used to cover a hole ◻ *a jacket with patches on the elbows* (**remendo**)

patch[2] /pætʃ/ VERB [**patches, patching, patched**] to repair a hole using a patch ◻ *We patched the hole in the roof.* (**remendar**)

patent /ˈpeɪtənt/ NOUN [plural **patents**] an official document that gives one person or company the right to make and sell a product and stops others from copying it (**patente**)

path /pɑːθ/ NOUN [plural **paths**] a narrow route across a piece of ground that people walk or ride a bicycle along ◻ *We walked along a narrow path through the woods.* ◻ *Dad was coming up the garden path.* 🔄 *There's a* cycle path *beside the canal.* (**caminho, trilha**)

pathetic /pəˈθetɪk/ ADJECTIVE an informal word meaning not at all useful, skilful or effective ◻ *This knife is pathetic. It won't cut anything!* 🔄 *She made a* pathetic attempt *to deny it.* (**patético**)

patience /ˈpeɪʃəns/ NOUN, NO PLURAL the ability to stay calm, especially when waiting for something, doing something for a long time or dealing with something or someone annoying ◻ *You need to have a lot of patience when dealing with young children.* 🔄 *I'm* losing *my* patience *with her silly behaviour.* (**paciência**)

patient[1] /ˈpeɪʃənt/ ADJECTIVE showing patience ◻ + **with** *I'm a slow learner and he's been very patient with me.* ◻ *I'm not a very patient person.* (**paciente**)

patient[2] /ˈpeɪʃənt/ NOUN [plural **patients**] someone who is being treated by a doctor or a nurse 🔄 *The clinic* treats patients *with eye problems.* ◻ *Every patient receives advice about healthy eating.* (**paciente**)

patrol[1] /pəˈtrəʊl/ VERB [**patrols, patrolling**/US **patroling, patrolled**/US **patroled**] to go around an area or building watching for any trouble or problems ◻ *Troops patrol the border.* (**patrulhar**)

patrol[2] /pəˈtrəʊl/ NOUN [plural **patrols**]
1 a group of soldiers or police officers who patrol an area 🔄 *a* police patrol (**patrulha**)
2 when someone patrols an area 🔄 *The soldiers were on a* routine patrol *when they were attacked.* (**patrulha**)

pattern /ˈpætən/ NOUN [plural **patterns**]
1 the way in which something normally happens or is organized ◻ + **of** *the pattern of the seasons* 🔄 *When we analyzed the data, a clear* pattern emerged. 🔄 *annual* weather patterns (**tendência, padrão**)
2 a design of shapes, colours, etc. repeated on a surface ◻ *The room was decorated in floral patterns.* ◻ *The boxes are carved with intricate patterns.* (**padrão**)
3 a set of instructions and shapes used for making something ◻ *a sewing pattern* (**modelo**)

pause[1] /pɔːz/ VERB [**pauses, pausing, paused**] to stop what you are doing for a short time ◻ + **todo**

something The actor paused to speak to fans. □ He paused for a moment before replying. (pausar, fazer uma pausa)

pause² /pɔːz/ NOUN [plural **pauses**] a short stop or rest 🔲 There was a *long pause* before anyone spoke. □ *+ for* He kept going with hardly a pause for breath. (pausa)

pave /peɪv/ VERB [**paves, paving, paved**] to make a layer of stones, bricks etc. on an area of ground □ The courtyard is paved with local stone. (calçar)
◆ IDIOM **pave the way for something** to do something that makes it possible for something else to happen □ This decision could pave the way for other legal cases.

pavement /ˈpeɪvmənt/ NOUN [plural **pavements**] a path next to a road which people walk along □ He waited on the pavement in front of the shop. (calçada)

paw /pɔː/ NOUN [plural **paws**] the foot of some animals, such as cats and dogs (patas)

pay¹ /peɪ/ VERB [**pays, paying, paid**]
1 to give money in order to buy something or because you owe someone □ *+ for* I'll pay for the meal. 🔲 He offered to *pay* the *bill*. □ I don't pay tax in this country. □ *+ by* Can I pay by credit card? (pagar)
2 to give someone money for work that they do □ I need the money to pay the builder. □ I get paid on the 15th of each month. (pagar)
3 pay attention to concentrate on something □ She paid great attention to his words. (prestar atenção)
4 pay someone a compliment to say something nice about someone (elogiar)
5 pay someone/something a visit to visit someone or something (visitar)
◆ PHRASAL VERB **pay someone back** to do something bad to someone because of something bad they have done to you

➤ Note that you pay **for** the thing that you are buying:
✓ Camille paid for the watch.
✓ Camille paid £120 for the watch.
✗ Camille paid the watch.

➤ **THESAURUS:** To pay means to give money in order to buy something or because you owe someone, or to give someone money for work that they do. To *earn* means to get money for work that you do. To *win* means to get something because you have been successful in a game, competition etc. To *spend* means to use money to buy things.

pay² /peɪ/ NOUN, NO PLURAL someone's pay is the amount of money they are paid by their employer □ The job's boring, but the pay's good. 🔲 I asked him for a *pay rise*. 🔲 Many workers are facing *pay cuts*. (remuneração)

payment /ˈpeɪmənt/ NOUN [plural **payments**]
1 money paid for something 🔲 We *make* monthly *payments*. □ All payments will be made to your bank account. 🔲 He received a *cash payment* of £200. (pagamento)
2 no plural when you pay for something □ *+ of* He was involved with the payment of bribes. (pagamento)

PC /ˌpiːˈsiː/ ABBREVIATION
1 personal computer (computador pessoal)
2 police constable; used before a police officer's name □ *PC Evans* (título e identificação da polícia)

pea /piː/ NOUN [plural **peas**] a small round green vegetable (ervilha)

peace /piːs/ NOUN, NO PLURAL
1 a situation in which there is no war or violence □ The two countries have been at peace for 50 years. 🔲 We are seeking to *bring peace* to the region. 🔲 The police were at the demonstration to *keep the peace*. 🔲 *peace talks* 🔲 a *peace deal* (paz)
2 a situation which is quiet and calm □ I want a little peace to get on with my homework. □ She goes to the library for a bit of *peace and quiet*. (paz)

peaceful /ˈpiːsfʊl/ ADJECTIVE
1 not involving war or violence □ a peaceful protest 🔲 It says its nuclear programme is for *peaceful purposes*. (pacífico)
2 quiet and calm □ She felt more peaceful than she had all day. □ a peaceful seaside town (tranquilo)

peach /piːtʃ/ NOUN [plural **peaches**] a round fruit with a soft skin, pale orange flesh and a large stone inside (pêssego)

peak /piːk/ NOUN [plural **peaks**]
1 the highest, greatest or most successful level □ the peak of the holiday season 🔲 She *reached the peak* of her career in the 1990s. 🔲 The trains are very crowded at *peak times*. (apogeu, pico)
2 the pointed top of a mountain or hill 🔲 snow-covered *mountain peaks* (pico)
3 the flat part at the front of a cap (= soft hat) that sticks out (pala)

peanut /ˈpiːnʌt/ NOUN [plural **peanuts**] a type of nut that grows underground in a shell and can be eaten (amendoim)

pear /peə(r)/ NOUN [plural **pears**] a fruit with green, yellow or brown skin and white flesh which is round at the bottom and narrower at the top (pera)

pearl /pɜːl/ NOUN [plural **pearls**] a round, white object, formed inside the shell of an oyster (= sea creature), and used for making jewellery □ a pearl necklace (pérola)

peasant /ˈpezənt/ NOUN [plural **peasants**] a poor person who works on the land in a poor country □ *a peasant farmer* (**camponês**)

peck /pek/ VERB [**pecks, pecking, pecked**] if a bird pecks, it hits something or picks something up with its beak □ *Birds pecked at the crumbs.* (**bicar**)

peculiar /pɪˈkjuːlɪə(r)/ ADJECTIVE strange or not expected, sometimes in an unpleasant way □ *a very peculiar smell* □ *It seems peculiar that no one noticed.* □ *That would explain his peculiar behaviour recently.* (**estranho, singular**)

pedal /ˈpedəl/ NOUN [plural **pedals**] a part that you push with your foot, such as on a bicycle, in a car or on a machine ▣ *the brake pedal* (**pedal**)

pedestrian /pɪˈdestrɪən/ NOUN [plural **pedestrians**] someone who is walking and not travelling in a vehicle □ *Pedestrians and cyclists are given priority in the city centre.* (**pedestre**)

peel[1] /piːl/ VERB [**peels, peeling, peeled**]
1 to remove the skin of a vegetable or a piece of fruit □ *She was peeling potatoes.* □ *+ off Let the peppers cool then peel off the skin.* (**descascar**)
2 if paint or skin peels, it comes off in small pieces □ *The paint was peeling off the walls.* (**descascar**)

peel[2] /piːl/ NOUN, NO PLURAL the skin of some fruit and vegetables □ *orange peel* (**casca**)

peer /pɪə(r)/ VERB [**peers, peering, peered**] to look at something carefully, usually because it is difficult to see □ *He peered through a downstairs window.* (**esquadrinhar**)

pen /pen/ NOUN [plural **pens**]
1 an object used for writing with ink ▣ *a ball point pen* □ *Have you got a pen and paper?* (**caneta**)
2 a small area surrounded by a fence and used for keeping animals in (**cercado**)

pence /pens/ PLURAL OF **penny** □ *a ten pence coin* (ver **penny**)

pencil /ˈpensəl/ NOUN [plural **pencils**] a long thin wooden object for writing or drawing, with a black or coloured substance in the centre □ *coloured pencils* □ *a pencil drawing* (**lápis**)

penetrate /ˈpenɪtreɪt/ VERB [**penetrates, penetrating, penetrated**] to get into or through something □ *Rain could not penetrate those thick trees.* □ *The knife penetrated his heart.* (**penetrar**)

pen friend /ˈpen ˌfrend/ NOUN [plural **pen friends**] a friend you write letters to, but do not meet (**correspondente**)

penguin /ˈpeŋgwɪn/ NOUN [plural **penguins**] a black and white bird that cannot fly but uses its wings to swim under water (**pinguim**)

penis /ˈpiːnɪs/ NOUN [plural **penises**] the male organ for urinating and producing babies. A biology word. (**pênis**)

penknife /ˈpen naɪf/ NOUN [plural **penknives**] a small knife with blades that fold into the handle (**canivete**)

penny /ˈpeni/ NOUN [plural **pence** or **pennies** or **p**] a small British coin worth one hundredth of £1 □ *Crisps cost 40 pence.* (**pêni**)

> Note that when you are saying how much something costs, the plural **pence** is used. When you are talking about the coins themselves, use the plural **pennies**: □ *It cost me fifty pence.* □ *I only had a few pennies left in my purse.*

pension /ˈpenʃən/ NOUN [plural **pensions**] an amount of money that a government or company regularly gives someone when they are too old to work ▣ *My grandma gets a state pension* (= a pension that a government gives people). ▣ *a company pension* (= a pension that a company gives to former employees) ▣ *The company has a good pension scheme.* (**pensão**)

pensioner /ˈpenʃənə(r)/ NOUN [plural **pensioners**] someone who gets a pension (**pensionista**)

people /ˈpiːpəl/ PLURAL NOUN men, women and children □ *young people* □ *How many people have you invited to your party?* □ *People don't like being criticized.* (**pessoas**)

> Remember that the noun **people** always takes a plural verb: □ *People are generally happy with the government.*

> Remember also that you do not say 'all people' or 'every people'. Instead you say **everyone** or **everybody**:
> ✓ *Everyone feels sad sometimes.*
> ✗ *All people feel sad sometimes.*

pepper /ˈpepə(r)/ NOUN [plural **peppers**]
1 *no plural* a powder with a strong taste which is added to food ▣ *He sprinkled salt and pepper on his food.* ▣ *freshly ground black pepper* (**pimenta**)
2 a hollow red, green or yellow vegetable which is eaten raw or cooked □ *a sliced red pepper* (**pimentão**)

per /pɜː(r)/ PREPOSITION for each □ *The meal will cost £20 per person.* □ *He was driving at 65 miles per hour when the crash happened.* □ *How much are the apples per kilo?* (**por**)

percent or **per cent** /pəˈsent/ ADVERB, ADJECTIVE, NOUN, NO PLURAL in or for every 100, shown by the symbol □ *Sales have increased by ten percent.* □ *There has been five percent fall in the number of people who are unemployed.* □ *Sixty percent of schoolchildren felt that they got too much homework.* (**porcento**)

percentage /pəˈsentɪdʒ/ NOUN [plural **percentages**] a number that is expressed as a number in 100 ▣ *A high percentage* of students *got top grades.* □ *What percentage of children have a television in their bedrooms?* (porcentagem)

perch /pɜːtʃ/ VERB [perches, perching, perched]
1 if something is perched somewhere, it is on the top or edge of something □ *The house is perched on a hillside next to the lake.* (empoleirar)
2 to sit on the edge of something □ *She perched on a stool next to me.* (empoleirar)

perfect¹ /ˈpɜːfɪkt/ ADJECTIVE
1 without any mistakes or faults □ *Emma has perfect teeth.* □ *Your English is perfect.* □ *This building is a perfect example of 1930s architecture.* (perfeito)
2 exactly right for something □ *Jones was the perfect choice for the role.* □ *South Beach is the perfect place for a holiday.* (perfeito)

> **THESAURUS:** Something that is perfect has no mistakes or faults. Something that is pure is not mixed with anything else. You can talk about pure gold or pure water. Something that is excellent is extremely good or of a very high quality.

perfect² /ˈpɜːfɪkt/ NOUN, NO PLURAL **the perfect** the tense of a verb in English is formed with *has/have/had* and the past participle □ *'He has played tennis for years'* is in the perfect. (perfeito)

perfect³ /pəˈfekt/ VERB [perfects, perfecting, perfected] to make something perfect □ *The hills are ideal for skiers determined to perfect their technique.* (aperfeiçoar)

perfection /pəˈfekʃən/ NOUN, NO PLURAL the state of being perfect □ *Some people try to achieve physical perfection.* □ *The meat was cooked to perfection* (= it was cooked perfectly). (perfeição)

perfectly /ˈpɜːfɪktli/ ADVERB
1 in an extremely good way □ *The children behaved perfectly.* □ *His arrival was perfectly timed because the meal was just ready.* (perfeitamente)
2 completely □ *It was perfectly obvious that he was lying.* □ *The equipment is old but it's perfectly safe.* (perfeitamente)

perform /pəˈfɔːm/ VERB [performs, performing, performed]
1 to do a task □ *Surgeons perform operations.* □ *He found it difficult to perform simple tasks after the accident.* (executar)
2 to act in a play, sing a song, etc. with people watching you □ *It was the first time we'd performed the song.* □ *I love performing in front of a live audience.* (representar)
3 perform well/poorly/badly etc. to do something well or badly □ *His team performed poorly in both games.* □ *The business has performed well* (= it has been successful) *in difficult circumstances.* (desempenhar)

performance /pəˈfɔːməns/ NOUN [plural performances]
1 an occasion when someone acts in a play, sings a song, etc. with people watching them ▣ *The show included a live performance by several bands.* ▣ *Kylie gave a great performance.* □ **+ of** *We went to a performance of Mozart's 'Magic Flute'.* (apresentação)
2 the level of success that someone or something has ▣ *The team needs to improve its performance.* ▣ *Her poor performance in the exams was very disappointing.* (desempenho)

performer /pəˈfɔːmə(r)/ NOUN [plural performers] a singer, actor, etc. who performs □ *She's a great performer.* □ *a circus performer* (intérprete)

perfume /ˈpɜːfjuːm/ NOUN [plural perfumes] a liquid that women put on their skin to make them smell nice ▣ *She always wears perfume.* □ *I could smell her perfume.* (perfume)

perhaps /pəˈhæps/ ADVERB possibly □ *I can't find Leo. Perhaps he's left.* □ *Perhaps I shouldn't have told him.* (talvez)

period /ˈpɪəriəd/ NOUN [plural periods]
1 an amount of time □ *The work was done over a two-year period.* ▣ *Rachel has learned a lot in a short period of time.* ▣ *He had spent long periods in prison.* □ **+ of** *He lived there for a period of several years.* (período)
2 a time in history □ *the Victorian period* □ *one of the earliest geological periods* (período)

perish /ˈperɪʃ/ VERB [perishes, perishing, perished] a formal word meaning to die □ *Four children perished in the fire.* (perecer)

permanent /ˈpɜːmənənt/ ADJECTIVE lasting forever or for a very long time □ *The accident left him with permanent brain damage.* □ *Ella has been offered a permanent job.* □ *We need a permanent solution to the problem.* (permanente)

> **THESAURUS:** Something that is permanent lasts forever or for a long time. You might have a permanent job or a permanent home, for example. Something that is constant never stops. For example you might talk about constant pain or constant noise. Something that is stable does not change over a period of time. For example, the price of something such as oil or gold might be stable.

permanently /ˈpɜːmənəntli/ ADVERB in a way that lasts forever or for a very long time □ *Her sight had been permanently damaged.* □ *Many new mothers feel permanently tired.* (permanentemente)

permission /pəˈmɪʃən/ NOUN, NO PLURAL if you have permission to do something, someone says you can do it ▣ *A doctor can't operate on you unless you give permission.* ▣ *You need to get permission from your teacher if you want to leave the class early.* □ *Rob had taken his Dad's car* *without permission.* □ **+ to do something** *I asked her permission to use the phone.* (**permissão**)

> Remember that you **get permission** or **give permission** to do something. You do not 'get/give *a* permission':
> ✓ I **got permission** from my teacher to leave early.
> ✗ I got a permission from my teacher to leave early.

permit¹ /pəˈmɪt/ VERB [**permits, permitting, permitted**] a formal word meaning to allow something □ *Smoking is not permitted anywhere in the building.* (**permitir**)

permit² /ˈpɜːmɪt/ NOUN [*plural* **permits**] an official document that allows you to do something □ *a work permit* (**licença**)

persist /pəˈsɪst/ VERB [**persists, persisting, persisted**] if something bad persists, it continues □ *If the problem persists, talk to your doctor.* (**persistir**)

persistent /pəˈsɪstənt/ ADJECTIVE
1 continuing to do something even when it is difficult or when someone tells you to stop □ *I said I wasn't interested but the salesman was quite persistent.* (**persistente**)
2 if something unpleasant is persistent, it continues for a long time □ *persistent rain* (**persistente**)

person /ˈpɜːsən/ NOUN [*plural* **people**] a man, woman or child □ *Heather's a really nice person.* □ *Tatsuya was the first person in his family to go to university.* □ *How many people were at the party?* ⧉ *Jeremy is the kind of person who knows everything.* (**pessoa**)

> Note that the plural of person is usually **people**. The plural 'persons' is sometimes used in formal writing but it is not used generally:
> ✓ Most **people** here own a car.
> ✗ Most **persons** here own a car.

personal /ˈpɜːsənəl/ ADJECTIVE
1 belonging to, or to do with one particular person □ *a personal opinion* □ *personal belongings* ⧉ *I know from personal experience that the exam is very difficult.* (**pessoal**)
2 private and to do with your health, relationships, etc. ⧉ *The singer's personal life has been quite troubled.* □ *Never give out personal information to a company on the phone.* (**pessoal**)

personal computer /ˌpɜːsənəlkəmˈpjuːtə(r)/ NOUN [*plural* **personal computers**] a small computer that is designed to be used by one person (**computador pessoal**)

personality /ˌpɜːsəˈnælətɪ/ NOUN [*plural* **personalities**]
1 someone's character and the qualities they have ⧉ *Artie has a very outgoing personality.* □ *The accident had changed his personality.* (**personalidade**)
2 a famous person ⧉ *He's one of America's best-known TV personalities.* (**personalidade**)

personally /ˈpɜːsnəlɪ/ ADVERB
1 used when stating your own opinion □ *Personally, I don't like him.* (**pessoalmente**)
2 done by you and not by anyone else □ *He wrote to everyone personally.* (**pessoalmente**)

personnel /ˌpɜːsəˈnel/ NOUN, NO PLURAL the people who work for a particular company or organization □ *army personnel* (**pessoal**)

persuade /pəˈsweɪd/ VERB [**persuades, persuading, persuaded**] to make someone agree to do something by telling them why they should do it □ **+ to do something** *I tried to persuade Tanya to come with us.* (**persuadir**)

persuasion /pəˈsweɪʒən/ NOUN, NO PLURAL when you persuade someone ⧉ *After a little gentle persuasion, he agreed to come with us.* (**persuasão**)

pest /pest/ NOUN [*plural* **pests**]
1 an animal or insect that destroys crops (**praga**)
2 an informal word for an annoying person, often a child (**peste**)

pesticide /ˈpestɪsaɪd/ NOUN [*plural* **pesticides**] a chemical used for killing insects which destroy crops (**pesticida**)

pet /pet/ NOUN [*plural* **pets**] an animal that you keep in your home ⧉ *Do you have any pets?* □ *Dogs and cats are very popular pets.* □ *Adam has a pet rabbit.* (**animal de estimação**)

petal /ˈpetəl/ NOUN [*plural* **petals**] one of the coloured parts of a flower □ *rose petals* (**pétala**)

petition /pɪˈtɪʃən/ NOUN [*plural* **petitions**] a piece of paper that a lot of people sign to try to get a government or someone in authority to do something ⧉ *We signed a petition against the closure of the post office.* (**petição**)

petrol /ˈpetrəl/ NOUN, NO PLURAL a fuel for cars, made from oil □ *I've just filled the car up with petrol.* □ *petrol prices*

> **THESAURUS:** Oil is a thick, dark liquid from under the ground. Fuel is a general word for a substance that burns to give heat, light or power. Petrol is a fuel for cars, made from oil. Diesel is a heavy type of oil that is used as a fuel. Buses and lorries usually use diesel. Gas is a substance that is not liquid or solid and moves about in the air. We often use gas for cooking or heating. Gas is also the American word for petrol.

petrol station /ˈpetrəl ˌsteɪʃən/ NOUN [*plural* **petrol stations**] a place where you buy petrol for a car (**posto de gasolina**)

pharmacist /ˈfɑːməsɪst/ NOUN [*plural* **pharmacists**] someone who prepares and sells medicines (**farmacêutico**)

pharmacy

pharmacy /ˈfɑːməsɪ/ NOUN [plural **pharmacies**]
a shop where medicines are prepared and sold □ *You can get most medicines at your local pharmacy.* (farmácia)

phase /feɪz/ NOUN [plural **phases**] a stage in the development of a thing or person □ *The first phase of the project was to interview 100 students.* □ *Children go through so many phases.* (fase)

PhD /ˌpiːeɪtʃˈdiː/ ABBREVIATION Doctor of Philosophy; the highest university degree □ *He's doing a PhD in applied mathematics.* (PhD)

philosopher /fɪˈlɒsəfə(r)/ NOUN [plural **philosophers**] someone who studies ideas about life (filósofo)

philosophy /fɪˈlɒsəfɪ/ NOUN, NO PLURAL the study of ideas about life □ *She did philosophy at university.* (filosofia)

phone¹ /fəʊn/ NOUN [plural **phones**]
1 a telephone ▣ *Here's my phone number.* ▣ *The phone was ringing.* ▣ *Can you answer the phone please?* □ *You can order a pizza by phone.* (telefone)
2 on the phone using the telephone □ *Mum's on the phone at the moment.* □ *I talk to my cousins on the phone every week.* (no telefone)

phone² /fəʊn/ VERB [**phones, phoning, phoned**]
to speak to someone using a telephone □ *I phoned my grandma last night.* □ *+ up I'll phone up and find out when the library opens.* (telefonar)

> Note that you **phone** a person or place. You do not 'phone to' a person or place:
> ✓ *I'll phone Javier.*
> ✗ *I'll phone to Javier.*
> ✓ *I'll phone the hospital.*
> ✗ *I'll phone to the hospital.*

◆ PHRASAL VERB **phone (someone) back** to call someone again using a telephone, because you could not talk to them the first time □ *I'm busy just now. I'll phone you back later.*

phone call /ˈfəʊn ˌkɔːl/ NOUN [plural **phone calls**]
when you speak to someone using a telephone ▣ *I'm just going to make a quick phone call.* (telefonema)

phone number /ˈfəʊn ˌnʌmbə(r)/ NOUN [plural **phone numbers**] the series of numbers that you use to call a particular telephone □ *What's your phone number?* (número de telefone)

photo /ˈfəʊtəʊ/ NOUN [plural **photos**] a photograph □ *digital photos* □ *Who's that woman in the photo?* ▣ *She took a photo of Clare and me on the beach.* ▣ *They showed us their wedding photos.* □ *+ of There were photos of the children all over the house.* (foto)

photocopy /ˈfəʊtəʊkɒpɪ/ NOUN [plural **photo copies**] a copy of a document that you make using a photocopier (= a machine that copies a document by taking a photograph of it) ▣ *He made a photocopy of the instructions.* (fotocópia)

photograph¹ /ˈfəʊtəɡrɑːf/ NOUN [plural **photographs**] a picture made with a camera ▣ *I took a photograph using my new camera.* □ *+ of a photograph of Lake Geneva* (fotografia)

photograph² /ˈfəʊtəɡrɑːf/ VERB [**photo graphs, photographing, photographed**] to make a picture of something using a camera □ *She photographed me in the school play.* (fotografar)

photographer /fəˈtɒɡrəfə(r)/ NOUN [plural **photographers**] someone who takes photographs, especially as their job □ *He's a professional photographer.* □ *a press photographer* (= photographer for a newspaper) □ *a fashion photographer* (fotógrafo)

photography /fəˈtɒɡrəfɪ/ NOUN, NO PLURAL the art of taking photographs ▣ *digital photography* □ *John teaches photography at the college.* (fotografia)

phrasal verb /ˌfreɪzəl ˈvɜːb/ NOUN [plural **phrasal verbs**] a verb that you use with an adverb or preposition, which has a different meaning from the verb used alone □ *'Give up' and 'get on' are examples of phrasal verbs.* (verbo frasal)

phrase /freɪz/ NOUN [plural **phrases**] a group of words that have a particular meaning ▣ *She used the phrase 'unwelcome attention' several times.* (frase)

> **THESAURUS:** A **phrase** is a group of words that have a particular meaning. A **sentence** is a group of words that usually includes a verb and expresses a statement or question. An **expression** is a word or phrase. An **idiom** is a phrase that has a meaning that you cannot understand simply by knowing the meaning of the separate words. A **saying** is a phrase or sentence that people often use, giving advice or saying something that many people believe is true.

physical /ˈfɪzɪkəl/ ADJECTIVE
1 to do with the body □ *These children have low levels of physical activity.* (físico)
2 to do with real things that you can see or touch, and not things that exist only in your mind □ *There was no physical evidence to link him to the crime.* (físico)

physicist /ˈfɪzɪsɪst/ NOUN [plural **physicists**] someone who studies physics, usually as their job (físico)

physics /ˈfɪzɪks/ NOUN, NO PLURAL the scientific study of natural forces, for example, heat, light, sound and electricity (físico)

pianist /ˈpɪənɪst/ NOUN [plural **pianists**] someone who plays the piano □ *a concert pianist.* (pianista)

piano / pilot

piano /pɪˈænəʊ/ NOUN [plural **pianos**] a musical instrument that you play by pressing the black and white keys on a long keyboard (**piano**)

pick¹ /pɪk/ VERB [**picks, picking, picked**]
1 to choose a person or thing from a group □ Jones has been picked for the England team. □ Pick any card from the pack. (**escolher**)
2 to take fruit, flowers or vegetables from the plant or tree they are growing on □ The children picked a bunch of wild flowers for their mum. □ I picked a few strawberries for tea. (**catar, colher**)
♦ PHRASAL VERBS **pick on someone** to treat one particular person unkindly or unfairly □ Please stop picking on your brother. **pick someone/something up** to go and collect someone or something from somewhere □ Could you pick me up at the airport tomorrow? □ I need to pick up my dry cleaning. **pick something up 1** to lift something □ She picked up the phone and started to dial. □ They asked us to pick up the litter. **2** to learn something by watching or listening instead of having lessons □ I just picked the language up while I was living in Mexico.

pick² /pɪk/ NOUN, NO PLURAL **have/take your pick** to choose what you want from a group □ You can take your pick from a wide range of cheeses. (**escolha**)

picnic¹ /ˈpɪknɪk/ NOUN [plural **picnics**] a meal that you take with you to eat outdoors 🔊 We had a picnic on the beach. 🔊 There's a beautiful picnic area in the forest. (**piquenique**)

> Note that you **have** a picnic. You do not 'make' a picnic:
> ✓ We had a picnic in the park.
> ✗ We made a picnic in the park.

picnic² /ˈpɪknɪk/ VERB [**picnics, picnicking, picnicked**] to have a picnic (**fazer piquenique**)

picture¹ /ˈpɪktʃə(r)/ NOUN [plural **pictures**] a painting, drawing or photograph □ The walls were covered with pictures of his family. 🔊 Draw a picture of your house. 🔊 Can I take a picture (= take a photograph) of your garden? (**retrato**)

> THESAURUS: Picture is a general word. A painting is a picture that someone has made using paint. A drawing is a picture done with a pencil or pen. A sketch is a drawing that is done quickly. An illustration is a picture in a book, magazine etc.

picture² /ˈpɪktʃə(r)/ VERB [**pictures, picturing, pictured**] to form an image of something in your mind □ I just couldn't picture my mother as a young girl. (**imaginar**)

pie /paɪ/ NOUN [plural **pies**] food such as meat, vegetables or fruit, baked in a covering of pastry □ apple pie and custard □ chicken and mushroom pie (**torta**)

piece /piːs/ NOUN [plural **pieces**]
1 an amount or example of something of a particular type □ a piece of wood □ Use a fresh piece of paper for each answer. □ Let me give you a piece of advice. (**pedaço, fragmento**)
2 one of the parts that join together to make a particular thing □ a jigsaw with 300 pieces □ Cut the pizza into eight pieces. 🔊 He took the clock to pieces to repair it. 🔊 I just touched the stool and it fell to pieces. (**peça, pedaço**)
3 a coin of a particular value □ a 50p piece (**moeda**)

pier /pɪə(r)/ NOUN [plural **piers**] a long wooden or metal structure built out over the sea that people can walk along (**cais**)

pierce /pɪəs/ VERB [**pierces, piercing, pierced**] if a sharp object pierces something, it makes a hole in it 🔊 I've just had my ears pierced. (**perfurar**)

pig /pɪɡ/ NOUN [plural **pigs**] a farm animal with a fat body, small eyes and a curly tail, kept for meat (**porco**)

pigeon /ˈpɪdʒɪn/ NOUN [plural **pigeons**] a grey bird that is often seen in towns or kept for racing (**pombo**)

pile¹ /paɪl/ NOUN [plural **piles**] a number of things one on top of the other □ a pile of leaves □ Dirty dishes were stacked in piles around the room. (**pilha**)

> THESAURUS : A pile or a stack is a number of things one on top of the other. A heap is an untidy pile of things. A mound is a small hill or pile of earth or stones.

pile² /paɪl/ VERB [**piles, piling, piled**] to put things on top of each other in a pile □ They piled all the chairs against the wall. (**empilhar**)

pilgrim /ˈpɪlɡrɪm/ NOUN [plural **pilgrims**] a person who is travelling to a holy place (**peregrino**)

pilgrimage /ˈpɪlɡrɪmɪdʒ/ NOUN [plural **pilgrimages**] a journey to a holy place □ They went on a pilgrimage to Mecca. (**peregrinação**)

pill /pɪl/ NOUN [plural **pills**] a small piece of solid medicine that you swallow □ antihistamine pills (**pílula**)

pillar /ˈpɪlə(r)/ NOUN [plural **pillars**] a tall, strong structure, usually made of stone, used to support something □ The statue is on top of a stone pillar. (**pilar**)

pillow /ˈpɪləʊ/ NOUN [plural **pillows**] a bag full of feathers or other soft material that you rest your head on when you are in bed (**travesseiro**)

pilot /ˈpaɪlət/ NOUN [plural **pilots**] someone who flies a plane or other aircraft □ an airline pilot □ a pilot's licence (**piloto**)

> THESAURUS: Someone who flies a plane or other aircraft is called a pilot. Someone who drives a car or other motor vehicle is called a driver. Someone who sits on and controls a bicycle, motorbike or horse is called a rider. Someone who is walking and not using a vehicle is called a pedestrian.

pin¹ /pɪn/ NOUN [plural pins]
1 a very thin, pointed piece of metal used for holding together pieces of cloth when you are sewing (alfinete)
2 a thin piece of metal or wood, used for holding things together □ He's had a pin in his leg since the accident. (pino)

> THESAURUS: A pin is a very thin, pointed piece of metal used for holding together pieces of cloth when you are sewing. A needle is a small, pointed piece of metal used for sewing. A nail is a thin, pointed piece of metal used to join things together, especially pieces of wood. A screw is a small, pointed metal object used to fix things together by turning it around into a hole. A clip is a small object that fastens something together or to something else. For example, you might wear a hair clip to keep your hair tidy and a paper clip holds paper together.

pin² /pɪn/ VERB [pins, pinning, pinned]
1 to fasten something in place with a pin □ She pinned the flower to her dress. (alfinetar)
2 to hold someone somewhere firmly so that they cannot move □ The policemen pinned him against the wall. (encurralar)

pinch¹ /pɪntʃ/ VERB [pinches, pinching, pinched]
1 to press someone's skin or flesh tightly between your thumb and finger, especially in order to hurt them □ Tom pinched me, Mum! (beliscar)
2 an informal word that means to steal something □ Have you pinched my magazine? (roubar)

pinch² /pɪntʃ/ NOUN [plural pinches]
1 a small amount of something that you pick up between your finger and thumb 🔂 Add a pinch of salt. (pitada)
2 when you pinch someone □ She gave him a pinch on the arm. (beliscão)

pine¹ /paɪn/ NOUN [plural pines] a tall tree with needles (= thin pointed leaves). (pinheiro)

pine² /paɪn/ VERB [pines, pining, pined] to feel sad, usually because you are not with a person that you love (definhar)

pineapple /ˈpaɪnæpəl/ NOUN [plural pineapples] a large fruit with sweet yellow flesh and a thick brown skin with sharp points on it □ pineapple juice (abacaxi)

pink¹ /pɪŋk/ ADJECTIVE having the colour you get if you mix red and white □ She wore a pink dress. □ His cheeks were pink from running. (cor-de-rosa)

pink² /pɪŋk/ NOUN, NO PLURAL the colour you get if you mix red and white (cor-de-rosa)

pint /paɪnt/ NOUN [plural pints] a unit for measuring liquid, equal to 0.57 litres 🔂 a pint of milk/beer (unidade de medida, quartilho)

pioneer¹ /ˌpaɪəˈnɪə(r)/ NOUN [plural pioneers]
1 one of the first people to develop a new idea, skill or method □ Charles Babbage was one of the pioneers of computer technology. (pioneiro)
2 one of the first people to go to a new country to live and work there □ the American pioneers (pioneiro)

pioneer² /ˌpaɪəˈnɪə(r)/ VERB [pioneers, pioneering, pioneered] to be one of the first people to do or make something □ The hospital is pioneering new surgical techniques. (ser pioneiro)

pip /pɪp/ NOUN [plural pips] a small seed in a fruit such as an apple or lemon (semente)

> THESAURUS: A seed is the thing that a plant produces and that new plants grow from. A pip is a small seed in a fruit such as an apple or a lemon. The hard piece in the middle of fruits such as cherries or peaches is called a stone.

pipe /paɪp/ NOUN [plural pipes]
1 a metal or plastic tube through which water or gas can flow 🔂 A pipe had burst and there was water everywhere. (cano)
2 a tube with a hollow bowl at one end used for smoking tobacco 🔂 Grandpa used to smoke a pipe. (cachimbo)

pipeline /ˈpaɪplaɪn/ NOUN [plural pipelines] a long pipe that crosses the land or sea and carries oil or gas (duto)
♦ IDIOM in the pipeline being planned or organized, or about to happen □ Further job losses are in the pipeline.

pirate /ˈpaɪrət/ NOUN [plural **pirates**] someone who steals things from ships while they are at sea ▫ *As a boy, he loved stories about pirates.* (**pirata**)

pistol /ˈpɪstəl/ NOUN [plural **pistols**] a small gun that is held in one hand (**pistola**)

pit /pɪt/ NOUN [plural **pits**]
1 a large, deep hole dug in the ground ▫ *The dead animals were buried in a pit.* (**cova**)
2 a deep mine, especially a coal mine ▫ *His father and grandfather had both worked at the pit.* (**poço de mina, mina**)

pitch¹ /pɪtʃ/ NOUN [plural **pitches**]
1 an area of ground, often with lines marked on it, where people play games like football or cricket ▫ *a football pitch* (**campo**)
2 how high or low a sound is (**entoação**)

> THESAURUS: A **pitch** is an area of ground where people play games such as football, rugby, or cricket. A **course** is a piece of land that a race is run over or where a game of golf is played. A **court** is an area where you play a sport such as tennis or basketball. A **ground** is an area where a sport is played, but includes the seats as well as the pitch.

pitch² /pɪtʃ/ VERB [**pitches, pitching, pitched**] **pitch a tent** to put up a tent so that it is ready to use (**armar**)

pity¹ /ˈpɪti/ NOUN, NO PLURAL
1 sadness you feel for other people who are suffering or in trouble ▫ *She felt a wave of pity for the poor old man, abandoned by his family.* (**pena**)
2 it's a pity... used for saying that you feel sorry or disappointed about a situation ▫ *It's a pity that John couldn't come.* (**é uma pena**)
3 take pity on someone to feel so sorry for someone that you help them ▫ *Mark took pity on me and gave me a lift home.* (**ter pena**)

pity² /ˈpɪti/ VERB [**pities, pitying, pitied**] to feel pity for someone ▫ *I really pity her, having a mother like that.* (**lamentar, ter pena**)

pizza /ˈpiːtsə/ NOUN [plural **pizzas**] a flat round piece of bread with cheese, vegetables or meat on top that is baked in an oven ▫ *a mushroom pizza* ▫ *Would you like another slice of pizza?* (**pizza**)

place¹ /pleɪs/ NOUN [plural **places**]
1 a particular area, position, town, building, etc. ▫ *We rented a place by the sea.* ▫ *I imagine Beijing is a very interesting place.* ▫ *She broke her arm in three places.* ▫ *Make sure you keep the money in a safe place.* ▫ *Smoking is not allowed in public places.* (**lugar**)
2 the position where something should be, or where something or someone usually is ▫ *Put the books back in their proper place on the shelf.* (**lugar**)
3 take place to happen ▫ *The election is due to take place next month.* ▫ *The wedding took place in secret.* (**lugar**)
4 a seat on a public vehicle or in a public building ▫ *Please go back to your places and sit down.* ▫ *Would you save my place while I get a coffee?* (**lugar**)
5 a position in a queue (= line of people waiting) ▫ *Now I've lost my place in the queue.* (**lugar**)
6 in first/third/last, etc. place used to show someone's position at the end of a race or competition (**lugar**)
7 in place in the correct position ▫ *Make sure the safety harness is in place.* (**no lugar**)
8 in place of someone/something instead of someone/something ▫ *Pat is here today, in place of Marc, who is ill.* (**em vez de**)

> THESAURUS: A **place** is a particular position, or the position where something should be, or where something or someone usually is. A **site** is a place where something happens or happened, or a place used for a certain purpose. For example, you can talk about the **site** where a battle took place or the **site** of a new hospital (where it will be built). A **spot** or a **location** is a place or position. **Spot** is a more informal word. You might talk about a nice **spot** for a picnic, or the **location** where a film is made.

place² /pleɪs/ VERB [**places, placing, placed**]
1 to put something somewhere, usually with care ▫ *He placed his hand on her shoulder.* ▫ *She placed a flower on the grave.* (**colocar**)
2 to cause someone or something to be in a particular situation or state ▫ *He had placed me in a very difficult situation by promising that I would go to the party.* ▫ *Money worries placed a great strain on their marriage.* ▫ *The government has placed restrictions on public pay rises.* (**colocar**)

plain¹ /pleɪn/ ADJECTIVE [**plainer, plainest**]
1 obvious ▫ *She made it quite plain that she didn't like me.* (**evidente**)
2 in one colour or without any decoration or pattern ▫ *a plain white tablecloth* (**simples**)
3 simple or ordinary ▫ *He likes fairly plain cooking.* (**simples**)
4 a plain person is not attractive (**comum**)

plain² /pleɪn/ NOUN [plural **plains**] a large flat area of land (**planície**)

plan¹ /plæn/ VERB [**plans, planning, planned**]
1 to decide what you are going to do and how you are going to do it ▫ *We spent months planning the wedding.* ▫ *Always plan your essay before you start writing.* ▫ *We got a designer in to plan the garden.* (**planejar**)
2 to hope and expect to do something in the future ▫ *+ to do something Natasha is planning to go to university next year.* ▫ *+ on doing something They're planning on taking a year off to travel.* (**planejar**)

plan² /plæn/ NOUN [plural **plans**]
1 an idea or arrangement for something you hope to do in the future ▫ *What are your plans for the future?* ▫ *+ to do something We have no plans to move house at the moment.* ▫ *There's been a change of plan. We're going out on Friday instead.* (**plano**)

2 a drawing that shows how a building, town, machine, etc. will be built ◻ *The council is showing its plans to develop the city centre.* (**planta**)

plane /pleɪn/ NOUN [*plural* planes] an aeroplane (**avião**)

planet /ˈplænɪt/ NOUN [*plural* planets] any of the large objects in space that move around a sun or star ◻ *the planet Venus* (**planeta**)

plank /plæŋk/ NOUN [*plural* planks] a long flat piece of wood (**tábua**)

plant¹ /plɑːnt/ NOUN [*plural* plants] any living thing that grows from the ground and has a stem, roots and leaves ◻ *Young plants must be protected from frost.* ◻ *a tobacco plant* (**planta**)

plant² /plɑːnt/ VERB [plants, planting, planted] to put seeds or plants in soil so that they grow ◻ *They're planting trees along the roadside.* (**plantar**)

plaster¹ /ˈplɑːstə(r)/ NOUN [*plural* plasters]
1 a piece of soft sticky cloth that you put over a cut to keep it clean (**emplastro**)
2 *no plural* a substance that is put on walls and dries to form a hard, smooth surface (**reboco**)
3 in plaster if your arm, leg etc. is in plaster, it has a hard cover around it to protect a broken bone (**engessado**)
plaster² /ˈplɑːstə(r)/ VERB [plasters, plastering, plastered] to put plaster on walls (**rebocar**)

plastic¹ /ˈplæstɪk/ NOUN [*plural* plastics] a light strong substance made from chemicals and used to make many different things ◻ *toys made of plastic* (**plástico**)

plastic² /ˈplæstɪk/ ADJECTIVE made of plastic ◻ *plastic bags* (**de plástico**)

plate /pleɪt/ NOUN [*plural* plates] a flat dish for eating or serving food from ◻ *a paper/plastic plate* ◻ *Pass your plates.* (**prato**)

platform /ˈplætfɔːm/ NOUN [*plural* platforms]
1 the area next to the tracks at a railway station, where passengers get on and off trains ◻ *The 9:45 service to Leeds will leave from platform 4.* (**plataforma**)
2 a raised area of floor where performers and speakers stand so that the audience can see them (**estrado**)

platinum /ˈplætɪnəm/ NOUN, NO PLURAL a very valuable silver metal that is used to make jewellery (**platina**)

play¹ /pleɪ/ VERB [plays, playing, played]
1 to spend time enjoying yourself with games or toys ◻ *The children were playing in the garden.* (**brincar**)
2 to take part in a sport or game ◻ *He plays cricket on Saturdays.* ◻ *Luke played well in the last match.* ◻ **+ for** *He used to play for the national team.* (**jogar**)
3 to make music with a musical instrument, or to perform a piece of music ◻ *Do you play the piano?* ◻ *He played all the Beethoven sonatas.* (**tocar**)
4 if you play a CD, DVD, etc., you put it in a machine to make it produce sound or images (**tocar**)
5 to act as a character in a film, play, etc. ◻ *She plays the part of Harry's daughter.* (**representar**)

play² /pleɪ/ NOUN [*plural* plays]
1 a story that is performed by actors in a theatre ◻ *Our school is putting on a play.* (**peça**)
2 *no plural* the activity of enjoying yourself with games and toys ◻ *Young children learn best through play.* (**jogo**)

player /ˈpleɪə(r)/ NOUN [*plural* players]
1 someone who plays a sport or game (**jogador**)
2 someone who plays a musical instrument (**músico**)
3 a machine for playing DVDs, CDs, etc. (**aparelho de som, DVD, CD, etc**)

playground /ˈpleɪɡraʊnd/ NOUN [*plural* playgrounds] an area, often next to a school or in a public park, where children play ◻ *Harry fell and hurt his knee in the playground.* (**playground**)

playing card /ˈpleɪɪŋ ˌkɑːd/ NOUN [*plural* playing cards] one of a set of 52 rectangular pieces of card used for playing games (**cartas**)

playing field /ˈpleɪɪŋ ˌfiːld/ NOUN [*plural* playing fields] an area of land used for playing sports such as football ◻ *the school playing fields* (**quadra**)

plea /pliː/ NOUN [*plural* pleas] when someone asks for something in a serious and emotional way ◻ *I couldn't ignore this plea for help.* (**apelo**)

pleasant

pleasant /ˈplezənt/ ADJECTIVE nice or enjoyable □ *We had a very pleasant evening at Sarah's.* □ *It was very pleasant, sitting out in the garden.* □ *Our new neighbours seem very pleasant.* (**agradável**)

pleasantly /ˈplezəntli/ ADVERB in a pleasant way □ *She smiled very pleasantly at us.* ▣ *I was pleasantly surprised by his attitude.* (**agradavelmente**)

please¹ /pliːz/ EXCLAMATION
1 used as a polite way of asking for something □ *Could I have a glass of water, please?* □ *Please could you turn the music down?* □ *Would you please leave?* (**por favor**)
2 yes, please used as a polite way of accepting an offer □ *'Would you like another biscuit?' 'Yes, please.'* (**por favor**)

please² /pliːz/ VERB [pleases, pleasing, pleased] to make someone happy by doing what they want □ *You can't please everyone.* □ *My mother is quite hard to please.* (**contente**)

pleased /pliːzd/ ADJECTIVE happy or satisfied with something □ **+ with** *He was pleased with the way the garden looked.* □ **+ at** *We were all pleased at the result.* □ **+ to do something** *She looked pleased to see him.* □ *She wasn't pleased when he told her he'd lost the tickets.* (**contente**)

pleasure /ˈpleʒə(r)/ NOUN [plural pleasures]
1 no plural a feeling of enjoyment or satisfaction ▣ *She took pleasure in cooking.* ▣ *It gives me great pleasure to be here today.* (**prazer**)
2 something that you enjoy □ *He enjoys the simple pleasures of life.* ▣ *It's a great pleasure to welcome you back.* (**prazer**)

pledge /pledʒ/ NOUN [plural pledges] a serious promise ▣ *The government has made a pledge to improve school food.* □ *He has received pledges of support from all over the world.* (**promessa**)

plenty /ˈplenti/ PRONOUN, ADVERB a lot of something, as much as you need or more than you need □ **+ of** *You'll have plenty of time to complete the test.* □ *Remember to drink plenty of water.* ▣ *There's plenty more bread in the freezer if we run out.* (**bastante, suficiente**)

plot¹ /plɒt/ NOUN [plural plots]
1 the story of a play, book or film □ *the plot of a novel* □ *The film's plot is based on a true story.* (**trama**)
2 a secret plan, especially to do something bad □ *They discovered a plot to kidnap a soldier* (**trama**)
3 a piece of land to be used for a particular purpose □ *a vegetable plot* □ *a plot of land* ∟ *go to* **lose** *the plot* □ *a vegetable plot* □ *a plot of land* ∟ *go to* **lose** *the plot* (**lote**)

plot² /plɒt/ VERB [plots, plotting, plotted] to plan to do something bad or illegal □ *The group may be plotting more attacks.* (**tramar**)

plough /plaʊ/ VERB [ploughs, ploughing, ploughed] to turn over soil with a plough (**arar**)

plug¹ /plʌg/ NOUN [plural plugs]
1 an object attached to a piece of electrical equipment by a wire which connects it to an electricity supply (**plugue**)
2 an object that you use for blocking a hole, especially in a bath or sink □ *a bath plug* (**tampão**)

plug² /plʌg/ VERB [plugs, plugging, plugged] to push something into a hole to block it □ *We need to plug the leak in the boat.* (**tapar**)
♦ PHRASAL VERBS **plug something in** to connect a piece of electrical equipment to the electricity supply □ *I plugged in my laptop.* **plug something into something 1** to connect one piece of electrical equipment to another □ *Plug the camera into your computer to download pictures.* **2** to connect a piece of electrical equipment to the electricity supply □ *Don't leave your phone charger plugged into a socket when you're not using it.*

plum /plʌm/ NOUN [plural plums] a soft red, purple or yellow fruit with a smooth skin and a large seed in the middle (**ameixa**)

plunge /plʌndʒ/ VERB [plunges, plunging, plunged]
1 to fall suddenly and with force □ *The bus plunged off a mountain road.* (**precipitar-se, lançar-se**)
2 to jump, especially into water □ *They plunged into the cool water.* (**afundar, mergulhar**)
3 to push something violently into something □ *He plunged a knife into her stomach.* (**afundar**)

pluperfect /ˌpluːˈpɜːfɪkt/ NOUN, NO PLURAL the tense of a verb that shows that an action finished before a particular time or event in the past, formed using *had* and a past participle (**mais-que-perfeito**)

plural¹ /ˈplʊərəl/ NOUN [plural plurals] the form of a noun, pronoun or verb that you use when there is more than one of something (**plural**)

plural² /ˈplʊərəl/ ADJECTIVE in the plural form □ *a plural noun* (**plural**)

plus¹ /plʌs/ PREPOSITION
1 added to □ *8 plus 2 is 10.* □ *He charges $50 an hour, plus travel expenses.* (**mais**)
2 as well as □ *There are six children, plus two adults.* (**mais**)

plus² /plʌs/ NOUN [plural pluses] a mathematical symbol (+) showing that a number is to be added to another (**mais**)

PM /ˌpiːˈem/ ABBREVIATION **prime minister (primeiro-ministro)**

pm or **p.m.** /ˌpiːˈem/ ABBREVIATION added after the time to show that it is in the afternoon or the evening **(p.m.)**

pocket /ˈpɒkɪt/ NOUN [plural **pockets**] an extra piece of cloth sewn into a piece of clothing or a bag, used for keeping small things in □ *It was in my jeans pocket.* □ *He pulled his wallet from his back pocket.* **(bolso)**

pocket money /ˈpɒkɪt ˌmʌni/ NOUN, NO PLURAL money that parents regularly give their children to buy small things □ *They spent all their pocket money on sweets.* **(mesada)**

podcast /ˈpɒdkɑːst/ NOUN [plural **podcasts**] a recording that you get from a website and then listen to on a computer or MP3 player (= small piece of computer equipment) **(podcast)**

poem /ˈpəʊɪm/ NOUN [plural **poems**] a piece of writing using interesting language, arranged in short lines, often using words with the same sounds □ *a love poem* ▣ *He wrote a poem for her.* **(poema)**

poet /ˈpəʊɪt/ NOUN [plural **poets**] someone who writes poems □ *He was a poet and nove list.* **(poeta)**

poetry /ˈpəʊɪtri/ NOUN, NO PLURAL poems in general □ *a book of poetry* **(poesia)**

point¹ /pɔɪnt/ NOUN [plural **points**]
1 an idea, opinion, or thing you want to say ▣ *He made the point that some people wouldn't be able to afford the service.* ▣ *I do take your point* (= understand your opinion) *about the high fence.* ▣ *'Meg says it's not fair for the girls to do all the work.' 'Well, she does have a point* (= her opinion is worth considering).' **(opinião)**
2 the reason for something or the purpose of some thing ▣ *What's the point of going home if you just have to go straight back out again?* ▣ *I can't really see the point of exercising.* ▣ *There's no point in asking her – she won't come.* **(razão)**
3 the most important thing about what has been said ▣ *The point is, we can't afford a holiday.* ▣ *She talked for so long, I thought she'd never get to the point.* **(questão)**
4 a particular time in an event or process ▣ *At that point, we decided to leave.* ▣ *I've reached the point with my studies where I'd like to specialize more.* ▣ *At some point today, I need to phone Miriam.* **(instante)**
5 a particular place □ *Drinks are available at several points along the route.* □ *This is the highest point in England.* **(ponto)**
6 a feature or characteristic ▣ *I know you don't like Mike, but he does have some good points.* **(característica)**
7 the sharp end of something □ *Make a small hole with the point of a needle.* **(ponta)**
8 the mark '.' that is used in numbers that have a part less than one, e.g. 5.34 **(ponto)**
9 a unit for showing the score in a game or a competition ▣ *Who got the highest number of points?* ▣ *You score 2 points for each correct answer.* **(ponto)**
10 be at the point of doing something to be going to do something very soon □ *We were at the point of signing the contract when the buyers pulled out.* **(ponto)**

point² /pɔɪnt/ VERB [**points, pointing, pointed**]
1 to show someone something by holding your finger or a thin object towards it □ + *at He pointed at a man in black.* □ *She pointed towards the door with her umbrella.* **(apontar)**
2 to face in a particular direction, or to make something face a particular direction □ + *at He pointed the gun at the target.* □ *The sign pointed north.* □ *What time is it when the little hand points to the three?* **(apontar)**
◆ PHRASAL VERB **point something out** to make someone aware of a fact □ *He pointed out that he had been waiting for over an hour.*

pointed /ˈpɔɪntɪd/ ADJECTIVE with a sharp end □ *a pointed stick* **(pontudo)**

pointless /ˈpɔɪntləs/ ADJECTIVE having no purpose or meaning □ *a pointless argument* □ *It's pointless asking him – he'll never come.* **(inútil)**

point of view /ˌpɔɪnt əv ˈvjuː/ NOUN [plural **points of view**]
1 a way of considering or judging a situation □ *From a practical point of view, I see nothing wrong.* **(ponto de vista)**
2 an opinion about something □ *They have different points of view.* **(ponto de vista)**

poison¹ /ˈpɔɪzən/ NOUN [plural **poisons**] a substance that causes death or illness when you eat, drink or breathe it □ *a deadly poison* □ *rat poison* **(veneno)**

poison² /ˈpɔɪzən/ VERB [**poisons, poisoning, poisoned**] to kill or harm someone with poison □ *They were poisoned by carbon monoxide fumes.* **(envenenar)**

poisonous /ˈpɔɪzənəs/ ADJECTIVE containing poison □ *This cleaning liquid is poisonous.* **(venenoso)**

poke /pəʊk/ VERB [**pokes, poking, poked**]
1 to quickly push something or someone with your finger or with something sharp □ *He poked me in the stomach.* **(cutucar)**
2 to appear through a hole or from behind something □ *She poked her head through the curtains.* □ *His hair was poking out from under his hat.* **(aparecer)**

poker /ˈpəʊkə(r)/ NOUN [plural **pokers**] a card game played for money **(pôquer)**

polar /ˈpəʊlə(r)/ ADJECTIVE to do with the north or south pole (= areas at the top and bottom of the Earth) ▫ *a polar region* ▫ *polar ice* (**polar**)

polar bear /ˈpəʊləˌbeə(r)/ NOUN [*plural* **polar bears**] a large white bear that lives near the North Pole (**urso polar**)

pole /pəʊl/ NOUN [*plural* **poles**]
1 a long thin stick of metal or wood, often used for supporting something ▫ *an aluminium tent pole* (**poste, vara**)
2 one of the two areas at the most northern and southern points of the Earth (**polo**)

police /pəˈliːs/ NOUN, NO PLURAL the people whose job is to make people obey the law and to catch people who break the law ▣ *One of his neighbours called the police.* ▫ *Last night police were questioning four men.* ▣ *the police force* ▣ *a police investigation* (**polícia**)

policeman /pəˈliːsmən/ NOUN [*plural* **policemen**] a male police officer (**policial**)

police officer /pəˈliːs ˌɒfɪsə(r)/ NOUN [*plural* **police officers**] a member of the police ▫ *an armed police officer* (**policial**)

police station /pəˈliːs ˌsteɪʃən/ NOUN [*plural* **police stations**] a building where the police have their offices (**posto policial**)

policewoman /pəˈliːsˌwʊmən/ NOUN [*plural* **policewomen**] a female police officer (**policial**)

policy /ˈpɒləsi/ NOUN [*plural* **policies**] a plan about how to deal with something by a government, political party, business, etc. ▫ *government policies* ▣ *US foreign policy* ▫ *the party's policy on immigration* (**política**)

polish¹ /ˈpɒlɪʃ/ VERB [**polishes, polishing, polished**] to rub something until it shines ▫ *Remember to polish your shoes.* (**polir**)

polish² /ˈpɒlɪʃ/ NOUN [*plural* **polishes**] a substance used to polish something ▣ *shoe polish* ▫ *furniture polish* (**polidor**)

polite /pəˈlaɪt/ ADJECTIVE [**politer, politest**] behaving in a pleasant way towards other people, for example, saying 'thank you' and 'please' ▫ *Her children are very polite.* ▫ *+ to She was polite to hospital staff.* ▫ *+ to do something He was too polite to interrupt.* (**educado, polido**)

politely /pəˈlaɪtli/ ADVERB in a polite way ▫ *'Would you like a seat?' he asked her politely.* ▫ *She politely declined the invitation.* (**educado, polido**)

political /pəˈlɪtɪkəl/ ADJECTIVE to do with politics, politicians or government ▣ *a political party* ▣ *a political leader* ▫ *a political and economic crisis* (**político**)

politician /ˌpɒlɪˈtɪʃən/ NOUN [*plural* **politicians**] someone whose job is politics, especially someone who has been elected to a parliament ▫ *People don't seem to trust politicians.* (**político**)

politics /ˈpɒlɪtɪks/ NOUN, NO PLURAL
1 ideas or activities to do with governing a country ▫ *He's very interested in politics.* (**política**)
2 the job of being a politician ▣ *He entered politics after leaving university.* (**política**)

poll /pəʊl/ NOUN [*plural* **polls**]
1 when a number of people are asked their opinion on a particular subject ▣ *The poll showed that about 55% of people are against the war.* ▣ *The poll was conducted for a local newspaper.* (**pesquisa de opinião**)
2 a political election in which people vote ▣ *Voters go to the polls* (= vote) *on 24 November.* (**eleição**)

pollute /pəˈluːt/ VERB [**pollutes, polluting, polluted**] to allow harmful substances to go into the air, soil or water ▫ *We need to find energy sources which don't pollute the environment.* (**poluir**)

pollution /pəˈluːʃən/ NOUN, NO PLURAL
1 harmful substances in the air, soil or water ▣ *the health effects of air pollution* ▣ *a major source of pollution* ▫ *+ from We need to reduce pollution from traffic.* (**poluição**)
2 when harmful substances are allowed into the air, soil or water ▫ *+ of We need to take action against the pollution of the oceans.* (**poluir**)

pond /pɒnd/ NOUN [*plural* **ponds**] a small area of water, smaller than a lake ▫ *a garden pond* ▫ *a fish pond* (**lagoa**)

pony /ˈpəʊni/ NOUN [*plural* **ponies**] a small horse (**pônei**)

pool /puːl/ NOUN [*plural* **pools**]
1 an area of water made for swimming in ▫ *The hotel has an indoor pool.* ▫ *a heated pool* (**piscina**)
2 a small area of liquid ▫ *There was a small pool of blood on the floor.* (**poça**)

poor /pʊə(r)/ ADJECTIVE [**poorer, poorest**]
1 having little money and owning few things ▫ *a poor country* ▫ *His family were very poor.* (**pobre**)
2 of a low standard ▣ *The paper was of poor quality.* ▣ *He's in very poor health.* ▫ *It was a poor performance by the team generally.* (**frágil**)
3 used to show that someone or something deserves sympathy ▫ *Poor you! You sound so ill.* ▫ *The poor little thing is all wet.* (**pobre**)

poorly /ˈpʊəli/ ADVERB badly or not well enough ▫ *a poorly paid job* ▫ *He performed fairly poorly in both matches.* (**pobremente**)

pop¹ /pɒp/ NOUN [*plural* **pops**]
1 *no plural* modern music with short, simple songs and a strong beat ▣ *pop music* ▣ *a pop star* ▣ *a pop song* (**pop**)
2 a short sound like something exploding ▫ *They heard a loud pop.* ▫ *The bottle opened with a pop.* (**estouro**)

pop² /pɒp/ VERB [pops, popping, popped]
1 to go somewhere quickly, for a short time □ + *out* *I just popped out for a few minutes.* □ + *into* *I need to pop into the office.* (ir rápido)
2 to put something somewhere quickly □ *I'll just pop the pizza in the oven.* □ *Karen popped her head around the door.* (enfiar)
3 to make a short sound like something exploding □ *The fire crackled and popped.* 🔄 *I could hear balloons popping in the background.* (estourar)
◆ PHRASAL VERB **pop up** to suddenly appear □ *Bars and cafe's are popping up all over the place.*

Pope /pəʊp/ NOUN [plural Popes] the leader of the Catholic Church (papa)

poppy /'pɒpɪ/ NOUN [plural poppies] a tall, red flower that grows in fields (papoula)

popular /'pɒpjʊlə(r)/ ADJECTIVE liked by a lot of people □ *a popular tourist destination* □ *She was a very popular student.* □ + *with* *The beach is popular with tourists.* 🔄 *Podcasts are becoming increasingly popular.* (popular)

population /ˌpɒpjʊ'leɪʃən/ NOUN [plural populations]
1 all the people who live in an area, country, etc. 🔄 *The troops are there to protect the local population.* □ *More than half the world's population live in cities.* (população)
2 the number of people who live in an area, country, etc. □ + *of* *The city has a population of around two million.* (população)

> THESAURUS: Population means all the people who live in an area, country, etc. Society is all the people who live in a group or in a particular country or area. We often use society to talk about the opinions and beliefs of the people in an area. The public means people generally. A citizen is someone who has the right to live in a country permanently.

pore /pɔː(r)/ NOUN [plural pores] one of the very small holes in your skin that sweat comes out of. A biology word. (poro)

pork /pɔːk/ NOUN, NO PLURAL meat from a pig □ *roast pork* (porco)

port /pɔːt/ NOUN [plural ports] a place where ships can stop on the coast, and the town or city around it □ *the Israeli port of Haifa* □ *a major shipping port* □ *It's a small fishing port on the south coast.* (porto)

portable /'pɔːtəbəl/ ADJECTIVE small enough to be carried easily □ *a portable television* □ *a portable DVD player* (portátil)

porter /'pɔːtə(r)/ NOUN [plural porters]
1 someone whose job is to carry bags for people at a station, hotel, etc. □ *The porter will take your bags up to your room.* (carregador)
2 someone whose job is to look after a building □ *the night porter at the hotel* (porteiro)

portion /'pɔːʃən/ NOUN [plural portions] a part of a total amount □ *She spends a large portion of her income on clothes.* (porção)

portrait /'pɔːtreɪt/ NOUN [plural portraits] a painting or photograph of a person, especially of their face □ *a portrait of the prince* 🔄 *a portrait painter* (retrato)

posh /pɒʃ/ ADJECTIVE [posher, poshest]
1 an informal word meaning expensive and comfortable □ *a posh hotel* □ *a posh London restaurant* (chique)
2 an informal word meaning from a high social class □ *a posh accent* (chique)

position /pə'zɪʃən/ NOUN [plural positions]
1 a way of standing, sitting or lying □ *I must have been sleeping in an awkward position.* (posição)
2 the place where something is, or the way in which it has been put there □ *His pipe was in its usual position, beside his chair.* □ *Push the lever to the 'on' position.* (localização)
3 the situation that someone is in 🔄 *Our team is in a strong position to win the championship.* 🔄 *Her demands put me in a very difficult position.* □ *Unfortunately, I am not in a position* (= I am not able) *to help you.* □ *In her position, I'd hire a really good lawyer.* (posição)
4 a job or post □ *He applied for a teaching position.* 🔄 *Our marketing manager left, and we have not yet filled his position.* (posto)

positive /'pɒzɪtɪv/ ADJECTIVE
1 completely certain □ + *that* *Are you absolutely positive that he's German?* □ + *about* *Jack has seen the letter. I'm positive about that.* (seguro)
2 feeling happy about a situation and believing that the future will be good 🔄 *He has a very positive attitude to life.* 🔄 *It can be difficult to remain positive when you have so many problems.* (positivo)

possess /pə'zes/ VERB [possesses, possessing, possessed] a formal word meaning to have something □ *He was charged with possessing an illegal weapon.* □ *Candidates should possess strong communication skills.* (possuir)

possession /pə'zeʃən/ NOUN [plural possessions] something you own or have 🔄 *They packed up their personal possessions.* (possuir)

possessive¹ /pə'zesɪv/ ADJECTIVE
1 not wanting to share your things with other people □ *Children are very possessive with their toys.* (possessivo)
2 in grammar, showing who or what a person or thing belongs to □ *a possessive pronoun such as 'mine'* (possessivo)

possessive

possessive² /pəˈzesɪv/ NOUN [plural possessives] in grammar, a word that shows who or what a person or thing belongs to (**possessivo**)

possibility /ˌpɒsəˈbɪləti/ NOUN [plural possibilities]
1 the chance that something might happen □ + of We were warned about the possibility of flooding. □ + that There's a strong possibility that the tour will be cancelled. (**possibilidade**)
2 something that might happen ▣ Civil war is now a real possibility. (**possibilidade**)

possible /ˈpɒsəbəl/ ADJECTIVE
1 something that is possible can happen or be done □ + to do something It isn't possible to see the doctor today. ▣ Try to avoid the area if possible. (**possível**)
2 something that is possible may be true □ + that It's possible that I made a mistake. □ That doesn't seem possible. ▣ There are several possible explanations. (**possível**)
3 as soon/quickly, etc. as possible as soon, quickly, etc. as you can □ We need the work done as quickly as possible. (**possível**)

possibly /ˈpɒsəbli/ ADVERB perhaps □ It could take about 5 days, possibly longer. (**possivelmente**)

post¹ /pəʊst/ NOUN [plural posts]
1 the service which collects and delivers letters and packages, or the letters and packages sent □ I sent it by post. □ Has the post arrived yet? (**correio**)
2 a job □ the post of finance director □ a teaching post ▣ He held a senior post at the bank. (**emprego**)
3 a long piece of wood fixed into the ground ▣ a fence post ▣ a goal post (**poste**)
4 a message which has been put on a website. A computing word □ a blog post □ She announced the tour in a post on her website. (**mensagem**)

post² /pəʊst/ VERB [posts, posting, posted]
1 to send a letter or package by post ▣ I posted the letter yesterday. (**postar**)
2 to put a message, video, picture, etc. on a website. A computing word □ He posted a message to fans on his website. □ A video of the interview was posted on the Internet. (**postar**)

postbox /ˈpəʊstbɒks/ NOUN [plural postboxes] a container in a public place where letters can be posted (**caixa de correio**)

postcard /ˈpəʊstkɑːd/ NOUN [plural postcards] a card with a picture on one side. You write on the other side and send the card by post without an envelope □ a picture postcard □ I'll send you a postcard from Tokyo. (**cartão-postal**)

post code /ˈpəʊstkəʊd/ NOUN [plural post codes] a series of letters and numbers at the end of an address (**código postal**)

pound

poster /ˈpəʊstə(r)/ NOUN [plural posters] a large notice or picture used for advertising, for decorating a wall, or for giving information □ She has posters of movie stars all over her bedroom walls. (**pôster**)

postman /ˈpəʊstmən/ NOUN [plural postmen] someone whose job is to deliver letters and packages to houses or offices □ Has the postman been yet? (**carteiro**)

post office /ˈpəʊst ˌɒfɪs/ NOUN [plural post offices] a shop where you can post letters and packages, and buy stamps (**agência dos correios**)

postpone /pəʊstˈpəʊn/ VERB [postpones, postponing, postponed] to decide to do something at a later time than planned □ We had to postpone our trip to Paris. (**adiar**)

pot /pɒt/ NOUN [plural pots] a round container used for cooking, for storing things in, or for growing plants in □ + of a pot of paint ▣ a pile of dirty pots and pans (= containers used for cooking) ▣ a flower pot (= container for growing plants) (**panela, pote, vaso**)

potato /pəˈteɪtəʊ/ NOUN [plural potatoes] a very common white, round vegetable that grows underground with a brown or yellow skin □ mashed potato □ roast potatoes (**batata**)

pottery /ˈpɒtəri/ NOUN, NO PLURAL
1 objects such as bowls and cups made from clay (**olaria, cerâmica**)
2 the job or activity of making things from clay (**olaria, cerâmica**)

poultry /ˈpəʊltri/ NOUN, NO PLURAL
1 birds such as chickens that are kept for people to eat (**aves domésticas**)
2 the meat from these birds (**aves**)

pounce /paʊns/ VERB [pounces, pouncing, pounced] to jump or move forward suddenly to attack or catch someone or something □ The cat pounced on the mouse. (**saltar, dar o bote**)

pound¹ /paʊnd/ NOUN [plural pounds]
1 the main unit of money in Britain. The written symbol is £. □ They cost just a few pounds each. □ a multi-million pound contract (**libra esterlina**)

2 a coin worth one pound (**libra**)
3 a unit for measuring weight, equal to 0.454 kilograms. This is often written lb. (**libra**)

pound² /paʊnd/ VERB [pounds, pounding, pounded] to hit something hard repeatedly □ Someone was pounding at the door, trying to get in. (**bater**)

pour /pɔː(r)/ VERB [pours, pouring, poured]
1 to make a liquid flow out of a container □ + **into** She poured the orange juice into a glass. □ + **out** She poured out the tea. □ + **over** Pour the sauce over the chicken. (**fluir**)
2 to rain very hard ▣ It's pouring with rain outside. □ The rain was pouring down. (**chover torrencialmente**)
3 to flow out of something fast and in large quantities □ Water was pouring through the ceiling. □ The sweat poured down his face. (**escorrer**)

poverty /ˈpɒvəti/ NOUN, NO PLURAL the state of being poor □ Many families are living in poverty. □ a campaign to reduce global poverty (**pobreza**)

powder /ˈpaʊdə(r)/ NOUN [plural powders] a substance in the form of very small dry pieces, like dust □ chilli powder □ washing powder □ She sprinkled some cocoa powder on the top. (**pó**)

power /ˈpaʊə(r)/ NOUN [plural powers]
1 the ability to control or influence people or things □ economic/military power □ + **over** The big factory owners had a lot of power over local people. □ They really understand the power of the media. (**poder, capacidade**)
2 energy used for working machines, or the supply of this energy ▣ nuclear power ▣ We are looking at new ways to generate power. ▣ Electricity companies are working day and night to restore power to the area. (**energia**)
3 a country with a lot of influence in the world □ He says that Western powers are failing to deal with climate change. (**potência**)
4 strength or force □ The power of the blast knocked me over. (**potência**)
5 the official right to do something □ + **to do something** We don't have the power to issue visas. □ The committee's powers are limited. (**autoridade**)

powerful /ˈpaʊəfʊl/ ADJECTIVE
1 having the ability to control or influence people or things □ a powerful politician □ a powerful nation (**poderoso**)
2 having a lot of physical force □ a powerful earthquake (**poderoso**)
3 very effective, being able to do a lot □ Computers have become more powerful. (**poderoso**)

practical¹ /ˈpræktɪkəl/ ADJECTIVE
1 to do with real situations, not ideas ▣ They provide practical advice. (**prático**)
2 useful and suitable ▣ It's the most practical solution to the problem. □ It's not practical to cycle in a long skirt. (**prático**)
3 good at repairing things and doing things with your hands □ He's not a very practical person. (**prático**)
4 able to make sensible decisions □ She's much more practical than her sister. (**prático**)

practical² /ˈpræktɪkəl/ NOUN [plural practicals] a lesson or an exam in which students learn or use practical skills (**prático**)

practically /ˈpræktɪkəli/ ADVERB almost □ It was practically full. □ Practically everything was destroyed. (**praticamente**)

practice¹ /ˈpræktɪs/ NOUN [plural practices]
1 when you do something often so that you get better at it □ He'll soon learn to play the violin with a bit more practice. □ He goes to choir practice on Mondays. (**treino, exercício**)
2 an activity, especially one that people have been doing for a long time □ They campaigned to end the practice of torture. □ She studied their religious practices. (**prática**)
3 be out of practice to not have done something for a long time □ I'd love to play in your hockey team, but I'm a bit out of practice. (**fora de forma**)

practice² /ˈpræktɪs/ VERB [practices, practicing, practiced] the US spelling of **practise**

practise /ˈpræktɪs/ VERB [practises, practising, practised] to do something again and again so that you get better at it □ + **ing** Practise breathing through your nose. □ To become a good musician, you must practise regularly. (**treinar, exercitar**)

> Remember that in British English, **practise** with an **s** is a verb. **Practice** with a **c** is a noun: □ This gave me a chance to practise my language skills. □ I have football practice tonight.

praise¹ /preɪz/ VERB [praises, praising, praised] to say how well someone has done and how you admire them □ + **for** He was widely praised for his work. □ The prime minister praised the rescue effort. (**elogiar**)

praise² /preɪz/ NOUN, NO PLURAL when you praise someone □ + **for** She received praise for her handling of the incident. ▣ He won praise from the team coach. (**elogiar**)

pray /preɪ/ VERB [prays, praying, prayed] to speak to a god □ + **for** She knelt down and prayed for forgiveness. □ + **to** He prayed to Allah. (**rezar**)

prayer /preə(r)/ NOUN [plural prayers]
1 the words that you use when you pray to a god □ the Lord's prayer ▣ He said a prayer of thanks. □ They went to the mosque for Friday prayers. (**oração, reza**)
2 no plural when you pray to a god □ They knelt in prayer. (**oração**)

preach /priːtʃ/ VERB [preaches, preaching, preached] to talk to a group of people about a religious subject, usually as part of a church service ◨ *Father Andrew will preach the sermon.* (pregar)

preacher /ˈpriːtʃə(r)/ NOUN [plural preachers] someone who talks to people about a religious subject at a church service (pregador)

precaution /prɪˈkɔːʃən/ NOUN [plural precautions] something you do to avoid an accident or a problem happening ◨ *We're taking all necessary precautions.* ◨ *They stopped work on the site as a safety precaution.* (precaução)

precious /ˈpreʃəs/ ADJECTIVE
1 very valuable and rare ▫ *precious stones* ▫ *In many parts of the world, water is a precious resource.* (precioso)
2 very important to someone ▫ *His books are very precious to him.* (precioso)

precise /prɪˈsaɪs/ ADJECTIVE
1 exact ▫ *the precise location* ▫ *He didn't give any precise details.* ◨ *At that precise moment, the bell rang.* (preciso)
2 careful and accurate ▫ *Her work is very precise* (preciso)

precisely /prɪˈsaɪslɪ/ ADVERB
1 exactly or accurately ▫ *We need to find out precisely what happened.* ▫ *It arrived at precisely 12.34.* (precisamente)
2 used to strongly agree with someone's opinion (exatamente)

predator /ˈpredətə(r)/ NOUN [plural predators] an animal that hunts and eats other animals (predador)

predict /prɪˈdɪkt/ VERB [predicts, predicting, predicted] to say that you think something will happen in the future ▫ *They're predicting snow for next week.* (predizer)

prediction /prɪˈdɪkʃən/ NOUN [plural predictions] when you say that you think something will happen in the future, or what you think will happen ◨ *I don't want to make any predictions yet.* (predição)

prefer /prɪˈfɜː(r)/ VERB [prefers, preferring, preferred] to like or to want one thing more than something else ▫ *I prefer the red dress to the black one.* ▫ *+ to do something We'd prefer to stay near the beach.* ▫ *He prefers not to talk about his family in public.* ▫ *+ ing I prefer working from home.* ▫ *You can bring you own food if you prefer.* (preferir)

preference /ˈprefərəns/ NOUN [plural preferences] when you prefer one thing to another, or something that you like or prefer ▫ *The children showed a preference for sweet foods.* (preferência)

pregnancy /ˈpregnənsɪ/ NOUN [plural pregnancies] the period when a woman or a female animal carries a developing baby inside her ▫ *Smoking during pregnancy can harm the baby.* (gravidez)

pregnant /ˈpregnənt/ ADJECTIVE if a woman or a female animal is pregnant, she is carrying a developing baby inside her ◨ *a pregnant woman* ▫ *+ with She was pregnant with twins.* ◨ *She got pregnant again quite quickly.* (grávida)

prehistoric /ˌpriːhɪˈstɒrɪk/ ADJECTIVE to do with the time in the past before history was written down ▫ *prehistoric times* ▫ *prehistoric animals* (pré-histórico)

prejudice /ˈpredʒudɪs/ NOUN [plural prejudices] when someone has an unfair opinion or dislike of someone or something without knowing or understanding them ◨ *racial prejudice* ▫ *There is still prejudice against people with mental disabilities.* (preconceito)

premature /ˈpremətjuə(r)/ ADJECTIVE a premature baby is born before the time it should have been born (prematuro)

premier /ˈpremjə(r)/ ADJECTIVE best, most successful or most important ▫ *France's premier resort* ▫ *one of the world's premier sports events* (principal)

premiere /ˈpremɪeə(r)/ NOUN [plural premieres] the first public showing or performance of a film, play, etc. ◨ *the world premiere of the new James Bond film* (estreia)

preparation /ˌprepəˈreɪʃən/ NOUN [plural preparations]
1 *no plural* when you get ready for something ▫ *+ for This is ideal preparation for next week's game.* ◨ *We did some shopping in preparation for the trip.* ▫ *Make sure the food preparation area is clean.* (preparativo)
2 something you do to get ready for something ▫ *How are the wedding preparations going?* ◨ *We're making the final preparations for the show.* (preparação)

prepare /prɪˈpeə(r)/ VERB [prepares, preparing, prepared] to get ready for something or to make something ready ▫ *+ for We need to prepare for the long journey.* ▫ *+ to do something They are preparing to open a new shop.* ▫ *He prepared a report on the company.* ▫ *We have to prepare students for working life.* ◨ *Prepare yourself for a shock when you see him.* (preparar)

preposition /ˌprepəˈzɪʃən/ NOUN [plural prepositions] a word or phrase used before a noun or a pronoun to show things like position, time or method. For example, *in*, *by* and *out of* are prepositions. (preposição)

prescribe /prɪˈskraɪb/ VERB [prescribes, prescribing, prescribed] to tell a patient to take a particular medicine ▫ *Doctors often prescribe antibiotics for infections.* (prescrever)

prescription /prɪˈskrɪpʃən/ NOUN [plural prescriptions] a written instruction from a doctor saying that someone needs a particular medicine ▫ *+ for a prescription for sleeping pills* ◨ *a prescription drug* (= medicine that must be prescribed by a doctor) (prescrição)

presence /ˈprezəns/ NOUN, NO PLURAL the fact of someone or something being somewhere ▫ *Tests* *indicated the presence of the disease.* ▣ *He was questioned in the presence of a lawyer.* (**presença**)

present¹ /ˈprezənt/ NOUN [plural **presents**]
1 something you give to someone, for example for their birthday ▫ *I've got a present for you.* ▣ *a birthday present* ▣ *The children opened their Christmas presents.* (**presente**)
2 the present the time now (**presente**)
3 at present now ▫ *He doesn't have a job at present.* (**atual**)

present² /ˈprezənt/ ADJECTIVE
1 being in a particular place ▫ *Both men were present at the meeting.* ▫ *Vitamin D is present in small quantities in food.* (**presente**)
2 to do with the time now ▫ *The present system isn't working.* ▣ *We'll look at fashion from the 50s to the present day.* (**atual**)

present³ /prɪˈzent/ VERB [**presents, presenting, presented**]
1 to give something to someone formally, often at a ceremony ▫ *She presented the best actor award.* ▫ *The captain was presented with the trophy.* (**apresentar**)
2 to introduce a radio or television show ▫ *She presents the news on the BBC.* (**apresentar**)

presentation /ˌprezənˈteɪʃən/ NOUN [plural **presentations**]
1 a talk to a group of people explaining or describing something ▣ *She gave a presentation on her research.* (**apresentação**)
2 when something, such as a prize, is formally given to someone ▫ *a presentation ceremony* (**apresentação**)

presenter /prɪˈzentə(r)/ NOUN [plural **presenters**] someone who introduces the parts of a radio or television programme ▫ *the presenter of Radio 4's Today Programme* (**apresentador**)

present participle /ˌprezənt ˈpɑːtɪsɪpəl/ NOUN [plural **present participles**] the form of a verb ending in -*ing*, usually used after the verb be. For example, *going* in I was going. (**particípio presente**)

present tense /ˌprezənt ˈtens/ NOUN [plural **present tenses**] a form of a verb used to show that the action is happening now (**tempo presente**)

preserve /prɪˈzɜːv/ VERB [**preserves, preserving, preserved**] to keep something the same, stopping it from being lost or destroyed ▫ *We try to preserve our traditions and culture.* ▫ *ancient fossils preserved in rocks* (**preservar**)

president /ˈprezɪdənt/ NOUN [plural **presidents**]
1 the elected leader of a country that has no king or queen ▫ *the Russian president* ▫ + *of* *the president of Pakistan* ▫ *President Bush* (**presidente**)
2 the person with the highest position in a company or an organization ▫ + *of* *He became president of General Motors in 1920.* (**presidente**)

press¹ /pres/ VERB [**presses, pressing, pressed**] **1** to push something, or to push something firmly against something else ▫ *Press the red button.* ▫ *Orla pressed her lips together.* ▫ *Nothing's happening – try pressing harder.* (**apertar**)
2 to make clothes flat by ironing them (**passar o ferro**)

press² /pres/ NOUN [plural **presses**]
1 the press newspapers and magazines, and the people who write for them ▫ *He issued a statement to the press.* ▫ *Press reports suggested that he was sacked from the post.* ▫ *She was mocked in the press.* (**imprensa**)
2 a push against something ▫ *I gave the button a press and a bell rang.* (**pressão, aperto**)
3 a machine that prints books, newspapers, etc. (**impressora**)

press conference /ˈpres ˌkɒnfərəns/ NOUN [plural **press conferences**] an official meeting at which someone gives information to people who work in television and on newspapers and answers their questions ▣ *The police are holding a press conference this afternoon.* (**entrevista coletiva**)

pressure /ˈpreʃə(r)/ NOUN [plural **pressures**]
1 *no plural* when someone tries to persuade or force someone to do something ▫ + **to do something** *The government are under pressure to change the law.* ▣ *Her father put pressure on her to study medicine.* ▣ *I don't want to put you under pressure.* (**pressão**)
2 *no plural* the force on or against a surface from something pressing on it ▫ *Applying pressure to the wound will stop the bleeding.* (**pressão**)
3 *no plural* the force that a liquid or gas has when it is inside something ▫ *air pressure* ▫ *high blood pressure* (**pressão**)
4 difficulties and problems that cause you to worry ▫ *the pressures of work* (**pressão**)

presumably /prɪˈzjuːməblɪ/ ADVERB used for saying something that you think is probably true ▫ *Presumably the picnic will be cancelled if it rains.* (**presumivelmente**)

pretend /prɪˈtend/ VERB [**pretends, pretending, pretended**]
1 to try to make someone believe something that is not true ▫ + *that* *She closed her eyes and pretended that she was asleep.* ▫ + **to do something** *Chris was sitting at the table, pretending to do his homework.* (**fingir**)
2 to imagine that something is true as part of a game ▫ + **to do something** *The children were pretending to be robots.* (**fingir**)

pretty¹ /ˈprɪtɪ/ ADJECTIVE [**prettier, prettiest**] people and things that are pretty are attractive, often in a delicate way ▫ *His girlfriend is very pretty.* ▫ *She was wearing a pretty white dress.* ▫ *What pretty flowers!* (**bonito**)

pretty² /ˈprɪtɪ/ ADVERB
1 quite ▫ *Eight out of ten is a pretty good mark.* (**muito**)
2 very ▣ *That's a pretty good salary, if you ask me!* (**bastante**)

prevent /prɪˈvent/ VERB [**prevents, preventing, prevented**] to stop something happening or someone doing something ▫ *Police are working*

prevention

hard to prevent gun crime. □ + *from* *They were prevented from leaving the building.* (impedir)

prevention /prɪ'venʃən/ NOUN, NO PLURAL when you prevent something 🔄 *crime prevention* □ *the prevention of infection* (prevenção)

preview /'pri:vju:/ NOUN [plural **previews**]
1 a showing or performance of a film, play, etc. to a small group of people before it is shown to everyone □ *Previews of the musical start this week.* (pré-estreia)
2 a short piece of a film, programme, etc. used to advertise it (pré-estreia)

previous /'pri:viəs/ ADJECTIVE happening or existing before □ *Please write down your previous address.* □ *I have some previous experience of working with children.* (anterior)

previously /'pri:viəsli/ ADVERB before □ *I'd met Sven a few months previously.* □ *He previously worked in a bank.* (anteriormente)

prey /preɪ/ NOUN, NO PLURAL an animal or bird that another animal hunts, kills and eats (presa)

price /praɪs/ NOUN [plural **prices**] the amount of money that something costs 🔄 *Food prices continue to rise.* 🔄 *House prices are falling.* (preço)

priceless /'praɪsləs/ ADJECTIVE extremely valuable □ *priceless works of art* (inestimável)

pride /praɪd/ NOUN, NO PLURAL
1 a feeling of pleasure because you have achieved something or because someone such as your child has achieved something □ *There was such pride in his face as he looked at his baby daughter.* (orgulho)
2 respect for yourself 🔄 *Jenny always took pride in her appearance.* (orgulho)

priest /pri:st/ NOUN [plural **priests**] someone who performs religious services in some religions □ *a Roman Catholic priest* (padre)

primary /'praɪməri/ ADJECTIVE main □ *Heart disease is still one of the primary causes of early death.* (principal)

primary school /'praɪməri,sku:l/ NOUN [plural **primary schools**] a school for children between the ages of four and eleven (escola primária)

prime minister /,praɪm 'mɪnɪstə(r)/ NOUN [plural **prime ministers**] the leader of the government in Britain and in many other countries of the world □ *the Irish prime minister* (primeiro ministro)

primitive /'prɪmɪtɪv/ ADJECTIVE belonging to the earliest stages of development □ *primitive man* □ *a primitive computer* (primitivo)

prince /prɪns/ NOUN [plural **princes**] the son or male grandchild of a king or queen, or the male ruler of a small state or country □ *Prince Charles* (príncipe)

prisoner

princess /prɪn'ses/ NOUN [plural **princesses**] the daughter or female grandchild of a king or queen, or the wife of a prince □ *Princess Caroline of Monaco* (princesa)

principal¹ /'prɪnsɪpəl/ ADJECTIVE main □ *Steel-making was the principal industry in the area.* (principal)

principal² /'prɪnsɪpəl/ NOUN [plural **principals**] the person in charge of a school, college or university (diretor escolar)

principle /'prɪnsɪpəl/ NOUN [plural **principles**]
1 a general rule or idea about how something is done □ *The government has drawn up principles of good practice for landlords.* (princípio)
2 a general rule that you base your behaviour on because you think it is morally right 🔄 *It was against his principles to borrow money.* (princípio)

print¹ /prɪnt/ VERB [**prints, printing, printed**]
1 to produce words, pictures, etc. on paper or another surface using a machine □ *We printed 500 copies of the letter.* □ *Cooking instructions are printed on the back of the label.* □ *All our reference books are printed in Italy.* □ *Is this document ready to print?* (imprimir)
2 to write words without joining the letters together □ *Print your name at the top of the form.* (escrever com letra de forma)
♦ PHRASAL VERB **print something out** to make a printed copy of a document or image from a computer □ *I printed out the map.*

print² /prɪnt/ NOUN [plural **prints**]
1 words, pictures, etc. that are produced on paper or another surface using a machine □ *She can only read books with large print.* □ *I was so excited to see my name in print.* (impressão)
2 a mark that is left when something has pressed on a surface □ *Prints from his boots could still be seen in the mud.* (impressão)
3 a fingerprint (= mark left when someone has touched something) (impressão digital)

printer /'prɪntə(r)/ NOUN [plural **printers**]
1 a machine that prints words and pictures from a computer (impressora)
2 a person or company whose business is printing books, newspapers, etc. (impressor)

prison /'prɪzən/ NOUN [plural **prisons**] a building where criminals are kept □ *Her father is in prison.* 🔄 *If he commits another crime he will be sent to prison.* 🔄 *He was released from prison last month.* (prisão)

prisoner /'prɪzənə(r)/ NOUN [plural **prisoners**]
1 someone who is kept in prison as a punishment □ *Four prisoners share each cell.* (preso)
2 someone who is kept in a place and cannot get out 🔄 *Her father kept her prisoner in the cellar for over 20 years.* (prisioneiro)

> **THESAURUS:** A **prisoner** is someone who is kept in prison as a punishment. **Convict** has a similar meaning. A **captive** is someone who is a prisoner, but a **captive** may or may not be in a prison. A **hostage** is someone who is kept as a prisoner until the people holding them get what they want. For example, someone who has been kidnapped or in a hijack might be a **hostage**.

privacy /ˈprɪvəsi, ˈpraɪvəsi/ NOUN, NO PLURAL
being alone where people cannot see or hear you □ *A higher fence will give us a bit more privacy.* (privacidade)

private¹ /ˈpraɪvɪt/ ADJECTIVE
1 belonging to or used by only one person, or a small group of people □ *a private beach* □ *The prince flew in on his private plane.* (privado)
2 where other people cannot see or hear you □ *Can we find somewhere more private?* (privado)
3 to do with relationships, family and the things that people do when they are not working ▣ *He never discusses his private life in interviews* □ *I never make private calls from the office.* (privado)
4 owned and managed by people or companies, not by the government □ *private industry* □ *a private hospital* (privado)

private² /ˈpraɪvɪt/ NOUN, NO PLURAL **in private**
with no one else present □ *Could I speak to you in private for a moment?* (particular)

privately /ˈpraɪvɪtli/ ADVERB
1 away from other people □ *Can we talk privately?* (privadamente)
2 a privately owned company is owned by a person or business and not by the government (privadamente)

private school /ˌpraɪvɪt ˈskuːl/ NOUN [plural **private schools**] a school which parents must pay to send their children to (escola particular)

privilege /ˈprɪvɪlɪdʒ/ NOUN [plural **privileges**]
a special right or advantage given to only one person, or to only a few people □ *The directors have special privileges such as their own dining room.* (privilégio)

prize /praɪz/ NOUN [plural **prizes**] something won in a competition or given as a reward for good work ▣ *The first prize was a trip to France.* ▣ *Adam won a prize in the competition.* (prêmio)

probable /ˈprɒbəbəl/ ADJECTIVE something that is probable is probably true or will probably happen □ *A cigarette was the probable cause of the fire.* □ *It now seems probable that we will go to war.* (provável)

probably /ˈprɒbəbli/ ADVERB used for saying that something will almost certainly happen or is almost certainly true □ *I'll probably be late.* □ *He'll probably lose it anyway.* (provavelmente)

problem /ˈprɒbləm/ NOUN [plural **problems**]
1 a situation that is causing difficulties □ *financial problems* □ **+ with** *There's a problem with the car.* ▣ *He's having problems with someone at work.* ▣ *I don't want to cause any problems for you.* □ *We had problems finding a hotel.* (problema)
2 no problem (a) used for agreeing to do something for someone □ *'Could you get some milk on the way home, please?' 'Sure, no problem.'* (b) used when someone thanks you for something □ *'Thanks for lending me your bike.' 'No problem.'* (problema)
3 a question that you have to answer or solve □ *maths problems* (problema)

> Note that you 'have problems **doing** something'. You do not have problems 'to do something':
> ✓ *We had problems finding the house.*
> ✗ *We had problems to find the house.*

> A very bad problem is a **serious** problem and not an 'important' problem:
> ✓ *Debt is a very serious problem.*
> ✗ *Debt is a very important problem.*

proceed /prəˈsiːd/ VERB [**proceeds, proceeding, proceeded**]
1 to continue something. A formal word. □ *She has decided not to proceed with her application.* (seguir, prosseguir)
2 proceed to do something to do something next, especially something annoying □ *He said he wasn't hungry and proceeded to eat two slices of cake.* (continuar)

process /ˈprəʊses/ NOUN [plural **processes**]
1 a series of actions or events that have a particular result □ *the production process* □ *Getting a visa is a lengthy process.* (processo)
2 a series of changes □ *the ageing process* (processo)

procession /prəˈseʃən/ NOUN [plural **processions**]
a line of people or vehicles moving along slowly, one behind the other □ *a funeral procession* (cortejo, desfile)

proclaim /prəˈkleɪm/ VERB [**proclaims, proclaiming, proclaimed**] to state something publicly or officially □ *He proclaimed his innocence.* (proclamar)

produce¹ /prəˈdjuːs/ VERB [**produces, producing, produced**]
1 to make, grow or create something □ *The new factory will produce goods for export.* □ *The plum tree didn't produce much fruit last year.* □ *The sun produces both light and heat.* (produzir)
2 to have a particular effect □ *This style of teaching produces better results.* (produzir)
3 to organize the actors, equipment and money, etc. that are needed for a film, programme, play or musical recording □ *a film produced by George Lucas* (produzir)
4 to show something so that people can see it □ *The conjuror produced a rabbit from a hat.* □ *The diary was produced as evidence at the trial.* (apresentar)

produce

produce² /ˈprɒdjuːs/ NOUN, NO PLURAL things that are grown or produced on farms, especially food 🔲 *The village shop sells local produce.* (**produção**)

producer /prəˈdjuːsə(r)/ NOUN [plural **producers**] someone who organizes the actors, equipment and money, etc. that are needed for a film, programme or musical recording □ *an independent producer* (**produtor**)

product /ˈprɒdʌkt/ NOUN [plural **products**] something that is produced in large numbers for selling 🔲 *dairy products* □ *household cleaning products* (**produto**)

production /prəˈdʌkʃən/ NOUN [plural **productions**]
1 no plural making, growing or producing something, or the amount that is produced □ *the production of organic food* □ *We now have this type of car in production.* □ *We have increased production by 30%.* (**produção**)
2 a performance or number of performances of a play or show □ *He played the lead in the school production of 'Grease'.* (**produção**)

profession /prəˈfeʃən/ NOUN [plural **professions**] a type of job that needs special qualifications and training, for example, medicine, law and teaching □ *He is considering going into the legal profession.* (**profissão**)

professional /prəˈfeʃənəl/ ADJECTIVE
1 to do with a type of job that needs special qualifications and training □ *professional training* (**profissional**)
2 doing something for money instead of as a hobby or for pleasure □ *a professional footballer* (**profissional**)

professor /prəˈfesə(r)/ NOUN [plural **professors**]
1 in the UK, the most important teacher in a university department (**professor**)
2 in the US, a teacher in a university or college (**professor**)

profit /ˈprɒfɪt/ NOUN [plural **profits**] money you make by selling something for more than you paid for it □ *The company is looking for ways to increase its profits.* 🔲 *We made a profit when we sold the house.* (**lucro**)

> Note that you **make** a profit. You do not 'gain' a profit:
> ✓ *We made a big profit on the sale.*
> ✗ *We gained a big profit on the sale.*

program¹ /ˈprəʊɡræm/ NOUN [plural **programs**]
1 a set of instructions put into a computer to make it perform a task. A computing word. □ *a word processing program* (**programa**)
2 the US spelling of **programme** (**programa**)

program² /ˈprəʊɡræm/ VERB [**programs, programming, programmed**]
1 to put a set of instructions into a computer or piece of electronic equipment to make it do something. A computing word. (**programar**)

promise

programme /ˈprəʊɡræm/ NOUN [plural **programmes**]
1 a television or radio show □ *an arts programme* (**programa**)
2 a thin book that gives information about an event or performance (**programa**)

progress¹ /ˈprəʊɡres/ NOUN, NO PLURAL
1 improvement of skills or knowledge 🔲 *Freya has made a lot of progress in the last year.* (**progresso**)
2 in progress happening or being done now □ *Work is now in progress to develop the site.* (**progresso**)
3 movement forwards or towards something □ *The bus made very slow progress through the crowds.* (**progresso**)

progress² /prəˈɡres/ VERB [**progresses, progressing, progressed**]
1 to develop □ *The work is progressing well.* □ *As the disease progresses, the patient requires more care.* (**progredir**)
2 if a period of time progresses, it continues □ *As the evening progressed, I felt more and more tired.* (**avançar**)
3 to go forward □ *They progressed slowly up the icy ridge.* (**avançar**)

prohibit /prəˈhɪbɪt/ VERB [**prohibits, prohibiting, prohibited**] to not allow people officially to do something □ *Smoking is prohibited in most public places.* (**proibido**)

project /ˈprɒdʒekt/ NOUN [plural **projects**]
1 a piece of work that is planned with a particular aim □ *a research project* □ *a major construction project* (**projeto**)
2 a piece of work done by a student, often involving collecting information on a subject and writing about it 🔲 *Hannah's doing a project on Henry VIII.* (**projeto**)

prominent /ˈprɒmɪnənt/ ADJECTIVE
1 important and known by a lot of people □ *a prominent member of the government* (**notável**)
2 sticking out or easily seen □ *a prominent landmark* (**proeminente**)

promise¹ /ˈprɒmɪs/ VERB [**promises, promising, promised**] to tell someone that you will certainly do something □ **+ to do something** *I've promised to help Rebecca with the food.* □ **+ that** *I promise that I'll pay you back.* □ *But you promised me you'd come!* (**prometer**)

> **THESAURUS:** If you promise something, you tell someone that you will certainly do something. If you **guarantee** something, you make a promise that something will happen or be done. If you **assure** someone, you tell them that something is certainly true or will certainly happen. If you **swear** something, you make a promise.

promise² /ˈprɒmɪs/ NOUN [plural **promises**] something that someone promises to do 🔲 *I'm not making any promises.* 🔲 *I try to keep my promises* (= do what I have said I will do). 🔲 *The unions accused the government of breaking its promise to them* (= not doing what it said it would). (**promessa**)

promote /prəˈməʊt/ VERB [**promotes, promoting, promoted**]
1 to give someone a more important job or a job that earns more money in the same organization 🔲 *Jack's been promoted to store manager.* (**promover**)
2 to tell people about something in order to persuade them to buy it or use it 🔲 *The book stores are all promoting her latest novel.* (**promover**)

promotion /prəˈməʊʃən/ NOUN [plural **promotions**]
1 a move to a more important job or a job that earns more money in the same organization 🔲 *Let's hope she gets her promotion.* (**promoção**)
2 *no plural* activities and materials which tell people about something in order to persuade them to buy it or use it (**promoção**)

prompt /prɒmpt/ ADJECTIVE doing something or happening without delay or at exactly the right time 🔲 *Thank you for your prompt reply to my letter.* (**pronto, pontual**)

prone /prəʊn/ ADJECTIVE often suffering from something 🔲 *He's always been prone to headaches.* 🔲 *an injury-prone football player* (**propenso**)

pronoun /ˈprəʊnaʊn/ NOUN [plural **pronouns**] a word that can be used in place of a noun. For example, in the sentence *Sara ate the ice cream*, *Sara* and *the ice cream* could be changed to pronouns and the sentence would be *She ate it.* (**pronome**)

pronounce /prəˈnaʊns/ VERB [**pronounces, pronouncing, pronounced**] to say the sound of a word or letter 🔲 *The two z's in pizza are pronounced 'tz'.* 🔲 *How do you pronounce your surname?* (**pronunciar**)

pronunciation /prəˌnʌnsɪˈeɪʃən/ NOUN [plural **pronunciations**] the way that a word is pronounced 🔲 *The pronunciation of some Arabic words is very difficult for English speakers.* (**pronúncia**)

proof /pruːf/ NOUN, NO PLURAL facts or objects which prove that something is true 🔲 *+ that Do we have any proof that she was actually there?* 🔲 *I was asked to provide proof of identity.* (**prova**)

propaganda /ˌprɒpəˈgændə/ NOUN, NO PLURAL ideas, information or opinions that are spread by a political group or by one side in a war, in order to influence people (**propaganda**)

proper /ˈprɒpə(r)/ ADJECTIVE
1 correct and suitable 🔲 *The staff hadn't received proper training.* 🔲 *The proper procedures were followed.* (**correto, adequado**)
2 real or good enough 🔲 *This is my first proper meal for days.* (**adequado**)

properly /ˈprɒpəli/ ADVERB correctly or well 🔲 *You're not properly dressed for the cold.* 🔲 *Come on, children, sit up properly.* (**corretamente**)

property /ˈprɒpəti/ NOUN [plural **properties**]
1 a house and the land it is on 🔲 *Private property - keep off!* 🔲 *property prices* (**propriedades**)
2 *no plural* the things that belong to you 🔲 *Customers must look after their personal property.* (**propriedade**)

> Remember that **property** meaning 'the things that belong to you' is not used in the plural:
> ✓ Stolen **property** is returned to the rightful owners.
> ✗ Stolen properties are returned to the rightful owners.

prophet /ˈprɒfɪt/ NOUN [plural **prophets**] in some religions, a man chosen by God to teach people and give them his messages 🔲 *the Prophet Isaiah* (**profeta**)

proportion /prəˈpɔːʃən/ NOUN [plural **proportions**]
1 a part of a whole amount or total 🔲 *A small proportion of old people live in care homes.* (**proporção**)
2 the number or amount of two groups or things when compared with each other 🔲 *The proportion of women to men in the company has risen.* (**proporção**)

proposal /prəˈpəʊzəl/ NOUN [plural **proposals**]
1 a plan or suggestion 🔲 *The council has a new proposal to ease traffic congestion.* (**proposta**)
2 when someone asks another person to marry them (**pedido de casamento**)

propose /prəˈpəʊz/ VERB [**proposes, proposing, proposed**]
1 to suggest a plan or idea 🔲 *I propose that we hold the meeting at a later date.* (**propor**)
2 to ask someone to marry you (**pedir em casamento**)

> Note that **propose** meaning 'to suggest a plan or idea' is followed by *that* and not 'to do something':
> ✓ I propose *that* we discuss this with Maria tomorrow.
> ✗ I propose to discuss this with Maria tomorrow.

prosecute /ˈprɒsɪkjuːt/ VERB [**prosecutes, prosecuting, prosecuted**] to accuse someone of a crime and take them to court 🔲 *She is being prosecuted for fraud.* (**processar**)

prosper /ˈprɒspə(r)/ VERB [**prospers, prospering, prospered**] to succeed, especially by making a lot of money (**prosperar**)

prosperity /prɒsˈperɪti/ NOUN, NO PLURAL success, especially having a lot of money (**prosperidade**)

protect /prəˈtekt/ VERB [**protects, protecting, protected**] to keep someone or something safe from harm or danger 🔲 *A mother will always protect her children.* 🔲 *+ from Protect the young plants from frost.* (**proteger, amparar**)

protection — public transport

protection /prəˈtekʃən/ NOUN, NO PLURAL when someone or something is protected □ **+ against** *A good diet provides protection against some diseases.* (proteção)

protein /ˈprəʊtiːn/ NOUN [plural **proteins**] a substance in foods such as eggs, meat and milk that is necessary for strength and growth (proteína)

protest¹ /prəˈtest/ VERB [**protests, protesting, protested**] to march or stand with a group of other people to show that you disagree with something □ *Thousands marched to protest about the war.* (protestar)

protest² /ˈprəʊtest/ NOUN [plural **protests**] a strong statement saying that something is wrong, or an organized action against something □ *Several MPs resigned in protest at the cuts.* □ *Students organized a peaceful protest against the regime.* (protesto)

> **THESAURUS:** A **protest**, **demonstration** or **march** is an event where a group of people march together to show that they support or disagree with something. A **riot** is a time when a large crowd of people behave wildly in a public place. A **strike** is a period of time when workers refuse to work because of an argument with their employer.

Protestant /ˈprɒtɪstənt/ ADJECTIVE to do with Protestants or their church (protestante)

protester /prəˈtestə(r)/ NOUN [plural **protester**] someone who does something to show that they do not agree with something □ *Anti-airport protesters blocked the roads.* (manifestante)

proud /praʊd/ ADJECTIVE [**prouder, proudest**]
1 feeling pleased about your achievements or about the achievements of someone such as your child □ *She felt very proud when her son got the award.* ▣ *Holding the winner's trophy was a really proud moment for me.* □ **+ of** *I'm proud of the fact that I carried on and didn't give up.* □ **+ to do something** *He was very proud to play for the national team.* (orgulhoso)
2 thinking that you are better than other people, in a way that annoys people (orgulhoso)

prove /pruːv/ VERB [**proves, proving, proved**] to show that something is true ▣ *Carter was determined to prove his innocence.* □ **+ that** *DNA tests proved that he was guilty.* (provar)

provide /prəˈvaɪd/ VERB [**provides, providing, provided**] to give or supply something □ *The hospital provides information on the treatments available.* □ *School provides an opportunity for children to learn and develop.* □ **+ with** *The refugees were provided with food and shelter.* (suprir)

provided /prəˈvaɪdɪd/ or **providing** /prəˈvaɪdɪŋ/ CONJUNCTION used when saying that one thing will happen only if another thing happens □ *You'll do well in the test, provided that you work hard.* □ *Providing you have no objection, I'd like you to work next Sunday.* (contanto que)

province /ˈprɒvɪns/ NOUN [plural **provinces**] one of the parts that some countries are divided into □ *Sichuan province in China* (província)

provoke /prəˈvəʊk/ VERB [**provokes, provoking, provoked**] to cause a particular reaction or feeling, often an angry one □ *His remarks have provoked a lot of criticism.* (provocar)

PS /ˌpiːˈes/ ABBREVIATION postscript; you write PS when you want to add something to the end of a letter □ *PS Say hi to David from me.* (pós-escrito)

PTO /ˌpiːtiːˈəʊ/ ABBREVIATION please turn over; written at the bottom of a page to show that someone should turn the page and read the other side (vide verso)

pub /pʌb/ NOUN [plural **pubs**] a place where people buy and drink alcoholic drinks, especially in the UK (**pub, bar**)

> **THESAURUS:** A **pub** is a place where people buy and drink alcoholic drinks, especially in the UK. A **bar** is also a place that sells alcoholic drinks, especially in a city or town. A **restaurant** is a place where you can buy and eat a meal. A **café** is a small restaurant that serves drinks and things to eat, but not usually alcoholic drinks. A **cafeteria** is a restaurant where the customers buy food and drink and take it to a table to eat it. Companies and schools often have a **cafeteria**.

public¹ /ˈpʌblɪk/ ADJECTIVE
1 to do with the people generally of a country ▣ *There has been a change in public opinion on this issue.* ▣ *There is a lot of public support for the idea.* (público)
2 available for everyone □ *a public park* □ *public libraries* □ *public events* (público)

public² /ˈpʌblɪk/ NOUN, NO PLURAL
1 the public people generally ▣ *A member of the public called the police* ▣ *The product will go on sale to the general public tomorrow.* (o público)
2 in public in a place where anyone can see □ *He was embarrassed when his parents kissed in public.* (em público)

publication /ˌpʌblɪˈkeɪʃən/ NOUN [plural **publications**]
1 *no plural* the process of printing and selling a book, magazine, etc. □ *The publication of the images provoked a strong reaction.* (publicação)
2 something such as a magazine or newspaper that is printed and sold (publicação)

publicity /pʌbˈlɪsəti/ NOUN, NO PLURAL attention that something gets from newspapers, television, etc. ▣ *The affair attracted a lot of publicity.* (publicidade)

public school /ˌpʌblɪk ˈskuːl/ NOUN [plural **public schools**]
1 in the UK, a school that you pay to go to, often where you stay as well as study (escola particular)
2 in the US, a school that the government pays for

public transport /ˌpʌblɪk ˈtrænspɔːt/ NOUN, NO PLURAL trains and buses that people can use □ *We* need to encourage more people to use public transport. (**transporte público**)

publish /'pʌblɪʃ/ VERB [**publishes, publishing, published**]
1 to print a book, magazine, etc. so that people can buy it □ *The book was published in September.* (**publicar**)
2 to make information available to people generally □ *The company does not publish sales information.* (**anunciar, tornar público**)

publisher /'pʌblɪʃə(r)/ NOUN [*plural* **publishers**] a person or company that publishes books, newspapers or magazines (**editor**)

pudding /'pʊdɪŋ/ NOUN [*plural* **puddings**] sweet food eaten at the end of a meal □ *We've got ice cream for pudding.* (**sobremesa**)

puddle /'pʌdəl/ NOUN [*plural* **puddles**] a small pool of rain on the ground □ *Young children love splashing in puddles.* (**poça**)

puff¹ /pʌf/ VERB [**puffs, puffing, puffed**] to breathe quickly because you have been exercising ▣ *John was puffing and panting as he came up the hill.* (**ofegar**)

puff² /pʌf/ NOUN [*plural* **puffs**] a small amount of breath, wind, air or smoke □ *a puff of air* (**lufada**)

pull¹ /pʊl/ VERB [**pulls, pulling, pulled**]
1 to hold something and move it towards you □ *He pulled the door open.* ▣ *Stop pulling my hair!* □ + **at** *He kept pulling at my sleeve.* (**puxar**)
2 if a machine, vehicle, etc. pulls something, it is attached to it and moves it □ *We had to get a tractor to pull our car out of the mud.* (**puxar**)
3 to separate the pieces of something or to damage something □ + **apart** *We pulled apart the curtains and looked inside.* □ + **down** *The old houses will be pulled down.* □ + **off** *He pulled off the insect's wings.* L *to pull your socks up* (**despedaçar, demolir, arrancar**)
◆ PHRASAL VERBS **pull over** if a vehicle pulls over, it moves to the side of the road and often stops □ *Pull over at the lights and I'll get out there.* **pull up** if a vehicle pulls up, it stops

pull² /pʊl/ NOUN [*plural* **pulls**] when you hold something and move it towards you □ *give the handle a pull* (**paixão**)

pulse /pʌls/ NOUN [*plural* **pulses**] your pulse is the regular movement that you feel on your lower arm or neck, caused by your heart pushing blood through your body ▣ *The nurse took my pulse* (= counted the number of movements in one minute). (**pulso**)

pump¹ /pʌmp/ NOUN [*plural* **pumps**] a piece of equipment that makes a gas or liquid move into or out of something □ *She got a bicycle pump and put some air in the tyres.* ▣ *a petrol pump* (= for putting petrol into a car) □ *a water pump* (**bomba**)

pump² /pʌmp/ VERB [**pumps, pumping, pumped**] to force liquid or gas to move somewhere □ *Your heart pumps blood around your body.* □ *Water is pumped from the well.* (**bombear**)

◆ PHRASAL VERB **pump something up** to put air into something using a pump □ *Ellie was pumping her bike tyres up.*

pumpkin /'pʌmpkɪn/ NOUN [*plural* **pumpkins**] a large, round, orange vegetable with a thick skin (**abóbora**)

punch¹ /pʌntʃ/ VERB [**punches, punching, punched**]
1 to hit someone or something with your closed hand □ *He punched the man in the face.* (**socar**)
2 to make a small hole in something using a special tool ▣ *The tool is used for punching holes in metal.* (**furar**)

punch² /pʌntʃ/ NOUN [*plural* **punches**] a hit using your closed hand (**soco**)

punctual /'pʌŋktʃuəl/ ADJECTIVE arriving at exactly the arranged time and not late □ *Robert was always very punctual.* □ *Switzerland has punctual and reliable trains.* (**pontual**)

punctuation mark /ˌpʌŋktʃuˈeɪʃən ˌmɑːk/ NOUN [*plural* **punctuation marks**] one of the marks such as , . ! which are used in writing (**sinal de pontuação**)

punish /'pʌnɪʃ/ VERB [**punishes, punishing, punished**] to make someone suffer because they have done something wrong □ + **for** *He was punished for his crimes.* □ + **by/with** *People who drop litter will be punished with fines.* (**punir**)

punishment /'pʌnɪʃmənt/ NOUN [*plural* **punishments**] something that is done to punish someone ▣ *He had to stay behind after school as a punishment.* □ + **for** *The maximum punishment for murder was life in prison.* ▣ *The old man escaped punishment after promising never to drive again.* (**punição**)

pupil /'pjuːpəl/ NOUN [*plural* **pupils**]
1 a student in a school □ *primary school pupils* □ *former pupils of the school* (**aluno**)
2 the small black circle in the middle of your eye ▣ ▣ *Pupils dilate to let in more light.* (**pupila**)

puppet /'pʌpɪt/ NOUN [*plural* **puppets**] a toy in the shape of an animal or person that you move by pulling strings or by putting it on your hand ▣ *The children enjoyed the puppet show.* (**fantoche**)

puppy /'pʌpi/ NOUN [*plural* **puppies**] a young dog (**filhote de cachorro**)

purchase₁ /'pɜːtʃəs/ VERB [**purchases, purchasing, purchased**] a formal word meaning to buy something □ *Tickets may be purchased in advance.* (**comprar**)

purchase₂ /'pɜːtʃəs/ NOUN [*plural* **purchases**]
1 a formal word meaning something you have bought □ *I was admiring your purchases.* (**compra**)
2 *no plural* a formal word meaning the act of buying something □ *There has been an increase in the purchase of household goods.* (**compra**)

pure /pjʊə(r)/ ADJECTIVE [**purer, purest**]
1 not mixed with anything else □ *pure gold* □ *pure oxygen* (**puro**)
2 clean □ *pure water* (**puro**)

purely /ˈpjʊəlɪ/ ADVERB only or simply □ *She is criticized purely because of her appearance.* (**puramente**)

purple¹ /ˈpɜːpəl/ ADJECTIVE having the colour you get if you mix red and blue □ *The carpet was dark purple.* □ *His face was purple with rage.* (**púrpura**)

purple² /ˈpɜːpəl/ NOUN, NO PLURAL the colour you get if you mix red and blue (**púrpura**)

purpose /ˈpɜːpəs/ NOUN [plural **purposes**]
1 what you intend to achieve when you do something □ *+ of The main purpose of the trip was to improve students' French.* □ *The website can be used for educational purposes too.* (**propósito**)
2 on purpose deliberately □ *He broke the vase on purpose to annoy me.* (**de propósito**)

purse /pɜːs/ NOUN [plural **purses**]
1 a small container that women carry money in □ *She had a lot of money in her purse.* □ *Mary opened her purse and got out some coins.* (**porta-níquel**)
2 the US word for **handbag** (**bolsa**)

pursue /pəˈsjuː/ VERB [**pursues, pursuing, pursued**] to chase someone or something in order to catch them □ *Should the police pursue stolen cars at high speed?* (**perseguir**)

push¹ /pʊʃ/ VERB [**pushes, pushing, pushed**] to press against someone or something with your hands or body, so that they move □ *I had to push him up the hill in his wheelchair.* □ *The new tooth is pushing the old one out.* □ *She pushed the door open.* □ *He pushed back his chair.* (**perseguir**)
◆ PHRASAL VERB **push someone/something over** to push someone or something so that they fall □ *He pushed his friend over in the playground.*

push² /pʊʃ/ NOUN [plural **pushes**] when you press against someone or something with your hands or body, so that it moves □ *The door's a bit stiff – give it a good push.* (**empurrar**)

put /pʊt/ VERB [**puts, putting, put**]
1 to move something to a place or position □ *Put the shopping on the table.* □ *He put his hands in the air.* □ *She put her arms around me.* (**pôr**)
2 to write something □ *Where do I put my address?* □ *I need to leave her a message, but I'm not sure what to put.* (**pôr**)
L go to **put your feet up**
◆ PHRASAL VERBS **put something away** to put something in the place where it is kept □ *He never puts his clothes away.* **put something back** to put something in the place where it came from □ *Could you put the milk back in the fridge?* **put someone/something down** to put someone or something onto a surface □ *He put down the gun.* **put off something** to delay doing something □ *I know I'll need an operation on my shoulder, but I'm trying to put it off as long as possible.* **put something on 1** to start wearing something □ *You'd better put on a coat.* **2** to make a machine or piece of equipment start working □ *Shall we put the heating on?* **put something out 1** to make a fire stop burning □ *Firefighters were called to put out the blaze.* **2** to turn a light off **put someone through** to connect someone to the person they want to speak to on the telephone □ *Just a moment, I'll put you through to the accounts department.* **put up with someone/something** to accept a situation or someone's behaviour although you do not like it □ *I can't put up with his laziness any longer!*

puzzle¹ /ˈpʌzəl/ NOUN [plural **puzzles**]
1 a game or toy that gives you a problem to solve 🖼 *Ben was doing a jigsaw puzzle.* (**quebra-cabeça**)
2 something that is difficult to understand 🖼 *Researchers hope to solve the puzzle of why some children develop the disease.* (**enigma**)

puzzle² /ˈpʌzəl/ VERB [**puzzles, puzzling, puzzled**] if something puzzles you, you feel confused because you do not understand it □ *Their unexplained deaths puzzled police for years.* (**confundir**)

pyjamas /pəˈdʒɑːməz/ PLURAL NOUN loose trousers and a shirt that you wear in bed 🖼 *He was wearing a pair of pyjamas.* □ *silk pyjamas* (**pijama**)

pyramid /ˈpɪrəmɪd/ NOUN [plural **pyramids**] a solid shape with a square base and triangular sides which form a point at the top (**pirâmide**)

Q q

Q or **q** /kjuː/ the 17th letter of the alphabet (a décima sétima letra do alfabeto)

quack /kwæk/ VERB [quacks, quacking, quacked] to make the sound of a duck (= a water bird with short legs and a wide, flat beak) (grasnar)

qualification /ˌkwɒlɪfɪˈkeɪʃən/ NOUN [plural qualifications] an exam you have passed or a course you have completed ▣ *He has no formal academic qualifications.* ▣ *She gained her teaching qualification at Leeds University.* (qualificação)

qualify /ˈkwɒlɪfaɪ/ VERB [qualifies, qualifying, qualified] to pass an exam or to complete a course needed to do a job □ + *as He qualified as a lawyer.* □ + *in She qualified in medicine in London.* (habilitar-se)

quality /ˈkwɒlɪti/ NOUN [plural qualities]
1 *no plural* how good or bad something is ▣ *All our courses are of a very high quality.* □ + *of The quality of her work is much better now.* ▣ *Your health affects your quality of life.* ▣ *We are taking measures to improve air quality.* (qualidade)
2 a part of someone's character □ *Her best qualities are her kindness and honesty.* (qualidade)

quantity /ˈkwɒntɪti/ NOUN [plural quantities] the amount or number of something □ + *of We only need a small quantity of paper.* □ *People throw away huge quantities of food.* ▣ *It can be produced cheaply and in large quantities.* ▣ *We need to improve both the quantity and quality of facilities.* (quantidade)

quarry /ˈkwɒri/ NOUN [plural quarries] a place where stone is dug out of the ground □ *a limestone quarry* (pedreira)

quarter /ˈkwɔːtə(r)/ NOUN [plural quarters]
1 1/4; one of four equal parts of something □ *We cut the cake into quarters.* (quarto)
2 quarter past/to 15 minutes after/before the hour □ *He arrived at quarter past three.* (quinze minutos)
3 quarter after/of the US phrase for 15 minutes after/before the hour (quinze minutos)

quarter-final /ˌkwɔːtəˈfaɪnəl/ NOUN [plural quarter-finals] the part of a competition involving the last eight teams or players □ *She reached the quarter-finals of Wimbledon.* (quartas de final)

quay /kiː/ NOUN [plural quays] a hard area built next to the water where things are put onto and taken off ships (cais)

queen /kwiːn/ NOUN [plural queens]
1 a woman who rules a country which has a royal family □ *Queen Elizabeth II* □ + *of the Queen of Denmark* (rainha)
2 the wife of a king (rainha)

query /ˈkwɪəri/ NOUN [plural queries] a question □ *Please phone me if you have any queries.* (pergunta)

quest /kwest/ NOUN [plural quests] a search for something or an attempt to do something, especially a long and difficult one □ *He vowed to continue his quest for justice.* (busca)

question¹ /ˈkwestʃən/ NOUN [plural questions]
1 the words you say or write when you want to ask something ▣ *After the talk, some people asked questions.* ▣ *He refused to answer my question.* (pergunta)
2 a situation or problem that needs to be discussed or solved □ *There is the question of how much to pay him.* ▣ *Toni raised the question of transport.* (questão)
3 be a question of something used to talk about the most important fact in a situation □ *It's a question of cost.* (questão)
4 out of the question if you say that something is out of the question, you are emphasizing that it is not possible □ *A pay rise is out of the question at the moment.* (fora de questão)

question² /ˈkwestʃən/ VERB [questions, questioning, questioned]
1 to ask someone questions, often officially □ *She was questioned by the police.* □ *He questioned me about where I had found the jewels.* □ *He questioned why I had decided to leave my job.* (perguntar)
2 to express doubts about something □ *They questioned the truth of his statement.* (questionar)

question mark /ˈkwestʃən ˌmɑːk/ NOUN [plural question marks] the mark (?) that you write after a sentence which is a question (ponto de interrogação)

questionnaire /ˌkwestʃəˈneə(r)/ NOUN [plural questionnaires] a list of questions to be answered by several people to get information ▣ *The students were asked to complete a short questionnaire.* (questionário)

queue¹ /kjuː/ NOUN [plural queues] a line of people waiting for something □ + *of There was a long queue of people waiting for taxis.* ▣ *We joined the queue for tickets.* (fila)

queue

queue² /kjuː/ VERB [queues, queuing, queued]
to stand in a queue □ *We had to queue for three hours to get the tickets.* (**fazer/ficar na fila**)

quick /kwɪk/ ADJECTIVE [quicker, quickest] taking a short time □ *Can we take a quick break?* □ *I had a quick look at the website.* (**rápido**)

> **THESAURUS:** Quick and **fast** are general words to describe something that takes a short time. **Rapid** is similar in meaning, but is often used to talk about changes or movements that happen quickly. For example, you might talk about a **rapid** change in the economy. We also use the word **swift** to talk about movements. **Swift** is also used to talk about a process or an event that happens quickly. Something that is **brief** is short. For example, you can say that a meeting is **brief** if it does not take much time.

quickly /ˈkwɪkli/ ADVERB
1 in a short time or immediately □ *I get bored quickly.* □ *He quickly realized his mistake.* 🔹 *I need to sort this out as quickly as possible.* (**depressa, imediatamente**)
2 fast □ *He had to move quickly.* □ *The fire quickly spread.* (**depressa, imediatamente**)

quiet¹ /ˈkwaɪət/ ADJECTIVE [quieter, quietest]
1 making little noise or no noise □ *a quiet voice* 🔹 *He asked everyone to be quiet.* 🔹 *He kept quiet, not wanting to disturb her.* □ *He was quite quiet and shy.* (**quieto**)
2 calm and without much activity □ *It was a quiet street with little traffic.* □ *It had been a very quiet week.* (**tranquilo**)

> **THESAURUS:** Something or someone that is quiet is making little or no noise. A **soft** sound is not loud. For example, you can talk about a **soft** voice or **soft** music. A **low** sound is near the bottom of the range of sounds. A **low** voice is quiet.

quiet² /ˈkwaɪət/ NOUN, NO PLURAL a quiet situation or time □ *She returned to the quiet of her room.* 🔹 *All he wanted was a bit of peace and quiet.* (**calma**)

quietly /ˈkwaɪətli/ ADVERB with little or no noise □ *She slipped quietly from the room.* □ *'It's okay,' she said quietly.* (**calmamente**)

quote

quit /kwɪt/ VERB [quits, quitting, quit]
1 to leave a job, school, etc. □ *He's quit his job.* □ *She quit university to become a singer.* (**abandonar**)
2 to stop doing something □ *I'm going to quit smoking.* (**abandonar**)

quite /kwaɪt/ ADVERB
1 to some degree but not very or completely □ *I'm quite hungry but I don't mind waiting.* □ *I'm quite nervous about it.* □ *They're quite likely to win.* (**bastante, razoavelmente**)
2 completely □ *I'm afraid I'm not quite ready.* □ *She made her opinion quite clear.* □ *It had quite the opposite effect.* (**completamente**)
3 quite a bit/a few/a while, etc. a large amount, a long time, etc. compared to what is normal or expected □ *He lost quite a bit of money.* □ *It took us quite a while.* (**um tanto**)

quiz /kwɪz/ NOUN [plural quizzes] a competition in which you have to answer questions □ *a general knowledge quiz* (**jogo de perguntas**)

quota /ˈkwəʊtə/ NOUN [plural quotas] an amount that someone is allowed to have or has to do □ *EU fishing quotas* □ *We all have to achieve our quota of sales.* (**cota**)

quotation /kwəʊˈteɪʃən/ NOUN [plural quotations] a set of words taken from a speech or piece of writing □ *a quotation from Shakespeare* (**citação**)

quotation marks /kwəʊˈteɪʃən mɑːks/ PLURAL NOUN the symbols ' ' or " " used in writing to show that someone's words are being repeated exactly (**aspas**)

quote¹ /kwəʊt/ VERB [quotes, quoting, quoted]
to repeat someone's words exactly as they said or wrote them □ *He quoted a passage from the Bible.* □ *One newspaper quoted him as saying: 'People are only interested in price.'* (**citar**)

> **THESAURUS:** If you **repeat** something, you say it again. If you **quote** someone, you repeat their words exactly as they said or wrote them. If you **copy** something, you write down words or information that you have found somewhere. If you **dictate** something, you say words for someone to write down.

quote² /kwəʊt/ NOUN [plural quotes] someone's words which are repeated exactly as they said or wrote them □ *a famous quote from Adam Smith* (**citação**)

Rr

R or r /ɑː(r)/ the 18th letter of the alphabet (a décima oitava letra do alfabeto)

rabbit /ˈræbɪt/ NOUN [plural rabbits] a small animal with long ears and soft fur, which people keep as a pet, or which lives in holes in the ground □ *She let me stroke her pet rabbit.* (coelho)

race¹ /reɪs/ NOUN [plural races]
1 a competition to see who can get somewhere fastest or do something fastest □ *I'm running in a race this weekend.* 🔁 *Lewis won the race.* (corrida)
2 one of the groups that people can be divided into according to their skin colour and physical characteristics □ *It's our hope that people of all races can live together in peace.* (raça, etnia)

race² /reɪs/ VERB [races, racing, raced]
1 to compete against someone in a race □ *I'll race you to the postbox.* □ **+ against** *His horse will be racing against some of the best horses in the country.* (apostar corrida)
2 to go somewhere very quickly, or to move someone or something very quickly □ **+ to** *Ambulances raced to the scene of the accident.* □ *Emma raced down the stairs to answer the door.* □ *He was raced to hospital with a suspected heart attack.* (correr)

> THESAURUS: If you race somewhere, you go there very quickly, or move someone or something very quickly. There are several other words with a similar meaning. You can also say that you *rush*, *hurry* or *speed* somewhere, or *rush* someone somewhere.

racial /ˈreɪʃəl/ ADJECTIVE to do with a person's race □ *racial discrimination* (racial)

racing /ˈreɪsɪŋ/ NOUN, NO PLURAL the sport of racing animals or vehicles 🔁 *Dad watches horse racing on the television.* 🔁 *He's one of the most famous people in motor racing.* 🔁 *a racing driver* (corrida)

racism /ˈreɪsɪzəm/ NOUN, NO PLURAL unfair treatment of someone or dislike of someone because they belong to a different race □ *The scheme aims to tackle racism in schools.* □ *He was a victim of racism.* (racismo)

racist¹ /ˈreɪsɪst/ NOUN [plural racists] someone who dislikes people or treats them unfairly because they belong to a different race (racista)

racist² /ˈreɪsɪst/ ADJECTIVE to do with unfair treatment of someone or dislike of someone because they belong to a different race □ *racist remarks* (racista)

rack /ræk/ NOUN [plural racks] a place where things are kept, usually made of narrow pieces of wood or metal □ *I put my bag in the luggage rack.* (estante, prateleira)

racket /ˈrækɪt/ NOUN [plural rackets] a piece of equipment that you use for hitting the ball in games such as tennis □ *a tennis racket* (raquete)

radar /ˈreɪdɑː(r)/ NOUN [plural radars] a system or piece of equipment that uses radio waves to find the position of aeroplanes, ships, etc. (radar)

radical /ˈrædɪkəl/ ADJECTIVE
1 believing that there should be big political and social changes □ *radical views* (radical)
2 big and important □ *radical changes* (radical)

radio /ˈreɪdiəʊ/ NOUN [plural radios]
1 a piece of equipment that you use for listening to programmes which are broadcast 🔁 *Raj switched the radio on to hear the news.* □ *He bought a digital radio.* (rádio)
2 *no plural* programmes that you listen to using a radio 🔁 *I enjoy listening to the radio.* 🔁 *The local radio station broadcasts travel news.* 🔁 *a radio show* □ *James is a radio presenter.* (rádio)
3 *no plural* a system of broadcasting that uses sound

waves instead of wires to send messages □ *He gave orders by radio.* ⊞ *They lost radio contact with the crew.* (**rádio**)

radioactive /ˌreɪdiəʊˈæktɪv/ ADJECTIVE sending out harmful radiation (= energy from a nuclear reaction). A physics word □ *radioactive substances* (**radioativo**)

raft /rɑːft/ NOUN [plural **rafts**] a flat boat made from large pieces of wood tied together (**jangada**)

rag /ræg/ NOUN [plural **rags**] an old piece of cloth □ *an oily rag* (**trapo**)

rage /reɪdʒ/ NOUN, NO PLURAL extreme anger that you cannot control □ *He killed his wife in a fit of jealous rage.* ⊞ *I've never seen him fly into a rage* (= become extremely angry) *like that before.* (**fúria**)

raid¹ /reɪd/ NOUN [plural **raids**]
1 a sudden military attack □ *a bombing raid* (**ataque**)
2 a sudden unexpected visit from the police, who enter a building and search it □ *Guns were found during a police raid on the house.* (**batida policial**)
3 a violent attack on a bank, shop, etc. to steal things □ *He was arrested for a £250,000 raid on a jeweller's shop.* (**assalto**)

raid² /reɪd/ VERB [**raids, raiding, raided**]
1 to attack a place using weapons □ *Troops raided villages.* □ *Armed robbers raided her home.* (**invadir**)
2 to use force to enter a place in order to search it □ *Police raided the factory and questioned staff.* (**fazer batida policial**)

rail /reɪl/ NOUN [plural **rails**]
1 no plural the railway system □ *Travelling by rail is more relaxing than driving.* ⊞ *Rail fares have increased again.* (**trem**)
2 a bar for hanging things on ⊞ *a towel rail* (**viga, barra**)
3 one of the two long metal bars that form a track for trains (**trilho**)

railing /ˈreɪlɪŋ/ NOUN [plural **railings**] a fence made of vertical metal bars, or the bar that goes along the top of a fence like this □ *He was leaning on the railings.* (**grades**)

railway¹ /ˈreɪlweɪ/ NOUN [plural **railways**]
1 a track for trains to travel on □ *Glasgow has Scotland's only underground railway.*
2 the railway the system and organizations to do with trains □ *We need to encourage more people to use the railway.*

railway² /ˈreɪlweɪ/ ADJECTIVE to do with trains and the tracks they use ⊞ *I'll meet you at the railway station.* □ *Children should be told about the danger of playing on railway lines.* □ *a railway bridge* (**ferrovia**)

rain¹ /reɪn/ NOUN, NO PLURAL water that falls from the sky □ *The children didn't want to go out in the rain.* ⊞ *Heavy rain* (= a large amount of rain) *has caused flooding in the area.* ⊞ *500mm of rain fell last month.* ⊞ *It was pouring with rain* (= a lot of rain was falling) *outside.* (**chuva**)

> **THESAURUS:** Water that falls from the sky is called **rain**. A mixture of snow and rain is called **sleet**. Small white balls of frozen ice that fall from the sky are called **hail**. A short period of rain is called a **shower**. A time when there is suddenly a lot of rain and wind is called a **storm**. One piece of rain is called a **drop** of rain.

rain² /reɪn/ VERB [**rains, raining, rained**] when it rains, water falls from the sky ⊞ *It's raining so take an umbrella.* ⊞ *It rained heavily* (= a lot of rain fell) *all night.* (**chover**)

rainbow /ˈreɪnbəʊ/ NOUN [plural **rainbows**] a curved line of colours that you see in the sky when it is raining and sunny at the same time (**arco-íris**)

raincoat /ˈreɪnkəʊt/ NOUN [plural **raincoats**] a light coat that you wear when it rains □ *She was wearing a blue raincoat.* (**capa de chuva**)

rainfall /ˈreɪnfɔːl/ NOUN, NO PLURAL the amount of rain that falls in a particular place over a particular period of time ⊞ *Heavy rainfall lead to widespread flooding.* (**precipitação**)

rainforest /ˈreɪnfɒrɪst/ NOUN [plural **rainforests**] a tropical forest with very tall trees which are close together, in an area where it rains a lot. A geography word. □ *the Amazon rainforest* (**mata tropical**)

rainy /ˈreɪni/ ADJECTIVE [**rainier, rainiest**] raining a lot □ *a rainy day* (**chuvoso**)

raise /reɪz/ VERB [**raises, raising, raised**]
1 to lift something to a higher position □ *Raise your hand if you know the answer.* □ *The wreck was slowly raised from the sea bed.* □ *She raised her eyebrows in surprise.* (**levantar**)
2 to increase the amount or level of something □ *They've raised the rent again.* □ *We are trying to raise standards in the school.* □ *This case has raised awareness of the disease.* (**elevar**)
3 to collect money for a particular purpose □ *We're raising money for charity.* (**levantar, reunir**)
4 if you raise children, you look after them until they are adults □ *My wages are not enough to raise a family.* (**criar**)

> Note that **raise** is always followed by an object: □ *She raised her hand.* □ *They have raised taxes.* The verb **rise** has the same meaning but is used without an object:
> ✓ *Taxes have risen.*
> ✗ *Taxes have raised.*

raisin /ˈreɪzən/ NOUN [plural **raisins**] a dried grape (= small round fruit) (**uva passa**)

rake /reɪk/ VERB [rakes, raking, raked] to use a rake to collect dead leaves or to make soil smooth (ancinho)

rally /ˈrælɪ/ NOUN [plural rallies]
1 a large public meeting to support something or to complain about something □ *Over 1000 people attended an anti-war rally.* (assembleia)
2 a car race on public roads □ *a rally driver* (rali)

Ramadan /ˌræməˈdæn/ NOUN, NO PLURAL the ninth month of the Islamic year, when Muslims do not eat anything during the day (ramadã)

ramp /ræmp/ NOUN [plural ramps] a sloping surface that joins two places that are at different levels □ *We should be able to get the wheelchair up the ramp quite easily.* (ramp)

ran /ræn/ PAST TENSE OF **run¹** (ver **run**)

ranch /rɑːntʃ/ NOUN [plural ranches] a large farm where cows or horses are kept (rancho)

random /ˈrændəm/ ADJECTIVE
1 done without a plan or a system □ *a random selection* (casual)
2 at random without a plan or system □ *The killer chose his victims at random.* (ao acaso)

rang /ræŋ/ PAST TENSE OF **ring²** (ver **ring²**)

range¹ /reɪndʒ/ NOUN [plural ranges]
1 a group of things of a similar type □ + **of** *The shop stocks a huge range of toys and games.* 🔄 *There is a wide range of courses to choose from.* (variedade)
2 all the ages, numbers, etc. that are included within fixed limits 🔄 *Most of the sofas we sell are in the £500–£1,0 00 price range.* 🔄 *The programme is aimed at children in the 10–13 age range.* (faixa, extensão)
3 the distance from which something can be seen, heard or reached 🔄 *Spectators have to stand well out of range of the arrows.* 🔄 *He shot the man at close range* (= from a position that is very close). (alcance)
4 a group of hills or mountains 🔄 *a mountain range* (cadeia de montanhas)

range² /reɪndʒ/ VERB [ranges, ranging, ranged] to include both things that are mentioned, and other things between them □ + **from** *The company has accommodation ranging from hostels to luxury hotels.* □ *Prices range from £70–£150 per night.*

□ + **between** *The dancers' ages ranged between 16 and 40.* (variar)

rank¹ /ræŋk/ NOUN [plural ranks] someone's level in an organization or in society 🔄 *A private is the lowest rank in the British army.* 🔄 *A duchess has a very high social rank.* □ + **of** *He held the rank of colonel.* □ *There are now more women in the senior ranks of the profession.* (posto, classe)

rank² /ræŋk/ VERB [ranks, ranking, ranked] to have a certain position that shows how good, bad, important, etc someone or something is □ + **as** *He ranks as one of the world's best actors.* □ + **among** *The country ranks among the world's poorest.* (classificar)

ransom /ˈrænsəm/ NOUN [plural ransoms] an amount of money that is paid to a criminal so that they will give back a person they have taken as a prisoner 🔄 *They paid a ransom of over $1 million.* (resgate)

rap /ræp/ NOUN [plural raps]
1 a quick hard hit □ *There was a rap on the window.* (golpe seco)
2 a type of pop music with words that are spoken in rhythm (rap)

rapid /ˈræpɪd/ ADJECTIVE done, happening or moving quickly □ *There has been a rapid growth in air travel.* (rápido)

rare /reə(r)/ ADJECTIVE [rarer, rarest] not happening or existing often □ *This type of attack is extremely rare.* □ *This is a rare example of a blue diamond.* □ *On rare occasions, errors are made.* □ + **to do something** *It's rare to find a vase like this in perfect condition.* (raro)

rarely /ˈreəlɪ/ ADVERB not often □ *I rarely see him.* □ *He's a keen football fan and rarely misses a game.* (raramente)

rash /ræʃ/ NOUN [plural rashes] an area of red spots on your skin, often caused by an illness 🔄 *I came out in a rash* (= developed a rash). (erupção)

raspberry /ˈrɑːzbərɪ/ NOUN [plural raspberries] a small soft red fruit that grows on bushes (framboesa)

rat /ræt/ NOUN [plural rats] an animal that looks like a large mouse with a long tail (rato)

rate /reɪt/ NOUN [plural rates]
1 how often something happens, or the number of people or things it happens to □ *Unemployment rates have fallen.* □ *We need to lower crime rates.* □ *The birth rate has risen.* (taxa)
2 the speed at which something happens □ *The rate of progress has been very slow.* □ *The disease is spreading at a tremendous rate.* 🔄 *At this rate, we'll have eaten all the food before lunch time.* (velocidade)
3 an amount of money that is paid for something □ *They charge very high rates for their services.* □ *Rates of pay have risen.* □ *The exchange rate is in our favour at the moment.* □ *The banks have raised interest rates.* (tarifa)
4 at any rate used to say that at least one part of what you have said is certain □ *He's gone to see his cousin or someone – a relative at any rate.* (de qualquer modo)

rather /ˈrɑːðə(r)/ ADVERB
1 slightly □ *It's rather cold in here, isn't it?* □ *He felt rather tired after such a long journey.* (um tanto)
2 rather than instead of □ *Many people choose to rent rather than buy houses.* □ *Rather than punishment, some children need support to improve their behaviour.* (em vez de)
3 would rather used when saying what you would prefer to do □ *I would rather talk about this later if you don't mind.* □ *I'd rather go swimming.* (preferir)

ratio /ˈreɪʃiəʊ/ NOUN [plural **ratios**] the relationship between two numbers or amounts that shows how much bigger one is than the other □ *Our nursery has a ratio of one member of staff to three children.* (proporção)

rational /ˈræʃənəl/ ADJECTIVE reasonable and sensible □ *a rational decision* (racional)

rattle¹ /ˈrætəl/ VERB [**rattles, rattling, rattled**]
1 if something rattles, it makes a noise by hitting against something else repeatedly □ *The windows were rattling in the wind.* (chocalhar)
2 to shake something so that it makes a noise □ *She rattled the door but it was locked.* (chacoalhar)

rattle² /ˈrætəl/ NOUN [plural **rattles**]
1 a baby's toy that makes a noise when you shake it (chocalho)
2 the noise that something hard and loose makes when it is shaken □ *There's a bad rattle coming from the engine.* (barulheira)

raw /rɔː/ ADJECTIVE [**rawer, rawest**]
1 raw food is not cooked □ *raw vegetables* □ *raw meat* (cru)
2 a raw substance is still in its natural state 🖼 *raw materials* 🖼 *Raw sewage had been pumped into the river.* (bruto)

ray /reɪ/ NOUN [plural **rays**] a beam of light □ *a ray of sunlight* (raio)

razor /ˈreɪzə(r)/ NOUN [plural **razors**] a sharp tool that you use for shaving hair from your face and body □ *He uses an electric razor.* 🖼 *a razor blade* (navalha, barbeador)

re- /riː/ PREFIX re- is added to the beginning of words to mean 'again' □ *reappear* □ *rearrange* (prefixo)

reach¹ /riːtʃ/ VERB [**reaches, reaching, reached**]
1 to arrive somewhere □ *We didn't reach the cottage until after dark.* □ *The train reached London at 10.34.* □ *My letter never reached him.* (chegar a)
2 to be able to touch or hold something □ *I can't reach the top shelf.* (alcançar)
3 to stretch out your arm to touch or hold something □ *He reached over me to get some bread.* □ **+ for** *As I reached for the fruit, I fell off the ladder.* (estender o braço)

> Note that **reach** meaning 'to arrive somewhere' is never followed by 'to':
> ✓ *It was midnight by the time we reached London.*
> ✗ *It was midnight by the time we reached to London.*

reach² /riːtʃ/ NOUN, NO PLURAL
1 beyond/out of (someone's) reach (a) too far away to touch or hold □ *Keep all medicines out of reach.* (b) not possible for someone to have or achieve □ *They feel that a university education is beyond their reach.* (alcance)
2 within (someone's) reach (a) close enough for someone to touch or hold □ *I made sure all his equipment was within reach.* (b) possible for someone to get or achieve □ *Suddenly, the gold medal seems within her reach.* (alcance)

react /riˈækt/ VERB [**reacts, reacting, reacted**]
to behave or feel a particular way because of something that has happened or something someone has said □ *How did Helen react when she heard the news?* □ **+ to** *He reacted angrily to their criticism.* □ **+ by** *He reacted by sacking 10 workers.* (reagir)

reaction /riˈækʃən/ NOUN [plural **reactions**]
behaviour or feelings that are a result of something that has happened or something someone has said □ *Did you see his reaction when he found out?* □ **+ to** *There has been a huge reaction to his death.* (reação)

read /riːd/ VERB [**reads, reading, read**]
1 to look at words and understand them □ *He was reading a novel.* □ *I read about the court case in the papers.* □ **+ that** *I read that they were going to open a new store.* (ler)
2 to look at words and say them aloud □ *I always read a story to the children at bedtime.* (ler)
♦ PHRASAL VERBS **read something out** to read something aloud □ *He read out the list of names.*
read something through to read the whole of something, often to check for mistakes □ *Make sure you read through your essay and correct your spelling.*

> THESAURUS: Read is a general word. If you read something very quickly, you can say that you **scan** it. For example, you might scan a telephone directory to find a number. If you read something slowly and carefully, you can say that you **study** it. For example, you might study a timetable to find out which train you need to catch.

reader /ˈriːdə(r)/ NOUN [plural **readers**] a person who reads □ *Regular readers will recognize this name.* (leitor)

reading /ˈriːdɪŋ/ NOUN, NO PLURAL the activity of looking at and understanding written words □ *How does the school teach reading?* □ *The course will help you improve your reading skills.* (leitura)

ready /ˈredi/ ADJECTIVE
1 prepared for something 🖼 *He was getting ready to leave.* □ **+ for** *Are the children ready for bed?* (pronto)
2 prepared and available to use, eat, etc. □ *Dinner's ready.* □ *The report should be ready by the end of the year.* (pronto)

3 willing □ + *to do something* He was always ready to help. (disposto)

real /rɪəl/ ADJECTIVE
1 existing, and not invented or imaginary ▣ *In real life* the actor is a quiet family man. □ The story is based on real events. (real)
2 true and not pretended □ Everyone calls her 'Sunny' but her real name is Barbara. □ The real reason he missed the class was that he had forgotten to bring his homework. (verdadeiro)
3 not artificial □ The seats are made of real leather. □ The diamond looked real. (verdadeiro)

realistic /rɪəˈlɪstɪk/ ADJECTIVE accepting or based on the true facts of a situation ▣ The team has a *realistic chance* of winning the competition. □ + *about* Navarez seems realistic about his future. (realista)

reality /rɪˈælɪti/ NOUN [plural **realities**]
1 the true facts of a situation □ We must face reality. (realidade)
2 in reality used when saying what the true situation is, especially when it seems different □ Everyone thought she was very successful, but in reality she was almost bankrupt. (na verdade)

realize or **realise** /ˈrɪəlaɪz/ VERB [**realizes, realizing, realized**] to know and understand something that you did not know or understand before ▣ *I suddenly realized* that he wasn't joking. □ I didn't realize he was so ill. (compreender)

really /ˈrɪəli/ ADVERB
1 very or very much □ I really like Dan. □ I'm really excited about the holiday. □ I don't really like fish. (realmente)
2 used for saying what the true situation is □ Did you really mean what you said? □ He doesn't really have much choice. (realmente)
3 not really no or not completely □ 'Are you ready for your trip?' 'Not really, there are still a lot of things I need to do.' (não totalmente)
4 Really? used when you are surprised or interested by what someone has just said □ 'Mrs Robinson is leaving the school in July.' 'Really?' (é mesmo?)

reap /riːp/ VERB [**reaps, reaping, reaped**] to cut and collect a crop (colher, ceifar)

rear¹ /rɪə(r)/ NOUN, NO PLURAL **the rear** the back part of something □ They were sitting at the rear of the plane. (fundos, retaguarda)

rear² /rɪə(r)/ VERB [**rears, rearing, reared**] if you rear children or animals, you look after them as they grow (criar)

rear³ /rɪə(r)/ ADJECTIVE at the back of something □ The rear wheels of the car were stuck in mud. (traseiro)

reason /ˈriːzən/ NOUN [plural **reasons**]
1 the reason for something is why it happened, exists or is true □ + *for* No one knows the reason for his disappearance. □ + *that* The reason that I phoned was to see if you want to meet for lunch. ▣ There are many *good reasons* for taking up a sport. ▣ He did not *give* any *reason* for his lateness. ▣ That is the *reason why* I moved to Paris. (razão)
2 no plural a good cause for something □ + *to do something* We have reason to suspect he is guilty. ▣ There is *no reason* to be afraid. ▣ She could *see no reason* to apologize. (motivo)

reasonable /ˈriːzənəbəl/ ADJECTIVE
1 sensible and fair □ I suppose it's a reasonable decision. □ Any reasonable person would agree with that. (razoável)
2 if something is reasonable, there are good reasons why you think it is true or correct □ They made the reasonable assumption that we would be late. □ These figures seem reasonable to me. (sensato)
3 not very expensive □ Their clothes are very reasonable. (razoável)

reassure /ˌriːəˈʃɔː(r)/ VERB [**reassures, reassuring, reassured**] to say or do something to make someone feel less worried □ He tried to reassure me that everything would be all right. (tranquilizar)

rebel /ˈrebəl/ NOUN [plural **rebels**]
1 someone who fights against a government □ Rebels have clashed with government troops. (rebelde)
2 someone who refuses to obey rules or people in authority □ He was always a bit of a rebel at school. (rebelde)

rebellion /rɪˈbeljən/ NOUN [plural **rebellions**] the use of violence to try to change a government □ The government tried to crush the rebellion. (rebelião)

receipt /rɪˈsiːt/ NOUN [plural **receipts**] a piece of paper you get when you buy something or when you have paid money to someone □ Make sure you keep the receipt. □ a credit card receipt □ + *for* The receipt for the clothes was still in the bag. (recibo)

receive /rɪˈsiːv/ VERB [**receives, receiving, received**] to get or be given something □ + *from* She received a letter from her aunt. □ She has been receiving treatment for cancer. □ The story received a lot of attention. □ He received an award for his work. (receber)

receiver /rɪˈsiːvə(r)/ NOUN [plural **receivers**] the part of a telephone that you hear and speak through □ 'Goodbye,' he said, and replaced the receiver. (fone)

recent /ˈriːsənt/ ADJECTIVE happening only a short time ago □ recent events □ The most recent figures show that violent crimes are increasing. □ Thes e changes are relatively recent. (recente)

recently /ˈriːsəntli/ ADVERB a short time ago □ I saw Ann quite recently. □ He recently bought a new car. □ Recently, the situation has become worse. (recentemente)

reception /rɪˈsepʃən/ NOUN [plural **receptions**]
1 a big, formal party ▣ The *wedding reception* was at a hotel. ▣ Government leaders will *attend a reception* hosted by the Queen. □ + *for* a reception for the French president (recepção)
2 no plural the place where people go when they arrive at a hotel, office building, etc. □ He was checking in at reception. ▣ She walked up to the

reception desk. The hotel has a large *reception area.* (recepção)

recession /rɪˈseʃən/ NOUN [plural **recessions**] a time when a country's economy is not successful □ *The rise in oil prices could cause a recession.* (recessão)

recipe /ˈresɪpi/ NOUN [plural **recipes**] a set of instructions for how to cook something ▣ *a recipe book* □ + *for This is a delicious recipe for chocolate cake.* (receita)

reckless /ˈrekləs/ ADJECTIVE doing something without caring or thinking about the results of your actions □ *reckless driving* (imprudente)

reckon /ˈrekən/ VERB [**reckons, reckoning, reckoned**]
1 to think that something is true □ *I reckon we'll win.* (crer, pensar que)
2 to calculate □ *The cost of restoring the painting is reckoned at £8,000.* (calcular)

recognition /ˌrekəɡˈnɪʃən/ NOUN, NO PLURAL
1 the fact of knowing someone or something because you have seen them before □ *a smile of recognition* (reconhecimento)
2 agreement that something is true or important □ *There is a growing recognition that play is important in children's development.* (reconhecer)

recognize or **recognise** /ˈrekəɡnaɪz/ VERB [**recognizes, recognizing, recognized**]
1 to know who or what someone or something is because you have seen them before □ *I recognized his face but couldn't remember his name* □ *Emma hadn't seen him for 50 years, but recognized him immediately.* (reconhecer)
2 to accept that something is true □ *We recognize the importance of research.* □ + *that Most people recognize that there is no easy solution to the problem of global warming.* (reconhecer)

recommend /ˌrekəˈmend/ VERB [**recommends, recommending, recommended**]
1 to advise someone to do something □ + *that Health experts recommend that you eat at least five portions of fruit or vegetables every day.* □ *We don't recommend the use of this drug.* (recomendar)
2 to suggest to someone that they would like something □ + *to My sister recommended this book to me.* (recomendar)

> Note that **recommend**, meaning 'to advise' is followed by a noun or is followed by **that...** It is not followed by 'to do something':
> ✓ She recommended new glasses.
> ✓ She recommended that I buy new glasses.
> ✗ She recommended me to buy new glasses.

recommendation /ˌrekəmenˈdeɪʃən/ NOUN [plural **recommendations**]
1 something that someone advises you to do □ *The school will consider the inspector's recommendations.* (recomendação)
2 something that a person suggests you would like □ *I bought the game on my friend's recommendation.* (recomendação)

record[1] /ˈrekɔːd/ NOUN [plural **records**]
1 a piece of information that has been stored in a document or on a computer ▣ *They keep records of all sales.* ▣ *Records show that crime has risen.* ▣ *medical/dental records* ▣ *She now has a criminal record.* (registro, documentação)
2 the best achievement ever in a particular activity, especially a sport ▣ *He holds the record for the high jump.* ▣ *She broke the previous record by 2 seconds.* ▣ *He has set a new record for sailing the Atlantic.* (recorde)
3 a round flat piece of plastic that music and speech can be stored on □ *I found a pile of old jazz records.* (disco)

record[2] /ˈrekɔːd/ ADJECTIVE bigger, better, faster, etc. than has ever happened or existed before □ *Record temperatures have led to water shortages.* ▣ *He finished the race in record time.* (recorde)

record[3] /rɪˈkɔːd/ VERB [**records, recording, recorded**]
1 to put sounds or images on a CD, video, etc. ▣ *I phoned her, but all I got was a recorded message.* □ *The band recorded their first album in 1982.* (gravar)
2 to keep information about something in a document or on a computer □ *All their addresses are recorded in a central database.* (registrar)

recorder /rɪˈkɔːdə(r)/ NOUN [plural **recorders**] a simple musical instrument made from a wooden pipe with holes that you cover with your fingers as you blow (registrar)

recording /rɪˈkɔːdɪŋ/ NOUN [plural **recordings**] sounds or images that have been recorded □ *I have a recording of the poet's own voice.* (gravação)

recover /rɪˈkʌvə(r)/ VERB [**recovers, recovering, recovered**]
1 to get better after being ill, injured or upset □ *The doctor says I am recovering very well.* □ + *from He is recovering from a serious illness.* □ *Most parents never recover from the death of a child.* (recuperar)
2 to return to a normal condition after problems or damage □ *The sea can take years to recover after an oil spillage.* □ *There are signs that the economy is recovering.* (recuperar)

recovery /rɪˈkʌvəri/ NOUN [plural **recoveries**]
1 the process of getting better after being ill, injured or upset ▣ *He made a miraculous recovery.* ▣ *She is expected to make a full recovery from her injuries.* (recuperação)
2 the process of returning to a normal condition after problems or damage □ *economic recovery* (recuperação)

recreation /ˌrekriˈeɪʃən/ NOUN, NO PLURAL a formal word meaning enjoyable things that you do in your free time □ *outdoor recreation* (recreação)

recruit[1] /rɪˈkruːt/ VERB [**recruits, recruiting, recruited**]

recruit to find new people to work for a company or join an organization ☐ *The company recruits a few school-leavers each year.* (**recrutar**)

recruit² /rɪˈkruːt/ NOUN [plural **recruits**] someone who has recently joined a company or organization 🔾 *New recruits are given a tour of the building.* (**recrutar**)

rectangle /ˈrektæŋɡəl/ NOUN [plural **rectangles**] a shape with four straight sides and four angles of 90 degrees. The opposite sides are of the same length, but two sides are longer than the other two. (**retângulo**)

rectangular /rekˈtæŋɡjʊlə(r)/ ADJECTIVE having the shape of a rectangle ☐ *a rectangular table* (**retangular**)

recycle /riːˈsaɪkəl/ VERB [**recycles, recycling, recycled**] to save something so that it can be used again or to do something to a substance so that it can be used again ☐ *I keep the bags in this drawer and recycle them.* ☐ *Most plastics can be recycled.* (**reciclar**)

recycling /riːˈsaɪklɪŋ/ NOUN, NO PLURAL the process of dealing with things which have been used so that they can be used again ☐ *We need to encourage recycling.* (**reciclagem**)

red¹ /red/ ADJECTIVE

1 having the colour of blood ☐ *She drives a red car.* 🔾 *He was wearing a bright red shirt.* 🔾 *The carpet was dark red.* (**vermelho**)

2 red hair is an orange colour (**ruivo**)

red² /red/ NOUN [plural **reds**] the colour of blood ☐ *The walls were painted a deep red.* (**vermelho**)

reduce /rɪˈdjuːs/ VERB [**reduces, reducing, reduced**] to make something smaller or less ☐ *Eating a healthy diet significantly reduces your risk of heart disease.* ☐ *We need to reduce pollution.* ☐ *+ to We have reduced the number of classes from six to four.* (**reduzir**)

▶ **THESAURUS:** If you reduce, cut or decrease something, you make it smaller or less. You can also say that something decreases if it becomes smaller or less. For example, you can say that the risk of disease decreases if you stop smoking. Cut is a slightly more informal word. If you lower something, you make it smaller in amount or degree. For example, a shop might cut, lower, reduce or decrease its prices. You might lower your voice to make it quieter.

reduction /rɪˈdʌkʃən/ NOUN [plural **reductions**] a decrease in the size, number, or amount of something 🔾 *We're offering huge price reductions.* ☐ *+ in There has been a significant reduction in the number of deaths on our roads.* (**redução**)

reef /riːf/ NOUN [plural **reefs**] a line of rocks, sand or coral (= hard substance made from small sea creatures) near the surface of the sea. A geography word. (**recife**)

refer /rɪˈfɜː(r)/
◆ PHRASAL VERBS [**refers, referring, referred**] **refer to someone/something** to mention someone or something 🔾 *She referred to the wedding several times.* ☐ *+ as He referred to the man as 'Robert'.* **refer to something**

1 a formal word meaning to look at something in order to get information ☐ *Please refer to the catalogue for more details.* (**consultar**)

2 to be about something ☐ *The figures refer to the period between 1990 and 2000.* (**referir-se**)

referee¹ /ˌrefəˈriː/ NOUN [plural **referees**] the person in a game such as football, who makes sure the players obey the rules ☐ *The referee blew his whistle to end the game.* (**árbitro**)

referee² /ˌrefəˈriː/ VERB [**referees, refereeing, refereed**] to be a referee during a game ☐ *Dixon refereed the match.* (**arbitrar**)

reference /ˈrefrəns/ NOUN [plural **references**]

1 a remark that mentions someone or something 🔾 *She made no reference to what had happened the day before.* (**referência**)

2 no plural the process of looking at something to get information, or the thing you look at 🔾 *He filed the documents away for future reference.* (**referência**)

3 a written report on your character that someone reads before offering you a job ☐ *You'll need a reference from your previous employer.* (**referendo**)

referendum /ˌrefəˈrendəm/ NOUN [plural **referenda** or **referendums**] when the people of a country vote on a political question 🔾 *We promise to hold a referendum on the issue.* (**referendo**)

reflect /rɪˈflekt/ VERB [**reflects, reflecting, reflected**]

1 if something is reflected, you can see an image of it in a surface like a mirror ☐ *+ in She caught sight of herself reflected in a shop window.* (**refletir**)

2 to be a sign of something ☐ *+ question word Her face reflected how she felt inside.* 🔾 *The price reflects the fact that the house is in a very popular area.* (**refletir**)

3 to think carefully about something, especially something that has happened ☐ *+ on I need time to reflect on my experiences.* (**refletir**)

reflexive /rɪˈfleksɪv/ ADJECTIVE to do with words that show that the subject of a verb is the same as its object ☐ *'Hurt yourself' is a reflexive verb.* ☐ *'Himself' is a reflexive pronoun.* (**reflexivo**)

reform¹ /rɪˈfɔːm/ VERB [**reforms, reforming, reformed**] to make changes to something in order to improve it ☐ *There are plans to reform the exams system.* (**corrigir**)

reform² /rɪˈfɔːm/ NOUN [plural **reforms**] changes that are made to improve something, or the process of making these changes ☐ *There were calls for reform of the tax system.* (**reforma**)

refresh /rɪˈfreʃ/ VERB [**refreshes, refreshing, refreshed**]
1 to make you feel cooler or less tired ▫ *The cool air refreshed him a bit.* ▫ *She woke up feeling refreshed and rested.* (**refrescar, revigorar**)
2 to change what is on a computer screen so that you can see the latest information. A computing word. (**atualizar**)

refreshing /rɪˈfreʃɪŋ/ ADJECTIVE making you feel cooler or less tired ▫ *a refreshing drink* (**refrescante**)

refreshments /rɪˈfreʃmənts/ PLURAL NOUN food and drink ▫ *Are refreshments available inside the park?* ▫ *Light refreshments will be provided.* (**lanche**)

refrigerator /rɪˈfrɪdʒəreɪtə(r)/ NOUN [plural **refrigerators**] a machine that you can store food or drink in to keep it cold and fresh (**geladeira**)

refuge /ˈrefjuːdʒ/ NOUN [plural **refuges**] protection from danger ▫ *The family took refuge from the fighting in a church.* (**refúgio**)

refugee /ˌrefjuˈdʒiː/ NOUN [plural **refugees**] a person who goes to another country because they are not safe in their own country ▫ *a refugee camp* (**refugiado**)

refund¹ /rɪˈfʌnd/ VERB [**refunds, refunding, refunded**] to give someone back some money that they have paid ▫ *We'll refund your money if you're not completely satisfied.* (**reembolsar**)

refund² /ˈriːfʌnd/ NOUN [plural **refunds**] money you have paid that is given back to you ▫ *He got a refund from the airline.* (**reembolso**)

refusal /rɪˈfjuːzəl/ NOUN [plural **refusals**] when you refuse to accept or to do something ▫ *His refusal to discuss the problem led to more bad feeling.* (**reembolso**)

refuse¹ /rɪˈfjuːz/ VERB [**refuses, refusing, refused**] **1** to say that you will not do something ▫ *He refused to help me.* ▫ *She refused a request for an interview.* (**recusar**)
2 to say that you will not accept something you are offered ▫ *Gerry refused a cup of tea but took a glass of water.* (**recusar**)

refuse² /ˈrefjuːs/ NOUN, NO PLURAL a formal word for rubbish that people throw away ▫ *household refuse* (**recusar**)

regard¹ /rɪˈɡɑːd/ VERB [**regards, regarding, regarded**] to think about someone or something in a particular way ▫ *My mother still regards me as a child.* ▫ *He was regarded with suspicion by many.* (**considerar**)

regard² /rɪˈɡɑːd/ NOUN, NO PLURAL respect or care for someone or something ▫ *They went ahead without regard for our opinion.* (**respeito, consideração**)

regarding /rɪˈɡɑːdɪŋ/ PREPOSITION about ▫ *I'd like to talk to you regarding next weekend.* ▫ *Police have appealed for information regarding the incident.* (**com respeito a**)

regardless /rɪˈɡɑːdləs/ ADVERB without paying any attention to something ▫ *Regardless of the cost, I'm determined to take this holiday.* ▫ *We warned them, but they carried on regardless.* (**independentemente**)

regards /rɪˈɡɑːdz/ PLURAL NOUN
1 used when sending good wishes to someone ▫ *Give my regards to Fiona when you see her.* (**saudações**)
2 used at the end of a friendly but polite letter or e-mail (**saudações**)

regiment /ˈredʒɪmənt/ NOUN [plural **regiments**] a large group of soldiers in an army (**regimento**)

region /ˈriːdʒən/ NOUN [plural **regions**] a large area of land such as a part of a country with a particular characteristic ▫ *We visited some of the wine-making regions of Spain.* ▫ *The region's economy is growing steadily.* (**região**)

> **THESAURUS:** Area is a general word for a part of a place. A region is a large area of land such as a part of a country with a particular characteristic. A district is a part of a country or a city. District is often used to talk about areas where people work, for example, a business district, or where a particular thing is done, for example a mining district. A neighbourhood is an area of a town or city, especially one where people live.

register¹ /ˈredʒɪstə(r)/ VERB [**registers, registering, registered**]
1 to put your name on an official list ▫ + **for** *We registered for the swimming class.* ▫ + **with** *Make sure you register with the embassy.* ▫ *You must register your son's birth in the next week.* (**registrar**)
2 if a device registers a measurement, it shows it ▫ *The earthquake registered 8.6 on the Richter scale.* (**registrar**)

register² /ˈredʒɪstə(r)/ NOUN [plural **registers**] an official list of names ▫ *Our teacher takes the register every morning.* ▫ *a register of births and deaths* (**registro**)

registration /ˌredʒɪˈstreɪʃən/ NOUN [plural **registrations**] when you put your name on an official list ▫ + **for** *Registration for next term's classes starts on the 20th.* ▫ *a registration fee* ▫ *You need to complete a registration form.* (**registro**)

regret¹ /rɪˈɡret/ VERB [**regrets, regretting, regretted**] to wish that something had not happened and to feel sorry about it ▫ *He regretted his decision.* ▫ + **ing** *Yes I'm sorry, I regret saying that.* ▫ *I regret not working harder at school.* ▫ + **that** *He now regrets that he didn't do more.* (**arrepender-se**)

regret² /rɪˈɡret/ NOUN [plural **regrets**] a sad feeling about something that has happened ▫ *Marion had no regrets about leaving home.* ▫ *He expressed regret for his actions.* ▫ *It is with great regret that I am leaving the club.* (**pesar, arrependimento**)

regular /ˈreɡjʊlə(r)/ ADJECTIVE
1 happening often or doing something often ▢ *We all know the benefits of regular exercise.* ▢ *I keep in regular contact with my family.* ▢ *He writes to me on a regular basis.* ▢ *She was a regular visitor to the museum.* (**regular**)
2 having the same amount of time or space between each thing ▢ *He has a regular heartbeat.* ▢ *I still see the doctor at regular intervals.* (**regular**)
3 following the usual rules of grammar ▢ *'Cat' has a regular plural.* ▢ *'Pick' is a regular verb.* (**regular**)
4 a US word meaning usual ▢ *My regular doctor was away.* (**habitual**)

regularly /ˈreɡjʊləlɪ/ ADVERB
1 often ▢ *We regularly have to call the police on a Saturday night.* ▢ *Patients are regularly denied medical care.* (**regularmente**)
2 with the same amount of time or space between each thing ▢ *The flowers were planted regularly along the border.* ▢ *All the equipment is regularly checked.* (**regularmente**)

rehearsal /rɪˈhɜːsəl/ NOUN [plural **rehearsals**] a practice for a performance ▢ *We are starting rehearsals for the new show.* (**ensaio**)

rehearse /rɪˈhɜːs/ VERB [**rehearses, rehearsing, rehearsed**] to practise performing something ▢ *Can we rehearse that last bit again?* (**ensaiar**)

reign[1] /reɪn/ VERB [**reigns, reigning, reigned**] to rule over a country as a king or queen ▢ *Queen Victoria reigned for over sixty years.* (**reinar**)

reign[2] /reɪn/ NOUN [plural **reigns**] the time when someone is the king or queen of a country ▢ *in the reign of King John* (**reinado**)

rein /reɪn/ NOUN [plural **reins**] a long piece of leather which goes around a horse's neck and is used to control it ▢ *He held the horse's reins tightly.* (**rédea**)

reinforce /ˌriːɪnˈfɔːs/ VERB [**reinforces, reinforcing, reinforced**] to make something stronger ▢ *reinforced glass* ▢ *The concrete walls have been reinforced with steel.* (**reforçar**)

reject /rɪˈdʒekt/ VERB [**rejects, rejecting, rejected**]
1 to refuse to accept something ▢ *The machine rejected my coin.* ▢ *Unions rejected the offer.* (**rejeitar**)
2 to decide not to accept someone for a job, a course, etc. ▢ *He was rejected for the job.* ▢ *Her application was rejected.* (**rejeitar**)
3 to not give someone enough love or attention ▢ *He felt rejected by his family.* (**rejeitar**)

relate /rɪˈleɪt/ VERB [**relates, relating, related**]
1 to show a connection between two things ▢ *The study attempted to relate mobile phone use to headaches.* (**relacionar**)
2 to tell a story or to say what happened ▢ *They related their strange experience to their friends.* (**relatar**)

◆ PHRASAL VERB **relate to someone/something** to be connected with someone or something ▢ *The charges relate to the death of a man last November.* ▢ *The figures relate to the period 2004–2005.*

> Remember that one thing is **related to** another thing. It is not 'related with' another thing:
> ✓ *Health is very much related to diet.*
> ✗ *Health is very much related with diet.*

relation /rɪˈleɪʃən/ NOUN [plural **relations**]
1 a connection between things ▢ *+ between Scientists established the relation between smoking and lung cancer.* ▢ *Most movies bear no relation to (= are nothing like) reality.* (**relação**)
2 someone in your family ▢ *All our friends and relations were there.* ▢ *+ of He's a distant relation of Tolstoy.* (**parente**)

relationship /rɪˈleɪʃənʃɪp/ NOUN [plural **relationships**] the way people or groups feel about each other and deal with each other ▢ *+ with Anne felt she had a good relationship with her brother.* ▢ *+ between There's a close relationship between our two countries.* ▢ *They had a father-son relationship.* (**relação**)

relative[1] /ˈrelətɪv/ NOUN [plural **relatives**] a member of your family ▢ *We invited all our friends and relatives.* ▢ *She has no close relatives.* ▢ *He's a distant relative of the prime minister.* (**parentes**)

relative[2] /ˈrelətɪv/ ADJECTIVE compared with similar people or things ▢ *We are in a period of relative calm.* ▢ *It compares the relative merits of the two education systems.* (**relativo**)

relatively /ˈrelətɪvlɪ/ ADVERB quite, compared with similar people or things ▢ *It's a relatively easy journey.* (**relativamente**)

relax /rɪˈlæks/ VERB [**relaxes, relaxing, relaxed**] to rest and become calmer and less worried ▢ *We spent the afternoon relaxing by the pool* ▢ *Relax– the children are quite safe.* ▢ *A holiday will help to relax you.* (**relaxar**)

relaxation /ˌriːlækˈseɪʃən/ NOUN, NO PLURAL when you relax or relax a part of your body ▢ *We practised relaxation techniques.* ▢ *I need a little rest and relaxation.* (**relaxamento**)

relaxed /rɪˈlækst/ ADJECTIVE feeling calm, comfortable and not worried ▢ *People are relaxed and enjoying themselves.* ▢ *a relaxed atmosphere* (**relaxado, calmo**)

relaxing /rɪˈlæksɪŋ/ ADJECTIVE making you feel relaxed ▢ *We had a relaxing break in the country.* ▢ *a relaxing massage* (**relaxante**)

release[1] /rɪˈliːs/ VERB [**releases, releasing, released**] to allow a person or an animal to go free ▢ *Three more prisoners have been released.* ▢ *+ from He was released from prison in 2004.* (**liberar**)

release[2] /rɪˈliːs/ NOUN [plural **releases**] when someone or something is allowed to go free ▢ *+of The government demanded the release of the*

hostages. □ + *from* I met him just after his release from prison. (**liberação**)

relevant /ˈreləvənt/ ADJECTIVE connected to or important for a subject, situation, etc. □ *Is this answer relevant to the question?* 🗎 *They sent us all the relevant information.* (**relevante**)

reliable /rɪˈlaɪəbəl/ ADJECTIVE
1 a reliable person can be trusted to do what they say they will do or to do something well □ *We need to find a reliable supplier of spare parts.* □ *He's one of the team's most reliable players.* (**confiável**)
2 a reliable system, piece of equipment, vehicle, etc. works well and does not often stop working □ *I need a reliable car to get me to work.* □ *The trains aren't very reliable.* (**confiável**)

relief /rɪˈliːf/ NOUN, NO PLURAL a good feeling because something bad or unpleasant stops or does not happen 🗎 *He gave a sigh of relief.* □ *It was a relief to be outside in the fresh air again.* □ *To my relief, no one was hurt.* (**alívio**)

relieve /rɪˈliːv/ VERB [**relieves, relieving, relieved**] to stop pain, suffering or a problem or to make it less □ *The drug is used to relieve pain.* □ *The new clinic will relieve pressure on the hospital.* □ *He read magazines to relieve the boredom.* (**aliviar**)

relieved /rɪˈliːvd/ ADJECTIVE feeling good because something bad or unpleasant stops or does not happen □ *I'm so relieved that you're home safely.* □ *She looked relieved.* (**aliviado**)

religion /rɪˈlɪdʒən/ NOUN [plural religions]
belief in a god or gods, and the activities and traditions to do with this belief □ *What is the role of religion in our society?* □ *We teach respect for different religions and cultures.* (**religião**)

religious /rɪˈlɪdʒəs/ ADJECTIVE
1 to do with religion □ *a religious service* 🗎 *a religious leader* 🗎 *religious beliefs* (**religioso**)
2 having strong beliefs about a god or gods 🗎 *He was a deeply religious man.* □ *I'm not particularly religious.* (**religioso**)

rely /rɪˈlaɪ/
◆ PHRASAL VERB [**relies, relying, relied**] **rely on someone/something**
1 to need someone or something in order to exist or be successful □ *We rely on the help of parents and friends.* 🗎 *The system relies heavily on computer technology.* (**depender de, contar com**)
2 to trust someone or something to do what they say they will do or what they should do □ *You can rely on our support.* □ *We can rely on Alan to sort it out.* □ *You can't rely on the trains in this country.* (**contar com**)

remain /rɪˈmeɪn/ VERB [**remains, remaining, remained**]
1 to continue to be in the same state or condition □ *He remained silent on the issue.* □ *His location remains a mystery.* □ *I won't vote for them while he remains leader.* (**permanecer**)
2 to be left when everything or everyone else has gone □ *All that remains in the fireplace is a pile of ash.* □ *The chemotherapy kills the cancer cells that remain after surgery.* (**restar**)

remainder /rɪˈmeɪndə(r)/ NOUN, NO PLURAL **the remainder** what is left of something after some of it has gone □ *He spent the remainder of his life in London.* □ *I tipped the remainder of the liquid away.* (**resto**)

remaining /rɪˈmeɪnɪŋ/ ADJECTIVE continuing to be there after other people or things have gone, been used, etc. □ *The remaining contestants will perform tonight.* □ *We can use the remaining time to tidy up.* (**restante**)

remains /rɪˈmeɪnz/ PLURAL NOUN parts of something that are left after the main part has gone □ *People returned to the remains of their burnt homes.* □ *the remains of a Roman temple* (**restos**)

remark¹ /rɪˈmɑːk/ VERB [remarks, remarking, remarked]
to express an opinion or a thought □ + *that* Tim remarked that he liked Di's hat. □ + *on* She didn't remark on the new painting. (**observar, comentar, notar**)

remark² /rɪˈmɑːk/ NOUN [plural remarks]
something you say when expressing an opinion or a thought □ + *about* He made a nasty remark about my writing. □ + *on* The President's remarks on immigration caused controversy. 🗎 *He made a racist remark.* (**observação**)

remarkable /rɪˈmɑːkəbəl/ ADJECTIVE surprising or noticeable, usually in a way that you admire □ *It's a remarkable story.* □ *It's remarkable how quickly she recovered.* (**notável**)

remarkably /rɪˈmɑːkəbli/ ADVERB in a very surprising or noticeable way □ *Remarkably, there were no injuries.* □ *They looked remarkably similar.* (**notavelmente**)

remedy /ˈremədi/ NOUN [plural **remedies**]
1 something that treats an illness 🗎 *a herbal remedy* □ *This is a traditional remedy for toothache.* (**remédio**)
2 something that solves a problem □ *Their policies are seen as a remedy for the country's economic crisis.* (**solução**)

remember /rɪˈmembə(r)/ VERB [remembers, remembering, remembered]
1 to have something from the past in your mind or to bring something back to your mind □ *I couldn't remember her name.* □ + *question word* I don't remember why we chose it. □ + *that* She suddenly remembered that she'd left the window open. □ + *ing* He remembered seeing a young girl outside. □ + *as* He will be remembered as a great player. (**lembrar**)
2 not to forget to do something □ + *to do something* Remember to take your key with you. (**lembrar**)

> **THESAURUS:** If you remember something, you don't forget to do it. If you make someone else remember to do something, you **remind** them to do it. If you remember who or what someone or something is because you have seen them before, you can say that you **recognize** the person or thing. If you remember how to do something because you have studied it carefully, you can say that you **learn** it. For example, you must **learn** the rules of English grammar.

remind /rɪˈmaɪnd/ VERB [reminds, reminding, reminded] to make someone remember something □ **+ to do something** Remind me to close the window before I go out. □ She reminded herself why she was there. □ **+ that** I want to remind everybody that the bus will leave at four o'clock. □ **+ of** She sent an email reminding students of the new timetable. (lembrar, fazer lembrança)

◆ PHRASAL VERB **remind someone of someone/something**

1 to make you think about someone or something from the past □ That picture reminds me of our holiday last year. (renovar)

2 to make you think about someone or something because of being similar to them □ Thomas reminded her of her father. (renovar)

> Note that if someone or something makes you think about someone or something from the past, they **remind** you **of** them. **Remind** in this sense is always followed by **to**:
> ✓ She **reminds** me **of** my sister.
> ✗ She reminds me my sister.

remote /rɪˈməʊt/ ADJECTIVE [remoter, remotest] a remote place is very far away from other places □ a remote village (remoto)

removal /rɪˈmuːvəl/ NOUN [plural removals] when something is removed □ He called for the removal of foreign troops. □ Doctors advised the removal of the tumour. (remoção)

remove /rɪˈmuːv/ VERB [removes, removing, removed] to take something away or to get rid of some thing □ The police have removed the car. □ Doctors removed the tumour. □ **+ from** Remove the pan from the heat and stir in the cream. (renovar)

renew /rɪˈnjuː/ VERB [renews, renewing, renewed]

1 to start doing something again after a break, often with more energy □ We'll renew our attempt to get the rules changed.

2 to make or to pay for something to continue for another period of time □ You can renew your bus pass at the office. (renovar)

renewable /rɪˈnjuːəbəl/ ADJECTIVE describes a type of natural energy such as power from the sun which can be replaced quickly and which will not end (renovável)

rent¹ /rent/ VERB [rents, renting, rented]

1 to pay someone money so that you can use a house or other building □ We rented a villa near the beach. (alugar)

2 to allow other people to pay to use something you own □ **+ out** They rent out the building for weddings. □ **+ to** We'll rent the house to students while we're away. (alugar)

3 a mainly US word meaning to pay someone money to use something such as a car or tools for a short time □ She rented a car for the week. (alugar)

> Note that in British English, **rent** is mainly used for houses and other buildings. The verb **hire** means 'to pay someone money to use something such as a car or tools for a short time'.

rent² /rent/ NOUN [plural rents] money you pay to the owner of a house or other building to use it ⓗ He's struggling to pay the rent. (aluguel)

repaid /riːˈpeɪd/ PAST TENSE AND PAST PARTICIPLE OF **repay** (pagar)

repair¹ /rɪˈpeə(r)/ VERB [repairs, repairing, repaired] to fix something that is damaged or not working □ Can the washing machine be repaired? ⓗ It will cost millions to repair the damage done by the storms. (reparar)

repair² /rɪˈpeə(r)/ NOUN [plural repairs] something you do to repair something □ The ship needed extensive repairs. (reparo)

repay /riːˈpeɪ/ VERB [repays, repaying, repaid] to pay back money that you have borrowed □ They are struggling to repay the loans. (pagar)

repeat /rɪˈpiːt/ VERB [repeats, repeating, repeated]

1 to say something again □ Could you repeat your name please? □ She repeated her request. □ I don't want to repeat myself (= say the same thing again). (repetir)

2 to do something again or to happen again □ I hope this mistake will never be repeated. □ The programme is repeated on Friday at 10pm. (repetir)

repeated /rɪˈpiːtɪd/ ADJECTIVE done or happening several times □ After repeated attempts to phone him, I finally went round to his office. (repetido)

repeatedly /rɪˈpiːtɪdli/ ADVERB again and again □ The victim had been stabbed repeatedly. (repetidamente)

replace /rɪˈpleɪs/ VERB [replaces, replacing, replaced]

1 to take the place of another thing or person □ The company bought new computers to replace the old ones. □ The cinema was demolished and replaced by a supermarket. □ **+ with** The phone has been replaced with a newer version. □ **+ as** He was replaced as chairman last year. (substituir)

2 to put something back where it was before or in its correct position □ *Make sure you replace the books in exactly the right order.* (**recolocar**)

replacement /rɪˈpleɪsmənt/ NOUN [plural **replacements**] a person or thing that replaces another one □ *This is broken so I'd like a replacement, please.* ▣ *They will have to find a replacement for the injured goalkeeper.* (**substituto**)

replay /ˈriːpleɪ/ NOUN [plural **replays**] a sports match that is played again because nobody won the first time □ *He scored in the second-round replay.* (**partida decisiva**)

reply¹ /rɪˈplaɪ/ VERB [**replies, replying, replied**] to answer □ *'No, I don't!' he replied angrily.* □ **+ that** *He replied that he was planning to stay another week.* □ **+ to** *You haven't replied to my question yet.* (**replicar, responder**)

reply² /rɪˈplaɪ/ NOUN [plural **replies**] an answer □ **+ to** *We've had a number of replies to our advertisement.* □ *In reply, Phoebe gave a nod.* ▣ *He received no reply to his letters.* (**resposta**)

report¹ /rɪˈpɔːt/ NOUN [plural **reports**]
1 a description of something that has happened □ **+ of** *Reports of an accident are just coming in.* ▣ *a television news report* (**relatório, informação**)
2 a teacher's written description of a student's progress ▣ *a school report* (**relatório**)

report² /rɪˈpɔːt/ VERB [**reports, reporting, reported**]
1 to tell people about an event or situation on television, on radio, in newspapers, etc. □ *The whole story was reported in the papers.* □ **+ on** *Tonight we'll be reporting on religious education.* (**relatar, fazer relatório**)
2 to tell someone officially that something has happened □ **+ to** *Did you report the incident to the police?* (**denunciar**)

reported speech /rɪˌpɔːtɪd ˈspiːtʃ/ NOUN, NO PLURAL the words you use when you say what someone has said without using their exact words (**discurso indireto**)

reporter /rɪˈpɔːtə(r)/ NOUN [plural **reporters**] a person whose job is to describe events for newspapers, television or radio news programmes, etc. ▣ *a newspaper reporter* (**repórter**)

represent /ˌreprɪˈzent/ VERB [**represents, representing, represented**]
1 to speak or to act officially for someone else □ *Our MPs represent us in the government.* □ *He was represented by a lawyer.* (**representar**)
2 to be a symbol or an example of something □ *The crown represents the king or queen.* □ *The black lines on the map represent railways.* (**representar**)

representative¹ /ˌreprɪˈzentətɪv/ NOUN [plural **representatives**] someone who represents someone else □ *a union representative* □ *There were representatives of several international organizations at the meeting.* (**representante**)

representative² /ˌreprɪˈzentətɪv/ ADJECTIVE typical of a group of people or things □ *a representative sample* □ *These statistics are representative of the overall population.* (**representativo**)

reproduce /ˌriːprəˈdjuːs/ VERB [**reproduces, reproducing, reproduced**]
1 to make something again or to copy something □ *The child had reproduced his father's signature.* □ *Other scientists failed to reproduce the same results.* (**reproduzir**)
2 to produce babies, young animals or plants. A biology word. □ *The virus reproduces quickly.* (**reproduzir-se**)

reproduction /ˌriːprəˈdʌkʃən/ NOUN [plural **reproductions**]
1 a copy of something □ *a reproduction of the painting* (**reprodução**)
2 the process of producing babies or young animals or plants. A biology word. □ *human reproduction* (**reprodução**)

reptile /ˈreptaɪl/ NOUN [plural **reptiles**] an animal with cold blood that produces eggs, such as a snake. A biology word. (**réptil**)

republic /rɪˈpʌblɪk/ NOUN [plural **republics**] a country with no king or queen, but with an elected government and usually a president (= elected leader) (**república**)

reputation /ˌrepjuˈteɪʃən/ NOUN [plural **reputations**] the opinion that most people have of someone or something based on experience □ *The restaurant has a very good reputation* □ **+ for** *He has a reputation for being a very tough player.* □ **+ as** *The country has built a reputation as a tourist destination.* (**reputação**)

request¹ /rɪˈkwest/ NOUN [plural **requests**] when someone politely asks for something ▣ *I've got a request to make.* □ **+ for** *There were hundreds of requests for information.* □ **+ to do something** *The man refused repeated requests to leave.* (**pedido**)

request² /rɪˈkwest/ VERB [**requests, requesting, requested**] to ask politely for something □ *The committee requested additional information.* □ *The pilot requested permission to land.* (**pedir, requerer, solicitar**)

> Note that you **request** something. You do not 'request for' something:
> ✓ *He requested an invitation.*
> ✗ *He requested for an invitation.*

require /rɪˈkwaɪə(r)/ VERB [**requires, requiring, required**] to need something □ *Do you require any further information?* □ *He required treatment for an ankle injury.* (**precisar**)

requirement /rɪˈkwaɪəmənt/ NOUN [plural **requirements**] something that you need or want ▣ *Each kitchen is designed to meet customer requirements.* (**exigências**)

rescue[1] /ˈreskjuː/ VERB [rescues, rescuing, rescued] to save someone from danger ▫ + *from* Firefighters rescued the people from the burning house. (salvar, resgatar)

rescue[2] /ˈreskjuː/ NOUN [plural rescues] when someone is saved from danger ▫ They were lost with no hope of rescue. ▫ Fire fighters made several *rescue attempts*. ▫ A passing driver *came to her rescue*. (salvamento)

research[1] /rɪˈsɜːtʃ, ˈriːsɜːtʃ/ NOUN [plural researches] when you study a subject carefully to find new information ▫ + *into* They fund research into causes of cancer. ▫ The *research was carried out* in 2005. ▫ The *research shows* little educational benefit to homework. (pesquisa)

research[2] /rɪˈsɜːtʃ, ˈriːsɜːtʃ/ VERB [researches, researching, researched] to study a subject carefully to find new information ▫ She is researching her family history. ▫ I was researching a book about Einstein. (pesquisar)

• **researcher** /rɪˈsɜːtʃə(r)/ NOUN [plural researchers] a person who researches something (pesquisador)

resemblance /rɪˈzembləns/ NOUN [plural resemblances] when things or people look or seem similar in some way ▫ Can you see the resemblance between the brothers? ▫ The film *bears* little *resemblance to* (= is quite different from) the original book. (semelhança)

resemble /rɪˈzembəl/ VERB [resembles, resembling, resembled] to look similar or to seem similar in some way ▫ Tom resembles his father. ▫ The website resembles the front page of a newspaper. (parecer-se)

resent /rɪˈzent/ VERB [resents, resenting, resented] to feel angry or unhappy about something you think is unfair ▫ She resented being interrupted. ▫ He resented his sister because of the attention she received. (ressentir-se)

reservation /ˌrezəˈveɪʃən/ NOUN [plural reservations] an arrangement to keep a place for you in a restaurant, hotel, plane, etc. ▫ + *for* We have a reservation for dinner. ▫ I'd like to *make a reservation* for two double rooms, please. (reserva)

reserve[1] /rɪˈzɜːv/ VERB [reserves, reserving, reserved]
1 to ask a hotel, restaurant, etc. to keep a place for you ▫ I'd like to reserve a table for dinner tonight, please. ▫ We reserved seats in a no-smoking section. (reservar)
2 to keep something for a particular use or person ▫ + *for* Some seats are reserved for elderly or disabled passengers. ▫ Mix in half the sugar, reserving the rest for the icing. (reservar)

reserve[2] /rɪˈzɜːv/ NOUN [plural reserves]
1 an amount of something you have available to use in the future ▫ the world's oil reserves ▫ She seems to have amazing reserves of energy and patience. (reserva)
2 someone or something available to be used if another person or thing is not available ▫ He was a reserve in the England team. ▫ He managed to open his reserve parachute. (reserva)
3 an area of land where plants or animals are protected ▫ a *nature reserve* (reserva)

reservoir /ˈrezəvwɑː(r)/ NOUN [plural reservoirs] a large lake where water is collected and stored in order to be used by people in an area (reservatório)

resign /rɪˈzaɪn/ VERB [resigns, resigning, resigned] to officially say that you are leaving your job ▫ She resigned from her post as finance director. (demitir-se)

◆ PHRASAL VERB **resign yourself to something** to accept something unpleasant that you cannot change ▫ He had resigned himself to defeat. ▫ They're resigned to losing the house.

resignation /ˌrezɪɡˈneɪʃən/ NOUN [plural resignations]
1 when you officially say that you are leaving your job ▫ a letter of resignation ▫ There have been calls for the minister's resignation. ▫ He's *handed in* his *resignation*. (demissão)
2 no plural a feeling of accepting something unpleasant that you cannot change ▫ a look of resignation (resignação)

resist /rɪˈzɪst/ VERB [resists, resisting, resisted]
1 to try to stop something from happening or to refuse to accept something ▫ The bank resisted pressure to cut interest rates. (resistir)
2 to stop yourself from doing or having something you want ▫ She resisted the *temptation* to take a look. ▫ The opportunity was too good to resist. (resistência)
3 to fight against someone or something, especially when they are attacking you. ▫ They couldn't resist the attackers. ▫ He *resisted arrest*. (resistir)

resistance /rɪˈzɪstəns/ NOUN, NO PLURAL
1 when you refuse to accept something ▫ The plans have *met stiff resistance*. (resistência)
2 when you fight against someone or something ▫ armed resistance (resistência)

resort /rɪˈzɔːt/ NOUN [plural resorts]
1 a place where people go on holiday ▫ a popular seaside resort ▫ a ski resort (local de férias, resort)
2 *a last resort* something you do only when everything else has failed ▫ I suppose we could borrow the money as a last resort. (último recurso)

◆ PHRASAL VERB [resorts, resorting, resorted] **resort to something** to do something you do not want to do in order to solve a problem ▫ The worst thing would be to resort to violence.

resource /rɪˈsɔːs/ NOUN [plural resources] something that you have and are able to use ▫ the country's *natural resources* ▫ He blamed a lack of resources for the delays. (recurso)

respect[1] /rɪˈspekt/ NOUN [plural respects]
1 the feeling of admiring someone or something because of their behaviour or their achievements ▫ + *of* She earned the respect of her colleagues. (respeito)

2 polite behaviour towards someone □ + *for* *Their behaviour shows a lack of respect for others.* ⮞ *He treats everyone with respect.* (**respeito**)
3 a part of something or a way of thinking about it □ *In many respects, the two boys are very similar.* □ *The plan was good in every respect.* (**aspecto**)

respect² /rɪˈspekt/ VERB [respects, respecting, respected] because of their behaviour or achievements □ *I respect her enormously.* ⮞ *He was highly respected in the local community.* (**respeitar**)

respectable /rɪˈspektəbəl/ ADJECTIVE
1 accepted by society as good, correct, honest, etc. □ *Simon comes from a respectable family.* (**respeitável**)
2 quite good □ *a perfectly respectable score* (**respeitável**)
• **respectably** /rɪˈspektəbli/ ADVERB in a socially acceptable way □ *She was respectably dressed.* (**respeitavelmente**)

respond /rɪˈspɒnd/ VERB [responds, responding, responded] to answer or to react □ *If someone hits you, you tend to respond by hitting back.* □ *'That's not my problem,' Gina responded.* □ *Police responded quickly to the call.* (**responder, reagir**)

response /rɪˈspɒns/ NOUN [plural responses] an answer or a reaction □ *His response was a shake of his head.* □ *What was the response of his colleagues to his announcement?* (**resposta**)

responsibility /rɪˌspɒnsəˈbɪləti/ NOUN [plural responsibilities]
1 something that you must do or deal with □ + *for* *The manager has responsibility for all the business.* □ + *of* *The first responsibility of a government is to protect its citizens.* □ + *to do something* *It's my responsibility to make sure all the doors are locked.* □ *They share the childcare responsibilities.* (**responsabilidade**)
2 blame for doing something, usually something bad ⮞ *I take full responsibility for the mistake.* (**responsabilidade**)

responsible /rɪˈspɒnsəbəl/ ADJECTIVE
1 if you are responsible for something, you are the person who must do it or deal with it □ + *for* *Who is responsible for keeping the money?* □ *the minister responsible for transport* (**responsável**)
2 if you are responsible for something which happens, you are to blame for it □ + *for* *Is human activity responsible for global warming?* ⮞ *He felt partly responsible for the mess.* (**responsável**)

rest¹ /rest/ NOUN [plural rests]
1 the rest the part of something that is left, or the people or things that are left □ *I don't want to spend the rest of my life here.* □ *The rest of the country will have showers.* □ *I want half of you in this room and the rest outside.* (**resto**)
2 a time when you relax or sleep ⮞ *Why don't you have a rest before dinner?* (**descanso**)

rest² /rest/ VERB [rests, resting, rested]
1 to relax or sleep after an activity □ *You should rest every few minutes when you're lifting such heavy weights.* (**descansar**)
2 to be supported by something, or to put something on something else for support □ *He left his spade resting against a wall.* □ *Mo rested her hands on the piano keys for a moment.* (**apoiar, pousar**)

restart /riːˈstɑːt/ VERB [restarts, restarting, restarted] to turn a computer off and then on again □ *Have you tried restarting your computer?* (**reiniciar**)

restaurant /ˈrestrɒnt/ NOUN [plural restaurants] a place where you can buy and eat a meal □ *a Chinese restaurant* (**restaurante**)

restless /ˈrestlɪs/ ADJECTIVE not able to stay still or quiet because you are nervous, worried or bored □ *The audience began to get restless after about an hour.* (**inquieto, impaciente**)

restrain /rɪˈstreɪn/ VERB [restrains, restraining, restrained]
1 to stop someone from doing something, often using force □ *He attacked the man as friends tried to restrain him.* (**conter**)
2 to control your emotions or behaviour □ *We had to restrain ourselves from laughing.* (**conter**)

restrict /rɪˈstrɪkt/ VERB [restricts, restricting, restricted] to limit something □ *We are restricting people to one ticket each.* □ *Parents can restrict children's access to certain websites.* (**restringir**)

restriction /rɪˈstrɪkʃən/ NOUN [plural restrictions] a limit on something □ *Are there any parking restrictions on this road?* ⮞ *Airlines imposed restrictions on hand luggage.* (**restrição**)

result¹ /rɪˈzʌlt/ NOUN [plural results]
1 what happens because of something else □ +*of* *This could be another result of global warming.* ⮞ *He died as a result of the accident.* ⮞ *He tried to play again too quickly, with the result that he made the injury worse.* (**resultado**)
2 the score or the winner at the end of a competition, an election, an exam etc. □ *the election result* □ + *of* *Do you know the result of yesterday's match?* ⮞ *She got good exam results.* (**resultado**)

result² /rɪˈzʌlt/ VERB [results, resulting, resulted] to happen because of something else □ *The fire apparently resulted from a dropped cigarette.* (**resultar**)

◆ PHRASAL VERB **result in something** to cause something □ *The changes will result in the loss of 300 jobs.*

resume /rɪˈzjuːm/ VERB [resumes, resuming, resumed] a formal word meaning to start again □ *Normal train services will resume next week.* (**recomeçar**)

retire /rɪˈtaɪə(r)/ VERB [retires, retiring, retired] to stop working because you are old □ *Many people retire at 65.* □ + *from* *She has just retired from a career in nursing.* □ + *as* *He retired as director in 2005.* (**aposentar-se**)

> **THESAURUS:** If you retire, you stop working because you are old. If you **resign**, you officially say that you are leaving your job, perhaps because you have a new job to go to. You can also say that you **quit** your job or **leave** your job. If you lose your job because you have done something wrong, you **get the sack**.

retired /rɪˈtaɪəd/ ADJECTIVE no longer working because you are old □ *a retired teacher* (**aposentado**)

retirement¹ /rɪˈtaɪəmənt/ NOUN [plural **retirements**] the period of time after you stop working because you are old □ *I hope you enjoy your retirement.* (**aposentadoria**)

retirement² /rɪˈtaɪəmənt/ ADJECTIVE to do with the time when you stop working because you are old ▣ *He is close to retirement age.* □ *a retirement party* (**aposentadoria**)

retreat¹ /rɪˈtriːt/ NOUN [plural **retreats**] when an army moves back because it does not want to fight □ *a strategic retreat* (**retirada**)

retreat² /rɪˈtriːt/ VERB [**retreats, retreating, retreated**] if an army retreats, it moves back because it does not want to fight (**retirar-se**)

return¹ /rɪˈtɜːn/ VERB [returns, returning, returned]

1 to go or come back to a place □ *We fly out on Friday and return the following Wednesday.* □ *+ to We all returned to our classrooms.* □ *+ from He returned from his skiing holiday with a broken leg.* ▣ *All the air crew have returned safely.* (**voltar**)

2 to take, put or send something back □ *Please return your books by Friday.* □ *+ to All sports equipment should be returned to the gym.* (**devolver**)

return² /rɪˈtɜːn/ NOUN [plural returns]

1 when someone comes or goes back to a place □ *+ to On my return to the house, I found the door wide open.* □ *+ from After his return from Africa, he settled in London.* ▣ *They celebrated the safe return of the climbers.* (**volta**)

2 when something is taken, put or sent back □ *+ of We are delighted at the safe return of the stolen paintings.* (**volta**)

3 a ticket that allows you to travel to a place and back again □ *I'd like a return to Glasgow, please.* (**passagem de ida e volta**)

reunion /ˌriːˈjuːnjən/ NOUN [plural **reunions**] a meeting of people such as friends or family members who have not seen each other for a long time □ *a family reunion* (**reunião**)

reveal /rɪˈviːl/ VERB [**reveals, revealing, revealed**]

1 to tell someone something that is secret or surprising □ *He refused to reveal details of the project.* (**revelar**)

2 to show something that you could not see before □ *The mobile phone has a screen which slides back to reveal the keyboard.* (**revelar**)

revenge /rɪˈvendʒ/ NOUN, NO PLURAL when you hurt or upset someone because they have hurt or upset you or someone that you love ▣ *Ben had ruined her life and she was determined to get revenge.* ▣ *a revenge attack* (**vingança**)

reverse /rɪˈvɜːs/ VERB [**reverses, reversing, reversed**]

1 if a vehicle reverses, it moves backwards □ *A car was reversing.* (**dar ré, inverter**)

2 to make a vehicle move backwards □ *She reversed the car into the parking space.* (**inverter**)

3 to change something so that it is the opposite of what it was before ▣ *The government has reversed its decision.* (**revogar, voltar atrás**)

review¹ /rɪˈvjuː/ VERB [reviews, reviewing, reviewed]

1 to examine something again, often in order to decide if changes should be made □ *The company is reviewing its safety procedures following the accident.* □ *Lawyers are reviewing the case.* (**rever**)

2 to write your opinion of a new book, play, etc. □ *She reviewed the book for the New York Times.* (**resenhar**)

review² /rɪˈvjuː/ NOUN [plural reviews]

1 when something is examined again, often in order to decide if changes need to be made □ *+ of The government is conducting a review of the policy.* (**rever**)

2 an article which gives someone's opinion of a new book, play, etc. □ *a film review* ▣ *The play got some good reviews.* □ *+ of He wrote a review of the book.* (**resenhar**)

revise /rɪˈvaɪz/ VERB [revises, revising, revised]

1 to study for an exam by looking again at the work you have done □ *+ for Guy was busy revising for his Chinese exam.* (**rever**)

2 to change something, often in order to improve it □ *The revised edition of the dictionary has hundreds of new words in it.* □ *We've had to revise our plans.* (**resenha, crítica**)

revision /rɪˈvɪʒən/ NOUN [plural **revisions**] work that you do before an exam, by looking at work you have already done ▣ *I need to do some revision for my history test.* (**revisão**)

revive /rɪˈvaɪv/ VERB [**revives, reviving, revived**] to make someone conscious again □ *Doctors were unable to revive him.* (**reanimar, ressuscitar**)

revolt /rɪˈvəʊlt/ NOUN [plural **revolts**]

1 when a group of people use violence in order to change a government (**revolta**)

2 when people refuse to accept the authority of a leader □ *The leader is facing a revolt by members of his party.* (**revolta**)

revolting /rɪˈvəʊltɪŋ/ ADJECTIVE extremely unpleasant □ *a revolting smell* (**nojento**)

revolution /ˌrevəˈluːʃən/ NOUN [plural **revolutions**]

1 a time when people use violence to change a government □ *the French Revolution of 1789* (**revolução**)

revolutionary

2 a complete change in something such as an industry or society ◻ *Computers have led to a revolution in the way we work.* ◻ *the Industrial Revolution* (**revolução**)

revolutionary¹ /ˌrevəˈluːʃənəri/ ADJECTIVE
1 completely new and different ◻ *revolutionary technology* (**revolucionário**)
2 to do with a time when people use violence to change a government ◻ *Castro's revolutionary movement* (**revolucionário**)

revolutionary² /ˌrevəˈluːʃənəri/ NOUN [plural **revolutionaries**] someone who is involved in using violence to change a government (**revolucionário**)

revolve /rɪˈvɒlv/ VERB [**revolves, revolving, revolved**] to move in a circle around something ◻ *The Earth revolves around the sun.* (**girar**)

revolver /rɪˈvɒlvə(r)/ NOUN [plural **revolvers**] a type of small gun (**revólver**)

reward¹ /rɪˈwɔːd/ NOUN [plural **rewards**] something you get for doing something good or useful ◻ *financial rewards* ◻ **+ for** *The victim's family are offering a £5,000 reward for any information that helps catch the killer.* ◻ *He got his reward for all his hard work when the team scored a goal.* (**recompensar**)

reward² /rɪˈwɔːd/ VERB [**rewards, rewarding, rewarded**] to give someone something good for something they have done ◻ **+ for** *He was rewarded for all his hard work.* ◻ **+ with** *The baby rewarded me with a smile as I picked her up.* (**recompensar**)

rhino /ˈraɪnəʊ/ NOUN [plural **rhinos**] an informal word for **rhinoceros**

rhinoceros /raɪˈnɒsərəs/ NOUN [plural **rhinoceroses**] a large, grey animal from Africa and Asia that has thick skin and a horn on its nose (**rinoceronte**)

rhyme¹ /raɪm/ VERB [**rhymes, rhyming, rhymed**] if words rhyme, they end with the same sound ◻ *'Ghost' rhymes with 'toast'.* (**rima**)

rhyme² /raɪm/ NOUN [plural **rhymes**]
1 a word that sounds like another, or a pair of words that have a similar sound ◻ *I don't think there is a rhyme for 'orange'.* (**rima**)
2 a short poem or song using words which rhyme ◻ *a book of children's rhymes* (**poema**)

ride

rhythm /ˈrɪðəm/ NOUN [plural **rhythms**] a repeated pattern of sounds or movements ◻ *He had an irregular heart rhythm.* ◻ **+ of** *Amy's foot was tapping to the rhythm of the music.* 🔊 *She has a good sense of rhythm.* (**ritmo**)

rib /rɪb/ NOUN [plural **ribs**] one of the curved bones in your chest, around your heart and lungs (**costela**)

ribbon /ˈrɪbən/ NOUN [plural **ribbons**] a long, narrow piece of cloth, used for example to tie your hair up, or as a decoration on a present (**fita**)

rice /raɪs/ NOUN, NO PLURAL brown or white grains that you cook and eat as food ◻ *boiled rice* 🔊 *a grain of rice* ◻ *brown rice* ◻ *rice fields* (**arroz**)

rich¹ /rɪtʃ/ ADJECTIVE [**richer, richest**]
1 having a lot of money ◻ *Her Dad's very rich.* ◻ *rich countries* 🔊 *He was looking for ways to get rich* (= become rich). (**rico**)
2 full of something good 🔊 *Nuts and seeds are a rich source of iron.* ◻ **+ in** *Oranges are rich in vitamin C.* (**rico**)
3 rich food contains a lot of butter or cream ◻ *The cake was very rich so I only ate a small piece.* (**rico**)

rich² /rɪtʃ/ NOUN, NO PLURAL **the rich** people who have a lot of money ◻ *She enjoyed reading about the lifestyles of the rich and famous.* (**rico**)

riches /ˈrɪtʃɪz/ PLURAL NOUN a word used in stories meaning a lot of money and expensive things (**riqueza**)

> **THESAURUS: Money** is a general word for coins and paper notes that you use for buying things. **Riches** is a literary word meaning a lot of money and expensive things. For example, you might talk about a king's riches in a story. Someone's **wealth** is all the money and expensive things that they have. A **fortune** is a very large amount of money.

rid /rɪd/ ADJECTIVE
1 get rid of something (a) to throw something away or give it to someone else ◻ *My parents got rid of the old sofa and bought a new one.* (b) to make something go away that you do not want ◻ *I opened the window to get rid of the smell.* ◻ *I can't seem to get rid of this cold.* (**livrar-se, desembaraçar-se**)

2 get rid of someone to make someone go away ◻ *He arrived at 7 o'clock and we couldn't get rid of him.* (**livrar-se**)

ridden /ˈrɪdən/ PAST PARTICIPLE OF **ride¹** (ver **ride¹**)

ride¹ /raɪd/ VERB [**rides, riding, rode, ridden**]
1 to travel on a bicycle, motorcycle or horse ◻ *I learned to ride a bike when I was six.* ◻ *Do you ride* (= ride a horse)? ◻ *He turned and rode off.* (**montar, andar a/de**)
2 to travel in or on a vehicle ◻ *She had been riding around in the car all day.* (**andar a/de**)

ride² /raɪd/ NOUN [plural **rides**] a journey in or on a vehicle □ *It was a short bus ride from the airport to the hotel.* 🔑 *We went for a bike ride.* □ + *in* I had a ride in her new car. □ + *on* Can I have a ride on your bike? (**passeio, volta**)

rider /ˈraɪdə(r)/ NOUN [plural **riders**] someone sitting on and controlling a bicycle, motorcycle or horse □ *horse riders* (**ciclista, motociclista, cavaleiro, motorista**)

ridge /rɪdʒ/ NOUN [plural **ridges**] a long narrow piece of high land □ *mountain ridges* (**cadeia, estrutura**)

ridiculous /rɪˈdɪkjuləs/ ADJECTIVE very silly □ *It's a ridiculous idea!* (**ridículo**)

rifle /ˈraɪfl/ NOUN [plural **rifles**] a type of long gun (**rifle**)

right¹ /raɪt/ ADJECTIVE

1 correct □ + *about* He was right about the train being late. □ *Make sure you sign in the right place.* □ *Are we going in the right direction?* 🔑 *I got most of the answers right.* 🔑 *'I hear you're leaving.' 'That's right, I've got a new job.'* (**correto**)

2 suitable or in the condition that you want or expect □ + *for* He is not the right person for the job. □ *We didn't have the right clothes for the weather.* 🔑 *I need a new table, and this one looks just right.* □ *As soon as I saw her, I knew that something wasn't right.* (**certo**)

3 fair or acceptable □ *It doesn't seem right that so many people in the world are hungry.* □ + *todo something* It's not right to tax the poor. (**certo**)

4 on or to the side that is towards the east when you are facing north □ *I write with my right hand.* □ *We sat on the right side of the church.* (**direito**)

right² /raɪt/ NOUN [plural **rights**]

1 something that you are allowed to do or have, either officially or because it is acceptable □ + *to* Everyone has a right to a decent education. □ *These laws protect their religious rights.* 🔑 *You have no right to speak to me like that.* (**direito**)

2 the side or direction that is on or towards the right side of your body □ *There's a chemist over there on the right.* (**direita**)

3 behaviour that is morally good □ *These children do not know right from wrong.* (**certo**)

> Note (noun, sense 1) that you have a **right to** something or the **right to do** something. You do not have the 'right of' something:
> ✓ *Everybody has a right to healthcare.*
> ✗ *Everybody has a right of healthcare.*

right³ /raɪt/ ADVERB

1 towards the direction that is to the east when you are facing north □ *Now turn right.* (**à direita**)

2 exactly □ *Don't move – stay right there.* □ *We were right in the middle of dinner.* □ *Stay right behind me.* (**exatamente**)

3 immediately □ *I'll come right after lunch.* 🔑 *I want the work done right now.* (**imediatamente**)

4 all the way □ *This road goes right round the outside of the park.* □ *I watched the film right to the end.* (**totalmente**)

5 correctly □ *Can't you do anything right?* (**corretamente**)

6 used to get someone's attention before you speak or start to do something □ *Right, shall we go outside?* (**certo, bem**)

right-handed /ˌraɪtˈhændɪd/ ADJECTIVE using your right hand to do things, especially to write □ *Are you right-handed?* □ *a right-handed tennis player* (**destro**)

rigid /ˈrɪdʒɪd/ ADJECTIVE

1 unwilling to change or impossible for someone to change □ *a rigid schedule* □ *The rules are very rigid.* (**rígido**)

2 stiff and impossible to bend □ *a rigid frame* (**rígido**)

rim /rɪm/ NOUN [plural **rims**] the edge of something round, such as a cup, bowl or wheel (**borda**)

ring¹ /rɪŋ/ NOUN [plural **rings**]

1 a round piece of jewellery that you wear on your finger 🔑 *a wedding ring* □ *I was wearing a diamond ring.* (**anel**)

2 something in the shape of a circle *The children sat in a ring around the story-teller.* □ *The house was surrounded by a ring of fire.* (**círculo**)

3 give someone a ring to telephone someone □ *I'll give you a ring tomorrow.* (**telefonar**)

4 the sound a bell makes □ *Did I hear a ring at the door?* (**toque**)

ring² /rɪŋ/ VERB [**rings, ringing, rang, rung**]

1 if a bell rings, it produces a sound, and if you ring a bell, you make it produce a sound □ *I think I heard the doorbell ring.* (**tocar**)

2 to telephone someone □ *I'm ringing about the car you have for sale.* (**tocar**)

> Note that you **ring** (= telephone) a person or place. You do not 'ring to' a person or place:
> ✓ *I'll just ring my sister.*
> ✗ *I'll just ring to my sister.*

◆ PHRASAL VERBS **ring (someone) back** to telephone someone after they have telephoned you □ *I'm a bit busy – can I ring you back later?* **ring someone up** to telephone someone □ *She rang me up in the middle of the night.*

rinse /rɪns/ VERB [**rinses, rinsing, rinsed**] to remove dirt or soap from something by putting it in clean water □ *Rinse your hair well after shampooing it.* (**enxaguar**)

riot /ˈraɪət/ NOUN [plural **riots**] a time when a large crowd of people behave violently in a public place □ *His election caused riots in the capital.* 🔑 *Riot police were brought in to control the crowd.* (**tumulto**)

rip¹ /rɪp/ VERB [**rips, ripping, ripped**]

1 to tear something roughly □ *She ripped sheets into strips and used them as bandages.* □ *Steve ripped his trousers on the barbed wire.* (**rasgar**)

2 to remove something quickly and forcefully □ *The storm ripped the roof off their house.* (**arrancar**)

◆ PHRASAL VERB **rip something up** to tear something into small pieces □ *I ripped the letter up and put it in the bin.*

rip   289   roast

rip² /rɪp/ NOUN [plural **rips**] a rough tear □ *There was a rip in my sleeve where the handle had caught it.* (**rasgo**)

ripe /raɪp/ ADJECTIVE [**riper**, **ripest**] ripe fruit is ready to be picked or eaten □ *The plums were ripe and juicy.* □ *ripe tomatoes* (**maduro**)

ripple /ˈrɪp(ə)l/ NOUN [plural **ripples**] a small movement on the surface of water □ *Tiny fish were causing ripples in the water.* (**ondulação**)

rise¹ /raɪz/ VERB [**rises, rising, rose, risen**]
1 to go up □ *A column of smoke rose above the village.* □ **+ up** *The balloon rose up into the air.* □ *The sun rises in the east.* □ *Ahead, the ground rose steeply.* (**elevar-se, levantar-se**)
2 to increase in level □ *Prices have risen this year.* ▣ *Profits rose sharply in the second half of the year.* □ *The government has tried to calm rising panic about fuel costs.* (**aumentar**)
3 to stand up □ *We all rose when the judge entered.* (**levantar-se**)

> Note that **rise** has no object after it. If you want to say 'to make something go up' or 'to make something increase in level', use the verb **raise**. Raise is always followed by an object:
> ✓ *She raised her hand.*
> ✗ *She rose her hand.*
> ✓ *They raised prices.*
> ✗ *They rose prices.*

rise² /raɪz/ NOUN [plural **rises**] an increase in level □ *There has been a rise in the number of homeless people.* (**aumento**)

risk¹ /rɪsk/ NOUN [plural **risks**]
1 a possibility that something bad will happen □ **+ of** *We face the risk of losing our homes.* □ **+ that** *There's a risk that the whole project might be called off.* ▣ *If you give up your job, you will be taking a big risk.* (**risco**)
2 at risk in a situation where something bad might happen □ *Their traditional way of life is at risk.* □ *These children are at risk of violence.* (**risco, perigo**)

risk² /rɪsk/ VERB [**risks, risking, risked**]
1 to put yourself in a situation where something bad could happen to you □ *He risked punishment by entering the room.* □ **+ ing** *She risked failing her exams.* (**arriscar**)
2 to take the chance of damaging or losing something ▣ *Soldiers are risking their lives every day.* □ *We have risked a lot of money on this business.* (**arriscar**)
3 to do something although you know there is a possibility that something bad will happen □ *I risked a glance at the document.* □ **+ ing** *She couldn't risk phoning him.* (**arriscar**)

> Note that the verb **risk** is followed by **doing something** and never by 'to do something':
> ✓ *I wouldn't risk telling him.*
> ✗ *I wouldn't risk to tell him.*

rival¹ /ˈraɪv(ə)l/ NOUN [plural **rivals**] a person or organization that competes against another □ *The two teams are bitter rivals.* (**rival**)

rival² /ˈraɪv(ə)l/ ADJECTIVE competing against each other □ *rival gangs* □ *rival political parties* (**rival**)

rivalry /ˈraɪvəlri/ NOUN, NO PLURAL when people or organizations compete against each other □ *There's a lot of rivalry between the twins.* (**rivalidade**)

river /ˈrɪvə(r)/ NOUN [plural **rivers**] a large stream of water that flows across land □ *There were several boats on the river.* ▣ *He crossed the river using the main bridge.* □ *the River Nile* (**rio**)

> THESAURUS: A river is a long line of water that flows across land to the sea. A **stream** is a very narrow river. A **canal** is a long passage filled with water, for boats to travel along. **Canals** are made by man. A **channel** is a narrow piece of sea. For example, the English **Channel** is the narrow piece of sea between Britain and France.

road /rəʊd/ NOUN [plural **roads**]
1 a hard, level surface for vehicles to travel along □ *There were a lot of cars parked in the road.* ▣ *Children need to learn how to cross the road safely.* ▣ *The accident happened on the main road between Pula and Porec.* ▣ *We live on a very busy road.* ▣ *He died in a road accident.* (**estrada**)
2 by road in a vehicle that travels on the road □ *The journey to London is three hours by road.* (**estrada**)
3 over/across the road on the opposite side of a road □ *Mark and Carrie live across the road from us.* (**estrada**)
4 down/along the road further on the same road □ *My school is just down the road.* (**estrada**)

roam /rəʊm/ VERB [**roams, roaming, roamed**] to walk or travel around a place without a particular aim ▣ *You see youths roaming the streets at night.* (**vaguear**)

roar¹ /rɔː(r)/ VERB [**roars, roaring, roared**]
1 when a lion roars, it makes a loud sound. (**rugir**)
2 to make a continuous loud sound □ *Planes roared overhead.* (**zunido**)

> THESAURUS: When a lion roars, it makes a loud sound. When a dog makes a loud sound, you can use the word **bark**. When a dog or a wolf makes a long, high noise, we say that it **howls**. When an animal such as a dog or a bear makes a deep, threatening noise in its throat, we say that it **growls**. When an animal such as a dog makes an angry sound and shows its teeth, we say that it **snarls**.

roar² /rɔː(r)/ NOUN [plural **roars**]
1 the call or sound that a lion makes (**rugir**)
2 a loud deep sound □ *the roar of the engine* (**roncar, troar**)

roast¹ /rəʊst/ VERB [**roasts, roasting, roasted**]
1 to cook meat or vegetables in an oven or over a fire □ *Roast the potatoes at the same time as the turkey.* (**assaer**)

2 meat or vegetables roast when they cook in an oven or over a fire ◻ *The sauce can be made while the vegetables are roasting.* (assar)

roast² /rəʊst/ NOUN [plural **roasts**] a piece of meat that has been cooked in the oven ◻ *We're having a roast tonight.* (assado)

roast³ /rəʊst/ ADJECTIVE cooked in the oven ◻ *roast potatoes* ◻ *roast beef* (assado)

rob /rɒb/ VERB [**robs, robbing, robbed**] to steal something from a place or person ▣ *They robbed a bank.* ◻ **+ of** *The family were robbed of jewellery worth at least £1 million.* (roubar)

▶ Remember that thieves **rob** people and places. They **steal** money and objects: ◻ *My parents were robbed in the street.* ◻ *They had robbed a bank.* ◻ *They stole my father's wallet.* ◻ *They stole five hundred pounds from her.*

robber /ˈrɒbə(r)/ NOUN [plural **robbers**] a person who steals ▣ *Armed robbers broke into his house.* ▣ *a bank robber* (ladrão)

robbery /ˈrɒbəri/ NOUN [plural **robberies**] the crime of stealing something from a person or place ▣ *He committed several robberies.* ▣ *a bank robbery* ▣ *He was in prison for armed robbery.* (roubo)

▶ THESAURUS: Theft is a general word for the crime of stealing something. Robbery is the crime of stealing something from a person or a place. Robbery often involves violence or threats. For example, if someone goes into a bank with a gun and demands money, this is called a bank robbery. Burglary is the crime of going into a building and stealing things. For example, if someone comes into your house at night and steals things, this is called a burglary.

robe /rəʊb/ NOUN [plural **robes**] a long loose piece of clothing ◻ *a priest's robes* (manto, toga, roupão)

robin /ˈrɒbɪn/ NOUN [plural **robins**] a small brown bird with a red chest (papo-roxo)

robot /ˈrəʊbɒt/ NOUN [plural **robots**] a machine that can do things like a person (robô)

robust /rəʊˈbʌst/ ADJECTIVE strong ◻ *a robust economy* ◻ *He was in robust health.* (robusto)

rock¹ /rɒk/ NOUN [plural **rocks**]
1 *no plural* the hard stone substance that the Earth is made of ◻ *volcanic rock* ◻ *The team were digging a tunnel through solid rock.* (rocha)
2 a large stone ◻ *Protesters threw rocks at the police.* (rocha)
3 a type of music with a strong beat that is played on electric guitars and drums ◻ *He played in a rock band.* (rock)

▶ THESAURUS: Rock is the hard substance that the Earth is made of. Caves are made of rock. A large piece of this substance is also called a rock. A smaller piece of rock is called a stone. Children often enjoy throwing stones into water. We also use the word stone to talk about the substance that rock is made of. For example, you might live in a house made of stone. A very large rock is called a boulder.

rock² /rɒk/ VERB [**rocks, rocking, rocked**] to move or move something gently backwards and forwards or from side to side ◻ *She was rocking the baby in her arms.* ◻ *The boats rocked gently in the harbour.* (embalar, balançar)

rocket /ˈrɒkɪt/ NOUN [plural **rockets**]
1 a long thin spacecraft ◻ *The Ariane rocket was launched from the EU space centre.* (foguete)
2 a long thin weapon with a bomb in it which is fired from a plane or ship ◻ *Rockets were fired across the border.* ◻ *a rocket attack* (foguete)
3 something which explodes high in the sky and makes bright lights for entertainment (rojão)

rock music /ˈrɒk ˌmjuːzɪk/ NOUN, NO PLURAL a type of music with a strong beat that is played on electric guitars and drums (música de rock)

rocky /ˈrɒki/ ADJECTIVE [**rockier, rockiest**] made of rock, or covered with rocks ◻ *the rocky slopes of the mountains* (rochoso)

rod /rɒd/ NOUN [plural **rods**] a long thin pole ▣ *a fishing rod* (vara, haste)

rode /rəʊd/ PAST TENSE OF **ride** (ver **ride¹**)

rogue /rəʊg/ NOUN [plural **rogues**] a dishonest or badly behaved man or boy ▣ *He's a lovable rogue* (= someone who behaves badly but you still like them). (vigarista, maroto)

role /rəʊl/ NOUN [plural **roles**]
1 the character that an actor is in a play or film ▣ *Daniel Radcliffe played the role of Harry Potter in the film.* ▣ *It was his first starring role* (= important role) *in a Hollywood movie.* (papel)
2 the job or purpose that someone or something has ▣ *Diet plays an important role in good health.* ◻ **+ of** *The role of women has changed greatly over the last century.* (papel)

roll¹ /rəʊl/ VERB [**rolls, rolling, rolled**]
1 to move along like a ball, or to make something move in this way ◻ **+ down/along, etc.** *Rocks sometimes rolled down the hills.* ◻ *She rolled the ball along the ground.* (rolar)
2 to move on wheels, or to make something on wheels move ◻ *Take the brake off and let the car roll forwards.* ◻ **+ into** *The train rolled into the station.* ◻ *I rolled the bike into the garage.* (rodar)
3 to turn your body when you are lying down, or to turn someone else's body when they are lying down ◻ **+ over** *My back hurts every time I roll in bed.* ◻ *She rolled the baby onto his tummy.* (virar-se)

4 to fold something so that it forms the shape of a ball or a tube ◻ *She rolled her clothes in tissue paper before packing them.* ◻ **+ up** *Roll the sleeping bag up tightly and tie the string around it.* **(enrolar)**

▸ PHRASAL VERB **roll something up 1** to make a piece of clothing shorter by folding it ◻ *She rolled her sleeves up so they didn't get wet.* **2** to fold something so that it forms the shape of a ball or tube ◻ *The carpet had been rolled up.*

> **THESAURUS:** If something **rolls**, or if you roll it, it moves along like a ball, or you make it move in this way. If something **revolves**, it moves in a circle around something. For example, the Earth **revolves** around the sun. If something **spins**, or if you **spin** it, it turns round and round very quickly, or you make it do this. For example, dancers sometimes **spin**. If something **rotates**, or if you **rotate** it, it moves around like a wheel.

roll² /rəʊl/ NOUN [plural **rolls**]
1 a small round piece of bread for one person, often with something such as meat or cheese in it ◻ *I had a cheese roll for lunch.* **(pãozinho)**
2 something that has been rolled into the shape of a tube ◻ **+ of** *a roll of toilet paper* ◻ *We'll need 12 rolls of wallpaper for this room.* **(rolo)**

roller skate /ˈrəʊləˌskeɪt/ NOUN [plural **roller skates**] a boot with two pairs of wheels on the bottom, used for skating **(patim de rodas)**

Roman Catholic¹ /ˌrəʊmən ˈkæθlɪk/ NOUN [plural **Roman Catholics**] a member of the part of the Christian church that has the Pope for a leader **(católico)**

Roman Catholic² /ˌrəʊmən ˈkæθlɪk/ ADJECTIVE to do with, or belonging to, the Roman Catholic Church **(católico)**

romance /rəʊˈmæns/ NOUN [plural **romances**]
1 no plural the feelings connected with being in love ◻ *They met at college and romance soon blossomed* **(romance)**
2 a short relationship between people who are in love ⊞ *The couple had a whirlwind romance* (= short and exciting relationship). **(romance)**
3 a love story ◻ *She read mainly romances.* **(romance)**

romantic /rəʊˈmæntɪk/ ADJECTIVE to do with feelings of love ⊞ *a romantic relationship* ⊞ *His latest film is a romantic comedy.* ◻ *a romantic dinner for two* **(romântico)**

roof /ruːf/ NOUN [plural **roofs**] the part that covers the top of a building or vehicle ◻ *The house has a red tiled roof.* ◻ **+ of** *He climbed onto the roof of the building.* **(romântico)**

room /ruːm, rʊm/ NOUN [plural **rooms**]
1 one of the areas a building is divided into inside ◻ *We have three rooms downstairs and four upstairs.* ◻ *She got up and left the room.* ⊞ *He went back to his hotel room.* **(cômodo)**

2 no plural space for something ◻ **+ for** *Is there room for another chair?* ◻ *There wasn't enough room in the car for everyone.* ◻ **+ to do something** *They had no room to move.* **(espaço)**

root /ruːt/ NOUN [plural **roots**] the part of a plant that grows underground ◻ **+ of** *of the roots of the tree* **(raiz)**

rope /rəʊp/ NOUN [plural **ropes**] very thick strong string **(corda)**

> **THESAURUS: Thread** is a long, thin piece of cotton, wool, etc. used for sewing. **String** is strong thread, used for tying things. **Rope** is very thick strong string, which is also used for tying things. Strong rope made of metal is called **cable**. Metal made into long, thin pieces, used for fastening things together, or to make fences, etc. is called **wire**.

rose¹ /rəʊz/ NOUN [plural **roses**] a garden plant with sharp points on the stems and flowers that smell sweet **(rosa)**

rose² /rəʊz/ PAST TENSE OF **rise** ◻ *The temperature rose steadily as the day wore on.* **(ver rise¹)**

rot /rɒt/ VERB [**rots, rotting, rotted**] to decay or to make something decay ◻ *The leaves fall on the forest floor and gradually rot into the soil.* ◻ *Sugar rots the teeth.* **(apodrecer)**

rotate /rəʊˈteɪt/ VERB [**rotates, rotating, rotated**] to turn around like a wheel, or to make something turn around like a wheel ◻ *Each wheel rotates on its own axle.* **(girar, rodar)**

rotten /ˈrɒtən/ ADJECTIVE
1 decayed or decaying ◻ *rotten eggs* ◻ *a rotten floorboard* **(podre)**
2 an informal word meaning very bad or unpleasant ◻ *We had a rotten meal there.* ◻ *I felt rotten when I woke up.* **(ruim, péssimo)**

rough /rʌf/ ADJECTIVE [**rougher, roughest**]
1 not smooth ◻ *We drove along a rough track.* ◻ *I get very rough skin on my feet.* **(áspero)**
2 not gentle ◻ *Rugby is a rough game.* **(bruto, rude)**
3 not exact ◻ *a rough guess/estimate* **(rudimentar)**

roughly /ˈrʌfli/ ADVERB
1 approximately ◻ *There were roughly ten thousand people in the stadium.* ⊞ *They're roughly the same size.* ◻ *Her name roughly translates as 'white flower'.* **(aproximadamente)**
2 in a quick way, without being careful or gentle ◻ *If you handle the flowers roughly, you'll damage them.* ◻ *roughly chopped onions* **(brutalmente)**

round¹ /raʊnd/ ADVERB, PREPOSITION
1 on all sides ◻ *We sat round the table.* ◻ *We tied a rope round the tree.* **(em volta)**
2 moving in a circle or along the edges of something ◻

The Moon goes round the Earth. 🔁 *We drove round and round in circles.* (em círculos)
3 to face the opposite direction □ *If you look round, you can see the clock.* 🔁 *He turned round and waved.* (sentido oposto)
4 to the other side of something □ *We were allowed to go round the back of the theatre.* 🔁 *I saw Jo coming round the corner.* (na virada)
5 in or to different parts of a place □ *We travelled all round Spain.* (por)
6 to someone's home 🔁 *Why don't you come round for supper?* 🔁 *I'm going round to Fred's after school.* (em vista)
7 from one person or place to another □ *The news got round pretty quickly.* □ *Please pass the books round to everyone.* (de pessoa para pessoa)

round² /raʊnd/ ADJECTIVE [**rounder, roundest**] having the shape of a circle or a ball □ *a round table* □ *The Earth is round.* (redondo)

roundabout /ˈraʊndəbaʊt/ NOUN [plural **roundabouts**]
1 a place where several roads meet and the traffic must go around a circle in the same direction before turning onto the next road □ *Turn left at the roundabout.* (praça circular)
2 a round structure that children sit on while it turns round (carrossel)

route /ruːt/ NOUN [plural **routes**] a way of getting from one place to another 🔁 *Which route do you take to work?* □ *a bus route* □ **+ of** *There were police all along the route of the march.* □ *It's the main route between London and Bristol.* (caminho)

routine¹ /ruːˈtiːn/ NOUN [plural **routines**] the usual things that you do and they way you do them 🔁 *Exercise should be part of your daily routine.* □ *They settled into a routine of family life.* (rotina)
routine² /ruːˈtiːn/ ADJECTIVE normal and done regularly □ *a routine inspection* (rotineiro)

row¹ /rəʊ/ NOUN [plural **rows**] a number of people or things arranged next to each other in a line □ *the front row of seats* □ *Sow the seeds in a straight row.* □ *a row of figures* (fila, fileira)

> THESAURUS: A **row** or a **line** is a number of things or people arranged next to each other. A **queue** is a line of people who are waiting for something. In American English, the word **line** is also used with this meaning.

row² /rəʊ/ VERB [**rows, rowing, rowed**] to pull a boat through water using oars (= long wooden poles) (remar)
row³ /raʊ/ NOUN [plural **rows**] a noisy argument or strong disagreement 🔁 *Tom had a row with his girlfriend.* □ *The incident caused a political row.* □ *They went on strike in a row over pay.* (briga)
row⁴ /raʊ/ VERB [**rows, rowing, rowed**] to argue noisily □ *They were always rowing and falling out.* (brigar)

> Notice the different pronunciations. **row¹** and **row²** are pronounced the same and rhyme with **low**. **row³** and **row⁴** are pronounced differently and they rhyme **with how**.

royal /ˈrɔɪəl/ ADJECTIVE to do with a king or queen or their family 🔁 *the Danish royal family* □ *a royal wedding* (real)

royalty /ˈrɔɪəlti/ NOUN, NO PLURAL all the members of the king or queen's family (realeza)

rub /rʌb/ VERB [**rubs, rubbing, rubbed**] to move your hand or an object backwards and forwards over a surface □ *He was rubbing his eyes.* □ *She rubbed her cheek against the velvet.* (esfregar, friccionar)
♦ PHRASAL VERB **rub something out** to remove words or pictures by rubbing them with a piece of rubber or a cloth □ *Copy these words off the board before I rub them out.*

rubber /ˈrʌbə(r)/ NOUN [plural **rubbers**]
1 *no plural* a strong substance that stretches and bends easily, made from tree juices □ *shoes with rubber soles* □ *a pair of rubber gloves* (borracha)
2 a small block that you rub on paper in order to remove pencil marks (borracha)

rubbish /ˈrʌbɪʃ/ NOUN, NO PLURAL
1 things that have been thrown away because they are no longer wanted □ *Put the rubbish in the bin.* □ *More household rubbish could be recycled.* 🔁 *a rubbish bin* (lixo)
2 an informal word for something someone says that is not true or is stupid 🔁 *He's talking rubbish.* (bobagem)
3 an informal word for something of very bad quality □ *Her new chat show is absolute rubbish.* (porcaria)

> THESAURUS: **Rubbish** is things that have been thrown away because they are no longer wanted. **Litter** is paper and other rubbish that people have thrown on the ground in a public place. **Waste** is rubbish or other material that cannot be used for anything. You can talk about industrial **waste**, for example, which might include chemicals. **Junk** is old things with little use or value.

rubble /ˈrʌbəl/ NOUN, NO PLURAL the broken pieces that are left when a building falls down □ *a pile of rubble* (entulho, pedregulho)

rude /ruːd/ ADJECTIVE [**ruder, rudest**]
1 insulting and not polite □ **+ to** *She was very rude to hotel staff.* □ *I don't mean to be rude, but isn't it a bit old?* □ **+ to do something** *It would be rude to ignore them.* (rude, grosseiro)
2 embarrassing or offensive and not acceptable in a polite situation □ *rude jokes* □ *a rude word* (grosseiro)

> Note that someone is **rude to** someone else and not 'rude with' someone else:
> ✓ He was very rude to my mother.
> ✗ He was very rude with my mother.

rug /rʌg/ NOUN [plural **rugs**] a cover for the floor which is not fixed □ *a sheepskin rug* (**tapete**)

rugby /'rʌgbɪ/ NOUN, NO PLURAL a sport played by two teams in which the players throw and run with an oval ball 🔲 *a rugby player* 🔲 *He plays rugby.* (**rúgbi**)

rugged /'rʌgɪd/ ADJECTIVE rough with a lot of rocks □ *a rugged coastline* (**acidentado**)

ruin¹ /'ruːɪn/ VERB [**ruins, ruining, ruined**] to spoil something completely □ *The rain ruined my hairstyle.* □ *The injury threatens to ruin her athletics career.* (**estragar, arruinar**)

ruin² /'ruːɪn/ NOUN [plural **ruins**]
1 something such as an old building that has fallen down □ *a Roman ruin* □ *the ancient Inca ruins of Machu Picchu* (**ruína**)
2 in ruins destroyed or completely spoilt □ *The city was in ruins after the earthquake.* (**em ruínas**)

rule¹ /ruːl/ NOUN [plural **rules**]
1 an instruction about what is allowed or what is not allowed □ *It's against the rules to move your feet when you're holding the ball.* 🔲 *She was disqualified from the competition for breaking the rules.* 🔲 *You must follow (= obey) all the rules carefully.* 🔲 *There are strict rules about employing staff.* (**regra**)
2 the person or group that controls a country or an area 🔲 *The country is under military rule.* (**governo, poder, controle**)

rule² /ruːl/ VERB [**rules, ruling, ruled**] to control a country or an area □ *He ruled France in the 18th century.* □ *She is a minister in the ruling socialist party.* (**governar**)

ruler /'ruːlə(r)/ NOUN [plural **rulers**]
1 a person who controls a country or an area □ *Gandhi never became ruler of India.* (**dirigente**)
2 a flat strip of wood, plastic or metal, used to draw straight lines or for measuring short lengths (**régua**)

rumble /'rʌmbəl/ VERB [**rumbles, rumbling, rumbled**] to make a low continuous sound □ *Thunder rumbled in the distance.* (**estrondar**)

rumor /'ruːmə(r)/ NOUN [plural **rumors**] the US spelling of **rumour**

rumour /'ruːmə(r)/ NOUN [plural **rumours**] information that people tell each other, although it may not be true □ *I heard a rumour that Jen was leaving.* 🔲 *Someone has been spreading rumours.* (**rumor, boato**)

run¹ /rʌn/ VERB [**runs, running, ran, run**]
1 to move with very fast steps □ *We had to run for the bus.* □ *They ran down the street screaming.* (**correr**)
2 to run in a race or as a sport □ *I'm hoping to run a marath on.* □ *He runs every morning.* (**correr**)
3 to control or organize an organization, event or activity □ *She runs a successful transport business.* □ *The college runs part-time courses.* □ *The party is not ready to run the country.* (**dirigir**)
4 if a machine or a piece of equipment is running, it is being used □ *I left the engine running while I ran into the house.* □ **+ on** *The heating runs on solar energy.* (**funcionar**)
5 if a liquid runs somewhere, it flows in that direction □ *I had tears running down my face.* □ *Water ran over the side of the bath.* (**correr, escorrer**)
6 if buses and trains are running, they are travelling and people can use them □ *The number 5 bus runs every 10 minutes.* 🔲 *The trains never run on time.* (**circular**)
7 if something runs in a particular direction or position, that is where it is □ *A path ran behind the house.* □ *Wires ran overhead.* (**passar**)
♦ PHRASAL VERBS **run away** to leave a place secretly 🔲 *I ran away from home several times.* **run someone/something down** to knock someone or something over with a vehicle □ *The lorry driver simply ran him down.* **run into someone** to meet someone by chance □ *I ran into Jake at the supermarket.* **run into something** to drive a vehicle into an object □ *I lost control and ran into a wall.* **run out 1** to use the whole amount of something □ *We have run out of money.* **2** to be completely used □ *The milk has run out.* **run someone/something over** to drive over someone or something in a vehicle □ *I reversed and ran over his bike.*

run² /rʌn/ NOUN [plural **runs**]
1 when you run in a race or as a sport 🔲 *I always go for a run before breakfast.* □ *That run was fast enough to give him a place in the Olympic team.* (**corrida**)
2 when you move with very fast steps 🔲 *When she saw Terry, she broke into a run (= started running).* (**corrida**)
3 a point that a player wins in a game like cricket or baseball 🔲 *He scored 58 runs.* (**pontos**)

rung¹ /rʌŋ/ NOUN [plural **rungs**] a step on a ladder (= a piece of equipment with steps you climb up to reach a high place) (**degrau**)

rung² /rʌŋ/ PAST PARTICIPLE OF **ring** □ *Have you rung your mother?* (ver **ring²**)

runner /'rʌnə(r)/ NOUN [plural **runners**] a person or animal that runs □ *He's a very fast runner.* □ *a marathon runner* (**corredor**)

runner-up /ˌrʌnər'ʌp/ NOUN [plural **runners-up**] the person who finishes in second place in a competition 🔲 *She finished runner-up in last year's race.* (**segundo colocado**)

running /'rʌnɪŋ/ ADJECTIVE
1 used to say that something happens a number of times, one directly after another □ *The album is at number one for the third week running.* (**consecutivo**)

2 running water water which comes through pipes from a water supply ◻ *The cottage has no running water or electricity.* (**água corrente**)

runway /'rʌnweɪ/ NOUN [*plural* **runways**] the long, wide road at an airport that aeroplanes take off from and land on (**pista**)

rural /'rʊərəl/ ADJECTIVE to do with the countryside 🔁 *She grew up in a rural area.* ◻ *a rural community* (**rural**)

rush¹ /rʌʃ/ NOUN [*plural* **rushes**]
1 a sudden, strong movement or feeling ◻ *a rush of cold air* 🔁 *She felt a rush of excitement.* (**ímpeto, investida**)
2 a hurry ◻ *It was a bit of a rush but we got there in time.* (**pressa**)
3 be in a rush to be hurrying ◻ *I was in a rush to get to the airport on time.* (**pressa**)

rush² /rʌʃ/ VERB [**rushes, rushing, rushed**]
1 to move or to do something quickly and suddenly ◻ *Firefighters rushed to the scene.* ◻ *Several colleagues rushed to help the woman.* (**correr, apressar-se**)
2 to take someone or something somewhere very quickly 🔁 *He was rushed to hospital in an ambulance.*
3 to do something too quickly and without enough care ◻ *I don't want to rush things.* (**precipitar**)

rush hour /'rʌʃ ˌaʊə(r)/ NOUN [*plural* **rush hours**] the time when there is most traffic because people are travelling to or from work 🔁 *the morning rush hour* 🔁 *Trains are packed during the evening rush hour.* (**hora do rush**)

rust¹ /rʌst/ NOUN, NO PLURAL a brown substance that forms on iron and other metals if they are in air and water (**ferrugem**)

rust² /rʌst/ VERB [**rusts, rusting, rusted**] to become covered in rust ◻ *The equipment was just left to rust.* (**enferrujar**)

rusty /'rʌsti/ ADJECTIVE [**rustier, rustiest**] covered in rust (= a reddish-brown substance that forms on metal) ◻ *rusty nails* (**enferrujado**)

ruthless /'ruːθlɪs/ ADJECTIVE cruel and trying to achieve what you want without caring how your behaviour affects others ◻ *a ruthless dictator* (**impiedoso**)

Ss

S¹ or **s** /es/ the 19th letter of the alphabet (**a décima nona letra do alfabeto**)

S² /es/ ABBREVIATION **south** (ver **south²**)

sack /sæk/ NOUN [plural **sacks**]
1 a large bag made of strong material used for carrying or storing things ◻ *a sack of potatoes* (**saco**)
2 the sack when you lose your job 🔂 *He got the sack for being late all the time.* 🔂 *They'll give her the sack if she doesn't work harder.* (**despedido**)

sacred /ˈseɪkrɪd/ ADJECTIVE
1 holy, or to do with God ◻ *a sacred shrine* (**sagrado**)
2 to do with religion ◻ *sacred music* (**sagrado**)

sacrifice¹ /ˈsækrɪfaɪs/ NOUN [plural **sacrifices**]
1 giving up something important to you in order to achieve something that is more important, or the thing that you give up in this way 🔂 *We had to make sacrifices in order to be able to buy a house.* (**sacrifício**)
2 the act of killing someone or something and offering them to a god, or the person or animal that is killed in this way (**sacrifício**)

sacrifice² /ˈsækrɪfaɪs/ VERB [**sacrifices, sacrificing, sacrificed**]
1 to give up something that is important to you in order to achieve something that is more important ◻ *He sacrificed his life to save his fellow soldiers.* (**sacrificar**)
2 to kill someone or something and offer them to a god (**sacrificar**)

sad /sæd/ ADJECTIVE [**sadder, saddest**]
1 unhappy 🔂 *I felt sad saying goodbye to them.* ◻ **+ to do something** *I'll be sad to leave the company after so many years.* (**triste**)
2 making you feel unhappy ◻ *a sad film* ◻ *a sad story* (**triste**)

saddle /ˈsædəl/ NOUN [plural **saddles**]
1 a leather seat for putting on a horse's back (**sela**)
2 a seat on a bicycle or motorcycle (**selim, assento**)

sadness /ˈsædnɪs/ NOUN, NO PLURAL a feeling of unhappiness ◻ *It is with great sadness that we announce the death of our mother, Nancy.* (**tristeza**)

safe¹ /seɪf/ ADJECTIVE [**safer, safest**]
1 unlikely to cause harm or damage ◻ *That ladder doesn't look very safe.* ◻ **+ to do something** *Is it safe to drink the water?* 🔂 *We need a safe place to rest.* (**seguro**)
2 not in danger of being harmed, damaged, lost, etc. ◻ *You must keep these documents safe.* ◻ **+ from** *Nobody is safe from the disease.* (**salvo**)
3 not damaged, harmed, stolen, etc ◻ *Thank goodness you're safe!* (**salvo**)

safe² /seɪf/ NOUN [plural **safes**] a strong box with a lock, where money or valuable objects are kept (**cofre**)

safely /ˈseɪfli/ ADVERB without risk or danger ◻ *Drive safely.* ◻ *We got everyone home safely.* (**em segurança**)

safety /ˈseɪfti/ NOUN, NO PLURAL being safe, not being in danger or dangerous ◻ *The safety of passengers is our first concern.* ◻ *Tests will ensure the safety of the drugs.* (**segurança**)

sag /sæg/ VERB [**sags, sagging, sagged**] to hang down or not be firm ◻ *The mattress has begun to sag in the middle.* (**ceder, arquear, vergar**)

saga /ˈsɑːgə/ NOUN [plural **sagas**] a long story, especially one about a group of people over many years ◻ *a family saga* (**saga**)

said /sed/ PAST TENSE AND PAST PARTICIPLE OF **say** ◻ *She said she was coming.* ◻ *They have said I can come back any time.* (ver **say**)

sail¹ /seɪl/ VERB [**sails, sailing, sailed**]
1 to travel somewhere in a ship or a boat ◻ *They're sailing off the coast of Sweden.* (**navegar**)
2 to start a journey in a ship ◻ *The ferry sails at noon.* (**zarpar**)

sail² /seɪl/ NOUN [plural **sails**] a sheet of strong cloth attached to a boat, which catches the wind and carries the boat along (**vela**)

sailor /ˈseɪlə(r)/ NOUN [plural **sailors**]
1 someone who works on a ship ◻ *a merchant sailor* (**marinheiro**)
2 someone who goes sailing ◻ *Joe's a keen sailor.* (**marinheiro**)

saint /seɪnt/ NOUN [plural **saints**] a dead person that the Christian church believes was especially holy ◻ *Saint Francis* (**santo**)

sake /seɪk/ NOUN [plural **sakes**]
1 for someone's sake in order to help someone ◻ *For his mother's sake, he wanted to be there.* ◻ *Please don't go to any trouble just for my sake.* (**por amor a**)
2 for the sake of something in order to get or achieve something ◻ *I gave in for the sake of peace.* (**a bem de, em consideração a**)

salad /ˈsæləd/ NOUN [plural **salads**] a mixture of usually raw vegetables that sometimes includes other food, such as fish or cheese ◻ *a mixed salad* ◻ *rice salad* (**salada**)

salary /ˈsæləri/ NOUN [plural **salaries**] an amount of money that a person is paid for doing their job each month or year □ *The job offers an annual salary of £35,000.* (**salário**)

sale /seɪl/ NOUN [plural **sales**]
1 *no plural* the process of selling things for money □ *the sale of houses* (**venda**)
2 a time when goods are sold at cheaper prices than usual □ *the January sales* (**liquidação**)
3 for sale available for someone to buy □ *Are these paintings for sale?* ▣ *They've just put their house up for sale.* (**à venda**)
4 on sale offered for sale □ *The DVD is on sale now.* (**à venda**)

salesman /ˈseɪlzmən/ NOUN [plural **salesmen**] a man whose job is to sell goods or services to customers (**vendedor**)

saleswoman /ˈseɪlzwʊmən/ NOUN [plural **saleswomen**] a woman whose job is to sell goods or services to customers (**vendedora**)

salmon /ˈsæmən/ NOUN [plural **salmon**]
1 a large silver fish that swims up rivers to produce its eggs (**salmão**)
2 the orange-pink flesh from this fish eaten as food (**salmão**)

salt /sɔːlt/ NOUN, NO PLURAL a white substance that comes from the ground or the sea and is used often for giving flavour to food ▣ *salt and pepper* ▣ *Add a pinch of salt.* (**sal**)

salty /ˈsɔːlti/ ADJECTIVE [**saltier, saltiest**] containing salt or tasting very strongly of salt □ *I thought the soup was too salty.* (**salgado**)

salute /səˈluːt/ NOUN [plural **salutes**] a movement that shows respect to someone you meet, especially a military officer □ *The Queen returned the salute.* (**continência, saudação, salva**)

same¹ /seɪm/ ADJECTIVE, PRONOUN
1 the same (a) the person or thing mentioned, not a different one □ *He won the lottery and left his job on the same day.* ▣ *We both started speaking at the same time.* (b) exactly like someone or something else ▣ *I was wearing the same jacket as Barbara.* ▣ *He broke his own mobile phone and now he's done the same thing to mine!* □ *You know I'd do the same for you.* (c) not changed □ *I thought she might have grown up a bit since leaving home, but she's just the same.* (**o mesmo, igual**)
2 at the same time used to say that another thing is also true □ *He needs to keep active, but at the same time he should be careful of his knees.* (**ao mesmo tempo**)

same² /seɪm/ ADVERB in the same way □ *We tend to dress the same.* □ *We treat all our children the same.* (**do mesmo modo**)

sample /ˈsɑːmpəl/ NOUN [plural **samples**] a small amount or number of something that shows what the rest is like ▣ *The magazine came with a free sample of chocolate.* ▣ *This was a random sample of consumers.* (**amostra**)

sand /sænd/ NOUN, NO PLURAL very small grains of rock that are found on beaches and in deserts (**areia**)

sandal /ˈsændəl/ NOUN [plural **sandals**] a light open shoe for wearing when the weather is warm (**sandália**)

sandwich NOUN [plural **sandwiches**] two pieces of bread with food between them □ *a ham sandwich* □ *a toasted sandwich* (**sanduíche**)

sandy ADJECTIVE [**sandier, sandiest**] covered with sand, or with sand inside □ *a sandy beach* □ *sandy shoes* (**arenoso**)

sane ADJECTIVE [**saner, sanest**] not mentally ill □ *The judge was told that Foster was sane at the time of the murder.* (**são, lúcido**)

sang PAST TENSE OF **sing** (ver **sing**)

sank PAST TENSE OF **sink** □ *The ship sank in rough waters.* (ver **sink¹**)

Santa Claus or **Santa** NOUN an imaginary old man with a white beard in a red coat who children believe brings presents on Christmas Eve □ *What did Santa bring you?* (**Papai Noel**)

sat PAST TENSE AND PAST PARTICIPLE OF **sit** □ *He sat down.* □ *I've sat here for an hour waiting for you!* (ver **sit**)

satellite NOUN [plural **satellites**] a piece of equipment that is put in space to travel around the Earth in order to send and receive information □ *a satellite link* □ *a weather/ communications satellite* (**satélite**)

satisfaction /ˌsætɪsˈfækʃən/ NOUN, NO PLURAL a feeling of pleasure at having achieved something or got something good □ *She looked at the finished work with satisfaction.* □ **+ from doing something** *I get a lot of satisfaction from cooking.* ▣ *Job satisfaction is extremely important.* (**satisfação**)

satisfactory ADJECTIVE of a good enough standard □ *Her progress in maths was described as satisfactory.* □ *We are still waiting for a satisfactory outcome to the situation.* (**satisfatório**)

satisfied /ˈsætɪsfaɪd/ ADJECTIVE pleased because you have achieved something or got something good □ **+ with** *Are you satisfied with the progress on the project?* □ *You're never satisfied – that's your problem.* □ *a satisfied customer* (**satisfeito**)

satisfy /ˈsætɪsfaɪ/ VERB [**satisfies, satisfying, satisfied**] to make someone pleased by giving them what they want or need □ *The resort should satisfy even the most experienced skiers.* □ *This proposal is unlikely to satisfy campaigners.* (**satisfazer**)

Saturday /ˈsætədi/ NOUN [plural **Saturdays**] the day of the week after Friday and before Sunday □ *On Saturday, we went shopping.* □ *What are you doing next Saturday?* (**sábado**)

sauce /sɔːs/ NOUN [plural **sauces**] a liquid food with a particular flavour that you put on other food □ *She had spaghetti with tomato sauce.* □ *ice cream with chocolate sauce* (**molho**)

saucepan /'sɔːspən/ NOUN [plural **saucepans**] a round metal container with a handle, used for cooking food on top of an oven (**caçarola**)

saucer /'sɔːsə(r)/ NOUN [plural **saucers**] a small plate that goes under a cup □ *a cup and saucer* (**pires**)

sausage /'sɒsɪdʒ/ NOUN [plural **sausages**] a long tube of meat mixed with spices (**linguiça ou salsicha**)

savage /'sævɪdʒ/ ADJECTIVE very violent and cruel □ *savage beatings* (**feroz, selvagem**)

save /seɪv/ VERB [**saves, saving, saved**]
1 to stop someone or something being harmed, killed or destroyed □ *The firefighters saved everyone in the building.* □ *Switch off lights and help save the planet.* □ *+ from A shelter of branches and leaves saved them from freezing.* 🔊 *The correct equipment could save your life.* (**salvar**)
2 to avoid using something, or to use less of it than usual □ *You can save 40 minutes by taking the motor way.* (**economizar**)
3 to keep something so that you can use it later □ *Save any food that's left over and heat it up later.* □ *We're saving our energy for tomorrow's walk.* (**economizar**)
4 to keep money, usually in a bank, so that you can use it later □ *We have saved regularly all our lives.* (**poupar**)
5 to make a computer store information. A computing word. □ *Make sure you save your work regularly.* (**salvar**)
6 to not allow the ball to go in the net in sports such as football □ *He saved a penalty.* (**defender, evitar**)
◆ PHRASAL VERB **save up** to keep money so that you can use it in the future □ *+ for I'm saving up for a new car.*

savings /'seɪvɪŋz/ PLURAL NOUN money that you have saved in a bank □ *Joe's going to spend all his savings on a drum kit.* (**economias**)

saw¹ /sɔː/ NOUN [plural **saws**] a tool with a thin blade used for cutting through wood or metal (**serra**)

> THESAURUS: A **blade** is the sharp part of a tool which cuts. We often use a saw to cut through wood or metal, for example if we are building something. If you are cutting wood for a fire, you might use an **axe**. A **knife** is a smaller tool with a blade and a handle, used especially for cutting food.

saw² /sɔː/ VERB [**saws, sawing, sawed, sawn**] to cut through wood or metal using a saw (**serrar**)

saw³ /sɔː/ PAST TENSE OF **see** □ *I saw Paolo last week.* (ver **see**)

say /seɪ/ VERB [**says, saying, said**]
1 to express something in words □ *I asked her about the rumours, but she wouldn't say anything.* □ *I asked for more money, but my boss said no.* □ *+ that Officials say that the death toll has reached 30.* □ *+ about Did she say anything about the wedding?* (**dizer**)
2 to give information in words or signs □ *What does the notice say?* □ *My watch said six.* (**dizer**)

> Remember that you **say** something but you do not 'say someone something':
> ✓ *She said she was leaving.*
> ✗ *She said me she was leaving.*

> THESAURUS: If you **say** something, you express it in words. If you **tell** someone something, you give them information by speaking. If you **speak** or **talk**, you say words in order to communicate. When more than one person is having a conversation, we usually use the word **talk**, not speak.

saying /'seɪɪŋ/ NOUN [plural **sayings**] a phrase or sentence that people often use, giving advice or saying something that many people believe is true □ *Gran's favourite saying was 'an apple a day keeps the doctor away'.* (**dito, ditado**)

scale /skeɪl/ NOUN [plural **scales**]
1 the general size or level of something □ *The hurricane has caused destruction on a huge scale.* □ *Experts warn that the scale of the problem is increasing.* (**escala**)
2 a series of numbers or marks used for measuring the level of something □ *The earthquake measured 3.2 on the Richter scale.* □ *Patients are asked to grade the pain they feel on a scale of one to ten.* (**escala**)
3 the size of something such as a model or a map, compared to the real size of the thing it represents □ *What's the scale of the map?* (**escala**)
4 scales an instrument for weighing things 🔊 *a set of kitchen scales* 🔊 *I weighed myself on the bathroom scales.* (**balança**)
5 a series of musical notes that goes up in order □ *the scale of G major* 🔊 *I try to practise my scales each day.* (**escala**)

6 one of the small thin pieces covering the skin of a fish or snake (escama)

scalp /skælp/ NOUN [plural **scalps**] the skin on the part of the head where the hair grows (**couro cabeludo**)

scan¹ /skæn/ VERB [**scans, scanning, scanned**]
1 to use a piece of equipment to copy a picture of something onto a computer □ *Scan the photo and then e-mail it to me.* (**escanear**)
2 to read something very quickly □ *Lou scanned the jobs section of the paper, looking for anything suitable.* (**correr os olhos por**)

scan² /skæn/ NOUN [plural **scans**] a medical process in which a special machine produces an image of the inside of your body □ *a brain scan* (**exame com escâner**)

scandal /ˈskændəl/ NOUN [plural **scandals**]
1 a situation in which important people behave in a way that is morally very wrong □ *a political/financial scandal* (**escândalo**)
2 talk or writing in the newspapers, etc. about behaviour that shocks people (**escândalo**)

scanner /ˈskænə(r)/ NOUN [plural **scanners**] a machine that copies a picture or document into a computer. A computing word. (**escâner**)

scar¹ /skɑː(r)/ NOUN [plural **scars**] a mark that is left on skin from an injury 🔁 *The surgery left a small scar.* (**cicatriz**)

scar² /skɑː(r)/ VERB [**scars, scarring, scarred**] to cause a scar □ *He was badly scarred by the fire.* (**marcar com cicatriz**)

scarcely /ˈskeəslɪ/ ADVERB almost not at all □ *The place had scarcely changed.* □ *I could scarcely believe it.* (**assustar**)

scare¹ /skeə(r)/ VERB [**scares, scaring, scared**] to frighten or to worry someone □ *We don't want to scare people.* □ *The reports are intended to scare us into driving more carefully.* (**assustar**)

scare² /skeə(r)/ NOUN [plural **scares**]
1 a situation in which a lot of people are frightened or worried about something □ *a public health scare* 🔁 *There was a bomb scare at the airport.* (**pânico**)
2 when something frightens or worries you for a short time 🔁 *It gave us all a scare when Maria fainted.* (**susto**)

scared /skeəd/ ADJECTIVE frightened □ *I'm scared of spiders.* □ *She's scared of her teacher.* □ *She lay in bed, too scared to move.* 🔁 *I'm scared stiff* (= very frightened) *of heights.* 🔁 *I was scared to death* (= very frightened) *of messing it up.* (**assustado, com medo**)

> **THESAURUS:** If you are **worried** or **anxious**, you are thinking a lot about problems or bad things that could happen. If you are **scared**, **frightened** or **afraid**, you are very worried about something.

scarf /skɑːf/ NOUN [plural **scarves**] a piece of cloth that you wear around your neck or head to keep warm or to look attractive □ *a silk scarf* □ *a thick woollen scarf* (**cachecol**)

scatter /ˈskætə(r)/ VERB [**scatters, scattering, scattered**] to spread something in a lot of places over a wide area □ *Scatter the seeds evenly over the prepared soil.* (**espalhar**)

scene /siːn/ NOUN [plural **scenes**]
1 the place where an event happens □ + *of the scene of the accident* 🔁 *a crime scene* □ *An ambulance was very quickly on the scene.* (**cena**)
2 part of a play, a book or a film that happens in one place □ *We'll have to film the scene on the beach next.* □ + *from It was like a scene from a Hollywood movie.* (**espalhar**)
3 a place or situation as someone sees it □ + *of Before me was a scene of celebration.* □ *Rescuers described a scene of utter devastation.*

scenery /ˈsiːnərɪ/ NOUN, NO PLURAL
1 what you see around you, especially the countryside □ *You get to see some wonderful scenery from the train.* □ *We stopped to take in the stunning scenery.* 🔁 *He needed a change of scenery* (= to go somewhere different). (**cenário**)
2 the large pictures used in the theatre behind the actors (**cenário**)

scent /sent/ NOUN [plural **scents**]
1 a good smell □ *The scent of lilies can fill a whole room.* (**perfume, aroma**)
2 the smell of an animal that other animals can follow (**vestígio, pista**)

schedule¹ /ˈʃedjuːl/ NOUN [plural **schedules**] a plan that shows when things should happen or be done □ *a flight schedule* □ *He has a very busy work schedule.* □ *The building work finished on schedule* (= when planned). □ *The project is already six months behind schedule.* (**programa**)

schedule² /ˈʃedjuːl/ VERB [**schedules, scheduling, scheduled**] to plan that something will happen at a particular time □ *The meeting has been scheduled for next Wednesday.* (**programar**)

scheme /skiːm/ NOUN [plural **schemes**] a plan or system for doing something □ *a national training scheme* □ *a pension scheme* (**projeto**)

school /skuːl/ NOUN [plural **schools**]
1 a place where children go to learn 🔁 *You'll go to school when you're five years old.* □ *We walked home from school together.* (**escola**)

2 *no plural* the time when you are at school □ *He plays football after school on a Wednesday.* ⧉ *She left school at sixteen.* **(escola)**
3 a place where people go to learn a particular skill ⧉ *a language school* **(curso)**
4 in the US, a college or university □ *Where did you go to school?* **(faculdade, universidade)**

> ➤ THESAURUS: A place where children go to learn is called a school. A school for children under five is called a **kindergarten**. A **nursery** is a place where babies and small children are looked after while their parents are at work. A **college** is a place where people go to learn after they have left school. Often people learn a skill or how to do a particular job at **college**. A **university** is a place where you go to study at the highest level after leaving school.

schoolgirl /'sku:lgɜ:l/ NOUN [*plural* **schoolgirls**] a girl who goes to school **(aluna)**

science /'saɪəns/ NOUN, NO PLURAL the study and knowledge of the physical world and the way things happen in it ⧉ *He studied science and mathematics.* □ *Few now question the science behind climate change.* **(ciência)**

science fiction /ˌsaɪəns 'fɪkʃən/ NOUN, NO PLURAL stories and films that take place in an imagined future or in other parts of the universe □ *a science fiction novel* **(ficção científica)**

scientific /ˌsaɪən'tɪfɪk/ ADJECTIVE to do with science ⧉ *scientific research* ⧉ *a paper in a scientific journal* **(científico)**

scientist /'saɪəntɪst/ NOUN [*plural* **scientists**] someone who studies science or who works in science □ *Scientists believe the condition is genetic.* □ *a team of forensic scientists* **(cientista)**

scissors /'sɪzəz/ PLURAL NOUN a cutting tool that you hold in one hand that has two blades joined in the middle ⧉ *a pair of scissors* □ *She cut them up using kitchen scissors.* **(tesoura)**

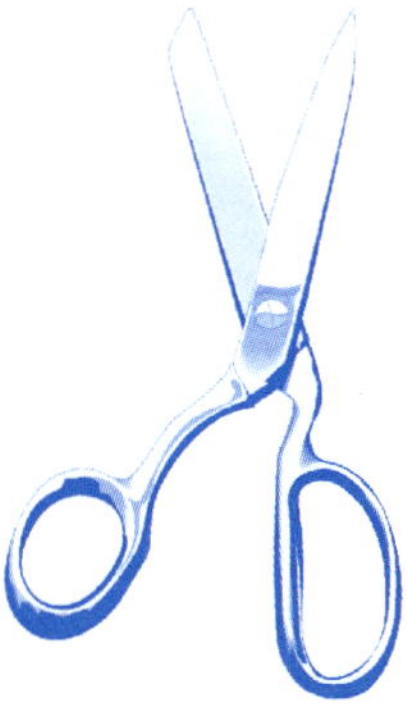

> ➤ *Remember that* **scissors** *is a plural noun:*
> ✓ *You'll need* **some scissors**.
> ✗ You'll need a scissors.

scoop /sku:p/ VERB [**scoops, scooping, scooped**] to lift or to remove something in your curved hands or with a large spoon or similar tool □ *She scooped up a handful of water.* □ *Scoop out the seeds with a teaspoon.* **(cavar)**

scooter /'sku:tər(r)/ NOUN [*plural* **scooters**]
1 a smaller and less powerful motorcycle ⧉ *Young men ride by on motor scooters.* **(lambreta)**
2 a child's toy with two wheels at either end of a board and a tall handle, which you stand on and push yourself along **(patinete)**

score[1] /skɔ:(r)/ VERB [**scores, scoring, scored**] to get a point in a game, test or competition ⧉ *Ronaldo scored the winning goal.* ⧉ *Racing drivers score 10 points for a win.* □ + **for** *Hamilton has scored again for the Rovers.* □ + **against** *He scored against Brazil in the World Cup.* **(marcar)**

score[2] /skɔ:(r)/ NOUN [*plural* **scores**] the number of points that you get in a game, test or competition ⧉ *What was the final score?* ⧉ *What's the highest score you can get?* ⧉ *Katie's test scores weren't very good.* **(contagem, escore, placar)**

scout /skaʊt/ NOUN [*plural* **scouts**]
1 the Scouts an organization for young people that encourages activities outdoors and practical skills **(escotismo)**
2 a member of the Scouts ⧉ *a boy scout* **(escoteiro)**

scramble /'skræmbəl/ VERB [**scrambles, scrambling, scrambled**] to climb or move using your hands and feet, especially with difficulty □ *We scrambled up the side of the hill.* **(trepar, escalar)**

scrap /skræp/ NOUN [*plural* **scraps**] a small piece or amount of something ⧉ *I have his address written on a scrap of paper.* □ *There isn't a scrap of evidence against us.* **(pedaço)**

scrape /skreɪp/ VERB [**scrapes, scraping, scraped**] to get something off a surface by using something sharp or rough □ *Scrape the mud off your shoes before you come in.* **(raspar)**

scratch[1] /skrætʃ/ VERB [**scratches, scratching, scratched**]
1 to make a mark on a surface with something sharp or pointed □ *The car was quite badly scratched.* □ *Students had scratched their names on the desks.* **(arranhar, riscar)**
2 to rub your nails on your skin, usually because it feels uncomfortable □ *She scratched her nose.* □ *Try not to scratch the spots.* **(coçar)**

scratch[2] /skrætʃ/ NOUN [*plural* **scratches**]
1 a mark left on a surface or your skin by something **(arranhão)**

sharp □ He looked for scratches on the car. □ They escaped with minor scratches. (arranhão)
2 from scratch from the beginning □ They learn to cook simple, healthy meals from scratch. (do zero)

scream¹ /skri:m/ VERB [screams, screaming, screamed] to make a high, loud sound because you are frightened, excited or in pain □ **+ out** The woman screamed out and the man ran off. □ **+ in** The children screamed in terror. □ **+ with** He was screaming with pain. ▣ She *screamed at the top of her voice*. (berrar)

scream² NOUN [plural screams] a loud, high noise or shout □ **+ of** a scream of agony □ She let out a high-pitched scream. (berro)
♦ IDIOM **be a scream** to be very funny. An informal phrase.

screen /skri:n/ NOUN [plural screens]
1 the part of a computer, television or cinema that you watch images on ▣ *a computer screen* □ *a 17inch screen* ▣ *Fans watched on giant TV screens.* (tela)
2 a piece of wood, cloth, metal, etc. that divides one area from another or prevents something from being seen □ We were separated by a glass screen. (biombo, anteparo)

screw¹ /skru:/ NOUN [plural screws] a small, pointed, metal object used to fix things together by turning it around into a hole (parafuso)
screw² /skru:/ VERB [screws, screwing, screwed]
1 to fix a screw into something □ Screw the bits of wood together. (parafusar)
2 to attach to or fasten something with a turning movement □ Screw the lid on tightly. (parafusar)
♦ PHRASAL VERB **screw something up** to crush something, especially paper □ He screwed up her letter and dropped it in the bin.

scribble /'skrɪbəl/ VERB [scribbles, scribbling, scribbled]
1 to write very quickly and in an untidy way □ I scribbled his name down before I forgot it. (rabiscar)
2 to draw untidy lines and shapes □ The baby had a pen and was scribbling on the wall. (rabiscar)

script /skrɪpt/ NOUN [plural scripts] the words of a film, play, speech, etc. ▣ *a film script* □ She writes scripts for TV series. (roteiro)

scrub /skrʌb/ VERB [scrubs, scrubbing, scrubbed] to rub something hard to get it clean □ We'll need to scrub these stains off the floor. (esfregar)

sculpture /'skʌlptʃə(r)/ NOUN [plural sculptures]
1 an object that an artist makes using a material like clay, stone or wood □ 'The Kiss' is a famous sculpture by Rodin. (escultura)
2 no plural the art of making objects using materials like clay, stone or wood (escultura)

sea /si:/ NOUN [plural seas]
1 no plural the salt water that covers most of the Earth's surface □ They live by the sea. □ I love swimming in the sea. □ Australia is completely surrounded by sea. (mar)
2 a large area of salt water □ the Dead Sea (mar)

seafood /'si:fu:d/ NOUN, NO PLURAL fish and sea animals that you can eat, especially animals in shells (frutos do mar)

seal¹ /si:l/ NOUN [plural seals] a large animal with shiny fur that spends its time both in the sea and on land (foca)

seal² /si:l/ VERB [seals, sealing, sealed]
1 to stick the top part of an envelope down so that it is closed (selar)
2 to close a container or an area by covering it completely with something so that air or liquid cannot get into it or get out of it (vedar)

sea level /'si: ˌlevəl/ NOUN, NO PLURAL the average level of the sea's surface, used as the point from which the height of land is measured □ The summit is 4000 feet above sea level. (nível do mar)

seam /si:m/ NOUN [plural seams] a line of sewing that joins two pieces of cloth □ The seam has split. (costura)

search¹ /sɜ:tʃ/ VERB [searches, searching, searched] to look carefully for something or someone □ **+ for** I'm still searching for my keys. □ **+ through** Firefighters searched through the wreckage for survivors. (procurar)

search² /sɜ:tʃ/ NOUN [plural searches]
1 an attempt to find someone or something ▣ The police made a *thorough search* for the missing child. □ **+ for** We will not stop in our search for her. (procura, busca, investigação)
2 in search of in order to find □ They went off in search of somewhere to eat. (à procura)
3 an attempt to find information on the Internet. A computing word ▣ Have you *done a search* on his name? (busca)

search engine /'sɜ:tʃ ˌendʒɪn/ NOUN [plural search engines] a computer program that helps you to search for something on the Internet. A computing word. (buscador)

seaside /'si:saɪd/ NOUN, NO PLURAL a place near the sea where people go on holiday □ Let's have a day at the seaside. ▣ *a seaside resort* (beira-mar)

season /'si:zən/ NOUN [plural seasons]
1 one of the four main periods that the year is divided into, each having different weather □ Spring is my favourite season. (estação)
2 a period of the year when a particular thing happens □ the football season □ This hotel will be packed in the holiday season. (temporada)

seat /si:t/ NOUN [plural seats]
1 a piece of furniture for sitting on □ a garden seat □ He was in the passenger seat of the car. (assento)
2 a chair that you pay to sit on in a vehicle or in a theatre □ I've booked three seats for the theatre. □ I prefer window seats in aeroplanes. (lugar)

seat belt /ˈsiːt ˌbelt/ NOUN [plural **seat belts**] a strong belt in a car or plane that goes across your body ▢ *Please fasten your seat belts now.* (**cinto de segurança**)

second¹ /ˈsekənd/ NUMBER 2nd written as a word ▢ *Julia is their second daughter.* ▢ *Marta came second in the race.* ▢ *This programme is the second in a series of three.* (**segundo**)

second² /ˈsekənd/ NOUN [plural **seconds**]
1 one of 60 parts that a minute is divided into ▢ *He ran the race in 57 seconds.* (**segundo**)
2 a very short time ▢ *Just wait a second.* (**segundo**)

secondary /ˈsekəndəri/ ADJECTIVE secondary education is for students between the age of 11 and 18 (**secundário**)

secondary school /ˈsekəndəriˌskuːl/ NOUN [plural **secondary schools**] a school for students between the ages of 11 and 18 (**escola secundária**)

second-class¹ /ˌsekənd ˈklɑːs/ ADJECTIVE describes the less expensive way of travelling that most people choose and the less expensive way of sending post that is slower ▢ *a second-class compartment* ▢ *a second-class stamp* (**segunda classe**)

second-class² /ˌsekənd ˈklɑːs/ ADVERB using the cheapest type ▢ *I sent the letter second-class.* (**de segunda classe, inferior**)

second-hand /ˌsekənd ˈhænd/ ADJECTIVE, ADVERB used for describing things which someone else has owned before you ▢ *a second-hand car* ▢ *Kathryn buys all her clothes second-hand.* (**de segunda mão**)

secret¹ /ˈsiːkrɪt/ NOUN [plural **secrets**]
1 a piece of information that must not be told to other people 🔁 *I'll tell you a little secret.* 🔁 *She can't keep a secret* (= not tell someone a secret) (**segredo**)
2 in secret without other people knowing ▢ *They began to meet in secret.* (**em segredo**)

secret² /ˈsiːkrɪt/ ADJECTIVE not told or shown to other people ▢ *secret information* 🔁 *The facts of the case were kept secret.* ▢ *The talks were held at a secret location.* (**secreto**)

secretary /ˈsekrətəri/ NOUN [plural **secretaries**]
1 someone whose job is to type letters, arrange meetings and take notes at business meetings, etc. ▢ *Please leave a message with my secretary if I'm out.* (**secretário**)
2 someone who is in charge of a government department ▢ *the education secretary* ▢ *He's the former British foreign secretary.* (**secretário**)

sect /sekt/ NOUN [plural **sects**] a group of people who have different beliefs from a larger group, especially in a religion (**seita**)

section /ˈsekʃən/ NOUN [plural **sections**] one of the parts that together make up something ▢ *The table has three sections that fit together.* ▢ *the fiction section of the library* ▢ *the arts section of the newspaper* (**seção**)

secure /sɪˈkjʊə(r)/ ADJECTIVE
1 unlikely to fail or change ▢ *a secure job* ▢ *They are financially secure.* (**seguro**)
2 safe, confident and not worried ▢ *Children need to feel secure.* (**seguro**)
3 safe against attack or harm ▢ *You can make your home more secure by installing a burglar alarm.* (**seguro**)
4 a secure place is guarded so that only particular people can go into it or leave it ▢ *Police have taken the family to a secure location.* ▢ *a secure area of the airport* (**seguro**)
5 firmly fixed or fastened ▢ *Check that the ropes are secure.* (**seguro**)

security /sɪˈkjʊərəti/ NOUN, NO PLURAL
1 safety from danger or crime and the things that are done to achieve this 🔁 *We need to tighten airport security.* 🔁 *The policy was a threat to national security.* (**segurança**)
2 a feeling of safety and confidence or a situation that provides this 🔁 *A stable family background can give children a sense of security.* (**segurança**)
3 the situation when something is unlikely to fail or change 🔁 *Job security is very important for most people.* 🔁 *A lot of people are worried about financial security.* (**segurança**)

see /siː/ VERB [**sees, seeing, saw, seen**]
1 to look at someone or something and notice them ▢ *The dog goes mad whenever he sees a cat.* ▢ *I saw you coming.* ▢ *Can you see where the switch is?* (**ver**)
2 to meet someone or spend time with them ▢ *Have you seen Peter much lately?* ▢ *I'm seeing Billie at the weekend.* (**ver, encontrar**)
3 to watch a film, television programme, etc. ▢ *Did you see 'Pride and Prejudice'?* (**ver**)
4 to understand something 🔁 *Now I see what you mean.* 🔁 *I don't see why I should tidy up your mess.* 🔁 *'He couldn't come because he didn't have a ticket.' 'Oh, I see.'* (**compreender**)
5 to find out something by waiting for something to happen ▢ *I'll see what she says.* ▢ *Let's see how today's lesson goes.* ▢ *See if you can arrange a taxi.* (**ver**)
6 to find out information about something ▢ *Can you see what time the bank opens?* ▢ *As we have seen, Cromwell was hated by the Irish.* (**saber**)
7 I'll see/We'll see used to say that you will consider agreeing to what someone has asked, but will not decide immediately ▢ *'Can I have a new bike for my birthday?' 'We'll see.'* (**vamos ver**)
8 let me see used when you are trying to remember something ▢ *It must have been – let me see – at least fifteen years ago.* (**deixe-me ver**)
9 See you. an informal way of saying goodbye
→ go to **not see eye to eye** (**até mais**)

◆ PHRASAL VERBS **see someone off** to go with someone to say goodbye to them **see to something** to deal with something ▢ *Don't worry about the travel arrangements – I'll see to all that.*

> **THESAURUS:** If you see something, you use your eyes and notice it. If you **look at** something, you turn your eyes to see it. If you **watch** something, you look at it for a while. For example, we **watch** television.

seed /siːd/ NOUN [plural **seeds**] a thing that a plant produces and that new plants grow from ⊞ *Sow the seeds about two centimetres deep in the soil.* □ *sunflower seeds* (**semente**)

seek /siːk/ VERB [**seeks, seeking, sought**] a formal word meaning to try to find or achieve something □ *They were seeking a long-term solution.* (**buscar, tentar**)

> Note that **seek**, meaning 'to try to find' is only used in formal English. The usual phrase for this meaning is **look for**:
> ✓ *I'm looking for a good hairdresser.*
> ✗ *I'm seeking a good hairdresser.*

seem /siːm/ VERB [**seems, seeming, seemed**] to appear to be something □ *He seemed very pleased to see you.* ⊞ *She seemed like a very nice young woman.* ⊞ *It seems likely that he will be in hospital for several weeks.* □ *It seems strange we haven't heard from him.* □ **+ to do something** *Nothing seems to worry him.* (**parecer**)

> **THESAURUS:** If something **seems** to be true, or **appears** to be true, you think that it is probably true, although you cannot be sure. If something **sounds** or **looks** good, bad, etc., it seems that way from what you have heard or read.

seen /siːn/ PAST PARTICIPLE OF **see** (ver **see**)

seize /siːz/ VERB [**seizes, seizing, seized**] to take something into your hand quickly and firmly □ *Joel seized my hand and shook it.* (**agarrar**)

seldom /ˈseldəm/ ADVERB not often □ *He seldom travelled abroad.* □ *A teacher's job is seldom an easy one.* (**raramente**)

select /sɪˈlekt/ VERB [**selects, selecting, selected**] to choose someone or something □ *She selected some items and went to pay for them.* □ **+ for** *Hawthorne has been selected for the Olympic hockey team.* (**selecionar**)

selection /sɪˈlekʃən/ NOUN [plural **selections**] a range of things that you can choose from ⊞ *The shop has a wide selection of boots and shoes.* (**seleção**)

self /self/ NOUN [plural **selves**] your character ⊞ *He was worried about revealing his true self to her.* (**si mesmo**)

self-confidence /ˌselfˈkɒnfɪdəns/ NOUN, NO PLURAL being sure of yourself and your own abilities (**seguro**)

self-confident /ˌselfˈkɒnfɪdənt/ ADJECTIVE sure of yourself and your own abilities (**seguro**)

selfish /ˈselfɪʃ/ ADJECTIVE thinking only about yourself and not about what other people might want or need □ *He's a very selfish person.* □ *I decided to stay for purely selfish reasons.* (**egoísta**)

self-service /ˌselfˈsɜːvɪs/ ADJECTIVE involving customers getting or doing something themselves □ *a self-service restaurant* □ *The airline provides a self-service check-in.* (**self-service**)

sell /sel/ VERB [**sells, selling, sold**]
1 to give someone something in exchange for money □ **+ for** *They sold the house for £450,000.* □ **+ to** *She sold the business to a Chinese company.* □ *He sold me his bike.* (**vender**)
2 to have something available for people to buy □ *The shop sells handmade chocolates.* □ *Do you sell batteries?* (**vender**)
◆ PHRASAL VERB **sell out 1** if a shop sells out of something, there is none of it left for people to buy □ *I'm sorry, we've sold out of milk.* **2** if something sells out, there is none left for people to buy □ *When I got there, all the tickets had sold out.*

seller /ˈselə(r)/ NOUN [plural **sellers**] someone who is selling something □ *ticket sellers* (**vendedor**)

semicircle /ˈsemɪsɜːkəl/ NOUN [plural **semicircles**] half a circle (**semicírculo**)

semicolon /ˌsemɪˈkəʊlən/ NOUN [plural **semicolons**] a mark (;) used to separate different parts of a sentence or list (**ponto e vírgula**)

semi-final /ˌsemɪˈfaɪnəl/ NOUN [plural **semifinals**] one of the two games in a competition which are played just before the last game ⊞ *Sweden reached the semi-final of the 1994 World Cup.* (**semifinal**)

send /send/ VERB [**sends, sending, sent**]
1 to arrange for something to go somewhere □ *He sent me an e-mail.* □ *Sophia sent him a birthday card.* □ **+ to** *I sent a text message to my Dad.* (**enviar**)
2 to make someone go somewhere □ *He was sent home from school because he was sick.* □ **+ to** *The doctor took one look and sent me straight to hospital.* □ *The government sent a team of rescue workers to the area.* (**mandar, enviar**)
◆ PHRASAL VERBS **send for someone** to ask for someone to come to you □ *They sent for a doctor.* **send off for something** to write to an organization and ask them to send you something □ *I sent off for a catalogue.*

senior[1] /ˈsiːniə(r)/ ADJECTIVE
1 having a higher position in an organization □ *senior government officials* □ *She has a very senior position in the company.* (**superior, mais antigo**)
2 older □ *senior members of the family* □ *senior players* (**mais velho**)

senior[2] /ˈsiːniə(r)/ NOUN [plural **seniors**] **be 5/10 etc. years someone's senior** to be 5/10 etc. years older than someone □ *My brother is six years my senior.* (**mais velho**)

sensation /sen'seɪʃən/ NOUN [plural sensations]
1 a physical feeling, or the ability to have physical feelings ☐ *He had a burning sensation in his chest.* ▣ *She lost all sensation in the right side of her face.* (sensação)

2 a state of excitement or shock ☐ *The announcement caused quite a sensation.* (sensação)

sense¹ /sens/ NOUN [plural senses]
1 no plural a feeling or belief about someone or something ☐ *People need work that gives them a sense of achievement.* ☐ *They have created a sense of calm in the building.* ☐ *I got the sense that he was worried about something.* (senso)

2 one of the 5 abilities of sight, touch, taste, hearing and smell ☐ *Janet lost her sense of smell after an illness.* (sentido)

3 no plural a natural quality ▣ *I don't think he has much of a sense of humour.* ☐ *She has a great sense of style.* (senso)

4 no plural the ability to understand things and make sensible decisions ▣ *Someone had the sense to call an ambulance.* ▣ *We were grateful for her good sense.* (sensatez)

5 the meaning of a word or of speech or writing ☐ *A single English word can have lots of different senses.* ☐ *You only have to understand the general sense of the passage.* (sentido)

6 make sense to have a clear meaning ☐ *Her explanations didn't make sense.* (fazer sentido)

sense² /sens/ VERB [senses, sensing, sensed]
to become aware of something without being told ☐ *+ that I sensed that not many people agreed with what I was saying.* (sentir)

sense of humour /ˌsens əv ˈhjuːmə(r)/ NOUN,
NO PLURAL your ability to understand things that are funny and to say funny things yourself ☐ *She's got a good sense of humour.* (senso de humor)

sensible /ˈsensɪbəl/ ADJECTIVE
showing good judgment and the ability to make good decisions ☐ *Lizzie's a very sensible girl.* ▣ *a sensible decision* ▣ *It's sensible to have insurance when you travel.* (sensato)

> Note that **sensible** does not mean 'very easily offended or upset'. for this, use the word **sensitive**.

sensitive /ˈsensɪtɪv/ ADJECTIVE
1 being aware of other people's feelings and careful not to upset them ☐ *he's a very sensitive, caring young man.* (sensível)

2 a sensitive situation or subject needs to be dealt with or spoken about carefully in order to avoid offending people ☐ *mental health is a sensitive issue.* (sensível)

3 very easily offended or upset ☐ *jamie's very sensitive about being bald.* ☐ *she was very sensitive to criticism.* (sensível)

4 very quickly and easily affected by something ☐ *fair skin is usually very sensitive to the sun.* (sensível)

sensor /ˈsensə(r)/ NOUN [plural sensors]
a device that notices things such as heat, light or movement ☐ *A sensor on the front of the camera measures how much light is available.* (sensor)

sent /sent/ PAST TENSE AND PAST PARTICIPLE OF send
(ver send)

sentence /ˈsentəns/ NOUN [plural sentences]
1 a group of words that usually includes a verb and expresses a statement or question ☐ *He hadn't finished his sentence before she interrupted him.* (sentença)

2 the punishment that a judge gives to someone who has committed a crime ▣ *Floyd received a five year prison sentence.* ▣ *He is serving a life sentence* (= in prison for the rest of his life) *for killing a police officer.* ▣ *Two of the killers were given a death sentence* (= a punishment of death). (sentença)

separate¹ /ˈsepərət/ ADJECTIVE
1 different and not the same ▣ *This is a completely separate matter.* ☐ *The children have separate bedrooms.* (distinto)

2 not touching something else or not joined to it ☐ *+ from Cycle paths keep bikes separate from traffic.* (separado)

• **separately** /ˈsepərətli/ ADVERB not together ☐ *Each of the suspects was interviewed separately by the police.*

separate² /ˈsepəreɪt/ VERB [separates, separating, separated]
1 to divide something into different parts ☐ *+ into The class was separated into two teams.* ☐ *+ from This article about his life separates fact from fiction.* (separar)

2 to be between two things so that they do not touch each other ☐ *The north and the south are separated by a range of high mountains.* ☐ *+ from Only a thin camping mat separated me from the hard ground.* (separar)

3 to keep people apart from each other ☐ *A teacher had to separate the boys who were fighting.* (separar)

September /sep'tembə(r)/ NOUN [plural Septembers]
the ninth month of the year, after August and before October ☐ *School starts again in September.* (setembro)

sequel /ˈsiːkwəl/ NOUN [plural sequels]
a book, play or film that continues an earlier story (sequência)

sequence /ˈsiːkwəns/ NOUN [plural sequences]
a series of things that happen one after the other ▣ *It was a remarkable sequence of events.* (sequência)

sergeant /ˈsɑːdʒənt/ NOUN [plural sergeants]
1 an officer of middle rank in the police ☐ *Sergeant Adam Cragg was the officer in charge.* (sargento)

2 an officer of middle rank in the army (sargento)

series /ˈsɪəriːz/ NOUN [plural series]
1 a series of something several similar things that happen or are done one after the other ☐ *a series of accidents* ☐ *They held a series of meetings.* (série)

2 a set of television or radio programmes with the same subject or the same characters ▣ *They're* filming a new TV series. ▫ a comedy series ▫ + of an old series of 'Cheers' (série)

serious /ˈsɪəriəs/ ADJECTIVE

1 very bad ▫ a serious accident ▫ serious injuries ▫ Noy was involved in several killings and other serious crimes. (sério, grave)
2 important and needing attention ▫ The report raises serious questions about the quality of education. ▫ Obesity is becoming a serious health issue. (sério)
3 meaning what you are saying and not joking or pretending ▫ I can never tell when he's joking and when he's being serious. ▫ + about Are you serious about becoming a teacher? (sério)
4 a serious person is sensible, quiet, and does not laugh much ▫ William was a very serious little boy. (sério)

seriously /ˈsɪəriəsli/ ADVERB

1 very badly ▫ Her father is seriously ill. ▫ Jan was seriously injured in the accident. (seriamente)
2 in a way that shows you think something is important ▫ We're taking these threats very seriously. (seriamente)

sermon /ˈsɜːmən/ NOUN [plural **sermons**] a speech that a priest makes in a church (sermão)

servant /ˈsɜːvənt/ NOUN [plural **servants**] someone who works in a big house and does jobs such as cooking and cleaning for the person who owns the house (empregado)

serve /sɜːv/ VERB [serves, serving, served]

1 to give someone food or drink ▫ I'll serve the soup and you can give out the spoons. ▫ Serve the cheese with crusty bread. (servir)
2 to sell things to customers in a shop ▫ Are you being served? (atender)
3 to work for a person or an organization ▫ Brown had served the family for fifty years. ▫ As a soldier, he served in Egypt. ▫ + as He served as treasurer for three years. (servir)
4 to provide something for people or an area ▫ This hospital serves nearly a million local people. ▫ There is no bus network serving these villages. (servir, atender)
5 serve someone right if a bad situation or result serves you right, you deserve it ▫ If you're sick, it serves you right for eating too much chocolate. (bem-feito)

service /ˈsɜːvɪs/ NOUN [plural services]

1 a system to provide something that people need, or an organization that provides it ▫ There have been cuts in mental health services. ▫ The firm has promised to improve the bus service. ▫ The charity provides basic services to homeless people. ▫ We are offering a free e-mail service. (serviço)
2 no plural the help that someone gives you in a place such as a hotel or shop ▫ I love the things they sell, but the service is awful. (serviço)
3 no plural the period of time that you work for a business or organization ▫ She resigned after 25 years' service in the company. ▫ He has 30 years of military service. (serviço)
4 a religious ceremony ▫ The queen attended a service to remember the dead. (serviço)
5 the services a country's military organizations (forças armadas)

session /ˈseʃən/ NOUN [plural **sessions**] a period of time that is used for doing something ▫ He missed last night's training session. (sessão)

set¹ /set/ VERB [sets, setting, set]

1 to put something somewhere ▫ Set the tray down on the table. (colocar)
2 to decide the time or date of something ▫ Have they set a date for the meeting? ▫ The government has set a timetable for change. (estabelecer)
3 to decide on a level for something ▫ Prices were set too high. ▫ We need to set a limit on what we will spend. ▫ The company has set new targets for growth. (estabelecer)
4 if a book, film, etc. is set somewhere, that is where the story happens ▫ Her first novel is set in Berlin. (ambientar)
5 to make a piece of equipment ready to work at a particular time ▫ Don't forget to set the DVD to record. ▫ Did you set the alarm? (ajustar)
6 the sun sets when it goes down (pôr-se)
7 if a teacher sets work or sets an exam, they tell the students to do it ▫ The teacher doesn't set my children enough homework. (dar)
8 set an example to behave in a way that other people may copy ▫ I try to set the children a good example by wearing my cycle helmet. (dar um exemplo)
9 set someone/something free to allow a person or an animal to leave of the place where they are being kept (libertar)
10 if a substance sets, it becomes solid ▫ Wait an hour or so for the jelly to set. (endurecer)
◆ PHRASAL VERBS **set off** to start a journey ▫ We need to set off early tomorrow. **set out** to start a journey ▫ We set out after breakfast. **set something up** to start a business, organization or group ▫ A tribunal was set up to hear the case. ▫ He set up his firm in 2003.

set² /set/ NOUN [plural sets]

1 a group of people or things that belong together or are used together ▫ a set of chairs ▫ a chess set (conjunto, coleção)
2 a radio or television ▫ We have a technical problem; please do not adjust your set. (aparelho)
3 the place where actors perform in a play, film, etc. ▫ He had to wear the wig all the time on set. (cenário)

setback /ˈsetbæk/ NOUN [plural **setbacks**] a problem that stops you making progress ▫ The project suffered a major setback when the manager resigned. (atraso)

setting /ˈsetɪŋ/ NOUN [plural **settings**] the place where something is or where something happens ▫ The hotel is the perfect setting for a wedding reception. (cenário)

settle /ˈsetəl/ VERB [settles, settling, settled]

1 if you settle an argument, you end it by agreeing something ▫ I wish they would settle their differences. ▫ The case was settled out of court. (resolver, acertar)

settlement | 305 | **shadow**

2 to decide on something or to arrange something ⮕ *That settles it – I'm leaving!* ⮕ *That's settled – we'll all meet next Tuesday.* (**resolver, aceitar**)
3 to become relaxed and comfortable in a situation □ *Harry settled into his armchair and fell asleep.* □ *Settle back and enjoy the show!* (**assentar**)
4 to go somewhere and make your home there □ *The family settled in New South Wales.* □ *They may not settle permanently in the UK.* (**estabelecer-se**)
5 to pay money that you owe □ *The bill can be settled in cash or with a cheque.* ⮕ *This money helped us settle our debts.* (**saldar**)
◆ PHRASAL VERBS **settle down** to start to live a life with less change, for example by staying somewhere for a long time or staying in a relationship □ *I'm not ready to settle down and have kids yet.* **settle (someone) down** to become calm or make someone calm after being nervous or excited □ *Settle down now, it's time to do some work.* **settle in** to start to feel happy and confident in a new situation □ *She's finding it difficult to settle in at her new school.*
settlement /ˈsetəlmənt/ NOUN [plural **settlements**]
1 an agreement that ends an argument ⮕ *The two sides have failed to reach a settlement.* ⮕ *a divorce settlement* (**acordo**)
2 a place where people have come and built homes □ *New settlements have grown up in the desert.* (**colônia**)

seven /ˈsevən/ NUMBER [plural **sevens**] the number 7 (**sete**)

seventeen /ˌsevənˈtiːn/ NUMBER the number 17 (**dezessete**)

seventeenth /ˌsevənˈtiːnθ/ NUMBER 17th written as a word (**décimo sétimo**)

seventh¹ /ˈsevənθ/ NUMBER 7th written as a word □ *the seventh day of the week* (**sétimo**)

seventh² /ˈsevənθ/ NOUN [plural **sevenths**] 1/7; one of seven equal parts of something (**um sétimo**)

seventieth /ˈsevəntiəθ/ NUMBER 70th written as a word (**septuagésimo**)
seventy /ˈsevənti/ NUMBER [plural **seventies**]
1 the number 70 (**setenta**)
2 the seventies the years between 1970 and 1979 (**os anos 1970**)

several /ˈsevərəl/ DETERMINER, PRONOUN more than a few but not a lot □ *I met him several years ago.* □ *Several people admired her dress.* □ **+ of** *Several of my friends have dogs.* □ *Would you like one of these leaflets? I've got several.* (**vários**)

➤ If you want to say 'a very small number' do not use the word **several**. Instead, use the phrase **a few**:
✓ *I've got a lot of friends but only a few close friends.*
✗ *I've got a lot of friends but only several close friends.*

severe /sɪˈvɪə(r)/ ADJECTIVE
1 very bad □ *severe weather conditions* □ *He suffered severe head injuries in the accident.* □ *She has severe health problems.* (**grave**)
2 extreme □ *severe punishments* □ *severe criticism* (**severo**)
3 not friendly or kind □ *a severe expression* (**severo**)

➤ THESAURUS: A **severe** person is not friendly or kind. A **strict** person expects people to obey their rules. A teacher might be **strict** with pupils, for example. A **tough** person is physically or mentally strong. A **difficult** person is not friendly or easy to please.

sew /səʊ/ VERB (**sews, sewing, sewed, sewn**) to use a needle and thread to join things together □ *He sewed the button back on his shirt.* (**costurar**)

sex /seks/ NOUN [plural **sexes**]
1 *no plural* the act in which a man puts his penis into a woman's vagina (**sexo**)
2 the fact of being male or female □ *It is now technically possible for couples to choose the sex of their baby.* □ *There are laws against sex discrimination.* (**sexo**)

sexual /ˈsekʃuəl/ ADJECTIVE
1 to do with or involving the activity of sex □ *a sexual relationship* □ *sexual behaviour* (**sexual**)
2 to do with the differences between men and women □ *sexual equality* (**sexual**)

shade¹ /ʃeɪd/ NOUN [plural **shades**]
1 *no plural* an area which is cooler and darker because there is no light from the sun □ *He was lying in the shade of a tree.* □ *On hot days I prefer sitting in the shade.* □ *This plant prefers shade.* (**sombra**)
2 an object that goes around a light and prevents the light being too bright □ *a lamp with a purple shade* (**quebra-luz, guarda-sol**)
3 a particular type of a colour □ **+ of** *The wall was painted in a deep shade of green.* (**matiz**)

shade² /ʃeɪd/ VERB [**shades, shading, shaded**] to protect something from the sun □ *A row of trees shaded the path.* (**proteger**)

shadow /ˈʃædəʊ/ NOUN [plural **shadows**] a dark shape on a surface caused when an object is between the surface and a bright light □ *There was a shadow on the wall.* ⮕ *The candle cast shadows around the room.* (**sombra**)

➤ THESAURUS: A **shadow** is a dark shape on a surface caused when an object is between the surface and a bright light. **Shade** is an area which is cooler and darker because there is no light from the sun. For example, you might sit in the **shade** on a very hot day. A **shelter** is a building or other structure that provides protection from harm or bad weather. For example you might sit in a **shelter** while you are waiting for a bus.

shady /ˈʃeɪdi/ ADJECTIVE [shadier, shadiest] a shady place has little light because it is covered by something □ *The plant will grow best in a shady spot.* (sombreado)

shake¹ /ʃeɪk/ VERB [shakes, shaking, shook, shaken]
1 to make many quick small movements from side to side or up and down □ *The whole area shook when the bomb landed.* □ *Mina was shaking with fear.* □ *His hands were shaking as he tried to sign his name.* (tremer)
2 to make something move quickly from side to side or up and down several times □ *The wind was shaking the trees and rattling the windows.* □ *A huge explosion shook the building.* □ *Shake the bottle before opening.* (sacudir, agitar)
3 shake your head to move your head from side to side as a way of saying 'no' □ *I asked if she was coming and he just shook his head.* (balançar a cabeça)
4 shake hands to hold someone's hand and move it up and down when you meet them for the first time or when making an agreement □ *He shook hands with the Prime Minister.* □ *We shook hands and the deal was done.* (apertar as mãos)

> **THESAURUS:** If something or someone **shakes**, they make many quick small movements from side to side or up and down. If someone **shivers** or **trembles**, they shake slightly because they are frightened. You can also **shiver** if you are cold or ill. If something **sways** it moves slowly from side to side. Trees **sway** in the wind.

shake² /ʃeɪk/ NOUN [plural shakes] a quick movement from side to side or backwards and forwards ▸ *Give the bottle a quick shake.*

shall /ʃæl/ MODAL VERB
1 used to make a suggestion or an offer □ *Shall we play chess?* □ *Shall I open the window?* (que tal...?)
2 how/what/when, etc. shall used to ask someone what to do □ *What shall I cook for dinner?* □ *When shall we phone him?* (dever fazer algo)
3 used as a formal way of saying what you will do in the future □ *I shall make an official complaint.* □ *I shall never forget this moment.* (determinação de fazer algo)

shallow /ˈʃæləʊ/ ADJECTIVE [shallower, shallowest] not deep ▸ *shallow water* ▸ *The children were playing in the shallow end of the pool.* □ *The lake was quite shallow.* □ *a shallow dish* (raso)

shame /ʃeɪm/ NOUN, NO PLURAL
1 it's/what a shame used when saying that you are disappointed about something □ *What a shame that you can't come to the party.* □ *It's a shame we can't stay longer.* □ *It would be a great shame if you had to give up playing the violin.* (vergonha)
2 the embarrassing feeling you have when you know you have done something wrong ▸ *Emma felt a sense of shame about the things she had done.*
□ *+ of He had suffered the shame of being arrested in front of his friends.* (vergonha)

shampoo /ʃæmˈpuː/ NOUN [plural shampoos] liquid soap used especially for washing your hair □ *a bottle of shampoo* (xampu)

shan't /ʃɑːnt/ a short way to say and write shall not □ *I shan't be late.* (ver **shall**)

shape¹ /ʃeɪp/ NOUN [plural shapes]
1 the form that is made by the outer edge of something □ *She made a cake in the shape of a piano.* □ *His body has changed shape dramatically.* □ *The children stuck coloured shapes onto the card.* □ *What shape is the window?* (formato)
2 the health or condition of someone or something ▸ *The team is in good shape for Saturday's match.* ▸ *He leaves the company in better shape than he found it.* ▸ *I'm getting a bit out of shape* (= not strong and healthy). ▸ *He runs every day to keep in shape* (= stay strong and healthy). (forma)

shape² /ʃeɪp/ VERB [shapes, shaping, shaped] to make something a particular shape □ *He shapes the clay pots on the potter's wheel.* (modelar)

share¹ /ʃeə(r)/ VERB [shares, sharing, shared]
1 to divide something between two or more people + **between** *We had two pizzas to share between 7 people.* □ + **among** *I shared the sweets among the children.* (dividir)
2 to have or use something at the same time as someone else □ *There aren't enough books to go round so some of you will have to share.* □ *She shares a home with her elderly mother.* □ *We must all share the blame for the accident.* (compartilhar)
3 to allow someone to have part of something that is yours or to use something that is yours □ *She kindly shared her lunch with me.* □ *William wouldn't share his toys.* (partilhar)
♦ PHRASAL VERB **share something out** to divide something between each person in a group *We shared out the food between us.*

share² /ʃeə(r)/ NOUN [plural shares]
1 a part of a total number or amount of something that is divided between people □ *I took my share of the cake.* ▸ *We hope to increase our share of the market.* ▸ *She wants a larger share of the profits.* (porção)
2 one of the equal parts of the value of a company that you can buy or sell □ + **in** *She has shares in the bank.* ▸ *I bought shares in his business.* ▸ *Shares rose/fell* (= increased/lost value) *at the news.* (ação)

shareholder /ˈʃeəhəʊldə(r)/ NOUN [plural shareholders] someone who owns shares in a company (acionista)

shark /ʃɑːk/ NOUN [plural sharks] a large sea fish with very sharp teeth (tubarão)

sharp¹ /ʃɑːp/ ADJECTIVE [sharper, sharpest]
1 having a thin edge or a pointed end that can cut things easily □ *a sharp knife* □ *sharp teeth* (afiado)

sharp

2 a sharp decrease or increase is sudden and large 🔹 *There has been a sharprise in crime.* (**acentuado**)
3 a sharp bend or turn is one that changes direction suddenly (**brusco**)
4 a sharp pain is sudden, short and painful (**agudo**)
5 a sharp image is clear ▫ *I can get a really sharp focus with this camera.* (**nítido**)
6 clever and quick to notice things (**perspicaz**)
7 if your hearing or eyesight (= how well you can see) is sharp, you can hear or see very well (**aguçado**)
8 showing anger ▫ *She received a sharp answer from her mother.* (**ríspido**)

sharp² /ʃɑːp/ NOUN [plural **sharps**] in written music, a sign (#) that makes a note higher by half a note (**sustenido**)

sharp³ /ʃɑːp/ ADVERB
1 5 o'clock, 6.15, etc. sharp at exactly 5 o'clock, 6.15, etc. (**em ponto**)
2 with a sudden change of direction ▫ *Turn sharp left at the next set of traffic lights.* (**abruptamente**)

sharpen /ˈʃɑːpən/ VERB [**sharpens, sharpening, sharpend**] to make something sharp or sharper ▫ *The lion was sharpening its claws on a tree.* ▫ *I need to sharpen this pencil.* (**apontar, afiar**)

sharpener /ˈʃɑːpənə(r)/ NOUN [plural **sharpeners**] a device that you use to make pencils or knives sharp (**apontador, afiador**)

sharply /ˈʃɑːpli/ ADVERB
1 suddenly and by a large amount 🔹 *Temperatures fall sharply at night.* (**agudamente**)
2 in a strong and angry way ▫ *The report sharply criticized his behaviour.* (**rispidamente**)

shatter /ˈʃætə(r)/ VERB [**shatters, shattering, shattered**] to break into lots of very small pieces or to break something into lots of very small pieces ▫ *He dropped the glass and it shattered.* ▫ *The explosion shattered windows.* (**estilhaçar**)

shave¹ /ʃeɪv/ VERB [**shaves, shaving, shaved**] to use a razor (= thin, sharp piece of metal) to cut away hair that is growing on your face or body ▫ *He shaved and showered, then got dressed.* ▫ **+ off** *He shaved off his beard.* (**barbear-se**)

shave² /ʃeɪv/ NOUN [plural **shaves**] when you shave ▫ *You need a shave and a haircut.* (**fazer a barba**)

shaver /ˈʃeɪvə(r)/ NOUN [plural **shavers**] an electrical tool for shaving hair (**fazer a barba**)

she /ʃiː/ PRONOUN used to talk or write about a woman, girl or female animal that has already been mentioned ▫ *Madeleine is funny. She really makes me laugh.* (**ela**)

shed¹ /ʃed/ NOUN [plural **sheds**] a simple wooden or metal building used for working in or for storing things 🔹 *a garden shed* (**barracão**)
shed² /ʃed/ VERB [**sheds, shedding, shed**] to make or allow clothes, skin, leaves etc. to fall or drop off ▫ *Snakes shed their skin.* (**mudar, soltar**)

she'd /ʃiːd/ a short way to say and write she had or she would ▫ *She'd forgotten her umbrella.* ▫ *She'd rather not say.* (ver **would, she had**)

sheep /ʃiːp/ NOUN [plural **sheep**] a farm animal with a thick wool coat 🔹 *a flock of sheep* (**carneiro**)

> Remember that the plural form of **sheep** is the same as the singular form: ▫ *He has a lot of sheep.*

sheer /ʃɪə(r)/ ADJECTIVE
1 used to emphasize the degree, size, strength, etc. of something ▫ *The sheer scale of the building is breathtaking.* ▫ *The first problem is the sheer size of the city.* (**puro**)
2 complete or only ▫ *It was sheer luck that no one was hurt.* ▫ *He ate four bags of crisps. It was just sheer greed.* (**mero**)
3 very steep or vertical ▫ *There were sheer cliffs on either side of the beach.* (**íngrime**)

sheet /ʃiːt/ NOUN [plural **sheets**]
1 a large, flat piece of cloth used to cover a bed ▫ *I'll just change the sheets on your bed.* (**lençol**)
2 a single piece of paper or a document on a single piece of paper ▫ **+ of** *an A4 sheet of paper* ▫ *She gave him a fact sheet about diabetes.* (**folha**)
3 a large thin flat piece of metal, plastic, glass, etc. ▫ **+ of** *a sheet of aluminium foil* ▫ *They covered it with a plastic sheet.* (**lâmina**)

shelf /ʃelf/ NOUN [plural **shelves**] a flat piece of wood, metal, etc. fixed horizontally to a wall or as part of a cupboard, used for putting things on ▫ *She stood on a chair to reach the top shelf of the kitchen cupboard.* 🔹 *He got a job stacking supermarket shelves.* (**prateleira**)

shell /ʃel/ NOUN [plural **shells**]
1 a hard covering on an egg or a nut ▫ *Remove the hard outer shell of the nut.* (**concha, casca, carapaça**)
2 a hard covering that protects the body of some sea creatures or other animals ▫ *a snail shell* (**carcaça**)

she'll /ʃiːl/ a short way to say and write she will □ *She'll be back in a minute.* (ver **she will**)

shelter[1] /ˈʃeltə(r)/ NOUN [plural **shelters**]
1 a building or other structure that provides protection from harm or bad weather □ *an underground bomb shelter* □ *Earthquake victims are living in temporary shelters.* (abrigar)
2 no plural protection from danger or bad weather ⚐ *It was pouring with rain, so we took shelter in a shop doorway.* □ *The explosion sent people running for shelter.* (abrigo)

shelter[2] /ˈʃeltə(r)/ VERB [**shelters, sheltering, sheltered**]
1 to stay in a place where you are protected from harm or bad weather □ *We sheltered from the rain under a tree.* □ *Thirty people sheltered in the basement.* (abrigar)
2 to protect someone from harm □ *The family were accused of sheltering criminals.* (abrigar)

shelves /ʃelvz/ PLURAL OF **shelf**

shepherd /ˈʃepəd/ NOUN [plural **shepherds**] someone whose job is to look after sheep (pastor)

she's /ʃiːz/ a short way to say and write she is or she has □ *She's my friend.* □ *She's always been my friend.* (ver **be, has**)

shield[1] /ʃiːld/ NOUN [plural **shields**] a large, flat object that is carried to protect someone's body from an attack □ *They were faced by police carrying riot shields.* (escudo)

shield[2] /ʃiːld/ VERB [**shields, shielding, shielded**] to protect someone or something from harm or danger □ *He had his hand over his eyes, shielding them from the strong sun.* (proteger)

shift[1] /ʃɪft/ VERB [**shifts, shifting, shifted**] to move something or to change position □ *Tom shifted uncomfortably in his seat.* □ *She shifted her weight from foot to foot.* (mudar)

shift[2] /ʃɪft/ NOUN [plural **shifts**]
1 a change from one thing to another □ *This represents a major shift in policy.* (mudar)
2 the period of time when one group of people works ⚐ *The miners worked 12-hour shifts.* ⚐ *Who's on the night shift this week?* (turno)

shift key /ˈʃɪft ˌkiː/ NOUN [plural **shift keys**] the key on a computer that allows you to write capital letters (= large letters, for example at the beginning of sentences). A computing word. (tecla shift)

shine /ʃaɪn/ VERB [**shines, shining, shone**]
1 to send out or reflect light ⚐ *The sun's shining – let's eat outside.* □ *We could see the lights of the city shining below us.* (brilhar)
2 to point a light on something □ *Don't shine your torch in my face.* (brilhar)
3 to be bright and shiny □ *She polished the pans until they shone.* (brilhar)

shining /ˈʃaɪnɪŋ/ ADJECTIVE **a shining example of something** someone or something that is very good at something □ *She's a shining example of growing old gracefully.* (brilhante)

shiny /ˈʃaɪni/ ADJECTIVE [**shinier, shiniest**] with a smooth surface that reflects light □ *shiny hair* □ *a shiny new bicycle* (brilhante)

ship /ʃɪp/ NOUN [plural **ships**] a large boat that carries passengers or goods on sea journeys □ *Her ship sails from Southampton tomorrow.* □ *They travelled from South Africa by ship.* (navio)

shirt /ʃɜːt/ NOUN [plural **shirts**] a piece of clothing for the top half of your body, often made from cotton, with long or short sleeves, a collar, and buttons down the front (camisa)

> **THESAURUS:** Both men and women wear shirts. A **blouse** is a woman's shirt. A **T-shirt** is a piece of clothing made from soft cotton which you wear on the top part of your body. A **T-shirt** can have long or short sleeves, but does not usually have buttons down the front.

shiver /ˈʃɪvə(r)/ VERB [**shivers, shivering, shivered**] to shake slightly because you are cold or frightened □ *She shivered in her thin cotton dress.* (estremecer, arrepiar-se)

shock[1] /ʃɒk/ NOUN [plural **shocks**]
1 no plural a strong and unpleasant reaction you have when something bad happens that you do not expect □ *The whole town is in shock at the news of the closures.* □ *You gave me such a shock bursting in like that!* ⚐ *I got quite a shock when I saw the bill.* (choque)
2 something that happens and makes you very surprised or upset □ *The news of his arrest was a terrible shock to his family.* (choque)
3 a current of electricity that passes through your body ⚐ *I got an electric shock when I unplugged the iron.* (choque)

shock[2] /ʃɒk/ VERB [**shocks, shocking, shocked**] to surprise and upset someone very much □ *I was shocked to see how ill he looked.* (chocar)

shocking /ˈʃɒkɪŋ/ ADJECTIVE making you feel surprised and upset □ *The news report contained some shocking scenes of the war.* (chocante)

shoe /ʃuː/ NOUN [plural **shoes**] something made of leather or a similar material that you wear on your foot □ *high-heeled shoes* 🖻 *a pair of shoes* □ *a shoe shop* (**sapato**)

shone /ʃɒn/ PAST TENSE AND PAST PARTICIPLE OF **shine** (**ver shine**)

shook /ʃʊk/ PAST TENSE OF **shake**¹ (**ver shake**)

shoot¹ /ʃuːt/ VERB [**shoots, shooting, shot**]
1 to fire a gun or other weapon □ *I shot an arrow in the air.* □ *Stop or I'll shoot!* (**atirar**)
2 to kill or injure a person or animal with a gun □ *He had been shot three times in the chest.* 🖻 *A passer-by was shot dead in the incident.* (**abater a tiros, fuzilar**)
3 to go somewhere very quickly □ *The rocket shot up into the air.* □ *Pain shot through his body.* (**lançar**)
4 to make a film or video, or take a photograph □ *They're shooting some scenes at Alnwick Castle.* (**fotografar, filmar**)

shoot² /ʃuːt/ NOUN [plural **shoots**] a new part of a plant or a very young plant □ *bamboo shoots* (**broto**)

shop¹ /ʃɒp/ NOUN [plural **shops**] a place where goods are sold or a particular service is provided □ *a flower shop* □ *We spent the afternoon going around the shops at the mall.* (**loja**)

> THESAURUS: Shop is a general word for a place where goods are sold or a particular service is provided. A store is the same as a shop. The word store is more common in American English. A department store is a large shop that has different departments which sell different types of product. A supermarket is a large shop that sells food and other goods.

shop² /ʃɒp/ VERB [**shops, shopping, shopped**] to buy things in shops □ *I hate shopping for clothes.* (**fazer compras**)

shop assistant /ˈʃɒp əˌsɪstənt/ NOUN [plural **shop assistants**] someone who sells things and looks after customers in a shop (**vendedora**)

shopkeeper /ˈʃɒpkiːpə(r)/ NOUN [plural **shopkeepers**] someone who owns or manages a shop (**lojista**)

shopping /ˈʃɒpɪŋ/ NOUN, NO PLURAL
1 the activity of going around shops to buy things 🖻 *Let's go shopping tomorrow.* (**compra**)
2 the things you buy at the shops □ *Can you get the shopping out of the boot?* (**compra**)

shopping centre /ˈʃɒpɪŋ ˌsentə(r)/ NOUN [plural **shopping centres**] an area or large building with a lot of different shops (**shopping center**)

shore /ʃɔː(r)/ NOUN [plural **shores**] the area of land next to the sea or next to a lake (**praia**)

short /ʃɔːt/ ADJECTIVE [**shorter, shortest**]
1 small in height, length or distance □ *a short skirt* □ *The school is a short walk from here.* □ *She has short hair.* □ *My brother is very short.* (**baixo, curto**)
2 continuing for a small period of time □ *We watched a short film about whales.* □ *We'll take a short break now.* (**curto**)
3 not having many words or pages □ *Can you give us a short description of the house?* □ *It's quite a short book.* (**curto**)
4 not having enough of something □ **+ of** *The troops are short of equipment.* 🖻 *Water was in short supply.* (**desprovido**)
5 be short for something to be a shorter way of saying or writing something □ *'Jon' is short for 'Jonathan'.* (**abreviação**)

shortage /ˈʃɔːtɪdʒ/ NOUN [plural **shortages**] when there is not enough of something □ *People in the region face severe food shortages.* (**escassez, falta**)

shorten /ˈʃɔːtən/ VERB [**shortens, shortening, shortened**] to make something shorter or to become shorter □ *We're working hard to shorten the waiting list for the operation.* □ *The days are shortening.* (**encurtar**)

shortly /ˈʃɔːtli/ ADVERB
1 soon □ *We'll shortly be arriving at Waverley Station.* (**logo**)
2 shortly before/after within a short period of time before or after something □ *The bomb exploded shortly before midday.* (**logo antes, depois**)

shorts /ʃɔːts/ PLURAL NOUN
1 short trousers that stop above your knees □ *a pair of shorts* (**shorts**)
2 a mainly US word for underwear for men (**calção**)

shot¹ /ʃɒt/ NOUN [plural **shots**]
1 the act of firing a gun or the sound of it being fired □ *I heard a shot out in the street.* 🖻 *Someone took a shot at me!* (**tiro**)
2 a kick, hit or throw of the ball to try to score a point or points □ *It was an excellent shot that just missed the goal.* (**jogada**)

3 a photograph or an image in a film □ *I managed to get some good shots of the mountains.* (**fotografia**)

shot² /ʃɒt/ PAST TENSE AND PAST PARTICIPLE OF **shoot¹** (ver **shoot¹**)

should /ʃʊd/ MODAL VERB
1 used to say what is the best or right thing to do □ *He said that we should all go home.* □ *Should I write her a letter?* □ *You shouldn't eat too much chocolate.* (**dever**)
2 used to say that you expect something to be true □ *The train should be arriving in a couple of minutes.* □ *The children should be asleep by eight.* (**dever**)
3 should have used to say what would have been the right thing to do when you have done something different □ *I should have helped him.* □ *I'm late – I should have taken a taxi.* (**deveria ter**)

shoulder /'ʃəʊldə(r)/ NOUN [plural shoulders]
one of the two parts of your body between your neck and your arms (**ombro**)

shouldn't /ʃʊdənt/ a short way to say and write should not □ *You shouldn't wait out in the rain.* (**abreviação de should not**)

should've /ʃʊdəv/ a short way to say and write should have □ *You should've seen him!* (**abreviação de should have**)

shout¹ /ʃaʊt/ VERB [shouts, shouting, shouted]
to say something very loudly or to make a loud noise with your voice □ *Someone was shouting my name.* □ *There's no need to shout.* □ + *at She's always shouting at the children.* (**gritar**)

shout² /ʃaʊt/ NOUN [plural shouts]
a loud cry or call □ *There were shouts of approval from the crowd.* (**grito**)

shove /ʃʌv/ VERB [shoves, shoving, shoved] to push someone or something hard or roughly □ *Someone shoved me in the back.* (**empurrar**)

shovel /'ʃʌvəl/ NOUN [plural shovels] a tool for digging or moving earth, sand, snow, etc. □ *a garden shovel* (**pá**)

show¹ /ʃəʊ/ VERB [shows, showing, showed, shown]
1 to prove that something exists or is true □ + *that The evidence shows that he could not have committed the crime.* □ *Polls show an increase in support for the president.* 🕮 *This incident shows why it is important to follow safety regulations.* (**mostrar**)
2 to allow someone to see something or to cause them to see it □ *Show me your new bike.* □ *Young people were shown images of knife wounds.* □ *His website shows pictures of him with his family.* (**mostrar**)
3 to express your feelings □ *I try to show an interest in his work.* □ *The man showed no emotion as the judge read his sentence.* (**mostrar**)
4 to tell someone where to go or where someone is, by explaining, pointing or taking them there □ *I showed her where to put her coat.* □ + *to I'll show you to your room.* (**acompanhar**)
5 to allow someone to watch you doing something so that they learn how to do it □ *Can you show me how to work the DVD player?* (**mostrar**)
6 to be able to be noticed □ *The scar hardly shows.* □ *I tried not to let my disappointment show.* (**aparecer**)

◆ PHRASAL VERBS **show off** to behave in a way that makes people notice you, or to talk a lot about something that you own, because you want people to admire you □ *He's always showing off about his cars.* **show up** to arrive □ *She showed up an hour late.*

show² /ʃəʊ/ NOUN [plural shows]
1 a performance in the theatre or on radio or television □ *He is starring in a new comedy show on the BBC.* (**espetáculo**)
2 an event where people or businesses can show things to the public □ *We went to a boat show.* □ *a fashion show* (**exposição**)
3 on show able to be seen □ *Some of her statues are on show in New York.* (**exposto**)

shower /'ʃaʊə(r)/ NOUN [plural showers]
1 a piece of bathroom equipment that produces a flow of water that you stand under to wash yourself □ *Adam's in the shower.* (**chuveiro**)
2 an act of washing yourself under a shower 🕮 *I had a shower to cool off.* (**chuveirada**)
3 a short period of rain □ *We got caught in a shower.* (**aguaceiro**)

shown /ʃəʊn/ PAST PARTICIPLE OF **show¹** (ver **show¹**)
shrank /ʃræŋk/ PAST TENSE OF **shrink** (ver **shrink**)
shriek /ʃriːk/ VERB [shrieks, shrieking, shrieked] to make a loud high noise or speak in a loud high voice because you are afraid, excited, etc. □ *She shrieked when she saw the mouse.* □ *'Watch out!' he shrieked.* (**guinchar, gritar**)

shrine /ʃraɪn/ NOUN [plural shrines] a religious place where people go to pray, often because it has something to do with a holy person □ *a shrine to the Virgin Mary* (**santuário**)

shrink /ʃrɪŋk/ VERB [shrinks, shrinking, shrank, shrunk] to get smaller or to make something smaller in size, amount or value □ *My sweater shrank in the wash.* □ *The number of honey bees has shrunk dramatically.* (**encolher**)

shrug /ʃrʌɡ/ VERB [shrugs, shrugging, shrugged] to raise and lower your shoulders in a movement that shows you do not know something or that you do not care about it 🕮 *She shrugged her shoulders and said 'I don't mind.'* (**dar de ombros**)

> ▶ **THESAURUS:** If you **shrug** your shoulders, you raise and lower your shoulders in a movement that shows you do not know something or that you do not care about it. If you **nod** your head, you move it up and down, especially to agree or to say 'yes'. If you **shake** your head, you move it from side to side as a way of saying 'no'.

shrunk /ʃrʌŋk/ PAST PARTICIPLE OF **shrink** (ver **shrink**)

shudder /'ʃʌdə(r)/ VERB [**shudders, shuddering, shuddered**] to shake suddenly, usually because of shock or disgust □ *She shuddered when she thought of his injuries.* (**estremecer**)

shuffle /'ʃʌfəl/ VERB [**shuffles, shuffling, shuffled**]
1 to walk slowly, sliding your feet along the ground without lifting them □ *The old woman shuffled slowly into the hall.* (**arrastar os pés**)
2 to mix up a set of playing cards before playing a game □ *Whose turn is it to shuffle?* (**embaralhar**)

shut¹ /ʃʌt/ VERB [**shuts, shutting, shut**]
1 to close something or to become closed □ *Could you please shut the window?* □ *I heard the door shut as he left.* □ *She shut her eyes and tried to remember his face.* (**fechar**)
2 to close a business for the day or for a short period of time □ *The shop shuts at 6 every evening.* (**fechar**)
♦ PHRASAL VERBS **shut (something) down** if a business, factory, shop etc. shuts down, or if someone shuts it down, it closes □ *The factory shut down several years ago.* **shut (someone) up** an informal word meaning to stop talking or make someone stop talking □ *I wish he'd shut up for once.* □ *Once she gets on to the old days, nothing will shut her up.*

shut² /ʃʌt/ ADJECTIVE
1 closed □ *All the windows were shut.* (**fechar**)
2 if a business is shut, it has closed for the day or for a short period of time □ *The swimming pool is shut for repairs.* (**fechar**)

shuttle /'ʃʌtəl/ NOUN [**plural shuttles**] an air, train or other transport service that goes backwards and forwards between two places □ *There's a shuttle bus to the airport.* (**ponte aérea**)

shy /ʃaɪ/ ADJECTIVE [**shyer, shyest**] nervous and not confident when meeting and speaking to people 🔲 *My brother is painfully shy* (= very shy). (**tímido**)

sibling /'sɪblɪŋ/ NOUN [**plural siblings**] a brother or sister □ *Most younger children tend to copy their older siblings.* (**irmão ou irmã**)

sick /sɪk/ ADJECTIVE [**sicker, sickest**]
1 sick people or animals are ill □ *He looks after his sick mother.* 🔲 *I got sick on holiday.* (**doente**)
2 feel sick to feel as if you are going to vomit □ *The smell made me feel physically sick.* (**enjoado**)
3 be sick to vomit 🔲 *He was violently sick.* (**enjoado**)
4 off sick not at work because you are ill (**ausente por doença**)
5 sick of something/someone an informal phrase meaning angry about something or bored with some thing □ *I'm sick of having to do all his work for him.* □ *I'm sick of salad – can't we have a hot meal?* (**farto, cansado**)
6 make someone sick (a) to make someone angry and upset □ *It makes me sick the way she expects* everyone to do what she wants all the time. (b) to make someone very jealous □ *She does everything well – it makes me sick!* (**deixar irritado, aborrecido**)

sickness /'sɪknɪs/ NOUN, NO PLURAL when someone is ill □ *He had a lot of time off work due to sickness.* (**doença**)

side /saɪd/ NOUN [**plural sides**]
1 the outer surface or edge of something, especially one that is not the top, bottom, front or back □ *He built a house by the side of the river.* □ *Go round the side of the building.* □ *Write on both sides of the paper.* □ *We sat on opposite sides of the table.* 🔲 *The two soldiers stood on either side of* (= both sides of) *the king.* (**lado**)
2 the area of something that is near the edge □ *Could you move to the side, please?* □ *He put the pasta to one side and started making the sauce.* (**lado**)
3 one of the parts or areas of something when it is divided □ *In the UK, people drive on the left hand side of the road.* □ *We live in the north side of town.* 🔲 *Australia is on the other side of the world.* (**lado**)
4 an edge or flat surface of a shape □ *How many sides does a hexagon have?* (**face**)
5 the left or right part of someone's body □ *She stood by his side all day.* □ *Could you lie on your side, please?* (**lado**)
6 side by side next to each other □ *They sat side by side on the sofa.* (**lado a lado**)
7 one of the people or groups who are arguing □ *Both sides agree that discussions are needed.*
8 one of the teams in a competition □ *He was chosen to captain the England side.* (**lado**)
9 if you are on someone's side, you support them in an argument 🔲 *Why do you always take Mum's side?* (**lado**)

sidewalk /'saɪdwɔːk/ NOUN [**plural sidewalks**] the US word for **pavement** (**calçada**)

siege /siːdʒ/ NOUN [**plural sieges**] a situation in which an army surrounds a place and stops supplies from getting in or people from getting out □ *The port was under siege.* (**cerco**)

sigh¹ /saɪ/ VERB [**sighs, sighing, sighed**] to breathe out noisily, because you feel tired, disappointed, unhappy, etc. □ *She sighed wearily as she looked at the pile of ironing she had to do.* (**suspirar**)

sigh² /saɪ/ NOUN [**plural sighs**] a long noisy breath out, often because you are tired, disappointed, unhappy, etc. □ *'I'm afraid there's still no news', he said with a sigh.* 🔲 *When Phil finally got home we all breathed a huge sigh of relief.* (**suspiro**)

sight /saɪt/ NOUN [**plural sights**]
1 *no plural* the ability to see □ *He lost his sight in an explosion.* (**vista**)
2 *no plural* when you see something □ *He fainted at the sight of blood.* 🔲 *I caught sight of him, hurrying round a corner.* (**visão, vista**)
3 *no plural* the place or area you are able to see □ *We watched the ship until it disappeared from sight.* 🔲 *We waved until their car was out of sight.* (**vista**)

4 something that you see □ *Foxes are a familiar sight round here.* □ *I'll never forget the sight of all those people waving flags.* (vista)
5 the sights interesting places to visit in a country or area □ *He offered to show me the sights of Hong Kong.* (vista)
→ *go to* **lose sight of something**

sightseeing /ˈsaɪtsiːɪŋ/ NOUN, NO PLURAL
travelling around looking at interesting things and places □ *The hotel organized a sightseeing trip to the Roman amphitheatre.* (circuito turístico)

sign¹ /saɪn/ NOUN [plural signs]
1 something that shows that something is happening or will happen or that something exists □ **+ of** *There is no sign of spring arriving yet.* □ **+ that** *There are signs that the economy is recovering.* ▣ *My boss is showing signs of stress.* ▣ *I can't see much sign of progress.* ▣ *The fact that he is eating well is a good sign.* (sinal)
2 an object in a public place with words, symbols or pictures that gives information □ *The sign said 'No smoking'.* □ *Follow the signs to the car park.* (tabuleta, placa)
3 a symbol with a particular meaning □ *a dollar sign* (sinal)

sign² /saɪn/ VERB [signs, signing, signed]
to write your name on something, for example to agree officially to something, or to prove that something was done by you □ *Please sign the contract and return it to us.* □ *The letter was not signed.* □ *The painting is a signed original.* (assinatura)

signal¹ /ˈsɪɡnəl/ NOUN [plural signals]
a sign, action or sound that sends a message to someone ▣ *When I give the signal, turn on the music.* □ **+ to do something** *The troops waited for the signal to attack.* (sinal)

signal² /ˈsɪɡnəl/ VERB [signals, signalling/US signaling, signalled/US signaled]
to make a sign, sound or movement to tell someone something □ *You must signal well before the junction.* □ **+ to** *Jo was signalling to us from across the room.* (sinalizar, fazer sinal)

signature /ˈsɪɡnətʃə(r)/ NOUN [plural signatures]
your name, written by you, for example on the bottom of a letter or on a document □ *Someone had forged my signature on the form.* (assinatura)

significance /sɪɡˈnɪfɪkəns/ NOUN, NO PLURAL
the meaning or importance of something □ *I didn't understand the significance of what he said at the time.* (significado)

significant /sɪɡˈnɪfɪkənt/ ADJECTIVE
large or important □ *A significant number of children are failing to reach the required standard.* □ *She is now recognized as one of the most significant novelists of the 20th century.* (significativo)

signpost /ˈsaɪnpəʊst/ NOUN [plural signposts]
a sign by a road showing which direction to go to get to a particular place (placa de sinalização)

silence /ˈsaɪləns/ NOUN [plural silences]
1 no plural when it is completely quiet and no sound can be heard □ *For a moment there was absolute silence in the theatre.* (silêncio)
2 a period when there is no sound or no one speaks □ *The players observed two minutes' silence for their former teammate.* (silêncio)

silent /ˈsaɪlənt/ ADJECTIVE
1 not speaking or making any noise ▣ *The crowd fell silent.* (calado)
2 completely quiet □ *the silent churchyard* (silencioso)

silk /sɪlk/ NOUN [plural silks]
a soft smooth cloth made from the very soft thin threads produced by a special insect (called a silkworm) □ *The dress was made of ivory silk.* □ *a silk kimono* (seda)

silver¹ /ˈsɪlvə(r)/ NOUN [plural silvers]
1 no plural a valuable shiny grey metal, used to make jewellery □ *This tray is made of solid silver.* (prata)
2 a silver medal (= prize for coming second in a competition or race) (prata)

silver² /ˈsɪlvə(r)/ ADJECTIVE
1 made of silver □ *a pair of silver earrings* (de prata, prateado)
2 having the colour of silver □ *silver paint*

similar /ˈsɪmɪlə(r)/ ADJECTIVE
two things are similar when they are like each other but not exactly the same □ **+ to** *An alligator is similar to a crocodile, but smaller.* (similar, semelhante)

similarity /ˌsɪmɪˈlærəti/ NOUN [plural similarities]
a characteristic that two people or things share □ *There are several similarities between the two novels.* (similaridade)

simmer /ˈsɪmə(r)/ VERB [simmers, simmering, simmered]
to cook food slowly by boiling it very gently (aferventar)

simple /ˈsɪmpəl/ ADJECTIVE [simpler, simplest]
1 easy to do, solve or understand □ *a simple sum* □ *The dishwasher came with a set of simple instructions.* □ *This mobile phone is very simple to use.* (simples, fácil)
2 basic or not complicated □ *Stone Age men could make simple tools.* □ *The simple truth is he's too old for the job.* (simples)
3 plain or without any decoration □ *a simple design* □ *I like simple home cooking.* (simples)

simply /ˈsɪmpli/ ADVERB
1 only □ *Now, it's simply a question of waiting until something happens.* (simplesmente)
2 in a way that is not difficult or complicated □ *I'll explain it simply so that you all understand.* (de maneira simples, simplesmente)
3 with no decorations or extra details □ *a simply furnished apartment* (simplesmente, com simplicidade)

sin /sɪn/ NOUN [plural **sins**] a very bad thing to do, especially one that breaks a religious law □ the sin of pride ▣ He felt that he had committed a sin. (**pecado**)

since¹ /sɪns/ CONJUNCTION
1 from a particular time or event in the past until the present □ Ann's been a lot happier since she changed jobs. □ He's put on weight since I saw him last. (**desde que**)
2 because □ I decided to go shopping, since I had some free time. (**já que**)

since² /sɪns/ ADVERB
1 from the time that has already been mentioned until the present □ She joined the choir last month and has been going to practice regularly since. ▣ I came to London in 1995, and I've lived here ever since. (**desde**)
2 at a later time than the time first mentioned □ They met last year and have since become friends. (**desde**)

since³ /sɪns/ PREPOSITION from a particular time in the past until the present □ The little girl has been missing since Christmas. □ We've been living here since 1986. □ I haven't spoken to Gretta since last week. (**desde**)

sincere /sɪnˈsɪə(r)/ ADJECTIVE honest and saying what you really think □ I'm never sure he's being sincere with me. (**sincero**)

sincerely /sɪnˈsɪəli/ ADVERB
1 in a way that is sincere □ I sincerely hope you're right about this. (**sinceramente**)
2 Yours sincerely used at the end of a letter when you have used the name of the person you are writing to (**atenciosamente**)

sing /sɪŋ/ VERB [**sings, singing, sang, sung**] to make musical sounds with your voice □ She sings in a choir. □ I asked him to sing my favourite song. (**cantar**)

singer /ˈsɪŋə(r)/ NOUN [plural **singers**] a person who sings, especially as their job □ a folk singer (**cantor**)

singing /ˈsɪŋɪŋ/ NOUN, NO PLURAL the activity of making musical sounds with your voice □ a singing teacher (**canto**)

single¹ /ˈsɪŋɡəl/ ADJECTIVE
1 only one □ I didn't get a single card on my birthday. □ A single shelf held all her belongings. (**único**)
2 talking about each thing in a group ▣ He rang me every single day while he was away. (**cada**)
3 not married □ a club for single women (**solteiro**)
4 for use by one person □ a single room □ a pair of single sheets (**de solteiro**)
5 a single ticket is used for a journey in one direction (**de ida**)

single² /ˈsɪŋɡəl/ NOUN [plural **singles**]
1 a ticket for a journey you make in one direction but not back again □ How much is a single to York? □ Two singles to Kings Cross. (**bilhete de ida**)
2 a musical CD or record with only one or two songs on it ▣ a hit single (= very popular song) (**CD ou gravação musical**)

singular¹ /ˈsɪŋɡjʊlə(r)/ ADJECTIVE in grammar, a singular form of a word is the form used to talk about one person, thing or group □ 'Child' is the singular form of 'children'. (**singular**)

singular² /ˈsɪŋɡjʊlə(r)/ NOUN **the singular** the form of a noun, pronoun, adjective or verb that you use to talk about one person, thing or group □ The singular is 'sheep' and the plural is also 'sheep'. (**singular**)

sink¹ /sɪŋk/ VERB [**sinks, sinking, sank, sunk**]
1 to drop below the surface of water and move down to the bottom, or to make something do this □ The boat sank in a storm. □ She fell in and sank below the surface of the water. (**afundar**)
2 to move to a lower position or level □ The sun was sinking towards the horizon. □ + **into** He sank to his knees. (**baixar**)

sink² /sɪŋk/ NOUN [plural **sinks**] a bowl fixed to the wall in a kitchen or bathroom, used for washing in ▣ She put the dirty cups in the kitchen sink. (**pia**)

sip¹ /sɪp/ VERB [**sips, sipping, sipped**] to drink something slowly taking only a small amount at a time □ Russell sipped his coffee. (**sorver**)

sip² /sɪp/ NOUN [plural **sips**] when you sip a drink ▣ She took a sip of water. (**pequeno gole**)

sir /sɜː(r)/ NOUN [plural **sirs**]
1 a polite way of speaking or writing to a man, especially one you do not know □ Excuse me, sir. Can I help you? (**senhor, cavaleiro**)
2 Dear Sir a way of beginning a formal letter to a man when you do not know his name (**senhor, cavaleiro**)
3 a title used before the name of a knight (= a man with a high social rank) □ Sir Paul McCartney (**sir**)

siren /ˈsaɪərən/ NOUN [plural **sirens**] a device that makes a very loud noise to warn people of something □ I heard police sirens outside. (**sirene**)

sister /ˈsɪstə(r)/ NOUN [plural **sisters**]
1 a girl or woman who has the same parents as you ▣ He had two older sisters. ▣ She was walking to school with her younger sister. (**irmã**)
2 a female nurse who is in charge of part of a hospital □ a ward sister (**enfermeira-chefe**)
3 a nun (= a member of a female religious group), often used as a title □ Sister Dorothy (**freira**)

sister-in-law /ˈsɪstərɪnˌlɔː/ NOUN [plural **sisters-in-law**] your brother's wife, or your husband's or wife's sister (**cunhada**)

sit /sɪt/ VERB [**sits, sitting, sat**]
1 to be in a position where your weight is supported on your bottom, not your legs □ I sat next to my friend. ▣ Would you please sit still while I get the books out? □ + **on** He was sitting on the sofa. □ + **down** They were sitting down waiting for me. (**sentar**)
2 to move your body into a position where your weight is supported on your bottom □ He came in

and sat on the floor. □ **+ down** *Sit down now, and get on with your work, please.* **(sentar-se)**
3 if you sit an exam, you do an exam □ *She's sitting her GCSEs next term.* **(fazer)**
◆ PHRASAL VERB **sit up 1** to move from a lying position to a sitting position □ *Can you manage to sit up?* **2** to sit with your back straight 🔲 *Sit up straight and pay attention!*

site /saɪt/ NOUN [plural **sites**]
1 a place where something happens or happened, or a place used for a certain purpose □ **+ of** *the site of a battle* 🔲 *He works on a construction site.* □ *It is one of the most visited archaeological sites in Europe.* □ *The minister visited the crash site.* **(local, sítio)**
2 a website. A computing word 🔲 *an Internet site* □ *The film is posted on video sharing sites like YouTube.* **(website)**

sitting room /ˈsɪtɪŋ ˌruːm/ NOUN [plural **sitting rooms**] a room, usually in a house, for sitting and relaxing **(sala de estar)**

situation /ˌsɪtjuˈeɪʃən/ NOUN [plural **situations**] the things that are happening in a place or affecting someone at a particular time 🔲 *We're in a difficult situation.* 🔲 *She handled the situation very well.* □ *They're trying to improve the situation for parttime workers.* **(situação)**

six /sɪks/ NUMBER [plural **sixes**] the number 6 **(seis)**

sixteen /ˌsɪksˈtiːn/ NUMBER the number 16 **(dezesseis)**
sixteenth /ˌsɪksˈtiːnθ/ NUMBER 16th written as a word **(décimo sexto)**

sixth[1] /sɪksθ/ NUMBER 6th written as a word **(sexto)**

sixth[2] /sɪksθ/ NOUN [plural **sixths**] 1/6; one of six equal parts of something **(sexto)**

sixtieth /ˈsɪkstiəθ/ NUMBER 60th written as a word **(sexagésimo)**
sixty /ˈsɪksti/ NUMBER [plural **sixties**]
1 the number 60 **(sessenta)**
2 the sixties the years between 1960 and 1969 **(a década de 1960)**

size /saɪz/ NOUN [plural **sizes**]
1 how big, small, long, wide, etc. something is, □ **+ of** *The hole was the size of a tennis ball.* □ *They are less than 2 centimetres in size.* □ *We were disappointed by the small size of the bedrooms.* 🔲 *It's about the same size as a credit card.* 🔲 *There were boats of every size and shape.* □ *The government wants to reduce class sizes.* **(tamanho, dimensão)**
2 one of the measurements that clothes, shoes and other objects are made in □ *Can I try a smaller size?* □ *I'm a size 12.* **(tamanho)**

skate[1] /skeɪt/ NOUN [plural **skates**]
1 an ice skate **(patim de gelo)**
2 a roller skate **(patim de roda)**
skate[2] /skeɪt/ VERB [**skates, skating, skated**] to move wearing skates □ *The Russian pair skated well.* **(patinar)**

skateboard /ˈskeɪtbɔːd/ NOUN [plural **skateboards**] a long narrow board with wheels on the bottom which you ride by standing on it **(skate)**

skating /ˈskeɪtɪŋ/ NOUN, NO PLURAL the sport or activity of moving over ice wearing ice skates (= boots with a metal blade on the bottom) **(patinação)**

skeleton /ˈskelɪtən/ NOUN [plural **skeletons**] the frame of bones inside the body of a person or an animal □ *They found a nearly complete dinosaur skeleton.* **(esqueleto)**

sketch /sketʃ/ NOUN [plural **sketches**] a drawing that is done quickly □ *a pencil sketch* □ *He drew a rough sketch of the house.* **(esboço, croqui)**

ski[1] /skiː/ NOUN [plural **skis**] one of two long narrow strips of wood or metal that you attach to boots and use for moving over snow 🔲 *a pair of skis* **(esqui)**

ski[2] /skiː/ VERB [**skis, skiing, skied**] to move over snow on skis □ *They skied down together.* □ *I'm just learning to ski.* **(esquiar)**

skier /ˈskiːə(r)/ NOUN [plural **skiers**] someone who skis **(esquiador)**

skiing /ˈskiːɪŋ/ NOUN, NO PLURAL the sport or activity of moving over snow on skis 🔲 *I would love to go skiing.* 🔲 *a skiing holiday* **(esqui)**

skilful /ˈskɪlful/ ADJECTIVE showing the ability to do something well □ *He's a very skilful player.* □ *She's very skilful at handling the media.* **(habilmente)**

skilfully /ˈskɪlfuli/ ADVERB in a skilful way □ *They had skilfully avoided being caught.* □ *a skilfully edited programme* **(habilmente)**

skill /skɪl/ NOUN [plural **skills**]
1 an ability to do something that you develop through training and practice 🔲 *It helps children develop their social skills.* 🔲 *Effective communication skills are essential.* 🔲 *They lack basic computer skills.* **(habilmente, experiência, competência)**
2 no plural the ability to do something very well □ *His skill as a writer is in creating interesting characters.* □ **+ in** *He showed great skill in handling the situation.* □ **+ at** *She was known for her skill at motivating workers.* **(habilidade)**

skilled /skɪld/ ADJECTIVE a skilled person is very good at what they do □ *Amanda's a skilled pianist.* 🔲 *a highly skilled employee* **(especializado, perito)**

skin /skɪn/ NOUN [plural **skins**]
1 no plural the outside layer of your body 🔲 *She had blonde hair and very pale skin.* 🔲 *People with dark skin don't burn as easily in the sun.* 🔲 *A moisturizing cream will help prevent dry skin.* □ *skin cancer* **(pele)**
2 the outside layer of some fruits and vegetables □ *banana skins* □ *grape skin* **(casca)**
3 the outside layer of a dead animal which is used for making something □ *the illegal trade in tiger skins* **(pele)**

skinny · slice

> **THESAURUS:** The outside layer of some fruits and vegetables is called the skin. Peaches, tomatoes and cherries have a skin. The skin of some fruits and vegetables is called the peel. Oranges, lemons, and bananas have peel. For some things, for example apples and potatoes, you can talk about either the skin or the peel. In general, when you remove the skin, we usually use the word peel, but when you eat the skin, we usually use the word skin. The hard covering on a nut or an egg is called the shell.

skinny /'skɪnɪ/ ADJECTIVE [skinnier, skinniest]
very thin □ *She's too skinny.* (**magrelo**)

skip /skɪp/ VERB [skips, skipping, skipped]
1 to move forward by jumping from one foot to the other foot □ *He skipped down the road.* (**saltitar**)
2 to jump over a rope that you are turning □ *The girls were skipping in the playground.* (**pular corda**)
3 to not do something that you should do □ *Children who skip breakfast find it more difficult to concentrate in class.* □ *He was being bullied and regularly skipped school.* (**pular**)

> **THESAURUS:** If you jump, you push yourself off the ground or other surface with your legs. If you skip, you move forward by jumping from one foot to the other foot, or jump over a rope that you are turning. If you hop, you jump on one leg. When an animal hops, it moves by jumping. Frogs, rabbits and kangaroos all hop.

skirt /skɜːt/ NOUN [plural skirts] a piece of clothing for girls or women that hangs from the waist 🔁 *Anja was wearing a black skirt.* □ *a short skirt* (**saia**)

skull /skʌl/ NOUN [plural skulls] the structure of bones that form your head □ *He fell out of a tree and fractured his skull.* (**crânio**)

sky /skaɪ/ NOUN [plural skies] the area above the Earth where you can see the stars, sun, moon, and clouds □ *There was a beautiful clear blue sky.* □ *She looked up at the cloudy sky.* □ *There were several stars in the sky.* (**céu**)

skyscraper /'skaɪskreɪpə(r)/ NOUN [plural skyscrapers] a very tall building (**arranha-céu**)

slam /slæm/ VERB [slams, slamming, slammed]
1 to shut quickly with a loud noise, or to shut something quickly with a loud noise 🔁 *She walked angrily out of the room and slammed the door.* 🔁 *The gate slammed shut.* (**bater, tombar**)
2 to put something somewhere with a loud noise □ *He slammed the books down on the table.* (**bater, trombar**)

slap¹ /slæp/ VERB [slaps, slapping, slapped] to hit something or someone with the flat part of your hand □ *She slapped him across the face.* (**estapear**)

slap² /slæp/ NOUN [plural slaps] a hit made with the flat part of your hand (**tapa**)

♦ IDIOM **a slap in the face** something someone does which upsets or insults you □ *The fare increases are a slap in the face for commuters.*

slaughter¹ /'slɔːtə(r)/ VERB [slaughters, slaughtering, slaughtered]
1 to kill an animal, usually for its meat (**abater**)
2 to kill a lot of people very violently (**massacrar**)

slaughter² /'slɔːtə(r)/ NOUN, NO PLURAL the act of killing a lot of people violently, or of killing animals for meat □ *Officials carried out a mass slaughter of cows to prevent the spread of the disease.* □ *The war has seen the slaughter of innocent civilians.* (**massacre, abate**)

slave /sleɪv/ NOUN [plural slaves] someone who is owned by another person and has to work for them without being paid □ *My parents treat me like a slave.* (**escravo**)

slavery /'sleɪvərɪ/ NOUN, NO PLURAL
1 the system of owning people and making them work without being paid □ *The US did not abolish slavery until 1865.* (**escravatura**)
2 the state of being a owned by another person □ *He had been sold into slavery.* (**escravidão**)

sleep¹ /sliːp/ NOUN, NO PLURAL
1 the state when you are resting with your eyes closed and are naturally unconscious □ *I really need some sleep.* 🔁 *I couldn't get to sleep.* (**sono**)
2 go to sleep (a) to begin to sleep (b) if part of your body goes to sleep, you lose the feeling in it (**ir dormir**)

sleep² /sliːp/ VERB [sleeps, sleeping, slept] to become naturally unconscious and rest with your eyes closed □ *I hardly slept at all last night.* □ *She slept through the fire alarm* (= did not wake up). 🔁 *After their long walk, they slept soundly* (= slept well). (**ir dormir**)

sleepy /'sliːpɪ/ ADJECTIVE [sleepier, sleepiest] feeling tired and wanting to sleep (**sonolento**)

sleet¹ /sliːt/ NOUN, NO PLURAL a mixture of rain and snow (**saraiva**)

sleet² /sliːt/ VERB [sleets, sleeting, sleeted] if it is sleeting, sleet is falling (**saraivar**)

sleeve /sliːv/ NOUN [plural sleeves] the part of a piece of clothing that covers your arm or part of your arm □ *a dress with wide sleeves* (**manga**)
♦ IDIOM **have something up your sleeve** to have a secret plan □ *I haven't persuaded them to come yet, but I've still got a few things up my sleeve.*

slender /'slendə(r)/ ADJECTIVE thin in an attractive way □ *a slender figure* (**esguio**)

slept /slept/ PAST TENSE AND PAST PARTICIPLE OF **sleep²** (ver **sleep²**)

slice¹ /slaɪs/ NOUN [plural slices] a thin or smaller piece cut from a larger piece of food □ *He cut himself a thick slice of chocolate cake.* □ *a slice of ham* (**fatia**)

slice² /slaɪs/ VERB [slices, slicing, sliced] to cut something into thin pieces ◻ *Slice the onions thinly.* ◻ *a tin of sliced peaches* (fatiar)

slide¹ /slaɪd/ VERB [slides, sliding, slid] to move over a surface quickly and in a smooth way, or to make something do this ◻ *The kids enjoyed sliding on the ice.* ◻ *a sliding door* ◻ *We slid the poles into place.* (escorregar, deslizar)

> **THESAURUS:** If you slide, you move over a surface quickly and smoothly, or make something do this. If you **slip**, you slide and lose your balance or fall. For example, you might slip on an icy path or a wet floor. If you **trip**, you hit your foot on something and fall, or almost fall. For example, you might trip on the edge of a carpet.

slide² /slaɪd/ NOUN [plural slides]
1 a piece of play equipment on which children climb up steps and slide down a smooth sloping surface ◻ *Megan loves playing on the slide.* (escorregar)
2 a small transparent photograph that you shine light through to look at an image on a screen ◻ *a slide show* (slide)
3 a small clear piece of glass or plastic which you put something on so that you can look at it using a microscope (= scientific instrument for examining things) (lâmina)

slight /slaɪt/ ADJECTIVE [slighter, slightest] small or not important ◻ *a slight increase in temperature* ◻ *There's a slight problem with your application.* ◻ *Lewis has a slight cold.* (leve, ligeiro)

slightly /ˈslaɪtli/ ADVERB by only a small amount ◻ *Adam is slightly taller than Alex.* ◻ *I only know her slightly.* (ligeiramente)

slim¹ /slɪm/ ADJECTIVE [slimmer, slimmest] thin in an attractive way ◻ *His sister's a tall, slim girl with blonde hair.* (esbelto)

slim² /slɪm/ VERB [slims, slimming, slimmed] to become or try to become thinner ◻ *I can't have any cake, I'm slimming.* (emagrecer)

slip¹ /slɪp/ VERB [slips, slipping, slipped]
1 to slide and lose your balance or fall ◻ *Gran slipped on the ice and broke her hip.* (escorregar)
2 to fall out of position or out of your hands ◻ *The knife slipped and I nearly cut myself.* ◻ *I'm sorry, the cup just slipped out of my hands.* (escorregar)
3 to put something somewhere quickly ◻ *Dad slipped a £10 note in my pocket.* (enfiar)
4 to go somewhere quietly and without anyone noticing you ◻ *I saw Polly slip out of the room.* ◻ *They must have slipped away while we were watching the show.* (escapar)

◆ PHRASAL VERB **slip up** to make a mistake or do something wrong ◻ *I'm afraid you slipped up on the first question.*

slip² /slɪp/ NOUN [plural slips]
1 a small piece of paper ◻ *a slip of paper* ◻ *Fill in the green slip and give it back to me.* (pedaço de papel)
2 a small mistake ◻ *She made a couple of slips in her dance routine.* (lapso)

slipper /ˈslɪpə(r)/ NOUN [plural slippers] a soft shoe for wearing indoors (chinelo)

slippery /ˈslɪpəri/ ADJECTIVE a slippery surface is smooth, wet or shiny and not easy to walk on or hold ◻ *The floor was slippery with grease.* (escorregadio)

slogan /ˈsləʊgən/ NOUN [plural slogans] a phrase that is easy to remember and is used to advertise something or to emphasize the opinions of political parties, etc. ◻ *advertising slogans* (slogan)

slope¹ /sləʊp/ VERB [slopes, sloping, sloped] to have one end higher than the other ◻ *The garden slopes upwards.* ◻ *a sloping roof* (inclinar [-se])

slope² /sləʊp/ NOUN [plural slopes] a surface that slopes ◻ *a steep slope* ◻ *a ski slope* (declive)

sloppy /ˈslɒpi/ ADJECTIVE [sloppier, sloppiest]
1 careless or untidy ◻ *a sloppy piece of work* (desleixado)
2 sloppy clothes are loose and do not have a clear shape ◻ *a sloppy jumper* (mole)

slot /slɒt/ NOUN [plural slots] a small narrow opening, especially one that you put coins or bank cards into ◻ *There's a pound coin stuck in the slot.* (fenda)

slow¹ /sləʊ/ ADJECTIVE [slower, slowest]
1 not fast or not moving or acting quickly ◻ *a slow march* ◻ *a slow reader* ◻ *We made slow progress through the crowds.* (lento, vagaroso)
2 not doing something immediately ◻ **+ to do something** *Social services were slow to take any action to protect the child.* ◻ **+ in** *He was very slow in coming to the phone.* (lento, vagaroso)
3 if a clock or watch is slow, it shows a time earlier than the correct time ◻ *I think your clock's five minutes slow.* (atrasado)

slow² /sləʊ/ VERB [slows, slowing, slowed]
◆ PHRASAL VERB **slow (something) down** to become slower or to make something slower ◻ *You should slow down as you approach the bend.*

slowly /ˈsləʊli/ ADVERB at a slow speed ◻ *He drove slowly past the house.* ◻ *She speaks very slowly.* (lentamente)

slug /slʌg/ NOUN [plural slugs] a creature with a long soft body and no legs, that moves slowly and eats plants ◻ *Slugs had attacked our bean plants.* (lesma)

slum /slʌm/ NOUN [plural slums] a part of a town or city where the buildings are dirty and in bad condition ◻ *She sang about her childhood in the slums of Naples.* (periferia)

slump /slʌmp/ VERB [slumps, slumping, slumped]
1 to quickly go down to a much lower level ◻ *Business has slumped in the last few months.* (baixar repentinamente)

smack

2 to fall or sit down suddenly because you feel weak, ill or tired ▫ *He was slumped over his desk, fast asleep.* ▫ *She suddenly slumped back in her chair.* (despencar)

smack /smæk/ VERB [smacks, smacking, smacked] to hit someone with your hand flat ▫ *It is wrong to smack children.* (dar palmada)

small /smɔːl/ ADJECTIVE [smaller, smallest]
1 little ▫ *a small country* ▫ *This coat is too small for you now.* ▫ *We're only interviewing a small number of applicants.* (pequeno)
2 very young ▫ *a playground for small children* ▫ *I used to love these books when I was small.* (pequeno)
3 not important or serious ▫ *a small problem* (pequeno)

smart /smɑːt/ ADJECTIVE [smarter, smartest]
1 clean and tidy ▫ *a pair of smart black shoes* ▫ *She looked really smart in her uniform.* (elegante)
2 clever ▫ *a smart answer* ▫ *He's one of the smartest guys I know.* (esperto)

smash /smæʃ/ VERB [smashes, smashing, smashed]
1 to break something into pieces, for example by dropping it ▫ *She smashed one of our best glasses.* ▫ *Mum, I've smashed a window.* ▫ *Police had to smash the door down.* (estraçalhar)
2 to break into pieces ▫ *The vase fell off the table and smashed.* (estraçalhar)

smear¹ /smɪə(r)/ VERB [smears, smearing, smeared] to spread a soft or dirty substance on a surface ▫ *Her face was smeared with mascara.* (lambuzar)

smear² /smɪə(r)/ NOUN [plural smears] a dirty mark made by spreading something sticky on something ▫ *smears of paint* (mancha)

smell¹ /smel/ VERB [smells, smelling, smelled or smelt]
1 to notice or recognize something by using your nose ▫ *Can you smell burning?* ▫ *I could smell his sweaty trainers from across the room.* (cheirar)
2 to have a particular smell ▫ *Those scones smell delicious.* ▫ *+ of The sheets smelled of lavender.* ▫ *This chicken smells funny.* (cheirar)
3 to have a bad smell ▫ *His breath smells.* (cheirar)

> **THESAURUS:** When you smell something, you notice or recognize it by using your nose. When you **breathe**, you take air into and out of your lungs. If you **sniff**, you breathe in through your nose in order to smell something. You might sniff a piece of food to decide if it smells bad.

smell² /smel/ NOUN [plural smells]
1 the quality you notice by smelling ▫ *a strong smell of garlic* ▫ *These lilies have a lovely smell.* (cheiro)
2 no plural the ability to smell things ▫ *The virus made him lose his sense of smell.* (olfato)

smelly /ˈsmeli/ ADJECTIVE [smellier, smelliest] having a strong or bad smell ▫ *smelly feet* (malcheiroso)

smooth

smelt /smelt/ PAST TENSE AND PAST PARTICIPLE OF **smell¹** (ver smell¹)

smile¹ /smaɪl/ VERB [smiles, smiling, smiled] to show you are happy or think something is funny by making the corners of your mouth go up ▫ *The little girl smiled happily up at him.* (sorrir)

> Remember that you **smile at** someone. You do not 'smile to' someone:
> ✓ *She turned and smiled at me.*
> ✗ *She turned and smiled to me.*

> **THESAURUS:** If you smile, you show you are happy or think something is funny by making the corners of your mouth go up. If you **grin**, you give a big smile. If you **laugh**, you make a sound of enjoyment when you think something is funny. If you **giggle**, you laugh in a silly or nervous way.

smile² /smaɪl/ NOUN [plural smiles] an expression in which the corners of your mouth go up to show you are happy ▫ *a broad smile* ▫ *'Can I help you?' she said with a smile.* (sorriso)

smoke¹ /sməʊk/ NOUN, NO PLURAL the grey or black gas that something produces when it is burning ▫ *I can smell smoke.* ▫ *cigarette smoke* ▫ *Firefighters battled thick smoke to rescue the children.* ▫ *A cloud of smoke rose into the air.* (fumaça)

smoke² /sməʊk/ VERB [smokes, smoking, smoked]
1 someone who smokes sucks smoke from cigarettes ▫ *My parents don't smoke.* ▫ *Dan was smoking a cigarette.* (fumar)
2 to produce smoke ▫ *The chimney was smoking.* (fumegar)

smoker /ˈsməʊkə(r)/ NOUN [plural smokers] someone who smokes cigarettes ▫ *He used to be a heavy smoker* (= someone who smokes a lot of cigarettes). (fumante)

smoking /ˈsməʊkɪŋ/ NOUN, NO PLURAL the habit of smoking cigarettes ▫ *My Dad wants to stop smoking.* ▫ *In England smoking is banned in public buildings.* (fumar, tabagismo)

smoky /ˈsməʊki/ ADJECTIVE [smokier, smokiest] filled with smoke ▫ *a smoky bar* (enfumaçado)

smooth /smuːð/ ADJECTIVE [smoother, smoothest]
1 having an even surface ▫ *She ran her fingers along the smooth surface of the wood.* ▫ *Babies have beautifully smooth, soft skin.* (liso)
2 a smooth substance has no lumps ▫ *Stir the ingredients until a smooth paste is formed.* (homogêneo)
3 happening without any problems ▫ *Young people want a smooth transition from school to work.* ▫ *His recovery from the operation was relatively smooth.* (suave)

4 having no sudden movements □ *Larger boats provide a smoother ride than rowing boats.* □ *In one smooth movement, he climbed onto the horse.* (**suave**)

smother /'smʌðə(r)/ VERB [**smothers, smothering, smothered**]
1 to cover something with a substance □ *The little boy's hands were smothered in chocolate.* □ *She smothered him with kisses.* (**cobrir, sufocar**)
2 to kill someone by putting something over their nose and mouth (**sufocar**)

smuggle /'smʌɡəl/ VERB [**smuggles, smuggling, smuggled**] to bring something into a country illegally □ *The weapons had been smuggled into the country.* (**contrabandear**)

smuggler /'smʌɡlə(r)/ NOUN [**plural smugglers**] someone who brings something into a country illegally (**contrabandista**)

snack /snæk/ NOUN [**plural snacks**] a small meal, or a small amount of food that you eat between meals ▣ *She had a snack during the morning.* ▣ *Some people eat too many snack foods such as crisps and biscuits.* (**lanche, refeição ligeira**)

snail /sneɪl/ NOUN [**plural snails**] a small creature with a soft body and a shell on its back (**caracol, lesma**)

snake /sneɪk/ NOUN [**plural snakes**] a long thin animal with no legs, which slides along the ground □ *There are several poisonous snakes in the region.* (**cobra**)

snap¹ /snæp/ VERB [**snaps, snapping, snapped**]
1 to break with a sudden, sharp noise or to break something with a sudden, sharp noise □ *The twig snapped.* □ *He snapped off a piece of his biscuit.* (**quebrar com estalo**)
2 to speak to someone in an angry way □ *When I asked for a break, he snapped at me.* (**falar bruscamente**)
3 if an animal snaps, it tries to bite someone or something (**tentar morder**)

snap² /snæp/ NOUN [**plural snaps**]
1 a sudden, short sound □ *She shut her purse with a snap.* (**estalo**)
2 an informal word for a photograph ▣ *holiday snaps* (**fotografia instantânea**)

snarl /snɑːl/ VERB [**snarls, snarling, snarled**]
1 to say something in an angry or threatening way □ *'I have no comment,' he snarled.* (**rosnar**)
2 if an animal snarls, it makes an angry sound and shows its teeth □ *The dog snarled every time he tried to move.* (**rosnar**)

snatch /snætʃ/ VERB [**snatches, snatching, snatched**] to take something from someone suddenly and roughly □ *He snatched the book out of my hand.* (**agarrar, arrebatar**)

sneak /sniːk/ VERB [**sneaks, sneaking, sneaked**] to go somewhere quietly and secretly □ *Maggie sneaked out of the house.* (**esgueirar-se**)

sneaker /'sniːkə(r)/ NOUN [**plural sneakers**] a US word for a type of sports shoe ▣ *Farooq was wearing a pair of sneakers.* (**tênis**)

sneeze /sniːz/ VERB [**sneezes, sneezing, sneezed**] to suddenly blow out air from your nose and mouth in a way that you cannot control □ *Dust always makes me sneeze.* (**espirrar**)

> **THESAURUS:** You might sneeze because you have a cold or if you have dust in your nose. When you **yawn**, you open your mouth very wide and breathe in, because you are feeling tired or bored. If you **snore**, you make a loud noise when you breathe while you are sleeping.

sniff /snɪf/ VERB [**sniffs, sniffing, sniffed**]
1 to breathe in air through your nose noisily □ *He was crying and sniffing.* (**fungar**)
2 to breathe in through your nose in order to smell something □ *Tess sniffed the air.* (**farejar**)

snore /snɔː(r)/ VERB [**snores, snoring, snored**] to make a loud noise when you breathe while you are sleeping □ *My Dad snores and you can hear it all round the house.* (**ronear**)

snow¹ /snəʊ/ NOUN, NO PLURAL soft white pieces that fall from the sky when it is very cold ▣ *15 centimetres of snow fell in many areas.* ▣ *Heavy snow affected much of the country.* ▣ *The snow was starting to melt.* (**neve**)

snow² /snəʊ/ VERB [**snows, snowing, snowed**] if it snows, snow falls from the sky □ *It's been snowing all night.* (**nevar**)

snowball /'snəʊbɔːl/ NOUN [**plural snowballs**] a ball of snow that children make and throw at each other ▣ *The children were throwing snowballs.* ▣ *a snowball fight* (**bola de neve**)

snowboarding /'snəʊbɔːdɪŋ/ NOUN, NO PLURAL a sport in which you move over snow while standing on a board (**snowboarding**)

snowman /'snəʊmæn/ NOUN [**plural snowmen**] a model of a person which children make from snow ▣ *The children have built a snowman.* (**boneco de neve**)

snowy /ˈsnəʊi/ ADJECTIVE [snowier, snowiest] covered with snow, or involving snow ◻ *snowy hills* ◻ *snowy weather* (**nevoso**)

so¹ /səʊ/ ADVERB
1 used to emphasize the word that follows ◻ *I was so happy to see her.* ◻ *I've never seen so many children.* ◻ *Thank you so much for all your help.* (**tão, tanto, muito**)
2 used to avoid repeating something that has just been said ◻ *'Are you coming to the party?' 'I hope so.'* ◻ *'How do you know Emma's going camping?' 'Because she said so.'* ▣ *When she won the competition, she was the first person over 40 to do so.* (**isso**)
3 used to say that something is true for something or someone else ◻ *She's tired and so am I.* ◻ *The accommodation was dreadful, and so was the food.* (**também**)
4 used to agree with something that you have just been shown or told ◻ *'Look, our tomato seeds are coming up.' 'Oh, so they are!'* (**de fato**)
5 or so used to show that a number or amount is not exact ◻ *There were forty people or so at the party.* ◻ *I've been feeling ill for the last week or so.* (**aproximadamente**)
6 and so on used to show that other similar things could be added to what you have just said ◻ *Make sure you have plenty of pens, pencils, paper and so on.* (**e assim por diante**)
7 so far until now ◻ *I'm enjoying the job so far.* (**por enquanto, até agora**)
8 So what? used to show that you do not think something is important ◻ *'Sam will be cross if we're late.' 'So what? He can't do anything to us.'* (**e daí?**)

so² /səʊ/ CONJUNCTION
1 used to show that something was the reason for something else ◻ *He asked me to come, so I did.* ◻ *So they got married and lived happily ever after.* (**então**)
2 so (that) in order to make something happen ◻ *I've washed my jeans so that I can wear them tomorrow.* (**para que**)

soak /səʊk/ VERB [soaks, soaking, soaked]
1 to put something in liquid for a period of time ◻ *If you soak your blouse, the stain might come out.* (**deixar de molho**)
2 to make someone or something very wet ◻ *Heavy rain soaked the city.* (**encharcar**)
♦ PHRASAL VERB **soak something up** if something soaks up a liquid, it takes it in ◻ *I used a towel to soak up the spilt milk.* (**e daí?**)

soap /səʊp/ NOUN [plural soaps] a substance that you use for washing ▣ *a bar of soap* ◻ *He washed his face with soap and water.* (**sabão**)

soar /sɔː(r)/ VERB [soars, soaring, soared]
1 to increase very quickly to a high level ◻ *The price of petrol has soared over the last ten years.* (**subir**)
2 to fly high in the air ◻ *An eagle soared high above their heads.* (**voar alto**)

sob /sɒb/ VERB [sobs, sobbing, sobbed] to cry noisily ◻ *Lisa lay on her bed, sobbing.* (**soluçar**)

sober /ˈsəʊbə(r)/ ADJECTIVE not drunk (**sóbrio**)

soccer /ˈsɒkə(r)/ NOUN, NO PLURAL football ◻ *The children were playing soccer.* ◻ *a soccer ball* (**futebol**)

social /ˈsəʊʃəl/ ADJECTIVE
1 to do with society ◻ *The programme is designed to tackle crime and other social problems.* ◻ *The school attracts students from all social backgrounds.* (**social**)
2 to do with meeting and being friendly with other people ◻ *I always feel nervous in social situations.* ◻ *a social club* ▣ *He didn't have very good social skills.* (**social**)

social networking /ˌsəʊʃəl ˈnetwɜːkɪŋ/ NOUN, NO PLURAL using websites to meet people and talk to them (**rede social**)

society /səˈsaɪəti/ NOUN [plural societies]
1 all the people who live in a group or in a particular country or area ◻ *Racism still exists in British society.* ◻ *Australia is a more multicultural society.* ▣ *We have a responsibility to support the weaker members of society.* (**sociedade**)
2 an organization for people with a particular interest ◻ *She joined the university's debating society.* (**sociedade**)

sock /sɒk/ NOUN [plural socks] a covering for your foot that you wear inside your shoe ▣ *a pair of socks* ▣ *She was wearing black socks.* (**meia**)
♦ IDIOM **pull your socks up** to try to improve your behaviour or work ◻ *You'll have to pull your socks up if you want to pass the exam.*

socket /ˈsɒkɪt/ NOUN [plural sockets] the place on a wall where you connect electrical equipment to the electricity supply ◻ *an electric socket* (**tomada**)

> **THESAURUS:** The thing that you connect to a socket is called a **plug**. A **plug** is attached to a piece of electrical equipment by a **wire**. A **switch** is a thing that you press to make something work or stop working. Many sockets also have a **switch**.

sofa /ˈsəʊfə/ NOUN [plural sofas] a long, comfortable seat for more than one person ◻ *Dan and Clare were sitting on the sofa watching television.* (**sofá**)

soft /sɒft/ ADJECTIVE [softer, softest]
1 not hard or firm ◻ *a nice soft cushion* ◻ *soft ground* (**macio**)
2 smooth and pleasant to touch ◻ *She had soft silky hair.* ◻ *soft leather* (**macio**)
3 not loud ◻ *a soft voice* (**suave**)
4 not bright ◻ *Her bedroom is decorated in soft pastel colours.* ◻ *a soft light* (**suave**)

soft drink /ˌsɒft ˈdrɪŋk/ NOUN [plural soft drinks] a cold drink that does not contain alcohol (**bebida não alcoólica**)

soften /ˈsɒfən/ VERB [softens, softening, softened] to become soft or to make something soft □ *Soften the clay by working it with your hands.* (**suavizar**)

softly /'sɒftli/ ADVERB gently or quietly □ *Snow was falling softly in the moonlight.* □ *She stroked the cat softly.* (**suavemente**)

software /'sɒftweə(r)/ NOUN, NO PLURAL computer programs. A computing word. 🔲 *We've installed new software.* 🔲 *Users need to download a piece of software.* (**software**)

soil /sɔɪl/ NOUN, NO PLURAL the top layer of the ground, that you can grow plants in □ *a soil sample* □ *Rice and corn grow well in the rich soil.* □ *He brushed the red, sandy soil off his trousers.* (**terra**)

solar /'səʊlə(r)/ ADJECTIVE
1 to do with the sun □ *a solar eclipse* (**solar**)
2 to do with energy from the sun □ *solar panels* (**solar**)

solar system /'səʊlə ˌsɪstəm/ NOUN [plural **solar systems**] the sun and the planets that move around it (**sistema solar**)

sold /səʊld/ PAST TENSE AND PAST PARTICIPLE OF **sell** (ver **sell**)

soldier /'səʊldʒə(r)/ NOUN [plural **soldiers**] someone who is in the army □ *Two soldiers from the same regiment were captured.* (**soldado, militar**)

sole[1] /səʊl/ ADJECTIVE only □ *Her sole ambition was to be famous.* □ *A young boy was the sole survivor of the accident.* (**único**)

sole[2] /səʊl/ NOUN [plural **soles**] the bottom part of your foot or of a shoe 🔲 *The sand was hot on the soles of her feet.* (**sola**)

sole[3] /səʊl/ NOUN [plural **sole**] a flat fish that people can eat (**linguado**)

solemn /'sɒləm/ ADJECTIVE serious and sometimes sad □ *a solemn expression* □ *a rather solemn little boy* (**sério**)

solicitor /sə'lɪsɪtə(r)/ NOUN [plural **solicitors**] someone whose job is to give advice to people about the law and help them with legal work □ *a firm of solicitors* (**advogado**)

solid[1] /'sɒlɪd/ ADJECTIVE
1 firm and with a fixed shape, not in the form of a liquid or a gas 🔲 *They scrambled through the mud to more solid ground.* □ *The river froze solid.* (**sólido**)
2 not hollow or with no spaces inside □ *a solid chocolate egg* 🔲 *They had to cut through solid rock.* (**maciço**)
3 solid gold, silver, etc. made only of gold, silver, etc. □ *a solid gold pendant* (**maciço**)

> **THESAURUS:** If something is **firm**, it is not soft. Something which is **solid** is firm and has a fixed shape, or does not have any spaces inside. Something which is **hollow** has an empty space inside. A football is **hollow**. Something which is **hard** is firm and is not easy to bend or break. Something which is **stable** is strong and does not move easily.

solid[2] /'sɒlɪd/ NOUN [plural **solids**] something that is not a liquid or a gas □ *This element changes from a solid to a gas when heated.* (**sólido**)

solo[1] /'səʊləʊ/ NOUN [plural **solos**] a piece of music or a song for one person to play or sing □ *a guitar solo* □ *Emma sang a solo in the Christmas concert.* (**solo**)

solo[2] /'səʊləʊ/ ADJECTIVE done or performed by one person alone □ *a solo flight* □ *a solo album* □ *He went on to have a career as a solo artist.* (**solo**)

solution /sə'luːʃən/ NOUN [plural **solutions**] an answer to a problem or a question □ **+ to** *It's difficult to offer simple solutions to a complex problem.* 🔲 *We must try to find a peaceful solution.* (**solução**)

> Remember that 'solution' is followed by the preposition **to**:
> ✓ *There is no easy solution to the problem.*
> ✗ *There is no easy solution of the problem.*

solve /sɒlv/ VERB [**solves, solving, solved**] to find an answer to a problem or a difficult question □ *Solve the puzzle to win a prize.* 🔲 *A new bridge won't solve the traffic problem.* 🔲 *This information could help us to solve the crime.* (**resolver**)

solvent[1] /'sɒlvənt/ NOUN [plural **solvents**] something that dissolves another substance. A chemistry word. (**solvente**)

solvent[2] /'sɒlvənt/ ADJECTIVE having enough money to pay what you owe □ *At last they were financially solvent.* (**solvente**)

some /sʌm/ DETERMINER, PRONOUN
1 used to talk about a number or an amount without saying exactly how many or how much □ *It's all right; I've got some money.* □ *Would you like some more milk?* □ *I've made a cake – would you like some?* (**algum, um pouco**)
2 used to talk about part of a larger amount or number of things or people □ **+ of** *Some of the apples were rotten.* □ *Some people have brought rain coats and some haven't.* (**algum**)
3 used to talk about a person or a thing when you do not know exactly who or what they are □ *He mentioned some letter that he had received.* □ *Some silly person forgot to close the gate.* (**algum**)

somebody /'sʌmbədi/ PRONOUN used to talk about a person when you do not know who they are or it is not necessary to say their name □ *Somebody knocked at the door.* □ *They get money every time somebody downloads a song.* □ *She's somebody who's popular at school.* 🔲 *Let somebody else* (= another person) *do it for a change.* (**alguém**)

somehow /'sʌmhaʊ/ ADVERB in a way that is not known or you do not understand □ *Don't worry, we'll manage somehow.* □ *She'd somehow managed to get her finger caught in the mechanism.*

☐ *Somehow, it didn't seem very important.* ☐ *He'll succeed in the end, somehow or other.* (**de algum jeito**)

someone /'sʌmwʌn/ PRONOUN used to talk about a person when you do not know who they are or it is not necessary to say their name ☐ *We'll have to find someone to replace him.* ☐ *I was having a conversation with someone at work about it.* ☐ *It could save someone's life.* ☐ *It's good to have someone else* (= another person) *to blame.* (**alguém**)

something /'sʌmθɪŋ/ PRONOUN
1 used to talk about a thing or a fact when you do not know what it is, or when it is not necessary to say what it is ☐ *I've got something in my eye.* ☐ *Let's have something to eat before we go.* ☐ *She told me something else as well.* ☐ *The roof's leaking and we need to do something about it.* (**alguma coisa**)
2 used to show that what you have said is only a guess or an example ☐ *I think he's an actor or something like that.* ☐ *She speaks something like ten different languages.* ☐ *We could take her some flowers or something.* (**algo assim**)

sometimes /'sʌmtaɪmz/ ADVERB at times, but not always ☐ *I still see him sometimes.* ☐ *Sometimes I feel like giving up my job and moving away.* (**às vezes**)

somewhat /'sʌmwɒt/ ADVERB quite or slightly ☐ *The wind had died down somewhat.* (**algo**)

somewhere /'sʌmweə(r)/ ADVERB used to talk about a place when you do not know where it is, or when it is not necessary to say where it is ☐ *Let's go away somewhere for a few days.* ☐ *They live somewhere near Oxford.* ☐ *It must be around here somewhere.* ☐ *Put it somewhere safe.* ☐ *If you don't like it, we can go somewhere else* (= to another place). (**algum lugar**)

son /sʌn/ NOUN [plural **sons**] someone's male child ☐ *They have two young sons.* ☐ *Her eldest son, Dave, is at university.* ☐ *+ of He's the son of Algerian immigrants.* (**filho**)

song /sɒŋ/ NOUN [plural **songs**]
1 a piece of music with words that you sing ☐ *a pop song* ☐ *This is one of my favourite songs.* ☐ *She mostly sings folk songs.* (**canção**)
2 no plural songs in general or the activity of singing ☐ *A blackbird suddenly burst into song.* ☐ *a song and dance routine* (**canto**)

son-in-law /'sʌnɪnˌlɔː/ NOUN [plural **sons-in-law**] your daughter's husband (**genro**)

soon /suːn/ ADVERB [**sooner, soonest**]
1 in a short time from now ☐ *It will soon be summer.* ☐ *I hope to see you soon.* ☐ *Soon we'll be reaching Liverpool* ☐ *I'd like the work done by Friday, or sooner if you can.* ☐ *I'll do it as soon as I can.* (**logo**)
2 as soon as immediately ☐ *As soon as I saw her, I knew something was wrong.* ☐ *He started shouting at us as soon as we arrived.* (**logo que**)

3 sooner or later used to say that you are certain that something will happen at some time in the future ☐ *Sooner or later there's going to be an accident.* (**mais cedo ou mais tarde**)
4 too soon too early ☐ *It's too soon to tell whether she'll recover.* ☐ *Help arrived not a moment too soon.* (**muito cedo**)

soothe /suːð/ VERB [**soothes, soothing, soothed**]
1 to make someone feel calmer or happier ☐ *She was unable to soothe her crying baby.* (**acalmar**)
2 to make pain less strong ☐ *I had a bath to soothe my sore muscles.* (**aplacar, aliviar**)

sophisticated /sə'fɪstɪkeɪtɪd/ ADJECTIVE
1 knowing a lot about the world, culture, fashion, etc. ☐ *a highly sophisticated audience* ☐ *It's a sophisticated and cosmopolitan city.* (**sofisticado, refinado**)
2 using new and clever ideas ☐ *highly sophisticated software* (**elaborado, complexo**)

sore¹ /sɔː(r)/ ADJECTIVE [**sorer, sorest**] if a part of your body is sore, it is painful ☐ *a sore finger* ☐ *She woke up with a sore throat.* ☐ *My legs feel sore today.* (**dolorido**)

sore² /sɔː(r)/ NOUN [plural **sores**] a red, painful place on your skin ☐ *The horse had a nasty sore on its leg.* (**ferida**)

sorry /'sɒrɪ/ ADJECTIVE [**sorrier, sorriest**]
1 (I'm) sorry (a) something that you say when you have done something wrong, hurt someone, upset someone, etc. ☐ *Sorry, I didn't mean to hurt you.* ☐ *I'm so sorry – I've spilt tea on your carpet.* ☐ *He broke my chair and he never even said sorry.* (b) something you say to be polite when you have to tell someone something they may not like ☐ *Sorry, the shop's closing now.* ☐ *I'm sorry, but this work just isn't good enough.* (**desculpa**)
2 ashamed about something that you have done and wishing you had not done it ☐ *She knows how much she upset us, and she's not even sorry.* ☐ *+ that I'm really sorry that I lied to you.* ☐ *+ about I'm sorry about forgetting your birthday.* ☐ *+ for He's truly sorry for spoiling your party.* (**arrependido**)
3 feeling sympathy for someone ☐ *I was sorry to hear about your father.* ☐ *+ for I feel really sorry for Anna, having to travel on her own.* ☐ *+ that I was sorry that you didn't get the job.* (**triste, ter pena**)
4 used to say that you wish a situation could have been different ☐ *+ that I was sorry that I never met her.* ☐ *+ to do something I think they were sorry to leave.* (**desolado**)

sort¹ /sɔːt/ NOUN [plural **sorts**]
1 a type of thing or person ☐ *+ of What sort of books do you read?* ☐ *We won't tolerate that sort of behaviour here.* ☐ *It's the sort of shop that might sell matches.* ☐ *There were all sorts of people there.* ☐ *She needs to take up a hobby of some sort.* ☐ *He enjoys skiing and that sort of thing.* (**tipo**)
2 sort of similar, but not exactly what has been said ☐ *I think she'd sort of forgotten about us by then.* ☐ *The house was sort of cut out of the rock.* (**meio**)

sort² /sɔːt/ VERB [sorts, sorting, sorted] to arrange things or people into groups or into a particular order □ + **into** *We sorted the books into piles by subject*. (separar, classificar)

◆ PHRASAL VERB **sort something out** to arrange or deal successfully with something □ *We've sorted out a new system for feeding the cattle*. □ *Did you manage to sort out Jackie's problem with her computer?*

so-so /ˈsəʊsəʊ/ ADJECTIVE not very good but not very bad □ *The restaurant looked nice but the meal was so-so*. (mais ou menos)

sought /sɔːt/ PAST TENSE AND PAST PARTICIPLE OF **seek** (ver seek)

soul /səʊl/ NOUN [plural **souls**]
1 the part of a person that is not their body but which some people believe continues to exist after they die □ *the souls of the dead* □ *God rest his soul*. (alma)
2 a type of pop music that expresses strong emotions, especially played by Black Americans 🔊 *a soul singer* 🔊 *He grew up listening to soul music*. (soul)

sound¹ /saʊnd/ NOUN [plural **sounds**] something that you can hear 🔊 *I could hear a faint sound*. □ + **of** *We heard the sound of breaking glass*. 🔊 *Elspeth made a sound of disgust*. □ *There isn't a sound coming from the children's bedroom*. (som, barulho)

sound² /saʊnd/ VERB [sounds, sounding, sounded]
1 if something sounds good, bad, etc., it seems that way from what you have heard or read □ *Tom's holiday sounds wonderful*. □ *I don't want to sound too negative*. □ *I don't think that sounds right. Are you sure?* 🔊 *That sounds like a good idea*. (parecer)
2 used to talk about a noise that you hear □ *His voice sounded shaky*. □ *All their songs sound exactly the same*. 🔊 *That sounds like Zoe's voice in the kitchen*. (soar)
3 to make a noise □ *Sound your horn before you turn the corner*. □ *If the fire alarm sounds, leave the building immediately*. (tocar)

sound³ /saʊnd/ ADVERB **sound asleep** if someone is sound asleep, they are sleeping and it is difficult to wake them □ *At ten o'clock I was still sound asleep*. (profundamente adormecido)

sound⁴ /saʊnd/ ADJECTIVE [sounder, soundest]
1 strong, firm, or healthy □ *The walls of the old church were still sound*. □ *Her health was pretty sound*. (forte)
2 good, sensible and that you can trust 🔊 *It seemed like sound advice*. □ *The recommendations are based on scientifically sound evidence*. (sólido, consistente)

soup /suːp/ NOUN [plural **soups**] a liquid food made from meat, fish, or vegetables □ *a bowl of chicken soup* (sopa)

sour /ˈsaʊə(r)/ ADJECTIVE [sourer, sourest] sour food has a bitter taste like a lemon, sometimes because it is bad □ *sour plums* □ *a sour taste* 🔊 *The milk had gone sour in the sun*. (azedo, ácido)

▶ THESAURUS: Sweet food tastes like sugar, or contains sugar. Salty food contains salt, or tastes of salt. Bitter food has a strong taste such as the taste of strong coffee or dark chocolate. Sour food has a sharp taste, like the taste of a lemon. Sometimes sour food tastes unpleasant because it has gone bad, for example sour milk.

source /sɔːs/ NOUN [plural **sources**] where something begins or comes from 🔊 *renewable energy sources* □ *Nuts are a rich source of protein*. □ *Tourism is the island's main source of income*. (fonte, origem)

south¹ /saʊθ/ NOUN, NO PLURAL the direction that is to your right when you are facing towards the rising sun (sul)

south² /saʊθ/ ADJECTIVE, ADVERB in or towards the south □ *the south coast* □ *The river flows south into the sea*. (para o sul)

south-east¹ /ˌsaʊθˈiːst/ NOUN, NO PLURAL the direction between south and east (sudeste)
south-east² /ˌsaʊθˈiːst/ ADJECTIVE, ADVERB in or towards the south-east □ *the south-east coast* (para o sudeste)

southern /ˈsʌðən/ ADJECTIVE in or from the south □ *the southern states of the USA* (meridional, sul)

South Pole /ˌsaʊθ ˈpəʊl/ NOUN **the South Pole** the point on the Earth that is furthest South (polo sul)
south-west¹ /ˌsaʊθˈwest/ NOUN, NO PLURAL the direction between south and west (sudoeste)
south-west² /ˌsaʊθˈwest/ ADJECTIVE, ADVERB in or towards the south-west (para o sudoeste)

souvenir /ˌsuːvəˈnɪə(r)/ NOUN [plural **souvenirs**] something that you buy to help you remember a particular place or occasion □ + **of** *We brought back some shells as souvenirs of our holiday*. 🔊 *a souvenir shop* (lembrança)

sow¹ /səʊ/ VERB [sows, sowing, sowed, sown] to put seeds on or in the ground so that they will grow (semear)
sow² /saʊ/ NOUN [plural **sows**] a female pig (porca)

▶ This meaning of **sow** rhymes with **how**.

space¹ /speɪs/ NOUN [plural **spaces**]
1 *no plural* the area available to be used □ *There isn't enough space to hold a party here*. 🔊 *Can you make space for one more person?* 🔊 *We created more space by removing all the shelves*. 🔊 *I don't have enough disk space*. (espaço)
2 an empty area □ *Write your name in the space at the top of the sheet*. 🔊 *I couldn't find a parking space*. 🔊 *It is important for cities to have plenty of open spaces*. (lugar)

space | specific

3 *no plural* the area outside the Earth's atmosphere, where the planets and stars are □ *Another rocket was launched into space yesterday.* (space)

> Remember that when you say 'space' meaning 'the area outside the Earth's atmosphere', you do not use the word 'the' before it:
> ✓ He's always been very interested in space.
> ✗ He's always been very interested in the space.

space² /speɪs/ VERB [spaces, spacing, spaced] to arrange things so that they have a particular distance or amount of time between them □ *Plants were spaced at intervals of roughly 50 centimetres.* □ *The journeys were spaced over a five year period.* (espaçar)

spacecraft /ˈspeɪskrɑːft/ NOUN [plural spacecraft or spacecrafts] a vehicle that can travel into space (nave espacial)

space shuttle /ˈspeɪs ˌʃʌtəl/ NOUN [plural space shuttles] a vehicle like a plane that can travel into space and come back to Earth to be used again (ônibus espacial)

spade /speɪd/ NOUN [plural spades]
1 a tool with a wide flat part that you use for digging (pá)
2 spades one of the four types of playing card, which have the symbol (♠) printed on them □ *the ace of spades* (espadas)

spaghetti /spəˈɡeti/ NOUN, NO PLURAL a type of pasta that is like long thin string □ *spaghetti with tomato sauce* (espaguete)

spam /spæm/ NOUN, NO PLURAL e-mails that you do not want, especially e-mails trying to sell you things. A computing word. (spam)

span¹ /spæn/ NOUN [plural spans] the length of time that something lasts □ *The country had changed completely within a span of twenty years.* □ *Most toddlers have a very short attention span.* (período)

span² /spæn/ VERB [spans, spanning, spanned]
1 to last for a particular period of time □ *His singing career spanned three decades.* (durar)
2 to go across an area □ *An old wooden bridge spans the river.* (atravessar)

spare¹ /speə(r)/ ADJECTIVE
1 extra and available to be used □ *I stayed in Fiona's spare room.* □ *I've got a spare ticket for Saturday's concert, if you'd like it.* □ *Neither of us had any spare cash.* (de reserva)
2 spare time time when you do not have to work and can do what you want □ *What do you do in your spare time?* (disponível)

spare² /speə(r)/ VERB [spares, sparing, spared] to be able to give or lend something to someone because you do not need it yourself □ *Could you spare me a few pounds?* □ *We can't spare anyone to help out today.* (dispensar)

spark /spɑːk/ NOUN [plural sparks] a very small burning piece that is sent out from a fire or made by rubbing two hard surfaces together □ *A shower of sparks shot out of the bonfire.* (faísca)

sparkle /ˈspɑːkəl/ NOUN [plural sparkles] points of bright light □ *the sparkle of the sea* (brilho)

speak /spiːk/ VERB [speaks, speaking, spoke, spoken]
1 to say something □ *+ to Could I speak to you for a moment?* □ *+ about He never spoke publicly about his marriage.* □ *She was so tired she could hardly speak.* □ *We all sat there, and nobody spoke.* (falar)
2 to be able to talk in a particular language □ *Do you speak Greek?* (falar)
3 Speaking. something you say when someone on the telephone asks to speak to you □ *'May I speak to Mrs Kennedy?' 'Speaking.'* (falando)
◆ PHRASAL VERB **speak up 1** to say something more loudly □ *Could you speak up, please?* **2** to tell people your opinion about something □ *We all thought our boss was being unfair, but nobody was brave enough to speak up.*

speaker /ˈspiːkə(r)/ NOUN [plural speakers]
1 a piece of equipment that the sound from a radio, CD player, etc. comes out of (alto-falante)
2 someone who gives a speech □ *Our guest speaker tonight is from Oxfam.* (orador, locutor)

spear /spɪə(r)/ NOUN [plural spears] a long thin weapon with a sharp metal point (lança, arpão)

special /ˈspeʃəl/ ADJECTIVE
1 unusual, and usually better than what is normal □ *We've been saving this wine for a special occasion.* □ *My boyfriend always makes me feel really special.* □ *We've all been making a special effort to be friendly.* (especial)
2 meant for or having a particular purpose □ *Special trains will take fans to the match.* □ *a special tool for making rugs* (especial)

specialist /ˈspeʃəlɪst/ NOUN [plural specialists] someone who knows a lot about a particular subject □ *My GP has referred me to a heart specialist.* (especialista)

specially /ˈspeʃəli/ ADVERB for one particular purpose □ *Jo's had her costume specially made for the party.* (especialmente)

species /ˈspiːʃiːz/ NOUN [plural species] a group of animals or plants whose members have similar features and that can produce young together □ *a rare species of orchid* (espécie)

specific /spəˈsɪfɪk/ ADJECTIVE
1 giving all the details about something in a clear way □ *Sarah's directions weren't very specific.* (específico)
2 exactly as has been stated or described □ *Each child has his own specific jobs to do.* (específico)

specimen /ˈspesɪmən/ NOUN [plural **specimens**] a small amount of blood etc. that can be tested by doctors or scientists □ *a specimen of urine* (**amostra, espécime**)

spectacle /ˈspektəkəl/ NOUN [plural **spectacles**] something that is interesting, exciting or surprising to see □ *The opening ceremony of the games was a wonderful spectacle.* (**espetáculo**)

spectacular /spekˈtækjulə(r)/ ADJECTIVE very interesting, exciting or surprising □ *a spectacular firework display* □ *The scenery was absolutely spectacular.* (**espetador**)

spectator /spekˈteɪtə(r)/ NOUN [plural **spectators**] someone who is watching an event □ *United won the match in front of more than 60,000 spectators.* (**espetador**)

sped /sped/ PAST TENSE AND PAST PARTICIPLE OF **speed**² □ *A bullet sped past his ear.* (**ver speed²**)

speech /spiːtʃ/ NOUN [plural **speeches**]
1 a talk that you give in front of a group of people ▣ *The bride's father usually makes a speech.* (**discurso**)
2 no plural the ability to speak ▣ *He seemed to have lost the power of speech.* (**linguagem**)
3 no plural the particular way that someone speaks □ *She was so tired that her speech was slurred.* (**modo de falar**)

> Note that when you speak formally in front of a group of people, you **make a speech**. You can also **give a speech**:
> ✓ *I had to make/give a speech at the wedding.*
> ✗ *I had to do a speech at the wedding.*

speed¹ /spiːd/ NOUN [plural **speeds**]
1 how quickly someone or something moves □ *He was driving at a speed of about 30 miles per hour.* □ *The train was travelling at speed when it hit the rocks on the track.* ▣ *What's the top speed of this model?* (**velocidade**)
2 how quickly someone or something works or something happens □ *Our new programs offer accuracy and speed.* □ *The managers are very pleased with the speed of her progress.* ▣ *You'll gradually pick up speed as you learn the job.* (**rapidez**)

speed² /spiːd/ VERB [**speeds, speeding, sped** or **speeded**] to move, go or pass quickly □ *He sped off down the road on his bike.* □ *The hours sped by as we sat and chatted.* (**ir em alta velocidade**)
♦ PHRASAL VERB **speed (something) up** to go faster or make something faster □ *Accepting online applications should speed up the recruitment process.*

speedy /ˈspiːdɪ/ ADJECTIVE [**speedier, speediest**] quick or fast □ *Thanks for the speedy reply to my letter.* (**rápido**)

spell¹ /spel/ VERB [**spells, spelling, spelt** or **spelled**] to say or write the letters of a word in the correct order □ *Could you spell your name for me?* □ *Adam was always good at spelling.* (**soletrar**)

spell² /spel/ NOUN [plural **spells**] a set of words that are used to make something magic happen ▣ *The wicked witch cast a spell on Snow White.* (**fórmula mágica**)

spelling /ˈspelɪŋ/ NOUN [plural **spellings**]
1 the way that a word is spelt □ *'Donut' is the American spelling of 'doughnut'.* (**ortografia**)
2 no plural the ability to spell □ *His spelling is terrible.* (**soletrar**)

spend /spend/ VERB [**spends, spending, spent**]
1 to use money to buy things ▣ *We spent a lot of money on our holiday.* □ *Try to cut down how much you spend.* (**gastar**)
2 to pass time doing something ▣ *Do you spend much time on the computer?* ▣ *I used to spend hours reading in my room.* ▣ *I spent ages decorating that cake.* □ *We spent the weekend at my sister's.* (**passar**)

> Note that you spend money **on** someone or something:
> ✓ *She spends a lot of money on clothes.*
> ✗ *She spends a lot of money for clothes.*

sperm /spɜːm/ NOUN [plural **sperm** or **sperms**] a cell from a man that joins with the egg from a woman to make a baby. A biology word. (**espermatozoide**)

sphere /sfɪə(r)/ NOUN [plural **spheres**] a solid object that is the shape of a ball (**esfera**)

spice /spaɪs/ NOUN [plural **spices**] a substance made from a plant that adds flavour to food □ *herbs and spices* □ *Ginger is a spice.* (**condimento**)

spicy /ˈspaɪsɪ/ ADJECTIVE [**spicier, spiciest**] tasting hot on your tongue □ *spicy food* (**apimentado**)

spider /ˈspaɪdə(r)/ NOUN [plural **spiders**] a small creature with eight legs that uses very thin threads to make a web (= very thin net) for catching insects (**aranha**)

spike /spaɪk/ NOUN [plural **spikes**] a hard, sharp point, usually made of metal or wood □ *There were sharp spikes on top of the wall.* (**ponta, espigão**)

spill /spɪl/ VERB [**spills, spilling, spilt** or **spilled**] to come out of a container by accident or to make something, especially a liquid, do this □ *Careful! You're going to spill your tea.* □ *She spilt a can of paint all over the carpet.* □ *The sack burst and the rice spilled out onto the floor.* (**derramar, transbordar, espalhar**)

> THESAURUS: If something **spills**, it comes out of a container by accident or you make something, especially a liquid, do this. If you **pour** a liquid, you make it come out of a container such as a jug or bottle. For example, you might **pour** a glass of orange juice from a bottle. If you **tip** a liquid somewhere, you pour it out of a container. If you **tip**, something, it is often less careful than **pouring**. For example, you might **tip** water into a sink when you have finished using it.

spin /spɪn/ VERB [spins, spinning, spun]
1 to turn round and round very quickly or make something do this □ *The ballerina spun round and round on her toes.* □ *He can spin the basketball on his finger.* (girar, rodopiar)
2 to make long, thin threads out of cotton, wool, or other material by pulling it and twisting it (fiar)

spinach /ˈspɪnɪdʒ/ NOUN, NO PLURAL a vegetable with large dark green leaves (espinafre)

spinal /ˈspaɪnəl/ ADJECTIVE to do with the line of bones down the back of a person or animal. A biology word. □ *a spinal injury* (espinhal)

spine /spaɪn/ NOUN [plural spines] the line of bones down the back of a person or animal. A biology word. (coluna vertebral, espinha)

spiral /ˈspaɪərəl/ NOUN [plural spirals] a shape formed by a line that curves round and round a centre point □ *The shell formed a perfect spiral.* (espiral)

spirit /ˈspɪrɪt/ NOUN [plural spirits]
1 your attitude or the attitude of a group of people □ *+ of The celebration was held in a spirit of friendship.* □ *Her adventurous spirit took her all over the world.* □ *Our town has a strong community spirit.* (espírito)
2 spirits your mood 🗏 *She was in really high/low spirits* (= a happy/sad mood). (humor, ânimo)
3 a strong alcoholic drink, for example whisky (bebida alcoólica forte)
4 the part of a person that some people believe continues to live after the body dies (espírito)

spiritual /ˈspɪrɪtʃuəl/ ADJECTIVE to do with someone's spirit, emotions and thoughts and not their body □ *an intensely spiritual experience* (espiritual)

spit /spɪt/ VERB [spits, spitting, spat] to force liquid or food out of your mouth □ *She took one mouthful and then spat it out on to her plate.* (cuspir)

spite /spaɪt/ NOUN, NO PLURAL
1 in spite of used to say that a fact or event makes something else that happens surprising □ *We decided to go to the seaside in spite of the rain.* □ *He passed his exam in spite of doing no revision.* (apesar de, a despeito de)
2 a feeling of wanting to hurt or upset someone □ *He threw my picture away out of spite.* (rancor)

splash¹ /splæʃ/ VERB [splashes, splashing, splashed]
1 to put liquid on something with a quick movement □ *Kate splashed some cold water on her face.* (salpicar)
2 to move water around in a noisy way □ *The baby was splashing happily in his bath.* (espirrar, borrifar)

splash² /splæʃ/ NOUN [plural splashes] the sound that water makes when something hits it □ *Kurt fell into the pool with a loud splash.* (chape)

splendid /ˈsplendɪd/ ADJECTIVE very good □ *a splendid idea* (esplêndido)

split¹ /splɪt/ VERB [splits, splitting, split]
1 to break or tear apart □ *Your trousers have split down the back.* (rachar)
2 to break something or tear it apart □ *The lightning had split the tree in two.* (rachar)
3 to divide a group of people into smaller groups □ *I split the children into two groups.* (dividir)
4 to end a marriage or relationship □ *I was three when my parents split.* □ *I've just split up with my boyfriend.* (separar)

split² /splɪt/ NOUN [plural splits] a tear or break in something □ *There's a long split in the wood.* (rachadura)

spoil /spɔɪl/ VERB [spoils, spoiling, spoilt or spoiled]
1 to make something less good □ *I had an argument with Adrian and it spoilt the whole evening.* □ *Low cloud spoilt the view of the mountains.* □ *The weather was fairly awful but we didn't let it spoil our fun.* (estragar)
2 to always allow a child to have or do what they want and cause them to become badly behaved □ *She spoils those children.* (mimar)

spoilt /spɔɪlt/ PAST TENSE AND PAST PARTICIPLE OF **spoil** (ver spoil)

spoke¹ /spəʊk/ PAST TENSE OF **speak** (ver speak)

spoke² /spəʊk/ NOUN [plural spokes] one of the thin metal pieces that connect the centre of a wheel with the edge (raio)

spoken /ˈspəʊkən/ PAST PARTICIPLE OF **speak** (ver speak)

sponge /spʌndʒ/ NOUN [plural sponges] a soft object, made from natural or artificial material, that you use to wash your body (esponja)

sponsor¹ /ˈspɒnsə(r)/ VERB [sponsors, sponsoring, sponsored]
1 to pay for something such as an event or television programme, often as a way of advertising your company □ *A local company sponsors our football team.* (patrocinar)
2 to agree to give someone money for a school, organization, etc. if they do something difficult □ *Will you sponsor me to run in the race?* (patrocinar)

sponsor² /ˈspɒnsə(r)/ NOUN [plural sponsors]
1 a company that gives money to someone or something as a way of advertising the company □ *The company is the official sponsor of the 2008 European Cup.* (patrocinar)
2 a person who gives money to a charity (= organization that helps people) if someone else does something difficult □ *How many sponsors have you got?* (patrocinador)

• **sponsored** /ˈspɒnsəd/ ADJECTIVE **a sponsored swim/walk, etc.** a swim or walk, etc. that you do to get money for a school or charity (= organization that helps people), in which people agree to give you money if you are successful

• **sponsorship** /ˈspɒnsəʃɪp/ NOUN, NO PLURAL when someone sponsors someone or something 🗏 *Toyota announced a five-year sponsorship deal with the American Football League.*

spoon /spu:n/ NOUN [plural **spoons**] an object with a handle and a curved part at one end that you use for lifting liquid food to your mouth □ *a soup spoon* □ *a wooden spoon* (colher)

spoonful /'spu:nfʊl/ NOUN [plural **spoonfuls**] the amount a spoon will hold □ *Jamila put a spoonful of sugar in her coffee.* (colherada)

sport /spɔːt/ NOUN [plural **sports**]
1 a particular game or activity □ *Football is a very popular sport.* □ *My Dad has played sports all his life.* □ *We have very good sports facilities at our school.* (esporte)
2 no plural games and physical activities like football, tennis, and swimming □ *Adam loves all kinds of sport.* □ *She watches a lot of sport on the television.* (esporte)

sports car /spɔːts kɑː(r)/ NOUN [plural **sports cars**] a small fast car that has two seats and no roof (carro esporte)

spot¹ /spɒt/ NOUN [plural **spots**]
1 a place or position □ *This is a lovely spot for a picnic.* □ *X marks the spot where the treasure is buried.* □ *She hopes to retain her number one spot in the championship.* (lugar)
2 a round shape that is often part of a pattern □ *She wore a pink dress with white spots.* (pinta)
3 a red raised mark on your skin □ *Teenagers often suffer from spots.* (marca)

spot² /spɒt/ VERB [**spots, spotting, spotted**] to see or notice something or someone □ *I suddenly spotted Ian over by the window.* □ *Social workers spotted signs of neglect in the girl.* (avistar)

spouse /spaʊs/ NOUN [plural **spouses**] a formal word meaning your husband or wife (cônjuge)

sprang /spræŋ/ PAST TENSE OF **spring²** (ver **spring²**)

spray¹ /spreɪ/ VERB [**sprays, spraying, sprayed**] to cause a liquid to come out of a container in many very small drops □ *She sprayed herself with perfume.* (borrifar)

spray² /spreɪ/ NOUN [plural **sprays**]
1 many very small drops of liquid in the air □ *The spray from the waterfall wet their hair.* (borrifo)
2 liquid in a container which is forced out in very small drops □ *a perfume spray* (spray)

spread /spred/ VERB [**spreads, spreading, spread**]
1 to cover a larger area or to affect more and more people, or to make something do this □ *The cancer has spread to his lungs.* □ *The virus spread rapidly in the crowded conditions.* □ *I don't want to spread alarm.* □ *Fire spread throughout the building.* (espalhar)
2 to arrange something so that it covers a large area □ **+ out** *I spread the map out on the table.* □ *The bird spread its wings and flew off.* □ *Bits of machinery were spread all over the floor.* (abrir)
3 if information spreads, or you spread it, it becomes known by more and more people □ *Rumours spread very quickly in this little village.* □ *News of his death spread rapidly.* (espalhar)
4 to put a layer of a soft substance onto a surface □ *She spread her toast thickly with butter.* (cobrir)

spring¹ /sprɪŋ/ NOUN [plural **springs**]
1 the season between winter and summer when plants start to grow □ *Daffodils flower in spring.* □ *There will be an election next spring.* □ *spring sunshine* (primavera)
2 a twisted piece of wire which goes back to its original shape after you have pushed or pulled it □ *The chair had some broken springs in it.* (mola)
3 a place where water flows out of the ground □ *a mountain spring* □ *spring water* (fonte)

spring² /sprɪŋ/ VERB [**springs, springing, sprang, sprung**] to move or jump quickly □ *He sprang out of bed to answer the door.* (saltar, pular)

sprinkle /'sprɪŋkəl/ VERB [**sprinkles, sprinkling, sprinkled**] to put small drops or pieces of something over a surface □ *She sprinkled chocolate chips onto the cake.* (salpicar, borrifar)

sprout /spraʊt/ VERB [**sprouts, sprouting, sprouted**] to start to grow, or to produce new leaves or flowers □ *Buds were sprouting on the sycamore tree.* (brotar)

spruce /spruːs/ NOUN [plural **spruces**] a tall tree with leaves that look like needles (abeto vermelho)

sprung /sprʌŋ/ PAST PARTICIPLE OF **spring²** (ver **spring²**)

spun /spʌn/ PAST TENSE AND PAST PARTICIPLE OF **spin** (ver **spin**)

spy¹ /spaɪ/ NOUN [plural **spies**] someone whose job is to discover secret information about another country or company □ *a former Russian spy* (espião)

spy² /spaɪ/ VERB [**spies, spying, spied**] to work as a spy □ *Both men had been spying for the government.* (espionar)
♦ PHRASAL VERB **spy on someone** to secretly watch what someone is doing □ *Hetty spent a lot of time spying on her neighbours.*

square¹ /skweə(r)/ NOUN [plural squares]
1 a flat shape with four equal sides and four angles of 90 degrees (**quadrado**)
2 an open space with buildings on all four sides □ *a tree-lined square* □ *There was a clock in the market square.* □ *Trafalgar Square* (**praça**)
3 the result of multiplying a number by itself. A mathematics word □ *The square of 4 is 16.* (**quadrado**)

square² /skweə(r)/ ADJECTIVE
1 shaped like a square □ *a square table* (**quadrado**)
2 measuring a particular amount on each side □ *The room was about 3 metres square.* (**quadrado**)
3 a square metre/foot/mile, etc. the area of a square which has sides which are a metre, a mile, etc. long □ *The tiles cost £20 a square metre.* □ *The building offers 65,000 square metres of office space.* (**quadrado**)

squash¹ /skwɒʃ/ VERB [squashes, squashing, squashed]
1 to press something until it is flat □ *Juliet squashed the empty can.* ▣ *All the strawberries got squashed at the bottom of the bag.* (**espremer, esmagar**)
2 to put a lot of people or things into a small space □ *I was squashed in the back seat of the car with three other people.* □ **+ into** *12 of us squashed into two cars to travel into town.* (**espremer**)

squash² /skwɒʃ/ NOUN, NO PLURAL
1 a game in which you hit a small rubber ball against the walls of a court (**squash**)
2 a sweet cold drink with a fruit flavour □ *a glass of orange squash* (**suco de**)

squeak /skwi:k/ NOUN [plural squeaks] a very high sound (**guincho**)

squeeze /skwi:z/ VERB [squeezes, squeezing, squeezed]
1 to press something tightly □ *She squeezed my hand encouragingly.* (**comprimir, apertar**)
2 to try to move somewhere where there is very little space □ *The cat tried to squeeze itself under the sofa.* □ *He was trying to squeeze into some very tight jeans.* (**espremer**)
3 to press something in order to get something out □ *He squeezed the last of the toothpaste out of the tube.* □ *Emma was squeezing a lemon.* (**espremer**)

> **THESAURUS:** If you **press** something, you push it, or push it firmly against something else. You might **press** a doorbell, for example. If you squeeze something, you press it tightly. For example, you squeeze a lemon to remove the juice. If you **squash** something, you press it until it is flat. You might **squash** a box before you put it into the bin, for example. If you **crush** something, you press it so that it is broken or in small pieces. You might **crush** biscuits to use in a cake.

squirrel /'skwɪrəl/ NOUN [plural squirrels] a small grey or red animal with a long, thick tail that lives in trees and eats nuts (**esquilo**)

St /seɪnt, stri:t/ ABBREVIATION
1 saint (ver **saint**)
2 street (ver **street**)

stab /stæb/ VERB [stabs, stabbing, stabbed] to kill or to injure someone by pushing a knife or other sharp object into them □ *The woman was stabbed with a knife.* (**apunhalar**)

stable¹ /'steɪbəl/ ADJECTIVE
1 firm, strong and not moving □ *This will help to keep the shelf stable.* (**firme**)
2 not changing over a period of time ▣ *The price has remained relatively stable over recent years.* ▣ *He's in a stable condition in hospital.* (**estável**)

stable² /'steɪbəl/ NOUN [plural stables] a building to keep horses in (**estábulo**)

stack¹ /stæk/ NOUN [plural stacks] a pile of things □ *a stack of books* (**pilha, meda**)

stack² /stæk/ VERB [stacks, stacking, stacked] to put things into a stack □ *Stack the dishes in the sink and I'll wash them later.* ▣ *He got a job stacking shelves in a supermarket.* (**empilhar**)

stadium /'steɪdiəm/ NOUN [plural stadiums or stadia] a large open area for playing sports, with seats around it ▣ *a football stadium* □ *They will face Real Madrid at the Bernabeu Stadium in the semi-finals.* (**estádio**)

staff /stɑ:f/ NOUN, NO PLURAL the people who work for a particular organization ▣ *Six new members of staff are joining the school this term.* □ *The company has a staff of 150.* □ *There is a shortage of medical staff in many hospitals.* (**pessoal, quadro de funcionários**)

stage /steɪdʒ/ NOUN [plural stages]
1 the raised area in a theatre where the actors and other performers perform □ *This is their first appearance on stage together.* ▣ *I loved the stage show.* (**palco**)
2 one part of a process, or a period of time in the development of something □ **+ of** *The designs are at various stages of development.* ▣ *The work is still in its early stages.* ▣ *It's hard to predict what will happen at this stage.* (**estágio, fase**)

stagger /'stægə(r)/ VERB [staggers, staggering, staggered] to walk moving from side to side in a way that looks as if you might fall □ *He staggered across the room and fell into a chair.* (**cambalear**)

stain¹ /steɪn/ VERB [stains, staining, stained] to leave a mark that is difficult to remove □ *The coffee you spilt has stained the carpet.* □ **+ with** *His uniform was stained with blood.* (**manchar**)

stain² /steɪn/ NOUN [plural stains] a dirty mark on something that is difficult to remove □ *His overalls were covered in oil stains.* (**mancha**)

stair /steə(r)/ NOUN [plural **stairs**]
1 stairs a set of steps that go from one level in a building to another ▣ *I climbed the stairs to the second floor.* ▣ *A flight of stairs led down to the cellar.* (escada)
2 one of these steps ▫ *Alice sat on the bottom stair.* (degrau)

staircase /'steəkeɪs/ NOUN [plural **staircases**] a set of stairs ▣ *a spiral staircase* (= stairs which curl round and round) (escadaria)

stale /steɪl/ ADJECTIVE [**staler, stalest**] not fresh ▫ *stale bread* ▫ *The air smelt stale inside the room.* (velho)

stalk /stɔːk/ NOUN [plural **stalks**] the stem of a flower, leaf or fruit ▫ *an apple stalk* (haste)

stall /stɔːl/ NOUN [plural **stalls**] a table or a small open shop where people sell things ▣ *a market stall* ▫ *a roadside food stall* ▫ *The stalls sell fresh fruit and vegetables.* (banca)

stamp¹ /stæmp/ NOUN [plural **stamps**]
1 a small printed piece of paper that you buy and stick on letters before you post them ▣ *a first-class stamp* ▫ *I noticed the Canadian stamp on the envelope.* (selo)
2 a tool that you use to stamp words, numbers, or a design on something, or the mark it makes ▣ *a rubber stamp* ▫ *a date stamp* (carimbo)

stamp² /stæmp/ VERB [**stamps, stamping, stamped**]
1 to bring your foot down firmly on the ground ▫ *+ on He stamped on the brake.* ▣ *She stamped her feet to keep them warm.* (pisar)
2 to print letters, numbers, or a design on something ▫ *The official stamped her passport.* ▫ *+ with Each letter is stamped with the date we receive it.* (carimbar)

stand¹ /stænd/ VERB [**stands, standing, stood**]
1 to be in a vertical position on your feet, not sitting or lying ▫ *I was so tired I could barely stand.* ▫ *I stood on a chair to reach the shelf.* ▫ *He was standing next to his brother.* (ficar em pé)
2 to get up onto your feet after sitting or lying ▫ *Everyone stood when the queen entered.* ▫ *+ up Stand up and let me look at you.* (levantar[-se])
3 to be in a particular position ▫ *The train stood outside Waterloo for nearly an hour.* ▫ *Durham stands on the River Wear.* (permanecer, ficar)
4 to put something in a particular position ▫ *I stood the jug on the table.* (pôr)
5 to be able to accept someone or some thing ▣ *I can't stand her brother, Mark.* ▫ *Marie couldn't stand hearing her parents arguing any more.* (aguentar)
6 to continue to exist or to be used ▫ *The judge ordered that the sentence should stand.* ▫ *His offer of money still stands.* (permanecer)

♦ PHRASAL VERBS **stand back** to move a short distance away from someone ▫ *Stand back, please, so that the doctors can get through.* **stand by 1** to be ready to do something ▫ *Teams of doctors are standing by with medical equipment.* **2** to do nothing to prevent an unpleasant action or situation ▫ *The government is just standing by while its people starve.* **stand for something** if letters stand for something, that thing begins with those letters ▫ *What does BBC stand for?* **stand out** to be very easy to see or notice ▫ *The yellow flowers really stood out against the green background.* **stand up** to get up onto your feet after sitting or lying ▫ *She stood up and left the room.* **stand up for someone/ something** to support someone or something that is being criticized or attacked ▫ *My brother always stands up for me when my parents tell me off.*

stand² /stænd/ NOUN [plural **stands**]
1 rows of seats where people sit to watch sports ▫ *Spectators were cheering from the stands.* (arquibancada)
2 something that an object stands on ▫ *a large mirror on a stand* (suporte)

standard¹ /'stændəd/ NOUN [plural **standards**]
1 a level of quality ▫ *+ of We hope to improve the standard of medical care.* ▣ *The club has set high standards for itself this season.* ▣ *Living standards have risen dramatically.* ▣ *Stan dards have been slipping* (= getting worse) *recently.* (padrão)
2 standards principles about what is acceptable behaviour ▫ *He has high moral standards.* (padrões)

standard² /'stændəd/ ADJECTIVE normal or usual ▫ *the standard charge for postage* ▣ *All of this is standard police procedure.* ▫ *Chemotherapy is now a standard treatment for cancer.* (padrão)

staple¹ /'steɪpəl/ NOUN [plural **staples**] a type of food or product that you use a lot of ▫ *staples such as milk and bread* (gêneros de primeira necessidade)
staple² /'steɪpəl/ ADJECTIVE a staple food or product is one of the most basic and important ones ▣ *Their staple diet is rice.* (produto principal)
staple³ /'steɪpəl/ NOUN [plural **staples**] a bent piece of wire that you push through papers to fasten them together (grampo)
staple⁴ /'steɪpəl/ VERB [**staples, stapling, stapled**] to fasten papers together with a staple ▫ *Staple the pages together.* (grampear)
• **stapler** /'steɪplə(r)/ NOUN [plural **staplers**] a small tool for stapling papers together

star¹ /stɑː(r)/ NOUN [plural **stars**]
1 a mass of burning gas in the sky that you can see at night as a point of light ▫ *the brightest star in the night sky* ▫ *There are billions of stars in our galaxy.* (estrela)

2 a famous person, especially a performer ▸ *a film star* ▸ *a pop star* ▸ *He became one of Hollywood's biggest stars.* □ **+ of** *He was married to Jennifer Aniston, star of the TV show 'Friends'.* (estrela)
3 a shape with five or more points □ *a six-pointed star* □ *The EU symbol is a circle of gold stars on a blue background.* (estrela)

star² /stɑː(r)/ VERB [stars, starring, starred]
to have the main part in a film □ *Tom Cruise is to star in the sequel.* □ *a new film starring Kate Winslet* (estrelar)

stare¹ /steə(r)/ VERB [stares, staring, stared]
to look at someone or something for a long time □ *What are you staring at?* (fitar)

stare² /steə(r)/ NOUN [plural stares]
when you look at someone or something for a long time ▸ *Tony gave him a blank stare.* (olhar fixo)

start¹ /stɑːt/ VERB [starts, starting, started]
1 to begin doing something □ **+ to do something** *Suddenly, a bird started to sing.* □ **+ ing** *What time did you start working this morning?* □ *I'm starting a new job next week.* (começar)
2 to begin to happen or exist, or to make something happen or exist □ *Work on the new bridge has started at last.* □ *He started an online art gallery.* □ *The fire started in the kitchen.* (por para funcionar)
3 to begin to work or to make a machine or a vehicle begin to work □ *The car wouldn't start.* □ *I couldn't start the engine.* (por para funcionar)
◆ PHRASAL VERB **start (something) off** to begin an activity or an event □ *Let's start off with some gentle exercises.*

start² /stɑːt/ NOUN [plural starts]
1 the beginning of something ▸ *Right from the start, I knew I'd be happy here.* □ **+ of** *The runners lined up for the start of the race.* (início)
2 make a start to begin doing something □ *I'm going to make a start on the cooking.* (começar a)
3 for a start used to give the first of a list of reasons □ *For a start, I'm fed up with sharing a room with my sister.* (primeiro)

startle /ˈstɑːtəl/ VERB [startles, startling, startled]
to suddenly frighten or shock someone □ *He was startled by a loud noise.* (assustar)

starvation /stɑːˈveɪʃən/ NOUN, NO PLURAL
when people are very hungry and have not got enough to eat □ *Thousands of people die of starvation every year.* (inanição)

starve /stɑːv/ VERB [starves, starving, starved]
to die or to suffer because you have not got enough to eat ▸ *If they don't get food aid, these people are going to starve to death.* (morrer de inanição)

state¹ /steɪt/ NOUN [plural states]
1 the condition that someone or something is in □ *The house was in a very poor state.* □ **+ of** *She's always complaining about the state of our public transport.* ▸ *I'm still in a state of shock.* (estado)
2 a country □ *the state of Israel* ▸ *There was a meeting between heads of state* (= leaders of countries). (estado)
3 the state the government of a country □ *The state should provide help for the sick and elderly.* (estado)
4 a part of a country that has its own government □ *New York state* □ **+ of** *the southern Indian state of Andhra Pradesh* (estado)
5 the States the US □ *He spent six weeks in the States.* (estado)

state² /steɪt/ VERB [states, stating, stated]
to formally say or write something □ *The letter clearly states that you must bring some identification with you.* □ *They were given an opportunity to state their views.* (declarar)

statement /ˈsteɪtmənt/ NOUN [plural statements]
something that you say or write, especially formally or officially ▸ *The police asked me to make a written statement of what I saw.* □ *A statement on his website said he had no plans to leave the band.* (declaração)

station /ˈsteɪʃən/ NOUN [plural stations]
1 a building where trains or buses stop to allow people to get on and off ▸ *a railway station* ▸ *a bus station* □ *I'll meet you at the station.* (estação)
2 a building where some types of work take place ▸ *He was taken to the local police station.* ▸ *a fire station* ▸ *We stopped at a petrol station* (= a place that sells petrol). ▸ *a nuclear power station* (posto)
3 a company which makes and broadcasts television or radio programmes ▸ *a local radio station* ▸ *The interview was broadcast by a Spanish television station.* (estação)

statue /ˈstætʃuː/ NOUN [plural statues]
a large model of a person or animal made out of stone, metal or wood □ **+ of** *a huge statue of the Buddha* □ *a life-size bronze statue* (estátua)

stay¹ /steɪ/ VERB [stays, staying, stayed]
1 to remain in a place □ *Make sure you stay inside the house.* □ *Would you like to stay for dinner?* ▸ *He agreed to stay home and look after the children.* ▸ *Stay there/here!* □ *I stayed in the same job for nearly twenty years.* (ficar)
2 to continue to be in a particular condition □ *She tried to stay calm as they waited.* □ *I could hardly stay awake.* □ *Things can't stay the same for ever.* ▸ *At the moment we are very happy together, and I hope it will stay that way.* (ficar)
3 to spend a period of time in a place □ **+ with** *I'm going to stay with my sister for a few days.* □ **+ in** *We stayed in a wonderful hotel.* ▸ *I stayed the night at a friend's house.* (ficar)
◆ PHRASAL VERBS **stay in** to remain in your house □ *I stayed in on Saturday and watched TV.* **stay out** to not come home at night, or to come home very late □ *My parents don't like me staying out late.* **stay up** to not go to bed until later than usual □ *We stayed up to watch the election results.*

stay² /steɪ/ NOUN [plural **stays**] a period of time that you spend at a place ▫ *The trip includes an overnight stay in Bangkok.* (**estrada**)

steady /'stedɪ/ ADJECTIVE [**steadier, steadiest**]
1 firm and not shaking ▫ *You need a steady hand.* ▫ *Can you hold it steady for me?* (**firme**)
2 continuous and gradual ▫ *We're making steady progress.* (**constante**)
3 not changing ▫ *I tried to keep a steady pace.* (**constante**)

steak /steɪk/ NOUN [plural **steaks**] a thick piece of meat or fish, especially meat from a cow ▫ *He was eating steak and chips.* ▫ *tuna steaks* (**bife**)

steal /stiːl/ VERB [**steals, stealing, stole, stolen**] to take something without the owner's permission ▫ *The thieves stole money and jewellery.* ▫ *It's wrong to steal.* ▫ + **from** *Several valuable paintings were stolen from the house.* ▫ *a stolen car* (**roubar**)

> Remember that thieves **steal** money and objects. They **rob** people and places: ▫ *They stole his money and his watch.* ▫ *They were robbed in the street.* ▫ *They robbed a bank.*

steam¹ /stiːm/ NOUN, NO PLURAL the gas that is formed when you heat water ▫ *Steam was rising from the coffee pot.* (**vapor**)

steam² /stiːm/ VERB [**steams, steaming, steamed**]
1 to produce steam ▫ *A kettle was steaming on the stove.* ▫ *a steaming bowl of soup* (**exalar vapor**)
2 to cook food in steam ▫ *steamed vegetables* (**cozer no vapor**)

steel¹ /stiːl/ NOUN, NO PLURAL a very hard metal that is a mixture of iron and carbon ▫ *Many knives and forks are made from stainless steel* (= steel that stays shiny). (**aço**)

steel² /stiːl/ ADJECTIVE
1 made from steel ▫ *steel knives* (**de aço**)
2 to do with making steel and steel objects ▫ *the steel industry* (**de aço**)

steep /stiːp/ ADJECTIVE [**steeper, steepest**] a steep hill or slope goes up or down very quickly ▫ *a steep hill* ▫ *The path was too steep for me to cycle up.* ▫ *It was a steep climb to the top of the hill.* (**escarpado**)

steer /stɪə(r)/ VERB [**steers, steering, steered**] to control the direction that a vehicle moves in ▫ *He steered the car through the narrow streets.* ▫ *The captain steered out of the harbour.* (**dirigir, conduzir**)

steering wheel /'stɪərɪŋ ˌwiːl/ NOUN [plural **steering wheels**] the wheel a driver holds to control a car's direction (**volante**)

stem /stem/ NOUN [plural **stems**] the long thin part of a plant, which the leaves grow on (**caule, haste**)

step¹ /step/ NOUN [plural **steps**]
1 one of a series of actions involved in doing or achieving something ▫ *These talks are an important step in bringing peace to the region.* ▫ *For me, that school play was the first step towards becoming an actor.* ▫ *Step by step* (= gradually) *she is learning to speak again.* (**passo**)
2 the action of lifting your foot off the ground and putting it down again in walking, running or dancing ▫ *He took a step forward.* ▫ *I'm sure I heard steps* (= the sound that steps make) *outside.* (**passo**)
3 a flat surface that you walk on to go up or down to a different level, often one of a series ▫ *The postman left the parcel on the front step.* ▫ *We climbed the steep steps to the castle.* (**degrau**)

step² /step/ VERB [**steps, stepping, stepped**]
1 to take a step ▫ *He opened the door and stepped out.* (**caminhar**)
2 to put your foot on something, often by accident ▫ + **on** *He stepped on my toe!* ▫ + **in** *I stepped in some mud.* (**pisar**)

step- /step/ PREFIX step- is added to the beginning of words to show that people are related to you by a second marriage ▫ *stepfather* ▫ *stepdaughter* ([**prefixo**] **por casamento**)

stepbrother /'stepbrʌðə(r)/ NOUN [plural **stepbrothers**] the son of a person who has married your mother or father, but who is not your brother (**meio-irmão**)

stepdaughter /'stepdɔːtə(r)/ NOUN [plural **stepdaughters**] the daughter of your husband or wife, who is not your daughter (**enteada**)

stepfather /'stepfɑːðə(r)/ NOUN [plural **stepfathers**] the man who is married to your mother but is not your father (**padrasto**)

stepmother /'stepmʌðə(r)/ NOUN [plural **stepmothers**] the woman who is married to your father but is not your mother (**madrasta**)

stepsister /'stepsɪstə(r)/ NOUN [plural **stepsisters**] the daughter of a person who has married your mother or father, but who is not your sister (**meia-irmã**)

stepson /'stepsʌn/ NOUN [plural **stepsons**] the son of your husband or wife, who is not your son (**enteado**)

stereotype /'steriətaɪp/ NOUN [plural **stereotypes**] an idea about what a particular type of person is like, which may be wrong or unfair ▫ *The programme aims to challenge racial stereotypes.* (**estereótipo**)

stern /stɜːn/ ADJECTIVE [**sterner, sternest**] very serious and slightly angry ▫ *He had a stern expression on his face.* ▫ *a stern warning* (**severo**)

steward /'stjuəd/ NOUN [plural **stewards**] a man whose job is to look after passengers on an aeroplane or ship (**comissário**)

stick[1] /stɪk/ VERB [sticks, sticking, stuck]
1 to push something thin or sharp into something, or to be pushed into something ▫ *We stuck pins into the cushion.* ▫ *Stop sticking your elbows into me!* ▫ *There was a thorn sticking in my skin.* ▫ *He stuck his fingers in his ears.* (**espetar**)
2 to fix something to something else, or to become fixed to something ▫ *Never mind, we can always stick the pieces back together.* ▫ *We stuck labels on the jam jars.* ▫ *He had a piece of paper stuck on his back.* (**colar**)
3 an informal word meaning to put something some where ▫ *Just stick the shopping on the floor.* ▫ *He stuck his head round the door to say hello.* (**colocar**)
4 to become unable to move ▫ *The car stuck in the mud.* ▫ *This drawer keeps sticking.* (**emperrar, atolar**)
L go to **stick your nose in/into something**
◆ PHRASAL VERBS **stick out** to come out further than a surface or an edge ▫ *His ears stick out.* ▫ *I could see an umbrella sticking out of her bag.* L go to **stick out like a sore thumb stick something out** to stretch a part of your body forward ▫ *They stuck out their hands for food.* ▫ *She stuck her tongue out at me.* **stick to something** if you stick to a plan, decision, etc., you do not change it ▫ *They promised to stick to our original agreement.*

stick[2] /stɪk/ NOUN [plural sticks]
1 a thin piece of wood that has come from a tree ▫ *We searched for sticks to make a fire.* (**graveto**)
2 a long thin piece of wood used for a particular purpose ▫ *a walking stick* ▫ *a hockey stick* (**vara**)
3 a long thin piece of something ▫ *a stick of rhubarb* (**haste**)

sticky /ˈstɪki/ ADJECTIVE [stickier, stickiest]
designed to stick to another surface, or covered with something that can stick to things ▫ *Mend the book with some sticky tape.* ▫ *sticky fingers* (**colante, grudento**)

stiff /stɪf/ ADJECTIVE [stiffer, stiffest]
1 difficult to bend ▫ *stiff cardboard* ▫ *stiff material* (**rijo**)
2 if part of your body is stiff, it hurts when you move it ▫ *I've got a stiff neck.* ▫ *stiff joints* (**duro, rígido**)

still[1] /stɪl/ ADVERB
1 up to a particular time and continuing ▫ *Are you still living in Tokyo?* ▫ *By Sunday she still hadn't replied to the invitation.* ▫ *I'm still hungry.* (**ainda**)
2 despite what you have just said or done ▫ *She's treated me badly but she's still my daughter and I love her.* ▫ *It was raining but we still decided to go.* (**mesmo assim**)
3 used for saying that something is possible even now ▫ *You can still catch the bus if you leave now.* (**ainda**)

still[2] /stɪl/ ADJECTIVE [stiller, stillest]
1 not moving ▫ *Keep still while I brush your hair!* (**quieto**)
2 a still drink is without bubbles ▫ *still lemonade* (**sem gás**)

sting[1] /stɪŋ/ VERB [stings, stinging, stung]
1 if an insect or plant stings you, it hurts your skin when it touches you ▫ *I was badly stung by the plant.* ▫ *Bees can sting.* (**picar**)
2 to feel a sudden pain in your eyes or skin, or to make someone feel a sudden pain in their eyes or skin ▫ *The shampoo made her eyes sting.* ▫ *Smoke stung his eyes.* (**arder**)

sting[2] /stɪŋ/ NOUN [plural stings]
1 the sudden pain you feel when an insect or plant stings you ▫ *a wasp sting* (**picada**)
2 a sudden pain in your eyes or skin (**picada, ferida**)

stir /stɜː(r)/ VERB [stirs, stirring, stirred]
1 to mix something with a circular movement ▫ *He put sugar in his tea and stirred it.* (**mexer**)
2 to move slightly, or to make something move slightly ▫ *The baby stirred in its sleep.* ▫ *The breeze stirred her hair.* (**mexer, agitar**)

stitch[1] /stɪtʃ/ NOUN [plural stitches]
1 a piece of thread on cloth that has been sewn ▫ *She sewed up the hole with small neat stitches.* (**ponto**)
2 a piece of thread that a doctor uses to repair injuries to your skin ▫ *He cut his hand and needed stitches in it.* (**ponto**)

stitch[2] /stɪtʃ/ VERB [stitches, stitching, stitched]
to sew ▫ *I stitched the button on to my coat.* (**costurar**)

stock[1] /stɒk/ NOUN [plural stocks]
1 the goods that a shop has available ▫ *Buy now while stocks last!* (**estoque**)
2 out of/in stock not available/available to buy in a particular shop ▫ *I'm sorry but the item is out of stock at the moment.* (**disponível/indisponível**)
3 stocks shares in a company, which you can buy. (**ações**)

stock[2] /stɒk/ VERB [stocks, stocking, stocked] to have something available to buy ▫ *Most supermarkets now stock organic products.* (**estocar**)

stocking /ˈstɒkɪŋ/ NOUN [plural stockings] a very thin piece of clothing for a woman's foot and leg ▫ *a pair of stockings* (**meia-calça**)

stock market /ˈstɒk ˌmɑːkɪt/ NOUN [plural stock markets] a place where company shares are bought and sold (**mercado financeiro**)

stole /stəʊl/ PAST TENSE OF **steal** (ver **steal**)
stolen /ˈstəʊlən/ PAST PARTICIPLE OF **steal** (ver **steal**)

stomach /ˈstʌmək/ NOUN [plural stomachs]
1 the part inside your body where food goes when you have eaten it (**estômago**)
2 the front part of your body below your chest ▫ *a flat stomach* (**barriga**)

stomachache /ˈstʌməkˌeɪk/ NOUN [plural stomachaches] a pain in the stomach (**dor de barriga**)

stone[1] /stəʊn/ NOUN [plural stones]
1 a small piece of rock ▫ *The boys were throwing stones into the water.* (**pedra**)
2 no plural the hard substance that rocks are made of ▫ *The house was built of stone.* (**pedra**)

stone

3 a small piece of valuable rock, used for making jewellery ▢ *The necklace was made of gold and precious stones* (= valuable and rare stones). (pedra)
4 [plural **stone**] a unit for measuring weight, equal to 6.35 kilograms ▢ *I weigh nine stone.* (stone)
5 the hard piece in the middle of some fruits ▢ *a peach stone* (caroço)

stone² /stəʊn/ ADJECTIVE made of stone ▢ *stone walls* ▢ *a stone floor* (de pedra)

stood /stʊd/ PAST TENSE AND PAST PARTICIPLE OF **stand¹** (ver **stand¹**)

stool /stuːl/ NOUN [plural **stools**] a seat without a back ▢ *She was sitting on a stool in the kitchen.* (tamborete, banco)

stop¹ /stɒp/ VERB [**stops, stopping, stopped**]
1 to prevent something happening or existing or someone from doing something ▢ **+ ing** *He'll never succeed but that won't stop him trying.* ▢ **+ from** *The barriers stop the crowd from pouring into the street.* ▢ *Nothing seems to stop the violence.* (impedir, deter)
2 to no longer do something ▢ **+ ing** *The wound has stopped bleeding.* ▢ *Please stop this nonsense.* ▢ *Stop it! I'm trying to concentrate.* (parar)
3 to not happen or exist anymore ▢ *It was lovely when the noise stopped.* ▢ *We're waiting for the rain to stop.* (parar)
4 to no longer move or to make something finish moving ▢ *A car stopped outside the house.* ▢ *He stopped the ball with his foot.* (parar)
5 if a public vehicle stops somewhere, it stays there for a short time for people to get on and off ▢ *Does this train stop at Chester?* (parar)
6 to no longer work ▢ *My watch has stopped.* (parar)

stop² /stɒp/ NOUN [plural **stops**]
1 a place where a public vehicle stops ▢ *This train calls at all stops to Glasgow.* (parada)
2 come to a stop to stop moving ▢ *The train came to a stop just outside Hull.* (parada)

store¹ /stɔː(r)/ NOUN [plural **stores**]
1 a shop ▢ *the village store* ▢ *an online store* ▢ *The company opened its first store in 1930.* ▢ *The store sells cards and gifts.* (armazém)
2 a supply of something which you keep to use when you need it ▢ **+ of** *Squirrels keep a store of food.* (provisão)

store² /stɔː(r)/ VERB [**stores, storing, stored**] to keep something somewhere ▢ *Store the chocolate in a cool dry place.* ▢ **+ away** *The books had been carefully stored away.* (guardar)

storey /ˈstɔːri/ NOUN [plural **storeys**] one of the levels in a building ▢ *a four-storey carpark* (andar)

storm /stɔːm/ NOUN [plural **storms**] a time when there is suddenly a lot of wind and rain ▢ *A huge storm hit New Orleans.* ▢ *She waited indoors until the storm had passed.* ▢ *a tropical storm* (tempestade)

stormy /ˈstɔːmi/ ADJECTIVE [**stormier, stormiest**] with a lot of strong winds and rain ▢ *stormy weather* ▢ *a stormy night* (tempestuosa)

story /ˈstɔːri/ NOUN [plural **stories**]
1 a description of events, which can be real or invented ▢ *The teacher was reading a story to the class.* ▢ *The film is based on a true story.* ▢ *The children were telling each other ghost stories.* ▢ **+ of** *The book is the story of his life.* ▢ **+ about** *It's a story about a Jewish boy growing up in London.* (história)
2 the US spelling of **storey**

straight¹ /streɪt/ ADJECTIVE [**straighter, straightest**]
1 not bent or curved ▢ *a straight line* ▢ *straight hair* (reto)
2 completely horizontal or vertical ▢ *That picture isn't straight.* (direito)
3 honest ▢ *Give me a straight answer!* (direto)

straight² /streɪt/ ADVERB
1 in a straight line ▢ *I was so tired, I couldn't walk straight.* ▢ *The lion ran straight towards him.* ▢ *She was looking straight at me.* (em linha reta)
2 straight on without changing direction ▢ *Go straight on at the traffic lights.* (diretamente)
3 immediately ▢ *I came straight here.* (imediatamente)
4 straight away immediately ▢ *Could you come to my office straight away, please?* (imediatamente)

straighten /ˈstreɪtən/ VERB [**straightens, straightening, straightened**] to become straight or to make something straight ▢ *The road curved then straightened.* ▢ *He straightened his tie.* (endireitar)

straightforward /ˌstreɪtˈfɔːwəd/ ADJECTIVE easy ▢ *a straightforward task* (simples)

strain¹ /streɪn/ VERB [**strains, straining, strained**]
1 to injure part of your body by using it too much ▢ *You'll strain your eyes reading in the dark.* (forçar)
2 to try hard to do something ▢ *He strained to look through a small hole in the wall.* (esticar, forçar)
3 to separate solid parts from a liquid ▢ *Now strain the pasta.* (filtrar, coar)

strain² /streɪn/ NOUN [plural **strains**]
1 an injury to part of your body because you have used it too much ▢ *a muscle strain* (estiramento, distensão)
2 no plural when something has a lot of pressure on it ▢ *The dam had burst under the strain.* (tensão)
3 no plural the bad effects on your mind and body when you have too much work or too many worries ▢ *The strain of looking after four young children was too much for her.* ▢ *He's been under a lot of strain recently.* (tensão)

strand /strænd/ NOUN [plural **strands**] a thin piece of something such as hair or thread ▢ *a strand of hair* (fio, cordão)

stranded /ˈstrændɪd/ ADJECTIVE being in a place that you cannot leave ▢ *She was left stranded without money or passport.* (retido, preso)

strange

strange /streɪndʒ/ ADJECTIVE [stranger, strangest]
1 unusual ▫ *She's a very strange woman.* ▫ + *that It's strange that he hasn't called.* ▫ *The strange thing is that the burglars ignored all her jewellery.* ▫ *That's strange – I wonder why she didn't tell you?* (**estranho**)
2 not familiar ▫ *Being ill in a strange country was quite frightening.* (**estranho**)

strangely /ˈstreɪndʒli/ ADVERB
1 in a strange way ▫ *She looked at me strangely.* (**estranhamente**)
2 used for saying that something is surprising ▫ *Strangely enough, some actors are quite shy.* (**estranho**)

stranger /ˈstreɪndʒə(r)/ NOUN [plural strangers]
1 someone who you do not know ▫ *Children should never talk to strangers.* ▫ *How many people would give £5000 to a complete stranger?* (**estranho**)
2 someone who is in a place they do not know ▫ *I'm afraid I don't know where the station is. I'm a stranger here myself.* (**forasteiro**)
3 **be no stranger to something** to have a lot of experience of something ▫ *She is no stranger to public attention.* (**estar acostumado**)

> Remember that a **stranger** is a person you do not know. It is not a person from another country. (The word for this is **foreigner**.)
> ✓ Foreigners are usually very welcome in this region.
> ✗ Strangers are usually very welcome in this region.

strangle /ˈstræŋgəl/ VERB [strangles, strangling, strangled] to kill someone by putting something around their throat ▫ *She had been strangled with a piece of rope.* (**estrangular**)

strap¹ /stræp/ NOUN [plural straps] a long narrow piece of leather or cloth used to hold things, fasten things or hang things on ▫ *a watch strap* ▫ *The bag had a shoulder strap.* (**correia**)

strap² /stræp/ VERB [straps, strapping, strapped] to fasten something with a strap ▫ *I usually strap my bag to my bike.* (**prender com correia**)

strategy /ˈstrætɪdʒi/ NOUN [plural strategies] a plan for achieving something ▫ *a business strategy* ▫ *He had developed his own strategies for dealing with stress.* (**estratégia**)

straw /strɔː/ NOUN [plural straws]
1 no plural long dried stems of crops which animals eat or sleep on ▫ *The cows need fresh straw.* (**palha**)
2 a thin tube used for sucking up a drink (**canudo**)
◆ IDIOM **the last/final straw** the last in a series of unpleasant events, which makes you feel angry or makes you want to stop doing something ▫ *They all started laughing at her, and it was the last straw.*

strength

strawberry /ˈstrɔːbəri/ NOUN [plural strawberries] a soft red fruit with many very small seeds on its surface ▫ *fresh strawberries* ▫ *strawberry ice cream* (**morango**)

stray /streɪ/ NOUN [plural strays] a cat or dog that has no home (**animal desgarrado**)

streak /striːk/ NOUN [plural streaks] a long thin line or mark ▫ *hair with blonde streaks* ▫ *There were dirty streaks on the window.* (**risco, traço**)

stream /striːm/ NOUN [plural streams]
1 a very narrow river ▫ *The children were paddling in the stream.* (**riacho**)
2 a flow of something ▫ *The museum had a steady stream of visitors.* ▫ *There was a constant stream of traffic.* (**corrente**)

street /striːt/ NOUN [plural streets] a road with buildings such as houses and shops on one or both sides ▫ *Lincoln's main street was full of shoppers.* ▫ *There are a lot of shops on this street.* ▫ *She walked down the street to the library.* ▫ *I live at 32 Montgomery Street.* (**rua**)

> THESAURUS: A **road** is a hard, level surface for vehicles to travel along. Road is a general word. A street is a road with buildings such as houses and shops on one side or both sides. A **lane** is a narrow road, especially in the country. A lane is also a strip of road separated by painted lines. Most roads have two lanes. A **motorway** is a wide road for vehicles travelling fast over long distances. Most motorway shave 3 or more lanes.

strength /streŋθ/ NOUN, NO PLURAL
1 when someone or something is strong ▫ *He didn't have the strength to lift the box.* ▫ *The soup gave her a little more strength.* ▫ *They tested the strength of the metal.* (**força**)
2 how successful, good or powerful something is ▫ *The strength of the dollar has caused problems for some companies.* ▫ *The government should not underestimate the strength of the army.* (**poder**)

strengthen /ˈstrɛŋθən/ VERB [strengthens, strengthening, strengthened] to become stronger or to make something stronger ▫ *He did exercises to strengthen his muscles.* ▫ *The wind strengthened.* (reforçar, fortalecer)

stress¹ /strɛs/ NOUN [plural stresses]
1 no plural the bad effect on your mind or body when you have too much work or too many worries ▫ *A lot of headaches are caused by stress.* ▫ *He was suffering from stress and exhaustion.* ▫ *Exercise is an effective way to reduce stress.* ▫ *Students often have high stress levels around the time of exams.* (estresse)
2 be under stress to have too much work or too many worries ▫ *I've been under a lot of stress recently.* (sob tensão)
3 the emphasis of a particular part of a word when you are saying it ▫ *In the word 'bedroom' the stress is on 'bed'.* (ênfase, acento)

stress² /strɛs/ VERB [stresses, stressing, stressed]
1 to say that something is important ▫ *Her speech stressed the need for change.* ▫ + **that** *She stressed that she did not blame her father.* (enfatizar)
2 to emphasize part of a word ▫ *When 'object' is a noun you stress the 'ob'.* (enfatizar, acentuar)

stretch /strɛtʃ/ VERB [stretches, stretching, stretched]
1 to make something longer or wider, especially by pulling ▫ *Stretch this rope between the two posts.* (esticar)
2 to become longer or wider ▫ *This material stretches.* ▫ *New shoes usually stretch a little.* (esticar)
3 to push your arms or legs as far as you can ▫ *Amy got out of bed and stretched.* ▫ *She stretched her arms over her head.* ▫ + **over/across, etc.** *He stretched across me to get the book.* (espreguiçar, alongar)
4 to cover a large area ▫ *The mountains stretch from the north to the south of the country.* (estender)

stretcher /ˈstrɛtʃə(r)/ NOUN [plural stretchers] a bed for carrying an ill or injured person ▫ *The stretcher was put into the back of the ambulance.* (maca)

strict /strɪkt/ ADJECTIVE [stricter, strictest] expecting people to obey your rules ▫ *a strict teacher* ▫ + **with** *He's very strict with the students.* (rigoroso)

strictly /ˈstrɪktli/ ADVERB
1 exactly ▫ *It's not strictly true.* ▫ *They are not refugees, strictly speaking* (= used for emphasizing that you are being exact). (rigorosamente)
2 strictly prohibited/forbidden/banned used to emphasize that something is not allowed ▫ *Smoking is strictly prohibited.* (estritamente)

stride /straɪd/ NOUN [plural strides] a long step you take when you walk (passo largo)
◆ IDIOM **take something in your stride** to deal with something difficult and not allow it to affect you ▫ *She's had a lot of health problems but she's taken them all in her stride.*

strike¹ /straɪk/ VERB [strikes, striking, struck]
1 to hit someone or something ▫ *The bomb struck its target.* ▫ *My head struck the table.* ▫ *The house was struck by lightning.* (bater)
2 if a thought strikes you, you suddenly think of it ▫ + **that** *It suddenly struck me that the road would be closed.* (ocorrer)
3 to refuse to work because of an argument with your employer ▫ + **for** *They were striking for higher wages.* ▫ + **over** *They are striking over their working conditions.* (fazer greve)
4 if a clock strikes, it makes a number of sounds to show the time ▫ *The clock struck three.* (soar, tocar)
◆ PHRASAL VERB **strike someone as something** to seem to someone to have a particular quality ▫ *He didn't strike me as particularly shy.*

strike² /straɪk/ NOUN [plural strikes] a period of time when workers refuse to work because of an argument with their employer ▫ *The train drivers are threatening to go on strike.* (greve)

string /strɪŋ/ NOUN [plural strings]
1 no plural strong thread, used for tying things ▫ *a ball of string* (barbante, fio)
2 a string of something (a) a series of things or a group of things ▫ *a string of disasters* ▫ *They have opened a string of nightclubs across Europe.* (b) several things which are on a piece of string ▫ *a string of beads* (uma série de)
3 a piece of wire used to make a sound on a musical instrument (corda)

strip¹ /strɪp/ NOUN [plural strips] a long narrow piece of something ▫ + **of** *a strip of paper* ▫ *a narrow strip of land* ▫ *Slice the peppers into strips.* (faixa, tira)

strip² /strɪp/ VERB [strips, stripping, stripped]
1 to remove a layer or covering from something ▫ + **off** *You need to strip off the old paint first.* (tirar)
2 to remove your clothes ▫ *He stripped and dived into the water.* ▫ + **off** *They stripped off their jackets.* (despir)

stripe /straɪp/ NOUN [plural stripes] a line of colour ▫ *a T-shirt with black and white stripes* (listra)

strive /straɪv/ VERB [strives, striving, strove, striven] a formal word meaning to try very hard to achieve something ▫ *The airline must strive to remain competitive.* (empenhar [-se])

stroke¹ /strəʊk/ NOUN [plural strokes]
1 a sudden illness in the brain that affects someone's ability to move and speak ▫ *She had a stroke in August.* (derrame cerebral, ataque)
2 a way of moving your arms and legs when you swim ▫ *I usually do breast stroke.* (braçada, movimento)
3 a stroke of luck something you are not expecting which is lucky ▫ *Police solved the crime by an incredible stroke of luck.* (golpe de sorte)

stroke² /strəʊk/ VERB [strokes, stroking, stroked] to rub something gently with your hand ▫ *She was stroking the cat.* (afagar)

stroll /strəʊl/ VERB [strolls, strolling, strolled] to walk in a slow, relaxed way □ *We strolled down to the beach.* (**perambular, passear**)

strong /strɒŋ/ ADJECTIVE [stronger, strongest]
1 physically powerful □ *He is very strong.* □ *I have strong legs from cycling.* (**forte**)
2 not easy to damage or break □ *We tied the branches together with a strong rope.* □ *They have a very strong relationship.* (**forte**)
3 believed, felt or expressed in a deep and forceful way □ *He has very strong opinions about climate change.* □ *There has been strong opposition to the new airport.* (**forte**)
4 having or using a lot of power or force □ *I felt a strong pull on the rope.* strong winds (**forte**)
5 very noticeable *There was a strong smell of fish in the room.* □ *She speaks with a strong French accent.* (**forte**)
6 a strong drink has a lot of a particular substance in it □ *He drinks really strong coffee.* (**forte**)

struck /strʌk/ PAST TENSE AND PAST PARTICIPLE OF **strike¹** (ver **strike¹**)

structure /ˈstrʌktʃə(r)/ NOUN [plural structures]
1 the way that the parts of something are arranged or organized □ **+ of** *the structure of the story* □ *Crick and Watson discovered the structure of DNA.* □ *a new management structure* (**estrutura**)
2 something that has been built □ *The bridge was a massive steel structure.* (**construção**)

struggle¹ /ˈstrʌɡəl/ VERB [struggles, struggling, struggled]
1 to try hard to do something that is difficult □ *She struggled to finish the work on time.* (**lutar contra**)
2 to turn and twist your body in order to try to escape □ *The child struggled in his arms.* (**debater [-se]**)

struggle² /ˈstrʌɡəl/ NOUN [plural struggles] a fight □ *the country's struggle for independence* (**luta por**)

stubborn /ˈstʌbən/ ADJECTIVE refusing to change your mind or do what other people tell you □ *a stubborn man* □ *I was frustrated by Tom's stubborn refusal to make any changes.* (**teimoso**)

stuck /stʌk/ PAST TENSE AND PAST PARTICIPLE OF **stick¹** (ver **stick¹**)

student /ˈstjuːdənt/ NOUN [plural students] someone who is studying, especially at a college or university □ *a law student* *a part-time university student* □ **+ at** *He's a student at Harvard University.* (**estudante**)

studio /ˈstjuːdiəʊ/ NOUN [plural studios]
1 a room from which radio or television programmes are broadcast *a TV studio* □ *The programme's recorded in front of a live studio audience.* (**estúdio**)
2 a place where films are made, or a company that makes films *an independent film studio* □ *Hollywood studios* (**estúdio**)
3 the room that an artist or photographer works in □ *She set up her own photographic studio.* (**estúdio**)

study¹ /ˈstʌdi/ NOUN [plural studies]
1 when you spend time examining something to find out more about it □ *a scientific study* *Researchers conducted a study on the effects of mobile phones.* *A new study shows coffee-drinking does not increase the risk of heart disease.* **2** when you spend time learning about a subject
□ **+ of** *the study of history* □ *He completed his undergraduate studies.* (**estudo**)
3 a room used for studying or quiet work □ *She sat reading in her study.* (**escritório**)

study² /ˈstʌdi/ VERB [studies, studying, studied]
1 to spend time learning about a subject □ *I'm studying French.* □ **+ for** *Sophie is studying for a degree in politics.* □ **+ to do something** *She's studying to be a teacher.* (**estudar**)
2 to look at something carefully □ *He studied the railway timetable.* (**examinar**)

stuff¹ /stʌf/ NOUN, NO PLURAL used to talk about a substance, material or a group of objects □ *What's that black oily stuff on the beach?* □ *I've got too much stuff to carry.* □ *I need to buy some stuff for the party.* (**substância, tralha**)

stuff² /stʌf/ VERB [stuffs, stuffing, stuffed]
1 to push something into a space, often in a quick, careless way □ *He stuffed the letter into his pocket.* □ *I stuffed tissue in my ears to block out the noise.* □ *All his old letters were stuffed into drawers.* (**empanturrar**)
2 to fill something completely □ *She used feathers to stuff the cushions.* □ *Her suitcase was stuffed with clothes.* (**rechear, encher**)

stumble /ˈstʌmbəl/ VERB [stumbles, stumbling, stumbled] to almost fall while you are walking □ *He stumbled along the track in the dark.* (**tropeçar**)

stump /stʌmp/ NOUN [plural stumps] the part of something left after the main part has been taken away *She sat on a tree stump.* (**toco**)

stun /stʌn/ VERB [stuns, stunning, stunned]
1 if you are stunned by something, it surprises or shocks you very much □ *We were all stunned by the news of the accident.* (**atordoar**)
2 to make someone unconscious, usually by hitting them on the head (**deixar sem sentidos**)

stung /stʌŋ/ PAST TENSE AND PAST PARTICIPLE OF **sting¹** (ver **sting¹**)

stunning /ˈstʌnɪŋ/ ADJECTIVE extremely attractive □ *She looked stunning.* (**impressionante**)

stunt /stʌnt/ NOUN [plural stunts] something dangerous and exciting that someone does, especially in a film □ *The actor performs all his own stunts.* (**proeza**)

stupid /ˈstjuːpɪd/ ADJECTIVE silly and not clever □ *It was a stupid thing to do!* □ *a stupid idea* □ *I felt rather stupid.* (**estúpido, bobo**)

stupidly /ˈstjuːpɪdli/ ADVERB in a stupid way ▫ *I'd rather stupidly forgotten to bring a coat.* ▫ *Stupidly, I agreed to do it.* (estupidamente)

sturdy /ˈstɜːdi/ ADJECTIVE [sturdier, sturdiest] strong ▫ *sturdy shoes* (vigoroso, resistente)

sty[1] /staɪ/ NOUN [plural sties] a place where pigs are kept (chiqueiro)

sty[2] or **stye** /staɪ/ NOUN [plural sties or styes] an infection near your eye that makes it painful and swollen (terçol)

style /staɪl/ NOUN [plural styles]

1 a particular way of doing something ▫ *a mix of musical styles* ▫ **+ of** *She has a wonderful style of writing.* (estilo)

2 the design of something, especially clothes or buildings ▫ **+ of** *a new style of shoe* ▫ *We stayed in a traditional style cottage.* (moda)

stylish /ˈstaɪlɪʃ/ ADJECTIVE attractive and fashionable ▫ *It's one of the city's most stylish hotels.* ▫ *She looked stylish in a simple black dress.* (estiloso, elegante)

subject /ˈsʌbdʒɪkt/ NOUN [plural subjects]

1 the person or thing that a story, a conversation, etc. is about ▫ **+ of** *The affair has been the subject of many rumours.* ▫ *He raised the subject of* (= started talking about) *security at the jail.* ▫ *Can we change the subject* (= talk about something different), *please?* (assunto)

2 something that you study and learn about at school, university, etc. ▫ *French is my favourite subject at school.* ▫ *Fewer students are now studying science subjects.* (matéria)

3 in grammar, the subject of a sentence is the person or thing that does something ▫ *In the sentence 'John plays tennis', 'John' is the subject.* (sujeito)

submarine /ˌsʌbməˈriːn/ NOUN [plural submarines] a ship that travels under water (submarino)

subscribe /səbˈskraɪb/ VERB [subscribes, subscribing, subscribed] to get a product or service by regularly paying money ▫ *One in three Americans subscribe to cable television.* (assinar)

subsequent /ˈsʌbsɪkwənt/ ADJECTIVE happening after something else ▫ *The story is about the soldier's capture and subsequent escape.* (assinar)

substance /ˈsʌbstəns/ NOUN [plural substances] a liquid, a solid or a gas ▫ *Glue is a sticky substance.* ▫ *a toxic substance* (substância)

substitute /ˈsʌbstɪtjuːt/ NOUN [plural substitutes]

1 a person or thing used instead of another ▫ *Use lemons as a substitute for limes.* (substituto)

2 a player who replaces another player in a team during a game ▫ *James came on as a substitute at half-time.* (substituto)

subtle /ˈsʌtəl/ ADJECTIVE [subtler, subtlest] slight and difficult to notice or to describe ▫ *There have been subtle changes.* ▫ *There is a subtle difference between the two birds.* (sutil)

subtract /səbˈtrækt/ VERB [subtracts, subtracting, subtracted] to take one number away from another. A mathematics word. ▫ **+ from** *If you subtract 4 from 6, you get 2.* (subtrair)

> **THESAURUS:** If you **subtract**, you take one number away from another. If you **add** two numbers, you put them together. If you add 2 and 3, you get 5. If you **multiply** two numbers, you increase one number by adding it to itself a particular number of times. If you multiply 3 by 5, you get 15. If you **divide** a number, you find out how many times that number contains another number. If you divide 12 by 3, you get 4.

suburb /ˈsʌbɜːb/ NOUN [plural suburbs] an area of houses at the edge of a town or city ▫ *a suburb of Liverpool* (subúrbio)

suburban /səˈbɜːbən/ ADJECTIVE to do with areas of houses at the edge of a town or city ▫ *suburban housing* (suburbano)

subway /ˈsʌbweɪ/ NOUN [plural subways]

1 a path under a busy road or railway (passagem subterrânea)

2 the US word for **underground**[2] (= a railway under the ground) (metrô)

succeed /səkˈsiːd/ VERB [succeeds, succeeding, succeeded] to achieve something, or to have the effect you want ▫ *If you try hard, I'm sure you'll succeed.* ▫ *Ravana's clever plan had succeeded.* ▫ **+ in** *She succeeded in getting the job.* (ter êxito)

> Note that **succeed** is followed by **in doing** something:
> ✓ *She finally succeeded in persuading him.*
> ✗ *She finally succeeded to persuade him.*

success /səkˈses/ NOUN [plural successes]

1 *no plural* the achievement of what you tried to achieve ▫ *Her success is due to determination and hard work.* ▫ *He tried, without success, to pull her out of the water.* ▫ *The project had little chance of success.* ▫ **+ in** *Have you had any success in finding a job?* (sucesso)

2 something that is popular or has the result that you want ▫ *The party had been a great success.* ▫ *The film was a huge success.* (sucesso)

successful /səkˈsesfʊl/ ADJECTIVE

1 having the result you wanted ▫ *a successful election campaign* ▫ *The policy has been very successful.* ▫ **+ in** *He was successful in his attempt to buy the business.* (bem-sucedido)

2 earning or achieving a lot in your work ▫ *a successful businessman* ▫ *Houlahan had a highly successful career training horses.* (bem-sucedido)

such /sʌtʃ/ DETERMINER, PRONOUN
1 such a used before a phrase with a noun for emphasizing a statement □ *I was such a fool to believe him.* □ *This is such a waste of time.* □ *She's such a nice person.* (**tão**)
2 such as used for giving an example □ *Citrus fruits such as oranges and lemons contain a lot of vitamin C.* (**tal, assim**)
3 similar to someone or something that has already been mentioned □ *Such things are difficult to find.* (**tal**)
4 such ... that used for saying what the result of something is □ *It was such an awful hotel that we decided to leave.* (**tal... que**)

suck /sʌk/ VERB [sucks, sucking, sucked]
1 to take something into your mouth by pulling in air □ *She was sucking lemonade through a straw.* □ *+ in Gerald sucked in his breath.* (**sugar**)
2 to hold something in your mouth while making pulling movements with your lips and tongue □ *My sister still sucks her thumb.* □ *She was sucking a sweet.* □ *+ on The baby was sucking on a dummy.* (**chupar**)

sudden /'sʌdən/ ADJECTIVE
1 happening quickly and unexpectedly □ *The sudden death of his mother changed everything.* □ *Pat felt a sudden urge to laugh.* □ *The attack was so sudden that he wasn't able to defend himself.* (**súbito**)
2 all of a sudden suddenly □ *All of a sudden, he started to run towards the door.* (**de repente**)

suddenly /'sʌdənli/ ADVERB quickly and unexpectedly □ *Suddenly a woman ran into the room, shouting.* □ *I suddenly felt very tired.* (**subitamente**)

sue /suː/ VERB [sues, suing, sued] to start a law case to try to get money from a person or organization that has harmed you □ *He sued the company for racial discrimination.* (**processar, acionar**)

suffer /'sʌfə(r)/ VERB [suffers, suffering, suffered]
1 to feel pain or unpleasant feelings ▣ *She suffered a lot of pain after the accident.* □ *I couldn't bear to see him suffering like that.* (**sofrer**)
2 suffer from something to have a particular illness □ *Her brother suffers from depression.* (**sofrer**)

suffering /'sʌfərɪŋ/ NOUN, NO PLURAL pain or unpleasant feelings ▣ *Years of civil war and drought have caused widespread human suffering.* (**sofrimento**)

sugar /'ʃʊɡə(r)/ NOUN, NO PLURAL white or brown grains that you add to food and drink to make them taste sweeter ▣ *Do you take sugar in your tea?* (**açúcar**)

suggest /sə'dʒest/ VERB [suggests, suggesting, suggested]
1 to mention something as a possibility □ *He suggested a picnic.* □ *+ that I suggest that we have lunch now.* □ *+ ing She suggested meeting outside the theatre.* (**sugerir**)
2 to tell someone about something that they might like or find useful □ *Can you suggest a nice place to stay in Paris?* □ *+ for She suggested me for the job.* (**sugerir**)

> Notice the examples in 'suggest' (sense 1). You **suggest that** someone **does** something, or you **suggest doing** something. You do not suggest 'to do' something.
> ✓ *I suggest that we start now.*
> ✓ *I suggest starting now.*
> ✗ *I suggest to start now.*

suggestion /sə'dʒestʃən/ NOUN [plural suggestions] an idea that you mention ▣ *He made several helpful suggestions.* ▣ *Do you have any suggestions about where we could go for a holiday?* □ *+ that He rejected suggestions that he had lied.* (**sugestão**)

suicide /'suːɪsaɪd/ NOUN [plural suicides] the act of killing yourself deliberately ▣ *He committed suicide by jumping off a bridge.* (**suicídio**)

suit¹ /suːt/ NOUN [plural suits]
1 a jacket and trousers or a jacket and skirt which are made of the same cloth and are worn together ▣ *He was wearing a suit and tie.* (**terno, conjunto, tailleur**)
2 one of the four types of cards in a set used for playing games □ *The four suits are hearts, diamonds, clubs and spades.* (**naipe**)

suit² /suːt/ VERB [suits, suiting, suited]
1 if something suits you, it makes you look nice □ *Blue really suits her.* □ *That dress suits you.* (**combinar com**)
2 to be convenient for someone □ *Would it suit you if I called round this evening?* (**convir a**)

suitable /'suːtəbəl/ ADJECTIVE right for a purpose, person or occasion □ *Finding suitable accommodation wasn't easy.* □ *+ for High-heeled shoes aren't suitable for walking in the country.* (**adequado**)
• **suitably** /'suːtəbli/ ADVERB in a way that is suitable □ *Are you suitably dressed for the cold weather?* (**convenientemente**)

suitcase /'suːtkeɪs/ NOUN [plural suitcases] a big case with a handle, that you carry your clothes in when you are travelling ▣ *He packed his suitcase and went to the airport.* ▣ *I unpacked my suitcase as soon as I arrived.* (**mala**)

sulk /sʌlk/ VERB [sulks, sulking, sulked] to show that you are angry by being silent □ *He's sulking because I said he couldn't go out.* (**amuar**)

sum /sʌm/ NOUN [plural sums]
1 an amount of money ▣ *Huge sums were spent on repairing the building.* ▣ *Some footballers earn vast sums of money.* (**soma**)
2 a simple calculation □ *I was never any good at sums.* (**cálculo, conta**)

3 the total when you add numbers together □ +of *The sum of 2, 3 and 4 is 9.* (soma)

summer /ˈsʌmə(r)/ NOUN [plural **summers**] the season between spring and autumn when the weather is warmest □ *People buy more ice cream in summer.* □ *My sister got married last summer.* □ *summer clothes* □ *summer holidays* □ *Summers are getting hotter.* (verão)

summit /ˈsʌmɪt/ NOUN [plural **summits**] the top of a hill or mountain ▣ *He reached the summit of Mount Everest in 1970.* (cume)

summon /ˈsʌmən/ VERB [**summons, summoning, summoned**] to order someone to come □ *The headteacher summoned me to her office.* (convocar)

sun /sʌn/ NOUN, NO PLURAL
1 the sun the yellow thing in the sky which gives light and heat to the Earth ▣ *The sun shone brightly into the room.* ▣ *The sun rose at 7.12 am.* ▣ *The sun set at 8.24 pm.* □ *The Earth goes round the sun.* (sol)
2 the light and heat from the sun □ *We sat in the sun.* (sol)

sunbathe /ˈsʌnbeɪð/ VERB [**sunbathes, sunbathing, sunbathed**] to lie or sit in the sun so that your skin becomes darker □ *Lots of people were sunbathing on the beach.* (tomar sol)

Sunday /ˈsʌndɪ/ NOUN [plural **Sundays**] the day of the week after Saturday and before Monday □ *I always go to church on Sundays.* (domingo)

sung /sʌŋ/ PAST PARTICIPLE OF **sing** (ver **sing**)

sunglasses /ˈsʌnglɑːsɪz/ PLURAL NOUN dark glasses that protect your eyes from the sun □ *She was wearing a pair of sunglasses.* (óculos de sol)

sunk /sʌŋk/ PAST PARTICIPLE OF **sink**¹ (ver **sink**¹)

sunlight /ˈsʌnlaɪt/ NOUN, NO PLURAL the light from the sun ▣ *Driving can be difficult in bright sunlight* ▣ *Keep babies out of direct sunlight.* (luz do sol)

sunny /ˈsʌnɪ/ ADJECTIVE [**sunnier, sunniest**] full of light from the sun ▣ *It's sunny outside.* ▣ *It's a lovely sunny day.* □ *sunny weather* (ensolarado)

sunrise /ˈsʌnraɪz/ NOUN [plural **sunrises**] the time when the sun appears in the morning □ *I was up at sunrise.* (alvorada)

sunset /ˈsʌnset/ NOUN [plural **sunsets**] the time when the sun starts to disappear in the evening □ *We left the beach at sunset.* (pôr do sol)

sunshine /ˈsʌnʃaɪn/ NOUN, NO PLURAL the light and heat of the sun ▣ *He was squinting in the bright sunshine.* (luz do sol)

suntan /ˈsʌntæn/ NOUN [plural **suntans**] a brown skin colour that you get because you have been in the sun (bronzeamento)

super /ˈsuːpə(r)/ ADVERB an informal word meaning very □ *I exercise a bit but I'm not super fit.* (super)

superb /suːˈpɜːb/ ADJECTIVE extremely good □ *a superb performance* (magnífico)

superior¹ /suːˈpɪərɪə(r)/ ADJECTIVE better than something else ▣ *This product is far superior to earlier versions.* (superior)

superior² /suːˈpɪərɪə(r)/ NOUN [plural **superiors**] a person who has a higher rank than you at work □ *He made complaints to his superiors.* (superior)

superlative¹ /suːˈpɜːlətɪv/ ADJECTIVE in grammar, the superlative form of an adjective or adverb is the form that usually ends with -est or is formed with *most*. For example, *hardest, worst* and *most difficult* are superlative forms. (superlativo)

superlative² /suːˈpɜːlətɪv/ NOUN [plural **superlatives**] a superlative form of an adjective or adverb (superlativo)

supermarket /ˈsuːpəmɑːkɪt/ NOUN [plural **supermarkets**] a large shop that sells food and other goods (supermercado)

superstar /ˈsuːpəstɑː(r)/ NOUN [plural **superstars**] a very famous actor, singer, person who plays sport, etc. (superastro, superstar)

supervise /ˈsuːpəvaɪz/ VERB [**supervises, supervising, supervised**] to be in charge of a person or activity □ *Someone has to be there to supervise the children.* □ *He was supervising the road repair work.* (supervisionar)

supervision /ˌsuːpəˈvɪʒən/ NOUN, NO PLURAL the act of being in charge of a person or activity □ *The prisoner was kept under close supervision.* (supervisão)

supper /ˈsʌpə(r)/ NOUN [plural **suppers**] a meal that you eat in the evening □ *He ate his supper and went to bed.* (jantar)

supply¹ /səˈplaɪ/ NOUN [plural **supplies**]
1 an amount of something that you can use ▣ *The lack of rain is affecting the city's water supply.* ▣ *There is a limited supply of housing in the area.* □ *+ of a supply of food* (suprimento)
2 supplies food, clothes, medicines, etc. that you need to live or to do something □ *A military plane landed with medical supplies for the refugees.* (suprimento)

supply² /səˈplaɪ/ VERB [**supplies, supplying, supplied**] to provide something □ *Wind power could supply up to 20% of the country's electricity.* □ *+ with The farm supplies several major supermarkets with milk.* □ *+ to He supplied information to the police.* (suprir, abastecer)

support¹ /səˈpɔːt/ VERB [**supports, supporting, supported**]
1 to agree with an idea, person, etc. and want them to succeed □ *I support the idea in principle.* □ *Teachers did not support the proposal.* (apoiar)
2 to be under something and stop it from falling □ *The roof was supported by wooden beams.* (sustentar, apoiar)
3 to like a particular sports team and want them to win □ *Which football team do you support?* (torcer)

4 to provide money for someone or something □ *She supports her family on a very low wage.* (sustentar)

support² /sə'pɔːt/ NOUN [plural **supports**]
1 *no plural* encouragement and help 🔲 *He called to offer support as soon as he heard about my accident.* (suporte, apoio)
2 an object under something, which stops it from falling □ *One of the supports of the bridge collapsed.* (suporte)
3 *no plural* agreement with an idea or person and wanting them to succeed 🔲 *The idea has received strong support from all the parties.* 🔲 *Klinsmann eventually won massive public support in Germany.* □ **+ for** *There was not much support for the war.* (apoio)

supporter /sə'pɔːtə(r)/ NOUN [plural **supporters**]
1 someone who likes a sports team and wants them to win □ *a Liverpool supporter* (torcedor)
2 someone who agrees with an idea or person and wants them to succeed 🔲 *He was a strong supporter of government policy.* (defensor, partidário)

suppose /sə'pəʊz/ VERB [**supposes, supposing, supposed**]
1 to think that something is probably true □ **+ that** *I suppose that all the tickets have been sold now?* 🔲 *I don't suppose we'll see him again.* □ *I suppose you'll be going to the concert.* (supor)
2 be supposed to do something (a) to be expected to do something, especially because of a rule □ *I'm supposed to look after my little sister on Saturdays.* □ *You're not supposed to walk on the grass.* (b) to be intended or expected to have a particular result or to happen in a particular way □ *The belts are supposed to support your back.* □ *He wasn't supposed to arrive until next week.* (dever, ser considerado)
3 I suppose so (a) used to agree to something that you do not want to do or to happen □ *'Could you do the shopping this week?' 'I suppose so.'* (b) used to agree that something is possible, true or correct, but in a way that shows that you are not sure or happy about it □ *'We could always hire a gardener.' 'I suppose so, but it would be rather expensive.'* (creio que sim)
4 I suppose used to say that you think something is possible, true or correct, although you are not sure or happy about it □ *We could get a taxi, I suppose.* □ *I suppose I deserve his criticism.* □ *I suppose the weather might improve.* (eu suponho)
5 be supposed to be something to be considered by many people to have a particular quality □ *That area is supposed to be really beautiful.* □ *He's supposed to be good at maths.* (ser considerado)

supreme /suːˈpriːm/ ADJECTIVE most powerful □ *the supreme ruler* (supremo)

sure /ʃʊə(r)/ ADJECTIVE
1 certain □ **+ that** *I'm sure that we've met before.* □ **+ about** *Alex is coming, but I'm not sure about Dan.* □ **+ question word** *I'm not sure why he was so angry.* □ **+ of** *I'll phone you when I'm sure of the date.* □ *Are you sure you want to leave?* (certo, seguro)
2 make sure (a) to do something to make it certain that something happens □ *Can you make sure all the doors are locked?* (b) to check that something is true □ *I think his birthday's on Saturday, but I'll look in the diary to make sure.* (ter certeza de)
3 sure to do something certain to happen or be the result of something □ *He's sure to win.* (certo)

surely /ˈʃʊəli/ ADVERB
1 used to show surprise about something □ *Surely you're going to wash that fruit before you eat it!* □ *Surely he didn't just leave her there!* (certamente)
2 used to show that you think something will probably happen □ *Surely they'll phone if they're not coming.* (com certeza)

surf /sɜːf/ NOUN, NO PLURAL the white part at the top of waves on the sea (espuma)

surface /ˈsɜːfɪs/ NOUN [plural **surfaces**] the outside or top layer of something □ *The leaves had a rough surface.* □ *The temperature of the Earth's surface has risen.* □ **+ of** *A light wind rippled the surface of the lake.* (superfície)

surfing /ˈsɜːfɪŋ/ NOUN, NO PLURAL the sport of balancing on a board and moving on the sea's waves 🔲 *We went surfing in Cornwall.* (surfe)

surgeon /ˈsɜːdʒən/ NOUN [plural **surgeons**] a doctor who does operations (cirurgião)

surgery /ˈsɜːdʒəri/ NOUN [plural **surgeries**]
1 *no plural* medical treatments which involve cutting into someone's body □ *heart surgery* (cirurgia)
2 a place where you go to see a doctor or a dentist (consultório)

surname /ˈsɜːneɪm/ NOUN [plural **surnames**] your last name or family name □ *Smith is a common English surname.* □ *What's your surname?* (sobrenome)

surplus /ˈsɜːpləs/ NOUN [plural **surpluses**] an extra amount that is more than you need □ *This country produces a surplus of grain.* (excedente)

surprise¹ /səˈpraɪz/ NOUN [plural **surprises**]
1 *no plural* the feeling caused by something sudden or unexpected □ *He stared at her in surprise.* 🔲 *To my surprise, I passed my driving test.* (surpresa)
2 something sudden or unexpected □ *Your letter was a nice surprise.* (surpresa)
3 take/catch someone by surprise to happen unexpectedly, and make you feel surprised □ *The message had taken her by surprise.* (pegar de surpresa)

surprise² /səˈpraɪz/ VERB [**surprises, surprising, surprised**]
1 to make someone feel surprise □ *He surprised me by turning up without calling.* (surpreender)
2 to attack someone suddenly and without warning □ *They surprised the enemy from the rear.* (surpreender)

surprised /səˈpraɪzd/ ADJECTIVE having a feeling of surprise ◨ *Anna looked surprised when I told her.* ◨ + *that I'm surprised that he agreed to come.* ◨ + *to do something I was very surprised to hear that he had left.* ◨ + *at/by She was surprised by the news.* (**surpreso**)

> Notice the prepositions that follow the word **surprised**. You are **surprised at** or **by** something:
> ✓ I was surprised at/by his decision.
> ✗ I was surprised about his decision.

surprising /səˈpraɪzɪŋ/ ADJECTIVE making you feel surprise ◨ *A surprising number of people voted for him.* ◨ *It's surprising how many people believe in ghosts.* (**surpreendente**)

surrender /səˈrendə(r)/ VERB [surrenders, surrendering, surrendered] to stop fighting or trying to escape because you know you will not be successful ◨ *They surrendered to the enemy.* (**render-se**)

surround /səˈraʊnd/ VERB [surrounds, surrounding, surrounded] to be or go all around something or someone ◨ *Fans surrounded the players.* ◨ *The city is surrounded by hills.* (**cercar**)

surroundings /səˈraʊndɪŋz/ PLURAL NOUN the area around a person or place ◨ *The hotel is set in beautiful surroundings.* ◨ *He was glad to be back in his own surroundings.* (**cercanias**)

survival /səˈvaɪvəl/ NOUN, NO PLURAL the fact of continuing to live or exist ◨ *His survival depended on finding fresh water.* (**sobrevivência**)

survive /səˈvaɪv/ VERB [survives, surviving, survived] to continue to live after something bad has happened ◨ *He didn't survive long after the accident.* ◨ *Amazingly, the diver survived the shark attack.* (**sobreviver**)

survivor /səˈvaɪvə(r)/ NOUN [plural survivors] someone who continues to live after something bad has happened to them ◨ *He was the only survivor of the crash which killed the princess.* (**sobrevivente**)

suspect¹ /ˈsʌspekt/ NOUN [plural suspects] someone who may have committed a crime ◨ *terrorist suspects* ◨ *He's the prime suspect in the murder of Rachel Smith.* (**suspeito**)

suspect² /səˈspekt/ VERB [suspects, suspecting, suspected]
1 to think that someone may have committed a crime ◨ *He's suspected of murdering two women.* (**suspeito**)
2 to think that something might be true ◨ *I suspect that she is hiding her true feelings.* (**suspeitar**)

suspend /səˈspend/ VERB [suspends, suspending, suspended]
1 to stop something for a period of time ◨ *All business will be suspended until after New Year.* (**suspender**)
2 to hang something ◨ *The meat was suspended from a hook.* (**pendurar**)

suspicion /səˈspɪʃən/ NOUN [plural suspicions]
1 a feeling or a belief that someone has done something wrong or illegal ◨ *He was arrested on suspicion of burglary.* (**suspeita**)
2 a feeling that something is true ◨ *I had a strong suspicion that it was broken.* (**suspeita**)

suspicious /səˈspɪʃəs/ ADJECTIVE
1 making you think that you do not completely trust someone ◨ *She gave him a suspicious glance.* (**desconfiado**)
2 making you think that a crime might be involved ◨ *He died in suspicious circumstances.* (**suspeito**)

swallow¹ /ˈswɒləʊ/ VERB [swallows, swallowing, swallowed] to make food or drink go down your throat ◨ *Try to swallow the pill.* ◨ *She swallowed a large mouthful of water.* (**engolir**)

swallow² /ˈswɒləʊ/ NOUN [plural swallows] a small bird with long pointed wings and a tail with two points (**andorinha**)

swam /swæm/ PAST TENSE OF **swim¹** (ver **swim¹**)

swamp /swɒmp/ NOUN [plural swamps] an area of land that is always very wet (**pântano**)

swan /swɒn/ NOUN [plural swans] a large white bird with a long neck which lives on rivers and lakes (**cisne**)

swap¹ /swɒp/ VERB [swaps, swapping, swapped] to exchange one thing for another thing ◨ *I took the dress back to the shop and swapped it for a bigger size.* (**trocar**)

swap² /swɒp/ NOUN [plural swaps] when you swap one thing for another ◨ *He suggested that we do a swap.* (**troca**)

sway /sweɪ/ VERB [sways, swaying, swayed] to move from side to side ◨ *The trees swayed in the wind.* (**balançar [-se]**)

swear /sweə(r)/ VERB [swears, swearing, swore, sworn]
1 to use words that are offensive ◨ *He was sent off for swearing at the referee.* (**xingar**)
2 to promise ◨ *She swore never to do it again.* (**jurar**)

sweat¹ /swet/ NOUN, NO PLURAL the salty liquid that comes out of your skin when you are hot ◨ *He was dripping with sweat after his run.* (**suor**)

sweat² /swet/ VERB [sweats, sweating, sweated] to give out sweat ◨ *Exercise makes you sweat.* (**suar**)

sweater /ˈswetə(r)/ NOUN [plural sweaters] a piece of clothing for the top part of your body that you pull over your head ◨ *He was wearing a blue sweater and jeans.* (**suéter, pulôver**)

> **THESAURUS:** A **jumper** is the same as a sweater. Sweaters and **jumpers** are often made of wool. A **sweatshirt** is a piece of clothing for the top part of your body, made of thick, soft cotton. A **cardigan** is a piece of clothing for your upper body that is made from wool and fastens with buttons down the front.

sweatshirt /'swetʃɜːt/ NOUN [plural **sweatshirts**] a piece of clothing for the top part of your body, made of thick, soft cotton (**blusão de moleton**)

sweep /swiːp/ VERB [**sweeps, sweeping, swept**]
1 to clean something using a brush □ He swept the floor. □ **+ up** She swept up the broken glass. (**varrer**)
2 to move someone or something somewhere with a quick, strong movement □ **+ away** Whole villages were swept away by the flood. □ Tonnes of mud were swept down the hillside. (**assolar**)

sweet[1] /swiːt/ ADJECTIVE [**sweeter, sweetest**]
1 tasting like sugar □ He loves sweet food. (**doce**)
2 kind and friendly □ She seems very sweet. ▣ It was sweet of him to offer. (**doce**)
3 pleasant in smell or sound □ the sweet smell of flowers (**doce, suave**)
4 attractive and making you feel affection □ a sweet little boy (**doce**)

sweet[2] /swiːt/ NOUN [plural **sweets**]
1 a small piece of sweet food, for example chocolate □ a packet of sweets (**doce**)
2 something sweet that people eat at the end of a meal (**sobremesa**)

swell /swel/ VERB [**swells, swelling, swelled, swollen**] to become bigger in size □ The wasp sting made her finger swell. □ **+ up** My feet swelled up. (**inchar [-se]**)

swept /swept/ PAST TENSE AND PAST PARTICIPLE OF **sweep** (ver **sweep**)

swerve /swɜːv/ VERB [**swerves, swerving, swerved**] to suddenly move to the right or left when you are driving □ The driver had to swerve to avoid hitting a dog. (**desviar**)

swift /swɪft/ ADJECTIVE [**swifter, swiftest**] quick □ I hope she makes a swift recovery. (**rápido, veloz**)

swim[1] /swɪm/ VERB [**swims, swimming, swam, swum**] to move through water using your arms and legs □ Can you swim? □ He swam across the river. (**nadar**)

swim[2] /swɪm/ NOUN [plural **swims**] when you swim ▣ I think I'll go for a swim. (**nado**)

swimmer /'swɪmə(r)/ NOUN [plural **swimmers**] someone or something that swims □ an Olympic swimmer ▣ She was a strong swimmer (= able to swim well). (**nadador**)

swimming /'swɪmɪŋ/ NOUN, NO PLURAL the activity or sport of moving through water using your arms and legs □ Swimming is excellent exercise. ▣ We went swimming at the local pool. (**natação**)

swimming costume /'swɪmɪŋ ˌkɒstjuːm/ NOUN [plural **swimming costumes**] a piece of clothing that women and girls wear for swimming (**maiô**)

swimming pool /'swɪmɪŋ ˌpuːl/ NOUN [plural **swimming pools**] an area of water made for swimming in (**piscina**)

swimming trunks /'swɪmɪŋ ˌtrʌŋks/ PLURAL NOUN a piece of clothing that men and boys wear for swimming (**maiô, calção**)

swimsuit /'swɪmsuːt/ NOUN [plural **swimsuits**] a piece of clothing that women and girls wear for swimming (**maiô**)

swing[1] /swɪŋ/ VERB [**swings, swinging, swung**]
1 to move backwards and forwards through the air, or to make something do this □ You swing your arms when you walk. □ The children were swinging on a rope. (**balançar**)
2 to move in a smooth, wide curve, or to make something do this ▣ The door swung open. □ She sat up and swung her legs over the side of the bed. (**balançar**)

swing[2] /swɪŋ/ NOUN [plural **swings**] a seat hanging from ropes or chains, that children sit on and move backwards and forwards (**balanço**)

switch[1] /swɪtʃ/ VERB [**switches, switching, switched**] to change from one thing to another thing □ We switched channels to watch the news. □ **+ from** She switched from English to French with no difficulty. □ **+ to** Many families have switched to cheaper gas suppliers. (**mudar**)

◆ PHRASAL VERB **switch (something) on/off** to turn something on or off using a switch □ I switched the light on. □ He'd forgotten to switch off the microphone.

> **THESAURUS:** If you turn something on, you move a switch or a device so that a machine starts working or a supply of something starts. You can turn on a light or turn on a tap, for example. If you switch something on, you turn it on, using a switch. You switch on a light, but you cannot switch on a tap. When you open something, you move it to a position that is not shut or fastened. You open a door or a window, for example.

switch[2] /swɪtʃ/ NOUN [plural **switches**] a device that you press to make something work or stop working ▣ I can't find the light switch. (**interruptor**)

swollen[1] /'swəʊlən/ ADJECTIVE bigger than usual □ He had a swollen ankle after falling downstairs. □ Several swollen rivers burst their banks. (**inchado**)

swollen[2] /'swəʊlən/ PAST PARTICIPLE OF **swell** (ver **swell**)

swoop /swuːp/ VERB [**swoops, swooping, swooped**] to suddenly and quickly move down □ The owl swooped down on its prey. (**mergulhar sobre**)

sword /sɔːd/ NOUN [plural **swords**] a weapon with a long blade (**espada**)

swore /swɔː(r)/ PAST TENSE OF **swear** (ver **swear**)

sworn /swɔːn/ PAST PARTICIPLE OF **swear** (ver **swear**)

swum /swʌm/ PAST PARTICIPLE OF **swim**[1] (ver **swim**[1])

syllable /ˈsɪləbəl/ NOUN [plural **syllables**] a word or part of a word that is a single sound. For example, *pen* has one syllable and *pen-cil* has two syllables. (**sílaba**)

symbol /ˈsɪmbəl/ NOUN [plural **symbols**]
1 something that represents a more general idea □ + *of* *The dove is a symbol of peace.* 🔲 *The statue became a symbol of freedom.* (**símbolo**)
2 a written sign or a letter that represents some thing □ + *for* *His chemical symbol for hydrogen* (**símbolo**)

sympathetic /ˌsɪmpəˈθetɪk/ ADJECTIVE feeling or showing sympathy □ *a sympathetic smile* (**simpático, solidário**)

sympathy /ˈsɪmpəθi/ NOUN [plural **sympathies**] when you feel sorry for someone who is unhappy or suffering □ + *for* *I have great sympathy for the victims.* □ *She received many letters of sympathy when her husband died.* □ *He expressed his sympathies to the family.* (**compaixão, condolência**)

symptom /ˈsɪmptəm/ NOUN [plural **symptoms**] a sign that someone has a particular illness □ *Sore throat, blocked nose, and sneezing are the usual symptoms of a cold.* (**sintoma**)

synagogue /ˈsɪnəgɒg/ NOUN [plural **synagogues**] a building where Jewish people go to pray (**sinagoga**)

syrup /ˈsɪrəp/ NOUN [plural **syrups**] a thick, sticky substance made from sugar (**xarope, calda**)

system /ˈsɪstəm/ NOUN [plural **systems**]
1 an way of organizing or doing something 🔲 *the country's education system* 🔲 *the US legal system* □ + *for* *We have a new system for processing applications.* (**sistema**)
2 pieces of equipment that work together □ *a computer operating system* □ *There's a problem with the central heating system.* (**sistema**)

T t

T or t /tiː/ the 20th letter of the alphabet (**a vigésima nona letra do alfabeto**)

table /ˈteɪbəl/ NOUN [plural **tables**]
1 a piece of furniture with a flat surface that you put things on ◘ *They were sitting at the dining room/kitchen table.* (**mesa**)
2 a set of numbers or words that are arranged in rows ▫ *The table below shows which schools have the best results.* (**tabela**)

tablecloth /ˈteɪbəlklɒθ/ NOUN [plural **tablecloths**] a cloth for covering a table. (**toalha**)

tablespoon /ˈteɪbəlspuːn/ NOUN [plural **tablespoons**] a large spoon, often used for measuring things when you are cooking. (**colher de sopa**)

tablet /ˈtæblɪt/ NOUN [plural **tablets**] a pill ◘ *She took a vitamin tablet.* ▫ *She takes sleeping tablets.* (**comprimido**)

table tennis /ˈteɪbəl ˌtenɪs/ NOUN, NO PLURAL a game in which people hit a ball over a net which is attached to a table (**pingue-pongue, tênis de mesa**)

tabloid /ˈtæblɔɪd/ NOUN [plural **tabloids**] a small newspaper with lots of pictures and not much serious news (**tabloide**)

tackle /ˈtækəl/ VERB [tackles, tackling, tackled]
1 to deal with something difficult ◘ *The policy is designed to tackle the problem of pollution.* ▫ *The government has failed to tackle poverty.* (**atacar, enfrentar**)
2 to try to get the ball from another player in games such as football (**desarmar**)

tactic /ˈtæktɪk/ NOUN [plural **tactics**] a way of doing something to achieve what you want ◘ *The companies had used the same tactics for promoting their products.* ▫ *I've got a new tactic for persuading the children to walk.* (**tática**)

tag /tæɡ/ NOUN [plural **tags**] a small piece of paper, plastic, etc. with information on it which is attached to something else ◘ *She looked at the price tag on the jacket.* (**etiqueta**)

tail /teɪl/ NOUN [plural **tails**] the part that sticks out from the end of an animal's body ◘ *The dog wagged its tail.* (**rabo**)

take /teɪk/ VERB [takes, taking, took, taken]
1 to get something and often move it from one place to another ▫ *I took him some food.* ▫ *Make sure you take a coat with you.* ▫ *Who's taken all the milk?* ▫ **+ away** *His passport was taken away from him.* ▫ **+ back** *I must take Jo's book back.* ▫ **+ out** *He opened the case and took out a jacket.* (**pegar, tirar**)
2 to accept something that you have been offered ▫ *She took a biscuit.* ▫ *Are you going to take the job?* ▫ *Do you take credit cards?* (**aceitar**)
3 to go somewhere with someone, especially to look after them or to provide transport for them ▫ *I took my mother to the hospital.* ▫ *I take my son swimming every week.* (**levar**)
4 to do or have a particular thing ▫ *Take a deep breath.* ▫ *Take a look at his work.* ▫ *She won't take any responsibility for the business.* ▫ *Sometimes, you have to take a chance.* (**fazer, aceitar, arriscar**)
5 to need a particular amount of time to be done ▫ *I just need to finish this letter – it won't take long.* ▫ *It took him five years to finish his novel.* (**levar, tomar**)
6 to need something ▫ **+ to do something** *It takes a lot of courage to oppose your friends.* ▫ *It took five people to lift the piano.* (**necessitar**)
7 to travel somewhere using a particular form of transport ▫ *I took a ferry to Stockholm.* (**pegar, tomar**)
8 to swallow medicine ▫ *I have to take these antibiotics for a week.* (**tomar**)
9 if you take a photograph, you use your camera to make a picture (**tirar**)
⇨ go to **take your breath away, take your mind¹ off something**

◆ PHRASAL VERBS **take after someone** to be like an older person in your family ▫ *She's so emotional – she takes after her father.* **take something down** to write something ▫ *He took down our names.* **take something off** to remove a piece of clothing ▫ *He took off his jacket.* **take off** if an aircraft takes off, it leaves the ground at the beginning of a flight **take over (something) 1** to start doing something that someone else was doing ▫ *Could you take over the cooking while I make a phone call?* ▫ **+ from** *She took over from Annie as*

secretary. **2** to take control of something □ *The business was taken over by a French company.*
take something up 1 to start doing an activity □ *I've taken up judo.* **2** to use a particular amount of time or space □ *His piano takes up most of the front room.*

> **THESAURUS:** If you take something, you get something and often move it from one place to another. If you take something violently or suddenly, you can say that you grab it or snatch it. If you grasp something, you take hold of it tightly. If you catch something, you stop and hold something that is moving through the air. You might catch a ball, for example. If you hold something, you have it in your hand or hands.

taken /ˈteɪkən/ PAST PARTICIPLE OF **take** (ver **take**)

take-off /ˈteɪkɒf/ NOUN [plural take-offs] the time when an aeroplane leaves the ground and goes up into the air □ *Please keep your seat belt fastened during take-off.* (**decolagem**)

takeover /ˈteɪkəʊvə(r)/ NOUN [plural takeovers] when a company takes control of another company ▣ *The company accepted a takeover bid.* (**aquisição**)

tale /teɪl/ NOUN [plural tales] a story, often one that is difficult to believe □ *tales of great adventures* (**história, conto**)

talent /ˈtælənt/ NOUN [plural talents] a natural ability to do something well □ *Sarah had a talent for acting.* (**talento**)

talented /ˈtæləntɪd/ ADJECTIVE having the ability to do something well □ *She's a talented young artist.* (**talentoso**)

talk[1] /tɔːk/ VERB [talks, talking, talked] to say words in order to communicate □ + *to I talked to Molly on the phone yesterday.* □ + *about He's always talking about football.* □ *I like him, but he talks too much.* (**falar, discutir**)

talk[2] /tɔːk/ NOUN [plural talks]
1 a conversation ▣ *I need to have a talk with Julie.* □ + *about We had a brief talk about school.* (**conversa**)
2 when someone talks to a group of people about a particular subject ▣ *He gave a talk about his work with gorillas.* (**palestra, conferência**)
3 talks formal meetings between people such as politicians, especially to try to make plans or solve arguments ▣ *Ministers will be holding talks in Geneva.* □ + *between Talks between unions and employers have broken down.* (**conversas, discussões**)

tall /tɔːl/ ADJECTIVE [taller, tallest]
1 bigger in height than most people or things ▣ *a tall building* □ *He's tall for his age.* □ *tall trees* (**alto, grande**)
2 used when talking about the height of someone or something □ *She's less than five feet tall.* (**de altura**)

tame /teɪm/ ADJECTIVE [tamer, tamest] a tame animal is no longer wild, and has been trained to be near people (**domesticado**)

tan[1] /tæn/ VERB [tans, tanning, tanned] to get darker skin because you have been in the sun □ *She tans very easily.* (**bronzear-se**)

tan[2] /tæn/ NOUN [plural tans] a brown colour on your skin because you have been in the sun □ *Many people want to get a tan even though it is bad for your skin.* (**bronzeado**)

tangle /ˈtæŋɡəl/ NOUN [plural tangles] a mass of wires, hair, string, etc. which are twisted together (**emaranhado, bagunça**)

tank /tæŋk/ NOUN [plural tanks]
1 a large container for liquids or gases ▣ *The car's fuel tank was empty.* □ *an oxygen tank* (**tanque, reservatório**)
2 a large military vehicle with a gun on top, which moves on metal belts over wheels (**tanque de guerra**)

tanker /ˈtæŋkə(r)/ NOUN [plural tankers] a ship or truck which carries liquids or gases ▣ *an oil tanker* (**petroleiros, caminhões-tanque**)

tap[1] /tæp/ NOUN [plural taps]
1 a device you use for controlling the flow of water or gas from a pipe ▣ *She turned on the tap to wash her hands.* ▣ *The tap is dripping.* ▣ *I always drink tap water rather than bottled water.* □ *the hot/cold tap* (**torneira**) (**torneira**)
2 a light knock □ *He felt a tap on his shoulder.* (**batidas leves**)

tap[2] /tæp/ VERB [taps, tapping, tapped]
1 to knock gently □ + *on He tapped on the window.* □ *She tapped me on the arm.* (**batida leve, tapinha**)
2 to hit your fingers or feet gently against something ▣ *He tapped his foot in time with the music.* (**batucar, marcar o compasso**)

tape[1] /teɪp/ NOUN [plural tapes]
1 a long, thin piece of plastic for recording sounds or pictures, or the case that it is kept in ▣ *They played a tape of the police interview.* (**fita**)
2 no plural a long, thin piece of plastic that is sticky on one side, used for fastening things □ *The door was sealed with yellow police tape.* (**fita**)

tape[2] /teɪp/ VERB [tapes, taping, taped]
1 to record sounds and pictures onto tape □ *I taped the show to watch later.* (**gravar**)
2 to fasten something somewhere using tape □ *The note was taped to the car's windscreen.* (**prender com fita**)

target /ˈtɑːɡɪt/ NOUN [plural targets]
1 a level that you are trying to achieve ▣ *The company won't reach its sales targets.* (**alvo**)
2 a mark or object that people aim at when they

are shooting 🔁 I practised until I could hit the target. (alvo)
3 a person or thing that someone attacks 🔁 Old people are an easy target for thieves. ☐ It is believed that the White House was the intended target of the attack. (alvo)

task /tɑːsk/ NOUN [plural tasks] a job that you have to do 🔁 The school is facing the difficult task of trying to raise money. 🔁 He was so ill that he couldn't even perform simple tasks. ☐ **+ of** The teacher gave me the task of helping her to carry the books. (tarefa)

> **THESAURUS: Job** is a general word for the work that someone does regularly for money, or for a piece of work. A **task** is a piece of work that you have to do. A **duty** is something that you do because other people expect you to do it, or because it is morally right to do it. An **exercise** is a piece of written work that you do when you are studying.

taste¹ /teɪst/ NOUN [plural tastes]
1 the flavour of something, especially food or drink ☐ The seeds have a bitter taste. (gosto)
2 *no plural* the ability to recognize flavours ☐ Smoking can affect your sense of taste. (paladar)
3 *no plural* the ability to judge if something such as clothing, art or behaviour is good and suitable for a situation 🔁 He has extremely good taste. (gosto)

taste² /teɪst/ VERB [tastes, tasting, tasted]
1 to have a particular flavour ☐ This sauce tastes salty. (ter gosto de)
2 to experience the flavour of something ☐ Can you taste the herbs in this? (sentir o gosto)
3 to try a small amount of food or drink to judge its flavour ☐ Have you tasted this cheese? (experimentar)

> **THESAURUS:** If you **taste** food, you try a small amount of it to judge its flavour. If you **chew** food, you break it up inside your mouth with your teeth. If you **swallow** food, you make it go down your throat. If you **eat** food, you put it in your mouth and swallow it.

tasty /teɪsti/ ADJECTIVE [tastier, tastiest] having a good flavor (saboroso)

tattoo /tæˈtuː/ NOUN [plural tattoos] a permanent picture made on someone's skin with ink (tatuagem)

taught /tɔːt/ PAST TENSE AND PAST PARTICIPLE OF **teach** (ver **teach**)

tax¹ /tæks/ NOUN [plural taxes] money you pay to the government from your income or that is added to the price of goods you buy to pay for public services 🔁 Most pensioners don't pay tax.
☐ **+ on** A company pays tax on its profits. 🔁 income tax rates (taxa, imposto)

tax² /tæks/ VERB [taxes, taxing, taxed] to charge tax on something ☐ There are plans to tax the profits of oil companies. ☐ Their income will be taxed at 40%. (taxar)

taxi /ˈtæksi/ NOUN [plural taxis] a car with a driver that you pay to take you from one place to another 🔁 They took a taxi to the airport. 🔁 Don't worry, I'll get a taxi home. 🔁 a taxi driver (táxi)

tea /tiː/ NOUN [plural teas]
1 a drink made by pouring boiling water on dried leaves, or the leaves you use to make this drink 🔁 Can I have a cup of tea? 🔁 She sat and drank her tea. ☐ Two teas and a coffee, please. ☐ Do you serve peppermint tea? (chá)
2 *no plural* a light meal with tea that some people have in the afternoon ☐ We stopped in a cafe for afternoon tea. (chá)
3 *no plural* used by some people to refer to the meal they have in the early evening (chá)

teach /tiːtʃ/ VERB [teaches, teaching, taught]
1 to give lessons at a school, college or university ☐ She taught at the local school. ☐ He teaches maths. ☐ Students are taught in small classes. (ensinar)
2 to pass your knowledge, skills or experience on to another person ☐ **+ to do something** Parents should teach their children to behave properly. ☐ **+ question word** Will you teach me how to sail a yacht? ☐ **+ about** They teach the children about healthy eating. (ensinar)

> **THESAURUS: Teach** is a general word for passing your knowledge, skills or experience on to another person. If you **instruct** or **train** someone, you tell them how to do something, especially something practical. You might **train** or **instruct** someone to use a new computer, for example. **Train** and **coach** are used to talk about helping people to improve a skill, often a sport. For example, a person might **train** or **coach** an athlete to compete in the Olympic Games.

teacher /ˈtiːtʃə(r)/ NOUN [plural teachers] someone who teaches, usually as their job ☐ She's an English teacher. ☐ He's the head teacher at the local school. (professor)

teaching /ˈtiːtʃɪŋ/ NOUN, NO PLURAL the work of a teacher ☐ teaching methods ☐ language teaching materials ☐ We want to improve the quality of teaching in schools. (ensino)

team /tiːm/ NOUN [plural teams]
1 a group of people who play together against another group in a game or a sport ☐ the England cricket team ☐ Which football team do you

support? ▫ He was selected for the national team. (**time**)
2 a group of people who work together ▫ *+ of* *a team of engineers* ▫ *the senior management team* (**equipe**)

tear¹ /teə(r)/ VERB [tears, tearing, tore, torn]
1 to damage paper, cloth, etc. by pulling it apart or making a hole in it ▫ *You've torn your sleeve on that barbed wire.* ▫ *The cat tore a hole in the curtain.* (**rasgar, arrancar**)
2 to pull or to remove something using force ▫ *a page torn from a notebook* ▫ *Liz tore open the envelope.* ▫ *He tore off a large chunk of bread.* (**rasgar, arrancar**)

◆ PHRASAL VERB **tear something up** to pull a piece of paper into many small pieces ▫ *She tore up the letter.* (**picar, rasgar, despedaçar**)

tear² /teə(r)/ NOUN [plural tears] the place where something has been torn ▫ *There was a large tear in the fabric.* (**rasgos**)

tear³ /tɪə(r)/ NOUN [plural tears]
1 a drop of liquid that comes from your eyes when you cry ▫ *His mum burst into tears* (= started crying). ▫ *They cried tears of joy.* (**lágrimas**)
2 in tears crying ▫ *We were all in tears at the end of the film.* (**aos prantos**)

tease /tiːz/ VERB [teases, teasing, teased] to say or do something to make someone angry or embarrassed, or to make them believe something that is not true, either as a joke or to make them angry ▫ *I didn't mean what I said. I was only teasing.* ▫ *Stop teasing the dog!* (**provocar, irritar**)

teaspoon /ˈtiːspuːn/ NOUN [plural teaspoons] a small spoon used for mixing sugar in tea or for measuring small amounts (**colher de chá**)

technical /ˈteknɪkəl/ ADJECTIVE to do with science and technology ▫ *Does he have any technical training?* (**técnico**)

technician /tekˈnɪʃən/ NOUN [plural technicians] someone whose job is to do practical work in a laboratory or to use special equipment (**técnico**)

technique /tekˈniːk/ NOUN [plural techniques] a particular method of doing something ▫ *traditional painting techniques* ▫ *We've been using a new technique.* ▫ *+ for* *There are improved techniques for language testing.* (**técnica**)

technological /ˌteknəˈlɒdʒɪkəl/ ADJECTIVE to do with technology ▫ *technological advances* (**tecnológico**)

technology /tekˈnɒlədʒi/ NOUN [plural technologies] scientific knowledge, methods or equipment used in practical ways ▫ *The system uses wireless technology.* ▫ *The company is investing in new technology.* (**tecnologia**)

teenage /ˈtiːneɪdʒ/ ADJECTIVE aged between 13 and 19 ▫ *a teenage girl* ▫ *a group of teenage boys* ▫ *They have a teenage son.* (**adolescente**)

teenager /ˈtiːneɪdʒə(r)/ NOUN [plural teenagers] someone who is aged between 13 and 19 ▫ *She's just a typical teenager.* ▫ *The site's popular with teenagers and young adults.* (**adolescente**)

teens /tiːnz/ PLURAL NOUN the years of your life between the ages of 13 and 19 ▫ *He was in his teens when the family moved.* ▫ *The audience were mostly in their late teens and early twenties.* (**adolescência**)

teeth /tiːθ/ PLURAL OF **tooth** ▫ *Look after your teeth.* (**dentes**)

telephone¹ /ˈtelɪfəʊn/ NOUN [plural telephones]
1 no plural a system for speaking to someone in another place, using equipment connected by wires ▫ *I spoke to him by telephone yesterday.* ▫ *Kennedy made a telephone call.* (**telefone**)
2 a piece of equipment that you use to make telephone calls ▫ *The telephone rang.* ▫ *Isabelle answered the telephone.* ▫ *Can I use your telephone?* (**telefone**)

telephone² /ˈtelɪfəʊn/ VERB [telephones, telephoning, telephoned] to contact someone using the telephone ▫ *Her mother telephoned the police when she didn't return home.* (**telefonar**)

telescope /ˈtelɪskəʊp/ NOUN [plural telescopes] a piece of equipment with lenses (= curved pieces of glass) and mirrors inside that makes objects that are far away seem closer or larger (**telescópio**)

television

television /ˈtelɪvɪʒən/ NOUN [plural televisions]
1 no plural a system for sending images and sounds in the form of electrical signals, or programmes broadcast in this way ▣ Children watch too much television. ☐ Is there anything good on television tonight? (**televisão**)
2 the equipment which receives these pictures and sounds ☐ a new flat-screen television ▣ an old black-and-white television set ▣ He switched on the television. (**televisão**)

> Remember that people and things appear on television:
> ✓ He's often on television these days.
> ✗ He's often in television these days.

tell /tel/ VERB [tells, telling, told]
1 to give someone information by speaking ☐ Don't tell Mum I've lost my key. ☐ + that He told the court that he was abroad at the time. ☐ + question word Can you tell us why you disagree? ▣ He promised to tell the truth. ▣ She accused us of telling lies about her. (**contar, dizer**)
2 to order someone to do something ☐ + to do something He told me to sit down. ▣ I wish you would do as you are told! (**mandar**)
3 if you can tell something, you know that it is true or recognize the characteristics of someone or something ▣ I couldn't tell if he was joking or not. ☐ + that I could tell that she was upset. ▣ Can you tell the difference between butter and margarine? (**dizer**)
4 tell the time to be able to understand the information on a clock or watch (**dizer a hora**)

> Note that when you use the word tell, meaning 'to speak to someone', you must say the person that you are speaking to:
> ✓ I told Peter I would come.
> ✓ I told him I would come.
> ✗ I told that I would come.

◆ PHRASAL VERB **tell someone off** to speak angrily to someone who has done something wrong ☐ + for He told me off for wasting water. (**repreender**)

temper /ˈtempə(r)/ NOUN [plural tempers]
1 when someone becomes angry very easily ▣ My father had a really bad temper. ☐ He was known for his violent temper. (**gênio forte**)
2 lose your temper to become angry ☐ I'm afraid I lost my temper and shouted at him. (**perder o controle**)
3 a person's mood ☐ Don't ask him until he's in a better temper. (**temperamento**)

temperature /ˈtemprətʃə(r)/ NOUN [plural temperatures]
1 how hot or cold a place or a thing is ☐ Average temperatures in spring are 19–24°C. ☐ + of a temperature of minus 10°C (**temperatura**)
2 how hot or cold a person's body is ▣ Flora woke up with a headache and a high temperature. ▣ A nurse came in to take his temperature (= to measure it). (**temperatura**)
3 have a temperature if someone has a temperature, their body is hotter than it should be because they are ill (**estar com febre**)

temple /ˈtempəl/ NOUN [plural temples]
1 a building in which the members of some religions show respect for a god by praying, having religious ceremonies, etc. ☐ a Hindu temple (**templo**)
2 the area on the side of your head between the side of your eye and your hair ☐ He rubbed his temples. (**têmpora**)

temporarily /ˈtempərərɪli/ ADVERB for a short or limited time only ☐ The road was temporarily closed. ☐ He'd repaired the roof temporarily with a piece of plastic. ☐ The noise seems to have stopped, at least temporarily. (**temporariamente, provisoriamente**)

temporary /ˈtempərəri/ ADJECTIVE lasting or used only for a short or limited time ☐ a temporary job ☐ The firm hires temporary workers in the summer. ▣ Some families are living in temporary accommodation. (**temporário**)

> **THESAURUS:** A temporary job only lasts for a short time. A part-time job is a job where you only work for part of the day or part of the working week. A permanent job is a job which lasts forever or for a long time. A full-time job is one where you work for all of the hours of a normal job, not part of the time.

tempt /tempt/ VERB [tempts, tempting, tempted] to make someone want to do something or to have something ☐ I was very tempted by their offer. ☐ Special deals are tempting people to switch banks. (**tentar**)

ten /ten/ NUMBER [plural tens] the number 10 (**dez**)

tenant /ˈtenənt/ NOUN [plural tenants] someone who pays rent to the owner of a house, building or land to use it ☐ The table was left by the previous tenants. (**inquilino**)

tend /tend/ VERB [tends, tending, tended] tend to do something to often do something, happen, or be a particular way ☐ She tends to be a bit moody. ☐ People tend not to talk about financial problems. (**tender**)

tender /ˈtendə(r)/ ADJECTIVE
1 tender meat and vegetables are soft and easy to cut ☐ Cook the beans until tender. (**macio, tenro**)
2 kind and gentle ☐ They shared a tender moment. (**terno**)
3 slightly painful when touched ☐ The skin is tender and red. (**sensível**)

tennis /ˈtenɪs/ NOUN, NO PLURAL
a game played on a court with a net across the middle in which the players hit a small ball over the net using rackets (= objects held in the hand) 🔹 We *play tennis* every weekend. 🔹 a professional *tennis player* 🔹 a *tennis court* (**tênis**)

tense¹ /tens/ NOUN [plural tenses]
a form of a verb which shows if the action of the verb happens now (the present tense), in the past (the past tense), or in the future (the future tense) (**tempo**)

tense² /tens/ ADJECTIVE [tenser, tensest]
1 feeling nervous and unable to relax ☐ *He looked tense and exhausted.* (**tenso**)
2 stretched tight ☐ *tense muscles* (**tenso**)

tense³ /tens/ VERB [tenses, tensing, tensed]
if you tense your muscles, you stretch them tight (**retesar**)

tent /tent/ NOUN [plural tents]
a frame covered with cloth which you sleep in when you are camping 🔹 We *pitched the tent* (= put it up) *next to the river.* (**tenda, barraca**)

tenth¹ /tenθ/ NUMBER
10th written as a word (**décimo**)

tenth² /tenθ/ NOUN [plural tenths]
1/10; one of ten equal parts of something (**um décimo**)

term /tɜːm/ NOUN [plural terms]
1 one of the periods of time that the school or college year is divided into ☐ *Students do exams in the summer term.* (**período**)
2 a limited period of time ☐ *the president's term of office* ☐ + **of** *He was sent to prison for a term of 15 years.* (**período**)
3 a word or expression with a particular meaning or used in a particular subject 🔹 *Patients don't understand complicated medical terms.* ☐ + **for** *What is the term for someone who collects coins?* ☐ + **of** *'Darling' is a term of affection.* (**termo**)
4 terms the rules of an agreement ☐ *Under the terms of his contract, he is eligible for a payment of £2 million.* (**termos**)

> **THESAURUS:** A **word** is a unit of language that is written as a group of letters with spaces on either side. A **term** is a word or expression with a particular meaning or used in a particular subject. For example, you might talk about a scientific term or a cookery term. An **expression** is a word or a phrase. You might talk about a German **expression**, or a humorous **expression**, for example.

terminal /ˈtɜːmɪnəl/ NOUN [plural terminals]
a building where planes, boats, trains or buses arrive at and leave from 🔹 *Smoking is not allowed in the terminal building.* ☐ *Developers want to build a new terminal at the airport.* (**terminal**)

terrace /ˈterəs/ NOUN [plural terraces]
1 an area next to a building or on the roof of a building where you can sit ☐ *They sat and drank coffee on the terrace at the Hotel Duomo.* (**terraço**)
2 a row of houses that are joined to each other (**fileira de casas**)
3 one of a series of flat areas cut into the side of a hill, where crops are grown (**terraço**)

terrain /teˈreɪn/ NOUN, NO PLURAL
a particular type of land ☐ *rough terrain* (**terreno**)

terrible /ˈterəbəl/ ADJECTIVE
very bad or of very low quality ☐ *a terrible smell* ☐ *He made a terrible mistake.* ☐ *I'm terrible at remembering names.* 🔹 *I feel terrible about lying to my parents.* (**terrível, horrível**)

terribly /ˈterəbli/ ADVERB
1 extremely ☐ *I'm terribly sorry I broke your vase.* ☐ *I feel terribly guilty about it.* (**extremamente**)
2 very badly ☐ *His death has affected us terribly.* (**terrivelmente**)

terrific /təˈrɪfɪk/ ADJECTIVE
excellent ☐ *He's done a terrific job as team captain.* ☐ *The party was terrific.* (**excelente, extraordinário**)

terrified /ˈterɪfaɪd/ ADJECTIVE
very frightened ☐ *I was terrified of my history teacher.* ☐ *He is absolutely terrified that someone will break into the house.* (**aterrorizado**)

terrify /ˈterɪfaɪ/ VERB [terrifies, terrifying, terrified]
to make someone feel very frightened ☐ *The thought of dying terrifies me.* (**aterrorizar**)

territory /ˈterətəri/ NOUN [plural territories]
1 the land that a particular country controls 🔹 *The army was in enemy territory.* ☐ *The plane wasn't allowed to land on British territory.* (**território**)
2 the area that an animal thinks is its own ☐ *Cats don't like other cats going into their territory.* (**território**)

terror /ˈterə(r)/ NOUN, NO PLURAL
a feeling of great fear ☐ *He ran away in terror.* (**terror**)

terrorism /ˈterərɪzəm/ NOUN, NO PLURAL
violence used by illegal groups to achieve political aims ☐ *There has been a rise in global terrorism.* (**terrorismo**)

terrorist /ˈterərɪst/ NOUN [plural terrorists]
someone who uses violence to achieve political aims 🔹 *a terrorist organization* ☐ *a suspected terrorist* (**terrorista**)

test¹ /test/ NOUN [plural tests]
1 an exam, usually a short one ☐ *a spelling test* 🔹 *You will need to pass a simple maths test.* 🔹 *I had to take a test to prove my French was good enough.* 🔹 *He failed his driving test.* (**exame, prova**)
2 something you do to check that something works correctly, is safe, etc. 🔹 *They will be conducting tests on the new aircraft next year.* 🔹 *nuclear tests* ☐ *an eye/blood test* (**teste**)

> Remember that you **do** or **take** a test (exam). You do not 'make' a test:
> ✓ *I had to do a test in my interview.*
> ✗ *I had to make a test in my interview.*

> **THESAURUS:** A **test** is a short examination, or something you do to check that something works correctly. An **experiment** is a scientific test to discover or prove something. An **investigation** is an attempt to find out about something such as an accident or a crime. The police conduct an **investigation** when a crime has taken place.

test² /test/ VERB [tests, testing, tested]
1 to do something to check that something works correctly, is safe, etc. □ *After driving through water, you should test the brakes.* □ **+ on** *The drugs are tested on volunteers.* □ *I need to get my eyes tested.* (**testar, examinar**)
2 to give someone an exam, usually a short one □ **+ on** *Can you test me on my verb endings?* (**testar**)

text¹ /tekst/ NOUN [plural texts]
1 a written message sent to a mobile phone □ *I sent a text to my sister.* □ *She got a text from her boyfriend.* (**mensagem**)
2 no plural the writing in a book □ *The pictures were nice but the text wasn't very interesting.* (**texto**)
3 a book or piece of writing that people study □ *India's ancient texts* (**texto, matéria**)

text² /tekst/ VERB [texts, texting, texted]
to send a written message to someone's mobile phone □ *Text me when you get to the station.* (**mandar uma mensagem**)

textbook /'tekstbʊk/ NOUN [plural textbooks] a book about a subject which you use at school or college □ *a biology textbook* (**livro escolar**)

text message /'tekst ˌmesɪdʒ/ NOUN [plural text messages] a **text¹** (= written message sent to a mobile phone) (**mensagem de texto**)

texture /'tekstʃə(r)/ NOUN [plural textures] the way something feels when you touch it □ *the smooth texture of a baby's skin* (**textura**)

than /ðæn/ CONJUNCTION
used when comparing things □ *The test was easier than I expected.* □ *He can swim better than me.* □ *The dress cost more than £200.* (**que, do que**)

thank /θæŋk/ VERB [thanks, thanking, thanked]
to tell someone that you are grateful for something □ **+ for** *He thanked me for the birthday present* □ *I must thank Emma for helping me.* (**agradecer**)

thanks¹ /θæŋks/ EXCLAMATION
1 something you say to show that you are grateful □ *'I've made you a drink.' 'Thanks.'* □ *'Here's an invitation to the party.' 'Oh, thanks very much.'* □ **+ for** *Thanks for the present. It's lovely.* □ *Thanks for driving me to the airport.* (**obrigado**)
2 no thanks used as a polite way of saying you do not want something □ *'Do you want to come with us?' 'No thanks, I'm busy on Saturday.'* (**não, obrigado**)

thanks² /θæŋks/ PLURAL NOUN
1 something you say or do to show that you are grateful □ *He expressed his thanks to everyone who helped.* □ *I got no thanks for helping him.* (**agradecimento**)
2 thanks to someone/something because of someone or something □ *We finished the project on time, thanks to everyone's hard work.* □ *Thanks to the strike, our flight was cancelled.* (**graças a**)

Thanksgiving /'θæŋksˌgɪvɪŋ/ NOUN, NO PLURAL
a holiday in the US and Canada in autumn, when families eat a special meal together (**dia de Ação de Graças**)

thank you /'θæŋkjuː/ EXCLAMATION
1 something you say to someone when you are grateful for something they have done or given you □ *'I've made you a cup of coffee.' 'Oh, thank you very much.'* □ **+ for** *Thank you for the flowers. They're beautiful.* □ *Thank you for helping me yesterday.* (**obrigado**)
2 used when answering a question in a polite way □ *'How are you?' 'I'm fine, thank you.'* (**obrigado**)
3 used as a polite way of accepting or refusing someone's offer □ *'Would you like to come for a meal with us?' 'Thank you. That would be lovely.'* □ *'Do you want another biscuit?' 'No, thank you.'* (**obrigado**)

> Note that you say **thank you for** something or **thank you for + doing** something: □ *Thank you for your help.* □ *Thank you for helping.*

that¹ /ðæt/ CONJUNCTION
1 used after some verbs, adjectives and nouns to start a new part of a sentence □ *He said that he hated sports.* □ *We must make sure that we invite enough people.* □ *The fact that he earns so much means he can afford a big house.* (**que**)
2 used instead of 'who' or 'which' at the beginning of a clause (= part of a sentence) □ *People that know her well say she is very unhappy.* □ *We are working with organizations that provide emergency aid.* (**que**)

that² /ðæt/ ADVERB
to the amount or degree mentioned □ *It's a kilometre to the shops. I can't walk that far.* □ *The film wasn't that bad.* (**tão**)

that³ /ðæt/ PRONOUN [plural those]
1 used to talk about something that you can see

or that you have already talked about □ *I don't want to know that.* □ *Who is that at the door?* **(aquele, aquilo, isso)**
2 that's it (a) used to say that someone has done something correctly □ *Put the wire through the hole – that's it.* (b) used to show that you are angry and will not continue with something □ *That's it! You can cook your own meals from now on!* **(é isso, já chega)**

that⁴ /ðæt/ DETERMINER [*plural* those] used to talk about a person or thing that you can see or that you have already talked about □ *Who is that girl over there?* □ *Pass me that towel, please.* □ *I left that job a year ago.* **(aquele, esse)**

that'd /ˈðætəd/ a short way to say and write that had or that would □ *That'd never happened before.* □ *That'd be nice.* **(abreviação de that had ou that would)**

that'll /ˈðætəl/ a short way to say and write that will □ *That'll be too big for you.* **(abreviação de that will)**

that's /ðæts/ a short way to say and write that is □ *That's not what I meant.* **(abreviação de that is)**

the /ðə/ DETERMINER
1 used before a noun to refer to a particular person or thing that has been mentioned or is known about □ *The bus arrived late, as usual.* □ *I opened the letter and read it.* □ *The men rode on horses and the women walked.* **(o, a, os, as)**
2 used before a noun when there is only one of that thing □ *The moon was shining.* □ *Balloons floated up into the air.* **(o, a, os, as)**
3 used to refer to part of a thing □ *Hold the box at the bottom.* □ *Come to the back of the building.* **(o, a, os, as)**
4 used in dates □ *the third of June* □ *July the fourth*
5 used before nouns referring to groups of people or things of the same kind □ *the poor* (= poor people) □ *the English* (= English people) **(o, a, os, as)**

theater /ˈθɪətə(r)/ NOUN [*plural* theaters]
1 the US spelling of theatre **(teatro)**
2 the US word for cinema **(cinema)**

theatre /ˈθɪətə(r)/ NOUN [*plural* theatres] a building where plays are performed 🔁 *We went to the theatre last night.* **(teatro)**

theft /θeft/ NOUN [*plural* thefts] the crime of stealing something 🔁 *car thefts* □ **+ of** *The theft of a computer is a serious matter.* □ *She was jailed for theft.* **(roubo)**

their /ðeə(r)/ DETERMINER belonging to or to do with them □ *Do you know their address?* **(seu, dele, sua, dela)**

theirs /ðeəz/ PRONOUN used to talk or write about things belonging to or to do with a group of people or things that have already been mentioned □ *They say it belongs to them, but I know it's not theirs.* **(seus, deles, suas, delas)**

them /ðem/ PRONOUN
1 used for talking about two or more people or things that you have already mentioned □ *The girls waved to me and I waved back to them.* □ *'Do you like strawberries?' 'Yes, I love them.'* **(eles, elas, os, as)**
2 used to avoid saying 'him' or 'her' □ *If anyone asks where I am, can you tell them I've gone to the dentist's.* **(eles, elas, os, as)**

theme /θiːm/ NOUN [*plural* themes] the main idea or subject in a book, film, discussion, etc. 🔁 *The country's history is the central theme of the book.* **(assunto, tema)**

theme park /ˈθiːm ˌpɑːk/ NOUN [*plural* theme parks] a place where you go for fun, where the entertainments and machines you ride on are based on one subject □ *Disney theme parks* **(parque temático)**

themselves /ðəmˈselvz/ PRONOUN
1 the reflexive form of they □ *They'd made themselves a cosy little shelter.* **(eles, elas, eles mesmos, elas mesmas)**
2 used to show that two or more people do something without any help from other people □ *They'll have to work it out themselves.* 🔁 *They built the shelter all by themselves.* **(sozinhos)**
3 used to emphasize the pronoun they □ *They themselves are innocent.* **(eles, elas, próprios, próprias)**
4 by themselves not with or near other people □ *They sat by themselves and didn't talk to anyone else.* **(sozinhos)**

then /ðen/ ADVERB
1 at that time, in the past or future □ *I didn't know you then.* 🔁 *The rest of the kids should be here by then.* 🔁 *They can deliver the car by March, but we really need it before then.* 🔁 *Max and I met up in June, but I haven't seen him since then.* **(então)**
2 after that time or next □ *I went for a swim, and then I went home.* □ *Mix in the flour and then the fruit.* **(então, depois)**
3 because of that □ *If you can't be quiet, then you'll have to leave the room.* □ *'This carpet will last longer.' 'I think we'll buy it then.'* **(então)**

theory /ˈθɪəri/ NOUN [*plural* theories] an idea which tries to explain why something happens □ **+ about** *There are many theories about why children are getting fatter.* □ **+ of** *Newton's theory of gravity* **(teoria)**

there¹ /ðeə(r)/ PRONOUN used to start a statement about something that exists or happens □ *There is a mouse somewhere in this* *house.* □ *There's too much noise.* □ *There is plenty of milk in the fridge.* (**haver**)

there² /ðeə(r)/ ADVERB
1 at, in or to a place □ *I know someone who lives there.* □ *I'm going there tomorrow.* □ *When I got to work, Clive was already there.* (**lá**)
2 used to show someone something you are pointing to or want them to look at □ *You can leave your coats there.* □ *There's Dad.* (**ali, lá**)

therefore /ˈðeəfɔː(r)/ ADVERB because of that □ *She had been awake all night and therefore was very tired.* (**por isso**)

thermometer /θəˈmɒmɪtə(r)/ NOUN [plural thermometers] an instrument for measuring the temperature of something or someone □ *The nurse used a thermometer to take his temperature* (**termômetro**)

these¹ /ðiːz/ DETERMINER used to talk about people or things that you have already talked about, or things that you can see, usually near you □ *These cups are dirty.* □ *These athletes train very hard.* □ *These problems could have been avoided.* (**estes**)

these² /ðiːz/ PRONOUN used to talk about things that you have already talked about, or that you can see, usually near you □ *I can't eat these.* □ *Are these yours?* (**estes**)

they /ðeɪ/ PRONOUN
1 used to talk or write about two or more people or things that have already been mentioned □ *Apes are not monkeys. They don't have tails.* □ *What did they think of your idea?* (**eles**)
2 people em general, or people in authority □ *They say it's going to be a hot summer.* □ *They've raised taxes again.* (**partícula '-se'**)

they'd /ðeɪd/ a short way to say and write they had or they would □ *They'd all had their lunch.* □ *They'd like to come with us* (ver **had, would**)

they'll /ðeɪl/ a short way to say and write they will or they shall □ *They'll be here tomorrow.* (ver **will, shall**)

they're /ðeə(r)/ a short way to say and write they are □ *They're going to the park after school.* (ver **are**)

they've /ðeɪv/ a short way to say and write they have □ *They've never been skating before.* (ver **have**)

thick /θɪk/ ADJECTIVE [thicker, thickest]
1 wide between the opposite sides or surfaces □ *Make sure you wear a thick coat.* □ *There was a thick layer of snow on the ground.* (**grosso, espresso**)
2 having a particular width between sides or surfaces □ *The ice was 20 centimetres thick.* (**de espessura**)
3 made up of many parts that are very close together □ *thick hair* (**denso, abundante**)
4 a thick liquid does not flow easily □ *thick soup* (**grosso, denso**)
5 thick smoke, fog, etc. fills the air and is difficult to see through (**cerrado**)
6 an informal word meaning stupid (**tolo**)

thief /θiːf/ NOUN [plural thieves] someone who steals things □ *car thieves* □ *Thieves stole her handbag.* (**ladrão**)

thigh /θaɪ/ NOUN [plural thighs] the top part of your leg above your knee (**coxa**)

thin /θɪn/ ADJECTIVE [thinner, thinnest]
1 not wide from one side to the other □ *He spread a thin layer of jam on the cake.* □ *Cut the potato into thin slices.* (**fino**)
2 a thin person or animal does not have much fat on their body □ *She is small and thin.* (**magro**)
3 a thin liquid flows very easily □ *They were given a bowl of thin soup.* (**ralo**)

thing /θɪŋ/ NOUN [plural things]
1 used to refer to an object without using its name □ *I bought a few things for the party when I was in town.* □ *Where's the thing for opening bottles?* (**coisa**)
2 an action or event □ *I hope I haven't done the wrong thing.* □ *The same thing happened to me once.* (**coisa**)
3 a fact, belief or idea □ *She said lots of nice things about you.* □ *He asked me a few things about my work.* (**coisa**)
4 your things the objects that belong to you □ *He packed up his things and left.* (**suas coisas**)

think /θɪŋk/ VERB [thinks, thinking, thought]
1 to have an opinion about someone or something □ *I think there's too much salt in this soup.* □ *+ that I think that you should ask him to leave.* □ *+ about What do you think about the death penalty?* □ *+ of What do you think of his new girlfriend?* (**pensar, achar**)

2 to believe that something is true, although you are not certain ◻ *I think Anna will be here soon.* ◻ **+ that** *We thought that there would be more people there.* ▣ *'Do the trains run on Sunday?' 'I think so.'* (**pensar, achar**)

3 to consider something, especially in order to understand it or to decide what to do ◻ **+ about** *You need to think very carefully about what you do.* ◻ **+ of** *We need to think of a way to raise money.* (**pensar**)

4 to remember someone or something ◻ **+ about** *I was just thinking about your birthday party.* ◻ **+ of** *I often think of my mother.* (**pensar**)

5 to express words to yourself in your mind ◻ *I kept thinking, 'I must stay calm.'* (**pensar**)

6 if you are thinking of doing something, you are considering doing it ◻ **+ of** *I'm thinking of starting my own business.* ◻ **+ about** *They're thinking about moving to Australia.* (**pensar, refletir**)

third¹ /θɜːd/ NUMBER 3rd written as a word ◻ *That's the third time he's called today.* ◻ *She came third in an art competition.* (**terceiro**)

third² /θɜːd/ NOUN [*plural* thirds] 1/3; one of three equal parts of something ◻ *The bottle holds a third of a litre.* (**um terço**)

Third World¹ /ˌθɜːd ˈwɜːld/ NOUN, NO PLURAL the Third World a slightly old-fashioned name for the countries of the world that are the poorest and least developed ◻ *The work aims to improve health in the Third World.* (**terceiro mundo**)

Third World² /ˌθɜːd ˈwɜːld/ ADJECTIVE to do with the countries of the Third World ▣ *a Third World country* (**de terceiro mundo**)

thirst /θɜːst/ NOUN, NO PLURAL the feeling that you need something to drink ◻ *He was dying of thirst.* (**sede**)

thirsty /ˈθɜːsti/ ADJECTIVE [thirstier, thirstiest] feeling that you need something to drink ◻ *They were tired, hungry and thirsty.* ▣ *I felt incredibly thirsty.* (**sedento**)

thirteen /ˌθɜːˈtiːn/ NUMBER the number 13 (**treze**)

thirteenth /ˌθɜːˈtiːnθ/ NUMBER 13th written as a word (**décimo terceiro**)

thirtieth /ˈθɜːtiəθ/ NUMBER 30th written as a word (**trigésimo**)

thirty /ˈθɜːti/ NUMBER [*plural* thirties]
1 the number 30 (**trinta**)
2 the thirties the years between 1930 and 1939 (**os anos 1930**)

this¹ /ðɪs/ DETERMINER [*plural* these]
1 used to talk about a person or thing that you have already talked about, or something that you can see, usually near you ◻ *This apple is sour.* ◻ *I've lived in this country for five years.* ◻ *This argument went on for weeks.* (**este, esta, isto**)
2 used to refer to a present period of time, or the one that comes next ◻ *I went shopping this morning.* ◻ *I'll be seeing her this weekend.* (**este, esta**)

this² /ðɪs/ ADVERB to the amount or degree mentioned ◻ *It wasn't this hot yesterday.* ◻ *I didn't know we'd used this much fuel already.* (**tão, tanto**)

this³ /ðɪs/ PRONOUN
1 used to talk about something that you have already talked about, or that you can see, usually near you ◻ *I can't eat this.* ◻ *Where are you going after this?* ◻ *This is my bedroom.* (**este, esta, isto**)
2 used to say who you are on the telephone ◻ *Hello, this is Ollie.*

thorough /ˈθʌrə/ ADJECTIVE done carefully, paying attention to every detail ◻ *He made a thorough search.* ▣ *We are conducting a thorough investigation into this incident.* (**minucioso**)

thoroughly /ˈθʌrəli/ ADVERB
1 with great care and attention to every detail ◻ *Clean all the kitchen surfaces thoroughly.* ◻ *The book has been thoroughly researched.* (**minuciosamente**)
2 completely ▣ *We thoroughly enjoyed ourselves.* ◻ *She was feeling thoroughly fed up.* ◻ *They thoroughly deserve this victory.* (**completamente**)

those¹ /ðəʊz/ DETERMINER used to talk about several people or things already mentioned or that you can see, usually not near you ◻ *Who are those two boys?* ◻ *In those days, people didn't have cars.* (**aqueles, esses**)

those² /ðəʊz/ PRONOUN used to talk about several things already mentioned or that you can see, usually not near you ◻ *What are those?* ◻ *Those are just some of the problems we face.* (**aqueles**)

though¹ /ðəʊ/ ADVERB used to show that what you have just said is surprising or different from what you said before ◻ *It's a pity we didn't win. It was an exciting match, though.* (**contudo**)

though² /ðəʊ/ CONJUNCTION
1 but ◻ *We only waited for half an hour, though it seemed like hours.* ◻ *He will continue his political work, though not with the same party.* (**mas**)
2 despite the fact that ◻ *He went out, though I told him not to.* (**embora**)

thought¹ /θɔːt/ NOUN [*plural* thoughts]
1 an idea, opinion, word or image that you have in your mind ◻ **+ on** *Do you have any thoughts on the problem of transport?* ◻ **+ about** *I had a sudden thought about the garden.* ◻ **+ of** *I can't bear the thought of leaving you all.* (**pensamento**)

thought

2 no plural the activity of thinking □ *This issue needs some careful thought.* (**reflexão**)

thought² /θɔːt/ PAST TENSE AND PAST PARTICIPLE OF think (ver **think**)

thoughtful /'θɔːtfʊl/ ADJECTIVE
1 a thoughtful person is kind and thinks of other people □ *It was very thoughtful of you to phone.* (**atencioso**)
2 if someone looks thoughtful, they look as if they are thinking (**pensativo**)

thoughtfully /'θɔːtfʊli/ ADVERB in a thoughtful way □ *She stared thoughtfully at the letter.* □ *She'd very thoughtfully left drinks and sandwiches on the kitchen table for us.* (**atenciosamente**)

thousand /'θaʊzənd/ NUMBER [plural thousands] the number 1.000 (**mil**)

thousandth¹ /'θaʊzəntθ/ NUMBER 1,000ᵗʰ written as a word (**milésimo**)

thousandth² /'θaʊzəntθ/ NOUN [plural thousandths] 1/1,000; one of a thousand equal parts of something (**milésimo**)

thread¹ /θred/ NOUN [plural threads]
1 a long, thin piece of cotton, wool, etc. used for sewing □ *fine silk threads* □ *His name was embroidered in red thread.* (**linha, fio**)
2 a series of messages on a website about a particular subject (**ideia, concepção central**)

thread² /θred/ VERB [threads, threading, threaded] to push something long and thin through a hole □ *He threaded a piece of wire through a hole in the top.* (**enfiar**)

threat /θret/ NOUN [plural threats]
1 a warning that someone might hurt you or harm you, especially if you do not do what they say 🔊 *She has received death threats.* □ **+ against** *Rebel leaders have made threats against the president.* (**ameaça**)
2 something that might cause harm or problems □ **+ to** *These actions are a threat to international peace.* (**ameaça**)

threaten /'θretən/ VERB [threatens, threatening, threatened]
1 to say that someone will be harmed or hurt, especially if they do not do something □ *His wife was threatened with a knife.* □ **+ to do something** *The kidnappers have threatened to kill the hostages.* (**ameaçar**)
2 to make problems or harm probable □ *Government cuts threaten the future of the service.* (**ameaçar**)

three /θriː/ NUMBER [plural threes] the number 3 (**três**)

threw /θruː/ PAST TENSE OF throw¹ (ver **throw¹**)

throw

thrill¹ /θrɪl/ VERB [thrills, thrilling, thrilled] to make someone feel excited and very pleased □ *He thrilled the crowd with some dramatic shots.* (**emocionar, fazer vibrar**)

thrill² /θrɪl/ NOUN [plural thrills] a feeling of excitement and pleasure, or the thing that gives you that feeling □ *She felt a thrill of excitement.* □ *Getting this job was a real thrill.* (**vibrações, emoções**)

thriller /'θrɪlə(r)/ NOUN [plural thrillers] a book, film or play with an exciting story, full of danger and frightening events 🔊 *He stars in a new crime thriller set in New York.* (**thriller**)

thrive /θraɪv/ VERB [thrives, thriving, thrived] to grow strong and healthy, or to become successful □ *The business is thriving.* □ *These guys thrive on competition.* (**desenvolver-se**)

throat /θrəʊt/ NOUN [plural throats]
1 the top part of the tube that goes from your mouth down to your stomach □ *My throat felt dry and I couldn't speak.* □ *He got a piece of food stuck in his throat.* 🔊 *I had a headache and a sore throat.* (**garganta**)
2 the front part of your neck □ *He put his hands round her throat.* (**pescoço**)

throne /θrəʊn/ NOUN [plural thrones] a special chair that a king or queen sits on (**trono**)

through /θruː/ PREPOSITION
1 from one end or side of something to the other □ *He walked through the door.* □ *The pole fits through this hole.* □ *We walked through the woods.* (**através de**)
2 because of something or using something □ *He failed his exams through laziness.* □ *He contacted people through his website.* (**por, por causa de**)
3 for the whole of a period of time or activity □ *We drove through the night.* □ *We left half way through the film.* □ *She has lived through some terrible events.* (**durante**)

throughout /θruː'aʊt/ PREPOSITION
1 during a whole period of time □ *It rained throughout June and July.* □ *There will be regular news reports throughout the day.* (**durante**)
2 in every part of something □ *They have stores throughout the country.* (**por**)

throw¹ /θrəʊ/ VERB [throws, throwing, threw, thrown]
1 to make something move through the air by pushing it with your hand □ *He threw the ball to me.* □ *They were throwing stones into the water.* (**jogar, lançar**)
2 to put something somewhere very quickly and without care □ *She threw her bag down and switched on the TV.* □ *I threw a few clothes into a case and set off.* (**jogar**)

3 to move your body or part of your body into a position quickly and with force □ *She threw herself to the floor.* □ *He threw his arms around me.* (lançar)

♦ PHRASAL VERBS **throw something away 1** to get rid of something you do not want □ *I threw away the rest of the food.* **2** to waste something □ *She threw away her career to follow her boyfriend.* **throw something out** to get rid of something that you do not want □ *I've thrown out all my old books.* **throw someone out** to force someone to leave a place □ *My parents threw me out when I was seventeen.*

throw² /θrəʊ/ NOUN [plural throws] an act of throwing something □ *That was a great throw!* (lance)

thrust /θrʌst/ VERB [thrusts, thrusting, thrust] to push something somewhere quickly and with force □ *He thrust his hands into his pockets.* □ *Someone thrust a microphone at him.* (enfiar)

thug /θʌɡ/ NOUN [plural thugs] a violent man □ *a gang of thugs* (valentão, brigão)

thumb /θʌm/ NOUN [plural thumbs] the short, thick finger that is on the side of your hand □ *He injured his right thumb.* □ *She held it carefully between her thumb and forefinger.* (polegar)

thump /θʌmp/ VERB [thumps, thumping, thumped] to hit someone or something hard, usually with your hand □ *He thumped the table for emphasis.* (bater)

thunder /ˈθʌndə(r)/ NOUN, NO PLURAL the loud, deep sound that you hear in a storm after a flash of lightning (= bright light in the sky) 🔊 *thunder and lightning* 🔊 *There was a loud clap of thunder.* (trovão)

thunderstorm /ˈθʌndəstɔːm/ NOUN [plural thunderstorms] a storm with thunder and lightning (= bright light in the sky) □ *Thunderstorms were forecast for the afternoon.* □ *We arrived in the middle of a thunderstorm.* (tempestade de trovões)

Thursday /ˈθɜːzdɪ/ NOUN [plural Thursdays] the day of the week after Wednesday and before Friday □ *My piano lessons are on Thursday.* (terça-feira)

tick¹ /tɪk/ NOUN [plural ticks]
1 a small written mark (✓) used to show that something is correct or to show which things on a list have been dealt with 🔊 *He put a tick in the box marked 'No'.* □ *The girl put a tick next to her name.* (tique)
2 the regular noise that a clock makes □ *+ of I could hear the tick of the clock in the hall.* (tique-taque)

tick² /tɪk/ VERB [ticks, ticking, ticked]
1 to write a tick 🔊 *You just tick the boxes.* (ticar)
2 to make a regular noise like a clock □ *a ticking clock* (tiquetaquear)

ticket /ˈtɪkɪt/ NOUN [plural tickets] a small piece of printed paper that shows you have paid to do something 🔊 *She bought an airline ticket to Paris.* 🔊 *a single/return ticket* □ *+ for He's got free tickets for the match.* (bilhete, passagem)

> **THESAURUS:** You usually need a ticket to travel on a public vehicle, and to go to the theatre or the cinema. A pass is a ticket that allows you to go into a place or to travel on a vehicle. For example, if you travel by train every day, you might buy a pass instead of buying a new ticket every day. Some people need a pass to show that they work in a particular building and are allowed to enter it. A card is a small flat piece of plastic that you can use in shops and machines to pay for things.

tickle /ˈtɪkəl/ VERB [tickles, tickling, tickled]
1 to touch someone's body lightly so that they laugh □ *She tickled him under the arms.* (fazer cócegas)
2 if something tickles you, it causes an uncomfortable, light feeling on your skin □ *The grass tickled her nose.* (coçar)

tide /taɪd/ NOUN [plural tides] the regular rise and fall of the level of the sea 🔊 *At high tide, the rocks are completely covered.* 🔊 *You can walk out to the island at low tide.* (maré)

tidy¹ /ˈtaɪdɪ/ ADJECTIVE [tidier, tidiest]
1 carefully ordered or arranged with everything in its correct place □ *Everything looked tidy.* 🔊 *He keeps his room tidy.* (em ordem, arrumado)
2 a tidy person likes to keep things ordered and in their correct place □ *She's the tidiest person I know.* (organizado)

tidy² /ˈtaɪdɪ/ VERB [tidies, tidying, tidied] to put things back in their correct places and to make something tidy 🔊 *Anne was tidying the kitchen.* □ *+ up Are you going to tidy up the mess you've made?* □ *+ away He tidied away his tools.* (arrumar)

tie¹ /taɪ/ VERB [ties, tying, tied]
1 to join or to fasten things together using string, rope, etc. □ *+ together We tied the boats together.* □ *+ with a box tied with white ribbon* □ *+ to The riders tied their horses to a tree.* □ *She tied her long hair in a ponytail.* □ *Their hands were tied behind their backs.* (amarrar)
2 to twist pieces of rope, string, etc. together to make a knot 🔊 *Tie a knot in the end of the thread.* □ *He bent down to tie his shoe lace.* □ *+ around She had a silk scarf tied around her neck.* (amarrar)

3 if two teams or players tie, they each have the same number of points □ *+ for* They tied for second place. (empatar)

♦ PHRASAL VERB **tie someone/something up** to fasten someone or something with rope, etc. so that they cannot move □ *The boat's tied up in the harbour.* □ *The kidnappers tied them both up.*

tie² /taɪ/ NOUN [plural ties]
1 a narrow piece of cloth worn round your neck under your shirt collar and tied in a knot □ *I have to wear a suit and tie for work* (gravata)
2 a situation in which two teams or players each have the same number of points □ *+ for* There was a tie for third place. (empate)

tiger /'taɪɡə(r)/ NOUN [plural tigers]
a large wild animal related to the cat with yellow fur and black stripes (tigre)

tight /taɪt/ ADJECTIVE [tighter, tightest]
1 fitting very closely and difficult to move □ *I was wearing very tight jeans.* □ *The top on this jar is very tight.* (apertado)
2 very firm and strong □ *a tight knot* (apertado)

tighten /'taɪtən/ VERB [tightens, tightening, tightened]
to become firmer and stronger or to make something firmer and stronger □ *He tightened his grip on my arm.* □ *I tightened up the screws.* (apertar)

tightly /'taɪtli/ ADVERB
in a firm and strong way □ *She held her purse tightly.* □ *I pulled the door tightly shut.* (firmemente)

tights /taɪts/ PLURAL NOUN
a piece of women's clothing covering the feet, legs and bottom made of very thin material □ *a pair of tights* (meia-calça)

tile /taɪl/ NOUN [plural tiles]
a piece of hard, flat material such as clay or stone, used for covering roofs, walls or floors □ *red roof tiles* □ *shiny floor tiles* (telha, azulejo)

till¹ /tɪl/ PREPOSITION, CONJUNCTION
until □ *We'll probably stay here till the end.* □ *It doesn't get dark till 10 o'clock in the summer.* (até)

till² /tɪl/ NOUN [plural tills]
a machine in a shop for counting what customers need to pay and for putting money in □ *She works at a supermarket behind the till.* (caixa)

tilt /tɪlt/ VERB [tilts, tilting, tilted]
to move something so that one side is lower than the other, or to move like this □ *He tilted his head to one side.* (inclinar)

timber /'tɪmbə(r)/ NOUN, NO PLURAL
wood that is used for building things such as houses, or a piece of this wood (madeira)

time¹ /taɪm/ NOUN [plural times]
1 no plural the way we measure minutes, hours, days, etc. □ *I was hardly aware of time passing.* (tempo)
2 a particular moment in a day □ *What's the time?* □ *What would be a good time to meet?* □ *What time does the show start?* □ *Excuse me, have you got the time* (= can you tell me what time it is)? □ *Can Dina tell the time* (= be able to read a clock) yet? (hora)
3 no plural an amount of time □ *Do you spend a lot of time in London?* □ *Ironing sheets is a complete waste of time.* □ *We spent a long time talking about the past.* □ *It takes a lot of time to learn a language well.* (tempo)
4 a particular occasion □ *Do you remember the time Michael fell in the river?* □ *I've been to Morocco several times.* □ *Next time you see Billy, can you ask him to call me?* □ *The first time we met, I thought he was really rude.* (vez)
5 no plural if it is time to do something or for something to happen, it should be done or happen now □ *It's time the children were in bed.* □ *Is it time to plant the tomatoes yet?* (tempo, época)
6 in time not too late □ *We got there just in time to see the queen.* □ *I hope the present arrives in time for his birthday.* (a tempo)
7 on time not early or late □ *The trains are usually on time.* (na hora)
8 a long enough period □ *We don't have time to contact everyone.* □ *We can play tennis if there's time later.* (tempo)
9 an experience, or a period in someone's life □ *Did you have a nice time in Brighton?* (tempo)
10 all the time (a) continuously □ *We monitor our staff all the time.* (b) very often □ *I love Crete – we go there all the time.* (o tempo todo, sempre)
11 one/two etc. at a time one/two etc. on a particular occasion □ *He ran up the steps three at a time.* □ *One at a time, we went to the front of the class.* (um/dois de cada vez)
12 in a hour's/day's/year's, etc. time after a particular period of time □ *The work should be complete in three week's time* (em uma hora/dias/semanas/anos etc.)

> ➤ Note that you have a good/great, etc. time somewhere. You do not 'spend' a good/great, etc. time somewhere:
> ✓ *We had a great time in Paris.*
> ✗ *We spent a great time in Paris.*

time² /taɪm/ VERB [times, timing, timed]
1 to arrange for something to happen at a particular time □ *The meeting was timed to coincide with his visit.* (escolher o momento de)
2 to measure how long something takes □ *He timed me running a mile.* (cronometrar)

times /taɪmz/ PREPOSITION
used in mathematics between the numbers you are multiplying □ *Two times four is eight.* (vezes)

timetable /'taɪmteɪbəl/ NOUN [plural timetables]

1 a list of the times when public vehicles such as trains or buses arrive or leave (**horário**)
2 a list of the lessons at a school, college, etc. and the times they happen 🔊 *We want to see more practical subjects on the school timetable.* (**horário**)

> **THESAURUS:** A **timetable** is a list of the times when public vehicles such as trains or buses arrive or leave, or a list of the lessons at a school and the times they happen. A **schedule** is a plan that shows when things should happen or be done. You might have a **schedule** for doing a particular job. An **agenda** is a list of things to be discussed at a meeting. A **calendar** is a thing that shows all the days, weeks and months of the year.

tin /tɪn/ NOUN [plural tins]
1 a closed metal container which food is sold in □ **+ of** *a tin of tuna* □ *He opened a tin of tomato soup.* (**lata**)
2 a metal container with a lid, which you store food or other things in □ **+ of** *a tin of biscuits* □ *a tin of paint* (**lata**)
3 no plural a soft, silver metal □ *the tin roof of the garage* □ *a tin bucket* (**folha de flandres**)

tin opener /ˈtɪn ˌəʊpənə(r)/ NOUN [plural tin openers] a small tool for opening metal containers of food (**abridor de latas**)

tiny /ˈtaɪni/ ADJECTIVE [tinier, tiniest] extremely small □ *a baby's tiny hands and feet* 🔊 *a tiny amount of water* (**minúsculo**)

tip¹ /tɪp/ NOUN [plural tips]
1 the point at the end or the top of something □ *They used arrows with poison tips.* □ *Point to it with the tip of your finger.* (**ponta**)
2 a small extra amount of money for someone who has done a job for you 🔊 *Did you leave a tip?* (**gorjeta**)
3 a piece of helpful advice □ *He gave me some useful tips on laying floor tiles.* (**dica**)

tip² /tɪp/ VERB [tips, tipping, tipped]
1 to move something so that it is not flat or vertical, or to move in this way □ *Tip the chairs forward against the tables.* □ *The vehicle tipped onto its side.* (**inclinar**)
2 to pour something from a container □ *They just tip the rubbish over the side of the ship.* □ *She tipped a bucket of water on my head.* (**despejar**)
3 to give a small extra amount of money to someone who has done a job for you □ *She tipped the taxi driver.* (**dar gorjeta**)

◆ PHRASAL VERB **tip (something) over** to push something onto its side or to fall on one side □ *She tipped her drink over.*

tire /ˈtaɪə(r)/ VERB [tires, tiring, tired] to start feeling that you need a rest □ *Grandma tires easily nowadays.* (**cansar-se**)

◆ PHRASAL VERBS **tire someone out** to make someone feel tired □ *Let's go to the park and tire the children out a bit.*

tired /ˈtaɪəd/ ADJECTIVE
1 feeling that you need a rest □ *You must be tired after your journey.* 🔊 *I was getting really tired.* 🔊 *He felt too tired and ill to continue.* (**cansado**)
2 bored and often annoyed □ **+ of** *I'm tired of wearing the same clothes every day.* □ *I'm tired of people asking me questions.* (**cansado**)

tissue /ˈtɪʃuː/ NOUN [plural tissues] a thin, soft piece of paper for cleaning your nose, etc. □ *She took out a tissue to wipe her nose.* (**lenço de papel**)

title /ˈtaɪtəl/ NOUN [plural titles]
1 the name of something such as a book, song or film □ **+ of** *What's the title of your poem?* □ *How did you choose the book's title?* (**título**)
2 a word that you can use before your name, for example Ms or Professor □ *Her title is 'Doctor', not 'Mrs'.* (**título**)

> **THESAURUS: Name** is a general word for the word or words that you use to refer to a person, animal, place or thing. A **title** is the name of something, such as a book, song or film. You can also use **title** to talk about the subject of an essay. A **headline** is the words that are printed in large letters at the top of a newspaper article.

to¹ /tuː/
1 used before a verb to make the infinitive form □ *I want to leave now.* □ *I forgot to tell him.* (**indica o tempo verbal infinitivo**)
2 used as part of the infinitive to show the purpose of something □ *I went to get a drink.* □ *I phoned her to invite her to the party.* (**para**)

to² /tuː/ PREPOSITION
1 used to say where someone or something goes □ *We went to the shops.* □ *I go to work by bus.* □ *The cup fell to the floor.* (**para, a, em**)
2 used to say who is given something, told something, etc. □ *Give the letter to Clara.* □ *I spoke to her several times.* (**para, com**)
3 connected or fixed □ *The cake was stuck to the tin.* □ *We nailed the picture to the wall.* (**a**)
4 facing or going in a particular direction □ *He had his back to me.* □ *Keep to the side of the woods.* □ *He pointed to the sign.* (**para**)
5 used to say how someone's actions affect someone or something □ *He was always kind to me.* □ *What have you done to my car?* (**para, a**)
6 **from... to** (a) used to show a period of time □ *We are open from 9 to 6.* (b) used to show a range of something □ *Everyone was there, from young to old.* (**até**)
7 used for saying the time up to 30 minutes before an hour □ *It's ten to three.* (**para**)

toast /təʊst/ NOUN [plural toasts]
1 no plural bread that has been made hard and slightly brown by heating ☐ *I had toast and honey for breakfast.* 🔊 *a piece of toast* (**torrada**)
2 when people lift their glasses and drink together to express good wishes to someone 🔊 *I'd like to propose a toast to the bride and groom.* (**brinde**)

toaster /'təʊstə(r)/ NOUN [plural toasters] a machine for heating bread until it is hard and slightly brown (**torradeira**)

tobacco /tə'bækəʊ/ NOUN, NO PLURAL the leaves of a plant that are dried and used for smoking ☐ *tobacco smoke* ☐ *the tobacco industry* (**tabaco**)

today[1] /tə'deɪ/ ADVERB
1 on this day ☐ *I can't come today.* 🔊 *I spoke to Alan earlier today.* 🔊 *My parents are coming over later today.* (**hoje**)
2 at or around the present time ☐ *People are taller today than they were a hundred years ago.* (**hoje**)

today[2] /tə'deɪ/ NOUN, NO PLURAL this day ☐ *Today is Tuesday.* ☐ *Today's announcement comes as no surprise.* (**hoje**)

toe /təʊ/ NOUN [plural toes] one of the five parts at the end of your foot ☐ *Reach up high, standing on your toes.* 🔊 *He injured his left big toe.* 🔊 *She stubbed (= hit) her toe on the end of the bed.* (**dedo do pé**)

together /tə'geðə(r)/ ADVERB
1 with or near each other ☐ *We work together.* ☐ *They spent the evening together watching television.* 🔊 *The houses are quite close together.* (**junto**)
2 touching, joined or mixed with each other ☐ *Mix the sugar and eggs together in a bowl.* ☐ *She pressed her hands together.* ☐ *Add all the numbers together.* (**junto**)
3 at the same time ☐ *All these things happened together.* (**junto**)

toilet /'tɔɪlɪt/ NOUN [plural toilets]
1 a large bowl that you sit on to get rid of waste from your body 🔊 *I need to go to the toilet.* 🔊 *He flushed the toilet and washed his hands.* (**vaso sanitário**)
2 a room with a toilet in it 🔊 *a public toilet* ☐ *Excuse me, where are the ladies' toilets?* (**toalete**)

> **THESAURUS:** A lavatory or a WC is the same as a toilet. Lavatory is a formal word, and quite old-fashioned, and WC is usually used to talk about public toilets. A bathroom is the room where you wash yourself, and usually also contains a toilet.

told /təʊld/ PAST TENSE AND PAST PARTICIPLE OF tell (ver **tell**)

tolerance /'tɒlərəns/ NOUN, NO PLURAL when you are willing to accept other people's ideas and behaviour, even when they are different from yours ☐ *Everyone needs to show tolerance.* 🔊 *His speech was about religious tolerance.* (**tolerância**)

tolerate /'tɒləreɪt/ VERB [tolerates, tolerating, tolerated] to accept something even if you do not like it or agree with it ☐ *I can't tolerate this noise for much longer.* ☐ *We will not tolerate aggressive behaviour.* (**tolerar**)

tomato /tə'mɑːtəʊ/ NOUN [plural tomatoes] a soft, red fruit with a lot of juice that is used like a vegetable in salads, sauces, etc. ☐ *pasta with tomato sauce* ☐ *a cheese and tomato sandwich* (**tomate**)

tomb /tuːm/ NOUN [plural tombs] a place where a dead body is buried, often with a stone structure (**túmulo**)

tomorrow[1] /tə'mɒrəʊ/ NOUN, NO PLURAL the day after today ☐ *Tomorrow is Wednesday.* 🔊 *He's arriving early tomorrow morning.* 🔊 *Will he be fit for the game tomorrow night?* 🔊 *I'll be back the day after tomorrow.* (**amanhã**)

tomorrow[2] /tə'mɒrəʊ/ ADVERB on the day after today ☐ *Let's have our meeting tomorrow.* ☐ *We'll be here tomorrow.* (**amanhã**)

ton /tʌn/ NOUN [plural tons]
1 a unit for measuring weight, equal to 1016 kilograms in Britain or 907 kilograms in America ☐ *a truck carrying 60 tons of coal* (**tonelada**)
2 tons of an informal phrase meaning a lot of something ☐ *She's got tons of clothes to choose from.* ☐ *I've got tons of things to do.* (**um monte de**)

tone /təʊn/ NOUN [plural tones] the quality of a sound or of someone's voice 🔊 *I could tell she was angry from her tone of voice.* ☐ *a cello with a soft gentle tone* (**tom**)

tongue /tʌŋ/ NOUN [plural tongues] the soft part inside your mouth that you can move and that you use to speak, eat and taste □ *He ran his tongue across his teeth.* 🔊 *Tim stuck his tongue out at me.* (**língua**)

tonight¹ /təˈnaɪt/ NOUN, NO PLURAL the night or evening of today □ *I'll have to miss tonight's class, I'm afraid.* (**hoje à noite**)

tonight² /təˈnaɪt/ ADVERB on the night or evening of today □ *I'm going to bed early tonight.* □ *The show is on BBC1 at 9pm tonight.* (**hoje à noite**)

tonne /tʌn/ NOUN [plural tonnes] a unit for measuring weight, equal to 1000 kilograms (**tonelada**)

too /tuː/ ADVERB
1 more than necessary or more than is sensible □ *If the water is too hot, add some cold.* □ *The offer was too good to refuse.* □ *Don't spend too much.* 🔊 *You're driving much too fast!* (**demais**)
2 also □ *Can I come too?* □ *I was really shocked and I think Maria was too.* (**também**)

> Note that if something is **too** heavy/hot/old, etc. it is bad. It means that something is more heavy/hot/old, etc. than you want it to be: □ *It's too heavy – I can't lift it.* □ *The weather is too hot – I like it a bit cooler.*

took /tʊk/ PAST TENSE OF take (ver **take**)

tool /tuːl/ NOUN [plural tools] a piece of equipment that you hold in your hand and use to do a particular job □ *a set of gardening tools* 🔊 *Keep a basic tool kit in the car.* (**ferramenta**)

> THESAURUS: There are many different types of tool. A **hammer** is a tool with a heavy metal or wooden part at the end of a handle, used for hitting nails etc. A **drill** is a tool for making holes in something hard. **Drills** are often electric. A **saw** is a tool with a thin blade used for cutting through wood or metal.

tooth /tuːθ/ NOUN [plural teeth]
1 one of the hard, white parts in your mouth that you use for biting □ *He has one front tooth missing.* 🔊 *I brushed my teeth and washed my face.* 🔊 *That cat's got sharp teeth.* (**dente**)
2 one of the row of sharp points that form one side of an object such as a comb (= thing used to tidy hair) (**dente**)

toothache /ˈtuːθeɪk/ NOUN, NO PLURAL a pain in or around your tooth 🔊 *I had terrible toothache.* □ *He went to the dentist with toothache.* (**dor de dentes**)

toothbrush /ˈtuːθbrʌʃ/ NOUN [plural toothbrushes] a small brush that you use for cleaning your teeth (**escova de dentes**)

toothpaste /ˈtuːθpeɪst/ NOUN, NO PLURAL a cream that you use to clean your teeth (**creme dental**)

top¹ /tɒp/ NOUN [plural tops]
1 the highest point or part of something □ *We climbed to the top of the tower.* □ *They were waiting at the top of the steps.* □ *Start reading at the top of the page.* (**topo, cume, alto, copa**)
2 the top the most successful position 🔊 *He's determined to get to the top of his profession.* (**topo**)
3 on (the) top on the upper surface of something □ *I keep his photograph on top of the TV.* □ *I like pizza with lots of olives on top.* (**sobre**)
4 the lid or cover of a container □ *Screw the top back on tightly.* (**tampa**)
5 a piece of clothing for the upper half of your body □ *She was wearing green trousers and a black top.* (**blusa**)

top² /tɒp/ ADJECTIVE
1 most important or successful □ *Safety is our top priority.* 🔊 *He came top in the exam.* □ *a top fashion designer* (**primeiro, principal**)
2 in the highest part of something □ *My office is on the top floor.* (**superior**)

topic /ˈtɒpɪk/ NOUN [plural topics] a subject to study, write or talk about □ **+ of** *The storms were the main topic of conversation.* □ *A range of topics was discussed.* □ *Immigration can be a sensitive topic.* (**tópico, assunto**)

topple /ˈtɒpəl/ VERB [topples, toppling, toppled] to fall over or to make something fall over □ *I knocked into a table and it toppled over.* □ *High winds toppled trees.* (**derrubar, cair**)

torch /tɔːtʃ/ NOUN [plural torches] a small electric light that you carry in your hand 🔊 *Someone shone a torch into the tent.*

tore /tɔː(r)/ PAST TENSE OF tear¹ (ver **tear¹**)

torn /tɔːn/ PAST PARTICIPLE OF tear¹ (ver **tear¹**)

tornado /tɔːˈneɪdəʊ/ NOUN [plural tornadoes] a violent storm with a powerful wind with a circular movement that causes a lot of damage (**tornado**)

torture /ˈtɔːtʃə(r)/ VERB [tortures, torturing, tortured] to hurt someone in a cruel way, usually as a punishment or to get information from them □ *He was tortured by his guards.* (**torturar**)

toss /tɒs/ VERB [tosses, tossing, tossed]
1 to throw something lightly or without care □ *Toss the keys over here, would you?* □ *He tossed aside the magazine.* (**lançar, jogar**)
2 to move repeatedly from side to side 🔊 *Alice spent the night tossing and turning restlessly.* (**revirar-se**)
3 to throw a coin up in the air to see which side it falls on, in order to make a choice □ *We decided to toss for the front seat.* 🔊 *Why not just toss a coin?* (**jogar cara ou coroa**)

total **town**

total¹ /ˈtəʊtəl/ ADJECTIVE
1 complete ☐ *She was a total stranger.* ☐ *He showed a total lack of respect.* ☐ *The job must be done in total secrecy.* (**total**)
2 including everything ▣ *Two more people arrived yesterday, bringing the total number of guests to 12.* ☐ *the total cost of the project* (**total**)

total² /ˈtəʊtəl/ NOUN [plural totals] the number or amount you get when you add everything together ☐ **+ of** *We've got a total of fifteen cats.* ▣ *They raised a grand total of £940.* ☐ *There were thirty people in total.* (**total**)

total³ /ˈtəʊtəl/ VERB [totals, totalling/US totaling, totalled/US totaled] to be a particular number or amount when added together ☐ *Our collection totalled £320.* (**totalizar**)

totally /ˈtəʊtəli/ ADVERB completely ☐ *Is she totally deaf?* ☐ *I agree with you totally.* (**totalmente**)

> **Totally** is only used before adjectives with very strong meanings. Before adjectives with less strong meanings, use **very** or **extremely**: ☐ *I was totally exhausted.* ☐ *I was very tired.* ☐ *It's totally ridiculous.* ☐ *It's very silly.*

touch¹ /tʌtʃ/ VERB [touches, touching, touched]
1 to put your hand or fingers on something ☐ *Please do not touch the items on the shelf.* ☐ *Can you touch the ceiling?* (**tocar**)
2 if things touch, there is no space between them ☐ *We stood in a line with our shoulders touching.* (**tocar**)

touch² /tʌtʃ/ NOUN [plural touches]
1 when you put your hands or fingers on something ☐ *You can start the engine at the touch of a button.* ☐ *I felt a touch on my shoulder.* (**toque**)
2 no plural the ability to feel ☐ *The fur was smooth to the touch.* (**tato**)
3 in touch if you are in touch with someone, you communicate with them ☐ *I wish Sally would get in touch with me.* ☐ *I hope we can stay in touch.* (**em contato**)
4 lose touch to stop communicating with someone, usually not deliberately ☐ *We lost touch after we left university.* (**perder contato**)

tough /tʌf/ ADJECTIVE [tougher, toughest]
1 difficult to deal with ☐ *It was a tough decision.* ☐ *He had a tough time in that job.* (**duro**)
2 very severe ☐ *Tough new measures have been introduced to reduce crime.* ☐ *We're very tough on students who do not work hard enough.* (**duro**)
3 physically or mentally strong ☐ *You need to be tough to succeed in business.* (**resistente**)
4 not easy to cut or damage ☐ *You'll need a tough pair of shoes for climbing.* ☐ *The meat was a bit tough.* (**duro, resistente**)

tour¹ /tʊə(r)/ NOUN [plural tours] a visit somewhere, stopping several times at places of interest ☐ **+ of** *We went on a tour of the region.* ▣ *He takes visitors on guided tours of the city.* (**viagem, excursão**)

tour² /tʊə(r)/ VERB [tours, touring, toured] to go on a tour ☐ *We're going to tour the wine-making regions of France.* ☐ *We've hired a car to tour the city.* (**viajar**)

tourism /ˈtʊərɪzəm/ NOUN, NO PLURAL travelling to and visiting places for enjoyment, or the business of providing holiday services ▣ *the tourism industry* ☐ *We are trying to promote tourism on the island.* (**turismo**)

tourist /ˈtʊərɪst/ NOUN [plural tourists] a person who is travelling for enjoyment or on holiday ☐ *a group of foreign tourists* ▣ *a tourist attraction* (**turista, turístico**)

tournament /ˈtʊənəmənt/ NOUN [plural tournaments] a number of sports matches that make up a big competition ▣ *a golf tournament* ▣ *the US Open tennis tournament* (**torneio**)

tow /təʊ/ VERB [tows, towing, towed] to pull something behind you with a rope or chain ☐ *The car broke down and we had to be towed home.* (**rebocar**)

towards /təˈwɔːdz/ PREPOSITION
1 in the direction of someone or something ☐ *I ran towards her.* ☐ *The sign points towards the east.* ☐ *He moved his chair towards the window* (**para**)
2 used to talk about the way someone feels about someone or something ☐ *I found his attitude towards money strange.* ☐ *She feels a lot of anger towards her family.* (**para com, com respeito a**)
3 near something ☐ *The bit about Cromwell is towards the end of the book.* ☐ *I hope to finish my book towards the end of the year.* (**perto de**)
4 in order to help to pay for something ☐ *He made a donation towards the new roof.* (**pelo**)

towel /ˈtaʊəl/ NOUN [plural towels] a piece of soft, thick cloth for drying yourself ▣ *a bath towel* ☐ *She picked up the wet towel from the bathroom floor.* ▣ *She dried her hands using a paper towel.* (**toalha**)

tower /ˈtaʊə(r)/ NOUN [plural towers] a tall narrow building or part of a building ☐ *a church tower* ☐ *the Eiffel Tower* (**torre**)

town /taʊn/ NOUN [plural towns] a place where people live and work, bigger than a village and smaller than a city ▣ *She comes from a small town* in Ohio. 🔊 *The wedding was in her home town of Hobart.* (cidade)

town hall /ˌtaʊn ˈhɔːl/ NOUN [plural town halls] a building that contains local government offices (prefeitura)

toxic /ˈtɒksɪk/ ADJECTIVE poisonous 🔊 *toxic chemicals* 🔊 *The river is polluted with toxic waste.* (tóxico)

toy /tɔɪ/ NOUN [plural toys] an object made for someone, especially a child, to play with (brinquedo)

trace¹ /treɪs/ VERB [traces, tracing, traced]
1 to find someone or something by following information about where they have been □ *The man has been traced to a village in the south of the country.* (rastrear)
2 to copy a picture by covering it with a sheet of thin paper and drawing over the lines you can see through it (calcar)

trace² /treɪs/ NOUN [plural traces] a mark or sign that someone or something leaves behind 🔊 *He disappeared without trace.* (vestígio, sinal)

track¹ /træk/ NOUN [plural tracks]
1 a rough path or road □ *We followed a narrow track along the edge of the field.* (trilha)
2 a mark on the ground left by a person, animal or thing that has been there □ *They followed the bear's tracks through the forest.* (rastro)
3 the long metal pieces that a train moves along □ *Repairs were needed to the track.* (trilhos)
4 an area of ground used for racing, often with a circular path □ *The runners were training on the track.* (pista)
5 keep track to continue to have enough information about something □ *I can't keep track of all the new rules.* (manter contato)
6 lose track to no longer have enough information about something □ *I've lost track of the number of times I've given her money.* (perder contato)

track² /træk/ VERB [tracks, tracking, tracked] to follow a person, animal or vehicle by looking for their marks or using special equipment □ *They use radar to track the aircraft's movements.* (rastrear)
♦ PHRASAL VERB **track someone/something down** to find someone or something after looking for them for a long time □ *I'm trying to track down an old friend.* □ *The shop has tracked down the book you ordered.* (localizar)

tractor /ˈtræktə(r)/ NOUN [plural tractors] a powerful vehicle with large wheels, used on farms (trator)

trade¹ /treɪd/ NOUN [plural trades]
1 no plural the buying and selling of goods, services or shares (= parts of a company that you can sell or buy) □ *international trade* (comércio)
2 a particular area of business □ *She works in the diamond trade.* (negócio)
3 a job using your hands that involves skill and training 🔊 *He learned the trade from his father.* (ofício)

trade² /treɪd/ VERB [trades, trading, traded] to buy or sell goods, services or shares (= parts of a company that you can sell or buy) □ **+ with** *We will not trade with corrupt regimes.* (comerciar)

trademark /ˈtreɪdmɑːk/ NOUN [plural trademarks] a name, word or symbol that a company uses on its products and which legally belongs to that company (marca registrada)

trader /ˈtreɪdə(r)/ NOUN [plural traders] a person or company that buys and sells things (comerciante)

tradition /trəˈdɪʃən/ NOUN [plural traditions] a custom that has continued for a long time □ *Having special birthday meals is a family tradition.* □ *He does not follow any religious tradition.* (tradição)

traditional /trəˈdɪʃənəl/ ADJECTIVE based on customs that have existed for a long time □ *They wore traditional costumes.* (tradicional)

traffic /ˈtræfɪk/ NOUN, NO PLURAL vehicles that are travelling 🔊 *We were stuck in heavy traffic* (= a lot of traffic). (tráfico)

> THESAURUS: **Vehicle** is a general word for something that carries people or goods, especially on roads. Cars, trucks and buses are all vehicles. **Traffic** is vehicles that are travelling. **Transport** is vehicles or a system used for taking goods and people from one place to another. For example, public transport includes buses and trains, and any other vehicle which carries people who buy a ticket to travel.

traffic jam /ˈtræfɪk ˌdʒæm/ NOUN [plural traffic jams] a long line of vehicles that cannot move because the road is blocked (engarrafamento)

traffic lights /ˈtræfɪk ˌlaɪts/ PLURAL NOUN a set of red, yellow and green lights that tell vehicles when to stop or go (semáforo)

traffic warden /ˈtræfɪk ˌwɔːdən/ NOUN [plural traffic wardens] a person whose job is to check that vehicles have been parked legally (guarda)

tragedy /ˈtrædʒədi/ NOUN [plural tragedies]
1 a very sad event, often where people die □ *The train driver did not cause the tragedy.* (tragédia)
2 a story that has a sad ending, especially when the main character dies □ *She is a character in a Shakespeare tragedy.* (tragédia)

tragic /ˈtrædʒɪk/ ADJECTIVE very sad, often because of a death 🔊 *His death was a tragic* *accident.* ☐ *Her actions had tragic consequences.* (**trágico**)

trail /treɪl/ NOUN [plural **trails**]
1 a series of marks or objects that someone or something leaves when they move somewhere ☐ *They left a trail of litter behind them.* (**pista, rastro**)
2 a path through the countryside (**trilha**)

train[1] /treɪn/ NOUN [plural **trains**] a vehicle that moves on a railway and carries passengers ☐ *I prefer to travel by train.* 🔊 *I caught the early train.* (**trem**)

> **THESAURUS: Train** is a general word for a vehicle that moves on tracks and carries pasengers. An **underground** is a railway that is underground, usually in a large city. The underground railway system in London is often called the **tube**. In American English, an underground is usually called a **subway**. A **tram** is a type of electric bus that runs on metal tracks in the street.

train[2] /treɪn/ VERB [**trains, training, trained**]
1 to teach a person or animal to do something ☐ *+ to do something Veronica has trained her dog to carry her handbag.* (**treinar**)
2 to learn to do a particular job ☐ *+ as Andrew trained as a nurse when he left school.* (**treinar, instruir**)
3 to prepare for a sports event ☐ *The team trains for three hours every day.* (**treinar**)

trainer /ˈtreɪnə(r)/ NOUN [plural **trainers**]
1 someone who teaches people or animals to do something (**treinador, adestrador**)
2 trainers soft shoes that are used for sport (**tênis**)

training /ˈtreɪnɪŋ/ NOUN, NO PLURAL
1 the process of training people or being trained ☐ *+ in We received very little training in how to use the equipment.* 🔊 *They run training courses for diving instructors.* (**formação**)
2 preparation for a sports event ☐ *The team will be in training for the World Cup.* (**treinamento**)

trait /treɪt/ NOUN [plural **traits**] a particular characteristic or quality that someone or something has ☐ *The test is supposed to reveal your character traits.* (**traços, características**)

traitor /ˈtreɪtə(r)/ NOUN [plural **traitors**] a person who is not loyal to their friends or country (**traidor**)

tram /træm/ NOUN [plural **trams**] a type of electric bus that runs on metal tracks in the street ☐ *Trams run from the station to the city centre every 5 minutes.* (**bonde**)

transfer[1] /trænsˈfɜː(r)/ VERB [**transfers, transferring, transferred**] to move someone or something from one place to another ☐ *She transferred all her photos onto a CD.* ☐ *I transferred some money into his account.* (**transferir**)

transfer[2] /ˈtrænsfɜː(r)/ NOUN [plural **transfers**]
1 when someone moves to another job or place of work in the same organization ☐ *The sergeant has asked for a transfer.* (**transferência**)
2 the act of moving someone or something from one place to another ☐ *I am responsible for the transfer of supplies to the new base.* (**transferência**)

transform /trænsˈfɔːm/ VERB [**transforms, transforming, transformed**] to change something completely ☐ *We could transform this room with a few tins of paint.* (**transformar**)

transitive /ˈtrænzɪtɪv/ ADJECTIVE a transitive verb always has an object ☐ *In the sentence 'I can see Mary.', 'see' is a transitive verb.* (**transitivo**)

translate /trænsˈleɪt/ VERB [**translates, translating, translated**] to change words into a different language ☐ *+ into Can you translate this into French?* (**traduzir**)

translation /trænsˈleɪʃən/ NOUN [plural **translations**]
1 writing or speech that has been changed into a different language ☐ *+ of This is a new translation of her novel.* (**tradução**)
2 no plural the process of changing words into a different language (**tradução**)

translator /trænsˈleɪtə(r)/ NOUN [plural **translators**] someone whose job is to change words into a different language (**tradutor**)

transparent /trænsˈpærənt/ ADJECTIVE if something is transparent, you can see through it ☐ *The box is made of transparent plastic so that you can see what's inside.* (**transparente**)

transplant /ˈtrænsplɑːnt/ NOUN [plural **transplants**] an operation to put an organ from one person's body into someone else 🔊 *He had a heart transplant.* (**transplante**)

transport[1] /ˈtrænspɔːt/ NOUN, NO PLURAL
1 vehicles or a system used for taking people and goods from one place to another 🔊 *Older people have free travel on public transport.* 🔊 *Paris has a very efficient transport system.* 🔊 *Trains are a*

very safe form of transport. (transporte)
2 moving people or things from one place to another ▫ *The price includes the cost of transport.* ▫ *+ of The transport of farm animals was banned.* (transporte)

> ➤ Remember that transport cannot be used in the plural:
> ✓ *Public transport is very good in the capital.*
> ✗ *Public transports are very good in the capital.*
> To talk about one particular type of transport, use the phrase **form of transport**: ▫ *Train is probably the greenest form of transport.*

transport² /trænsˈpɔːt/ VERB [transports, transporting, transported] to move something from one place to another ▫ *The planes were used to transport prisoners.* ▫ *Red blood cells transport oxygen around the body.* (transportar)

trap¹ /træp/ NOUN [plural traps]
1 a piece of equipment for catching animals ▫ *a mouse trap* (armadilha)
2 a clever plan that is designed to trick someone 🔁 *Police set a trap for the thief.* (cilada)

trap² /træp/ VERB [traps, trapping, trapped]
1 if you are trapped in a bad place or situation, you cannot escape from it ▫ *Passengers were trapped in the burning bus.* ▫ *He was trapped in a loveless marriage.* (estar preso)
2 to catch an animal in a trap ▫ *The animals were trapped for their fur.* (capturar com armadilha)

trash /træʃ/ NOUN, NO PLURAL the US word for **rubbish** (= things that have been thrown away)

trauma /ˈtrɔːmə/ NOUN [plural traumas] a very unpleasant experience that upsets someone a lot and for a long time ▫ *She never recovered from the trauma of losing her son.* (trauma)

travel¹ /ˈtrævəl/ VERB [travels, travelling/US traveling, travelled/US traveled]
1 to go from one place to another ▫ *Holly spent the summer travelling in the United States.* ▫ *Some people have to travel long distances to get to school.* 🔁 *She travels the world in her job.* ▫ *+ by I like travelling by train.* (viajar)
2 to move at a particular speed ▫ *How fast does light travel?* ▫ *The vehicle was travelling too fast.* (deslocar-se)

travel² /ˈtrævəl/ NOUN, NO PLURAL the activity of going from one place to another 🔁 *Cheap air travel has encouraged more people to fly.* 🔁 *Make sure you have travel insurance if you go abroad.* (viagem)

travel agency /ˈtrævəl ˌeɪdʒənsɪ/ NOUN [plural travel agencies] a shop or business where you can buy holidays (agência de viagens)

travel agent /ˈtrævəl ˌeɪdʒənt/ NOUN [plural travel agents]
1 a person whose job is to arrange holidays for people (agente de viagens)
2 a travel agent's a travel agency (agente de viagens)

traveler /ˈtrævələ(r)/ NOUN [plural travelers] the US spelling of traveller (viajante)

traveler's check /ˈtrævələz ˌtʃek/ NOUN [plural traveler's checks] the US spelling of traveller's cheque (traveler cheques)

traveller /ˈtrævələ(r)/ NOUN [plural travellers] a person who is on a journey 🔁 *Air travellers faced delays due to bad weather.* (viajante)

traveller's cheque /ˈtrævələz ˌtʃek/ NOUN [plural traveller's cheques] a cheque for a fixed amount that you can change for local money when you are abroad (traveler cheques)

tray /treɪ/ NOUN [plural trays] a flat object for carrying food, plates, cups, etc. on ▫ *The waiter was carrying a tray of drinks.* (bandeja)

tread /tred/ VERB [treads, treading, trod, trodden]
1 to put your foot on something ▫ *Don't tread on the flowers.* (pisar)
2 tread water to stay in one place in water by moving your legs up and down (boiar em pé)

treason /ˈtriːzən/ NOUN, NO PLURAL the crime of not being loyal to your country, for example by giving away secret information (traição)

treasure /ˈtreʒə(r)/ NOUN, NO PLURAL valuable objects, especially if they have been hidden % *The children were hoping to find some buried treasure.* (tesouro)

treat¹ /triːt/ VERB [treats, treating, treated]
1 to behave in a particular way towards someone ▫ *I think Debbie treated Steve really badly.* ▫ *They treat their staff well.* (tratar)
2 to deal with something in a particular way ▫ *+ as He treated my remark as a joke.* ▫ *We treat any form of racism very seriously.* (tratar)
3 to give medicine or medical care to someone who is ill or injured ▫ *Doctors use all the latest methods to treat their patients.* ▫ *+ for She is being treated for shock.* (tratar)
4 to buy or do something special for someone ▫ *+ to I treated the children to a pizza on the way home.* (oferecer)

treat² /triːt/ NOUN [plural treats] something special that you do or buy for someone 🔁 *We're having dinner in front of the TV as a special treat.* (regalo)

treatment /ˈtriːtmənt/ NOUN [plural treatments]
1 medicine or medical care ▫ *My treatment will last for about a month.* 🔁 *He is receiving treatment for a heart condition.* ▫ *They are trying*

treaty 363 **triumph**

out a new treatment for cancer. (tratamento)
2 no plural the way you behave towards someone or deal with something □ *Will I get special treatment if I pay more?* (tratamento)

treaty /ˈtriːtɪ/ NOUN [plural treaties] an official agreement between countries 🔊 *The two countries have signed a peace treaty.* (tratado)

tree /triː/ NOUN [plural trees] a very tall plant with branches and leaves □ *We planted lots of trees in the garden last autumn.* □ *an apple tree* □ *an oak tree* 🔊 *We planted a new tree.* 🔊 *The children were climbing trees.* 🔊 *a tree trunk* (árvore)

tremble /ˈtrembəl/ VERB [trembles, trembling, trembled] to shake because you are frightened or excited □ *Joe's hand trembled as he dialled the number.* □ *She was trembling with fear.* (tremer)

tremendous /trɪˈmendəs/ ADJECTIVE
1 very great □ *The car was travelling at a tremendous speed.* (enorme)
2 very good □ *That's tremendous news!* (fantástico)

trench /trentʃ/ NOUN [plural trenches] a long narrow hole dug in the ground (trincheira)

trend /trend/ NOUN [plural trends] a gradual change or development □ *There's a new trend towards healthy eating.* (tendência)

trial /ˈtraɪəl/ NOUN [plural trials]
1 a legal process in which a court has to decide if someone is guilty of a crime □ *a murder trial* 🔊 *She's on trial for the killing of her husband.* 🔊 *He was not given a fair trial.* (julgamento)
2 a test that is done to find out how good or effective something is □ *The company is carrying out trials on new drugs.* (prova)

triangle /ˈtraɪæŋɡəl/ NOUN [plural triangles] a flat shape with three sides and three angles □ *a right-angled triangle* (triângulo)

triangular /traɪˈæŋɡjʊlə(r)/ ADJECTIVE in the shape of a triangle □ *a triangular shape* □ *a triangular piece of cloth* (triangular)

tribal /ˈtraɪbəl/ ADJECTIVE to do with a group of families who have the same culture and language and have a traditional way of living a long way from cities □ *tribal ceremonies* (tribal)

tribe /traɪb/ NOUN [plural tribes] a group of families who have the same culture and language and have a traditional way of living a long way from cities □ *the Christian Arab tribes of the Syrian desert* (tribo)

tribute /ˈtrɪbjuːt/ NOUN [plural tributes]
1 a speech or action that shows you admire someone □ *The film will be shown as a tribute to its star who died last week.* (tributo)

2 pay tribute to someone/something to praise someone or something in public □ *They wanted to pay tribute to all the soldiers who had died in the war.* (homenagear)

trick¹ /trɪk/ NOUN [plural tricks]
1 an unfair or unpleasant thing that you do to someone as a joke, or in order to get an advantage for yourself 🔊 *The children were playing tricks on each other.* (truque)
2 something that looks like magic which you do to entertain people 🔊 *a magic trick* 🔊 *Ella was doing card tricks.* (truque)

trick² /trɪk/ VERB [tricks, tricking, tricked] to make someone do what you want by using clever but unfair methods □ *+ into She was tricked into signing the papers.* (enganar)

trickle /ˈtrɪkəl/ VERB [trickles, trickling, trickled] to flow in a slow, thin stream □ *Sweat trickled down his face.* (pingar)

tricky /ˈtrɪkɪ/ ADJECTIVE [trickier, trickiest] difficult to do or to deal with □ *a tricky situation* (complicado)

tried /traɪd/ PAST TENSE AND PAST PARTICIPLE OF try¹ (ver **try**¹)

trigger¹ /ˈtrɪɡə(r)/ NOUN [plural triggers] the part you pull to fire a gun 🔊 *He pointed the gun and pulled the trigger.* (gatilho)

trigger² /ˈtrɪɡə(r)/ VERB [triggers, triggering, triggered] to make something start to happen □ *The announcement triggered violent protests around the country.* (desencadear)

trillion /ˈtrɪljən/ NUMBER [plural trillions] the number 1,000,000,000,000 (trilhão)

trim /trɪm/ VERB [trims, trimming, trimmed] to cut a small amount off something □ *Get your hair trimmed.* □ *You'll need to trim that photo to get it into the frame.* (aparar)

trio /ˈtriːəʊ/ NOUN [plural trios] a group of three people or things, especially musicians (trio)

trip¹ /trɪp/ NOUN [plural trips] a journey to a place and back again □ *There are boat trips around Lake Geneva.* 🔊 *a shopping trip* 🔊 *He has made several trips to Japan.* □ *+ to We went on a trip to the zoo.* (viagem)

trip² /trɪp/ VERB [trips, tripping, tripped]
1 to hit your foot on something and fall, or almost fall □ *+ over Caroline tripped over the edge of the carpet.* □ *Mind you don't trip on the step.* (tropeçar)
2 to make someone fall by putting your foot in front of them □ *+ up One of the boys tripped me up.* (fazer tropeçar)

triumph /ˈtraɪəmf/ NOUN [plural triumphs] a great success in a competition or fight □ *It was* *another triumph for the champions.* □ *England's only World Cup triumph was in 1966.* (**triunfo**)

trod /trɒd/ PAST TENSE OF tread (ver **tread**)

trodden /'trɒdən/ PAST PARTICIPLE OF tread (ver **tread**)

trolley /'trɒlɪ/ NOUN [plural trolleys] a container on wheels, used for carrying things □ *a supermarket trolley* (**carrinho**)

troops /truːps/ PLURAL NOUN soldiers □ *The US sent troops to Darfur.* (**soldados**)

trophy /'trəʊfɪ/ NOUN [plural trophies] a prize such as a silver cup that you get for winning a trophy competition □ *Helen won the junior tennis trophy last year.* (**troféu**)

tropical /'trɒpɪkəl/ ADJECTIVE in or to do with hot areas near the equator (= line round the middle of the world) □ *a tropical rainforest* (**tropical**)

tropics /'trɒpɪks/ PLURAL NOUN the tropics the hot areas near the equator (= line round the middle of the world). A geography word. (**trópico**)

trot /trɒt/ VERB [trots, trotting, trotted] if a horse trots, it moves more quickly than walking, but does not run □ *The horse trotted down the road.* (**trotar**)

trouble¹ /'trʌbəl/ NOUN [plural troubles]

1 problems, difficulties or worries □ + *ing She has trouble sleeping.* □ *He had financial troubles.* ▣ *You'll have no trouble finding a better job.* (**problema**)

2 no plural extra effort ▣ *He took the trouble to thank everyone.* ▣ *They went to so much trouble to make our visit pleasant.* (**esforço**)

3 no plural a problem with your health or with a machine or piece of equipment □ *She has heart trouble.* □ *The car had engine trouble.* (**problema**)

4 no plural a situation where people are behaving badly, fighting, causing difficulties, etc. ▣ *Some people at the back of the hall started to cause trouble.* (**distúrbio**)

5 no plural a difficult or dangerous situation ▣ *Their ship got into trouble during a storm.* ▣ *The business is in deep trouble.* (**problema**)

6 no plural a situation where you will be punished or blamed ▣ *We got into trouble for talking in class.* ▣ *If I'm late home, I'll be in big trouble.* (**problema**)

7 no plural the thing about something that causes problems ▣ *The trouble is, I already have a meeting on that day.* (**problema, questão**)

trouble² /'trʌbəl/ VERB [troubles, troubling, troubled] if something troubles you, it worries you □ *They were troubled by reports of violence in the area.* (**perturbar**)

trousers /'traʊzəz/ PLURAL NOUN a piece of clothing for the lower half of your body that covers each leg ▣ *She was wearing a pair of black trousers.* (**calça**)

truce /truːs/ NOUN [plural truces] an agreement to stop fighting or arguing ▣ *The political parties called a truce.* (**trégua**)

truck /trʌk/ NOUN [plural trucks] a large road vehicle for carrying goods □ *He drove the truck into the yard.* □ *Her Dad's a truck driver.*

true /truː/ ADJECTIVE [truer, truest]

1 real and not invented ▣ *Is it a true story?* □ + *that Is it true that you're moving to Tokyo?* (**verdadeiro**)

2 real and not pretended □ *Ben never showed his true feelings.* □ *She's a true friend.* □ *He had finally found true love.* □ *He had a false passport to hide his true identity.* (**real, verdadeiro**)

3 come true if something comes true, the thing you have spoken about really happens □ *My wish to travel round the world has finally come true.* (**realizar**)

truly /'truːlɪ/ ADVERB really □ *Tell me what you truly want to do.* □ *I'm truly sorry.* (**sinceramente, realmente**)

trumpet /'trʌmpɪt/ NOUN [plural trumpets] a metal musical instrument that you blow into □ *Millie is learning to play the trumpet.* (**trombeta**)

trunk /trʌŋk/ NOUN [plural trunks]

1 the thick main stem of a tree ▣ *a tree trunk* (**tronco**)

2 an elephant's long nose (**tromba**)

3 a large box for storing things (**baú**)

4 the main part of a person's body, not including their head, arms or legs (**tronco**)

5 the US word for boot (= part of a car) (**porta-malas**)

trust¹ /trʌst/ VERB [trusts, trusting, trusted]

1 to believe that someone is honest and loyal □ *The officer picked ten men he knew he could trust.* (**confiar**)

2 to feel confident that someone will do something correctly and well or will look after something well □ + *to do something I know I can trust you to choose a suitable present.* (**confiar**)

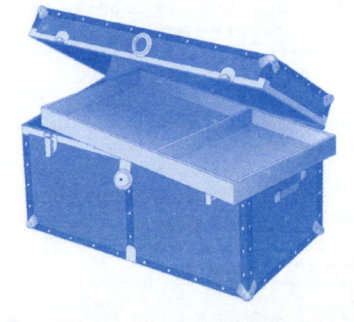

trust[2] /trʌst/ NOUN, NO PLURAL the belief that someone is honest and loyal ◻ *The new manager will have to gain the trust of her staff.* (confiança)

trustworthy /'trʌstwɜːði/ ADJECTIVE able to be trusted ◻ *I'm sure he's a trustworthy person.* (digno de confiança)

truth /truːθ/ NOUN [plural truths]
1 the truth the true facts ◻ *I don't think he is telling the truth.* ◻ **+ about** *I don't think we'll ever know the truth about what happened.* (verdade)
2 no plural the quality of being true ◻ **+ in** *Is there any truth in the rumours that he is leaving?* (verdade)

> Note that you tell the truth. You do not 'say the truth':
> ✓ *Tell me the truth: Do you like her?*
> ✗ *Say the truth: Do you like her?*

try[1] /traɪ/ VERB [tries, trying, tried]
1 to make an effort or an attempt to do something ◻ **+ to do something** *Please try to understand.* ◻ *He failed the exam, but he can always try again next year.* (tentar)
2 to do or use something to see if you like it or if it works or is effective ◻ *Try this powder for a cleaner wash.* ◻ *I've never tried Chinese food.* ◻ **+ ing** *You could try phoning him.* (experimentar)
3 to find out if someone committed a crime by hearing all the evidence (= facts or statements given in a court of law) ◻ *They will be tried in the European Court of Human Rights.* ◻ **+ for** *She was tried for murder.* (julgar)
◆ PHRASAL VERB **try something on** to put on a piece of clothing to see if it fits or what it looks like on you ◻ *I tried on three summer dresses but I didn't like any of them.*
⇨ go to **try your luck**

try[2] /traɪ/ NOUN [plural tries] an attempt to do something ◻ *I couldn't get the tyre off – could you have a try?* (tentativa)

T-shirt /'tiːʃɜːt/ NOUN [plural T-shirts] a piece of clothing made from soft cotton which you wear on the top part of your body ◻ *She was wearing jeans and a white T-shirt.* (camiseta)

tsunami /tsuːˈnɑːmi/ NOUN [plural tsunamis] a very high, fast wave that is caused by an earthquake (= when the ground shakes) under the sea (tsunami)

tub /tʌb/ NOUN [plural tubs]
1 a container with a lid which has food in it ◻ *a tub of ice cream* (pote)
2 a round, deep container ◻ *The tub was full of bright red flowers.* (tina)

tube /tjuːb/ NOUN [plural tubes]
1 a long, thin pipe ◻ *He was in hospital with a feeding tube in his stomach.* (cano, tubo)
2 a container for a soft substance which you press to get the substance out ◻ **+ of** *a tube of toothpaste* (tubo)
3 no plural an underground railway system, especially in London ◻ *We can easily get there by tube.* ◻ *a tube station* (metrô)

tuck /tʌk/ VERB [tucks, tucking, tucked] to push the edge of something somewhere to make it tidy or firm ◻ *Tuck your shirt into your trousers.* ◻ *She tucked the flap into the envelope.* (enfiar)
◆ PHRASAL VERB **tuck someone in/up** to make someone comfortable in bed by putting the sheets over them ◻ *She went upstairs to tuck the children in.*

Tuesday /'tjuːzdɪ/ NOUN [plural Tuesdays] the day of the week after Monday and before Wednesday ◻ *Kay's coming on Tuesday.* (terça-feira)

tug[1] /tʌɡ/ VERB [tugs, tugging, tugged] to pull something suddenly and firmly ◻ *She tugged her hand away from mine.* ◻ *James tugged on the rope.* (puxar)

tug[2] /tʌɡ/ NOUN [plural tugs] a sudden firm pull ◻ *I gave his arm a tug and he looked at me angrily.* (puxão)

tuition /tjuːˈɪʃən/ NOUN, NO PLURAL teaching something, especially to one person or a small group ◻ *His parents paid for him to have private tuition in English.* ◻ *Students have to pay tuition fees.* (aula, ensino)

tumble /'tʌmbəl/ VERB [tumbles, tumbling, tumbled] to fall somewhere ◻ *He tripped and tumbled down the stairs.* (levar um tombo)

tummy /'tʌmɪ/ NOUN [plural tummies] an informal word for stomach (estômago)

tumour /'tjuːmə(r)/ NOUN [plural tumours] a group of cells in your body which are not growing in a normal way ◻ *He had an operation to remove a brain tumour.* (tumor)

tune[1] /tjuːn/ NOUN [plural tunes] a series of musical notes that sound nice ◻ *She was playing some tunes on the piano.* ◻ *a catchy tune* (= one that is easy to remember) (melodia)

tune[2] /tjuːn/ VERB [tunes, tuning, tuned] to make small changes to a musical instrument so that it sounds right ◻ *Ben was tuning his guitar.* (afinar)

tunnel[1] /'tʌnəl/ NOUN [plural tunnels] a long underground passage ◻ *There is a rail tunnel linking England and France.* ◻ *There were plans to build a tunnel through the Alps.* (túnel)

tunnel[2] /'tʌnəl/ VERB [tunnels, tunnelling/US tunneling, tunnelled/US tunneled] to make an underground passage ◻ *Will they tunnel under the river or build a bridge over it?* (escavar)

turkey /'tɜːkɪ/ NOUN [plural turkeys]
1 a large bird that lives on farms and is eaten as food (peru)

2 no plural the meat from this bird □ *roast turkey* □ *a turkey sandwich* (peru)

turmoil /'tɜːmɔɪl/ NOUN, NO PLURAL a state of worry and confusion □ *Her mind was in turmoil.* □ *political turmoil* (alvoroço)

turn¹ /tɜːn/ VERB [turns, turning, turned]
1 to move your body or part of your body to face in another direction □ *He turned and walked away.* □ *+ around I turned around to look at them.* □ *+ to She turned to her neighbour and whispered something.* □ *He turned his head slightly.* (virar-se)
2 to move something so that it faces in another direction, or to move like this □ *The car turned upside down.* □ *+ over You must not turn the cards over before the game starts.* □ *+ round He turned the book round to show us the picture.* (virar)
3 to make a circular movement around a central point, or to make something do this □ *The wheels began to turn.* □ *Turn the handle to the right.* (virar)
4 if you turn the page of a book, you move it so that you can see the next page □ *She took one look and turned pale.* □ *Things turned nasty when the police arrived.* (tornar-se)
⇨ go to **turn** your **nose** up at something

♦ PHRASAL VERBS **turn** something **down** to make a machine produce less sound, heat, etc. □ *Could you turn the music down, please?* □ *I've turned down the heating.* **turn** someone/something **down** to not accept an offer □ *He asked her to marry him but she turned him down.* □ *I turned down a job in his company.* **turn (someone/ something) into** someone/something to change into something different or to make someone or something do this □ *His book is being turned into a movie.* □ *The caterpillar turns into a butterfly.* **turn** something **off** to move a switch so that a machine stops working or a supply of something is stopped □ *Don't forget to turn off the lights.* **turn** something **on** to move a switch so that a machine starts working or a supply of something is started □ *I've turned on the heating.* **turn out** to be found to have a particular reason, quality or result □ *It turned out that she'd never received the letter.* □ *The hotel turned out to be really bad.* **turn up** to arrive □ *He didn't turn up for work this morning.*

turn² /tɜːn/ NOUN [plural turns]
1 the time when you can or must do something, before or after someone else □ *It's your/my turn next.* □ *Josh hasn't had a turn yet.* (vez)
2 take turns/take it in turns if people take turns, each person does something, one after the other □ *We took it in turns to use the computer.* (revezar)
3 in turn one after the other □ *He tried each of the dishes in turn.* (alternadamente)
4 a change of direction or a curve or corner in a road or path □ *Take the first turn on the right.* □ *a left/right turn* (esquina)
5 when something is moved in a circle around a central point □ *I gave the screw another turn.* (volta)

turning /'tɜːnɪŋ/ NOUN [plural turnings] a place where a car can leave a road and go onto another road □ *Take the second turning on the right.* □ *We took a wrong turning and ended up on a mud track.* (rua transversal, esquina, desvio)

turtle /'tɜːtəl/ NOUN [plural turtles] an animal that usually lives in water and has a hard shell (tartaruga)

tutor /'tjuːtə(r)/ NOUN [plural tutors] a teacher who teaches one person or a small group □ *He hired a private tutor to help him learn Japanese.* (monitor)

TV /ˌtiːˈviː/ NOUN [plural TVs] television □ *She switched the TV on.* □ *What's on TV tonight?* □ *I think the children watch too much TV.* (tevê)

twelfth /twelfθ/ NUMBER 12th written as a word (décimo segundo)

twelve /twelv/ NUMBER [plural twelves] the number 12 (doze)

twentieth /'twentiəθ/ NUMBER 20th written as a word (vigésimo)

twenty /'twenti/ NUMBER [plural twenties]
1 the number 20 (vinte)
2 the twenties the years between 1920 and 1929 (os anos 1920)

twice /twaɪs/ ADVERB two times □ *He sneezed twice.* □ *I could eat twice that amount.* □ *I visit my grandmother twice a week.* (duas vezes)

twilight /'twaɪlaɪt/ NOUN, NO PLURAL the time in the evening just before it becomes completely dark (lusco-fusco)

twin¹ /twɪn/ NOUN [plural twins] one of two children born to the same mother at the same time □ *Paul and Jo are twins.* □ *Our children are identical twins* (= they look exactly the same). (gêmeo)

twin | **tyre**

twin² /twɪn/ ADJECTIVE twin sister/brother/daughters, etc. a sister, brother, etc. who is a twin □ *Bella's my twin sister.* (**irmão gêmeo**)

twist¹ /twɪst/ VERB [twists, twisting, twisted]
1 to turn something using your hands □ *Twist the handle hard and then pull it.* □ *She twisted the lid of the jar.* (**girar, torcer**)
2 to turn the top half of your body □ **+ round/around** *Gregory twisted round in his chair to look at me.* (**girar, torcer**)
3 to bend something out of its correct shape □ *The front wheel of the bike twisted when it hit the wall.* (**torcer, retorcer**)
4 twist your ankle/knee, etc. to hurt your ankle, knee, etc. by turning it suddenly (**torcer**)
5 if a road or river twists, it has a lot of curves in it □ *The road twisted and turned up the mountain.* (**serpentear**)

> THESAURUS: If you twist something, you turn it, using your hands. You might twist a lid to remove it, for example. If you wind something, you twist or wrap it around something else. For example, you might wind a bandage around your arm if you hurt yourself. If you curl something, you make it form curves. Some women curl their hair.

twist² /twɪst/ NOUN [plural twists]
1 a piece of something that has been bent □ *She put a twist of lemon in the drink.* (**pedacinho**)
2 a movement in which you turn something □ *Give the lid a twist.* (**torção**)
3 a curve in a road or river (**dobra, curva**)
4 a sudden and unexpected change in a story or situation □ *This announcement added a strange new twist to his sudden death.* (**virada**)

twitch /twɪtʃ/ VERB [twitches, twitching, twitched] if part of your body twitches, it moves slightly in a way you cannot control □ *Her eyelid twitched.* (**crispar-se**)

two /tu:/ NUMBER [plural twos] the number 2 (**dois**)

type¹ /taɪp/ NOUN [plural types]
1 used for talking about people or things that have similar qualities and can be considered as a group 🔲 *Research of this type has never been done before.* □ **+ of** *He's the type of person who never worries about anything.* □ *What type of dog have you got?* □ *There are many different types of cancer.* (**tipo**)
2 no plural printed letters and numbers □ *The title should be in bold type.* (**letra, tipo**)

type² /taɪp/ VERB [types, typing, typed] to write something using a keyboard on a computer □ *Type your name and then your password.* (**digitar**)

typical /ˈtɪpɪkəl/ ADJECTIVE having the usual qualities of a particular person or thing 🔲 *This is a typical example of a 17th-century cottage.* □ *Beth is a typical teenager.* □ *On a typical day, there are over 100,000 lorries on Britain's roads.* □ **+ of** *It was typical of Emily to offer to help.* (**típico**)

typically /ˈtɪpɪkəli/ ADVERB as you would expect from a particular person or thing □ *Typically, Tracy arrived late.* □ *He was behaving in a typically aggressive way.* (**tipicamente**)

tyrant /ˈtaɪrənt/ NOUN [plural tyrants] a ruler who uses power in a cruel and unfair way (**tirano**)

tyre /ˈtaɪə(r)/ NOUN [plural tyres] a piece of rubber around the edge of a wheel, which has air in it 🔲 *We had a flat tyre.* (**pneu**)

U u

U or **u** /juː/ the 21st letter of the alphabet (a vigésima primeira letra do alfabeto)

ugly /ˈʌɡli/ ADJECTIVE [**uglier, ugliest**] not pleasant to look at □ *an ugly building* □ *a big ugly monster* (**feio**)

> People do not often use the word **ugly** to describe people as it sounds unkind. Sometimes the word **plain** (which has the same meaning) is used instead as it sounds less unkind.

UK /ˌjuːˈkeɪ/ ABBREVIATION **United Kingdom** (abreviação de **Reino Unido**)

ulcer /ˈʌlsə(r)/ NOUN [plural **ulcers**] a small sore area on your skin or inside your body □ *a mouth ulcer* (**úlcera**)

umbrella /ʌmˈbrelə/ NOUN [plural **umbrellas**] a frame with cloth over it that you hold above you for shelter when it rains (**guarda-chuva**)

umpire /ˈʌmpaɪə(r)/ NOUN [plural **umpires**] the person in a game such as cricket, who makes sure the players obey the rules (**árbitro**)

UN /ˌjuːˈen/ ABBREVIATION **United Nations** (abreviação de **Nações Unidas**)

un- /ʌn/ PREFIX un- is used at the beginning of words to mean 'not' □ *untidy* □ *unkind* (**in-, a-**)

unable /ʌnˈeɪbəl/ ADJECTIVE **unable to do something** not able to do something □ *He stood completely still, unable to take his eyes off the bear.* (**incapaz**)

unacceptable /ˌʌnəkˈseptəbəl/ ADJECTIVE something unacceptable cannot be allowed to happen, exist or continue because it is wrong or not of a high enough standard □ *His behaviour is totally unacceptable.* □ *The bank decided that the financial risk was unacceptable.* (**inaceitável**)

unanimous /juːˈnænɪməs/ ADJECTIVE agreed by everyone □ *a unanimous decision* (**unânime**)

unbelievable /ˌʌnbɪˈliːvəbəl/ ADJECTIVE
1 used to emphasize how bad, good, extreme, etc. something is □ *Seeing the whales was an unbelievable experience.* (**inacreditável**)
2 difficult to believe □ *an unbelievable story* (**inacreditável**)

uncertain /ʌnˈsɜːtən/ ADJECTIVE
1 not sure what to decide □ *+ about I was uncertain about what to do next.* (**incerto**)
2 not known □ *The future is uncertain.* (**incerto**)

uncle /ˈʌŋkəl/ NOUN [plural **uncles**]
1 the brother of one of your parents □ *My aunt and uncle live in Scotland.* □ *Uncle Douglas came to visit.* (**tio**)
2 your aunt's husband (**tio**)

unclear /ʌnˈklɪə(r)/ ADJECTIVE not obvious or easy to understand □ *It's unclear why she left her job.* □ *The writing was rather unclear.* (**obscuro, incerto**)

uncomfortable /ʌnˈkʌmftəbəl/ ADJECTIVE
1 not feeling comfortable □ *We were uncomfortable in the heat.* (**desconfortável**)
2 causing you to feel uncomfortable □ *The seats were really uncomfortable.* (**desconfortável**)
3 slightly embarrassed or slightly embarrassing □ *+ about I feel uncomfortable about accepting money from her.* □ *There were a lot of uncomfortable silences.* (**constrangido**)

> THESAURUS: Something which is uncomfortable does not feel comfortable. For example, a chair might be uncomfortable, or shoes that do not fit properly. If something is **painful**, it causes you pain. You might describe a toothache as **painful**. If something is **awkward**, it is difficult to manage or use. If you write with your left hand, scissors may be **awkward** to use.

uncomfortably /ʌnˈkʌmftəbli/ ADVERB in an uncomfortable way □ *Tom shifted uncomfortably in his seat.* (**desconfortavelmente**)

unconscious /ʌnˈkɒnʃəs/ ADJECTIVE in a state like sleep where you are not aware of what is happening around you, because you are seriously ill or injured ◘ *A brick hit his head and he was knocked unconscious.* (**inconsciente**)

uncontrollable /ˌʌnkənˈtrəʊləbəl/ ADJECTIVE not possible to control ◘ *She suddenly had an uncontrollable urge to kick something.* (**incontrolável**)

uncount noun /ˈʌnkaʊnt ˌnaʊn/ or **uncountable noun** /ʌnˌkaʊntəbəl ˈnaʊn/ NOUN [plural **uncount nouns** or **uncountable nouns**] in grammar, a noun that does not have a plural form, e.g. *happiness, water* or *advice* (**substantivo incontável**)

uncover /ʌnˈkʌvə(r)/ VERB [uncovers, uncovering, uncovered]
1 to discover something that had been secret or hidden ◘ *Police have uncovered new evidence about the murder.* (**descobrir**)
2 to remove a cover from something (**descobrir**)

under[1] /ˈʌndə(r)/ PREPOSITION
1 below something ◘ *The bag is under the table.* ◘ *We walked under the bridge.* (**sob, embaixo de**)
2 covered by something ◘ *I found my glasses under a cushion.* ◘ *The mountains were under a thick layer of snow.* (**sob, embaixo de**)
3 less than an amount, level or age ◘ *All the clothes are under £20.* ◘ *The competition is open to anyone under 30.* (**menos de**)
4 controlled by a particular person, government, organization, etc. ◘ *The country was under military control.* (**sob**)
5 having a particular thing done, or affected by a particular thing ◘ *Our troops came under attack.* ◘ *He was under pressure to resign.* ◘ *I think you should show her some sympathy under the circumstances* (= because of the situation). (**sob**)

> **THESAURUS:** Below means in a lower place or position. A plane might fly below the clouds, or you could stand on the top of a hill and look at what is below you. If something is under something else, it is directly below it. You might put a saucer under a cup, for example. Beneath has a similar meaning to under.

under[2] /ˈʌndə(r)/ ADVERB
1 in or to a lower place ◘ *We watched the divers go under.* (**abaixo, para baixo**)
2 less than an amount, level or age ◘ *The play equipment is for children aged 6 and under.* (**abaixo, para baixo**)

undercover /ˈʌndəkʌvə(r)/ ADJECTIVE working or done secretly ◘ *an undercover police operation* (**clandestino**)

undergo /ˌʌndəˈgəʊ/ VERB [undergoes, undergoing, underwent, undergone] to experience something ◘ *He underwent an operation to mend his broken leg.* (**passar por**)

undergraduate /ˌʌndəˈgrædʒuət/ NOUN [plural **undergraduates**] someone who is studying at a university and has not yet done their degree (= qualification) (**não graduado**)

underground[1] /ˈʌndəgraʊnd/ ADJECTIVE, ADVERB below the surface of the ground ◘ *Moles live underground.* ◘ *an underground stream* (**subterrâneo**)

underground[2] /ˈʌndəgraʊnd/ NOUN [plural **undergrounds**] a railway that is under the ground, usually in a large city ◘ *the London Underground* (**metrô**)

underline /ˌʌndəˈlaɪn/ VERB [underlines, underlining, underlined] to draw a line under something ◘ *Underline all the adjectives in these sentences.* (**sublinhar**)

underpants /ˈʌndəpænts/ PLURAL NOUN underwear that men and boys wear under their trousers (**cueca**)

understand /ˌʌndəˈstænd/ VERB [understands, understanding, understood]
1 to know what something means ◘ *I can't understand the instructions.* ◘ *Do you understand German?* (**compreender**)
2 to know why something happens, how something works, or the effect or importance of something ◘ **+ question word** *Doctors still don't understand how the disease spreads.* ◘ *We didn't understand the importance of his words at the time.* (**compreender, entender**)
3 to know why someone behaves and feels the way they do ◘ *I'll never understand him.* ◘ *I understood her anger.* ◘ *I don't understand what you are trying to do.* (**entender**)

> **THESAURUS:** If you understand something, you know what it means, or why it happens or is important. If you realize something, you understand something that you did not know or understand before. If you recognize something, you accept that it is true. If you follow someone, you understand what they are saying. For example, it can be difficult to follow what people say on television if you do not speak the language very well.

understanding[1] /ˌʌndəˈstændɪŋ/ NOUN, NO PLURAL knowledge about something ◘ *Scientists are trying to gain a better understanding of the disease.* (**conhecimento**)

understanding[2] /ˌʌndəˈstændɪŋ/ ADJECTIVE able to understand other people's feelings or to forgive someone because of their situation □ *The illness makes me bad-tempered at times, but my family have been very understanding.* (compreensivo)

understood /ˌʌndəˈstʊd/ PAST TENSE AND PAST PARTICIPLE OF understand (ver **understand**)

undertake /ˌʌndəˈteɪk/ VERB [undertakes, undertaking, undertook, undertaken] undertake to do something a formal word meaning to promise to do something □ *I undertook to ensure their safety.* (comprometer-se)

underwater /ˌʌndəwɔːˈtə(r)/ ADJECTIVE, ADVERB under the surface of water ⁒ *an underwater creature* □ *Can you swim underwater?* (subaquático, embaixo d'água)

underway /ˌʌndərˈweɪ/ ADJECTIVE happening or having started ▣ *Work on the new motorway got underway last week.* (encaminhado, em andamento)

underwear /ˈʌndəweə(r)/ NOUN, NO PLURAL clothes you wear next to your skin and under your other clothes (roupa de baixo)

> **THESAURUS:** Underwear is a general word for any clothes that you wear under your clothes next to your skin. Pants are underwear that covers your bottom. Both men and women wear pants. Pants for women are also called knickers. A bra is a piece of underwear that women wear to support their breasts. A vest is a piece of underwear without sleeves that covers the top part of your body.

underwent /ˌʌndəˈwent/ PAST TENSE OF undergo (ver **undergo**)

undid /ʌnˈdɪd/ PAST TENSE OF undo (ver **undo**)

undo /ʌnˈduː/ VERB [undoes, undoing, undid, undone] to open something that is fastened □ *He undid his jacket.* (desfazer)

unemployed /ˌʌnɪmˈplɔɪd/ ADJECTIVE without a job □ *My Dad's unemployed at the moment.* □ *unemployed miners* (desempregado)

unemployment /ˌʌnɪmˈplɔɪmənt/ NOUN, NO PLURAL

1 the number of people who do not have a job ▣ *Unemployment has risen again.* (desemprego)
2 not having a job (desemprego)

unexpected /ˌʌnɪkˈspektɪd/ ADJECTIVE surprising because of not being expected □ *an unexpected visitor* □ *an unexpected development* (inesperado)

unfair /ʌnˈfeə(r)/ ADJECTIVE

1 not right or reasonable □ *Some of her criticism was very unfair.* (injusto)
2 when a situation is unfair, people are not treated in an equal way, or do not have equal opportunities ▣ *His father's fame gives him an unfair advantage.* (injusto, desleal)

unfairly /ʌnˈfeəli/ ADVERB in a way that is unfair □ *We have been very unfairly treated.* (injustamente)

unfasten /ʌnˈfɑːsən/ VERB [unfastens, unfastening, unfastened] to open something that was fastened □ *She unfastened her coat.* (desprender, desatar)

unfit /ʌnˈfɪt/ ADJECTIVE

1 not suitable or not good enough □ *The water is unfit to drink.* (inapto, inapropriado)
2 not in good physical condition, especially because of not doing enough exercise (fora de forma)

unfold /ʌnˈfəʊld/ VERB [unfolds, unfolding, unfolded] to spread out something that was folded (desdobrar)

unfortunate /ʌnˈfɔːtʃənət/ ADJECTIVE caused by bad luck □ *an unfortunate accident* (infeliz)

unfortunately /ʌnˈfɔːtʃənətli/ ADVERB used to show that you wish something had not happened or been true □ *Unfortunately, I lost the ring.* (infelizmente)

unfriendly /ʌnˈfrendli/ ADJECTIVE not friendly □ *His sister was very unfriendly.* (antipático)

unhappiness /ʌnˈhæpɪnɪs/ NOUN, NO PLURAL the state of being unhappy (infelicidade)

unhappy /ʌnˈhæpi/ ADJECTIVE [unhappier, unhappiest]

1 sad or causing sadness ▣ *Ben has been feeling unhappy for a long time.* □ *an unhappy marriage* (triste, infeliz)
2 not pleased or not satisfied □ + **about** *He was unhappy about the result of the meeting.* ▣ *We were deeply unhappy about the quality of their work.* (descontente)

unhealthy /ʌnˈhelθi/ ADJECTIVE [unhealthier, unhealthiest]

1 someone who is unhealthy is ill, or does not have good health □ *He looks very unhealthy.* (doentio)
2 harmful for your health □ *an unhealthy lifestyle* (insalubre, mórbido)

uniform /ˈjuːnɪfɔːm/ NOUN [plural uniforms] a set of clothes that shows you belong to a particular organization, job or school □ *a bus driver's uniform* ▣ *school uniform* (uniforme)

union /ˈjuːnjən/ NOUN [plural unions]

1 an organization of workers that tries to get good pay and conditions for its members (sindicato)

unique

2 a group of countries, organizations, etc. that join together (**união**)

unique /juːˈniːk/ ADJECTIVE completely different from anyone or anything else (**único**)

> ▸ THESAURUS: A unique person is different from all other people in some way. A **single** person is a person who is not married. A **lone** person is acting on their own. So a **lone** parent looks after their children without a husband or wife, and a **lone** criminal commits a crime without any other people. A **lonely** person is unhappy because they are alone with no friends around them.

unit /ˈjuːnɪt/ NOUN [plural **units**]
1 a measure used to show an amount or level □ A metre is a unit of length. □ What is the unit of currency in Ecuador? (**unidade**)
2 a single thing that can be part of a larger group of things □ The book is divided into ten units. (**unidade**)

unite /juːˈnaɪt/ VERB [unites, uniting, united]
1 if people or groups unite, they join together, often to achieve something □ Workers have united to oppose the pay cuts. (**unir-se**)
2 to join people or groups together, often making them feel that they belong together and have the same opinions □ We need a new leader to unite the party. (**unir-se**)

United Kingdom /juːˌnaɪtɪd ˈkɪŋdəm/ NOUN the United Kingdom England, Scotland, Wales and Northern Ireland (**Reino Unido**)

United Nations /juːˌnaɪtɪd ˈneɪʃənz/ NOUN the United Nations an organization of people from most countries of the world, that works to try to solve world problems (**Organização das Nações Unidas**)

United States of America /juːˈnaɪtɪd ˌsteɪts əv əˈmerɪkə/ NOUN the United States of America the 50 states that make the country of North America (**Estados Unidos da América**)

unity /ˈjuːnəti/ NOUN, NO PLURAL when people agree on things and act together □ She has called for unity within the party. (**unidade**)

universal /ˌjuːnɪˈvɜːsəl/ ADJECTIVE
1 affecting or including everyone in the world □ English may become a universal language that everyone can learn and use. (**universal**)
2 relating to everyone in a group □ There was universal approval of the decision. (**universal**)

universe /ˈjuːnɪvɜːs/ NOUN the universe everything that exists anywhere, including the Earth, the sun and all the other planets and stars in space □ Somewhere in the universe there might be another world like ours. (**universo**)

unpleasant

university /ˌjuːnɪˈvɜːsəti/ NOUN [plural **universities**] a place where you go to study at the highest level after leaving school 🔂 I am hoping to go to university. □ university students (**universidade**)

unkind /ˌʌnˈkaɪnd/ ADJECTIVE [unkinder, unkindest] cruel and not kind □ It was unkind of you to tease her. (**cruel, duro**)

unknown /ˌʌnˈnəʊn/ ADJECTIVE
1 not known □ The man's identity is unknown. (**desconhecido**)
2 not famous □ an unknown actor (**desconhecido**)

unleaded /ˌʌnˈledɪd/ ADJECTIVE unleaded petrol does not have lead (= a soft, grey metal) added to it and so causes less harm to the environment (**sem chumbo**)

unless /ənˈles/ CONJUNCTION except when, or except if □ We always go for a walk on Sundays, unless it's raining. □ Don't come unless I phone you. (**a menos que, a não ser que**)

unlike /ˌʌnˈlaɪk/ PREPOSITION different from □ I never saw twins who were so unlike each other. (**diferente**)

unlikely /ˌʌnˈlaɪkli/ ADJECTIVE not expected to happen □ + that It's unlikely that she'll come. □ + to do something We're unlikely to finish the work today. 🔂 A victory for England now seems highly unlikely. (**improvável**)

unload /ˌʌnˈləʊd/ VERB [unloads, unloading, unloaded] to take things off or out of a vehicle □ After we got back from the trip, we had to unload the car. (**descarregar**)

unlock /ˌʌnˈlɒk/ VERB [unlocks, unlocking, unlocked] to open something that is locked □ Unlock this door now! (**destrancar**)

unlucky /ˌʌnˈlʌki/ ADJECTIVE having bad luck, causing bad luck or caused by bad luck □ I'm very unlucky at cards. □ It was an unlucky defeat. (**azarado**)

unmarried /ˌʌnˈmærɪd/ ADJECTIVE not married □ unmarried couples (**solteiro**)

unnecessary /ˌʌnˈnesəsəri/ ADJECTIVE not needed □ Any unnecessary clothing can be given to charity. (**desnecessário**)

unofficial /ˌʌnəˈfɪʃəl/ ADJECTIVE not done or allowed by anyone in authority □ Unofficial estimates suggest unemployment is still rising. (**extraoficial**)

unpleasant /ˌʌnˈplezənt/ ADJECTIVE
1 if something is unpleasant, you do not like it or enjoy it □ an unpleasant smell □ I found skiing a thoroughly unpleasant experience. (**desagradável**)

2 not polite, friendly or kind □ + *to He was rather unpleasant to his students.* (desagradável)

unpopular /ʌnˈpɒpjələ(r)/ ADJECTIVE disliked by many people □ *He is very unpopular at school.* (impopular)

unreasonable /ˌʌnˈriːzənəbəl/ ADJECTIVE not fair, often because of wanting too much □ *It's unreasonable to expect students to do so much homework.* □ *He accused the unions of making unreasonable demands.* (irracional)

unreliable /ˌʌnrɪˈlaɪəbəl/ ADJECTIVE not able to be trusted to do something □ *He's totally unreliable.* □ *My car's a bit unreliable.* (não confiável)

unsafe /ˌʌnˈseɪf/ ADJECTIVE dangerous □ *unsafe practices* (perigoso, inseguro)

unstable /ˌʌnˈsteɪbəl/ ADJECTIVE
1 changing or may change over a period □ *a politically unstable region* (instável)
2 not firm or strong □ *This chair seems a bit unstable.* (instável)

unsuccessful /ˌʌnsəkˈsesfʊl/ ADJECTIVE not managing to do something you are trying to do ▣ *Thieves made an unsuccessful attempt to steal the car.* □ *I tried to contact him but was unsuccessful.* (malsucedido)

unsuitable /ˌʌnˈsuːtəbəl/ ADJECTIVE not right for a purpose or occasion □ *unsuitable clothing* (impróprio, inoportuno)

unsure /ˌʌnˈʃɔː(r)/ ADJECTIVE not certain □ *I was unsure of the spelling.* □ *I asked if she was coming but she seemed unsure.* (inseguro)

untidy /ˌʌnˈtaɪdi/ ADJECTIVE [untidier, untidiest]
1 not carefully ordered or arranged □ *His flat is always untidy.* (desarrumado)
2 an untidy person does not keep their home, office, etc. tidy (desleixado)

until /ənˈtɪl/ PREPOSITION, CONJUNCTION
1 continuing to a particular time but not after that □ *He'll be here until midday.* □ *I waited until she left.* (até)
2 continuing as far as somewhere □ *Carry on walking until you get to a bridge.* (até)
3 not... until not before □ *I won't start until you tell me.* (não... até)

untrue /ˌʌnˈtruː/ ADJECTIVE false, not true □ *His story was completely untrue.* (falso)

unused[1] /ˌʌnˈjuːzd/ ADJECTIVE not having been used or not used now □ *unused stamps* (não usado)

unused[2] /ˌʌnˈjuːst/ ADJECTIVE **be unused to sth** to have little experience of something □ *I'm unused to cooking my own meals.* (não acostumado)

unusual /ʌnˈjuːʒʊəl/ ADJECTIVE not normal or not ordinary ▣ *It's unusual for him to arrive late.* □ *They make some lovely, quite unusual jewellery.* (incomum)

unwilling /ʌnˈwɪlɪŋ/ ADJECTIVE not wanting to do something □ + *to do something They seem unwilling to help.* (relutante)

up[1] /ʌp/ ADVERB, PREPOSITION
1 towards or in a higher position □ *I walked up the stairs.* □ *We went up in a helicopter.* □ *He looked up and saw her.* □ *She threw the ball up in the air.* (para cima)
2 to a greater amount or level □ *Prices have gone up again.* □ *Could you turn the volume up a bit?* (para cima)
3 if you stand up or sit up, you move your body to a vertical position (para cima)
4 up to less than or as much as a particular amount or level □ *The hall can hold up to 200 people.* (até)
5 up to him/you, etc. if an action or decision is up to you, you are responsible for doing it or making it □ *It's up to you whether you come or not.* (depende de)
6 used after verbs to show that something is finished or completely used □ *Eat up all your vegetables.* (tudo, completamente)
7 if you go up to someone, you move close to them, often in order to speak to them □ *He came up to me and asked if I needed any help.* (até)
8 further along a road, river, etc. □ *He lives just up the road from me.* (adiante)
9 be up to something to be doing something, usually something wrong or secret □ *The children are very quiet – what are they up to?* (estar ocupado)

up[2] /ʌp/ ADJECTIVE
1 not in bed □ *He's not up yet.* □ *I've been up half the night.* (acordado, fora da cama)
2 if an amount or level is up, it is higher □ *Profits are up by 25% this year.* (acima de)
3 if the sun is up, it has risen (alto)
4 if something is up, there is a problem. An informal word ▣ *What's up with you today?* □ *As soon as we reached the house, I knew something was up.* (estar acontecendo)

up[3] /ʌp/ VERB [ups, upping, upped] to increase something □ *The doctors have upped his dose of painkillers.* (elevar, aumentar)

update[1] /ʌpˈdeɪt/ VERB [updates, updating, updated]
1 to add the latest information to something □ *When did we last update the website?* (atualizar)
2 to change something to make it more modern □ *I need to update my wardrobe.* (atualizar)

update² /ˈʌpdeɪt/ NOUN [plural updates] the latest information about a subject 🔹 *Dan gave me an update on the situation.* (**informação atualizada**)

upgrade /ˈʌpgreɪd/ NOUN [plural upgrades] a piece of software that makes a computer more powerful. A computing word. (**atualização**)

uphill /ˈʌphɪl/ ADJECTIVE
1 going upwards □ *an uphill part of the track* (**íngreme, elevado**)
2 very difficult 🔹 *We face an uphill struggle to finish the job.* (**difícil**)

uphold /ʌpˈhəʊld/ VERB [upholds, upholding, upheld] to support or agree with a decision, especially in a court of law □ *The court upheld his complaint.* (**confirmar**)

upon /əˈpɒn/ PREPOSITION on. A formal word □ *a castle upon a high cliff* (**sobre, a**)

upper /ˈʌpə(r)/ ADJECTIVE
1 being the higher of two things that are the same □ *my upper lip* (**superior**)
2 at the top or towards the top □ *the upper floors of the building* (**superior**)

upset¹ /ʌpˈset/ VERB [upsets, upsetting, upset]
1 to make someone sad or worried □ *I didn't mean to upset you.* (**perturbar**)
2 to stop something from happening in the right way □ *I don't want to upset your plans.* (**contrariar**)
3 to knock something over by accident (**derrubar**)

upset² /ʌpˈset/ ADJECTIVE
1 sad or worried about something that has happened □ *He looked upset.* □ + *that She's upset that no one invited her.* 🔹 *She got upset looking at his photos.* (**incomodado, contrariado**)
2 upset stomach/tummy an illness affecting the stomach (**embrulhado**)

upside down /ˌʌpsaɪd ˈdaʊn/ ADJECTIVE, ADVERB with the top part where the bottom should be and the bottom part where the top should be □ *He was holding the book upside down.* (**de cabeça para baixo**)

▶ THESAURUS: If something is upside down, the top part is where the bottom part should be and the bottom part is where the top part should be. If something, especially clothes, is inside out, the part that should be on the inside is on the outside. If something is back to front, the part that should be at the back is at the front.

upstairs¹ /ʌpˈsteəz/ ADVERB to or on a higher level of a building □ *I went upstairs to bed.* (**no andar de cima**)

upstairs² /ʌpˈsteəz/ ADJECTIVE on a higher level of a building □ *an upstairs bedroom* (**andar de cima**)

upward /ˈʌpwəd/ ADJECTIVE towards a higher place or position □ *an upward climb* (**ascendente**)
• **upwards** /ˈʌpwədz/ or **upward** /ˈʌpwəd/ ADVERB towards a higher place or position □ *He looked upwards and saw the sun.* (**para cima**)

urban /ˈɜːbən/ ADJECTIVE to do with a town or city □ *urban areas* □ *urban planning* (**urbano**)

urge¹ /ɜːdʒ/ VERB [urges, urging, urged] to advise someone strongly to do something □ *I urge you to fill in the form as soon as possible.* (**insistir**)

urge² /ɜːdʒ/ NOUN [plural urges] a sudden, strong feeling of wanting to do something □ *I felt an urge to shake him.* 🔹 *I resisted the urge to tell her* (= did not tell her although I wanted to). (**ímpeto**)

urgent /ˈɜːdʒənt/ ADJECTIVE very serious and needing action now 🔹 *There is an urgent need for water and food supplies in the region.* 🔹 *He has called for urgent action to stop the killing.* (**urgente**)

urinate /ˈjʊərɪˌneɪt/ VERB [urinates, urinating, urinated] to pass urine out of your body. A formal word. (**urinar**)

US /juːˈes/ ABBREVIATION the **United States**

us /ʌs/ PRONOUN used as the object in a sentence to talk or write about yourself and at least one other person □ *Do you want to come with us?* □ *They gave us coffee.* □ *The news surprised all of us.* (**nós**)

USA /juːesˈeɪ/ ABBREVIATION the **United States of America**

use¹ /juːz/ VERB [uses, using, used]
1 to do something with something for a particular purpose □ *Use a knife to open it.* □ *He used words like 'disappointing' and 'shocking'.* □ + *for I use these boxes for storing apples.* □ + *as Dad uses this room as his office.* (**usar**)
2 to take an amount of something from a supply in order to do something with it □ *I've used all the milk now.* □ *You can use the wood from the garage.* (**usar**)
♦ PHRASAL VERB **use something up** to use all of a supply of something □ *We've used up all the paper.*

use² /juːs/ NOUN [plural uses]
1 no plural when you use something □ + *of We do not allow the use of calculators in the exam.* 🔹 *We were able to make use of the sports facilities.* (**uso**)
2 the purpose for which something is used □ *This knife has a lot of uses.* □ *They deny that the uranium is for military use.* (**uso**)

3 no plural if something is of use, it is useful or effective □ *Is this coat of any use to you?* 🔂 *It's no use asking him for help – he's always busy* (utilidade)
4 no plural the right or ability to use something □ **+ of** *He offered me the use of his car while he's away.* □ *She lost the use of her legs.* (uso)

used /juːzd/ ADJECTIVE something that is used has been owned and used by someone else □ *He sells used cars.* (usado)

used to¹ /ˈjuːst tuː/ MODAL VERB used to talk about things that happened regularly in the past or things that were true in the past, especially when they no longer happen or are true □ *I used to visit her a lot when she lived in Germany.* □ *The fence used to be painted white.* □ *I used to be a teacher.* (costumava, havia)

> If you use **used to** in a question or a negative, you should use the form **use to**: □ *Did you use to play the piano?* □ *I didn't use to like many vegetables.*

used to² /ˈjuːst tuː/ ADJECTIVE if you are used to something, you have often seen it or experienced it before, so it does not seem strange, difficult, etc. □ *I'm used to living on my own.* 🔂 *Working nights is difficult, but you get used to it.* (acostumado)

useful /ˈjuːsfʊl/ ADJECTIVE helpful for doing something or achieving something □ *The book gave me some useful information.* □ **+ for** *These little pots are useful for growing seeds.* (útil)

useless /ˈjuːsləs/ ADJECTIVE having no purpose, or not effective or working correctly □ *This knife's useless – it's completely blunt.* □ *It's useless trying to explain to them.* □ *She wastes her money on useless things.* (inútil)

user /ˈjuːzə(r)/ NOUN [plural **users**] a person who uses something □ *users of public transport* (usuário)

usual /ˈjuːʒuəl/ ADJECTIVE
1 done or happening most often □ *I had my usual coffee this morning.* □ *'What did you talk about?' 'Oh, the usual things.'* □ *My walk to work took longer than usual.* (habitual, costumeiro)
2 as usual as happens most often □ *He was late as usual.* (como de costume)

usually /ˈjuːʒuəli/ ADVERB normally, on most occasions □ *I usually drink tea.* □ *We usually go on holiday in August.* □ *Usually I'm in bed by ten o'clock.* (habitualmente)

utter¹ /ˈʌtə(r)/ VERB [**utters, uttering, uttered**] to say something □ *She didn't utter a single word.* (pronunciar)
utter² /ˈʌtə(r)/ ADJECTIVE complete □ *utter silence*
• **utterly** /ˈʌtəli/ ADVERB completely □ *I feel utterly exhausted.* (absoluto, total)

V¹ or **v** /viː/ the 22nd letter of the alphabet (a vigésima segunda letra do alfabeto)

V² /viː/ ABBREVIATION volt; a unit for measuring how strong an electric current is (voltagem, V)

v /viː/ ABBREVIATION

1 *versus*; used for saying which two players or teams are competing against each other ◻ *Arsenal v Manchester United* (abreviação de *versus*)

2 *very* ◻ *v good* (= very good) (abreviação de muito)

vacancy /ˈveɪkənsɪ/ NOUN [*plural* **vacancies**]

1 an available room in a hotel ◻ *Sorry, no vacancies.* (vaga)

2 an available job (vaga)

vacant /ˈveɪkənt/ ADJECTIVE

1 if something is vacant, it is available because no one else is using it ◻ *a vacant seat* ◻ *a vacant office* (vago)

2 if a job is vacant, it is available because no one is doing it (vago)

vacation /vəˈkeɪʃən/ NOUN [*plural* **vacations**]

1 the US word for holiday 🔲 *We're taking a vacation in the mountains this summer.* (férias)

2 on vacation taking a holiday. A US phrase. (em férias)

3 a part of the year when a university is closed ◻ *the summer vacation* (férias)

vaccinate /ˈvæksɪneɪt/ VERB [**vaccinates, vaccinating, vaccinated**] to put a substance containing bacteria or a virus into someone's body to protect them from a disease (vacinar)

vaccination /ˌvæksɪˈneɪʃən/ NOUN [*plural* **vaccinations**] the process of putting a substance containing bacteria or a virus into someone's body in order to protect them from disease (vacinação)

vaccine /ˈvæksiːn/ NOUN [*plural* **vaccines**] a substance containing bacteria or a virus, which is put into someone's body in order to protect them against a disease (vacina)

vacuum¹ /ˈvækjuəm/ NOUN [*plural* **vacuums**] a space with no air or other gases in it (vácuo)

vacuum² /ˈvækjuəm/ VERB [**vacuums, vacuuming, vacuumed**] to clean a floor using a vacuum cleaner (passar aspirador de pó)

vacuum cleaner /ˈvækjuəm ˌkliːnə(r)/ NOUN [*plural* **vacuum cleaners**] an electrical machine that sucks dust up from the floor (aspirador de pó)

vagina /vəˈdʒaɪnə/ NOUN [*plural* **vaginas**] the passage in a woman's body that connects her womb (= organ where a baby grows) to the outside of her body. A biology word. (vagina)

vague /veɪɡ/ ADJECTIVE [**vaguer, vaguest**]

1 not clear and without details 🔲 *I have a vague idea of where he lives.* 🔲 *He had a vague memory of seeing her there.* (vago)

2 explaining something in a way that is not clear and has no details ◻ *He was a bit vague about their plans.* (vago, indeciso)

vain /veɪn/ ADJECTIVE [**vainer, vainest**]

1 very pleased with your appearance and paying too much attention to it (vaidoso)

2 unsuccessful 🔲 *I made a vain attempt to reach her.* (vão)

3 in vain without achieving what you want to ◻ *I tried in vain to persuade him.* (em vão)

valid /ˈvælɪd/ ADJECTIVE

1 legally or officially acceptable and able to be used ◻ *a valid passport* ◻ *a valid ticket* (válido)

2 reasonable and acceptable ◻ *a valid excuse* ◻ *a valid argument* (válido)

valley /ˈvælɪ/ NOUN [*plural* **valleys**] an area of low land between hills, often with a river running through it (vale)

valuable /ˈvæljuəbəl/ ADJECTIVE
1 worth a lot of money □ *valuable jewellery* (valioso)
2 very useful □ *valuable advice* □ *She's a valuable member of the team.* (valioso)

> Note that **valuable** does not have the same meaning as 'expensive'. If something is valuable, you could sell it for a lot of money. If something is expensive, it costs a lot of money: □ *valuable antiques/paintings* □ *expensive food/clothes*

value¹ /ˈvælju:/ NOUN [plural values]
1 the amount of money that something is worth □ *The paintings had an estimated value of $1.4 billion.* □ *The house has increased in value.* (valor)
2 *no plural* how useful and important something is □ *This food has very little nutritional value.* (valor)
3 *no plural* the quality or amount of something compared to its price 🔊 *I thought the hotel was very good value.* (preço)

> **THESAURUS:** The cost of a thing is the amount of money you need in order to buy it. If something is worth a particular amount of money, that is how much it would cost to buy. The value of a thing is how much money it is worth. So you can say that a diamond ring has a value of £1000 or that it is worth £1000.

value² /ˈvælju:/ VERB [values, valuing, valued]
1 to think something is important and worth having □ *I really value my free time.* □ *I value your advice on the matter.* (valorizar)
2 to say how much something is worth □ *The jewels were valued at three thousand dollars.* (avaliar)

valve /vælv/ NOUN [plural valves]
something that opens and shuts to control the flow of liquid, air or gas through a pipe (válvula)

vampire /ˈvæmpaɪə(r)/ NOUN [plural vampires]
in stories, a dead person who comes out at night and sucks blood from people's necks (vampiro)

van /væn/ NOUN [plural vans]
a road vehicle, like a small truck, used for carrying goods (furgão)

> **THESAURUS:** A lorry or a truck is a large vehicle for carrying heavy goods by road. A van is a road vehicle like a small truck, used for carrying goods. People like plumbers or electricians often use a van to carry their tools and equipment.

vanilla /vəˈnɪlə/ NOUN, NO PLURAL
a flavour that is used in a lot of sweet foods □ *vanilla ice cream* (baunilha)

vanish /ˈvænɪʃ/ VERB [vanishes, vanishing, vanished]
to disappear suddenly, leaving nothing behind □ *He was standing in front of me a moment ago and suddenly he vanished.* (sumir)

variety /vəˈraɪəti/ NOUN [plural varieties]
1 *no plural* a lot of different types □ *+ of The chairs are available in a variety of colours.* (variedade)
2 *no plural* the quality of having many different things □ *You need variety in your diet.* (variedade)
3 a type that is different from other similar things □ *a new variety of rose* (variedade)

various /ˈveəriəs/ ADJECTIVE
many different □ *There were various types of cheese.* □ *There's been flooding in various parts of the country.* (variedade)

vary /ˈveəri/ VERB [varies, varying, varied]
1 if things of the same type vary, they are all different in some way □ *Prices vary from shop to shop.* (variar)
2 if something varies, it changes at different times □ *Snowfall varies throughout the season.* (variar)
3 to change something slightly □ *You can vary the quantity that you order.* (variar)

vase /vɑ:z/ NOUN [plural vases]
a decorative container for flowers (vaso)

vast /vɑ:st/ ADJECTIVE
extremely big □ *a vast area of land* (vasto)

VAT /væt, ˌvi:eɪˈti:/ ABBREVIATION
value added tax; a tax on goods and services in the UK (value added tax – imposto sobre bens e services no Reino Unido)

veal /vi:l/ NOUN, NO PLURAL
meat from a baby cow (vitela)

vegetable /ˈvedʒtəbəl/ NOUN [plural vegetables]
a plant that you can eat, especially one that is not sweet □ *vegetables such as potatoes and carrots* (hortaliça)

> Note that although the word 'fruit' cannot be used in the plural, the word **vegetable** can:
> ✓ *Eat more fruit and vegetables.*
> ✗ *Eat more fruit and vegetable.*

vegetarian¹ /ˌvedʒɪˈteəriən/ NOUN [plural vegetarians]
someone who does not eat meat or fish (vegetariano)

vegetarian² /ˌvedʒɪˈteəriən/ ADJECTIVE
not eating or containing meat or fish □ *vegetarian cookery* (vegetariano)

vehicle /ˈvi:ɪkəl/ NOUN [plural vehicles]
something that carries people or goods, especially on roads, for example a car or a truck (veículo)

veil /veɪl/ NOUN [plural **veils**] a piece of material that covers a woman's head or face (**véu**)

vein /veɪn/ NOUN [plural **veins**] one of the thin tubes inside the body that carry blood back to the heart (**veia**)

velvet /'velvɪt/ NOUN, NO PLURAL a thick cloth that feels very soft on one side (**veludo**)

venue /'venjuː/ NOUN [plural **venues**] the place where an event happens □ *The castle is used as a wedding venue.* (**local, lugar**)

verb /vɜːb/ NOUN [plural **verbs**] a word that says what someone or something does. For example, eat, speak and be are verbs. (**verbo**)

verbal /'vɜːbəl/ ADJECTIVE spoken and not written □ *a verbal agreement* □ *verbal communication* (**verbal**)

verdict /'vɜːdɪkt/ NOUN [plural **verdicts**] a decision made in a court of law saying if someone is guilty or not guilty of committing a crime 🔁 *Eventually the jury reached a verdict.* (**veredito**)

verge /vɜːdʒ/ NOUN [plural **verges**] the area at the edge of a road, usually covered in grass. (**beira, borda**)

♦ IDIOM on the verge of something going to do something very soon □ *The company is on the verge of collapse.* (**prestes a, à beira de**)

verse /vɜːs/ NOUN [plural **verses**]
1 a set of lines that form one part of a song or poem (**estrofe**)
2 *no plural* poetry and not ordinary writing (**poesia**)

version /'vɜːʃən/ NOUN [plural **versions**]
1 one form of something when other forms of it exist □ *I know three versions of this song.* (**versão**)
2 one person's description of something that happened 🔁 *I've only heard Debbie's version of events.* (**versão**)

versus /'vɜːsəs/ PREPOSITION used for saying which two players or teams are competing against each other □ *It's Scotland versus France tonight.* (**versus**)

vertical /'vɜːtɪkəl/ ADJECTIVE pointing straight up, at an angle of 90° to the ground □ *vertical lines* (**vertical**)

very /'veri/ ADVERB
1 to a great degree □ *I'm very tired.* □ *She was very pleased.* □ *It all happened very quickly.* (**muito**)
2 not very good/nice/pleased, etc. not good/nice/pleased, etc. □ *She wasn't very pleased.* (**não muito**)

➤ Very is not used before adjectives which have a strong meaning:
✓ I was very tired.
✗ I was very exhausted.
If you are using an adjective with a strong meaning, put an adverb such as completely or absolutely before it: □ *I was completely exhausted.*

vest /vest/ NOUN [plural **vests**]
1 a piece of underwear without sleeves that covers the top part of the body (**camiseta**)
2 the US word for waistcoat (**colete**)

vet /vet/ NOUN [plural **vets**] someone whose job is to treat animals that are ill or injured (**veterinário**)

veto /'viːtəʊ/ NOUN [plural **vetoes**] when someone officially stops something from happening (**veto**)

via /'vaɪə/ PREPOSITION travelling through a place □ *The train goes to London via Birmingham.* (**por**)

vicar /'vɪkə(r)/ NOUN [plural **vicars**] in the Church of England, a priest (**pároco**)

vice /vaɪs/ NOUN [plural **vices**] a bad habit □ *vices such as smoking* (**vício**)

vice-president /ˌvaɪsˈprezɪdənt/ NOUN [plural **vice-presidents**] the person who is next in rank after a country's president (= elected leader of a country) □ *the vice-president of the United States* (**vice-presidente**)

vicious /'vɪʃəs/ ADJECTIVE extremely cruel and violent □ *a vicious attack* (**cruel, feroz**)

victim /'vɪktɪm/ NOUN [plural **victims**] someone who is harmed or killed by something bad, such as a crime, disease, flood, etc. □ *victims of crime* □ *victims of the bombing* □ *murder victims* (**vítima**)

victorious /vɪkˈtɔːriəs/ ADJECTIVE successful in a fight or competition (**vitorioso**)

victory /'vɪktəri/ NOUN [plural **victories**] success in a fight or competition □ *victory in the Cup Final* □ **+ for** *The game ended in victory for France.* (**vitória**)

video¹ /'vɪdiəʊ/ NOUN [plural **videos**]
1 a recording of a film or television programme made on videotape (**vídeo**)
2 a recording of an event that has been made using a video camera (**vídeo**)
3 a machine for playing videos (**aparelho de vídeo, videocassette**)

video² /'vɪdiəʊ/ VERB [**videos, videoing, videoed**]
1 to record a television programme onto videotape (**gravar em vídeo**)
2 to film an event using a video camera (**filmar**)

video camera /ˈvɪdiəʊ ˌkæmərə/ NOUN [plural **video cameras**] a piece of equipment that you use to record events onto videotape (**câmera de vídeo**)

video game /ˈvɪdiəʊ ˌɡeɪm/ NOUN [plural **video games**] an electronic game in which players move images on a computer or television screen (**vídeo-game**)

videotape /ˈvɪdiəʊteɪp/ NOUN [plural **videotapes**] magnetic tape (= long, thin piece of plastic) that pictures and sounds can be recorded on (**videoteipe**)

view
view /vjuː/ NOUN [plural **views**]
1 your opinion □ + **on** What's your view on wind farms? □ + **about** He made his views about the government very clear. (**opinião**)
2 your ability to see things from a place □ The tall man spoilt my view of the concert. 📷 Eventually, the lion came into view. (**visão**)
3 the things you can see from a place □ There's a fantastic view from the top of the hill. (**vista**)

viewer /ˈvjuːə(r)/ NOUN [plural **viewers**] someone who watches television □ The programme attracted more than a million viewers. (**espectador**)

vigorous /ˈvɪɡərəs/ ADJECTIVE very active and energetic □ vigorous exercise (**vigoroso**)

villa /ˈvɪlə/ NOUN [plural **villas**] a large house, especially one used for holidays (**casa de passeio**)

village
village /ˈvɪlɪdʒ/ NOUN [plural **villages**] an area where people live in the countryside, which is smaller than a town □ She lives in a village just outside Stratford. (**aldeia**)

> **THESAURUS:** A village is an area in the countryside where people live. A town is a place where people live and work, which is bigger than a village. A city is a large important town. Manchester, Bristol and London are all cities. A capital or capital city is the city where the government of a state or country is. London is the capital of the UK, Paris is the capital of France and Beijing is the capital of China.

villager /ˈvɪlɪdʒə(r)/ NOUN [plural **villagers**] someone who lives in a village (**aldeão**)

villain /ˈvɪlən/ NOUN [plural **villains**] a bad person in a story, film, etc. (**vilão**)

> **THESAURUS:** A bad person in a story or a film is called a villain. A criminal is someone who has committed a crime. A rogue is a dishonest or badly behaved man or boy.

vine /vaɪn/ NOUN [plural **vines**] a plant that grapes (= small green or red fruit that grows in groups) grow on (**videira**)

vinegar /ˈvɪnɪɡə(r)/ NOUN, NO PLURAL a sour liquid that is used for giving flavour to food (**vinagre**)

vineyard /ˈvɪnjəd/ NOUN [plural **vineyards**] a place where grapes (= small green or red fruit that grows in groups) are grown to produce wine (**vinha, vinhedo**)

violence
violence /ˈvaɪələns/ NOUN, NO PLURAL
1 actions intended to hurt or kill someone or to damage something □ Something must be done to stop the violence. □ + **against** violence against women (**violência**)
2 force and strength, often causing damage □ The violence of the storm shocked everyone. (**violência**)

violent
violent /ˈvaɪələnt/ ADJECTIVE
1 involving actions intended to hurt or kill someone or to damage something □ violent crime □ a violent film (**violento**)
2 with a lot of force and strength, causing damage □ a violent storm □ a violent explosion (**violento**)

violently /ˈvaɪələntli/ ADVERB in a violent way (**violentamente**)

violet /ˈvaɪələt/ ADJECTIVE having a pale purple colour (**violeta**)

violin
violin /ˌvaɪəˈlɪn/ NOUN [plural **violins**] a musical instrument with four strings, which you hold under your chin and play by pulling a bow (= long, thin piece of wood with hair stretched along it) across the strings (**violino**)

VIP /ˌviːaɪˈpiː/ ABBREVIATION very important person; someone who is treated very well because they are powerful or famous (**VIP**)

virtual /ˈvɜːtʃuəl/ ADJECTIVE
1 almost a particular thing □ He was a virtual prisoner in his own home. (**virtual**)
2 using computer images to make something that is not real seem real. A computing word. □ a virtual tour of the museum (**virtual**)

virtue /ˈvɜːtʃuː/ NOUN [plural **virtues**]
1 a good quality in a person's character □ Patience is a virtue. (**virtude**)
2 a way of behaving that is morally good. A formal word. □ a woman of virtue (**virtude**)

virus
virus /ˈvaɪrəs/ NOUN [plural **viruses**]
1 a very small living thing that can enter the body and cause disease. A biology word. (**vírus**)
2 an illness caused by a virus □ He's been off work all week with a virus. (**vírus**)
3 a computer program that can send itself to many computers, for example by e-mail, and can destroy files on those computers. A computing word. (**vírus**)

visa — vulnerable

visa /ˈviːzə/ NOUN [plural **visas**] a document that you need to travel to and work in some countries (**visto**)

visible /ˈvɪzəbəl/ ADJECTIVE able to be seen □ *Is the house visible from the road?* (**visível**)

vision /ˈvɪʒən/ NOUN [plural **visions**]
1 your ability to see □ *poor vision* (**visão**)
2 an idea of how something should be in the future □ *He talked about his vision for the school.* (**visão**)

visit[1] /ˈvɪzɪt/ VERB [**visits, visiting, visited**] to go and see a place or person □ *We're going to visit my aunt while we're in York.* □ *We visited a couple of museums.* (**visitar**)

visit[2] /ˈvɪzɪt/ NOUN [plural **visits**] the act of visiting a place or person ◘ *I'm going to pay him a visit.* (**visita**)

visitor /ˈvɪzɪtə(r)/ NOUN [plural **visitors**] someone who visits a place or person ◘ *She had two visitors yesterday.* (**visitante, visita**)

visual /ˈvɪʒuəl/ ADJECTIVE to do with seeing □ *visual signals* (**visual**)

vital /ˈvaɪtəl/ ADJECTIVE necessary or extremely important □ *vital information* □ *He played a vital role in the project.* (**vital**)

vitamin /ˈvɪtəmɪn/ NOUN [plural **vitamins**] a substance in food that you need to stay healthy □ *Oranges contain vitamin C.* (**vitamina**)

vivid /ˈvɪvɪd/ ADJECTIVE
1 producing very clear ideas and pictures in your mind □ *a vivid description* □ *vivid memories* (**vívido**)
2 very bright □ *vivid colours* (**vívido**)

vocabulary /vəˈkæbjulərɪ/ NOUN [plural **vocabularies**]
1 the range of words that someone knows and uses □ *She has a good vocabulary for a child of her age.* (**vocabulário**)
2 all the words in a language (**vocabulário**)

voice /vɔɪs/ NOUN [plural **voices**] the sound you make when you speak or sing □ *She has quite a low voice.* □ *Her singing voice is beautiful.* □ *I thought I heard voices.* (**voz**)

volcano /vɒlˈkeɪnəʊ/ NOUN [plural **volcanoes**] a mountain that sometimes sends out hot lava (= liquid rock) through a hole in its top (**vulcão**)

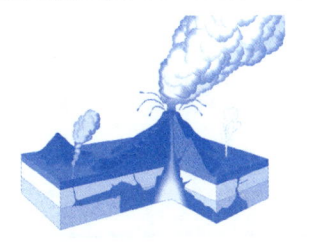

volleyball /ˈvɒlɪbɔːl/ NOUN, NO PLURAL a game in which two teams hit a ball over a high net with their hands (**voleibol**)

volume /ˈvɒljuːm/ NOUN [plural **volumes**]
1 the level of sound that something makes ◘ *Can you turn the volume down on the TV, please?* (**volume**)
2 the space that something takes up or the amount of space that a container has (**volume**)
3 a book, especially a book that is part of a set (**volume**)

voluntary /ˈvɒləntərɪ/ ADJECTIVE
1 done by choice and not because you have to □ *She took voluntary redundancy.* (**voluntário**)
2 done without payment ◘ *voluntary work* (**voluntário**)

volunteer[1] /ˌvɒlənˈtɪə(r)/ NOUN [plural **volunteers**]
1 someone who offers to do something □ *Do I have any volunteers to help me tidy up?* (**voluntário**)
2 someone who does work for no payment (**voluntário**)

volunteer[2] /ˌvɒlənˈtɪə(r)/ VERB [**volunteers, volunteering, volunteered**] to offer to do something □ *Dana volunteered to take the children swimming.* (**oferecer-se como voluntário**)

vomit /ˈvɒmɪt/ VERB [**vomits, vomiting, vomited**] to bring food back up from your stomach through your mouth (**vômito**)

vote[1] /vəʊt/ VERB [**votes, voting, voted**] to make a formal choice by secretly marking a piece of paper or putting your hand up to be counted □ **+ for** *Which candidate did you vote for in the elections?* □ **+ to do something** *They voted to reject the offer.* (**votar**)

• **voter** /ˈvəʊtə(r)/ NOUN [plural **voters**] someone who votes in an election (**eleitor**)

vote[2] /vəʊt/ NOUN [plural **votes**] a choice you make by marking a piece of paper or putting your hand up to be counted ◘ *The party that plans to lower taxes will get my vote.* (**voto**)

vowel /ˈvaʊəl/ NOUN [plural **vowels**]
1 one of the letters a, e, i, o or u (**vogal**)
2 a speech sound you make that does not use your lips, teeth, or tongue to stop the flow of air (**vogal**)

voyage /ˈvɔɪɪdʒ/ NOUN [plural **voyages**] a long journey by sea or in space (**viagem**)

vulnerable /ˈvʌlnərəbəl/ ADJECTIVE easily hurt, upset or made ill □ *the protection of vulnerable children* □ *After surgery, people are more vulnerable to infection.* (**vulnerável**)

Ww

W¹ or **w** /'dʌbəlju:/ the 23rd letter of the alphabet (a vigésima terceira letra do alfabeto)

W² /west/ ABBREVIATION **west²** (oeste)

wade /weɪd/ VERB [wades, wading, waded] to walk through water or mud □ *We waded across the stream.* (avançar penosamente)

wag /wæg/ VERB [wags, wagging, wagged] if an animal wags its tail, it moves it from side to side □ *The dog ran backwards and forwards, wagging its tail.* (abanar)

wage /weɪdʒ/ NOUN [plural **wages**] money that someone is paid for doing their job □ *They pay our wages on Fridays.* □ *a wage increase/cut* □ *What's the average wage?* (salário)

wail /weɪl/ VERB [wails, wailing, wailed] to cry loudly □ *A small child was wailing in the next room.* (gemer)

waist /weɪst/ NOUN [plural **waists**] the middle part of your body, where you wear a belt (cintura)

waistcoat /'weɪskəʊt/ NOUN [plural **waistcoats**] a short jacket with no sleeves and usually with buttons up the front that is worn over a shirt (colete)

wait¹ /weɪt/ VERB [waits, waiting, waited]
1 to stay in a place until something happens, something or someone is ready, etc. □ **+ for** *Several people were already waiting for the bus.* □ *He asked us to wait outside.* □ *We waited patiently for the show to begin.* (esperar)
2 to not do something until something happens, someone arrives, etc. □ *I will wait until it stops raining before I leave.* □ **+ for** *We'd better wait for Jasmine before we start.* (esperar)
3 to not do something or get something for a particular period of time □ *I had to wait 6 months for my operation.* □ *I decided to wait a while before making a decision.* (esperar)
4 can't wait/can hardly wait if you can't wait to do something or for something to happen, you are very excited about it □ *I can't wait for our holiday!* (não ver a hora)
5 wait a minute/second used to tell someone to stop what they are doing or stay where they are for a short time □ *Wait a minute – I need to get my keys.* (esperar)
♦ PHRASAL VERB **wait up** to not go to bed until someone comes home □ *I'll be late tonight – don't wait up for me.*

wait² /weɪt/ NOUN [plural **waits**] a period of time when you are waiting □ *We had a long wait for the bus.* (espera)

> **THESAURUS:** A **wait** is a period of time when you are waiting. A **delay** is the extra time you have to wait if something happens later than expected. For example, if your train is late, you might have a ten minute **delay**. A **pause** is a short stop or rest. If someone stops talking, there might be a **pause** before someone replies. An **interval** is a period of time between two things. If you go to the theatre, there is often an **interval** in the middle of the play when you can have a drink.

waiter /'weɪtə(r)/ NOUN [plural **waiters**] someone who brings food to customers in a restaurant (garçom)

waiting list /'weɪtɪŋ ˌlɪst/ NOUN [plural **waiting lists**] a list of people who are waiting to get or do something □ *hospital waiting lists* (lista de espera)

waitress /'weɪtrɪs/ NOUN [plural **waitresses**] a woman who brings food to customers in a restaurant (garçonete)

wake /weɪk/ VERB [wakes, waking, woke, woken] to stop sleeping, or to make someone stop sleeping □ *We woke the children early and set off.* (acordar, despertar)
♦ PHRASAL VERB **wake (someone) up** to stop sleeping, or to make someone stop sleeping □ *We were woken up by the dogs.*

walk¹ /wɔːk/ VERB [walks, walking, walked] to move by putting one foot in front of the other □ *The door opened and Simon walked in.* □ *I think I'll walk to work today.* (andar, passear)
♦ PHRASAL VERB **walk out** to leave a place because you are angry or upset □ *I was so angry in the meeting that I walked out.*

> **THESAURUS: Walk** is a general word. If you **march**, you walk in an angry, confident or determined way. **March** is also used to describe soldiers walking together with the same, regular steps. If you walk slowly, sliding your feet along the ground without lifting them, you **shuffle**. To **crawl** means to move on your hands and knees. Babies crawl before they learn to walk.

walk

walk² /wɔːk/ NOUN [plural **walks**] a journey made by walking 🔹 *They went for a walk on the beach.* ☐ *It's just a short walk to the shops.* ☐ *I need to take the dog for a walk.* (**passeio, caminhada**)

wall /wɔːl/ NOUN [plural **walls**]
1 any of the sides of a room or building ☐ *She hung the new clock on the kitchen wall.* (**parede**)
2 a structure made of brick or stone that separates two areas or goes around an area ☐ *A high wall surrounds the school.* (**muro, muralha**)

wallet /ˈwɒlɪt/ NOUN [plural **wallets**] a flat container for money and cards, usually made of leather (**carteira**)

> THESAURUS: Men usually carry a wallet. Women often carry money and cards in a purse. A handbag is a woman's bag for carrying things like money and keys. You might carry a purse in your handbag.

wander /ˈwɒndə(r)/ VERB [**wanders, wandering, wandered**] to go from one place to another without any clear plan or purpose ☐ *We spent the summer wandering all around southern Italy.* (**vaguear**)

want¹ /wɒnt/ VERB [**wants, wanting, wanted**]
1 to feel that you would like to have something or do something, or to wish that something will happen ☐ *Do you want some cake?* ☐ *Nobody wants higher taxes.* ☐ **+ to do something** *I didn't want anyone to know.* (**querer**)
2 to need something ☐ *Your hands want a good wash.* (**precisar**)
3 used to give someone advice or a warning ☐ *Maps? You want to try the library.* ☐ *She has a lot of influence. You don't want to upset her.* (**procurar**)

want² /wɒnt/ NOUN, NO PLURAL the state of being very poor or not having the things you need to live ☐ *Many families are living in severe want.* (**escassez, carência**)

war /wɔː(r)/ NOUN [plural **wars**]
1 fighting between two countries or groups, involving armies 🔹 *War broke out* (= started) *between the two countries.* 🔹 *That was the year that war was declared* (= announced). ☐ **+ between** *the war between Britain and Argentina* (**guerra**)
2 at war fighting a war ☐ *The two countries had been at war for years.* (**em guerra**)

ward /wɔːd/ NOUN [plural **wards**] a room with beds in a hospital ☐ *the children's ward* (**ala, enfermaria**)

warden /ˈwɔːdən/ NOUN [plural **wardens**] someone who is in charge of a building and the people in it (**guardião**)

wardrobe /ˈwɔːdrəʊb/ NOUN [plural **wardrobes**] a tall cupboard that you hang clothes inside (**guarda-roupa**)

warning

warehouse /ˈweəhaʊs/ NOUN [plural **warehouses**] a big building where businesses store large amounts of things ☐ *a furniture warehouse* (**depósito, armazém**)

warfare /ˈwɔːfeə(r)/ NOUN, NO PLURAL fighting in a war ☐ *modern warfare* (**guerra**)

warm¹ /wɔːm/ ADJECTIVE [**warmer, warmest**]
1 quite hot in a way that is pleasant ☐ *a nice warm bath* ☐ *Are you warm enough?* 🔹 *I tried to keep warm by jumping up and down.* (**quente**)
2 warm clothes make you feel warm ☐ *a warm winter coat* (**quente**)
3 friendly and showing good feelings towards other people 🔹 *a warm welcome* ☐ *She's a very warm person.* (**caloroso**)

warm² /wɔːm/ VERB [**warms, warming, warmed**] to make someone or something warm ☐ *She warmed her hands on the radiator.* ☐ *I'll just warm the sauce.* (**aquecer, esquentar**)

♦ PHRASAL VERBS **warm (someone/something) up** to become warm, or to make someone or something warm ☐ *Put a sweater on and you'll soon warm up.* ☐ *Could you warm up the soup?* **warm up** to make your body ready to do a sport by doing gentle exercises ☐ *It's important to warm up before a run.*

warmly /ˈwɔːmli/ ADVERB
1 in a warm way ☐ *Make sure you're warmly dressed for the walk.* (**calorosamente**)
2 showing good feelings ☐ *She spoke very warmly of him.* (**calorosamente**)

warmth /wɔːmθ/ NOUN, NO PLURAL
1 pleasant heat, or the state of being pleasantly warm ☐ *the warmth of the fire* (**calor**)
2 when someone is friendly and shows good feelings towards other people ☐ *the warmth of her welcome* (**calor**)

warn /wɔːn/ VERB [**warns, warning, warned**] to tell someone about a possible danger or something bad that may happen so that they can avoid it or prepare for it ☐ **+ about** *I warned her about the icy roads.* ☐ **+ that** *He warned me that it would be expensive.* ☐ **+ to do something** *I warned you to be careful!* (**prevenir, advertir, avisar**)

warning /ˈwɔːnɪŋ/ NOUN [plural **warnings**]
1 a statement that tells you about a possible danger or something bad that may happen 🔹 *There are health warnings on all bottles of alcohol.* ☐ *There are flood warnings for the region.* (**aviso, advertência**)
2 without warning if something bad happens without warning, it happens suddenly so that you do not know it is going to happen ☐ *The volcano erupted without any warning.* (**aviso, alerta**)

> THESAURUS: Warning is a general word. A threat is a warning that someone might hurt you or harm you, especially if you do not do what they say. An alarm is a loud noise to warn people about something, for example a fire. An alert is a warning about something. For example, if there is going to be very bad weather, there may be an alert to warn people about it.

warrant /ˈwɒrənt/ NOUN [plural **warrants**] a document that gives the police the right to arrest someone or search their property **(mandato)**

warrior /ˈwɒrɪə(r)/ NOUN [plural **warriors**] especially in the past, a soldier **(guerreiro)**

wary /ˈweərɪ/ ADJECTIVE [**warier, wariest**] not wanting to do something or trust someone because you think it might cause problems ☐ *I am very wary of lending her money.* **(cauteloso)**

was /wɒz/ VERB the past tense of the verb **be**[1] (ver **be**[1]) when it is used with **I, he, she** or **it** ☐ *I was surprised to see Rosie there.* ☐ *Mr Brock was my favourite teacher.* (ver **be**[1])

wash[1] /wɒʃ/ VERB [washes, washing, washed]

1 to clean something with water and soap ☐ *His mum still washes his clothes.* 🔁 *Wash your hands before dinner.* **(lavar)**

2 if water washes against something, it flows against it ☐ *Gentle waves were washing against the boat.* **(bater contra)**

◆ PHRASAL VERBS **wash something away** if something such as a building, tree or car is washed away, the force of the water carries it away ☐ *Whole trees were washed away in the storm.* **wash (something) up** to wash the plates, dishes, etc. that you have used for eating ☐ *It's my turn to wash up.*

> THESAURUS: If you clean something, you remove the dirt from it. If you wash something, you clean it with soap and water. If you rinse something, you remove dirt or soap from it by putting it in clean water. You rinse your hair to remove the shampoo from it, and you rinse clothes after you have washed them.

wash[2] /wɒʃ/ NOUN [plural **washes**]

1 when you wash yourself or wash something 🔁 *I'll just have a wash.* ☐ *Could you give this shirt a wash?* **(banho, lavagem)**

2 no plural all the clothes that need to be washed ☐ *Your red shirt is in the wash.* **(lavagem)**

washbasin /ˈwɒʃbeɪsən/ NOUN [plural **washbasins**] a bowl with taps (= objects you turn to get water) for washing your hands and face in **(pia)**

washing /ˈwɒʃɪŋ/ NOUN, NO PLURAL all the clothes that need to be washed **(roupas para lavar)**

washing machine /ˈwɒʃɪŋ məˌʃiːn/ NOUN

[plural **washing machines**] a piece of electrical equipment that you wash clothes in **(máquina de lavar)**

washing-up /ˌwɒʃɪŋˈʌp/ NOUN, NO PLURAL

1 all the dishes, plates, etc. that need to be washed after cooking or eating **(louça para lavar)**

2 the activity of washing dishes and plates, etc. after cooking or eating 🔁 *I'll do the washing-up.* **(lavagem de louça)**

wasn't /ˈwɒzənt/ a short way to say and write was not ☐ *He wasn't there.* **(abreviação de was not)**

wasp /wɒsp/ NOUN [plural **wasps**] an insect with a thin black and yellow body that can sting you (= hurt you when it touches your skin) **(vespa)**

waste[1] /weɪst/ VERB [wastes, wasting, wasted]

1 to use too much of something, often in a way that means some of it is thrown away ☐ *I'm trying not to waste any paper.* ☐ *We waste too much food.* **(desperdiçar)**

2 to use something, especially time or money, in a way that does not have good results 🔁 *You're wasting your time.* 🔁 *He wastes so much money.* **(desperdiçar)**

waste[2] /weɪst/ ADJECTIVE waste products or

materials have no use now and can be thrown away ☐ *waste paper* **(resíduo)**

waste[3] /weɪst/ NOUN, NO PLURAL

1 when too much of something is used, often so that some of it is thrown away ☐ *You should never throw away food – it's such a waste.* **(desperdício)**

2 when something, especially time or money, is used in a way that does not have good results 🔁 *I'm not going to clean this area – it's just a waste of time.* 🔁 *The whole course was a complete waste of money.* **(desperdício)**

3 rubbish or material that cannot be used for anything ☐ *industrial waste* **(refugo, resíduo)**

watch[1] /wɒtʃ/ VERB [watches, watching, watched]

1 to look at someone or something for a while ☐ *Max is watching the football.* ☐ *I watched the children dancing.* **(assistir, olhar)**

2 to be careful about something ☐ *Watch you don't trip over that step.* **(tomar cuidado)**

3 to look after someone or something ☐ *Could you watch the baby for me while I go and wash my hands?* **(olhar, tomar conta)**

◆ PHRASAL VERB **watch out** used for telling someone to be careful ☐ *Watch out! Don't bang your head!*

watch[2] /wɒtʃ/ NOUN [plural **watches**]

1 a small clock that you wear on your lower arm **(relógio)**

2 keep a watch on something/someone to pay attention to something or someone, often to make sure that nothing bad happens (**vigiar alguém**)

water¹ /'wɔːtə(r)/ NOUN, NO PLURAL a clear liquid that falls from the sky as rain and is used for drinking, washing, etc. ☐ *a glass of water* (**água**)

water² /'wɔːtə(r)/ VERB [waters, watering, watered]

1 to water a plant is to pour water on it so it will live and grow (**aguar, regar**)

2 if your eyes water, they produce tears ☐ *The smoke made her eyes water.* (**lacrimejar**)

waterfall /'wɔːtəfɔːl/ NOUN [plural waterfalls] a place where a river or stream falls over a high rock onto rocks below (**cascata, cachoeira**)

waterproof /'wɔːtəpruːf/ ADJECTIVE waterproof material does not allow water through it (**impermeável**)

waters /'wɔːtəz/ PLURAL NOUN used for talking about large areas of water, especially areas of the sea which belong to a particular country ☐ *The boat had entered Australian waters.* (**mares**)

watt /wɒt/ NOUN [plural watts] a unit of electrical power. This is often written W. (**watt**)

wave¹ /weɪv/ NOUN [plural waves]

1 a raised line of water that moves across the sea or other area of water ☐ *The waves were huge.* (**onda**)

2 a movement of the hand to say hello or goodbye or to attract someone's attention 🔆 *She gave a wave as the train left the station.* (**aceno**)

3 the form that sound or light takes as it travels through the air ☐ *sound waves* (**onda**)

wave² /weɪv/ VERB [waves, waving, waved]

1 to move your hand in order to say hello or goodbye or to attract someone's attention 🔆 *She waved goodbye and then got on the train.* (**acenar**)

2 to move in the wind ☐ *Flags were waving in the breeze.* (**ondular**)

3 to move something from side to side in the air ☐ *She waved a handkerchief at me.* (**acenar**)

wavelength /'weɪvleŋθ/ NOUN [plural wavelengths] the length of radio wave that a radio station uses to broadcast programmes (**comprimento de onda**)

♦ IDIOM **be on the same wavelength** to think in the same way as someone else so you are able to understand them ☐ *My mother and I are just not on the same wavelength.* (**estar em sintonia**)

wax /wæks/ NOUN, NO PLURAL a solid substance such as bees make, which becomes liquid when you heat it (**cera**)

way /weɪ/ NOUN [plural ways]

1 a method of doing something, or how someone does something ☐ + *of We are trying out new ways of working.* ☐ + *to do something The best way to make new friends is to join a club.* ☐ + *hat I like the way that she sings.* 🔆 *I've found a way to make cakes without eggs.* (**jeito, maneira**)

2 used to talk about a particular feature or characteristic of something 🔆 *He's like his father in many ways.* 🔆 *In some ways I'd prefer to work full time.* (**aspecto**)

3 a route from one place to another ☐ + *to Do you know the way to the station?* 🔆 *Sorry I'm late – I lost my way.* 🔆 *Can you manage to find your way to the main hall?* (**caminho**)

4 a distance, or a journey or movement from one place to another 🔆 *It's quite a long way to the coast.* 🔆 *They have come all the way from Brazil* (**distância**)

5 an amount of time 🔆 *The wedding still seems a long way off.* (**longe**)

6 on his/its/my, etc. way coming towards a place ☐ *Karen is on her way.* ☐ *Dinner is on its way.* (**a caminho**)

7 in/out of the way in/not in a position that stops someone seeing something or being able to move easily ☐ *I couldn't see the stage – there was a pillar in the way.* ☐ *Could you get out of the way while I'm cooking, please?* (**ficar/sair do caminho, atrapalhar**)

8 used to talk about how much of something has happened or been done 🔆 *We were half way through our dinner when the phone rang.* (**caminho**)

9 by the way used to add a piece of information ☐ *By the way, have you heard the news about Alex?* (**aliás, a propósito**)

10 no way (a) certainly not. An informal phrase. ☐ *'Are you giving any money towards Carlo's present?' 'No way!'* (b) no possibility ☐ *There's no way we'll be finished before June.* (c) used to show surprise. An informal phrase. ☐ *They're getting married? No way!* (**de jeito nenhum**)

11 way of life the things that someone usually does □ *Marriage had changed his whole way of life.* (**modo de vida**)

way out /ˌweɪ 'aʊt/ NOUN [plural **ways out**] a door you go through to leave a public building (**saída**)

WC /ˌdʌbəljuːˈsiː/ NOUN [plural **WCs**] a toilet (**WC, toalete**)

we /wiː/ PRONOUN
1 used to talk or write about yourself and at least one other person □ *We left home at about nine o'clock.* (**nós**)
2 people in general □ *We need to do more about global warming.* (**nós**)

weak /wiːk/ ADJECTIVE [**weaker, weakest**]
1 not physically strong □ *His illness has left him feeling very weak.* □ *She suffers from a weak heart.* (**fraco**)
2 not powerful □ *a weak government/leader* (**fraco**)
3 not strong in character □ *She's too weak to stand up to her boss.* (**fraco**)
4 easy to break □ *The metal bolts were too weak to hold the structure.* □ *a weak bridge* (**fraco**)
5 weak liquids contain a lot of water, do not have a strong taste, or do not contain much alcohol □ *a cup of weak tea* (**fraco**)

weaken /ˈwiːkən/ VERB [**weakens, weakening, weakened**] to become weak or to make someone or something weak □ *The metal has weakened because of rain and age.* □ *The illness weakened her heart.* (**enfraquecer, gastar**)

weakness /ˈwiːknɪs/ NOUN [plural **weaknesses**]
1 no plural when something or someone is not strong or forceful □ *The weakness of the frame made the building dangerous.* □ *I was ashamed of my weakness.* (**fraqueza, fragilidade**)
2 a feature of something that is not of a high quality or standard □ *His main weakness is that he is lazy.* □ *The plan has several major weaknesses.* (**fraqueza**)

wealth /welθ/ NOUN, NO PLURAL when someone has a lot of money and expensive things □ *The wealth of these people is amazing.* (**fortuna, riqueza**)

wealthy /ˈwelθi/ ADJECTIVE [**wealthier, wealthiest**] rich □ *a wealthy businessman* (**rico**)

weapon /ˈwepən/ NOUN [plural **weapons**] something that is used for fighting, such as a gun or a knife □ *The murder weapon was never found.* (**arma**)

wear /weə(r)/ VERB [**wears, wearing, wore, worn**]
1 to have clothes, jewellery, etc. on your body □ *Ann was wearing a red hat.* □ *How long have you worn glasses?* □ *He doesn't wear a wedding ring.* (**usar**)
2 if a material or surface wears, it gradually becomes thinner because of being used or rubbed, and if something wears it, it makes it thinner □ *His sleeves had worn through at the elbows.* 🔂 *My chair has worn a hole in the carpet.* (**gastar**)

> Note that to **wear** clothes is to have them on your body. To say 'to start to wear clothes', use the phrasal verb put on:
> ✓ *I put on my coat and left.*
> ✗ *I wore my coat and left.*

◆ PHRASAL VERBS **wear off** if a feeling or the effect of something wears off, it gradually disappears □ *The anaesthetic should soon wear off.* **wear (something) out** to use something so much that it becomes damaged and cannot be used any more, or to become damaged in this way □ *These shoes are completely worn out already.* **wear someone out** to make someone very tired □ *Walking so far completely wore me out.*

weary /ˈwɪəri/ ADJECTIVE [**wearier, weariest**] tired □ *He finally got home, weary after a long day.* (**cansado**)

weather /ˈweðə(r)/ NOUN, NO PLURAL the conditions outside, for example how hot, cold, wet or dry it is 🔂 *cold/hot weather* 🔂 *bad weather* □ *The weather's very warm for October.* (**tempo, clima**)

weave /wiːv/ VERB [**weaves, weaving, wove, woven**]
1 to make cloth by passing threads under and over each other on a frame called a loom (= a machine for making cloth) (**tecer**)
2 to make something by twisting long pieces of things together □ *She taught me how to weave baskets.* (**trançar**)

web /web/ NOUN [plural **webs**]
1 a very thin net that a spider makes for catching insects (**teia**)
2 the Web the World Wide Web; all the websites on the Internet. A computing word. (**rede mundial de computadores, internet**)

website /ˈwebsaɪt/ NOUN [plural **websites**] a group of connected pages on the Internet about a particular company, organization, subject, etc. A computing word. □ *Rowling's official website* □ *He has his own website.* (**website**)

we'd /wiːd/ a short way to say and write we had or we would □ *We'd better hurry up.* □ *We'd buy a new car if we had the money.* (**abreviação de we would**)

wedding /ˈwedɪŋ/ NOUN [plural **weddings**] a marriage ceremony □ *I met her at Lucy and John's wedding.* □ *a wedding present* (**casamento**)

Wednesday /ˈwenzdɪ/ NOUN [plural **Wednesdays**] the day of the week after Tuesday and before Thursday □ *Shall we meet again on Wednesday?* (**quarta-feira**)

weed /wiːd/ NOUN [plural **weeds**] a wild plant that is growing where you do not want it to □ *The garden was full of weeds.* (**erva-daninha**)

week /wiːk/ NOUN [plural **weeks**]
1 a period of seven days □ *Debbie teaches aerobics twice a week.* □ *I'll see you next week.*
2 in/during the week on the five days from Monday to Friday when many people go to work □ *I don't go out much during the week.* (**semana**)

weekday /ˈwiːkdeɪ/ NOUN [plural **weekdays**] any of the days from Monday to Friday □ *The office is only open on weekdays.* (**dia de semana, dia útil**)

weekend /ˌwiːkˈend/ NOUN [plural **weekends**] Saturday and Sunday □ *We're going to Oxford for the weekend.* □ *I like to go cycling at the weekend.* (**fim de semana**)

weekly¹ /ˈwiːklɪ/ ADJECTIVE happening or produced once every week □ *a weekly magazine* (**semanal**)

weekly² /ˈwiːklɪ/ ADVERB once every week □ *In those days I used to get paid weekly.* (**semanalmente**)

weep /wiːp/ VERB [**weeps, weeping, wept**] to cry □ *She wept when she heard the terrible news.* (**chorar**)

weigh /weɪ/ VERB [**weighs, weighing, weighed**]
1 to measure how heavy something is □ *Brenda weighs herself every day.* □ *Weigh the ingredients carefully.* (**pesar**)
2 to have a particular weight □ *My suitcase weighed 15 kilograms.* (**pesar**)

weight¹ /weɪt/ NOUN [plural **weights**]
1 no plural how heavy someone or something is □ *My luggage was above the weight limit.* ▣ *He has lost a lot of weight* (= got thinner) *recently.* ▣ *I've put on weight* (= got fatter) *since I stopped cycling.* (**peso**)
2 no plural the quality of being heavy □ *The shelf bent under the weight of all those books.* (**peso**)
3 weights heavy objects that you lift to make your muscles stronger □ *I spend ten minutes lifting weights.* (**peso**)

weight² /weɪt/ VERB [**weights, weighting, weighted**] to put something heavy into or onto something □ *We weighted the sheet down with rocks.* (**pôr lastro em**)

weird /wɪəd/ ADJECTIVE [**weirder, weirdest**] very strange □ *Something really weird just happened.* (**estranho**)

welcome¹ /ˈwelkəm/ ADJECTIVE
1 if someone or something is welcome, you are pleased about it □ *This fall in inflation is welcome news to home owners.* □ *We stopped for a very welcome rest.* (**bem-vindo**)
2 if you are welcome somewhere, people like you being there and make you feel happy and comfortable ▣ *They made us very welcome in their home.* □ *He is not welcome at his parent's house.* (**bem-vindo**)
3 welcome to do something if someone is welcome to do something, you are happy to allow them to do it □ *You're welcome to borrow my bike when I'm not using it.* (**ter liberdade para**)
4 You're welcome. used as a polite reply when someone has thanked you for something □ *'Thank you for all your help.' 'You're welcome.'* (**de nada, não há de quê**)

welcome² /ˈwelkəm/ EXCLAMATION used for welcoming someone who has arrived somewhere □ **+ to** *Welcome to London!* (**bem-vindo**)

welcome³ /ˈwelkəm/ NOUN [plural **welcomes**] the way that people treat someone when they arrive somewhere ▣ *We received a very warm welcome in Berlin.* (**acolhida, boas-vindas**)

welcome⁴ /ˈwelkəm/ VERB [**welcomes, welcoming, welcomed**]
1 to meet someone and make them feel that you are happy to see them □ *The whole family came to welcome us at the airport.* (**acolher, dar as boas-vindas**)
2 to be pleased about something □ *I would welcome the chance of a different job.* □ *We welcome these new plans.* (**receber com agrado**)

welfare /ˈwelfeə(r)/ NOUN, NO PLURAL health, happiness and safety □ *The police were concerned for the child's welfare.* (**bem-estar**)

well¹ /wel/ ADVERB [**better, best**]
1 in a satisfactory, successful or correct way □ *Janet speaks French very well.* □ *Federer played really well.* ▣ *My students are all doing well* ▣ *Our meetings went well.* (**bem**)
2 completely □ *Mix the butter and sugar well before adding the flour.* □ *I know Marie really well.* (**bem**)
3 as well in addition □ *I'd like an ice cream as well.* □ *As well as his family, a lot of his colleagues were there.* (**também**)
4 may as well/might as well used to make a suggestion because of a situation □ *If you're spending that much on rent, you might as well buy a flat.* □ *We may as well talk to them.* (**o melhor a fazer é**)
5 well done used to praise someone for something they have done □ *You passed? Oh, well done!* □ *Well done for remembering the map!* (**muito bem**)

6 used to form compound adjectives (= adjectives in two parts). When they are used before nouns, they usually have hyphens, e.g. a well-paid job □ *The business was very well run.* □ *Their staff are well paid.* (**bem**)

well² /wel/ EXCLAMATION

1 used at the beginning of a statement, especially a reply, often when you are explaining something, or expressing slight doubt or disagreement □ *'How did you make the sofa?' 'Well, I started with an old bed frame.'* □ *'Do you think he's suitable for the job?' 'Well, I've never worked with him, so it's hard to say.'* □ *'It's a great book, isn't it?' 'Well, I didn't enjoy it as much as you.'* (**bem**)
2 oh well used for accepting a bad situation □ *'Kiera is going to be late.' 'Oh well, we'll have to start without her.'* (**paciência**)

well³ /wel/ ADJECTIVE [**better, best**] healthy 🔊 *I don't feel very well.* 🔊 *You're looking well.* 🔊 *Get well soon!* (**bem**)

well⁴ /wel/ NOUN [*plural* **wells**] a deep hole in the ground where you can get water, oil or gas □ *an oil well* (**poço**)

we'll /wiːl/ a short way to say and write we will □ *I'm sure we'll meet again.* (**abreviação de we will**)

well-known /ˌwelˈnəʊn/ ADJECTIVE famous or known by many people □ *a well-known writer* (**conhecido, famoso**)

Welsh¹ /welʃ/ ADJECTIVE
1 belonging to or from Wales (**galês**)
2 to do with the Welsh language (**galês**)

Welsh² /welʃ/ NOUN, NO PLURAL
1 the Celtic language of Wales (**galês**)
2 the Welsh people of Wales (**galês**)

went /went/ PAST TENSE OF **go¹** (**ver go¹**)

wept /wept/ PAST TENSE AND PAST PARTICIPLE OF **weep** (**ver weep¹**)

were /wɜː(r)/ PAST TENSE OF **be¹** when it is used with you, we or they □ *We were so relieved to see him.* (**ver be¹**)

we're /wɪə(r)/ a short way to say and write we are □ *We're so pleased you could come.* (**abreviação de we are**)

weren't /wɜːnt/ a short way to say and write were not □ *Weren't the acrobats amazing?* (**abreviação de ver were**)

west¹ /west/ NOUN, NO PLURAL
1 the direction in which the sun goes down (**oeste**)
2 the countries in Europe and North America □ *The family moved to the West in 1998.* (**oeste**)

west² /west/ ADJECTIVE, ADVERB in or towards the west □ *the west coast of America* □ *We travelled west as far as the motorway.* (**oeste**)

western¹ /ˈwestən/ ADJECTIVE in or from the west □ *the western hills* (**do oeste, ocidental**)

western² /ˈwestən/ NOUN [*plural* **westerns**] a book or film about cowboys (= men who ride horses and look after cows) in North America (**western**)

westward /ˈwestwəd/ or **westwards** /ˈwestwədz/ ADVERB to or towards the west □ *We travelled westwards.* (**para o oeste, em direção ao oeste**)

wet¹ /wet/ ADJECTIVE [**wetter, wettest**]
1 full of water or covered with water □ *wet clothes* □ *It's easy to slip on a wet floor.* 🔊 *My trousers are* soaking *wet!* (**molhado**)
2 not dried □ *wet paint* (**molhado**)
3 raining □ *a wet afternoon* (**chuvoso**)

> **THESAURUS:** If something is **wet**, it is full of water or covered in water. If something is **damp** or **moist**, it is slightly wet. For example, a towel might be **damp** once you have used it after a bath. If something is **soaking**, it is very wet.

wet² /wet/ VERB [**wets, wetting, wet**] to make something wet □ *He wet his hair to flatten it down.* (**molhar**)

we've /wiːv/ a short way to say and write we have □ *We've got something to tell you.* (**ver have**)

whale /weɪl/ NOUN [*plural* **whales**] a very large mammal that lives in the sea (**baleia**)
> IDIOM **have a whale of a time** to enjoy yourself very much □ *The children had a whale of a time at the swimming pool.* (**divertir-se muito**)

what¹ /wɒt/ DETERMINER, PRONOUN

1 used for asking for information about something □ *What day is it today?* □ *What's your brother's name?* □ *What did that man want?* □ *What shall we do this evening?* (**que, o que, qual**)
2 used for referring to something □ *This bag is just what I wanted.* □ *I saw what you did.* □ *I had no idea what to do.* (**o que, para que**)
3 what for used to ask about the purpose of something or the reason for something □ *What's this handle for?* □ *What did you do that for?* (**para que**)
4 an informal word used when you have not heard someone and want them to repeat what they have said □ *'Could you pass the bread?' 'What?'* (**o quê?, como?**)
5 an informal word used to ask what someone wants when they speak to you or call to you □ *'Kate!' 'Yes, what?'* (**sim, pois não**)
6 used to emphasize your feelings about something □ *What a beautiful view!* (**que**)

what   387   **whichever**

what² /wɒt/ EXCLAMATION used to express surprise or shock ☐ *'The car repairs cost £400.' 'What! I had no idea it would be that much.'* (**o quê?!**)

whatever /wɒt'evə(r)/ PRONOUN, DETERMINER
1 any, anything or any amount ☐ *I can give you whatever money you need.* ☐ *Choose whatever you like from the menu.* (**tudo, qualquer coisa**)
2 used to say that something will always be true and will not be affected by anything else ☐ *You know we'll always love you, whatever happens.* ☐ *We'll be going, whatever the weather.* (**não importa**)
3 an informal word used to say that you do not care what happens or what you do ☐ *'Do you want to come with me to the party?' 'Whatever.'* (**tanto faz**)

what'll /'wɒtəl/ a short way to say and write what will ☐ *What'll happen to him?* (abreviação de **what will**)

what's /wɒts/ a short way to say and write what is or what has ☐ *What's that noise?* ☐ *What's she got in her hand?* (abreviação de **what is**)

what've /'wɒtəv/ a short way to say and write what have ☐ *What've you done with the phone?* (abreviação de **what have**)

wheat /wi:t/ NOUN, NO PLURAL a plant that produces grain that is used to make flour (**trigo**)

wheel¹ /wi:l/ NOUN [plural **wheels**] a round object under a vehicle that turns to make the vehicle move ☐ *There's a spare wheel in the boot.* (**roda**)

wheel² /wi:l/ VERB [**wheels, wheeling, wheeled**] to push something along on wheels ☐ *He wheeled the trolley through the airport.* (**rodar, girar**)

wheelchair /'wi:ltʃeə(r)/ NOUN [plural **wheelchairs**] a seat with wheels, used by people who cannot walk (**cadeira de rodas**)

when /wen/ ADVERB, CONJUNCTION
1 used for asking about the time something happened or will happen ☐ *When did you get home?* ☐ *When do you think they will arrive?* ☐ *When will the cakes be ready?* (**quando**)
2 used for talking about the time at which something happens or will happen ☐ *I'll go when I've had a shower.* ☐ *I'm not sure when the new store will open.* (**quando**)
3 used for talking about something that happens at the same time as something else ☐ *I was just going out when the phone rang.* ☐ *When I heard the news, I went straight to the airport.* ☐ *I was with her when she died.* (**quando**)

whenever /wen'evə(r)/ CONJUNCTION, ADVERB
1 at any time ☐ *You can borrow my book whenever you want to.* (**sempre que**)
2 every time ☐ *They go swimming whenever they get the chance.* (**sempre**)
3 used at the beginning of a question, especially to show that you are surprised ☐ *Whenever did you do all this?* (**quando, afinal**)

where /weə(r)/ ADVERB, CONJUNCTION
1 used for asking about a place or position ☐ *Where are we going?* ☐ *Where did you get that hat?* ☐ *Where can I park my car?* ☐ *Where do you come from?* (**onde**)
2 used for talking about a place or position ☐ *I know where you can buy really good fish.* ☐ *He told me where he lives.* ☐ *That is the place where I lost my camera.* (**onde**)

whereas /weər'æz/ CONJUNCTION used for comparing two things ☐ *He likes going out and meeting people, whereas I'm quite shy.* (**enquanto, ao passo que**)

where's /weəz/ a short way to say and write where is or where has ☐ *Where's the cat?* ☐ *Where's he gone?* (abreviação de **where has**)

where've /weəv/ a short way to say and write where have ☐ *Where've the children gone?* (abreviação de **where have**)

wherever /weər'evə(r)/ CONJUNCTION, ADVERB
1 to or in any place ☐ *Wherever he is, I am sure he will come back soon.* (**em qualquer lugar**)
2 to or in every place ☐ *He follows me wherever I go.* (**seja onde for**)
3 used to ask where someone or something is, especially when you are surprised or angry ☐ *Wherever did you get that hat?* (**onde**)

whether /'weðə(r)/ CONJUNCTION
1 used to show that there is a choice between two possibilities ☐ *I couldn't decide whether to have the salmon or the pork.* ☐ *I wasn't sure whether or not to tell her.* (**se**)
2 if ☐ *I'm not sure whether they're coming.* (**se**)

which /wɪtʃ/ ADJECTIVE, DETERMINER
1 used for asking or talking about a choice between two or more people or things ☐ *Which hand do you think the coin is in?* ☐ *Which person is tallest?* ☐ **+ of** *Which of these books is yours?* (**qual**)
2 used for referring to something ☐ *I saw the letter which was lying on the table.* ☐ *These are the ideas which we must discuss.* (**que**)
3 used for giving extra information about something ☐ *The cars, which were all luxury models, were available for us to use.* ☐ *I went to her party, which was very pleasant.* (**que, o que**)

whichever /wɪtʃ'evə(r)/ DETERMINER, PRONOUN
any of a group of things or people ☐ *Come on whichever day suits you.* (**qualquer um**)

while¹ /waɪl/ CONJUNCTION during the time that
☐ *Will you go to Disneyland while you are in Florida?* ☐ *I had a cup of coffee while I was waiting.* (**enquanto, quando**)

> Note that the word while, meaning 'during the time that' is never followed by a noun:
> ✓ *She got ill while we were on holiday.*
> ✗ *She got ill while the holiday.*

while² /waɪl/ NOUN a while a period of time
☐ *We waited inside for a while, but the rain didn't stop.* ☐ *I haven't seen her for quite a while* (= a long time). (**um tempo**)

whilst /waɪlst/ CONJUNCTION while ☐ *You could look at these magazines whilst you're waiting.* (**enquanto, quando**)

whine /waɪn/ VERB [whines, whining, whined]
1 to talk in a complaining voice ☐ *She's always whining about her job.* (**lamuriar-se**)
2 a dog or other animal whines when it makes a long high sound (**gemer, choramingar**)

whip¹ /wɪp/ NOUN [plural whips] a piece of leather or other material fastened to a handle and used to hit animals or people (**chicote**)

whip² /wɪp/ VERB [whips, whipping, whipped]
1 to hit someone or something with a whip (**açoitar**)
2 to mix food, especially cream, very quickly to make it become thick (**bater**)

> **THESAURUS:** Whip is used particularly to talk about cream. If you beat other food, such as eggs, or a cake mixture together very quickly, you can use the word **beat**. To **whisk** means to mix food together to get a lot of air into it, using a whisk (a kitchen tool with curved wire parts). You might **whisk** egg whites, for example.

whisk¹ /wɪsk/ NOUN [plural whisks] a kitchen tool with curved wire parts, used for mixing things like cream or eggs and getting a lot of air into them. (**batedor**)

whisk² /wɪsk/ VERB [whisks, whisking, whisked]
1 to mix food with a whisk (**bater**)
2 to make someone or something move somewhere quickly ☐ *They whisked us off to meet their cousins.* ☐ *She whisked away the plates.* (**tirar, mover, levar rapidamente**)

whisky /ˈwɪski/ NOUN [plural whiskies] a strong alcoholic drink made from grain, or a glass of this drink (**uísque**)

whisper¹ /ˈwɪspə(r)/ VERB [whispers, whispering, whispered] to talk very quietly so that other people cannot hear ☐ *My friend whispered the answer to me.* (**cochichar, sussurrar**)

whisper² /ˈwɪspə(r)/ NOUN [plural whispers] something said in a very quiet voice ☐ *She answered in a whisper.* (**murmúrio, sussurro**)

whistle¹ /ˈwɪsəl/ VERB [whistles, whistling, whistled]
1 to make a high sound or musical notes by blowing air through your lips ☐ *She was whistling a merry tune.* (**assoviar**)
2 to make a high sound using a whistle ☐ *The train whistled as it entered the tunnel.* ☐ *The referee whistled for the end of the game.* (**apitar**)

whistle² /ˈwɪsəl/ NOUN [plural whistles]
1 a small object that makes a high sound when you blow in it (**apito**)
2 a piece of equipment that makes a loud, high sound, for example on a train (**apito**)
3 the sound made when someone or something whistles (**assovio**)

white¹ /waɪt/ ADJECTIVE
1 having the colour of snow ☐ *He served the soup in large, white bowls.* ☐ *This powder will get your washing really white.* (**branco**)
2 white people are of a race that have pale skin ☐ *He married a white woman.* (**branco**)
3 white tea or coffee has milk in it (**com leite**)
4 white wine is a pale yellow colour (**branco**)

white² /waɪt/ NOUN [plural whites]
1 no plural the colour of snow ☐ *The white of the walls reflected the sunlight.* (**branco**)
2 the white of an egg is the clear substance around the yolk (= yellow part) which turns white if it is cooked (**clara de ovo**)

who /huː/ PRONOUN
1 used for asking about a person or people ☐ *Who is your favourite actor?* ☐ *Who left the door open?* ☐ *Who are you going to London with?* (**quem**)
2 used for referring to a person or people ☐ *It was Malcolm who told me the news.* ☐ *It was the Italians who invented pizza.* ☐ *I know who has been offered the job.* (**que**)
3 used for giving extra information about a person or people ☐ *Emily, who lives next door, is 12 years old.* (**que**)

who'd /huːd/ a short way to say and write who had or who would ☐ *It was my Dad who'd told him.* ☐ *Who'd like another biscuit?* (**ver would**)

whoever /huːˈevə(r)/ PRONOUN, CONJUNCTION
1 the person that has done something □ *Would whoever left the gate open please go and close it.* (**quem, aquele que**)

2 any person □ *Bring whoever you like to the party.* (**quem**)

3 used at the beginning of a question to show that you are surprised □ *Whoever told you I was a doctor?* (**quem, a quem**)

whole¹ /həʊl/ ADJECTIVE
1 containing or including every part of something □ *We spent the whole day on the beach.* □ *I drank a whole bottle of milk.* □ *Half the guests were late, and the whole thing was a disaster.* (**inteiro**)

2 not broken into parts □ *The cake is decorated with whole hazelnuts.* (**inteiro**)

whole² /həʊl/ ADVERB in one complete piece □ *He swallowed the egg whole.* (**todo**)

whole³ /həʊl/ NOUN, NO PLURAL

1 a complete thing, especially one that is made up of different parts □ *Two halves make a whole.* (**inteiro**)

2 the whole of something all of something □ *She spent the whole of her life in Wales.* □ *The Olympics will benefit the whole of the country.* (**todo o**)

3 on the whole used to talk about what something is usually or mostly like □ *On the whole, I enjoy school.* □ *People were very kind to us on the whole.* (**em conjunto, como um todo**)

who'll /huːl/ a short way to say and write who will □ *Who'll help me to carry this box?* (ver **will**)

whom /huːm/ PRONOUN a formal word, used instead of 'who' when it is the object of a verb or a preposition □ *He phoned his friend Andrew, whom he hadn't seen for years.* □ *To whom should I address the letter?* (**quem, a quem**)

who're /ˈhuːə(r)/ a short way to say and write who are □ *Who're you going with?* (ver **are**)

who's /huːz/ a short way to say and write who is or who has □ *Who's coming for a walk?* □ *Who's got the TV guide?* (ver **is**)

whose /huːz/ ADJECTIVE, PRONOUN
1 used to ask who something belongs to or is connected with □ *Whose bike is this?* □ *Whose is this coat?* (**de quem**)

2 used to say that something or someone belongs to someone or is connected to them □ *This is the boy whose family owns the farm.* □ *Cheeky, whose real name was Robert Ritchie, lived in Glasgow.* (**cujo, de quem**)

who've /huːv/ a short way to say and write who have □ *These are the members who've already paid their subscriptions.* (ver **have**)

why /waɪ/ ADVERB
1 used for asking and talking about the reason for something □ *Why were you late?* □ *Why didn't they phone us?* □ *She explained why she had made the decision.* □ *I have no idea why he was so angry.* (**por que**)

2 used for making a suggestion □ *Why don't you ask Claire to come with you?* □ *Why doesn't he ask a doctor about it?* (**por que**)

3 why not…? (a) used for making a suggestion □ *Why not make some soup with the vegetables?* (b) used for agreeing to a suggestion □ *'Shall we invite Peter?' 'Yes, why not?'* (**por que não?**)

why've /waɪv/ a short way to say and write why have □ *Why've we got to wait?* (ver **have**)

wicked /ˈwɪkɪd/ ADJECTIVE
1 evil or morally wrong □ *a wicked old witch* □ *Separating children from their parents is wicked.* (**mau, ruim**)

2 an informal word meaning very good □ *He scored a wicked goal.* (**ótimo**)

wide¹ /waɪd/ ADJECTIVE [wider, widest]
1 a large distance from side to side □ *a wide river* □ *Floods affected a wide area.* (**largo, amplo**)

2 having a particular width □ *The river is nearly a mile wide at some points.* (**de largura**)

3 including many different things 🔁 *They sell a wide range of products.* □ *The college offers a wide choice of subjects.* (**amplo**)

wide² /waɪd/ ADVERB [wider, widest]
1 with a large distance from top to bottom or side to side □ *The tiger opened his mouth wide, showing his enormous teeth.* 🔁 *The door was wide open.* 🔁 *She stood with her feet wide apart.* (**completamente, amplamente**)

2 wide awake completely awake (**bem aberto, arregalado**)

widely /ˈwaɪdli/ ADVERB
1 by many people or in many places □ *He was widely believed to be guilty.* □ *The tour was widely advertised.* (**amplamente, muito**)

2 by a large amount □ *Standards vary widely.* (**largamente, extensamente**)

widen /ˈwaɪdən/ VERB [widens, widening, widened] to make something wider or to become wider □ *The river widens as it reaches the sea.* (**alargar**)

widespread /ˈwaɪdspred/ ADJECTIVE found in a lot of places or among a lot of people □ *There is widespread use of these drugs.* □ *There has been widespread criticism of the law.* (**muito difundido**)

widow /ˈwɪdəʊ/ NOUN [*plural* widows] a woman whose husband has died (**viúva**)

widower /ˈwɪdəʊə(r)/ NOUN [*plural* widowers] a man whose wife has died (**viúvo**)

width /wɪdθ/ NOUN [plural **widths**] the width of something is how much it measures from side to side ▢ *This curtain material comes in several different widths.* (**largura**)

wife /waɪf/ NOUN [plural **wives**] the woman that a man is married to (**esposa**)

wig /wɪg/ NOUN [plural **wigs**] a covering of artificial hair that is worn on the head (**peruca**)

wild /waɪld/ ADJECTIVE [**wilder, wildest**]

1 wild animals or plants live in natural conditions and are not kept by human beings ▢ *wild salmon* ▢ *wild flowers* (**selvagem**)

2 not controlled, and often expressing strong emotions or a lot of energy and excitement ▢ *When he came on stage, the audience went wild.* ▢ *The children were wild with excitement.* ▢ *wild parties* (**louco**)

wilderness /ˈwɪldənɪs/ NOUN [plural **wildernesses**] a wild area of a country with no roads, houses, etc. (**selva, selvageria**)

wildlife /ˈwaɪldlaɪf/ NOUN, NO PLURAL wild animals, birds, insects and plants (**vida selvagem**)

will¹ /wɪl/ MODAL VERB

1 used to talk about the future ▢ *It will be winter soon.* ▢ *Will Tom be at the party?* ▢ *It won't take long to mend the hole.* (**indicativo de futuro**)

2 used to talk about if someone is willing to do something ▢ *Will you hold this for me?* ▢ *I'll carry that bag for you.* ▢ *He won't lend me any money.* (**oferecimento de ajuda/ Você poderia...?**)

3 used in conditional sentences that start with 'if' ▢ *If he is rude, I will leave straight away.* ▢ *If it rains, they will have to work indoors.* (**usado em orações condicionais começadas com if**)

> Notice that instead of **will not**, people often say or write the short form **won't**: ▢ *I won't tell her.*

will² /wɪl/ NOUN [plural **wills**]

1 the mental strength needed to achieve something ▢ *She has the will to succeed.* ▢ *He had a very strong will.* (**vontade**)

2 a legal document that says what you want to happen to your money and possessions when you die ▢ *Have you made a will?* (**testamento**)

will³ /wɪl/ VERB [**wills, willing, willed**] if you will something to happen, you try to make it happen by wishing for it very much ▢ *We were willing our team to win.* (**disposto a**)

willing /ˈwɪlɪŋ/ ADJECTIVE willing to do something if you are willing to do something, you will do it if you are asked to ▢ *He'll succeed if he's willing to work hard.* ▢ *She wasn't willing to accept responsibility.* (**disposto**)

win¹ /wɪn/ VERB [**wins, winning, won**]

1 to beat everyone else in a game, competition, election, etc. ▢ *We played tennis, and Sam won easily.* ▢ *They won the championship three times* (**ganhar**)

2 to defeat the other side in a war, argument, etc. (**ganhar**)

3 to get something because you have been successful in a game, competition, etc. ▢ *She won a gold medal at the 2008 Olympics.* ▢ *The film won two Oscars.* (**conquistar**)

win² /wɪn/ NOUN [plural **wins**] when someone wins a game, competition, etc. ▢ *This is the team's third win this season.* (**vitória**)

wind¹ /wɪnd/ NOUN [plural **winds**] a current of air ▢ *Strong winds prevented the aircraft from landing.* ▢ *The wind blew and snow fell.* (**vento**)

> THESAURUS: Wind is a general word. A light wind is called a **breeze**. A very strong wind is called a **gale**. A storm with very strong winds is called a **hurricane**. A **tornado** is a violent storm with a powerful wind with a circular movement. **Hurricanes** and **tornadoes** often cause a lot of damage.

wind² /waɪnd/ VERB [**winds, winding, wound**]

1 to twist or wrap something around something else ▢ **+ round** *A turban is a long piece of cloth that is wound round the head.* (**enrolar**)

2 if a road, path or river winds somewhere, it has a lot of curves or turns ▢ **+ through** *A narrow path wound through the valley.* (**serpentear**)

3 to turn a part of a machine or piece of equipment in order to make it work ▢ *This watch has a battery, so you don't need to wind it.* ▢ **+ up** *You wind up this toy car to make it go.* (**dar corda**)

◆ PHRASAL VERB **wind someone up** an informal word meaning to make someone upset or angry ▢ *It really winds me up when he's late.*

windmill /ˈwɪndmɪl/ NOUN [plural **windmills**] a building with large parts on the outside which are turned by the wind and provide power for crushing grain (**moinho de vento**)

window 391 with

window /ˈwɪndəʊ/ NOUN [plural **windows**]
1 an opening in the wall of a building or in a vehicle, with glass fitted in it 🔁 *Could you open/close the window, please?* (**janela**)
2 an area on a computer screen where you can work or see information. A computing word 🔁 *I opened a new window.* (**janela**)

windscreen /ˈwɪndskriːn/ NOUN [plural **windscreens**] the window at the front of a car or other vehicle (**para-brisa**)

windshield /ˈwɪndʃiːld/ NOUN [plural **windshields**] the US word for windscreen (**para-brisa**)

windsurfing /ˈwɪndsɜːfɪŋ/ NOUN, NO PLURAL the sport of moving across the surface of water standing on a narrow board with a sail attached to it (**windsurfe**)

windy /ˈwɪndi/ ADJECTIVE [**windier, windiest**] with a lot of wind 🔁 *a windy day* (**ventoso**)

wine /waɪn/ NOUN [plural **wines**] an alcoholic drink usually made from grapes (= small green or purple fruits) 🔁 *a glass of wine* 🔁 *red/white wine*

wing /wɪŋ/ NOUN [plural **wings**]
1 one of the parts of a bird or an insect's body that it uses to fly with 🔁 *The owl flapped its wings.* (**asa**)
2 one of the two long flat parts that stick out at either side of an aircraft (**asa**)

wink[1] /wɪŋk/ VERB [**winks, winking, winked**] to shut one of your eyes and open it again quickly, as a friendly or secret sign to someone (**piscar, dar uma piscadela**)

> **THESAURUS:** If you wink, you shut and open one eye. If you **blink**, you close and open your eyes quickly. If you **frown**, you look as if you are angry, worried or thinking a lot by moving your eyebrows down.

wink[2] /wɪŋk/ NOUN [plural **winks**] the action of shutting one of your eyes and opening it again quickly (**piscadela**)

winner /ˈwɪnə(r)/ NOUN [plural **winners**] someone who wins a race, competition, election, etc. 🔁 *This year's winner gets a £3,000 prize.* (**vencedor**)

winter /ˈwɪntə(r)/ NOUN [plural **winters**] the coldest season of the year, between autumn and spring 🔁 *the winter months* 🔁 *a winter coat* (**inverno**)

wipe /waɪp/ VERB [**wipes, wiping, wiped**]
1 to rub the surface of something to clean it or dry it 🔁 *I wiped my face with a tissue.* 🔁 *We wiped all the tables.* 🔁 *Please wipe your feet* (= clean the dirt off your shoes) *before you come in.* (**limpar, enxugar**)
2 to remove something, for example dirt or water, from the surface of something by rubbing it 🔁 *Wipe any mud off the potatoes.* (**limpar**)
◆ PHRASAL VERBS **wipe something out** to destroy something completely 🔁 *These elephants are in danger of being wiped out by hunters.* **wipe something up** to clean away a substance, often a liquid, with a cloth 🔁 *Could you wipe that milk up, please?*

wire /ˈwaɪə(r)/ NOUN [plural **wires**]
1 no plural metal that has been made into long, thin pieces, used for fastening things together, or for fences, etc. 🔁 *a wire fence* (**arame**)
2 a piece of wire used for carrying electricity or telephone signals (**fio**)

wisdom /ˈwɪzdəm/ NOUN, NO PLURAL when someone understands a lot about life and is able to make good decisions and give good advice (**sabedoria**)

wise /waɪz/ ADJECTIVE [**wiser, wisest**] a wise person understands a lot about life and is able to make good decisions and give good advice (**sábio**)

wish[1] /wɪʃ/ VERB [**wishes, wishing, wished**]
1 to want something to happen, especially to want a situation to change 🔁 *I wish it would stop raining.* 🔁 *+ that I wish that I could go with you.* (**desejar**)
2 wish to do something a formal word meaning to want to do something 🔁 *Do you wish to pay now or later?* (**vontade de fazer algo**)
3 used to say that you hope someone will have something or enjoy something 🔁 *We all wish you luck.* 🔁 *I wished her a happy birthday.* (**desejar**)

wish[2] /wɪʃ/ NOUN [plural **wishes**]
1 what you want to do or to happen 🔁 *We must respect his wishes* (= do what he wants). (**desejo**)
2 something that you want to happen by magic 🔁 *Blow out the candles and make a wish!* (**pedido**)
3 best wishes a polite way of ending a letter or email (**saudação cordial**)

wit /wɪt/ NOUN, NO PLURAL the ability to say funny and clever things (**senso de humor**)

witch /wɪtʃ/ NOUN [plural **witches**] a woman in stories who has evil magic powers (**bruxa**)

> **THESAURUS:** A witch is a woman with magic powers. A man with magic powers is called a **wizard**. A **fairy** is an imaginary creature which looks like a small person with wings.

with /wɪð/ PREPOSITION
1 if something or someone is in a place with something or someone else, or doing something with someone or something else, they are together 🔁 *Come with me.* 🔁 *She keeps her diary on the shelf with her other books.* 🔁 *He was playing football with his friends.* (**com**)

2 using ☐ *The board was stuck down with glue.* ☐ *I chopped up the wood with an axe.* ☐ *He covered the table with a sheet.* (com)

3 having ☐ *Who is that man with the curly hair?* ☐ *The meeting was in the room with the large table.* (com)

4 as the result of ☐ *He was crying with pain.* (de)

5 against ☐ *I'm always arguing with my parents.* ☐ *He was killed in the war with Spain.* (com)

6 used to describe how something happens or is done ☐ *She agreed with a smile.* ☐ *He stood with his hands behind his back.* (com)

7 holding or carrying ☐ *He arrived with a huge bunch of roses.* (com)

8 used to show what something refers to ☐ *What's wrong with your eye?* ☐ *I'm really pleased with my new computer.* (com)

withdraw /wɪðˈdrɔː/ VERB [withdraws, withdrawing, withdrew, withdrawn]

1 to take something away or to stop providing something ☐ *The council has withdrawn funding for the nursery.* ☐ *His father has withdrawn consent for the treatment.* (retirar)

2 to not take part in something, or to say that someone cannot take part in something ☐ *The government has withdrawn from the negotiations.* ☐ *He began to withdraw from public life.* (retirar)

3 to take money out of a bank account ☐ *I withdrew £100 for the weekend.* (sacar)

4 if an army withdraws or is withdrawn, it leaves an area 🔁 *We plan to withdraw our forces from the area.* (retirar)

wither /ˈwɪðə(r)/ VERB [withers, withering, withered] if a plant withers, it becomes dry and starts to die (murchar)

withhold /wɪðˈhəʊld/ VERB [withholds, withholding, withheld] to refuse to give something to someone 🔁 *She was accused of wit holding information from the police.* (recusar, reter)

within /wɪˈðɪn/ PREPOSITION

1 in less than a particular amount of time, or during a particular period of time ☐ *The police were called within minutes of the discovery.* ☐ *We'll be home within the hour.* ☐ *Within the last week there have been reports of fighting in the area.* (dentro de)

2 less than a particular distance or amount away from something ☐ *I have always lived within 20 miles of York.* ☐ *They are within two points of the championship.* (a menos de)

3 inside a place, group, organization or system ☐ *They took cover within the castle walls.* ☐ *I moved to another job within the same company.* (dentro)

without[1] /wɪˈðaʊt/ PREPOSITION

1 not having something ☐ *I prefer my coffee without milk.* ☐ *It's a kind of bicycle without pedals.* ☐ *They left us without any food or water.* 🔁 *We had to do without knives and forks.* (sem)

2 not with someone or something ☐ *Don't leave without me* (sem)

3 not doing something ☐ + **ing** *He left without saying goodbye.* (sem)

without[2] /wɪˈðaʊt/ ADVERB do/go without to manage when you do not have something ☐ *We only have two blankets, so the children will have to do without.* (fazer sem, ajeitar-se sem)

withstand /wɪðˈstænd/ VERB [withstands, withstanding, withstood] to not be harmed by something ☐ *The buildings are designed to withstand earthquakes.* (resistir)

witness[1] /ˈwɪtnɪs/ NOUN [plural witnesses]

1 someone who sees an event such as an accident or a crime happening, and can tell other people about it ☐ + **to** *Were there any witnesses to the accident?* (testemunha)

2 someone who answers questions in a court about what they know about a crime (testemunha)

witness[2] /ˈwɪtnɪs/ VERB [witnesses, witnessing, witnessed] to see something happening ☐ *Several people witnessed the shooting.* (testemunhar)

witty /ˈwɪti/ ADJECTIVE [wittier, wittiest] clever and funny ☐ *My brother is very witty.* ☐ *a witty remark* (brincalhão, espirituoso)

wives /waɪvz/ PLURAL OF **wife**

wizard /ˈwɪzəd/ NOUN [plural wizards] in stories, a man with magic powers (mágico)

woke /wəʊk/ PAST TENSE OF **wake**

woken /ˈwəʊkən/ PAST PARTICIPLE OF **wake**

wolf /wʊlf/ NOUN [plural wolves] a wild animal like a large dog (lobo)

woman /ˈwʊmən/ NOUN [plural women] an adult female person ☐ *There were three other women in the office.* (mulher)

womb /wuːm/ NOUN [plural wombs] the organ inside a woman's or female animal's body where her babies grow. A biology word. (útero)

won /wʌn/ PAST TENSE AND PAST PARTICIPLE OF **win**[1] (ver **win**[1])

wonder¹ /'wʌndə(r)/ VERB [wonders, wondering, wondered]

1 to want to know something ▫ + *question word* I wonder what Jack has bought me for Christmas. ▫ I wonder whether Susie is coming? (interrogar--se, perguntar-se)

2 used to ask someone something in a polite way ▫ I wonder if you could tell me where the post office is? (gostaria de saber)

wonder² /'wʌndə(r)/ NOUN [plural wonders]

1 no plural a feeling of great admiration and surprise ▫ The comet filled people with wonder. ▫ We stared in wonder at the castle. (maravilhamento, assombro)

2 something that makes you feel admiration and surprise ▫ Now we can keep in touch all the time, with the wonders of modern technology. (maravilha)

3 no wonder used to say that something does not surprise you ▫ It's no wonder she gets cross if you behave like that. (não é de admirar)

wonderful /'wʌndəfʊl/ ADJECTIVE extremely good ▫ We had a wonderful view of the mountains. ▫ This job is a wonderful opportunity for her. (maravilhoso)

won't /wəʊnt/ a short way to say and write will not ▫ He won't tell me what he saw. (abreviação de **will not**)

wood /wʊd/ NOUN [plural woods]

1 the hard substance that trees are made of ▫ a piece of wood ▫ a wood floor ▫ They were chopping wood for the fire. (madeira)

2 also **woods** an area where a lot of trees grow closely together ▫ We went for a walk in the woods. (bosque)

wooden /'wʊdən/ ADJECTIVE made of wood ▫ wooden toys ▫ a wooden chair (de madeira)

wool /wʊl/ NOUN, NO PLURAL cloth or thread made from the hair of sheep ▫ a ball of wool ▫ a wool coat (lã)

woollen /'wʊlən/ ADJECTIVE made of wool ▫ a woollen blanket (de lã)

word /wɜːd/ NOUN [plural words]

1 a unit of language that is written as a group of letters with spaces on either side ▫ She asked me how to pronounce the word 'catastrophe'. ▫ He always uses lots of long words. (palavra)

2 words something that someone says ▫ What were her exact words? ▫ Tell us what happened in your own words. (palavra)

3 no plural a short conversation ▫ I'll have a word with my Dad and see if we can borrow the car. ▫ I want a word with you. (palavra)

4 no plural a promise ▫ He gave me his word that he would be there. ▫ I will always keep my word. (palavra)

5 in other words used when you say something in a different way in order to explain it ▫ We are spending more than we earn at the moment. In other words, we need more money. (em outras palavras)

6 not believe/understand, etc. a word to not believe/understand, etc. any of what is said or written ▫ I couldn't hear a word of what he was saying. ▫ She doesn't speak a word of English. (palavra)

7 take someone's word for it to believe what someone says about something ▫ The movie's great, but you don't have to take my word for it – go and see it yourself. (acreditar em alguém)

8 word for word using exactly the same words ▫ He copied the essay word for word from the Internet. (palavra por palavra)

wore /wɔː(r)/ PAST TENSE OF **wear** (ver **wear**)

work¹ /wɜːk/ VERB [works, working, worked]

1 to do something that needs effort or energy ▫ + *on* She's working on another novel. ▫ + *to do something* We have been working to improve conditions for the homeless. ▫ We all need to work hard to make this event a success. (trabalhar)

2 to have a job that you are paid to do ▫ + *for* He works for a shipping company. ▫ + *as* I was working as a nurse at the time. (trabalhar)

3 to operate correctly ▫ My e-mail isn't working at the moment. (funcionar)

4 to be successful or effective ▫ The new treatment seems to be working. ▫ Our plan worked well. (funcionar)

5 to operate a machine or a piece of equipment ▫ I don't know how to work the heating. (trabalhar, fazer funcionar)

◆ PHRASAL VERBS **work out 1** if a plan or a situation works out, it is successful ▫ I hope everything works out for you. **2 to end in a particular way** ▫ The arrangement worked out well for me. **3 to do exercises** to make your body stronger ▫ I work out four times a week. **work something out 1** to be able to understand something or make a decision about something ▫ + *question word* There was a message on the back, but I couldn't work out what it said. ▫ I worked out how to put the tent up. **2 to calculate something** ▫ I've worked out how much tax I owe. ▫ The doctors have worked out the correct dose for me.

work² /wɜːk/ NOUN [plural works]

1 no plural an activity that needs effort ▫ It was hard work clearing up after the party. ▫ There's still a lot of work to do before the website will be ready. (trabalho)

2 no plural someone's job, or the place they go to do it ▫ I go to work at 8. ▫ I usually go to the gym before work. ▫ My work involves talking to doctors. (trabalho)

3 *no plural* the things that you create or do when you are working ☐ *I've done a lot of work with young people.* ☐ *Hand your work in to the teacher.* (trabalho)

4 something produced by an artist, musician, writer etc. ☐ *Her early works are quite different.* (obra)

5 get/set to work to start working ☐ *We set to work on the garden.* (mãos à obra)

worker /'wɜːkə(r)/ NOUN [*plural* workers] someone who works for a company or organization, but who is not a manager ☐ *steel workers* (trabalhador)

workforce /'wɜːkfɔːs/ NOUN, NO PLURAL all the people who work in a country or in a particular company (mão de obra)

working /'wɜːkɪŋ/ ADJECTIVE
1 to do with your job 🔁 *They demanded better working conditions.* 🔁 *He'd spent his whole working life in the same job.* 🔁 *He wanted to reduce his working hours.* (de trabalho)
2 having a job ☐ *working mothers* (ativo)

work of art /ˌwɜːk əv 'ɑːt/ NOUN [*plural* works of art] something which an artist has painted or made ☐ *The gallery owns the country's best-known works of art.* (obra de arte)

workout /'wɜːkaʊt/ NOUN [*plural* workouts] an occasion when you do exercises to make you stronger (treino)

workplace /'wɜːkpleɪs/ NOUN [*plural* workplaces] a building or room where people work (local de trabalho)

workshop /'wɜːkʃɒp/ NOUN [*plural* workshops]
1 a meeting to learn more about something by discussing it and doing practical exercises ☐ *a drama workshop* (oficina)
2 a place where things are built or repaired (oficina)

world /wɜːld/ NOUN [*plural* worlds]
1 the world the Earth or all the people living on it ☐ *He is the tallest man in the world.* ☐ *The whole world is affected by global warming.* ☐ *He longed to travel the world.* ☐ *She really wants to change the world.* (mundo)
2 the people and things involved in a particular activity ☐ *He is famous in the world of antiques.* (mundo)
3 an area of the world or a group of countries with a particular characteristic ☐ *the Arab world* ☐ *Many of the goods we import are from the developing world.* (mundo)

worm /wɜːm/ NOUN [*plural* worms] a long, thin, soft creature with no bones or legs which lives in soil (verme)

worn /wɔːn/ PAST PARTICIPLE OF wear (ver **wear**)

worried /'wʌrɪd/ ADJECTIVE thinking a lot about problems or bad things that could happen ☐ **+ about** *I'm worried about what will happen if I fail my exams.* ☐ **+ that** *He is worried that Amy won't like him.* (preocupado)

worry¹ /'wʌri/ VERB [worries, worrying, worried]
1 to keep thinking about a problem or something bad that might happen ☐ **+ about** *A lot of young people worry about the future.* (preocupar)
2 to make someone feel worried 🔁 *It worries me that I might not be able to find a job.* (preocupar)
3 Don't worry (a) said when trying to make someone feel less worried ☐ *Don't worry. I'm sure things will improve.* (b) used to tell someone that they do not need to do something ☐ *Don't worry about getting the milk. I can get it on my way home.* (não se preocupe)

worry² /'wʌri/ NOUN [*plural* worries]
1 something that makes you worried 🔁 *Lack of money is a real worry at the moment.* (preocupação)
2 no plural the feeling of being worried ☐ *Some medical tests can lead to unnecessary worry.* (preocupação)

worse¹ /wɜːs/ ADJECTIVE
1 of a lower standard, or more unpleasant 🔁 *The situation will get worse.* ☐ **+ than** *The damage was worse than expected.* (pior)
2 more ill ☐ *I felt worse yesterday.* (pior)

worse² /wɜːs/ ADVERB
1 more badly, or more severely ☐ **+ than** *His headache had returned worse than ever.* (pior)
2 not as well ☐ **+ than** *Some of the children were treated worse than others.* (pior)

worship¹ /'wɜːʃɪp/ VERB [worships, worshipping, worshipped]
1 to show respect for a god by praying, having religious ceremonies, etc. (adorar, cultuar)
2 to admire someone so much that you do not see their faults ☐ *She worshipped her husband.* (adorar)

worship² /'wɜːʃɪp/ NOUN, NO PLURAL religious services and other ways of showing respect for a god 🔁 *a place of worship* (= a church, mosque, etc.) (culto, adoração)

worst¹ /wɜːst/ ADJECTIVE the worst most severe, most unpleasant, or most difficult ☐ *It was the worst storm we'd ever seen.* (o pior)

worst² /wɜːst/ ADVERB most badly ☐ *I scored worst in the test.* ☐ *The area worst affected by the floods was the North.* (pior)

worth¹ /wɜːθ/ ADJECTIVE
1 having a particular value ☐ *The ring is worth £1000.* (equivalente)
2 used for saying that something is useful, important or enjoyable ☐ *The museum is worth a*

worth

visit. □ + *ing It is worth asking a solicitor for advice.* 🔑 *The project was hard work but it was worth it.* (**digno de**)

worth² /wɜːθ/ NOUN, NO PLURAL
1 £10/$50, etc. worth of something an amount of something that costs £10/$50, etc. to buy □ *£10,000 worth of jewellery was stolen in the robbery.* (**valor**)
2 a week's/a month's, etc. worth of something an amount for a week/month, etc. □ *A month's worth of rain fell in less than 24 hours.* (**inteiro**)
3 how useful someone or something is 🔑 *Since joining the team, he has proved his worth.* (**valor**)

worthless /ˈwɜːθləs/ ADJECTIVE
1 not important or not useful □ *He felt worthless.* (**sem valor, desvalorizado**)
2 having no financial value □ *The necklace is worthless.* (**sem valor, imprestável**)

worthwhile /ˌwɜːθˈwaɪl/ ADJECTIVE if something is worthwhile, it is useful or enjoyable although you have to spend time or effort doing it □ *a worthwhile project* (**que vale a pena**)

worthy /ˈwɜːði/ ADJECTIVE [worthier, worthiest]
1 deserving respect or support □ *The German team were worthy winners.* 🔑 *She gives a lot of money to worthy causes.* (**merecedor**)
2 be worthy of something a formal phrase meaning to deserve something □ *The offer is certainly worthy of consideration.* (**digno de consideração**)

would /wʊd/ MODAL VERB
1 used to say what might happen in a particular situation □ *What would you do if you won a million dollars?* □ *What would happen if there was a fire?*
2 used as the past tense of **will¹** to talk about what was going to happen □ *I didn't think she would agree.* □ *He said he would come later.* (**ver will¹**)
3 used as the past tense of **will¹** to talk about if someone or something was willing or able to do something □ *My camera wouldn't work.* □ *She wouldn't help me.*
4 used for talking about what you think is true, or what you think the reason for something is □ *You would find it hard to get another job.* □ *It would be difficult to manage without a car.* □ *Why would he want to hurt them?*
5 would you used in polite questions and offers □ *Would you like a drink?* □ *Would you mind helping me with these boxes?*
6 would like/prefer, etc. used to say what you want or what you want to do □ *I would like to see a different doctor.* □ *I would really like a hot shower.*

wouldn't /ˈwʊdənt/ a short way to say and write would not □ *She wouldn't go.* (**abreviação de would not**)

would've /ˈwʊdəv/ a short way to say and write would have □ *It would've been nice to see her.* (**abreviação de would have**)

wound¹ /waʊnd/ PAST TENSE AND PAST PARTICIPLE OF **wind²** (**ver wind²**)

wound² /wuːnd/ NOUN [plural wounds] an injury, especially where the skin is broken □ *gunshot wounds.* (**ferida, chaga**)

wound³ /wuːnd/ VERB [wounds, wounding, wounded] to injure a person or an animal, especially in a way that breaks their skin □ *She was seriously wounded in the attack.* (**ferir, machucar**)

wove /wəʊv/ PAST TENSE OF weave (**ver weave**)

woven /ˈwəʊvən/ PAST PARTICIPLE OF weave (**ver weave**)

wow /waʊ/ EXCLAMATION an informal word used to express surprise or admiration □ *Wow! You look great!* (**uau!**)

wrap /ræp/ VERB [wraps, wrapping, wrapped] to cover something by putting paper or another material around it □ *Would you like the chocolates wrapped?* □ *We wrapped all the glasses in paper.* (**embrulhar**)

◆ PHRASAL VERB **wrap something up** to cover something with paper or another material, especially a present □ *We wrapped up the toys.*

wreck¹ /rek/ VERB [wrecks, wrecking, wrecked]
1 to destroy or badly damage something □ *He wrecked all our new furniture.* □ *A knee injury has wrecked his chance of playing in the final.* (**destroçar**)
2 if a ship is wrecked, it is damaged and sinks (**destroçar**)

wreck² /rek/ NOUN [plural wrecks]
1 a ship that has sunk (**naufrágio**)
2 a badly damaged vehicle that has crashed (**destroço**)

wreckage /ˈrekɪdʒ/ NOUN, NO PLURAL the damaged pieces left after a vehicle has been destroyed □ *He was trapped in the wreckage for over an hour.* (**destroço**)

wrestle /ˈresəl/ VERB [wrestles, wrestling, wrestled] to fight with someone by holding them and trying to throw them to the ground (**lutar corpo a corpo**)

wriggle /ˈrɪɡəl/ VERB [wriggles, wriggling, wriggled] to make short, twisting movements □ *Stop wriggling about in your chair and sit still!* (**remexer, esquivar-se**)

wrinkle /ˈrɪŋkəl/ NOUN [plural wrinkles]
1 a line in your skin, caused by getting older (**ruga**)
2 a line where something such as a piece of cloth is slightly folded (**vinco, prega, dobra**)

wrist /rɪst/ NOUN [plural wrists] the part of your body where your arm joins your hand (**pulso**)

write /raɪt/ VERB [writes, writing, wrote, written]

1 to form letters, words or numbers, usually on paper using a pen or pencil □ *Write your name and address on the top of the paper.* **(escrever)**

2 to use words to make a story, essay, book, letter, song, etc. □ *She has written four novels.* □ *I wrote a note and left it on the table.* □ **+ *about*** *She writes about gardening.* **(escrever)**

3 to send a letter or a message to someone □ **+ *to*** *I wrote to the manager to complain.* □ *We'll write in a week or two.* **(escrever)**

4 if you write music, you put the symbols for the notes on special paper □ *He wrote his second symphony when he was fifteen.* **(compor)**

◆ PHRASAL VERB **write something down** to write something on a piece of paper, especially so that you do not forget it □ *I wrote down his phone number.*

writer /'raɪtə(r)/ NOUN [*plural* **writers**] someone who writes books, plays, newspaper articles, etc. as a job **(escritor)**

writing /'raɪtɪŋ/ NOUN [*plural* **writings**]

1 **no plural** the forming of letters and words on paper or other surfaces so that they can be read **(escrita)**

2 **no plural** your writing is the way you write **(escrita)**

3 the things that a writer has written **(escrita)**

written /'rɪtən/ PAST PARTICIPLE OF write **(ver write)**

wrong¹ /rɒŋ/ ADJECTIVE

1 if something is wrong, there is a problem □ **+ *with*** *Is there something wrong with David? He doesn't look happy.* □ *What's wrong? I thought you'd be pleased to see me.* **(errado)**

2 not correct □ *That was the wrong answer.* □ *We made the wrong decision.* □ *You're looking in the wrong place.* □ **+ about** He was wrong about Helen. **(errado)**

3 not morally right □ *She has done nothing wrong.* □ **+ *to do something*** *It would be wrong to deceive him.* **(errado)**

4 not suitable □ **+ *with*** *If you want flowers, what's wrong with roses?* □ **+ for** *The dress was wrong for a wedding.* **(errado, impróprio)**

wrong² /rɒŋ/ ADVERB

1 in a way that is not correct □ *I think I have spelt your name wrong.* □ *He guessed wrong.* **(de maneira errada)**

2 **go wrong** (a) to stop working correctly □ *My watch has gone wrong.* (b) to stop being successful □ *Everything went wrong after Nik left.* **(funcionar mal, dar errado)**

wrong³ /rɒŋ/ NOUN, NO PLURAL behaviour that is not morally correct ⧉ *He doesn't know the difference between* right and wrong. □ *I accept that I did wrong.* **(errado)**

wrongly /'rɒŋlɪ/ ADVERB not correctly □ *The plug had been fitted wrongly so the machine did not work.* □ *She was wrongly accused of fraud.* **(incorretamente)**

wrote /rəʊt/ PAST TENSE OF **write** (ver **write**)

Xx

X *or* **x** /eks/ the 24th letter of the alphabet (**a vigésima quarta letra do alfabeto**)

Xmas /'eksməs/ NOUN an informal short way of writing **Christmas**¹ (ver **Christmas**)

X-ray /'eksreɪ/ NOUN [*plural* **X-rays**] a special kind of photograph that shows the inside parts of someone's body (**radiografia**)

Y y

Y or **y** /waɪ/ the 25th letter of the alphabet (**a vigésima quinta letra do alfabeto**)

yacht /jɒt/ NOUN [plural **yachts**] a boat with sails that you use for racing or for pleasure (**iate**)

yard¹ /jɑːd/ NOUN [plural **yards**] a unit for measuring length, equal to 3 feet (**jarda**)

yard² /jɑːd/ NOUN [plural **yards**]
1 an area of land, often with a fence or wall around it, and often used for a particular purpose ▢ *The dogs have a large exercise yard.* (**pátio, quintal**)
2 a US word for a garden next to a house (**jardim**)

yawn /jɔːn/ VERB [**yawns, yawning, yawned**] to open your mouth very wide and breathe in, because you are feeling tired or bored (**bocejar**)

yeah /jeə/ EXCLAMATION an informal way of saying **yes**

year /jɪə(r)/ NOUN [plural **years**]
1 a period of 365 or 366 days, marking the length of time it takes for the Earth to go around the sun, especially the period from 1 January to 31 December ▢ *We're going to America next year.* ▢ *I spent a year working in Paris.* ▢ *In recent years, the building has not been used much.* (**ano**)
2 three/sixteen/fifty, etc. years old used to talk about the age of someone or something ▢ *He's only twelve years old.* ▢ *Our house is almost three hundred years old.* (**ano, idade**)
3 a three/sixteen/fifty year-old a person who is a particular age ▢ *You're acting like a five year-old!* (**ano**)
4 years a long period of time 🔁 *I haven't been to Madrid for years.* (**anos**)
5 the students at a school, college, etc. who start in the same year ▢ *He was in my year at school.* ▢ *We studied the Egyptians in year 3.* (**ano**)

> When saying how old someone is, do not say 'years'. Say only the number or a number + 'years old':
> ✓ *She is eight.*
> ✓ *She is eight years old.*
> ✗ *She is eight years.*

yearly /ˈjɪəli/ ADJECTIVE, ADVERB happening or done every year ▢ *our yearly holiday* ▢ *Accounts must be prepared yearly.* (**anual, anualmente**)

yeast /jiːst/ NOUN, NO PLURAL a substance that is used to make bread rise (**fermento**)

yell /jel/ VERB [**yells, yelling, yelled**] to shout something loudly ▢ *'Let me go!' she yelled.* (**berrar**)

yellow¹ /ˈjeləʊ/ ADJECTIVE
having the colour of the sun or a lemon ▢ *The garden was full of bright yellow flowers.* (**amarelo**)

yellow² /ˈjeləʊ/ NOUN, NO PLURAL
the colour of the sun or a lemon (**amarelo**)

yes /jes/ EXCLAMATION
1 used to agree with someone, agree to do something, or to give a positive answer ▢ *'Are these shoes all right?' 'Yes, they're lovely.'* ▢ *'Could you help me with my homework?' 'Yes, no problem.'* ▢ *'Would you like a cup of coffee?' 'Yes, please.'* (**sim**)
2 used to disagree with a negative statement ▢ *'You haven't washed your hair.' 'Yes I have.'* (**sim**)

yesterday /ˈjestədeɪ/ ADVERB, NOUN, NO PLURAL
the day before today ▢ *I saw Kim yesterday.* ▢ *He called me yesterday morning.* ▢ *Yesterday was her birthday.* (**ontem**)

yet¹ /jet/ ADVERB
1 used in questions or negative statements to mean before now or before the time you are talking about ▢ *Have you read her new book yet?* ▢ *We haven't paid them any money yet.* (**ainda, já, até agora**)
2 used in questions and negative statements to mean that something will not happen immediately but will happen in the future ▢ *Please don't leave yet.* ▢ *You can't go in yet.* (**ainda**)
3 used to emphasize how often something exists or happens 🔁 *Yet again, they have let us down.* 🔁 *Apparently, Richard has bought yet another bicycle.* (**outra vez, novamente**)

yet² /jet/ CONJUNCTION
used to say something surprising after what has been said before ▢ *He was pleasant, yet failed to offer any real help.* ▢ *We claim to live in a civilized society, and yet children live in poverty here.* ▢ *The decorations were colourful yet tasteful.* (**no entanto**)

yield

yield /jiːld/ VERB [yields, yielding, yielded]
1 to produce something useful ☐ *Discussions have failed to yield results.* ☐ *The investment yielded a good profit.* (**produzir**)
2 to produce a particular amount of a crop (**produzir**)
3 to be forced to do something or agree to something, or to be defeated ☐ *The government yielded to pressure and delayed the tax rise.* ☐ *The army yielded to enemy forces.* (**produzir, ceder**)

yoga /ˈjəʊgə/ NOUN, NO PLURAL a type of exercise for the body and the mind, which involves stretching your body and doing breathing exercises (**ioga**)

you /juː/ PRONOUN used to talk or write about the person or people that you are talking to ☐ *Do you like pizza?* ☐ *I'll ring you tomorrow night.* ☐ *Max is taller than you.* (**você, tu, vocês, vós**)

you'd /juːd/ a short way to say and write you had or you would ☐ *You'd better be careful.* ☐ *You'd be sorry if she left.* (abreviação de **you would**)

you'll /juːl/ a short way to say and write you will ☐ *You'll never guess what happened next!* (abreviação de **you will**)

young¹ /jʌŋ/ ADJECTIVE [younger, youngest] not old ☐ *a young boy* ☐ *You're too young to stay up so late.* (**jovem**)

young² /jʌŋ/ PLURAL NOUN
1 the babies that an animal or bird has ☐ *a bird feeding its young* (**filhote**)
2 the young young people (**os jovens**)

your /jɔː(r)/ DETERMINER
1 belonging to or to do with you ☐ *Can I borrow your pen?* (**seu, teu, vosso**)
2 belonging to or to do with people in general ☐ *Your school days are the happiest days of your life.* (**seu, teu, vosso**)

you're /jɔː(r)/ a short way to say and write you are ☐ *You're early!* (abreviação de **you are**)

yours /jɔːz/ PRONOUN
1 used to talk or write about things belonging to or to do with the person or people you are talking to ☐ *Which glass is yours?* (**seu, teu, vosso**)
2 used at the end of a letter, before your name ☐ *I look forward to hearing from you. Yours, Amy.* (**atenciosamente**)

yourself /jɔːˈself/ PRONOUN [*plural* yourselves]
1 the reflexive form of you ☐ *Careful you don't cut yourself on that knife.* ☐ *You'll have to dry yourselves on your T-shirts.* (**você mesmo**)
2 used to show that you do something without any help from other people ☐ *Did you really make that skirt yourself?* ☐ *Have you done this work all by yourself?* (**sozinho**)
3 used to emphasize the pronoun **you** ☐ *You can not film the concert yourselves, but you can buy a video.* (**sozinho**)
4 by yourself not with or near other people ☐ *It can be lonely living by yourself.* (**sozinho, só para você**)

youth /juːθ/ NOUN [*plural* youths]
1 a young man ☐ *a gang of youths* (**jovem, rapaz**)
2 no plural the time in your life when you are young ☐ *She spent most of her youth abroad.* (**juventude**)
3 no plural young people ☐ *the youth of today* (**juventude**)

you've /juːv/ a short way to say and write you have ☐ *You've left the door open again.* (ver **have**)

Zz

Z or z /zed/ the 26th letter of the alphabet (a última letra do alfabeto)

zebra /ˈzebrə/ NOUN [plural **zebras**] an animal like a horse with black and white stripes (**zebra**)

zebra crossing /ˌzebrə ˈkrɒsɪŋ/ NOUN [plural **zebra crossings**] a place where you can cross a road, marked with black and white stripes (**faixa de pedestres**)

zero /ˈzɪərəʊ/ NOUN [plural **zeros**]
1 nothing or the number 0 ◻ There are six zeros in one million. (**zero**)
2 no plural the temperature at which water freezes ◻ It was three degrees below zero. (**zero**)

zip[1] /zɪp/ NOUN [plural **zips**] a device for fastening clothes or bags that has two rows of small metal or plastic parts that fit tightly together when a sliding piece is pulled along them (**zíper, fecho**)

zip[2] /zɪp/ VERB [**zips, zipping, zipped**]
1 to fasten something with a zip ◻ Zip up your jacket; it's cold. (**fechar com zíper**)
2 to make the information on a computer file fit into a much smaller space, so that it can be sent or stored more easily. A computing word ◻ I'll zip the file before I send it to you. (**compactar, zipar**)
3 to move somewhere very quickly, or to do something very quickly ◻ The bullet zipped by his head. ◻ He zipped through the answers. (**sair correndo, mover com energia**)

zodiac /ˈzəʊdɪæk/ NOUN the zodiac the twelve signs of the groups of stars that some people believe influence your life ◻ What sign of the zodiac are you? (**zodíaco**)

zone /zəʊn/ NOUN [plural **zones**] an area that has a particular feature or where a particular thing happens ◻ This is a danger zone because of avalanches. ◻ a smoke-free zone ◻ a war zone (**zona, área**)

zoo /zuː/ NOUN [plural **zoos**] a place where wild animals are kept for people to look at (**zoológico**)

zoom /zuːm/ VERB [**zooms, zooming, zoomed**] to go somewhere very fast, especially with a loud noise ◻ The rocket zoomed up into the air. (**zunir, passar zunindo**)